ENCYCLOPEDIA OF THE THIRD REICH

LOUIS L. SNYDER

Professor of History
The City College and The City University of New York

Marlowe & Company
New York

Published in the United States by

Marlowe & Company
632 Broadway, Seventh Floor
New York, NY 10012

Reprinted by arrangement with McGraw-Hill, Inc.

Manufactured in the United States of America

Library of Congress Cataloging-in-Publication Data
Snyder, Louis Leo, 1907-
Encyclopedia of the Third Reich / Louis L. Snyder
p. cm.
Bibliography: p.
ISBN 1-56924-917-2 (pbk.)
1. Germany—History—1933–1945—Dictionaries. 2. National socialism—Dictionaries. I. Title.
[DD256.5.S92 1989]
943.086—dc19 88-14696
CIP

Preface

When McGraw-Hill assigned me the task of compiling this encyclopedia, I was given a choice of procedures: to farm out the entries, fully or partially, or write them all myself. I chose the latter course for several reasons. First, it seemed to me best to assure a consistency of style, especially for the biographies. Second, the time consumed in checking each contributor's facts would have approached that used in researching and writing the articles. And, finally, the work was of special interest to me: I have been fascinated by the phenomenon of Hitlerism since my student days from 1928 to 1931 in Germany. I was able at that time to witness at first hand the closing days of the Weimar Republic and the rise of National Socialism. My first book, *Hitlerism: The Iron Fist in Germany* (1931), written under the pseudonym Nordicus, was published a year before Hitler assumed political power. As a neophyte scholar, I did not understand at the time that historians should direct their attention to the past and not, like Nostradamus, to the future. Consequently, I made a number of wild predictions, all of which came true except the prophecy that France would fight a preventive war to block the Nazi road to power. The scope of the present work is different: it seeks to stay with the facts. Responsibility for accuracy, of course, is entirely mine.

The major area covered is the period from the rise of National Socialism to the fall of the Third Reich in 1945. There are selected entries from the time of the Weimar Republic, which preceded Hitler, and from the Bonn Republic, which succeeded him. These are included because they were closely associated with Hitler and the Nazi regime. Several thousand names of lesser National Socialists might well have been included, but this would have meant the production of a multivolume encyclopedia. The names of the biographees selected are those that would be recognized by most historians of the Third Reich as of some significance. The amount of space devoted to each entry was judged by its relative importance to historians of the era.

Much of the source material comes from my own collection, from pamphlets of the 1920s to archival documents of the 1970s. I wish to express my thanks to the staff of the Firestone Library at Princeton University and to its former director, University Librarian William S. Dix; to the helpful librarians at the New York Public Library; and to the staffs of the university and historical seminars at Heidelberg, Frankfurt am Main, Marburg, Giessen, Bochum, Bonn, Cologne, Göttingen, and the Free University of Berlin. I am indebted to the editors of *Der Spiegel* in Hamburg, who graciously tracked down some hard-to-find facts for me, to Edward Hine of the Imperial War Museum in London, and to the staff of the City College Library.

Above all, I wish to express my special appreciation to the Wiener Library in London and especially to two of its gifted librarians, Mrs. Marghita Johnson and Miss C. S. Wichman, who spent many hours with me tracing elusive facts. Founded by Dr. Alfred Wiener (q.v.) in Amsterdam in 1933 and transferred to London in 1939, the Wiener Library is a treasure trove of documentation on every phase of Nazi history, from a collection of beautifully designed cigarette cards portraying contemporary Nazi heroes to the valuable *Fuehrerlexikon*, now out of print. One can only repeat the words of H. R. Trevor-Roper (q.v.), Professor of Modern History at Oxford: "I know of no important work on the political science of the totalitarian era of Europe, whether primarily political or sociological in its emphasis, whose author does not acknowledge indebtedness to the Wiener Library."

The production of an encyclopedia of this kind becomes an enormous task without the able assistance of an inside editorial and production team. It is, therefore, with the greatest pleasure that I express my warm thanks to the staff of the McGraw-Hill Professional and Reference Book Division, especially Leonard Josephson, Robert A. Rosenbaum, Tobia L. Worth, Beatrice E. Eckes, and Maura E. Seger.

Finally, as always in the past, I want to express my sense of indebtedness to my wife, who devoted her efforts not only to the selection of entries but also to the important tasks of editing and proofreading throughout the life of the project. Again and again she rescued me from monumental errors, a service for which any writer is extremely grateful. Both of us hope that this encyclopedia, presented without praise or polemic, will give users the essential facts of the Third Reich.

LOUIS L. SNYDER
Princeton, New Jersey

Calendar of Significant Dates in the History of the Third Reich

1889

April 20. Birth of Adolf Hitler in Braunau am Inn, Austria.

1893

January 12. Birth of Hermann Goering in Rosenheim, Upper Bavaria.

1897

October 29. Birth of Paul Joseph Goebbels in Rheydt, in the Rhineland.

1900

October 7. Birth of Heinrich Himmler in or near Munich.

1914

August 3. Hitler petitions King Louis III of Bavaria for permission to volunteer in a Bavarian regiment for service in World War I.

1916

October 7. Hitler wounded in combat by a grenade splinter.

1917

September 17. Hitler awarded the Bavarian Service Cross.

1918

May 9. Hitler awarded a regimental diploma for courage beyond the call of duty.
August 4. Hitler awarded the Iron Cross (First Class).
October 13. Hitler wounded again. He temporarily loses his sight because of gas poisoning.
November 11. Armistice ending World War I signed at Compiègne.
November 12. Proclamation by Friedrich Ebert on the aims of the new German regime.
December 20. National conference of Communist Spartacists held in Berlin.

1919

January 5. Founding of the German Workers' party.
January 5. General strike and Communist uprising in Berlin.
January 15. Murder of Rosa Luxemburg and Karl Liebknecht by nationalists.
February 21. Murder of Kurt Eisner in Munich.
April 4. Soviet republic established in Bavaria.
April 27. Attempt by Red Guards to arrest Hitler.
May 2. Communist revolt in Munich smashed.
June 28. Signing of the Treaty of Versailles by German delegates.
July 31. Adoption of the Weimar Constitution.

1920

January 10. The Treaty of Versailles comes into effect.
February 24. First mass meeting of the NSDAP, at the Hofbräuhaus in Munich. Hitler makes the party program known.
March 12–17. Kapp *Putsch* a fiasco in Berlin.
August 26. Matthias Erzberger, Minister of Finance, murdered by rightist extremists.

1921

February 3. First great Nazi mass meeting, held in the Zirkus Krone, Munich.
July 29. Hitler made first chairman of the NSDAP.
November 4. Foundation of the SA.

1922

April 16. Treaty of Rapallo between Germany and the U.S.S.R.

June 24. Murder of Walther Rathenau, German statesman of Jewish descent.

December 26. Germany declared in default by the Allied Reparations Commission.

1923

January 11. Occupation of the Ruhr by French and Belgian forces.

January 28. First Nazi party day, held in Munich.

May 26. Execution of Albert Leo Schlageter as a saboteur by the French in the Rhineland.

November 8–9. Unsuccessful Hitler-Ludendorff *Putsch* in Munich.

November 11. Hitler arrested and held in Landsberg fortress.

November 15. End of German inflation; introduction of the *Rentenmark.*

1924

February 26. Beginning of the trial of Hitler for treason.

April 1. Hitler sentenced to five years' imprisonment in Landsberg fortress.

April 9. Dawes Plan on reparations issued.

Ca. April 15. Hitler begins work on *Mein Kampf.*

May 4. Reichstag elections: Nazis win 6.4 percent of the vote.

December 7. Reichstag elections: Nazi popular vote down to 3 percent.

December 20. Hitler released from prison.

1925

February 24. Refounding of the NSDAP.

February 28. Death of Ebert, first President of the Weimar Republic.

March 29. Presidential elections: Gen. Erich Ludendorff, supported by Nazis, wins only 211,000 of 27 million votes cast.

April 26. Field Marshal Paul von Hindenburg elected second President of the Weimar Republic in a runoff election

July 14. Beginning of the withdrawal of Allied occupation forces from the Ruhr.

July 18. Publication of Volume I of *Mein Kampf.*

October 16. Signature of the Locarno Pact.

December 8. Official publication date of *Mein Kampf.*

1926

July 3. Party day, held in Weimar.

September 8. Germany made a member of the League of Nations.

December 1. Goebbels appointed *Gauleiter* of Berlin by Hitler.

1927

March 10. Lifting of speaking ban on Hitler.
August 19. Party day, held in Nuremberg: march of 30,000 Brownshirts.

1928

May 20. Reichstag elections: Nazis return 12 out of 491 deputies, with 2.5 percent of the vote.
September 28. Lifting of speaking ban on Hitler in Prussia.
November 16. Speech by Hitler at an open meeting in Berlin.

1929

January 6. Himmler appointed *Reichsfuehrer-SS.*
June 7. Young Plan on reparations issued.
August 2. Party day, held in Nuremberg: 150,000 participants.

1930

January 23. Wilhelm Frick made minister of the interior of Thuringia.
February 23. Death of Horst Wessel.
June 30. French troops withdrawn from the Rhineland.
September 2. Hitler assumes the position of supreme SA leader.
September 14. Reichstag elections: Nazis return 107 out of 577 deputies, with 18 percent of the vote.
December 31. SS Central Office for Race and Resettlement set up by Richard-Walther Darré.

1931

January 16. A National Socialist elected as president of Bremen.
September 14. NSDAP vote doubled in an election in Hesse.
October 11. Harzburg Conference of representatives of rightist political parties, including German Nationalists, Stahlhelm leaders, and National Socialists, against the Weimar regime.
October 16. Large SA demonstration in Braunschweig.

1932.

January 27. Speech by Hitler to Rhineland industrialists in Düsseldorf.
February 25. German citizenship granted to Hitler.
March 13. Presidential elections: Hitler receives 13.7 million votes.
April 10. Hindenburg reelected President of the Weimar Republic in a runoff election.
April 14. The SA and SS banned by Chancellor Heinrich Bruening.

May 30. Resignation of Bruening as Chancellor.
June 1. Appointment of Franz von Papen as Chancellor.
June 16. Ban on the SA and SS lifted by Von Papen.
July 31. Reichstag elections: Nazis win 230 out of 608 seats.
August 13. Refusal by Hitler to accept President von Hindenburg's offer of a Cabinet post.
November 6. Reichstag elections: Nazis return 196 deputies, for a loss of 34 seats.
December 3. Appointment of Gen. Kurt von Schleicher as Chancellor.

1933

January 4. Secret meeting of Hitler and Von Papen at the Cologne home of the banker Kurt von Schroeder to discuss Hitler's role in a future German government.
January 28. Resignation of Chancellor von Schleicher.
January 30. Appointment of Hitler as Chancellor.
February 2. Beginning of the Second International Disarmament Conference. It ends on October 14.
February 22. Some 40,000 SA and SS men sworn in as auxiliary policemen.
February 27. The Reichstag fire.
February 28. Hitler given emergency powers by a presidential decree.
March 5. Reichstag elections: Nazis return 288 out of 647 deputies.
March 9. Himmler made police president of Munich.
March 13. Appointment of Goebbels as Reich Minister for Public Enlightenment and Propaganda.
March 16. Dr. Hjalmar Schacht named president of the Reichsbank.
March 17. Formation of the Leibstandarte-SS Adolf Hitler (SS Bodyguard Regiment Adolf Hitler) under Josef (Sepp) Dietrich.
March 21. Communist deputies forbidden to take seats in the new Reichstag.
March 21. Special courts established for the prosecution of political enemies.
March 24. Adoption of the Enabling Act (Law to Remove the Distress of People and State).
March 31. Individual states of the Reich stripped of power.
April 1. National boycott of Jewish business and professional people.
April 21. Designation of Rudolf Hess as Deputy Fuehrer of the NSDAP by Hitler.
April 26. Formation of the Gestapo.

May 2. Dissolution of the labor unions.
May 10. Burning of books in Berlin and throughout Germany.
May 14. Letter denouncing the Nazi regime sent by Romain Rolland to the editor of the *Kölnische Zeitung*.
May 17. Strikes prohibited throughout Germany.
June 9. The SD made the sole political and counterespionage agency for the NSDAP.
July 14. Law Concerning the Formation of New Parties.
July 20. Signing in Rome of a concordat between the Vatican and the Third Reich.
September 22. Reich Chamber of Culture set up under Goebbels.
October 14. German withdrawal from the League of Nations.
November 12. Reichstag elections: 93 percent of the vote cast for the NSDAP.

1934

January 26. Ten-year nonaggression pact signed by Germany and Poland.
January 30. Elimination of provinces in federal states.
January 30. Promulgation of the Law for the Reorganization of the Reich.
April 20. Himmler made acting chief of the Prussian Gestapo.
June 17. Vice-Chancellor von Papen denounces the continuing Nazi revolution.
June 30. Blood Purge: Ernst Roehm, SA chief, is killed with other advocates of a second revolution.
July 20. The SS made an independent unit from the SA.
July 25. Assassination of Chancellor Engelbert Dollfuss of Austria.
July 26. Appointment of Von Papen as German envoy to Austria.
August 2. Death of President von Hindenburg. Hitler declares himself Fuehrer of the German state. The armed forces are required to take a personal oath of loyalty to him.
August 19. Plebiscite on Hitler's new powers: 89.93 percent vote yes.

1935

January 13. Plebiscite in the Saar: 91 percent favor return to the Reich.
March 16. Introduction of military conscription.
April 11. Great Britain, France, and Italy, meeting in Stresa, protest the Nazi conscription decree.
May 21. Hitler's speech in the Reichstag giving his peace program.

June 18. Anglo-German naval agreement allowing the German Navy up to 35 percent of British strength.
June 26. Law Regarding Labor Service.
September 15. Nuremberg Laws disenfranchising Jews decreed.
October 3. Invasion of Ethiopia by Italy.

1936

March 7. Denunciation of the Locarno Pact by Hitler. German troops are sent into the demilitarized Rhineland.
March 12. Great Britain, France, Italy, and Belgium denounce the German breach of the Locarno Pact.
March 29. Expansion of the SS to 3,500 men.
June 17. Himmler appointed chief of the German Police.
July 11. German-Austrian agreement recognizing Austrian sovereignty signed.
August 23. German Evangelical Church manifesto.
September 9. Four-Year Plan proclaimed.
October 25. Announcement of Italo-German Axis pact.
November 25. Anti-Comintern Pact signed by Germany and Japan.
December 1. Law Making the Hitler Youth a State Agency.
December 19. Letter from the dean of the Philosophical Faculty of the University of Bonn striking the name of Thomas Mann from the list of honorary doctors.

1937

March 14. Encyclical of Pope Pius XI: *Mit brennender Sorge (With Deep Anxiety).*
April 27. Guernica bombed by German planes supporting the Insurgents in the Spanish Civil War.
September 7. Hitler declares the end of the Treaty of Versailles.
November 5. Hossbach Conference: In the Hossbach Memorandum, dated November 10, Hitler's plans to dominate Europe are outlined.
November 6. Italian adherence to the Anti-Comintern Pact.
November 19. Conference between Hitler and Lord Halifax.
December 11. Italian withdrawal from the League of Nations.

1938

February 2–4. Blomberg-Fritsch crisis.
February 4. Gen. Wilhelm Keitel appointed chief of the High Command of the armed forces.
February 4. Joachim von Ribbentrop named Foreign Minister.
February 12. Austrian Chancellor Kurt von Schuschnigg called to Berchtesgaden by Hitler.
February 15. Artur Seyss-Inquart appointed Austrian Minister of the Interior.

March 9. Designation by Chancellor von Schuschnigg of March 13 as the date for a plebiscite to decide on Austrian independence.

March 11. Resignation of Von Schuschnigg.

March 12. Crossing of the Austrian border by German troops.

April 24. Call for autonomy for the Sudeten Germans by Konrad Henlein, head of the Sudeten German party.

May 20. Partial mobilization of Czechoslovakia.

September 15. Flight of Prime Minister Neville Chamberlain to Berchtesgaden to maintain the peace.

September 22. Flight of Chamberlain to Bad Godesberg for a second meeting with Hitler.

September 26. Speech by Hitler in Berlin in which he states that the Sudetenland is his last territorial claim in Europe.

September 29–30. Munich Agreement between Hitler, Mussolini, Chamberlain, and French Premier Édouard Daladier agreeing to Germany's acquisition of the Sudetenland.

October 28. First deportation of Polish Jews from the Third Reich.

November 7. Ernst vom Rath, Third Secretary in the German Embassy in Paris, shot and mortally wounded by Herschel Grynszpan, a Polish Jew. He dies on November 9.

November 9. Crystal Night, in which mobs attack Jewish synagogues and stores throughout Germany.

November 12. German Jews fined 1 billion marks.

November 15. Expulsion of all Jewish pupils from German schools.

December 3. Decree for compulsory Aryanization of all Jewish enterprises and shops.

December 6. Nonaggression pact signed by Germany and France.

1939

January 20. Walther Funk named president of the Reichsbank.

March 15. Czechoslovakian President Emil Hácha forced to ask Hitler's protection. The Protectorate of Bohemia and Moravia is established.

March 23. German occupation of Memel.

March 28. Occupation of Madrid by Gen. Francisco Franco.

March 31. Anglo-French guarantee of Poland.

April 7. Italian seizure of Albania.

April 15. Appeal by President Franklin Delano Roosevelt to Hitler to respect the independence of European nations.

April 28.	Response by Hitler to President Roosevelt in a long speech before the Reichstag.
May 22.	Pact of steel: military alliance between Germany and Italy.
May 23.	Hitler informs generals that war with Poland is "inevitable."
May 31–June 7.	German nonaggression treaties with Estonia, Latvia, and Denmark.
July 4.	German Jews denied the right to hold government jobs.
July 21.	Adolf Eichmann appointed director of the Prague Office of Jewish Emigration.
August 23.	Soviet-German nonaggression pact signed in Moscow with a secret protocol on Poland.
August 24.	Appeal for peace by Pope Pius XII.
August 25.	Appeal to Hitler by President Roosevelt.
August 25.	British-Polish treaty.
August 26.	Appeal to Hitler by Premier Daladier.
August 31.	Polish announcement of readiness to negotiate.
September 1.	German invasion of Poland. Great Britain and France demand that Germany withdraw its troops.
September 1.	Beginning of SD activity in Poland.
September 1.	Jews in Germany forbidden to be outdoors after 8 P.M. in winter and 9 P.M. in summer.
September 3.	Declaration of war on Germany by Great Britain and France.
September 4.	Warsaw cut off by the German Army.
September 17.	Crossing of the Polish border by Soviet troops.
September 21.	Reinhard Heydrich's plans for ghettos in Poland presented.
September 23.	German Jews forbidden to own wireless sets.
September 27.	Fall of Warsaw.
October 6.	Peace offer by Hitler to Great Britain and France.
October 6.	Proclamation by Hitler on the isolation of Jews.
October 7.	Himmler appointed Reich Commissioner for the Consolidation of German Nationhood.
October 12.	Evacuation of Jews from Vienna.
October 12.	Hans Frank appointed chief civilian officer for occupied Poland.
November 8.	Attempted assassination of Hitler at the Bürgerbräu Keller in Munich.
November 21.	Beginning of a British blockade of German exports.
November 23.	Identity stars required to be worn by Jews in occupied Poland.
November 30.	Invasion of Finland by the Soviet Union. Helsinki is bombed.
December 17.	*Graf Spee* sunk off Montevideo.

1940

February 12. First deportation of Jews from Germany.
March 12. Soviet-Finnish peace treaty signed in Moscow.
March 21. Paul Reynaud named Premier of France, replacing Daladier.
April 9. Invasion of Denmark and Norway by Germany.
May 10. German invasion of Belgium, the Netherlands, and Luxembourg.
May 10. Resignation of Chamberlain. Winston Churchill is appointed Prime Minister of Great Britain.
May 14. Capitulation of the Dutch Army. Rotterdam is almost destroyed.
May 17. Occupation of Brussels.
May 18. Antwerp captured by Germans.
May 26. Start of the evacuation of Dunkirk.
May 28. Surrender of Belgium.
June 4. Dunkirk captured by Germans.
June 10. Declaration of war by Italy on Great Britain and France. President Roosevelt calls this a stab in the back.
June 14. Occupation of undefended Paris by the Germans.
June 14. German breakthrough of the Maginot Line south of Saarbrücken.
June 15–16. Soviet occupation of Lithuania, Latvia, and Estonia.
June 16. Resignation of Premier Reynaud. Marshal Henri Philippe Pétain is made Premier of France.
June 22. Truce signed at Compiègne by Germany and France.
July 10. Beginning of Nazi air attack on England.
August 13. Start of Battle of Britain.
August 15. Eichmann's Madagascar Plan for the Jews presented.
September 3. Exchange of fifty United States destroyers for naval base sites in British possessions in the Western Hemisphere.
September 6. Abdication of King Carol II of Romania.
September 7. Beginning of all-out air attack on London.
September 15. A total of 185 German planes shot down in the Battle of Britain.
September 17. Hitler postpones projected invasion of Britain.
September 27. Formation of the Rome-Berlin-Tokyo Axis.
October 7. Invasion of Romania by German troops.
October 16. First draft in the United States: 16.4 million men registered.
October 22. Deportation of Jews from Baden, the Saar, and Alsace-Lorraine.
October 28. Italian invasion of Greece.

November 11.	British Fleet Air Arm attack on Taranto.
November 14.	German air raid on Coventry.
November 15.	Warsaw ghetto sealed.
November 20–25.	Hungary, Romania, and Slovakia join the Tripartite Pact.
December 15.	British invasion of Italian Libya.
December 17.	United States proposal of lend-lease aid to Britain.

1941

January 6.	Address to Congress by President Roosevelt calling for a peace based on the Four Freedoms.
January 10.	Lend-lease bill introduced into Congress.
January 22.	Fall of Tobruk to the British.
January 31.	Attempt to set up a *Judenrat* in Frankfurt am Main.
February 6.	Benghazi captured by Australians.
February 12.	Arrival of Gen. Erwin Rommel in Tripoli to direct German forces in North Africa.
February 22.	Deportation of 400 Jewish hostages from Amsterdam.
March 1.	Bulgaria joins the Tripartite Pact.
March 2.	German troops march into Bulgaria.
March 7.	Employment of Jews for compulsory labor inside Germany.
March 11.	Lend-lease bill signed by President Roosevelt.
March 24.	German offensive in North Africa takes El Agheila.
March 27.	Revolution in Yugoslavia: Prince Regent Paul is overthrown, and King Peter II is installed.
March 28.	Battle of Cape Matapan: British defeat the Italian Fleet.
April 6.	German invasion of Yugoslavia and Greece.
April 11.	Beginning of the siege of Tobruk.
April 19.	German flanking move in the Pindus Mountains compels the British to retreat in Greece.
April 23–May 1.	Evacuation of Greek mainland by the British.
April 27.	German occupation of Athens.
May 10.	Landing of Hess in Scotland.
May 10.	German air raid damages Westminister Abbey, the Houses of Parliament, and the British Museum.
May 14.	Martin Bormann named successor to Hess.
May 14.	Approximately 3,600 Jews arrested in Paris.
May 16.	Broadcast by Marshal Pétain approving collaboration with Germany.
May 20.	German airborne attack on Crete.
May 27.	Sinking of the German battleship *Bismarck* in the North Atlantic.
May 27.	Proclamation by President Roosevelt of a national emergency.

June 1. Fall of Crete to the Germans.
June 2. Conference of Hitler and Benito Mussolini at the Brenner Pass.
June 5. Secretary of State Cordell Hull denounces Vichy collaboration with the Third Reich.
June 14. Freezing of Axis funds in the United States by President Roosevelt.
June 18. German-Turkish friendship agreement signed in Ankara.
June 22. German attack on the U.S.S.R. on a front from the Baltic to the Black Sea.
July 3. Policy of scorched earth instituted by Joseph Stalin.
July 12. Soviet-British mutual assistance pact signed in Moscow.
July 17. Appointment of Alfred Rosenberg as Reich Minister for the Eastern Occupied Territories.
July 21. Concentration camp in Maidanek constructed by Himmler.
July 31. Order by Goering to Heydrich to evacuate all Jews from German-occupied territory in Europe.
August 9–12. Meeting of Roosevelt and Churchill off Newfoundland.
August 14. Atlantic Charter announced.
September 1. Decree ordering all Jews to wear yellow stars.
September 8. Land connections of Leningrad with the rest of the U.S.S.R. cut by Germans.
September 17. Beginning of general deportation of German Jews.
September 19. German occupation of Kiev.
September 23. Tests for gassing at Auschwitz.
October 2. Beginning of the German drive on Moscow.
November 18. British counteroffensive in North Africa.
December 1. Soviet counterattack at Tula.
December 7. Pearl Harbor attacked by the Japanese.
December 8. Declaration of war by Japan on the United States and Great Britain.
December 10. British free Tobruk from German encirclement.
December 11. German and Italian declarations of war on the United States.
December 13. Hungarian and Bulgarian declarations of war on the United States.
December 19. Gen. Walther von Brauchitsch dismissed as commander in chief of the Wehrmacht. Command is assumed by Hitler.

1942

January 1. United Nations Declaration signed by twenty-six nations.

January 20. Wannsee Conference: decision for the "Final Solution" of Jewish problem.
January 21. Success of Rommel at El Agheila.
January 31. Capture of Benghazi by the Afrika Korps.
February 9. Albert Speer named Minister of Armaments and War Production to succeed Fritz Todt.
February 12. Escape of the *Gneisenau, Scharnhorst,* and *Prinz Eugen* from Brest.
March 15. Prediction by Hitler of victory over the Soviet Union by summer.
March 28. Fritz Sauckel named Chief of Manpower to expedite recruitment of slave labor.
March 29. First trains from Paris to Auschwitz.
April 20. Ban on the use of public transport by Jews.
May 26–31. Pastor Dietrich Bonhoeffer confers with the Bishop of Chichester in Stockholm.
May 27. German counteroffensive launched in North Africa.
May 29. Assault on Heydrich by Czech patriots.
May 30–31. Air raid on Cologne by 1,000 RAF bombers.
June 1. Jews required to wear yellow stars in France and the Netherlands.
June 4. Heydrich dies of his wounds.
June 10. German destruction of Lidice.
June 21. German capture of Tobruk.
June 23. First gassings in Auschwitz.
June 24. Gen. Dwight D. Eisenhower in command of United States forces in the European theater of operations.
June 25–27. Second Washington Conference between Roosevelt and Churchill.
July 16. Raids on Parisian Jews.
August 19. British-Canadian raid on Dieppe.
August 23. Beginning of German attack on Stalingrad.
August 26–28. 7,000 Jews arrested in Unoccupied France.
September 18. Reduction of food rations for Jews in Germany.
October 4. All Jews in concentration camps ordered to be sent to Auschwitz.
October 23. Attack by Gen. Bernard Law Montgomery on the Afrika Korps at El Alamein.
October 29. Approximately 16,000 Jews killed in Pinsk.
November 5. Rommel beaten at El Alamein.
November 7–8. Landing of American and British troops on the coast of northwest Africa.
November 11. Invasion of Unoccupied France by German troops.
November 19–22. Soviet counteroffensive at Stalingrad.
November 20. Capture of Benghazi by General Montgomery.
November 27. French Fleet scuttled at Toulon by its own crews.

December 24. Adm. Jean-François Darlan assassinated in North Africa.

1943

January 14. Beginning of Casablanca Conference.
January 18. Land connections between Leningrad and the rest of the Soviet Union reopened.
January 18. First resistance in the Warsaw ghetto.
January 20–26. Deportations to Auschwitz.
January 23. Entrance of the British Eighth Army into Tripoli.
January 24. Announcement of a policy of unconditional surrender at the Casablanca Conference.
January 30. Ernst Kaltenbrunner made chief of the Security Police and SD and head of the RSHA.
February 2. Stalingrad retaken by Soviet troops.
February 15. Rostov and Voroshilovgrad (Lugansk) recaptured by the Russians.
February 18. Student uprising in Munich. Hans and Sophie Scholl are arrested.
February 27. Jews employed in Berlin armaments industry sent to Auschwitz.
March 9. General Rommel recalled to Germany.
March 13. First new crematorium opened at Auschwitz.
March 13. Failure of attempt to assassinate Hitler on a flight from Smolensk.
March 21. Failure of attempt to assassinate Hitler at Heroes' Memorial Day ceremonies in Berlin.
March 27. Breaking of the Mareth Line by Montgomery in North Africa.
April 5. Arrest of Pastor Bonhoeffer.
April 7. Linking of American and British forces in Tunisia.
April 19. Beginning of the destruction of the Warsaw ghetto.
May 7. Tunis and Bizerte taken by the Allies.
May 12–25. Third Washington (Trident) Conference between Roosevelt and Churchill.
May 13. Surrender of the last German units in North Africa.
May 15. Third International (Comintern) dissolved in Moscow.
May 19. Berlin declared *Judenfrei* (cleansed of Jews).
June 12. Surrender of the island of Pantelleria, off Sicily, to the Allies.
July 10. Allied landings in Sicily.
July 19. Allied bombing of Rome.
July 25. Resignation of Mussolini. Gen. Pietro Badoglio is made Italian Premier.
August 17. Conquest of Sicily completed by the Allies.
August 17–24. First Quebec (Quadrant) Conference.

August. 25.	Himmler appointed Minister of the Interior "to combat defeatism."
September 3.	Landing of Allied troops on the Italian mainland.
September 8.	Announcement of the unconditional surrender of Italy.
September 9.	Allied landings at Salerno.
September 10.	German occupation of Rome.
September 11.	Beginning of Jewish family transports from Theresienstadt to Auschwitz.
September 13.	Rescue of Mussolini by Otto Skorzeny.
October 1.	Naples entered by the Allies.
October 13.	Italian declaration of war on Germany.
October 18.	First deportation of Jews from Rome to Auschwitz.
October 19–30.	Moscow Conference of Foreign Ministers (Hull, Anthony Eden, Vyacheslav M. Molotov).
November 6.	Kiev recaptured by the Russians.
November 9.	Establishment of the United Nations Relief and Rehabilitation Administration (UNRRA).
November 22–26	First session of Cairo (Sextant) Conference.
November 27.	Auschwitz crematorium blown up.
November 28 December 1.	Meeting of Roosevelt, Churchill, and Stalin at Teheran.
December 3–7.	Second session of Cairo Conference.
December 24.	General Eisenhower made supreme commander of the Allied invasion forces.
December 26.	German battleship *Scharnhorst* sunk off North Cape.
December 26.	Failure of attempt on Hitler's life by Lieut. Col. Claus Schenk Graf von Stauffenberg.

1944

January 3.	Soviet troops reach former Polish border.
January 16.	General Eisenhower assumes his new command in England.
January 19.	Twenty-nine-month siege of Leningrad lifted.
January 22.	Allied landings at Anzio, behind the German lines.
February 15.	Destruction of Monte Cassino by American bombers.
March 20.	Hungarian frontier crossed by German troops.
April 5.	Gen. Charles de Gaulle made head of the French Committee of National Liberation.
April 14.	First transport of Jews from Athens to Auschwitz.
April 22.	Invasion of Romania by Soviet forces.
May 11.	Beginning of an Allied offensive against the Gustav Line in Italy.
May 23.	Allies move out from the Anzio beachhead.

May 25. Germans yield entire coast from Terracina to Anzio.
June 4. Occupation of Rome by the United States Fifth Army.
June 6. D Day: Allied landings in Normandy.
June 12. First V-1 flying bombs exploded on England.
June 14. Return of De Gaulle to France.
July 3. Minsk recaptured by the Russians.
July 4–6. Wholesale arrests of former Communists and members of the Social Democratic party by the Gestapo.
July 9. Request by Rommel to withdraw his troops from Normandy refused. Rommel agrees to support the plot against Hitler.
July 11. Penetration of Lithuania and Latvia by Soviet forces.
July 16. Gen. Ludwig Beck and Von Stauffenberg have a final meeting in Berlin before the planned coup against Hitler.
July 18. German lines at Caen broken by the British Second Army.
July 20. July Plot: An unsuccessful attempt to assassinate Hitler at his Rastenburg headquarters.
July 24. Nazi salute substituted for the military salute in the German Army.
July 25–27. American breakthrough in France west of Saint-Lô.
August 1. Beginning of the Polish underground revolt in Warsaw.
August 4. Court of honor set up to dismiss convicted conspirators from the German Army.
August 7–8. Trial of conspirators before the People's Court.
August 8. Field Marshal Erwin von Witzleben and seven others hanged.
August 15. Allied invasion of the south coast of France.
August 21. United States forces reach the Seine north and south of Paris.
August 21–October 9. Dumbarton Oaks Conference on the formation of the United Nations.
August 23. Coup d'état in Romania. Surrender of Romania to Soviet forces.
August 25. De Gaulle enters Paris.
September 3. Liberation of Brussels by the British Second Army under Gen. Sir Miles Dempsey.
September 4. Armistice between Finland and the Soviet Union.
September 5. Soviet declaration of war on Bulgaria.
September 8. First V-2 bomb on England.
September 9. Armistice between Bulgaria and the Allies.
September 12. Invasion of Germany from the west.

September 17. Allied airborne landings at Arnhem. Operation is repelled by the Germans by September 26.

October 14. Suicide of Rommel.

October 20. Fall of Belgrade to the Russians.

November 16. All-out Allied offensive in the west (Operation Queen).

November 26. Order of Himmler for the destruction of the crematoria at Auschwitz.

December 4. Opening battle for the Saar Basin.

December 16. Counteroffensive under Field Marshal Gerd von Rundstedt through the Ardennes. The so-called Battle of the Bulge ends in January 1945, when the Germans are driven back to previous lines.

1945

January 14. Invasion of East Prussia by Soviet troops.

January 17. Liberation of Warsaw by the Russians.

January 17. Approximately 80,000 Jews freed by the Russians at Budapest.

January 20. Signing of an armistice by provisional government of Hungary.

January 27. Liberation of Memel, Lithuania.

February 4–11. Allied conference at Yalta.

February 13. Fall of Budapest to the Russians.

February 23. German Roer Line protecting Cologne breached by the Americans.

March 3. Declaration of war by Finland on Germany, predated as of September 15, 1944.

March 7. Fall of Cologne.

March 7. Crossing of the Rhine at Remagen by the Americans.

March 16. Allied attack on the Saar Basin.

March 23. British-American crossing of the Rhine in the north for a drive on the Ruhr.

April 10. More than 15,000 Jews freed at Buchenwald.

April 11. Essen captured by the Allies.

April 12. Death of President Roosevelt. The Presidency is assumed by Vice President Harry S. Truman.

April 13. Occupation of Vienna by the Russians.

April 15. Approximately 40,000 prisoners freed at Belsen by the British.

April 16. Russians on final push to Berlin.

April 23. Outskirts of Berlin reached by the Russians.

April 25. Refusal of Himmler's offer to arrange German surrender to the Allies.

April 25. Opening of the United Nations parley at San Francisco.

April 25. Meeting of American and Russian troops at Torgau, on the Elbe River south of Berlin.

April 28. Mussolini executed by Italian partisans near Lake Como.

April 30. Hitler a suicide in his Berlin bunker.

April 30. Approximately 33,000 inmates freed from concentration camps by the Americans.

May 2. Unconditional surrender of the German armies in Italy.

May 2. Adm. Karl Doenitz continues the Reich government at Flensburg-Mürwick, Schleswig-Holstein.

May 2. Capitulation of Berlin.

May 2. Concentration camp at Theresienstadt taken over by the Red Cross.

May 5. Surrender of German armies in the Netherlands, Denmark, and north Germany.

May 6. Occupation of Plzeň, Czechoslovakia, by the United States Third Army.

May 7. Unconditional surrender signed by Gen. Alfred Jodl at Reims.

May 8. V-E Day.

May 9. Field Marshal Keitel and Marshal Georgi K. Zhukov sign the German unconditional surrender documents in Berlin.

June 26. United Nations Charter signed by representatives of fifty nations in San Francisco.

July 17–August 2. Potsdam Conference.

November 20. Opening of the Nuremberg International Military Tribunal.

December 16–26. Meeting of Big Three Foreign Ministers in Moscow.

1946

January 10. Opening of the first session of the General Assembly of the United Nations in London.

January 17. Opening of the first session of the United Nations Security Council in London.

October 16. Executions of Nazi war criminals at Nuremberg.

A

A-MEN to AZIOLE

A-MEN. *See* AGENTEN.

AA. *See* AGRARPOLITISCHER APPARAT.

AB AKTION (Ausserordentliche Befriedungsaktion; Extraordinary Pacification Action). Code name for the liquidation of Polish intellectuals and leaders after the German invasion of Poland in 1939. The task was entrusted to Hans Frank as Governor-General and to his deputy, Artur Seyss-Inquart (qq.v.). More than 2,000 Polish men and women were apprehended from September 1939 to June 1940 and summarily executed. A ruthless killer, Frank kept thorough records of his work in a forty-two-volume journal. Many Jews were among the victims.

ABETZ, OTTO (1903–1958). German diplomat. Otto Abetz was born in Schwetzingen on May 26, 1903. From July 8, 1940 (after the fall of France), to 1944 he was German Ambassador to France. In July 1949 he was sentenced to twenty years' imprisonment as a war criminal. He was released from a French prison in April 1958.

ABSCHNITT (Section). A regional subdivision of the SS (q.v.) territorial organization. It was subordinate to the *Oberabschnitt* (q.v.), or higher section. The term *Abschnitt* was also used to denote a regional section of the SD (q.v.), the security service.

ABWEHR (Abw; Counterintelligence). Popular designation for the Amt/Ausland Abwehr, the foreign and counterintelligence department of the High Command of the armed forces. The Abwehr was headed by Adm. Wilhelm Canaris (q.v.), who was arrested as a spy in 1944 and hanged in 1945. After Canaris's arrest the Abwehr was in disgrace with the Fuehrer.

ABWEHR POLIZEI (Counterespionage Police). A police force detailed for special frontier service. It was controlled by the Gestapo (q.v.).

ACHSE (Axis). Code name for one of four military operations ordered by Hitler on July 31, 1943, to meet the expected invasion of Allied forces on the mainland of Italy (*see also* EICHE; SCHWARZ; STUDENT). Operation Achse called for the capture or destruction of the Italian Fleet. An earlier version, Alarich (q.v.), was superseded on September 9, 1943, one day after the announcement of Italy's surrender to the Allies. Operation Schwarz (military occupation of all Italy) and Operation Achse were combined into one undertaking.

ACTION CIRCLE. *See* TATKREIS.

ADAM, WILHELM (1877–1949). Chief of the *Truppenamt* (adjutant general). Wilhelm Adam was born in Anspach, Bavaria, on September 15, 1877. He served in World War I as an officer in the Bavarian Army. After the war he became a major in the Reichswehr (q.v.) and was promoted to lieutenant colonel in 1922 and colonel in 1927. A blunt and able officer, Adam acquired a reputation as the German "father of mountain troops" and as a highly efficient General Staff officer. In 1930 he was promoted to major general, and later that year Gen. Kurt Freiherr von

Gen. Wilhelm Adam. [*Picture Collection, The Branch Libraries, The New York Public Library*]

Hammerstein-Equord (q.v.) designated Adam his successor as *Chef des Truppenamtes* Adam was promoted to lieutenant general on December 1, 1931. In 1933 he was given command of Wehrkreis (Defense District) VII in Munich. In 1935, although nearing retirement, he was assigned to command of the new Wehrmachtakademie (Armed Forces Academy) in Berlin, whose purpose was to train officers of the various armed forces in interservice strategy and combined operations. He managed to survive the Blomberg-Fritsch crisis (q.v.) in early 1938 and was ordered to command an army group in Kassel.

Adam's relations with Hitler were cool, not only because of his own close association with Gen. Kurt von Schleicher (q.v.) but also because of his open criticism of the Fuehrer's plans. On June 26, 1938, Adam was summoned to Berghof (q.v.) to give Hitler a personal report on progress in building the West Wall (q.v.). In typically tactless fashion, he said that the wall was "not much yet," a judgment that angered the Fuehrer. On August 27, 1938, while on an inspection tour of the West Wall, Hitler approached Adam, who warned the Fuehrer again that he could not hold the wall with the troops at his disposal. Hitler went into a rage: "The man who could not hold these fortifications is a *Hundsfott* [lowly cur]!" Despite this scene, Adam was left in command of the west front for the time being. He was removed on November 27, 1938, even though he was the seventh ranking officer of the Army. He died in Garmisch on April 8, 1949.

ADENAUER, KONRAD (1876–1967). Politician and statesman who presided over the recovery of West Germany after the fall of the Third Reich. Konrad Adenauer was born in Cologne on January 5, 1876, to a Catholic family. After studying law and political economy, he entered the municipal administration of his birthplace in 1906. In 1909 he became deputy mayor of Cologne, and from 1917 to 1933 he served as lord mayor. He was an unsuccessful candidate for the chancellorship in 1926. In 1933 he was dismissed from his post in Cologne on the ground of his uncompromising hostility to Hitler and the philosophy of National Socialism. Because of his continued opposition he was arrested twice by the Gestapo (q.v.), in 1934 and again in 1944. After his second arrest he was committed to Brauweiler Prison. There he was told by his warden: "Now please do not commit suicide. You would cause me no end of trouble. You are sixty-eight years old, and your life is over anyway." Adenauer was to serve as Chancellor for two years longer than Hitler held the office.

Konrad Adenauer. [*Wide World Photos*]

After the fall of the Third Reich, Adenauer was the cofounder of the Christian Democratic Union. He became its presiding officer in 1946. He was elected Chancellor of the German Federal Republic in 1949 and was returned to that office in 1953, 1957, and 1961. From 1951 to 1955 he served as his own Foreign Minister. A patriarchical, strong-willed man, he was immensely popular with the German public, which fondly called him *der Alte* (the Old Fellow).

Adenauer's leadership transformed West Germany from a hopeless, defeated nation into a respected member of the world community. As the first Federal Chancellor he bent his efforts to reducing the restrictions imposed on Germany by the Allies. He promoted domestic stability, strengthened ties with France, cooperated in the movement for European integration, and won the support and confidence of the Western powers. He concluded the Paris peace pacts and made an agreement with the Soviet Union in 1955. His most spectacular achievement was the economic miracle of industrial recovery and expansion. Revered as the political and economic architect of his country, he retired from the chancellorship in 1963 because of his advanced age. He had taken over the post at the age of seventy-three and had served for fourteen years. He died in his villa at Rhöndorf on April 19, 1967, at the age of ninety-one.

Bibliography. Edgar Alexander, *Adenauer and the New Germany*, tr. by Thomas E. Goldstein, Farrar, Straus & Cudahy, Inc., New York, 1957.

ADLER UND FALKE (Eagle and Falcon). Early Nazi youth organization. It was banned in Thuringia but was allowed to resume activities after Wilhelm Frick (q.v.) was made minister of the interior.

ADLERANGRIFFE (Eagle Attacks). Code name for the air offensive by the Luftwaffe (q.v.) against England planned by Hermann Goering (q.v.). The assault was launched in mid-August 1940 with the objective of driving the Royal Air Force from the skies and making way for the projected invasion of the British Isles (*see* SEELÖWE). Operation Adlerangriffe failed, and Britain was spared a German invasion.

ADLERTAG (Eagle Day). Cover name for the opening day of Operation Adlerangriffe (q.v.), the projected air offensive against England.

ADOLF HITLER FUND. *See* ADOLF HITLER–SPENDE.

ADOLF HITLER–SCHULE (Adolf Hitler Schools). The first of three types of schools established by Hitler for the purpose of training a Nazi elite (for the other two types, *see* NATIONALPOLITISCHE ERZIEHUNGSANSTALTEN, the *Napolas*, or National Political Training Institutes; and ORDENSBURGEN, the Order Castles). Pupils for the Adolf Hitler Schools were preselected from the Hitler Jugend (q.v.), the Hitler Youth. During their second year in the Jungvolk, the junior branch of the Hitler Youth, potential candidates for the Adolf Hitler Schools were examined for their racial background and then sent to a youth camp for two weeks for the final selection. A main criterion of selection was physical appearance: the blond, blue-eyed youth had a better chance to be chosen. The training was military. Pupils were divided into squads. Teachers watched their charges at every stage of training, including bedmaking, deportment, and personal hygiene. Squads competed with one another and were judged collectively instead of by individual examination. There were five periods of physical training each week and one and one-half periods of study, especially of newspapers. Students were graduated at the age of eighteen and were considered qualified for entrance to a university. Many graduates of the Adolf Hitler Schools sought to obtain entrance to the *Ordensburgen* as the summit of training for the future Nazi elite.

ADOLF HITLER–SPENDE (Adolf Hitler Fund). A fund collected and administered by Martin Bormann (q.v.), who was in charge of Hitler's finances. Businessmen who profited from their association with the National Socialist party were expected to contribute "voluntarily" and liberally for the Fuehrer's favorite projects. Other party members hoped to establish similar funds for themselves, but Bormann discouraged them by obtaining from Hitler a monopoly for his special fund. Bormann made it a point to satisfy other leaders in the hierarchy by granting them certain rights for the fund. His administration of the Adolf Hitler Fund gave Bormann a strong power status in the Nazi hierarchy.

ADOLF LEGALITÉ (Adolf the Legal One). Popular term used to describe Hitler because of his repeatedly expressed desire to obtain political power only through "legal means." Hitler himself had only contempt for the current legal system (*see* JUSTICE IN THE THIRD REICH), but he was careful to maintain a public image as a strong proponent of law and order. The term *Adolf Legalité* was regarded as a tribute to the Fuehrer's sincerity.

AFRIKA KORPS. German elite motorized force that performed brilliantly in Hitler's North African campaigns from 1941 to 1943. Under the command of Erwin Rommel (q.v.), the Desert Fox, the Afrika Korps arrived in Tripoli in February 1941, quickly retrieved sagging Axis fortunes, and caused dismay in Allied headquarters until its ultimate liquidation in Tunisia two and a quarter years later, in May 1943. The performance of the Afrika Korps under difficult circumstances was phenomenal. It is generally agreed among historians that had Rommel been given the three extra divisions of tanks for which he asked Hitler and the OKW (Oberkommando der Wehrmacht, q.v.) in 1941, he would have reached Cairo and the Suez Canal by the beginning of 1942 and could then have cut the flow of American supplies going to the Soviet Union

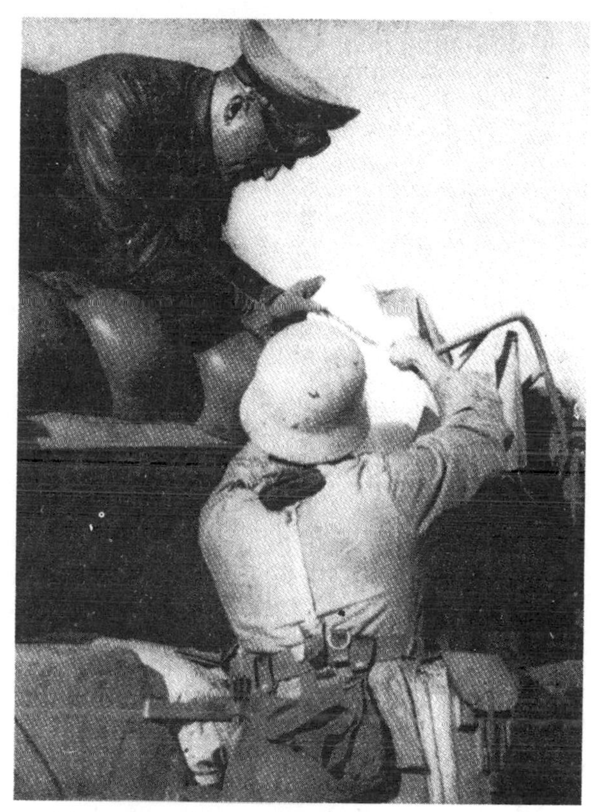

Field Marshal Erwin Rommel consulting a map during the Tunisian campaign. [*US Army*]

via the Persian Gulf route. The Allies were saved from disaster by Hitler's preoccupation with his main offensive against the U.S.S.R. and by his failure to take the African campaign seriously.

In early February 1941 Marshal Rodolfo Graziano's large Italian army in Cyrenaica was cut off and captured at Bedafomm by British mechanized forces. The Italian troops who remained in Tripolitania were so badly shaken by the disaster that they were in no condition to defend Mussolini's remaining foothold in North Africa. In this emergency Hitler decided to send Rommel to North Africa. As a junior officer in World War I, Rommel had helped smash the Italians at Caporetto in 1917. In 1939, at the outbreak of World War II, Rommel commanded Hitler's personal escort in Poland. In France in 1940 he led the 7th Panzer (Armored) Division and played a leading role in the destruction of the Anglo-French armies. He went to North Africa in the firm belief that defensive measures were not indicated and that the way to victory was through constant movement forward.

Rommel arrived in North Africa on February 12, 1941, with only modest elements of the Afrika Korps. He had only two advanced units, which he hurried to the front to conceal his weakness and to discourage the British from throwing the Italians out of Africa. It was not until mid-March that the *Panzer* regiment of his leading division of the Afrika Korps arrived at Tripoli. By the end of March the whole of the 5th Light (later, 21st Panzer) Division had not yet arrived. The second of Rommel's two divisions, the 15th Panzer, was not due until May. Despite this lack of strength, Rommel on April 3, 1941, ordered his one, as yet uncompleted, division into a probing counteroffensive against the British. He was even more successful than he had hoped. Within a fortnight he altered the balance in favor of the Axis. The Afrika Korps took Bardia in a few days and then stormed on to Tobruk. Gen. Archibald Wavell quickly retired to his Egyptian bases, leaving at Tobruk a strong garrison of Australians who had to withstand a ferocious siege. The Rats of Tobruk, in a remarkable display of raw courage, held out for eight months until relieved. The Afrika Korps was unable to take Tobruk, but it had drastically changed the balance of war in North Africa.

In May and again in June the British launched renewed offensives against the Germans, but each time Rommel and his Afrika Korps managed to repel them while still maintaining pressure on Tobruk. By this time Prime Minister Winston Churchill was gravely concerned by the performance of Rommel and the Afrika Korps. In November 1941 he replaced Wavell by Gen. Sir Claude Auchinleck as commander in chief of British forces in the Middle East. In December 1941 Auchinleck, now heading the British Eighth Army, launched a well-planned offensive against Rommel's lines and drove the Afrika Korps all the way back to El Agheila, liberating Tobruk in the process. The British forces outnumbered the Afrika Korps by 4 to 1 and held a superiority of 2 to 1 in tanks (the British had a total of 756 gun-armed tanks plus a third as many in reserve, while the Germans had 174 tanks as well as 146 obsolescent tanks). At the height of the British attack Churchill paid a rare tribute in the House of Commons to Rommel: "We have a very daring and skillful opponent against us, and, may I say across the havoc of war, a great general."

In the struggle Rommel and the Afrika Korps were forced to withdraw from Cyrenaica to the border of Tripolitania, from which they had advanced. Rommel managed to escape the snares set for him and at the same time kept the bulk of his armor intact. In early 1942 the Afrika Korps was moving again. A German convoy in the Mediterranean brought up Rommel's depleted tank strength from 50 to 100 tanks, apparently enough to send the Afrika Korps surging forward. It retook the El Gazala line in February. By late spring it was moving again. In May Rommel began a great counterattack that finally took Tobruk and went on into Egypt, moving past Sidi Barrani and Mersa Matruh, until he reached El Alamein, only about 60 miles west of Alexandria. The Desert Fox accomplished this remarkable feat with only 280 gun-armed tanks and 230 obsolescent Italian tanks against nearly 1,000 British tanks. In addition, the British had more than 150 new American Grant tanks, with heavier armament than their own. In two weeks the fast-moving Germans pushed the British Eighth Army back to its last shelter before the Nile Delta. Only there could the surging Germans be halted.

Despite this triumphant procession the Afrika Korps was exhausted by its efforts. During the advance its stocks of fuel had been seriously depleted. Replenishment was difficult. British planes and ships based at Malta struck savagely at German supply lines. Troops of the Afrika Korps were weakened by combat fatigue. Worst of all was the lack of reinforcements from home. Throughout its year of victories the Afrika Korps had comprised only its two small original divisions, consisting of two tank and three infantry battalions, added to an improvised light division made up of several infantry and artillery units. Hitler sent in another infantry division by air after the Afrika Korps was halted at El Alamein, but it was too late.

In August 1942, on the occasion of his first conference with Joseph Stalin in Moscow, Churchill stopped off in Cairo to appraise the situation in North Africa and the Middle East. He took advantage of his visit to reorganize the British command in the face of the crisis engendered by Rommel and his Afrika Korps. He named Gen. Sir Harold Alexander as the new commander in chief of the British Middle East forces. The new command of the Eighth Army was a problem. Lieut. Gen. W. H. E. (Strafer) Gott, who had been slated for the post, had been killed in a plane crash. After some thought Churchill chose Lieut. Gen. Bernard Law Montgomery. It was a momentous decision. Montgomery turned out to be the nemesis of the Afrika Korps.

Montgomery gathered every ounce of available strength and awaited the propitious moment for a death thrust. The British Eighth Army now had a superiority of 6 to 1 in both tanks and aircraft. In the moonlight of October 23, 1942, the British opened a massive artillery barrage on the Afrika Korps. Four hours later came the assault that finally turned the scales (*see* EL ALAMEIN). The Afrika Korps was thrown into a retreat that did not stop until the last Germans laid down their arms in Tunis six months later. In this extraordinary 2,000-mile retreat the outnumbered Afrika Korps was never cut off by the British. Hitler bombarded his troops with pleas to stand and die in their places.

Meanwhile, a great Allied fleet bore down on the Moroccan and Algerian coasts and on November 8, 1942, landed Allied troops at Casablanca, Oran, and Algiers. The Afrika Korps was finally caught in a trap, and any further recovery was impossible. North Africa was won to the Allied cause. At long last Hitler made frantic attempts to hold on by pouring reinforcements into Tunis and Bizerte, but they were too late. Rommel managed to mount an offensive against the Americans at Kasserine Pass and inflicted heavy casualties on them. The Americans recovered quickly, and in March and April, helped by the British Eighth Army, drove the Afrika Korps to the tip of Cape Bon Peninsula. Here a quarter of a million German troops finally surrendered in May 1943.

The relatively small Afrika Korps was beaten, but it had left its mark. It had drawn into the North African theater the equivalent of more than twenty divisions of British strength, half of Britain's operational power.

Bibliography. K. J. Macksey, *Afrika Korps,* Pan/Ballantine, London, 1972.

AGENTEN (Agents; A-Men). The fieldmen of the SD (q.v.), the security service.

AGRARPOLITISCHER APPARAT (aA; Office for Agriculture). Group of Nazi party officials responsible for agricultural matters.

AGRICULTURAL AUXILIARY SERVICE. Class of schoolchildren over fourteen years of age who went to the countryside as a group to help with the harvest during the holidays as well as in termtime.

AHNENERBE FORSCHUNGS- UND LEHRGEMEINSCHAFT (Society for Research and Teaching of Ancestral Heritage). An organization devoted to the study and spread of racial doctrine (q.v.). Its purpose was to investigate early German history in order to prove the value of pure Aryan blood. It was administered by the personal staff of Heinrich Himmler (q.v.), *SS-Reichsleiter* (SS Reich leader), the highest-ranking Nazi party official.

AHNENPASS (Ancestry Passport). An identification card supposed to be carried by every German during the National Socialist regime. The purpose was to demonstrate Aryan heritage and to identify those contaminated by Jewish blood. A lucrative business in the buying and selling of false identification cards took place.

AHNENSCHEIN (Genealogical Chart). A paper used by individuals to prove their correct Aryan descent.

AÏDA. Code name for an operation approved by Hitler in March 1942 for the offensive by Gen. Erwin Rommel (q.v.) eastward across North Africa to the Nile. The operation was not successful (*see* AFRIKA KORPS).

AIR CIRCUITS. *See* LUFTKREISE.

AIR FORCE. *See* LUFTFLOTTE; LUFTWAFFE.

AIR TRAVEL MINISTRY. *See* REICHSLUFTFAHRTMINISTERIUM.

ALARICH. Code name for the occupation of Italy in the summer of 1943. On July 25, 1943, King Victor Emmanuel III announced that he had "accepted the resignation from office of the Head of Government, Prime Minister and State Secretary tendered by Benito Mussolini" and had appointed Gen. Pietro Badoglio to the vacated office to carry on the war. For a time the Badoglio government made a pretense of maintaining Italy's alliance with Germany, but actually Badoglio was attempting to make peace with the Allies through agents in Lisbon. Meanwhile, Hitler made plans to meet the emergency. A series of actions for the occupation of Italy would be implemented immediately on release of the code word Alarich (later changed to Achse, or Axis). German troops would seize Italian positions in France, the Balkans, and Italy, and the Italian Fleet would be captured. *See also* ACHSE.

ALARMISTS AND CRITICS. *See* MIESSMACHER UND KRITIKASTER.

ALFARTH, FELIX (1901–1923). One of the first Nazi martyrs. Felix Alfarth was born in Leipzig on July 5, 1901. After completing his early schooling in 1917, he studied merchandising at the Siemens-Schuchert Works and in 1923 moved to Munich to begin his career as a merchant. An early and enthusiastic follower of Hitler, he took part in the march on the Feldherrn Halle (q.v.) on November 9, 1923 (*see* BEER-HALL PUTSCH), and was shot during the battle with the police. Alfarth became a folk hero in the Nazi lexicon. At the moment of his death, it was said, he was singing "Deutschland über Alles" ("Germany above All"). Alfarth headed the list alphabetically of the sixteen Nazis killed in the unsuccessful *Putsch*. The names were given a place of honor on an introductory page to Hitler's *Mein Kampf* (q.v.).

ALLGEMEINE-SS (General SS). The overall body of the SS (q.v.), composed of full-time, part-time, active, and inactive, or honorary, members. Many members of the Waffen-SS (q.v.) came from the ranks of the Allgemeine-SS, but the two were regarded as distinct organizations.

ALLGEMEINES WEHRMACHTSAMT (AWA; Armed Forces General Office). Special office in the Oberkommando der Wehrmacht (q.v.). It was concerned primarily with personnel, training, and equipment.

ALLKETT. The most important factory in Berlin for the production of tanks (*see* PANZER). Most of the main workshops were destroyed in an Allied air raid on November 26, 1943. Disturbed by this attack, Hitler issued a direct order to fire departments as far away as Potsdam and Brandenburg to move to Allkett and save as much as possible of the key factory.

ALPENFESTUNG (Alpine Redoubt). The area on the Obersalzberg to which Hitler originally intended to retreat and lead the final struggle against the Allies in World War II. On the order of Heinrich Himmler (q.v.), administration of the operation was entrusted to Ernst Kaltenbrunner (q.v.). Hitler later changed his mind and retreated to his specially built bunker in Berlin for his last days (*see* FUEHRERBUNKER).

ALPENVEILCHEN (Alpine Violet). Code name for German intervention in Albania. In a war council held on January 11, 1941, Hitler directed that German reinforcements be sent to Albania under Operation Alpenveilchen to help the Italians, who were bogged down there. He was anxious to avoid the danger of a collapse on the Albanian front.

ALPINE REDOUBT. *See* ALPENFESTUNG.

ALTE KÄMPFER (Old Guard). Literally "old fighters," the *Alte Kämpfer* were those early members of the Nationalsozialistische Deutsche Arbeiterpartei (q.v.) who were especially honored for their role in the rise of the National Socialist movement. Hitler often praised them for their services. He gave them preference for jobs in the bureaucracy and granted them civil service status. For example, in 1938 thirty-six *Alte Kämpfer* worked as technicians at opera houses in Berlin and Wiesbaden. Those who had been injured in street fights against Communists received the same benefits as the ones allowed to disabled war veterans.

The *Alte Kämpfer*. [*The Bettman Archive*]

ALTMARK. German auxiliary supply ship sunk by the British in Norwegian territorial waters. Some 300 British seamen captured by the *Graf Spee* (q.v.), for which the *Altmark* acted as supply ship, were being taken to Germany as prisoners of war on the *Altmark*. On February 14, 1940, the *Altmark* was observed by a British scouting plane as she proceeded southward in Norwegian territorial waters in the direction of Germany. The *Altmark* took refuge in Jøssing Fjord. Prime Minister Winston Churchill, apprised of the news, ordered an attack on the *Altmark*. On the night of February 16–17, a British destroyer, the *Cossack*, entered the fjord and sent a boarding party to the German ship. The assault party killed 4 Germans, wounded 5, and liberated 299 of their comrades. The Norwegian government protested this violation of its territorial waters, to which the British replied that Norway itself had violated international law by allowing its waters to be used by Germans to transport British prisoners to Germany. Hitler attacked Norway on April 9, 1940.

ALTONA. The cancellation code word for Operation Barbarossa (q.v.). *See also* DORTMUND.

AMANN, MAX (1891–1957). Hitler's sergeant during World War I and presiding officer of the Reich Press Chamber after the Nazis came to power. Max Amann was born in Munich on November 24, 1891, to a Catholic family. He attended public and business schools in his birthplace. He served throughout World War I in a Bavarian infantry regiment, was Hitler's company sergeant, and was awarded the Iron Cross (Second Class). Amann became one of Hitler's earliest followers. In 1921 he was made the first business manager of the Nationalsozialistische Deutsche Arbeiterpartei (q.v.) and after 1922 the director of the Eher Verlag (q.v.), the official Nazi publishing house. When Hitler, while in Landsberg Prison, wrote his blueprint for the future, he gave it the awkward title *Four and a Half Years of Struggle against Lies, Stupidity, and Cowardice*. Amann, as his publisher, changed the title to *My Struggle* (*Mein Kampf*, q.v.). Amann saw the book through scores of editions. Along with Heinrich Hoffmann (q.v.), Amann was responsible for Hitler's great wealth. Amann was the publisher of the daily *Völkischer Beobachter*, the weekly *Illustrierter Beobachter*, and the *Nationalsozialistische Monatshefte* (qq.v.). He saw to it that Hitler obtained huge fees for his contributions to the publications. Amann, too, enriched himself enormously in his service to the Nazi party. In November 1933 Hitler made Amann *Reichsleiter* (Reich leader) of the entire National Socialist press as well as head of the Reich Press Chamber. Amann died in Munich on March 30, 1957.

AMNESTY DECREE, 1934. A general amnesty order issued on August 7, 1934, under which certain prisoners in custody, especially members of the SA (q.v.), were released from prison. Five days earlier President Paul von Hindenburg (q.v.) had died, and Hitler had assumed the office of Reich President. The Fuehrer's purpose was to lessen anxiety among civil servants who had been frightened by the June 30, 1934, Blood Purge (q.v.).

AMNESTY DECREE, 1939. A secret amnesty decreed by Hitler on October 4, 1939, in favor of armed formations of the SS (q.v.). After the invasion of Poland, Hitler allowed his *SS-Einsatzgruppen* (task forces) to seize and liquidate Jewish organizations. Senior officers of the armed forces, outraged by the atrocities and degradations, intervened, in some cases with much severity. Hitler's secret decree was designed to put an end to Army interference in the actions of armed formations of the SS.

AMT/AUSLAND ABWEHR (Office of Foreign Intelligence). Branch of the Oberkommando der Wehrmacht (q.v.) responsible for foreign intelligence. The Chief of Amt/Ausland Abwehr from 1938 to 1944 was Adm. Wilhelm Canaris (q.v.), who was involved indirectly in the 1944 July Plot (q.v.) against Hitler. In 1938 and 1939 this office was known as Amtsgruppe Auslandsnachtrichten und Abwehr (Group Office for Foreign Information and Intelligence). *See also* ABWEHR.

AMTSGRUPPE ALLGEMEINE WEHRMACHTSANGELEGENHEITEN (Office for General Military Affairs). Branch of the Oberkommando der Wehrmacht (q.v.) responsible for general military matters. In 1938 and 1939 this office was called the Wehrwirtschaftsstab (Military Economics Staff).

ANCESTRY PASSPORT. *See* AHNENPASS.

ANGRIFF, DER (The Assault). Nazi newspaper founded by Dr. Paul Joseph Goebbels (q.v.). In 1927 there was scarcely any need for another party newspaper, for the principal organ of the Nazi movement, the *Völkischer Beobachter* (q.v.), was published daily in Munich and reached Berlin within twelve hours. But Goebbels insisted upon having his own newspaper in which he could write as he pleased. He regarded the name, *Der Angriff*, as effective propaganda and as "covering everything for which we aim." The subtitle was *For the Oppressed against the Oppressors.* Goebbels reserved the right-hand column of the front page for a short, sensational article always signed "Dr. G." The paper published anything to attract the attention of the public. There were many unsuccessful libel actions against *Der Angriff.* Goebbels's men often used strong-arm tactics in fighting news dealers on the streets. *Der Angriff* never attained the huge circulation of the party's official organ. It was more of a polemical pamphlet than a newspaper and served mostly as a vehicle for Goebbels's grievances.

ANGSTBROSCHE (Brooch of Fear). Derisory epithet applied by dissidents to the Nazi party badge.

ANSCHLUSS (Union). Movement for the political union of Germany and Austria. When the Austro-Hungarian Empire was forcibly dissolved by the Treaty of Saint-Germain-en-Laye (September 10, 1919), most of its German-speaking people supported the idea of eventual union with Germany. This was explicitly forbidden by the Treaty of Versailles, which at the same time denied the Bohemian (Sudeten) Germans the right to national self-determination. *Anschluss* became a burning issue during the 1920s as agitation continued for union. In March 1931 both the German and the Austrian governments proposed a customs union. Austria, weakened by the collapse of the Kreditanstalt (Loan Bank) and by politi-

German troops marching into Austria in March 1938. [*Imperial War Museum, London*]

cal anarchy, was especially anxious to implement this first step toward *Anschluss.* Both France and the Little Entente (Czechoslovakia, Yugoslavia, and Romania) denounced the proposed customs union. The plan was submitted to the International Court of Justice at The Hague, which by a vote of eight to seven decided that the suggested customs union was illegal. The drive for *Anschluss* was revived in 1933 as soon as Hitler acceded to power. Born in Austria, the Fuehrer regarded the union of Germany and Austria as a keystone of his foreign policy.

On July 25, 1934, Chancellor Engelbert Dollfuss (q.v.) of Austria was murdered in the Chancellery in Vienna by Austrian Nazis anxious to stage a coup d'état. Hitler backed the illegal Austrian Nazi party even though in 1936 he recognized the independence of Austria by treaty. Two years later he tore up his agreement. He invited Chancellor Kurt von Schuschnigg (q.v.) to Berchtesgaden in February 1938 and demanded concessions for the Austrian Nazis. Schuschnigg, aware that he could not count on the support of either Great Britain or France, was forced to yield. In a desperate attempt to forestall the inevitable, the Austrian Chancellor scheduled an immediate plebiscite on the question of Austrian independence. Hitler countered by sending German troops to the border. In an ultimatum on March 11, 1938, Hitler demanded Schuschnigg's resignation in favor of Artur Seyss-Inquart (q.v.), leader of the Austrian Nazis. Neither Schuschnigg's resignation nor cancellation of the proposed plebiscite satisfied the Fuehrer. Hermann Goering (q.v.) ordered Seyss-Inquart to send a telegram to Germany requesting invasion "to restore order." *Anschluss,* Hitler proclaimed, was at long last achieved.

Bibliography. Jürgen Gehl, *Austria, Germany, and the Anschluss, 1931–1938,* Oxford University Press, London, 1963.

ANSCHLUSS BALLOT. A plebiscite on the "reunion" of Austria and Germany. It was held on April 10, 1938. Voters were told to answer this question: "Do you agree to the reunion of Austria with the German Reich carried out on March 13 and do you vote for the [Reichstag] list of our Leader, Adolf Hitler?" The *Anschluss* was accepted by an affirmative vote of 99.07 percent in a total vote of 99.59 percent of the qualified electorate of Germany.

ANTI-JEWISH WORLD LEAGUE. An anti-Semitic organization with headquarters in Germany. Its members were united by hatred of Judaism and contempt for all Jews. In 1935 Julius Streicher (q.v.), editor of *Der Stürmer* and vociferous critic of the Jews, told a mass meeting of the Anti-Jewish World League that the Jews were preparing for the greatest ritual murder of all time—a new war. He called the Jews the eternal racial enemy of the Germans and accused them of representing both evil capitalism and evil Marxism. They were responsible, he said, for inflation, depression, and unemployment. He claimed that 90 percent of all prostitutes in Germany were brought to their profession by Jews, and he denounced the influx of Jews from the east. Members of the league were in agreement on these and additional accusations against the Jews living in the Third Reich.

ANTI-SEMIT (Anti-Semitic). A roll-your-own tobacco introduced by the growing Nazi movement in 1920. The trademark was designed to promote Nazi propaganda during the struggle for political power.

ANTI-SEMITISM. Name first applied to a movement of opposition to Jews in the second half of the nineteenth century. Anti-Semitism had been prevalent, however, throughout Europe in the Middle Ages and varied in intensity in different countries. The modern movement originated in Russia and Central Europe, which had large Jewish minorities. Antipathy toward Jews in its recent form was not due completely to their religion but was based on economic factors of wealth and power. Toward the latter part of the nineteenth century, anti-Semitism assumed a virulent form in imperial Russia and Hungary, where there were riots and murders. The publication of the *Protocols of the Elders of Zion* (q.v.) in the early twentieth century stimulated pogroms (attacks on Jews). Anti-Semitic political parties rose in Austria and Germany, and efforts were made to restrict the political rights of Jews.

A revival of anti-Semitism swept through Germany as soon as Hitler assumed political power. Jews, no matter what their class or reputation, were reviled and deprived of their livelihood. Germans of part-Jewish origin were included in the persecutions. Nazi anti-Semitism took the form of a political movement after Hitler promoted it as a basic part of his personal philosophy. In conformity with the teachings of Arthur Comte de Gobineau and Houston Stewart Chamberlain (qq.v.), Hitler made anti-Semitism an official movement in the Third Reich (*see* NUREMBERG LAWS ON CITIZENSHIP AND RACE). Nazi anti-Semitism led to the slaughter of 6 million Jews in the concentration camps and extermination camps (qq.v.). *See also* ARIERPARAGRAPH; AUSCHWITZ; BELSEN; DACHAU; HOLOCAUST; MAIDANEK; MEIN KAMPF; RACIAL DOCTRINE.

ANTON. Revised code name for the occupation of Unoccupied France (previously known under the code name Attila, q.v.) and the Iberian Peninsula (formerly known as Isabella, q.v.). Anton was specified by Hitler in a war directive dated May 29, 1942. On the defeat of France in 1940 the Pétain government agreed to German occupation of more than half of the country, including Paris, the northern areas, and the entire Atlantic coast to the Spanish border. The French were required to bear the costs of occupation and to maintain a regime friendly to the Third Reich. Hitler's code name Anton was reserved for possible acquisition of the remainder of the country. On November 7–8, 1942, when American and British troops began landing in North Africa, Hitler notified Gen. Gerd von Rundstedt (q.v.) that Anton was in effect.

AO. *See* AUSLANDSORGANISATION.

APA. *See* AUSSENPOLITISCHES AMT.

APPEASEMENT. The policy adopted by Prime Minister Neville Chamberlain and Premier Édouard Daladier (qq.v.) by giving in to Hitler in the Munich crisis of September 1938 (*see* MUNICH AGREEMENT).

"ARBEIT MACHT FREI" ("Labor Liberates"). Adage emblazoned on the camp gates at Auschwitz (q.v.), one of the extermination camps (q.v.). The purpose was to indicate to both the public and the inmates that the camps were dedicated to the useful goal of labor in the service of the Third Reich.

ARBEITERTUM (Work). A publication of the Deutsche Arbeitsfront (q.v.), the German Labor Front.

ARBEITSAMT (Labor Office). The local labor office for members of the Nationalsozialistische Deutsche Arbeiterpartei (q.v.).

ARBEITSDIENST. *See* REICHSARBEITSDIENST.

ARBEITSDIENSTFUEHRER (Labor Service Leader). An official responsible for labor performance in concentration camps (q.v.). He was generally under the supervision of an *Arbeitseinsatzfuehrer* (q.v.), a labor supervisor.

ARBEITSEINSATZFUEHRER (Labor Supervisor). Supervisor of labor in concentration camps (q.v.) during World War II. He was senior to the *Arbeitsdienstfuehrer* (q.v.), a labor service leader.

ARBEITSERZIEHUNGSLAGER (Workers' Educational Camps). Special camps set up for prisoners released from concentration camps (q.v.). These inmates were regarded as needing additional training to fit them for reentering industry.

ARBEITSFRONT. *See* DEUTSCHE ARBEITSFRONT.

ARBEITSGEMEINSCHAFT (Labor Community). An army group working in Nazi schools.

ARBEITSGEMEINSCHAFTSLEITER (Labor Community Leader). Division leader in the University Student Bund.

ARBEITSMAIDEN (Labor Maids). Young females in the Reich Labor Service. By a decree of September 6, 1936, the strength was set at 25,000 *Arbeitsmaiden* for the period from April 1937 to March 1938.

ARCHITECTURE IN THE THIRD REICH. More than any other art form in the Nazi era, architecture reflected the personal likes and dislikes of Hitler. "How I wish I had become an architect," he often stated. In October 1907, when he was eighteen years old, he moved to Vienna hoping to become a great artist. He was crushed when he failed to pass the entrance examinations for the Academy of Fine Arts. He remained in Vienna for the next five years. Architecture was one of his early passions. He was much impressed by the neobaroque buildings on the Ringstrasse, which he sketched in a notebook along with warships and weapons. Above all he liked massive buildings such as the Vienna Opera House ("This is the most magnificent opera house in the world!"). Later, he was to be attracted by the Paris Opera House ("Its stairwell is the most beautiful in the world!") and the ornate Palace of Justice in Brussels. His taste in architecture was always drawn back to the inflated baroque preferred by Emperor William II during the Second Empire from 1888 to 1914. Hitler's interest did not lessen for the rest of his life.

In the days of his drive for political power, Hitler regarded Paul Ludwig Troost (q.v.) as his favorite architect. In 1930 he assigned Troost to rebuild the Barlow

Hitler's sketch of a triumphal arch. [*Used with the permission of Macmillan Publishing Co., Inc. from* INSIDE THE THIRD REICH *by Albert Speer. Copyright © 1970 by Macmillan Publishing Co., Inc. Copyright © 1969 by Verlag Ullstein Gmbh.*]

Palace in Munich for the new Nazi party headquarters (*see* BRAUNES HAUS). Hitler's passion for architecture continued after he became Chancellor in 1933. He was anxious to spell out through architecture the substance of the new political, military, and economic power of the Third Reich. The only monuments to the past, he said, were to be found in architecture. Only through this art form could the greatness of Greek and Roman times be visualized. He would himself demonstrate the glory of his own work for future generations and transmit to them the spirit of the Third Reich through its monumental buildings. "Why always the biggest? I do this to restore to each individual German his self-respect. In a hundred ways I want to say to the individual—'We are not inferior; on the contrary, we are the complete equal of every nation.'" His new German architecture would show a union between the Greek Doric and the Germanic form, in his mind an ideal artistic combination.

From the opening days of the Third Reich, Nazi architects were motivated by what was called the Fuehrer's style, a combination of Troost's neoclassicism and Hitler's neobaroque preference, multiplied and exaggerated. In the autumn of 1933 Hitler commissioned Troost to rebuild and completely refurnish the Chancellery residence in Berlin. The old building had been neglected; its ceilings and floors were moldy, its wallpaper ruined, and its halls filled with an unbearable odor. Each day the Fuehrer, full of enthusiasm and followed by his adjutant, went to the site to observe the progress being made and to make suggestions for improvement. "If there is anything new, let me see it." After this came a flurry of construction. The complex of party headquarters around the Königplatz in Munich was extended to house the remains of Nazi martyrs. The party buildings in Nuremberg were adorned with Nazi symbolism. Troost and other Nazi architects planned and built state and municipal edifices throughout the country. There were new administrative offices, social buildings for workers, and bridges across the main highways. One of the constructions, the Olympic Stadium in Berlin (*see* OLYMPIAD XI), won the admiration of the world in 1936. On the other hand, only Nazis were satisfied with the new public housing with its exaggerated folklore treatment favored by Hitler. To please the sentimental Fuehrer, Nazi architects built thatched-roof cottages with wooden balconies and handmade oak beams, as well as whitewashed Tyrolean peasant houses in wooded areas of Berlin. Nazi architects also favored a new type of civic center. Instead of a central cathedral square as in medieval times, they constructed a *Stadtkrone* (city crown), a central urban community in which buildings were placed around a geometrically designed center to which enormous avenues led. The area was decorated with sculptures and ornaments of Nazi mythology.

Meanwhile, non-Nazi architects continued to work in traditional forms, especially the simplified Bauhaus architecture favored during the era of the Weimar Republic (q.v.). Untouched and uninfluenced by Hitler's accent on the colossal, these architects experimented in industrial design and produced many buildings that won international approval.

The rebuilding of Berlin became one of Hitler's most absorbing interests. "Berlin must change its face in order to adapt to the new mission." Together with a new favorite architect, Albert Speer (q.v.), the Fuehrer decided that the new Berlin would tell the world about the political, economic, and military power of the new Germany. Under Hitler's close supervision, Speer worked to produce an entirely new metropolis. He had the best cabinetmakers construct extensive illuminated models on a scale of 1 to 50, which reproduced in every detail what he had planned. Nearly every day the Fuehrer went to the Academy of Fine Arts to inspect and modify the reconstruction work.

Speer's new Berlin had two huge north-south and east-west axes. Colossal railroad stations were to be built in the north and south. The main plaza was crowned by an Arch of Triumph, planned to rival Napoleon's Arc de Triomphe in Paris. Sighting through its 260-foot opening, the visitor would see at the end of the 3-mile vista the Great Hall with its enormous dome. The grand boulevards and avenues were lined with great public buildings, such as the headquarters of eleven ministries, a Town Hall 1,500 feet in length, the new Police Headquarters, the War Academy, and the High Command of the Army. In addition, there would be a large House of the Nations for meetings, a hotel of twenty-one stories, a new opera house, a new concert hall, three theaters, a cinema holding 2,000 people, mass and luxury restaurants, a variety theater, and even an indoor swimming pool built like the old Roman baths with courtyards and colonnades.

Construction of the new metropolis was hindered and finally halted by the outbreak of war in 1939. Speer later agreed that the whole project was "lifeless and regimented," and he criticized its "monumental rigidity." Also dropped were two more projects planned by Hitler as memorials to the greatness of the Third Reich. On the Atlantic coast, facing west, were to be several *Totenburgen* (q.v.; castles of the dead), monumental memorials to soldiers who had died in "liberating the Continent from British influences." The Fuehrer also wanted similar massive towers in the east to symbolize the conquest of the "chaotic forces of the east."

Bibliography. Albert Speer, *Inside the Third Reich*, tr. by Richard and Clara Winston, George Weidenfeld & Nicolson, Ltd., London, 1970.

ARIERPARAGRAPH (Aryan Clause). Clause that banned Jews from all cultural activities such as any part of the film industry. It was announced on June 30, 1933, but clear warning had been given as early as the preceding April. Because of this clause many Jews took the opportunity to leave Germany.

The Aryan clause, also called the Aryan paragraph, was important in the relations of National Socialism and the Protestant churches. According to this decision, any member of a Protestant church who could not prove his ancestry to be Aryan up to two or three generations back must be excluded from the church. These persons were known in the Third Reich as *Juden-Christen* (q.v., Jew-Christian). The German Faith movement (Deutsche Glaubensbewegung, q.v.) accepted the Aryan paragraph, but the Bekenntniskirche (q.v.), the newly organized Confessional Church, opposed it. The theologian Karl Barth (q.v.) stated: "A Protestant Church that would exclude the Jew-Christians or would regard them as second-class Christians would cease to be a Christian Church."

ARMAMENTS COUNCIL. A committee organized by Hitler in 1942 to administer the armaments program in World War II. Hitler was careful to select important businessmen and industrialists for the council. The fundamental agreement between the Nazi regime and big business is indicated by the membership:

NAME	AFFILIATION
Hermann Bücher	Krupp
Philip Kessler	Elektro and Siemens
Paul Pleiger	Hermann Goering-Werke
Ernst Poensgen	Vereinigte Stahlwerke
Quant	Personal friend of Dr. Goebbels
Hermann Röchling	Röchlingwerke
Helmuth Röhnert	Hermann Goering-Werke
Albert Vögler	Vereinigte Stahlwerke
Wilhelm Zange	Mannesmann Rohrenwerke

ARMED FORCES. *See* WEHRMACHT.

ARMED FORCES COMMANDER. *See* WEHRMACHTSBEFEHLSHABER.

ARMED FORCES GENERAL OFFICE. *See* ALLGEMEINES WEHRMACHTSAMT.

ARMED FORCES OPERATIONS OFFICE. *See* WEHRMACHTSFUEHRUNGSAMT.

ARMED FORCES OPERATIONS STAFF. *See* WEHRMACHTSFUEHRUNGSSTAB.

ARMED SS. *See* WAFFEN-SS.

ARNDT, WALTHER (1891–1944). Physician and scientist doomed to death by an unfortunate chance remark. Walther Arndt, born on January 8, 1891, studied natural science at the University of Breslau and in 1914 received his degree in medicine. Taken prisoner by the Russians in October 1914 while serving as a noncommissioned officer in a field hospital, he was repatriated two and one-half years later in an exchange of medical personnel. After the war he turned to science and became in turn a curator and a professor. He made many exploring expeditions abroad, for which he received recognition both in foreign countries and in Germany. In 1940 he was made an honorary member of the German Zoological Society. Deeply devoted to his scientific work, he had little interest in politics, but his life was endangered by a slip of the tongue. After an air raid in 1944, he was denounced by two colleagues for saying: "This is the end of the Third Reich, and the guilty can now be brought to punishment." For that he was arrested and sentenced to death by the People's Court (*see* VOLKSGERICHT). He was executed on June 26, 1944.

A painting by Hermann Otto Heyer, typical of the art favored in the Third Reich, shown at the Greater Germany Art Exhibition of 1937. [*Ullstein*]

ART IN THE THIRD REICH. German artists contributed to all major forms of art in the twentieth century, including impressionism, expressionism, cubism, and Dada. In the early 1920s many outstanding artists living in Germany won worldwide recognition for their work. These included a major exponent of the new realism (Die Neue Sachlichkeit), George Grosz (q.v.); the Swiss-born expressionist Paul Klee (q.v.); and the Russian expressionist Wassily Kandinsky. These three, among others, worked at the famous Bauhaus to produce a significant post-World War I richness.

For Hitler, who considered himself a genuine artist despite his early failures in Vienna, the modern trend in German art was senseless and dangerous. In *Mein Kampf* (q.v.) he delivered a tirade against the "Bolshevization of art." He mistakenly attributed to the Russians the excesses of cubism and Dada. This art, he said, "is the sick production of crazy people." Its effects, he asserted, could be seen in the short period of the Bavarian Soviet Republic, when political posters featured a modernistic approach. "Pity the people who no longer are able to control this sickness." Throughout the years of his drive for political power, Hitler maintained this sense of opposition to modern art. In 1930 he supported the National Socialist Combat League of Alfred Rosenberg (q.v.), which was active in the campaign against "degenerate art." Hitler's own taste in painting was limited to the heroic and the realistic. True German art, he said, must never depict anguish or distress. Painters must not use colors "different from those perceived in Nature by the normal eye." He himself preferred the canvases of such Austrian romantics as Franz von Defregger, who specialized in genre pictures of Tyrolean peasant life, and minor Bavarian artists who depicted happy rustics and bibulous monks at work or play. Hitler made it plain that one day he would purge Germany of its decadent art in favor of "the true Germanic spirit."

Soon after Hitler became Chancellor in 1933, he set up the Reich Chamber of Culture (Reichskulturkammer, q.v.) under Dr. Paul Joseph Goebbels (q.v.), Minister for Public Enlightenment and Propaganda. There were seven subchambers (fine arts, music, theater, literature, press, radio, and films), all of which were expected to implement the policy of *Gleichschaltung* (q.v.), or coordination. Some 42,000 Nazi-approved artists were required to join the Reich Chamber of Visual Arts. The directives of this chamber had the validity of law. Any member could be expelled for "political unreliability." Artists were subjected to a series of bans: *Lehrverbot,* deprivation of the right to teach; *Ausstellungsverbot,* deprivation of the right to exhibit; and *Malverbot,* deprivation of the right to paint. Agents of the Gestapo (q.v.) made lightning raids on artists' studios. Owners of art stores were given lists of proscribed artists and forbidden to sell them art supplies.

Unable to work under such conditions, many of Germany's most prominent artists went into exile. Paul Klee returned to Switzerland; Wassily Kandinsky went to Paris and became a French citizen, Oskar Kokoschka (q.v.), whose violent expressionism annoyed Hitler, moved to England and took British citizenship; George Grosz emigrated to the United States; Max Beckmann (q.v.) settled in Amsterdam. Several famous artists decided to remain in Germany. The elderly Max Liebermann (q.v.) stayed in Berlin ("I cannot eat as much as I would like to vomit!") and died there. All these artists were denounced as purveyors of non-German art.

The first exhibit of "degenerate art," called Government Art, 1918–1933, was mounted at Karlsruhe in 1933 within months after Hitler assumed political power. In early 1936 Hitler appointed a purge tribunal of four Nazi artists, under the chairmanship of Professor Adolf Ziegler, President of the Reich Chamber of Visual Arts, to tour all the major galleries and museums of Germany for the purpose of removing all "decadent art." One of the judges, Count von Baudissen, made it clear what type of art he preferred: "The most perfect shape, the subtlest image that has recently been created in Germany, has not come from any artist's studio—it is the steel helmet." The jury removed 12,890 paintings, drawings, sketches, and sculptures by German and non-German artists, including Picasso, Gauguin, Cézanne, and Van Gogh. On March 31, 1937, these sequestered art works were exhibited in a special display of degenerate art in Munich. Huge crowds came to see the works rejected by Hitler (*see* ENTARTETE KUNST). A concurrent exhibition nearby, the Greater Germany Art Exhibition, at which some 900 works approved by Hitler were shown, drew considerably less enthusiastic crowds. The Fuehrer encouraged "German artists" by setting up several hundred prize competitions for art works suited to his own taste.

During World War II, Hermann Goering (q.v.), who was much more eclectic in his art tastes than Hitler, appropriated art works from the major museums of Europe following Nazi invasions. He gradually gathered a collection of enormous value which he regarded as his personal property. The Einsatzstab Rosenberg (q.v.), the so-called Rosenberg Task Force, was designated by Hitler to confiscate many art treasures of France and other occupied countries. More than 5,281 paintings, including works by Rubens, Rembrandt, Goya, Fragonard, and other masters, as well as thousands of other works of art, were sent back to the Third Reich. This looted treasure was returned to the original owners after the war.

ARTAMAN LEAGUE. An organization of young nationalists in the 1920s who were devoted to the concept of settling on the soil and to the idea of *Blut und Boden* (q.v.; blood and soil). Members of the league wanted to work on farms in lieu of military service. Originating in the *voelkisch* wing of the German youth movement (*see* VOELKISCH MOVEMENT), the Artamans were strongly anti-Slav and urged that Polish farmers living in Germany be returned to their own country. Many journeyed to farms in east Germany to defend the fatherland against the Slavs. Among the Artaman leaders in 1924 was Heinrich Himmler (q.v.), who, like others in the league, turned in the end to National Socialism. Eventually, the Artaman League disappeared as the new Nazi movement gained strength.

ARTICLE 48. Key clause of the Weimar Constitution. Although the Weimar Constitution is considered one of the most advanced constitutions in history, its effectiveness was invalidated by the very existence of Article 48, which permitted the Reich President to suspend temporarily all the fundamental rights of the citizen guaranteed by the constitution. Hitler, who had given his word to achieve and hold political power legally, governed by virtue of Article 48 and used it to his own advantage in seizing absolute power.

ARTICLE 231. The famous war guilt clause of the Treaty of Versailles. The article was placed under Part VI, Reparation, and its opening lines ran as follows:

> The Allied and Associated Governments affirm and Germany accepts the responsibility of Germany and her allies for causing all the loss and damage to which the Allied and Associated Governments and their nationals have been subjected as a consequence of the war imposed upon them by the aggression of Germany and her allies. . . .

The significance of this controversial clause lay in the fact that it placed moral responsibility upon Germany and its allies for causing the loss and damage of the war. For the first time in history a provision of this kind was included in a peace treaty as a basis for reparations. Hitherto, the mere fact of victory had been deemed sufficient, on the ground that to the victor belong the spoils.

All political parties in Germany during the Weimar Republic (q.v.) from 1918 to 1933 agreed in denouncing Article 231. For Hitler and Nazi ideologists it was a special target of satire and sarcasm. In Hitler's view, the entire Treaty of Versailles was dedicated to the "enslavement" of Germany. He strongly supported the stab-in-the-back theory (*see* DOLCHSTOSSTHEORIE), which held that Jews and Social Democrats on the domestic front had been the *Novemberverbrecher* (q.v.), the November traitors, who had driven Germany to defeat. In public addresses Nazi speakers continually referred to Article 231 as a disgraceful canard and demanded that Germans strike back at a wholly unwarranted charge of war guilt.

ARYAN CLAUSE (Aryan Paragraph). *See* ARIERPARAGRAPH.

ARYAN RACE. *See* RACIAL DOCTRINE.

ASCHAFFENBURG. One of the earliest Nazi concentration camps (q.v.). It was located at the river port and resort town of Aschaffenburg, Bavaria, 168 miles northwest of Munich. In 1933 a group of SS (q.v.) men killed a number of Jews at the camp and were arrested by local authorities. SS officials insisted that their men were not subject to civil authority. Heinrich Himmler (q.v.) demanded that no charges be brought against the men. This was the earliest instance in which the power of the SS took precedence over any rival government agency. A precedent was set for future mass murder in the concentration and extermination camps (q.v.).

ASSAULT, THE. *See* ANGRIFF, DER.

ASSOCIATE LEADER OF STUDENTS. *See* MITARBEITER IN DER STUDENTENFUEHRUNG.

ATLANTIC WALL. Fortifications constructed by Hitler along the eastern and northern coasts of France during the first year of World War II to counter an Allied landing on the Continent.

ATLANTIS. One of Hitler's deadliest sea raiders in World War II. Originally built by the Bremen Hansa Line as the 7,860-ton freighter *Goldenfels,* the *Atlantis* was 500 feet long and 60 feet wide, with a draft of 25 feet and a top speed of 17½ knots. Soon after the beginning of the war, she was placed in drydock and in fourteen weeks was converted into an armed cruiser. She was fitted with six 6-inch guns, a 3-inch warning gun, two twin 3.7-centimeter antiaircraft guns, and four 2-centimeter automatics, all invisible under clever camouflage. On both sides below the waterline amidships there was a torpedo tube. A special compartment held ninety-two magnetic mines. A real funnel could be lengthened or lowered, and a dummy funnel could be set up or stowed away.

On December 19, 1939, the *Atlantis* was commissioned and soon was on her way to the Atlantic. Her mission was to approach unsuspecting Allied merchant ships and either take them captive or sink them. Equipped for a voyage of two years and manned by a picked crew, she displayed various flags, including British, Dutch, Japanese, and Norwegian. Altogether, she sank more than 140,000 tons of Allied shipping and was credited as the most effective German raider of the war. On November 22, 1941, while refueling a German U-boat, she was trapped by a British cruiser, HMS *Devonshire,* and sunk.

The *Atlantis* was one of a number of German raiders that took a high toll during the war. The raider *Emden* destroyed 74,000 tons of Allied shipping. In February 1940 the raider *Altmark* (q.v.), with some 300 prisoners on board, was detected by a British plane as she headed along the Norwegian coast. When she entered an ice-filled Norwegian port, she became the prey of a British destroyer sent in after her. In an action reminiscent of Elizabethan days, sailors from the *Cossack* leaped to the deck of the German raider and after a hand-to-hand combat managed to release the prisoners.

Bibliography. Wolfgang Frank and Bernhard Rogge, *The German Raider Atlantis,* Ballantine Books, Inc., New York, 1956.

ATTILA. Code name for the occupation of Unoccupied France. On December 10, 1940, Hitler issued a war directive titled Operation Attila in which he noted: "In the event those parts of the French Colonial Empire now controlled by General Weygand should show signs of revolt, preparation will be made for the rapid occupation of the still unoccupied territory of continental France. At the same time it will be necessary to lay hands on the French home fleet and on those parts of the French Air Force in home bases, or at least prevent their going over to the enemy." Operation Attila, renamed Anton (q.v.), was put into force by Hitler as soon as he learned of the landing of American and British troops on the coastline of Northwest Africa on November 7–8, 1942. Vichy France was occupied. The French Fleet, to avoid seizure by the Germans, was scuttled by its own crews in Toulon harbor. Hitler was able to prevent Allied seizure of Tunisia, toward which Gen. Erwin Rommel (q.v.) was retreating.

AUF GUT DEUTSCH (In Plain German). Paper edited and published by Dietrich Eckart (q.v.), nationalist poet in early post-World War I Munich. In this blunt and somewhat coarse journal, which had a circulation of about 30,000, Eckart took a strongly nationalist, Pan-German, and anti-Semitic line. His columns contained bitter attacks on the Munich City Council.

AUFBAU OST (Buildup East). Code name for the preparations for the attack on the Soviet Union, a preliminary to Barbarossa (q.v.). On August 8, 1940, Hitler designated Col. Walther Warlimont (q.v.), deputy to Gen. Alfred Jodl (q.v.), chief of operations at the Oberkommando der Wehrmacht (q.v.), to prepare the deployment areas in the east for the coming assault on the Soviet Union. The transfer of large bodies of troops to the east was to be carried out in the greatest secrecy in order not to arouse Stalin's suspicions.

AUGSBURG. Code name for "Delay offensive in the west." In a war directive issued on November 20, 1939, Hitler ordered the armed forces to make preparations for conducting the campaign in the west. The code word Danzig (q.v.) meant "Proceed with offensive." Augsburg meant to halt offensive operations for the time being.

AUGUST WILHELM, PRINCE. *See* PREUSSEN, AUGUST WILHELM HEINRICH GÜNTHER, PRINZ VON.

AUSCHWITZ (Oświęcim). Extermination camp in Poland (*see* EXTERMINATION CAMPS). Situated on a marshy tract between the Vistula and its tributary, the Sola, 160 miles southwest of Warsaw, the camp was built in an unfavorable location surrounded by stagnant ponds, smelly and pestilential. The place was originally a military barracks and later a tobacco factory. It was opened in 1940, after the defeat of Poland, and later was greatly expanded. *Spezialeinrichtungen* (special installations) were added, including *Badeanstalten* (bathhouses) used for gassing and *Leichenkeller* (corpse cellars) for storage of bodies. An experienced concentration camp staff, composed of SS (q.v.) members, was sent to Auschwitz to carry out the Final Solution (*see* ENDLÖSUNG, DIE). The staff was composed of *Lagerältteste* (camp seniors), *Blockältteste* (block seniors), *Stubendienst* (room orderlies), and *Kapos* (foremen of the individual huts).

Death transports flowed to this large complex of buildings, including victims from all over Europe: 400,000 from Hungary, 250,000 from Poland and Upper Silesia, 100,000 from Germany, 90,000 from the Netherlands, 90,000 from Slovakia, 65,000 from Greece, and 11,000 from France. On May 1, 1940, *SS-Hauptsturmfuehrer* (Capt.) Rudolf Franz Hoess (q.v.) was transferred from Sachsenhausen (q.v.) to Auschwitz. The next year Heinrich Himmler (q.v.) inspected Auschwitz and gave orders to enlarge the camp and drain the swamps. At the same time he set up a new camp at nearby Birkenau (q.v.). The first Jews arrived from Slovakia and Upper Silesia in 1941. Those unfit for work were gassed in temporary chambers run by tank and automobile engines. Later special crematoria were set up to implement the Final Solution. It is estimated that from

The crematory at Auschwitz. [*Eastfoto*]

1 to 4 million persons died in gas ovens and by a variety of other methods at Auschwitz. The leading SS officers who worked at Auschwitz were tried at Frankfurt am Main from December 20, 1963, to August 20, 1965 (*see* FRANKFURT TRIAL).

AUSCHWITZ TRIAL. *See* FRANKFURT TRIAL.

AUSLAND-SD. The unit of the SD (q.v.) dealing with intelligence in foreign countries.

AUSLANDSDEUTSCHE (Germans in Foreign Countries). Germans who had spent their early and impressionable years in a German community abroad. National Socialist racial doctrine held that all such Germans retained their affiliation with the homeland. National Socialism appealed to many Germans living abroad, especially in the United States (*see* GERMAN-AMERICAN BUND) and Argentina. Such Germans were well organized in Argentina, where the Nationalsozialistische Deutsche Arbeiterpartei (q.v.) had some 60,000 members in 1939. *Auslandsdeutsche* in Argentina controlled shipping lines, a student exchange program, and a special news service (Transozean). In 1945, after World War II, escaping Nazis sent vast amounts of currency to Argentina. Many former members of the SS (q.v.) emigrated to Argentina and were absorbed in everyday life there.

AUSLANDSORGANISATION (AO; Organization for Foreigners). The special agency of the Nationalsozialistische Deutsche Arbeiterpartei (q.v.) responsible for the supervision of Germans abroad. It was considered to be the equivalent of a *Gau* (q.v.), or one territorial division of the Nazi party. Its leader issued such proclamations as: "A German day in Buenos Aires or Chicago concerns us just as deeply as the struggle of our brethren near our frontiers." *See also* AUSLANDSDEUTSCHE.

AUSSENPOLITISCHES AMT (APA; Foreign Policy Office). The foreign policy office of the Nationalsozialistische Deutsche Arbeiterpartei (q.v.), headed by Alfred Rosenberg (q.v.).

AUSSERORDENTLICHE BEFRIEDUNGSAKTION. *See* AB AKTION.

AUSTRIAN LEGION. An organization of Austrian National Socialists who agitated for *Anschluss* (q.v.), union between Austria and the Third Reich. Formed in the 1930s, the Austrian Legion was equipped with arms, including heavy guns, lived in camps, and in effect carried on war against its own government. Chancellor Engelbert Dollfuss (q.v.) suppressed the organization, arrested many of its members, and forced others to flee to Germany. He complained to the German Foreign Office, which replied that it could not intervene in what was an "internal affair." Berlin also informed Dollfuss that Austrian Nazis had the right to choose Hitler as their Fuehrer.

AUTARKIE (Autarchy). A term derived from the Greek *autarkeia* and indicating national self-sufficiency. Behind it was the implication that a country should produce everything it requires and that it should reduce imports from foreign countries. Hitler constantly affirmed the German will to *Autarkie*. German self-sufficiency, he said, had to be based on military considerations, and the Third Reich had to become immune to the type of blockade that had burdened Germany in World War I.

AUTOBAHN (Superhighway). *See* REICHSAUTOBAHN.

AUTUMN FOG. *See* HERBSTNEBEL.

AUTUMN JOURNEY. *See* HERBSTREISE.

AWA. *See* ALLGEMEINES WEHRMACHTSAMT.

AXIS. *See* ACHSE.

AXIS SALLY. *See* GILLARS, MILDRED.

AXMANN, ARTUR (1913–). Hitler Youth leader. Artur Axmann was born in Hagen on February 18, 1913. He joined the Hitler Jugend (q.v.), the Hitler Youth, in 1928 and became so active in its affairs that within four years he was called to a position of leadership in the organization. In 1933, after Hitler became Chancellor, Axmann was made chief of the Social Office of the Reich Youth Leadership. On August 8, 1940, he was named *Reichsjugendfuehrer der NSDAP* (Reich Youth Leader of the Nazi party) as successor to Baldur von Schirach (q.v.). In 1941 he served on the eastern front. Axmann was among those present in the *Fuehrerbunker* (q.v.) during Hitler's last days in April 1945 (*see also* GÖTTERDÄMMERUNG). According to William L. Shirer (q.v.), Axmann deserted his battalion of boys defending the Pichelsdorf Bridge in Berlin to save his own life. Axmann later claimed in a deposition that he had seen the body of Martin Bormann (q.v.) lying under the bridge where the Invalidenstrasse crossed the railroad tracks.

AZIOLE. Contraction of asoziale. A term meaning "antisocial." It was used to describe inmates of concentration camps (q.v.) who were said to be criminal or work-shy.

B

B-TAG
to
BV

B-TAG (B-Day). Military shorthand and cover term for the opening day of the Barbarossa (q.v.) attack. The date was changed several times and finally was rescheduled for June 22, 1941.

BABI YAR. Name of a ravine near Kiev where, in September 1941, thousands of Jews were slaughtered. On September 19, 1941, a German Army group, after hammering at the Soviet defenses at Kiev for forty-five days, finally entered the city. A few days later tremendous explosions rocked the Continental Hotel, which housed the headquarters of a German command post, and nearby areas. In the huge fires which then followed, many German soldiers lost their lives. The German military command decided that the Jews of Kiev were responsible for the heavy loss of German lives. In reprisal the Jews were marched in small groups to the outer limits of the city to the Babi Yar ravine. There some 35,000 were killed in two days of summary executions. The bodies were buried in a pit about 60 yards long and 8 feet deep.

At the Nuremberg Trial (q.v.), Col. Gen. Alfred Jodl (q.v.) denied the theory that land mines had been planted in Kiev by the Jewish population of the city. He recalled seeing a captured chart showing the location of fifty land mines prepared by the Russian troops before their retreat. Investigators later claimed that evidence had been discovered implicating Russians in the Babi Yar massacre, but the facts became obscured in the sand dunes.

The massacre was the subject of a poem by Yevgeny Yevtushenko, a young Russian poet who expressed his distress not only because of German behavior but also because of Russian anti-Semitism. The opening and closing lines are:

> No gravestone stands at Babi Yar,
> Only coarse earth heaped roughly on the gash.
> Such dread comes over me. Today I am a Jew. . . .
> No drop of Jewish blood flows in my veins,
> But anti-Semites with a dull, gnarled hate
> Detest me like a Jew.
> O know me truly Russian through their hate.
>
> Translated by Marie Syrkin.[1]

BACH-ZELEWSKI, ERICH VON DEM (1899–1972). High-ranking officer of the Waffen-SS (q.v.). Erich von dem Bach-Zelewski was born in Lauenburg, Pomerania, on March 1, 1899. A professional soldier, he served in World War I and joined the Nationalsozialistische Deutsche Arbeiterpartei (q.v.) in 1930. From 1932 to 1934 he was a member of the German Reichstag (q.v.), representing Wahlkreis (Electoral District) Breslau. In 1939 he was promoted to *SS-Obergruppenfuehrer* (general) and in 1941 to *General der Waffen-SS.* On July 21, 1943, he was designated for the special task of subduing the Polish partisans. In 1944 and 1945 he commanded various SS corps and at the end of the war was commander of an army group.

BACKE, HERBERT (1896–1947). Food Minister during the last year of the Third Reich. Herbert Backe was born in Batum, in the Caucasus, on May 1, 1896. After attending the Russian Tifliser Gymnasium from 1905 to 1914, he studied at the University of Göttingen. In 1923 and 1924 he was an assistant at the Technical College of Hannover. He spent the years from 1914 to 1918 as a prisoner of war in Russia. An expert in agrarian politics, he served as Reich Food Minister in Hitler's last Cabinet in 1944 and 1945. He committed suicide by hanging at Nuremberg Prison on April 6, 1947.

BAECK, LEO (1873–1956). Rabbinical scholar and leader of the Jewish community in Berlin during the era of the Third Reich. Leo Baeck was born in Lissa, Prussia (now Leszno, Poland), on May 23, 1873, the son of Rabbi Samuel Baeck. After study for the rabbinate, he served as a rabbi in Oppeln (Opole), Düsseldorf, and Berlin from 1912 to 1943. An army chaplain in World War I, he won a wide reputation after the war as a rabbinical scholar. He rejected Adolf von Harnack's Christian theology, which he described as a romantic philosophy in contrast to classical Judaism. Baeck was also known for his scientific

[1]By permission of Marie Syrkin.

essays. In Berlin he was active in the Union of German Rabbis and as presiding officer of B'nai B'rith. He refused to go into exile when Hitler came to political power in January 1933. Instead, he worked as the guiding force in the Reichsvertretung (*see* JUDENRÄTE), the representative body of German Jews, and devoted his energies to defending whatever rights remained to the Jews in the Third Reich. He declined all offers from abroad and announced that he would stay in Berlin until the last minyan (prayer quota).

Baeck was arrested in 1943 and sent to Theresienstadt (q.v.). In the concentration camp he was named head of the *Aelsterat* (council of elders) of the Jewish prisoners. He lectured on philosophy and theology. In this hostile milieu he continued to bear witness to his faith. When the camp was liberated in 1945, he prevented the lynching of the Nazi guards by embittered inmates. In London he became president of the Council of Jews of Germany and chairman of the World Union for Progressive Judaism. Later he served as professor of the history of religion at Hebrew Union College, Cincinnati. In 1954 he founded and became the first presiding officer of the Leo Baeck Institute, New York and London, which was devoted to research on the history of Jews in Germany. He died in London on November 2, 1956.

Bibliography. Leo Baeck, *The Essence of Judaism,* Schocken Books, Inc., New York, 1948.

BAEUMLER, ALFRED (1887–). Professor at the University of Berlin and leading academic philosopher of the Third Reich. Baeumler was the most important liaison academician between the German universities and the department headed by Alfred Rosenberg that was charged with the ideological education of the Nazi party. He performed the scholarly legerdemain of adopting Friedrich Nietzsche (q.v.) as a philosopher of Nazi heroism and champion of Nordic and soldierly valuation. Baeumler ignored the facts of Nietzsche's contempt for his fellow countrymen and his hostility to nationalism of any kind.

BAMBERG PARTY CONGRESS. A meeting of all party *Gaufuehrer* (district leaders) called by Hitler at Bamberg in southern Germany on February 14, 1926, to settle the Nazi party program. There had been a clash of opinion between northern and southern leaders, and Hitler was anxious to resolve the difficulties. He carefully selected a weekday, when it was difficult for the northerners to get away from their jobs. Only Gregor Strasser and Dr. Paul Joseph Goebbels (qq.v.) were able to speak for northerners against the majority of south Germans. The northerner Gregor Strasser represented the urban, socialist, revolutionary trend, while the southerner Gottfried Feder (q.v.) reflected rural, racialist, and populist ideas. Hitler was determined to move slowly between these two hostile groups, and he was not inclined to allow his fledgling party to turn in the direction of "undiluted socialist principles."

The issue came to a head at Bamberg on the matter of expropriating the property of the princely houses. Hitler made a two-hour speech telling the delegates why they should not vote for expropriation. National Socialism, he said, must not help Communist-inspired movements; expropriation would not stop with relegating the Wittelsbachs and other German dynasties to history's rubbish heap. Although Goebbels was supposed to represent the Strasser position, he sensed the outcome and quietly gravitated to the Hitler position. As a reward he won a post as *Gauleiter* (q.v.) of Berlin, which was the beginning of his successful career in the party. The split in the party between Nationalists and Socialists was finally resolved by the 1934 Blood Purge (q.v.).

BANSE, EWALD (1883–1953). Military writer well known in the Third Reich. Ewald Banse was born in Braunschweig on May 23, 1883. In February 1933 he was appointed professor of military science at Braunschweig Technical College. He had already won a reputation with several books on military and geographical subjects. One of his major works, *Raum und Volk im Weltkriege (Space and People in World War),* was translated into English by Alan Harris as *Germany Prepares for War: A Nazi Theory of "National Defense"* (1934) and was later widely distributed by the Allies as one of their most effective propaganda instruments in World War II. In this book Banse praised national sentiment as "self-respect and healthy egoism," and denounced internationalism as "self-abandonment and degeneration of the tissues." He stated that "the sword will come into its own again." He discussed war as a geographical phenomenon. Again and again he expressed war cult ideas: "War derives its nourishment from a country's spiritual and economic strength and translates it into military action through the agency of a leader; this in turn creates better opportunities for statesmanship than were previously forthcoming." Banse saw peace as an ideal state, but he insisted that it carries with it the risk of stagnation and somnolence; war on the contrary, he said, is a grand stimulant and uplifter.

The crux of Banse's thinking came in a passage in which he described the "actively warlike man" as the man who does not fight to live but lives to fight. Such a man, Banse wrote, has an eagle eye ever on the alert for the opportunities of fighting. This kind of born warrior hurls himself without thinking into the fight and, far from trying to avoid a quarrel, seeks one and greets it with joy. He is totally unfitted for civil life. He represents the "essential Nordic original aristocracy of the West," the kind of people who fight for the sake of fighting, not merely in defense of hearth and home.

Banse then contrasted the superb fighting man with the "peace-loving man, the pacifist." Such a man endures any humiliation in order to avoid war. His dim, lusterless eye betokens servility; his clumsy body is built only for work. This is the born stay-at-home. To this "bourgeois, or philistine," the warrior is the sworn foe, the deadly enemy. Banse dismissed with contempt this man of peace, "who values honor and renown less than his own little life."

Banse recommended a German renaissance with two principal missions: (1) to summon the soul of Germany from the depths to perform its national, cultural, and political task so that on German soil all thought, all action, and all speech would be German; and (2) to combine German territory throughout its whole extent into a unified and therefore powerful state, whose boundaries would be far wider than those of 1914. He urged that preparation for future wars must not stop at the creation, equipment, and training of an efficient army but must go on to train the minds of the whole people for the war and must employ all the resources of science to master the conditions governing the war itself and the possibility of endurance. In effect, Banse was giving the credo of a military expert to substantiate the ideas implicit in Hitler's *Mein Kampf* (q.v.). Banse died on October 31, 1953.

Bibliography. Ewald Banse, *Germany Prepares for War: A Nazi Theory of "National Defense,"* tr. by Alan Harris, Harcourt, Brace and Company, Inc., New York, 1934.

BÄR, HEINRICH (1913–1957). Ace fighter pilot for the Luftwaffe (q.v.) in World War II. Heinrich Bär was born in Leipzig on March 25, 1913. Beginning his career as a sergeant, he shot down his first enemy plane in September 1939. He served at various times with Jagdgeschwader (Fighter Groups) 51, 71, 1, and 3 and was promoted to lieutenant colonel. Bär scored a total of 220 kills, which gave him ninth place among Luftwaffe aces. He was the highest scorer on the western front (124 kills) against British and American fighter pilots.

BARBAROSSA (Red Beard). Code name, sometimes called Fall Barbarossa (Case Barbarossa), for the attack on the Soviet Union in 1941. In his War Directive 21 (*see* DIRECTIVE 21), issued on December 18, 1940, Hitler dropped the original cover name Fritz and substituted for it the term Barbarossa. He took the name from the German hero and Holy Roman emperor Frederick I (1123–1190), known as Barbarossa from the Italian for "red beard." On June 10, 1190, while clad in full armor on the Third Crusade through Asia Minor, Barbarossa was drowned in attempting to cross a stream. The legend arose that Barbarossa continued to live on, awaiting the call of his country, in a cave in the Kyffhäuser mountain range in the geographical center of Germany. It became a summer tradition for thousands of German schoolchildren to journey to the cave to see a marble statue of the legendary hero.

In August 1939 Hitler and Stalin agreed to a ten-year nonaggression pact. Nearly two years later, on June 22, 1941, the Fuehrer sent his war machine crashing across the frontiers of the U.S.S.R., unleashing a furious *Blitzkrieg* (q.v.). As a pretext for invasion, Hitler accused Stalin of treachery, of threatening to cross German frontiers, and of promoting anti-German propaganda. At his own choice Hitler opted for another two-front war. Although the invasion came as a surprise to many observers, those who had studied *Mein Kampf* (q.v.) knew of his hatred for bolshevism. The Fuehrer described the assault on Russia as a crusade against communism, but he obviously was motivated by a need for wheat, oil, and mineral supplies to enable him to defy the British blockade.

Bibliography. Barton Whaley, *Codeword Barbarossa,* The M.I.T. Press, Cambridge, Mass., 1973.

A cartoon based on Radio Moscow's characterization of Hitler: "This miserable ape of Napoleon." [*Bernard Partridge in* Punch, *September 24, 1941*] [*© 1941 Punch (Rothco)*]

BARKHORN, ERICH GERHARD (1919–). Ace fighter pilot for the Luftwaffe (q.v.) in World War II. Erich Gerhard Barkhorn was born in Königsberg on March 20, 1919. His flying career began in 1941, when he was posted to Jagdgeschwader (Fighter Group) 52 in Ostend as a 1st lieutenant. Promoted to captain in 1943 and to major in 1944, he was sent to the Russian front to fly Me 262s. He was officially credited by Luftwaffe statisticians with 301 kills, all on the Russian front, giving him second place to Maj. Erich Hartmann (q.v.), with 352 kills. Both Barkhorn and Hartmann survived the war.

BARRACK HUNDREDS. *See* KASERNIERTE HUNDERTSCHAFTEN.

BARTELS, ADOLF (1862–1945). Professor and literary historian who identified himself early with National Socialism. Adolf Bartels was born in Wesselburen on November 11, 1862. He was the author of historical novels, dramas, and poetry with a strong *voelkisch* character (*see* VOELKISCH MOVEMENT). He combined his literary works with an uncompromising anti-Semitism (q.v.) in such monographs as *Lessing und die Juden,* 1918 *(Lessing and the Jews).* On the formation of the Vereinigung Voelkischer Verleger (Alliance of Folkish Publishers) in 1920, Bartels became editor of its monthly journal, *Deutsches Schriftum (German Writings),* which featured anti-Semitic articles. In 1924 he praised the Nazi movement in his *Nationalsozialismus Deutschlands Rettung (National Socialism Germany's Deliverance),* for which he received high praise from Nazi leaders. Bartels died in Weimar on March 7, 1945.

BARTH, KARL (1886–1968). Leading figure in world

Protestantism and opponent of National Socialism. Karl Barth was born in Basel on May 10, 1886. A holder of professorships at the Universities of Göttingen, Münster, and Bonn, he was a prophet of New Testament thought. Barth's teaching emphasized the absolute difference between man and God, man's inability to solve his own problems, and his complete dependence on revelation. Because he refused to take an oath of allegiance to Hitler, Barth was removed from his post at the University of Bonn. Commanded to begin his lectures on God each day by raising his arm in salute and saying *"Heil Hitler!"* he denounced the order as blasphemy. He completed his academic career at the University of Basel and died in Basel on December 10, 1968.

BASSERMANN, ALBERT (1867–1952). German actor and refugee from the Third Reich. Albert Bassermann was born in Mannheim on September 7, 1867, the nephew of a theater director. Choosing an acting career, he went in 1895 to Berlin, where he worked at the Deutsches Theater from 1900 to 1909 and with Max Reinhardt (q.v.) from 1909 to 1914. A follower of the naturalistic school of acting, he gave a psychological orientation to his performances. In his early career he specialized in plays by Ibsen, and later he turned to classical roles as Mephisto, Egmont, Tell, and others. In 1934 he left Germany and subsequently went to the United States, where he was well known for his film roles. He died in Zürich on May 15, 1952.

BATTLE FOR BERLIN. The final battle of World War II in Europe. Hitler intended to make Berlin, the huge, sprawling metropolis on the Spree, the capital of his Nazi world empire. In the closing days of the war the Fuehrer retreated there for a last stand. Now worn out, he was determined to fight on "until five past midnight." He refused to surrender or leave, rejected the advice of his generals, and remained in his bunker in the Reich Chancellery to await the miracle that would save his empire (*see* GÖTTERDÄMMERUNG).

Berlin was protected on the east by a dense system of trenches. In the city proper, pillboxes, mines, and booby traps were placed at strategic points. The streets were barricaded. Slogans by Dr. Paul Joseph Goebbels (q.v.) covered the walls: *"Wir kapitulieren nie!"* ("We Shall Never Surrender!") "Every German Will Defend His Capital!" "We Shall Halt the Red Hordes at the Walls of Our Own Berlin!" "Victory or Siberia!" Despite this show of bravado, Berlin was already in its death throes. The great city was caught in a giant trap and was being pounded to pieces by Russian artillery from the east and by British and American air power from the west. British Lancasters and American Flying Fortresses and Liberators rained a hail of bombs on the metropolis. Between raids by the giant planes, fast British medium bombers called Mosquitoes droned over the doomed city in a psychological attack designed to give the residents little or no sleep.

The city was systematically destroyed as one famous landmark after another—the Opera, the Chancellery, the

Soviet soldiers raising their flag on the gutted Reichstag building on May 1, 1945. [*Sovphoto*]

Air Ministry—crumbled into dust. Flames poured from broken gas mains, lighting up the blackened shells of the buildings. Berliners cringed in cellars and subways. Boys in their teens and men in their sixties were rounded up for a final stand. Desperate housewives stole food from the stores. Loudspeakers in the streets appealed to the people to fight to the death.

In the final days of April 1945, Soviet troops broke through the suburbs and headed toward Unter den Linden in the center of the city. Powerful Russian tanks and rocket-firing trucks moved through the rubble-filled streets and smashed down the barricades. German suicide squads left their hiding places and attacked the Russian tanks with bottles filled with gasoline. Germans and Russians joined in hand-to-hand fighting with tommy guns, rifles, and pistols. The combat surged from corridors to rooftops and into the cellars, tunnels, and subways.

By April 25, eight Soviet armies were closing in on the city. By the evening of the next day the Russians cut off the last German force in Potsdam and pushed the Berlin defenders into a pocket 9½ miles long from east to west and 1 to 3 miles wide. In the center of the city the Russians drove spearheads from north to south to the governmental quarter. Soviet armies competed with one another for the honor of taking the Reichstag (q.v.), which they regarded as a symbol of the Third Reich even though it had been gutted by the 1933 fire (*see* REICHSTAG FIRE).

Berlin went down in a wave of destruction. Other cities had felt the lash of war. Leningrad had been subjected to cold and starvation, and Dresden and Hamburg to the devastation of fire bombs; Hiroshima and Nagasaki were later to feel the annihilating atomic bomb. But Berlin had been singled out for special torture. For months a despairing population, reduced to 1.7 million, mostly women, children, and the aged, had been forced underground into the air-raid shelters. They endured Soviet shells and rockets and Allied bombs as the city disintegrated above them.

Berlin formally surrendered on May 2, 1945. It was a terrible spectacle at the end. The city was reduced to a hollow shell. The streets were impassable because of the giant rubble heaps. For mile after mile grotesque skeletons of buildings swayed on their shaky foundations. The air was foul with the stench of dead people and animals in the streets. It was as if a giant scourge had leveled the metropolis.

Bibliography. Vasili I. Chuikov, *The Fall of Berlin*, Holt, Rinehart and Winston, Inc., New York, 1968; Cornelius Ryan, *The Last Battle*, Simon and Schuster, New York, 1966.

BATTLE OF BRITAIN. *See* LUFTWAFFE.

BAVARIAN JOE. A disreputable Berliner with whom Col. Gen. Werner Freiherr von Fritsch (q.v.), commander in chief of the Army, was accused of committing a homosexual offense in the Potsdam railroad station. On February 4, 1938, Hitler sent a letter to Von Fritsch accepting his resignation (*see* BLOMBERG-FRITSCH CRISIS).

BAYREUTH FESTIVAL. A season of musical entertainment held annually in Bayreuth, Bavaria, 122 miles north of Munich, to present the operas of Richard Wagner (q.v.). Wagner's home was in Bayreuth, and the composer was buried in the garden of his former villa. The composer's wife, Cosima (1837–1930), a daughter of Franz Liszt, was instrumental in obtaining funds for the Festspielhaus, which Wagner himself had designed. Beginning in 1876, Wagnerian operas were performed there. After the composer's death, Cosima became supervisor and régisseur. She was succeeded by her son, Siegfried Wagner (1869–1930), and on his death by his wife, Winifred Wagner (1894– , q.v.).

A fervent Wagnerite, Hitler was so deeply devoted to the festival that he made it a National Socialist annual event. He saw to it that performances continued during World War II to the summer of 1944. After the fall of the Third Reich, the festival was directed by Wieland Wagner, the composer's grandson. Following Wieland's death in 1966, his brother Wolfgang, helped by a governmental subsidy, continued the presentations.

BDM. *See* BUND DEUTSCHER MÄDEL.

BEAMTENBUND (Reichsbund Deutscher Beamter; Civil Service League). A monolithic body of civil servants closely allied with the Nazi party and under its control. A part of the system of *Gleichschaltung* (q.v.), it was designed to supersede the old professional civil service organizations. It was expected to implement all special decrees of the government. For example, by a decree of September 9, 1937, all Beamtenbund members were required to boycott those department stores then under attack. There were more than 1 million members who paid substantial dues and contributions, attended meetings after office hours, and observed all orders from the authorities.

BEAUTY OF LABOR. A section of the German Labor Front (*see* DEUTSCHE ARBEITSFRONT) organized to attract the support of workers of the Third Reich. Created by Robert Ley (q.v.) on January 30, 1934, the Beauty of Labor was designed as a welfare plan for holiday trips, festivals, factory celebrations, folk dancing, and political education. It existed alongside the similar Strength through Joy movement (*see* KRAFT DURCH FREUDE).

BECHER, KURT (1909–). Assistant to Heinrich Himmler (q.v.) in the SS (q.v.). Kurt Becher was born in Hamburg on September 12, 1909. Originally a grain dealer, he joined the Nationalsozialistische Deutsche Arbeiterpartei (q.v.) and rose to the rank of SS-*Standartenfuehrer* (colonel). He served as *Leiter* (leader) of the SS Horse Purchase Commission in Hungary. Because of his reputation as a successful horse trader, he was designated by Himmler in the winter of 1944–1945 to conduct negotiations to exchange Jews for money payments. He was not successful in this task.

BECK, LUDWIG (1880–1944). Chief of staff of the armed forces from 1935 to 1938 and a central figure in the Resistance (q.v.) and conspiracy movements against Hitler. Born in Biebrich, in the Rhineland, on June 29, 1880, he

Gen. Ludwig Beck. [*Picture Collection, The Branch Libraries, The New York Public Library*]

was attached to the General Staff in World War I. A brilliant officer, he was appointed on October 1, 1933, *Chef des Truppenamtes* (adjutant general), a key post in the Reichswehr (q.v.). From 1935 to 1938 Beck was chief of the Army General Staff, the elite of the military leadership responsible for the preparation and conduct of land warfare. In this post he was entitled to take a major role in all important military decisions. On May 30, 1938, Beck protested when Hitler made his decision to conquer Czechoslovakia in the foreseeable future. The Army was unprepared, he said, to deal with a general war. He was convinced that modern war should be limited and controlled mainly through a policy based on moral principles. Beck attempted to organize opposition to Hitler's policy by the Chiefs of Staff, but he failed. On August 18, 1938, he resigned his post as chief of the General Staff.

From then on Beck played a leading role in the German Resistance movement and became the recognized leader of the conspirators against Hitler. He was regarded as a possible head of state once Hitler had been removed from the scene. After the failure of the July Plot (q.v.) in 1944, Beck made two unsuccessful attempts on his life in the War Office at the Bendlerstrasse (q.v.). At his request a sergeant gave him the *coup de grâce.*

BECKMANN, MAX (1884–1950). Painter and etcher, denounced as a purveyor of degenerate art in Nazi Germany (*see* ENTARTETE KUNST). Max Beckmann was born in Leipzig on February 12, 1884. As a painter he moved from an early interest in impressionism to expressionism and symbolism. In 1925 he taught in an art school in Frankfurt am Main. Forced to flee from his native country in 1933, he settled in Amsterdam and spent the years of World War II there. In 1947 he went to the United States and became an art teacher at Washington University in St. Louis (1947) and at the Brooklyn Museum (1949). He died in New York on December 27, 1950.

BEEFSTEAK NAZIS. Term of derision used to describe those Communists and Socialists who for reasons of expediency joined the National Socialist party. Beefsteak Nazis were regarded as "brown on the outside and red on the inside." In June and July 1933, shortly after Hitler assumed political power, there were some SA (q.v.) units which were almost entirely Communist.

BEER-BOTTLE GUSTAV. *See* FLASCHENBIERGUSTAV.

BEER-HALL ATTEMPT. *See* BÜRGERBRÄU KELLER ATTENTAT.

BEER-HALL PUTSCH. Unsuccessful attempt by Hitler and his new Nazi party to seize power in the early stage of the National Socialist movement. On the evening of November 8, 1923, some 3,000 Germans were present in the Bürgerbräu Keller, a large beer hall in Munich, to hear a speech by Gustav Ritter von Kahr (q.v.), state commissioner of Bavaria. On the platform with him were local dignitaries such as Gen. Otto von Lossow, commander of the armed forces in Bavaria, and Col. Hans von Seisser, chief of the Bavarian State Police. While Von Kahr was delivering his talk, the hall was silently surrounded by 600 Storm Troopers. The SA (q.v.) men set up a machine gun outside with its muzzle pointed at the front door. In the darkness the Nazi leader, Adolf Hitler, surrounded by followers, hurried down the aisle, jumped on a chair, fired a shot at the ceiling, and in the sudden silence cried out: "The national revolution has broken out!" To the astonished audience he added: "The hall is filled with 600 armed men. No one is allowed to leave. The Bavarian government and the government at Berlin are hereby deposed. A new government will be formed at once. The barracks of the Reichswehr [q.v.] and the police barracks are occupied. Both have rallied to the swastika!"

Hitler then turned to the podium and gruffly ordered Von Kahr, Von Lossow, and Von Seisser to follow him to a small side room. Here he denounced his prisoners and informed them that he, together with Gen. Erich Ludendorff (q.v.), the war hero, was forming a new government. The three leaders of the Bavarian regime, still nervous but beginning to recover their wits, started to berate Hitler and demanded to know what he meant by this confounded nonsense. Hitler flew into a rage. He dashed back into the hall and shouted to the still-muttering crowd: "Tomorrow will find a national government in Germany, or it will find us dead!"

The huge crowd, puzzled by the spectacle, did not know what was coming next. At this critical moment a great cheer went up when General Ludendorff, known to everyone in the audience, appeared on the scene. Ludendorff at once denounced Hitler for presuming to start a revolution without clearing the matter with him in advance. Hitler, sensing enthusiasm in the audience, ignored the slight. Once again he mounted the podium, turned to the crowd, and informed it that victory was his. "I have at last fulfilled the oath I swore five years ago as a blind cripple in a military hospital."

What seemed to many in the crowd to be a comic opera being played before their eyes continued through the night. The struggle for control went on behind the scenes. One by one Von Kahr, Von Lossow, and Von Seisser managed to escape from Hitler's SA men. When the news was flashed to Berlin, Gen. Hans von Seeckt (q.v.), commander of the Reichswehr, pledged that he would smash the rebellion if the Munich authorities failed in their responsibilities. By early morning Hitler began to feel that his *Putsch* had misfired, but Ludendorff insisted that there be no retreat.

At 11 A.M. the assembled Nazis, bearing swastika ban-

Proklamation
an das deutsche Volk!
Die Regierung der November-
verbrecher in Berlin ist heute
für abgesetzt erklärt worden:
Eine provisorische deutsche
National-Regierung
ist gebildet worden.
Diese besteht aus
General Ludendorff, Adolf Hitler
General von Lossow, Oberst von Seisser

Proclamation of the Beer-Hall *Putsch:* "Proclamation to the German people! The regime of the November criminals is today declared deposed. A provisional German national government is formed. This consists of General Ludendorff, Adolf Hitler, General von Lussow, Colonel von Seisser." [*Author's collection*]

ners and war flags, began a demonstration march toward the Marienplatz in the center of Munich. At the head were Hitler, Ludendorff, Hermann Goering (q.v.), and Julius Streicher (q.v.). At first the marchers pushed aside the small police contingents sent to stop them. As the parade came to the Odeonplatz near the Feldherrn Halle (q.v.), the way was barred by a stronger detachment of police bearing carbines. About 100 police confronted 3,000 Nazis. Hitler called on the police to surrender. The response was a hail of lead. In seconds 16 Nazis and 3 policemen lay dead on the pavement, and others were wounded. Goering, who was shot through the thigh, fell to the ground. Hitler, reacting spontaneously because of his training as a dispatch bearer during World War I, automatically hit the pavement when he heard the crack of guns. Surrounded by comrades, he escaped in a car standing close by. Ludendorff, staring straight ahead, moved through the ranks of the police, who in a gesture of respect for the old war hero, turned their guns aside. *See also* MARTYRS, NAZI; MUNICH TRIAL.

On the surface the Beer-Hall *Putsch* seemed to be a failure, but actually it was a brilliant achievement for a political nobody. In a few hours Hitler catapulted his scarcely known, unimportant movement into headlines throughout Germany and the world. Moreover, he learned an important lesson: direct action was not the way to political power. It was necessary that he seek political victory by winning the masses to his side and also by attracting the support of wealthy industrialists. Then he could ease his way to political supremacy by legal means.

Bibliography. Richard Hanser, *Putsch*, Pyramid Books, New York, 1971.

BEFRISTETE VORBEUGUNGSHÄFTLINGE (BV; Prisoners in Limited-Term Preventive Custody). A category of concentration camp inmates, classed by the Gestapo (q.v.) as criminals who had already served several sentences.

BEGLEITKOMMANDO-SS (Escort Guard SS). A military guard assigned to keep watch over official buildings.

BEHRENDS, HERMANN (1907–1946). High Nazi officer and official. Hermann Behrends was the first leader of the Berlin SD (q.v.), the security service. Eventually he won the rank of *SS-Brigadefuehrer* (major general). Behrends was appointed leader of the Volksdeutsche Mittelstelle (q.v.; VOMI), the German Racial Assistance Office, in Yugoslavia. He was hanged in Belgrade in 1946.

BEKENNTNISKIRCHE (Confessional Church). A countermovement by Protestant theologians opposed to Hitler's German Faith movement (Deutsche Glaubensbewegung, q.v.). Its aim was to keep the Evangelical faith in pure form. Shortly after assuming political power in 1933, Hitler made it clear that he wanted a Reich church which supported his own doctrines of race and leadership. He included both Protestants and Catholics in his policy of coordination (*see* GLEICHSCHALTUNG), by which he intended to mold all elements of society in the Nazi way of life. He succeeded in concluding the Concordat of 1933 (q.v.) with the Vatican but was less successful in coming to an understanding with the Protestants. On July 14, 1933, a written constitution for the new Reich church was formally recognized by the Reichstag (q.v.). There was a struggle over the election of the first Reich bishop. Hitler supported Ludwig Müller (q.v.), whose views coincided with his own, and saw to it that Müller was elected to the post on July 23. To defend the traditional church, Martin Niemoeller (q.v.) and others organized the Bekenntniskirche, the Confessional Church, which declared that Christianity was incompatible with the Nazi *Weltanschauung* (q.v.). Some 7,000 of the 17,000 Protestant pastors in Germany joined the Confessional Church, but they were cut down quickly by Nazi persecution. Many pastors, including Dietrich Bonhoeffer (q.v.), were to pay with their lives for their opposition to Hitler.

"BELIEVE! OBEY! FIGHT!" Motto of the SS (q.v.). This slogan was borrowed from the Italian Fascist call: *"Credere! Obbedire! Combattere!"*

BELLO, HEINZ (1920–1944). Medical Corps sergeant executed for speaking out against National Socialism, militarism, and Nazi party informers. Heinz Bello was born in Breslau on September 5, 1920, the son of a tax collector. After completing his compulsory stint with the Deutsche Arbeitsdienst (q.v.), the German Labor Service, he was called to Army service at the outbreak of World War II in 1939. In January 1940 he was relieved of military service to study medicine at the University of Münster. Recalled in October 1940, he subsequently took part in the drive on Moscow and won the Iron Cross (Second Class), the East Medal, and the Badge for Wounded Soldiers. On March 18, 1944, he was brought before the Central Military Court in Berlin-Charlottenburg after being denounced by two "friends." On being detailed for fire watching, he had expressed his annoyance with some harsh words for National Socialism and militarism in general. He was found guilty of "undermining morale" and sentenced to "death, dishonor, and loss of civil rights for life." He was executed on the machine-gun range at Berlin-Tegel on June 29, 1944.

BELSEN (Bergen-Belsen). Concentration camp 10 miles Northwest of Celle, Hannover, near the village of Bergen on the road to Hamburg. Originally a small camp, Belsen was later enlarged and at one time included some 10,000 prisoners, including those jailed for political offenses. Staffed like the other camps (*see* CONCENTRATION CAMPS), Belsen had no gas chambers, but thousands of its inmates died from disease and starvation. The shortage of food was always acute, although the camp staff was well fed. Prisoners are said to have resorted to cannibalism. In late 1944 Belsen received a new commandant, Josef Kramer (q.v.), later known as the Beast of Belsen. Allied troops liberated Belsen in April 1945. A reporter, Patrick Gordon Walker, described the scene at Belsen:[1]

> I went to Belsen. It was a vast area surrounded by barbed wire. The whole thing was being guarded by Hungarian guards. They had been in the German Army and are now immediately and without hesitation serving us. They are saving us a large number of men for the time being. Outside the camp, which is amidst bushes, pines, and heather, all fairly recently planted, were great notices in red letters: DANGER—TYPHUS.
>
> We drove into what turned out to be a great training camp, a sort of Aberdeen, where we found the officers and Oxfordshire Yeomanry. They began to tell us about the concentration camp.
>
> It lies south of the training area and is behind its own barbed wire. The Wehrmacht is not allowed near it. It was entirely guarded by SS men and women. This is what I discovered about the release of the camp that happened about the fifteenth. I got this story from Derek Sington, political officer, and from officers and men of Oxfordshire Yeomanry.
>
> Typhus broke out in the camp, and a truce was arranged so that we could take the camp over. The Germans originally had proposed that we should bypass the camp. In the meanwhile, thousands and thousands of people would have died and been shot. We refused these terms, and demanded the withdrawal of the Germans and the disarmament of the SS guards. Some dozen SS men and women were left behind under the command of Higher Sturmführer Kramer, who had been at Auschwitz. Apparently they had been told all sorts of fairy tales about the troops, that they could go on guarding, and that we would let them free and so forth.
>
> We only had a handful of men so far, and the SS stayed there that night. The first night of liberty, many hundreds of people died of joy.
>
> Next day some men of the Yeomanry arrived. The people crowded around them, kissing their hands and feet—and dying from weakness. Corpses in every state of decay were lying around, piled up on top of each other in heaps. There were corpses in the compound in flocks. People were falling dead all around, people who were walking skeletons. One woman came up to a soldier who was guarding the milk store and doling the milk out to children, and begged for milk for her baby. The man took the baby and saw that it had been dead for days, black in the face and shriveled up. The woman went on begging for milk. So he poured some on the dead lips. The mother then started to croon with joy and carried the baby off in triumph. She stumbled and fell dead in a few yards. I have this story and some others on records spoken by the men who saw them.
>
> On the sixteenth, Kramer and the SS were arrested. Kramer was taken off and kept in the icebox with some stinking fish of the officers' home. He is now going back to the rear. The rest, men and women, were kept under guard to save them from the inmates. The men were set to work shoveling up the corpses into lorries.
>
> About thirty-five thousand corpses were reckoned, more actually than the living. Of the living, there were about thirty thousand.
>
> The SS men were driven and pushed along and made to ride on top of the loaded corpses and then shovel them into their great mass open graves. They were so tired that they fell exhausted amongst the corpses. Jeering crowds collected around them, and they had to be kept under strong guard.
>
> Two men committed suicide in their cells. Two jumped off the lorry and tried to run away and get lost in the crowd. They were shot down. One jumped into a concrete pool of water and was riddled with bullets. The other was brought to the ground, with a shot in the belly.
>
> The SS women were made to cook and carry heavy loads. One of them tried to commit suicide. The inmates said that they were more cruel and brutal than the men. They are all young, in their twenties. One SS woman tried to hide, disguised as a prisoner. She was denounced and arrested.
>
> The camp was so full because people had been brought here from East and West. Some people were brought from Nordhausen, a five-day journey, without food. Many had marched for two or three days. There was no food at all in the camp, a few piles of roots—amidst the piles of dead bodies. Some of the dead bodies were of people so hungry that though the roots were guarded by SS men they had tried to storm them and had been shot down then and there. There was no water, nothing but these roots and some boiled stinking carrots, enough for a few hundred people.
>
> Men and women had fought for these raw, uncooked roots. Dead bodies, black and blue and bloated, and skeletons had been used as pillows by sick people. The day after we took over, seven block leaders, mostly Poles, were murdered by the inmates. Some were still beating the people. We arrested one woman who had beaten another woman with a board.

[1]Courtesy United States War Department.

She quite frankly admitted the offense. We are arresting these people.

An enormous buried dump of personal jewelry and belongings was discovered in suitcases. When I went to the camp five days after its liberation, there were still bodies all around. I saw about a thousand.

In one place, hundreds had been shoveled into a mass grave by bulldozers; in another, Hungarian soldiers were putting corpses into a grave that was sixty feet by sixty feet and thirty feet deep. It was almost half full.

Other and similar pits were being dug. Five thousand people had died since we got into the camp. People died before my eyes, scarcely human, moaning skeletons, many of them gone mad. Bodies were just piled up. Many had gashed wounds and bullet marks and terrible sores. One Englishman, who had lived in Ostend, was picked up half dead. It was found that he had a great bullet wound in his back. He could just speak. He had no idea when he had been shot. He must have been lying half unconscious when some SS man shot him as he was crawling about. This was quite common. I walked about the camp. Everywhere was the smell and odor of death. After a few hours you get used to it and don't notice it any more. People have typhus and dysentery.

In one compound I went, I saw women standing up quite naked, washing among themselves. Near by were piles of corpses. Other women suffering from dysentery were defecating in the open and then staggering back, half dead, to their blocks. Some were lying groaning on the ground. One had reverted to the absolute primitive.

A great job had been done in getting water into the camp. It has been pumped in from the outside and carried by hoses all over the camp with frequent outlet points. There are taps of fresh clean water everywhere. Carts with water move around.

The Royal Army Service Corps has also done a good job in getting food in.

I went into the typhus ward, packed thick with people lying in dirty rags of blankets on the floor, groaning and moaning. By the door sat an English Tommy talking to the people and cheering them up. They couldn't understand what he said, and he was continually ladling milk out of a caldron. I collected together some women who could speak English and German and began to make records. An amazing thing is the number who managed to keep themselves clean and neat. All of them said that in a day or two more, they would have gone under from hunger and weakness.

There are three main classes in the camp: the healthy, who have managed to keep themselves decent, but nearly all of these had typhus; then there were the sick, who were more or less cared for by their friends; then there was the vast underworld that had lost all self-respect, crawling around in rags, living in abominable squalor, defecating in the compound, often mad or half mad. By the other prisoners they are called Mussulmen. It is these who are still dying like flies. They can hardly walk on their legs. Thousands still of these cannot be saved, and if they were, they would be in lunatic asylums for the short remainder of their pitiful lives.

There were a very large number of girls in the camp, mostly Jewesses from Auschwitz. They have to be healthy to survive. Over and over again I was told the same story. The parades at which people were picked out arbitrarily for the gas chambers and the crematorium, where many were burned alive. Only a person in perfect health survived. Life and death was a question of pure chance.

After the liberation of Belsen by the British on April 15, 1945, the bodies of dead victims are removed for burial. [*Imperial War Museum, London*]

Rich Jews arrived with their belongings and were able to keep some. There were soap and perfume and fountain pens and watches. All amidst the chance of sudden, arbitrary death, amidst work commandos from which the people returned to this tomb so dead beat that they were sure to be picked for the gas chamber at the next parade, amidst the most horrible death, filth, and squalor that could be imagined.

People at Auschwitz were saved by being moved away to work in towns like Hamburg and were then moved back to Belsen as we advanced. At Auschwitz every woman had her hair shaven absolutely bald.

I met pretty young girls whose hair was one inch long. They all had their numbers tattooed on their left arm, a mark of honor they will wear all their lives.

One of the most extraordinary things was the women and men—there were only a few—who had kept themselves decent and clean.

On the first day many had on powder and lipstick. It seems the SS stores had been located and looted and boots and clothes had been found. Hundreds of people came up to me with letters, which I have taken and am sending back to London to be posted all over the world. Many have lost all their relatives. "My father and mother were burned. My sister was burned." This is what you hear all the time. The British Army is doing what it can. Units are voluntarily giving up blankets. Fifty thousand arrived while I was there and they are being laundered. Sweets and chocolate and rations have been voluntarily given.

Then we went to the children's hut. The floors had been piled with corpses there had been no time to move. We collected a chorus of Russian girls from twelve to fourteen and Dutch boys and girls from nine to fifteen. They sang songs. The Russian children were very impressive. Clean and quite big children, they had been looked after magnificently amidst starvation. They sang the songs they remembered from before captivity. They looked happy now. The Dutch children had been in camp a long time and were very skinny and pale. We stood with our backs to the corpses, out in the open amidst the pines and the birch trees near the wire fence running around the camp.

Men were hung for hours at a time, suspended by their arms, hands tied behind their back, in Belsen.

Beatings in workshops were continuous, and there were many deaths there. Just before I left the camp a crematorium was discovered. A story of Auschwitz was told to me by Helen—and her last name, she didn't remember. She was a Czechoslovak.

When the women were given the chance to go and work elsewhere in the work zones like Hamburg, mothers with children were, in fact, given the choice between their lives and their children's. Children could not be taken along. Many preferred to stay with their children and face certain death. Some decided to leave their children. But it got around amongst the six-year-old children that if they were left there they would at once be gassed. There were terrible scenes between children and their mothers. One child was so angry that though the mother changed her mind and stayed and died, the child would not talk to her.

That night when I got back at about eleven o'clock very exhausted, I saw the Jewish padre again and talked to him as he was going to bed. Suddenly, he broke down completely and sobbed.

The next morning I left this hellhole, this camp. As I left, I had myself deloused and my recording truck as well. To you at home, this is one camp. There are many more. This is what you are fighting. None of this is propaganda. This is the plain and simple truth.

BELZEC (Bełżec). With Sobibór and Maidanek (qq.v.), one of the extermination camps (q.v.) in the Lublin district of Poland. Originally a labor camp, Belzec was founded by *SS-Brigadefuehrer* Odilo Globocnik (q.v.), who in 1941 became head of all the death camps in the General Government of Poland. There were no non-Jewish inmates, nor was there any industrial activity. The business of Belzec was the gassing of hundreds of thousands of Jews. Originally, the gassings took place in a shack known as the Heckenboldt Foundation after *Unterscharffuehrer* (Sergeant) Heckenboldt, who ran the diesel engine that distributed exhaust fumes used for gassing. In August 1942, Zyklon-B (q.v.; hydrocyanic, or prussic, acid fumes) was demonstrated for the first time at Belzec. It was declared to be more humane (effective) than engine exhaust fumes, not only at Belzec but also at Sobibór, Maidanek, and Treblinka (q.v.). Belzec was also known for its supply of euthanasia technicians.

BENDLERSTRASSE. Street in Berlin on which the Ministry of War was located. In popular parlance Bendlerstrasse was used as a synonym for the Ministry of War or for the High Command of the armed forces, just as Wilhelmstrasse was used to denote the Chancellery.

BENEŠ, EDUARD (1884–1948). Statesman who fought against the Third Reich to maintain the independence of Czechoslovakia. Eduard Beneš was born in Kožlany, Bohemia, on May 28, 1884, the son of a peasant. He was educated at the University of Prague and the Sorbonne. Early in his career he became a lecturer in economics and later in sociology at the University of Prague. When World War I started, he fled to Paris, where he worked with Tomáš G. Masaryk to start the Czechoslovak National Council. On the founding of the new state of Czechoslovakia in 1918 he became its first Foreign Minister, and then succeeded Masaryk as President in 1935. He was instrumental in the formation of the Little Entente between Czechoslovakia, Yugoslavia, and Romania, which aimed to prevent a Hapsburg or Hungarian attempt to upset the settlement made in 1919. Beneš played a central role during the negotiations that led to the Munich Agreement (q.v.) in 1938. In his meetings with Prime Minister Neville Chamberlain (q.v.), Hitler violently abused Beneš and Czechoslovakia for what he charged was the persecution of the Sudeten Germans (*see* SUDETENLAND). "The oppression of the Sudeten Germans," Hitler declared, "and the terror exercised by Beneš admit of no delay." The Fuehrer denounced Beneš as a warmonger: "Who speaks of force? Herr Beneš applies force against my countrymen. Herr Beneš mobilized in May, not I." Beneš tried desperately to save his homeland. He informed Chamberlain: "I beg that nothing may be done at Munich without Czechoslovakia being heard." He was unsuccessful in warding off the appeasement that ended the independence of his country. He resigned the Presidency in October 1938 after the signing of the Munich Pact.

Eduard Beneš. *[Roger-Viollet, Paris]*

Beneš went to Chicago as a university lecturer. After the start of World War II he moved to London, where he assumed the Presidency of the Czech government-in-exile. On the defeat of Germany in 1945 he returned to Prague and became head of the Second Czechoslovak Republic. In the elections of May 1946 the Communists were the leading party, and the next July Klement Gottwald, the Communist leader, became President. In February 1948 the Communists took power through a coup d'état. In June Beneš resigned his office and was succeeded by Gottwald, as Czechoslovakia became a Communist state. He died in Sezimovo Ústí, Bohemia, on September 3, 1948.

Bibliography. Sir Compton Mackenzie, *Dr. Beneš*, George G. Harrap & Co., Ltd., London, 1946.

BENN, GOTTFRIED (1886–1956). Doctor of medicine, lyric poet, and early admirer and later critic of the Nazi revolution. Gottfried Benn was born in Mansfeld on May 2, 1886. While practicing as a physician in Berlin, he turned to writing and became one of the leading literary expressionists during the Weimar Republic (q.v.). Influenced by Friedrich Nietzsche and Oswald Spengler (qq.v.), he combined the cold jargon of the physician and biologist with the grand flights of the lyric poet. Fascinated by the problem of breeding, he urged that the German "race" be safeguarded against degradation and emasculation by dangerous interbreeding. At first he saw the Nazi state as a genuine revival in German history and as an escape from the type of rationalism which he believed had paralyzed Western civilization. He praised Hitler's concept of a "mystical collectivity" and agreed that the individual "I" had to surrender itself to the more powerful "totality" advocated by Nazi philosophy.

Benn was soon disillusioned by the realities of Hitler's regime. His moral and aesthetic sensibilities were offended by Nazism in action, and he accused Nazi leaders of misunderstanding his own conception of "the law of vitality in the age of breeding." The Nazi revolution, he now believed, had not brought the expected new and heroic sentiment of life filled with the spirit of sacrifice. On their part, Nazi authorities resented Benn's description of the Germans as an exhausted people. In 1938 the Reichsschriftumskammer (q.v.), the National Socialist authors' association, banned Benn from further writing. At the outbreak of World War II he began military service as a doctor. He was posted to lonely garrisons in eastern Germany, where in relative isolation he poured out his despair in poems and essays.

After the war Benn defended his earlier support of Hitler on the ground that in 1933 no one took the Nazi program of anti-Semitism (q.v.) and racialism seriously. It was only later, he said, that the horrifying truth came to light. He now stated that the poet had no place on the political scene, and that above all the poet needed solitude and asceticism in order to create. Benn died in Berlin on July 7, 1956.

BERCHTESGADEN. German town in southeast Bavaria near the Austrian border, 74 miles southeast of Munich. Berchtesgaden was the site of Hitler's mountain retreat. Situated at a height of 1,700 feet in the Alps, it was near three majestic mountains, Watzmann (8,820 feet), Hochkalter (8,473 feet), and Hoher Göll (8,196 feet). With a population in 1933 of 3,919 (later expanded to 26,000), Berchtesgaden was known for its extensive mines of rock salt. A health and winter sports resort, it became a mecca for tourists during the Third Reich. Here the Fuehrer built the Berghof (q.v.), a large estate and chalet. At the foot of the steps leading up to the house, he received his famous guests.

BEREITSCHAFT (Emergency Force). An emergency detachment of the Nationalsozialistische Deutsche Arbeiterpartei (q.v.) or the police to be used on special occasions.

BERGEN-BELSEN. *See* BELSEN.

BERGER, GOTTLOB (1895–). *SS-Obergruppenfuehrer* (general) who specialized in security problems. Berger served in the Central Security Office (Reichssicherheitshauptamt, q.v.). In 1941, while in charge of the ministry of Alfred Rosenberg (q.v.) in occupied Russia, he was instrumental in publishing an instructional pamphlet titled *The Subhuman*, which called the people of the Soviet Union "the afterbirth of humanity existing spiritually on a lower level than animals." In August 1944 he was assigned command of military operations in Slovakia; in this post he was said to have imposed the peace of the graveyard after an uprising. Berger was tried at Nuremberg for the wartime murder of Jews and in April 1949 was sentenced to twenty-five years' imprisonment. He was released in 1951.

BERGHOF. Hitler's estate and chalet on the Obersalzberg high above the town of Berchtesgaden (q.v.), in southeastern Bavaria. This elaborate mountain retreat, constructed on the site of the original Haus Wachenfeld, was bought by the Fuehrer with his own funds acquired from the sales of *Mein Kampf* (q.v.). The Berghof reflected Hitler's passion for huge rooms, thick carpets, and a view of the mountain area. He planned the building himself, and he had it completed by slave labor. The central chalet, built in the midst of a compound containing barracks for some 20,000 troops, was protected by five rings of fortifications. Made of stone in the shape of a mushroom, the

The Eagle's Nest in the Berghof. [*Photo by Hugo Jaeger*, Look, *January 6, 1959*]

Berghof sat squarely on a mountaintop. Of the thirteen floors, only the top story was above the ground. On this floor was a series of large rooms from which there were magnificent views of the surrounding mountains and the valley below. Most impressive was the great reception room with a huge octagonal table and a massive picture window. Nearby was a rectangular banqueting hall. In the underground floors was a maze of guardrooms, bedrooms, kitchens, and food and wine cellars. There was also a special tower, the Eagle's Nest (q.v.), with a private elevator to the top, where the Fuehrer could resign himself to complete solitude.

In the vicinity of Hitler's chalet were smaller houses occupied by Hermann Goering, Dr. Paul Joseph Goebbels, and Martin Bormann (qq.v.). Goering insisted that his own estate be no more than 100 yards from Hitler's chalet. He persuaded the Bavarian Cabinet to give him a piece of land 100,000 meters square. In every direction were camps for the security troops. A special road led from Berchtesgaden to the Berghof.

Life at the Berghof was a model of *petit bourgeois* comfort. Hitler was indifferent to clothes and food; he never touched meat, nor did he smoke or drink. He took little exercise. He liked flowers in his room, cream cakes and sweets, dogs, and clever women. He was fond of motion pictures and often entertained his friends with the latest films. His vitality rose in the late evenings; he hated to go to bed because he found it difficult to sleep. After dinner he would assemble his household guests and visitors for late-night sessions around the fireplace, during which he would comment on every possible subject. Chewing peppermints or sipping herbal drinks, he would speak at length on his philosophy of life, often referring pleasantly to his *Kampfzeit* (q.v.), the years of struggle, and his *Alte Kämpfer* (q.v.), his old fighting comrades.

On September 15, 1938, Prime Minister Neville Chamberlain (q.v.) flew to Munich and then went by automobile to Berchtesgaden to discuss the critical Czechoslovakian situation with Hitler. The Fuehrer received him in the usual fashion at the foot of the steps leading to the Berghof. During World War II the compound was a special target for Allied air raids. The central chalets were wrecked, and the entire area after the bombing gave the appearance of a landscape on the moon.

BERGNER, ELISABETH (1897–   ). Stage and film actress and refugee from the Third Reich. Elisabeth Bergner was born in Drogobych, Galicia, on August 22, 1897. She performed her first stage roles in Vienna and then went to Berlin, where she was an outstanding success in such plays as *Saint Joan* (1924) by George Bernard Shaw, *Fräulein Else* (1927), and *Ariane* (1931). In 1933 she married the stage director Paul Czinner and left Germany for London.

BERLIN, BATTLE FOR. *See* BATTLE FOR BERLIN.

BERLIN PUTSCH. An attempt by the Resistance (q.v.) movement to overthrow Hitler in September 1938. The Fuehrer distrusted most of his generals, who had opposed him and National Socialism from the beginning. In all there were five occasions on which members of the military were implicated in the goal of ending Hitler's career: (1) the January 1933 Potsdam *Putsch,* (2) the September 1938 Berlin *Putsch,* (3) the November 1939 Zossen *Putsch,* (4) the January 1943 Stalingrad *Putsch,* and (5) the 1944 July Plot (qq.v.). In each case Hitler, either by careful planning or by good fortune, was able to outwit the conspirators and survive.

By 1938 the opposition to Hitler was transformed into a Resistance movement, including, in addition to the recalcitrant generals, civilians who were disgusted with the Nazi regime. The generals were infuriated by the Blomberg-Fritsch crisis (q.v.). The angry officers included Col. Gen. Ludwig Beck and Col. Gen. Kurt Freiherr von Hammerstein-Equord (qq.v.) Added to the military were such high-placed civilians as Hjalmar Schacht, Carl Friedrich Goerdeler, and Johannes Popitz (qq.v.); members of the Abwehr (q.v.), such as Adm. Wilhelm Canaris and Col. Hans Oster (qq.v.); and a younger group including Dietrich Bonhoeffer (q.v.), Fabian von Schlabrendorff, Hans von Dohnányi (q.v.), and Otto John. Other members of the Kreisau Circle (q.v.) joined later.

In the summer of 1938 General Beck resigned his post as chief of the General Staff and became active in the conspiracy against Hitler. The plan was to seize the Fuehrer as soon as he gave the order for Operation Green (*see* GRÜN), directed against Czechoslovakia. Hitler was to be taken alive and brought before a new People's Court, certified insane, and put away in a lunatic asylum. The conspirators attempted to make contacts in London for assistance. Meanwhile, Prime Minister Neville Chamberlain (q.v.) made his three trips by plane to Germany in an effort to maintain peace. Plans for the *Putsch* were shattered because of irresolute leadership, ineptitude in organization, and failure to act at the psychological moment. The leaders hesitated until the visits of Chamberlain destroyed all hope for success.

BERNADOTTE OF WISBORG, COUNT FOLKE (1895–1948). Swedish Red Cross official. Folke Bernadotte was born in Stockholm on January 2, 1895. In 1943 he became vice president, and in 1946 president, of the Swedish Red Cross. In the last days of the Third Reich, Heinrich Himmler (q.v.) attempted to use the services of Bernadotte as an intermediary to bring about an armistice. Altogether there were four interviews between Himmler and Bernadotte, on February 12, April 2, April 21, and April 23–24, 1945. Himmler was torn with indecision: on the one hand, he was moved by his loyalty to the Fuehrer, while on the other he wanted to save his own life in a rapidly deteriorating situation. The two discussed the possible transfer of the concentration camps (q.v.) to the International Red Cross. Himmler spoke of releasing Polish women from Ravensbrück (q.v.), but even here he insisted on obtaining Hitler's approval. Himmler hoped for direct negotiations with Gen. Dwight D. Eisenhower.

On April 27 Bernadotte brought back news that neither Himmler nor a limited surrender was acceptable to the Allies. When Hitler learned that his "faithful Heinrich" had attempted to negotiate behind his back, he flew into a rage and ordered that Himmler's claim to the succession be canceled. He also ordered the arrest of Himmler for treason: "A traitor must never succeed me as Fuehrer!" In

Count Folke Bernadotte. [*Picture Collection, The Branch Libraries, The New York Public Library*]

his political testament Hitler expelled Himmler from the party because of secret negotiations with the enemy as well as his "illegal" attempts to seize power. This, he charged, had brought "irreparable shame on the country and the whole people." *See also* HITLER'S POLITICAL TESTAMENT.

Count Bernadotte was killed by Jewish extremists in Jerusalem on September 17, 1948, while attempting to negotiate an armistice between Jews and Arabs.

Bibliography. Count Folke Bernadotte, *The Curtain Falls*, Alfred A. Knopf, Inc., New York, 1945.

BERNHARD, OPERATION. Code name for a plan to drop forged British banknotes on England by plane early in World War II. The scheme was devised by Alfred Helmut Naujocks, an assistant to Reinhard Heydrich (qq.v.). Naujocks for a time managed a section of the SD (q.v.) that specialized in forging passports and similar necessities for espionage agents.

BESITZBÜRGERTUM (Property-owning Bourgeoisie). Term applied to the bourgeoisie by the leftist wing of the Nazi party in the early days of the movement. After Ernst Roehm (q.v.) and his followers had been liquidated and the second revolution (q.v.) averted, Hitler turned his scorn on the educated middle class instead of the bourgeois business and financial leaders. He denounced intellectuals as "rejects of nature." Dr. Paul Joseph Goebbels (q.v.), Minister for Public Enlightenment and Propaganda, added that intellectuals were "a pack of prating parasites."

BEST, WERNER (1903–). National Socialist legal expert and, from 1940 to 1942, Reich Commissioner for occupied Denmark. Werner Best was born at Darmstadt on July 10, 1903, the son of a senior postmaster. He attended a humanistic *Gymnasium* (high school), first in Darmstadt and then in Mainz. At the age of sixteen he founded a national youth organization in Mainz. He studied law in Frankfurt am Main, Freiburg, Giessen, and Heidelberg, where he completed his doctorate in 1927. In 1929 he took his first legal position with the justice department in Hesse.

From 1930 on Best became active in the affairs of the Nationalsozialistische Deutsche Arbeiterpartei (q.v.). He was forced to resign his position in Hesse in 1931, when the Boxheim documents (q.v.), which served as a blueprint for the Nazi seizure of power, were found in his possession. In March 1933, shortly after Hitler became Chancellor, Best was appointed special commissioner of police for Hesse; within four months he was Governor of the state. In 1935 he was made section leader of the Secret State Police under Reinhard Heydrich (q.v.). Hitler depended upon Best to explain away the "many unfortunate accidents" in Gestapo (q.v.) prisons. Best presented a positive view: "As long as the police carries out the will of the leadership, it is acting legally."

Best served on the staff of the military commander in France from 1940 to 1942. From November 1942 to May 1945 he was Reich Commissioner for occupied Denmark. In this post he tried friendly methods in dealing with the Danes and made it a point to treat Niels Bohr, the Danish physicist, with consideration. Tried in Denmark in 1948, Best was sentenced to death, but the punishment was later commuted to a prison term. He was released in 1951.

BILDUNGSBÜRGERTUM (Bourgeoisie by Education). Term used to describe adherence to the middle class, or bourgeoisie, by virtue of education, as distinct from wealth.

BIRDS OF DEATH. *See* TOTENVÖGEL.

BIRDS OF PASSAGE. *See* WANDERVÖGEL.

BIRKENAU (Brzezinka). Extermination camp (*see* EXTERMINATION CAMPS) located in the Birkenau woods near Auschwitz (q.v.) in occupied Poland. Birkenau was constructed in 1941 on orders from Heinrich Himmler (q.v.) as a special killing center for 100,000 Russian prisoners. Two old farm buildings were made airtight by strong wooden doors. Prisoners were unloaded from nearby transports and separated into those fit for work and those to be liquidated. The latter were required to undress at the doors of the *Disinfektionsraum* (disinfection chamber) and were then sent in 250 at a time. After the doors were locked, tins of Zyklon-B (q.v.) gas were thrown into specially constructed apertures. Later the doors were opened, and the bodies were removed by prisoner details and burned in pits lined with rags soaked in paraffin. Six to seven hours were necessary to cremate 100 bodies in one burial pit.

BISMARCK. German superdreadnought, one of the most powerful warships ever launched, sunk by the British in World War II. Displacing 42,000 tons and measuring 791 feet at the waterline, she mounted a main battery of eight modern 15-inch guns, twelve 5.9-inch guns, and sixteen 4.1-inch guns. Her twin-shaft turbines gave her a speed of 30 knots. Her optical fire-control system was one of the best in the world, and her watertight compartments were believed to have made her virtually unsinkable. Winston Churchill pronounced her "a masterpiece of naval construction."

In May 1941 the giant warship, together with the *Prinz Eugen* and several other vessels, left anchorage in a fjord near Bergen with the assignment of raiding British con-

The *Bismarck*. [*Imperial War Museum, London*]

voys. British reconnaissance planes detailed specifically for the task quickly discovered the enemy raiders. The British Admiralty dispatched a strong force, including the battleship *Prince of Wales,* the battle cruiser *Hood,* the cruisers *Suffolk* and *Norfolk,* and several destroyers, to engage the *Bismarck*. The warships met off the coast of Greenland on May 24, 1941. In the first exchange of fire the *Bismarck* scored a direct hit on the twenty-one-year-old *Hood.* The British ship was covered with a bright sea of flame after the hit blasted her thinly armored magazine loaded with powder. Parts of her hull were thrown hundreds of feet into the air. In a few minutes all that was left was a patch of smoke on the water and some small bits of wreckage.

Meanwhile, the other British warships continued to rain shells on the *Bismarck.* Taking advantage of weather conditions, the German ships slipped away, probably heading for the safety of a French port. The *Bismarck* was lost for the next thirty-one hours. From the Admiralty in London came orders for every available warship from Newfoundland to Gibraltar to hunt the *Bismarck.* Two days later the air crew of a British plane spotted the *Bismarck* around 400 miles off the French coast and apparently in trouble. Heavy fleet units, including the aircraft carrier *Ark Royal,* were sent to the area. Torpedo-carrying planes from the *Ark Royal* harassed the German battleship until other ships could close in on her. One torpedo hit the *Bismarck* amidships, and a second crashed into her stern, crippling the steering mechanism and causing the ship to turn around and around in uncontrollable circles. Then other naval units, including destroyers led by the *Cossack,* caught up with the floundering giant and rained shells on her from every direction.

On the morning of May 27, 1941, the powerful *King George V* and the *Rodney* appeared on the scene to finish off the *Bismarck.* Salvos from 14- and 16-inch guns sliced through the armor of the German battlewagon. By this time the *Bismarck* was battered beyond recognition, her superstructure destroyed and her impotent guns pointing crazily in all directions. Hundreds of the crew, unable to survive on the blazing ship, jumped into the sea. The *Doretshire* closed in on the mortally wounded hulk and sent her remaining torpedoes speeding toward the target. Slowly, the *Bismarck* heeled over to port, turned upside down, and disappeared beneath the waves. In the rough seas British sailors lowered lines to survivors and rescued 100 crewmen, but broke off the operation when a submarine was reported in the vicinity. The destruction of the *Bismarck,* at a time when the Germans were inflicting heavy defeats on the British on land, was important for the Allied cause. Not only was the sinking of the *Hood* quickly avenged, but the demonstration of British naval power gave a psychological lift to the nations pledged to destroy Nazism.

Bibliography. C. S. Forester, *Sink the Bismarck,* Bantam Books, Inc., New York, 1959.

BLACK. *See* SCHWARZ.

BLACK BOOK, NAZI. *See* SONDERFAHNDUNGSLISTE-GB.

BLACK CORPS, THE. *See* SCHWARZE KORPS, DAS.

BLACK FRONT. *See* SCHWARZE FRONT.

BLACK ORDER. *See* SS.

BLACK REICHSWEHR. *See* FEHMEMORD.

BLACK WEDNESDAY. Name given to September 28, 1938, the day on which war seemed inevitable because of the unresolved Czechoslovakian crisis. At 2 P.M. Hitler, just as his ultimatum was about to expire, decided to postpone mobilization of his troops "at the request of my great friend and ally, Mussolini." Invitations were hastily sent to Prime Minister Neville Chamberlain, Premier Édouard Daladier, and Benito Mussolini (qq.v.) to meet the Fuehrer in Munich at noon of the following day to settle the Czech question. *See also* MUNICH AGREEMENT.

BLACKSHIRTS. Name given to members of the SS (q.v.).

BLASKOWITZ, JOHANNES (1883–1948). Senior Wehrmacht (q.v.) general during the Third Reich. Johannes Blaskowitz was born in Peterswalde, East Prussia, on July 18, 1883. A career officer in the Reichswehr (q.v.) after World War I, he was one of a group of officers who advocated an agreement with Soviet Russia so that Germany could prosecute a war against Poland, "a sacred though a sad duty." On December 1, 1935, he was promoted to general of infantry and the next year was given command of Wehrkreis (Defense District) II. With Generals Wilhelm List and Fedor von Bock (qq.v.), Blaskowitz managed to survive the military reorganization of early 1938 (*see* BLOMBERG-FRITSCH CRISIS) and was assigned as a field commander to Dresden. On March 15, 1939, he led the Third Army into Bohemia as Hitler took over Czechoslovakia. On the eve of World War II, at the age of fifty-six, he was seventh in seniority among generals of the Wehrmacht.

In September 1939 Blaskowitz led the Eighth Army to tie down the Polish forces in Poznań (Posen). At one point he incurred the Fuehrer's displeasure by ordering a temporary retreat, an action which Hitler regarded as virtually treasonable. Nevertheless, after the Polish campaign came to an end, Hitler on October 22, 1939, made Blaskowitz commander in chief of the army of occupation in Poland with headquarters in Spala. In this post Blaskowitz came into conflict with the Austrian Artur Seyss-Inquart (q.v.), who had been appointed by Hitler as civilian Governor-General. An officer of the old school, Blaskowitz objected to the excesses of the SS (q.v.) and the actions of German police against both Jews and the old Polish governing class. In a memorandum he warned that, judging from the conduct of members of the SS in Poland, "they might later turn on their own people in the same way." Urged to send the memorandum directly to Hitler, he hesitated and forwarded it through proper channels to Gen. Walther von Brauchitsch (q.v.), ranking senior officer. It was promptly lost.

Although Blaskowitz was unaware of it, members of his staff were involved in the conspiracy against Hitler. In 1944 he was given command of Army Group G under Gen. Gerd von Rundstedt (q.v.), and in early 1945 he commanded German troops in the Netherlands.

After the war Blaskowitz was indicted as a minor war criminal in Case 12 *(Wilhelm von Leeb, et al.)* by the American military tribunal in Nuremberg. On February 5, 1948, just before he was to be brought to trial, he committed suicide in the Nuremberg jail. Later a story of doubtful authenticity became current that Blaskowitz was murdered by disgruntled SS members who had become prison trusties.

BLAU (Blue). Code name for the war with Great Britain.

BLESSED WITH CHILDREN. *See* KINDERSEGEN.

BLITZKRIEG (Lightning War). Military tactics inaugurated by Hitler and carried out by such combat commanders as Gen. Heinz Guderian (q.v.) in the Polish and French campaigns of 1939 and 1940. The accent was no longer placed on endless columns of soldiers marching a few miles a day. Instead of the static lines of World War I, as in the bloodbath at Verdun, where opposing armies dug themselves like moles into the ground and hurled artillery shells at one another, *Blitzkrieg* emphasized mobility and fluidity. "The whole battlefield," said one observer, "becomes an amorphous permeation like a plague of vermin in a garden." It was a new kind of attack that threw defenders into hopeless confusion.

First, the way was prepared by activities of the fifth column (q.v.) behind enemy lines. Second, in a swift surprise blow, the opposing air force was destroyed on the ground, thus removing the prime obstacle to land attack. Third, the enemy was slowed down by bombing from the air all his means of communication and transportation. Fourth, troop concentrations were dive-bombed to keep them off balance and prevent them from striking back in strength. Fifth, light forces—motorcycle infantry, light tanks, motor-drawn artillery—were sent ahead. Sixth, heavy tanks followed them to carve out mechanized pockets in the rear. Finally, the regular infantry—foot soldiers, supported by artillery—were committed to mop up resistance and join up with advanced forces.

The theory of *Blitzkrieg* was suggested in 1934 by a forty-four-year-old French officer, Col. Charles de Gaulle, in *Vers l'armée de métier* (translated as *The Army of the Future*). In a plea for mechanization, De Gaulle favored the concentration of armored troops in armored divisions as against the French General Staff policy of parceling them out as army tank brigades in a supporting role. His ideas on the tactical employment of armor were opposed by conservative officers inured to the policies of Foch and Joffre. Frenchmen would not listen to De Gaulle's revolutionary ideas, but Hitler and his generals adopted them with scintillating success in the opening phases of World War II.

Bibliography. Larry H. Addington, *The Blitzkrieg Era and the German General Staff, 1865–1941*, Rutgers University Press, New Brunswick, N.J., 1971.

BLOCKWART (Block Warden). The lowest Nazi party official above the members of the rank and file.

BLOMBERG, WERNER VON (1878–1946). Minister of Defense and supreme commander of the armed forces in the early years of the Nazi regime. Werner von Blomberg was born in Stargard on September 2, 1878. A man of imposing presence, sometimes called "a Siegfried with a monocle," he seemed destined for a great military career. From 1927 to 1929 he was adjutant general of the Reichswehr (q.v.). While in this post he visited Soviet Russia,

Field Marshal Werner von Blomberg. [*Associated Press*]

where he received a favorable impression of the military. "I was not far short of becoming a complete Bolshevik myself," he wrote later. In 1929 he was given command of Wehrkreis (Defense District) I at Königsberg headquarters in East Prussia. He was impressed by Hitler, who visited Königsberg in August 1930, and came to the conclusion that the Nazi leader would eventually make the Reichswehr a truly popular army. Hitler in power, he believed, would do for Germany what the Red Army had accomplished for the Soviet Union.

Though not a convinced Nazi, Von Blomberg remained loyal to the Fuehrer and won rapid promotion. On January 1, 1933, a month before Hitler became Chancellor, Von Blomberg was named Minister of Defense. He retained that post after the Nazis came to political power and held it until his resignation in 1938. On August 2, 1934, immediately after the death of President Paul von Hindenburg (q.v.), Von Blomberg called on all officers of the Reichswehr to take a personal oath of loyalty to the Fuehrer. In May 1935 he was appointed supreme commander of the new Wehrmacht (q.v.). In this capacity he led the process of German rearmament. In 1936 Hitler made him the first general field marshal of the armed forces. Von Blomberg was one of the leading officers present at the Hossbach Conference (q.v.) of November 5, 1937, at which Hitler made known his plans for aggression. By this time relations between Hitler and Von Blomberg had cooled. On February 4, 1938, Von Blomberg was dismissed under especially embarrassing circumstances (*see* BLOMBERG-FRITSCH CRISIS). He died in an American prison in Nuremberg on March 4, 1946.

BLOMBERG-FRITSCH CRISIS. Hitler's dismissal in early 1938 of his two leading generals after distasteful personal scandals. The outcome allowed the Fuehrer to solidify his control over the Army and embark upon his program of aggression. When Hitler became Chancellor in 1933, he was merely tolerated by the Army as a political upstart. By the summer of 1934 he succeeded in extinguishing any spark of organized political opposition inside Germany. High army officers at first saw no reason to oppose him because he was obtaining precisely the results they desired. The Blomberg-Fritsch crisis shattered their illusions. Officers disgusted by Hitler's plans began to take a stand against him. Opposition ripened into Resistance (q.v.) and eventually into conspiracy. The military played an important role in all three movements.

Field Marshal Werner von Blomberg (q.v.), Minister of Defense and supreme commander of the Wehrmacht (q.v.), the new armed forces, and Col. Gen. Werner Freiherr von Fritsch (q.v.), commander in chief of the Army, were two of the highest officers in the new Third Reich. Both were present at the historic Hossbach Conference (q.v.) on November 5, 1937, when Hitler showed his hand and made clear his intention of achieving *Lebensraum* (q.v.), or living space, by force. Both were appalled and shaken, and both were out of office within three months. In each case the dismissal was accompanied by scandal, manipulated and used to destroy the careers of the two officers.

Toward the end of 1937 Von Blomberg, a widower, began to entertain seriously the thought of marrying his secretary, a Fräulein Eva Gruhn, despite her questionable past. This was not a marriage which the ranking member of the officers' corps could embark upon without severe repercussions. Nevertheless, the wedding took place on January 12, 1938, with Hitler himself and Hermann Goering (q.v.) present as witnesses. Almost immediately gossipmongers began to attack the name and reputation of the new *Frau Generalfeldmarschall.* There were complaints about Von Blomberg's "disgracing the officers' corps," and there were embarrassing comments in the press. Unhappily for him and his bride, there was some truth to the rumors.

Meanwhile, Wolf Heinrich Graf von Helldorf (q.v.), chief of the Berlin Police, had gathered a dossier on the field marshal's new wife, and it was not a favorable one. Von Helldorf took the dossier to Gen. Wilhelm Keitel (q.v.), Von Blomberg's immediate subordinate, but Keitel refused to have anything to do with the matter and suggested that Von Helldorf bring it to Goering. The latter, who regarded Von Blomberg as an obstacle to his own career, brought it to Hitler's attention. The Fuehrer, highly indignant and angered because he had attended the wedding, ordered Von Blomberg's dismissal. The resignation took effect on February 4, 1938. Hitler sent a letter to Von Blomberg praising him for his loyal service during the past five years in helping build the new Wehrmacht. The Fuehrer then appointed himself supreme commander of the armed forces, a post he regarded as vital to his plans. Von Blomberg and his bride went into exile to Capri and disappeared from the military scene in Germany.

Von Fritsch was involved in an even uglier situation. He, too, had opposed Hitler at the Hossbach Conference, and he, too, was slated for dismissal. He had to be eliminated in one way or another, and the means were found quickly. Von Fritsch's dossier contained what was said to be evidence that he was guilty of homosexual offenses under Section 175 of the Criminal Code. He was called before Hitler, Goering, and Heinrich Himmler (q.v.) to answer such charges. Himmler produced an obscure witness named Schmidt who was prepared to testify that he had observed Von Fritsch commit a homosexual offense with Bavarian Joe (q.v.), a *Lustknabe,* a young boy, near the Potsdam railroad station in November 1934. Stunned and humiliated, Von Fritsch hotly denied the charge. A lifelong bachelor who had never had much to do with the opposite sex, Von Fritsch was especially vulnerable to accusations of this kind. He demanded and obtained a trial before an army court of honor, which acquitted him "for proven innocence." His personal honor was vindicated, but his career was ended. On February 4, 1938, the same day on which he had written a cordial letter to Von Blomberg, Hitler sent an icy communication to Von Fritsch accepting his resignation. Von Fritsch was replaced by Gen. Walther von Brauchitsch (q.v.) as commander in chief of the Army.

On August 11, 1938, Von Fritsch was publicly rehabilitated. Preferring to remain in Germany, he declined offers to serve as military adviser in Spain or South America. In August 1939, just before the outbreak of World War II, he was recalled to command his old Artillery Regiment 12, to which he had been attached a decade earlier and which was now stationed in East Prussia. On September 22, 1939, only a few weeks after the beginning of the war, he was hit by a Polish machine-gun bullet while in a field on the outskirts of Warsaw. Many of his colleagues believed that, humiliated beyond endurance, he had deliberately sought death.

With the fall of Von Blomberg and Von Fritsch, Hitler succeeded in penetrating the closed society of the generals. As supreme commander of the armed forces the Fuehrer believed that he could pursue his plans for the creation of a Greater Germany without the annoying opposition of weak professionals.

BLONDI. Hitler's Alsatian dog, to which he was much attached. Blondi was a favorite in the household at the Berghof (q.v.). The Fuehrer turned for comfort in his last days in the Berlin bunker to the only two creatures on earth who he believed had remained loyal to him—Eva Braun (q.v.) and Blondi. He furiously rejected Heinrich Himmler and Hermann Goering (qq.v.) because he believed that they had deserted him at a critical hour. On the morning of April 30, 1945, the day of his suicide, Hitler called in one of his doctors to destroy Blondi with poison. At the same time two other dogs were shot by the sergeant assigned to take care of them.

BLOOD AND SOIL. *See* BLUT UND BODEN.

BLOOD BANNER. *See* BLUTFAHNE.

BLOOD ORDER. *See* BLUTORDEN.

BLOOD PURGE (also called Die Nacht der langen Messer, or Night of the Long Knives). A campaign of assassination unleashed by Hitler on the night of June 30, 1934, against the growing power of the SA (q.v.), the brownshirted Storm Troopers. From its beginning, the Nazi revolution was pulled in two directions. The very name of the party—National Socialist—spelled trouble between the two movements, nationalism and socialism. Eventually, Hitler was forced to choose between them.

The struggle revolved around the personality, career, and beliefs of Ernst Roehm (q.v.), Hitler's close friend for fifteen years. A hard, stocky little man, Roehm gave the appearance of being a tough character. Wounded three times in World War I, he faced the world with half his nose shot away and his cheek scarred by a bullet. In the immediate postwar years he was a professional freebooter, always looking for a fight. "Because I am a bad man," he was fond of saying, "war appeals to me more than peace." In the early days of the Nazi movement, Roehm created the SA, the "popular army" composed of patriots, street bullies, and gangsters. Under Roehm's direction, the SA won the battle of the streets against the Communists and played an important role in Hitler's rise to political power. A grateful Hitler said that he would never forget what Roehm had done for the movement. "I want to thank Heaven," Hitler said, "for having given me the right to call a man like you my friend and comrade-in-arms."

At the same time, Hitler began to be more and more seriously embarrassed by Roehm's political position. Roehm, together with Gregor Strasser (q.v.) and other early Nazis, formed a left-wing branch of the party and called for a second revolution (q.v.) in the direction of socialism. "The National Socialist struggle," Roehm said, "has been a Socialist Revolution. It has been a revolution of the workers' movement. Those who made this revolution must also be the ones to speak for it." The implication was that the SA would see to it that the Nazi revolution would not slow down.

This view placed Hitler in an uncomfortable dilemma. He wanted to retain Roehm's friendship and loyalty, but he also needed support from two other sources, both of which detested Roehm and his aggregation of misfits and roughnecks. Roehm hoped that one day his Storm Troopers would be absorbed into the regular Army, a view which infuriated high officers of the armed forces. Moreover, Hitler desperately needed financial support from the Rhineland industrialists, all of whom scorned the socialism of the Nazi left-wingers.

Hitler tried to reason with Roehm. On June 4, 1934, he sent for the SA leader, and in a five-hour conversation begged his good friend to keep in line. "Forget the idea of a Second Revolution. Believe in me. Don't cause any trouble." Hitler said that he did not intend to dissolve the SA, to which he owed so much, but he ordered it on leave for the month of August, during which time no uniforms were to be worn. Another conversation with Roehm was arranged for Bad Wiessee on July 1.

By this time Hitler had almost come to the conclusion that Roehm and his followers had to be eliminated for the good of the cause. He was joined in his determination by Hermann Goering (q.v.), the No. 2 Nazi, and Heinrich Himmler (q.v.), leader of the SS (q.v.). Dr. Paul Joseph Goebbels (q.v.), Hitler's propaganda expert, who at one time had flirted with the left wing, decided to cast his lot with Hitler. The time for vacillation was over.

On the morning of June 29, Hitler, who was staying at a hotel in Bad Godesberg overlooking the Rhine, summoned Viktor Lutze (q.v.), *SA-Obergruppenfueher* (general) of Hannover, to his presence and informed him abruptly that he was to succeed Roehm as *Stabschef* (chief of staff) of the SA. The astonished Lutze accepted. At the same time Goebbels flew in from Berlin to be at the Fuehrer's side at the right moment. He informed Hitler that Karl Ernst (q.v.), the SA chief in Berlin, was at that moment alerting his Storm Troopers, certainly for some ill purpose. It was a calculated canard: Ernst, who had just been married, with Roehm and Goering in attendance, was on his way to Bremen with his bride and was about to board a passenger ship for a honeymoon in Madeira.

At 1 A.M. on June 30, Hitler received urgent messages from Goering and Himmler confirming the rumor that an SA uprising was being synchronized in Berlin and Munich for the next day. This was to be the long-planned second revolution. Hitler now made the drastic decision to purge the traitors. He sent orders to Goering to take care of the situation in Berlin and to Adolf Wagner, Bavarian minister of the interior, to move in Munich. Wagner would have the assistance of two companies of the Leibstandarte-SS Adolf Hitler (q.v.) sent from Berlin under Josef (Sepp) Dietrich (q.v.).

Meanwhile, Hitler, accompanied by Goebbels and Lutze, flew from an airport near Bonn southward across Germany. At 4 A.M. the plane touched down in Munich. Hitler and his entourage proceeded to the Ministry of the Interior. Here two chiefs of the Bavarian SA, named Scheinhuber and Schmidt, were taken into custody. The prisoners saluted the Fuehrer, only to be greeted with an outburst of hysterical rage. Hitler tore off the insignia of rank from the shoulders of the astonished officers and screamed abuse at them. He drew his revolver, but was beaten to the draw by Emil Maurice (q.v.), one of his bodyguards, who shot at point-blank range. Hitler kicked one of the corpses and remarked: "These men were not the most guilty!"

Followed by his SS guards, Hitler set out in a hurry for Bad Wiessee. Here Roehm and several of his associates were staying at a private hotel. Roehm lay in bed, fast asleep. Hitler banged loudly on the door. "Who is there?" Roehm asked sleepily. "It's I, Hitler. Open up!" Roehm unbolted the door and said: "Already? I wasn't expecting you until tomorrow." "Arrest him," Hitler shouted to his aides. At the same time, a detachment of the SS kicked in the door of a neighboring room. There they found *SA-Obergruppenfuehrer* (Gen.) Edmund Heines (q.v.), a close associate of Roehm, in bed with his young chauffeur. Heines and his young friend were shot dead. Several other SA leaders were taken prisoner and, together with the protesting Roehm and the corpses of Heines and his friend, were pushed into a waiting automobile.

Back in Munich, Rudolf Hess (q.v.), the Deputy Fuehrer, who had arrived at the Brown House (Braunes Haus, q.v.), turned the building into a trap for SA officers. As Storm Troopers arrived, they were taken prisoner by an SS cordon. One after another the bewildered men were taken to Stadelheim Prison. Hitler went there and ordered additional executions.

Meanwhile, Hitler called Berlin and ordered Goering and Himmler to go ahead with their end of the bloodbath. More than 150 top SA leaders suspected of disloyalty to Hitler were arrested and placed in a coal cellar at the Lichterfelde Cadet School barracks. Most had no idea why they were being shot. Many went to their deaths shouting *"Heil Hitler!"* Four at a time the victims were led out to a wall in the courtyard. Then an SS man opened their shirts and with a piece of charcoal drew a black circle on the left part of the chest. This was the target. A few yards from the wall a firing squad of eight men pumped bullets into the doomed men. On it went, hour after hour. The firing squads had to be changed frequently because the executioners could not stand the strain for long. The victims lay screaming and writhing on the ground. An officer finished them off with a shot in the head. The bodies were taken away in a butcher's tin-lined truck.

Two days later Roehm died. Hitler had ordered that a revolver be left in his cell so that he could take the "honorable" way out within ten minutes. Roehm refused to believe the order and demanded that his friend come to see him. Two guards, acting on Sepp Dietrich's orders, then entered the cell and pumped bullets into the half-clad prisoner.

No one knows how many were killed in the blood purge. It is estimated that at least 77 leading Nazis died as well as at least 100 others. The massacre was directed primarily at the left wing of the party, but in the confusion some leading Nazis took advantage of the situation to settle old scores. Goering, jealous of the military rank and influence of Gen. Kurt von Schleicher (q.v.), was said to have placed his name on the death list. Von Schleicher, master of intrigue, who had been living in retirement since January 1933, had only contempt for Roehm and the SA, but he was to share their fate. While Hitler flew to Munich, a detachment of six SS men disguised in civilian clothes drew up in a car outside Von Schleicher's villa in Neubabelsberg, on the outskirts of Berlin. The men pushed into the house and confronted Von Schleicher, who was at breakfast with his wife and fourteen-year-old stepdaughter. The intruders pulled out their guns and fired bullets into Von Schleicher and his wife. They warned the girl that she would suffer the same fate if she told what she had seen.

Gregor Strasser was shot in his cell by an SS man who boasted: "I have killed the swine!" Vice Chancellor Franz von Papen (q.v.) was more fortunate: he was kept under surveillance for several days, but his principal secretary was gunned down at a desk, and his collaborator on the Marburg speech (*see* MARBURGER REDE) was murdered in prison. In Munich the seventy-five-year-old Gustav Ritter von Kahr (q.v.), who eleven years earlier had crushed Hitler's 1923 Beer-Hall *Putsch* (q.v.), was dragged from his home, beaten to death, and left in a swamp. There were some ghastly mistakes. Willi Schmid, a respected music critic, was confused with a man named Willi Schmidt, and died because of the coincidence. Rudolf Hess visited the widow to express an apology. Karl Ernst, the supposed organizer of the "SA plot," was seized by SS men near Bremen as he was about to sail on his honeymoon, flown back to Berlin, and executed there.

On July 1, the controlled press announced the execution of eight SA chiefs. Von Schleicher's death was described as "accidental." On July 2, the news was released that "the traitor Roehm, who had refused to take the consequences of his deeds," had been executed.

On July 13, 1934, Hitler addressed the Reichstag (q.v.) in a formal explanation of what had happened. It was an extraordinary speech. After the usual introduction denouncing his political predecessors and boasting of the accomplishments of his regime, the Fuehrer listed and described four dangerous dissident elements in the Third Reich: (1) Communists supported by Jews; (2) political leaders of the old parties; (3) a band of leftist revolutionaries headed by Roehm, "who wanted revolution for the sake of revolution"; and (4) self-appointed critics and rumormongers. "Though worthless in themselves, they are, nevertheless, dangerous because they are veritable bacillus-carriers of unrest and uncertainty, of rumors, assertions, lies and suspicion, of slanders and fear." Critics said that Hitler was apparently unaware of the fact that he was describing his own movement.

The Fuehrer went on to state that some months previously he had heard rumors of a plot against the new order. At first he had attributed the stories to his obvious enemies, but now he began to see plainly the hand of the SA dissidents. He accused them of leading disgraceful lives. They were guilty of "bad behavior, drunken excesses, molestation of decent people." "These men are not National Socialists, and they are in the highest degree detestable." Hitler insisted that his action in suppressing the plot was not illegal and barbaric but instead "belonged to a higher justice." "This was the Second Revolution. Their ghastly name for it was the 'Night of the Long Knives.'" In this way Hitler assigned to the "Roehm plot" the name that was to be given to his own purge. He went on to list the victims among the SA. He made no mention of those unconnected with the SA or the party who had lost their lives in the massacre.

Hitler concluded with these words: "In this hour I was responsible for the fate of the German people, and therefore I became the supreme Justiciar of the German people. . . . Everyone must know that in all future time if he raises his hand to strike at the State, then certain death will be his lot."

Wilhelm Frick (q.v.) framed an extraordinary law that declared all Hitler's actions in the purge to be legal and statesmanlike. It was passed quickly by the puppet Reichstag.

Bibliography. Nikolai Tolstoy, *Night of the Long Knives*, Ballantine Books, Inc., New York, 1972.

BLOOD SHAME. *See* BLUTSCHANDE.

BLUBO. Abbreviation of *Blut und Boden* (q.v.; blood and soil), a much-used Nazi propaganda phrase. The term was also employed to designate a palatial building in the Briennerstrasse in Munich, which was rebuilt and furnished according to the Fuehrer's plans.

BLUE. *See* BLAU.

BLÜCHER. Code name for a proposed attack from the Crimea in the Caucasus by Hitler's Eleventh Army. In a war directive dated July 11, 1942, Hitler ordered preparations to be made for a thrust on either side of the Caucasus in a southeasterly and easterly direction. The cover name Blücher was regarded as highly secret. The landing was to be known as B-1 Day. Hitler was confident that he could continue his Russian campaign to final success in 1942.

BLUMENKRIEGE (Flower Wars). Term used by Dr. Paul Joseph Goebbels (q.v.) to describe the German victory over Austria and the destruction of Czechoslovakia in 1938. "Not bullets but flowers greet our soldiers," said the Propaganda Minister as German troops moved toward Vienna and Prague. The implication was that these were not real wars worthy of German military strength. Hitler won his "flower wars" by using inside traitors and making threats of German power. Artur Seyss-Inquart in Austria and Konrad Henlein (qq.v.) in Czechoslovakia set a standard in the flower wars for the machinations of Vidkun Quisling and Pierre Laval (qq.v.) in World War II.

BLUMENTRITT, GÜNTHER (1892–). German general active in World War II. Günther Blumentritt was born in Munich on February 10, 1892. He began his army career early in 1911 and was commissioned in the 71st Infantry Regiment later that year. In 1938 he became chief of the department of training on the General Staff. On May 7, 1939, then a colonel and chief of operations for Gen. Gerd von Rundstedt (q.v.) on the General Staff, Blumentritt presented the plans for Operation White (*see* WEISS), the expected invasion of Poland. In 1939 and 1940 he commanded Army Group South. From 1940 to 1942 he was chief of staff of the Army. He was chief of staff of the Fourth Army at the invasion of Soviet Russia in June 1941.

Blumentritt's book (1952) on the life of his superior officer, Gerd von Rundstedt, gives an extraordinary account of the decline of morale in the top Army hierarchy during the unsuccessful campaign. Blumentritt was astonished both by the fighting qualities of the Russian soldier and by the Russian T-34 tank, a "terror weapon" so heavily armored that German antitank shells bounced harmlessly off it. He noted signs of despair as winter set in "and no winter clothing" was on hand. He remembered the ghosts of Napoleon's Grande Armée, which had taken the same road to Moscow. He agreed with Hitler's "instinctive order" not to retreat, because withdrawal over open Russian country without prepared positions in the rear would mean catastrophe.

In December 1944 Blumentritt joined Field Marshal Walther Model, Gen. Hasso Freiherr von Manteuffel, and SS Gen. Josef (Sepp) Dietrich (qq.v.) in attempting to break Hitler's resolve and end the war, but to no avail. In early 1945 Hitler appointed Blumentritt to command the First Parachute Army (Army Blumentritt) in the West, but it was far too late for a German victory.

Bibliography. Günther Blumentritt, *Von Rundstedt, the Soldier and the Man*, tr. by Cuthbert Reavely, Odhams Press, Ltd., London, 1952.

BLUT UND BODEN (Blood and Soil). The Nazi motif of common blood and soil, reflecting the antiurban animus of the movement in its early days. Hitler stressed the idea of a land-oriented socialism that connected city workers with farmers. Good German Aryan students were expected to do rural labor service as a patriotic duty. *See also* BLUBO.

BLUTFAHNE (Blood Banner). A special Nazi flag used at rituals. It derived its name from allegedly having been drenched in the gore of the Nazi martyrs killed during the abortive 1923 Beer-Hall *Putsch* (q.v.) in Munich. At the Nuremberg rallies (q.v.) held each year, Hitler consecrated new party colors by touching them with one hand while his other hand grasped the cloth of the bullet-riddled *Blutfahne*.

BLUTORDEN (Blood Order). The highest honorary decoration of the Nationalsozialistische Deutsche Arbeiterpartei (q.v.). Originated in 1933, the medal was awarded to 1,500 Nazis who had taken part in the November 1923 Beer-Hall *Putsch* (q.v.) in Munich. Worn on the right breast, the medal was made of silver and attached to a red band with a white enclosure. Such loyal party members as Wilhelm Frick (q.v.) were entitled to wear the badge.

BLUTSCHANDE (Blood Shame). Literally the German word for "incest." Hitler misused the term to indicate a violation of nature's law of racial purity by intermarriage with other races, and it was thus used by propagandists in the Third Reich. In highly emotional passages of *Mein Kampf* (q.v.), Hitler denounced the "racial conglomerate [in Vienna] with its peoples' mixture of Czechs, Poles, Hungarians, Ruthenians, Serbs, Croats, and above all the fission fungus [*Spaltpilz*] of mankind—Jews and again Jews." *"Mir erscheint die Riesenstadt als die Verkörperung der Blutschande"* ("To me the big city appears to be the personification of blood shame").

BOARDS OF SHAME. Signs erected in small communities on which were listed the names of those who "despite financial ability" refused to make donations to the Winterhilfe (q.v.), the Winter Relief organization. On occasion, the Winterhilfe itself placed ominous notices in the press.

BOCK, FEDOR VON (1880–1945). General field marshal in the armed forces of the Third Reich. Born in Küstrin, Brandenburg, on December 3, 1880, Fedor von Bock was the son of a distinguished general. After attending Potsdam Military Academy, he served as an officer on the General Staff in World War I. In 1917, as commander of an infantry battalion, he won the Pour le Mérite medal. In 1938 he was promoted to full general and commanded the forces that entered Austria. In 1939, at the outbreak of World War II and at the age of fifty-nine, he was third in seniority among the leading officers of the armed forces. In the eastern campaign of 1939 he commanded Army Group North in its invasion of Poland, and from October 5, 1939, to September 12, 1940, he moved Army Group B in the Netherlands, Belgium, and western France, leading the thrust along the lower Somme River. On July 19, 1940, after the defeat of France, with eleven other high officers he was made a general field marshal by Hitler. From April 1 to December 18, 1941, he was in command of Army Group Center in the campaign leading to an attack on Moscow. After the offensive broke down, he was dismissed from his command by an infuriated Fuehrer, only to be recalled from January 16 to July 15, 1942, as commander of Army Group South. After a difference on strategy with Hitler, he was finally relieved of his duties. Von Bock, a fanatical, harsh soldier of the old school, was killed in an air raid on May 4, 1945.

Bibliography. Alfred W. Turney, *Disaster at Moscow*, Cassel, London, 1971.

Field Marshal Fedor von Bock. [*Picture Collection, The Branch Libraries, The New York Public Library*]

BOGER, WILHELM (1906–   ). Guard at the Auschwitz (q.v.) extermination camp who was convicted of complicity in the murder of at least 1,000 inmates. Born on December 19, 1906, in Stuttgart-Zuffenhausen, the son of a local merchant, Boger was an early member of the National Socialist youth movement, which later became the Hitler Jugend (q.v.), the Hitler Youth. He joined both the Nazi party and the SA (q.v.) in 1929. In early 1933 he entered the SS (q.v.) and was soon assigned to police duty. At the outbreak of World War II in 1939 he was sent to the front; in March 1942 he was wounded. In December 1942 he was transferred to Auschwitz for duty as a member of the camp Gestapo (q.v.). Boger was placed in charge of the "escape department" and took pride in the fact that Auschwitz had the fewest escapes of any concentration camp. He remained there until the camp was evacuated.

Arrested by the American Military Police on June 19, 1945, Boger escaped extradition to Poland. On October 8, 1958, he was arrested and charged with complicity in the crimes at Auschwitz. He was tried in 1963–1965, when former SS men went before a German court in Frankfurt am Main (*see* FRANKFURT TRIAL). Boger was accused of having taken part in numerous selections and executions at Auschwitz as well as of having mistreated prisoners so severely during interrogation that they subsequently died. The court found him guilty of murder on at least 144 separate occasions, of complicity in the murder of at least 1,000 prisoners, and of complicity in the joint murder of at least 10 persons. "His rigorous interrogations on the Boger swing, which resulted in the death of at least five victims, were illegal even then. He approved of these tortures. He was proud of being called the devil of the camp." Boger was sentenced to life imprisonment and an additional five years at hard labor.

BOMBER GROUP. *See* KAMPFGESCHWADER.

BONHOEFFER, DIETRICH (1906–1945). Evangelical theologian executed because of his opposition to Hitler. Dietrich Bonhoeffer was born in Breslau on February 4, 1906, the son of Karl Bonhoeffer, a distinguished psychiatrist and university professor. Choosing a career in academic theology, he studied at Tübingen (1923) and Berlin (1924).

Dietrich Bonhoeffer. [*Stamp issued by the German Federal Republic*]

Klaus Bonhoeffer. [*From Annedore Leber (ed.),* Conscience in Revolt, *tr. by Rosemary O'Neill, Vallentine, Mitchell & Co., Ltd., London, 1957*]

He qualified for the licentiate in 1927 and took his first theological examination in 1928. In 1930 he went to New York to study at the Union Theological Seminary, and the next year he became a lecturer at the theological faculty in Berlin. In October 1933, after discovering that the German church was being used by Hitler, he took up a London pastorate. Bonhoeffer was not inclined to accept the institutional church, which was willing to be a tool of Hitler, and instead gave his support to the Confessional Church (Bekenntniskirche, q.v.). After visits to many Anglican communities, he returned to Germany to take a leading role in the activities of the Confessional Church. He wrote a book on ethics while struggling with the decision to become a counterspy and take part in the assassination of Hitler.

In 1938 Bonhoeffer made his first contacts with Maj. Gen. Hans Oster, chief of staff of the Abwehr; Col. Gen. Ludwig Beck, who had just resigned as chief of the Army General Staff; and Adm. Wilhelm Canaris of the Abwehr (qq.v.). Bonhoeffer became a double agent in Canaris's counterespionage service and as a courier maintained links abroad through visits to Sweden and Switzerland. On March 19, 1939, he journeyed to London for talks with Bishop George Bell, Reinhold Niebuhr, and Gerhard Leibholz (q.v.) and the next month went to the United States. On a visit to Sweden in 1942, Bonhoeffer carried proposals from the conspirators for peace terms with the Allies. He helped seven Jews to escape to Switzerland, an operation that nearly cost him his life. On January 17, 1943, his engagement to Maria von Wedemeyer was announced, but on April 5 he was arrested, placed in Tegel Prison, and charged with "subversion of the armed forces." After the 1944 July Plot (q.v.), in which Claus Schenk Graf von Stauffenberg (q.v.) made an unsuccessful attempt on Hitler's life, Bonhoeffer was removed to the Gestapo (q.v.) cellars in Prinz-Albrecht Strasse. On February 7, 1945, he was sent to Buchenwald (q.v.) concentration camp, and eventually to Flossenbürg (q.v.). All those who came into contact with him were impressed by his noble bearing and cheerfulness under painful conditions. Tried by summary court-martial, he was executed at Flossenbürg on April 9, 1945, only a few days before the end of the war in Europe. In theological circles and elsewhere Bonhoeffer is regarded as a contemporary martyr.

Bibliography. Eberhard Bethge, *Dietrich Bonhoeffer*, tr. by Eric Mosbacher and others, Harper & Row, Publishers, Incorporated, New York, 1970.

BONHOEFFER, KLAUS (1901–1945). Resistance (q.v.) leader executed by the Nazis. Klaus Bonhoeffer was born in Breslau on January 5, 1901, the son of a psychiatrist and university professor. He was a brother of Dietrich Bonhoeffer and a brother-in-law of Hans von Dohnányi (qq.v.), both of whom were active in the movement to rid Germany of Hitler. Klaus Bonhoeffer was admitted to the bar in 1930 and became legal adviser to the Lufthansa (q.v.), the German commercial air fleet, in 1936. From the beginning of his career he was convinced that the Nazi movement had stained the honor of his country. He therefore worked with various Resistance groups to eliminate it. Arrested by the Gestapo (q.v.), he was brought before the People's Court (*see* VOLKSGERICHT) on February 2, 1945, and found guilty of treason. He was shot by the SS (q.v.) on the night of April 22–23, 1945, just as the triumphant Russians entered Berlin.

BOOKS, BURNING OF THE. A symbolic incident in early Nazi Germany that provoked a wave of disgust throughout the world. On May 10, 1933, students and other young people invaded public and private libraries and collected books by Jewish, Marxist, bolshevist, and other "disrup-

The 1933 Nazi bonfire of books. [*Imperial War Museum, London*]

tive authors." The books were removed and publicly burned in huge bonfires. In Berlin the works of Karl Marx, Sigmund Freud, Thomas Mann, Maxim Gorky, Henri Barbusse, Lion Feuchtwanger, Walther Rathenau, Heinrich Heine, and many others were burned in front of the University of Berlin. Dr. Paul Joseph Goebbels (q.v.) made a short speech: "Spirits are awakening, oh, century; it is a joy to live!" The Propaganda Minister was careful, however, to instruct all German newspapers to minimize the event. The world press denounced the book burning as a descent into barbarism. *See also* LITERATURE IN THE THIRD REICH.

BORDER CONTROL POLICE. *See* GRENZPOLIZEI.

BORMANN, MARTIN (1900–?1945). Hitler's private secretary and close associate; the most important man next to the Fuehrer during the declining years of the Third Reich. Martin Bormann was born in Halberstadt, central Germany, on June 17, 1900, the son of a sergeant in a cavalry regiment who later became a civil servant. He attended a *Gymnasium* (high school) for a year but left without a diploma to work on an estate in Mecklenburg. Called up late in World War I, he served as a cannoneer in Field Artillery Regiment 55. After the war he returned to agriculture as an inspector of farmlands. At the same time he joined the rightist *Freikorps* (q.v.) unit Rossbach-Mecklenburg (*see* ROSSBACH GROUP) "to help liberate Germany from the traitors who had stabbed her in the back." With Rudolf Franz Hoess (q.v.), the future commandant of Auschwitz (q.v.), Bormann took part in the murder of Walther Kadow, his former teacher in elementary school, who allegedly had betrayed Albert Leo Schlageter (q.v.), later a Nazi martyr, to the French during the occupation of the Ruhr. In March 1924 Hoess was sentenced to ten years in prison; Bormann, as a collaborator in the crime, served one year in a Leipzig prison. After his release he joined the Nationalsozialistische Deutsche Arbeiterpartei (q.v.; NSDAP).

Bormann rose steadily in the Nazi hierarchy. In 1937 he was regional press officer for the NSDAP in Thuringia. The next year he was promoted to *Gauleiter* (district leader) and chief business manager of the party in Thuringia. At the same time he became a member of the supreme command of the SA (q.v.). In 1929 he married Gerda Buch, the daughter of a Reichstag deputy. Gerda Bormann was highly regarded by the Fuehrer, and like her husband she was a fanatical adherent of National Socialist ideology. Hitler was a witness at the wedding. Gerda Bormann bore ten children, the first being named Adolf after Adolf Hitler, his godfather. In 1930 Bormann was made administrator of the Hilfskasse (q.v.), a fund which he himself created to assist party members injured in the bloody street fighting with Communists.

Martin Bormann. [National Archives, Washington]

Shortly after Hitler became Chancellor in 1933, he appointed Bormann chief of staff to Deputy Fuehrer Rudolf Hess (q.v.). The following October Bormann became a Reich leader *(Reichsleiter)* of the Nazi party. He also served as a National Socialist deputy to the Reichstag (q.v.). It was clear that Bormann, a master of the arts of intrigue and political infighting, was headed for lofty eminence in the Third Reich. He took control of Hitler's financial affairs and functioned as an administrator of the Adolf Hitler–Spende (q.v.), a huge fund consisting of "suggested" contributions from industry. At the Fuehrer's orders he purchased the house in Braunau am Inn where Hitler was born, the home of the Fuehrer's parents in Leonding, and the entire complex of properties on the Obersalzberg (*see* BERGHOF).

During World War II Bormann was Hitler's closest collaborator. On May 12, 1941, two days after the Hess flight (q.v.), Hitler abolished Hess's post as Deputy Fuehrer and appointed Bormann to direct the newly created party chancellery. In this post Bormann worked to strengthen the party against both the Wehrmacht and the SS (qq.v.) and also found time to supervise attacks on Christianity. He wrote hundreds of memorandums dealing with Jews, Slavs, prisoners of war, and the behavior of *Gauleiters*.

Bormann's party comrades dubbed him the Brown Eminence; enemies called him "the Machiavelli behind the office desk." He was, indeed, the power behind Hitler's throne. Under his unprepossessing exterior was the classic manipulator, the anonymous power seeker who worked in secrecy and outmaneuvered all his rivals seeking Hitler's ear. Observers described him as a short, squat man in a badly fitting civil servant's uniform with his briefcase under his arm, always working to advance his own interests.

During the final days the school dropout exerted almost total power in the Third Reich. At a time when others deserted, Bormann remained faithful to the Fuehrer, who called him "my most loyal Party comrade." The now-isolated and crushed Fuehrer had his only contacts with the outside world through Bormann. The faithful paladin signed Hitler's political testament. He acted as witness to the wedding ceremony uniting Hitler and Eva Braun (q.v.). As one of his last acts, Hitler named Bormann Party Minister in the Cabinet. Bormann watched the flames devour Hitler's body in the courtyard of the Reich Chancellery. For a few hours he tried unsuccessfully to negotiate with the Allies. Then he vanished from the *Fuehrerbunker* (q.v.).

In 1946 the International Military Tribunal at Nuremberg sentenced Bormann *in absentia* to death (*see* NUREMBERG TRIAL). Since then efforts have been made to find him. He was reported as being seen as a monk in Italy and as a businessman in various countries of South America, favorite haunt of Nazi refugees. In 1973 the writer Ladislas Farago claimed that Bormann was living in Argentina as a millionaire. In April 1973 a West German court formally pronounced Bormann dead on the evidence of a skeleton unearthed half a mile from the site of Hitler's bunker between the Weidenhammer Bridge and the Lehrter Station in Berlin. The court ordered all search warrants to be quashed and future reports of Bormann sightings to be ignored. Simon Wiesenthal (q.v.), the head of the Documentation Center in Vienna, voiced his dissent: "Some doubts must remain whether the bones found in Berlin are really those of Bormann."

Bibliography. William Stevenson, *The Bormann Brotherhood,* Harcourt Brace Jovanovich, Inc., New York, 1973.

BORN, MAX (1882–1970). Winner of the Nobel Prize for physics and refugee from the Third Reich. Max Born was born in Breslau on December 12, 1882, the son of the anatomist Gustav Born. After studying physics, he lectured at Berlin (1915), Frankfurt am Main (1919), and Göttingen (1921). Because of his Jewish background he was dismissed from his post at Göttingen in 1933. He settled at first in England as Cavendish lecturer at Cambridge University. From 1936 to 1954 he was Tait professor for natural philosophy at the University of Edinburgh.

Max Born. [*German Information Center, New York*]

A close friend of Albert Einstein (q.v.), with whom he maintained a long correspondence, Born lectured on the special relativity theory. Born played an important role in the development of modern theoretical physics, especially with mathematical explanations of basic properties of matter. He did outstanding work on the quantum theory. Born was the first to recognize that Schrödinger's waves could be excluded as a statistical function in describing the behavior of a solitary molecule in time and space. Unlike Einstein, he started an important school of physics; his students at Göttingen included the famed physicist Werner Heisenberg. In 1954 Born, together with Walther Bothe, was awarded the Nobel Prize for physics for his work on the mathematical basis of quantum mechanics. Born was made a British citizen in 1939 but, again unlike Einstein, returned to Germany in his later years. He died in Bad Pyrmont on January 5, 1970.

BOUHLER, PHILIP (1899–1945). Business manager of the Nationalsozialistische Deutsche Arbeiterpartei (q.v.). Philip Bouhler was born in Munich on September 11, 1899. He served as a volunteer in World War I and was badly wounded. An early member of the Nazi party, he worked with the *Völkischer Beobachter* (q.v.) and from 1925 to 1934 was business manager of the party. In June 1933, as an *SS-Gruppenfuehrer* (lieutenant general), he was made a *Reichsleiter* (Reich leader) of the NSDAP and was elected to the Reichstag (q.v.) as a deputy for Wahlkreis (Electoral District) Westphalia. In 1934 he was appointed police president of Munich and also became chief of the Fuehrer's personal Chancellory (Hitler's personal affairs). He committed suicide in May 1945.

BOURGEOISIE BY EDUCATION. *See* BILDUNGSBÜRGERTUM.

BOXHEIM DOCUMENTS. A plan of action adopted by Nazi functionaries in 1931 and intended as a blueprint for the seizure of political power. The name comes from the Boxheim estate, near Worms, where a group of National Socialists held a series of conversations. The documents were signed by Werner Best (q.v.), who later became Reich Commissioner for occupied Denmark. The plan was to take power after a hypothetical Communist revolution had been thwarted by battle in the streets. The National Socialist party would execute anyone who opposed the new government. Hitler, at this time anxious to obtain funds from Rhineland industrialists and insistent that he would attain power only through legal means, publicly disavowed the Boxheim documents.

BOYS' EXAMINATION. *See* PIMPFENPROBE.

BRACK, VIKTOR (1904–1948). Bureaucrat in the Reich Chancellery. Viktor Brack was born in Haaren on November 9, 1904. Joining the Nationalsozialistische Deutsche Arbeiterpartei (q.v.), he rose in the Nazi ranks to *SS-Standartenfuehrer* (colonel) and Reich leader of the Nazi party. Serving in the Reich Chancellery, he was concerned with the construction of extermination camps (q.v.) in Poland. Sentenced to death by an American military tribunal at Nuremberg, he was hanged in Landsberg Prison on June 2, 1948.

BRAND, JOEL JENÖ (1906–1964). Leader of a Hungarian Jewish relief committee and unsuccessful negotiator in a large-scale attempt to exchange Jews for trucks. Joel Jenö Brand was born in Naszód, Hungary (now Năsăud, Romania), and moved to Erfurt in 1910. Active in left-wing politics, he was arrested in 1933 after Hitler came to power but was released in September 1934. Escaping from Germany, he went to Transylvania and then to Budapest. In 1938 he became active in a semiclandestine organization for helping Jewish refugees through secret contacts with Nazi agents in Hungary. On May 17, 1944, on orders from Adolf Eichmann (q.v.), he journeyed to neutral Turkey with a proposal for the Jewish Agency there. Eichmann agreed to prevent the extradition of Hungarian Jews destined for extermination camps (q.v.) in exchange for a huge supply of trucks and other equipment desperately needed in Germany. Brand was arrested in Aleppo, Syria, by the British, who suspected him of being a Nazi agent. He was taken to Cairo, then to Jerusalem, and was released on October 7, 1944. His mission was a failure. Hungarian Jews were transported to Auschwitz (q.v.), where they were gassed.

After the war Brand was active in tracking down suspected Nazi war criminals. In 1961 he testified at the Eichmann trial in Jerusalem as a witness for the prosecution. The story of his unsuccessful mission was dramatized in 1965 by Heinar Kipphardt in a play entitled *Die Geschichte eines Geschäftes (The History of a Business Deal).*

BRANDT, KARL (ca. 1904–1948). Personal physician to Hitler and to his staff *(Begleitarzt).* In August 1933, Karl Brandt, then a doctor aged twenty-nine, was summoned in Upper Bavaria to treat Hitler's niece and his adjutant, Wilhelm Brückner, who had been injured in an automobile accident. Dr. Brandt made so favorable an impression that he was invited to become one of Hitler's personal physicians. By 1934 he was a permanent member of the Obersalzberg circle (*see* BERGHOF). He was given the rank of major general in the Waffen-SS (q.v.) and, despite his limited experience, was appointed Reich Commissioner for Health and Sanitation. In his intimate contact with the Fuehrer, Brandt became suspicious of the ministrations of Dr. Theodor Morell (q.v.), who was injecting Hitler with large dosages of drugs and vitamins. There was danger, Brandt warned, of systemic poisoning, but Hitler would not listen and rejected any criticism of Dr. Morell.

Dr. Brandt retained Hitler's favor for many years. On April 16, 1945, just two weeks before his suicide, Hitler learned that Brandt had left his wife and child in Thuringia at a place where they could give themselves up to the advancing Americans. Furious, he dismissed Brandt and appointed a summary court-martial, consisting of Propaganda Minister Dr. Paul Joseph Goebbels, Reich Youth Leader Artur Axmann, and SS Maj. Gen. Gottlob Berger (qq.v.), to try Brandt on a charge of treason. Hitler even sent the court a letter accusing Brandt of losing faith in victory and, instead of sending his wife to Berchtesgaden, of seeking to use her as a courier for secret documents intended for the Americans. Brandt was condemned to death and brought to a villa in West Berlin. His life was saved by Heinrich Himmler (q.v.), who stalled the execution by calling for "new witnesses."

Dr. Brandt being sentenced to death. [*Public Information Photo Section, Office Chief of Counsel for War Crimes, Nuremberg*]

Dr. Brandt, however, did not escape the vigilance of the Allies. He was one of the main defendants in the trial of twenty-three SS physicians and scientists that began on December 9, 1946, in Nuremberg before American Military Tribunal No. 1 (*see* DOCTORS' TRIAL). He did his best to defend himself:

> PROSECUTOR: Herr Brandt, do you regard as criminal experimentations on human beings without their consent?
>
> DR. BRANDT: It depends on what kind of experiments are involved. In my opinion the question of consent plays an important part in judging the experiments as a whole—indeed an aggravating part if the experiments are qualified as criminal.
>
> PROSECUTOR: In your view were the freezing experiments dangerous?
>
> DR. BRANDT: Yes. Because death sometimes occurred, they were undoubtedly dangerous experiments.
>
> JUDGE SEBRING: Would an order which authorized or directed a subordinate medical officer to select subjects involuntarily and subject them to experiments, the execution of which that officer knew would likely result in the death of the subject, would such an order [be reasonable]?
>
> DR. BRANDT: That is a difficult question to answer, because it depends on a clear chain of command. If Himmler ordered a Dr. X to conduct a certain experiment, it is quite possible that such a Dr. X might be unwilling to carry out such an order. If he refused, he would surely have been called to account for his failure. In such a case—and here the authoritarian character of our system of government must be taken into account—any personal code of ethics must give way to the total character of the war.

The Court was unimpressed. Dr. Brandt was sentenced to death by hanging. Before his execution at Landsberg Prison he offered his own body for medical experiments similar to those he had conducted, but his offer was rejected. Like six other doctors who died with him, he refused religious solace. In his final speech he said: "It is no shame to stand upon this scaffold. This is nothing but political revenge. I have served my Fatherland as others before me. . . ." The black hood was placed over his head in midsentence, and he was hanged on June 2, 1948.

Bibliography. Alexander Mitscherlich and Fred Mielke, *Doctors of Infamy*, tr. by Heinz Norden, Henry Schuman, Inc., Publishers, New York, 1949.

BRANDT, WILLY (1913–   ). The first post-World War II Social Democratic Chancellor, serving from 1969 to 1974. Born in Lübeck on December 18, 1913, Willy Brandt was the illegitimate child of a mother named Frahm and an unknown father. He grew up under poor circumstances but with a sense of human dignity and social justice. Refusing to join the young followers of Hitler, he chose instead to fight the Nazis in the streets. In 1933,

Willy Brandt. [*Wide World Photos*]

when the Socialists were forced underground, Brandt left Lübeck to continue his struggle against Nazism abroad. He lost his German citizenship and became a Norwegian. Brandt continued to serve the socialist cause while in Scandinavia and on several occasions returned secretly to Berlin to work in the Social Democratic underground. He wore a Norwegian uniform, which prevented his discovery by the Gestapo (q.v.). On one occasion he went into hiding in a German prisoner-of-war camp and managed to escape to Sweden.

Although Brandt could have remained a Norwegian citizen after the war, he chose to return to his homeland. Serving a long apprenticeship, he worked his way up the political ladder. From 1955 to 1957 he was president of the House of Representatives in Berlin and from 1957 to 1966 mayor of Berlin. During this time Brandt won the confidence of Western statesmen. In 1964 he became chairman of the German Socialist party (SPD). He became Minister for Foreign Affairs and Vice-Chancellor in 1966 and was named Chancellor in 1969. Brandt represented his country's interests with courage and common sense. He did much to put West Germany on a firm democratic basis and in the democratic community of the Western world. He negotiated agreements on joint economic projects with Eastern European countries and pursued a general policy of nonaggression toward all the states of the Warsaw Pact. His efforts won him the Nobel Peace Prize in 1971. He resigned his office in 1974 after the discovery that an aide was an East German agent.

Bibliography. Hermann Otto Bolesch and Hans Dieter Leicht, *Der lange Marsch des Willy Brandt: Ein Porträt des deutschen Bundeskanzlers,* Erdmann, Tübingen and Basel, 1971.

BRAUCHITSCH, WALTHER VON (1881–1948). General field marshal in the armed forces of the Third Reich and ranking senior officer at the outbreak of World War II. Walther von Brauchitsch was born in Berlin on October 4, 1881. His earliest military assignment was as captain of artillery in World War I. He was promoted to *Generalleutnant* (lieutenant general) in 1931 and head of the artillery unit the next year. In 1933 he was given command of the 1st Division at Königsberg, East Prussia. On February 4, 1938, Hitler promoted him to *Generaloberst* (colonel general) and named him *Oberbefehlshaber des Heeres* (commander in chief of the Army) as successor to Gen. Werner Freiherr von Fritsch (q.v.).

From the beginning of his appointment as commander in chief Von Brauchitsch was aware of the conspiracy of army officers against Hitler. He looked with disapproval upon the Fuehrer's aggressive plans, but as a firm believer in the rule of law *(Rechtstaat)* he felt bound by his oath of loyalty to Hitler. He was approached again and again by Gen. Ludwig Beck (q.v.), key figure of the Resistance (q.v.), to cooperate with the conspirators, but he wavered between professional and domestic pressures. At the time of the 1938 Blomberg-Fritsch crisis (q.v.), Von Brauchitsch divorced his wife and married the daughter of a Silesian official. Hitler is said to have provided Von Brauchitsch with the necessary funds for settlement with his first wife. Von Brauchitsch's second wife was a fanatical Hitler supporter who urged her husband, already in awe of the Fuehrer, to stand with the National Socialists. Throughout the Czech crisis in 1938 Von Brauchitsch's support was sought by Beck and his fellow conspirators. On August 10, 1938, Hitler called his generals to the Berghof (q.v.) and angrily excoriated those who were reluctant to support him. Von Brauchitsch was overwhelmed by the Fuehrer's explosions of rage and said: "I am a soldier. It is my duty to obey." Beck resigned in disgust, but Von Brauchitsch stayed on. He figured intermittently in the plans of the Resistance movement but never played an active role in the conspiracy.

In World War II Von Brauchitsch was the formal leader of the campaigns against Poland, France, Yugoslavia, Greece, and the Soviet Union. After the early successes he became more and more subservient to Hitler. The almost uncanny victory over France removed all hope that he would support any conspiracy against Hitler. By this time he complied automatically with the Fuehrer's orders even against his own better judgment. On December 19, 1941,

Field Marshal Walther von Brauchitsch. [*Keystone*]

torn between his oath to Hitler and his integrity as a member of the officer class and plagued by severe illness, he retired. Hitler himself assumed command as supreme commander of the armed forces. From then on Von Brauchitsch lived with a cloud over his name. In 1944, when he learned of the July Plot (q.v.), he made a public statement condemning the conspirators. He died in Hamburg on October 18, 1948.

BRAUER, MAX (1888–1973). Social Democrat, former mayor of Hamburg, and refugee from the Third Reich. Max Brauer joined the Social Democratic party at the age of sixteen and entered local politics at the close of World War I. He began his active political career in Altona, then part of Schleswig-Holstein, and served as mayor of Hamburg from 1924 to 1933. Persecuted and imprisoned by the Nazis, he later emigrated from Germany. After a stay in China as a representative of the League of Nations, he settled in the United States. He returned to Hamburg on a trade union mission in 1946. Brauer again became mayor of Hamburg and supervised its reconstruction. Elected to the Bundestag in 1961, he retired in 1965. He died in Hamburg on February 2, 1973.

Max Brauer. [*dpa Bild*]

BRAUN, EVA (1912–1945). Hitler's mistress for twelve years and his wife for one day before their joint suicide. Eva Braun was born in Munich, the daughter of middle-class Bavarian parents (her father was a schoolteacher). In her late teens she was employed as an assistant by Heinrich Hoffmann (q.v.), Hitler's photographer, who introduced her to Hitler. Tall, slim, with regular features, pretty rather than beautiful, she was a devotee of physical culture, adept at swimming, gymnastics, skiing, and mountain climbing. She was extremely fond of dancing, which she had studied professionally. Reticent and somewhat shy, she had little interest in politics, preferring to devote most of her attention to sports, reading novels, and watching motion pictures. Her one goal in life was to serve her beloved Fuehrer.

Since the suicide of Angela (Geli) Raubal (q.v.) on September 18, 1931, Hitler had been unhappy in his relationships with women. He would surround himself with beautiful women, but he dreaded becoming too closely attached to any one of them. "A highly intellectual man," he said, "should have a primitive and stupid woman. Imagine if I had a woman to interfere with my work." He was frightened by the possibility of petticoat politics. For years Propaganda Minister Dr. Paul Joseph Goebbels (q.v.) tried to ingratiate himself with the Fuehrer by introducing him to strikingly handsome blondes with the proper Nordic features, but to no avail. Hitler instead turned to Eva Braun, the undemanding photographer's helper, who epitomized the bourgeois world of Nazism. He had total influence over her. He worried constantly about her health and forbade her to fly or to drive a fast automobile. He made her independently wealthy by assigning rights to his photographs to her and to Heinrich Hoffmann.

Eva Braun fitted well into the Alpine milieu of Hitler's Berghof (q.v.) at Berchtesgaden. Here she was installed as the Fuehrer's mistress, but she was kept in the background and surrounded by a wall of silence. The servants, forbidden to talk to her, referred to her only as "E. B." Although a part of the intimate circle, she was banished to her rooms whenever important guests were entertained. Very few Germans knew of her existence. Hitler did not allow her to go to Berlin until the last two years of her life. During the war years, when the Fuehrer was generally away at one of his military headquarters, Eva Braun remained at the Berghof, reading, exercising, writing letters and diary entries, and brooding. She could only unhappily await the return of her master. Her misery was so great that on several occasions she attempted suicide.

On April 15, 1945, Eva Braun arrived in Berlin to share in Hitler's death (*see* FUEHRERBUNKER). The Fuehrer had sent her to Munich, but she refused to stay there. When he ordered her to leave the bunker, she again declined. "A Germany without Adolf Hitler would not be fit to live in," she told a friend. Before his death Hitler decided to grant Eva Braun her dearest wish: he agreed to marry her. The formalities on April 29, 1945, were brief. Both declared that they were of Aryan descent and that they

Eva Braun. [*Courtesy of the Library of Congress*]

were free of any hereditary disease. They shook hands with the guests and had a wedding breakfast, and then Hitler went off to dictate his last will and political testament (*see* HITLER'S LAST WILL; HITLER'S POLITICAL TESTAMENT). Eva Braun's supreme moment came when a servant addressed her in the usual form as *Gnädiges Fräulein* (gracious lady). She cautioned the servant: "You may now safely call me Mrs. Hitler [*Gnädige Frau*]!" Shortly before half-past three on the afternoon of April 30, 1945, Eva Braun swallowed poison and died by the side of her husband.

Bibliography. Nerin E. Gun, *Eva Braun, Hitler's Mistress*, Leslie Frewin (Publishers) Ltd., London, 1969.

BRAUN, OTTO (1872–1955). Leading Social Democratic politician and statesman in the Weimar Republic. Otto Braun was born in Königsberg, East Prussia, on January 28, 1872, the son of a poverty-stricken regimental cobbler who later became a railroad workman. The young man managed to receive an education and set up a printing business. He became a member of the then-illegal Social Democratic party in East Prussia and remained with it for the rest of his life. In 1913 he was elected as a delegate to the Prussian Landtag (Legislature). In 1918 he headed the Prussian Ministry of Economics and the next year served as a member of the Weimar National Assembly. In March 1920 he became Minister-President of Prussia and remained in this post, with short interruptions in 1921 and 1925, until 1932–1933. After 1925 he headed a coalition of Social Democrats, Centrists, and Democrats. In July 1932 he was removed from office as the result of a coup d'état by Franz von Papen (q.v.). In March 1933, shortly after the rise of Hitler to power, Braun emigrated to Switzerland, where he spent the last two decades of his life. He never gave up hope for the reconstruction of Germany after the fall of National Socialism. He died in Lugano on December 14, 1955.

Bust of Otto Braun by Hermann Brachert. [*Internationaal Instituut voor Sociale Geschiedenis, Amsterdam*]

BRAUN, WERNHER FREIHERR VON (1912–1977). Rocket expert. Wernher von Braun was born in Wirsitz, Prussia (now Wyrzysk, Poland), on March 23, 1912. At the age of twenty he was engaged by the German Army to do rocket research. In 1937 he became technical director of the rocket weapon project at Peenemünde (q.v.). He did special work on constructing rocket model A-4, which developed into the V-2 used in 1944–1945 against England (*see* VERGELTUNGSWAFFEN). From 1945 on Von Braun lived and worked in the United States, where he played a major role in the development of the satellite program. He was responsible for, among other achievements, the Jupiter-C rocket, which was used to send the satellite *Explorer-1* into orbit in 1958. In 1960 he became Director of the George C. Marshall Space Flight Center in Huntsville, Alabama, and in this post had a vital part in the development of the Saturn rockets. He played an important role in all phases of the American moon flight program.

BRAUNAU AM INN. A small town on the German-Austrian border; birthplace of Adolf Hitler.

BRAUNER LADEN (Brown Store). A store specializing in the sale of Nazi party paraphernalia.

BRAUNES HAUS (Brown House). From 1931 on the headquarters of the Reich leadership of the Nationalsozialistische Deutsche Arbeiterpartei (q.v.). It was located at Briennerstrasse 45 in Munich. An early headquarters building had been opened in 1920 in a modest building on the Sternacker-Bräu in Munich. From 1922 to the breakup of the party on November 11, 1923, after the Beer-Hall *Putsch* (q.v.), Hitler and the Nazis used a small building at Corneliusstrasse 12 for meetings. After the party was reorganized on February 27, 1925, the movement used the facilities of the Eher Verlag (q.v.), a publishing firm at Thierstrasse 15, which was eventually to become the official National Socialist publishing house. Six months later Hitler moved the party rooms to the rear of Schellingstrasse 50, and then took over the entire house. With funds obtained from Rhineland industrialists, especially from Emil Kirdorf (q.v.), the party in 1928 bought the spacious old patrician mansion called the Barlow Palace at Briennerstrasse 45. The architect Paul Ludwig Troost (q.v.), under directions from Hitler, rebuilt the palace into a complex of offices. The large rooms and great halls were reduced to moderate-size rooms, and intermediate floors were added.

The Brown House, Munich. [*National Archives, Washington*]

BRAUNSCHWEIG (Brunswick). Cover name for Hitler's Caucasus offensive in the summer of 1942. In a war directive dated July 23, 1942, Hitler ordered his forces to destroy the enemy south of the Don River and then to occupy the entire eastern coastline of the Black Sea. In this way he hoped to prevent the enemy from using the Black Sea ports and the Black Sea fleet. Operation Brunswick was considered a companion undertaking to Blücher (q.v.).

BRAUNSTEINER, HERMINE (1920–). Female guard in Nazi death camps during World War II. In 1941 and 1942 she acted as supervisor of the Ravensbrück (q.v.) concentration camp in Germany (*see* CONCENTRATION CAMPS), and in 1943 she served as supervising warden in the extermination camp of Maidanek (q.v.), near Lublin in German-occupied Poland (*see* EXTERMINATION CAMPS). In 1949 she was convicted by an Austrian court of murder, including assassination, manslaughter, and infanticide, and sentenced to three years in prison. After her release an Austrian civil court granted her amnesty from further prosecution in that country.

In 1959 Fräulein Braunsteiner married Russell Ryan, an American electrical construction engineer. She went to the United States and settled in New York City, and in 1963 became an American citizen. At this time she was brought to court for a deportation hearing. Government testimony against her included evidence by survivors of concentration camps who identified her as a guard responsible for terrorizing, torturing, and murdering inmates. She was accused of assisting actively in the selection process that consigned women, children, and elderly persons to the gas chambers. Eyewitnesses testified that she supplied candidates for extermination who had been overlooked. One deposition charged her with a brutal, unprovoked assault on a female inmate who died the next day. Another asserted that Mrs. Ryan had ordered a young girl to stand on a stool and be hanged by SS (q.v.) guards. In her own defense she insisted that she had only performed the usual normal duties of a prison guard.

In 1971 the United States stripped Mrs. Ryan of her citizenship because she had failed to state on her application for American residence and citizenship that she had served in German concentration camps. On March 14, 1973, an extradition bench warrant was issued in Düsseldorf for Mrs. Ryan's return for trial before a German court. At the same time a similar request came from the Polish government. Seized at her home by United States marshals, she was held without bail and sent back to West Germany. She became the first United States resident whose extradition for alleged war crimes was granted.

BRECHT, BERTOLT (1898–1956). The most important German playwright of the twentieth century. Revolutionary poet, stage director, novelist, and ballad writer, Bertolt Brecht was a prominent refugee from the Third Reich. He was born in Augsburg, Bavaria, on February 10, 1898, into a family of mixed Roman Catholic and Protestant background. A patriot in 1914, he became an orderly in the German Army in 1917, but was disillusioned by the war. As a playwright he developed a type of epic theater (later called dialectical theater) that was designed to influence audiences to direct political judgment. One of his greatest successes was *Die Dreigroschenoper*, 1928 *(The Threepenny Opera)*, with music by Kurt Weill (q.v.). As a Marxist, Brecht became a target for Nazi persecution. Shortly after Hitler came to political power in 1933, Brecht emigrated to Denmark, where he lived until 1939, and then stayed briefly in Sweden and Finland. In 1941 he moved to the United States, where he wrote anti-Nazi plays. His one-act drama *Die Gewehre der Frau Carrar*, 1937 *(Senora Carrar's Rifles)*, dealt with the Spanish Civil War. All his works are distinguished by skepticism and irony. He dramatized emotionally the confrontations of modern life, especially between the individual and an evil society. In 1954 he received the Stalin Peace Prize, a high honor in the Soviet Union. Brecht died in East Berlin on August 14, 1956.

Bertolt Brecht. [*Stamp issued by the German Democratic Republic*]

Bibliography. Martin Esslin, *Brecht: A Choice of Evils*, Eyre & Spottiswoode (Publishers), Ltd., London, 1959.

BRENNESSEL, DIE (The Stinging Nettle). The humor sheet of the Nazi party.

BRIGADEFUEHRER-SS (Brif.). Major general in the SS (q.v.). This rank was equivalent to *Generalmajor* in the German Army, deputy *Gauleiter* in the Nationalsozialistische Deutsche Arbeiterpartei (q.v.), and *Generalmajor der Polizei* in the police force.

BROAD, PERCY (1921–). Guard at the Auschwitz (q.v.) concentration camp (*see* CONCENTRATION CAMPS). Percy Broad was born in Rio de Janiero on April 25, 1921, the son of a Brazilian businessman and a German mother. He was taken back to Germany by his mother soon after his birth. Attending primary and secondary schools in Berlin, he was an early member of the Hitler Jugend (q.v.), for which he was awarded a gold membership pin. He attended the Technische Hochschule (Technical College) of Berlin until December 1941, at which time he could not get his Brazilian passport renewed. He volunteered for Army service, but because of his nearsightedness he was sent to Auschwitz as a guard and later was transferred to the political section there. At the end of the war he was taken prisoner by the British, for whom he wrote an extensive report on the horrendous conditions at the camp. On December 20, 1963, he was brought to trial in Frankfurt am Main (*see* FRANKFURT TRIAL) with other SS (q.v.) men accused of having taken part in the Final

Solution (q.v.). He was accused of complicity in joint murder on at least twenty-two separate occasions, two involving the murder of at least 1,000 inmates. The judges found that his active contribution was comparatively minor. Broad was found guilty of complicity and was sentenced to a total of four years at hard labor.

BROOCH OF FEAR. *See* ANGSTBROSCHE.

BROWN BOOK OF THE HITLER TERROR AND THE BURNING OF THE REICHSTAG. A book published in 1933 by the World Committee for the Victims of German Fascism. It gave an account of the Nazi terror and accused National Socialists of having started the Reichstag fire (q.v.). A successor volume, *The Reichstag Fire Trial: The Second Brown Book of the Hitler Terror,* with an introduction by Georgi M. Dimitrov (q.v.), a Bulgarian Communist acquitted at the Reichstag Fire Trial (q.v.), was published by the same committee (London, 1934).

BROWN HOUSE. *See* BRAUNES HAUS.

BROWN STORE. *See* BRAUNER LADEN.

BROWNSHIRTS. *See* SA.

BRUENING, HEINRICH (1885–1970). Politician and one of the last statesmen of the Weimar Republic (q.v.). Heinrich Bruening was born in Münster, Westphalia, on November 26, 1885. After studying philosophy and political science, he served as business manager of the League of German Trade Unions from 1920 to 1930. A member of the Catholic Center party, he was a deputy in the Reichstag (q.v.) from 1924 to 1933. In 1929 he became chairman of his party group in that body. Bruening achieved a national reputation for his work in financial legislation. On March 28, 1930, he was named Chancellor. With the support of President Paul von Hindenburg (q.v.), he set up a Cabinet dominated by the bourgeois center. When the Reichstag refused to support his budget, he dismissed it on July 18, 1930. After the elections of September 14, 1930, had resulted in a triumph for the National Socialists, Bruening, with Von Hindenburg's assent, utilized Article 48 (q.v.) of the Weimar Constitution to rule by decree.

From 1930 to 1932 Bruening struggled unsuccessfully to resolve the deepening economic crisis. Unemployment rose to more than 6 million, and he was attacked bitterly by the Communists on the left and the National Socialists on the right. Despite the critical economic situation, he was able to bring an end to reparations at Lausanne in 1932. He also made some progress in his goal of achieving a revision of the Treaty of Versailles. In this way he hoped to diminish Hitler's mass appeal. Meanwhile, his relations with Von Hindenburg grew cooler as the Reich President came to be more and more deeply influenced by the right. At the instigation of Gen. Kurt von Schleicher (q.v.), Von Hindenburg began to look with favor on the now politically powerful Nazi party. On May 30, 1932, the President sent a brusque note to Bruening asking for his resignation. This key dismissal was a blow to the Weimar Republic. Either the military or the Nazis would take over political control.

Chancellor Bruening addressing a rally supporting the reelection of President Paul von Hindenburg. [*Ullstein*]

In July 1933 Bruening relinquished the chairmanship of the Catholic Center party. In 1934, aware of increasing danger for himself in the Third Reich, he emigrated to the United States, where he accepted a professorship at Harvard University. Returning to Cologne in 1951, he became professor of political science there. In 1954 he went to the United States again. He died in Norwich, Vermont, on March 30, 1970.

Bibliography. Bernhard Menne, *The Case of Dr. Bruening,* tr. by E. Fitzgerald, Hutchinson & Co. (Publishers), Ltd., London, 1942.

BRUNSWICK. *See* BRAUNSCHWEIG.

BRZEZINKA. *See* BIRKENAU.

BUCHENWALD. One of the major concentration camps (q.v.) in the Third Reich. Buchenwald was one of three camps set up in 1933 to form the nucleus of a concentration camp system: Sachsenhausen (q.v.) in the north, Dachau (q.v.) in the south, and Buchenwald in central Germany. Buchenwald was located on a wooded hill 4

Inmates of Buchenwald. [*The Bettman Archive*]

miles from Weimar, the shrine of German culture associated with the names of Goethe, Schiller, Herder, and Wieland. According to the report of a congressional committee sent to investigate Buchenwald: "It was an extermination factory and the means of extermination were starvation, beatings, tortures, incredibly crowded sleeping conditions, and sickness. The effectiveness of these measures was enhanced by the requirements that the prisoners work in an adjacent armaments factory for the manufacture of machine guns, small arms, ammunition, and other matériel for the German Army. The factory operated 24 hours a day, using two 12-hour shifts of prisoners."

On April 10, 1945, Buchenwald was liberated by the United States 80th Division. Five days later the American correspondent Edward R. Murrow delivered a famous CBS broadcast describing conditions at Buchenwald on the day of liberation:[1]

> I propose to tell you of Buchenwald. It's on a small hill, about four miles outside Weimar.
>
> This was one of the largest concentration camps in Germany . . . and it was built to last. As we approached it, we saw about a hundred men in civilian clothes, with rifles, advancing in open order across the fields.
>
> There were a few shots. We stopped to inquire. We were told that some of the prisoners had a couple of S.S. men cornered in there. We drove on, reached the main gate. The prisoners crowded up behind the wire. We entered. And now let me tell this in the first person, for I was the least important person there, as you can hear. There surged around me an evil-smelling crowd; men and boys reached out to touch me. They were in rags and the remnants of uniforms. Death had already marked many of them, but they were smiling with their eyes. I looked out over that mass of men to the green fields beyond, where well-fed Germans were ploughing.
>
> A German, Fritz Kirchenheimer, came up and said: "May I show you around the camp? I've been here ten years." An Englishman stood to attention, saying: "May I introduce myself? Delighted to see you. And can you tell me when some of our blokes will be along?" I told him "soon," and asked to see one of the barracks. It happened to be occupied by Czechoslovakians. When I entered, men crowded around, tried to lift me to their shoulders. They were too weak. Many of them could not get out of bed. I was told that this building had once stabled eighty horses. There were twelve hundred men in it, five to a bunk. The stink was beyond all description. When I reached the center of the barracks, a man came up and said: "You remember me, I'm Peter Zenkl, one-time Mayor of Prague." I remembered him, but did not recognize him. He asked about Beneš and Jan Masaryk.
>
> I asked how many men had died in that building during the last month. They called the doctor. We inspected his records. There were only names in the little black book . . . nothing more . . . nothing to show who had been where, what he had done or hoped. Behind the names of those who had died, there was a cross. I counted them. They totaled two hundred forty-two—two hundred forty-two out of twelve hundred, in one month.
>
> As I walked down to the end of the barracks, there was applause from the men too weak to get out of bed. It sounded like the handclapping of babies. They were so weak. The Doctor's name was Paul Heller. He had been there since 'thirty-eight. As we walked out into the courtyard, a man fell dead. Two others, they must have been over sixty, were crawling towards the latrine. I saw it, but will not describe it. In another part of the camp they showed me the children, hundreds of them. Some were only six. One rolled up his sleeves, showed me his number. It was tattooed on his arm . . . B-6030, it was. The others showed me their numbers. They will carry them until they die. An elderly man standing beside me said: "The children . . . enemies of the State!" I could see their ribs through their thin shirts. The old man said, "I am Professor Charles Richer, of the Sorbonne." The children clung to my arms and stared. We crossed to the courtyard. Men kept coming up to speak to me and to touch me . . . professors from Poland, doctors from Vienna, men from all Europe, men from the countries that made America.
>
> We went to the hospital. It was full. The doctor told me that two hundred had died the day before. I asked the cause of death. He shrugged and said: "Tuberculosis, starvation, fatigue, and there are many who have no desire to live. It is very difficult." Dr. Heller pulled back the blanket from a man's feet to show me how swollen they were. The man was dead.
>
> Most of the patients could not move.
>
> As we left the hospital, I drew out a leather billfold, hoping that I had some money that would help those who lived to get home. Professor Richer from the Sorbonne said: "I should be careful of my wallet, if I were you. You know there are criminals in this camp too." A small man tottered up, saying: "May I feel the leather, please. You see, I used to make good things of leather in Vienna." Another man said: "My name is Walther Roede (?). For many years I lived in Joliet, came back to Germany for a visit and Hitler grabbed me."
>
> I asked to see the kitchen. It was clean. The German in charge had been a Communist, had been at Buchenwald for nine years, had a picture of his daughter in Hamburg, hadn't seen her for almost twelve years . . . and if I got to Hamburg, would I look her up?

[1]By permission of the estate of Edward R. Murrow.

He showed me the daily ration: one piece of brown bread about as thick as your thumb, on top of it a piece of margarine as big as three sticks of chewing gum. That, and a little stew, was what they received every twenty-four hours.

He had a chart on the wall . . . very complicated it was. There were little red tabs scattered through it. He said that was to indicate each ten men who died. He had to account for the rations, and he added: "We're very efficient here."

We went again into the courtyard, and as we walked, we talked. The two doctors, the Frenchman and the Czech, agreed that about six thousand had died during March. Kirchenheimer, the German, added that back in the winter of 'thirty-nine, when the Poles began to arrive, without winter clothing, they died at the rate of approximately nine hundred a day. Five different men asserted that Buchenwald was the best concentration camp in Germany. They had had some experience in the others.

Dr. Heller, the Czech, asked if I would care to see the crematorium. He said it wouldn't be very interesting, because the Germans had run out of coke some days ago and had taken to dumping the bodies into a great hole nearby.

Professor Richer said perhaps I would care to see the small courtyard. I said yes. He turned and told the children to stay behind. As we walked across the square, I noticed that the Professor had a hole in his left shoe and a toe sticking out of the right one. He followed my eyes and said: "I regret that I am so little presentable, but what can one do?"

At that point, another Frenchman came to announce that three of his fellow-countrymen outside had killed three S.S. men and taken one prisoner.

We proceeded to the small courtyard. The wall was about eight feet high. It adjoined what had been a stable or garage. We entered. It was floored with concrete. There were two rows of bodies stacked up like cordwood. They were thin and very white. Some of the bodies were terribly bruised, though there seemed to be little flesh to bruise. Some had been shot through the head, but they bled but little. Only two were naked. I tried to count them as best I could, and arrived at the conclusion that all that was mortal of more than five hundred men and boys lay there in two neat piles. There was a German trailer, which must have contained another fifty, but it wasn't possible to count them. The clothing was piled in a heap against the wall. It appeared that most of the men and boys had died of starvation; they had not been executed.

But the manner of death seemed unimportant. Murder had been done at Buchenwald. God knows how many men and boys have died there during the last twelve years. Thursday, I was told that there were more than twenty thousand in the camp. There had been as many as sixty thousand. Where are they now?

As I left that camp, a Frenchman who used to work for Havas in Paris came up to me and said: "You will write something about this perhaps." And he added: "To write about this, you must have been here at least two years, and after that . . . you don't want to write any more."

I pray you to believe what I have said about Buchenwald. I reported what I saw and heard, but only part of it. For most of it, I have no words.

Dead men are plentiful in war, but the living dead—more than twenty thousand of them in one camp . . . and the country round that was pleasing to the eye, and the Germans were well-fed and well-dressed; American trucks were rolling towards the rear filled with prisoners. Soon they would be eating American rations, as much for a meal as the men at Buchenwald received in four days.

If I have offended you by this rather mild account of Buchenwald, I'm not in the least sorry. I was there on Thursday . . . and many men and many tongues blessed the name of Roosevelt. For long years, his name had meant the full measure of their hope. These men who had kept close company with death for many years did not know that Mr. Roosevelt would, within hours, join their comrades who had laid their lives on the scales of freedom.

Back in forty-one, Mr. Churchill said to me, with tears in his eyes: "One day the world and history will recognize and acknowledge what it owes to your President." I saw and heard the first installment of that at Buchenwald on Thursday. It came from men all over Europe.

Their faces, with more flesh on them, might have been found anywhere at home. To them the name Roosevelt was a symbol, a code-word for a lot of guys named Joe, who were somewhere out in the blue with the armor, heading east. At Buchenwald they spoke of the President just before he died. If there be a better epitaph, history does not record it.

BUILDUP EAST. *See* AUFBAU OST.

BUND DEUTSCHER MÄDEL (BdM; League of German Girls). The feminine branch of the German youth movement. The BdM was organized on parallel lines with the

Members of the Bund Deutscher Mädel. [*Ullstein*]

Hitler Jugend (q.v.), the Hitler Youth. It was under the supervision of *Reichsjugendfuehrer* (Reich Youth Leader) Baldur von Schirach (q.v.). There were two general age groups: the Jungmädel (q.v.), from ten to fourteen years of age, and older girls from fifteen to twenty-one. The smallest group was the *Mädelschaft*, two to four of which made up a *Mädelschar*. Two to four *Mädelscharen* constituted a *Gruppe*, and five *Gruppen* made up a *Ring*. From five to six *Ringe* formed an *Untergau*, of which there were 684. Then came the *Obergau*. Altogether, there were 125,000 leaders, who were trained in thirty-five provincial schools, most of them on a part-time basis.

All girls in the BdM were constantly reminded that the great task of their schooling was to prepare them to be "carriers of the National Socialist *Weltanschauung*" (q.v.), the Nazi world view. They were to dedicate themselves to comradeship, service, and physical fitness for motherhood. In parades they wore navy blue skirts, white blouses, brown jackets, and twin pigtails. When they reached seventeen, they were eligible for an organization called Glaube und Schönheit (q.v.), Faith and Beauty, in which they received advanced training in domestic science and preparation for marriage. By 1936 more than 2 million girls were enrolled in BdM.

Bibliography. Clifford Kirkpatrick, *Nazi Germany: Its Women and Family Life*, The Bobbs-Merrill Company, Inc., Indianapolis, 1938.

BUND OBERLAND. A paramilitary "Fatherland" organization in Munich in the early 1920s. An outgrowth of the Thule Gesellschaft (q.v.), it was once a *Freikorps* (q.v.) unit but now called itself a *Bund*, or league. Headed by Dr. Frederick Weber, a tall, thin veterinarian, the Oberländer wore a spray of edelweiss on their caps. They made a show of appearing in Bavarian mountain hats and high woolen stockings. As a unit in the Fighting Union, the Oberländer marched in Munich on November 9, 1923, in the Beer-Hall *Putsch* (q.v.).

BUNKER. *See* FUEHRERBUNKER.

BÜRCKEL, JOSEPH (1895–1944). National Socialist pioneer in the Palatinate and Nazi Governor of Austria. Joseph Bürckel was born in Lingenfeld, in the Palatinate, on March 30, 1895. After attending *Volksschule* (elementary school) in Speyer, he served at the front throughout the four years of World War I. After the war he took a teaching post but spent most of his time fighting the French occupation and the French efforts to set up a Rhineland republic. In 1925 he abandoned his teaching post to devote full time to building the National Socialist movement in his home area. In 1925 he became *Gauleiter* (district leader) of the Nationalsozialistische Deutsche Arbeiterpartei (q.v.) in the Rhineland-Palatinate. He set up his own newspaper, *Der Eisenhammer (The Iron Hammer)*, which was banned by the authorities on several occasions. He was elected to the Reichstag (q.v.) in 1930 to represent the Nazi party in the Saar region. In 1934 he succeeded Franz von Papen (q.v.) as Plenipotentiary for the Saar Territory, and the next year, when the Saar was returned to Germany, he was named its Reich Commissioner. After the *Anschluss* (q.v.) between Germany and Austria in 1938, he was appointed *Gauleiter* of Vienna and *Reichsstatthalter* (Governor) of Austria. He died, a probable suicide, on September 28, 1944.

BÜRGERBRÄU KELLER. *See* BEER-HALL PUTSCH.

BÜRGERBRÄU KELLER ATTENTAT (Beer-Hall Attempt). Unsuccessful attempt on Hitler's life shortly after the outbreak of World War II. On November 8, 1939, on the sixteenth anniversary of the 1923 Beer-Hall *Putsch* (q.v.), Hitler summoned his followers to Munich to celebrate that critical event in the history of the Nazi movement. Meanwhile, a bomb was planted in the pillar of the hall with a fuse that could be operated by a push button in an alcove near the street entrance. The Fuehrer's speech, which was concerned with the theme of British perfidy, was shorter than customary, and he left the hall earlier than usual. Twenty minutes later the bomb, which had been placed near the rear of the platform, exploded with tremendous force. The roof collapsed on the audience, killing seven and injuring sixty-three, all members of the *Alte Kämpfer* (q.v.), the old guard. Hitler offered a large reward for the apprehension of the conspirators and attended the funeral held for the victims.

The *attentat* remained a mystery. An official explanation accused Communists, Nazi deviationists, and the British Secret Service of planning the attempt on Hitler's life. Some observers, including Martin Niemoeller (q.v.), claimed that the incident had been planned by Heinrich Himmler (q.v.), with Hitler's approval, as a means of augmenting the Fuehrer's popularity and of stimulating war fever in the German people.

BURGFRIEDE (Public Peace). A moratorium or cessation of political acitivity. In 1923 the political situation in Germany, which was burdened by a runaway inflation, was chaotic. Spontaneously all political parties, with the exception of Hitler's National Socialists, accepted a political moratorium as a means of dealing with the critical situation. The spirit of the *Burgfriede* had been voiced also at the outbreak of World War I by Emperor William II when he announced: "I no longer know any parties. I know only Germany!"

BURNING OF THE BOOKS. *See* BOOKS, BURNING OF THE.

BÜRO DER ABGEORDNETEN (Office for Deputies). A special office for Nazi deputies in the Landtag (Legislature) of Prussia. This office was used by Hitler to camouflage the illegal activities of his party during the period when it was dissolved (1927–1928).

BURSCHENSCHAFT (Fraternity). A student fraternity at German universities in the pre-Hitler era.

BUSCH, ADOLF (1891–1952). Violinist and refugee from the Third Reich. Adolf Busch was born in Siegen, Westphalia, on August 8, 1891. After studying at the Cologne Conservatory, he headed several musical groups from 1919 on, especially a musical quartet that included his brother, Hermann Busch, a cellist, and his son-in-law, Rudolf Serkin, a pianist. Busch left Nazi Germany in 1933 for Switzerland and subsequently settled in the United States, where he continued his career as an interpreter of classical music and as a composer. He died in Brattleboro, Vermont, on June 9, 1952.

BUSCH, ERNST VON (1885–1945). General field marshal in the armed forces of the Third Reich and one of the high officers loyal to Hitler. Ernst von Busch was born in Essen-Steele on July 6, 1885. An army careerist, he remained outspokenly pro-Hitler from the day on which he took his oath of personal allegiance. On February 2, 1938, at the relatively early age of fifty-three and as a result of the Blomberg-Fritsch crisis (q.v.), he was one of eight major generals promoted to full general. He was given command of the Sixteenth Army and Wehrkreis (Defense District) VIII. Later in 1938, during the Czech crisis, he and Walther von Reichenau (q.v.) were the only two generals who opposed the warning about military disaster given by Col. Gen. Ludwig Beck (q.v.). At the beginning of World War II Von Busch saw service in the Polish

Field Marshal Ernst von Busch. *[Imperial War Museum, London]*

campaign. In 1940 he commanded the Sixteenth Army in the west, and the next year, on the invasion of Soviet Russia, he was shifted to the east. His army suffered heavy losses during the winter of 1942–1943. Nevertheless, his promotion to general field marshal came through on February 1, 1943, the very day on which Hitler swore that he would create no more general field marshals in the war. On June 27, 1944, broken and depressed by his unsatisfactory career, Von Busch was relieved of his command. On March 20, 1945, near the end of the war, he was detailed by Hitler to command the defense of the North Sea coast and Schleswig-Holstein against the British. He died on July 17, 1945, while a prisoner of the British.

BUSINESS IN THE THIRD REICH. Hitler, the consummate politician, was never reluctant to confess his lack of interest in economic matters. During his early career he was influenced by the bizarre economic views of Gottfried Feder (q.v.). Feder's ideas were expressed in general form in the original Twenty-five Points of the German Workers' party (Deutsche Arbeiterpartei, q.v.). The aim was to root out the old foundations of business and industry, especially *Zinsknechtschaft* (q.v.), or interest slavery. In Feder's view interest slavery was the main cause of Germany's economic distress.

Once Hitler began his drive for political power, he discarded eccentric economic notions and came to terms with current practice. He needed financial support for his budding political movement. At first most industrial and business magnates opposed Hitler's pretensions, but they began to help him as soon as they realized that he was on his way (*see* KIRDORF, Emil; KRUPP VON BOHLEN UND HALBACH, Gustav; STINNES, Hugo; THYSSEN, Fritz). At the same time Hitler relied on voting support from the middle class of independents *(Mittelstand),* such as shopkeepers and craftsmen. These small businessmen, who saw in Nazism a panacea for all their ills, were valuable allies for Hitler in his drive toward the chancellorship.

As soon as Hitler achieved political power, he made it clear to German businessmen that he expected their support to achieve his goals. His new state, he said, was neither occupational *(berufständisch)* nor corporative *(ständisch),* but was power-political *(machtständlich).* Businessmen were to think in ideological rather than economic terms, and they were expected to help him achieve *Lebensraum* (q.v.), or living space, for the German people. Like members of the civil service and the Army, all businessmen were expected to accept nazification and to agree to total control of the economy. It was the responsibility of the state to control prices and wages, credit, manpower, and production. The state would see to full employment, to the accumulation of foreign currency, and to the expanding export market. In return business, big and small, was expected to give full acquiescence to orders from above. In other words, business was subjected, along with every other activity in the Third Reich, to *Gleichschaltung* (q.v.), or coordination.

Hitler's first step was to remove Jewish influence from business. His wrath was directed primarily against those Jewish merchants who had pioneered and owned large department stores. Aware of the Fuehrer's intentions, party members who themselves were retailers and artisans rushed to profit from the elimination of Jewish businessmen. Jewish-owned stores were forced into sale at a fraction of their true value. Of the 3,700 Berlin shops owned by Jews at the time of the *Kristallnacht* (q.v.), the Night of the Broken Glass, at least 700 passed into the hands of waiting Nazis. There were immediate repercussions. The Aryanization of German business resulted in a 50 percent decrease in the number of textile and clothing enterprises.

Businessmen eagerly accepted the regimentation proposed by Hitler. They would be economic soldiers in the Fuehrer's peacetime mobilization. At the same time they were disturbed by the large-scale disorder that accompanied the process of coordination. Businessmen who thought in terms of competition were told to "think not of profit but of a strong, independent national economy." They were confused by orders from Nazi officials to "think of ideological goals," "eliminate competitors," "be careful of tax advantages." Those who tried to build up their enterprises received word from Berlin that they were expected to "emancipate themselves from capitalism." Expecting clear-cut directives, they received a host of conflicting orders. Early enthusiasm for the Nazi regime was followed by frustration and then by silence. Most businessmen decided that it was best not to cause waves that might rock the ship of state. One observer, perplexed by the status of business in the Third Reich, offered the analogy of the conductor of a runaway bus, who had no control over the actions of the driver but continued to collect fares from the passengers right up to the final crash.

BUTTER-OR-GUNS SPEECH. A talk delivered by Hermann Goering (q.v.) in 1936. In his speech Goering made it plain that if Germans were to make a choice between butter and guns, they must choose guns. The speech had a depressing effect in the world's capitals. The key passage follows:

Party comrades, friends, I have come to talk to you about Germany, our Germany. *Germany must have a place in the sun!* Rearmament is only a first step to make our people happy. For me rearming is not merely a goal in itself. I do not want to have rearmament for military ends or to oppress others. I want it solely for the freedom of Germany. Believe me, my friends, I am for international understanding. That is just why we are rearming. If we are weak, we shall be at the mercy of the world. What's the good of being in the concert of nations, if we are only allowed to play a comb?

I must speak clearly. There are those in international life who are hard of hearing. They listen only if the guns go off. We have no butter, my good people, but I ask you, would you rather have butter or guns? Should we import lard or metal ores? Let me tell it to you straight—preparedness makes us powerful. Butter merely makes us fat!

BV. *See* BEFRISTETE VORBEUGUNGSHÄFTLINGE.

C

CABINET, HITLER'S FIRST to CULTURE, NAZI

CABINET, HITLER'S FIRST. Hitler's original Cabinet, formed when he became Chancellor on January 30, 1933, was as follows:

Adolf Hitler	Chancellor
Franz von Papen	Vice-Chancellor
Wilhelm Frick (NSDAP)	Minister of the Interior
Hermann Goering (NSDAP)	Minister without Portfolio; later Minister for Air
Alfred Hugenberg (German Nationalist party	Minister of Economics
Gen. Werner von Blomberg (no party affiliation)	Minister of Defense
Franz Seldte (Stahlhelm federal leader; German Nationalist party)	Minister of Labor
Constantin Freiherr von Neurath (no party affiliation)	Foreign Minister
Lutz Graf Schwerin von Krosigk (no party affiliation)	Minister of Finance
Franz Gürtner (German Nationalist party)	Minister of Justice
Paul Freiherr von Eltz-Rübenach (no party affiliation)	Minister of Communications

"CALL ME MEIER!" Statement attributed to Hermann Goering, creator of the Luftwaffe (qq.v.). On August 9, 1939, just before the outbreak of World War II, Goering boasted about the strength of his air defenses: "Not a single bomb will fall on the Ruhr. If an enemy plane reaches the Ruhr, my name is not Hermann Goering—you can call me Meier!" Many Germans bitterly recalled this boast when, in the late stages of the war, cities throughout Germany were subjected to devastating British and American raids by thousands of planes.

CANADA. Term used by guards in the extermination camps (q.v.) to describe the great sorting house for booty taken from new prisoners. The railroad wagons which brought prisoners to the camps were cleaned out and used on the return journey to transfer anything of value taken from the inmates. Such articles were held temporarily in a building called Canada. Oswald Pohl (q.v.), chief of the Economic and Administrative Central Office (Wirtschafts- und Verwaltungshauptamt, q.v.) of the SS, reported that in February 1943 exactly 781 wagonloads had left Auschwitz (q.v.) for Germany; of these 245 were filled with clothing and 1 with varied human hair. Gold fillings retrieved from human ashes were melted down and sent in the form of ingots to the Reichsbank for the special Max Heiliger deposit account (q.v.).

CANARIS, WILHELM (1887–1945). Director of the Abwehr (q.v.), the counterintelligence department of the High Command of the armed forces, and leader in the conspiracy against Hitler. Wilhelm Canaris was born in Aplerbeck bei Dortmund on January 1, 1887. In 1915 and 1916 he carried out a secret mission in Spain for the German Navy. From 1924 to 1928 he was active in naval affairs, and in 1935 he took over control of the Abwehr in the Reich War Ministry. In 1938 he headed the foreign branch of the Oberkommando der Wehrmacht (q.v.), the High Command of the armed forces. Canaris gradually became an opponent of National Socialism and of Hitler's policies. He joined the Resistance (q.v.) movement but

Adm. Wilhelm Canaris. [*Picture Collection, The Branch Libraries, The New York Public Library*]

was always against any attempt to assassinate Hitler. In cooperation with Gen. Ludwig Beck (q.v.), Canaris organized Resistance cells. He maintained a social relationship with Reinhard Heydrich, deputy to Heinrich Himmler (qq.v.), while trying to protect his own men who opposed Hitler. According to a subordinate, Gen. Edwin Lahausen, Canaris had human qualities that placed him far above the usual military bureaucrat. He hated violence and was confused and uncomfortable in his double role. Under the strain he slowly broke down. Dismissed from his office in February 1944, he was arrested after the July Plot (q.v.) of 1944 and was hanged in the Flossenbürg (q.v.) concentration camp on April 9, 1945.

Bibliography. Hans Bernd Gisevius, *To the Bitter End,* Houghton Mifflin Company, Boston, 1947.

CANNED GOODS. Code name arranged in August 1939 for a plan to use the bodies of condemned criminals to justify the forthcoming attack on Poland. Conceived by Heinrich Himmler, Reinhard Heydrich, and Heinrich Müller (qq.v.), leaders of the Gestapo (q.v.), and approved by Hitler, the scheme was to dress a dozen condemned German criminals in Polish uniforms, order a Nazi doctor to give them fatal injections, cover them with gunshot wounds, and then place the bodies at a prearranged spot to make it appear that Polish soldiers had been attacking German troops. There were several such faked attacks by "Polish soldiers," the most important of which was the raid on the radio station at Gleiwitz (*see* GLEIWITZ RAID).

CARE. *See* PFLEGE.

CARPET CHEWER. *See* TEPPICHFRESSER.

CASSIRER, ERNST (1874–1945). Distinguished member of the neo-Kantian school of philosophy and a prominent refugee from the Third Reich. Ernst Cassirer was born in Breslau, Silesia, on July 28, 1874, the son of a wealthy Jewish merchant. Educated at the Universities of Berlin, Leipzig, and Heidelberg, he won a name for himself as an outstanding philosopher. Cassirer found it difficult to obtain a professorship because of his Jewish background. At the age of thirty he completed a two-volume history of epistemology and was invited to Berlin as a lecturer. In 1914 he was called to Harvard University but was unable to accept the appointment because of the outbreak of World War I. After the war he became a professor (1919–1930) and rector (1930–1933) at Hamburg. While at Hamburg he wrote his masterwork, *The Philosophy of Symbolic Forms* (1923–1929), in which he subjected mythical thinking to detailed analysis.

Cassirer resigned his position in disgust when Hitler became Chancellor in 1933. He was called to Oxford University (1933–1935) and then to the University of Göteborg in Sweden. In 1941 he went to Yale University as a guest professor. Meanwhile, he continued to write prolifically on political philosophy, the history of ideas, and physics. He died in Princeton, New Jersey, on May 13, 1945.

CASTLES OF THE DEAD. *See* TOTENBURGEN.

CELEBRATIONS. *See* HOLIDAYS, NAZI.

CELL LEADER. *See* ZELLENLEITER.

CENTRAL COMMITTEE OF THE COMMUNIST PARTY. *See* ZENTRALKOMITEE DER KOMMUNISTISCHEN PARTEI.

CENTRAL OFFICE FOR RACE AND RESETTLEMENT. *See* RASSE- UND SIEDLUNGSHAUPTAMT.

CENTRAL POLITICAL COMMISSION. *See* POLITISCHE ZENTRALKOMMISSION.

CHAIN. *See* KETTE.

CHAMBERLAIN, HOUSTON STEWART (1855–1927). Anglo-German author and precursor of Nazi ideology. Born in Southsea, a resort and yachting center in Hampshire, England, on September 9, 1855, Chamberlain was the son of a British admiral. He received his early education in Cheltenham and then studied various sciences at Geneva and aesthetics and philosophy at Dresden. He became a zealous partisan of Richard Wagner (q.v.), joined the Wagnerian circle, and married Eva Wagner, the composer's daughter. In 1908 he settled in Bayreuth. Chamberlain became more fanatically German than the Germans themselves. He admired the German way of life, which he found considerably more attractive than that of his homeland. In World War I he wrote anti-British propaganda for the German press and regularly denounced his own country. In England he was called "a turn-coat son of Britain" and "a renegade Englishman." His ideology was in close conformity with that of Hitler, as later expressed in *Mein Kampf* (q.v.). Chamberlain died on January 9, 1927, six years before the National Socialists assumed power.

Chamberlain was a prolific writer on philosophical and historical subjects. The work that made him famous was *Die Grundlagen des neunzehnten Jahrhunderts* (Munich, 1899), translated by John Lees as *The Foundations of the Nineteenth Century* (London, 1910). A rationalization of European history on a grand scale, the book was animated by an obscure sense of Christianity, an aristocratic scorn for the masses, and a highly romanticized conception of the Germans as a master race with a mission to rule the world. Chamberlain set for himself the task of revealing the bases on which the nineteenth century, "an inexhaustible theme," rested. European culture, he wrote, was the product of five forces: the art, literature, and philosophy of Greece; the law, statecraft, and citizenship of Rome; Christian revelation in its Protestant version; the creative, regenerative genius of the Teutons; and the alien, disruptive influence of Jews and Judaism.

In Volume I Chamberlain discussed events before 1200, the legacy of the ancient world. He called the birth of Christ the most important date in the history of mankind. "No battle, no dynastic change, no natural phenomenon, no discovery possesses an importance that could bear comparison with the short earthly life of the Galilean," for Christ brought a revolution in human feeling and action. With Hellenism came the rich blossoming of the human intellect. The Greeks were creative in language, religion, politics, philosophy, science, history, and geography. At

Houston Stewart Chamberlain. [*Picture Collection, The Branch Libraries, The New York Public Library*]

the central point of this creative genius stood Homer. But there were also clouds in the Hellenic inheritance: cruel, shortsighted democracies, a lack of lofty political conditions, an old and corrupt morality, and the decline of religion. The world owes to the Romans its rescue from the Semitic-Asiatic spell, permitting predominantly Indo-Teutonic Europe to become "the beating heart and thinking brain of all mankind." Greece gravitated toward Asia until Rome tore it away. But the Roman legacy forms a complicated and confused mass, for Rome lived for 2,500 years and allowed its impulses to disintegrate and frequently to neutralize one another. "The work of an incomparably energetic Indo-European race was revised and manipulated by the subtlest minds of the West-Asiatic mixed races, this again leading to the obliteration of unity of character."

Chamberlain turned now to the heirs of antiquity. At once there arose, he wrote, the study of race problems. He advised daring and cautiousness to steer safely between the Scylla of a science almost unattainable and the Charybdis of unstable and baseless generalizations. Rome transferred the center of gravity of civilization to the West, an unconsciously accomplished act of global importance. But Rome left an inextricable confusion of different races and types. In the midst of the chaos of the peoples (*Voelkerchaos,* q.v.) were the Jews, the one race which had chosen purity of blood. The Teutonic race entered history as an opposing force to the diminutive but influential Jewish race. "To this day these two powers—Jews and Teutons—stand, wherever the recent spread of the Chaos has not blurred their features, now as friendly, now as hostile, but always as alien forces face to face." Nothing, said Chamberlain, is so convincing as the consciousness of race. A man who belongs to a distinct, pure race never loses the sense of it. Race lifts a man above himself: it endows him with an extraordinary, almost superhuman power and distinguishes him from the individual who springs from the chaotic jumble of peoples drawn from all parts of the world. "The richer the blood that courses invisibly through the veins, the more luxuriant will be the blossoms of life that spring forth." The important secret of all history is that pure race is sacred. The raceless and nationless chaos of the late days of the Roman Empire was a pernicious, nearly fatal condition: the Teutonic peoples were to remedy this almost fatal condition.

In Volume II Chamberlain analyzed the rise of the new Germanic world and the struggle of the great powers for mastery. Three religious ideals sought domination: the East (Hellenic), the North (Teutonic), and Rome. At the opening of the thirteenth century this thousand-year struggle ended with what seemed to be the unconditional victory of Rome and the defeat of the Germanic North. But the Roman imperium was destined to sink as the free Teutons made ready to possess the world. In northern Italy the Teutons created a new culture. The work of Teutonism "is beyond all question the greatest that has hitherto been achieved by man." What is not Teutonic, Chamberlain wrote, consists of alien elements not yet exorcised. The Jews were the inheritors of Roman racial chaos; the Teutonic race was responsible for the spiritual salvation of mankind. All achievements in science, industry, political economy, and art were stimulated and propelled forward by the Teutons. Thus the nineteenth century rested upon a secure Teutonic foundation.

There are two basic themes in Chamberlain's *Foundations:* (1) the Teutons were the creators and bearers of civilization, and (2) the Jews were a negative racial force and a disrupting, degenerative influence in history. Chamberlain idealized the pure-blooded Teuton as alone responsible for all worldly progress. The Teutonic invaders of the crumbling Roman Empire were men with great radiant heavenly eyes, golden hair, gigantic stature, symmetrical development, lengthened skull, and an ever-active brain. They were the fresh and virile forest children who regenerated Western civilization and introduced new concepts of freedom. The state-building Teutons gave the individual a concept that hitherto had remained unknown—human liberty. Teutonism was the reforming force in Italy: it was responsible for Petrarch, Correggio, Galileo, Dante, Giotto, Donatello, Leonardo, and Michelangelo; in short, for the glorious Renaissance.

Against the creative genius of the Teutons, Chamberlain placed the low civilization of the Jews. The Jews were an alien people who in the nineteenth century had obtained a disproportionately important place in German life. They must be judged from the lofty heights of Teutonic superiority, not from the low depths of hatred and suspicion. The judgment could not possibly be favorable, because the Jew would deceive his neighbor and would not speak the truth. Great men, among them Cicero, Frederick the Great, Bismarck, Herder, and Goethe, had regarded the influence of Jews as pernicious. Almost all preeminent and free men, wrote Chamberlain, from Tiberius to Bismarck, had looked on the presence of the Jews as a social and political danger. Above all it must be made clear that Christ was not a Jew. He had not a single drop of Jewish blood in his veins. Christ opposed the Jewish dietary laws, never once mentioned fear of God, and often changed the meaning of words of Scripture. Anyone who regarded Christ as a Jew was ignorant or insincere. Chamberlain attributed Ernest Renan's statement "*Jésus était un juif*" to Jewish tyranny and influence.

Chamberlain's *Foundations* became an immediate best seller when Emperor William II pronounced it a study of the highest importance. German critics praised the book for its brilliant passages of lofty eloquence, its vast learning, and its critical acumen. Some reviewers hailed it as one of the most significant works of the century. Within three years of publication, three editions of the *Foundations* were exhausted in Germany, and by 1909 it had passed through eight editions. The reception in England was stormy; critics attacked the book in reviews ranging from mild satire to bitter invective. Chamberlain was described as "a street-corner preacher now assuming the toga of Roman oratory and now the robes of Christian ceremony" and as a man whose work was "the crapulous eructations of a drunken cobbler." The work was described as nothing more or less than "a clever synthesis of Schopenhauerism and Gobineauism reflecting the more brutal and audacious affirmations of the mystical alliance between Teutonism and the divinity of progress." In the United States the Nordic school hailed Chamberlain as the great architect of Nordic theory. In 1911 the former American president Theodore Roosevelt, while recognizing Chamberlain's brilliance and suggestiveness, wrote that his doctrines were based on foolish hatred and that "his brilliant lapses into sanity are fixed in a matrix of fairly bedlamite passion and non-sanity." "He likes David, so he promptly makes him an Aryan Amorite. He likes Michelangelo, and Dante, and Leonardo da Vinci, and he instantly says that they are Teutonic; but he does not like Napoleon, and so he says that Napoleon is the true representative of the raceless chaos."

Hitler's racial theories expressed in *Mein Kampf* were strongly influenced by Chamberlain's *Foundations.* Nowhere did he mention Chamberlain by name, but it is clear that if he had not read the *Foundations* he at least had imbibed its theories secondhand. Konrad Heiden classifies Hitler as an apostle of the apostles of Arthur Comte de Gobineau (q.v.) and Chamberlain, that is, of Hans F. K. Günther and Alfred Rosenberg (qq.v). Certainly Hitler would not have understood the involved metaphysics of the *Foundations,* much less have taken the time to read the two volumes. But *Mein Kampf* expressed in more elementary form precisely the same thesis of Teutonic superiority and Jewish decadence that Chamberlain advocated.

Bibliography. Martin Dippel, *Houston Stewart Chamberlain,* Deutscher Volksverlag, Munich, 1938.

CHAMBERLAIN, NEVILLE (1869–1940). British statesman closely concerned with the history of the Third Reich. Arthur Neville Chamberlain was born in Edgbaston, near Birmingham, on March 18, 1869, the son of Joseph Chamberlain, a successful industrialist and a progressive lord mayor of Birmingham. After working as a planter in the Bahamas from 1890 to 1897, he returned to England to pursue an industrial and political career. In 1918 he was elected as a Conservative to the House of Commons for Birmingham. Thereafter he held various governmental posts, including Postmaster General (1922), Minister of Health (1923), Chancellor of the Exchequer (1924–1929), and Minister of Welfare (1931–1937). In May 1937 he succeeded Stanley Baldwin as Prime Minister.

Although Chamberlain knew little about European politics, he assumed leadership in foreign affairs. Successful in social reform, economics, and finance, he was less effective in foreign relations. He was certain that he could settle German grievances by man-to-man talks with Hitler. During the Czechoslovakian crisis of 1938 he made his first flight to Berchtesgaden to meet Hitler and then a second one to Bad Godesberg. Chamberlain was one of the four major figures who concluded the Munich Agreement (q.v.). At the airport on his return to London, he

Prime Minister Neville Chamberlain (left) meeting at Berchtesgaden with Hitler, Joachim von Ribbentrop, and Ambassador Sir Nevile Henderson. [*Wide World Photos*]

waved a piece of paper which he said meant "peace in our time." Chamberlain abandoned his policy of appeasement only after the Germans occupied Prague in March 1939. He then offered guarantees of support to Poland, Romania, and Greece. Great Britain declared war on Germany on September 3, 1939. On May 10, 1940, Chamberlain resigned and was succeeded by Winston Churchill. Chamberlain died in Heckfield, Hampshire, on November 9, 1940.

Chamberlain's policy of appeasement led to a major historical controversy. On the one hand he was criticized for having given the dictators an opening for further aggression. On the other he was defended as acting with shrewd insight to gain time for an unprepared Britain to arm itself for the coming confrontation. Finally aware that Hitler's word was not to be trusted, Chamberlain took the initiative in declaring Poland's borders inviolable. The historical controversy over Chamberlain has not yet been resolved.

Bibliography. Iain Macleod, *Neville Chamberlain,* Frederick Muller, Ltd., London, 1962.

CHAOS OF PEOPLES. *See* VOELKERCHAOS.

CHEF DER SICHERHEITSPOLIZEI UND DES SD (CSSD; Chief of the Security Police and Security Service). Title conferred on Reinhard Heydrich until 1942 and then on Ernst Kaltenbrunner (qq.v.).

CHEŁMNO (Kulmhof). One of the main extermination camps (q.v.) in Poland. After the Wannsee Conference (q.v.) of January 20, 1942, on the Final Solution (*see* ENDLÖSUNG, DIE), *Reichsstatthalter* (Governor) Arthur Greiser (q.v.), in conjunction with the SS (q.v.) and Polish police, set up a killing center at Chełmno, in the middle of the Warta (Warthe) River region, as a strictly local enterprise for the Jews of his area. Chełmno later became one of the more important killing centers in occupied Poland.

There were no industrial activities in this camp, nor were there any non-Jewish inmates. From all over Poland "sick and sickly Jews" were resettled in Chełmno. The deportees were brought to a large mill in the nearby village of Zawadki and then taken in small groups by truck to Chełmno, where their clothes were collected and they were gassed. The camp guards received a bonus of 15 reichsmarks per day because of dangerous duty in that they were "exposed to infection." Chełmno achieved a special reputation among extermination camps because of its efficient *Knochenmühle* (bone-crushing machine). In the summer of 1942 Heinrich Himmler (q.v.) sent a special commando unit to Chełmno to destroy the mass graves by fire and dynamite.

CHIEF OF THE SECURITY POLICE AND SECURITY SERVICE. *See* CHEF DER SICHERHEITSPOLIZEI UND DES SD.

CHRISTIAN, GERDA (1913–). One of Hitler's private secretaries from 1933 to 1945. Gerda Christian, nee Daranowski, was born in Berlin on December 13, 1913. She worked closely with the Fuehrer and was accepted into his intimate evening circle of close associates. She was married to Eckard Christian, a young officer who eventually was promoted to general and chief of staff of the Luftwaffe (q.v.). With Frau Gertrud Junge (q.v.), she was one of two secretaries who remained in the *Fuehrerbunker* (q.v.) during Hitler's final days (*see* GÖTTERDÄMMERUNG). The two women were among those invited to Hitler's private suite to drink champagne after the wedding of the Fuehrer and Eva Braun (q.v.). In interviews after the fall of the Third Reich, Frau Christian was noncommittal about her service to Hitler during the Nazi era. She now lives in Düsseldorf.

CIRCLE OF FRIENDS OF HEINRICH HIMMLER. *See* FREUNDESKREIS HEINRICH HIMMLER.

CIRCUIT. *See* KREIS.

CIRCUIT LEADER. *See* KREISLEITER.

CIRCUIT LEADERSHIP. *See* KREISLEITUNG.

CITADEL. Code name for a final giant offensive by the Nazi armies in the war against the Soviet Union. On July 5, 1943, Hitler directed that Operation Citadel be launched against the Russian salient west of Kursk. Seventeen *Panzer* (q.v.) divisions with half a million men, the best of the German Army, were to be thrown into an assault from the southeast in the direction of Moscow. The offensive was a disastrous failure. It was stopped short by the Russians, who countered with a smashing offensive of their own.

CIVIL SERVICE LEAGUE. *See* BEAMTENBUND.

CLAN BOOK. *See* SIPPENBUCH.

CLEANSED OF JEWS. *See* JUDENFREI.

CLOTHES. *See* KLUFT.

COLDITZ. German prisoner-of-war camp in World War II. Colditz Castle was a fortresslike cluster of buildings dominating the small town of Colditz astride the Mulde River in Saxony. In the interior were two courtyards backing onto each other. The prisoners' courtyard, originating in the early days of the castle, was on one side, while the German administration buildings were located in the adjoining eighteenth-century yard. All around the castle the ground sloped away in terraces.

Colditz Castle was constructed originally in 1014 as a hunting lodge for the kings of Saxony. In the sixteenth century it belonged to the Danish princess Anna, who married Augustus, Elector of Saxony. Because Saxony was on the Protestant side in the Thirty Years' War (1618–1648), Colditz was sacked by the Imperial Army in 1634. Swedish troops retook the castle and remained there for several years. It was not used again by the Saxon dukes until 1753. The castle became a prison in 1800 and a lunatic asylum in 1828. Colditz was the site of one of the first concentration camps in 1933. Then it became a special work camp for the Hitler Jugend (q.v.).

In October 1939, shortly after the outbreak of World War II, Colditz was set up as a camp for Polish officers; later it was used for Belgian officers. It then became a *Sonderlager* (special camp) for captured officers held in strict surveillance under Article 48 of the Geneva Convention. It was supposed to hold a maximum of 200 officers, all classed as "undesirables," but many more were confined there. The number of guards usually equaled the number of prisoners.

There was a constant battle of wits between prisoners and guards. The inmates devised ingenious methods of escape, and the warders used every possible defensive means of foiling them. Those escapees who were recaptured were punished by solitary confinement. On about 130 occasions, inmates actually escaped from the castle grounds. Of these escapees, 30 (14 French, 9 British, 6 Dutch, and 1 Pole) managed to cross the frontier and reach safety.

Conditions in Colditz worsened in late 1944 as the Nazi regime was heading for collapse. By now its guard companies were formed exclusively of veterans between the ages of fifty and sixty-five. Food and fuel supplies steadily decreased, and escape attempts were more and more frequent. As American tanks approached Colditz, prisoners had almost completed preparations for a final bizarre attempt at escape: in the upper attic over the chapel a glider had been built in sections for eventual launching. Colditz fell to the Americans in mid-April 1945.

Bibliography. Reinhold Eggers, *Colditz: The German Story*, tr. by Howard Gee, Robert Hale, Ltd., London, 1961.

COLUMBIA-HAUS (Columbia House). The worst and most infamous of the Gestapo (q.v.) prisons set up in various parts of Berlin after Hitler became Chancellor on January 30, 1933. Columbia-Haus was notorious for its torture chambers in which Communists, Social Democrats, Jews, and other enemies of the Nazi regime were interrogated, beaten, and abused before being sent to concentration camps (q.v.). Its use was discontinued in 1936 in favor of Sachsenhausen (q.v.) concentration camp.

COMMANDER IN CHIEF. *See* OBERBEFEHLSHABER.

COMMANDER IN CHIEF OF THE AIR FORCE. *See* OBERBEFEHLSHABER DER LUFTWAFFE.

COMMANDER IN CHIEF OF THE ARMY. *See* OBERBEFEHLSHABER DES HEERES.

COMMANDO ORDER. A top-secret order, issued by Hitler on October 18, 1942, that called for the execution of Allied commandos captured in the west. As the tide of war began to turn against him, the Fuehrer, angered by Allied air attacks, decided that any captured fliers should be turned over to the SD (q.v.) for summary execution. Until this time captured enemy soldiers had been treated under the rule of the Geneva Convention. However, there never had been any question about Russian guerrillas or partisans: they were executed on the spot.

COMMISSAR DECREE. *See* KOMMISSAR ERLASS.

COMMITTEE OF SEVEN. A group set up in early 1938 in Vienna ostensibly for the purpose of bringing about peace between the Nazis and the Austrian government. Actually, the Committee of Seven was the central unit of the illegal Nazi underground working in Austria for Anschluss (q.v.). The Austrian police raided the headquarters of the Committee of Seven on January 25, 1938. They found documents initialed by Rudolf Hess (q.v.), Hitler's Deputy Fuehrer, calling for Austrian Nazis to stage a revolt in the spring. Following the revolt the German Army was to cross the border "to prevent German blood being spilled by Germans."

COMMITTEE OF THREE. A committee set up during the Stalingrad crisis in the winter of 1943 to ease Hitler's administration as chief of state. It consisted of Martin Bormann (q.v.), who for eight years had been Hitler's shadow; Field Marshal Wilhelm Keitel (q.v.), who had remained close to the Fuehrer; and Hans Heinrich Lammers (q.v.), Reich Minister and Chief of the Reich Chancery. Henceforth all orders to be signed by Hitler were to be cleared through this screen of three men. The committee divided its jurisdiction. Keitel was to be in charge of all orders relating to the armed forces, but problems arose immediately because the commanders of the Navy and the Air Force refused to accept his authority. All constitutional affairs and administrative problems were delegated to Lammers, while Bormann was supposed to handle all domestic matters. As it turned out, both Keitel and Lammers had to defer to Bormann, whose years of experience enabled him to have the final word in deciding who was to see Hitler. Bormann now could make top-level decisions once made by the Fuehrer himself.

COMMITTEES FOR EXAMINATION AND ADJUSTMENT. *See* UNTERSUCHUNGS- UND SCHLICHTUNGS-AUSSCHÜSSE.

COMMUNIST PARTY OF GERMANY. *See* KOMMUNISTISCHE PARTEI DEUTSCHLANDS.

COMMUNITY OF NEED, BREAD, AND FATE. *See* NOT-, BROT- UND SCHICKSALSGEMEINSCHAFT.

COMPIÈGNE. The place at which Hitler on June 21, 1940, after the defeat of France, handed French envoys the German terms of surrender. The Fuehrer chose the same railroad coach at exactly the same spot in a little clearing in the forest of Compiègne where, on November 11, 1918, the armistice that ended World War I had been signed. He ordered the German and French plenipotentiaries to meet in the railroad coach that had been used by Marshal Ferdinand Foch. As additional salt for the wounds of prostrate France, Hitler insisted that the same table be used and that he himself occupy the seat on which Foch had sat when the Frenchman had dictated terms to defeated Germany. Undoubtedly, Hitler had in mind what he conceived to be historic justice: in 1919 the victorious Allies had chosen the Hall of Mirrors at Versailles to dictate the peace to Germany—the same hall in which the Second German Empire had been proclaimed by Bismarck on January 18, 1871.

Hitler's hour of triumph was described to the listening world in a dramatic broadcast for the Columbia Broadcasting System by William L. Shirer (q.v.). Phrasing his reactions quickly, with no opportunity to polish his story, Shirer improvised from notes in what turned out to be one of the memorable reporting events of the war. The text of Shirer's broadcast follows:[1]

> ANNOUNCER: At this time, as the French government considers Germany's terms for an armistice, Columbia takes you to Berlin for a special broadcast by William Shirer in Germany. We take you now to Berlin. Go ahead, Berlin.
>
> SHIRER: Hello, America! CBS! William L. Shirer calling CBS in New York.
>
> William L. Shirer calling CBS in New York, calling CBS from Compiègne, France. This is William L. Shirer of CBS. We've got a microphone at the edge of a little clearing in the forest of Compiègne, four miles to the north of the town of Compiègne and about forty-five miles north of Paris. Here, a few feet from where we're standing, in the very same old railroad coach where the Armistice was signed on that chilly morning of November 11, 1918, negotiations for another armistice—the one to end the present war between France and Germany—began at 3:30 P.M., German summer time, this afternoon. What a turning back of the clock, what a reversing of history we've been watching here in this beautiful Compiègne Forest this afternoon! What a contrast to that day twenty-two years ago! Yes, even the weather, for we have one of those lovely warm June days which you get in this part of France close to Paris about this time of year.
>
> As we stood here, watching Adolf Hitler and Field Marshal Göring and the other German leaders laying down the terms of the armistice to the French plenipotentiaries here this afternoon, it was difficult to comprehend that in this rustic little clearing in the midst of the Forest of Compiègne, from where we're talking to you now, that an armistice was signed here on the cold, cold morning at five A.M. on November 11, 1918. The railroad coach—it was Marshal Foch's private car—stands a few feet away from us here, in exactly

[1]By permission of William L. Shirer.

the same spot where it stood on that gray morning twenty-two years ago, only—and what an "only" it is, too—Adolf Hitler sat in the seat occupied that day by Marshal Foch. Hitler at that time was only an unknown corporal in the German army, and in that quaint old wartime car another armistice is being drawn up as I speak to you now, an armistice designed like the other that was signed on this spot to bring armed hostilities to halt between those ancient enemies—Germany and France. Only everything that we've been seeing here this afternoon in Compiègne Forest has been so reversed. The last time the representatives of France sat in that car dictating the terms of the armistice. This afternoon we peered through the windows of the car and saw Adolf Hitler laying down the terms. That's how history reversed itself, but seldom has it done so as today on the very same spot. The German leader in the preamble of the conditions which were read to the French delegates by Colonel General von Keitel, Chief of the German Supreme Command, told the French that he had not chosen this spot at Compiègne out of revenge but merely to right a wrong.

The armistice negotiations here on the same spot where the last armistice was signed in 1918, here in Compiègne Forest, began at 3:15 P.M., our time; a warm June sun beat down on the great elm and pine trees and cast purple shadows on the hooded avenues as Herr Hitler with the German plenipotentiaries at his side appeared. He alighted from his car in front of the French monument to Alsace-Lorraine which stands at the end of an avenue about two hundred yards from the clearing here in front of us where the armistice car stands. That famous Alsace-Lorraine statue was covered with German war flags, so that you cannot see its sculptured works or read its inscriptions. I had seen it many times in the postwar years, and doubtless many of you have seen it—the large sword representing the sword of the Allies, with its point sticking into a large, limp eagle, representing the old empire of the Kaiser, and the inscription underneath in front saying, "To the heroic soldiers of France, defenders of the country and of right, glorious liberators of Alsace-Lorraine."

Through our glasses, we saw the Führer stop, glance at the statue, observe the Reich war flags with their big swastikas in the center. Then he strolled slowly toward us, toward the little clearing where the famous armistice car stood. I thought he looked very solemn: his face was grave. But there was a certain spring in his step, as he walked for the first time toward the spot where Germany's fate was sealed on that November day of 1918, a fate which, by reason of his own being, is now being radically changed here on this spot.

And now, if I may sort of go over my notes—I made from moment to moment this afternoon—now Hitler reaches a little opening in the Compiègne woods where the Armistice was signed and where another is about to be drawn up. He pauses and slowly looks around. The opening here is in the form of a circle about two hundred yards in diameter and laid out like a park. Cypress trees line it all around, and behind them the great elms and oaks of the forest. This has been one of France's national shrines for twenty-two years. Hitler pauses and gazes slowly around. In the group just behind him are the other German plenipotentiaries—Field Marshal Göring, grasping his Field Marshal baton in one hand. He wears the blue uniform of the air force. All the Germans are in uniform, Hitler in a double-breasted gray uniform with the Iron Cross hanging from his left breast pocket. Next to Göring are the two German army chiefs, Colonel General von

Hitler dances for joy on June 22, 1940, the day after the German terms are handed to the defeated French at Compiègne. [*Imperial War Museum, London*]

Keitel, Chief of the Supreme Command, and Colonel General von Brauchitsch, Commander-in-Chief of the German Army. Both are just approaching sixty, but look younger, especially General von Keitel, who has a dapper appearance, with his cap slightly cocked on one side. Then we see there Dr. Raeder, Grand Admiral of the German Fleet. He has on a blue naval uniform and the invariable upturned stiff collar which German naval officers usually wear. We see two nonmilitary men in Hitler's suite—his Foreign Minister, Joachim von Ribbentrop, in the field-gray uniform of the Foreign Office, and Rudolf Hess, Hitler's deputy, in a gray party uniform.

The time's now, I see by my notes, 3:18 P.M. in the Forest of Compiègne. Hitler's personal standard is run up on a small post in the center of the circular opening in the woods. Also, in the center, is a great granite block which stands some three feet above the ground. Hitler, followed by the others, walks slowly over to it, steps up, and reads the inscription engraved in great high letters on that block. Many of you will remember the words of that inscription. The Führer slowly reads them, and the inscription says, "Here on the eleventh of November, 1918, succumbed the criminal pride of the German Empire, vanquished by the free peoples which it tried to enslave." Hitler reads it, and Göring reads it. They all read it, standing there in the June sun and the silence. We look for the expression on Hitler's face, but it does not change. Finally he leads his party over to another granite stone, a small one some fifty yards to one side. Here it was that the railroad car in which the German plenipotentiary stayed during the 1918 armistice negotiations stood from November 8 to 11. Hitler looks down and reads the inscription, which merely says: "The German plenipotentiary." The stone itself, I notice, is set between a pair of rusty old railroad tracks, the very ones that were there twenty-two years ago.

It is now 3:23 P.M., and the German leaders stride over to the armistice car. This car, of course, was not standing on this spot yesterday. It was standing seventy-five yards down the rusty track in the shelter of a tiny museum built to house it by an American citizen, Mr. Arthur Henry Fleming of Pasadena, California. Yesterday the car was removed from the museum by the German army engineers and rolled back those seventy-five yards to the spot where it stood on the morning of November 11, 1918. The Germans stand outside the car, chatting in the sunlight. This goes on for two minutes. Then Hitler steps up into the car, followed by Göring and the others. We watch them entering the drawing room of Marshal Foch's car. We can see nicely now through the car windows.

Hitler enters first and takes the place occupied by Marshal Foch the morning the first armistice was signed. At his sides are Göring and General Keitel. To his right and left at the ends of the table we see General von Brauchitsch and Herr Hess at the one end, at the other end Grand Admiral Raeder and Herr von Ribbentrop. The opposite side of the table is still empty, and we see there four vacant chairs. The French have not yet appeared, but we do not wait long. Exactly at 3:30 P.M. the French alight from a car. They have flown up from Bordeaux to a near-by landing field and then have driven here in an auto.

They glance at the Alsace-Lorraine memorial, now draped with swastikas, but it's a swift glance. Then they walk down the avenue flanked by three German army officers. We see them now as they come into the sunlight of the clearing—General Huntziger, wearing a brief khaki uniform; General Bergeret and Vice-Admiral Le Luc, both in their respective dark-blue uniforms; and then, almost buried in the uniforms, the one single civilian of the day, Mr. Noël, French Ambassador to Poland when the present war broke out there. The French plenipotentiaries passed the guard of honor drawn up at the entrance of the clearing. The guard snapped to attention for the French but did not present arms. The Frenchmen keep their eyes straight ahead. It's a grave hour in the life of France, and their faces today show what a burden they feel on their shoulders. Their faces are solemn, drawn, but bear the expression of tragic dignity. They walked quickly to the car and were met by two German officers, Lieutenant Colonel Tippelskirch, Quartermaster General, and Colonel Thomas, Chief of the Paris Headquarters. The Germans salute; the French salute; the atmosphere is what Europeans call "correct"; but you'll get the picture when I say that we see no handshakes—not on occasions like this. The historic moment is now approaching. It is 3:32 by my watch. The Frenchmen enter Marshal Foch's Pullman car, standing there a few feet from us in Compiègne Forest. Now we get our picture through the dusty windows of the historic old *wagon-lit* car. Hitler and the other German leaders rise from their seats as the French enter the drawing room. Hitler, we see, gives the Nazi salute, the arm raised. The German officers give a military salute; the French do the same. I cannot see Mr. Noël to see whether he salutes or how. Hitler, so far as we can see through the windows just in front of here, does not say anything. He nods to General Keitel at his side. We can see General Keitel adjusting his papers, and then he starts to read. He is reading the preamble of the German armistice terms. The French sit there with marblelike faces and listen intently. Hitler and Göring glance at the green table top. This part of the historic act lasts but a few moments. I note in my notebook here this—3:42 P.M.—that is, twelve minutes after the French arrived—3:42—we see Hitler stand up, salute the three with hand upraised. Then he strides out of the room, followed by Göring, General von Brauchitsch; Grand Admiral Raeder is there, Herr Hess, and, at the end, von Ribbentrop. The French remain at the green-topped table in the old Pullman car, and we see General Keitel remains with them. He is going to read them the detailed conditions of the armistice. Hitler goes, and the others do not wait for this. They walk down the avenue back towards the Alsace-Lorraine monument. As they pass the guard of honor, a German band strikes up the two national anthems *Deutschland über Alles* and the *Horst Wessel Song*.

The whole thing has taken but a quarter of an hour—this great reversal of a historical armistice of only a few years ago.

CBS ANNOUNCER: You have just heard a special broadcast from the Compiègne Forest in France, where on the historic morning of November 11, 1918, representatives of the German army received from the Allies the terms of the armistice which ended the First World War, and where today, June 21, 1940, representatives of the French government received from Führer Adolf Hitler the terms under which a cessation of hostilities between Germany and France may be reached. As you know, the actual terms presented to the French plenipotentiaries have not yet been made public.

MUSIC: *Organ.*

ANNOUNCER: This is the Columbia Broadcasting System.

COMRADE. *See* KAMERAD.

CONCENTRATION CAMPS. Institutions used in the Third Reich and in occupied territories for imprisoning opponents of the Nazi regime. The term *concentration camp* was first used in the twentieth century to describe centers in South Africa in which Boer civilians were interned from 1900 to 1902 to prevent them from helping guerrillas. The camps became notorious because of inefficient administration and bad hygienic conditions. Hitler, too, regarded such camps as an effective tool. In a talk with Hermann Rauschning (q.v.) before he became Chancellor, he stated: "We must be ruthless! We must regain our clear conscience as to ruthlessness. Only thus shall we purge our people of their softness and sentimental philistinism, of their *Gemütlichkeit* [easygoing, genial nature] and their degenerate delight in beer-swilling. We have no time for fine sentiments. I don't want the concentration camps transferred into penitentiary institutions. Terror is the most effective instrument. I shall not permit myself to be robbed of it simply because a lot of stupid, bourgeois mollycoddlers choose to be offended by it." In accordance with this principle Hitler set up concentration camps shortly after he assumed political power in 1933. It was announced that the goal was to "reform" political opponents and to turn "anti-social members of society into useful members." The German public was convinced in the early stages that concentration camps were needed for the restoration of public order and security and that they were legal under Article 48 (q.v.) of the Weimar Constitution. A law dated February 28, 1933, suspended clauses of the constitution guaranteeing personal liberties and provided for *Schutzhaft* (protective custody) for dissenters.

The first three main camps were set up in the early days of the Nazi regime at Dachau, near Munich in the south; Buchenwald, near Weimar in central Germany; and Sachsenhausen (qq.v.), near Berlin in the north. The first inmates were Communists and Jews, but opposition to Nazi totalitarianism was so great that Socialists, Democrats, Catholics, Protestants, and even dissident Nazis were added to the camp population. Trade union leaders,

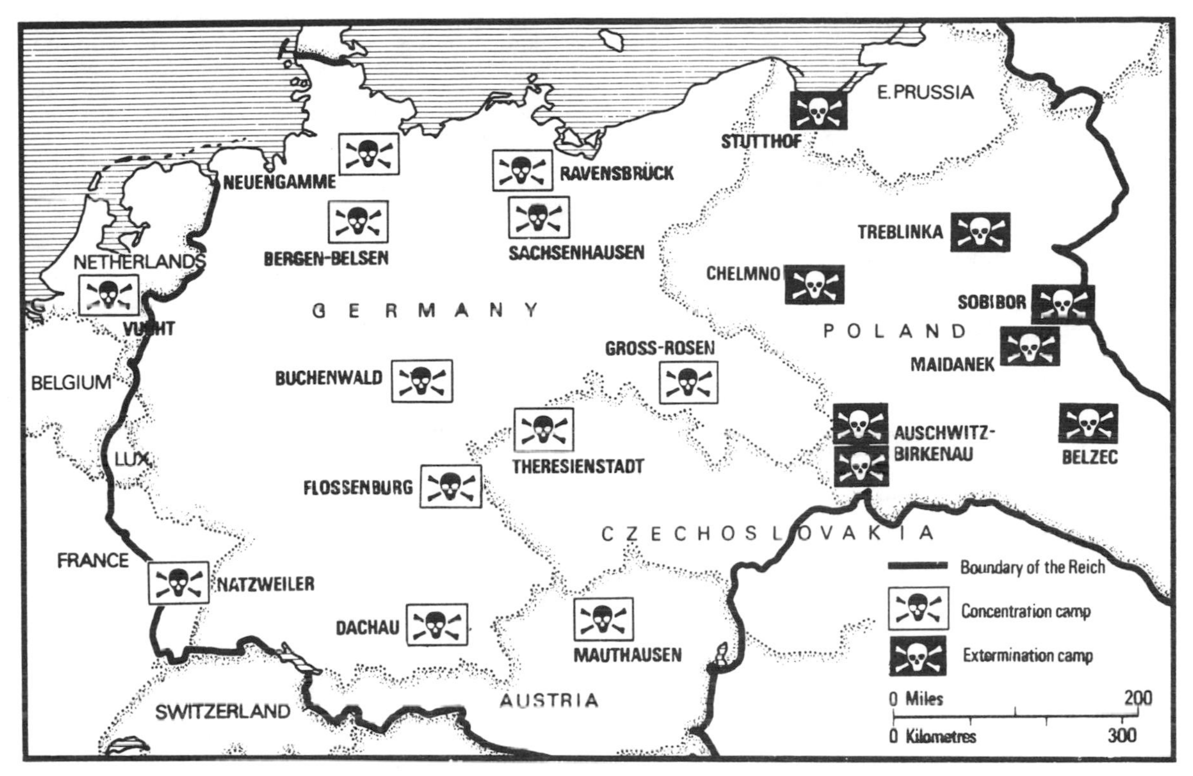

Sites of Nazi concentration camps.

clergymen, monks, pacifists, Jehovah's Witnesses—all were herded into the camps without trial and without the right of appeal. Other camps were added, including Ravensbrück, Belsen, Gross-Rosen, and Papenburg (qq.v.) in Germany; Mauthausen (q.v.) in Austria after the *Anschluss* (q.v.); and Theresienstadt (q.v.) in Bohemia. Some 200,000 inmates passed through the concentration camps between 1934 and 1939, and more than 50,000 were confined at the outbreak of war in 1939. The population multiplied rapidly after the beginning of the war.

After the conquest of Poland the camps at Auschwitz, Birkenau, Treblinka, and Maidanek (qq.v.) were transformed into extermination camps (q.v.). In these death camps a deliberate attempt was made to reduce the inmates to subhuman standards. The SS (q.v.) guards, recruited from the most ruthless Nazi elements, worked the inmates beyond their physical capacity and starved, humiliated, and tortured them beyond endurance. What originally were supposed to be "institutes for reform" became centers of genocide (q.v.), the deliberate destruction of a people.

Although conditions varied somewhat in camps throughout Germany, there were some general features common to most of them. The categories of prisoners consisted primarily of four groups: political opponents, members of "inferior races," criminals, and "shiftless elements" believed to be asocial. The second group, embracing Jews and Gypsies, was marked for special attention. All but an insignificant number of Gypsies perished in the camps. The Jews were the main target. They were divided among all four categories, although they remained segregated in special barracks. They were given the most menial jobs and were subject to cruel treatment by the SS guards. Criminals were divided into two groups. The *Befristete Vorbeugungshäftlinge* (prisoners in limited-term preventive custody) were those who had served several sentences before. They were generally known by the term *BV*. The *Sicherungsverwahrte* (prisoners in security custody) consisted of convicts who were actually serving sentences. These were commonly known as *SV*. The political opponents were members of anti-Nazi parties, former Nazi party members guilty of some infraction, foreign exchange violators, illegal radio listeners, grumblers, and Jehovah's Witnesses. Included among the "shiftless elements" were homosexuals, who were treated in ghastly fashion.

All inmates of the concentration camps had to wear prescribed markings on their clothing, including a serial number and colored triangles affixed to the left breast and the right trouser leg. At Auschwitz the serial number was tattooed on the left forearm. All political prisoners wore a red triangle; criminals, green; shiftless elements, black; homosexuals, pink; Gypsies, brown. Jews were required to wear a yellow triangle in addition to the classification triangle. The yellow triangle pointed up, the other down, thus forming the six-pointed Star of David. Any Jew who had defied the racial laws ("race defiler") had to wear a black border around the green or yellow triangle. Foreigners were identified by letters: *F* for France, *P* for Poland. The letter *K* indicated a war criminal *(Kriegsverbrecher)*. The letter *A* identified a labor disciplinary prisoner, from the German word *Arbeit* (work). The feebleminded were forced to wear the word *Blöd* (stupid). Inmates suspected of seeking to escape had to wear a red-and-white target sewn on chest and back. Some prisoners were decked out in a variety of colors.

When the victorious Allies swarmed into Germany from both east and west in mid-1945, they captured the concentration and extermination camps. Men hardened by battle were sickened by the sights, sounds, and stenches in the camps, and by cruelties so enormous as to be incomprehensible to the normal human mind. The revelation of the horrors shocked the world. Inmates testified to blows, beatings, and kicking as a part of daily life and described murder through injection, death in cesspools or on the electric barbed wires, and extermination by gas. After the war sentences were passed on SS (q.v.) officials responsible for administration in the camps.

Bibliography. Raul Hilberg, *The Destruction of the European Jews,* Quadrangle Books, Inc., Chicago, 1961; Nora Levin, *The Holocaust: The Destruction of European Jewry, 1933–1945,* Thomas Y. Crowell Company, New York, 1968.

CONCORDAT OF 1933. A treaty between the papacy and the Third Reich concerning ecclesiastical affairs. From April to July 1933 negotiations took place between the Papal Secretary of State, Eugenio Pacelli, the former Papal Nuncio in Berlin and the future Pope Pius XII (q.v.), and high German officials, including Franz von Papen (q.v.), concerning the status of the Catholic Church in the new Third Reich. On July 20, 1933, the concordat was formally signed and sealed by Pacelli and Von Papen in an elaborate ceremony at the Vatican. A rapprochement between the Third Reich and the Holy See was formally made. The preamble stated that the two contracting parties, led by "their reciprocal desire to consolidate and develop the amicable relations existing between the Holy See and the German Reich," had decided to conclude a solemn agreement. Article 1 guaranteed "freedom of the profession and the public exercise of the Catholic Religion," as well as the right of the church to regulate and administer freely its own affairs independently within the limit of laws applicable to all and to issue, within the framework of its own competence, laws and ordinances binding on its members. Other clauses reaffirmed diplomatic representation, the legal status of the clergy, the appointment of bishops, guarantees for the property of the church, the ecclesiastical right of veto over the appointment and continuation of Catholic teachers of religion, Catholic education, the appointment of a bishop for the armed forces, Catholic organizations, and the exclusion of the clergy from politics. A secret annex concerned the treatment of the clergy in the event that the government should introduce universal military training.

The concordat was regarded by world opinion as a great diplomatic victory for Hitler. In return for the assurance from Rome that it would not meddle in German politics, the Fuehrer granted Catholics freedom to practice their religion. He made the agreement for specific reasons: to undermine the strength of the Catholic Center party in German politics, to cut the influence of the Catholic labor unions, and to win public recognition for his new regime. It is questionable whether he intended to abide by the concordat. In the end Catholics as well as all others were to be subjected to total coordination (*see* GLEICHSCHALTUNG).

Bibliography. Guenther Lewy, *The Catholic Church and Nazi Germany,* McGraw-Hill Book Company, New York, 1964.

CONDOR LEGION. A unit of the Luftwaffe (q.v.) detailed for special duty during the Spanish Civil War. In November 1936, Hermann Goering (q.v.), head of the Luftwaffe and Minister of Aviation, assigned Maj. Gen. Hugo Sperrle (q.v.) to command the Condor Legion in its support of Gen. Francisco Franco and the Spanish Insurgents. The air unit was composed of several squadrons of Junker-52 bombers and Heinkel-51 fighters. In coordination with the German Mediterranean Fleet, which attacked Almería with heavy guns, Sperrle sent his planes against Spanish towns behind the Loyalist lines. On April 27, 1937, the Condor Legion attacked Guernica (q.v.) with heavy loss of civilian life. This devastating raid, which shocked the world, was immortalized by the artist Pablo Picasso in a powerful painting. In 1938 Sperrle's unit made a series of bombing attacks on Barcelona in a dress rehearsal for the raids on urban centers in World War II. Goering rotated the command of the Condor Legion in order to give his senior Luftwaffe officers combat experience. In November 1937 Sperrle was succeeded by Maj. Gen. Helmuth Volkmann (q.v.), and in November 1938 Brig. Gen. Wolfram Freiherr von Richthofen (q.v.), who had served as chief of staff to both Sperrle and Volkmann, was appointed the last commander of the Condor Legion.

CONFESSIONAL CHURCH. *See* BEKENNTNISKIRCHE.

CONTI, LEONARDO (1900–1945). Chief physician of the Third Reich. Leonardo Conti was born in Lugano, Switzerland, on August 24, 1900. After taking his medical degree, he settled in Berlin to practice medicine. One of the *Alte Kämpfer* (q.v.), the old guard of the Nazi party, he became an SA (q.v.) man and the first SA physician in Berlin in 1923. Responsible for building the Sanitation Corps of the SA, he was also the founder of the NS-Aerztebund, the National Socialist Doctors League, in Berlin. In 1932 he was named a delegate to the Prussian Landtag (Legislature).

In 1939 Hitler appointed Conti *Reichsgesundheitsfuehrer* (Reich Health Leader) and State Secretary for Health in the Reich and Prussia. In these posts he was responsible for the killing of a large number of Germans of unsound mind in the campaign to purify the Nordic race. He was elected to the Reichstag (q.v.) in 1941 and was promoted to *SS-Gruppenfuehrer* (lieutenant general). Conti committed suicide in Nuremberg Prison in 1945. On May 1, 1959, his estate was fined 3,000 marks by the Berlin *Spruchkammer* (denazification trial tribunal).

COORDINATION. *See* GLEICHSCHALTUNG.

CORINTH, LOVIS (1858–1925). Painter and etcher denounced by the Nazis for his "degenerate art" (*see* ENTARTETE KUNST). Lovis Corinth was born in Tapiau, East Prussia, on July 21, 1858. He studied art in Paris from 1884 to 1887, settled in Munich from 1890 to 1900, and then went to Berlin. He died in Zandvoort, the Netherlands, on July 17, 1925. On March 31, 1936, his paintings were shown at the Exhibit of Degenerate Art in Munich with such captions as "Painted after his first apoplectic fit."

CORPSE COMMANDO. *See* LEICHENKOMMANDO.

COUNCIL FOR A DEMOCRATIC GERMANY. An organization formed in the United States to unite all German refugees. The Council for a Democratic Germany originated from a meeting held in New York on November 4, 1943, under the chairmanship of Thomas Mann (q.v.). Among its chief promoters were Paul Hagen (also known as Karl Frank), Carl Zuckmayer (q.v.), the dramatist, and Paul Tillich (q.v.), the theologian. Former Nazis, but not former Communists or Communist sympathizers, were excluded. The official policy of the council was stated: "We believe only that we typify to some extent the various points of view on which the future democratic and peaceful Germany will be based." The Vansittartists (*see* VANSITTART, Robert Gilbert) and the Rex Stout group (Society for the Prevention of World War III) attacked the Council for a Democratic Germany on the grounds that it was propagating a "soft" peace and that it was a disguised Communist front.

COUNTERESPIONAGE POLICE. *See* ABWEHR POLIZEI.

COUNTERINTELLIGENCE. *See* ABWEHR.

COURT-MARTIAL. *See* STANDGERICHT.

COURTS. *See* JUSTICE IN THE THIRD REICH.

COVENTRY. English Midlands manufacturing city attacked by the Luftwaffe (q.v.) in a massive air raid on November 15, 1940. When the British refused to capitulate to Hitler's air attacks in September 1940, the Fuehrer turned to the ports of Dover, Bournemouth, Portsmouth, and Southampton. In November he shifted his attention to the industrial Midlands. On the night of November 15, there was a devastating raid on Coventry. Some 94 miles northwest of London, Coventry stands on a small hill at the confluence of several tributaries of the Avon. The home of one of the world's great cathedrals, Coventry was also a city of 200,000, a manufacturing center whose munitions and war materials took precedence over motorcars and art metalwork. It was a top priority target for the Luftwaffe. The greater part of the city was left in flames, and the brownstone cathedral was a smoking wreck. Only the big main spire, 303 feet high, was left standing; all the rest, built from 1373 to 1450, lay in a tangle of broken stone and crumpled debris. There were at least 1,000 dead and injured in the city. Frenzied rescuers tore at piles of brickwork and concrete covering the bodies of the dead. Houses as well as factories were wrecked, and essential services were paralyzed. Later in the war the Royal Air Force retaliated by similar attacks on German cities.

CRYSTAL NIGHT. *See* KRISTALLNACHT.

CSSD. *See* CHEF DER SICHERHEITSPOLIZEI UND DES SD.

CULT OF INSANITY. *See* MESCHUGGISMUS.

CULTURE, NAZI. *See* KULTUR, NAZI.

D

DACHAU to DÜSSELDORF SPEECH

DACHAU. Concentration camp located in Bavaria, 12 miles northwest of Munich on the Amper River, a tributary of the Isar (*see* CONCENTRATION CAMPS). Dachau was one of three camps set up in 1933 to form the nucleus of a concentration camp system: Dachau in the south, Buchenwald in central Germany, and Sachsenhausen (qq.v.) in the north. Known during World War II as one of the worst and most notorious camps, Dachau was the scene of the medical experiments carried out on hundreds of inmates. In 1941 and 1942 some 500 operations were performed on healthy persons. Inmates were subjected to malaria experiments and immersed for long periods in cold water to test the effect on their bodies. Among those killed in Dachau were captured American airmen. After the war the camp commandant and guards were tried before an American military tribunal and sentenced. Physicians who performed medical experiments at Dachau were also brought to trial (*see* DOCTORS' TRIAL).

In the postwar era Dachau was opened to the public with support from the Bavarian state government and the International Committee of Dachau Survivors. More than 2.6 million visitors, two-thirds of them non-Germans, visited Dachau to wander silently through the gray grounds and stare at the cold ovens.

Bibliography. Marcus J. Smith, *The Harrowing of Hell: Dachau*, The University of New Mexico Press, Albuquerque, 1972.

DAF. *See* DEUTSCHE ARBEITSFRONT.

DAG. *See* DEUTSCHE ANSIEDLUNGSGESELLSCHAFT.

DALADIER, ÉDOUARD (1884–1970). French statesman and Premier at the time of the Munich Agreement (q.v.). Édouard Daladier was born in Carpentras, Vaucluse Department, on June 18, 1884, the son of a baker, and became a schoolmaster, teaching history. He served with distinction in World War I. Daladier was a Radical Socialist throughout his life. He first took public office as a deputy elected for his *département* in 1919. From 1921 to 1924 he opposed the Ruhr policies of the French government, including the occupation of the Ruhr. In 1924 he was appointed Minister of Colonies in the government of Édouard Herriot. He held seven other portfolios before he served his own first term as Premier, from January to October 1933. In the premiership he was a party to a four-power peace pact between France, Great Britain, Germany, and Italy, concluded in July 1933.

Daladier held the office of Minister of War in the next two governments, serving from October 1933 to January 1934. He led his Radical Socialist party into the Popular Front with Socialists and Communists in 1935, and he served as Minister of Defense in Léon Blum's first govern-

Édouard Daladier. [*The French Ministry of Foreign Affairs*]

ment (June 1936–June 1937), Camille Chautemps's government (June 1937–March 1938), and Blum's second government (March–April 1938). When Daladier took over again as Premier in 1938, the immediate issues that led to World War II were already in existence. His signature on the Munich Agreement was opposed by the Communists and was not supported by the Socialists. Daladier feebly trailed behind Prime Minister Neville Chamberlain (q.v.) in his appeasement of Hitler and agreed to the latter's demands made under threat of war. The decisions taken at Munich meant the end of the Popular Front.

Daladier was at the helm when France declared war on Germany on September 3, 1939. On September 26, he dissolved the Communist party. He remained in power until March 1940, when Paul Reynaud took over after promising a more aggressive prosecution of the war. The German victory over France in June led to Reynaud's resignation, the end of the Third Republic, and the establishment of a new regime under Marshal Philippe Pétain (q.v.). Daladier was interned by the Vichy government on September 8, 1940, and brought to trial in Riom in February 1942. He was then handed over to the Germans and deported to Germany. Liberated in April 1945, he was elected in 1946 to the Constitutional Assembly and in 1947 to the National Assembly, where he served until 1958. From 1953 to 1958 he was lord mayor of Avignon. He died in Paris on October 10, 1970.

Bibliography. Stanton B. Leeds, *These Rule France*, The Bobbs-Merrill Company, Inc., Indianapolis, 1940.

DALUEGE, KURT (1897–1946). Engineer and Deputy Reich Protector of Bohemia and Moravia. Kurt Daluege was born in Kreuzburg on September 15, 1897. After World War I he joined the Rossbach group (q.v.), a freebooter *Freikorps* (q.v.) rightist unit. He was an early member of the Nationalsozialistische Deutsche Arbeiterpartei (q.v.) and founded the first SA (q.v.) unit in Berlin. From 1928 to 1933 he led an SS (q.v.) group. He served as a member of the National Socialist delegation to the Prussian Landtag (Legislature) in 1932. After Hitler assumed political power, Daluege received a series of high posts. In late 1933 he became a member of the Reichstag (q.v.), representing Wahlkreis (Electoral District) East Berlin. He also served that year as a ministerial director and as a Prussian state councillor. In 1936 he was appointed Chief of Security Police in the central office of the SD (q.v.). In 1942, as *SS-Oberstgruppenfuehrer* (colonel general), he was made Deputy Protector of Bohemia and Moravia as the successor to Reinhard Heydrich (q.v.), who had been assassinated. Daluege was hanged by the Czechs on October 24, 1946.

DANZIG. Code name for "Proceed with offensive in the west." Hitler's war directive of November 20, 1939, ordered the armed forces to be ready for attack in the west. Danzig gave the word for an immediate attack, whereas Augsburg (q.v.) meant "Delay offensive."

DARLEHEN. *See* EHESTANDSDARLEHEN.

DARRÉ, RICHARD-WALTHER (1895–1953). Agricultural expert in the Third Reich. Richard-Walther Darré was born in Belgrano, Buenos Aires, Argentina, on July 14, 1895. He attended the *Oberrealschule* (nonclassical secondary school) in Heidelberg and the Evangelical School in Bad Godesberg. In 1911 he was an exchange student at Wimbledon, near London. He served as a lieutenant in a field artillery regiment in World War I. After the war he turned to agriculture and began to organize farmers on behalf of the Nationalsozialistische Deutsche Arbeiterpartei (q.v.). On April 4, 1933, shortly after Hitler's assumption of political power, Darré was called to head the organization of German farmers. Hitler appointed him *Reichsbauernfuehrer* (Reich Agricultural Leader) and *Reichsernährungsminister* (Reich Food Minister). As as *SS-Gruppenfuehrer* (lieutenant general) he was also chief of the Rasse- und Siedlungshauptamt (q.v.; Central Office for Race and Resettlement) of the SS (q.v.). He was a prolific author on such subjects as the meaning of race, Marxism, and agriculture. He died in Munich in September 1953 of a liver disorder.

DAW. *See* DEUTSCHE AUSRÜSTUNGSWERKE.

DAWES PLAN. A report on reparations issued by a committee headed by Charles G. Dawes on April 9, 1924. A very severe economic problem was a contributory factor leading to the rise of Hitler and the Third Reich. Article 231 (q.v.), the war guilt clause, of the Treaty of Versailles, which held Germany and its allies responsible "for causing all the loss and damage" of World War I, was used as a basis for imposing reparations. In January 1921 the Allied Supreme Council set the figure at $56 billion. This sum was reduced to $16 billion in May 1921. The inability and unwillingness of the Germans to meet the annual installments led to French and Belgian occupation of the Ruhr in January 1923. Then came a crippling inflation and economic collapse.

The Dawes Plan was designed to balance Germany's budget and stabilize the mark. The recommendations included (1) a sliding scale of payments for five years, ranging from $250 million to $625 million; (2) the return of funds from mortgages on railways and industries and a transport tax; (3) stabilization of the German currency by means of a foreign loan; and (4) restoration of German fiscal and economic unity. The Germans were irritated by the plan because it called for foreign control of their finances. Most discouraging of all, the Dawes Plan set no final total of indebtedness. Germans felt that they would have to continue making large payments without knowing how long they were to pay. The Dawes Plan helped solve the immediate problem of inflation, but it gave political ammunition to such critics as the National Socialists. In his speeches Hitler hammered away at the fact that Germany was still subject to the control of foreign governments.

DAY OF THE SEIZURE OF POWER. *See* HOLIDAYS, NAZI.

DAY OF THE SUMMER SOLSTICE. *See* HOLIDAYS, NAZI.

DAY OF THE WINTER SOLSTICE. *See* HOLIDAYS, NAZI.

DEATH BOOK. *See* TOTENBUCH.

DEATH CAMPS. *See* EXTERMINATION CAMPS.

"DEATH TO JUDAISM!" *See* "JUDA VERRECKE!"

DEATH'S HEAD FORMATIONS. *See* SS-TOTENKOPFVERBÄNDE.

DEFENSE DISTRICT. *See* WEHRKREIS.

DEFENSE ECONOMY. *See* WEHRWIRTSCHAFT.

DEFENSE ECONOMY OFFICE. *See* WEHRWIRTSCHAFTSAMT.

DEFENSIVE LAND FORCES. *See* REICHSWEHR.

DEGENERATE ART. *See* ENTARTETE KUNST; VERFALLSKUNST.

DEGRELLE, LÉON (1906–). Pro-Hitler Belgian fascist politician. Léon Degrelle was born in Bouillon on June 15, 1906, into a family that produced many Jesuit priests. As a young man in the 1920s he was influenced by Charles Maurras, the French nationalist, and became a member of the reactionary Action Française. He was convinced that law, order, and responsibility rested on one keystone, the monarchy. A believer in racial purity, he denounced the Jews, "who never did want to be the true citizens of one country." In 1930, while managing a small publishing firm in Louvain, he founded Rex, a Belgian fascist equivalent of Mussolini's movement in Italy. Violently anticommunist, antisocialist, anti-Semitic, and antibourgeois, he launched a movement that in miniature imitated Nazi trappings: packed mass meetings, parades, banners, and bands. Flattered by the imitation, Hitler reportedly said: "If I had a son, I would want him to be like Degrelle."

The Belgian voters were not sympathetic to Degrelle's Rexist movement. He lost a key election in February 1937 when all other political parties combined against him. Rexism was revived in 1940 with the German occupation of Belgium. In 1941 Degrelle joined a legion of Walloon volunteers to fight for the Germans on the eastern front; of the original contingent of 850, only 3 men survived after three years of fighting. In 1945 Degrelle fled to Spain. A Belgian high court sentenced him to death *in absentia* for treason. In 1946 he went to Argentina and then returned to Spain. Found living in a luxurious apartment in Madrid by a Dutch television team in April 1973, Degrelle praised Hitler as the greatest statesman of his age. "I am only sorry I didn't succeed, but if I had the chance, I would do it all again, but much more forcefully."

Bibliography. Charles d'Ydewalle, *Degrelle, ou La triple imposture,* P. de Méyère, Brussels, 1968.

DELP, ALFRED (1907–1945). Member of the Kreisau Circle (q.v.) in the conspiracy against Hitler. Converted to Catholicism at the age of fifteen, he entered the Jesuit order three years later and was ordained a priest in 1937. Joining the Resistance (q.v.) in 1942, he prepared a draft for a Christian social order to replace the Nazi regime. He was arrested in late July 1944 after the failure of the July Plot (q.v.). Delp was brought before the dreaded People's Court (Volksgericht, q.v.) under the presidency of Roland Freisler (q.v.). Freisler heaped scorn on Delp and denounced him for allowing his quarters to be used by the conspirators. "You knew well that treason was taking place. But, of course, such a holy, consecrated fellow as you would be anxious to keep your tonsured scalp out of danger. No, you went off to pray that the plot would go along lines pleasing to God." Delp was condemned to death and hanged on February 2, 1945.

Alfred Delp. [*Stamp issued by the German Federal Republic*]

DENAZIFICATION (Entnazifizierung). The immensely complicated task of the Allies to eradicate Nazism after the fall of the Third Reich. In the early months of occupation each zone commander, Russian, American, British, and French, proceeded according to instructions from his own government. The Russians and French wanted summary removal of all Nazis from public positions, while the British and Americans, seeking to observe legal formalities, worked more slowly. By 1946 the process of denazification had become more systematic. In October of that year the Control Council issued a directive making a clear distinction between punishment of those who had committed war crimes and internment of potentially dangerous persons. Five categories of Nazis were defined: (1) major offenders (to be sentenced to death or life imprisonment); (2) activists, militarists, or profiteers (to be sentenced to a maximum of ten years in prison); (3) lesser offenders, such as young men who deserved leniency (to be placed on probation for two or three years); (4) followers who were nominal supporters of the Nazi regime (to be placed under police surveillance and obliged to pay a fine); and (5) exonerated individuals, such as former Nazis who had resisted the National Socialist government either actively or passively and who had themselves suffered from Nazi oppression.

Denazification proceeded slowly. In some cases those who deserved punishment were able to escape, but many others were arrested, found guilty, and punished.

DEPUTY HEALTH SERVICE OFFICER. *See* SANITÄTSDIENSTGEFREITER.

DER SCHÖNE ADOLF (The Handsome Adolf). Descriptive term applied to Hitler by girls and women in the Third Reich. Many regarded the Fuehrer as a strikingly handsome man and as an attractive sex symbol.

DESERT FOX. *See* ROMMEL, ERWIN.

DEST. *See* DEUTSCHE ERD- UND STEINWERKE, GMBH.

DEUTSCH, ERNST (1890–). Actor and refugee from the Third Reich. Ernst Deutsch was born in Prague on

September 16, 1890. After working as an actor in Vienna, Prague, and Dresden, he went to Berlin in 1920. There he became associated with Max Reinhardt (q.v.), the famous director. Deutsch was noted for playing such classic roles as Hamlet, Don Carlos, Shylock, Mephisto, and Nathan the Wise. He left Germany for the United States in 1933 after Hitler came to political power. After World War II he returned to Europe.

DEUTSCHE ANSIEDLUNGSGESELLSCHAFT (DAG; German Resettlement Society). An organization devoted to encouraging the resettlement of Germans as colonists in the conquered eastern territories during the opening years of World War II.

DEUTSCHE ARBEITERPARTEI (German Workers' Party). A small, obscure political group originating in Munich directly after World War I. A remnant of the once-powerful Pan-German Fatherland party, the new party was founded by Anton Drexler (q.v.), a toolmaker, and Dietrich Eckart (q.v.), a journalist. On September 19, 1919, Hitler became member No. 7 of the Deutsche Arbeiterpartei. Its first public meeting was held in a Munich beer hall on February 24, 1920. Although not yet the party leader, Hitler delivered an impassioned speech in which he demanded that the program of the Twenty-five Points be adopted. In April 1920 the name of the party was changed to Nationalsozialistische Deutsche Arbeiterpartei (q.v.; NSDAP), the National Socialist German Workers' party. The text of the Twenty-five Points follows:[1]

> The program of the German Workers' Party is limited as to period. The leaders have no intention, once the aims announced in it have been achieved, of setting up fresh ones, merely in order to increase the discontent of the masses artificially, and so ensure the continued existence of the party.
>
> 1. We demand the union of all Germans to form a Great Germany on the basis of the right of self-determination enjoyed by nations.
>
> 2. We demand equality of rights for the German people in its dealings with other nations, and abolition of the peace treaties of Versailles and Saint-Germain.
>
> 3. We demand land and territory (colonies) for the nourishment of our people and for settling our excess population.
>
> 4. None but members of the nation may be citizens of the state. None but those of German blood, whatever their creed, may be members of the nation. No Jew, therefore, may be a member of the nation.
>
> 5. Anyone who is not a citizen of the state may live in Germany only as a guest and must be regarded as being subject to foreign laws.
>
> 6. The right of voting on the leadership and legislation is to be enjoyed by the state alone. We demand therefore that all official appointments, of whatever kind, whether in the Reich, in the country, or in the smaller localities, shall be granted to citizens of the state alone. We oppose the corrupting custom of Parliament of filling posts merely with a view to party considerations, and without reference to character or capacity.
>
> 7. We demand that the state shall make it its first duty to promote the industry and livelihood of citizens of the state. If it is not possible to nourish the entire population of the state, foreign nationals (non-citizens of the state) must be excluded from the Reich.
>
> 8. All non-German immigration must be prevented. . . .
>
> 9. All citizens of the state shall be equal as regards rights and duties.
>
> 10. It must be the first duty of each citizen of the state to work with his mind or with his body. The activities of the individual may not clash with the interests of the whole, but must proceed within the frame of the community and be for the general good.
>
> We demand therefore.
>
> 11. Abolition of incomes unearned by work.
>
> 12. In view of the enormous sacrifice of life and property demanded of a nation by every war, personal enrichment due to a war must be regarded as a crime against the nation. We demand therefore ruthless confiscation of all war gains.
>
> 13. We demand nationalization of all businesses (trusts). . . .
>
> 14. We demand that the profits from wholesale trade shall be shared.
>
> 15. We demand extensive development of provision for old age.
>
> 16. We demand creation and maintenance of a healthy middle class, immediate communalization of wholesale business premises, and their lease at a cheap rate to small traders, and that extreme consideration shall be shown to all small purveyors to the state, district authorities, and smaller localities.
>
> 17. We demand land reform suitable to our national requirements. . . .
>
> 18. We demand ruthless prosecution of those whose activities are injurious to the common interest. Sordid criminals against the nation, usurers, profiteers, etc., must be punished with death, whatever their creed or race.
>
> 19. We demand that the Roman Law, which serves the materialistic world order, shall be replaced by a legal system for all Germany.
>
> 20. With the aim of opening to every capable and industrious German the possibility of higher education and of thus obtaining advancement, the state must consider a thorough reconstruction of our national system of education. . . .
>
> 21. The state must see to raising the standard of health in the nation by protecting mothers and infants, prohibiting child labor, increasing bodily efficiency by obligatory gymnastics and sports laid down by law, and by extensive support of clubs engaged in the bodily development of the young.
>
> 22. We demand abolition of a paid army and formation of a national army.
>
> 23. We demand legal warfare against conscious political lying and its dissemination in the press. In order to facilitate creation of a German national press we demand:
>
> (*a*) that all editors of newspapers and their assistants, employing the German language, must be members of the nation;
>
> (*b*) that special permission from the state shall be necessary before non-German newspapers may appear. These are not necessarily printed in the German language;
>
> (*c*) that non-Germans shall be prohibited by law from participation financially in or influencing German newspapers. . . .
>
> It must be forbidden to publish papers which do not

[1]Translated in *National Socialism*, United States Department of State Publication 1864, Washington, 1943, pp. 222–225.

conduce to the national welfare. We demand legal prosecution of all tendencies in art and literature of a kind likely to disintegrate our life as a nation, and the suppression of institutions which militate against the requirements above-mentioned.

24. We demand liberty for all religious denominations in the state, so far as they are not a danger to it and do not militate against the moral feelings of the German race.

The party, as such, stands for positive Christianity, but does not bind itself in the matter of creed to any particular confession. It combats the Jewish-materialist spirit within us and without us. . . .

25. That all the foregoing may be realized we demand the creation of a strong central power of the state; unquestioned authority of the politically centralized Parliament over the entire Reich and its organizations; and formation of chambers for classes and occupations for the purpose of carrying out the general laws promulgated by the Reich in the various states of the confederation.

The leaders of the party swear to go straight forward—if necessary to sacrifice their lives—in securing fulfillment of the foregoing points.

DEUTSCHE ARBEITSFRONT (DAF; German Labor Front). Monolithic labor organization allied to the Nazi party and set up by Hitler to take the place of the labor union system of the Weimar Republic (q.v.). The Nazi program called for the elimination of labor unions as the incarnation of the Marxian class struggle. At a workers' festival celebrated on May 1, 1933, early in the Hitler regime, it was announced that the task of "reestablishing social peace in the world of labor" would soon begin. The next day Dr. Robert Ley (q.v.) led a "committee of action for the protection of German labor" in occupying by force the offices of all the trade unions. Within a few days 169 trade organizations were under Nazi control. On May 10, the Deutsche Arbeitsfront was officially established. At first it included not only the members of former labor unions but also white-collar groups and management associations. In this way harmony was to be established between the legitimate interests of all concerned. "Discord," said Hitler, "will give way to a people's community. Commonweal before private gain!" Instead of strikes for better wages or employers' lockouts, the new system called for all laborers to work together for the common good. The new philosophy was epitomized in the Labor Charter (q.v.), promulgated on January 16, 1934, which resembled Mussolini's Charter of Labor.

The Deutsche Arbeitsfront comprised the entire labor world of the Third Reich. Including more than 20 million workers, it had a huge budget and owned extensive property. On September 13, 1935, Dr. Ley summarized its achievements to the foreign press: its management, he said, had been more economical than that of the trade unions. It distributed financial assistance, used its funds for workers' education and the construction of buildings, and stabilized wages. Several subsidiary units provided rest and relaxation for workers. The Strength through Joy movement (*see* KRAFT DURCH FREUDE) was designed to give paid vacation trips to workers with unblemished party records. The Beauty of Labor (q.v.) unit was formed to improve conditions in plants and factories.

Dr. Paul Joseph Goebbels (q.v.) and his Ministry for Public Enlightenment and Propaganda stressed the "gigantic achievements" of the Deutsche Arbeitsfront and praised it as a worthy substitute for the evil labor unions of the past. Fundamentally, the DAF tried to win the working class to the Nazi way of life. For a time it attracted many workers with its slogans, but it found it difficult to hide the fact of dictatorship. Labor problems remained alive throughout the days of the Third Reich, from rearmament to war.

DEUTSCHE AUSRÜSTUNGSWERKE (DAW; German Armament Works). An armaments enterprise set up in 1939 under the control of the SS (q.v.).

DEUTSCHE ERD- UND STEINWERKE, GMBH (DEST; German Excavation and Quarrying Co., Ltd.). An enterprise formed in 1938 by the SS (q.v.). Its workers were provided by the concentration camps (q.v.).

DEUTSCHE GESELLSCHAFT FÜR WEHRPOLITIK UND WEHRWISSENSCHAFT (German Society for Military Policy and Military Science). An organization designed to educate the German people for military preparedness and to help implement the ideas of Professor Ewald Banse (q.v.). It was composed of officers of the Reichswehr (q.v.), members of the Stahlhelm (q.v.), leaders of the SA (q.v.), and professors of military science at German universities. At a secret meeting of the society held in Berlin on October 6–7, 1933, members were allotted the assignment of solidifying the fighting spirit of German youth in accordance with Banse's teachings.

DEUTSCHE GLAUBENSBEWEGUNG (German Faith Movement). The neo-pagan church of the Third Reich. The movement consisted of sworn enemies of prior religions. Adherents were known as *Gottgläubige* (believers in God). An improvised offshoot of the Nazi movement in the spiritual sphere, the movement was designed to replace traditional Christianity. It proposed to convert Christmas into a pagan solstice festival as well as to dechristianize the rituals surrounding birth, marriage, and death. Nazi leaders of the Deutsche Glaubensbewegung banned nativity plays and carols from schools and called for an end to required daily prayers in the classroom. Efforts were made to have individual parishioners withdraw from their old churches. All those dependent on the regime such as civil servants and teachers were expected to join the German Faith movement. *See also* POSITIVE CHRISTIANITY.

DEUTSCHE RECHTS-PARTEI (DRP; German Rightist Party). An early neo-Nazi political party, founded shortly after World War II. *See also* NEO-NAZISM.

DEUTSCHE WIRTSCHAFTSBETRIEBE (German Economic Enterprises). A holding company designed to include all business and industry under the control of the SS (q.v.).

DEUTSCHER BLICK (German Glance). In popular parlance in Nazi Germany, a furtive rotation of the head and eyes to ensure the absence of eavesdroppers before opening a confidential topic of conversation. After the authorities designated *"Heil Hitler!"* (q.v.) as the official German greeting, skeptics and anti-Nazis adopted the German glance as a counterpart.

DEUTSCHKUNDE (Study of German Culture). A required subject of study in all Nazi schools as part of the training of children.

"DEUTSCHLAND ERWACHE!" ("Germany Awake!"). One of Hitler's favorite slogans. It was probably taken from the prose works of the composer Richard Wagner (q.v.), who was deeply revered by the Fuehrer. It became the title of one of the most popular German songs:

GERMANY AWAKE!

Storm, storm, storm, storm!
From tower to tower peal bells of alarm.
Peal out! Sparks fly as hammers strike.
Come Judas forth to win the Reich.
Peal out! The bloody ropes hang red.
Around our martyred hero dead.
Peal out—that thundering earth may know
Salvation's rage for honor's sake.
To people dreaming still comes woe.
Germany awake! Awake!

"DEUTSCHLAND ERWACHE! JUDA VERRECKE!" ("Germany Awake! Perish Judah!"). A variation of Hitler's favorite slogan, *"Deutschland Erwache!"* (q.v.). This type of incantation was regarded as desirable in the campaign against the Jews. It was shouted in unison by raiders who wanted to incite attacks on Jewish stores during the early years of the Nazi regime.

"DEUTSCHLAND IST HITLER! HITLER IST DEUTSCHLAND!" ("Germany Is Hitler! Hitler Is Germany!"). A slogan popular with Nazi speakers. After Hitler completed his speeches at party meetings, Rudolf Hess (q.v.), the Fuehrer's deputy, would introduce disciplined cheering with this slogan.

"DEUTSCHLAND ÜBER ALLES" ("Germany above All"). German national anthem. The lyrics were written by Hoffmann von Fallersleben in 1841 to an early melody by Joseph Haydn. Originally, the anthem was a plea for the unification of the conglomerate German states (there were exactly 1,789 states in 1789). During the Hitler regime the anthem was used to justify the call for *Lebensraum* (q.v.), or living space.

DEUTSCHLANDSENDER (Transmitter Germany). The German national radio station. Listeners had a choice between the programs of the regional stations and those of the Deutschlandsender. During World War II, at peak listening times on Sunday evenings, listeners could hear light music on local wavelengths or tune in on classical concerts relayed by the Deutschlandsender from Berlin or Vienna. *See also* RADIO IN THE THIRD REICH.

DIBELIUS, FRIEDRICH KARL OTTO (1880–1967). Evangelical theologian and opponent of Nazi coordination. Friedrich Karl Otto Dibelius was born in Berlin on May 15, 1880. From 1915 on he was a pastor in Berlin. In 1921 he became an advisory member of the Protestant Church, and in 1925 general superintendent of the Lutheran Church in Prussia. Opposed to the Nazis, he was dismissed from his post after Hitler became Chancellor in 1933. Dibelius made it clear that he would not submit to control by the government in the exercise of his spiritual and pastoral functions. In an open letter to Dr. Hans Kerrl (q.v.), Nazi Minister for Church Affairs, circulated in March 1937, Dibelius wrote:

> Let me ask you one question, *Herr Reichsminister*. If, in the morning's religious instruction, the children are told that the Bible is God's word that speaks to us in the Old and New Testaments and when, in the afternoon, young people have to memorize: "Which is our Bible? Our Bible is Hitler's *Mein Kampf*," who is to change his doctrine here? This is the decisive point. When you demand that the Evangelical Church shall not be a state within a state, every Evangelical Christian will agree. The Church must be a church and not a state within the state. But the doctrine which you proclaim would have the effect of making the state into the Church in so far as the state, supported by its coercive powers, comes to decision with regard to the sermons that are preached and the faith that is confessed. Here lies the root of the whole struggle between the state and the Evangelical Church. . . . As soon as the state endeavors to become Church and assumes power over the souls of men, . . . then we are bound by Luther's word to offer resistance in God's name. And that is what we shall do.

Dibelius was brought before a *Sondergericht* (q.v.), a special court, on a charge of treasonable attacks on the government. His acquittal caused great agitation among Nazi officials. Hitler himself asked the court for a copy of its reasons for the judgment, but he did not interfere.

After Hitler's fall, Dibelius was appointed Bishop of Berlin, a position he held until 1966. From 1949 to 1961 he was chairman of the board of the Evangelical Church in Germany, and from 1954 to 1961 he was one of five presidents of the World Council of Churches, the first German to hold this office. His criticism of any outside total influence on the Protestant Church was directed also against Communist East Germany: from 1960 on he was not allowed in the German Democratic Republic to perform his duties as bishop in Brandenburg. He died in Berlin on January 31, 1967.

DIELS, RUDOLF (1900–1957). Ministerial councillor and first chief of the Gestapo (q.v.). Rudolf Diels was born in Berghaus, in the Taunus, on December 16, 1900. As a student at the University of Marburg, he was a member of a highly popular student *Korps* (fraternity). He was known for his proficiency in beer drinking. It is reported that in 1932 he testified before a federal court that his superiors in the Socialist regime of Prussia had attempted a fighting alliance with the Communists—a historic perjury. A few days later the Socialists were removed from office in Prussia, and the chief witness against them emerged as an assistant minister. At this time Diels turned to Hermann Goering (q.v.) and the Nazis. When Goering took over control of Prussia, he was convinced by Diels that the only way to keep his enemies in subjection was to establish a secret police force. In June 1933 Goering appointed Diels chief of Department 1A in the Prussian State Police, attached to the Ministry of the Interior. This organization eventually became the Gestapo.

In his new post Diels was caught in a struggle between his patron, Goering, and Heinrich Himmler (q.v.), both of whom wanted to head a national unified secret police system. When Himmler assumed control of the Gestapo in 1934, he saw to it that Diels was dismissed. Diels, who was married to Goering's cousin, was forced to turn to other employment. Through his patron he was appointed to such posts as assistant police commissioner of Berlin (1934), administrative president of Cologne (1934), and inland shipping administrator of the Hermann Goering-Werke (Hermann Goering Works, 1934–1940). After the July Plot (q.v.) against Hitler in 1944, Diels was arrested and placed in a Gestapo prison. He was fortunate to survive the fall of the Third Reich. After World War II he was employed as a provincial administrator in Lower Saxony.

DIENSTSTELLE RIBBENTROP (Ribbentrop Bureau). A special office set up by Hitler as a rival, duplicate organization of the German Foreign Office. After Hitler became Chancellor on January 30, 1933, he regarded the old, conservative bureaucrat-ridden Foreign Office as an obstacle to his plans for German expansion. He appointed Constantin Freiherr von Neurath (q.v.) Minister for Foreign Affairs in his first Cabinet but paid little attention to him. In the spring of 1933 he established the so-called Ribbentrop Bureau. It was located opposite the Foreign Office in the Wilhelmstrasse, in the former house of the Prussian Foreign Minister. The Fuehrer preferred the compliant Joachim von Ribbentrop (q.v.), a former champagne salesman, as his adviser on foreign affairs. At first a small unit, the Ribbentrop Bureau soon numbered more than 300. On February 4, 1938, when Hitler reshuffled his administration and military leadership to gain more cooperative lieutenants, he made Von Ribbentrop Reich Minister for Foreign Affairs and abolished the special office.

DIET. *See* LANDTAG.

DIETRICH, JOSEF (SEPP; 1892–1966). High political and military figure in the Third Reich, described by William L. Shirer (q.v.) as one of its most brutal men. Sepp Dietrich was born in Hawangen, near Memmingen, on May 28, 1892. A butcher by trade, he served in the Imperial Army in 1911 and as a paymaster sergeant during World War I. After the war he went from one job to another, working as a farm laborer, waiter, policeman, foreman in a tobacco factory, customs officer, and gas station attendant. Burly and tough, he was quick to take offense. An early member of the Nationalsozialistische Deutsche Arbeiterpartei (q.v.), he came to Hitler's favorable attention and was made commander of Hitler's bodyguard in 1928. Nicknamed "Chauffeureska" by his patron, he accompanied Hitler on his automobile tours of Germany. Impressed by his hard Bavarian, Hitler found him a variety of jobs, including dispatcher for the publishing house of Franz Eher (*see* EHER VERLAG) in Munich and various SS (q.v.) posts. In 1930 Dietrich was elected to the Reichstag (q.v.) as a delegate for Wahlkreis (Electoral District) Lower Bavaria. By 1931 he had attained the rank of *SS-Gruppenfuehrer* (lieutenant general).

After the Nazis took power in 1933, the former butcher rose rapidly in the hierarchy of the party: *SS-Oberstgruppenfuehrer* (colonel general); commander of the Leibstandarte-SS Adolf Hitler (q.v.), Hitler's bodyguard regiment; general of the Waffen-SS (q.v.); and member of the Prussian State Council. He took an important part in the Blood Purge (q.v.) of 1934. At that time Hitler drew up a list of conspirators and dispatched Dietrich to the Ministry of Justice in Berlin to shoot the traitors. "Go back to the barracks," Hitler ordered, "select an officer and six men and have the SA (q.v.) leaders shot for high treason." Dietrich complied. The doomed men protested. One cried out: "Sepp, my friend, what is happening? We are completely innocent!" Dietrich replied: "You have been condemned to death by the Fuehrer. *Heil Hitler!*" The men were executed on the spot. The incident illustrated Dietrich's philosophy of life: "Human life matters little to the SS." He regarded it as his overwhelming duty to protect the person of Adolf Hitler.

In World War II Dietrich, noted for his fighting qualities, commanded a tank corps in the attack on Paris and later led an SS army on the Russian front. He was awarded many decorations. In the fall of 1943 he was sent to Italy on a mission to return Clara Petacci, Mussolini's mistress, to the Italian dictator. In December 1944, Hitler, still suspicious of most members of his High Command, gave Dietrich command of the Sixth Panzer Army in the belief that he could trust his own Waffen-SS troops. In a desperate gamble the Fuehrer committed his last reserves through the Ardennes to cut off the northern wing of the Allies from their supply base and wreck preparations for the coming Allied spring offensive. When Dietrich's army stalled, Hitler's offensive collapsed.

In April 1945 an angered Hitler, dissatisfied with the performance of his troops on the Russian front, ordered Dietrich's men stripped of their armbands. Infuriated, Dietrich announced in the presence of other officers that he would return all his decorations or shoot himself. "Let's take a chamber pot, put all our medals into it, and around it tie the ribbon of *Götz von Berlichingen* division." (Here Dietrich referred to the knight in Goethe's drama *Götz von Berlichingen,* who said to the Bishop of Bamberg: "You can kiss my backside!") The incident expressed perfectly the personality of Sepp Dietrich.

In early 1946 Dietrich was brought before an American military tribunal and accused, with forty-two other SS officers, of being responsible for the murder of seventy-one American prisoners of war near Malmédy on December 17, 1944, at the height of the Battle of the Bulge. He was sentenced to a prison term of twenty-five years. Dietrich was released after serving ten years and was then brought to Munich to be tried before a German court. On May 14, 1957, he was sentenced to nineteen months' imprisonment for his part in the 1934 Blood Purge. He died in Ludwigsburg on April 21, 1966.

DIETRICH, MARLENE (1904–). Film actress, singer, and anti-Nazi. Marlene Dietrich was born in Berlin on December 27, 1904. Beginning her career as an actress in 1922, she won worldwide attention in 1930 in the film *Der blaue Engel (The Blue Angel)* with Emil Jannings. From 1933 to 1945 she refused to return to Germany because of the Nazi regime. From 1937 on she lived most of the time in the United States and made many American films. Her instantly recognizable voice, theatrical rather than musical, was at its best in songs of despair and such war songs as "Lili Marlene" (*see* LILI MARLEEN).

DIETRICH, OTTO (1897–1952). Publicist and press chief of the Nazi regime. Otto Dietrich was born in Essen on August 31, 1897. After service in World War I, during which he was awarded the Iron Cross (First Class), he studied economics, philosophy, and political science at the Universities of Freiburg, Munich, and Frankfurt am Main. In 1928 he became business manager of the *Augsburger Zeitung* and in that post met many prominent Nazis. He married the daughter of the owner of the *Rheinisch-Westfälische Zeitung*, the mouthpiece of heavy industry, and through this connection acted as an intermediary for Hitler and the Rhineland industrialists, especially Emil Kirdorf (q.v.). Dietrich was appointed press chief of the Nationalsozialistische Deutsche Arbeiterpartei (q.v.) in 1931. On December 24, 1932, he became member No. 301,349 of the SS (q.v.), and in 1933 he was given the task of coordinating the German press. On June 30, 1934, he accompanied Hitler to Bad Wiessee to carry out the Blood Purge (q.v.) and the next day gave a bloodcurdling account of the slaughter to the press. He described Hitler's sense of shock at the moral degeneracy of his oldest comrades.

In 1938 Dietrich was promoted to Press Chief of the Reich and State Secretary to the Propaganda Ministry. His main task was to present the Nazi *Weltanschauung* (q.v.), or world view, to the German public. "The individual," he said, "has neither the right nor the duty to exist." At the outbreak of war in 1939 he issued a daily directive *(Tagesparole)* for newspapers on how to present the news from the front. He saw to it that the public received a steady diet of victory reports even after the tide had turned in favor of the Allies. When he learned of the flight of Rudolf Hess (q.v.) to Scotland on May 10, 1941, Dietrich at first reported that Hess was the victim of an accident over enemy territory. When Propaganda Minister Dr. Paul Joseph Goebbels (q.v.) protested violently, Dietrich changed his story to a charge that Hess had temporarily lost his mind: "He was motivated by pacifism. He was not a traitor, because there was nothing to betray." Dietrich's reports were not noted for accuracy. On October 8, 1941, when the Germans took Orel, a key city south of Moscow, Hitler sent Dietrich back to Berlin to announce that the last Russian armies were locked in two German steel traps. "For all military purposes," Dietrich reported, "Soviet Russia is finished. The British dream of a two-front war is dead."

In January 1943, when the forces led by Gen. Friedrich von Paulus (q.v.) were about to surrender to the Russians, Dietrich had a nervous breakdown. In 1944 he was in Rastenburg at the time of the July Plot (q.v.) on Hitler's life and reported by phone to Dr. Goebbels in Berlin that the Fuehrer was still alive. Dietrich was tried before Military Tribunal No. 4 in Nuremberg and on April 11, 1949, was sentenced to seven years' imprisonment. He was released in 1950 and died in 1952.

DIMITROV, GEORGI M. (1882–1949). Bulgarian Communist, defendant in the Reichstag Fire Trial (q.v.). Georgi Dimitrov was born in Radomir, Bulgaria, on June 18, 1882, the son of a Macedonian worker forced to flee from his native soil at the time of the Turkish massacres. At the age of twelve young Dimitrov started work in Sofia as a printer's apprentice. At sixteen he wrote his first revolutionary pamphlet and helped found the Printers Union. He joined the Bulgarian Social Democratic party and soon became the most prominent member of its left wing. Elected to the Bulgarian Sobranje in 1913, he served for ten years as a delegate representing the workers of Sofia. As an opponent of Bulgarian participation in World War I, he was held in prison for two years without trial. After the war he joined the Bulgarian Communist party and became its leader in demonstrations and strikes. During the 1920s he lived in exile in Moscow, Vienna, and Berlin.

Georgi Dimitrov. [*Stamp issued by the German Democratic Republic*]

Dimitrov was one of three Bulgarians, along with Blagoi Popov and Vassili Tanev, who were arrested after the Reichstag fire (q.v.) of February 27, 1933. He was the central figure at the subsequent trial, which attracted worldwide attention. Nothing, no threat of the presiding judge, no silence imposed on him for his outbursts in court, no expulsion from the proceedings, could move Dimitrov from the direction he regarded as necessary for his defense and that of the Communist party. His dramatic confrontation with Hermann Goering (q.v.) was the sensation of the trial. Obviously not guilty, he was acquitted of all charges. From that moment Dimitrov became a hero for Communists everywhere.

In 1935 Dimitrov was appointed general secretary of the Communist International (Comintern) in Moscow. After the occupation of Bulgaria by Soviet troops in 1944, he took over the leadership of Bulgarian Communists. He was made Premier of Bulgaria on November 6, 1946. In 1947 he concluded a friendship pact with Yugoslavia. The sovietization of Bulgaria is generally attributed to Dimitrov. In 1948 he became general secretary of the Bulgarian Communist party. He died in Moscow on July 2, 1949.

DIRECTIVE 21. War directive issued by Hitler for Barbarossa (q.v.), cover name for the invasion of the Soviet Union. On December 6, 1940, on the instructions of Hitler, Lieut. Gen. Alfred Jodl (q.v.), chief of operations, ordered his deputy, Maj. Gen. Walther Warlimont (q.v.), to prepare a general plan for operations against Soviet Russia. Six days later the draft was designated Directive 21, initially called Fritz. On December 18 Hitler issued the directive, which he renamed Barbarossa. The introductory lines were:

> The German Armed Forces must be prepared, even prior to the conclusion of the war against England, to crush Soviet Russia in a rapid campaign.
>
> The Army must employ all available formations to this end, with the reservation that occupied territories must be defended against surprise attacks. . . .
>
> It is of decisive importance that our intention to attack not be known.

Bibliography. H. R. Trevor-Roper (ed.), *Hitler's War Directives, 1939–1945,* Sidgwick & Jackson, Ltd., London, 1964.

DIRECTIVE 39. Order issued by Hitler on December 8, 1941, commanding his forces in Russia to go on the defensive. The Fuehrer had counted on completing his *Blitzkrieg* (q.v.) against the Soviet Union in one overwhelming summer campaign. He would "wipe Leningrad from the face of the earth," and he would smash through to Moscow. His generals insisted that they must dig in for the winter, but he demanded an attack despite the intensely cold weather. The assault failed, and Hitler was forced by circumstances to recognize that the war in the east, like that in the west, would be a long one. The introduction to his directive was as follows:

> The severe winter weather which has come surprisingly early in the East, and the consequent difficulties in bringing up supplies, compel us to abandon immediately all major offensive operations and to go over to the defensive.
>
> The way in which these defensive operations are to be carried out will be decided in accordance with the purpose which they are intended to serve, viz.:
>
> (*a*) To hold areas which are of great operational or economic importance to the enemy.
> (*b*) To enable forces in the East to rest and recuperate as much as possible.
> (*c*) Thus to establish conditions suitable for the resumption of large-scale offensive operations in 1942.

Bibliography. H. R. Trevor-Roper (ed.), *Hitler's War Directives, 1939–1945,* Sidgwick & Jackson, Ltd., London, 1964.

DIRKSEN, HERBERT (1882–1955). Diplomat. Herbert Dirksen was born in Berlin on April 2, 1882. He made his *Abitur* (final high school examination) at the König Wilhelm Gymnasium in Berlin and went on to study law. In 1905 he passed his examinations as *Referendar* (junior barrister) and in 1907 embarked on a round-the-world tour that took him to East Africa, India, Java, China, Japan, North America, Brazil, and Argentina. This trip was basic for his subsequent diplomatic career. After serving as an assistant judge in 1910, he made a four-month journey to German East Africa, Rhodesia, and Cape Colony. In World War I he served in the Army as a lieutenant and was awarded the Iron Cross (Second Class). After the war he entered the diplomatic service. From 1923 to 1925 he was German Consul at Danzig, and in 1928 he was appointed Ministerial Director of the East Division of the Foreign Office. That year he became German Ambassador to Moscow, and in 1933 Ambassador to Tokyo.

In his memoirs Dirksen revealed that his service for the Third Reich was an exercise in humiliation and frustration. His first interview with Hitler lasted two to three minutes. "Hitler moved uneasily in his chair, excused himself, and left abruptly. I was confounded and furious when I left him." Dirksen never became reconciled to the "insincerity, superficiality, and inefficiency" of the Foreign Office under Joachim von Ribbentrop (q.v.). He despised Von Ribbentrop as a parvenu and described him as "an unwholesome, half-comical figure." After the Munich Agreement (q.v.) he "gave up the idea of trying to convert Von Ribbentrop to a reasonable policy." Dirksen confessed: "That it was more honorable not to serve the Hitler régime altogether was a thought that lay far from me at the time."

Bibliography. Herbert von Dirksen, *Moskau-Tokio-London: Erinnerungen und Betrachtungen zu 20 Jahren deutscher Aussenpolitik, 1919–1939,* W. Hohlhammer, Stuttgart, 1950.

DISARMAMENT CONFERENCE. A conference of sixty nations, including such nonmembers of the League of Nations as the United States and the Soviet Union, held to bring about a reduction of national armaments as called for by the Covenant of the League. The meetings took place at intervals from 1932 to early 1934. There were two major reasons behind the failure of the conference: (1) French insistence that security be guaranteed before disarmament and (2) the military threat of the new Third Reich. Hitler abandoned the Disarmament Conference in October 1933.

DISTRICT. *See* GAU.

DISTRICT LEADER. *See* GAULEITER.

DISTRICT LEADERSHIP. *See* GAULEITUNG.

DISTRICT PROPAGANDA LEADERSHIP. *See* GAUPROPAGANDALEITUNG.

DISTRICT STUDENT LEADERSHIP. *See* GAUSTUDENTENFUEHRUNG.

DITTMAR, KURT (1891–1959). Army radio commentator. Kurt Dittmar was born in Magdeburg on March 5, 1891. A career soldier, he served in World War I, also for the Weimar Republic (q.v.), and throughout the Hitler regime. In 1941 he was promoted to general and named commander of the 169th Infantry Division. The next year he was made official radio commentator for the armed forces. He died on April 20, 1959.

DIVE BOMBER GROUP. *See* STURZKAMPFGESCHWADER.

DOCTORS' TRIAL. The trial of twenty-three Schutzstaffel (SS, q.v.) physicians and scientists held in Nuremberg before American Military Tribunal No. 1 beginning on December 9, 1946. The indictment specified four charges: (1) common design or conspiracy, (2) war crimes, (3) crimes against humanity, and (4) membership in criminal organizations. The accused were charged with such varied crimes as experiments involving high altitude, low temperature, and the drinking of seawater; experiments

NAME	PROFESSIONAL STATUS	MILITARY OR SS RANK	JUDGMENT
1. Becker-Freysing, Hermann	M.D.; specialist, aviation medicine	Captain, Medical Corps	Twenty years
2. Beigelböck, Wilhelm	M.D.; professor, University Clinic, Vienna	Captain, Medical Corps	Fifteen years
3. Blome, Kurt	Professor; Deputy Reich Health Leader; deputy chief, Reich Chamber of Medicine		Acquitted
4. Brack, Victor	Chief administrative officer, Reich Chancellery	Colonel, SS	Death
5. Brandt, Karl	M.D.; professor; personal physician to Hitler; Reich Commissioner for Health and Sanitation	Major general, Waffen-SS	Death
6. Brandt, Rudolf	LL.D.; chief of Ministerial Office, Ministry of the Interior	Colonel, SS	Death
7. Fischer, Fritz	M.D.; assistant surgeon, Hohenlychen	Major, Waffen-SS	Life imprisonment
8. Gebhardt, Karl	M.D.; professor, personal physician to Heinrich Himmler; chief surgeon to the Reich Physician, SS; president of the German Red Cross		Death
9. Genzken, Karl	M.D.; chief of Medical Service, Waffen-SS	Major general, SS	Life imprisonment
10. Handloser, Siegfried	M.D.; professor, chief of medical services of the armed forces; medical inspector of the Army	Lieutenant general, Medical Corps	Life imprisonment
11. Hoven, Waldemar	M.D.; camp physician, Buchenwald	Captain, SS	Death
12. Mrugowsky, Joachim	M.D.; professor, chief of the Institute of Hygiene, Waffen-SS	Colonel, SS	Death
13. Oberheuser, Herta	Only woman among the defendants; M.D.; assistant surgeon, Hohenlychen		Twenty years
14. Pokorny, Adolf	Urologist and dermatologist practicing in Munich		Acquitted
15. Poppendick, Helmut	M.D.; chief surgeon, Rasse- und Siedlungshauptamt, SS (Central Office for Race and Resettlement)	Colonel, SS	Ten years
16. Romberg, Hans Wolfgang	M.D.; section chief, German Experimental Institute for Aviation		Acquitted
17. Rose, Gerhart	M.D.; professor, chief of Division of Tropical Medicine, Robert Koch Institute	Brigadier general, Medical Corps	Life imprisonment
18. Rostock, Paul	M.D.; professor, chief of Berlin University Clinic; chief of medical science and research	Brigadier general, Medical Corps	Acquitted
19. Ruff, Siegfried	M.D.; chief of the Institute of Aviation Medicine, Berlin		Acquitted
20. Schäfer, Konrad	M.D.; assistant, chemotherapy laboratories, Schering Corporation	Noncommissioned medical officer	Acquitted
21. Schröder, Oskar	M.D.; chief of the Air Force Medical Service	Lieutenant general, Medical Corps	Life imprisonment
22. Sievers, Wolfram	Chief of the Institute for Military Scientific Research	Colonel, SS	Death
23. Welz, Georg August	M.D.; professor; chief of the Institute of Aviation Medicine	Lieutenant colonel, Medical Corps	Acquitted

The twenty-three defendants on trial in 1946–1947 for medical war crimes. Dr. Karl Brandt is at the left in the front row. [*UPI*]

with typhus and infectious jaundice; experiments with sulfa drugs, bone grafting, and mustard gas; the collection of skulls of Jews; euthanasia of undesirable racial groups (*see* EUTHANASIA PROGRAM); and mass sterilization. The trial was completed on August 20, 1947. The judgment found sixteen of the defendants guilty and seven not guilty. Seven were sentenced to death by hanging, five to life imprisonment, and four to long prison terms.

DODD, WILLIAM E. (1869–1940). United States Ambassador to the Third Reich from 1933 to 1937. William E. Dodd was born in Clayton, North Carolina. He was graduated from Virginia Polytechnic Institute and was awarded a doctorate at the University of Leipzig with a dissertation on Thomas Jefferson's return to politics in 1796 ("Jeffersons Rückkehr zur Politik"). After teaching for eight years at Randolph-Macon College, he was called in 1908 to the University of Chicago, where he began a distinguished career of teaching and research in American history. Among his major works were *Life of Nathaniel Macon* (1905), *Life of Jefferson Davis* (1907), *Statesmen of the Old South* (1911), *The Cotton Kingdom* (1919), *The Public Papers of Woodrow Wilson* (with Ray Stannard Baker, 1924–1926), and *Struggle for Democracy* (1937).

President Franklin D. Roosevelt selected Dodd to serve as American Ambassador at Berlin during the early years of the Hitler regime. By study, training, and disposition Dodd was within the tradition of other American historians sent to the embassy at Berlin, including George Bancroft, and such journalists as Bayard Taylor. In Berlin Dodd, who esteemed the life of the old Germany, sought to strengthen and rally moderate elements not yet completely subjected to *Gleichschaltung* (q.v.), or coordina-

Ambassador Dodd in the American Embassy in Berlin in 1933. [*Wide World Photos*]

tion. He was noted for bluntness and undiplomatic convictions. He had only contempt for the more blatant excesses of the Hitler government and from the beginning refused to attend the Nuremberg rallies (q.v.). Dodd did what he could to stop the persecution of the Jews, but with conspicuous lack of success. He was unable to effect the collection of debts due American creditors, and despite persistent attempts he could not break the deadlock in German-American business relations. As a historian, he saw more clearly than many of his colleagues that Germany was drifting into war under its aggressive Fuehrer. He opposed the policy of appeasement and fought as much as he could to stop it. He was recalled at the end of 1937.

Dodd's diary gives a remarkable picture of the Nazi regime before World War II. In a typical entry on March 7, 1934, Dodd wrote that the Nazi regime was composed of "three rather inexperienced and very dogmatic persons," all of whom had been connected with murderous undertakings in the preceding decade. He described the unique triumvirate as composed of Hitler, "less educated, more romantic," with a semicriminal record; and Goebbels and Goering, both moved by intense class and foreign hatreds and both willing to use ruthless methods. Dodd noted that they did not love one another but had to work together to maintain their power. The historian observed that there had been no such unique group in modern history, although there had been one in ancient Rome.

Bibliography. William E. Dodd, *Ambassador Dodd's Diary, 1933–1938*, ed. by William E. Dodd, Jr., and Martha Dodd, Harcourt, Brace and Company, Inc., New York, 1941.

DOENITZ, KARL (1891–1980). Grand admiral, builder of the German U-boat arm (*see* U-BOATS), and political successor to Hitler. Karl Doenitz was born in Grünau bei Berlin on September 16, 1891, the descendant of a long line of farmers who had lived in Westphalia for centuries and later moved to Magdeburg. After attendance at the *Realgymnasium* (semiclassical school) in Weimar, he joined the Imperial Navy and was first assigned to the light cruiser *Breslau*. He served on that ship when, together with the cruiser *Goeben*, she broke through the British Mediterranean Fleet to join the Turks against the Russian Fleet in the Black Sea in the first days of August 1914. He remained in Near Eastern waters until October 1916, when he was transferred to the submarine fleet. He served for a time as watch officer on the *U-39* and then commanded the *U-68*. In October 1918 his submarine was sunk after he had torpedoed a British merchant ship in a convoy near Malta, and he was a prisoner of war until July 1919. After the war he became an inspector of torpedo boats and then was assigned to naval headquarters in Berlin.

Doenitz was one of the few convinced National Socialists among high officers in the Navy. He praised Hitler in speeches to his sailors: "Heaven has sent us the leadership of the Fuehrer!" On one occasion he told a cheering crowd in Berlin that Hitler foresaw everything and made no misjudgments: "We are worms compared with him!" Hitler, on his side, had the utmost confidence in Doenitz. In 1939 the Fuehrer chose Doenitz to head the U-boat

Grand Adm. Karl Doenitz. [*Wide World Photos*]

service. In this post Doenitz was responsible for developing the tactics used by German submarines in World War II, especially the pack system in which U-boats worked in groups to prey on Allied shipping. In 1942 he was promoted to admiral, and on January 30, 1943, he was named grand admiral and successor to Adm. Erich Raeder (q.v.) as supreme commander of the Navy.

As in World War I, German U-boats were at first successful in destroying Allied shipping, but they were unable to drive the enemy from the seas. In May 1943 Doenitz was forced to withdraw his submarines, whereupon Hitler stormed: "There can be no letup in submarine warfare. The Atlantic is my first line of defense in the West." By autumn 1943 a U-boat was being sunk for every freighter torpedoed. Doenitz noted in his diary: "The enemy holds every trump card, covers all areas with long-range air patrols, and uses location methods of which we still have no warning. The enemy knows all our secrets and we know none of his."

In the closing days of his life Hitler named Doenitz as his successor. Between May 2 and 5, 1945, Doenitz set up a government under the chairmanship of Lutz Graf Schwerin von Krosigk (q.v.) at the Baltic enclave of Flensburg-Mürwick in Schleswig-Holstein. Hoping for an immediate end to the war, Doenitz wanted to allow as many Germans as possible to surrender to the British and Americans in order to save them from the Russians. He urged an end to Hitler's demolition policy and recommended to the German people that they start reconstruction as a means of counteracting the paralyzing horror of defeat. The new Chief of State was captured by the British on May 23, 1945. He had been Fuehrer of the Reich for exactly twenty-three days.

Doenitz was astonished when he was indicted with twenty-two other Nazi leaders by the International Military Tribunal at Nuremberg on October 20, 1945 (*see* NUREMBERG TRIAL). He attempted to dismiss the charges as something that did not concern him: "None of these indictments concerns me in the least. Typical American humor!" His judges decided that although he built and trained the German U-boat arm, he was not privy to the conspiracy to wage aggressive war, nor did he prepare and initiate such a war. He was absolved of killing shipwrecked survivors, but he was charged with responsibility for Hitler's order of October 18, 1942, by which members of an Allied motor torpedo boat crew were turned over to the SS (q.v.) and shot. Doenitz was found guilty on count 2 (crimes against peace) and count 3 (war crimes) and sentenced to ten years' imprisonment. He served his sentence in Spandau Prison in West Berlin and was released on October 1, 1956. He always kept with him a file of letters from Allied naval officers who had written to him expressing their sympathy and understanding.

DOHNÁNYI, HANS VON (1902–1945). Legal expert, brother-in-law of Dietrich Bonhoeffer (q.v.), and one of the key figures in the conspiracy against Hitler. Hans Dohnányi was born in Vienna on January 1, 1902, the son of a Hungarian concert pianist. A brilliant lawyer, he was appointed in May 1933 to the Ministry of Justice, where he worked on legal reform. After the 1934 Blood Purge (q.v.), he joined Carl Friedrich Goerdeler (q.v.) and the Resistance (q.v.) movement. In 1939 he was transferred to the Abwehr (q.v.), the counterintelligence agency under Adm. Wilhelm Canaris (q.v.), as *Sonderfuehrer OKW* (special leader in the High Command of the armed forces). In March 1943 he took part in an unsuccessful attempt on Hitler's life by Maj. Gen. Henning von Tresckow (q.v.) and Lieut. Fabian von Schlabrendorff, and was arrested the next month. He was released but was arrested again in 1944 immediately after the July Plot (q.v.) and accused of being the instigator of the movement to kill Hitler. Removed from a Gestapo (q.v.) cell, he was taken to Sachsenhausen (q.v.) concentration camp, where his treatment was especially severe. Paralyzed by brutal beatings, he was unable to wash himself or even turn over on his cot. In a note smuggled to his wife he wrote: "Sometimes I have faith that I will win through, even if the world is full of devils." It is believed that Von Dohnányi was executed at Flossenbürg (q.v.) on April 8, 1945, not long before the end of the war in Europe, but it is not known exactly what happened.

Hans von Dohnányi. [*From Annedore Leber (ed.),* Conscience in Revolt, *tr. by Rosemary O'Neill, Vallentine, Mitchell & Co., Ltd., London, 1957*]

DOLCHSTOSSTHEORIE (Stab-in-the-Back Theory). The theory that the German Army and Navy were defeated in World War I only because they were "stabbed in the back" by traitors, Social Democrats, and Jews at home. Hitler branded the Jews as "November criminals" (NOVEMBERVERBRECHER, q.v.) and never stopped calling them by that name. The National Socialist propaganda machine hammered away at the stab-in-the-back legend and regarded it as the gem in the mine of exploitable political issues. The German masses were willing to accept the charge because it enabled them to project all guilt for the defeat on Judaism. They identified the Weimar Republic (q.v.), and with it democracy in general, with the loss of the war. Hitler was successful in promoting an attitude of resentment that helped pave the way for his accession to power in the Third Reich.

The term *stab in the back* was first used in a report from England to the *Neue Zürcher Zeitung* of December 1, 1918: "As far as the German Army is concerned the general view is summarized in these words: It was stabbed in the back by the civil population." After the war a Reichstag (q.v.) commission investigated the problem of the German collapse in 1918. The following is a summary of the report by Gen. Hermann von Kuhl, which mildly criticized the stab-in-the-back concept but did not altogether reject it:

> The expression "stab-in-the-back" (*"Dolchstoss"*) in the oft-used sense, as if the country had attacked the victorious army in the rear and as if the war had been lost for this reason alone, is not accurate. We succumbed for many reasons.
>
> It is certain, however, that a pacifistic, international, anti-military, and revolutionary undermining of the army took place which contributed in no small measure to the harm done and the disintegration of the army. It originated at home, but the blame does not attach to the entire population, which in the four and a half years of war endured superhuman sufferings; it attaches only to the agitators and corrupters of the people and of the army who for political reasons strove to poison the bravely-fighting forces.
>
> The effects of this pernicious activity became especially apparent when, after the failure of our offensive in the summer of 1918, the war seemed hopelessly lost. But the subversive work had long before been systematically begun. One should therefore speak, not of a stab in the back, but of a *poisoning of the army*.
>
> The expression "stab-in-the-back" may, however, be applied to the sudden and devastating effects of the *revolution* itself. It literally attacked the army from the rear, disorganized the lines of communication, prevented the forwarding of supplies, and destroyed all order and discipline as if at a blow. It made all further fighting impossible and compelled the acceptance of any armistice terms. The revolution was not the result of the collapse of the offensive, although this substantially furthered its outbreak and its effects. On the contrary, the revolution was prepared long beforehand.
>
> The revolution further gave rise to the danger of the complete dissolution of the army during the retreat and thus of a monstrous catastrophe. This danger was averted only with the greatest difficulty.

STATEMENT OF CHAIRMAN ALBRECHT PHILIPP ON KUHL'S REPORT

In view of the many interpretations of the expression "stab-in-the back," it is better not to use this term for the influences which, coming from home, weakened the army's will to fight. That such influences were present in large number cannot be denied. Heavy blame doubtless lies with those circles which fostered the efforts to disintegrate or poison the armed forces. But the available factual material does not suffice to prove that these circles alone were to blame. Von Kuhl declares quite correctly: "We succumbed for many reasons." All those revolutionary efforts can be blamed, not for the circumstance that we had to evacuate the West and thus give up the prospects of winning the war, but for the way in which the end of the war overwhelmed Germany. The expression "stab-in-the-back" is absolutely correct as a criticism of the revolution as a single event, but it can be applied only with limitations to the motive powers of the development which prepared the ground for the German Revolution.

DOLLFUSS, ENGELBERT (1892–1934). Austrian politician. Engelbert Dollfuss was born in Texing, Lower Austria, on October 4, 1892. He started his career as secretary of the Lower Austrian Farmers League and in 1927 founded the Lower Austrian Agricultural Chamber. In 1931 he became general director of the Austrian railway system and then won Cabinet rank as Minister of Agriculture. He became Austrian Chancellor and Foreign Minister in May 1932. Aware of Hitler's goal of *Anschluss* (q.v.) between Germany and Austria, Dollfuss made no secret of his opposition. In order to thwart Nazi designs on his country he deemed it best not to call the Austrian Parliament after Hitler took power and instituted what amounted to a clerical-fascist dictatorship of his own. On February 12, 1934, government troops and fascist militia turned artillery on workers' apartments in Vienna, ostensibly to prevent a Social Democratic rebellion, and killed at least 1,000 persons while wounding many others. Dollfuss then turned on the rightist Fatherland Front.

Meanwhile, the Austrian Nazis, supported from Berlin, began a reign of terror, blowing up power stations, administration buildings, and railways and beating or killing supporters of Dollfuss. Exiled Austrians poured a stream of propaganda from Munich into Austria. On July 25, 1934, some 154 members of SS Standarte 89 (a formation roughly equivalent to a regiment), while dressed in Austrian Army uniforms invaded the Federal Chancellery. Dollfuss was shot in the throat. The invaders refused to permit any medical help, and the Austrian Chancellor was allowed to bleed to death on a sofa. The conspirators bungled the *Putsch,* however, and government forces, led by Dr. Kurt von Schuschnigg (q.v.), were able to gain control for the time being. When Mussolini hastily mobilized four divisions on the Brenner Pass, Hitler dropped his plan for immediate *Anschluss.*

Bibliography. John Duncan Gregory, *Dollfuss and His Times,* Hutchinson & Co. (Publishers), Ltd., London, 1935.

DORPMÜLLER, JULIUS (1869–1945). Reich Communications Minister from 1937 to 1945. Julius Dorpmüller was born in Elberfeld on July 24, 1869. After attending the *Gymnasien* (high schools) in Munich-Gladbach and Aachen, he studied engineering at the Aachen Technical College. From 1898 to 1907 he worked for the Prussian railroad system, from which he was granted leave to accept a post with the Imperial Railway in China. In 1914 he fled from China through Siberia and European Russia to return home under adventurous conditions. After World War I he continued his work with the German railroad system and in 1926 became general director of the Reichsbahn (Reich Railways). He was named *Reichsverkehrsminister* (Reich Minister of Communications) in 1937 and served until his death in Malente, Schleswig-Holstein, on June 5, 1945.

DORTMUND. Code word designed to call the Barbarossa (q.v.) operation into effect. *See also* ALTONA.

DRANG NACH OSTEN (Drive to the East). Phrase describing the historic area of German expansion. German boundaries during the past 1,000 and more years have changed many times in every century. The eastern boundary, especially, has always been fluid. From the early Middle Ages on, the line between Germans and Slavs shifted from generation to generation, depending upon such variables as diplomatic maneuvers, colonization, Christianization, and war. From the fourth to the seventh century the direction was westward during the *Völkerwänderung* (barbarian invasions), when Germanic tribes first infiltrated and then surged into the Roman Empire. Thereafter the trend was reversed. Charlemagne (ca. 742–814) initiated the *Drang nach Osten* by first subduing and Christianizing the neighboring Germanic tribes and then pushing eastward to the Elbe. During the ninth and tenth centuries the main direction of expansion was toward Austria. The high point of colonization came in the thirteenth and fourteenth centuries with the drive of the Teutonic Knights, facilitated by the temporary decline of the Polish kingdom, toward the northeast. In the eighteenth and nineteenth centuries there were further drives into Poland and to the southeast, where the Ottoman Empire was in decline. Emperor William II (1859–1941), while aware of and favoring the traditional *Drang nach Osten,* preferred a more aggressive colonial policy and urged German penetration of the Far East, the South Seas, the Near and Middle East, and North Africa. His proposed Berlin-to-Baghdad railway was planned as an overland route to India to compete with the British sea route through the Mediterranean and Suez Canal.

In *Mein Kampf* (q.v.) Hitler made it clear that he intended to revive the spirit of the *Drang nach Osten.* It was a mistake, he said, to seek colonies in Africa. "Territorial policy cannot be fulfilled in Africa but must be made today almost exclusively in Europe." Germany must seek her *Lebensraum* (q.v.; living space) toward the east instead of searching eternally in the south and west of Europe. The goal was Russia as well as the border states controlled by it. The "racially inferior" Russian Slavs had appropriated a disproportionately huge portion of the earth's surface. The Germanic element in Russia had been wiped out and its place taken by the Jews, "the ferment of decomposition." Now, wrote Hitler, Bolshevik Russia was ready for collapse. "Fate has made us witness to a catastrophe. And only the sword can win this ground. The new Reich must set itself on the march along the road of the Teutonic Knights to obtain by the German sword the sod for the German plow and the daily bread for the nation." In essence, Hitler's view of the *Drang nach Osten* coincided with the geopolitical theories of Karl Haushofer (q.v.), who regarded the Russian Ukraine as a necessary breadbasket and complement to industrial Germany.

DREXLER, ANTON (1884–1942). One of the intellectual fathers of the National Socialist movement. Anton Drexler was born in Munich on June 13, 1884. Bespectacled and unassuming, he was a locksmith and toolmaker who went to Berlin to make his fortune. There he was humiliated by having to play a zither in a restaurant. During World War I he joined the Fatherland party, an organization dedicated to the task of obtaining a fair peace for Germany. The Fatherland party was favored by both the High Command and industrialists. At this time Drexler had the idea of forming a nationally minded workers' party which he would place at the disposal of the General Staff. On March 7, 1918, he set up a Committee of Independent Workmen, a branch of a larger North German Association for the Promotion of Peace along Working-Class Lines. Regarding himself as a champion of the working class, he denounced the Marxism of the trade unions.

In January 1919, soon after the war, Drexler merged his small group with a larger one called the Political Workers' Circle, led by Karl Harrer, a journalist. The combined group called itself the German Workers' party (Deutsche Arbeiterpartei, q.v.). It had no letterheads, not even a rubber stamp, and its only assets were a cigar container serving as a cashbox and Harrer's briefcase. This was the group which Hitler met in Munich in 1919. He described it in *Mein Kampf* (q.v.):

> Herr Drexler, then chairman of the *Ortsgruppe*[1] Munich, was a simple worker, as speaker not very gifted, moreover no soldier. He had not served in the Army, and was not a soldier during the war, and because his whole being was weak and uncertain, he was not a real leader for us. He (and Herr Harrer) were not cut out to be fanatical enough to carry the movement in their hearts, nor did he have the ability to use brutal means to overcome the opposition to a new idea inside the party. What was needed was one fleet as a greyhound, smooth as leather, and hard as Krupp steel.

Hitler, nevertheless, was impressed with Drexler's ideas. He agreed wholeheartedly with the concept that there existed a diabolical Jewish-capitalistic-Masonic conspiracy which had to be counteracted. He believed that Drexler was right: on the one side there were the innocent German worker, farmer, and soldier; on the other there was the common enemy, "the plastic demon of the fall of mankind," the capitalistic Jews. From this germ came the essence of Hitler's Nazism. He joined the tiny group. Drexler wrote to a friend: "An absurd little man has become member No. 7 of our Party."

Drexler tried to keep Hitler under control, but he failed. Within a short time Hitler was *Ortsgruppenvorsitzender der Deutschen Arbeiterpartei* (chairman of the German Workers' party), and soon the group was merged into the new Nationalsozialistische Deutsche Arbeiterpartei (q.v.; NSDAP) under Hitler's sole control. Drexler was promoted to the innocuous post of honorary chairman of the NSDAP. After the 1923 Beer-Hall *Putsch* (q.v.), Drexler served a short prison term. He left the party in 1923 and was elected in April 1924 on the list of the People's Bloc in the Bavarian Landtag. After the reorganization of the NSDAP in February 1925, he avoided the party and opposed Hitler. There was a reconciliation in 1930, but Drexler never again took part in the movement he had generated. He died in Munich on February 24, 1942.

[1]The *Ortsgruppe* was a local group of the Nationalsozialistische Deutsche Arbeiterpartei, responsible for a town section.

DRITTE REICH, DAS (The Third Reich). A bimonthly magazine founded in 1974. According to its publisher, Alexander Jahr, *Das Dritte Reich* was designed to give the German people a vivid account of what took place during the Nazi era. "It is an open secret," he said, "that this subject gets treated very superficially in the schools or not at all." He held it to be necessary that all Germans, especially younger people, be given through the medium of a newsmagazine an accurate account of the mood and experiences of the Hitler regime. Editor Christian Zentner added that the magazine intended to explain how "a nation of poets and philosophers could become a nation of murderers and criminals."

The maiden issue of *Das Dritte Reich*, consisting of forty-eight pages, appeared in March 1974. Attractively designed and produced, it showed how National Socialism rose in the post-World War I depression and how it bloomed in the resurgence of nationalism promoted by Hitler and the Nazis. Illustrations devoted to the 1932–1933 period featured the film actress Marlene Dietrich (q.v.) and also the boxer Max Schmeling (q.v.) fighting the American Jack Sharkey for the world's heavyweight championship.

Officials of the German Federal Republic indicated displeasure at the publication of the new magazine. They feared that such nostalgia might trigger a new outburst of neo-Nazism (q.v.). They also condemned the promotional tactics used in the prepublication campaign. These included advertisements featuring posters of the 1930s, tiny swastika flags, and throwaway records of Hitler's speeches. Critics claimed that this technique tended to glorify the Nazi era instead of condemning it and that impressionable youngsters might see fun in "the good old Nazi days." On a Berlin court order, police raided newsstands and confiscated the items designed to attract customers for the magazine. The first issue sold 100,000 copies at $1.10 each.

DRIVE TO THE EAST. *See* DRANG NACH OSTEN.

DRP. *See* DEUTSCHE RECHTS-PARTEI.

DUEL. *See* MENSUR.

DUESTERBERG, THEODOR (1875–1950). Former professional soldier and one of the founders of the Stahlhelm (q.v.), the veterans' organization. Theodor Duesterberg was born in Darmstadt on October 19, 1875, and served in World War I as a lieutenant colonel. In 1918, with Franz Seldte (q.v.), he organized the Stahlhelm, which he regarded as the army of the new Germany. On

October 11, 1931, Duesterberg and Seldte represented the Stahlhelm in the Harzburg Front (q.v.), an unsuccessful attempt to combine all rightist organizations in one powerful political unit. Duesterberg ran as a candidate of the German Nationalist party in the presidential elections of March 13, 1932. During the course of the campaign, the Nazis struck at Duesterberg with a deadly weapon after discovering that his grandfather was Abraham Selig Duesterberg, a Jew. Badly shaken by the news, Duesterberg swore that he had not known of his Jewish origin. His quest for the Presidency was hopeless: he received 2,557,729 votes against 18,650,730 for Field Marshal Paul von Hindenburg (q.v.), honorary president of the Stahlhelm, and 11,339,285 for Hitler. The Nationalists withdrew Duesterberg's name from the runoff election of April 10, 1932, and urged their followers to vote for Hitler. Von Hindenburg was elected.

On January 30, 1933, Hitler apologized to Duesterberg for the charge of Jewish background that had been made by Nazi zealots and offered him a post in a projected coalition Cabinet. Duesterberg refused, whereupon the Nazi-controlled newspapers revived the charge about his Jewish grandfather and attacked him as having a racially unclean past. At this time Duesterberg broke with Seldte, his Stahlhelm colleague, who became an admirer and eventually a retainer of Hitler. Because Duesterberg continued to call the Nazis bandits, he was imprisoned temporarily in 1934. In 1943 he made contact with Carl Friedrich Goerdeler (q.v.), the civilian Resistance (q.v.) leader, but never joined the inner core of the conspiracy. Duesterberg died in Hameln on May 4, 1950.

DÜHRING, EUGEN KARL (1833–1921). Philosopher, political economist, and intellectual forerunner of National Socialism. Eugen Karl Dühring was born in Berlin on January 12, 1833. After practicing law until 1859, he became a *Privatdozent* (unsalaried lecturer) at the University of Berlin in 1864. Three years later, after a bitter quarrel with a colleague, he had his license to teach withdrawn. Dühring wrote many treatises on mathematics, physics, and literature, but he became known through his work in philosophy and economics. As a positivist philosopher, he held to the concept of reality expressed in scientific terms. As an economist, he stressed the national character of economic life. He was denounced by Friedrich Engels in the latter's famous textbook on Marxism, known as *Anti-Dühring*, because of what Engels called Dühring's "vulgar materialism."

Dühring carried on an emotional struggle against both Christianity and Judaism. In 1881 he published *Die Judenfrage als Rassen-, Sitten-, und Kulturfrage (The Jewish Question as a Racial, Moral, and Cultural Problem)*, which was one of the first books to base anti-Semitism (q.v.) on racialist theories. He recommended "interning" Jews under "international law." The tenacity of Judaism, he said, could be destroyed only by the destruction of the Jews themselves. It was the first duty of every Christian, he declared, to turn against Judaism with all the force at his command. In 1924 a Dühring Bund was organized to spread his ideas.

When the eighteen-year-old Adolf Hitler went to Vienna in October 1907 and remained there for the next five years, he was exposed to the racial teaching and arrogant nationalism of Dühring. Young Hitler was also influenced by others who held similar views, including Paul Anton de Lagarde, Julius Langbehn, Adolf Stoecker, Arthur Comte de Gobineau, and Houston Stewart Chamberlain (qq.v.). Hitler's stereotyped view of the "Jewish question" undoubtedly came from these ideologists. Dühring died in Potsdam on September 21, 1921.

DULLES, ALLEN WELSH (1893–1969). Head of the United States Office of Strategic Services (OSS) in Europe, which maintained contact with the German Resistance (q.v.) movement during World War II. Allen Welsh Dulles was born in Waterloo, New York, on April 7, 1893. After graduation from Princeton University, he entered the diplomatic service with a post in Vienna. The next year he was assigned to Bern, Switzerland. In December 1918 he worked in Paris with the American Commission to Negotiate Peace. In 1919 he was posted to Berlin and the next year was transferred to the Department of State. Dulles was Chief of the Division of Near Eastern Affairs from 1922 to 1926. After the United States entered the war in December 1941, he was given control of the OSS on the Continent. From November 1942 on he maintained continual contact with the German Resistance from Switzerland. His activities helped lead to the capitulation of Italy effective September 8, 1943.

Hans Bernd Gisevius (q.v.), one of the leaders of the Resistance, who worked for German counterintelligence from a base in Switzerland, reported: "Allen Dulles was the first intelligence officer who had the courage to extend his activities to the political aspect of war. He tried to establish contact with all the Resistance groups in Europe." Dulles's bureau on the Herrengasse in Bern became in time a center of European resistance to Hitler. Not only Germans but also Americans, Hungarians, Italians, Romanians, and Finns, as well as citizens of occupied countries, met there. Dulles was assisted by Gerd von Gaevernitz, a German-American living in Switzerland who was well informed on German conditions. Members of the German underground who visited Dulles urged him to convince the Western Allies that the policy of unconditional surrender, in lieu of decent treatment, would drive the Germans into the Russian camp. Dulles was head of the American Central Intelligence Agency (CIA) from 1953 to 1961. He died in Washington on January 29, 1969.

Bibliography. Robert Edwards, *A Study of a Master Spy, Allen Dulles*, Housmans, London, 1961.

DÜSSELDORF SPEECH. Talk delivered by Hitler in an attempt to win the support of German industrialists for the Nazi cause. It was one of the most important and effective speeches of the Fuehrer's career. On January 27, 1932, Hitler was invited to Düsseldorf, the heart of the German steel industry, to address the Industrieklub (q.v.; Industry Club), a wealthy group of Rhenish-Westphalian industrialists. It was the first time that German industrial leaders had met Hitler. At first their reception was cool. Hitler seized the opportunity to present his case to Germans who could further his political career. For two and one-half hours he harangued the assembled coal and steel barons. His approach was shrewd and impressive. He wanted big business to know that he and his Nazi followers could be trusted. He defended private property, attacked the Bolshevik menace, and praised National Socialism. His talk was tailored to the views of his audience.

The following condensation summarizes the salient points of this historic speech:

> The dominant consideration in politics today should not be foreign relations. I regard it as of the first importance that we break down the view that our destiny is conditioned by world events. The most important factor in national life is the inner worth of a people and its spirit. In Germany, this inner worth has been undermined by the false values of democracy and the supremacy of mere numbers in opposition to the creative principle of individual personality.
>
> Private property can only be justified on the ground that men's achievements in the economic field are unequal. But it is absurd to construct economic life on achievement of personality, while in political life this authority is denied, and thrust in its place is the law of the greatest number—democracy.
>
> Communism is more than just a mob storming about in our German streets. It is taking over the entire Asiatic world. Unemployment is driving millions of Germans to look on Communism as the logical theoretical counterpart of their actual economic situation. This is the heart of the German problem. We cannot cure this state of affairs by emergency decrees.
>
> There can only be one basic solution—the realization that a flourishing economic life must be protected by a flourishing, powerful state. Behind this economic life must stand the determined political will of the nation ready to strike, and strike hard.
>
> This same is true of foreign policy. The Treaty of Versailles is the result of our own inner confusion. It is no good appealing for national unity and sacrifice when only fifty per cent of the people are ready to fight for the national colors.
>
> Today we stand at a turning point in Germany's destiny. Either we shall succeed in working out a body-politic as hard as iron from this conglomeration of parties, or Germany will fall into final ruin. Today no one can escape the obligation to complete the regeneration of the German body-politic. Every one must show his personal sympathy, and every one must take his place in the common effort. I speak to you today not to ask for your votes or to induce you to do this or that for the party. No, I am here to present a point of view. I am convinced that victory for this point of view is the only starting-point for German recovery.
>
> Remember that it means sacrifice when today hundreds of thousands of SA and SS men mount their trucks, protect meetings, undertake marches, sacrifice themselves day and night, and then return in the grey dawn to workshop and factory, or, as jobless, take the pittance of a dole. It means sacrifice when these little men spend all their money to buy uniforms, shirts, badges, and even pay their own fares.
>
> But there is in all this the strength of an ideal—a great ideal. If the entire German nation today had this idealism, Germany would look far different in the eyes of the world than she does now!

When Hitler finished his oration, his audience rose and cheered him. It was a significant day in the history of Germany. The industrialists now had a champion to protect them against radicalism, communism, and the clamoring trade unions. For Hitler, too, the event was critical. Now he had access to the purse strings of Germany's moneyed industrialists. From this point on heavy contributions began to flow into the Nazi treasury. The way was prepared for the triumph of National Socialism.

E

EAGLE AND FALCON to EXTRAORDINARY PACIFICATION ACTION

EAGLE AND FALCON. *See* ADLER UND FALKE.

EAGLE ATTACKS. *See* ADLERANGRIFFE.

EAGLE DAY. *See* ADLERTAG.

EAGLE'S NEST. Hitler's isolated cabin on a mountaintop high above Berchtesgaden (q.v.). A hairpin road carved into the Bavarian mountainside led to a long underground passageway drilled into the rock. This in turn gave access to an elevator that rose 370 feet to the cabin perched at the top. From the Eagle's Nest the Fuehrer had a superb view of the surrounding scenery. He preferred to be there alone, but on occasion he brought visitors with him and took pleasure in impressing them with the view. On October 18, 1938, he was accompanied by French Ambassador André François-Poncet to his retreat. The French envoy later expressed his astonishment at the experience. He wondered if this structure could have been the product of a normal mind. *See also* BERGHOF.

EAST SUBVENTION SCANDAL. *See* OSTHILFE SKANDAL.

EASTERN INDUSTRIES, LTD. *See* OSTINDUSTRIE GMBH.

EASTERN MARCH. *See* OSTMARK.

EASTERN MEDAL. *See* OSTMEDAILLE.

EASTERN WORKER. *See* OSTARBEITER.

EBERT, FRIEDRICH (1871–1925). First President of the Weimar Republic (q.v.). Friedrich Ebert was born in Heidelberg on February 4, 1871. A saddler by trade, he became the editor of the Social Democratic organ, the *Bremer Bürgerzeitung*, in 1893. In 1905 he was made secretary of the Central Committee of the Social Democratic party, and in 1913 he succeeded Ferdinand August Bebel as its chairman. He played an important role in the late years of World War I as leader of the Majority Socialists. On February 11, 1919, Ebert was named Provisional President by the Weimar National Assembly. To avoid an election in critical days, Ebert was named President to serve until June 30, 1925, by a special constitutional amendment.

Friedrich Ebert. [*British Museum*]

In office he steered a middle course between left and right. He suppressed Communist uprisings on the left and the Kapp *Putsch* (1920) and the Beer-Hall *Putsch* (1923, qq.v.) on the right. For these actions he utilized the provisions of Article 48 (q.v.) of the Weimar Constitution to enable him to prevent the overthrow of the government. Although he won respect for his rational political leadership, he was attacked bitterly from the right. A court judgment of December 25, 1924, spoke of his "treason" for having taken part in the munitions strike of January 1918. Ebert was deeply wounded by this charge, especially because he had lost two sons in the war. He died in Berlin on February 28, 1925.

Bibliography. George Kotowski, *Friedrich Ebert*, F. Steiner, Wiesbaden, 1963.

ECKART, DIETRICH (1868–1923). Nationalist poet and central figure of Hitler's entourage in the early post-World War I years in Munich. Born on March 23, 1868, in Neumarkt, Upper Palatinate, he began his career as a poet and journalist. He opposed the German revolution of 1918, which he regarded as Jewish-inspired. His poem *Jeurjo* (1919) used the words *"Deutschland Erwache!"* ("Germany Awake!"), which later became a battle cry of the Nazi movement. With close contacts in rightist circles, Eckart joined the party of Anton Drexler (q.v.). He also began a close friendship with Hitler and introduced the awkward young politician to his friends in Munich. The two went to Berlin in 1920 at the time of the Kapp *Putsch* (q.v.). There they met Gen. Erich Ludendorff (q.v.), who was attracted by their views. In December 1920, with the help of funds obtained by Eckart, Hitler's followers were able to buy the *Völkischer Beobachter* (q.v.), which eventually became the Nazi party's official organ. Eckart, assisted by a young protégé, Alfred Rosenberg (q.v.), edited the paper for two years. The Bavarian Catholic poet and the Protestant Baltic journalist worked well together until Eckart lost the editorship to his assistant.

By 1923 Eckart's connections in Munich, added to Hitler's oratorical gifts, gave strength and prestige to the fledgling Nazi political movement. Eckart accompanied Hitler at rallies and was at his side in party parades. While Hitler stirred the masses, Eckart wrote panegyrics to his friend. The two were inseparable. Hitler never forgot his early sponsor. Volume 2 of *Mein Kampf* (q.v.) ends with the name of Dietrich Eckart in bold type. In Hitler's table talk (*see* TABLE TALK, HITLER'S), he mentioned Eckart's name more than any other. He spoke emotionally of his "fatherly friend," and there were often tears in his eyes when he mentioned Eckart's name. Eckart, he said, was his North Star, a teacher with whom he had begun his struggle in Bavaria, a man whose services to National Socialism were "inestimable."

Eckart's *Storm Song* (q.v.) was the oldest popular Nazi song. A few months before his death he published an uncompleted pamphlet, a *Zwiegespräch* (dialogue) between himself and Hitler. Titled *Der Bolshewismus von Moses bis Hitler (Bolshevism from Moses to Hitler)*, it was published by the Hohenreichen Verlag in Munich. Hitler's name did not appear in the text, but he was recognizable on every page. The author gave Hitler credit for discovering that the hidden force causing irregularities in history was the Jew. It was Hitler, according to Eckart, who took the fatal pessimism of Arthur Comte de Gobineau (q.v.) and transformed it into an aggressive optimism. Hitler was the first man, he said, to reveal that the Jews undertook a mass migration from Egypt because they had made a revolutionary, murderous, but unsuccessful assault on the Egyptian ruling class. Moses was the first leader of bolshevism. The anti-Semitic ideas (*see* ANTI-SEMITISM) expressed in this dialogue were used again and again by Hitler before and after assuming political power.

In his early years Eckart had been a morphine addict and had spent some time in an asylum for the mentally diseased. He was also a heavy drinker. He was already seriously ill before the 1923 Munich Beer-Hall *Putsch* (q.v.). He died on December 23, 1923, in Berchtesgaden of a heart attack. Nazi party propaganda asserted that his fatal illness was induced by the illegal treatment given him while he was in a Bavarian prison.

ECONOMIC AND ADMINISTRATIVE CENTRAL OFFICE. *See* WIRTSCHAFTS- UND VERWALTUNGSHAUPTAMT.

ECONOMIC AND ARMAMENT OFFICE. *See* WIRTSCHAFTS- UND RÜSTUNGSAMT.

EDELWEISS. Code name for a directive issued by Hitler on July 23, 1942, concerning a prospective attack by Army Group A on the Baku oil fields in the Caucasus. The army group occupying the area was to await the arrival of the Italian Alpine Corps. Situated on the western shore of the Caspian Sea, Baku was the center of a district of large oil fields with refineries and engineering industries. The Fuehrer regarded the success of Edelweiss as a prime necessity for continuing the war. The major German attack in September 1942 won Maikop, but it fell short of the oil fields at Grozny and never reached Baku.

EDUCATION IN THE THIRD REICH. For more than a century the German educational system had been a model for the world. German organization of study from kindergarten to university, the status of teachers, the nature of the curriculum, all these were admired everywhere. There was a catastrophic decline during the twelve years of the Third Reich, when education was revised to meet the standards of the dictatorship.

Hitler was convinced that "whoever has the youth has the future." He proposed definite ideas about education:

> I begin with the young. We older ones are used up. We are rotten to the marrow.
>
> But my magnificent youngsters! Are there any finer ones in the world? Look at these young men and boys! What material? With them I can make a new world.
>
> My teaching will be hard. Weakness will be knocked out of them. A violently active, dominating, brutal youth—that is what I am after. Youth must be indifferent to pain. There must be no weakness and tenderness in it. I want to see once more in its eyes the gleam of pride and independence of the beast of prey.
>
> I will have no intellectual training. Knowledge is ruin to my young men. I would have them learn only what takes their fancy. But one thing they must learn—self-command. They shall learn to overcome their fear of death under the severest tests.
>
> This is the heroic stage of youth. Out of it will come the creative man, the god-man!

Hitler's philosophy of education was based in large part on his antagonism to educational authority. He never forgot the terrible blow he had received in Vienna when, at the age of eighteen, he was turned down by the Academy of Fine Arts. Thereafter he was contemptuous of teachers and intellectuals. He wanted to break violently with the intellectualism of the Weimar Republic (q.v.). The first duty of the state, he said, was to care for the bodily development of the young. "The whole education in a national state must aim first of all not at stuffing the student with mere knowledge but by building bodies which are healthy to the core." The minds of the young must not be crammed with scientific knowledge. "Genius can never spring from a nation of degenerates." The new youth, like that of ancient Sparta, must be virile and strong. There were to be two basic educational ideas in his ideal state. First, there must be burnt into the heart and brains of youth the sense of race. Second, German youth must be made ready for war, educated for victory or death. The ultimate purpose of education was to fashion citizens conscious of the glory of country and filled with fanatical devotion to the national cause. National Socialism would furnish the necessary elite for the nation.

Hitler's hostility to teachers, professors, and intellectuals influenced the Nazi hierarchy to adopt similar sentiments. Dr. Robert Ley (q.v.), head of the Deutsche Arbeitsfront (q.v.), the German Labor Front, expressed the Nazi attitude: "A street cleaner sweeps a thousand microbes into the gutter with one stroke; a scientist preens himself on discovering a single microbe in the whole of his life." Julius Streicher (q.v.), anti-Semitic editor of *Der Stürmer* (*see* STURMER, DER), illustrated his attitude toward academicians in a talk to students at the University of Berlin. He drew two scales on the blackboard. The lower one, he said, contained the Fuehrer's brains, the upper one the *Dreck* (rubbish) of the professors' brains. *Das Schwarze Korps* (*see* SCHWARZE KORPS, DAS), publication of the SS (q.v.), labeled such scientists as Werner Heisenberg and Max Planck "white Jews in the sphere of science." Other Nazi leaders echoed Hitler's concern for a special type of education for the young. Dr. Paul Joseph Goebbels (q.v.), Minister for Public Enlightenment and Propaganda, said: "Youth belongs to us, and we will yield them to no one."

Soon after Hitler became Chancellor in 1933, he gave orders for the nazification of the entire school system, from the opening school years to the university. The schools were to be reformed in line with his own theories of education. In February 1933 he appointed Bernhard Rust (q.v.), an unemployed provincial schoolmaster, Prussian minister of education, and in April 1934 he promoted him to Reich Minister for Science, Education, and Culture. In this key post Rust transformed the German educational system into a pillar of the Nazi state.

In one respect Rust's efforts were eased: in both the Second Empire and the Weimar Republic the school establishment had already been dominantly nationalistic. Rust's problem was to turn that sense of nationalism into a Nazi asset. His first step was to purge all schools and universities of Jewish teachers. Within a short time 97 percent of the teachers were enrolled in the NS-Lehrerbund (q.v.), the NSLB, or National Socialist Teachers' Alliance. By 1936 some 32 percent of the NSLB teachers were Nazi party members. By 1938 two-thirds of all elementary school teachers were indoctrinated at special camps in a compulsory one-month training course of drills and lectures. What they learned at camp they were expected to pass on to their students.

The first book the German child saw after kindergarten was the *Primer*. On the cover was a caricature of a Jew, with the words: "Trust no fox on the green heath! Trust no Jew on his oath!" Inside were pictures of marching and camp life and accompanying text:

> He who wants to be a soldier,
> That one must have a weapon,
> Which he must load with powder,
> And with a good hard bullet.
> Little fellow, if you want to be a recruit,
> Take good care of this little song.

Sports received unprecedented attention in the curriculum from the grade schools through the high schools (*Gymnasien*) to the universities (*see* SPORTS IN THE THIRD REICH). The subjects upgraded were history, biology, and Germanics. The study of history was converted to historicism, or the use of history for political purposes. Students were expected to know about the glories of the 1923 Munich Beer-Hall *Putsch* (q.v.) and the martyr Horst Wessel (q.v.), as well as about the evils of the Weimar Republic (q.v.) and the contemptible Kurt Eisner, who had attempted to set up a soviet republic in Bavaria in 1919. Pre-teen-age youngsters learned about World War I epics in these terms: "Otto's bayonet slid gracefully between the Russian's ribs, so that he collapsed groaning. There it lay, simple and distinguished, before him, his dream's desire, the Iron Cross."

Biology in the schools emphasized Hitler's views on race and heredity (*see* RACIAL DOCTRINE). The approved textbook on race was Hermann Gauch's *New Elements of Racial Research*, with this typical passage: "The animal world can be classified into Nordic men and lower animals [Jews]. We are thus able to establish the following principle: there exist no physical or psychological characteristics which would justify a differentiation of mankind from the animal world. The only differences that exist are those between Nordic man, on the one hand, and animals, in general, including non-Nordic men, or sub-men (who are a transitional species), on the other hand" (*see* RASSENFORSCHUNG). Students were encouraged to measure their skills to determine their Aryan heritage.

The study of Germanics was motivated by the necessity of proving Teutonic greatness, with stress on Germans as a culture-producing race and Jews as a culture-destroying race. Teachers were urged to familiarize their pupils with heroic Nordic sagas and to require them to use Germanized versions of loanwords from other languages. Pupils were expected to regurgitate handouts from Dr. Goebbels's Propaganda Ministry. They received special credit for essays on such subjects as "The Educational Value of the Reich Labor Service."

There was not much change in the basic study of mathematics, except that emphasis was now placed on subliminal conditioning of pupils for war service. Mathematical questions revolved around artillery trajectories and fighter-to-bomber ratios. This was a typical question from a lower-grade mathematics text: "An airplane flies at the rate of 240 kilometers per hour to a place at a distance of 210 kilometers in order to drop bombs. When may it be expected to return if the dropping of bombs takes 7.5 minutes?"

Religious instruction was sharply reduced. By 1935, questions on religion were dropped from the school-leaving examinations, and attendance at school prayers was made optional. The erosion of religious instruction continued during the remaining years of the Nazi regime.

Despite the continuing nazification of the school system, Hitler preferred to pursue his educational reforms beyond the classroom into the major youth organizations. As a school dropout himself, he preferred the leagues and societies that acted as appendages to the Nazi party. "This new Reich will give its youth to no one, but will itself take over youth and give to youth its own education and its own upbringing." For this purpose he founded the Hitler Jugend (q.v.), the Hitler Youth, under the leadership of Baldur von Schirach (q.v.). Through this organization the Fuehrer expected German youth to become as hard as steel and to understand military order and discipline. In 1932 the Hitler Youth had an enrollment of just over 100,000; by 1938 it numbered 7,728,329. Similarly, the Bund Deutscher Mädel (q.v.), the League of German Girls, was expected to train girls to be mothers and to prepare for war. "The one absolute aim of female education," Hitler wrote in *Mein Kampf*, "must be with a view to the future mother." There were already too many people in Germany, which needed *Lebensraum* (q.v.), or living space; nevertheless, Hitler called for more and more children.

The Fuehrer also added to the educational system three types of schools for the training of a future Nazi elite to carry on the work and ideology of National Socialism. First were the *Adolf Hitler–Schule* (q.v.), the Adolf Hitler Schools, where young cadets were trained in physical exercise, racialism, and loyalty to the Fuehrer. Second were the *Nationalpolitische Erziehungsanstalten* (q.v.), the *Napolas*, or National Political Training Institutes, used to provide a type of education formerly given in Prussian military academies, with emphasis upon the soldierly spirit, duty, and discipline. Third were the *Ordensburgen* (q.v.), the Order Castles, dedicated to training the best of the Nazi elite. Here students especially chosen from the Adolf Hitler Schools and the *Napolas* underwent four years of study to be prepared for posts as future leaders of the Nazi party: first year—study of racial science; second year—athletics, mountain climbing, parachute jumping; third year—political and military instruction; fourth year—final political and military indoctrination.

The "reforms" instituted by Hitler in German education had catastrophic results. A system that had won global respect for its dignity and thoroughness became merely an appendage of the Propaganda Ministry. Standards declined precipitously in the German educational establishment all the way from the grade schools to the universities.

See also UNIVERSITIES IN THE THIRD REICH.

Bibliography. Erika Mann, *School for Barbarians: Education under the Nazis*, Modern Age Books, Inc., New York, 1938; Gregor Ziemer, *Education for Death*, Oxford University Press, New York, 1941.

EHER VERLAG. Munich publishing house owned originally by Franz Eher II and taken over by Max Amann (q.v.) in 1922. It issued the first and subsequent editions of *Mein Kampf* (q.v.) and became the official publishing house for leading National Socialists.

EHESTANDSDARLEHEN (Marriage Loan). Loan (*Darlehen*) to aid a married couple in setting up housekeeping. The providing of such loans was one of a series of legislative measures that sought to encourage marriage and raise the birthrate in the Third Reich. The Reich Statistical Office reported that between August 1933 and the end of 1936 the Nazi regime financed 694,367 marriages, to which 485,285 children were born. Similar measures included prizes for large families, gifts to newborn infants, financial privileges for large families, and a special tax on bachelors and childless couples.

EHRENFUEHRER (Honorary Leader). Title granted by Heinrich Himmler (q.v.) to selected leading members of the Nazi hierarchy. With it went the post of honorary SS (q.v.) general. The title, regarded as a special distinction, was given to such men as Martin Bormann and Joachim von Ribbentrop (qq.v.), who were nominally attached to Hitler's staff.

"EHRHARDT LIED" ("Ehrhardt Song"). The official song of Captain Ehrhardt's Volunteer Marine Brigade, one of the paramilitary units of the *Freikorps* (q.v.), the free corps of the post-1918 era. One of the most active terrorist units of the period, it expressed its spirit in this song:

> The Swastika in the helmet of steel,
> Black-white-red band,
> The Brigade of Ehrhardt,
> Is known around the land.
> Workman, workman, what will become of you
> When the Ehrhardt Brigade stands ready for the fight?
> The Ehrhardt Brigade knocks everything to bits,
> Woe to you, woe to you, workman son of a bitch!

Many members of the various *Freikorps* units turned to National Socialism because of its similar rightist goals.

EICHE (Oak). Code name for one of four operations ordered by Hitler on July 31, 1943, to meet the expected invasion by Allied forces onto the Italian mainland (*see also* ACHSE; SCHWARZ; STUDENT). Operation Eiche called for the rescue of Mussolini from captivity. On September 13, 1943, a party of German parachutists, led by Otto Skorzeny (q.v.), landed on the rocks of the Abruzzi Apennines, where Mussolini was imprisoned, and rescued him from his captors. The Duce then became Hitler's puppet ruler of German-occupied Italy.

EICHMANN, [KARL] ADOLF (1906–1962). SS (q.v.) officer charged with the destruction of millions of Jews. Karl Adolf Eichmann was born in Solingen on March 19, 1906. He spent his youth in Linz, Austria, where Hitler, too, lived during his early years. A lonely and melancholy boy, moody and withdrawn, Eichmann was called "*der kleine Jude*" ("the little Jew") by his playmates because of his dark complexion. After attendance at public school in Thuringia, he studied electrical engineering but was forced to leave school because of the inflation. Taking a job as a traveling salesman for an oil company in Vienna, he gradually learned to assert himself and developed into a talkative, hard-drinking extrovert who loved to show off his red motorcycle. He hated the Jews he met in Vienna, a sentiment stimulated by attendance at Nazi meetings. "Hitler was right," he said later, "when he charged that this one people had intrigued to link as many nations as possible against our country and bring about the terrible times we are going through." In 1927 Eichmann joined the youth section of the Austro-German Veterans' Organization, and in 1932 he became a member of the Austrian Nazi party. As a protégé of Ernst Kaltenbrunner (q.v.), he took part in Nazi activities, which brought him to the attention of the Austrian police.

Leaving Vienna for Berlin, Eichmann began to work for Austro-German *Anschluss* (q.v.). He moved to Bavaria, where an Austrian legion-in-exile was being formed. After starting as a lowly file clerk, he learned that there

Adolf Eichmann. [*Institute of Contemporary History and Wiener Library, London*]

was an opening in Heinrich Himmler's SD (Sicherheitsdienst), the information center for the Gestapo (qq.v.). Himmler, who believed that Eichmann could speak Hebrew, made him head of the Scientific Museum for Jewish Affairs. In 1937 Eichmann paid a short visit to Palestine to get in touch with Arab leaders, but he was ordered out of the country by the British. On his return to Germany he was promoted rapidly from *SS-Untersturmfuehrer* (2d lieutenant) to *Hauptsturmfuehrer* (captain) and then to *Obersturmbannfuehrer* (lieutenant colonel). After service in the Reich Central Office of Jewish Emigration, he was made chief of Subsection IV-B-4 of the Reichssicherheitshauptamt (q.v.; RSHA), the Reich Central Security Office, as an expert on Jewish affairs. He was present at the Wannsee Conference (q.v.) on January 20, 1942, when it was decided to deport Jews to the extermination camps (q.v.). In August 1944 Eichmann reported to Himmler that, although the death camps kept no exact statistics, 4 million Jews had died in them and that 2 million more had been shot or killed by mobile units.

Arrested at the end of World War II, Eichmann escaped unrecognized from an internment camp in the American zone in 1946 and disappeared. On May 11, 1960, the Israeli secret service found him in Argentina and smuggled him back to Israel. His trial, which took place in Jerusalem from April 11 to August 14, 1961, aroused worldwide attention. He was charged with crimes against the Jewish people, crimes against humanity, and war crimes. Found guilty, he was hanged at Ramle on May 31, 1962.

Bibliography. Hannah Arendt, *Eichmann in Jerusalem: A Report on the Banality of Evil,* The Viking Press, Inc., New York, 1963.

EICKE, THEODOR (1892–1943). First inspector of concentration camps (q.v.). Theodor Eicke was born in Hampont, Alsace-Lorraine, in 1892. In 1919 he gave up his career as a paymaster in the Imperial Army to join the police administration in Thuringia. He held various police jobs, all of which he lost because of his uncompromising hostility to the Weimar Republic (q.v.). In 1928, after a period of unemployment, he became a member of the Nationalsozialistische Deutsche Arbeiterpartei (NSDAP) and the SA and shortly afterward transferred to the SS (qq.v.). He was appointed an *SS-Standartenfuehrer* (colonel) in 1931. In March 1932 he was sentenced to two years' imprisonment for preparing political bomb attacks. He escaped to Italy and returned home when Hitler assumed power in 1933. In June of that year he became the new commander of Dachau (q.v.). In April 1934 Heinrich Himmler (q.v.) appointed Eicke inspector of concentration camps and SS guard formations and within a few weeks promoted him to *SS-Gruppenfuehrer* (lieutenant general).

Eicke's influence on the organization and spirit of the SS guard formations was second only to that of Himmler. His regulations included precise instructions on solitary confinement, corporal punishment, beatings, reprimands, and warnings. He informed his guards that any pity for enemies of the state was unworthy of SS men. Any SS man with a soft heart would do well "to retire quickly to a monastery." He said he could use only hard, determined men who would ruthlessly obey every order. At the opening of World War II he addressed his concentration camp commanders: "It is the duty of every SS man to identify himself body and soul with the cause. Every order must be sacred to him and he must carry out even the most difficult and hardest of them without hesitation."

Eicke was succeeded in 1940 by Richard Gluecks (q.v.) as chief inspector of concentration camps. In 1943 Eicke was promoted to *SS-Obergruppenfuehrer* (general) and general of the Waffen-SS (q.v.).

"EIN VOLK! EIN REICH! EIN FUEHRER!" ("One People! One Government! One Leader!"). Nazi battle cry popularized in the Third Reich by the propaganda machine of Dr. Paul Joseph Goebbels (q.v.). The slogan was popular before and after Hitler became Chancellor in 1933.

EINDEUTSCHUNG (Germanization). Term used to denote the process of turning foreign nationals into Germans.

EINSATZ REINHARD (Reinhard Pool). Code name for an assignment allocated to *SS-Brigadefuehrer* Odilo Globocnik (q.v.), head of extermination camps (q.v.) in Poland. The purpose was to annihilate all Polish Jews as a memorial to Reinhard Heydrich (q.v.) on June 4, 1942. Einsatz Reinhard resulted in the deportation of several hundred thousand Jews from Poland to death camps at Maidanek, Belzec, Sobibór, Treblinka, and Auschwitz (qq.v.).

EINSATZGRUPPEN (Task Forces). Special mobile formations charged with carrying out liquidations in occupied countries. They were attached to Amt (Office) IV of the RSHA (Reichssicherheitshauptamt, q.v.), the Reich Central Security Office. The individual detachment was called an *Einsatzkommando*, the operations staff was designated an *Einsatzstab*, and the smallest unit was called an *Einsatztrupp*. These formations were given the task of supervising the Final Solution (*see* ENDLÖSUNG, DIE) of the Jewish problem by extermination. Together with other elements of the Security Police, they were responsible for the deaths of 2 million of the estimated 6 million Jews killed.

EINSATZKOMMANDOS (Killer Units). Individual detachments of the *Einsatzgruppen* (q.v.), special formations of highly mobile killer units ("slaughterhouses on wheels"), charged with destroying Communists, partisans, saboteurs, and Jews on the eastern front. Their special task was to preserve rear communications in the campaign against the Soviet Union in World War II.

EINSATZSTAB (Staff Pool). Operational staff of the Security Police for use in occupied territory. *See also* EINSATZGRUPPEN.

EINSATZSTAB ROSENBERG (Rosenberg Task Force). An organization headed by Alfred Rosenberg (q.v.) and designated by Hitler to confiscate selections of the great art treasures in France and other occupied countries. Guided by Hermann Goering and Field Marshal Wilhelm Keitel (qq.v.), Rosenberg was ordered to transport to Germany "cultural goods which appear valuable to you and to safeguard them there." Rosenberg assumed that he had a free hand to sequester all "ownerless Jewish property." His official report to Hitler stated that between October 1940 and July 1944 he had appropriated the following art works: 21,903 art objects of all kinds, brought to Germany in twenty-nine shipments, including 137 freight cars. Among them were 5,281 paintings, including works by Rembrandt, Rubens, Goya, Gainsborough, Fragonard, and other masters; 5,825 handmade objects, such as porcelains, bronzes, and coins; several hundred icons; and 2,477 pieces of furniture of the seventeenth and eighteenth centuries. The art works from France, including those from the Louvre, were valued at $1 billion. The better works were selected by Goering for his own collections. The Vichy government, citing the Hague Convention, protested in vain. After the war these works of art were returned to their original owners.

At Nuremberg Rosenberg defended his acquisition of art works by presenting the argument that German property to the value of 25 billion marks had been expropriated after World War I. It was only historical justice, he said, that Jewish and Masonic property be sequestered in return. It was "the biggest art operation in history." His vast enterprise, he said, was designed to protect art from the vicissitudes of war, to make an exact inventory, and to see that great treasures were not destroyed. They were certainly not intended, he insisted, to be added to Goering's private collections. When reminded that several Dutch paintings had been found in his own home, Rosenberg replied that these had been gifts to his wife, who loved antiques.

EINSATZTRUPP (Troop Task Force). Smallest unit of the *Einsatzgruppen* (q.v.), the mobile task forces responsible for carrying out liquidations in occupied countries.

EINSTEIN, ALBERT (1879–1955). Leading twentieth-century physicist and the best-known critic of Nazism. Albert Einstein was born in Ulm, Württemberg, on March 14, 1879, of Jewish parentage. He was the son of Hermann Einstein, who in 1880 moved with his family to Munich, where he started a small electrochemical factory. As a shy child, Albert disliked formal instruction and was educated at home. He was fascinated by algebra and geometry. At the age of seventeen he began four years of study

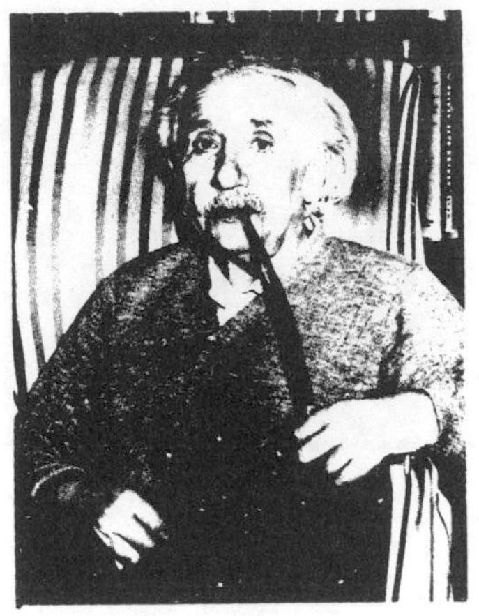

Albert Einstein. [*National Archives, Washington*]

at the Federal Polytechnic School in Zürich. He became a Swiss citizen. After his graduation in 1900, he received an appointment to a post in the patent office at Bern. In 1905 he published four papers of major importance in the *Annalen der Physik:* on the production and transformation of light, the Brownian movement, molecular dimensions, and the electrodynamics of moving bodies. In 1909 he was appointed adjunct professor of physics at Zürich and in 1911 professor of physics at Prague. In 1914 he was made director of the Kaiser Wilhelm Institute for Physics in Berlin, a post combined with a chair at the University of Berlin.

Meanwhile, Einstein published his general theory of relativity, which superseded Newton's dynamics. His predicted equivalence of mass (m) and energy (E) according to the relation $E = mc^2$, where c is the velocity of light, was soon verified and later demonstrated in the production of nuclear power and the explosion of atomic bombs.

Einstein was in California in January 1933 when Hitler came to power. As the most famous living Jew he became a prime target of Nazi hostility and was almost immediately deprived of his posts in Berlin. He moved to England and later to the United States, where he accepted a permanent position at the Institute for Advanced Study in Princeton, New Jersey. In 1939 he signed a letter to President Franklin D. Roosevelt calling attention to the progress of physics in Germany and warning of the real danger that the Nazis might develop a uranium bomb. Although of a mild and retiring nature, Einstein remained firm in his opposition to Hitler and Nazism. As a lifelong pacifist, a humanitarian, and a critic of unrestrained nationalism, he regarded the Third Reich as a throwback to barbarism and as a disaster for civilization. He died in Princeton on April 18, 1955.

Bibliography. Ronald William Clark, *Einstein: The Life and Times,* The World Publishing Company, New York, 1971.

EINTOPF (One-Pot Meal). Propaganda term used by Nazi officials during World War II to exhort the public to eat a weekly one-pot meal. The purpose was to conserve food, especially meat. Advertisements labeled the *Eintopf* "the meal of sacrifice for the Reich."

EISERNE FAUST (Mailed Fist). A paramilitary group in 1919. The purpose of the unit was to terrorize loyal followers of the Weimar Republic (q.v.). Among its members were Adolf Hitler and Ernst Roehm (qq.v.). While active in this group, Hitler, quite by accident he later said, met the members of a smaller party called the Deutsche Arbeiterpartei (q.v.), the German Workers' party, which he joined and eventually led.

EISERNE FRONT (Iron Front). A loose union of democratically minded anti-Nazi political parties, including the Social Democrats. The Eiserne Front was organized in March 1932 to support the reelection of President Paul von Hindenburg (q.v.). It was interested primarily in helping the victor of Tannenberg against Hitler, the politically rising candidate of the Nationalsozialistische Deutsche Arbeiterpartei (q.v.). Von Hindenburg won the second election of April 10, 1932, with 53 percent of the vote to Hitler's 36.8 percent. The Eiserne Front was never formally transformed into a political party or a union of parties.

EISERNES KREUZ (EK; Iron Cross). A military decoration for heroism. The Iron Cross was originated by King Frederick William III of Prussia on March 10, 1813. Originally, there were three classes: Iron Cross (Second Class), Iron Cross (First Class), and Grand Cross. In its special form of a gold breast star it was awarded only twice, to Gen. Gebhart Leberecht Prince Blücher von Wahlstatt, after the defeat of Napoleon at Waterloo (1815), and to Gen. Paul von Hindenburg (q.v.), the World War I hero (1918). By the original terms the Iron Cross was to be reinstituted at the outbreak of a major war: after 1813 this was done three times (1870, 1914, and 1939). On September 1, 1939, at the beginning of World War II, Hitler announced the revival of the medal, but he changed its grading, design, and ribbon. He introduced a new grade termed the *Ritterkreuz* (Knight's Cross; *see* RITTERKREUZ for a summary of the variation in grades). In World War II the following medals were awarded: Iron Cross, 6,973; Knight's Cross with Oak Leaves, 853; Knight's Cross with Oak Leaves and Swords, 150; Knight's Cross with Oak Leaves, Swords, and Diamonds, 27; Knight's Cross with Golden Oak Leaves, Swords, and Diamonds, awarded only to Col. Hans-Ulrich Rudel (q.v.).

The Iron Cross (Second Class).

In setting conditions for an award of the Iron Cross, Hitler abolished the decoration for noncombat service. Women were declared eligible, but only one woman received the medal in World War II. Hitler personally decorated Hanna Reitsch (q.v.) with the Iron Cross (Second Class) in March 1941 and the Iron Cross (First Class) in October 1942 for her services as a test pilot for military aircraft. Hitler himself had been awarded the Iron Cross (First Class) on August 4, 1918, for valor in combat. It was the main decoration he wore together with the Party Golden Badge and the Wound Badge of World War I.

EL ALAMEIN. One of the decisive battles of World War II. On July 1, 1942, Gen. Erwin Rommel (q.v.), known as the Desert Fox, ordered his men of the Afrika Korps (q.v.) to stop at El Alamein, a stony, waterless desert spot about 60 miles west of Alexandria. Early the next month, Prime Minister Winston Churchill placed Gen. Bernard Law Montgomery in charge of the British Eighth Army. Throughout the summer, reinforcements—jeeps, trucks, Sherman tanks, planes, and ammunition—were rushed to Montgomery from England and the United States. Montgomery waited to strike until he had superiority in armor and in the air. Reorganizing his army with extreme care, he used deception on a vast scale, convincing the Germans that he would strike in the south instead of in the north. He spoke coldly to his troops: "Kill Germans, even the *padres*—one per weekday and two on Sundays."

On October 23, 1942, Montgomery hurled his full strength against the Germans. First came a violent artillery attack. The whole horizon burst into tongues of flame. Then 41,000 troops, 9,000 vehicles of all kinds, and 1,000 tanks surged forward on the Afrika Korps. Australians, Englishmen, Scots, New Zealanders, and South Africans pushed forward. Rommel, at this time in Germany for medical attention, had drawn up defensive plans. At Hitler's urgent request he rushed back to North Africa by plane, only to find that the Battle of El Alamein was lost. When his counterattack failed, Rommel decided to withdraw on the night of November 2–3, 1942.

El Alamein was one of the great turning points of the war, a tremendous victory for the Allies and a disheartening defeat for Hitler. "It may almost be said," commented Churchill, "before Alamein we never had a victory, after Alamein we never had a defeat."

ELBE. Code name for an earlier version of Augsburg (q.v.; 1939) meaning "Delay offensive in the west."

ELECTORAL DISTRICT. *See* WAHLKREIS.

ELITE GUARD. *See* SS.

ELSAS, FRITZ (1890–1945). Lawyer, mayor of Berlin, and close friend of Carl Friedrich Goerdeler (q.v.), civilian leader of the Resistance (q.v.). Fritz Elsas was born in Bad Cannstatt, Württemberg, on July 11, 1890. Successful in public administration, he served as legal adviser to the

Fritz Elsas. [*From Annedore Leber (ed.),* Conscience in Revolt, *tr. by Rosemary O'Neill, Vallentine, Mitchell & Co., Ltd., London, 1957*]

city of Stuttgart, president of the German Association of Municipal Councils, and mayor of Berlin (1931). His career in public life ended in 1933 because of his Jewish descent. Arrested as an associate of Goerdeler, he was tortured in the Gestapo (q.v.) prison on the Lehrterstrasse and executed by the SS (q.v.) at Sachsenhausen on January 4, 1945.

ELTZ-RÜHENACH, PAUL FREIHERR VON (1875–1943). Reich Minister of Post and Communications in Hitler's original Cabinet. Paul von Eltz-Rühenach was born in Wahn, Mülheim am Rhein, on February 7, 1875, the son of a *Rittergutsbesitzer* (manorial lord). After attending a humanistic *Gymnasium* (high school), he served in World War I, first in the field and later at Supreme Headquarters as an expert on railroads. He was awarded the Iron Cross (First and Second Classes). After the war he worked with the German railway system and in 1921 became its president. He was named Reich Minister of Post and Communications in 1932 and was retained by Hitler in that office after the Nazi assumption of power. Eltz-Rühenach died in Linz in 1943.

EMERGENCY FORCE. *See* BEREITSCHAFT.

ENABLING ACT (Gesetz zur Erhebung der Not von Volk und Reich). The single law providing the constitutional foundation for Hitler's dictatorship. The Law to Remove the Distress of People and State, enacted on March 24, 1933, represented an alteration of the Weimar Constitution. The Reichstag (q.v.) passed the bill by a vote of 441 to 94. The text of the law follows:[1]

> The Reichstag has resolved the following law, which is, with the approval of the National Council, herewith promulgated, after it has been established that the requirements have been satisfied for legislation altering the Constitution.
>
> ARTICLE 1. National laws can be enacted by the National Cabinet as well as in accordance with the procedure established in the Constitution. This applies also to the laws referred to in article 85, paragraph 2, and in article 87 of the Constitution.
>
> ARTICLE 2. The national laws enacted by the National Cabinet may deviate from the Constitution so far as they do not affect the position of the Reichstag and National Council. The powers of the President remain undisturbed.
>
> ARTICLE 3. The national laws enacted by the National Cabinet are prepared by the Chancellor and published in the *Reichsgesetzblatt*. They come into effect, unless otherwise specified, upon the day following their publication. Articles 68 to 77 of the Constitution do not apply to the laws enacted by the National Cabinet.
>
> ARTICLE 4. Treaties of the Reich with foreign states which concern matters of national legislation do not require the consent of the bodies participating in legislation. The National Cabinet is empowered to issue the necessary provisions for the execution of these treaties.
>
> ARTICLE 5. This law becomes effective on the day of publication. It becomes invalid on April 1, 1937; it further becomes invalid when the present National Cabinet is replaced by another.
>
> Berlin, March 24, 1933
>
> *Reich President* VON HINDENBURG
> *Reich Chancellor* ADOLF HITLER
> *Reich Minister of the Interior* FRICK
> *Reich Minister for Foreign Affairs*
> BARON VON NEURATH
> *Reich Minister of Finances*
> COUNT SCHWERIN VON KROSIGK

[1]United States Department of State, *National Socialism: Basic Principles*, prepared by Raymond E. Murphy, F. B. Stevens, Howard Trivers, and Joseph M. Roland, Government Printing Office, Washington, 1943, pp. 217–218. Courtesy United States Government Printing Office.

ENDLÖSUNG, DIE (The Final Solution). The cover name *(Deckname)* of Hitler's plan to destroy all the Jews in Europe. Although estimates vary, about 6 million Jews were annihilated during World War II by officials of the Nazi regime.

In *Mein Kampf* (q.v.) Hitler called the Jews "destroyers of civilization" and urged a drastic solution of the long conflict between German Nordics and Jews (*see* RACIAL DOCTRINE). When he won political power in 1933, he immediately began an active program to purge the Third Reich of Jewish influence. As the process of *Gleichschaltung* (q.v.), or coordination, proceeded, Jews were driven from public life and were reduced to the status of second-class citizens. The process moved from exclusion to persecution, then to expulsion, and ultimately to annihilation. Every Nazi aggression in Europe diminished the possibility of Jewish escape or resistance.

The year 1941 marked a turning point in the anti-Jewish campaign. The invasion of the Soviet Union on June 22 unleashed Hitler's sense of destructive nihilism. Enmeshed in total war, he saw Jews in the way of victory. Several million Jews were incarcerated in Polish ghettos. Emigration was costly. A project initiated in 1940 to expel the Jews to Africa had failed (*see* MADAGASCAR PLAN). Hitler decided on a drastic move. At this time the idea of a "final solution," or what he called a "territorial solution," began to form in his mind. The plan called for the complete elimination of European Jewry. Hitler's *idée fixe* would be implemented at long last.

At the Wannsee Conference (q.v.), held on January 20, 1942, the course of action was completed: "In the course of the execution of the Final Solution, Europe will be combed from west to east" (*see* WANNSEE PROTOCOL).

Responsibility for the project was placed in the hands of Heinrich Himmler and his assistants in the Gestapo (qq.v.). Under their guidance the Nazi apparatus went into action. The extermination camps (q.v.) of Poland began to operate at full blast. Jews inside Germany, already under legal and economic restrictions, were rounded up and sent to labor camps regarded as way stations to extermination camps. The action was disguised as "resettlement in the East," and deception was used to lead doomed Jews to the gas chambers. Most were killed, although some managed to save their lives despite incredibly bad conditions in Nazi-founded ghettos.

The campaign spread from the ghettos of Poland to virtually every nation in Nazi-controlled Europe. Each country reacted in its own way, depending upon its special history, traditions, and attitude toward Jews and upon the strength of the Nazi pressure. Most of the Jewish citizens of Poland, the Netherlands, Greece, and Czechoslovakia were killed in the gas chambers. About half of the Jews in Romania and Hungary perished. Most Jews managed to survive in Denmark and Bulgaria, where the local population offered them protection and escape possibilities.

The campaign of destruction was unprecedented. There had been violence against Jews throughout history, but nothing to compare with the *Endlösung* in dimensions and total configuration. The uniqueness of the phenomenon required the coinage of a new word, genocide (q.v.), to describe it. *See also* HOLOCAUST.

Bibliography. Raul Hilberg, *The Destruction of the German Jews,* Quadrangle Books, Inc., Chicago, 1961; Nora Levin, *The Holocaust: The Destruction of European Jewry, 1933–1945,* Thomas Y. Crowell Company, New York, 1968; Gerald Reitlinger, *Die Endlösung,* Colloquium, Berlin, 1953.

ENEMIES OF THE PEOPLE. *See* VOLKSSCHÄDLINGE.

ENSIGN. *See* STANDARTE.

ENTARTETE KUNST (Degenerate Art). Forms of modern art to which Hitler objected. A frustrated artist himself, the Fuehrer leaned toward realism and rejected all modern art from expressionism to cubism as *Verfallskunst,* or *entartete Kunst* (degenerate art). In 1936 he authorized Professor Adolf Ziegler, president of the Reich Chamber of Visual Arts and a prominent painter, to head a purge tribunal to confiscate all specimens of decadent art from more than 100 museums in Germany. The jury collected 12,890 works of art, of which 700 were sold in Lucerne to obtain foreign currency for armaments. Expropriated were paintings by 112 artists, including 1,000 by Emil Nolde, 500 by Max Beckmann, 400 by Oskar Kokoschka, and 200 by George Grosz (qq.v.). There were also paintings by such non-German artists as Picasso, Gauguin, Matisse, Cézanne, Dufy, Chirico, and Van Gogh.

On March 31, 1937, the confiscated paintings were shown at the Exhibit of Degenerate Art in Munich. This was the most popular display ever staged in the Third Reich. More than 2 million visitors stared at the unframed paintings under such captions as: "Thus did sick minds view Nature!" and "German Peasants in the Yiddish Manner." Later, in March 1939, 4,829 of these paintings were burned at fire department headquarters in Berlin.

A concurrent exhibition, titled the Greater Germany Art Exhibition and composed of approved paintings, was held nearby in a specially constructed building designed in neoclassical style by the architect Paul Ludwig Troost (q.v.) and Hitler. Here some 900 works, mostly selected by Hitler from among 15,000 submitted, were exhibited. On the opening day thousands of Nazis turned out to gaze at the paintings, most of which stressed challenging heroism or soulful elevation. There were rustic family scenes, Storm Troopers marching with their banners, and fruit harvesting by bare-bosomed Amazons. Nazi critics spoke glowingly of the new Spartan, robust German art, "purged of pretentiousness and crazy rubbish."

See also ART IN THE THIRD REICH.

ENTNAZIFIZIERUNG. *See* DENAZIFICATION.

EPP, FRANZ XAVER RITTER VON (1868–1947). National Socialist politician and general. Franz von Epp was born in Munich on October 16, 1868. After service in World War I, he became a leader of a *Freikorps* (q.v.) unit, one of the postwar rightist freebooter bands. He was one of Hitler's earliest supporters. In 1921 he obtained the final 60,000 marks required by Hitler to purchase the Nazi party's first newspaper, the *Völkischer Beobachter* (q.v.). When the SA (q.v.) was reorganized in 1926, Von Epp became its area commander in Munich. He hoped to have the SA supplant the regular Army when Hitler came to power. He was in charge of a special "defense political" office called the *Wehrpolitisches Amt,* the five divisions of which were concerned with external and defense policy, defense forces, and the like. But neither he nor Hitler was ever able to make the SA anything better than a motley band of street brawlers. In 1928 Von Epp became a *Mitglied* (delegate) to the Reichstag (q.v.), representing Upper Bavaria–Swabia for the NSDAP (Nationalsozialistische Deutsche Arbeiterpartei, q.v.).

On March 9, 1933, shortly after Hitler became Chancellor but two weeks before the Enabling Act (q.v.) was adopted, Von Epp, on Hitler's order, dismissed the government of Bavaria and set himself up as *Statthalter* (Governor). He held this post until the fall of the Third Reich. That summer Hitler appointed him *Reichsleiter* (Reich leader) of the NSDAP. In 1934 he was made *Landesjägermeister* (master of the hunt) in Bavaria, and in 1936 he was appointed Reich leader of the Colonial Office. He died in an American internment camp in 1947.

ERBHÖFE (Hereditary Estates). Special farms set up under the Hereditary Farm Law of September 29, 1933.

ERBHOFGESETZ (Hereditary Farm Law). A special law adopted on September 29, 1933, designed to create a farmer aristocracy.

ERDMAN, LOTHAR (1888–1939). Socialist journalist beaten to death in Sachsenhausen (q.v.) concentration camp. Lothar Erdman was born in Halle on October 12, 1888, the son of a professor of philosophy. After studying history and philosophy at Bonn and Freiburg, he went to London for further study and there gave his allegiance to

Lothar Erdman. [*From Annedore Leber (ed.),* Conscience in Revolt, *tr. by Rosemary O'Neill, Vallentine, Mitchell & Co., Ltd., London, 1957*]

Fabian socialism. A company commander on the western front in World War I, he worked as a journalist and trade unionist after the war. After the Nazis took over the trade unions in 1933, he worked in straitened circumstances as a free-lance journalist. When World War II broke out in 1939, he was sent to Sachsenhausen "for preventative reasons." Protesting the treatment of fellow prisoners, he was kicked and beaten viciously and suffered internal injuries, from which he died on September 18, 1939. Erdman was one among many thousands who met with the same fate.

ERNST, KARL (1904–1934). Storm Trooper leader executed in the 1934 Blood Purge (q.v.). Born in Wilmersdorf, Berlin, Karl Ernst was a hotel bellhop and a bouncer in a café frequented by intellectuals. He joined the Nazi party in 1923 at the age of nineteen. A handsome young man, he attracted the attention of Capt. Ernst Roehm (q.v.), the SA (q.v.) leader, who added Ernst to his intimate circle of young men. On April 4, 1931, Roehm promoted Ernst to the post of supreme SA leader of Berlin and Brandenburg Province. Through Roehm's influence Ernst was elected *Mitglied* (delegate) to the German Reichstag (q.v.) in 1932. Early in 1934 he was promoted to *SS-Gruppenfuehrer* (lieutenant general) and was attached to the supreme leadership of the national SA. On June 30, 1934, Ernst drove to Bremen with his bride to board a ship for a honeymoon in Madeira. As his automobile neared Bremen, he was overtaken by SS gunmen, who fired on the car, wounding his bride and his chauffeur. Knocked unconscious, Ernst was flown back to Berlin and executed in the Blood Purge (q.v.).

ESCORT GUARD SS. *See* BEGLEITKOMMANDO-SS.

ESSER, HERMANN (1900–). Cofounder *(Gründungsmitglied)* of the NSDAP (Nationalsozialistische Deutsche Arbeiterpartei, q.v.), the Nazi party, prototype of the early Nazi, and one of Hitler's closest comrades-in-arms in the opening days of the Nazi movement. Hermann Esser was classed with Julius Streicher (q.v.) as one of the worst Jew baiters in the Third Reich, but unlike Streicher he was not brought to trial at Nuremberg. He owed his survival to the fact that his character, personality, and private life were too unsavory even for the Nazi hierarchy. Hitler was careful to keep him in posts of comparatively minor importance in which he could not cause too much damage to the party.

Hermann Esser was born in Rohrmoos, near Dachau in Bavaria, on July 29, 1900, the son of a civil servant. He studied at the humanistic *Gymnasium* (high school) in Kempten, Allgäu, and while still in his teens served in World War I. He returned from the war as a radical socialist, organized a revolutionary students' council, and then took a job as a reporter for a left-wing provincial newspaper. Together with Anton Drexler (q.v.), Esser formed the Deutsche Arbeiterpartei (q.v.), the German Workers' party, the forerunner of the Nazi party. The new political group's platform stressed extreme nationalism and anti-Semitism (q.v.).

As member No. 2 of the fledgling party, Esser formed an attachment to Adolf Hitler, who was member No. 7. Both were employed early in 1920 by the new Reichswehr (q.v.) dictatorship in Bavaria as speakers in the press office of the regional Army headquarters at Munich. The twenty-year-old Esser was an effective orator, the only real competitor as a speaker to Hitler in the early days of the movement. Both were rabble-rousers who made emotional attacks on the establishment.

Konrad Heiden describes Esser as "the arch-type of the National Socialist," who lacked the inhibitions that even Hitler had. Crude and uncultured, of low moral character, Esser was involved in one escapade after another. A brash, arrogant rowdy, he was arrested again and again for unlawful behavior. The scandals in his private life proved to be a liability even for the Nazi party. It was charged that, when a woman friend became pregnant, he refused to marry her until she appealed directly to Hitler. It was rumored that the latter ordered Esser to do his duty "for the sake of the honor of the Party and its leadership." Later Hitler became godfather to the couple's son.

The youthful Esser was a clever tactician in the political turmoil that engulfed Munich in the immediate postwar years. He was one of Hitler's most loyal supporters and the first publicly to call Hitler *"the* Leader." A gifted propagandist, he produced brutal posters for display on the streets. His eloquence brought many new members to the struggling political party. Consumed by ambition, he was always an opportunist. On one occasion, it was said that when he did not receive his salary punctually from the party, he became furious and threatened to bolt to the Communists. They would pay him well, he intimated, for revealing the innermost Nazi secrets. When told about this threat of defection, Hitler was not surprised: "I know that Hermann Esser is a rascal, but I must use him as long as he is of any use. I must keep him near me so that I can watch him." And again: "I can use him as a speaker for a certain type of public. But I shall never give him political responsibility."

Hitler's attitude toward Esser remained ambivalent. On the one hand, he preferred the company of Esser and old party comrades such as Dietrich Eckart (q.v.), Drexler, and Streicher. He felt closer to them than to the newer "intellectuals" of the movement, including Gottfried Feder, Rudolf Hess, and Alfred Rosenberg (qq.v.). On the other hand, Hitler was careful to see that although Esser was rewarded with minor posts, he would never rise to a position of real power. In 1920 Hitler made Esser editor of the *Völkischer Beobachter* (q.v.), the party's new official organ. From 1923 to 1925 Esser was a propaganda leader of the NSDAP.

Esser played a prominent role in the struggle for Munich, but he did not take part in the unsuccessful 1923 Beer-Hall *Putsch* (q.v.). Pleading illness, he remained in bed on that historic occasion, thereby earning from Hitler the label of "a conceited coward." Esser fled to Austria. When he returned to Germany in January 1924, he was sentenced to three months' imprisonment for breaching the peace. After his release, he successfully ingratiated himself with Hitler by visits to Landsberg Prison, where the Fuehrer was serving his own term.

At this time a violent feud broke out in party ranks between the Bavarian "conservatives," led by Esser and Streicher, and the north German "socialists," including Gregor and Otto Strasser (qq.v.) and Alfred Rosenberg (*see* SECOND REVOLUTION). Each side excoriated the other in the bitter political infighting. Gregor Strasser denounced Esser: "His private life is immoral. His actions are egotistic and *unvölkisch*. His behavior in November 1923 was cowardly and most unworthy of a real National Socialist." Esser replied in equally hostile terms. Hitler, who regarded the split as dangerous, angrily ordered his lieutenants to "end these squabbles."

In 1926 Esser quarreled with Streicher. The Fuehrer took Streicher's side and forbade Esser the right to continue using the familiar *Du*. Esser countered heatedly by threatening to disclose party secrets. Hitler bought him off by making him editor of the new *Illustrierter Beobachter* (q.v.). Esser held this post for six years. As editor in chief, he published scandals that titillated a wide audience but struck fear among blackmail-shy members of the Nazi hierarchy.

In 1928, when Gustav Stresemann (q.v.), then Minister of Foreign Affairs, went to Munich to deliver a speech on behalf of the government, Esser, at the head of 500 Storm Troopers (*see* SA), invaded the gallery and, shouting "*Juda Verrecke!*" (q.v.), prevented Stresemann from speaking. In 1928 Esser became a member of the county council of Upper Bavaria. The next year he began to serve on the Munich City Council, and in 1932 he became a delegate to the Bavarian Landtag (Legislature, or Diet). Shortly after Hitler assumed political power in 1933, Esser was appointed to several administrative posts: Bavarian minister of economics, chief of the Bavarian State Chancellery, delegate to and president of the Bavarian Landtag, and member of the German Reichstag (q.v.), representing Wahlkreis (Electoral District) Upper Bavaria–Swabia.

In his post as minister of economics, Esser was said to have forced Bavarian industrialists to contribute large sums to the state treasury. Esser came out second best in a bitter personal conflict with Adolf Wagner (q.v.), Bavarian minister of the interior. Hitler deposed Esser in March 1935, ostensibly because of "administrative reform" but more probably because of Esser's continuing scandalous personal life. It was alleged, among other charges, that Esser had assaulted a young girl, the daughter of a prominent Munich businessman, and that subsequently there had been a nasty public scene.

Even then Hitler did not drop the man who knew too much about the inside affairs of the party. On December 12, 1939, he made Esser Vice President of the Reichstag. The same year he appointed his difficult comrade to the relatively obscure post of Secretary of State for Tourist Traffic, an office connected with the Reich Ministry for Public Enlightenment and Propaganda. At this time Esser published a virulent anti-Semitic book, *The Jewish World Pest*, written in the style popularized by Streicher's *Der Stürmer* (*see* STÜRMER, DER).

During World War II Esser faded into the background. Now and then he appeared as a speaker on festive occasions, and on February 24, 1943, he was the main speaker at the twenty-third anniversary of the founding of the Nazi party celebrated by the *Alte Kämpfer* (q.v.) at a beer hall in Munich. Esser's attempts to regain Hitler's favor were unsuccessful. After the war Esser had reason to be grateful for his lack of prominence in the late days of the Third Reich. While other Nazi leaders had to stand trial at Nuremberg, Esser escaped attention. He was arrested by the Americans but, judged of minor importance, was released in 1947.

On August 8, 1949, a Munich denazification (q.v.) court declared Esser to be a major offender as one of the oldest propagators of Nazi ideology. He was sentenced *in absentia* to five years' forced labor, confiscation of all his property, and loss of civil rights for life. In 1949 Esser was publicized in the German press as the author of a series of newspaper articles on "The Great Lover—Adolf Hitler."

ETHNIC GERMANS. *See* VOLKSDEUTSCHE.

EUTHANASIA PROGRAM. Eugenic measures designed to improve the quality of the German "race" (*see* RACIAL DOCTRINE). On July 14, 1933, the Law for the Protection of Hereditary Health was promulgated for this purpose. This was the beginning of a development that culminated in enforced "mercy" deaths for the incurably insane and in plans for exterminating peoples said to be biologically inferior, such as Jews, Poles, Russians, and Gypsies. The program comprised three major classifications: (1) euthanasia for incurables, (2) direct extermination by *Sonderbehandlung* (special treatment), and (3) experiments in mass sterilization.

Hitler supported the program as a stimulus to "national health" and the "racial integrity of the German people." In 1935 he stated that if war came, he would implement the idea of euthanasia, "because I am of the opinion that such a program could be put into effect more smoothly and readily in time of war, that in the general upheaval of war the open resistance to be anticipated on the part of the Church would not play the part that might be expected." To ensure secrecy, only tried and trusted Nazis and SS (q.v.) leaders were enlisted to implement the program. In the course of World War II the Nazi leadership began to show less and less restraint in the destruction of Jews and captured Eastern peoples. Sterilization was induced by medication, x-ray, and intrauterine irritation. At the same time there were experiments involving high altitude, low temperature, and the drinking of seawater as well as experiments with typhus, infectious jaundice, bone grafting, and mustard gas.

On December 9, 1946, twenty-three SS physicians and scientists were brought to trial at Nuremberg before American Military Tribunal No. 1 for war crimes. Twenty of the defendants were physicians who stood at the top of the medical hierarchy of the Third Reich, while three occupied administrative posts. *See also* DOCTORS' TRIAL.

Bibliography. Alexander Mitscherlich and Fred Mielke, *Doctors of Infamy: The Story of the Nazi Medical Crimes,* by Heinz Norden, Henry Schuman, New York, 1949.

EXHIBIT OF DEGENERATE ART. *See* ENTARTETE KUNST.

EXTERMINATION CAMPS (Death Camps). Concentration camps (q.v.) that specialized in the execution of unwanted persons in the Third Reich. Originally, concentration camps were designed as prisons for "preventive custody." After the outbreak of World War II in 1939, some of the camps were transformed into extermination centers to implement the policy of genocide (q.v.; *see* ENDLÖSUNG, DIE). The more important extermination camps were located in occupied Poland, such as those at Auschwitz, Maidanek, and Treblinka (qq.v.). *See also* HOLOCAUST.

EXTRAORDINARY PACIFICATION ACTION. *See* AB AKTION.

F

"FAHNE HOCH, DIE" to FW-190

"FAHNE HOCH, DIE" ("Hold High the Banner!"). A name for the "Horst Wessel Lied" (q.v.), the official Nazi anthem. *Die Fahne Hoch* were the first three words of the opening verse.

FAITH AND BEAUTY. *See* GLAUBE UND SCHÖNHEIT.

FALKENHAUSEN, ALEXANDER FREIHERR VON (1878–1966). General of infantry. Alexander von Falkenhausen was born in the Blumenthal manor, Neisse District, on October 29, 1878. In World War I he won the coveted Pour le Mérite decoration for extraordinary courage in combat. After the war he commanded the School of Infantry at Dresden, where Erwin Rommel (q.v.) was one of his students. From 1934 to 1939 he served as the last of a succession of German military advisers to Chiang Kai-shek. Despite his protest, he was ordered by the Fuehrer to return with his staff to Germany. From 1940 to 1944 he was assigned the military command in Belgium and northern France. He had some sympathy for the Resistance (q.v.) movement, but the conspirators avoided him because of his record in the shooting of Belgian hostages. In 1944 he was arrested by the Gestapo (q.v.) after the July Plot (q.v.) and sent to Dachau (q.v.) concentration camp, from which he was liberated by American troops on April 28, 1945. He was subsequently rearrested by American military authorities and turned over to the Belgians. Tried by a Belgian military tribunal, he was accused of executing hostages and deporting Jews and Belgian workers. On March 9, 1951, he was sentenced to twelve years' penal servitude but was soon released. He died in Nassau on July 31, 1966.

FALLSCHIRMTRUPPEN (FST; Parachute Troops). Airborne troops used successfully by the Germans in *Blitzkrieg* (q.v.) tactics, especially in the attack on Crete on May 20, 1941.

FARMERS' ASSOCIATION. *See* LANDBUND.

FAULHABER, MICHAEL VON (1869–1952). Cardinal of the Roman Catholic Church in the Third Reich. Michael von Faulhaber was born in Klosterheidenfeld, Lower Franconia, on March 5, 1869. Ordained in the priesthood in 1892, he was appointed professor of Old Testament exegesis at Strassburg (Strasbourg) in 1903 and named Bishop of Speyer in 1911. He defended the German cause in World War I: "The war waged by Germany to avenge the murder at Sarajevo will go into the annals as the prototype of a just war." In 1917 he was appointed Archbishop of Munich-Freising, and in 1921 he became a cardinal. In his post Von Faulhaber was a firm leader of Bavarian Catholicism. He energetically defended his church and its teachings. Although he was aware that the Weimar Republic (q.v.) granted legal recognition to all denominations, he was not altogether satisfied with this recognition and criticized it in 1920 as "granting the same rights to truth and error."

The coming of the Hitler regime brought Von Faulhaber face to face with a dilemma. He tried to steer a middle course between the requirements of his church and the demands of the Nazi authorities. Several days after the March 1933 elections, he made his *ad limina* required visit to Rome to report to Pope Pius XI (q.v.) on the new situation in Germany. On his return he reported to a conference of Bavarian bishops that the Pope had publicly praised Chancellor Hitler for his stand against communism. Von Faulhaber gave the Pope a lengthy memorandum stressing the differences between the German and Italian Fascist movements.

The Cardinal was pleased by the conclusion of the Concordat of 1933 (q.v.) between the Third Reich and the Catholic Church. Almost immediately, however, it became clear that Hitler did not propose to abide strictly by the terms of this agreement. In November 1933, Von Faulhaber protested the threatening relapse into paganism, defended the Old Testament, and warned that "the individual must not be deprived of his own dignity or be treated as a slave without rights of his own." Informed in June 1936 that a Swiss Catholic had asked his children to

Michael Cardinal von Faulhaber. [*Ullstein*]

pray for the death of Hitler, Von Faulhaber ordered prayers for the Fuehrer: "Catholic men, we will now pray together a *paternoster* for the life of the Fuehrer."

Despite continuing attacks on the church, Von Faulhaber worked to smooth relations with the Nazi authorities. On November 4, 1936, he was received by Hitler at the Berghof (q.v.), the Obersalzberg retreat. In a conference lasting three hours the Fuehrer sought to allay the fears of the churchman. "The Catholic Church," Hitler warned, "should not deceive itself. If National Socialism does not succeed in defeating Bolshevism, then both Church and Christianity are also finished in Europe. Bolshevism is the mortal enemy of the Church as much as it is of Fascism." In 1938, at the time of the *Anschluss* (q.v.) with Austria, Von Faulhaber asked Catholics to pray for the peaceful cooperation of church and state in the Greater German Reich. In the Czech crisis of late 1938 he ordered German bishops to send a letter of congratulations to Hitler for "this great deed of safeguarding international peace." At the same time he tried to alleviate the suffering of victims of Nazism.

On November 9, 1938, during the anti-Jewish riots of the *Kristallnacht* (q.v.), the Night of the Broken Glass, Von Faulhaber revealed his sympathy for the Jews by providing a truck for the Chief Rabbi of Munich to rescue religious objects from his synagogue before it was demolished. Carl Friedrich Goerdeler (q.v.), one of the central figures of the Resistance (q.v.), tried to draw Von Faulhaber to his side and informed him of the plot against Hitler. The Cardinal made no commitment despite the recurrence of anti-Catholic incidents. After the failure of the July Plot (q.v.) in 1944, Von Faulhaber was questioned vigorously by the Gestapo (q.v.), especially about his conference with Goerdeler. Von Faulhaber denounced the assassination attempt and affirmed his personal loyalty to Hitler. He died in Munich on June 12, 1952.

See also RELIGION IN THE THIRD REICH.

Bibliography. Michael von Faulhaber, *Judaism, Christianity, and Germany*, tr. by G. D. Smith, The Macmillan Company, New York, 1935.

FEDER, GOTTFRIED (1883–1941). National Socialist party ideologist, a member of the *Alte Kämpfer* (q.v.), or old guard, and an early economics adviser to Hitler. Although Feder was influential in the early days, he remained a peripheral figure in the Third Reich. Born in Würzburg on January 27, 1883, he passed his examinations as an engineer in 1905 and settled in Munich, where he engaged in the construction of airplane hangars. Later he turned to political economy. Toward the end of World War I he became convinced that his country's economic ruin could be attributed to the manipulators of high finance. He favored retaining the capitalist system, especially such productive assets as factories, mines, and machines, but he would abolish the idea of interest because it created no value. The idea of "interest slavery" became the keynote of his teaching (*see* ZINSKNECHTSCHAFT). He formed an organization called the Deutscher Kampfbund zur Brechung der Zinsknechtschaft (German Alliance for the Destruction of Interest Slavery). He tried at first to interest Kurt Eisner, Communist leader of the Bavarian revolution in 1918, in his ideas but without success.

Early in 1919 Feder became a member of a tiny group called the Deutsche Arbeiterpartei (q.v.), the German Workers' party, under Anton Drexler (q.v.). Other early members were Capt. Ernst Roehm, Dietrich Eckart, Franz Xaver Ritter von Epp (qq.v.), and, later, Hitler. In May 1919 Hitler heard Feder speak before a meeting of the small party and was immediately converted. He told of the effect of the speech in *Mein Kampf* (q.v.): "For the first time in my life I saw the meaning of international capitalism. After I had heard Feder's first lecture, the thought flashed through my head that I had found the essential suppositions for the founding of a new party. . . . The development of Germany was clear enough to show me that the hardest battles of the future were to be fought not against enemy nations, but against international capital. I felt a powerful prophecy of this coming battle in Feder's lecture." For Hitler, Feder's separation between stock exchange capital and the national economy offered the possibility of going into battle against the internationalization of the German economy without threatening the founding of an independent national economy by a fight against capital. Best of all, from Hitler's point of view, was the fact that he could identify international capitalism as wholly Jewish-controlled. Hitler soon became a member of the German Workers' party, and Feder became his friend and guide.

Feder assisted Anton Drexler and Dietrich Eckart in writing the Twenty-five Points of the German Workers' party, which later became the program of the Nationalsozialistische Deutsche Arbeiterpartei (q.v.), the Nazi party. He was able to get the theme of his concept of interest slavery incorporated into the program.

From this point on Feder devoted his major activity to the Nazi cause, which he regarded as in sharp contrast to the current capitalism and its "Marxian satellites." He fell quickly into the National Socialist pattern, as witness these words:

> Fight for our life in the service of this powerful idea, fight for a New Germany. It would be no decent battle, if we did not have a symbol, a banner in the struggle! Our storm banners wave before our ranks. Always, young, beaming and brilliant, the *Hakenkreuz* [swastika], symbol of life awakening again, comes before our eyes. Our storm banners, our eagles, bear this symbol:

We are the army of the *Hakenkreuz*,
Wave the banners high,
We shall bring the German workers,
To the road of a new freedom!

Feder was the editor of the National Socialist Library, which included works attacking the Dawes Plan (q.v.), Freemasonry, capitalistic department stores, and the Jewish press evil. He edited *Die Flamme (The Flame)* in Nuremberg, *Der Streiter (The Fighter)* in Forchheim, and the *Hessenhammer (Hesse Hammer)* in Darmstadt. By this time he considered himself the highest intellectual arbiter of National Socialism.

In 1923, when Hitler returned from prison in Landsberg after the Munich Beer-Hall *Putsch* (q.v.), he found the party drawn toward two ideological factions. One was a populist, rural, racialist, anti-industrialist faction around Feder. The other was an urban, socialist, revolutionary faction gathered around the brothers Gregor and Otto Strasser (qq.v.). Feder promoted his own point of view vehemently in the Reichstag (q.v.), to which he was elected in 1924, and at party gatherings. On October 14, 1930, he introduced in the Reichstag a bill that would freeze interest rates at 4 percent and expropriate the property of those banking and stock exchange leaders who were Jews. For some years the Reichstag had paid no attention to such ideas, but the National Socialist party now had 107 representatives, or nearly one-third of its membership. Feder made it known that the party would create a belt of small peasant farms in the east, with "farm beside farm," and that he would smash the unprofitable large estates.

By this time Hitler, definitely on his way to political power, had become convinced that not only were Feder's populist views old-fashioned but they would hurt his own chance for supreme power. Dr. Hjalmar Schacht (q.v.) warned Hitler that Feder's economic planning apparatus would ruin the German economy. The Fuehrer had his choice between remaining with Feder's "old-fashioned ideas" and accepting support from such Rhineland industrialists as Gustav Krupp von Bohlen und Halbach and Fritz Thyssen (qq.v.) and the Siemens Company. As a matter of necessity, Hitler turned to the industrialists.

In July 1933, after Hitler assumed political power, Feder was rewarded with a humiliating minor position as Undersecretary in the Reich Ministry of Economics. In this post he was outranked by a Schacht man, Dr. Kurt Schmitt (q.v.), director of Germany's largest insurance company. Feder tried to organize a "rurban" (rural plus urban) settlement of farmers gathered around large cities, an activity that aroused the scorn of the Reichsnährstand, the leading farm organiztion. Further pressure was placed on Hitler, who at this time decided on rearmament and needed the goodwill and support of the Rhineland industrialists. The Fuehrer dismissed Feder from the Ministry of Economics in December 1934. Unlike the Old Bolsheviks, who were purged by Stalin, Feder was allowed to return to private life. Plaintively, he told Hitler that his ideas had won millions to the party but that millions who believed in his theories would now drift away. Feder saw the Third Reich as a revolution betrayed, but there was little he could do about it now. For his part the Fuehrer deserted the friend who dreamed of money reform. Feder died in Murnau on September 24, 1941.

Bibliography. Gottfried Feder, *Hitler's Official Programme and Its Fundamental Ideas*, George Allen & Unwin, Ltd., London, 1934.

FEGELEIN, HERMANN (1906–1945). Lieutenant general in the Waffen-SS (q.v.) and the liaison officer between Heinrich Himmler (q.v.) and Hitler. Hermann Fegelein was born in Ansbach, Middle Franconia, on October 30, 1906. Typical of the men who rose to prominence during the Nazi regime, he started his career as an unknown, almost-illiterate groom and then became a jockey. In this capacity he had the good fortune to meet Christian Weber, a horse fancier and an old comrade of Hitler's who had amassed a huge fortune through questionable means by contacts in the Nazi party. With Weber as his patron, Fegelein rose to a high level in the Nazi hierarchy. Because of his work with horses he was named leader of the first Reiter-SS (q.v.), a mounted cavalry brigade. From May to December 1942 he was inspector of cavalry and transport in the Reich Central Security Office (Reichssicherheitshauptamt, q.v.), and on December 2, 1942, was promoted to *SS-Oberfuehrer* (brigadier general). On October 30, 1943, he was wounded in combat. He was then sent to the Fuehrer's headquarters to act as liaison officer for Himmler. He rose still higher in the Nazi order when he married Gretl Braun, the sister of Eva Braun (q.v.).

Fegelein was a member of the group surrounding Hitler during the last days in the *Fuehrerbunker* (q.v.). Concerned for his own safety, he quietly slipped away on April 26, 1945, to his home in the Charlottenburg district of Berlin. The next day Hitler noted his disappearance and sent an armed SS (q.v.) search party to find him. Brought back to the Chancellery, Fegelein was stripped of his rank and placed under arrest. Fegelein's attempted escape aroused Hitler's suspicions of Himmler. On the evening of April 28 came word from Stockholm that Himmler was seeking to negotiate with the Allies behind the Fuehrer's back. Hitler raged at the incredible news that Himmler, "my loyal Himmler," had also deserted him in his hour of need. He ordered Himmler's arrest ("A traitor must never succeed me as Fuehrer!"). Unable to place his hands on the greatest traitor of them all, Hitler turned his full wrath on the available Fegelein. He had Fegelein brought to him from the guardhouse and questioned him brusquely on Himmler's betrayal. Fegelein insisted that he knew nothing about it and, moreover, had intended to come back to the bunker. Eva Braun, by this time preparing for her own ritual death, made no effort to save her brother-in-law. An SS squad took Fegelein out into the Chancellery garden and shot him.

FEHME MURDER. *See* FEHMEMORD.

FEHMEGERICHTE (Fehme Courts). Secret courts in the Weimar Republic (q.v.) composed of rightist members of paramilitary organizations. The name was taken from the medieval *Fehmegerichte*, courts that dispensed a brutal form of justice at a time when ordinary law courts were without power. The *Fehmegerichte* of the early 1920s were set up to punish those suspected of denouncing rightist nationalists either to the Reich disarmament authorities or to the Allied Control Commission. Because members of the *Fehmegerichte* were also connected with the Reichswehr (q.v.), they became known as the Black Reichswehr. Such freebooter Fehmists as Edmund Heines (q.v.) eventually transferred their allegiance to the growing Nazi movement.

FEHMEMORD (Fehme Murder). Murder committed in the early 1920s by members of rightist paramilitary *Fehme* bands, sometimes called the Black Reichswehr. *See also* FEHMEGERICHTE.

FEINDHÖRER (Listeners to Enemy Broadcasts). Persons who listened to enemy broadcasts during World War II. They were included in the category of *Volksschädlinge* (q.v.), or enemies of the people. Teen-agers were encouraged to denounce their parents who made a practice of listening to the British BBC or other Allied broadcasts. *See also* RADIO IN THE THIRD REICH.

FEININGER, LYONEL (1871–1956). American artist rated in Nazi Germany as a purveyor of "degenerate art." Lyonel Feininger was born in New York on July 17, 1871, the son of a violinist. In 1883 he was taken to Germany to study music but turned instead to painting. He studied art in Hamburg, Berlin, and Paris and later joined the staff of the Bauhaus in Dessau. His paintings are distinguished by a delicate geometric style with complex interlocking translucent planes. Feininger left Germany in 1933, when Hitler came to power. In 1936 his works were included in the Exhibit of Degenerate Art (*see* ENTARTETE KUNST) in Munich. He died in New York on January 13, 1956.

FELDHERRN HALLE (Hall of Heroes). A great hall constructed in the middle of Munich to honor German military heroes. The November 9, 1923, confrontation between Hitler's Nazis and the Bavarian police took place near the Feldherrn Halle (*see* BEER-HALL PUTSCH).

FELDJÄGERKORPS (Sharpshooter Corps). A shock formation of the SA (q.v.) used in the early days of the Nazi movement to fight the battle of the streets against the Communists. The Feldjägerkorps was disbanded in 1933 after Hitler became Chancellor and was incorporated into the regular police.

FELIX. Code name for the prospective capture of Gibraltar, the Spanish Canary Islands, and the Portuguese Cape Verde Islands. In a directive issued on November 12, 1940, Hitler spoke of destroying the British position in the western Mediterranean. Gen. Francisco Franco was anxious to profit from Hitler's patronage, but he was unwilling to pay any price for it. Hitler was attracted by the possibility of isolating the British and regarded Gibraltar as a key point in this area. His directive was clear-cut:

> SPAIN AND PORTUGAL
>
> Political measures to bring about the entry into the war of Spain in the near future have been instituted. The aim of German intervention in the Iberian peninsula (cover name Felix) will be to drive the English from the Western Mediterranean.
>
> (*a*) Gibraltar is to be captured and the Straits closed.
>
> (*b*) The English are to be prevented from gaining a foothold at any other point on the Iberian peninsula or in the Atlantic Islands.

Hitler's ambition to close the Mediterranean to the British Fleet was never achieved. Within a month of this directive he quietly ordered that Felix be dropped "because the political conditions no longer exist."

See also ISABELLA.

FELLGIEBEL, ERICH FRITZ (1886–1944). Career officer and member of the conspiracy against Hitler. Erich Fritz Fellgiebel was born in Pöpelwitz bei Breslau on October 4, 1886. From 1939 to 1944 he served as chief of communications for the armed forces with the rank of *Generaloberst*

Gen. Erich Fritz Fellgiebel. [*Ullstein*]

(colonel general). Alienated by the philosophy of National Socialism, he was one of the high officers who took part in the unsuccessful July Plot (q.v.) in 1944. He was present at Rastenburg (*see* RASTENBURG CONFERENCE), where it was his task to block the signal circuits. Arrested, he was charged with treason and was hanged in Berlin on September 4, 1944.

FELLOWSHIP CLUB. *See* KAMERADSCHAFTSKLUB.

FELLOWSHIP LEADER. *See* KAMERADSCHAFTSFUEHRER.

FEUCHTWANGER, LION (1884–1958). German author of best-selling novels on historical and political subjects, especially on Jews in positions of power. Lion Feuchtwanger was born in Munich on July 7, 1884. He studied philosophy at Berlin and Munich. Later he published *Die hässliche Herzogin* (1923), translated as *The Ugly Duchess; Jud Süss* (1925), translated as *Power;* and *Der jüdische Krieg* (1932), translated as *Josephus.* Feuchtwanger's writings were suppressed during World War I because of their revolutionary content. Because of his Jewish parentage and the nature of his work he was forced to flee Germany in the early stage of the Hitler regime. Feuchtwanger was one of the earliest critics of Hitler and the Nazis. From London in 1934 he issued a strong statement entitled "Murder in Hitler Germany." He died in Los Angeles on December 21, 1958.

Bibliography. Lion Feuchtwanger, *Moscow, 1937,* tr. by Irene Josephs, The Viking Press, Inc., New York, 1937.

FEUERZAUBER (Fire Magic). Code name for an earlier version of Nordlicht (q.v.), the projected capture of Leningrad.

FIFTH COLUMN. Hitler's network of secret sympathizers and supporters engaged in espionage, sabotage, and other subversive activities inside foreign countries. The term *fifth column* originally referred to Franco sympathizers inside Madrid during the Spanish Civil War, as described by Gen. Emilio Mola in a radio address on October 1 or 2, 1936, while he was leading a column of troops against the city. He referred to a fifth column of sympathizers inside Madrid. Shortly after Hitler became Chancellor in 1933, a rumor spread that the Nazis were creating a worldwide network of conspirators to conquer nations from the inside. Nazi success with the *Anschluss* in Austria and the Munich Agreement (qq.v.) in Czechoslovakia lent credence to the belief in a German fifth column. The swift conquest of Poland in 1939 and of Denmark, Norway, the Low Countries, and France in 1940 seemed to confirm the idea. Fear of the German fifth column spread ahead of the German armies that penetrated Yugoslavia, Greece, and the Soviet Union. Later historical analysis revealed that there were only two groups comparable to the fifth column most people were certain existed; these were in Poland and Yugoslavia. The popular belief was much exaggerated during the period when Hitler overextended himself in Europe. It is probable that unreasoning fear of the German fifth column achieved more for Hitler than the fifth column itself.

Bibliography. Louis de Jong, *The German Fifth Column in the Second World War,* The University of Chicago Press, Chicago, 1956.

FIGHTER AIRCRAFT LEADER. *See* JAGDFLIEGERFUEHRER.

FIGHTER BOMBER. *See* JAGDBOMBER.

FIGHTER GROUP. *See* JAGDGESCHWADER.

FILMS IN THE THIRD REICH. "I want to exploit the film as an instrument of propaganda." This statement was made by Dr. Paul Joseph Goebbels (q.v.), Minister for Public Enlightenment and Propaganda. At Hitler's instigation, Goebbels was directed to achieve *Gleichschaltung* (q.v.), or coordination, of all the arts and media of communication in the Third Reich. The prospect of controlling the film industry was a task Goebbels relished, for not only was he interested in films, he was obsessed by them. As a young man he had been fascinated by motion pictures. In his position of political power in Nazi Germany he was able to do more than indulge in his favorite pastime: he could place his imprint upon every phase of the industry from production to acting to distribution.

Even on his busiest day, the Propaganda Minister found time to see at least one film and to write about it. His predilection for film actresses was never a secret. The little man with the piercing eyes, crippled foot, deep, resonant voice, and turned-on charm exerted a tremendous appeal on established film actresses as well as on ambitious starlets. Many could advance their careers if they could win the attention of the Propaganda Minister with the insatiable appetite for attractive women. Goebbels would entertain them either in the privacy of his office at the Ministry or at parties held frequently at his estate in Schwanenwerder, near Berlin.

The German film industry had won a worldwide reputation for originality and creativeness during the existence of the Weimar Republic (q.v.). Such films as *The Cabinet of Dr. Caligari* (1919) had set a new standard for film making. But the entire industry, in the view of Hitler and Goebbels, was permeated with Jewish influence. Goebbels's first concern was to purge Jews from every level of film making. He would "lift the film industry out of the sphere of liberal and economic thought" and clothe it in National Socialist ideology.

Accordingly, as soon as the Nazis achieved political power, Goebbels moved to eliminate Jews and liberals from the production of films. The great figures of German films were forced into compulsory or voluntary exile. Among them were the directors Fritz Lang, Wilhelm Dieterle, and Ernst Lubitsch; the composers of film music Kurt Weill (q.v.), Friedrich Hollander, Hanns Eisler, and Mischa Spoliansky; the actors Fritz Kortner (q.v.) and Conrad Veidt; and the actresses Elisabeth Bergner, Marlene Dietrich (qq.v.), and Mady Christians. Conrad Veidt, although not a Jew, wrote the word *Jude* (Jew) across a racial questionnaire, packed his bags, and left Germany in disgust. Brigitte Helm was accused of "race defilement" because she had married a Jew.

The campaign against Jews in films persisted throughout the life of the Third Reich. A Jewish actor named Leo Reuss fled from Germany to Vienna, where he dyed his hair and beard blond and specialized in Aryan roles much praised by Nazis. He then revealed himself as a Jew and emigrated to Hollywood. The beautiful actress Renate Müller, hounded by the Gestapo (q.v.), committed suicide in 1937 at age thirty rather than yield to harassment by Goebbels's Propaganda Ministry. All Germany was stirred by the case of Joachim Gottschalk (q.v.), one of the nation's most popular actors. The handsome young actor, who had married a Jew, repeatedly refused to follow a suggestion from Nazi officials that he divorce his wife and leave his half-Jewish child. In 1940 the Gestapo gave the wife, accused of *Rassenschande* (q.v.), or race defilement, and her child one day to pack and join the Jewish exodus. When Gestapo agents finally raided the home, they found Gottschalk, his wife, and his child dead. The news spread quickly through Berlin's artistic quarter, and there was a near revolt in the film studios.

Some film stars made their peace with the Nazi regime and decided to remain in Germany. These included the actors Emil Jannings, Heinrich George, Werner Kraus, and Gustav Gründgens (q.v.) and the actresses Lil Dagover and Pola Negri. The actress Anny Ondra, who was married to the boxer Max Schmeling (q.v.), continued to work during the Nazi period.

Three major Nazi propaganda films were produced during 1933 after Hitler had been named Chancellor on January 30. *SA-Mann Brand* (q.v.), which was meant as a tribute to Nazi Storm Troopers, was made at a Bavarian studio with a second-rate cast of unknown actors and a third-rate director. There was an impressive opening night at the Gloria Palast in Berlin as thousands of SA

A still from *Triumph des Willens.* [*Leni Riefenstahl Productions*]

members lined the streets to the theater. Within a few days audiences dwindled as Berliners flocked to an American film, *I Am a Fugitive from a Chain Gang,* starring Paul Muni. A second Nazi film, *Hitlerjunge Quex,* was based on the case of Herbert Norkus, a young boy reportedly murdered by Communists in 1932. Although his father and mother were dedicated Communists, the lad was drawn to the National Socialists and was said to have been murdered by drunken, crazed Communists. The picture was previewed by Hitler in Munich on November 12, 1933. The third film, *Hans Westmar,* a cinematic biography of Horst Wessel (q.v.), the Nazi martyr, was scheduled to appear on the anniversary of his birth. An earlier version entitled *Horst Wessel* was scrapped, and the remade picture, renamed *Hans Westmar,* opened on December 12, 1933. The film showed how Horst Wessel went to live in the East Berlin Communist stronghold, how he won many Communists to the Nazi cause, and how he was brutally shot by his enemies. It was technically the best of the three propaganda films produced under Nazi auspices.

Nazi control of films increased to an even greater degree in 1934 and 1935. On April 25, 1935, Goebbels, anxious to win prestige for the Nazi state, was host to the International Film Congress held at the Kroll Opera House (q.v.) in Berlin. Some 2,000 delegates representing forty nations attended the programs. That same year marked the appearance of *Triumph des Willens* (q.v.; *Triumph of the Will*), an impressive documentary produced by Leni Riefenstahl (q.v.) on the party rally held in Nuremberg on September 4–10, 1934. By 1937 the German film industry was virtually nationalized. In 1938 another striking documentary, *Olympia,* concerning the Olympic Games of 1936 (*see* OLYMPIAD XI), was produced by Leni Riefenstahl. In 1939 there began a series of anti-Semitic films, including *Die Rothschilds Aktien von Waterloo* (*The Rothschilds' Shares in Waterloo,* 1940) and *Jud Süss* (*The Jew Süss,* 1940). During the early years of World War II, Nazi films were filled with scenes of triumph, glorification of the fighting man, and denunciations of the enemy. By this time the public was thoroughly satiated with second-rate productions designed as propaganda. By 1943 the tone began to change to a plea for sustained morale. In the latter part of the war, when British and American bombing raids crippled the Nazi film industry in Berlin, production was transferred to Amsterdam, Budapest, and Rome.

During the life of the Third Reich from 1933 to 1945, the German film industry produced 1,363 feature films. These films, as well as shorts, newreels, and documentaries, had to be passed by the Propaganda Ministry before public showing. Most feature films were designed for escapism. Only a few of them were selected for propaganda purposes, but these were carefully chosen. The public, annoyed by boring films, generally stayed away. Before the war German audiences preferred American films, even the poorer ones, and crowded the UFA Palast, the country's largest cinema, to see the latest importations from Hollywood. During the war audiences dwindled.

Bibliography. David Stewart Hull, *Film in the Third Reich*, Simon and Schuster, New York, 1973.

FINAL SOLUTION, THE. *See* ENDLÖSUNG, DIE. *See also* WANNSEE CONFERENCE; WANNSEE PROTOCOL.

FIRE MAGIC. *See* FEUERZAUBER.

FISCHREIHER (Heron). Secret code name for the attack by Army Group B on Stalingrad in 1942. In a war directive dated July 23, 1942, Hitler called for the continuation of Operation Braunschweig (q.v.) in the Stalingrad area. He ordered the special operation to be known by this secret cover name.

FLASCHENBIERGUSTAV (Beer-Bottle Gustav). Term of derision used by early Nazi orators to describe Gustav Stresemann (q.v.), whose authority as Chancellor was restored after the failure of Hitler's Beer-Hall *Putsch* (q.v.) in 1923. Stresemann had written his doctoral dissertation on the economics of the German brewery industry. Nazi speakers, from Hitler to local leaders, regarded Stresemann as an especially dangerous political enemy and often expressed their contempt for him.

FLASH. Code name for the attempt on Hitler's life on March 13, 1943. *See* SMOLENSK ATTENTAT.

FLATFOOT INDIANS. *See* PLATTFUSSINDIANERN.

FLICK, FRIEDRICH (1883–1972). Industrialist and early supporter of the Nazi movement. Friedrich Flick was born in Ernsdorf, Westphalia, on July 10, 1883. In 1913, at the age of thirty, he began to work in the iron industry, and he rapidly rose to a position of great wealth and influence. In 1932 the Flick firm gave 950,000 reichsmarks to the campaign to reelect President Paul von Hindenburg (q.v.) and at the same time contributed 50,000 reichsmarks to the Nazi movement. The next year Flick gave 100,000 reichsmarks to the Nationalist People's party and 120,000 reichsmarks to the Nazis. At this time he joined the Nationalsozialistische Deutsche Arbeiterpartei (q.v.) as member No. 5,918,393. He was a member of the Circle of Friends of Heinrich Himmler (Freundeskreis Heinrich Himmler, q.v.), whose members contributed heavily to the various activities of the SS (q.v.). In April 1947, with Gustav Krupp von Bohlen und Halbach and Fritz Thyssen (qq.v.), Flick was brought to trial on charges of having helped Hitler to achieve power and conquest. He was accused specifically of using slave labor for his many enterprises. The Flickgruppe lost most of its assets, but it was later built anew.

FLOSSENBÜRG. One of the smaller concentration camps, located in the Neustadt district of the Upper Palatinate of Bavaria. In the fifteenth century this territory had been acquired by the Wittelsbach dynasty. At the end of 1940 Flossenbürg was chosen to be visited by a medical commission to select prisoners for special experiments. On August 24, 1942, *SS-Obersturmbannfuehrer* (Lieutenant Colonel) Künstler, commander of Flossenbürg, was removed from his post because of drunkenness.

FLOWER WARS. *See* BLUMENKRIEGE.

FOCK, CARIN VON. *See* GOERING, CARIN VON KANTZOW.

FOCKE WULF-190 (Fw-190). Highly successful German combat plane. The Fw-190 was put on the production line in 1941, less than a year after the Messerschmitt-109 (q.v.) had been withdrawn following its defeat in the Battle of Britain. The Fw-190 was a superlatively designed aircraft that remained victorious in combat for two years. The Fw-190A-8 had a 1,700-horsepower air-cooled engine, a wingspan of 34.5 feet, a top speed of 408 miles per hour at 20,600 feet, and an armament of two 13-millimeter machine guns and four 20-millimeter cannon. Later designs were even faster. The plane quickly demonstrated its superiority to the British Spitfire by executing fast turns that would have torn the wings off any other fighter plane then in use. In June 1942 a Luftwaffe (q.v.) pilot in trouble landed his Fw-190 almost intact on British soil. British designers studied the remarkable German plane, copied most of its features, and on short order produced the Hawker Fury to fight back on equal terms.

The Focke Wulf-190. [*US Air Force*]

FOLLOWERS. *See* GEFOLGSCHAFT.

FOR THE SEMITE. *See* POUR LE SÉMIT.

FÖRDERNDE MITGLIED DER SS (Patron Member of the SS). Supporter of the Schutzstaffel (SS, q.v.), who was expected to pay a monthly contribution for its upkeep.

FOREIGN POLICY OFFICE. *See* AUSSENPOLITISCHES AMT.

FORSTER, ALBERT (1902–   ). Nazi Fuehrer of the free state of Danzig. Albert Forster served as *Gauleiter* (district leader) of the Nazi party in Danzig and later as its administrative leader. He held the honorary title of *SS-Gruppenfuehrer* (lieutenant general). On April 28, 1948, he was sentenced to death by a Gdańsk (Danzig) court. The sentence was commuted to life imprisonment.

FORTRESSES OF THE TEUTONIC KNIGHTS. *See* ORDENSBURGEN.

FOUNDATION DAY OF THE NSDAP. *See* HOLIDAYS, NAZI.

FOUNTAIN OF LIFE. *See* LEBENSBORN.

FOUR-YEAR PLAN. Hitler's scheme for national self-sufficiency, devised in the summer of 1936. On September 9, 1936, at the annual Nazi party rally held in Nuremberg, Hitler proclaimed a Four-Year Plan to alter the structure of German economic life. The proclamation, read by Adolf Wagner (q.v.) on behalf of the Fuehrer, contained these ideas:

> I [Hitler] today present the following as the new Four-Year Plan. In four years Germany must be wholly independent of foreign areas in those materials which can be produced in any way through German ability, through our chemical and machine industry, as well as through our mining industry. The re-building of this great German raw material industry will serve to give employment to the masses. The implementation of the plan will take place with National Socialist energy and vigor. But in addition, Germany cannot relinquish the solution of its colonial demands. The right of the German people to live is surely as great as that of other nations. . . .
>
> The success of this plan is merely a question of our energy and determination. National Socialists have never recognized the word "impossible."

Hitler entrusted the implementation of the Four-Year Plan to Hermann Goering (q.v.), who became more and more interested in economic matters. During the next two years, in 1937 and 1938, it became obvious that Goering, an amateur in economic affairs, was increasingly in conflict with the more conservative views of Dr. Hjalmar Schacht (q.v.), president of the Reichsbank and Minister of Economics. On November 15, 1937, Schacht tendered his resignation from the Economics Ministry, effective the next January 15. In January 1939 he was removed from the presidency of the Reichsbank. Both posts went to Walther Funk (q.v.), an economist who had been a close adviser of the Fuehrer.

The Four-Year Plan was continued into the war years under Goering's control, and the office was extended in the midst of the conflict. Again and again Goering utilized forced labor on behalf of the plan, justifying this practice on the ground that the German people were fighting for their very existence.

14F.13. Special code signal used in the euthanasia program (q.v.) administered by the National Coordinating Agency for Therapeutic and Medical Establishment (T-4, q.v.). This symbol, usually marked "special treatment 14f.13," was placed on falsified lunacy certificates and in the files of Jewish prisoners in concentration camps.

FRAGEBOGEN, DER (The Questionnaire). Book by Ernst von Salomon (q.v.), published in 1951, in which the author gave detailed answers in 791 pages to the 131 questions of the Allied military government's *Fragebogen*. After the defeat of Germany in 1945 the occupation authorities issued several detailed questionnaires to be used as a basis for denazification (q.v.; *Entnazifizierung*). The questionnaires were served on all Germans suspected of having directed, assisted, or collaborated with the National Socialist regime from 1933 to 1945. They were designed as a method of excluding from the future administration of Germany all those who had had any responsibility for the crimes of National Socialism.

In his book Von Salomon, a writer of ability and a former right-wing activist, sought to disassociate himself from any guilt for the excesses of Nazism. He minimized his early association with the *Freikorps* (q.v.), the freebooter paramilitary units that had a direct influence on the National Socialist movement and supplied it with much of its ideology, street tactics, and personnel. He admitted only that he possessed "the good, old-fashioned Prussian virtues." In long answers Von Salomon portrayed himself as a gay bohemian, contemptuous of dirty politics. Throughout, he adopted a tone of amused cynicism and mockery, attacking the naïve set of questions with a spirited defense of the German people against individual or collective guilt for the crimes of Nazism.

The book was enormously successful in Germany, where it sold a quarter of a million copies within three years. German critics condemned it strongly on both political and moral grounds and expressed the fear that it might have a deleterious effect on Germany's future. Outside Germany the book was denounced as evidence of deep-rooted tendencies of the German character that had not been eliminated by the fall of Hitler.

Bibliography. Ernst von Salomon, *Der Fragebogen*, Rowohlt Verlag, Hamburg, 1951. The ninth printing, of 207,000 to 212,000 copies, was published in March 1953. The English version, translated by Constantine Fitzgibbon, was titled *The Answers to the 131 Questions of the Allied Military Government "Fragebogen,"* Putnam & Co., Ltd., London, 1954.

FRANK, ANNE (1929–1945). A German-Jewish girl who with her family hid from the Gestapo (q.v.) in Amsterdam for two years and died in Belsen (q.v.) concentration camp. Anne Frank was born in Frankfurt am Main on June 12, 1929, the daughter of a businessman who could trace his family back to the seventeenth century. Her childhood in a comfortable apartment was secure in the love of her parents, sister, and relatives. In the summer of 1933 the Franks left Frankfurt for Amsterdam, where Otto Frank set up a food products business. For centuries the Netherlands had given refuge to the persecuted. The Dutch received German Jews just as they had taken in French Huguenots in the sixteenth century and English Puritans in seventeenth. The Germans invaded the Netherlands in 1940 and soon introduced anti-Jewish measures. In February 1941 the Nazi authorities began a roundup of Amsterdam's Jews for deportation to concentration camps (q.v.) in Germany. Dutch associates of the Frank family arranged a secret annex in a group of rooms at the top and back of a building that had served as a warehouse on the Prinsengracht canal. Here the Franks were joined by another family, Mr. and Mrs. Van Daan, their son Peter, who was about Anne's age, and a Mr. Dussel, an elderly dentist. Provided with food and other necessities by friends on the outside, the small group remained in the hideout for two years.

On August 4, 1944, there was the dreaded knock on the door. Five Gestapo agents rushed in and arrested the occupants, who had been betrayed by a Dutch informer. Otto Frank, who survived, later wrote: "The SS [q.v.] man picked up a portfolio and asked me whether there were any jewels in it. I told him there were only papers. He threw the papers, and Anne's diary, on the floor, and put our silverware and a candlestick used to celebrate *Hanukkah* [the Jewish Festival of Lights] into his brief case. If he had taken the diary with him, no one would ever have heard of my daughter." Anne was later taken to Belsen concentration camp, where in March 1945, only several months before the end of the war, she died.

A year later Otto Frank returned to the house on the Prinsengracht and found the diary lying on the floor where the SS man had thrown it. Published as *The Diary of Anne Frank,* it was an immediate sensation. The book was eventually translated into thirty-two languages and later became a successful stage play and motion picture. The conscience of the world was aroused by the tragic story of a normal, unusually intelligent girl, of warm spirit and sensitivity, passing through the critical years of adolescence before her early death. Anne Frank described the vicissitudes of people living together under dangerous circumstances, facing hunger and the ever-present threat of discovery, boredom, misunderstandings—all the cruelties and kindnesses of human behavior.

In the opening lines of her diary Anne Frank expressed the hope that she could confide completely in the reader and added that she hoped the reader would be a great support and comfort to her. In the final passage she stated that if she were watched, she first became snappy, then unhappy, and finally twisted her heart around again "so that the bad is on the outside and the good is on the inside." She would keep on seeking a way to become what she would like to be and what she could be if "there weren't any other people living in the world."

Today the secret annex in the office building on the Prinsengracht is visited daily by hundreds, especially teen-agers, who see in Anne Frank an extension of all youth. Many young Germans, similarly affected by the nobility of the young girl's spirit, go to Belsen each year to pray for the soul of Anne Frank.

Bibliography. *Anne Frank: The Diary of a Young Girl,* Doubleday & Company, Inc., Garden City, N.Y., 1952.

FRANK, HANS (1900–1946). Hitler's lawyer and later Governor-General of occupied Poland. Hans Frank was born in Karlsruhe on May 23, 1900. Because of his youth he served for only one year in World War I. After the war he joined a *Freikorps* (q.v.) unit to fight the Communists who ruled Munich for a few days in April 1919. That year he joined the Deutsche Arbeiterpartei, and he became a Nazi when it was absorbed into the Nationalsozialistische Deutsche Arbeiterpartei, or NSDAP (qq.v.). He took part in the 1923 Beer-Hall *Putsch* (q.v.) in Munich as a Storm Trooper (*see* SA). In 1926 he passed the state bar examinations and began practice as an attorney in Munich. He was active in defending Brownshirts who had been arrested in street fighting with Communists (some 40,000 such trials were held between 1925 and 1933). While conducting one of these cases, Frank called Hitler as a witness for a client. In his appearance Hitler lectured the court on the patriotism and selfless motives of his Nazi followers and predicted that heads would roll when he took power

Hans Frank. [*Ullstein*]

legally from "the degenerate Weimar Republic [q.v.]."

Hitler retained Frank as his own attorney and made him leader of the legal division of the NSDAP. The young lawyer represented Hitler in some 150 lawsuits. He was also entrusted with the research to prove that Hitler had no Jewish blood. Frank was a member of the German Reichstag (q.v.) from 1930 on. When Hitler became Chancellor in 1933, he appointed Frank to a number of high offices: Bavarian minister of justice, Reich Minister of Justice, and Reich Minister without Portfolio (1934). Still in his early thirties, Frank became *Reichsleiter* (Reich leader) of the NSDAP, president of the Academy of German Law, founder of the Institute of German Law, and president of the "International Chamber of the Law."

On October 12, 1939, after Hitler conquered Poland, he appointed Frank chief civilian officer for occupied Polish territory and then Governor-General of occupied Poland. Frank described his policy in this post: "Poland shall be treated like a colony: the Poles will become the slaves of the Greater German Empire." He destroyed Poland as a national entity and exploited its human and material resources for the German war effort. Frank ran Poland in imitation of the Nazi state. He declared German to be the official language; he warned that Jews and Poles could be sentenced to death for any act of force against a German or for damage to a public installation; he confiscated Jewish and Polish property; he expropriated valuable paintings, including a Leonardo da Vinci and a Rembrandt, for his own home at Schliersee in southern Germany; and he allowed huge quantities of food to be smuggled from Poland to Germany. At a time when most of Europe was hungry, Frank set an elaborate table at the Governor's palace in Cracow. By December 1942 more than 85 percent of the Jews in Poland had been transported to extermination camps (q.v.).

Brought before the International Military Tribunal at Nuremberg after the fall of the Third Reich, Frank announced his conversion to Catholicism, abjectly confessed his guilt, and begged the forgiveness of God. The man who had sent thousands of helpless people to their deaths fought doggedly for his own life. "I regard this trial," he said, "as a God-willed world court, destined to examine and put an end to the terrible era of suffering under Adolf Hitler." He now attacked Hitler as a betrayer of the trust and devotion of millions of Germans. "The testimony I have heard in this courtroom has shaken me." The judges were not impressed either by Frank's conversion or by his confession. They found him guilty of count 3 (war crimes) and count 4 (crimes against humanity). He was hanged at Nuremberg on October 16, 1946.

Bibliography. Stanislaw Piotrowski (ed.), *Hans Frank's Diary*, Państwowe Wydawn, Naukowe, Warsaw, 1961.

FRANKFURT TRIAL. A trial, held at Frankfurt am Main, of the chief SS (q.v.) officers who worked at the extermination camp of Auschwitz (q.v.). Also known as the Auschwitz Trial, it took place from December 20, 1963, to August 20, 1965, the longest legal case in German records. Robert Karl Mulka and other SS defendants came mostly from middle-class families. Eight had a higher education. Most claimed that they were as innocent as their victims: "I knew only one mode of conduct: to carry out the orders of superiors without reservations" (Boger). "I had nothing to do with it" (Höcker). "I believed in the Fuehrer. I wanted to serve my people" (Stark). "I naturally sought to save as many Jewish lives as possible" (Dr. Lucas). "No one died by my hand" (Hantl).

The testimony brought out such items as these:

Barracks were horse stables with a capacity for 500 people, into which 1,200 prisoners were crammed.

Clerks worked night and day in shifts at seven typewriters making out death reports.

The lockers of SS men contained a fortune in jewelry belonging to the victims.

A main concern of the SS guards was that "new-born infants should have a prisoner number tattooed on their thighs immediately because the arm of an infant was too small."

Jewish prisoners in the yard of the crematories circled the doctor who was making selections for life or death, all eager to read the least wish on his face.

Women and children on their knees cried: "Take pity, take pity on us!"

No mother let her child go alone to the gas chambers. All mothers went with their children.

Above the front gate through which new arrivals marched was written the slogan *"Arbeit Macht Frei"* (q.v.), or "Labor Liberates."

The charges and punishments of the accused are listed on the opposite page.

FRATERNITY. *See* BURSCHENSCHAFT.

FRAUENFRONT (Women's Front). *See* FRAUENSCHAFTEN.

FRAUENLAGER (Women's Camp). Official name for a concentration camp whose inmates were exclusively women (*see* CONCENTRATION CAMPS).

FRAUENSCHAFTEN (Women's Organizations). National Socialist women's auxiliaries. Founded as early as October 1, 1931, they had as their main task after Hitler came to political power the coordination (*see* GLEICHSCHALTUNG) of all women's organizations, including professional groups, into a National Socialist Frauenfront (Women's Front). Other women's organizations, especially the democratic, humanitarian societies, were accused of Marxism, enmity to the family, advocacy of abortion, and lack of patriotism. They were all brought into line with Nazi ideology. Hitler regarded any kind of feminism or women's liberation movement as forbidden activity. He expected women to play an inferior role in society (*see* KINDER, KIRCHE, KÜCHE). Above all, women were to be responsible for the task of bearing and rearing future leaders of the National Socialist state.

FREE CORPS. *See* FREIKORPS.

FREIBURG KREIS (Freiburg Circle). One of the Resistance (q.v.) movements opposed to Hitler. Composed of intellectuals at the University of Freiburg and led by the historian Gerhard Ritter (q.v.), the Freiburg Circle regarded Hitler and the Nazis as a disgrace to the name of Germany. Its members attacked Hitler's nihilism and condemned him for perverting and misleading the masses. Nazism, they said, did not have its source in German history but rather in the democratization of the masses inaugurated in the French Revolution. They took a strongly nationalistic line: while they supported Dietrich Bonhoeffer (q.v.) and others who were opposed to Hitler, they refused to take the position that their fatherland should be defeated in World War II. They also rejected such kindred Resistance groups as the Rote Kapelle (q.v.), which they accused of passing military information to the Soviet Union.

FREIKORPS (Free Corps). Paramilitary units which after the defeat of Germany in 1918 became the available "force in being" for the formation of the new German Army. The name was taken from the first *Freikorps*, a voluntary corps organized by a Major Lützow in 1813 as the kernel of an army designed to win liberation from Napoleon. After 1919 a new *Freikorps*, composed of former officers, demobilized soldiers, military adventurers, fanatical nationalists, and unemployed youths, was organized by Capt. Kurt von Schleicher (q.v.). Rightist in political philosophy, blaming Social Democrats and Jews for Germany's plight, the *Freikorps* called for the elimination of "traitors to the Fatherland." *Freikorps* units began to spring up all over Germany. At first Paul von Hindenburg (q.v.) and other generals supported the formation of these freebooter squads, but the behavior of the volunteers eventually made them obnoxious to the old military clique. *Freikorps* units fought with Allied approval against the Bolsheviks in Lithuania and Latvia in 1919. Later, after the formation of a national army, remnants of the *Freikorps* formed murder squads to attack officials of the Weimar Republic (q.v.).

Bibliography. Harold J. Gordon, Jr., *The Reichswehr and the German Republic, 1919–1926*, Princeton University Press, Princeton, N.J., 1956.

RESULTS OF THE FRANKFURT TRIAL

NAME OF ACCUSED	DATE OF BIRTH	DUTY AT AUSCHWITZ	VERDICT OF GUILT	PUNISHMENT
1. Baretzski, Stefan	1919	Block leader	5 murders; 11 joint murders; complicity in deaths of 3,000 persons	Life plus five years' hard labor
2. Bednarek, Emil	1907	Prisoner	14 murders	Life at hard labor
3. Boger, Wilhelm	1906	Camp Gestapo	144 murders; 10 joint murders; complicity in deaths of 1,000 persons	Life plus five years' hard labor
4. Breitwieser, Johann	1910	Disinfection section		Acquitted
5. Broad, Percy	1921	Camp Gestapo	22 joint murders; complicity in deaths of 1,000 persons	Four years' hard labor
6. Capesius, Dr. Victor	1907	Head, camp pharmacy	Complicity in joint murder on at least four separate occasions of 2,000 deaths each	Nine years' hard labor
7. Dylewski, Klaus	1916	Guard unit	Complicity in joint murder on at least thirty-two separate occasions, two involving the murder of 750 persons each	Five years' hard labor
8. Frank, Dr. Willi	1903	Chief, dental station	Complicity in joint murder on at least six separate occasions of at least 1,000 deaths each	Seven years' hard labor
9. Hantl, Emil	1902	Medical section	Complicity in joint murder on at least forty separate occasions of at least 170 deaths each	Three years six months at hard labor
10. Höcker, Karl		Adjutant to camp commander	Complicity in murder of at least 1,000 persons each on three separate occasions	Seven years' hard labor
11. Hofmann, Franz	1906	Officer in charge	1 murder; 30 joint murders; joint murder on three separate occasions of 750 deaths each	Life at hard labor
12. Kaduk, Oswald		Roll-call leader	10 murders; joint murder of 1,000 persons	Life at hard labor
13. Klehr, Joseph	1904	Medical section	475 murders	Life plus fifteen years' hard labor
14. Lucas, Dr. Franz	1911	Camp medical officer	Complicity in murder of 1,000 persons	Three years three months at hard labor
15. Mulka, Robert Karl	1895	Adjutant to Camp Commander Hoess	Complicity in murder of 750 persons	Fourteen years' hard labor
16. Nubert, Gerhard			Case severed because of illness	
17. Schatz, Dr. Willi	1905	Dental station		Acquitted
18. Scherpe, Herbert		Medical section	Complicity in joint murder of 700 persons	Four years six months at hard labor
19. Schlage, Bruno	1902	Prison bunker guard	Complicity in joint murder on eighty separate occasions	Six years' hard labor
20. Schoberth, Johann				Acquitted
21. Stark, Hans	1921	Camp Gestapo	Joint murder on forty-four separate occasions, one involving 200 persons and one involving at least 100 persons	Ten years

Roland Freisler [*Bundesarchiv*]

FREISLER, ROLAND (1893–1945). Dreaded "hanging judge" of the Volksgericht (q.v.), the People's Court in Berlin, from 1942 to 1945. Roland Freisler was born in Celle on October 30, 1893, to an old Hessian farmer family. Volunteering for service in World War I, he was captured by the Russians and imprisoned in Siberia for five years. He mastered the Russian language but developed a supreme contempt for communism. Pretending to cooperate with his captors by posing as a fanatical Bolshevik, he managed to escape in 1920 and return to Germany. He studied law at Jena, passed his examinations *summa cum laude,* and opened a law office in Kassel in 1923. After serving the city government for the Socialist bloc, he joined the Nazis in 1925 and began a lifelong affiliation with them. He was elected in 1932 as a National Socialist delegate to the Prussian Landtag (Legislature), and the next year to the Reichstag (q.v.) for Wahlkreis (Electoral District) Hessen-Nassau. At the same time he became director of personnel for the Prussian Ministry of Justice. On May 29, 1934, he was appointed a state secretary with the special duty of combating sabotage. On January 20, 1942, he participated in the Wannsee Conference (q.v.) in Berlin, at which extermination of all Jews in Europe was proposed (*see* ENDLÖSUNG, DIE).

From 1942 to 1945 Freisler headed the Volksgericht, the most feared tribunal in the Third Reich. In this post he put into practice Soviet Russian techniques of eliminating the Old Bolsheviks. Shrewd and cold-blooded, he was an unmerciful judge. He excoriated the prisoners brought before him and heaped abuse upon them before sending them to the gallows. He was especially vindictive toward the leaders of the July Plot (q.v.) of 1944. On February 3, 1945, while presiding over a treason trial, Freisler was killed by a bomb dropped from an American plane (*see* SOLF TEA PARTY).

FREUNDESKREIS HEINRICH HIMMLER (Circle of Friends of Heinrich Himmler). A group of wealthy patrons drawn from the top echelons of industry, banking, and insurance that acted as a connecting link between the holders of political and economic power in the Third Reich. The group played a major role in such matters as financing the crucial 1932–1933 election campaigns and supplying Waffen-SS (q.v.) units with arms and uniforms during World War II. Both Heinrich Himmler (q.v.) and his circle of friends benefited from mutual interests. Industrialists and businessmen found it not only a matter of prestige to be included in the Himmler circle but also a practical advantage, for they might be allocated scarce labor from the concentration camps (q.v.). Those who contributed to the fund were often rewarded with high rank in the SS (q.v.). They neither expected nor received any accounting. The circle met every second Monday in Berlin, and Himmler kept careful records of attendance ("Count von Bismarck has been absent three times"). Moneys received in the fund were to be used for expenses that Himmler could not finance from his own budget, such as cultural activities and medical experiments in the concentration camps.

FRICK, WILHELM (1877–1946). Jurist and one of Hitler's closest comrades during the early years of struggle for political power. Wilhelm Frick was born in Alsenz, in the Palatinate, on March 12, 1877, the son of a schoolteacher and a farmer's daughter. He attended *Volksschule* (grammar school) and *Gymnasium* (high school) in Kaiserslautern, studied law at Munich, Göttingen, and Berlin, and took his doctorate at Heidelberg. In 1912 he went to Munich to practice law. Because of weak lungs Frick did not take part in World War I. He headed the Munich police section from 1919 to 1923 and the criminal section until 1925. Frick learned to know Hitler intimately when the fledgling Nazi leader applied for permission to hold political meetings in Munich. Converted to Nazi ideology, he became Hitler's contact in police headquarters. On at least one occasion he saw to it that Hitler was freed after an arrest. In *Mein Kampf* (q.v.) Hitler wrote that Frick and the former municipal police president Ernst Poehner, both firm rightists who detested the Communists, were the only two men he knew "who had the courage to be Germans first and then officials."

Just before the Beer-Hall *Putsch* (q.v.) in Munich on November 8–9, 1923, Hitler assigned Frick and Poehner to take over police headquarters for the revolutionists. Frick, who was at Hitler's side during the street march, was arrested and held for four months under interrogation. He was eventually sentenced to fifteen months' imprisonment. However, the judgment was suspended in 1924, and Frick returned to his duties at police headquarters as if nothing had happened. That year he was elected to the Reichstag (q.v.) as a Nazi party delegate.

In 1930, after the Nationalsozialistische Deutsche Arbeiterpartei (q.v.) had returned six members to the Thuringian Diet, Frick was appointed minister of the interior in Thuringia, the first Nazi to hold an important provincial post. In this capacity he made Thuringia a hotbed of opposition to the Social Democratic government in Berlin. He purged the police force of officers suspected of republican sympathies. He also introduced a spoils system favoring Nazi candidates for office and filled police ranks with Nazis. Frick's activities brought him into conflict with the Social Democratic Minister of the Interior, Carl Severing, who threatened to withdraw financial support from the Thuringian police system if Frick did not cease his illegal activities. Frick replied that he would dismiss the entire police force and create a vigilante body composed solely of Storm Troopers (*see* SA). The affair was brought to a conclusion with a temporary victory for Frick when the Leipzig Supreme Court issued a decision forcing Berlin to continue its financial support.

Frick's actions in Thuringia, prefiguring similar activities later on in his capacity as Reich Minister of the Interior, brought him praise from Hitler and acclaim by Nazis. He called for the release of the murderers of Matthias Erzberger and Walther Rathenau, accusing the murdered men of "historical crimes" and insisting that the act of killing them was not so serious as their own crimes. He banned *Im Westen nichts Neues (All Quiet on the Western Front)*, an antiwar film of the novel by Erich Maria Remarque (q.v.), which had been passed by the Berlin censors. In Frick's view, "it shamefully [depicted] Germans as cowards." He allowed National Socialist newspapers to resume publication, and he created a special chair of social anthropology at the University of Jena for the National Socialist professor Hans F. K. Günther (q.v.), the intellectual apostle of racialism. Both Hitler and Frick were present at Günther's *Eintrittsvorlesung* (inaugural lecture), which they compared to the opening talk by the great poet Schiller at the same university.

The future quality of Nazi nationalism was indicated in the special prayers introduced by Frick for the schools of Thuringia:

Vater im Himmel!
Ich glaube an deine Allmacht, Gerechtigkeit und Liebe.
Ich glaube an mein liebes deutsches Volk und Vaterland.
Ich weiss, dass Gottlosigkeit und Vaterlandsverrat unser Volk zerriss und Vernichtete.
Ich weiss, dass trotzdem in den Besten die Sehnsucht und die Kraft zur Freiheit wohnt.
Ich glaube, dass diese Freiheit kommen wird, durch die Liebe des Vaters im Himmel, wenn wir an unsere eigene Kraft glauben.

(Father in Heaven!
I believe in thy almightiness, justice and love.
I believe in my beloved German people and Fatherland.
I know that godlessness and treason to the Fatherland have torn and destroyed our people.
I know that in spite of this the desire and power for liberty dwells in the spirit of the good.
I believe that this liberty will come, through the love of our Father in Heaven, if we believe in our own power.)

Vater im Himmel!
Ich glaube an deine allmächtige Hand,
Ich glaube an Volkstum und Vaterland,
Ich glaube an der Ahnen, Kraft und Ehr,
Ich glaube, du bist uns Waffe und Wehr,
Ich glaube, du strafst unseres Landes Verrat
Und segnest der Heimat befreiende Tat!
Deutschland, erwache zur Freiheit!

(Father in Heaven!
I believe in thy almighty Hand,
I believe in nation and Fatherland,
I believe in my ancestors, power and honor,
I believe thou art our weapon and defense,
I believe that thou shalt punish our nation's traitors,
And bless the deed that brings us liberty!
Germany, awake to liberty!)

Immediately after becoming Chancellor in 1933, Hitler appointed Frick, by this time his favorite bureaucrat, to the key post of Reich Minister of the Interior. Frick at once submitted to the Cabinet a statement showing that most judges and lawyers in Berlin were Jews. He removed the local government in Bavaria and set up a Nazi regime there. On March 31, 1933, just a week after the Enabling Act (q.v.) had been adopted, Frick used it for the first time to dissolve the diets of all states except Prussia and ordered them reconstituted on the basis of votes cast in the last Reichstag elections. This meant that there would be no Communist members. On June 19, 1933, he dissolved the Social Democratic party as subversive. Meanwhile, he made certain that all new *Reichsstatthälter* (Reich Governors) were Nazis. On April 7, 1933, he sponsored enactment of the Law for the Restoration of the Civil Service, and he saw to it that his party comrades would be favored. On September 15, 1935, he drew up the Nuremberg Laws on citizenship and race, forcing Jews to register, forbidding them to marry Germans, and in general relegating them to second-class citizenship. By this time Frick was responsible for sending at least 100,000 persons to concentration camps (q.v.).

At the Nuremberg Trial (q.v.), Frick was charged with being largely responsible for bringing Germany under Nazi control. He was accused of drafting, signing, and activating numerous laws abolishing political parties, suppressing trade unions, and preparing the way for the Gestapo (q.v.) and the concentration camp system. He was also charged with drafting, signing, and administering laws designed to eliminate Jews from German life and the national economy. He was found guilty on count 2 (crimes against peace), count 3 (war crimes), and count 4 (crimes against humanity). On October 16, 1946, he was hanged at Nuremberg.

A colorless civil servant, Frick brought the mind of a trained bureaucrat to the Nazi movement. Deeply devoted to his leader, he carried out Hitler's slightest wish. A master of legal verbiage, he was able to cover the Fuehrer's amoral actions with a cloak of legality. His ideology was simple: "*Recht* [Right] is what benefits the German people, *Unrecht* [wrong] is what harms them." For his Fuehrer, Frick was the devoted crypto-Nazi who would ease the revolutionary way to total power. "We must put an end," he said in 1933, "once and for all to the spirit of subversion that has gnawed long enough at Germany's heart." He was the loyal servant who knew how to implement Hitler's plans.

FRIEDEBURG, HANS GEORG VON (1895–1945). Admiral and final supreme commander of the German Navy. Hans Georg von Friedeburg was born in Strassburg (Strasbourg) on July 15, 1895. He served as a cadet in the Imperial Navy in 1914 and transferred to the U-boat service in 1917 (*see* U-BOATS). In 1933 he was promoted to lieutenant commander and the next year, through the intercession of Heinrich Himmler (q.v.), was appointed to the High Command. For eight days, from May 1 to 9, 1945, he was supreme commander of the Navy and in this capacity was a signatory of Germany's unconditional surrender at Reims on May 7, 1945. He committed suicide in Mürwick on May 23, 1945.

FRITSCH, WERNER FREIHERR VON (1880–1939). Commander in chief of the German Army until 1938 and a victim of Hitler's campaign to obtain complete control of the armed forces. Werner von Fritsch was born in Benrath on August 4, 1880. Entering the Army at the age of eighteen, he displayed qualities that won the attention of superior officers on the General Staff. In 1901, when he was only twenty-one, he was transferred to the War Academy. In 1911, as a 1st lieutenant, he was appointed to a coveted position on the General Staff. Von Fritsch spent the war years from 1914 to 1918 in various tasks of increasing importance. He served the Reichswehr (q.v.) in the Weimar Republic (q.v.) with equal success. Like his colleague Werner von Blomberg (q.v.), he was an ardent supporter of liaison with Soviet Russia. Reserved, patient, and duty-conscious, he was interested chiefly in his Army career. He had few relationships with women and never married. In 1930 he commanded a cavalry division at Frankfurt an der Oder and became a leading figure in General Staff circles. He received his promotion to lieutenant general in July 1932.

Von Fritsch was shocked by the lawlessness of Hitler's colleagues as well as by the Nazi suppression of civil liberties, but he refrained from open criticism. What worried him most of all was the possibility that Hitler's antibolshevism might lead to an unwanted war with the Soviet Union. He was inclined to attribute the excesses of Hitlerism to "youthful exuberance." In 1934 he was made chief of the High Command of the Army and the next year promoted to commander in chief. With Von Blomberg he participated in rearmament and the building of the new Wehrmacht (q.v.). Von Fritsch was among the leading officers present at the Hossbach Conference (q.v.) on November 5, 1937, when Hitler clearly revealed his aggressive intentions. Like Von Blomberg, he was appalled by Hitler's plan to wage war at a time when the Army was not ready.

Accused by Hermann Goering and Heinrich Himmler (qq.v.) of homosexual activities, Von Fritsch was forced to resign on February 4, 1938. He was replaced by Gen. Walther von Brauchitsch (q.v.) as commander in chief of the Army. Acquitted by an honor court of officers, he was recalled to the Army just before the outbreak of World War II. He died in combat near Warsaw on September 22, 1939. It was believed that he deliberately sought his death on the battlefield. *See also* BLOMBERG-FRITSCH CRISIS.

Bibliography. Johann Adolf Kielmansegg, *Der Fritschprozess, 1938*, Hoffmann und Campe, Hamburg, 1949.

Col. Gen. Werner Freiherr von Fritsch. [*Picture Collection, The Branch Libraries, The New York Public Library*]

FRITZ. Initial cover name for the planned invasion of the Soviet Union. On December 6, 1940, Lieut. Gen. Alfred Jodl (q.v.) instructed his deputy, Maj. Gen. Walther Warlimont (q.v.), to prepare a draft for a general plan to invade Russia. On December 12 the first draft was given the code name Fritz. Six days later Hitler dropped the term Fritz and substituted for it Barbarossa (q.v.), the cover name by which the plan was to be known thereafter.

FRITZSCHE, HANS (1900–1953). Radio propaganda chief in the Ministry for Public Enlightenment and Propaganda, headed by Dr. Paul Joseph Goebbels (q.v.). Hans Fritzsche was born in Bochum, Westphalia, on April 21, 1900, the son of a postal official. After attending the humanistic *Gymnasien* (high schools) in Halle, Breslau, and Leipzig, he served as a private in the latter part of World War I. After the war he studied history, economics, and philosophy at several universities but did not complete his doctorate. In 1923 he became editor of the *Preussische Jahrbücher*, a monthly journal. From 1924 to 1932 he was an editor of the Telegraphen Union and editor in chief of the International News Service, a division of the vast Hugenberg press empire (*see* HUGENBERG, Alfred). In 1932 he became head of the Rundfunk (q.v.), the German wireless news service.

On May 1, 1933, Goebbels, who needed the cooperation of able newsmen, made Fritzsche head of the news service in the Press Section of the Propaganda Ministry. Fritzsche's main duty was to tell German editors what they could print. In November 1942 he left the Press Section and became head of the Radio Division, one of the twelve sections of the Ministry, with the title Plenipotentiary for the Political Organization of the Greater German Radio. In this post he had an audience of listeners who sat before 16 million radio sets. His broadcasts, beginning *"Hier spricht Hans Fritzsche!"* ("Hans Fritzsche speaking!") and presented regularly on the radio network of Greater Germany, made him one of the best-known commentators in the Third Reich. His articulate booming voice and his carefully reasoned arguments appealed to Germans who were repelled by ordinary Nazi spellbinders. Although the two men collaborated in presenting propaganda to the German people, Fritzsche and his immediate superior, Goebbels, never developed an intimate relationship. Goebbels admired his assistant's work but never his personality.

In addition to his work in radio news broadcasting, Fritzsche, as head of the German Press Section, was responsible for the wire services to foreign countries and for some 2,000 daily newspapers and magazines. All these news outlets were subjected to *Gleichschaltung* (q.v.), the coordination demanded by Hitler. Fritzsche conducted frequent briefings for several hundred representatives of the most important German papers and met smaller groups of selected journalists to present the official Nazi propaganda line.

With Goebbels, Fritzsche emphasized the main points of Hitler's ideology as expressed in *Mein Kampf* (q.v.): the conspiracy of world Jewry, the plutocratic democracies, the Bolshevik danger, living space, and the leadership principle (*Fuehrerprinzip*, q.v.). Before the war Fritzsche delivered encomiums on the genius of the Fuehrer. No one in German history, he wrote, had brought the Reich so much territory and prestige as had Hitler in the space of five years. And, added Fritzsche, the Fuehrer had never fired a shot in the process. This great German had demolished the paper tigers of Versailles and restored Germany's position in Europe. In the early years of World War II, Fritzsche reported dazzling victories for the Third Reich; in the later years he was faced with the much more difficult task of stimulating morale in a time of bitter setbacks. Every German was threatened not only by the Russians but by the West. Fritzsche quoted the London *News Chronicle:* "We are for destroying every living being in Germany: man, woman, and child, bird and insect." He was at the microphone until the last hours of the war.

Brought to trial before the International Military Tribunal at Nuremberg in 1946, Fritzsche admitted that he had been wrong in his estimate of Hitler and Nazism and that he had finally come to realize that the Fuehrer was determined to exterminate not only the Jews but also the German people. "It is the most terrible indictment of all times. Only one thing is more terrible: the indictment the German people will make for the abuse of their idealism." The court accepted his defense: "It appears that Fritzsche sometimes made strong statements of a propagandistic nature in his broadcasts. But the Tribunal is not prepared to hold that they were intended to incite the German people to commit atrocities on conquered peoples, and he cannot be said to have been a participant in the crimes charged." On October 1, 1946, he was found not guilty.

On February 4, 1947, Fritzsche was brought before a German denazification (q.v.) court on charges that he had strengthened anti-Semitism (q.v.), given the German people false information, and urged them to continue fighting after the war had been lost. He was freed on September 29, 1950. Fritzsche died in Cologne on September 27, 1953, still fervent in his belief that he had served his country well.

Bibliography. Hans Fritzsche, *Es sprach Hans Fritzsche*, Thiele, Stuttgart, 1949.

FROMM, ERICH (1900–). Social philosopher, psychoanalyst, and prominent refugee from the Third Reich. Erich Fromm was born in Frankfurt am Main on March 23, 1900. After taking his doctorate at Heidelberg in 1922, he studied at the Psychoanalytic Institute in Berlin. He lectured at Frankfurt from 1929 to 1932, but he left Germany in 1933, when Hitler came to political power. In the United States he continued his career as one of the nation's most distinguished psychoanalysts. He lectured at many universities and held a post as fellow of the William Alanson White Institute. His publications include such best sellers as *The Sane Society* (1955), *Sigmund Freud's Mission* (1958), *The Heart of Man* (1964), and *The Anatomy of Human Destructiveness* (1973).

FROMM, FRIEDRICH (1888–1945). Commander in chief of the German Reserve Army and chief of armament from September 1, 1939, to July 20, 1944. Friedrich Fromm was born in Berlin on October 8, 1888, and spent his early years in the normal routine of a military career. He was aware of the July Plot (q.v.) against Hitler in 1944, but he was undecided whether to participate in it. He was sure that the war was lost, but he decided not to join the Resistance (q.v.) movement until it could demonstrate its success.

Gen. Friedrich Fromm. [*Bundesarchiv*]

Fromm was stationed at the headquarters of the Ministry of War on the Bendlerstrasse (q.v.) on July 20, 1944, when news arrived about the bombing attempt on Hitler's life at Rastenburg, the eastern field headquarters (*see* RASTENBURG CONFERENCE). He immediately telephoned Rastenburg and by accident learned from Gen. Wilhelm Keitel (q.v.) that the coup had failed and that Hitler was alive. Col. Claus Schenk Graf von Stauffenberg (q.v.), who had just arrived by air from Rastenburg, informed Fromm that the Fuehrer was dead. Fromm ordered Von Stauffenberg's arrest. The latter said coldly: "General Fromm, I myself detonated the bomb. No one in that room could possibly be alive." Fromm replied: "Count Stauffenberg, the assassination attempt has failed. You should shoot yourself at once." Von Stauffenberg said: "I shall do nothing of the kind." Then followed a tragic comedy of arrests. The conspirators arrested Fromm, but officers loyal to Hitler quickly turned the tables and took the plotters into custody. Fromm ordered the summary execution of Von Stauffenberg and three of his immediate entourage. He then induced Gen. Ludwig Beck (q.v.), who was the leader of the conspiracy, to commit suicide. These measures did not win Fromm the safety he wanted. He was arrested, tried, and executed in March 1945.

FRONT EXPERIENCE. *See* FRONTERLEBNIS.

FRONTBANN (Front Union). One of the illegal organizations of the old SA (q.v.), the Storm Troopers. The Frontbann remained active after the unsuccessful Beer-Hall *Putsch* (q.v.) in Munich in 1923.

FRONTERLEBNIS (Front Experience). A type of writing on war experiences. The *Fronterlebnis* school, favored by Nazi authorities, stressed the camaraderie and homoeroticism of wartime. Novelists of this persuasion always described the coalescence at the front of a motley of self-centered atoms into "an oath-bound band of brothers." This genre turned out to be a maudlin mixture of nationalism and eroticism. *See also* LITERATURE IN THE THIRD REICH.

FSTR. *See* FALLSCHIRMTRUPPEN.

FRÜHLINGSERWACHEN (Spring Awakening). Code name for a projected operation aimed at the destruction of the Soviet Army in Hungary in the spring of 1945. The German attack was halted on March 17, 1945, when the Soviet troops launched a large-scale counteroffensive. Within twenty-four hours the Russians recaptured all the territory the Germans had taken in the previous two weeks and then advanced on Austria.

FUEHRER, DER (The Leader). Title used by Hitler to signify his role as supreme head of the Third Reich. It was equivalent to such designations as Duce, describing Benito Mussolini (q.v.) as head of Fascist Italy; Caudillo, used by Gen. Francisco Franco as chief of the Spanish state and commander in chief of the Army; and Generalissimo, the title assumed by Joseph Stalin as supreme commander in chief of the Soviet armed forces.

FUEHRER ELITE. *See* FUEHRER-KORPS.

FUEHRER-KORPS (Leaders' Corps). Term used to describe the large number of high leaders in the Nazi state. The *Fuehrerprinzip* (q.v.), the Fuehrer principle, was considered of basic importance in the Third Reich. It meant rule by an authoritarian leader. National Socialism was supposed to be a mass movement, but it had little trust in the masses. Its ideology denounced civilian methods of elections, negotiation, and compromise as horse trading and called for authority of command, discipline, and obedience. The Fuehrer principle became identical with the elite principle. The Fuehrer elite were regarded as independent of the will of mass followers.

This attitude of respect for the strong man led to the appearance of many Fuehrers of different types and grades. The Fuehrer hierarchy was composed of upper leaders and lower leaders, all of whom had a place in the pecking order. Appointments, power, and length of tenure always depended upon the whim of the Fuehrer at a slightly higher level. In every case the leader considered himself something more than a civilian. Eventually, there were so many Fuehrers in the higher ranks that they were given the distinction of belonging to a *Fuehrer-Korps*. There was intense rivalry for promotion to this party aristocracy.

See also FUEHRER WORSHIP.

FUEHRER PRINCIPLE. *See* FUEHRER-KORPS; FUEHRERPRINZIP.

FUEHRER WORSHIP (Leader Worship). The practice during the Third Reich of presenting a larger-than-life image of the leader as an idol endowed with superhuman qualities. The Fuehrer was depicted to his people as a teetotaler, vegetarian, nonsmoker, and asexual bachelor, as a man without human ties of love or friendship. In popular legend he exemplified his people's yearning for greatness.

Germany became a vast camp of Hitler saluters. The new German greeting was *"Heil Hitler!"* (q.v.). This most frequent adaptation to Nazi ritual was an obligation for all citizens on every possible occasion. Everyone used the greeting: the butcher, the baker, the janitor, the bus conductor, the high official. Every child in the Third Reich was expected to use the greeting throughout the day. Boys and girls were told to denounce their own parents for failure to use the greeting or for reducing the salute to an infinitesimal movement of the right arm accompanied by an inarticulate mumble.

Dr. Paul Joseph Goebbels (q.v.), Minister for Public Enlightenment and Propaganda, led the campaign of national devotion. He popularized such descriptions as this: "We are witnessing the greatest miracle in history. A genius is building the world!" And again: "We heard his voice while Germany slept. His hand has made us a nation again. His hand has led us back to the Fatherland. Our whole life we give to the Fuehrer!" And again: "He alone is never mistaken. He is always right. Amazing how great the Fuehrer is in his simplicity and how simple is his greatness. He is above us all. He is always like a great star above us."

Other leaders of the Nazi hierarchy vied with one another in praise of the great leader. Rudolf Hess (q.v.) spoke of his master in biblical terms: "And then unto us was born a child in Braunau." His praise approached hysteria:

> What he does is necessary,
> Whatever he does is necessary,
> Whatever he does is successful. . . .
> Clearly the Fuehrer has divine blessing.

Dr. Robert Ley, chief of the Reichsarbeitsdienst (qq.v.), the State Labor Service, maintained: "The Lord God has sent us Adolf Hitler." Leaders of the church praised Hitler's secular attributes. Michael Cardinal von Faulhaber (q.v.) saw Hitler as possessing "greater diplomatic finesse and social grace than a true-born king." One leader of the German Faith movement (Deutsche Glaubensbewegung, q.v.) claimed: "God has manifested himself not in Jesus Christ but in Adolf Hitler." Special efforts were made to win the attention of German youth to their Fuehrer, as in this text on a Hitler Jugend (q.v.; Hitler Youth) poster:

> We all believe on this earth in Adolf Hitler, our Leader.
> We believe that National Socialism will be the only creed for our people.
> We believe that there is a God in Heaven who created us, leads, and directs us.
> And we believe that this God has sent us Adolf Hitler so that Germany should be a foundation stone in all eternity.

Hitler's picture was everywhere, in classrooms, offices, railroad stations, street corners. A German could scarcely go anywhere without seeing the face of the Fuehrer staring down at him. Millions of postcards showing the Fuehrer as a giant Siegfried, sailing godlike through the air on his way to slay his dragon enemies, were printed.

Fuehrer worship persisted to a point at which it drew on reserves of self-pity and feelings of paranoia and persecution. When the sun appeared in a cloudless sky at a Nuremberg rally (*see* NUREMBERG RALLIES), the weather was popularly described as "Fuehrer weather." To German womanhood Hitler appeared as an Adonis. He was often called *"der schöne Adolf"* (q.v., "the handsome Adolf"). He received thousands of letters from female admirers, many of them begging him to father their children. The extraordinary Hitler worship induced in the female mind was exemplified when women fainted from ecstasy in his presence. When a press photograph showing Hitler at a reception bent over the hand of the actress Olga Tschechova was published, there was an overwhelming fan mail: "It is good to know that you will marry Adolf Hitler." "At last he has found his true love!" "Make him happy—he deserves it!" One enamored woman lecturer insisted that her dog could say the words "Adolf Hitler" because his small canine brain recognized his Fuehrer. Another charmed woman cried out: "It is not with the gushing gratitude of youth that I witness the miracle of your approach. I am overwhelmed with humble gratitude."

War added a new dimension to Fuehrer worship. Goebbels extolled Hitler as the greatest general of all time. The Fuehrer's voice came over the radio to raise the morale of soldiers at the front. The most popular slogan devised by Goebbels was *"Hitler ist der Sieg!"* ("Hitler Is Victory Itself!"). Through the country spread a rumor that when an Allied bomb demolished a house, it spared the wall with the portrait of Hitler on it. In response to an appeal by Goebbels, millions of Germans lighted candles in "Hitler corners" in their homes. The news of Hitler's death on April 30, 1945, was accompanied by a wave of suicides. Thousands of panic-stricken people dissolved into tears. Many Germans refused to accept the finality of Hitler's death and continued to believe that he would rise phoenixlike from the ashes of Berlin.

The elevation of Hitler into the spiritual realm was not a unique phenomenon in the age of dictatorships. Benito Mussolini (q.v.) in Fascist Italy and Stalin in Soviet Russia were similarly endowed with superhuman qualities as a means of maintaining the totalitarian state. The personality cult was designed deliberately to appeal to the diseased side of the human psyche, above all to the capacity for resentment. A cluster of myths formed around the leader's name. Hitler's image, especially, had an extraordinary influence on Germans, who were affected hypnotically by the Fuehrer's transfixing gaze displayed everywhere in photographs.

FUEHRERBUNKER (Leader's Bunker). Subterranean headquarters below the Chancellery and its garden in Berlin where Hitler spent his last days, from April 20 to 30, 1945. The *Fuehrerbunker* was constructed during World War II some 50 feet below the ground. It could be reached through the New Chancellery by descending a stairway from the butler's pantry. There were two levels. On the upper level was a dining passage separating six rooms on each side. On one side were the kitchens; on the other, the servants' quarters and three additional guest rooms. At the end of the central passage a curved stair led down to Hitler's own deeper bunker. This area had seventeen rooms, all small, cramped, and uncomfortable: Hitler's suite of three rooms, a map room used for conferences, the dressing room and bedroom of Eva Braun, the bedroom of Dr. Paul Joseph Goebbels, the rooms of Dr. Ludwig Stumpfegger (qq.v.), lavatories and bathrooms, an emergency telephone exchange, a drawing room, guardrooms, an anteroom and cloakroom, and a "dog bunker." From the cloakroom an emergency exit led up four flights into the Chancellery garden.

From April 22 to May 1, 1945, the following were present in the bunker:

Albrecht: *SS-Brigadefuehrer* (major general)
Axmann, Artur: *Reichsjugendleiter* (Reich Youth Leader)
Baur, Hans: *SS-Gruppenfuehrer* (lieutenant general), Hitler's personal first pilot
Beetz: *SS-Standartenfuehrer* (colonel), Hitler's personal second pilot
Below, Nicholaus von: Hitler's liaison in the Reich Chancellery and assistant to General Burgdorf
Blondi: Hitler's Alsatian bitch, with her four puppies
Boldt, Capt. Gerhard: Orderly officer and aide-de-camp to Major Freytag-Loringhoven
Bormann, Martin: Hitler's trusted assistant
Braun, Eva: Hitler's companion and, later, his wife for one day
Burgdorf, Gen. Wilhelm: Wehrmacht adjutant at the Fuehrer's headquarters
Christian, Frau Gerda: One of Hitler's two final secretaries
Fegelein, Hermann: *SS-Gruppenfuehrer* (lieutenant general), Eva Braun's brother-in-law
Freytag-Loringhoven, Maj. Bernd von: Adjutant to General Krebs
Goebbels, Dr. Paul Joseph: Minister for Public Enlightenment and Propaganda
Goebbels, Frau Magda: Goebbels's wife, with her six young children
Guensche, Otto: *SS-Sturmbannfuehrer* (major), Hitler's SS adjutant
Hewell, Walther: Joachim von Ribbentrop's personal liaison officer
Hitler, Adolf
Hoegl: *SS-Standartenfuehrer* (colonel), deputy to *SS-Brigadefuehrer* Rattenhuber
Johannmeier, Maj. Willi: Wehrmacht attaché at the Fuehrer's headquarters and assistant to General Burgdorf
Junge, Frau Gertrud: One of Hitler's two final secretaries
Karnau, Hermann: Security guard on duty in the bunker
Kempka, Erich: *SS-Sturmbannfuehrer* (major), Hitler's personal chauffeur and transport officer
Krebs, Gen. Hans: Chief of staff
Krueger, Fräulein Else: Martin Bormann's secretary
Linge, Heinz: *SS-Sturmbannfuehrer* (major), Hitler's valet
Lorenz, Heinz: Representative of the Press Service of the Ministry for Public Enlightenment and Propaganda
Mansfeld, Erich: *SS-Hauptscharfuehrer* (master sergeant), guard on duty in the bunker
Manzialy, Fräulein: Hitler's vegetarian cook
Matthiesing, Heinz: Batman to Von Below
Mueller, Willi Otto: Tailor in the Reich Chancellery
Müller, Heinrich: Chief of the Gestapo
Naumann, Werner: Assistant to Dr. Goebbels in the Ministry for Public Enlightenment and Propaganda
Poppen, Hilco: Guard on duty in the bunker
Rattenhuber, Johann: *SS-Brigadefuehrer* (major gen-

eral), head of the detective force responsible for the Fuehrer's safety
Schwaegermann, Günther August Wilhelm: *SS-Hauptsturmfuehrer* (Captain)
Stumpfegger, Dr. Ludwig: Hitler's personal physician
Varo, Baroness von
Voss, Admiral: Liaison officer for Grand Adm. Karl Doenitz
Weidling, General: Commandant of Berlin
Weiss, Lieutenant Colonel: Aide-de-camp to General Burgdorf
Zander, Wilhelm: *SS-Standartenfuehrer* (colonel), Martin Bormann's deputy

The following were the major visitors to the bunker from April 20 to April 25, 1945:

Christian, Eckard: Luftwaffe general
Doenitz, Karl: Grand admiral and successor to Hitler
Greim, Robert Ritter von: Luftwaffe general and last field marshal appointed by Hitler
Jodl, Alfred: General and chief of the Leadership Staff of the armed forces, 1939–1945
Keitel, Wilhelm: General and Hitler's chief military adviser
Reitsch, Hanna: Well-known woman test pilot
Ribbentrop, Joachim von: Foreign Minister
Schoerner, Ferdinand: General field marshal
Speer, Albert: Architect and Minister for Armaments and War Production

See also GÖTTERDÄMMERUNG.

FUEHRERHAUPTQUARTIER (Leader's Field Headquarters). Operational headquarters used by Hitler during World War II. Rastenburg, in East Prussia, one of the *Fuehrerhauptquartiere*, was the scene of the July Plot (q.v.) of 1944.

FUEHRERLEXIKON. The Nazi *Who's Who*. Published in 1934, it gave brief accounts of the Nazi party leaders and hierarchy, especially those who had taken part in the political drive for power. The lexicon gave the names of National Socialist fighters, martyrs, politicians, industrial managers, civil servants, lawyers, and technologists. There were some omissions, notably the name of Joachim von Ribbentrop (q.v.), who at the time was regarded as a parvenu. Included also were the names of many third-rate, comparatively unknown Nazis. No women were mentioned, nor were there many names of the older military figures. A second edition was contemplated, but it never appeared.

FUEHRERPRINZIP (Leadership Principle). Concept, outlined by Hitler in *Mein Kampf* (q.v.), that the new Germany must be an authoritarian state with power emanating from the leader at the top. As early as July 1921 Hitler insisted that the *Fuehrerprinzip* (Fuehrer principle) be the law of the Nazi party. In *Mein Kampf* he denounced democracy as nonsense and made it clear that the coming Third Reich would be a dictatorship. "Every man will have advisers to help him, but the decision will be made by one man." "Irresponsible parliamentarianism" would be succeeded by the absolute responsibility of a leader and an elite of assistant leaders. The principle was applied to all National Socialist organizations; thus Frau Gertrud Scholtz-Klink (q.v.) became Fuehrerin of the National Socialist *Frauenschaften* (q.v.).

See also FUEHRER-KORPS.

FUEHRERSTAAT (Leader State). Descriptive term for the Third Reich. The *Fuehrerstaat* was a state in which the will of the leader was the highest law of the land. The term was popular among National Socialists.

FUEHRERTREU (Loyal to the Leader). Phrase applied to those who remained utterly faithful to the leader under all circumstances. In the Third Reich the man who was *Fuehrertreu* was regarded as the noblest of human beings.

FUEHRUNGSHAUPTAMT-SS (Operational Headquarters–SS). Main office of the SS (q.v.), responsible for training its members.

FUNK, WALTHER (1890–1960). National Socialist politician, Minister of Economics, and president of the Reichsbank. Walther Funk was born in Trakehnen, East Prussia, on August 18, 1890, to a family of businessmen. He was a man of many talents in a wide variety of subjects, including economics, philosophy, literature, and music. At the University of Berlin he studied philosophy, law, and economics. Drafted into the Army in 1916, he was discharged because of ill health. Working on the conservative *Berliner Boersenzeitung*, he became chief editor of its business section in 1920 and served as editor from 1922 until 1932. He was a fervent nationalist and strongly anti-Marxist. Through Gregor Strasser (q.v.) he met Hitler in 1931 and joined the Nazi party. Within a short time he was Hitler's personal economics adviser and chief of the party office for the private economy. To relieve the economic depression he proposed public works, a large road-building program, mechanization of farms, and intensified automobile manufacture. He was elected to the Reichstag (q.v.) in July 1933.

In March 1933, after Hitler was named Chancellor, Funk was appointed Press Chief of the Reich government, Undersecretary of the Reich Ministry for Public Enlightenment and Propaganda under Dr. Paul Joseph Goebbels (q.v.), and chairman of the board of directors of the Reich Broadcasting Company. In 1938 he succeeded Dr. Hjalmar Schacht (q.v.) as Minister of Economics. Within two years he had taken over Schacht's posts as president of the Reichsbank and Plenipotentiary of the War Economy. In this dual role he became responsible for the economic and financial leadership of Germany. Schacht, who had only contempt for his successor, denounced him as "a harmless homosexual and alcoholic." In 1942 Funk entered into an agreement with Heinrich Himmler (q.v.) whereby the Reichsbank was to receive gold, jewels, and currency taken from Jews killed in the extermination camps (q.v.); no questions were to be asked.

Throughout his career Funk never opposed any measure that Hitler favored. He devoted his pen and his glib journalistic mind completely to the service of the Fuehrer because he believed that no one else was able to rescue the fatherland from either bankruptcy or communism. He has been called a weak, not very intelligent man who willingly went along with a movement that gave him high rank and material benefits.

On October 20, 1945, Funk, along with twenty-one other Nazi leaders, was indicted by the International Military Tribunal at Nuremberg (*see* NUREMBERG TRIAL). With great emotion he protested his innocence: "I have never in my life consciously done anything which could contribute to such an indictment. If I have been made guilty of those acts, through error or ignorance, then my guilt is a human tragedy and not a trial." The Tribunal, however, found that he either knew what was being received by the Reichsbank from the so-called Max Heiliger deposit account (q.v.) or was deliberately closing his eyes. He was found guilty on count 2 (crimes against peace), count 3 (war crimes), and count 4 (crimes against humanity) and sentenced to life imprisonment. In 1957 he was released from Spandau Prison because of illness. He died in Düsseldorf on May 31, 1960.

FURTWÄNGLER, WILHELM (1886–1954). Widely recognized as one of the great musical conductors of the twentieth century, Wilhelm Furtwängler was born in Berlin on January 25, 1886. After study at Munich, he became a conductor at Strassburg (Strasbourg), Lübeck, Mannheim, Vienna, Frankfurt am Main, and Berlin. He led the Berlin Philharmonic from 1922 to 1945 and again from 1950 to 1954. From 1937 on he directed the Bayreuth Festival (q.v.), dedicated to the composer Richard Wagner (q.v.). He also led concert orchestras elsewhere, including the New York Philharmonic in 1926 and 1927 and the Vienna Philharmonic from 1927 to 1930. When Hitler became Chancellor in 1933, many leading literary figures went into exile, but musicians, the least politically minded of artists, did not feel oppressed by the new regime. Furtwängler stayed in Germany, a decision for which he was roundly criticized in other countries. For a time he was out of favor in the Third Reich because he defended the composer Paul Hindemith (q.v.), whose works Nazi officialdom regarded as decadent. Furtwängler remained in Berlin and led the Berlin State Opera in 1933 and 1934. In 1946 a German denazification (q.v.) tribunal accepted Furtwängler's application to have his name and record cleared. He claimed that he had misunderstood conditions in Nazi Germany and that he had always opposed its excesses. He died in Baden-Baden on November 30, 1954.

FW-190. *See* FOCKE WULF-190.

G

GALEN, CLEMENS AUGUST GRAF VON to GÜRTNER, FRANZ

GALEN, CLEMENS AUGUST GRAF VON (1878–1946). Cardinal-Archbishop of Münster. Clemens August Graf von Galen was born in Dinklage on March 16, 1878. He started his career in the Catholic Church in 1904 as bishop's chaplain in Münster. He became a priest in Berlin in 1919 and an archbishop in Münster in 1933. That year he issued a pastoral letter against the National Socialist racial doctrine (q.v.). Thereafter, he criticized the Nazi government for practices he regarded as inconsistent with Christianity. In 1941 he publicly denounced the execution of mentally ill persons. Cardinal von Galen died in Münster on March 22, 1946.

Clemens August Cardinal Graf von Galen. [*Ullstein*]

GALLAND, ADOLF (1911–   ). Fighter ace and Luftwaffe (q.v.) organizer. Adolf Galland was born in Westerholt, Recklinghausen District, in 1911 and educated in Hindenburg (now Zabrze, Poland). An expert glider pilot

Adolf Galland. [*Imperial War Museum, London*]

at the age of nineteen, he joined the Lufthansa (q.v.), Germany's commercial airline, in 1932. In 1935 he was badly injured in an air crash, but he returned to flying as a pilot for the new Luftwaffe. Galland took part in 300 missions with the Condor Legion (q.v.) in the Spanish Civil War. In the opening months of World War II he was a training officer, but later he was transferred to Jagdgeschwader (Fighter Group) 26 as a pilot. Active in almost every theater of operations, including the British Isles during the Battle of Britain, he was credited by Luftwaffe statisticians with 103 air kills and was awarded many decorations. He was the second Luftwaffe pilot to win the Knight's Cross with Oak Leaves, Swords, and Diamonds. In November 1941 he succeeded Werner Moelders (q.v.) as general of fighters. Galland retained this post until January 1945, when Hermann Goering (q.v.) virtually relieved him of his duties by sending him on leave without naming a successor.

On April 26, 1945, Galland was shot down in combat with an American P-51 Mustang pilot, but he survived. After the war he attributed the failure of the Luftwaffe in the Battle of Britain to the fact that it was used as a strategic instead of a tactical force. Moreover, he said, the squadron commanders and leaders, the group commanders of the years to come, all died in the air battle over Britain.

GAU (District). Main territorial unit in the intricate Nazi party structure. When reorganized in the mid-1920s, the

Nationalsozialistische Deutsche Arbeiterpartei (q.v.; NSDAP) was divided into units corresponding roughly to the old Reichstag (q.v.) electoral districts. The *Gau* was also identical with a civil defense region. Each *Gau* was headed by a *Gauleiter* (district leader), appointed by Hitler and responsible to him. In turn, the *Gau* was broken down into *Kreise* (circuits; *see* KREIS), each being administered by a *Kreisleiter* (q.v.). The next-smallest party unit was the *Ortsgruppe* (local group). In the cities the *Ortsgruppen* were subdivided into street cells *(Zellen)*. This party structure was maintained basically after Hitler came to power. Additional *Gaue* were set up in 1938 for Austria and Czechoslovakia. In all, there were forty-two *Gaue*. The Auslandsorganisation (q.v.), which supervised Germans abroad, was regarded as the forty-third *Gau*. A list of *Gaue* with figures for 1942 follows:[1]

[1]Adapted from Erich Stockhorst, *Fünftausendköpfe*, Blick & Bild Verlag, Velbert and Kettweg, 1967, p. 26.

GAU	GAULEITER	SEAT	NUMBER OF KREISE	NUMBER OF ORTSGRUPPEN
1. Baden	Robert Wagner	Karlsruhe	27	1,040
2. Bayreuth	Fritz Wächtler	Bayreuth	39	1,531
3. Berlin	Paul Joseph Goebbels	Berlin W9	10	269
4. Danzig–West Prussia	Albert Forster	Danzig		
5. Düsseldorf	Friedrich Karl Florian	Düsseldorf	7	156
6. Essen	Josef Terboven	Essen	9	180
7. Franconia	Karl Holz	Nuremberg	18	193
8. Halle-Mersenburg	Joachim Albrecht Eggeling	Halle	17	683
9. Hamburg	Karl Kaufmann	Hamburg	19	195
10. Hesse-Nassau	Jakob Sprenger	Frankfurt am Main	26	1,279
11. Carinthia	Friedrich Rainer	Klagenfurt	8	222
12. Cologne-Aachen	Joseph Grohé	Cologne	18	287
13. Hesse-Kassel	Karl Weinrich	Kassel	15	332
14. Magdeburg-Anhalt	Rudolf Jordan	Dessau	18	560
15. Main-Franconia	Otto Hellmuth	Würzburg	14	317
16. Mark Brandenburg	Emil Stürtz	Berlin W35	31	1,582
17. Mecklenburg	Friedrich Hildebrandt	Schwerin	13	589
18. Moselland	Gustav Simon	Koblenz	18	725
19. Munich–Upper Bavaria	Paul Giesler	Munich	25	562
20. Lower Danube	Hugo Jury	Vienna	24	926
21. Lower Silesia	Karl Hanke	Breslau		
22. Upper Danube	August Eigruber	Linz	16	548
23. Upper Silesia	Fritz Bracht	Kattowitz		
24. East Hannover	Otto Telschow	Lüneburg	16	453
25. East Prussia	Erich Koch	Königsberg	37	613
26. Pomerania	Franz Schwede-Coburg	Stettin	31	974
27. Saxony	Martin Mutschmann	Dresden	27	1,420
28. Salzburg	Gustav Ad. Scheel	Salzburg	5	139
29. Schleswig-Holstein	Heinrich Lohse	Kiel	21	793
30. Swabia	Karl Wahl	Augsburg	15	637
31. Styria	Siegfried Uiberreither	Graz	17	322
32. Sudetenland	Konrad Henlein	Reichenberg	39	3,164
33. South Hannover–Brunswick	Hartmann Lauterbacher	Hannover	26	782

(continued)

GAU	GAULEITER	SEAT	NUMBER OF KREISE	NUMBER OF ORTSGRUPPEN
34. Thuringia	Fritz Sauckel	Weimar	21	1,363
35. Tyrol-Vorarlberg	Franz Hofer	Innsbruck	10	208
36. Wartheland	Arthur Greiser	Posen		
37. Weser-Ems	Paul Wegener	Oldenburg	22	515
38. Westphalia North	Alfred Meyer	Münster	19	690
39. Westphalia South	Albert Hoffmann	Bochum	18	385
40. Westmark	Joseph Bürckel	Neustadt	18	494
41. Vienna	Baldur von Schirach	Vienna	10	426
42. Württemberg-Hohenzollern	Wilhelm Murr	Stuttgart	35	1,036
43. Auslandsorganisation	Ernst Wilhelm Bohle	Berlin		

GAU AGRICULTURAL EXPERT. *See* LANDWIRTSCHAFTLICHER GAUFACHBERATER.

GAUCH, HERMANN. *See* RASSENFORSCHUNG.

GAUFUEHRER. *See* GAULEITER.

GAUGER, MARTIN (1905–1941). Member of the Kreisau Circle (q.v.) and victim of the Nazi regime. In 1934, as a lawyer in the office of the public prosecutor in Munich-Gladbach, Gauger refused to take the required oath of allegiance to Hitler and resigned from the civil service. In a subsequent post as legal adviser to the Bekenntniskirche (q.v.), he devoted himself to the Resistance (q.v.) movement. In May 1940 he fled to the Netherlands by swimming across the icy waters of the Rhine River, arriving just as Hitler's SS (q.v.) troops marched into the neutral country. Captured, he was taken to Buchenwald (q.v.) concentration camp, where he died on July 14, 1941.

GAULEITER (District Leader). The highest-ranking Nazi party official below the top Reich leadership. Sometimes called a *Gaufuehrer*, the *Gauleiter* was responsible for all political and economic activities, civil defense, and the mobilization of labor in his district. Most district leaders were appointed directly by the Fuehrer. For example, in the early days of the Nazi movement Hitler made the youthful Dr. Paul Joseph Goebbels (q.v.) *Gauleiter* of Berlin (October 1926) as a reward for his support at the Bamberg Party Congress (q.v.). In some areas the *Gauleiter* took on police duties. Below the *Gauleiter* in the Nazi hierarchy was the *Kreisleiter* (q.v.), the circuit leader. All were required to swear unconditional allegiance to Hitler.

GAULEITUNG (GL; District Leadership). Administration responsible for the leadership of a *Gau* (q.v.), a district.

GAUPROPAGANDALEITUNG (GPL; District Propaganda Leadership). Administration responsible for propaganda in a *Gau* (q.v.), a district.

GAUSTUDENTENFUEHRUNG (District Student Leadership). Administration responsible for leadership in the Nationalsozialistischer Deutscher Studentenbund (q.v.), the National Socialist German Students' League.

GDVG. *See* GROSSDEUTSCHE VOLKSGEMEINSCHAFT.

GEFOLGSCHAFT (Followers). Term used by Hitler to describe those who were governed by fidelity to the Fuehrer. Hitler adopted the ideal of military leadership and discipline as the most effective means of creating an orderly state. He insisted that for the people to be led was to cooperate voluntarily and not to be commanded. He regarded himself as an official carrying out the will of the people. Fuehrer and followers were expected to be faithful to each other. *See also* FUEHRER WORSHIP.

Gefolgschaft was also the official name of the retinue provided by the Hitler Jugend (q.v.). This organization was expected to furnish loyal support for the Fuehrer. Everything the youngsters did, even their play, was regarded as an important part of their ideological training as the *Gefolgschaft* of the leader. In 1935 a book of tales was published for the Hitler Jugend *Gefolgschaft* with this battle cry for its young readers: "No one shall live after the Fuehrer's death!"

GEHEIME FELDPOLIZEI (Secret Field Police). Special police assigned to the Abwehr (q.v.) for security duty in the armed forces. By 1942 its duties had been taken over by the SD (q.v.).

GEHEIME STAATSPOLIZEI. *See* GESTAPO.

GEHEIMER KABINETTSRAT (Secret Cabinet Council). A special secret cabinet set up by Hitler on February 4, 1938, to guide him in the conduct of foreign affairs. That day the Fuehrer dropped Constantin Freiherr von Neurath as Foreign Minister and replaced him with Joachim von Ribbentrop (qq.v.), who was more agreeable to a policy of aggression. Von Neurath was named presiding officer of the new cabinet. Its members included the chiefs of the three armed services as well as Gen. Wilhelm Keitel (q.v.), chief of the Oberkommando der Wehrmacht (q.v.). Nazi propaganda attempted to depict the council as Hitler's supercabinet. Actually, it never functioned at all. At Nuremberg Hermann Goering (q.v.) denied the existence "even for a minute" of any such cabinet.

GELB (Yellow). Secret code name for the attack on France and the Low Countries in May 1940. On October 9, 1939, Hitler issued a war directive giving provisional orders for such an attack, known by the cover name Fall Gelb (Case Yellow). "I have decided, without further loss of time, to go over to the offensive. Any further delay will not only entail the end of Belgian and perhaps of Dutch neutrality, to the advantage of the Allies, but it will also increasingly strengthen the military power of the enemy, reduce the confidence of the neutral nations in Germany's final victory, and make it more difficult to bring Italy as a full ally into the war." Operation Yellow was implemented in May 1940 with notable success.

GEMPP, WALTER (1878–1939). Chief of the Berlin fire brigade and victim of Nazi vengeance. For twenty-seven years Walter Gempp served the Berlin Fire Department and as its chief made it a highly respected institution. Immediately after the Reichstag fire (q.v.) of February 27, 1933, he incurred the wrath of Nazi officials by reporting that the fire brigade had been warned too late, that Hermann Goering (q.v.) had forbidden him to make full use of his men and equipment, and that enough incendiary material had been found in the undamaged rooms of the Reichstag (q.v.) to fill a truck. A month later Gempp was accused of "Marxist subversive and inflammatory activities," but he nevertheless testified at the Reichstag Fire Trial (q.v.). His damaging evidence was never forgotten by the top Nazi leaders. Arrested in September 1937 for malpractice, he was convicted but appealed the verdict. On May 2, 1939, before his new trial was to begin, he was found strangled in his cell.

GENEALOGICAL CHART. *See* AHNENSCHEIN.

GENERAL FIELD MARSHAL. *See* GENERALFELDMARSCHALL.

GENERAL GOVERNMENT. *See* GOUVERNEMENT-GÉNÉRALE.

GENERAL QUARTERMASTER. *See* GENERALQUARTIERMEISTER.

GENERAL SS. *See* ALLGEMEINE-SS.

GENERAL STAFF OF THE ARMY. *See* GENERALSTAB DES HEERES.

GENERALFELDMARSCHALL (GFM; General Field Marshal). The highest rank in the German armed forces. In addition to the prestige of an exalted rank, the *Generalfeldmarschall* received an annual salary of 36,000 reichsmarks plus allowances, all of it exempt from income tax. The honor had been used sparingly before the era of the Third Reich. In World War I only five general field marshals were named by Emperor William II, and not even Gen. Erich Ludendorff (q.v.) was given the honor. In a flush of enthusiasm at the collapse of France, Hitler on July 19, 1940, created twelve new general field marshals: Walther von Brauchitsch, Wilhelm Keitel, Gerd von

Hitler with his general field marshals at the Reich Chancellery in 1940: (left to right) Wilhelm Keitel, Gerd von Rundstedt, Fedor von Bock, Hermann Goering, Hitler, Walther von Brauchitsch, Wilhelm Ritter von Leeb, Wilhelm List, Günther Hans von Kluge, Erwin von Witzleben, Walther von Reichenau. [*Associated Press*]

Rundstedt, Walther von Reichenau, Fedor von Bock, Wilhelm Ritter von Leeb, Wilhelm List, Günther Hans von Kluge, Erwin von Witzleben, and Luftwaffe (q.v.) Generals Erhard Milch, Albert Kesselring, and Hugo Sperrle (qq.v.). In naming these officers to the highest military rank the Fuehrer had the additional motive of strengthening his hold over the conservative military caste, which he mistrusted.

On January 31, 1943, Hitler conferred the honor on Gen. Friedrich von Paulus (q.v.) in the hope that his besieged general would hold out at Stalingrad. By this time Hitler was furious with the officers who had disappointed him in the Russian campaign. The next day he told a war conference at his field headquarters: "This is the last Field Marshal that I shall appoint in this war." Ironically, that very day orders came through for the naming of three more: Ernst von Busch, Ewald von Kleist, and Maximilian Freiherr von Weichs (qq.v.). Four more were subsequently named: Walther Model, Ferdinand Schoerner, Wolfram Freiherr von Richthofen, and Robert Ritter von Greim (qq.v.). Erwin Rommel (q.v.) was made a field marshal in 1942. Gen. Erich von Manstein (q.v.), who held the rank himself, testified at Nuremberg that, of the many active general field marshals who took part in World War II, ten were sent home during the war and three lost their lives for being implicated in the July Plot (q.v.) of 1944.

GENERALQUARTIERMEISTER (GenQu; General Quartermaster). Principal staff officer responsible for supply at the Oberkommando des Heeres (q.v.), the High Command of the Army, and at the Oberkommando der Luftwaffe (q.v.), the High Command of the Air Force.

GENERALSTAB DES HEERES (GenStdH; General Staff of the Army). Highest administrative staff of the Army in the Third Reich.

GENOCIDE. Use of a deliberate, systematic policy designed to eliminate an entire racial, political, or cultural group of a nation or a people. The word was formed from the Greek *genos* (race, kind) and *-cide* (killing). It was first applied to the attempted extermination of the Jews in the Third Reich and elsewhere. Genocide was considered part of Hitler's program of "blood, selection, and austerity" toward the goal of maintaining the purity of "Aryan-Nordic-Germanic blood." *See also* CONCENTRATION CAMPS; EXTERMINATION CAMPS.

GENQU. *See* GENERALQUARTIERMEISTER.

GENSTDH. *see* GENERALSTAB DES HEERES.

GENTLEMEN'S CLUB. *See* HERRENKLUB.

GEORGE, STEFAN ANTON. *See* GEORGE-KREIS.

GEORGE-KREIS (George Circle). An exclusive group of literary cultists who had profound influence on German life during the Weimar Republic (q.v.) and who unconsciously prepared the way for Hitler and the Third Reich. Their leader was the poet Stefan Anton George (1868–1933), called "the embodiment of Roman culture on Rhenish soil" and "Napoleon at the court of the Muses." Stefan George looked upon every German poet as a priest and prophet of the nation, a man of "heroic vitality" who was destined to set the pace for his fellow countrymen. His own poems were filled with imagery and artifices of punctuation and spelling; it was virtually impossible to translate them into other languages.

Although predominantly a poet, George was also interested in political and social issues. He preferred spiritual to material values and had an aristocratic disdain for the philistines of his day. Drawn to Nietzsche's philosophy, George was impressed by the image of the superman. A neoromantic, he was hostile to rationalism and preferred guidance by the emotions. He was attracted by the idea of ruthless, unlimited power. Above all, he loved ancient Teutonic lore and called for its revival. One day, he predicted, there would come a hero who would lead the rebirth of Germany, Europe, and all the world. That superman would burst the chains of a backward society, bring order to the ruins, and plant the seeds of a new Reich. Wearing black clothes of a clerical cut, George moved from city to city, presenting his views to small audiences of the faithful.

Around George there gathered a worshipful cult of followers, including Friedrich Gundolf (q.v.), Ludwig Klages, Karl Wolfskehl, and Alfred Schuler. Calling themselves the Cosmics, they formed a kind of secular priesthood and imitated George in dress, facial expression, and argument. One of the Cosmics, Schuler, who was the first to use the swastika (*Hakenkreuz*, q.v.) as a symbol, attempted to give the movement an anti-Semitic tone (*see* ANTI-SEMITISM), a step that George himself deplored.

The teachings of the George-Kreis spread rapidly in academic circles in the period immediately preceding World War I. When an impoverished Hitler went to Munich in early 1923, he found the bohemian atmosphere of the taverns and cafés to his liking. Here he attended the lectures of Alfred Schuler and was much impressed by their tone of anti-Semitism and virulent nationalism.

GEREKE, GÜNTHER (1893–). Opponent of National Socialism. Günther Gereke was born in Grüna on October 6, 1893. In 1932 Chancellor Franz von Papen (q.v.) appointed him Commissioner for Work Procurement, a post that was continued after Hitler came to power. Because of Gereke's opposition to National Socialism, he was arrested on unfounded charges of speculation, bribery, and misappropriation of public funds. Gereke was a friend of Dr. Johannes Popitz and Field Marshal Erwin von Witzleben (qq.v.), both of whom joined the conspiracy against Hitler, and he himself was arrested again after the July Plot (q.v.) of 1944. He was freed by the Allies.

GERMAN-AMERICAN BUND. A pro-Nazi organization in the United States during the early years of the Third Reich. Of the numerous American Nazi groups that emerged in the 1930s the largest was the Friends of the New Germany, which in 1935 became the German-American Bund. Under the leadership of Fritz Kuhn the German-American Bund organized camps for its members and children in New Jersey and held mass meetings at Madison Square Garden in New York. Proud of his contacts with leading figures of the Third Reich, Kuhn con-

Members of the German-American Bund at a meeting in Madison Square Garden in 1939. [*Wide World Photos*]

veyed to friends inside Germany a somewhat exaggerated picture of the strength and influence of his organization in the United States. The Steuben Society, a conservative German-American organization, warned Hitler that the American people were angered by the activities of the German-American Bund on their soil. The Fuehrer had ambivalent feelings about the Bund: on the one hand it supported the racial ties he so vehemently espoused, but on the other hand he was concerned about possible effects on American public opinion. Officially Hitler disavowed the German-American Bund after protests were received from the American Ambassador in Berlin. The Fuehrer denied that German-Americans owed allegiance to Germany and promised "to throw any official into the North Sea who sent Nazi propaganda to the United States." The Bund made little headway in the United States and vanished during World War II.

GERMAN ARMAMENT WORKS. *See* DEUTSCHE AUSRÜSTUNGSWERKE.

GERMAN CULTURE, STUDY OF. *See* DEUTSCHKUNDE.

GERMAN ECONOMIC ENTERPRISES. *See* DEUTSCHE WIRTSCHAFTSBETRIEBE.

GERMAN EXCAVATION AND QUARRYING CO., LTD. *See* DEUTSCHE ERD- UND STEINWERKE, GMBH.

GERMAN FAITH MOVEMENT. *See* DEUTSCHE GLAUBENSBEWEGUNG.

GERMAN GLANCE. *See* DEUTSCHER BLICK.

GERMAN GREETING. *See* "HEIL HITLER!"

GERMAN LABOR FRONT. *See* DEUTSCHE ARBEITSFRONT.

GERMAN RACIAL ASSISTANCE OFFICE. *See* VOLKSDEUTSCHE MITTELSTELLE.

GERMAN RESETTLEMENT SOCIETY. *See* DEUTSCHE ANSIEDLUNGSGESELLSCHAFT.

GERMAN RIGHTIST PARTY. *See* DEUTSCHE RECHTS-PARTEI.

GERMAN SOCIAL DEMOCRATIC PARTY. *See* SPD.

GERMAN SOCIETY FOR MILITARY POLICY AND MILITARY SCIENCE. *See* DEUTSCHE GESELLSCHAFT FÜR WEHRPOLITIK UND WEHRWISSENSCHAFT.

GERMAN WORKERS' PARTY. *See* DEUTSCHE ARBEITERPARTEI.

GERMAN YOUTH MOVEMENT. *See* BUND DEUTSCHER MÄDEL; HITLER JUGEND.

GERMANISCHE-SS (Germanic SS). Units of the Waffen-SS (q.v.) composed of native Germans in such occupied territories as Norway and Denmark.

GERMANIZATION. *See* EINDEUTSCHUNG.

GERMANS IN FOREIGN COUNTRIES. *See* AUSLANDSDEUTSCHE.

"GERMANY ABOVE ALL." *See* "DEUTSCHLAND ÜBER ALLES."

"GERMANY AWAKE!" *See* "DEUTSCHLAND ERWACHE!"

"GERMANY AWAKE! PERISH JUDAH!" *See* "DEUTSCHLAND ERWACHE! JUDA VERRECKE!"

"GERMANY IS HITLER! HITLER IS GERMANY!" *See* "DEUTSCHLAND IST HITLER! HITLER IST DEUTSCHLAND!"

GESAMT-SS (Total SS). Term used to describe all the SS (q.v.) branches.

GESCHWADER (Groups). Operational units of the Luftwaffe (q.v.). The *Geschwader* were named for such national heroes as Von Hindenburg, Von Richthofen, Immelmann, and Horst Wessel.

GESETZ ZUR ERHEBUNG DER NOT VON VOLK UND REICH. *See* ENABLING ACT.

GESTAPO (Geheime Staatspolizei; Secret State Police). A secret police force dedicated to the task of maintaining the National Socialist regime. Hitler deemed it necessary to protect the existence of the Third Reich by a political police that would track down and eliminate all dissidents, complainers, and opponents. He regarded any individual, no matter what his status, as a potential suspect. His Gestapo became a symbol of the Nazi reign of terror.

In the early days of the Nazi movement Hitler was protected by a personal bodyguard called the Stabswache (q.v.), the Headquarters Guard. In the late 1920s this small group was enlarged into the SS, all of whose units were combined in 1929 under Heinrich Himmler (qq.v.). In April 1933 Hermann Goering (q.v.) incorporated the political police of Prussia into the Gestapo as Amt (Office) IV of the Reichssicherheitshauptamt (q.v.), the Central Security Office of the Third Reich. He set up headquarters in a suitable group of buildings on Prinz Albrechtstrasse in Berlin, formerly occupied by an arts and crafts school and not far from his own reconstructed palace.

Meanwhile, a struggle for power in the party took place between Goering and Himmler. Each wanted to be head of a unified political police force. At the time the meek-looking but overwhelmingly ambitious Himmler held a secondary post as police president of Munich. One of his assistants was Heinrich Müller (q.v.), later to head the Gestapo. Himmler prepared the way by gradually taking control of the political police in a series of German states. Finally, in April 1934, he headed the entire unified political police force.

The Gestapo organization was extended throughout Germany and developed into the most important security organ of the state. It became autonomous and set up its own legal system, with power far exceeding that of any law court in the Third Reich, and began to exercise its right to assume control over the lives, freedom, and property of all Germans. In working for "the annihilation of the enemy," it could and did use any methods it deemed necessary. It hunted down Jews, Marxists, and Bolsheviks. It interrogated and imprisoned anyone who told an anti-Nazi joke. It made reports on persons who dared to celebrate Emperor William II's birthday, for they were considered dangerous monarchists opposed to National Socialism. The average citizen was in dread of the Gestapo because of rumors about those who disappeared into its headquarters and suffered tortures in its cellars.

Gestapo methods were crude but effective. Any person suspected of opposition to the Hitler regime was first given a warning. If that did not work, he was taken into custody "for the security of the State." The usual form of punishment was assignment to a concentration camp (*see* CONCENTRATION CAMPS). If the victim was considered really dangerous, he was arrested, interrogated, and sometimes beaten to death. Where it was necessary to provide a semblance of legality, the accused was brought before the Volksgericht (q.v.), the People's Court. Here justice was dispensed on an assembly line.

The Gestapo played a role in virtually all the major developments of the Nazi movement. It was at the fulcrum of events before and after Hitler became Chancellor. It was in the background of such important occurrences as the Blomberg-Fritsch crisis (q.v.), the *Anschluss* (q.v.) between Germany and Austria, and the acquisition of Czechoslovakia. During World War II it was instrumental in breaking down resistance in the occupied countries. Gestapo agents were active during the terror in Poland, in the execution of Russian prisoners of war, and in the arrest and slaughter of the conspirators of July 1944 (*see* JULY PLOT). Not only was the Gestapo a formidable organization inside the Third Reich, but it extended its activities throughout Europe and even to distant parts of the world. It followed the German armed forces into occupied countries and used its own tested methods to destroy all elements hostile to Nazi rule. Everywhere it was regarded as one of the cruelest police forces of modern times.

After the war the International Military Tribunal at Nuremberg, in judging National Socialist leaders and organizations, linked the Gestapo and the SD (q.v.) in this judgment:

> They were first linked together on June 26, 1936, by the appointment of Heydrich, who was the Chief of the S.D., to the position of Chief of the Security Police, which was defined to include both the Gestapo and the Criminal Police.
>
> From a functional point of view both the Gestapo and the S.D. were important and closely related groups within the organization of the Security Police and the S.D. The Security Police and S.D. was under a single command, that of Heydrich and later Kaltenbrunner, as Chief of the Security Police and S.D.; it had a single headquarters, the R.S.H.A.; it had its own command channels and worked as one organization both in Germany, in occupied territories and in the areas immediately behind the front lines. During the period with which the Tribunal is primarily concerned applicants for positions in the Security Police and S.D. received training in all its components, the Gestapo, Criminal Police and S.D.
>
> The Security Police and S.D. was a voluntary organization. It is true that many civil servants and administrative officials were transferred into the Security Police. The claim that this transfer was compulsory amounts to nothing more than the claim that they had to accept the transfer or resign their positions, with a possibility of having incurred official disfavour. During the war a member of the Security Police and S.D. did not have a free choice of assignments within that organization, and the refusal to accept a particular position, especially when serving in occupied territory, might have led to serious punishment. The fact remains, however, that all members of the Security Police and S.D. joined the organization voluntarily under no other sanction than the desire to retain their positions as officials.
>
> The Gestapo and S.D. were used for purposes which were criminal under the Charter involving the persecution and extermination of the Jews, brutalities and killings in concentration camps, excesses in the administration of occupied territories, the administration of the slave labour programme and the mistreatment and murder of prisoners-of-war. The defendant Kaltenbrunner, who was a member of this organization, was among those who used it for these purposes. In dealing with the Gestapo the Tribunal includes all executive and administrative officials of Amt IV of the R.S.H.A. or concerned with Gestapo administration in other departments of the R.S.H.A. and all local Gestapo officials serving both inside and outside of Germany, including the members of the Frontier Police, but not including the members of the Border and Customs Protection or the Secret Field Police, except such members as have been specified above. At the suggestion of the prosecution the Tribunal does not include persons employed by the Gestapo for purely clerical, stenographic, janitorial or similar unofficial routine tasks. In dealing with the S.D. the Tribunal includes Amts III, VI and VII of the R.S.H.A. and all other members of the S.D. including all local representatives and agents, honorary or otherwise,

whether they were technically members of the S.S. or not.

The Tribunal declares to be criminal within the meaning of the Charter the group composed of those members of the Gestapo and S.D. holding the positions enumerated in the preceding paragraph who became or remained members of the organization with knowledge that it was being used for the commission of acts declared criminal by Article 6 of the Charter, or who were personally implicated as members of the organization in the commission of such crimes. The basis for this finding is the participation of the organization in war crimes and crimes against humanity connected with the war; this group declared criminal cannot include, therefore, persons who had ceased to hold the positions enumerated in the preceding paragraph prior to September 1, 1939.

Bibliography. Edward Crankshaw, *The Gestapo,* Putnam & Co., Ltd., London, 1956.

GESUNDHEITSAMT (Health Office). Nazi health office with branches throughout Germany. Its special interest was to maintain the health of all Aryan citizens.

GHETTO LAWS. *See* NUREMBERG LAWS ON CITIZENSHIP AND RACE.

GIEHSE, THERESE (1898–). Actress and refugee from the Third Reich. Working on the stage from the age of twenty, Therese Giehse was well known in Germany for her performances as Mother Courage in the play of the same name by Bertolt Brecht (q.v.). In 1926 she began an engagement at the famous Munich Kammerspiel. Just before Hitler became Chancellor in 1933, the *Völkischer Beobachter* (q.v.) praised the actress. "At last we can see a genuine German woman on the Jewish stage," was the verdict of one of its critics. The judgment did not last long. Soon it was discovered that Therese Giehse was a Bavarian of Jewish descent. Her life was endangered when she continued singing satirical songs at the cabaret Die Pfeffermühle (The Pepper Mill). She fled to Zürich, where she presented another version of the cabaret. Angered Swiss Nazis soon put a stop to what they regarded as subversive agitation. Therese Giehse was engaged, nevertheless, as an actress by the Zürich Schauspielhaus. After World War II she returned to Germany.

GILLARS, MILDRED (1901–). American-born "Axis Sally" of World War II. Mildred Gillars was a dropout from Ohio Wesleyan, where in 1920 she was the first woman student to wear knickers. She went to Germany in the 1920s as a music student. During World War II she broadcast Nazi propaganda from Berlin, greeting American troops with such statements as "Go home and forget the war!" American GIs, who enjoyed the jazz records she played, dubbed her Axis Sally and paid little attention to her propaganda line. Arrested by Allied authorities after the war, she was sentenced to twelve years in a federal prison for women. She was paroled in 1961. After teaching German, French, and music in a suburban Roman Catholic convent in Columbus, Ohio, she returned to Ohio Wesleyan and completed her bachelor's degree in speech in 1973 at the age of seventy-two.

GIRAUD, HENRI (1879–1949). French general who was involved in a remarkable escape from a Nazi prison. Henri Giraud was born in Paris on January 18, 1879, of Alsatian descent and was educated at the Saint-Cyr Military Academy. A captain of Zouaves in World War I, he was wounded in battle, left for dead, and captured by the Germans. Within a few weeks he escaped from a hospital and made his way to the Netherlands. He was active in the North African colonial wars from 1922 to 1933. In 1939, at the outbreak of World War II, he was given command of the Seventh Army Group. Once again, in May 1940, he was captured by the Germans, who this time placed him in the fortress of Königstein, a maximum-security prison perched on a sheer cliff with all entrances double-guarded and numerous sentries passing every few minutes.

For two years Giraud carefully planned his escape. He learned German until he could speak almost without accent, and he memorized every contour of a stolen map of the countryside. On April 17, 1942, he lowered himself down the side of the mountain fortress and reached the ground. Donning a raincoat and a Tyrolean hat, he shaved his moustache and headed toward the town of Schandau, 5 miles to the south, where a contact was waiting. Escaping a motorcycle search party, he leaped aboard a moving train, changed trains at Stuttgart, and through a series of fortunate ruses managed to reach the French border 40 miles away.

Giraud's spectacular escape captured the imagination of a defeated and humiliated France, and he became a public idol. Infuriated, Heinrich Himmler (q.v.) sent secret orders to Gestapo (q.v.) headquarters in Paris to "find Giraud and assassinate him." German agents swarmed into Unoccupied France in search of the missing general. Giraud finally escaped from France by boarding a British submarine and joined Adm. Jean-François Darlan in North Africa. He fought alongside the Americans in Tunisia. In May 1943 he began to work with Gen. Charles de Gaulle and the French Committee of National Liberation, but differences with De Gaulle led to his resignation in November. He served as commander in chief of the Free French Forces until 1944. From 1944 to 1948 he was vice president of the Conseil Supérieur de la Guerre (Supreme Council of War). He was awarded the Médaille militaire for his escape from Königstein. Giraud died in Dijon on March 11, 1949.

Bibliography. Jacques Grunier, *Un général a disparu,* Presse de la Cité, Paris, 1971.

GIRLS' GROUP LEADER. *See* GRUPPENLEITERIN.

GISEVIUS, HANS BERND (1904–1974). Diplomat and writer. Hans Bernd Gisevius was born in Arnsberg on July 14, 1904. Entering the diplomatic service, he held various posts from the beginning of the Nazi regime in 1933. Gisevius was involved in a number of plots to overthrow Hitler. From 1940 to 1944 he served as Vice Consul in Zürich, and in this capacity he conferred frequently with Allen Welsh Dulles (q.v.) of the United States Office of Strategic Services. After the failure of the July Plot (q.v.) in 1944, Gisevius took refuge in Switzerland. He was a leading prosecution witness at the Nuremberg Trial (q.v.). Gisevius spent several years in the United States and West Berlin after the war, but he returned to Switzerland to make his home there. He died in West Germany on February 23, 1974.

In his memoirs Gisevius described the leading personalities of the Third Reich and the attempts to assassinate Hitler. He was appalled by the immorality of the Nazi regime, especially by the events of the *Kristallnacht* (q.v.), the Night of the Broken Glass. He indicated that the word *pogrom* was not strong enough to describe what had happened in Germany: "Not a Jewish home remained unmolested, not a Jewish business unplundered, not a synagogue unburned." Gisevius reported that anyone who experienced those terrible hours would never forget them: "Incited to a pitch of insanity, the mob vented its emotion on defenseless people."

Gisevius absolved the "overwhelming majority who had no part in the hideous affair." The Nazi instigators of the riots stopped them abruptly and with significant haste began to clean up. Gisevius revealed that although Heinrich Himmler and Reinhard Heydrich (qq.v.) signed the orders, "the Fuehrer himself inaugurated these frightful and portentous excesses." The cowed middle class, Gisevius wrote, "stared at the Nazi monster like a rabbit at a snake."

Bibliography. Hans Bernd Gisevius, *To the Bitter End*, tr. by Richard and Clara Winston, Houghton Mifflin Company, Boston, 1947.

GL. *See* GAULEITUNG.

GLAGAU, OTTO (1834–1892). Anti-Semitic journalist and forerunner of National Socialist ideology. With Wilhelm Marr (q.v.), Otto Glagau was one of the German journalists who influenced public opinion against the Jews. After the financial crash of 1873, he wrote a series of articles attributing a Berlin stock exchange swindle to the Jews. They were, he charged, the spearhead of capitalism, an alien race that was sucking the marrow from the bones of the German people. Manchester liberalism, he said, had given the Jews an opportunity to create havoc. Like Marr, Glagau preached a combination of nationalism and a vague socialism, which eventually became the philosophy of National Socialism.

GLAUBE UND SCHÖNHEIT (Faith and Beauty). A special branch of the Bund Deutscher Mädel (q.v.), the League of German Girls. Established by Baldur von Schirach (q.v.) in 1937, Glaube und Schönheit was intended to develop the spiritual and physical graces of girls from the ages of seventeen to twenty-one. They received special training in the domestic sciences and fashion design and were supposed to be prepared for marriage. The girls were to become prize exhibits for the National Socialist conception of ideal womanhood. The Glaube und Schönheit handbook for 1943 included recipes, the birth dates of Nazi heroes, and pictures of Von Schirach and Hitler's mother.

GLEICHSCHALTUNG (Coordination). The complete coordination of all political and other activities by the National Socialist regime. To consolidate his dictatorship, Hitler was determined to fuse every element of German life into a functioning Nazi social machine. For example, trade unions with differing political views and aims had hitherto existed side by side; now they were consolidated into one body with the military name German Labor Front (Deutsche Arbeitsfront, q.v.). *Gleichschaltung* became a national pursuit with its collection of fronts, including a German Shoe Front and a German Milk Front.

GLEIWITZ RAID (also called Operation Himmler). A simulated assault on a German radio station by "Polish" troops on the evening before the German invasion of Poland on September 1, 1939. In early August 1939 Reinhard Heydrich (q.v.), chief of the Gestapo, called in Alfred Helmut Naujocks (q.v.) and outlined to him details of a fictitious Polish attack on a small German radio station at Gleiwitz, just 1 mile from the Polish border. The idea was to make it appear that the attacking force consisted of Poles. Practical proof was needed, said Heydrich, for such attacks by Poles "for the foreign press as well as for propaganda." Naujocks, an adventurous daredevil, was delighted by the assignment. Leading a force of six SS (q.v.) men, he went to Gleiwitz and waited fourteen days to study the situation. There he was told that he would be supplied with an expendable condemned criminal from one of the concentration camps (q.v.), who would be dressed in a Polish uniform and left dead at the scene as "evidence" (*see* CANNED GOODS).

At 7:30 on the evening of August 31, Naujocks and his commandos, clad in Polish uniforms, stormed into the radio station, fired a fusillade of shots, and with pistol butts slugged the employees. One of the raiders seized an emergency transmitter and barked out in perfect Polish: "People of Poland! The time has come for war between Poland and Germany! Unite and smash down any German, all Germans, who oppose your war. Trample all resistance! The time has come!" The commandos fired more shots that could be heard by Radio Gleiwitz listeners. Then they fled, leaving the blood-soaked body (in civilian clothes) of the unfortunate camp inmate shot by them at the site of the raid.

The next day, in a high state of excitement, Chancellor Hitler informed the German people that they were at war with Poland. Among the reasons he gave for his invasion was "the attack by regular Polish troops on the Gleiwitz transmitter."

GLOBKE, HANS (1898–1973). Prussian civil service bureaucrat who wrote the official commentary on the law placing German Jews outside German society. Born in Aachen, the son of a cloth dealer, Hans Globke studied law and in 1925 began a civil servant's career as deputy to the police commissioner of his hometown. In 1929 he became an administrative adviser to the Prussian Ministry of the Interior and in the late thirties directed the citizenship department of the ministry. An efficient organizer, Globke served Hitler with the same loyalty and discretion that he had exhibited in working for the Weimar Republic (q.v.). Although he never joined the Nationalsozialistische Deutsche Arbeiterpartei (q.v.), he was accused by critics of playing a major role in writing the anti-Jewish legislation of the Third Reich.

After World War II, Chancellor Konrad Adenauer (q.v.), though a firm opponent of Nazism, retained Globke at his post as State Secretary of the Chancellery from 1953 to 1963 and rejected Globke's five offers of resignation.

Meanwhile, an anti-Globke campaign continued. An East German court tried him *in absentia* on the charge of having been a key figure in the campaign against the Jews and sentenced him to life imprisonment. A few months later Globke resigned his position in the Chancellery. Adenauer maintained that Globke's involvement was never more than "an objective interpretation of the racial laws" and that he had in fact sought to soften the impact of the legislation. Globke retired in 1963 and moved to Switzerland but maintained a residence in Bonn.

GLOBOCNIK, ODILO (d. 1945). *SS-Brigadefuehrer* (major general) and head of all the extermination camps (q.v.) in Poland during World War II. Globocnik won Nazi approval as early as 1938 by working for the seizure of Austria through the *Anschluss* (q.v.). As a reward he was made *Gauleiter* (q.v.) of Vienna, but his behavior in that post was so scandalous that he was demoted to a lesser position in the SS (q.v.). As police head of Lublin in occupied Poland, he founded Belzec, Maidanek, and Sobibór, three extermination camps in the Lublin district, as well as Treblinka (qq.v.). In 1941 he was made head of all death camps in Poland. Arrested in Austria by Allied troops in early May 1945, he committed suicide.

GLOEDEN, LILO (1903–1944). Housewife beheaded for giving shelter to a high army officer accused of treason. Lilo Gloeden was born in Cologne on December 19, 1903, the daughter of a physician. In 1938 she married an architect and settled in Berlin with him and her daughter. Opponents of the Nazi dictatorship, she and her husband did what they could to help those persecuted by the authorities. Among others, Dr. Carl Friedrich Goerdeler (q.v.), civilian leader of the Resistance (q.v.) movement, was given shelter in their home. After the July Plot (q.v.) of 1944, Gen. Fritz Lindemann, for whose arrest the Gestapo had offered a reward of 500,000 marks, was sheltered by the Gloedens for six weeks even though they were aware of the charge of treason against him. Both Lilo Gloeden and her mother were arrested and subjected to torture under interrogation. On November 30, 1944, she, her husband, and her mother were all beheaded at intervals of two minutes at Plötzensee Prison. Nazi authorities publicized their fate as a warning to anyone attempting to shield traitors to the Third Reich.

GLUECKS, RICHARD (1889–1945). Head of the concentration camp inspectorate (*see* CONCENTRATION CAMPS). A former Düsseldorf businessman and an artillery officer in World War I, Gluecks joined the Nationalsozialistische Deutsche Arbeiterpartei (q.v.) in its early days. In 1936 he was assigned to the staff of Theodor Eicke (q.v.), the first inspector of concentration camps. In early 1940 Eicke was promoted to a post in which he was charged with toughening occupation forces. Gluecks, now a lieutenant general in the Waffen-SS (q.v.), was named to succeed him. On February 21, 1940, Gluecks reported to his superior, Heinrich Himmler (q.v.), that he had found a suitable site for a new quarantine camp at a damp, marshy town called Auschwitz (q.v.), which formerly had been used as an Austrian cavalry barracks. More than 2 million victims were slaughtered in this camp. Gluecks was last seen in early May 1945 at a naval hospital near Flensburg at the Danish border, where he was being treated for shock after an Allied air bombardment. He then vanished without a trace.

GOBINEAU, [JOSEPH] ARTHUR COMTE DE (1816–1882). French diplomat and publicist, one of the most influential forerunners of Nazi racialism (*see* RACIAL DOCTRINE). Gobineau was born on July 14, 1816, in Ville-d'Avray, near Paris, to an old patrician family. He began his career as a journalist and came to the attention of Alexis de Tocqueville, who as French Foreign Minister made Gobineau chief of his secretariat during his short term of office in 1848–1849. After De Tocqueville's fall in 1849, Gobineau served in various diplomatic posts in Bern, Hannover, Frankfurt am Main, Teheran, Athens, Rio de Janeiro, and Stockholm. Forced by circumstances to retire, he left Stockholm in 1877 and spent the rest of his days in Rome. His works on ethnology, politics, and philosophy, published in the form of historical studies, travel books, short stories, and lyric verse, brought him worldwide fame.

Always the uncompromising aristocrat, Gobineau had the misfortune of living in a France that was moving in the opposite direction from aristocracy and absolutism. His fellow countrymen, while impressed by his reputation as a scholar, were undecided as to whether he was to be accepted as a pioneer of French philosophy or as a charlatan. He was complimented as a politico-literary thinker, but Frenchmen declined to be impressed by his racial creed. De Tocqueville was attracted by Gobineau's ingenuity in blending race and language, but he rejected his racialism as demonstrably false. "At best," De Tocqueville told him, "your fame will be an echo from across the Rhine."

Gobineau's fame rested primarily on his four-volume work *Essai sur l'inégalité des races humaines (Essay on the Inequality of Human Races)*, published in two parts in 1853 and 1855. Written by a conservative advocate of the cult of ancestor worship, the *Essai* passed almost unnoticed upon its publication in France. By the end of the century, however, it had made Gobineau's name known throughout Europe and especially in Germany.

Gobineau's thesis was simple: all human races are unequal, anatomically, physically, and psychologically. The course of civilization reveals that every assemblage of man, however ingenious the network of social relations that protects it, acquires on the day of its birth the seed of inevitable death. Degeneration inevitably begins when the primordial race unit of a civilization is so broken and swamped by the influx of foreign elements that its effective qualities are destroyed. As long as the blood and institutions of a nation keep to a sufficient degree the impress of the original nation, that nation will continue to exist.

After considering the concept of "racial degeneration," Gobineau went on to claim that there are real differences in the relative value of human races. His first step was to find a foundation of fact and argument capable of supporting such a vast structure. The idea of an original, clear-cut, and permanent inequality of races is, in Gobineau's view, one of the oldest and most widely held opinions in the world. Every people, great or small, began its life by accepting the idea of inequality. As soon as isolated groups grew great and civilized, when most of the people had mixed blood flowing in their veins, they first asserted that men are equal. But all are not equal. If it be true, Gobineau asked, that the Huron Indian had in undeveloped form an intellect as great as that of an Englishman, then why did he not in the course of the ages invent printing or steam power? If it be true that human societies are equal, Gobineau further asked, then why is it that every nation adds to the names of others epithets that suggest their unlikeness from itself?

Gobineau's next step was to examine the problem of whether the development of peoples is affected by climate, soil, or geography. He found that nations, whether progressive or stagnant, are independent of the regions in which they live. Nowhere is the soil more fertile or the climate milder than in certain parts of the Americas, yet the greater part of this land is occupied by peoples who have not succeeded to the slightest extent in exploiting their treasures. Nor does a nation derive its value from its geographical situation. It is the people who have always given, and always will give, the land its moral, economic, and political status. Thus, no external force is powerful enough to turn the congenital barrenness of a people into fertility. One must search in biology for the answers.

Gobineau maintained that Christianity neither created nor changed the capacity for civilization. He admitted that all human races are gifted with an equal capacity for being received into the bosom of Christian communion. But he warned that the universal power of recognizing the truths of Christianity and following its concepts must not be confused with the "very different faculty" that leads one race, and not another, to understand the early conditions of social improvement and so climb from one rung of the ladder of civilization to another. Christianity, in Gobineau's view, was not a civilizing power and, because of the inherent inequality of races, had excellent reasons for not being a civilizing power.

Civilization, Gobineau said, is not an event but rather a series, a chain of events linked more or less logically and brought about by the interaction of ideas that are often themselves very complex. Every human activity, whether moral or intellectual, has its original source in one or another of two currents, the "male" materialistic current and the "female" intellectual current. Only the races that have one of these elements in abundance, without of course altogether lacking the other, can reach a high level of civilization. The civilization of the mid-nineteenth century is not superior to those that have gone before. This civilization was created by the mingling of the Germanic tribes with the races of the ancient world, "the union of preeminently male groups with races and fragments clinging to the decayed remnants of ancient ideas." "The richness, variety, and fertility of invention for which we honor our modern societies, are the natural, and more or less, successful result of the maimed and disparate elements which our Germanic ancestors instinctively knew how to use, temper, and disguise."

Having set the framework for his racial theory, Gobineau then discussed in some detail views on the origin of the races of mankind as expressed by such scholars as Peter Camper, Johann Friedrich Blumenbach, Samuel George Morton, Carl Gustav Carus, and Ernst Heinrich Weber and found them all of doubtful value. The human species did not have multiple origins. Racial differences are permanent. The various races are physiologically separated, and different varieties have resulted from their intermixture, all unequal in strength and beauty. There are three races, and three only: the white (Caucasian, Semitic, or Japhetic); the black (Hamitic); and the yellow (Altaic, Mongol, Finnish, and Tatar). Gobineau rejected Blumenbach's twenty-eight varieties and James Cowles Prichard's seven because they included "notorious hybrids." The three major races are distinguished by peculiar features. Races are physically different: they are always unequal in beauty and muscular strength. In strength of fist the English are superior to all other European races; the French and Spanish have a greater power of resisting fatigue and privation. "The French have certain physical qualities that are superior to those of the Germans, which allow them to brave with impunity the snows of Russia as well as the burning sands of Egypt."

Gobineau maintained that languages, too, are unequal and always correspond in relative merit to the races that use them. Philology confirms all the facts of physiology and history on the special character of the races. It is a universal axiom, Gobineau wrote, "that the hierarchy of languages is in strict correspondence with the hierarchy of races."

Among the three races, Gobineau held, the white race is superior, and within this type the Aryan is in the most elevated position. All civilizations derive from the white race, and none can exist without its help. A society is great and brilliant only insofar as it preserves the blood of the noble group that created it, provided that this group itself belongs to the most illustrious of the species. There is no true civilization among the European peoples where the Aryan branch is not prominent. European peoples degenerate only in consequence of the various admixtures of blood that they undergo; their degeneration corresponds exactly to the quantity and quality of the new blood.

In summary, civilizations rise or perish because of race. The degeneration of noble races is brought about by intermixture with inferior races. Human races have always been unequal in physiological character and mental capacity, and the whole course of history may be explained from this point of view.

Although Gobineau's doctrines failed to influence intellectual France, they were supported by French nationalists, who found in them a justification for the continuing existence of the old nobility in the face of rising democratic institutions.

The story was different in Germany, where Gobineau's theories received widespread acceptance. The composer Richard Wagner (q.v.) saw in Gobineau's view precisely the right sort of argument for his own romanticism. Ludwig Schemann (q.v.), who popularized the *Essai* in Germany, said: "All good Germans regard Gobineau as one of the most extraordinary men of the nineteenth century, one of the greatest God-inspired heroes, saviors, and liberators sent by Him across the ages." The Gobineau Vereinigung (Gobineau Society), founded by Schemann at Freiburg in 1891, was the first of a host of similar societies. The cult of Gobineauism was used to support the rising anti-Semitism (q.v.). The great success of Bismarck's Second Reich was hailed as a vindication of the type of racial supremacy preached by Gobineau.

Gobineau's ideas were appropriated by Houston Stewart Chamberlain, Alfred Rosenberg, and Hitler in *Mein Kampf* (qq.v.). Chamberlain, the Germanicized Englishman, agreed that race is the most important factor in history and repeated many of Gobineau's hypotheses. Although Gobineau differed on some points, such as the attitude toward Christianity, Chamberlain saw in the passage of fifty years from the publication of Gobineau's *Essai* to his own era a clarification of the riddle of race. Gobineau's work, he said, was astonishingly rich in intuitive ideas, "which later have been verified." Similarly, Alfred Rosenberg, in *The Myth of the Twentieth Century*, spoke of the inherent superiority of the German Nordic race and urged that it be kept free from the disruptive influences of Etrusco-Syrio-Judaeo-Asiatic-Catholic dominance. In *Mein Kampf* Hitler insisted that it was the business of the state to place race at the center of attention and to keep the race clean. The racial ideology of *Mein Kampf*, with its emphasis on "culture-bearing" and "culture-destroying" races, came directly from Gobineau's *Essai*. The philosophy of a French racialist became the foundation stone for race ideology in the Third Reich.

Bibliography. Gerald H. Spring, *The Vitalism of Count de Gobineau*, Columbia University Press, New York, 1932.

GOEBBELS, PAUL JOSEPH (1897–1945). High-ranking National Socialist politician, close friend of Hitler, and propaganda expert of the Third Reich. Paul Joseph Goebbels was born in Rheydt, in the Rhineland, on October 29, 1897, the son of a manual worker in a strict Roman Catholic family. He attended *Bürgerschule* (grammar school) and *Gymnasium* (high school) in Rheydt. Goebbels was rejected for Army service in World War I because of a crippled foot and a permanent limp. From 1917 to 1921, with financial help from the Catholic Albertus Magnus Verein (Albertus Magnus Society), he studied Germanics, history, literature, and philosophy at the Universities of Freiburg, Bonn, Würzburg, Cologne, Munich, and Heidelberg. At Heidelberg he studied with Professor Friedrich Gundolf (q.v.), the Jewish historian of literature, who introduced him to Goethe and Shakespeare.

Throughout his life Goebbels suffered from what he regarded as the stigma of being unable to serve his country in time of war. He was always conscious of his deformity and physical inadequacy. Despite his piercing intelligence and demagogic brilliance, he resented the stares and the suspected comments. It was especially galling for this crippled little man, with his slight frame and black hair, "a pupil of the Jesuits and a half-Frenchman," to appear in public and preach the virtues of a tall, healthy, blue-eyed Aryan race. He was aware that his well-built, feeble-brained comrades condescendingly called him "the little mouse-doctor" and ridiculed him behind his back. It is probable that deep-rooted hatreds stemmed in large part from his resentment because of his physical condition.

After World War I Goebbels tried his hand unsuccessfully at poetry and drama. He joined the Nationalsozialistische Deutsche Arbeiterpartei (q.v.; NSDAP) in 1922. In 1924 he wrote *Der Wanderer (The Wanderer)*, a somewhat pathetic play, which was rejected by the Frankfurt Schauspielhaus. He moved to the Ruhr district in 1924

Goebbels demanding the return of the Saar to Germany in a speech delivered in March 1934. [*Wide World Photos*]

and started a career in journalism as editor of the *Völkische Freiheit (People's Freedom)* in Elberfeld. The next year he was made business manager of the Rhineland-North *Gau* (district) of the NSDAP. At the same time he became editor for the publications of Gregor Strasser (q.v.), including the *NS-Briefe* (q.v.).

While working with Strasser and his brother Otto Strasser (q.v.), Goebbels became embroiled in the controversy between the Strassers and Hitler on the extent of socialism in the National Socialist movement. At the height of the struggle Goebbels made his famous demand that "the bourgeois Adolf Hitler shall be expelled from the National Socialist Party." However, in 1926 he changed his mind and opted for Hitler, a decision that was to have enormous consequences both for himself and for the party. He began to regard Hitler "as either Christ or St. John." "Adolf Hitler, I love you!" he wrote in his diary. One of his first books was "dedicated respectfully" to Hitler. His praise was glowing: "Before the court at Munich you grew before us into the figure of a leader. What you said there is the greatest statement spoken in Germany since Bismarck's death. God gave you the words to describe what is ailing in Germany. You began at the bottom like every truly great leader. And like every leader you grew greater as your task grew greater."

Such words drew Hitler's favorable attention. In 1926 he made Goebbels *Gauleiter* (district leader) of the NSDAP in Berlin-Brandenburg. In the capital city the young Rhinelander began to demonstrate his talents for agitation and propaganda. From 1927 to 1935 he edited his own weekly newspaper, *Der Angriff (The Assault; see* ANGRIFF, DER), devoted to spreading the philosophy of National Socialism. In public speaking he showed himself, with his deep, booming voice, to be almost the equal of Hitler. At mass meetings and demonstrations he hurled sarcasm and insults at the Berlin city government, Communists, and Jews. The little man with the long nose and glittering eyes, always wearing a trench coat too big for him, won attention for himself, for Hitler, and for the party. He discovered a political martyr in Horst Wessel (q.v.), a Nazi who had been killed in a brawl, and promoted Wessel's doggerel verse as the official party song and later gave it the status of a national anthem. In 1928 Goebbels was elected to the Reichstag (q.v.) to represent Wahlkreis (Electoral District) Berlin for the NSDAP.

Hitler was so greatly impressed with Goebbels's work in Berlin that he appointed him *Reichspropagandaleiter der NSDAP* (Reich propaganda leader of the Nazi party) in 1929. In this capacity Goebbels was more responsible than any other individual for Hitler's rise to power. In 1932 he organized Hitler's two campaigns for the Presidency and revitalized the party campaigns for seats in the Reichstag, doubling its percentage of the votes cast. His propaganda was decisive in the year preceding Hitler's assumption of the chancellorship.

Goebbels was a master of modern propaganda techniques. A student of American advertising and promotion methods, he successfully applied them with modifications to the German scene. His Ten Commandments for National Socialists, written in the early days of the Nazi movement, revealed an understanding of the psychology of propaganda:

> 1. Your Fatherland is called Germany. Love it above all and more through action than through words!
> 2. Germany's enemies are your enemies. Hate them with your whole heart!
> 3. Every national comrade, even the poorest, is a piece of Germany. Love him as yourself!
> 4. Demand only duties for yourself. Then Germany will get justice!
> 5. Be proud of Germany. You ought to be proud of a Fatherland for which millions have sacrificed their lives!
> 6. He who abuses Germany, abuses you and your dead. Strike your fist against him!
> 7. Hit a rogue more than once! When one takes away your good rights, remember that you can only fight him physically!
> 8. Don't be an anti-Semitic knave. But be careful of the *Berliner Tageblatt!*
> 9. Make your actions that you need not blush when the New Germany is mentioned!
> 10. Believe in the future. Only then can you be a victor!

In his polemical pamphlets Goebbels used the technique of simple phraseology and extensive capitalization employed on the editorial pages of some newspapers in the United States:

> What we demand is NEW, CLEAR-CUT and RADICAL, therefore in the long run REVOLUTIONARY. . . . The upheaval we want is to be achieved first of all IN THE SPIRIT OF THE PEOPLE. . . . We know no IF OR BUT, we know only EITHER . . . OR!
>
> We demand: the RESTORATION OF GERMAN HONOR. WITHOUT HONOR NO RIGHT TO LIVE. . . . In the LOSS OF OUR HONOR lies the origin of the LOSS OF OUR LIBERTY.
>
> In place of the SLAVE-COLONY the rebuilding of a German NATIONAL STATE. The STATE is for us nothing in itself, it is only a MEANS TOWARD AN END. The end is NATIONALITY, that is the sum of all living and creative powers in the nation. The picture that calls itself the GERMAN REPUBLIC to-day is no longer the protector of our inherited worth. . . . We want the destruction of the SLAVE-COLONY and a substitution of a NATIONAL FREE STATE.
>
> For every working man WORK AND BREAD! Every production is to be rewarded on the grounds of ABILITY. More means of LIVELIHOOD for the German worker!
>
> For the people LIVING QUARTERS AND BREAD, AND AFTERWARDS REPARATIONS! No democrat, no republican has the right to deny these. We want ACTION!
>
> FIRST THE MOST VITAL NECESSITIES FOR THE PEOPLE, and then LUXURY AND TRIFLES. WORK for those who want to work! LAND for the farmer! The German foreign political policy, which is ruining us to-day, must be changed so that something can be done about the lack of ROOM in the Fatherland.
>
> Peace among the workingmen! Every person must do his duty and help the general welfare; in return the STATE TAKES OVER THE PROTECTION OF THE INDIVIDUAL and guarantees him the reward due for his work. . . .
>
> War against profiteers, peace with the workers! Destruction of all capitalistic influences on the political system of the country.
>
> SOLUTION OF THE JEWISH QUESTION. Rejection of all foreign races from public life of all kinds. Clean distinction between GERMAN AND NON-GERMAN, based upon race and not upon changed nationality or religion.
>
> An END TO THE DEMOCRATIC PARLIAMENT! Creation of a PROFESSIONAL PARLIAMENT, that takes care of the fate of PRODUCTION. . . .
>
> RESTORATION OF TRUTH in industrial life. Make good the injustice by which millions of Germans were robbed during the war, WITHOUT RESERVATION.
>
> THE RIGHT OF THE PERSONALITY above the mob. THE GERMAN ALWAYS BEFORE THE FOREIGNER AND JEW!
>
> FIGHT against the withering poison of the international-Jewish spirit! Conscious strengthening of German power and German customs! Extirpation of the foul Semitic immorality and racial destruction.
>
> DEATH SENTENCE FOR CRIMES AGAINST THE PEOPLE! THE GALLOWS FOR PROFITEERS AND USURERS!

On March 13, 1933, shortly after Hitler became Chancellor, he made Goebbels *Reichsminister für Volkserklärung und Propaganda* (Reich Minister for Public Enlightenment and Propaganda) with orders to use the full resources of the state for National Socialist *Gleichschaltung* (q.v.), or coordination. In this work Goebbels showed no regard for principles or morals. He brought every element of national life—press, films, theater, radio, sports—into the Nazi sphere and became in effect the dictator of the cultural life of the nation. To satisfy Hitler he directed his severest onslaughts against the Jews. With Heinrich Himmler and, later, Martin Bormann (qq.v.), he became one of Hitler's most intimate and influential advisers. His wife, Magda Quant, divorced from a Jewish businessman, and their six children were special favorites in the Fuehrer's private circle at Berchtesgaden (q.v.). His liaisons with a series of stage and film actresses were widely publicized. On one occasion he was beaten by an outraged film star who objected to Goebbels's attentions to his wife. His affair with Lida Baarova, a Czech actress, nearly led to a divorce until Hitler intervened. Goebbels was constantly at odds with other leading Nazis, especially Hermann Goering and Joachim von Ribbentrop (qq.v.), both of whom resented his intimacy with the Fuehrer.

In World War II Goebbels was given the task of maintaining morale behind the lines. His propaganda machine pointed to discontent in Soviet Russia and urged the Germans to hold on until eventual victory. The assignment became more and more difficult as the tide of war changed in favor of the Allies. Goebbels worked energetically to bolster the fighting spirit of the Germans by reminding them of their fate if they surrendered. After the failure of the July Plot (q.v.) in 1944, Hitler made Goebbels *Generalbevollmächtiger für den totalen Kriegsanstalt* (General Plenipotentiary for the Mobilization of Total War) and authorized him to gather all manpower and reserves for a last-ditch fight. But it was far too late: Germany was on the verge of collapse.

In April 1945, true to his sense of mystical egotism, Goebbels advised Hitler to remain in Berlin at the *Fuehrerbunker* (q.v.) and, if necessary, to leave the earth in a blinding *Götterdämmerung* (q.v.). Only in this way, Goebbels argued, could the great Hitler legend be maintained. The Fuehrer, fearful of being exhibited naked in a circus cage by the Russians, agreed. One by one the other original Nazi leaders deserted Hitler, but Goebbels stayed. When President Franklin D. Roosevelt died on April 12, Goebbels, in a burst of euphoria, compared the event to a similar one in the life of Frederick the Great, which ended in victory. Hitler's spirits were raised for a few moments. In Hitler's political testament (q.v.) Goebbels was appointed the Fuehrer's successor as Reich Chancellor. Goebbels added an appendix in a propaganda gesture (*see* GOEBBELS'S FINAL TESTAMENT). Immediately after Hitler's suicide, Goebbels and Bormann made a last attempt to negotiate with the Russians. When it became clear that this was impossible, Goebbels decided to commit suicide. Magda Goebbels poisoned their six children and killed herself. Goebbels then ended his own life.

See also PROPAGANDA, NAZI.

Bibliography. Paul Joseph Goebbels, *The Goebbels Diaries*, ed. and tr. by Louis P. Lochner, Hamish Hamilton, Ltd., London, 1948; id., *Vom Kaiserhof zum Reichskanzlei*, Eher Verlag, Munich, 1934; Roger Manvell and Heinrich Fraenkel, *Doctor Goebbels: His Life and Death*, Simon and Schuster, New York, 1960.

GOEBBELS'S FINAL TESTAMENT. On April 29, 1945, Dr. Goebbels added his signature as a witness to Hitler's political testament (q.v.). He then wrote an appendix to the Fuehrer's testament in which he gave his own personal apologia. The text follows:

> The Fuehrer has ordered me, should the defense of the Reich capital collapse, to leave Berlin, and to take part as a leading member of a government appointed by him.
>
> For the first time in my life I must categorically refuse to obey an order of the Fuehrer. My wife and children join me in this refusal. Otherwise—quite apart from the fact that feelings of humanity and loyalty forbid us to abandon the Fuehrer in his hour of greatest need—I should appear for the rest of my life as a dishonorable traitor and common scoundrel, and should lose my self-respect together with the respect of my fellow citizens; a respect I should need in any future attempt to shape the future of the German Nation and State. . . .
>
> For this reason, together with my wife, and on behalf of my children, who are too young to speak for themselves, but who would unreservedly agree with this decision if they were old enough, I express an unalterable resolution not to leave the Reich capital, even if it falls, but rather, at the side of the Fuehrer, to end a life which will have no further value to me if I cannot spend it in the service of the Fuehrer, and by his side.

Bibliography. H. R. Trevor-Roper, *The Last Days of Hitler*, The Macmillan Company, New York, 1947.

GOERDELER, CARL FRIEDRICH (1884–1945). Jurist, lord mayor of Leipzig, and civilian leader in the conspiracy against Hitler. Carl Friedrich Goerdeler was born in Schneidemühl (now Piła, Poland) on July 31, 1884, the son

Carl Friedrich Goerdeler in the People's Court. [*From Annedore Leber (ed.),* Conscience in Revolt, *tr. by Rosemary O'Neill, Vallentine, Mitchell & Co., Ltd., London, 1957*]

of a conservative Prussian district judge. After studying law, he turned to a career in local administration, serving in 1922 as second mayor of Königsberg and in 1930 as lord mayor of Leipzig. A man of almost puritanical character, Goerdeler was a commanding figure who was known for his ability to bring others to his own point of view. In the early Nazi regime he accepted a post as Reich Commissioner of Prices. He attempted without success to win Hitler's support for major reforms in local administration. In November 1936, while Goerdeler was abroad, the Nazi councillors of Leipzig removed the statue of the composer Felix Mendelssohn from its position opposite the Gewandhaus concert hall. On his return Goerdeler resigned in protest as mayor of Leipzig.

From this point on Goerdeler became active in the opposition to Hitler, progressing gradually to Resistance (q.v.) and then to conspiracy. He took a position as financial adviser to the Stuttgart firm of Robert Bosch primarily because the industrialist was anti-Nazi. Traveling for his firm, he became a tireless propagandist against National Socialism. It was agreed among the conspirators that Goerdeler would become Chancellor of a provisional government (q.v.) after Hitler's fall. One of the main leaders of the July Plot (q.v.) of 1944, he was denounced, arrested, sentenced, and executed at Plötzensee Prison on February 2, 1945.

GOERING, CARIN VON KANTZOW (born Carin von Fock; d. 1931). First wife of Hermann Goering (q.v.), the No. 2 Nazi. She was the fourth daughter of a Swedish colonel. After World War I Goering, who had taken a post as a transport pilot in Sweden, met the beautiful Carin von Kantzow at the home of Count Eric von Rosen, her brother-in-law. The mother of an eight-year-old son and four years older than Goering, she was unhappily married and spent most of her time with relatives. She suffered severely from epilepsy. Carin von Kantzow dissolved her marriage and married the impecunious German pilot. In many ways she dominated her husband's life, directly while she was alive and indirectly after her death. Her family, horrified by Goering's behavior as a morphine addict, for a time refused to have anything to do with him. After a long illness Carin Goering died of tuberculosis on October 17, 1931. Goering, who loved his wife deeply, was crushed. He brought the body of his deceased wife to his sumptuous new estate in the Schorfheide, north of Berlin, which he named Karinhall (q.v.) in her honor.

GOERING, EMMY SONNEMANN (1893–1973). Second wife of Hermann Goering (q.v.) and unofficial first lady of the Third Reich. A provincial actress in her youth, Emmy Sonnemann became the second Frau Goering on April 10, 1935. Because the Fuehrer was unmarried, Frau Goering often took over the direction of social affairs among the leading National Socialist hierarchy. In 1948, two years after Goering's suicide, Frau Goering was convicted of being a Nazi and was barred from the stage for five years. Unable to revive her career, she lived out her days in a small apartment in Munich with her only daughter, Edda (named after Mussolini's daughter). Emmy Sonnemann Goering died on June 8, 1973.

GOERING, HERMANN [WILHELM] (1893–1946). No. 2 Nazi, Hitler's heir apparent, and high military and economic leader of the Third Reich. Hermann Wilhelm Goering was born in Rosenheim, Upper Bavaria, on January 12, 1893, the son of a colonial official. As a young man he attended the cadet college at Karlsruhe. At the beginning of World War I he served as a lieutenant of infantry in Alsace-Lorraine and later was transferred to the Air Force as a combat pilot. In 1918 he became commander of the Flying Circus *Jagdgeschwader* (q.v.; fighter group) made famous by Baron Manfred von Richthofen. Much decorated, Goering received the Pour le Mérite medal and the Iron Cross (First Class). By the end of the war he had won tremendous popularity as a romantic knight of the skies.

Goering was one of many German officers who found it difficult to adjust to civilian life after the war. For two years he worked for the Fokker Aircraft Works. He became an adviser to the Danish government, a stunt pilot, and a commercial pilot for Svenska Lufttraffik in Sweden. There he met Carin von Kantzow (born Carin von Fock; *see* GOERING, Carin von Kantzow), whom he married in Munich after her divorce. Through her he met Hitler in the fall of 1922 and decided to join the rising young politician. Hitler was delighted: "Splendid! A war ace with Pour le Mérite—imagine it! Excellent propaganda! Moreover, he has money and doesn't cost me a cent." In December Hitler made Goering supreme commander of the SA (q.v.). At the 1923 Beer-Hall *Putsch* (q.v.) in Munich, Goering was at Hitler's side and was severely wounded. Arrested, he managed to escape to Austria and then lived in Italy and Sweden. During his long recovery, he became addicted to morphine, for which he was jailed.

After the political amnesty of 1926 Goering returned to Germany and quickly reestablished his contacts with Hitler. In 1928 he was one of the first Nazis to be elected to the Reichstag (q.v.) and in 1930 was reelected. He served as Hitler's political agent in Berlin. After the Nazi victory in the elections of 1932, Goering became President of the Reichstag, and he played an important role in the involved negotiations preceding Hitler's assumption of power on January 30, 1933.

Goering won rapid promotion in the Nazi hierarchy. Within a short time after Hitler became Chancellor, Goering took on a number of high posts: Reich Minister without Portfolio, Reich Commissioner for Air, Prussian Minister President, and Prussian Minister of the Interior. In the last-named position he consolidated Nazi power by filling the Prussian administration with party members. He founded the political police of Prussia, who in 1934 were incorporated into the Gestapo (q.v.) under the leadership of Heinrich Himmler and Reinhard Heydrich (qq.v.). He also created the first concentration camp at Oranienburg (*see* CONCENTRATION CAMPS). At first it was widely assumed that Goering was involved in the Reichstag fire (q.v.) on February 27, 1933, because there was a tunnel from his office to the Reichstag, but historians later were inclined to cast doubt on this charge. Shortly after the fire Goering had some 4,000 Communists and Social Democrats arrested and the Marxist press banned. On June 30, 1934, he was responsible for directing operations in Berlin for the Blood Purge (q.v.), which resulted in the elimination of the leader of the SA, Capt. Ernst Roehm, and in the decline of the SA itself. On March 1, 1935, Goering was named *Oberbefehlshaber der Luftwaffe* (commander in chief of the Air Force), and in that post he organized the production of military aircraft and the training of pilots. By this time he was, next to Hitler, the most important man in the Third Reich. He could now afford to live in luxury at a small palace in Berlin and a hunting lodge north of the city, named Karinhall (q.v.), where he kept the remains of his first wife. In 1935 he married an actress (*see* GOERING, Emmy Sonnemann).

The personality and character of Goering stood out in Hitler's collection of bizarre eccentrics, including the sadist Heinrich Himmler, the pornographer Julius Streicher, the fanatical intellectual Paul Joseph Goebbels, and the fawning champagne salesman Joachim von Ribbentrop (qq.v.). A German version of Falstaff, fat, glamorous, and magnetic, Goering was the charming hero with impeccable manners who gave tone and taste to Nazism in its early drive for power. A massive egoist, he regarded himself as "the last Renaissance man." He was a mixture of adventurer and sybarite, who showed naïve joy in his great power and wealth. He had his own reservations about Nazism: "I joined the Party because I was a revolutionary, not because of any ideological nonsense." He was careful, however, to follow Hitler's orders to the letter. A mass of contradictions, he was entranced by the pleasures of the hunt; yet he turned away in disgust when the King of Italy ordered that animals be forced into a small enclosure for easy killing. He loved children but had no compunctions about blood purges and extermination camps (q.v.).

Goering's massive figure and extraordinary vitality made him a great hero with the German public. Countless stories were told about his love for uniforms and his lusty, often-infantile behavior. The masses identified with this jolly extrovert who roared with good humor at jokes about himself. They liked him as much as they were repelled by the caustic Goebbels, the moody Rudolf Hess (q.v.), and the sour Himmler. He understood the phenomenon: "The people want to love and the Fuehrer was often too far from the broad masses. Then they clung to me." Most Germans never lost their high regard for this charming swashbuckler. Even when numbed by defeat, they were delighted by the way Goering committed suicide just before he was to be hanged at Nuremberg: "Our Hermann has done it again!"

In 1936 Hitler made Goering a full general. Annoyed by the caution of Hjalmar Schacht (q.v.), the Fuehrer appointed Goering Plenipotentiary for the Implementation of the Four-Year Plan (q.v.). In effect the economic dictator of the Third Reich, with vast power for acquiring property and directing industry, Goering was responsible for the rearmament of Germany. From 1937 on he amassed a huge fortune through the Reichswerke–Hermann Goering (q.v.), a state-owned mining and industrial enterprise. At the same time he began to acquire a great personal art collection, which became even larger through expropriations in conquered countries in World War II. Goering engineered the proceedings that resulted in the Blomberg-Fritsch crisis (q.v.) of February 4, 1938, and the removal of the Army's two leading generals. He was the

Hitler congratulates Goering on his forty-fifth birthday, January 12, 1938. [*Ullstein*]

central figure in the *Anschluss* (q.v.), the union of Germany and Austria in 1938, and he subsequently threatened to bomb Prague if the Czechs did not submit to Hitler. To satisfy Hitler he condoned the persecution of the Jews and did his best to force them out of German economic life.

While Goering supported Hitler's aggressive policies, in the days before the outbreak of World War II he foresaw the dangers of an attack on Poland and tried unsuccessfully to negotiate with Prime Minister Neville Chamberlain (q.v.) through Birger Dahlerus, a Swedish intermediary. On August 30, 1939, Hitler made Goering Chairman of the Reich Council for National Defense. The next day he designated Goering as his successor in the event that he, Hitler, met death in the uniform he was going to wear until victory or death. Goering commanded the Luftwaffe in the *Blitzkrieg* (qq.v.), or lightning war, attacks on Poland and France, and on June 19, 1940, he was made *Reichsmarschall* (Reich marshal). Meanwhile, his economic dictatorship was extended to the occupied countries in the east.

The Battle of Britain in the summer marked a change in the fortunes of Goering. His failure to dominate the skies over Britain forced Hitler to abandon plans for an invasion across the English Channel in Operation Sea Lion (Seelöwe, q.v.). Later, Goering's Luftwaffe proved to be unable to defend Germany itself against ever-increasing Allied air power. Discredited, he saw his relations with Hitler steadily deteriorate. Beginning to lose his initiative as well as his sense of humor, he lapsed into subservience. He came away crushed by stormy quarrels in the Fuehrer's headquarters. His prestige in party councils sank as that of Goebbels, Himmler, and Martin Bormann (q.v.) grew. Goering had begun his career as Hitler's showpiece, and he was to end it as his scapegoat. In his *Fuehrerbunker* (q.v.), living the life of a troglodyte preparing for his *Götterdämmerung* (q.v.), Hitler became hysterical when he learned that Goering had made a last-minute attempt to seize power for himself. The enraged Fuehrer ordered his once-faithful paladin to be deprived of all his offices and shot. Later, Goering protested that he had always remained loyal to his chief and was proceeding in a manner to which Hitler had agreed beforehand. When he heard of Hitler's suicide, Goering exclaimed to his wife: "He's dead, Emmy! Now I shall never be able to tell him that I was true to the end!"

Goering was captured by troops of the United States Seventh Army on May 9, 1945, and vainly demanded a "man-to-man talk" with Gen. Dwight D. Eisenhower. In 1946 he was brought before the International Military Tribunal at Nuremberg. Goering defended himself with skill and aggressiveness. He regarded himself as the ranking officer in the prisoners' dock and insisted that all the accused follow his orders. He demanded that he not be questioned about the party's program because, he said, he knew nothing about it. The judges were not impressed. "There is nothing," ran the decision, "to be said in mitigation. His guilt is unique in its enormity. The record discloses no excuses for this man." He was found guilty on all four counts: count 1, conspiracy to commit crimes alleged in other counts; count 2, crimes against peace; count 3, war crimes; count 4, crimes against humanity. He was then sentenced to death. In a last letter to his wife he expressed his confidence in posthumous rehabilitation: "In 50 or 60 years there will be statues of Hermann Goering all over Germany. Little statues, maybe, but one in every German home."

On October 15, 1946, two hours before he was to be hanged at Nuremberg, Goering took a vial of poison that somehow had escaped the vigilance of his guards. At the order of the court his ashes were thrown into the last remaining incinerator at Dachau (q.v.).

Bibliography. Willi Frischauer, *The Rise and Fall of Hermann Goering,* Houghton Mifflin Company, Boston, 1951.

GOERING-WERKE. *See* REICHSWERKE HERMANN GOERING.

GOLDEN PHEASANTS. *See* GOLDFASANEN.

GOLDENES PARTEIABZEICHEN (Party Golden Badge of Honor). A special gold decoration given by Hitler personally to those who had performed outstanding services for the Nationalsozialistische Deutsche Arbeiterpartei (q.v.; NSDAP). It was given to all NSDAP members who held Party numbers below 100,000. The lower the number, the closer to the Fuehrer (No. 1) the wearer supposedly was. The badge came in two sizes: large, for uniforms, and small, for civilian wear. Some recipients were Albert Speer, Hitler's favorite architect; Adm. Eroch Raeder, commander-in-chief of the German Navy; and Dr. Hjalmar Schacht (qq.v.), president of the Reichsbank and Minister of Economics before WW II.

GOLDFASANEN (Golden Pheasants). Term of ridicule applied to gaudily uniformed Nazi party functionaries in the occupied territories during World War II. Many of these administrators were corrupt. The common soldier regarded them as ostentatious and filled with a sense of self-importance. The term *golden pheasants* derived from the fact that the German eagle was usually portrayed on the party uniform, which led to a plethora of ornithological nicknames for party officials. *See also* TOTENVÖGEL.

GOLLOB, GORDON (1912–). Fighter ace of the Luftwaffe (q.v.) in World War II. Gordon Gollob was born in Vienna on June 16, 1912. In 1941 and 1942 he commanded Jagdgeschwader (Fighter Group) 3, and from 1942 to 1944 he led Jagdgeschwader 77. He was officially credited by Luftwaffe statisticians with 160 kills, most of which were on the eastern front. Gollob was promoted to *General der Jagdflieger* (general of fighter pilots). He was the third Luftwaffe officer to be awarded the high decoration of Knight's Cross with Oak Leaves, Swords, and Diamonds (*see* RITTERKREUZ).

GÖTTERDÄMMERUNG (Twilight of the Gods). Term used to describe the last days of Hitler in his Berlin bunker in late April 1945 (*see* FUEHRERBUNKER). The word was taken from the final part of Hitler's favorite opera, *Der Ring des Nibelungen* by Richard Wagner (q.v.), which ends in an orgy of destruction. On April 1, the Fuehrer shifted his headquarters to a retreat just behind the old section of the Chancellery. Great clouds of smoke hovered in the midday sky over doomed Berlin. Russian artillery shells exploded incessantly, and gunfire thundered through the canyons of rubble. In the bunker, which was two stories deep and stocked with food, was gathered the remainder of Hitler's court.

The historian H. R. Trevor-Roper (q.v.) described the scene as a "cloud cuckoo-land." On April 21, Hitler ordered one last effort to throw the Russians back from Berlin. "Any commander who holds his men back," Hitler shouted, "will forfeit with his life within five hours." By this time the Fuehrer was deploying imaginary battalions and disposing of formations that existed only in his own mind. At a conference held the next day he went into a rage, crying that he had been deserted, surrounded by traitors, and smothered with lies and corruption. The end had come at last. His Third Reich had been a failure, and there was nothing left for him to do but die. His face, formerly tanned by the sun, was puffy and florid. He wore dark trousers, a field-gray tunic, a white collar with a black tie, and the Iron Cross as his only decoration.

Hitler gave way to despair: "My friends, I see that all is lost. I shall remain in Berlin. I shall fall here in the Reich Chancellery. I can serve the German people best in that way. There is no sense in continuing any longer." He urged the others to flee: "Get out, get out! Go to South Germany. I'll stay here. It is all over anyhow." Gen. Wilhelm Keitel (q.v.) cut in: "We won't leave you. I'd be ashamed to face my wife and children if I deserted you." Hitler waved him aside. Martin Bormann (q.v.) added his objection: "This would be the first time I ever disobeyed you. I won't go." Gen. Alfred Jodl (q.v.) spoke up calmly: "I shall not stay in this mouse hole. We are soldiers. Give us an army group and orders to fight wherever possible. But I won't stay in this mouse hole." On other days Hitler would have had Jodl shot for this remark. Now he shrugged and said: "Do what you wish—it doesn't mean anything to me any more."

Then came successive shocks for the Fuehrer. On April 23, Hermann Goering (q.v.) sent a telegram to Hitler:

> *My Fuehrer!* In view of your decision to remain at your post in the fortress of Berlin, do you agree that I take over, at once, the total leadership of the Reich, with full freedom of action, at home and abroad, as your deputy, in accordance with your decree of 29 June 1941? If no reply is received by ten o'clock tonight, I shall take it for granted that you have lost your freedom of action, and shall consider the conditions of your decree as fulfilled, and shall act for the best interests of our country and our people. You know what I feel for you in this gravest hour of my life. Words fail me to express myself. May God protect you, and speed you quickly here in spite of all. Your loyal
>
> HERMANN GOERING

After this blow Hitler learned that Heinrich Himmler (q.v.) had been attempting on his own to start negotiations with the Allies. Hitler's rage was monumental at these evidences of treason by his closest associates. The news was now given him that the Allies had raided Obersalzberg (*see* BERGHOF) from the air and had left the Berghof looking like a landscape on the moon. Hermann Fegelein, the brother-in-law of Eva Braun (qq.v.), attempted to escape from the bunker, but he was captured at Hitler's orders, taken out into the Chancellery yard, and shot.

On April 29, 1945, Hitler married Eva Braun in an underground ceremony. He dictated his last will and his political testament (*see* HITLER'S LAST WILL; HITLER'S POLITICAL TESTAMENT). The next afternoon, in the quiet of the bunker, he shot a bullet into his mouth. Eva Braun ended her life beside him. Following his instructions, his body was drenched with fuel and burned. After putting to death their six daughters, Dr. Paul Joseph Goebbels (q.v.) and his wife committed suicide.

Bibliography. H. R. Trevor-Roper, *The Last Days of Hitler*, The Macmillan Company, New York, 1947.

GOTTSCHALK, JOACHIM (1904–1941). Actor driven to suicide in the Third Reich. Joachim Gottschalk was born on April 10, 1904, the son of a physician. After working at sea for three years, he became an actor and gradually built a reputation at Leipzig and Frankfurt am Main. Called to Berlin in 1938, he won recognition for his work in films and enjoyed wide popularity. His career was endangered, however, because his wife was Jewish, and he refused to leave her despite the suggestion by the Nazi authorities that he do so. He turned down an offer to go on tour with the Kraft durch Freude (q.v.), the Strength through Joy organization. The strain became so great that Gottschalk and his wife agreed on suicide. After killing their child with veronal, both took their own lives. In his last letter, Gottschalk repeated the words of the poet Heinrich von Kleist before his own suicide: "The truth is that there was no help for me on this earth." *See also* FILMS IN THE THIRD REICH.

GOUVERNEMENT-GÉNÉRALE (General Government). Official name for Nazi-occupied Poland.

GOVERNMENT COUPONS. *See* STAATSKASSENGUTSCHEINE.

GPL. *See* GAUPROPAGANDALEITUNG.

GR. *See* GRUPPE.

GRAF, HERBERT (1903–1973). Stage director and prominent German refugee from the Third Reich. Herbert Graf, son of a Viennese critic and writer on music, received his doctorate from the University of Vienna in 1925. He originally wanted to be a singer, but after writing his dissertation, titled "Richard Wagner as Stage Director," he turned to stage directing. Graf began his career in Münster and then went on to Breslau, Frankfurt am Main, Basel, and Prague. His staging of works by Handel attracted considerable attention. In 1934 he went to the United States to escape Nazi persecution. After making his American debut as stage director of the Philadelphia Orchestra opera series in the 1934–1935 season, in 1936 he joined the Metropolitan Opera, for which he staged many works. His final production for the company was Strauss's *Elektra*, which was introduced in the 1966–1967 season. He died in Geneva on April 6, 1973.

GRAF, HERMANN (1920–). Fighter pilot ace of the Luftwaffe (q.v.) in World War II. A factory worker and a passionate football player; Herman Graf joined the Luftwaffe in 1939 as an officer cadet at the Wildpark Flying School. Within a short time he had demonstrated unusual skill as a fighter pilot, and in 1941 he was posted to Romania and Greece. In 1944 he became the last commander of Jagdgeschwader (Fighter Group) 52, the most successful Air Force unit in World War II. By the end of the war he was one of Germany's leading aces, credited by Luftwaffe statisticians with 202 victories, all on the eastern front. He was awarded the Knight's Cross with Oak Leaves, Swords, and Diamonds (*see* RITTERKREUZ). On April 4, 1945, he was shot down and captured by the Russians, who kept him in a prisoner-of-war camp for five years. After his return to Germany he ran an electronics firm in Bremen.

GRAF, ULRICH (1878–). One of Hitler's comrades during the early days of National Socialism. Ulrich Graf was born in Bachhagel on July 6, 1878. A miller and butcher by vocation, he was one of the founders of the Nationalsozialistische Deutsche Arbeiterpartei (q.v.) and from 1920 to 1923 was Hitler's personal companion. He was badly wounded at the 1923 Beer-Hall *Putsch* (q.v.) in Munich. In 1925 he was made a member of the Munich City Council, and in 1936 he was elected to the Reichstag (q.v.) as a representative of the Nazi party. In World War II he served as an *SS-Brigadefuehrer* (major general).

GRAF SPEE. German pocket battleship, the pride of Nazism and symbol of Hitler's rising naval power. It was named after Graf Maximilian von Spee (1861–1914), German naval hero of World War I, who was defeated by a British squadron on December 8, 1914, in the Battle of the Falkland Islands and who went down with his flagship, the *Scharnhorst.* Launched at Wilhelmshaven in 1934, the *Graf Spee* was the third and last of the German pocket battleships designed by naval technicians to circumvent the Treaty of Versailles. She was a miracle of naval construction, a fast, light, heavily armored warship noted for firepower and speed. As long as three New York City blocks and as wide as a four-lane superhighway, she was protected by a belt of armor. She had six 11-inch guns, eight 6-inch rifles, and eight 19.7-inch torpedo tubes. Able to cruise at 26 knots, she could outrun any ship she could not outshoot.

At the outbreak of World War II, the *Graf Spee,* under the command of Capt. Hans Langsdorff and with a crew of 1,107, moved to the southern seas to prey on Allied commerce. The neutral nations of South America had drawn a 300-mile safety belt, which no belligerent warships were supposed to penetrate, but Hitler paid no attention. For several months the *Graf Spee* cruised through the South Atlantic and sank at least nine ships. For the British Admiralty this was a serious challenge. In early December it urged Brazilian authorities to allow the sale of British fuel to Nazi freighters at Brazilian ports. The British guessed that these fuel-laden freighters were on missions to refuel Nazi raiders at sea. They could be followed.

On the morning of December 13, 1939, the *Graf Spee* approached the coast of Uruguay. Waiting were three British cruisers patiently on the search for her, the fast 8,300-ton *Exeter,* the 7,030-ton *Achilles,* and the 6,985-ton *Ajax.* The three British ships surrounded the *Graf Spee* and sent volley after volley against her. Captain Langsdorff turned his batteries on the largest British warship, the *Exeter,* and in four hours put her out of action. Below deck, imprisoned in the *Graf Spee*'s holds, were sixty British seamen who had been captured in raids on merchant ships. The British sailors cheered wildly as the German ship shuddered violently from the impact of British shells.

The struggle continued for fourteen hours. The *Graf Spee* was doing well, but Captain Langsdorff, concerned about the pounding from the *Ajax* and the *Achilles,* ordered forced draft and turned southwest in search of a haven. Thirty of his crew had been killed, and some sixty of his seamen were wounded. Followed by the British warships, Captain Langsdorff sought refuge in the neutral waters of Montevideo harbor. In Montevideo he buried thirty-six of his crew and hospitalized the wounded. His damage control crew then went to work to repair the battered ship. He requested fifteen days to complete repairs, but the Uruguayan government informed him that he had to leave within two days or be interned with his crew. Meanwhile, the British cruisers waited outside the harbor. Though days away, British reinforcements sped toward Montevideo under forced draft. British radio reports spoke of overwhelming naval forces converging on the scene.

By this time the attention of the entire world was riveted on the sensational drama taking place at Montevideo. At 6 P.M. on Sunday, December 17, the *Graf Spee* weighed anchor and moved uncertainly along the Río de la Plata. Thousands of spectators on shore awaited the battle in the fading daylight. Suddenly the large warship stopped, and her accompanying tugboats moved away. A pillar of smoke from midships shot skyward. There were bursts of flame as explosions shattered the ship. Within three minutes she sank to the bottom of the harbor. Captain Langsdorff, his entire crew, and the captive British seamen reached shore safely and were interned. Three days later the depressed Captain Langsdorff, wrapped in the flag of the old Imperial Navy, put a bullet into his head. Hitler himself had given the order to scuttle the *Graf Spee* rather than see her humiliated in defeat. For the British the destruction of the powerful German warship was a hopeful sign at a time of little good news from the battlefronts.

GREATER GERMAN EMPIRE. *See* GROSSDEUTSCHES REICH.

GREATER GERMAN LEAGUE. *See* GROSSDEUTSCHER BUND.

GREATER GERMAN PEOPLE'S COMMUNITY. *See* GROSSDEUTSCHE VOLKSGEMEINSCHAFT.

GREEN. *See* GRÜN.

GREIF (Snatch). Code name for a German operation that employed special troops dressed in American uniforms to capture the bridges over the Meuse River during the Battle of the Bulge in December 1944. Using captured American tanks and jeeps, the disguised German troops were supposed to misdirect traffic, cut communications, and in general create chaos in the American lines. The operation was never successfully implemented.

GREIM, ROBERT RITTER VON (1892–1945). Luftwaffe (q.v.) general and the last field marshal appointed by Hitler. Born in Bayreuth on June 22, 1892, Robert Ritter von Greim served in World War I as a fighter pilot. In 1935 Hermann Goering (q.v.) appointed him as the first squadron leader of the newly created Luftwaffe. In 1939 Von Greim was made chief of personnel of the Luftwaffe. In the opening campaigns of World War II he led various fighter groups. From February 1943 on he commanded a *Luftflotte* (air force) on the eastern front, compiling an outstanding record as one of the best pilots of the Luftwaffe. Von Greim and Hanna Reitsch (q.v.), a well-known woman test pilot, were the last two visitors to Hitler in the *Fuehrerbunker* (q.v.), the underground headquarters during the last days of the Third Reich.

On April 24, 1945, Hitler sent a telegram from his bunker to Von Greim, then in command of Luftflotte VI in Munich, and ordered him to report to the Reich Chancellery. It was a difficult task to get there, but Von Greim,

Gen. Robert Ritter von Greim. [*Imperial War Museum, London*]

accompanied by Hanna Reitsch, managed it. Early on the morning of April 25, they arrived at Rechlin, where they intended to board a helicopter and land in the garden of the Chancellery or on a nearby street. Finding the only helicopter damaged, the two requisitioned a Focke Wolfe-190 (q.v.) and ordered its sergeant pilot to take them to the bunker. Hanna Reitsch, small of figure, was stuffed into the tail of the plane, in a cramped emergency opening. Accompanied by protective fighter planes, the aircraft hedgehopped through Russian flak to the airfield at Gatow. Here Von Greim attempted unsuccessfully to telephone the Chancellery. Finding an old training plane, an Arado-60, the two flew at treetop level toward their goal. Over the Tiergarten in Berlin a Russian antiaircraft shell injured Von Greim's foot. Hanna Reitsch leaned over, grabbed the controls, and landed the plane on the east-west axis near the Chancellery.

Hitler welcomed the two visitors to his bunker. He went to the surgery, where Von Greim's wound was being dressed, and told his visitor: "I have called you because Hermann Goering has betrayed both me and the Fatherland. Behind my back he has made contact with the enemy. I have had him arrested as a traitor, deprived him of all his offices, and removed him from all organizations. That is why I have called you." Hitler named the startled Von Greim as the new commander in chief of the Luftwaffe, with the rank of field marshal. The Fuehrer could well have made the promotion by radio, but by now he was acting irrationally. Three days later he ordered Von Greim and Fräulein Reitsch to depart with the argument that the new air force commander was needed at headquarters. Both Von Greim and Fräulein Reitsch begged to be allowed to stay in the bunker and sacrifice their lives for the honor of the Luftwaffe, but Hitler would not agree. The two flew out of Berlin as they had entered it, escaping miraculously through explosions and a sea of flames. They went to Plön, the headquarters of Adm. Karl Doenitz (q.v.). When they saw Heinrich Himmler, they told him that Hitler had denounced him for treason. Von Greim committed suicide at Salzburg on May 24, 1945.

GREISER, ARTHUR (1897–1946). Nazi leader in Danzig. Arthur Greiser was born in Schroda, Posen Province (now Środa, Poznań Province), on January 22, 1897. An aviator in World War I, he was the cofounder of the Stahlhelm (q.v.), the veterans' organization, in Danzig. In 1929 he joined the Nationalsozialistische Deutsche Arbeiterpartei and the SA, and in 1930 the SS (qq.v.) He was President of the Danzig Senate and also *Gauleiter* (district leader) of the Wartheland (Posen-Łódź) in 1939. In July 1940 he was elected to represent that district in the Reichstag (q.v.), and in 1943 he was promoted to *SS-Obergruppenfuehrer* (general). Arrested after the war, he was hanged at Poznań on June 20, 1946.

GRENZPOLIZEI (Border Control Police). The frontier police under the administration of the Gestapo (q.v.).

GRESE, IRMA (ca. 1921–1946). Concentration camp guard (*see* CONCENTRATION CAMPS), variously called the Belle of Auschwitz, Angel of Death, and Blond Angel of Hell. Irma Grese became a camp guard at the age of nineteen, and at twenty-two was placed in charge of 18,000 female prisoners at Auschwitz (q.v.). Described by some of her victims as of surpassing beauty and by others as a frowzy blonde, she acquired a reputation as a sadist who beat prisoners without mercy and who spent hours transfixed as she watched medical experiments, especially the removal of breasts. She was said to have had love affairs with Josef Kramer (q.v.), the camp commandant, and Dr. Josef Mengele (q.v.), the head camp physician. After the war she was tried as a war criminal, condemned to death, and dragged screaming to the gallows.

GRIMM, HANS (1875–1959). The Third Reich's most celebrated nationalist author. Hans Grimm was born in Wiesbaden on March 22, 1875. He studied political science at Lausanne, Munich, and Hamburg and then took a post in the Colonial Institute at Hamburg. He lived for fifteen years in the German colony of South-West Africa and in South Africa, where he developed a lively interest in Germany's colonial expansion. Preoccupied with his "German dream world," Grimm was a zealous advocate of *voelkisch* nationalism (*see* VOELKISCH MOVEMENT) and racialism, to which he turned his poetic attention.

Grimm came to public notice in 1926 with the publication of his political novel *Volk ohne Raum (People without Space)*. The book attracted immediate attention and sold a half million copies. The secret of its success was Grimm's ability to give literary expression to a sentiment that until then had not been stated in popular terms. Attached to traditional conservatism and advocating social imperialism, Grimm was convinced that Germany was fated to breed itself into starvation and extinction if it were not allowed to expand overseas. This became an *idée fixe* which he promoted throughout his writing career. He doubted that the old upper classes had the vitality and ability to bring about a thorough reform of German conditions.

Grimm's attitude toward the Nazi way of life was ambiguous. He agreed with Hitler's diagnosis of the evils besetting the German fatherland, with Hitler's elitism, and with his call for a purified German "race." At the same time, he distrusted Nazi revolutionary radicalism, *petit bourgeois* leadership, and the idea of a mass following. Declaring that he wrote from a position of independence, Grimm supported the Nazis, jubilantly greeted their accession to political power, and hailed Hitler's early successes such as the *Anschluss* (q.v.), the union with Austria. The Nazis, in turn, venerated Grimm as a leading "literary prophet of the German transformation." They appropriated the title of his book as their powerful slogan *"Volk ohne Raum"* (q.v.). Hitler, especially, was impressed not only with Grimm's imperialism, racialism, and nationalism but even more deeply with his insistence that literature was not concerned primarily with artistic merit but with political aims.

After the fall of the Third Reich, Grimm began to write about "new insights" into the historical meaning of National Socialism in what amounted to the most systematic postwar justification of Hitler and Nazism. In his *Answer of a German* (1949), prompted by a message broadcast to the German people by the Archbishop of Canterbury in November 1945, Grimm made his apology: "To this day the benefit which [National Socialism] has bestowed on Europe is that it protected the awakening German people, and with it the crowded Central European masses, from mass desertions to Communism." He died in Lippoldsberg an der Weser on September 27, 1959.

GRINDING. *See* SCHLEIFEREI.

GROENER, WILHELM (1867–1939). High army officer active in the Weimar Republic (q.v.). Wilhelm Groener was born in Ludwigsburg, Württemberg, on November 22, 1867. Joining the Army at seventeen, he became a career soldier and in 1899 was attached to the General Staff. In 1912 he was appointed chief of the railroad division of the General Staff, and in this post he organized the efficient transportation system that was used to good effect in the deployment of troops during World War I. He was promoted to lieutenant colonel in 1916. As chief of the new *Kriegsamt* (war office) for arming troops, he came into conflict with Gen. Erich Ludendorff (q.v.), was dismissed in August 1917, and was given a frontline assignment. On October 26, 1918, he succeeded Ludendorff as senior quartermaster general. He played an important role in Germany's final capitulation and led the retreat and demobilization of the German armies.

After the war Groener became a loyal supporter of the democratic Weimar Republic, working doggedly to promote his political aim of healing the breach between Army tradition and the new democratic constitutionalism. In June 1919 he opposed the officers' corps when it criticized the signing of the Treaty of Versailles. From 1920 to 1923 he served several times as Reich Communications Minister, from 1928 to 1932 as Reich Minister of Defense, and in 1931 and 1932 as Reich Minister of the Interior. In the last-named office he worked closely with his protégé, Gen. Kurt von Schleicher (q.v.), who owed his rapid rise in both the Army and politics to his patron. Groener was the strong man in the Cabinet of Chancellor Heinrich Bruening (q.v.). In April 1932 he banned the SA and SS (qq.v.) and thereby came into sharp conflict with Von Schleicher, who wanted Hitler's support for his own political career. On May 10, ill with diabetes and distressed by Von Schleicher's desertion, Groener rose in the Reichstag (q.v.) to defend his ban on Nazi organizations, only to be violently attacked by Hermann Goering (q.v.) and other Nazi deputies. Groener's resignation was a grave setback for the tottering Weimar Republic. He died in Bornstedt, Potsdam, on May 3, 1939.

GROPIUS, WALTER (1883–1969). One of the most important architects of the twentieth century and a refugee from the Third Reich. Walter Gropius was born in Berlin on May 18, 1883, a great-nephew of Martin Gropius, the nineteenth-century classical architect. After study in Berlin and Munich with Peter Behrens, he practiced privately. In 1919 he founded and became director at Weimar of the Bauhaus, the first major school of design and architecture to unite art with industry and daily life. In 1925 the school was transferred to Dessau. Gropius left Germany in 1934 and worked for two years in London in collaboration with E. Maxwell Fry. In 1937 he moved to the United States, where he was named professor of architecture at Harvard University. His main creations included pavilions at the Cologne Exhibition (1914), a factory at Alfeld (1914), a theater at Jena (1922), the Bauhaus at Dessau, and the Harvard Graduate Center (1950). As a leading advocate of the new architecture, Gropius influenced innovations throughout the world. He died in Boston following heart surgery on July 5, 1969.

Walter Gropius. [*Picture Collection, The Branch Libraries, The New York Public Library*]

GROSS, NIKOLAUS (1898–1945). Trade union worker implicated in the July Plot (q.v.) of 1944 on Hitler's life.

Nikolaus Gross. [*From Annedore Leber (ed.),* Conscience in Revolt, *tr. by Rosemary O'Neill, Vallentine, Mitchell & Co., Ltd., London, 1957*]

Nikolaus Gross was born in the Ruhr district on September 30, 1898. After attending elementary school, he went into the mines and became a trade union secretary and editor of the *Westdeutsche Arbeiterzeitung (West German Workers' Journal)*. Gross was a determined opponent of Nazism from its inception. He helped build a network among trade unions and Catholic workingmen's associations in preparation for the attempt to kill Hitler. Arrested on August 12, 1944, he was executed January 23, 1945.

GROSS-ROSEN. A small concentration camp (*see* CONCENTRATION CAMPS) located near Striegau (now Strzegom) in Silesia. Gross-Rosen was added to the system after three main camps had been established, in the south at Dachau, in central Germany at Buchenwald, and in the north at Sachsenhausen (qq.v.). Gross-Rosen was visited in January 1942 by a medical commission to select prisoners for special experimentation.

GROSSDEUTSCHE VOLKSGEMEINSCHAFT (GDVG; Greater German People's Community). An organization of the southern division of the Nazi party during the period from 1924 to 1926.

GROSSDEUTSCHER BUND (Greater German League). A group of nationalistic youth organizations in the Weimar Republic (q.v.). Led by Adm. Adolf von Trotha (1868–1940), a friend of President Paul von Hindenburg (q.v.), the young patriots had an annual *Lager* (encampment) at which they sang patriotic songs and listened to nationalistic speeches. On June 17, 1933, the first encampment after Hitler took political power was surrounded by police and SS (q.v.) men, and the boys were sent home. The same day the Grossdeutscher Bund was ordered dissolved, and Baldur von Schirach (q.v.) was named Reich Youth Leader. When Admiral von Trotha protested, his home was searched and he was listed as a suspicious person for opposing Nazi *Gleichschaltung* (q.v.), or coordination. In 1936, however, he accepted honorary membership in the navy division of the Hitler Jugend (q.v.), the Hitler Youth.

GROSSDEUTSCHES REICH (Greater German Empire). Designation of an expanded Germany that was intended to include all German-speaking people in one political entity. The idea originated in the early nineteenth century with the beginning of the German national movement and was presented originally by Ernst Moritz Arndt (1769–1860). Arndt called for a single strong, proud realm including all Germans. The matter came to a head during the Revolution of 1848. The Frankfurt Assembly was hampered both by the wishes of the multinational Austrian movement and by the Prussian urge to lead Germany. Was there to be a Greater German *(grossdeutsch)* or a Little German *(kleindeutsch)* settlement? The latter solution would mean Prussian hegemony. German unification was achieved by Otto von Bismarck in 1871 in conformity with the *kleindeutsch* concept.

For Hitler, an Austrian by birth, the Third Reich could have no meaning unless Austria were included, nor could the Greater German program be successful without absorbing Czechoslovakia. He pushed the idea of expansion from the beginning of his regime: he regained the Saar region; he withdrew from the League of Nations; he remilitarized the Rhineland; he discarded the Treaty of Locarno; he won *Anschluss* (q.v.) with Austria; and he absorbed Czechoslovakia. Greater Germany included most of Western Europe during the early years of World War II. By 1944, German postage stamps were changed to read *"Grossdeutsches Reich"* instead of *"Deutsches Reich."* For the triumphant Hitler this was an achievement that had been desired throughout a century of German history.

GROSSEN-WANNSEE CONFERENCE. *See* WANNSEE CONFERENCE.

GROSZ, GEORGE (1893–1959). German painter and graphic artist and a prominent refugee from the Third Reich. George Grosz was born Georg Ehrenfried in Berlin on July 26, 1893. After studying at Dresden, he was influenced by the spirit of revolt among German artists following World War I. In a highly personalized style he satirized militarism, capitalism, and the bourgeoisie. His favorite targets were the church, East Prussian Junkers, big industrialists, and generals. His *Ecce Homo*, depicting Christ on the Cross wearing a gas mask and Army boots, led to a trial for blasphemy Leader of the German school of the new realism (Die Neue Sachlichkeit), he won global attention. Sensing the drift to Nazism in Germany, he emigrated in 1932, went to the United States, and became a naturalized American citizen. Most of his work in the Third Reich disappeared, although some of it was exhibited in Hitler's display of "degenerate art" (*see* ENTARTETE KUNST). In the United States Grosz continued to create works symbolic of tortured mankind and acidly criticizing the establishment. He died in Berlin on July 7, 1959.

GROUP LEADER. *See* GRUPPENLEITER.

GROUPS. *See* GESCHWADER.

GRUF. *See* GRUPPENFUEHRER-SS.

GRÜN (Green). Code name for Hitler's plan to conquer Czechoslovakia. In March 1938 the Fuehrer ordered Konrad Henlein (q.v.), leader of the Sudeten German party in Czechoslovakia, to accelerate his campaign of disobedience and harassment inside the country. He then conferred with his generals and drew up plans to fabricate a pretext for war. On May 30, 1938, Hitler added this introductory paragraph to the text of Fall Grün (Case Green): "It is my unalterable decision to smash Czechoslovakia by military action in the near future. To wait for, or bring about, the moment which is politically and militarily suitable is the task of military leadership." The military leaders were reluctant to follow the Fuehrer in this dangerous scheme. For Hitler himself, the policy of appeasement, adopted by both Great Britain and France, was an uncomfortable barrier to be overcome by direct action.

GRÜNDGENS, GUSTAF (1899–1963). Nazi Germany's best-known and most popular actor. Under the sponsorship of Hermann Goering (q.v.), Gründgens was given control of the Prussian State Theater in Berlin. The arts were completely under the control of Dr. Paul Joseph

Goebbels (q.v.), but a legislative quirk made Goering responsible for the Prussian State Theater. Gründgens had been a member of a theatrical circle with Communist sympathies, but he refused to leave Germany in 1933. He died in Manila in 1963.

GRUPPE (Gr; Wing). A unit in the Luftwaffe (q.v.) consisting of about forty planes in three *Staffeln* (*see* STAFFEL).

GRUPPENFUEHRER-SS (GRUF). A lieutenant general in the SS (q.v.).

GRUPPENLEITER (Group Leader). A Nazi party functionary.

GRUPPENLEITERIN (Leader of a Girls' Group). Highest official in a Nazi women's auxiliary.

GRYNSZPAN, HERSCHEL (1921–ca. 1940). Polish-Jewish youth whose assassination of a German diplomat resulted in an intensified anti-Semitic campaign in Germany. Herschel Grynszpan was born in Hannover in 1921, the son of Polish-Russian parents who had fled from anti-Semitism (q.v.) just before World War I. Herschel left Germany in 1936, intending to emigrate to Palestine, but went instead to Paris. He had a precarious and rootless existence in the French capital. In late 1938 he received a letter from his sister, who had remained in Germany with the rest of the family. The letter stated that the Grynszpan family, together with all Polish Jews living in Hannover, had been arrested without warning and deported to Poland under especially harrowing circumstances. Brooding on the suffering of his family, Herschel became obsessed by a desire for revenge. On November 7, 1938, he bought a revolver and went to the German Embassy, where he was admitted to the office of a third secretary, Ernst vom Rath. Uttering a cry of vengeance for his people, Grynszpan shot and mortally wounded the young German diplomat.

Inside the Third Reich, where Nazi persecution of Jews had been increasing steadily, the murder of Vom Rath by a Jew caused an immediate sensation. It pushed Hitler and Dr. Paul Joseph Goebbels into extreme action. Throughout Germany on the night of November 9, 1938, Jewish shops and homes were burned and looted, synagogues destroyed, and thousands of Jews arrested. The event passed into history as the *Kristallnacht* (q.v.), the Crystal Night, or the Night of the Broken Glass, from the tons of glass strewn on the pavements of German cities wherever the mobs attacked.

Grynszpan was charged with murder in France. The legal steps in his case dragged on until long after the outbreak of World War II in 1939. After the fall of France in 1940, he was taken by Nazi authorities and sent back to Germany. In his defense he claimed that he had had a homosexual relationship with Vom Rath. Although the charge was not substantiated, the Nazis did not risk a show trial, which could have been diverted into a scandal. Grynszpan, in Nazi custody, disappeared in the early 1940s.

Bibliography. Rita Thalmann and Emmanuel Feinermann, *Crystal Night*, Thames & Hudson, Ltd., London, 1974.

Col. Gen. Heinz Guderian. [*National Archives, Washington*]

GUDERIAN, HEINZ (1888–1954). German tank expert who, with Gen. Charles de Gaulle and Gen. J. F. C. Fuller, is regarded one of the principal creators of modern mechanized warfare. Heinz Guderian was born in Kulm (now Chełmno, Poland) on June 17, 1888. After service in World War I, he specialized in developing the Panzer (Tank or Armored) Corps of the armed forces (*see* PANZER). A plebeian officer, he was elevated to important field commands. In 1935, as a brigadier general on the staff of Oswald Lutz, general of *Panzer* troops, he attracted Hitler's attention. In February 1938 he was made corps commander as successor to Lutz, and in November of that year he was promoted to general and named chief of motorized troops on the Army General Staff. During the 1938 Blomberg-Fritsch crisis (q.v.), Guderian was regarded as pro-Nazi and as a result went quickly up the military ladder. He commanded the new 16th Corps of motorized troops during the critical days of *Anschluss* (q.v.) with Austria in 1938. His tanks started a motorized dash to Vienna, but at least a third of them came to grief on the roads. In 1939 Guderian's *Panzers* took part in the invasion of Poland as an integral part of *Blitzkrieg* (q.v.) tactics, destroying thousands of artillery pieces as well as several Polish infantry divisions. Hitler visited Guderian on the battlefield and was impressed by his successful tank expert. In 1940 Guderian's *Panzer* group headquarters was shifted to Paris. In May his thrust to the coast at Abbeville cut the Allied armies in two.

After the defeat of France, Guderian favored a Mediterranean strategy, but he was not able to convince Hitler, who was already committed to an assault on Soviet Russia. When, on June 22, 1941, Hitler began his attack on the U.S.S.R., Guderian's tanks were there to push on to Moscow. When the mechanized assault broke down in autumn and winter conditions, the angry Fuehrer forced Guderian to resign (December 1941) and demoted him to inspector of *Panzer* training.

The conspirators of the July Plot (q.v.) of 1944 made several attempts to win Guderian to their side, but they were never successful in making him an active member. Although they feared that he might betray them because they had divulged too much to him, he cautiously said nothing. At the time of the attempt on Hitler's life, Guderian was inspecting troops in East Prussia. Two days later, after being appointed to the General Staff of the armed forces, he issued an order of the day denouncing the conspirators as cowards and weaklings who had preferred the road of disgrace to the only road open to the honest soldier, "the road of duty and honor." Hitler appointed Guderian to the court of honor, along with Field Marshals Wilhelm Keitel and Gerd von Rundstedt (qq.v.), to investigate the conduct of the officers arrested in the conspiracy. The three judges expelled the conspirators from the Army and transferred them for trial to the Volksgericht (q.v.), the notorious People's Court, which meant almost certain execution.

In early 1945 Guderian made several halfhearted attempts to persuade Joachim von Ribbentrop, Hermann Goering, and Heinrich Himmler (qq.v.) that an immediate armistice with the Allies was essential, but he refrained from making the same recommendation to Hitler. He died in Schwangau bei Füssen, Bavaria, on May 15, 1954.

GUERNICA. Spanish town attacked by the Condor Legion (q.v.) in a bombing from the air. Situated in the province of Vizcaya in the Basque country, on an outlet to the Bay of Biscay, Guernica was a town of 5,000 population, a religious center without military importance. In its center was an oak tree where the traditional liberties of the Basques were periodically confirmed in local celebrations. On April 27, 1937, at 4:30 on a cloudless Monday afternoon, German airmen descended on Guernica in a devastating raid. The bombing was denounced throughout the world as unnecessary. Critics charged that the Germans were testing the joint effect of explosive and incendiary bombs on civilians. In his memoirs the German fighter ace Adolf Galland (q.v.), who arrived in Spain shortly before the raid, called the bombing accidental and attributed it to inexperienced crews. The Condor Legion, he insisted, was under orders to spare civilians as much as possible. The destruction of Guernica, he said, caused great depression among members of the Condor unit.

The bombing of Guernica was memorialized in a great painting. At the time of the air raid the artist Pablo Picasso (1881–1973) was engaged by the Loyalist government to paint a mural for its pavilion at a Paris fair to be held later that year. The attack on Guernica gave him his subject, and within a month he completed an extraordinary painting. The monochromatic mural, in black, gray, and white, is considered one of the great paintings of the twentieth century. Critics have praised the simplicity of *Guernica*, which makes it a picture easily understood, and have pointed to the forms that are divested of all complications which could distract from their meaning. One critic has spoken of "signs as unmistakable as those used by primitive artists." The painting, retained by the artist in trust for the Spanish nation, was shown in the Museum of Modern Art in New York. Picasso stipulated that it was not to be returned to his native country as long as Gen. Francisco Franco was alive.

Bibliography. Rudolf Arnheim, *Picasso's Guernica*, University of California Press, Berkeley, 1962.

GUNDOLF, FRIEDRICH (1880–1931). Poet, professor of literature at the University of Heidelberg, and teacher of Dr. Paul Joseph Goebbels (q.v.). Of half-Jewish background, he was born Friedrich Gundolfinger in Darmstadt on June 20, 1880. From 1899 on he was a member of the George-Kreis (q.v.), a group of aesthetes who regarded great poetry as the summit of the arts. Tall, handsome, but extremely withdrawn, Gundolf began to teach at Hei-

Picasso's *Guernica*. [*Collection, The Museum of Modern Art, New York*]

delberg in 1911. He was appointed to the chair of literary history in 1920. Gundolf believed that the artist and his work formed an inseparable unity. His call for an absolute aestheticism had an important effect on German literary research. His work on Shakespeare and his influence on the German classics won widespread recognition. Gundolf was a firm German nationalist. He justified World War I by depicting Germany as the sole qualified representative of the idea of Germans as "the master people." He described the enemies of Germany as "mediocre braggarts" and "blinded mobs." "The culture of the future is destined to be created by the German mind." He saw culture as neither chattel nor enjoyment: "Culture consists in being, in acting, in changing; it is creation, destruction, metamorphosis, and Attila is nearer to culture than all the Shaws, Maeterlincks, d'Annunzios, and their like."

Such ideas fascinated his student Goebbels, who went to Heidelberg after World War I. Goebbels was captivated by Gundolf's lectures on the past world of German romanticism. He hoped to become a member of the George-Kreis through Professor Gundolf, but the latter was only mildly impressed by the young Rhinelander and eventually rejected him. Goebbels wrote his doctoral thesis, "Wilhelm von Schuetz: Ein Beitrag zur Geschichte des Dramas der Romantischen Schule" ("Wilhelm von Schuetz: A Contribution to the History of the Romantic Drama"), under the sponsorship of Professor von Waldberg. Gundolf quarreled with Stefan George and was expelled from the George-Kreis. He died on July 12, 1931.

GUNS-BEFORE-BUTTER SPEECH. *See* BUTTER-OR-GUNS SPEECH.

GÜNTHER, HANS F. K. (1891–1968). Social anthropologist and political publicist. Hans F. K. Günther was born in Freiburg on February 16, 1891, and taught at the Universities of Jena, Berlin, and Freiburg. His numerous works on race combined scientific insights with exaggerated hero-building mysticism. His book *A Short Ethnology of the German People* (1929) sold more than 275,000 copies and went through many editions. Günther's teachings played an important role in providing an ideological foundation for National Socialist racism. In 1931, despite strong faculty opposition, he was appointed professor of *Rassenkunde* (ethnology; *see* RASSENFORSCHUNG) in a newly established chair of racial research at the University of Jena. The main theme of his teaching regarded the Nordic as the ideal racial type, to be contrasted with the Jews as an ignoble mixture of races.

According to Günther, there were five European races: the Nordic, Mediterranean, Dinaric, Alpine, and East Baltic. Among these the great creative force of history was the Nordic race. The Jewish race did not even belong to Europe but was an outside race, "a thing of ferment and disturbance, a wedge driven by Asia into the European structure." The Jews were one of those non-Nordic races responsible for such disintegrative movements as democracy, parliamentarianism, and liberalism. It was the task of the creative Nordic race to increase its own valuable hereditary tendencies. "We wish to keep the thought always before us that, if our race is not to perish, it is a question of not only choosing a Nordic mate, but over and above this, of helping our race through our marriage to a victorious birth rate." Youth, he warned, must strive for an organic philosophy of life springing from the people and the native land. That philosophy must accord with the laws of life and be opposed to all individualism. It must always seek models for its spiritual guidance from the old Germanic world, "which was the expression of the Nordic nature."

Günther saw World War I as really a civil war, comparable to the Peloponnesian War in its racially destructive effects. He offered the Nordic idea to a world on the brink of disaster. If it took root in the proper nation, Nordicism would lead to an era of harmony and peace. "The Nordic idea must widen out into the All-Nordic ideal. In its object and nature the All-Nordic ideal would necessarily be at the same time the ideal of the sacredness of peace among the peoples of Germanic speech." The will of Nordic-minded men must span the centuries, halt the bastardization and mongrelization threatening real civilization, and eugenically purge Nordic ranks of all disintegrative elements. "The Nordic movement in the end seeks to determine the spirit of the age, and more than this spirit, from out of itself. If it did not securely hold this confident hope, there would be no meaning or purpose in any longer thinking the thoughts of Gobineau."

Günther's theory of race eventually became the foundation stone on which the Third Reich rested (*see* RACIAL DOCTRINE). His views, similar to those of Arthur Comte de Gobineau and Houston Stewart Chamberlain (qq.v.), became National Socialist doctrine, and he was regarded as the official spokesman for Nazi ideology. He died in Freiburg on September 25, 1968.

GÜRTNER, FRANZ (1881–1941). Reich Minister of Justice in Hitler's original Cabinet. Franz Gürtner was born in Regensburg on August 26, 1881, the son of a locomotive engineer. After attendance at the *Gymnasium* (high school) in Regensburg, he studied law at the University of Munich. He served in World War I, first on the western front against France and then in Palestine as a captain, receiving the Iron Cross (First and Second Classes). After the war he pursued a successful legal career. In the decade from 1922 to 1932, as a member of the German Nationalist party, he was state minister of justice in Bavaria. In this capacity he did much to promote Hitler's career. At the time of the Hitler-Ludendorff Beer-Hall *Putsch* (q.v.) in 1923, Gürtner became Hitler's protector and used his influence to win a light sentence for the Nazi leader. He obtained Hitler's release from Landsberg Prison despite the opposition of the state attorney's office. Gürtner later persuaded the Bavarian Cabinet to allow Hitler to speak again in public and also to legalize the forbidden Nazi party. In June 1932 Gürtner was made Minister of Justice in the coalition Cabinet of Chancellor Franz von Papen (q.v.), and he took a similar post in Hitler's first Cabinet in 1933.

As Hitler's Minister of Justice, Gürtner was charged with the *Gleichschaltung* (q.v.), or coordination, of jurisprudence in the Third Reich. He nominated all judges, public prosecutors, and officers of the law; the Fuehrer appointed them and swore them in himself. Gürtner merged the older Association of German Judges with the new National Socialist Lawyers' Association (NS-Rechtswahrerbund, q.v.). He was careful to remove legal safeguards for persons who opposed Hitler. Immediately after the 1934 Blood Purge (q.v.), Gürtner proposed a law, which was adopted by the Cabinet, proclaiming Hitler's actions "justified as a means of State defense." In the opening months of World War II he set up a system of courts (*Ständegerichte*) to try Jews and Poles in the occupied lands of the east. He played an important role in giving official sanction to any act of the dictatorship. The Fuehrer, always insistent on strict legality, relied on his Minister of Justice to find legal grounds for his government's actions. An example was the Nacht- und Nebel Erlass (q.v.), the decree of December 7, 1941, that enabled Nazi authorities to seize persons "endangering Germany's security," who were to vanish into the "night and fog."

Gürtner retained his post as Minister of Justice until his death in Berlin on January 29, 1941.

H

H-MEN
to
HUNTING UNITS

H-MEN. *See* HELFERSHELFER.

HÁCHA, EMIL (1872–1945). President of Czechoslovakia when it became a protectorate of the Third Reich. Born on July 12, 1872, in Schweinitz (now Trhové Sviny), Bohemia, Emil Hácha studied law and in 1925 became the first President of the Czechoslovak Supreme Administration Court. On November 30, 1938, he succeeded Eduard Beneš (q.v.) as President of Czechoslovakia. Hácha's task was to maintain the independence of his country after the loss of the Sudetenland (q.v.). In early March 1939, as German forces were poised along the perimeter of Bohemia, he requested an interview with Hitler, who summoned him to Berlin. Despite a heart condition Hácha, together with Frantisek Chvalkovsky, his Foreign Minister, left Prague and arrived at Berlin on the evening of March 14. They were received with military honors. At 1:15 A.M. on March 15 the two Czechs were summoned to Hitler's study for a dramatic confrontation. Hácha attempted to please his host by saying that he had little use for Beneš and Tomáš G. Masaryk, the founders of the Czechoslovak Republic, and that the destiny of his country was safeguarded in Hitler's hands. He literally begged the Fuehrer to spare his people, because "they have a right to live a national life."

Then began one of those extraordinary scenes for which Hitler was notorious. He replied to Hácha's groveling appeal with a display of arrogant browbeating. He insisted that he had no enmity toward the people of Czechoslovakia but that the Beneš "tendencies" had not disappeared. He had, therefore, given orders for the invasion of Czechoslovakia by German troops and the incorporation of the country into the Third Reich. The troops would move within a few hours. He was almost ashamed to say it, he said, but for every Czech battalion there was a German division. Hitler then walked out, leaving the two Czechs to Hermann Goering and Joachim von Ribbentrop (qq.v.). The two Nazis demanded that Hácha immediately sign an instrument of surrender; otherwise, Prague would be annihilated within a few hours. Hácha fainted. He was brought back to consciousness by Dr. Theodor Morell (q.v.), Hitler's physician and a specialist in injections. At 4 A.M. Hácha capitulated and signed the death warrant of his country. The Fuehrer "accepted" the declaration and ordered German troops to enter Prague. Czechoslovakia ceased to exist as a sovereign state.

Hitler allowed Hácha to remain in office nominally as *Staatspräsident des Reichsprotektorat Böhmen und Mähren* (State President of the Reich Protectorate of Bohemia and Moravia). In reality a puppet ruler, Hácha urged his countrymen to support the Third Reich. Throughout the German occupation, however, the Czech people continued to look to Beneš as their rightful leader. Most remained hostile to the Nazi regime. Hácha continued his passive role until Czechoslovakia was invaded by the Russians. He died in a Prague prison on June 27, 1945.

HAEFTEN, WERNER VON (1908–1944). Adjutant to Col. Claus Schenk Graf von Stauffenberg (q.v.). Werner von Haeften was born in Berlin on October 9, 1908. He began his career as a corporation lawyer for a large bank in Hamburg. Serving in World War II, he was wounded in the winter of 1942 and then detailed to duty at the General Quartermaster's Office of the Oberkommando des Heeres (q.v.), the High Command of the Army, in Berlin. In this capacity he was adjutant to Graf von Stauffenberg, who was at the center of the conspiracy to kill Hitler (*see* JULY PLOT). On July 20, 1944, Von Stauffenberg wrapped a 2-pound bomb in a shirt and placed it in a briefcase holding his reports for Hitler. Von Haeften concealed a similar bomb in his own briefcase. He waited in the open as Von Stauffenberg entered the conference hut at the Fuehrer's field headquarters. After Von Stauffenberg had planted his bomb inside the hut, he and his adjutant moved quickly by automobile through two checkpoints to a nearby airfield. On the way Von Haeften took apart his own bomb and threw sections of it along the roadside as the car sped along. In Berlin Von Haeften was arrested at the Bendlerstrasse (q.v.) by Col. Gen. Friedrich Fromm (q.v.) and executed later on July 20.

Werner von Haeften was the younger brother of Hans Bernd von Haeften (1905–1944), an official of the Foreign

Office, who was executed on August 15, 1944, on the same charge of treason.

"HAIL HITLER!" *See* "HEIL HITLER!"

"HAIL HITLER! DEATH TO JUDAISM!" *See* "HEIL HITLER! JUDA VERRECKE!"

"HAIL HITLER TO THEE!" *See* "HEIL HITLER DIR!"

"HAIL TO VICTORY!" *See* "SIEG HEIL!"

HAKENKREUZ (Swastika). The most important Nazi symbol. The hooked, or crooked, cross is a rectilinear cross with oblique arms that turn clockwise. The symbol was adopted by Hitler as the official emblem of the Nationalsozialistische Deutsche Arbeiterpartei (q.v.), the Nazi party, both before and after its rise to political power.

The swastika shown on a postage stamp issued under the Third Reich.

The swastika is one of the most ancient and popular of all ornamental forms. It appeared again and again among different peoples in both hemispheres. It was used on ceramics in Iran as early as the fourth millennium B.C., and it appeared later in Troy, Greece, India, Tibet, and Japan. Sometimes it served as a religious symbol or as a charm against the "evil eye." The American Indians often used the swastika in their handicraft work. On occasion it was employed to denote the movement of the sun. As early as 1910 the swastika was used in Germany to denote "the superior Aryan race." The propaganda machine of Dr. Paul Joseph Goebbels (q.v.) popularized the swastika as the official Nazi emblem.

HALDER, FRANZ (1884–1972). Chief of the General Staff of the German Army from 1938 to 1942. Franz Halder was born in Würzburg on June 30, 1884, to a family that had contributed high-ranking soldiers to Germany for three centuries. He served as a General Staff officer in World War I and remained in the Army in the 1920s. In 1926 he was appointed senior quartermaster of the Reichswehr (q.v.), the 100,000-man Army to which Germany was restricted by the Treaty of Versailles. In October 1936 Hitler retained him in the same post in the new Wehrmacht (q.v.). On August 27, 1938, Halder was made chief of the General Staff to replace Gen. Ludwig Beck (q.v.), who had been forced to resign.

From the beginning of his installation at the Bendlerstrasse (q.v.) as chief of the General Staff, Halder was aware of the deep resentment of army officers toward Hitler. Like most of the upper core of the military and the greater part of the population, he was disgusted by the senseless terrorism of the Storm Troopers (q.v.). Moreover, he disapproved of Nazi party interference in military matters. Like his superior officer, Commander in Chief Gen. Walther von Brauchitsch (q.v.), Halder was torn between his opposition to Nazism and his oath of loyalty to the Fuehrer. Halder indicated that he was inclined to support a coup d'état by army officers, but he would not hear of any attempt to assassinate Hitler. He was the leader of the first officers' Resistance (q.v.) plot (*see* HALDER PLOT). In late 1938, after the Munich Agreement (q.v.), he, like Von Brauchitsch, virtually withdrew from the Resistance. He now felt that the overthrow of the Nazi regime would have to await some outstanding reversal, a diplomatic or military defeat that would destroy Hitler's prestige with troops and people: "A breach of my oath to the Fuehrer is not justified."

Gen. Franz Halder. [*Imperial War Museum, London*]

Halder was opposed to the war that began in 1939, but he chose to follow the orders of the Fuehrer. At the same time he continued to resist the strategy that Hitler expressed in high-level conferences. He was dismissed on September 24, 1942. Arrested after the July Plot (q.v.) against Hitler in 1944, he was kept in a concentration camp (*see* CONCENTRATION CAMPS) until the end of the war. On April 28, 1945, he was liberated by American forces at Niederdorf. In 1949 Halder stated that the German High Command had been hamstrung by Hitler's interference. Germany, he said, might not have won the war but at least it could have avoided the stigma of defeat. The country had been stabbed in the back, he charged, not by Social Democrats this time but by Adolf Hitler.

HALDER PLOT. The first Resistance (q.v.) movement within the officers' corps designed to remove Hitler from power. The leader was Gen. Franz Halder (q.v.), who on August 27, 1938, succeeded Gen. Ludwig Beck (q.v.) as chief of the General Staff of the Army. Soon after taking up his post, Halder made contact with several sympathizers: Maj. Gen. Hans Oster (q.v.), chief of staff of the Abwehr (q.v.), the counterintelligence unit; Hans Bernd Gisevius (q.v.), who worked for the Abwehr; and Dr. Hjalmar Schacht (q.v.), who had been removed from his office as president of the Reichsbank. The group enlisted Maj. Gen. Erwin von Witzleben (q.v.), a senior officer in the Wehrmacht (q.v.), the armed forces. The conspirators proposed to seize the government by a military *Putsch* in Berlin and to install a parliamentary regime, but the plot never went beyond the discussion stage. Halder made an effort to enlist Gen. Walther von Brauchitsch (q.v.), commander in chief of the Wehrmacht, but he was unsuccessful in obtaining the support of that key figure. The plan was dealt a severe blow when Prime Minister Neville Chamberlain (q.v.) made his flights to Germany to appease Hitler. When the Munich Agreement (q.v.) was signed on September 30, 1938, the Halder Plot was swept away.

HALL BATTLES. *See* SAALSCHLACHTEN.

HALL OF HEROES. *See* FELDHERRN HALLE.

HAMILTON, DUKE OF (1900–1971). Premier peer of Scotland who became the object of Rudolf Hess's flight for peace in 1941 (*see* HESS, Rudolf; HESS FLIGHT). Douglas Douglas-Hamilton, the 14th Duke, was the head of Clan Douglas, which had provided Scotland with leaders for more than 700 years. Educated at Eton and Balliol College, Oxford, he represented the university in rowing and boxing. Elected to the House of Commons, he served as a Conservative for a decade before being forced to resign on succeeding to the dukedom. At the 1936 Olympic Games in Berlin (*see* OLYMPIAD XI), he met the Anglophile Albrecht Haushofer, son of Professor Karl Haushofer (qq.v.), theoretician of geopolitics. Albrecht Haushofer spoke to Hess about the British nobleman. In September 1940 Hess asked Haushofer to write to the duke proposing a meeting in Portugal to discuss possible peace negotiations. Hess was disturbed because Germany and England, "two Aryan master races," were at war with each other. The duke, at the suggestion of British Intelligence, was preparing to reply when Hess suddenly flew to Scotland on May 10, 1941, to meet him.

After a crash landing, Hess asked to be directed to the duke's estate. He was under the impression that the duke could influence Prime Minister Winston Churchill to make instant peace with the Third Reich and enter into an alliance with Germany against the Soviet Union. He informed the duke: "Hitler is willing to meet Britain to stop this war with honor." The British jailed Hess, and a furious Hitler publicly pronounced him insane.

Bibliography. James Leasor, *Rudolf Hess: The Uninvited Envoy*, George Allen & Unwin, Ltd., London, 1962.

HAMMERSTEIN-EQUORD, KURT FREIHERR VON (1878–1943). General in the armed forces and, with Gen. Ludwig Beck (q.v.), a senior officer who rejected Hitler and worked in the conspiracy against him. Kurt von Hammerstein was born in Hinrichshagen, Waren District, on September 26, 1878. In World War I he was attached to the General Staff, and in 1930 he was called to succeed Gen. Wilhelm Heye as chief of the Army Command of the Reichswehr (q.v.), the armed forces of the Weimar Republic (q.v.). Respected for his integrity, courage, and patriotism, Von Hammerstein was also noted for his indolence. He laughingly told friends that the only thing that hampered his career was "a need for personal comfort." He regarded himself as a servant of the state, not of political parties. From the beginning he was outspoken in his contempt for Hitler and the Nazis. In the winter of 1930 he made it clear that he was ready for action if the Nazis moved to take political control. "The Reichswehr," he said, "will not allow Hitler to come to power." He supported Field Marshal Paul von Hindenburg (q.v.) for the Presidency in 1932 as the one chance of thwarting Hitler. Von Hammerstein managed to hold his post until February 1, 1934, when he resigned.

Gen. Kurt Freiherr von Hammerstein-Equord. *[Imperial War Museum, London]*

On general mobilization in 1939, Von Hammerstein was recalled to the active list and given command of Army Section A in the defense of the West Wall (q.v.). Later he claimed that he had tried to entice Hitler to come to Cologne, where he intended to seize him: "I would have rendered him harmless, even without judicial proceedings." He was transferred temporarily to command Wehrkreis (Defense District) VIII in Silesia, only to be permanently retired by Hitler, who had learned of his anti-Nazi sentiments. Von Hammerstein became active in the Resistance (q.v.), working with Carl Friedrich Goerdeler (q.v.), the civilian head of the conspiracy. His son, Ludwig von Hammerstein, was one of the younger officers who were determined to unseat Hitler. General von Hammerstein's death in Berlin on April 25, 1943, deprived the Resistance of one of its most valuable members.

HANDSOME ADOLF, THE. *See* DER SCHÖNE ADOLF.

HANFSTAENGL, ERNST FRANZ SEDGWICK (1887–1975). Hitler's unofficial jester in the early days of the Nazi movement. Ernst Hanfstaengl was born in Munich in 1887 of mixed German-American parentage. His father was a well-known art dealer. His maternal grandmother, a member of a New England family, was a cousin of Gen. John Sedgwick, who fell at Spotsylvania Court House in the American Civil War. His grandfather was William Heine, another Civil War general. Ernst was educated at the Royal Bavarian Wilhelm-Gymnasium (high school), where his form master was the father of Heinrich Himmler (q.v.). Designated to take over control of the branch of the family business on Fifth Avenue in New York, Ernst was sent to Harvard University in 1905 and was graduated there in 1909. He spent the four years of World War I in the United States and was disappointed in his inability to serve his fatherland during the crisis. He returned to Munich after the war. Hanfstaengl had left Germany at the height of its imperial glory and returned to find the country crushed and miserable in defeat.

A towering 6-foot, 4-inch giant with an enormous head, a pugnacious jaw, and thick hair, Hanfstaengl endured the nickname Putzi throughout his career. He was a gifted pianist who used his huge hands to pound out the more flamboyant passages of Liszt and Wagner. In the politically chaotic Munich of the early 1920s, he formed an attachment to Hitler, then an aspiring but unknown agitator. Hanfstaengl, the only literary member of Hitler's inner circle, introduced the coarse Austrian to the Munich milieu of art and culture and attempted to make him socially acceptable. After the 1923 Beer-Hall *Putsch* (q.v.), Hitler fled for sanctuary to the Hanfstaengl villa in the Bavarian Alps. Hanfstaengl visted Hitler during the prison term at Landsberg am Lech and helped to reestablish his political career after his release.

Both before and after the Nazi accession to political power in 1933, Hanfstaengl remained a favorite of Hitler's immediate entourage. The tall Bavarian was a gay and amusing companion on political campaigns. With his practical jokes and broad sense of humor, he was regarded as a kind of Shakespearean jester whose main task was to provide relaxation for the harried leader. He performed by the hour. He was rewarded with the nominal post of foreign press chief of the Nationalsozialistische Deutsche Arbeiterpartei (q.v.), the Nazi party. In this position, which he held until he left Germany, he was expected to win goodwill for the Nazi cause among his many important foreign friends.

In late 1934 relations between Hitler and Hanfstaengl became considerably cooler. The latter attempted in subtle ways to influence the Fuehrer to moderate his political, religious, and racial views, while Hitler on his side resented any interference. On one occasion at a crowded reception, Hanfstaengl loudly called Dr. Paul Joseph Goebbels (q.v.), Minister for Public Enlightenment and Propaganda, a swine. This kind of frankness did not endear him to the Nazi establishment. In March 1937, Hanfstaengl, sensing that he was in danger, fled from Germany. He learned later that a plot had been organized to liquidate him by dropping him from a plane. On April 19, 1937, Hermann Goering (q.v.) wrote to Hanfstaengl to assure him that the whole affair was intended as a harmless joke: "We wanted to give you an opportunity of thinking over some rather over-audacious utterances you have made. Nothing more was intended. I assure you on my word of honor that you can remain here amongst us as you have always done in complete freedom. Forget your suspicions and act reasonably. I expect you to accept my word." Hanfstaengl was not inclined to take Goering's word of honor and remained in exile.

During World War II Hanfstaengl served at the American White House as an expert on Nazi affairs. After the war he was interned. Released, he returned to his homeland. He died in Munich on November 6, 1975.

Bibliography. Ernst Hanfstaengl, *Hitler: The Missing Years*, Eyre & Spottiswoode (Publishers), Ltd., London, 1957.

HANKE, KARL (1903–1945). High-ranking Nazi official. Karl Hanke was born in Lauban (Lubań), Lower Silesia, on August 24, 1903. A miller by trade, he was attracted early to the Nazi movement and by 1932 represented the Nationalsozialistische Deutsche Arbeiterpartei (q.v.) in the Reichstag (q.v.) for Wahlkreis (Electoral District) Berlin-East. From 1933 to 1941 he was adjutant and personal assistant to Dr. Paul Joseph Goebbels (q.v.) in the Ministry for Public Enlightenment and Propaganda. In 1941 he was named *Gauleiter* (district leader) of the party in Lower Silesia. During his last days in his Berlin bunker, Hitler, infuriated by what he regarded as treason, named Hanke to succeed Heinrich Himmler (q.v.) in all his offices. Hanke was shot by Czech partisans in July 1945.

HARNACK, ERNST VON (1888–1945). Government official, Social Democrat, and member of the conspiracy against Hitler. Ernst von Harnack was born in Berlin on July 15, 1888, the son of Adolf von Harnack, the well-known religious historian. After study at Marburg, he served in World War I. In the early postwar years he occupied various posts in the Prussian civil administration but was discharged in 1933 when Hitler reorganized the civil service. Denouncing the Nazi regime as "government without goodness or grace," Von Harnack joined the Resistance (q.v.) movement. He was assigned the task of informing other countries about the secret forces inside Germany working against Hitler. Arrested after the July Plot (q.v.) in 1944, he was sentenced to death by the

Ernst von Harnack. [*From Annedore Leber (ed.),* Conscience in Revolt, *tr. by Rosemary O'Neill, Vallentine, Mitchell & Co., Ltd., London, 1957*]

Volksgericht (q.v.), the dreaded People's Court, and was executed on March 3, 1945.

HARNIER, ADOLF VON (1903–1945). Lawyer and member of the Resistance (q.v.) movement against Hitler. Adolf von Harnier, Freiherr (Baron) von Regendorf, was born in Bavaria on April 14, 1903, the son of a landowner. He took his degree as doctor of law in 1934 and settled in Munich as a lawyer. Von Harnier rejected Nazism and was converted to Catholicism. Denounced by a Gestapo (q.v.) informer, he was arrested in 1939 and remanded until 1944 while his case was being investigated. Tried for treason, he was sentenced to ten years in prison. On May 12, 1945, just as American troops reached the prison in Straubing, Von Harnier died of typhoid fever.

HARTMANN, ERICH (1922–). Fighter pilot of the Luftwaffe (q.v.). Major Hartmann, credited by Luftwaffe statisticians with 352 kills, was the German ace of aces in World War II. His career started in 1942 on the Russian front, where he was known as Bubi and the Black Devil. At first he served in Jagdgeschwader (Fighter Group) 52 and in 1944 was promoted to squadron commander of Jagdgeschwader 53. Hartmann was awarded many decorations, and he was the sixth Luftwaffe pilot to win the coveted Knight's Cross with Oak Leaves, Swords, and Diamonds (*see* RITTERKREUZ). The claim of 352 kills was disputed by Allied airmen, who pointed to the records of the top American ace, Richard I. Bong (40), and the leading Briton (38). In defense, Luftwaffe statisticians replied that the record was made on the eastern front, where German fighter pilots did not have formidable opposition. In 1944 Hartmann was captured by the Russians and confined to a prisoner-of-war camp. He was released in 1955.

HARVEST THANKSGIVING DAY. *See* HOLIDAYS, NAZI.

HARZBURG FRONT. A projected alliance of rightist nationalists in 1931 in opposition to the government of Chancellor Heinrich Bruening (q.v.). In 1928 Alfred Hugenberg (q.v.), leader of the German Nationalists and one of the most powerful tycoons of heavy industry, urged Hitler to join him in a battle against the Young Plan (q.v.) on reparations. Hugenberg was anxious to use the strength of the National Socialists, who had won twelve seats in the Reichstag (q.v.) in the elections of May 20, 1928, receiving some 800,000 votes. At this time Hitler was torn between the rightist and leftist wings of his party.

On October 11, 1931, in the little town of Bad Harzburg in Braunschweig, a conclave of rightist parties convened for the purpose of ousting Chancellor Bruening and establishing a "truly national Government." In this gathering were represented such varied groups as Nationalists, Pan-Germans, Junkers, Stahlhelm (q.v.) members, generals, admirals, spokesmen for heavy industry, and National Socialists. Among the individuals present were Hugenberg; Fritz Thyssen (q.v.), director of the United Steel Works; Franz Seldte (q.v.), head of the Stahlhelm; Hjalmar Schacht (q.v.), banker and economics expert; and Hitler. Hugenberg, demanding that Germany be rescued from the Bolshevik peril and from bankruptcy, urged Bruening's resignation and new elections. Hitler, pleased by being included in this distinguished gathering, spoke along similar lines and predicted that Germany would turn either to nationalism or to bolshevism.

The Harzburg Front represented money, influence, and political power, and with Hitler and his Nazis it would have mass support. Between the Harzburg combination and political power stood only the venerable President Paul von Hindenburg (q.v.), who could keep a minority in power as long as he invoked the authority of Article 48 (q.v.) of the Weimar Constitution. The Harzburg Front was not successful in its goal, primarily because Hitler had no intention of diminishing his own strength by combining with the Nationalists. He suspected that Hugenberg wanted to use him for the interests of the Nationalist party, and he was resolved not to allow that. Hitler felt himself to be too close to political power to dilute his position in German politics.

HASSELL, CHRISTIAN ALBRECHT ULRICH VON (1881–1944). Career diplomat and leading diplomat of the Resistance (q.v.) movement. Born in Anklam, Pomerania, on November 12, 1881, to a patrician family, Ulrich von Hassell entered the diplomatic service at an early age. He married the daughter of Grand Adm. Alfred von Tirpitz, naval hero of World War I. After serving as Ambassador in Copenhagen (1926–1930) and Belgrade (1930–1932), he became envoy to Rome in 1933. In his new post he opposed both the Rome-Berlin Axis (q.v.) and the Anti-Comintern Pact. In 1937 he was recalled because of disagreements with Joachim von Ribbentrop (q.v.) in the Foreign Office. He then joined the Resistance movement and became one of its most active members. Hans Bernd Gisevius (q.v.) described Von Hassell's role in the Resistance as an important one. According to Gisevius, Von Hassell was highly esteemed by Col. Gen. Ludwig Beck (q.v.) and by almost everyone else in the opposition. Von Hassell was noted, Gisevius said, for his trenchant humor, his diplomatic finesse, and his unshakable political principles.

Von Hassell's diaries, which he hid in a tea chest buried in the garden of his home in Ebenhausen, Bavaria, are a main source of information about the Resistance movement. Published posthumously, they give an extraordinary picture of the daily activities and dangers of those who served in the attempt to remove Hitler. After Von Hassell's retirement, he traveled widely in Europe. Supposed to report on economic activities, he kept in touch with those who had been sympathetic to the Resistance. Eventually he was arrested, tried before the Volksgericht (q.v.), the People's Court, and found guilty. He was hanged at Plötzensee Prison on September 8, 1944.

Bibliography. *The Von Hassell Diaries*, Hamish Hamilton, Ltd., London, 1948.

HAUPTMANN, GERHART [JOHANN] (1862–1946). Novelist, poet, and dramatist known for his writings of social protest and for his submission to the Nazi regime. Gerhart Johann Hauptmann was born in Obersalzbrunn, Silesia (now Szczawno Zdrój, Poland), on November 15, 1862, the son of an innkeeper. After working for a time as a farmer, he went to Breslau to study art and continued his education at the University of Jena. At first a pioneer

Gerhart Hauptmann. [*Stamp issued by the German Democratic Republic*]

in German literary naturalism, he wrote plays dealing with the evil conditions of the working class, such as *Vor Sonnenaufgang* (*Before Dawn*, 1889) and *Die Weber* (*The Weavers*, 1892), his most famous drama. Later he turned from the drama of social mass revolution to a neoromanticism distinguished by poetic mysticism. Among his neoromantic works are *Hanneles Himmelfahrt* (*Hannele's Journey to Heaven*, 1893), *Die versunkene Glocke* (*The Sunken Bell*, 1896), and *Der arme Heinrich* (*Poor Henry*, 1902). Widely regarded as the patriarch of modern German literature, Hauptmann was awarded the Nobel Prize for Literature in 1912.

Hauptmann was one of the few great German literary figures who remained in Nazi Germany after the rise of Hitler to political power. Whereas Thomas Mann (q.v.) and others of his stature went into exile, Hauptmann stayed and became more and more submissive to the Nazi state. His silence was variously interpreted as opportunism or possibly agreement with the symbolism and mysticism of the Nazi way of life. He died in Agnetendorf (Jagniątków) on June 6, 1946.

Bibliography. Frederick W. J. Heuser, *Gerhart Hauptmann*, Niemeyer, Tübingen, 1961.

HAUPTSTURMFUEHRER-SS. Captain in the SS (q.v.).

HAUSHOFER, ALBRECHT (1903–1945). Teacher, poet, dramatist, and member of the Resistance (q.v.) movement against Hitler. Son of the geopolitician Karl Haushofer (q.v.), Albrecht Haushofer was born in Munich on January 7, 1903. He wrote several dramatic works, including *Scipio* (1934) and *Sulla* (1938). A co-worker in his father's specialty, he became professor of political geography at the University of Berlin in 1940. From 1940 on he worked in the Foreign Office. Regarding Nazism as a calamity for the German people, Haushofer joined the Resistance. He was arrested after the July Plot (q.v.) of 1944 and imprisoned. His *Moabiter Sonette*, written in prison, preserved by accident, and published later, bears witness to the spirit of the conspirators. Albrecht Haushofer was shot on April 23, 1945, while being transferred from Berlin-Moabit Prison, just a few days before the end of the war in Europe.

HAUSHOFER, KARL (1869–1946). Founder of German geopolitics. Karl Haushofer was born in Munich on August 27, 1869. From 1887 on he traveled on various diplomatic missions through Southeast Asia, and from 1908 to 1910 he was in Japan. In World War I he served as a brigadier general. In 1921 he became professor of geography at the University of Munich, where he founded the Institute for Geopolitics. He was the teacher and friend of Rudolf Hess (q.v.), then a poverty-stricken young student, who was deeply moved by Haushofer's teachings. Hess later passed them on to Hitler.

Haushofer was the main exponent in Germany of geopolitics, a modern version of political geography or anthropogeography, calling for a fusion of geography and politics. The idea was by no means new. Herodotus and Thucydides recognized the dependence of political events on the character of the earth, a concept later taken up by Montesquieu, the French legalist, and Ranke, the German historian. The idea was developed by Sir Halford John Mackinder (1861–1947), a Scotsman, who wrote of the value of geography as a factor in social reconstruction, and by Adm. Alfred Thayer Mahan (1840–1914), an American, who saw world politics as essentially a conflict between oceanic and continental powers. Haushofer utilized much of this past work and contributed his own data in support of the principles of geopolitics. Other scholars considered part of his work to be sound science, but some critics dismissed it as immature pseudoscience, equipped with a flashy terminology and filled with half-truths.

Haushofer believed that the British Empire, a naval power, was in decline, and that it was the turn of a Continental power to take over the leadership. Otherwise, space would be controlled by Eurasians. Germany, which needed *Lebensraum* (q.v.), or living space, had to expand, especially toward the east, where the agricultural Ukraine should be appended to the industrial German *Herzland* (heartland). Haushofer warned, however, that Britain must remain a cornerstone of German politics. When Hess flew to Scotland on May 10, 1941, on his peace

Karl Haushofer. [*Picture Collection, The Branch Libraries, The New York Public Library*]

mission (*see* HESS FLIGHT), he carried with him the visiting cards of Karl Haushofer and his son Albrecht Haushofer (q.v.). Hess claimed that the idea of flying to Britain came to him from Professor Haushofer, who told him of a dream in which he had seen Hess striding through the tapestried walls of English castles on a mission to bring the two Nordic nations together.

In Nazi Germany geopolitics became a new fashion, and Haushofer won a reputation as the "man behind Hitler." The Fuehrer used the political aspects of geopolitics as a rationalization for national expansion. He borrowed from Haushofer one of his favorite expressions, "space as a factor of power." The eagerness with which National Socialists embraced his theories embarrassed Haushofer. Added to his discomfort was the fact that he was forced to ask Hess's help as a protective hand for Frau Haushofer, who was of Jewish background. Abroad he was regarded as a leading Nazi, and his role in the creation of Nazi ideology was exaggerated. Haushofer was arrested after the anti-Hitler July Plot (q.v.) of 1944, in which his son was implicated. Grieving for his son, who was shot by the Gestapo (q.v.), and disillusioned by National Socialism, Haushofer committed suicide at Pähl bei Weilheim on March 13, 1946.

Bibliography. Karl Haushofer, *Wehr-Geopolitik*, Junker und Dünnhaupt, Berlin, 1941.

HAW-HAW, LORD. *See* JOYCE, WILLIAM.

HAY ACTION. *See* HEU AKTION.

HEADQUARTERS GUARD. *See* STABSWACHE.

HEALTH OFFICE. *See* GESUNDHEITSAMT.

HEIDEGGER, MARTIN (1889–1976). Philosopher who looked with favor on the Nazi cause. Martin Heidegger was born in Messkirch, Baden, on September 26, 1889, to an old Swabian farm family. He attended *Gymnasien* (high schools) in Konstanz and Freiburg and took his doctorate in philosophy at the University of Freiburg in 1913. In 1915 he became a *Privatdozent* (lecturer without fixed remuneration) at Freiburg, and in 1923 was given a post at Marburg. Heidegger was named successor to Edmund Husserl at Freiburg in 1928 and made *Rektor* (chancellor) of the university in 1933. In his inaugural address he spoke of "the glory and greatness of the revolution of 1933." He stated: "The much-praised academic freedom of German universities will be cast out." Heidegger died at Messkirch on May 26, 1976.

"HEIL HITLER!" ("Hail Hitler!"). The new Nazi "German greeting" designed to take the place of the familiar *"Guten Tag!"* ("Good Day!"). Originally, *"Heil!"* meant "salvation" and was used in describing relations between man and his God. One could speak of *ewiges Heil* (eternal salvation); the adjective *heilig* (holy) is derived from the noun. During the Third Reich there was a new usage, and the old neutral greeting was succeeded by a new formula required by law. Adults greeted one another with *"Heil Hitler!"* School study periods were opened with the greeting, and every child was expected to say *"Heil Hitler!"* 50 to 150 times a day. Along with the greeting went the "big" Hitler salute (q.v.), with the right arm raised as high as it would go.

"HEIL HITLER DIR!" ("Hail Hitler to Thee!"). Title of a popular marching song of the SA (q.v.), the brown-shirted Storm Troopers.

"HEIL HITLER! JUDA VERRECKE!" ("Hail Hitler! Death to Judaism!"). Two favorite Nazi slogans, generally used in combination. The juxtaposition was supposed to indicate the relative importance of each slogan.

HEILIGER GRUND UND BODEN (Holy Ground and Soil). A favorite slogan of Nazi propaganda to encourage German nationalism.

HEILMANN, ERNST (1881–1940). Social Democratic politician who died at Buchenwald (q.v.) concentration camp (*see* CONCENTRATION CAMPS). Ernst Heilmann was born in Berlin on April 13, 1881, the son of middle-class Jewish parents. He joined the Social Democratic party in 1903 and served it as a delegate to the Prussian Landtag (Legislature) from 1924 to 1928 and as a deputy to the German Reichstag (q.v.) from 1928 to 1933. Considered a dangerous enemy by the Nazis, he was arrested in 1933 and confined in such concentration camps as Papenburg, Dachau (qq.v.), and Buchenwald. Heilmann was subjected to harsh treatment throughout his imprisonment, and on one occasion he was attacked by bloodhounds that mangled his arms and hands. Despite beatings and constant humiliation, however, he never gave in to Nazi brutality. On April 3, 1940, at the age of fifty-nine, he died at Buchenwald. The medical report called his death "a clear case of weakness and old age."

HEIMABEND (Home Evening). Special evening meeting held for Nazi boys and girls under the supervision of the Nazi party.

HEIMATROMAN (Regional Novel). Literary form that emphasized the national mystique of regional Germanness. This type of novel was favored by Hitler and the Nazi authorities as a means of building German nationalism. *See also* LITERATURE IN THE THIRD REICH.

HEIMTÜCKE GESETZ (Treason Law). Special law designed to punish wartime offenders. It was intended to control political dissenters, many of whom were arrested by the Gestapo (q.v.) and sent to concentration camps (q.v.). Often such prisoners were sent to lunatic asylums after their release.

HEINES, EDMUND (1897–1934). Member of the intimate circle of SA (q.v.) leader Ernst Roehm (q.v.). Born on July 21, 1897, Edmund Heines served as a junior officer in World War I. After the war he became an adjutant to Gerhard Rossbach, leader of the Rossbach group (q.v.), one of the many companies of the restless *Freikorps* (q.v.), or freebooters. Distinguished by a girlish face on the body of a truck driver, Heines took part in numerous street brawls with opponents during the era of the Weimar Republic (q.v.). Like many other *Freikorps* members, he joined the Nazi party early, and he soon became a close colleague of Roehm. In May 1927 Hitler expelled Heines from the party, ostensibly for "loose morals" but actually because he had called Hitler a dishrag and had tried to arouse other SA members against the party leadership. On Roehm's energetic protest, Hitler retreated and sent Heines a letter thanking him heartily for his achievements and services to the cause of National Socialism. In 1929 Heines was sentenced to five years' imprisonment for a *Fehme* murder (*see* FEHMEMORD) but was soon released in a general amnesty. In 1933 he was appointed *SA-Obergruppenfuehrer* (general) assigned to Silesia and was made commissioner of police at Breslau.

On June 30, 1934, Hitler and a small entourage went to the Hanselbauer Sanatorium in Bad Wiessee on the shores of the Tegernsee, where Roehm, Heines, and their circle were recuperating from "illnesses." In a room next to that of Roehm, Hitler found Heines in bed with a young boy. According to eyewitnesses, the Fuehrer ordered the "ruthless extermination of this pestilential tumor." Heines and his companion were dragged from the room and shot, the first victims of the Blood Purge (q.v.). Shortly afterward, Heines's younger brother, suffering from tuberculosis and convalescing while in custody in the Silesian mountains, was also executed. Some weeks later Heines's mother sent an awkwardly written letter to the authorities pleading that her second son, whom she described as her sole support, be released. When an investigation revealed that she had already been sent the ashes of Edmund Heines, the ashes of her second son were also forwarded to her.

HELDENGEDENKTAG ATTENTAT (Heroes' Memorial Day Attempt). An attempt on Hitler's life made on March 21, 1943, by the Resistance (q.v.). After the failure of the Smolensk *attentat* (q.v.) on March 13, the conspirators decided to try again a week later. The day selected was one dedicated to commemorate the dead of World War I. A ceremony was held annually at the Zeughaus on Unter den Linden, Berlin. It was Hitler's custom to attend the ceremony, this time to see a collection of weapons captured from the Russians. Maj. Gen. Henning von Tresckow (q.v.), operational chief of the plot, selected a colleague, Maj. Gen. Rudolf Christian Freiherr von Gersdorff, for the task of killing Hitler. Von Gersdorff was supposed to use a ten-minute fuse for the bomb, but he was unable to find one in time and decided to abandon the plot. Ironically, Hitler remained for just eight minutes after the ceremony.

HELFERSHELFER (H-Men; Secondary Informants). Members of a special unit of the SD (q.v.), the security service, usually informants who acted from highly questionable and selfish motives.

HELLDORF, WOLF HEINRICH GRAF VON (1896–1944). Police president of Berlin and member of the conspiracy against Hitler. Wolf Heinrich von Helldorf was born in Merseburg on October 14, 1896. Just eighteen years old at the outbreak of World War I, he served as an officer and in 1916 as the leader of a machine-gun company. Von Helldorf was awarded the Iron Cross (First and Second Classes). After the war he joined the Rossbach group (q.v.), one of the freebooter *Freikorps* (q.v.) units, and

Wolf Heinrich Graf von Helldorf. [*Ullstein*]

fought in street battles against the Communists in the Rhineland. After taking part in the rightist Kapp *Putsch* (q.v.) in 1920, he was exiled to Italy. Returning to Germany in 1924, he was elected to the Prussian Landtag (Legislature). In 1926 he joined the Nationalsozialistische Deutsche Arbeiterpartei (q.v.) and in 1931 became an SA (q.v.) leader in Berlin. In 1933, after Hitler became Chancellor, Von Helldorf was named to high posts in both the SA and the SS (q.v.) in Berlin-Brandenburg, serving as *SA-Gruppenfuehrer* (lieutenant general) and *SS-Obergruppenfuehrer* (general). On November 11, 1933, he was elected to the Reichstag (q.v.) as a Nazi deputy. From March 1933 to July 1935 he served as police president of Potsdam and from 1935 on as police president of Berlin.

From the beginning Graf von Helldorf had reservations about the National Socialist regime. He was absent from Berlin on Crystal Night (*see* KRISTALLNACHT), November 9, 1938, but on his return called a conference of police officers and berated them for their passivity during the riots against the Jews. To the dismay of his listeners he stated that had he been present he would have ordered his men to shoot all rioters and looters. Von Helldorf took part in the July Plot (q.v.) against Hitler in 1944, after which he was arrested, tortured for days, and finally executed on August 15.

HELPERS. *See* HILFSWILLIGE.

HENLEIN, KONRAD (1898–1945). Sudeten German politician. Konrad Henlein was born in Maffersdorf (Vratislavice nad Nisou), Bohemia, on May 6, 1898. Early in his career he was a bank clerk. In 1931 he was placed in charge of the German Gymnastics Association of Czechoslovakia. On October 1, 1933, after the accession of Hitler to power, he founded a small political party that eventually became the Sudeten Deutsche Partei (SdP), the strongest political party in Czechoslovakia. From the beginning Henlein's party was supported financially by the Nazi regime. In 1933, for example, the party's newspaper received 120,000 Czech crowns from the Third Reich to pay its debts. That year Rudolf Hess (q.v.) granted Henlein a subsidy of 8 million crowns. Henlein's followers, hiding under the name of Sport Abteilung (its initials corresponded with those of the German SA, q.v.), began agitation for Sudeten German independence.

In October 1934 Henlein's party held its first mass meeting, at which 20,000 people were present. In the Czech elections of 1935 it returned forty-four deputies, or 60 percent of the representatives of the German-speaking population in Czechoslovakia. The Berlin Foreign Office then began paying a fixed subsidy of 12,000 reichsmarks per month to Henlein and his followers. On March 28, 1938, Hitler informed Henlein in an interview: "I will stand by you. Tomorrow you will be my viceroy [*Sie sind auch morgen mein Statthalter*]." The next month Henlein announced the eight Karlsbad (Karlovy Vary) demands, asking for virtually complete autonomy for the Sudeten Germans. In May he journeyed to London, where he gave his word of honor that he had never received orders or even recommendations from Berlin.

After the Munich Agreement (q.v.), Henlein was appointed *Reichskommissar* (State Commissioner) for the Sudetenland. On May 1, 1939, he became *Gauleiter* (district leader) and *Reichsstatthalter* (Reich Governor, or State Viceroy), the head of the civil administration in Czechoslovakia. Captured in May 1945 by the United States Seventh Army, Henlein committed suicide in an Allied internment camp on May 10.

HENRICI, SIEGFRIED (1889–). Career officer. Siegfried Henrici was born in Soest, Westphalia, on November 11, 1889. Joining the Imperial Army as an ensign *(Fahnenjunker)* in 1907, he was promoted to lieutenant two years later. After serving in World War I, he retired in 1919. During the era of the Weimar Republic (q.v.) he worked in various capacities in the Prussian security service and the Ministry of the Interior. Returning to the Army in 1935, he was made a major general on June 1, 1939. Henrici commanded the 12th Corps in the west in 1940, the 43d Corps in Russia as a lieutenant general in 1941, the Fourth Army in Russia from 1942 to May 1944, the First Panzer Army in 1944–1945, and Army Group West, covering Berlin, in March 1945. On April 28, 1945, Henrici led the Third Tank Army, which was supposed to be on its way to Berlin, northward against the strictest orders of Marshal Wilhelm Keitel (q.v.). Keitel, his face purple, accused Henrici of insubordination, treason, cowardice, and sabotage. Henrici waited quietly until Keitel's shouting stopped. Then he pointed to his soldiers without rifles, guns, ammunition, and armor, exhausted and hopeless. "Marshal Keitel," he said, "if you want these men to be shot, please begin!" Keitel, who had not seen the front until that day, repeated his order to march on to Berlin and then drove off. Henrici was imprisoned after being captured by the Russians on May 9, 1945.

HERBSTNEBEL (Autumn Fog). Code name for Hitler's counteroffensive in the Ardennes in December 1944.

HERBSTREISE (Autumn Journey). Code name for a large-scale feint to be undertaken in conjunction with Operation Sea Lion (Seelöwe, q.v.). In early August 1940 Hitler issued a directive for the conduct of air and naval warfare against England. Late that month he gave additional orders for a series of deceptions to be carried out with Sea Lion, of which Herbstreise was one. Four large passenger liners, including the *Europa* and the *Bremen*, together with ten transports and four accompanying cruisers, were to leave Norwegian waters and head for the British coast between Newcastle and Aberdeen. There would be only necessary crews aboard the armada, which would move toward the British coast two days before the contemplated invasion and then turn back home in the darkness. The entire plan of Operation Sea Lion was canceled the next month, when the Luftwaffe (q.v.) received a sound beating in the Battle of Britain.

HERCULES. Code name for the proposed capture of Malta by German parachute troops in the spring of 1942. The operation was postponed when large British forces got through to the island on June 16, 1942. British aircraft soon drove the Luftwaffe (q.v.) from the skies around Malta, and British planes based on the island sank most of the supply ships seeking to reach Gen. Erwin Rommel (q.v.) in North Africa.

HEREDITARY ESTATES. *See* ERBHÖFE.

HEREDITARY FARM LAW. *See* ERBHOFGESETZ.

HERMANN GOERING NATIONAL WORKS. *See* REICHSWERKE HERMANN GOERING.

HEROES' MEMORIAL DAY ATTEMPT. *See* HELDENGEDENKTAG ATTENTAT.

HERON. *See* FISCHREIHER.

HERRENKLUB (Gentlemen's Club). A social club in Berlin whose members considered themselves to be among the country's elite. Among the organizers and leading members was Franz von Papen (q.v.), Chancellor in June 1932 and Vice-Chancellor in Hitler's first Cabinet.

HERRENMENSCH (Master Man). In Nazi ideology any individual belonging to the *Herrenvolk* (q.v.), the master race. *See also* RACIAL DOCTRINE.

HERRENVOLK (Master Race). The Nazi conception of the Germans as a superior race among the *Voelkerchaos* (q.v.), the chaos of peoples. *See also* RACIAL DOCTRINE.

HESS, [WALTER RICHARD] RUDOLF (1894–1987). Deputy to the Fuehrer and at one time Hitler's appointed successor after Hermann Goering (q.v.). Rudolf Hess was

Rudolf Hess in Spandau Prison. [*Wide World Photos*]

born in Alexandria, Egypt, on April 26, 1894, the son of a German importer. He attended schools in Alexandria, Bad Godesberg, Neuchâtel, and Hamburg. In World War I he served first on the western front as a shock-troop leader in the same regiment as Hitler and later as a lieutenant in the Air Force. He was wounded at Verdun. In 1919 he joined the Thule Gesellschaft, a unit of the freebooter *Freikorps* (q.v.) under the command of Gen. Franz Xaver Ritter von Epp (q.v.). As a student at the University of Munich, he worked closely with Professor Karl Haushofer (q.v.), whose theory of geopolitics (q.v.) made a deep impression on him. Hess was at Hitler's side in the Beer-Hall *Putsch* (q.v.) in Munich in 1923 and managed to escape to Austria. Returning to Germany, he was sentenced to seven months in Landsberg Prison (*see* LANDSBERG AM LECH). While in custody, he aroused Hitler's interest in geopolitics and took down much of Hitler's dictation for *Mein Kampf* (q.v.).

After the reorganization of the Nationalsozialistische Deutsche Arbeiterpartei (q.v.) in 1925, Hess became Hitler's private secretary. He was soon elevated to high posts in the party. In December 1932 Hitler made him chairman of the Central Political Commission of the party. In 1932 Hess became a Nazi delegate to the Reichstag (q.v.) and was promoted to *SS-Obergruppenfuehrer* (general). On April 21, 1933, shortly after Hitler became Chancellor, Hess was appointed Deputy Fuehrer. He was named Reich Minister without Portfolio on June 29. On September 24, 1935, he was given the right to take part in the appointment of all high Nazi officials. On February 4, 1938, when Hitler reorganized the military and political administration, Hess was made a member of the Secret Cabinet Council (Geheimer Kabinettsrat, q.v.). On August 30, 1939, he became a member of the Ministerial Council for the Defense of the Reich. At this time he was named the successor to Hitler after Goering.

Hess was instantly recognizable because of his deep-set eyes in a square-cut face. His loyalty to the Fuehrer was absolute. He had a doglike devotion to the man who had lifted him from obscurity as a purposeless student to posts of high leadership in the Third Reich. Introverted, without superior intelligence or demagogic talent, he knew only unconditional faith in his Fuehrer. "Hitler," he said, "is simply pure reason incarnate." Newsreels revealed a religious fervor in his eyes and voice when he introduced Hitler at mass meetings. In 1934 he said: "With pride we see that one man remains beyond all criticism. This is because everyone feels and knows that Hitler is always right, and that he will always be right." In one of Hess's lucid moments at Nuremberg he showed that he had never lost faith: "It was granted me for many years to live and work under the greatest son whom my nation has brought forth in the thousand years of its history."

On May 10, 1941, Hess astonished an incredulous world by flying alone from Augsburg and parachuting to earth in Scotland. This was a classic case of disobedience by a hitherto-obedient servant who believed he was acting in his master's interest. The purpose of Hess's fantastic trip has never been explained, but it is assumed that he hoped to reach Tory appeasers in England who would make peace with Hitler as soon as the Fuehrer attacked the Soviet Union. Hitler promptly pronounced Hess insane. *See also* HESS FLIGHT.

In 1946 Hess was brought to trial before the International Military Tribunal at Nuremberg. Throughout the trial he remained in a state of total or feigned amnesia. He replied to all questions with the repeated phrase "I can't remember!" He was emaciated and broken, his eyes staring vacantly into space. The court found that Hess, as deputy to the Fuehrer, was the chief man in the Nazi party, with responsibility for handling all party matters and authority to make decisions in Hitler's name on all questions of party leadership. On September 27, 1938, at the time of the Munich crisis (*see* MUNICH AGREEMENT), Hess had arranged with Gen. Wilhelm Keitel (q.v.) to make the machinery of the Nazi party available for a secret mobilization. "That Hess acts in an abnormal manner, suffers from a loss of memory, and has mentally deteriorated during his trial, may be true. But there is nothing to show that he does not realize the nature of the charges against him, or is incapable of defending himself. He was ably represented at the trial by counsel appointed for that purpose by the Tribunal. There is no suggestion that Hess was not completely sane when the acts charged against him were committed." He was found guilty on count 1 (conspiracy to commit crimes alleged in other counts) and count 2 (crimes against peace) and sentenced to life imprisonment.

Hess was sent to Spandau Prison (q.v.), where after 1966 the last of the other six leading Nazis were released after serving their terms. Although there was a movement in the West for his release, he was retained at Spandau as the only prisoner because the Russians insisted that a life term meant just that. On August 17, 1987, after 41 years, the 93-year-old inmate reportedly hanged himself. British authorities said he had used an electrical cord and the cause of death was asphyxiation.

Bibliography. Ilse Hess, *Gefangener des Friedens,* Drufel-Verlag, Leoni am Starnberger See, 1955; James Leasor, *Rudolf Hess: The Uninvited Envoy,* George Allen & Unwin, Ltd., London, 1962; J. R. Rees (ed.), *The Case of Rudolf Hess,* William Heinemann, Ltd., London, 1947.

HESS FLIGHT. The airplane flight of Rudolf Hess (q.v.), Deputy Fuehrer of the Third Reich, to Scotland to seek British collaboration against the Russians. On May 10, 1941, the No. 3 Nazi parachuted safely into Scotland following an 800-mile forbidden flight from Germany. After the outbreak of World War II in 1939, Hess, who had operated closely in the shadow of the Fuehrer, was gradually relegated to the background. Fretting about his bad fortune, he began to devise plans to regain Hitler's attention by a magnificent act of sacrifice. It was a tragedy, he believed, for Germans and British, "Aryan blood brothers," to fight one another in the war. He would fly alone to the British Isles, arrange a peace with the British, and get them to join in the war that the Fuehrer would soon begin against Bolshevik Russia. Hess was certain that he would be welcomed in Britain. During the Olympic Games held at Berlin in 1936 (*see* OLYMPIAD XI), he had met a British aristocrat who later became the Duke of Hamilton (q.v.). After the war began, Hess wrote to the duke and presented a peace feeler, but the latter, acting on government instructions, did not reply. Hess nevertheless believed that if he could get to Scotland, the duke, as lord steward to the royal family, would lead him directly to the King and help him on his mission of peace.

Hess prepared carefully for the flight. He had been forbidden by the Fuehrer to fly, but he managed to induce Willy Messerschmitt (q.v.), the aircraft designer, to give him facilities for long-distance–flying training inside Germany. He concentrated on learning air navigation. On May 10, 1941, he took off from Augsburg in an unarmed plane without fuel for a return trip. He was dressed as a Luftwaffe (q.v.) flight lieutenant and carried a map on which he had penciled his course. His navigation was remarkable. He had intended to land the plane near the estate of the Duke of Hamilton, but he was unable to find a suitable spot. Stalling for a crash, he bailed out and floated down on a Scottish farm. Unarmed and unresisting, he allowed himself to be captured by a farmer armed with a pitchfork. Suffering from a broken ankle but otherwise unharmed, the smiling Hess was removed to a Glasgow hospital. At first he gave his name as Horn but later admitted that he was Rudolf Hess and showed various photographs of himself at different ages in order to establish his identity.

Hess was astonished when high British officials, apparently at a loss for what to make of the flight, declined to talk to him. To an officer of the Foreign Office, who had known him before the war and now came to the hospital to see him, Hess gave his personal message. If the British would only halt hostilities, they could join their brothers in Germany in a crusade against bolshevism. Hitler would give the British a free hand in their empire, while Germany would maintain control of the European continent. There were some conditions: Germany's colonies, which had been stolen from her by the Treaty of Versailles, must be returned; Iraq must be evacuated; and the British must conclude an armistice with Mussolini. This was the price for peace. Moreover, the British must know that the Fuehrer would not negotiate with Prime Minister Winston Churchill and that it would be best if Churchill were forced to resign.

From Germany came anguished cries of disbelief and disavowal. Hitler ordered Propaganda Minister Dr. Paul Joseph Goebbels (q.v.) to inform the world that Hess had taken leave of his senses. The press release was explicit: "It seemed that Party Member Hess lived in a state of hallucination, as a result of which he felt he would bring about an understanding between England and Germany. . . . The National Socialist Party regrets that this idealist fell a victim to his hallucination. This, however, will have no effect on the continuance of the war which has been forced on Germany."

Churchill ordered that Hess be treated with dignity, as if he were an important general who had fallen by accident into British hands. The prisoner was eventually moved to the Tower of London, where he was held until October 6, 1945, when he was transferred to a cell at Nuremberg. Later Churchill stated that, whatever his moral guilt because as a German he stood by Hitler, Hess had atoned for this by "his completely devoted and frantic deed of lunatic benevolence." The British Prime Minister believed that Hess had come to England of his own free will and that although without any authority, he had something of the quality of an envoy. Churchill concluded that Hess was a medical and not a criminal case and should be so regarded.

Bibliography. Joseph Bernard Hutton, *Hess: The Man and His Mission*, The Macmillan Company, New York, 1970.

HEU AKTION (Hay Action). An order by Alfred Rosenberg (q.v.), Reich Minister for the Eastern Occupied Territories, for a quota of foreign workers to be sent to Germany. Issued on June 12, 1944, Heu Aktion called for the apprehension of 40,000 to 50,000 youths, aged ten to fourteen, for shipment to the Reich. At Nuremberg Baldur von Schirach (q.v.), although he had ceased to be head of the Hitler Jugend (q.v.), the Hitler Youth, in 1940, was accused of complicity in this kidnapping action.

HEUSINGER, ADOLF (1897–). Lieutenant general and chief of operations of the Army High Command in World War II. Adolf Heusinger was born in Holzminden on August 4, 1897. From 1931 to 1944 he served on the General Staff and from 1939 to 1944 as chief of operations. He had little use for Nazi ideology and especially for the anti-Semitic campaign, which he regarded as "a military imbecility that needlessly added to the difficulties in fighting the enemy." Heusinger was aware of the conspiracy against Hitler, but the extent of his role in the plot is not clear. He was present at the conference at Hitler's headquarters at Rastenburg, East Prussia, on July 20, 1944, when the unsuccessful attempt was made on Hitler's life (*see* RASTENBURG CONFERENCE). At Hitler's immediate right, he was in the midst of a melancholy report on the Russian breakthrough when the bomb exploded. Heusinger was slightly wounded. He was taken into custody and tried before the Volksgericht (q.v.), the People's Court, on August 7, 1944. At his trial he was implicated in the conspiracy by Gen. Helmuth Stieff (q.v.), staff officer of the Army High Command, who as one of the plotters stated that he had revealed the imminence of the attempt to Heusinger. The latter wrote an explanatory memorandum to Hitler, who responded: "I thank you for it. It is the most comprehensive critical assessment of my war measures that I have come by." Heusinger was then released. *See also* JULY PLOT.

Heusinger took a leading role in the military affairs of the Federal Republic from 1952 on. From 1957 to 1961 he served as general inspector of the Bundeswehr, the armed forces of West Germany, and from April 1961 to February 1964 he was chairman of the armed forces of the North Atlantic Treaty Organization (NATO) in Washington.

"HEUTE DEUTSCHLAND! MORGEN DIE WELT!" ("Today Germany! Tomorrow the World!"). Slogan popular among Nazis during their drive for political power.

HEYDRICH, REINHARD [TRISTRAN EUGEN] (1904–1942). Head of the Reich Security Service, Deputy Reich Protector of Bohemia and Moravia, administrator of the concentration camps (q.v.), and a specialist in Nazi terror. In inner Nazi circles Reinhard Heydrich was regarded as a possible successor to the Fuehrer. Born in Halle, Saxony, on March 7, 1904, he was the son of Bruno Richard Heydrich, a gifted musician and founder of the First Halle

Conservatory for Music, Theater, and Teaching. In 1916 Bruno Heydrich was described in Hugo Riemann's *Musiklexikon* as "Heydrich, Bruno, real name Süss." This entry, intimating that the elder Heydrich was Jewish, was to plague Reinhard Heydrich for the rest of his life. Again and again he brought legal suit for racial slander against anyone who accused him of having "Jewish blood."

In his early twenties Heydrich served as an officer in the German Navy, from which he was dismissed in 1931 after a court-martial for an affair with a young girl. In 1932 he joined the SS (q.v.) and quickly rose to the top of that organization. From the beginning he attracted the attention of Heinrich Himmler (q.v.), who made him his closest associate. To Himmler the tall blond athletic Heydrich was in outward appearance the very model of the blond Nordic then being popularized by Nazi ideologists. Heydrich played a leading role in the 1934 Blood Purge (q.v.). On June 17, 1936, he was made chief of the Sicherheitspolizei (q.v.), the Security Police, and of the SD (q.v.). In 1940 he was elected to the presidency of the International Criminal Police Commission, in which capacity he sought to develop a system of German espionage in other countries. He was promoted to *Obergruppenfuehrer-SS* (general) in 1941.

By this time Heydrich had established the first ghetto for Jews and become the first administrator of concentration camps. On September 27, 1941, Hitler appointed him Deputy Reich Protector for Bohemia and Moravia. At the Wannsee Conference (q.v.), held on January 20, 1942, Heydrich was chosen to administer the "Final Solution" of the Jewish question (*see* ENDLÖSUNG, DIE). His pacification measures in Czechoslovakia, carried out with cynical brutality, led to widespread resistance. Czechoslovakian exiles in London decided to strike back. On May 27, 1942, two young men of the Czech resistance were dropped by parachute to the vicinity of Prague. Two days later, on May 29, they waited for Heydrich's automobile at the edge of the city. As the car slowed down, one of them, Jan Kubis, threw a bomb that exploded under the vehicle. Heydrich was critically wounded and died a week later.

The reaction in Germany was bitter. Baldur von Schirach (q.v.), head of the youth movement, charged that the British had encouraged Czech resistance. In retaliation, he proposed that German planes bomb an English cultural center. An enraged Hitler looked upon Heydrich's assassination as a "lost battle." In a funeral speech he called Heydrich "the Man with the Iron Heart." Some 860 Czechs were condemned to death by court-martial at Prague and 395 at Brno. The entire village of Lidice (q.v.) was obliterated and its inhabitants executed or scattered on the charge that they had harbored the assassins. The murder of Heydrich also resulted in an intensified campaign against the Jews.

The character and personality of Heydrich have attracted intense interest. In his cold sadism, amorality, and greed for power, he ranks with the great criminals of all time. Cynical, brutal, the embodiment of suspicion, he trusted no one. He had only contempt for human life, no compassion, no sense of pity, no feeling of decency or justice. Yet this cold, harsh human being was a passionate lover of music, who devoted much of his time to chamber music and especially to the works of Mozart and Haydn.

Reinhard Heydrich. [*Imperial War Museum, London*]

At the core of his character was a gnawing suspicion that his own body was tainted by Jewish blood. He was never free of the torment occasioned by this belief. It is possible that his savage conduct in dealing with Jewish victims may have been dictated by a kind of perverse racial compensation. Certainly it reflected his morbid self-hatred. One of his colleagues reported that on coming home intoxicated one evening Heydrich suddenly saw his own image reflected in a large wall mirror. Instantaneously, in cold rage, he whipped out his pistol and fired two shots at his image.

Both Hitler and Himmler were aware of Heydrich's self-contempt because of his Jewish problem, but both regarded him as too valuable a functionary to ruin his career. Hitler, especially, looked upon Heydrich as indispensable to the movement and held that his possible non-Aryan origin was useful in the sense that Heydrich would be eternally grateful to the Nazi leadership for keeping him. This kind of man, Hitler thought, would obey orders blindly. For the colorless, narrow-minded Himmler, his charismatic assistant, with his blond appearance and explosive energy, was an ideal front man in the business of exterminating the Jews. Heydrich, in turn, was obligingly obsequious to his superior officer and carried out his orders with unflagging zeal. Carl Jacob Burckhardt fittingly labeled Heydrich "a young evil god of death."

Bibliography. Charles Wighton, *Heydrich, Hitler's Most Evil Henchman,* Odhams Press, Ltd., London, 1962.

HIAG. *See* HILFSGEMEINSCHAFT AUF GEGENSEITIGKEIT.

HIGH COMMAND OF THE AIR FORCE. *See* OBERKOMMANDO DER LUFTWAFFE.

HIGH COMMAND OF THE ARMED FORCES. *See* OBERKOMMANDO DER WEHRMACHT.

HIGH COMMAND OF THE ARMY. *See* OBERKOMMANDO DES HEERES.

HIGH COMMAND OF THE SS. *See* REICHSFUEHRUNG-SS.

HIGHER EDUCATION. *See* UNIVERSITIES IN THE THIRD REICH.

HIGHER SECTION. *See* OBERABSCHNITT.

HILFERDING, RUDOLF (1877–1941). One of the best-known Social Democratic theorists of his generation and a victim of Nazi vengeance. Rudolf Hilferding was born in Vienna on August 10, 1877, the son of a wealthy businessman. He became a physician but never practiced medicine because of his overwhelming interest in problems of political economy. As early as 1902 he published studies on socialism, and in 1906 he taught economics and political economy at the Social Democratic school in Berlin. His *Finanzkapital (Finance Capital),* published in 1910, was praised as the most important theoretical contribution by a Socialist since Karl Marx's *Das Kapital.* Lenin praised Hilferding's work and used it in his own studies on imperialism.

On the fall of the Second Reich in 1918, Hilferding became chief editor of *Freiheit (Freedom),* a Social Democratic organ noted for its lively style. After the murder of Hugo Haase on November 7, 1919, Hilferding became the spiritual leader of the Social Democratic party, especially in its ideological struggles with the Communists and the Third International. Throughout his life Hilferding regarded socialism without freedom and democracy as altogether unsatisfactory. From 1924 on he was a member of the German Reichstag (q.v.). He served the Weimar Republic (q.v.) twice as Finance Minister, first in August 1923 in the Stresemann Cabinet, when he was instrumental in the currency reform associated with the *Rentenmark,* by which the mark was stabilized on a new basis of landed values. He also served as Finance Minister in 1928 under Chancellor Herman Müller. Hilferding was widely regarded as one of the most able Cabinet members in recent German history.

Strongly anti-Nazi in the 1920s, Hilferding worked zealously to oppose Hitler and the National Socialist movement. In 1932 he took part in a debate in the Reichstag with Gregor Strasser (q.v.), one of Hitler's chief propagandists. On Hitler's accession to political power in 1933, Hilferding went into exile, first in Denmark, then in Switzerland, and finally in France. He continued his efforts to alert the free world to the aggressive intentions of Hitler. At the outbreak of World War II a despairing Hilferding moved to southern France. As a Socialist and as a Jew he was *persona non grata* to the Vichy regime. Friends tried to get him out of France, but they were not successful. The French police promised him immunity, then brought him to the border of occupied France and turned him over to the Gestapo (q.v.). Brutually handled by the secret police, he died from his injuries on the night of February 11, 1941.

HILFSGEMEINSCHAFT AUF GEGENSEITIGKEIT (HIAG; Mutual Aid Association). Welfare organization for former Waffen-SS (q.v.) members, formed after World War II for the purpose of helping Waffen-SS personnel in need. Its headquarters was set up in Lüdenscheid, Westphalia.

HILFSKASSE (Relief Fund). A special account used to help Nazi party members who had been injured in street fighting with Communists. The fund was set up in 1930 by Martin Bormann (q.v.) and administered by him.

HILFSWERK MUTTER UND KIND (Mother and Child Welfare). A special office set up for the benefit of mothers and children. It was connected with the Nationalsozialistische Volkswohlfahrt (q.v.), the National Socialist People's Welfare Organization.

HILFSWILLIGE (HIWI; Helpers). Foreigners, especially Russians, who joined the German Army during the late days of World War II. Thousands of Russians, including prisoners of war, voluntarily retreated with the German armies when the Russians took the offensive. These "helpers" manned antiaircraft guns and performed noncombatant jobs. In return, the *Hilfswillige* received preferential treatment.

HIMMLER, HEINRICH (1900–1945). Leading National Socialist politician and ruthless practitioner of Nazi terrorism. Born in or near Munich on October 7, 1900, the son of a secondary school master, Heinrich Himmler was brought up in a devout Roman Catholic home. He was educated in the *Gymnasium* (high school) at Landshut, Bavaria. At the age of seventeen he joined the 11th Bavarian Infantry as a cadet-clerk. After World War I he studied at Munich Technical College and obtained a diploma in agriculture. As a member of a rightist paramilitary nationalist organization he came to the attention of Hitler, who made him business manager of the Nationalsozialistische Deutsche Arbeiterpartei (q.v.) in Bavaria. Himmler took part in the Beer-Hall *Putsch* (q.v.) in Munich in 1923 at the side of Ernst Roehm (q.v.). For a time he served as secretary to Gregor Strasser (q.v.) in the socialist wing of the party. In 1925 he became acting *Gauleiter* (q.v.), or district leader, in Lower Bavaria, and in 1926 in Upper Bavaria. From 1925 to 1930 he was acting propaganda leader of the party. In 1928 he married the daughter of a West Prussian landowner, Margarete Boden, who was seven years his senior. His wife awakened his interest in homeopathy, mesmerism, and herbalism. Meanwhile, neglecting his own family, he fathered several illegitimate children.

In 1928 Himmler became a poultry farmer near Munich. On January 6, 1929, Hitler appointed him head of the

Schutzstaffel (SS, q.v.), the Fuehrer's personal bodyguard, then called the Black Guard and consisting of 300 men. This appointment became the foundation of Himmler's later exalted position of power. By 1933 he had demonstrated his ability as an organizer by extending the membership of the SS to more than 50,000. Himmler patiently worked his way up in the Nazi hierarchy. He studied the records of other party chieftains and accumulated a mass of information that was to give him great power over their careers. From 1931 to 1933, at a time when the SS was nominally under Roehm's SA (q.v.), Himmler organized his own secret civilian security organization, the Sicherheitsdienst (SD, q.v.), under Reinhard Heydrich (q.v.). In 1933 Himmler was named chief of police at Munich and in that capacity, at Hitler's order, set up the first concentration camp (*see* CONCENTRATION CAMPS), at Dachau (q.v.). On April 20, 1934, Hermann Goering (q.v.) made Himmler acting chief of the Gestapo (q.v.) in Prussia.

The date of June 30, 1934, was crucial for Himmler's career. He had already prepared a list of those to be executed or imprisoned in Hitler's Blood Purge (q.v.). Now he let loose his SS commandos in a three-day massacre that eliminated the left wing of the Nazi movement. Three weeks later Hitler elevated the SS, until then subordinate to the SA, to the status of an independent organization. On June 17, 1936, Hitler designated Himmler as head of the unified police system of the Third Reich as *Reichsfuehrer* of the SS and leader of the Gestapo. Himmler was now in control of a vast machine of political oppression.

The outbreak of World War II in 1939 saw Himmler at the apex of his power. In October Hitler made him *Reichskommissar für die Festigung deutschen Volkstums* (Reich Commissar for the Consolidation of German Nationhood). In this post Himmler devised methods of mass murder based on a rationalized extermination process. His task was to eliminate "racial degenerates" such as Jews, Poles, Russians, and Czechs—all those who, in Hitler's estimation, stood in the way of Germany's regeneration. Himmler was responsible for fifth-column activities (*see* FIFTH COLUMN) whenever and wherever the opportunity arose. After the invasion of the Soviet Union in June 1941, he controlled the political administration of the occupied territory. He expanded the SS from three to thirty-five divisions, until it rivaled the Wehrmacht (q.v.) itself. Made Minister of the Interior on August 25, 1943, he strengthened his grip on the civil service and the courts. Meanwhile, he enlarged the concentration camps and the extermination camps (q.v.), organized a supply of expendable labor, and authorized pseudomedical experiments in the camps.

After the July Plot (q.v.) of 1944 on Hitler's life, Himmler became, next to the Fuehrer himself, the most powerful man in the Third Reich. On July 21, 1944, Hitler made him supreme commander of the Volkssturm (q.v.), the People's Army. In early 1945, as the Russians closed in on Berlin, Himmler was designated head of the Volkssturm defending the German capital and chief of the Werwolf (q.v.) unit that was expected to carry on a last-ditch fight in the Bavarian mountains. By now, however, he was losing his influence with Hitler and beginning to think in terms of personal safety. In April he made clumsy approaches to the Allies through the Swedish internationalist Count Folke Bernadotte of Wisborg (q.v.) by offering to free Jews from the concentration and extermination camps and calling for a capitulation. Infuriated by the news, relayed to him in his *Fuehrerbunker* (q.v.) in Berlin, Hitler ordered Himmler's arrest.

On May 21, 1945, after the German surrender, Himmler left Flensburg in disguise with his moustache shaved and a black patch over one eye and posing in the uniform of Heinrich Hitzinger, a discharged Gestapo agent. Himmler was apparently unaware that any member of an organization associated with his name was subject to immediate arrest. He was captured at Bremervörde, northeast of Bremen, by British troops. On May 23, while being examined by a British doctor at Lüneburg, Himmler swallowed a vial of cyanide of potassium that he had concealed in his mouth. He died almost instantaneously.

Many attempts have been made to unravel Himmler's personality and character. There is general agreement about his appearance. Observers described him as having the look of an intelligent schoolteacher rather than that of a man of violence. His gray-blue eyes looked out from behind pince-nez glasses. His moustache was trimmed neatly below a straight, well-shaped nose and above thin lips and a receding chin. One acquaintance noted his

Heinrich Himmler with Hitler. [*Photograph captured at SS headquarters*]

"slender, pale and almost girlishly soft hands covered with blue veins." Himmler's outward appearance was that of a meek, gentle man who would not harm a fly, but behind the exterior were a quite different personality and character. Erich Fromm (q.v.), in *The Anatomy of Human Destructiveness* (1973), depicts Himmler as "an example of the sadistic authoritarian who developed a passion for unlimited control over others."

Himmler typified the extreme mysticism of the National Socialist movement. He believed implicitly in the Nazi *Weltanschauung* (q.v.) in all its manifestations, especially in theories of race and hostility to the Jews. Behind the colorless exterior was a fanatical, sadistic nature. *Gnadelos* (merciless) was one of his favorite words. Throughout his life Hitler's Grand Inquisitor and master of destruction suffered from psychosomatic illnesses, including severe headaches and stomach spasms, undefined pains, and hysteria. He was aware of his evil reputation: "I know that there are people in Germany who feel sick when they see this black tunic. We can understand that." He made certain not to remain alive in Allied hands.

Bibliography. Willi Frischauer, *Himmler*, Odhams Press, Ltd., London, 1953.

HIMMLER, OPERATION. *See* GLEIWITZ RAID.

HIMMLER-KERSTEN AGREEMENT. A late agreement signed by Heinrich Himmler and Dr. Felix Kersten (qq.v.), his personal physician, on the treatment of concentration camp prisoners (*see* CONCENTRATION CAMPS). On March 12, 1945, at a time when the Third Reich was coming to its end, Himmler and Kersten, in a darkened room of the SS (q.v.) sanatorium at Hohenlychen, signed the following statement. Himmler himself added the heading:

AGREEMENT IN THE NAME OF HUMANITY

It was decided:

1. That concentration camps will not be blown up.
2. On the approach of Allied troops, a white flag will be hoisted.
3. No more Jews will be killed, and Jews will be treated like other prisoners.
4. Sweden is allowed to send food parcels to individual Jewish prisoners.

(Signed) Himmler
Kersten

HIMMLER'S CIRCLE OF FRIENDS. *See* FREUNDESKREIS HEINRICH HIMMLER.

HINDEMITH, PAUL (1895–1963). Leading German composer of the generation after Richard Strauss and prominent exile from the Third Reich. Paul Hindemith was born in Hanau, near Frankfurt am Main, on November 16, 1895. After studying the violin and composition, he served as concertmaster of the Frankfurt Opera Orchestra from 1915 to 1923. He played the viola in the Amar-Hindemith Quartet until 1929 and taught at the Berlin Hochschule für Musik (College School for Music) from 1927 to 1937. When the Nazis objected to his music as decadent, he left Germany in 1938, settling first in Switzerland and in 1940 in the United States, of which he became a citizen in 1946. He became head of the department of music at Yale University in 1942 and returned to Switzerland in 1953. One of the most prolific composers of the twentieth century, Hindemith represented a reaction against romanticism. He revived the early polyphonic and baroque styles and combined them with his own distinctive sense of modern harmony. Hindemith established a form called *Gebrauchmusik* (music for use), practical music making by amateurs. He opposed the twelve-note system of Arnold Schoenberg and insisted that harmony should retain a fundamental tonal basis. He died in Frankfurt am Main on December 28, 1963.

HINDENBURG, OSKAR VON (1883–1960). Son of and military aide to President Paul von Hindenburg (q.v.). Oskar von Hindenburg was born in Königsberg on January 31, 1883. Without political ambition, he at first played an inconspicuous role in his father's service, but later, as military aide, he acted in the important capacity of liaison between his father and the Army, and he did what he could to ease his father's work. In physical decline the old man became more and more dependent on his son. Oskar von Hindenburg was involved in the *Osthilfe Skandal* (q.v.), the East Subvention scandal, as the owner of an East Prussian baronial estate that had been presented to his father in Oskar's name in order to avoid inheritance taxes. On January 22, 1933, Hitler had a secret conversation with Oskar von Hindenburg. It was rumored that in this interview Hitler informed Oskar von Hindenburg that if he were not made Chancellor, he would disclose the scandal of tax evasion at Neudeck (q.v.) and work for the impeachment of President von Hindenburg. According to the rumor Oskar von Hindenburg was forced to submit to this blackmail and convinced his father that it might be best to take Hitler into the government. Seven months after Hitler became Chancellor, some 5,000 acres were added to Neudeck tax-free.

President von Hindenburg died on August 2, 1934. On August 15 his political testament, in which the marshal had high praise for "my Chancellor Adolf Hitler and his movement," was published. Hitler decreed that presidential functions be sanctioned by the German people in a "free and secret" plebiscite to be held on August 19, 1934. On the eve of the voting Oskar von Hindenburg broadcast a radio appeal to the country:

> The late Reich President and General Field Marshal, having concluded his compact with Adolf Hitler on January 30 of last year and having confirmed it during that sacred hour in the *Garnisonkirche* at Potsdam on March 21, always supported Adolf Hitler and approved all the important decisions of Hitler's Government. . . . My father himself saw in Adolf Hitler his direct successor as head of the German state, and I am acting in accordance with my father's wishes when I call upon all German men and women to vote for the transfer of my father's office to the Fuehrer and Chancellor.

The plebiscite produced an overwhelming majority of 90 percent of the vote in Hitler's favor. Oskar von Hindenburg died in Bad Harzburg on February 12, 1960, at the age of seventy-seven.

HINDENBURG, PAUL [LUDWIG HANS VON BENECKENDORFF UND] VON (1847–1934). General field marshal, Germany's outstanding military leader in World War I, and the second President of the Weimar Republic (q.v.). Paul von Hindenburg was born in Posen (now Poznań, Poland) on October 2, 1847. Entering the Prussian Army, he served in the Austro-Prussian War of 1866 and the Franco-Prussian War of 1870–1871. He rose steadily to commanding general of the Fourth Army in Magdeburg in 1903 and retired in 1911. However, this was only the first stage of a remarkable triple career. On August 22, 1914, he was recalled to active duty as supreme commander on the eastern front. Gen. Erich Ludendorff (q.v.) was his chief of staff. Together the two were credited with outstanding victories over the Russians in August and September 1914 at the Battles of Tannenberg and the Masurian Lakes, although the contributions of Gen. Max Hoffmann (1869–1927), first General Staff officer of the Eighth Army, were of decisive importance. On November 1, 1914, Von Hindenburg was promoted to supreme commander in the east, and on November 27 was named general field marshal.

After further engagements against the Russians, Von Hindenburg became the most popular field commander of the German Army. The public elevated him to the status of a major folk hero as *Der eiserne Hindenburg* (the Iron Hindenburg). On August 29, 1916, he was appointed by Emperor William II to supreme military commander, succeeding Gen. Erich von Falkenhayn, chief of the General Staff, who had failed to achieve the expected German victory. Von Hindenburg was transferred to the western front, where the Germans had incurred heavy losses at Verdun and the Somme. He was able to ease the situation somewhat by withdrawing German armies to the defensive Hindenburg Line. At the end of September 1918, when the military situation became hopeless, Von Hindenburg urged William II to abdicate. He led the withdrawal of German armed forces into the homeland and then retired to his estate at Neudeck (q.v.), in East Prussia. According to the Treaty of Versailles, he was to be tried as a war criminal, but he was never indicted. In his retirement he avoided all political activity.

Then came the third stage of Von Hindenburg's career. Following the death on February 28, 1925, of Friedrich Ebert (q.v.), the first President of the Weimar Republic, Von Hindenburg agreed to become the candidate for the Presidency of a coalition of rightist parties. He was successful in a runoff election held on April 26, 1925, receiving 14.6 million votes to 13.8 million for Wilhelm Marx, the candidate of the Liberals, Catholics, and Socialists. The result caused consternation in the victorious Allied countries, where it was felt that this was but the first step in the eventual restoration of the Hohenzollern monarchy. This fear disappeared when Von Hindenburg, under the influence of Otto Meissner (q.v.), Chief of the Reich Chancellery, made it clear that he would be impartial in the deepening political crisis and that he would adhere strictly to the Weimar Constitution. Gradually, however, Von Hindenburg came under the influence of a camarilla of Junker army officers, who schemed to win control over him. On March 28, 1930, he appointed Heinrich Bruening (q.v.), leader of the Catholic Center party, to whom he had taken a great liking, to the office of Chancellor. As economic conditions worsened, Von Hindenburg allowed Bruening to rule more and more by decree, in a procedure

President von Hindenburg not long before his death. Behind him are Hitler and Goering, who exercise actual power. [*Brown Brothers*]

that was legal under Article 48 (q.v.) of the Weimar Constitution.

In the runoff elections of April 10, 1932, Von Hindenburg received 53 percent of the votes cast (Von Hindenburg, 19,359,650; Hitler, 13,418,011; Ernst Thaelmann, 3,706,655). Two months later, after he had been persuaded by the military camarilla that Bruening was about to expose Junker thefts of state relief funds by introducing legislation against them (*see* OSTHILFE SKANDAL), Von Hindenburg dismissed the Chancellor and appointed Franz von Papen (q.v.) in his place. Von Papen immediately set up a "Cabinet of barons" at the head of a conservative minority government. Meanwhile, Von Hindenburg was caught in a power struggle between Von Papen and Kurt von Schleicher (q.v.), both ambitious Junkers, who each in his own way hoped to contain Hitler and the rising Nazis and assure Junker and military control. In the two Reichstag (q.v.) elections of July and November 1932, the Nationalsozialistische Deutsche Arbeiterpartei (q.v.) emerged as the strongest political party in Germany. The problem of handling Hitler became critical. Von Hindenburg, who had little use for "that Bohemian corporal," had to decide whether he would set up a coalition government that would include Hitler and the Nazis (*see* HINDENBURG-HITLER INTERVIEW).

Von Hindenburg had clung to political office long after his mental and physical powers waned. He was far too senile to realize what was happening. It was said at the time that no bureaucrat dared to leave a sandwich paper near the President for fear that the aged man would mistake it for a state paper and sign it. His only son, Oskar von Hindenburg (q.v.), was in a precarious position because he had allowed the family estate at Neudeck to be registered in his own name in order to avoid inheritance taxes. He feared that Hitler and his followers, who were well aware of the situation, might broadcast charges against both father and son. As a result he was quite willing to work with Von Papen in influencing his father on Hitler's behalf.

On December 3, 1932, Von Papen was relieved as Chancellor and succeeded by Von Schleicher. On January 4, 1933, through the mediation of the banker Kurt Freiherr von Schroeder (q.v.), Von Papen met Hitler in secret and offered him the support of Rhineland industrialists provided that he, Hitler, agreed to include him in his Cabinet as Vice-Chancellor. Hitler agreed. Von Papen and Oskar von Hindenburg then prevailed upon the President to dismiss Von Schleicher. On January 30, 1933, in a constitutionally legal move, Von Hindenburg made the Nazi leader Chancellor. On April 5, Hitler sent Von Hindenburg a letter justifying his opposition to the Jews.

From this point on Von Hindenburg's political activity declined. He retired to Neudeck and allowed Hitler, with his coalition of rightists, to run the government. For a short time Hitler made good use of Von Hindenburg's name and prestige but then began to disregard him altogether as he solidified his own political position. On June 30, 1934, the day of the Blood Purge (q.v.), Hitler received a wire, presumably from Von Hindenburg, congratulating him for "nipping treason in the bud and saving the German nation from serious danger."

Von Hindenburg died in Neudeck on August 2, 1934. He was buried in a mausoleum, the Marshal's Tower, at Tannenberg, the scene of his greatest victory. In 1944, as the Russians closed in on the national memorial, Von Hindenburg's body was removed from its mausoleum. On April 27, 1945, American troops found it, together with the corpses of Frederick the Great and Frederick William I, in a flag-draped underground vault at Bernterode, near Mühlhausen.

Bibliography. Rudolph Weterstetten and A. M. K. Watson, *The Biography of President von Hindenburg,* The Macmillan Company, New York, 1930; John W. Wheeler-Bennett, *Hindenburg: Wooden Titan,* The Macmillan Company, London, 1932.

HINDENBURG-HITLER INTERVIEW. Interview in which Reich President Paul von Hindenburg (q.v.) offered Hitler a post in the Cabinet and was refused. In the Reichstag (q.v.) elections of July 31, 1932, the Nazis returned 230 deputies, but in the following November 6 elections they won seats for 196 deputies, sustaining a loss of 34 seats. Nevertheless, an attempt was made to appease the Nazi leader. On August 13, 1932, Hitler was received by Chancellor Franz von Papen (q.v.), who invited him to be interviewed by President von Hindenburg. A chilly affair, the interview lasted only fifteen minutes. Von Hindenburg offered Hitler a Cabinet post. To the question whether he and the Nationalsozialistische Deutsche Arbeiterpartei (q.v.) were ready to enter the Von Papen Cabinet, Hitler replied: "We are ready to take over full responsibility for German political policies in every form, provided that that means unequivocal leadership of the government. If that is not the case, then the National Socialist movement can accept neither power nor responsibility. Specifically, it declines entrance into a cabinet headed by Von Papen." To Von Hindenburg this meant "all or nothing at all." The Nazis claimed, to the contrary, that the Fuehrer never demanded "complete power" but only "unequivocal leadership of the government." Whatever the attitude, Von Hindenburg broke off the negotiations as fruitless. Both sides were contemptuous. Von Hindenburg had already said several times: "Hitler—Chancellor? Never, as long as I live, and certainly not by these indelicate, blackmailing methods." Hitler now began to repeat his own favorite refrain: "Hindenburg? He is 85 years old, I am 45. I can wait!"

HIRT, AUGUST (1898–). Anthropologist and surgeon. August Hirt was born in Mannheim on April 29, 1898. After taking a medical degree, he taught for a time at Heidelberg. He met Heinrich Himmler (q.v.) in 1936 and joined the SS (q.v.) as a *Hauptsturmfuehrer* (captain) in 1939. Assigned by Himmler to find an antidote to mustard gas, Hirt experimented both on dogs and on himself, ending up in a hospital with bleeding lungs. He then began experiments on prisoners, twenty of whom went blind and died in agony.

Himmler, as president of the Society for Research and Teaching of Ancestral Heritage (Ahnenerbe Forschungs- und Lehrgemeinschaft, q.v.), was anxious to obtain "scientific support" for his racial theories. He appointed Hirt to head the new Anatomy Institute at the University of Strassburg. To obtain a satisfactory collection of skulls, Hirt worked closely with those who could send him a supply, including Josef Kramer (q.v.), known as the Beast of Belsen, and Wolfram Sievers, the Nazi Bluebeard, business manager of the Ancestral Heritage Society. Hirt described his work in a memorandum to Himmler dated February 9, 1942: "By procuring the skulls of the Jewish-Bolshevist Commissars, who represent the prototype of the repulsive but characteristic subhuman, one has the chance to obtain palpable scientific data. The best practical method is to turn over alive all such individuals. Following induced death of the Jew, the head, which should not be damaged, should be separated from the body and sent in a hermetically sealed tin can filled with preservative fluid." At Strassburg Hirt studied pathological features of the skulls, such as form and size of brain.

In the summer of 1944, as American and French troops converged on Strassburg, Hirt asked Himmler's advice as to disposition of his skull collection. Himmler advised its destruction. American troops found a supply of headless bodies in Hirt's storeroom. Hirt himself vanished and was never found. He may have committed suicide.

HITLER, ADOLF (1889–1945). Austrian-born politician who became Fuehrer (leader) and Chancellor of the Third Reich from 1933 until his death in 1945. He rose from peasant origin to become dictator of Germany and conqueror of most of Europe. Taking advantage of the wave of European fascism after World War I, he constructed a German regime unparalleled as an instrument of tyranny. He won startling success in identifying his own morbid emotions with the needs of the German people. His rule resulted in temporary advantage for a rearmed Germany, the ruin of much of the European structure, and the extermination of some 6 million Jews. He was eventually smashed down by a global alliance, but not before he had brought Western civilization to the brink of destruction.

Early years. Adolf Hitler was born in the small village of Braunau, on the Inn River between Austria and Germany, on April 20, 1889, the son of an Austrian customs official aged fifty-two, Alois Schickelgruber Hitler, and a peasant girl still in her twenties, Klara Poelzl Hitler (qq.v.). Both sides of the family came from the Waldviertel (Woodlands) of Lower Austria, a back-country section of hills and woods housing a hardworking community of small peasants. The unfriendly people were as harsh as the land they inhabited and suspicious of the city folk in Vienna, 50 miles away. Little is known about Hitler's ancestry. His grandfather, Johann Georg Hiedler, was a wandering miller who formed a relationship with a peasant girl, Anna Marie Schickelgruber, a household servant in Graz. In 1837 Anna Marie gave birth to an illegitimate son, Alois. Five years later Johann Hiedler and Anna Marie were married. Alois used the name Schickelgruber until 1876, when he had it legally changed to Hitler because he had been reared in the house of his uncle, Johann Nepomuk Hiedler. Alois married three times. His third wife, Klara Poelzl, twenty-three years his junior, bore him five children, only two of whom lived to maturity, Adolf and his younger sister, Paula.

Hitler's mother was a quiet, hardworking woman with a solemn, pale face and large, staring eyes. She kept a clean household and labored diligently to please her husband. Hitler loved his indulgent mother, and she in turn considered him her favorite child, even if, as she said, he was "moonstruck." Later, he spoke of himself as his mother's darling. She told him how different he was from other children. Despite her love, however, he developed into a discontented and resentful child. Psychologically, she unconsciously made him, and through him the world, pay for her own unhappiness with her husband. Adolf feared his strict father, a hard and difficult man who set the pattern for the youngster's own brutal view of life. Miserable and lonely, with three unhappy marriages, Alois Hitler sought solace in drink. Many times the young Hitler had to bring his tipsy parent home. Adolf later pictured his father as an inebriated sadist who squandered the family income. This sour, hot-tempered man was master inside his home, where he made the children feel the lash of his cane, switch, and belt. Alois snarled at his son, humiliated him, and corrected him again and again. There was deep tension between two unbending wills. It is probable that Adolf Hitler's later fierce hatreds came in part from this hostility to his father. He learned early in life that right was always on the side of the stronger one.

In 1895, just before he reached the age of six, Adolf entered the *Volksschule* (public school) in the village of Fischlham. Two years later his highly religious mother sent him to the monastery school at Lambach, where she hoped that he would eventually become a monk. He was expelled after he was caught smoking on the monastery grounds. The family then moved to Leonding, a small suburb of Linz, where young Adolf at first did well in school. He was noted among his comrades for his insistence on playing the game "Follow the Leader," in which he was always the leader. From 1900 to 1904 he attended the *Realschule* (high school for science) at Linz and in 1904–1905 at Steyr. His performance in high school was less than mediocre. "The things which pleased me, I learned," he wrote later. "Above all, everything that I thought would be of use to me later as a painter. The things which seemed to me meaningless in this respect or which did not appeal to me, I sabotaged completely." Adolf left school at sixteen without being graduated.

For two years Adolf did nothing, remaining at home, roaming the streets, or spending hours in the public library reading German history and mythology. He dreamed about becoming an artist and was talented in the art of evading responsibilities. He developed a lifelong contempt for educated people. "Most of my teachers," he said, "had something wrong with them mentally, and quite a few of them ended their days as honest-to-God lunatics." The only teacher he admired was a Dr. Leopold Poetsch, a fervent Pan-Germanist, who taught the young man to despise the Hapsburgs and support the cause of German nationalism. Adolf's only friend was August Kubizek (q.v.), an upholsterer's helper, who served as a one-man audience for his flights into mysticism.

In October 1907, when he was eighteen, Hitler left his mother, who was incurably ill with cancer, and went to Vienna to make his way in the world. He suffered a

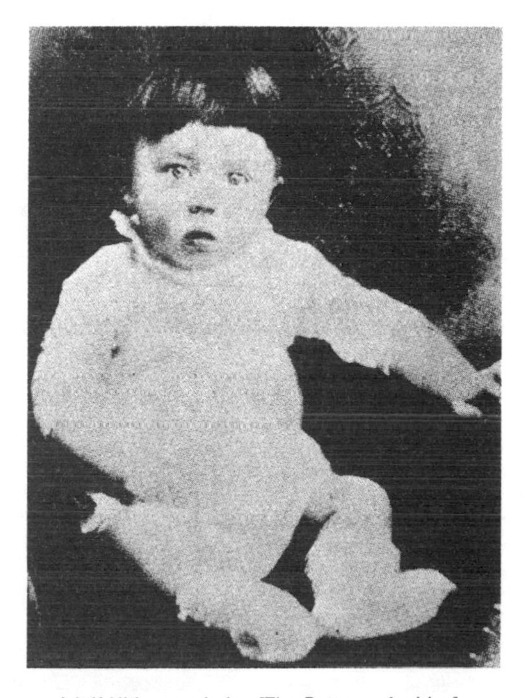

Adolf Hitler as a baby. [*The Bettman Archive*]

Hitler in a crowd at the Odeonplatz in Munich cheering the outbreak of war in 1914.

terrible setback when the Vienna Academy of Fine Arts failed him on the admission examination. He never recovered from this blow to his pride, which he blamed on "those stupid professors." In December 1908 his mother died, another crushing event in his life. For the next five years he lived on charity, occasional odd jobs, and the sale of his sketches. "Five years of misery and woe in Vienna," he wrote later. "Five years, in which I earned my living first as apprentice and then as unknown painter. Hunger was my faithful companion. It never left me for a moment." He made daily rounds of the cafés and picture framers, trying to sell his drawings so that he could eat. Looking like an untidy vagabond, he seldom shaved and wore a filthy black derby and a long overcoat reaching down to his ankles.

In Vienna Hitler learned to hate. He rejected the teachings of Karl Marx and remained anti-Marxist throughout his life. Influenced by the writings of Karl Lueger (q.v.), he began to hate the Jews as "rats, parasites, and bloodsuckers." One day on a street in Vienna, he saw a Jew in a caftan and asked himself: "Could this be a German?" Then followed what he called a soul-searching battle between feeling and reason. Jews, he decided, together with Marxists, had combined in a union to destroy the world. "If the Jew wins over the world with the help of the Marxists, then this crown will be the wreath of death for mankind." He also began to despise democracy. He found relief in dreams of a great and glorious Germany that would in time take over the weak Hapsburg monarchy. In cheap cafés he gave political harangues directed against his pet hatreds. People began to listen to the sickly, harried young man with the hypnotic eyes. He left Vienna in May 1913 for Munich, a German city. There, too, he was depressed and embittered, a lonely stranger in a gay, throbbing metropolitan center.

Military service. In February 1914 Hitler was temporarily recalled to Austria to be examined for military service, but he was rejected as "too weak, and unfit to bear arms." When war broke out in August 1914, he wrote to the King of Bavaria and asked to serve in his army. He was assigned to the 16th Bavarian Infantry (List Regiment), composed mostly of student volunteers. With only a few weeks of training, he was sent to the front. He proved to be an able and courageous soldier. Until 1916 he served as an orderly and later as a dispatch bearer. In four years he took part in forty-seven battles, often in the thick of the fighting. He was wounded twice. On October 7, 1916, he was brought to the hospital at Hermis with a wounded leg. Two years later, only four weeks before the end of the war, he was badly gassed, and he spent three agonized months in a small hospital near Berlin. He received his first decoration, the Iron Cross (Second Class) in 1914, and he was given the Iron Cross (First Class), a rare award for a common soldier in the Imperial German Army, on August 4, 1918. The latter medal was for the capture of an enemy officer and fifteen men. However, Hitler was never promoted beyond the rank of lance corporal.

The war had a profound influence on Hitler's life. It gave him, at long last, the purpose for which he had dreamed. He learned about violence and its use. Later, he told how the creeping gas began to eat into his eyes during the last days of the war. When he began to weaken under the terror of blindness, a voice thundered, "Miserable fool, you want to weep while thousands are worse off than you." Hitler recounted that the more he tried to understand the great events of the hour, the more his brow burned with shame: "I knew everything was lost. Only fools—liars or criminals—could hope for mercy from the enemy. In these nights my hatred grew against the men who had brought about this crime. I, however, decided to go into politics."

Rise to party leadership. After Germany's humiliating defeat in World War I, Hitler returned to Munich. Angered by the revolution in Germany and the rise of the Weimar Republic (q.v.), he turned to politics to work against both the Treaty of Versailles and the new German democracy. Remaining on the roster of his old regiment, he was assigned to spy on political parties. In September

1919 he was ordered to investigate a small group of nationalistic veterans of the German Workers' party (Deutscher Arbeiterpartei, q.v.). The party had no program and no plan of action (it was just against the government), and it had only $2 in its treasury, but Hitler was much impressed by its few definite ideas, which coincided with his own. He joined the party as member No. 55 and later was made No. 7 of its Executive Committee. He had finally found the right outlet for his talents in political agitation and organization, and he lost no chance to talk before a crowd wherever he could find one: "I could speak! After 30 minutes the people in the tiny room were electrified!"

Within two years Hitler advanced to leadership of the little party. He changed its name to the Nationalsozialistische Deutsche Arbeiterpartei (q.v.), the National Socialist German Workers' party, later to be known everywhere as the NSDAP. The word *Nazi* was an acronym of the words *NAtional SoZIalist*. Hitler left the Army to devote all his time to building the new party. Conditions were favorable: there was economic discontent, and there was strong resentment against the victorious Allies. In his program of Twenty-five Points, announced on February 24, 1920, Hitler emphasized the ideas he had absorbed in Vienna: anti-Semitism (q.v.), extreme nationalism, the concept of Aryan racial supremacy (*see* RACIAL DOCTRINE), contempt for liberal democracy, and the principle of leadership (*see* FUEHRERPRINZIP). The program was designed to appeal to everyone with a grievance of some kind. Most of Hitler's ideas were not new, but he colored them with extraordinary showmanship and eloquence. He gave the Nazi party the swastika symbol (*see* HAKENKREUZ) and the "*Heil!*" ("Hail!") greeting, both borrowed from older racial groups. He managed to acquire a party newspaper, the *Völkischer Beobachter* (q.v.), or *Racial Observer*, to represent the party's views. As a trained militia to guard his meetings, he organized the Sturmabteilung (SA, q.v.), the brown-shirted Storm Troopers, under the command of a close friend, Capt. Ernst Roehm (q.v.). A second unit, the Schutzstaffel (SS, q.v.), was a black-shirted, highly disciplined personal bodyguard for Hitler himself, pledged to fight to the death for him.

By late 1923 Hitler was convinced that the Weimar Republic was on the verge of collapse and that he now could fulfill his promise to "march on Berlin" and strike down the government of "Jewish-Marxist traitors." With the support of the Army he would bring Germany under nationalist control. As a front man he brought into the plan Gen. Erich Ludendorff (q.v.), the reactionary militarist of World War I. In the Beer-Hall *Putsch* (q.v.) held in Munich on November 8, 1923, Hitler and Ludendorff took advantage of the chaotic political situation to force the leaders of the local government in Munich and the local Reichswehr (q.v.) commander to proclaim a national revolution. Holding a captive audience in the beer hall, Hitler, in wild excitement, jumped on a chair, fired a pistol into the air, and announced the revolution: "Tomorrow will find a national government in Germany, or it will find us dead!" The next day the Nazis marched through the streets of Munich to the War Ministry, but a cordon of police fired on them and dispersed the column. The *Putsch* collapsed.

On February 26, 1924, Hitler was brought to trial on a charge of high treason. He took advantage of the occasion to convert the proceedings into a propaganda triumph. Acting as his own lawyer, he put on a dazzling display of oratory. He took full blame for planning the *Putsch*. "This is my attitude: I would rather be hanged in a Bolshevik Germany than perish under the rule of French swords." The hour would come when the masses, who stood on the streets with their swastika banners, would unite with those who would fire on them. The companies would grow into battalions, the battalions into regiments, the regiments into divisions. "Even if you judge us guilty a thousand times, the goddess of the eternal court of history will laugh and tear up the verdict of this court, but she pronounces us not guilty." Hitler was sentenced to five years' imprisonment. His courtroom behavior made a deep impression on Germans, who began to regard him as a great national hero. He himself learned a vital lesson from the inglorious *Putsch:* it was necessary above all that his movement achieve political power by legal means.

Hitler served only nine months of his sentence at Landsberg am Lech (q.v.). He settled down in a comfortable cell and began to ponder on his mistakes. He ate breakfast in bed, lectured to his fellow prisoners, and walked in the garden of what was more a sanatorium than a prison. He also dictated to Rudolf Hess (q.v.) the first volume of *Mein Kampf* (q.v.), which became the political bible of the Nazi movement. In this crude, turgid, disorganized book, Hitler gave the story of his life, his philosophy, and the blueprint of the program he intended to achieve for Germany. The basic theme was social Darwinism: individuals and nations are both subject to a continuous struggle for life. Power was preeminent, and morality was foolish. The racially superior German people were threatened by Jews, "the plastic demon of the fall of mankind," by Marxists, Bolsheviks, and liberals, and by humanists or humanitarians of any kind. Germany could become great again only if it waged relentless warfare against these internal enemies. Under a dictatorship supported by the people, a new, powerful Germany would seek *Lebensraum* (q.v.), the living space denied it by external enemies. The new Nazi movement would prepare the strategy for world domination. *Mein Kampf* was a wordy, repetitious book, but it eventually became a best seller. By 1939 it had been translated into eleven languages, and more than 5.2 million copies had been sold. The royalties made Hitler a rich man.

Rebuilding the Nazi party. The collapse of the 1923 *Putsch* resulted in the temporary disintegration of the Nazi party, but Hitler, released from Landsberg Prison under an amnesty in December 1924, was soon hard at work reconstructing his movement. Assisted by two close followers, Dr. Paul Joseph Goebbels, a propaganda wizard, and Capt. Hermann Goering (qq.v.), a World War I flying ace, Hitler went about the critical business of winning mass support. His immediate problem was to decide between the socialist left of his followers in Berlin and the nationalist right in Munich, between the northern party members led by Gregor Strasser (q.v.) and his own comrades in Bavaria. At a party conference held in February 1926, Hitler outmaneuvered Strasser and stripped him of any influence on the growing Nazi movement (*see* BAMBERG PARTY CONGRESS). Meanwhile, with rare political acumen, he used his oratorical skill to attract both left and right. His propaganda appealed to the lower classes hard-hit by the economic depression. At the same time, his insistence upon attaining power by legal means, which won him the name *Adolf Legalité* (q.v.; Adolf the Legal One), gave him prestige with the military, the nationalists, and the conservatives. This combination of insight into mass psychology and willingness to work with the conservative right was a powerful factor in elevating Hitler to supreme political power. He gradually recovered the ground he had lost since the abortive Beer-Hall *Putsch*. By 1930 he was the undisputed head of the Nazi movement. Funds began to flow into the party's coffers from wealthy Rhineland industrialists, who saw in Hitler their best safeguard against the annoying unions and the inroads of communism. At the same time Hitler drew increasing support from solid bourgeois elements as well as from discontented workers, to both of whom he promised security and relief from despoliation by Jewish financiers.

Rise to political power. In the 1928 Reichstag (q.v.) elections the Nazis won only 12 seats to the Communists' 54. During the economic depression starting in 1929 Hitler made an alliance with the Nationalist Alfred Hugenberg (q.v.) in a united campaign against the Young Plan (q.v.). Through newspapers controlled by Hugenberg, Hitler was able for the first time to address a considerable national audience. Moreover, he was now able to reach greater numbers of industrial and business magnates who could easily place his party on a secure financial basis. In the 1930 elections the NSDAP won more than 6 million votes and 107 delegates to the Reichstag, thereby becoming the second largest party in the country. The number of Communist representatives rose to 77. Hitler's drumbeating tactics had won him the attention of the German electorate.

After acquiring German citizenship through the state of Braunschweig on February 25, 1932, Hitler decided to test his party's strength by running for the Presidency. The aging incumbent, Paul von Hindenburg (q.v.), had the support of the Socialists, Catholics, and labor. There were two other candidates: Theodor Duesterberg (q.v.), an army officer, and Ernst Thaelmann, the Communist party leader. Hitler staged an energetic campaign for the presidential elections of March 13, 1932, winning more than 30 percent of the vote and depriving Von Hindenburg of an absolute majority. In the runoff elections of April 10, the popular old war hero was returned the victor with 53 percent of the vote (Von Hindenburg, 19,359,650; Hitler, 13,418,011; Thaelmann, 3,706,655). In the elections of July 1932 the Nazis won 230 seats in the Reichstag and became the largest political party in Germany. The following November Hitler received a slight setback when the number of Nazi deputies dropped to 196, as that of the Communists rose to 100. There followed a deadly battle in the streets between the Brownshirts and the Red Front.

Meanwhile, the political situation was deteriorating rapidly. Chancellor Heinrich Bruening (q.v.), although liberal and moderate in outlook, felt himself compelled to govern by decree. It was an unfortunate decision that actually prepared the way to dictatorship. On May 30, 1932, Von Hindenburg dismissed Bruening from office. There began a bitter political battle behind the scenes between the Junkers in the east, the wealthy industrialists in the west, and Reichswehr officers. These three groups took over the Cabinet, first headed by Franz von Papen (q.v.), a shrewd politician and a master of intrigue, and then by Gen. Kurt von Schleicher (q.v.), an army officer who preferred a military dictatorship. Von Papen made a political deal with Hitler. The two met secretly on January 4, 1933, and decided to work together for a government in which Hitler would be Chancellor and Von Papen's associates would hold important ministries. They also agreed to eliminate Social Democrats, Communists, and Jews from political life. Hitler promised to renounce the socialist part of his program, while Von Papen pledged that he would obtain further subsidies from the industrialists for Hitler's use. The final problem was to win the support of the elderly President, who had little use for the crude upstart lance corporal of World War I. Both Oskar von Hindenburg (q.v.), the President's son, who was worried about the family estate at Neudeck (q.v.) in the east, and a wealthy banker, Kurt Freiherr von Schroeder (q.v.), urged the President to go along with Von Papen. On January 30, 1933, with great reluctance Von Hindenburg named Hitler German Chancellor with a coalition Cabinet but refused him extraordinary powers. It was a great moment for the little man who had been an unwashed tramp on the streets of Vienna. He had achieved his goal without a *Putsch*, without revolution, in the constitutional way he had promised.

Beginning of the Third Reich, 1933–1934. Hitler promised that the Third Reich, which began in 1933, would last for 1,000 years. Once in power, he moved rapidly to establish and consolidate an absolute dictatorship. He obtained Von Hindenburg's agreement for new elections because a majority could not be obtained in the Reichstag. His first concern was to alert the country to the dangers of the red terror. He would consolidate his own position at the expense of the Communists. The Reichstag fire (q.v.) on the night of February 27, 1933, provided him with the excuse he needed to destroy his opponents and set the ground for his system of totalitarianism. The fire was apparently the work of a weak-minded twenty-four-year-old Dutch vagabond, Marinus van der Lubbe (q.v.), who had once belonged to a Communist club in Holland, but some observers concluded that the Nazis themselves had set the fire and blamed it on the Communists. It was charged that a group of Storm Troopers entered the Reichstag by way of a tunnel running from Hermann Goering's headquarters, prepared the fire by soaking the curtains and rugs with inflammable liquids, and then brought in the simpleminded ex-Communist Dutchman to start small fires of his own. The question of responsibility for the fire is still the subject of controversy among historians.

Whether or not the Nazis set the Reichstag fire, it served Hitler well. Not only did it make the imposing edifice a blazing inferno, but it also gave Hitler a reason for crushing his opponents. In the elections of March 5, 1933, the Nazis increased their representation in the Reichstag from 196 to 288 and their popular vote from 11,737,000 to 17,277,200, or some 44 percent of the total. With support from the Nationalists, Hitler now had a 52 percent majority. On March 24, 1933, the Reichstag passed the so-called Enabling Act (q.v.), the Law to Remove the Distress of People and State (Gesetz zur Erhebung der Not von Volk und Reich). In five brief para-

Hitler, seated at left, in Landsberg Prison in 1923. Rudolf Hess is second from the right. [*Imperial War Museum, London*]

graphs it took away from the Reichstag the powers of legislation, including control of the budget, initiation of constitutional amendments, and approval of treaties with foreign nations, and gave them to the Reich Cabinet for a period of four years. Within a few months all other political parties were banned, Nazi *Statthalter* (governors) were in control of the German states, trade unions were dissolved, and all elements of the population were organized into party-controlled units.

Hitler consolidated his power by a premeditated system of brutality and terror. Those who dared to speak up against his regime were beaten or disappeared by assassination, arrest, or imprisonment. Although he carefully avoided offending powerful interests, Hitler astutely pushed the conservatives aside while handling the radicals roughly. He revealed a superb mastery of Machiavellian politics in his campaign to harry, arrest, and deprive opponents of their rights and lives. He made government, law, education, and religion subservient to National Socialism. Like Mussolini, he would watch over his people from cradle to grave. *"Heil Hitler!"* became the obligatory form of greeting, the swastika the symbol of the Nazi state, the "Horst Wessel Lied" (q.v.) its official anthem, and bread and circuses the daily fare of the German people. Under the guidance of Dr. Paul Joseph Goebbels a cult of Fuehrer worship (q.v.) was propagated. In 1934 the chancellorship and the Presidency were united in the person of Hitler.

Consolidation of the dictatorship. Only one thing remained in the way of absolute dictatorship—the radical element within the party centering in the SA and its leader, Capt. Ernst Roehm. Thus far Hitler had maintained an alliance with the business and military leaders who had paved the way for his own rise to political power, and for the time being he wanted to avoid a radical solution to the problem of Germany's ills. But Roehm and his impatient followers called for a "continuing revolution." The *Alte Kämpfer* (q.v.), Hitler's old comrades, demanded a larger role in Army affairs. The German generals made it plain to Hitler that he would lose their support unless he corrected the behavior of the Storm Troopers. Hitler was forced to choose between the national and socialist sides of his movement. He survived by adopting a hard solution. Rallying behind him the party and Army leaders and especially the SS led by Heinrich Himmler (q.v.), he struck furiously in the Blood Purge (q.v.) of June 30, 1934. He flew to Bad Wiessee in Upper Bavaria, where Roehm and several of his followers were staying at the Hanselbauer Sanatorium, a private hotel. Hitler entered the room quietly, awakened Roehm, and arrested him. Two days later he ordered the SA leader to kill himself within ten minutes. An unbelieving Roehm refused, whereupon he was shot down in his cell.

Meanwhile, 150 top SA leaders were arrested in Berlin, and most of them were massacred 4 at a time. No one knows how many were slaughtered in the purge. Six assassins killed former Chancellor Kurt von Schleicher in his villa. In Munich the seventy-two-year-old Gustav von Kahr (q.v.), who a decade earlier had crushed Hitler's Beer-Hall *Putsch*, was dragged from his home, murdered, and left in a swamp. "In those hours," Hitler said, "I was the supreme judge of the German people." When the purge ended, Hitler emerged as the undisputed dictator of the Third Reich.

The rule of traditional law was now finished. On the death of Von Hindenburg on August 2, 1934, Hitler assumed the titles of Fuehrer and *Kanzler* (Chancellor) after rejecting the designation *Reichspräsident* (Reich President). All army officers were required to take an oath of allegiance, not to the constitution but to Hitler himself.

From this point on Hitler paid relatively little attention to domestic affairs. He made his broad lines of policy clear to his subordinates, with the understanding that they would carry out the system of terror he deemed necessary to maintain the existence of his regime. Each of these officials—Goering, Goebbels, Himmler, and others—exercised arbitrary power within his own domain by setting up a special office of his own. The Fuehrer watched them carefully and saw to it that no one private organization could become strong enough to challenge his own authority. He encouraged Himmler to construct a concentration camp system (*see* CONCENTRATION CAMPS) to deal with domestic enemies. Through the Nuremberg Laws on citizenship and race (q.v.) of 1935 he deprived Jews of their citizenship and banned marriage between Aryans (Germans) and non-Aryans (Jews). He supported restrictive laws that led to a massive emigration of Jews, socialists, and intellectuals, who found it difficult to survive in the closed society of the Third Reich.

Germany became a vast prison camp. Gestapo (q.v.) agents raided homes in the middle of the night. Some captives vanished forever; others were taken to dungeons, where they were beaten and tortured to extract confessions. Crimes—from holdups to murders—were called "politics" in the name of the "national revolution." There was a scramble to mount the Nazi bandwagon: those who had low numbers in the party, showing early membership, took advantage of their good luck by appropriating jobs in the civil service. Famous professors were dismissed from their posts in favor of incompetent Nazi successors. Great mass meetings were held at Nuremberg to stir the emotions of the people (*see* NUREMBERG RALLIES). Flags and standards merged in a riot of color as marchers headed for the stadium to hear the words of the master. Meanwhile, Goebbels's propaganda machine glo-

Hitler with President von Hindenburg on January 30, 1933, after he has been named Chancellor of Germany. [*Brown Brothers*]

rified the Fuehrer: "We are witnessing the greatest miracle in history. A genius is building the world!" And again: "We heard his voice while Germany slept. His hand has made us a nation again!" "He alone is never mistaken!" "He is always like a star above us!"

The road to war, 1935–1939. Certain that his position in Germany was now consolidated by terrorism, Hitler began his campaign to restore German power in Europe and achieve the goals he had outlined in *Mein Kampf*. His first concern was to rearm the country. At first secretly and then openly, he violated the provisions of the Treaty of Versailles for German disarmament. With huge expenditures on arms and the unemployed drained off into the Army, the economy improved.

Shortly after he became Chancellor, Hitler adopted an aggressive foreign policy. His treaties with the Vatican (*see* CONCORDAT OF 1933) and Poland (1934) were designed to conceal his intentions. In October 1933 he withdrew Germany from the League of Nations. He attempted to move into Austria in the summer of 1934 but retreated when the Italian dictator Mussolini sent troops to the frontier to guard Austria's independence. In March 1935 Hitler announced that Germany would build a peacetime army of thirty-six divisions, or 550,000 men, in direct violation of the Treaty of Versailles. The Great Powers protested only mildly. A year later, in March 1936, Hitler sent his troops marching into the demilitarized Rhineland, while at the same time denouncing the Locarno Pact (q.v.).

When, in July 1936, civil war broke out in Spain, Hitler gave aid to Gen. Francisco Franco and the Spanish fascists. He sent his Luftwaffe (q.v.) to Spain to gain experience in what amounted to a dress rehearsal for World War II. In the Rome-Berlin Pact of October 25, 1936, Germany and Italy joined in a common front against bolshevism and the Western powers. Hitler saw this solid bloc of 115 million people as ready to obtain "living space" for the "have-not" nations. During this period of military preparation coupled with economic reorientation aiming at self-sufficiency (*see* AUTARKIE), Hitler adopted the technique of deliberately lying in order to lull his future victims into a false sense of security. While preparing for war, he spoke publicly of his yearning for peace. The bigger the lie, he said, the more people would believe it.

By the end of 1937 Hitler's expansionist policy was in full force. On November 5, 1937, almost two years before the invasion of Poland, he called a meeting with his military leaders, since known as the Hossbach Conference (q.v.), at which he made it clear that he intended to solve the German space problem "no later than 1943–1945." By various stratagems he got rid of two members of the High Command, Field Marshal Werner von Blomberg and Col. Gen. Werner Freiherr von Fritsch (qq.v.), both of whom were present at the Hossbach Conference and both of whom opposed his aggressive designs (*see* BLOMBERG-FRITSCH CRISIS). In 1938 Hitler achieved *Anschluss* (q.v.) with Austria by manipulating a crisis in Austro-German relations and then sending the German Army across the frontier to incorporate Austria forcibly into the Third Reich. A plebiscite held under Nazi direction won 99.59 percent approval of *Anschluss*. "This is the proudest hour of my life," said Hitler.

A greater test of Hitler's policy came later in 1938 when he began a campaign to liberate the Sudeten Germans of Czechoslovakia (*see* SUDETENLAND). This was an attack on a sovereign state whose independence had been guaranteed by the Western powers and by ties with the Soviet Union. After Nazi-inspired riots inside Czechoslovakia, Hitler promised the Sudeten Germans that he would not neglect them. The saber rattling frightened British Prime Minister Neville Chamberlain and French Premier Édouard Daladier (qq.v.), who went to Germany and signed the humiliating Munich Agreement (q.v.). These bloodless victories elevated Hitler's prestige among Germans. Within less than a year he had added 10 million people to the Third Reich. After each victory he proclaimed that he had no further territorial claims to make. The one-time mendicant adventurer of Vienna was now the most powerful dictator in Europe since the Napoleonic era. His people regarded him as a consummate statesman, even greater than Bismarck, while diplomats in the Western countries feared him as a persistent aggressor.

Poland was Hitler's next designated victim. He now claimed the Polish Corridor and Danzig, the loss of which he attributed to the Treaty of Versailles. The Western powers, in response to Poland's appeal, guaranteed Polish independence. Meanwhile, Hitler began negotiations with Moscow with the excuse that it was vital to avoid war on two fronts, as he had pointed out in *Mein Kampf*. On August 23, 1939, Nazi Germany and Soviet Russia, mortal enemies, signed a pact of friendship agreeing to divide Poland between them (*see* HITLER-STALIN PACT). This was Stalin's reply to the diplomats of the West, whom he suspected of trying to turn Hitler against him. Prime Minister Chamberlain, appalled by this diplomatic bombshell, informed Hitler that Britain would not hesitate to fulfill its obligations to Poland. An angered Hitler made no reply but said privately: "I am 50 years old, and prefer war now to when I shall be 53 or 60."

Early domination of World War II. From this stage on, Hitler's life and career merged with the cascading events of World War II. He put on his soldier's tunic and announced that he would not change it until Germany was triumphant. In the first weeks of the war, starting on September 1, 1939, Poland was crushed between German and Russian forces. Hitler insisted that he was neither at war nor at peace, a convenient fiction leaving him with the initiative both on the battlefield and in diplomacy. In an extraordinary speech to the Reichstag on October 6, 1939, he suggested peace to Britain and France—his "last offer." But by now it was realized everywhere that his word could not be trusted. A month later, on the anniversary of the 1923 Beer-Hall *Putsch*, he announced that he was giving orders for a five-year war that would end only in victory for the Third Reich.

Then came the *Sitzkrieg* (q.v.), the sit-down war, lasting through the winter of 1939–1940, when neither Hitler nor his enemies in the west attempted an attack. The French stayed behind their Maginot Line (q.v.), while British pilots bombed Germany with leaflets. In his New Year address of 1940, Hitler declared that he was fighting for a "new order" in Europe (*see* NEUORDNUNG). In March 1940 he met his ally, Mussolini, on the Brenner Pass to reveal his plans. Suddenly, on April 9, Hitler moved against Denmark and Norway with the explanation that the British had laid mines in Norwegian waters. A month later he sent his troops in a *Blitzkrieg* (q.v.) on Belgium, the Netherlands, Luxembourg, and France. "This battle will decide the fate of Germany for a thousand years." On June 22, 1940, a triumphant Hitler required the French to agree to an armistice in the same railway car at Compiègne (q.v.) in which the Germans had been forced to sign the armistice in 1918. The Fuehrer returned to Berlin as a conquering hero. The events of the preceding weeks had confirmed the average German's belief in Hitler's genius. He was given the major credit for the overall planning of a brilliant military campaign. For the Allies it was a disastrous defeat.

Hitler's next step was to subjugate Britain by aerial bombardment, to be followed by invasion in Operation Sea Lion (Seelöwe, q.v.). The expected surrender of Britain failed to materialize, however, as RAF pilots struck back at Hitler's great air armadas. On August 15, 1940, the British shot down 180 German aircraft. Without air control Hitler could not invade Britain. His strategy now turned to the east. Mussolini, annoyed at being kept in ignorance of Hitler's plans, invaded Greece, but his conspicuous failure there made it necessary for Hitler to turn his attention to the Balkans and North Africa. On April 6, 1941, Hitler attacked Greece and Yugoslavia and then sent his Afrika Korps (q.v.) hurtling toward Egypt. Success of this plan depended on the neutrality of Soviet Russia.

Hitler now made the most critical decision of his career. He had 250 divisions of German troops and about 100 divisions from satellite countries. He decided to attack the Soviet Union in the belief that he could complete the task in six weeks. He would then separate Russia from its Western allies by stressing his own anti-Bolshevik crusade. On June 22, 1941, German troops crossed the border and surged into the Soviet Union on a front extending from the Baltic to the Black Sea. At first Hitler was successful, as his troops covered two-thirds of the distance to Moscow in twenty-six days. The Russians, using a defense-in-depth strategy, retreated. "Today," said Hitler on October 2, 1941, "begins the last, great decisive battle of the war." He was partly right: it was decisive in favor of the Russians. Although he boasted that he had smashed Russia, his final desperate assault on the Caucasus was a disastrous failure. On December 19, 1941, after the catastrophe at Moscow, Hitler dismissed his commander in chief, Field Marshal Walther von Brauchitsch (q.v.), and assumed control of all military operations himself. By this time the United States had entered the war, and four-fifths of the world was ranged against Nazi Germany.

Hitler's New Year message of 1942 showed a marked decline in his usual euphoric and confident mood. His armies were still winning victories in the Ukraine and in North Africa, but the great impulse of *Blitzkrieg* was no longer working effectively. He retreated into his field headquarters, constantly quarreling with his military advisers on strategy and tactics. Hitler continued to make errors of judgment. On the eastern front he moved haphazardly from one objective to another or ordered his armies to stand and fight when their position was hopeless. He neglected the Mediterranean area at a time when a relatively small additional effort might have brought decisive results.

Meanwhile, Hitler paid less and less attention to politics and diplomacy. He ordered Heinrich Himmler to prepare the framework for his New Order in Europe, consisting of the countries annexed by the Third Reich, the territories of Czechoslovakia and Poland, France and Belgium under Nazi governors, and Norway and Holland in a loose union. In all the occupied countries there arose powerful resistance movements, which Hitler attempted to smash by the same kind of terror he had used successfully in Germany. He imported vast numbers of foreign workers to supply his armies. He ordered Himmler to expand both the concentration camps and the extermination camps (q.v.) to deal with dissidents and to cleanse the Aryan race by destroying the Jews and other "inferior" elements.

The turning point came in the fall of 1942. By this time Gen. Erwin Rommel (q.v.) was routed at El Alamein (q.v.). In November Hitler's Sixth Army, commanded by Gen. Friedrich von Paulus (q.v.), began to stall and break down before Stalingrad. "I won't leave the Volga," Hitler shouted and ordered the encircled Sixth Army to be known as Fortress Stalingrad. In February 1943, Von Paulus surrendered. This was a disaster and meant the loss of the war. Hitler had publicly promised to capture Stalingrad but had allowed his armies to bleed to death in attempting to redeem his pledge. Until this time he had been successful in achieving the goals he had set for himself. Now he began to speak less of victory than of the inability of his enemies to defeat him. He retreated into his own world of fantasy and isolated himself from those who would warn him of the consequences of defeat. His health began to decline as he depended more and more upon the injections given by Dr. Theodor Morell (q.v.), whose drugs were having a serious effect on his health. Hitler's days of glory were ended.

Military decline. Unwilling to concede defeat, Hitler ordered total mobilization of the German economy in a final effort to extricate himself. There was one crisis after another to plague him. In July 1943 Mussolini's regime collapsed in Italy, and Hitler had to assume the responsibility of rebuilding it. He hoped that the tremendous pounding of German cities by Allied air power would rekindle the fighting spirit of his people. Germany would never capitulate: "She will go on fighting past 12 o'clock!"

Blows began to rain in on the Fuehrer from all directions. The Allies smashed his armies in North Africa. In Russia his troops were pushed back from village to village to their own soil. Anglo-American forces invaded Sicily and then the mainland of Italy, reaching Naples on October 1, 1943, and Rome on June 4, 1944. On June 6 came the supreme event of 1944, Operation Overlord, the Allied invasion of France. One of the most remarkable expeditions in military history, it was accomplished with complete initial surprise. Soon a million Allied troops were pushing the Germans eastward, bypassing Paris and cutting the Germans to pieces in their own version of a *Blitzkrieg*. Hitler was caught in a giant trap as the Allied armies moved across the Rhine and the Russians drove on relentlessly from the east. Goering's Luftwaffe was unable to protect German cities and industrial centers from the effects of shattering Allied air bombardments. The U-boat campaign was a failure (*see* U-BOATS).

All these factors in a desperate military situation

Hitler visits an armaments factory on his fifty-fourth birthday, April 20, 1943. [*US Army*]

encouraged the small anti-Hitler movement inside Germany to take action. Criticism of the Fuehrer had moved in several stages from opposition to resistance to conspiracy. The several small and loosely connected German opposition groups were never organized into a strong mass movement. Apparently, they did not have the mass strength of the underground fighters in the occupied countries who waged war against the Nazis. The German Resistance (q.v.), however, did make several attempts to eliminate Hitler. On July 20, 1944, a number of high military and civilian officials, including Field Marshal Erwin von Witzleben, Carl Friedrich Goerdeler, mayor of Leipzig, and the thirty-seven-year-old Col. Claus Schenk Graf von Stauffenberg (qq.v.), executed a long-planned plot against Hitler at his eastern front headquarters. Surviving the bombing with some injuries, Hitler took vicious vengeance on the conspirators (*see* JULY PLOT).

Hitler's last days. With the war hopelessly lost, Hitler moved his headquarters to Berlin. Here in the *Fuehrerbunker* (q.v.), built underground below the Chancellery garden, he passed his last days. In the midst of his lackeys the Nazi dictator played out the final act of his life. He spent hours before giant war maps, shifting colored pins about to locate units that no longer existed. By this time he was in a state of extreme nervous exhaustion: although only fifty-six, he moved as if he were prematurely senile. His health grew even worse under the ministrations of his doctors. With the exception of Goebbels and Martin Bormann (q.v.), his secretaries, and several others, his lieutenants began to desert him. He denounced Goering for trying to usurp his leadership and Himmler for seeking to negotiate with the Allies. Albert Speer (q.v.), his Minister of Armaments and War Production, refused to carry out his orders for a scorched-earth policy. At last acknowledging defeat, the Fuehrer decided to leave the world in a gesture of Wagnerian self-immolation. Germany, too, he said should commit suicide, for the Germans had been unworthy of his genius and had been defeated in the struggle for life. Two further acts remained for him. In the early hours of April 29, 1945, he married Eva Braun (q.v.), his mistress, and immediately afterward dictated his last will and political testament, in which he justified his life and work (*see* HITLER'S LAST WILL; HITLER'S POLITICAL TESTAMENT). The next day he retreated into his suite and shot himself, while Eva took poison to end her life. In accordance with his instructions, the bodies were dumped into a trough in the Chancellery garden, doused with gasoline, and burned. *See also* GÖTTERDÄMMERUNG.

Personality and character. Hitler's personality is a familiar one in every German *Bierstube* (taproom). Self-educated, shrewd, arrogant, the German of this type holds forth on every subject under the sun, from food to world politics, from music to cleansing the race. Pompous, omniscient, he refuses to discuss ideas but instead issues dicta and ukases. He mistakes his own intuitions for scientific fact. He knows all the answers to the meaning of history. He lives in a curious dream world and dismisses as nonsense any idea opposed to his judgments and disconnected monologues.

Hitler's unguarded all-night off-the-record table talk (*see* TABLE TALK, HITLER'S) gives clues to his personality and character. Race: "It's our duty continually to arouse the forces that slumber in our people's blood." Self-glorification: "There was a time when there was *only* one Prussian in Europe and he lived in Rome. There was a second Prussian. He lived in Munich, and was myself." Sense of grandeur: "When one enters the Reich Chancellery, one should have the feeling that he is visiting the master of the world." Suspicions: "I never met an Englishman who didn't say that Churchill was off his head." "There's no doubt about it—Roosevelt is a sick brain." Hostility: "There's nobody more stupid than the Americans. They can never fight like heroes."

The mind of Hitler has fascinated psychiatrists, psychoanalysts, psychologists, and historians. It is now generally agreed that he suffered from lack of mental stability, and some believe that he was burdened by several types of insanity. His character was molded in his early years by an accumulation of frustrations, hostility, and hatreds attributable to the obscurity and failures of his early days. The British historian H. R. Trevor-Roper (q.v.) described Hitler's mind in a striking sentence: "A terrible phenomenon, imposing indeed in its granite harshness and yet infinitely squalid in its miscellaneous cumber—like some huge barbarian monolith, the expression of giant strength and savage genius, surrounded by a festering heap of refuse—old tins and dead vermin, ashes and eggshells and ordure—the intellectual detritus of centuries."[1]

Historical significance. Dispassionate observers agree on the importance of Hitler's role not only in the history of the twentieth century but in the annals of modern times. He won his way to political power by a mixture of violence and deceit and used the same device to destroy other nations. By the time he committed suicide he had broken the structure of the world in which he lived and had led the way to even greater possibilities for destruction. The enormous power he wielded was unprecedented, especially in the technical resources he controlled. His ideas were old and shopworn, but his methods, while Machiavellian, took on the trappings of modern technology. Both in his drive to power and during his chancellorship he used lies, terror, and extreme cruelty to gain his end. In the eyes of the world he became the incarnation of evil. His legacy is the memory of one of the most horrible tyrannies in the course of civilization.

There are three levels of value judgments on the life and career of Hitler. To German nationalists of similar persuasion he was the great national hero who fought against an unjust Carthaginian peace and lifted Germany once more to the pinnacle of prestige and international power. To a small group of revisionist historians he was a unique political genius who was able to respond effectively to the mistakes of other, less able diplomats, in the way that Frederick the Great took advantage of Maria Theresa's errors. To the largest group of observers, however, Hitler is regarded as an amoral evil genius who brought Western civilization to its nadir and nearly destroyed it in the process. He alone was responsible, they say, for the horror and barbarism of the Third Reich. A disturbed neurotic himself, he found in the tortured state of mind of the German people after the shock of defeat in World War I a mirror of his own morbid emotions, of extreme frustration and hostility. Throughout his life he, an Austrian, insisted on identifying himself with the German people and, by inflaming them with his hypnotic oratory and shrewd propaganda, found an outlet for his own hatreds and ambitions. His intuitive understanding of the German mind was extraordinary. He achieved one startling success after another and later was able to construct a massive tyranny among a people who in the past had contributed much to the best in European culture. A complex concatenation of circumstances elevated him from the soapbox to the seat of power in Germany; it took a worldwide coalition of powers to strike him down.

The true monument to Hitler was the devastation of the nation he ruled with such cruelty and terror. He made his own unwitting epitaph in these prophetic words to Hermann Rauschning (q.v.): "We must be prepared for the hardest struggle which a nation has ever had to face. Only through this test of endurance can we become ripe for the dominion to which we are called. It will be my duty to carry on this war regardless of losses. The sacrifice of lives will be immense. . . . We shall have to abandon much that is dear to us and today seems irreplaceable. Cities will become heaps of ruins; noble monuments of architecture will disappear forever. This time our sacred soil will not be spared. But I am not afraid of this."

Bibliography. Alan Bullock, *Hitler: A Study in Tyranny*, Harper & Row, Publishers, Incorporated, New York, 1964; Konrad Heiden, *Der Fuehrer*, tr. by Ralph Manheim, Houghton Mifflin Company, Boston, 1948; Henri Lichtenberger, *The Third Reich*, tr. by Koppel S. Pinson, The Greystone Press, New York, 1937; William L. Shirer, *The Rise and Fall of the Third Reich*, Simon and Schuster, New York, 1960; H. R. Trevor-Roper, *The Last Days of Hitler*, The Macmillan Company, New York, 1947.

HITLER, ALOIS SCHICKELGRUBER (1837–1903). Father of Adolf Hitler (q.v.). Alois Schickelgruber was born in Strones, Lower Austria, on June 7, 1837, the illegitimate son of Johann Georg Hiedler, a wandering miller, and Anna Marie Schickelgruber, a peasant girl. The parents were married five years later, in May 1842, at Döllersheim. Alois, who was not legitimized, continued to be known by his mother's name until he was nearly forty. He was raised by his father's brother, Johann Nepomuk Hiedler,

[1]Introduction by H. R. Trevor-Roper to Adolf Hitler, *Hitler's Secret Conversations, 1941–1944*, Farrar, Straus & Young, New York, 1953, pp. xxix–xxx.

who in 1876 took steps to legitimize the young man who had grown up in his home. From the beginning of 1877, some twelve years before Adolf was born, Alois used the name Hitler.

At the age of thirteen Alois left his uncle's home to work as a cobbler's apprentice. At eighteen he joined the Imperial Customs Service, and he spent the remainder of his working life as a customs officer in Braunau and other towns of Lower Austria. His appointment to this post meant that Alois had moved several steps upward in the social scale from his peasant origins. Resplendent in his uniform with its shiny gold buttons and gold-rimmed velvet cap and pistol at his belt, he appeared to be a paragon of lower-middle-class respectability.

Alois Schickelgruber's private life was morose and unhappy. In 1864 he married Anna Glasl, the daughter of another customs official, who suffered a long siege of illness and died in 1883. A month later he married Franziska Matzelberger, a young hotel servant who had already borne him a son out of wedlock. The second marriage ended when Franziska died of tuberculosis. On January 7, 1885, after obtaining an episcopal dispensation for a marriage between second cousins, Alois married Klara Poelzl, who was twenty-three years younger than he (*see* HITLER, KLARA POELZL). Klara became the mother of Adolf Hitler.

In 1895, when Adolf was six years old, Alois retired from governmental service at the early age of fifty-eight. For the next four years he moved restlessly from one district to another near Linz, buying and selling farms, raising bees, and spending most of his time drinking and brooding at village inns. Angry, obstinate, and hot-tempered, Alois was master in his own home. Adolf felt the lash of his father's cane, dog whip, and belt. On many occasions young Adolf had to take his tipsy father home from the local inn. There was continuous conflict between the sixty-four-year-old father and the twelve-year-old son. Alois wanted the boy to be a civil servant and was shocked when Adolf indicated a preference for the arts. The father's reaction was violent: "No! No! Never as long as I shall live!" Alois died suddenly in Leonding on January 3, 1903, of a lung hemorrhage. His widow was left with a small pension to care for herself and the two living children.

Adolf Hitler never called himself by any other name. Opponents attempted to label him with the name Adolf Schickelgruber and hinted that he had changed it because the term *"Heil Schickelgruber!"* lacked euphonius appeal. It was also suggested that Adolf Hitler's grandfather was a Jew, but here, too, there is no evidence to substantiate the claim.

HITLER, KLARA POELZL (1860–1908). Mother of Adolf Hitler (q.v.). Klara Poelzl was born in Spital on August 20, 1860, the daughter of Johanna Poelzl and the granddaughter of Johann von Nepomuk Hütler. As a young peasant girl she spent an unhappy childhood with her impoverished family. At fifteen, in the place of a daughter, she was taken into the household of Alois Schickelgruber Hitler (q.v.). Because his second wife was gravely ill, Alois Hitler decided to take his young foster daughter as his wife on the death of his spouse. Alois and Klara, second cousins by marriage, were married on January 7, 1885. She was pregnant, and their first child was born four months and ten days later. Klara Poelzl was quiet, earnest, and hardworking. Photographs show her with a solemn, pale face, and large, staring eyes. Though unhappy with her husband, who was addicted to alcohol, she kept his home spotless and tried in every possible way to please him. Neighbors reported that she had "nothing to smile about." She bore five children, three of whom died at an early age: Gustav (1885–1887), Ida (1886–1888), Adolf (1889–1945), Edmund (1894–1900), and Paula (1896–). Adolf, who resembled her, was her favorite child. Later he admitted that he was "mother's darling"; others called him *Muttersöhnchen* (mama's boy). Klara deeply loved her son even though she believed him to be "moonstruck" and different from other children. Despite his mother's love for him, he became an unhappy, resentful child.

Alois Hitler died suddenly in Leonding on January 3, 1903, of a lung hemorrhage at the age of sixty-five when Adolf was nearly fourteen. His mother moved to an apartment in Urfahr, a suburb of Linz, where she attempted to maintain herself and her two surviving children on a modest pension. All along she had been bewildered by Adolf's desire to become an artist. Highly religious, she had hoped that he would become a monk, but he was little interested in an ecclesiastical career. His father had preferred a civil servant's career for his son, but here, too, Adolf rebelled. Klara endured severe hardships for three years to support the young man. Ill for a long time, she died of cancer in Linz-Urfahr on December 21, 1908. The nineteen-year-old Adolf hurried home for the funeral. "It was a dreadful shock. I had honored my father, but my mother I had loved." Klara was buried in Leonding beside her husband.

HITLER CHAMBER. *See* HITLER KAMMER.

HITLER JUGEND (HJ; Hitler Youth). The male branch of the German youth movement. It was regarded as a *Gliederung* (limb) of the Nazi party. Hitler believed that the survival of his Third Reich for 1,000 years depended upon the education of youth. "A violently active, dominating, brutal youth—that is what I am after. Youth must be indifferent to pain. . . . I will have no intellectual training. Knowledge is ruin to my young men." *See also* EDUCATION IN THE THIRD REICH.

To promote this educational goal, Hitler set up two state-controlled organizations in 1933, the Hitler Jugend (Hitler Youth) and the Bund Deutscher Mädel (q.v.), the League of German Girls. All the youth clubs existing at the time were brought into the new German organization. By 1935 the Hitler Youth was a huge organization comprising almost 60 percent of German youth. It was placed under the direction of *Reichsjugendfuehrer* (Reich Youth Leader) Baldur von Schirach (q.v.). At the September 1935 Nazi party rally at Nuremberg (*see* NUREMBERG RALLIES), 54,000 representatives of the Hitler Jugend marched before Hitler. The Fuehrer addressed them in glowing tones. What was desired of youth, he said, was quite unlike what former generations wanted. The dull philistine youth of yesterday was succeeded by the lanky athlete, "swift as the greyhound, tough as leather, and hard as Krupp steel." National Socialism would replace yester-

A member of the Hitler Youth is greeted by the Fuehrer in this propaganda postcard. [*Photo Hoffmann, Munich*]

day's degenerate and would educate the new youth in strict discipline and perfect self-respect.

The education of the Hitler Jugend was carefully regulated. At first came the preliminary steps. By March 15 of the year in which he would celebrate his tenth birthday, every German youngster had to register with the Reich Youth Headquarters. After a thorough investigation of the boy's record and that of his family, with special attention to his "racial purity," he was admitted free of taint in the year's group of initiates to the Deutsches Jungvolk (German Young People; *see* JUNGVOLK). This section included boys aged from ten through thirteen years. The honor took place in a ceremony on the Fuehrer's birthday, April 20, in the presence of a high party functionary. The Hitler Jugend accepted youngsters from fourteen to eighteen. At the age of eighteen the young man was graduated from the youth organizations into the National Socialist party and eventually into the SA (q.v.). At the age of nineteen young Nazis were called for six months into the Reichsarbeitsdienst (q.v.), the State Labor Service, in which they were subjected to manual labor and strict discipline. After this stage they went into the Wehrmacht (q.v.), the armed forces, for their two years of military service. In this way the Nazi party never relinquished its hold on German youngsters from the age of ten to twenty-one.

On December 1, 1936, the Hitler Jugend was made a state agency. Every young German was expected to belong to the Hitler Jugend. The organization had something for everyone: arts and crafts, model planes, journalism, and music. Its activities took precedence over any kind of formal education. The routine filled the entire week. Boys went on camping and hiking trips, spent evenings together in youth homes, attended public demonstrations in uniform, and went on long trips to foreign countries. When World War II began, boys collected blankets and clothes for the troops and bones and paper for the war effort. Every free hour was monopolized, and the youngsters scarcely had a moment for their families. Parents dared not object to this kind of conformity and Spartan regime. The failure of any boy to join the Hitler Jugend was regarded as a violation of civic responsibility. Youngsters, living more and more with their comrades, were gradually weaned from their families.

Bibliography. Howard Becker, *German Youth: Bond or Free*, Oxford University Press, New York, 1946.

HITLER KAMMER (Hitler Chamber). An organization concerned with euthanasia (*see* EUTHANASIA PROGRAM), the elimination of people regarded as of inferior racial quality. *See also* UNTERMENSCHEN.

HITLER PUTSCH (Hitler-Ludendorff Putsch). *See* BEER-HALL PUTSCH.

HITLER SALUTE. The special form of greeting between Nazis. Early in the movement Hitler instituted the regular military salute, hand to cap, in the belief that his followers formed a military unit. But the younger Storm Troopers (*see* SA), who had had no military training, regarded the traditional salute with the bent elbow as too great a strain. They started the practice of greeting their comrades with a simple wave of the hand. Later this salute stiffened into a quick upward thrust, similar to that used by Mussolini's Fascists. The Hitler salute was generally accompanied by the phrase *"Heil Hitler!"* (q.v.; "Hail Hitler!").

HITLER-STALIN PACT. Agreement between Nazi Germany and Soviet Russia. It was signed on August 23, 1939, in Moscow by German Foreign Minister Joachim von Ribbentrop (q.v.) and Soviet Commissar for Foreign Affairs Vyacheslav M. Molotov. The pact provided that the two countries would not support any third power in the event that it attacked either of the two signatories, that they would consult with each other on matters of common interest, and that each would refrain from associating with any grouping of powers aimed at the other. A secret protocol, made public in 1948, divided Eastern Europe into German and Soviet spheres, and each signatory was given territorial gains in lands lying between them.

The signing of the pact was a political bombshell. For years there had been a war of ideologies between the two hostile countries. In *Mein Kampf* (q.v.) and in many speeches Hitler had excoriated bolshevism as the archenemy of civilization, and in turn Stalin had denounced the Nazis as fascist beasts. The surprising end to the war of words came because both dictators saw benefits in the agreement.

Stalin regarded the pact as advantageous. He had long dreaded a combination of Britain, France, and Germany directed against his country. He would not allow London and Paris to channel fascist expansion eastward. Moreover, the Soviet Union, weakened by military purges and uncertain of British and French intentions, needed time to complete the military industrialization envisioned in the Third Five-Year Plan. In late September 1938, at the time of the Munich Agreement (q.v.), the U.S.S.R. was left alone in Europe. What Stalin feared most was that the four partners at Munich might form a coalition directed against Russia. In early 1939 negotiations began between Russia and the Western states. When Britain suggested that the Soviet Union make a unilateral guarantee of assistance to any neighboring state that wanted such a pledge, Stalin replied with a suggestion that made clear the price the Western democracies would have to pay. In addition to a mutual assistance agreement and a military convention, they would have to guarantee as a defensive barrier against Nazi aggression all the states between the Baltic and the Black Sea (Poland, Romania, Finland, the Baltic states, Bulgaria, Yugoslavia, and Greece). This was far too great a price for Prime Minister Neville Chamberlain and Premier Édouard Daladier (qq.v.), who believed that such

The British cartoonist David Low comments on the Nazi-Soviet Pact of August 1939. [*From Low's* Autobiography, *Simon and Schuster, New York, 1957*]

an agreement would give the Russians a huge zone of influence which would soon be occupied by Soviet troops. In turning to Germany, Stalin was accepting a second choice for the security he needed.

For Hitler the pact was an achievement of the first order. Above all it relieved him of the fate of Emperor William II, who had been caught between two fronts in World War I. The Fuehrer saw no difficulty in assigning to Russia the Balkan states and parts of Poland and Romania. He did not want to concern himself with the eastern front in the event that Britain and France really came to Poland's aid. True, he had emphasized the Bolshevik menace as long as Britain and France had allowed him to win victories in Spain, Austria, and Czechoslovakia. He would turn *for the time being* to Soviet Russia. Later, after he had defeated the democracies, he could attend to matters in the east.

The following sequence of events led to the agreement:

March 10, 1939. Before the Eighteenth Congress of the Communist party, Stalin announces that he has decided not to allow Soviet Russia to be drawn into conflict by warmongers "who are accustomed to get others to pull the chestnuts out of the fire for them." For Hitler this is a signal of extraordinary importance.

April 3. Hitler issues Case White (Weiss, q.v.), a top-secret directive calling for operations against Poland. The target date is September 1. The Fuehrer signed a ten-year friendship pact with Poland in January 1934, but this does not affect his plans.

April 28. In a major speech Hitler drops all criticism of Marxism and bolshevism.

May 3. Maxim M. Litvinov, Soviet Foreign Commissar noted for his anti-German stance, is relieved of his post in favor of Vyacheslav M. Molotov.

May 20. Molotov requests better economic and political relations with the Third Reich.

May 23. At a military conference with his chief aides in the Chancellery at Berlin, Hitler says that he will attack at the earliest opportunity and adds: "It is not ruled out that Russia might disinterest herself in the destruction of Poland."

August 3. Hitler sends a message to Stalin that Germany is now ready "to recast German-Russian relations."

August 10. A Franco-British military commission arriving in Moscow is courteously received but subjected to mysterious delays and obstructions.

August 12. Stalin informs Hitler that he is ready "to discuss by degrees" all political questions including the question of Poland.

August 14. The Fuehrer asks Stalin to receive Foreign Minister Joachim von Ribbentrop to discuss "joint territorial questions in Eastern Europe [the partition of Poland]."

August 15. The German Ambassador in Moscow informs the Kremlin that "ideological contradictions should not prohibit reasonable cooperation of a new and friendly type."

August 16. Hitler informs Stalin that he is willing to sign a nonaggression pact.

August 18. Von Ribbentrop requests Stalin to receive him at once.

August 19. Stalin informs the Politburo that he intends to conclude a pact with Hitler.

August 20. Hitler requests Stalin to receive Von Ribbentrop: "The tension between Germany and Poland has become intolerable."

August 21. Stalin agrees. Hitler is wildly enthusiastic at the news: "I have the world in my pocket!"

August 23. The pact is signed in Moscow as Stalin drinks to Hitler's health.

August 24. Von Ribbentrop is received by Hitler as "a second Bismarck."

There was consternation in London and Paris. Chamberlain could only say: "Whatever may prove to be the nature of the German-Soviet agreement, it cannot alter Great Britain's obligations." Poland, which had been a buffer state against Russian expansion to the west, was doomed.

HITLER YOUTH. *See* HITLER JUGEND.

HITLER'S FIRST CABINET. *See* CABINET, HITLER'S FIRST.

HITLER'S LAST WILL. On the morning of April 29, 1945, as Berlin was engulfed in a sea of flames, Hitler married Eva Braun (q.v.) in his underground bunker at the Chancellery (*see* GÖTTERDÄMMERUNG). While the wedding was being celebrated, Hitler sent for his secretary, Frau Gertrud Junge (q.v.), and dictated two documents, his last will and his political testament (*see* HITLER'S POLITICAL TESTAMENT). In his private will Hitler explained his marriage, disposed of his property, and announced his impending death. The next day at 3:30 P.M., Hitler and his wife committed suicide. The bodies were burned and then buried in the Chancellery garden or taken away by the Russians. The text of the will follows:[1]

> As I did not consider that I could take responsibility, during the years of struggle, of contracting a marriage, I have now decided, before the closing of my earthly career, to take as my wife that girl who, after many years of faithful friendship, entered, of her own free will, the practically besieged town in order to share her destiny with me. At her own desire she goes as my wife with me into death. It will compensate us for what we both lost through my work in the service of my people.
>
> What I possess belongs—in so far as it has any value—to the Party. Should this no longer exist, to the State; should the State also be destroyed, no further decision of mine is necessary.
>
> My pictures, in the collections which I have bought in the course of years, have never been collected for private purposes, but only for the extension of a gallery in my home town of Linz on Donau.
>
> It is my most sincere wish that this bequest may be duly executed.
>
> I nominate as my Executor my most faithful Party comrade,
>
> Martin Bormann
>
> He is given full legal authority to make all decisions. He is permitted to take out everything that has a sentimental value or is necessary for the maintenance of a modest simple life, for my brothers and sisters,

[1]Translated in the Office of United States Chief of Counsel for the Prosecution of Axis Criminality, *Nazi Conspiracy and Aggression*, Government Printing Office, Washington, 1946–1948, vol. VI, pp. 259–260.

also above all for the mother of my wife and my faithful co-workers who are well known to him, principally my old Secretaries Frau Winter etc. who have for many years aided me by their work.

I myself and my wife—in order to escape the disgrace of deposition or capitulation—choose death. It is our wish to be burnt immediately on the spot where I have carried out the greatest part of my daily work in the course of a twelve years' service to my people.

Given in Berlin, 29th April 1945, 4:00 A.M.

[*Signed*] A. Hitler

[*Witnesses*]
Dr. Joseph Goebbels
Martin Bormann
Colonel Nicholaus von Below

HITLER'S POLITICAL TESTAMENT. After writing his last will (*see* HITLER'S LAST WILL), Hitler wrote a political testament in which he defended his work and career. In the first part he maintained that he had not wanted to go to war in 1939 and placed the blame for the conflict on "International Jewry." In the second part he expelled from the party the men who he decided were traitors to his cause, including Hermann Goering and Heinrich Himmler (qq.v.), appointed his successors, and outlined the form of government that they should adopt.

The authenticity of Hitler's political testament was challenged by a writer to the London *Daily Telegraph*, who noted the "un-German" characteristics of the typescript. H. R. Trevor-Roper (q.v.), the British historian, regards the validity of the testament as established beyond doubt by a mass of internal and circumstantial evidence, including expert scrutiny of the signatures and the testimony of Frau Gertrud Junge (q.v.), who typed the documents. Trevor-Roper characterizes this last advertisement of the Nazi movement, designed as a valedictory to the world and a message to later generations, as "nothing but the old claptrap, the negative appeal, the purposeless militarism, of the Revolution of Destruction. . . ." The text of the testament follows:[1]

First Part of the Political Testament

More than thirty years have now passed since I in 1914 made my modest contribution as a volunteer in the first world war that was forced upon the Reich.

In these three decades I have been actuated solely by love and loyalty to my people in all my thoughts, acts, and life. They gave me the strength to make the most difficult decisions which have ever confronted mortal man. I have spent my time, my working strength, and my health in these three decades.

It is untrue that I or anyone else in Germany wanted the war in 1939. It was desired and instigated exclusively by those international statesmen who were either of Jewish descent or worked for Jewish interests. I have made too many offers for the control and limitation of armaments, which posterity will not for all time be able to disregard for the responsibility for the outbreak of this war to be laid on me. I have further never wished that after the first fatal world war a second against England, or even against America, should break out. Centuries will pass away, but out of the ruins of our towns and monuments the hatred against those finally responsible whom we have to thank for everything, International Jewry and its helpers, will grow.

Three days before the outbreak of the German-Polish war I again proposed to the British ambassador in Berlin a solution to the German-Polish problem—similar to that in the case of the Saar district, under international control. This offer also cannot be denied. It was only rejected because the leading circles in English politics wanted the war, partly on account of the business hoped for and partly under influence of propaganda organized by International Jewry.

I have also made it quite plain that, if the nations of Europe are again to be regarded as mere shares to be bought and sold by these international conspirators in money and finance, then that race, Jewry, which is the real criminal of this murderous struggle, will be saddled with the responsibility. I further left no one in doubt that this time not only would millions of children of Europe's Aryan people die of hunger, not only would millions of grown men suffer death, and not only hundreds of thousands of women and children be burnt and bombed to death in the towns, without the real criminal having to atone for this guilt, even if by more humane means.

After six years of war, which in spite of all setbacks, will go down one day in history as the most glorious and valiant demonstration of a nation's life purpose, I cannot forsake the city which is the capital of this Reich. As the forces are too small to make any further stand against the enemy attack at this place and our resistance is gradually being weakened by men who are as deluded as they are lacking in initiative, I should like, by remaining in this town, to share my fate with those, the millions of others, who have also taken upon themselves to do so. Moreover I do not wish to fall into the hands of an enemy who requires a new spectacle organized by the Jews for the amusement of their hysterical masses.

I have decided therefore to remain in Berlin and there of my own free will to choose death at the moment when I believe the position of the Führer and Chancellor itself can no longer be held.

I die with a happy heart, aware of the immeasurable deeds and achievements of our soldiers at the front, our women at home, the achievements of our farmers and workers and the work, unique in history, of our youth who bear my name.

That from the bottom of my heart I express my thanks to you all, is just as self-evident as my wish that you should, because of that, on no account give up the struggle, but rather continue it against the enemies of the Fatherland, no matter where, true to the creed of a great Clausewitz. From the sacrifice of our soldiers and from my own unity with them unto death, will in any case spring up in the history of Germany, the seed of a radiant renaissance of the National Socialist movement and thus of the realization of a true community of nations.

Many of the most courageous men and women have decided to unite their lives with mine until the very last. I have begged and finally ordered them not to do this, but to take part in the further battle of the Nation. I beg the heads of the Armies, the Navy and the Air Force to strengthen by all possible means the spirit of resistance of our soldiers in the National Socialist sense, with special reference to the fact that also I

[1]Translated in the Office of the United States Chief of Counsel for the Prosecution of Axis Criminality, *Nazi Conspiracy and Aggression*, Government Printing Office, Washington, 1946–1948, vol. VI, pp. 260–263.

myself, as founder and creator of this movement, have preferred death to cowardly abdication or even capitulation.

May it, at some future time, become part of the code of honor of the German officer—as is already the case in our Navy—that the surrender of a district or of a town is impossible, and that above all the leaders here must march ahead as shining examples, faithfully fulfilling their duty unto death.

Second Part of the Political Testament

Before my death I expel the former Reichsmarschall Hermann Göring from the party and deprive him of all rights which he may enjoy by virtue of the decree of June 29th, 1941; and also by virtue of my statement in the Reichstag on September 1st, 1939, I appoint in his place Grossadmiral Dönitz, President of the Reich and Supreme Commander of the Armed Forces.

Before my death I expel the former Reichsführer-SS and Minister of the Interior Heinrich Himmler, from the party and from all offices of State. In his stead I appoint Gauleiter Karl Hanke as Reichsführer-SS and Chief of the German Police, and Gauleiter Paul Giesler as Reich Minister of the Interior.

Göring and Himmler, quite apart from their disloyalty to my person, have done immeasurable harm to the country and the whole nation by secret negotiations with the enemy, which they have conducted without my knowledge and against my wishes, and by illegally attempting to seize power in the State for themselves. . . .

Although a number of men, such as Martin Bormann, Dr. Goebbels, etc., together with their wives, have joined me of their own free will and did not wish to leave the capital of the Reich under any circumstances, but were willing to perish with me here, I must nevertheless ask them to obey my request, and in this case set the interests of the nation above their own feelings. By their work and loyalty as comrades they will be just as close to me after death, as I hope that my spirit will linger among them and always go with them. Let them be hard but never unjust, but above all let them never allow fear to influence their actions, and set the honor of the nation above everything in the world. Finally, let them be conscious of the fact that our task, that of continuing the building of a National Socialist State, represents the work of the coming centuries, which places every single person under an obligation always to serve the common interest and to subordinate his own advantage to this end. I demand of all Germans, all National Socialists, men, women and all the men of the Armed Forces, that they be faithful and obedient unto death to the new government and its President.

Above all I charge the leaders of the nation and those under them to scrupulous observance of the laws of race and to merciless opposition to the universal poisoner of all peoples, International Jewry.

Given in Berlin, this 29th day of April 1945, 4:00 A.M.

Adolf Hitler

[*Witnesses*]

Dr. Joseph Goebbels   Wilhelm Burgdorf[1]
Martin Bormann   Hans Krebs[2]

HIWI. *See* HILFSWILLIGE.

[1]Gen. Wilhelm Burgdorf, Wehrmacht adjutant at the Fuehrer's headquarters.

[2]Gen. Hans Krebs, chief of staff.

HJ. *See* HITLER JUGEND.

HOEPNER, ERICH (1886–1944). General in the armed forces and a leading member of the Resistance (q.v.) against Hitler. Erich Hoepner was born in Frankfurt an der Oder on September 14, 1886. In 1938 he was one of the senior officers who were skeptical of Hitler's plans for aggression, and he was convinced that the Fuehrer was a menace to the country. As commander of an armored division in Thuringia in 1938, Hoepner was ready to intercept the Munich SS (q.v.) should it go to the defense of Berlin. In 1941 he was given command of Armored Group 4 on the Russian front. In this capacity he called for a withdrawal in defiance of Hitler's orders and was dismissed without a court-martial. His degradation was announced publicly in an order of the day, which referred to the "former [*ehemaliger*] Colonel-General Erich Hoepner." From then on Hoepner took an active role in the plot against Hitler.

Slated for high office after the overthrow of the Nazi regime, Hoepner was to take command of the Home Army and then the entire Army. He was also considered for a post as War Minister in a new provisional government. He was arrested after the July Plot (q.v.) of 1944 and tried by the Volksgericht (q.v.), the People's Court. Found guilty, he was executed in Berlin on August 8, 1944. Before his death he was offered a pistol for a ceremonial suicide, but he rejected it with the words: "I am not a swine that I should have to condemn myself."

HOESS, RUDOLF FRANZ (1900–1947). Commandant of the extermination camp at Auschwitz (q.v.; *see* EXTERMINATION CAMPS). Rudolf Franz Hoess was born in Baden-Baden on November 25, 1900, the son of Franz Xaver Hoess, a shopkeeper. The elder Hoess, a pious Catholic, hoped that his son would become a priest. In World War I, Rudolf Hoess, not yet fifteen, managed secretly to join the Army and was sent to the Turkish front. Wounded several times, he was decorated with the Iron Cross (First and Second Classes). After the war he joined the *Freikorps* (q.v.), the freebooter units consisting mostly of returning soldiers uprooted by the conflict. In 1923 he was arrested, along with Martin Bormann (q.v.), for the murder of Walther Kadow, a teacher who had been accused of denouncing Albert Leo Schlageter (q.v.) to the French (Schlageter was later to become a Nazi folk hero). In prison Hoess remained close to Bormann, who later helped him in his career. In 1928 Hoess was released under a general amnesty, after which he became a farm worker and then a member of the SS (q.v.). Hitler's assumption of political power in 1933 was a turning point in Hoess's career. In 1934 he was attached to the SS at Dachau, and in 1940 he was given the rank of *SS-Hauptsturmfuehrer* (captain) in command at the Auschwitz camp.

At Auschwitz Hoess was responsible for the execution of more than 2.5 million inmates, not counting a half million who were allowed to starve to death. He performed his job so well that he was commended in a 1944 SS report that called him "a true pioneer in this area because of his new ideas and educational methods." In 1945, at the recommendation of Bormann, Hoess was made deputy to *SS-Obergruppenfuehrer* (Gen.) Richard

Gluecks (q.v.), head of the inspectorate of concentration camps (q.v.). On March 29, 1947, Hoess was sentenced to death at Warsaw and was executed several days later at Auschwitz.

The personality and character of Hoess have fascinated students of abnormal psychology. He regarded himself as a perfectly normal man who led an uneventful family life while carrying out his orders to the best of his ability. Believing that he was more sensitive than most people, he tried to conceal this defect with an icy exterior. He felt that he had a difficult but necessary job to perform and that he had to undertake the assigned task without sympathy and without pity. "I must admit," he said later, "that the gassing process had a calming effect on me. I always had a horror of the shootings, thinking of the number of people, the women and children. I was relieved that we were spared these blood baths." At Nuremberg he explained the improvements he had made at Auschwitz over other extermination camps: "We tried to fool the victims into believing that they were going through a delousing process. Of course, at times they realized our true intentions and we sometimes had riots and difficulties. Frequently women would hide their children under their clothes, but we found them and we sent the children to be exterminated. We were required to carry out these exterminations in secrecy, but the foul and nauseating stench from the continued burning of bodies permeated the whole area and all the people living around Auschwitz knew what was going on." When his wife told him that she had heard rumors of the gassings and asked him if they were true, he admitted that they were. He even waxed poetical: "In the Spring of 1942 many blossoming people walked under the blossoming trees of the farmstead, and most of them went with no premonition of their deaths."

Others regarded this most sinister of the underlings of Heinrich Himmler as a mass murderer. In attempting to understand him, they say that he was the perfect example of the individual who could renounce his own mind in favor of total obedience. He felt at home only in the world of command and understood only the SS slogan: "Believe! Obey! Fight!" In his autobiography Hoess gave a clue to this overriding characteristic:

> I had been brought up by my parents to be respectful and obedient towards all grown-up people, and especially the elderly, regardless of their social status. I was taught that my highest duty was to help those in need. It was constantly impressed upon me in forceful terms that I must obey promptly the wishes and commands of my parents, teachers, priests, etc., and indeed of all grown-up people, including servants, and that nothing must distract me from this duty. Whatever they said was always right.
>
> These basic principles on which I was brought up became part of my flesh and blood. I can still clearly remember how my father, who on account of his fervent Catholicism was a determined opponent of the Reich Government and its policy, never ceased to remind his friends that, however strong one's opposition might be, the laws and decrees of the State had to be obeyed unconditionally.
>
> From my earliest youth I was brought up with a strong awareness of duty. In my parents' house it was insisted that every task be exactly and conscientiously carried out. Each member of the family had his own special duties to perform.

Added to Hoess's compulsion to follow orders was the fact that he had been brought up to believe that anti-Semitism (q.v.) was a form of pest control. To him the business of exterminating Jews was strictly an impersonal, mechanical system with the precision of modern industry. His work was to him hygienic and clinically clean. Most of all, his orders relieved him in his own mind of any personal responsibility. Those who knew him testified to Hoess's sentimental love for animals.

Bibliography. Rudolf Hoess, *Commandant at Auschwitz*, Popular Library, Inc., New York, 1961.

HOFACKER, CAESAR VON (1896–1944). A member of the officers' conspiracy against Hitler. Caesar von Hofacker was born on March 11, 1896. An industrialist, he was attached as a colonel to the staff of Gen. Karl Heinrich von Stuelpnagel (q.v.) in the German military command in Paris after the fall of France in 1940. In this post he played an active role as liaison agent with the conspirators inside Germany. He maintained close relations with his cousin, Lieut. Col. Claus Schenk Graf von Stauffenberg (q.v.), the central figure in the July Plot (q.v.) of 1944. At a meeting held at Von Stauffenberg's home at Wannsee on July 16, 1944, at which the final determination to kill Hitler was made, Von Hofacker reported on the imminent breakdown of the German armies in the west. He was arrested after the failure of the July Plot and, under Gestapo (q.v.) torture in the Prinz-Albrecht Strasse, revealed the name of Field Marshal Erwin Rommel (q.v.) as implicated in the conspiracy ("Tell the people in Berlin they can count on me"). Hitler immediately decided to purge Rommel. Von Hofacker was brought before the Volksgericht (q.v.), the People's Court in Berlin, found guilty of treason, and executed on December 20, 1944.

HOFFMANN, HEINRICH (1885–1957). Court photographer to Hitler and the National Socialist party and, with Max Amann (q.v.), the man responsible for the Fuehrer's wealth. Heinrich Hoffmann was born in Fürth on September 12, 1885, the son of a successful photographer. As a young man he learned his trade after school in his father's shop, and in World War I he served as a photographer in the Bavarian Army. In 1919 he published his first book of photographs, *A Year of Bavarian Revolution*.

Hoffmann's personal and political relationships with Hitler began in Munich in the early days of the National Socialist movement. The photographer, sensing a brilliant future for the budding politician, became his constant companion. For some time he belonged to Hitler's inner circle. Hitler often visited the Hoffmann home in Munich-Bogenhausen, where he felt he could relax from his hectic political life. In 1935, when Hoffmann became critically ill, he sought the medical attention of an old friend, Dr. Theodor Morell (q.v.), who cured him with sulfanilamides obtained from Hungary. On Hoffmann's repeated recommendations, Morell became the Fuehrer's physician and plied him with drugs that were to have a negative effect on his health. Hitler respected Hoffmann's taste in art. He was much amused when Hoffmann brought him paintings by Eduard Grützner of tipsy monks and inebriated butlers. The Fuehrer gave Hoffmann the task of sifting through paintings for the Annual Grand Art Show.

In his small sedan Hoffmann often drove Hitler to see

his friend Frau Winifred Wagner, daughter-in-law of Richard Wagner (qq.v.). Hoffmann introduced Hitler to Eva Braun (q.v.), who worked in his photography shop and who eventually was to become Hitler's wife for one day before his death. A loyal party member, Hoffmann was pleased when his daughter was courted by Baldur von Schirach (q.v.), the Reich Youth Leader.

To this personal friendship was added a profitable business relationship. Much of Hitler's early popularity was due to Hoffmann's superb photography. For some time Hoffmann was the only man permitted to take pictures of the Fuehrer. When Hitler objected to a photographic proof, he knew that Hoffmann would not print it. In late June 1940 Hoffmann photographed Hitler in Paris gazing down on the tomb of Napoleon at the Invalides. "That," he said to Hoffmann, "was the greatest and finest moment of my life." Hoffmann and Martin Bormann (q.v.) insisted that Hitler's photograph on many postage stamps of different denominations deserved royalties, a decision that led to the accumulation of an enormous fund. The photographer who wagered on the success of the National Socialist movement became a millionaire.

Hoffmann published a long series of picture books, including *Germany Awakened, The Brown House,* and *Hitler Unknown,* all of which had heavy sales. In 1933 he was elected to the Reichstag (q.v.), and in 1938 Hitler conferred the title of professor on him. He rose in party circles when his daughter Henrietta was married to Baldur von Schirach, but the marriage ended in divorce before World War II.

In 1947 Hoffmann was tried before a West German court as a Nazi profiteer. He was sentenced to ten years' imprisonment, all his wealth with the exception of 3,000 marks was confiscated, and the title of professor was withdrawn. The next year the sentence was reduced to three years, only to be raised again in 1950 to five years. Hoffmann died in Munich on December 16, 1957, at the age of seventy-two.

Bibliography. Heinrich Hoffmann, *Hitler über Deutschland,* Eher Verlag, Munich, 1932.

HOHEITSABZEICHEN (National Badge). Nazi insignia for the Army, Navy, and Luftwaffe (q.v.). The badge, which portrayed the Nazi eagle, was usually worn on hats over the cockade or on tunics and blouses over the right breast. Army generals and naval officers were given gold badges; others wore silver ones. Enlisted men of the Army and Luftwaffe were issued badges of silver-gray wool; Navy ratings, yellow wool. A similar emblem made of aluminum was permitted for use on civilian clothes.

"HOLD HIGH THE BANNER!" *See* "FAHNE HOCH, DIE."

HOLIDAYS, NAZI. A cycle of red-letter days designed to inculcate a note of reverence for the National Socialist party. The festivals were also expected to serve as substitutes for religious high holy days. The following days were set aside for special celebrations:

January 30: Day of the Seizure of Power. This day was observed because Hitler had assumed the chancellorship on January 30, 1933.

February 24: Foundation Day of the NSDAP. Although the Nazi party received its name on April 1, 1920, the date of February 24, 1920, was chosen as Foundation Day.

March 16: National Day of Mourning. Before 1933 the National Day of Mourning was linked with care of German war cemeteries. The Nazis gave it a new name, Heroes' Remembrance Day. The date was fixed permanently for March 16, instead of the customary fifth Sunday before Easter. A major success, such as the reintroduction of conscription in 1935 and the remilitarization of the Rhineland in 1936, was always honored on this day.

April 20: Hitler's Birthday. One of the most important days in the ritual of Fuehrer worship (q.v.), Hitler's birthday was celebrated by the public display of millions of photographs of the Fuehrer, red, white, and black bunting on house fronts, and extensive ceremonies. There were torchlight parades, mass choruses, and mass initiation rites.

May 1: National Labor Day. The Nazis appropriated May Day from the Socialists and used it to observe a holiday for their own workers. Maypole dances and huge bonfires, as well as parades, were held every year in the Third Reich. *See also* NATIONAL LABOR DAY.

Second Sunday in May: Mothering Sunday. On this occasion crosses of honor were awarded to prolific mothers at public ceremonies (*see* HONOR CROSS OF THE GERMAN MOTHER).

Summer: Day of the Summer Solstice. This special day was celebrated with evening bonfires into which wreaths dedicated to party martyrs or war heroes were thrown. Then the participants leaped across the flames, lit torches from the fires, and joined a procession homeward. Special *Feuersprüche* (fire speeches) were made by party dignitaries to celebrate the day.

September: Reich Party Rally at Nuremberg. The annual celebrations always came to a climax with a three-day festival held in the old city of Nuremberg. There were long marches past Hitler, a consecration of party colors, and the climax, a speech by the Fuehrer. *See also* NUREMBERG RALLIES.

Autumn: Harvest Thanksgiving Day. A day set aside to celebrate the harvest and to pay tribute to the German farmer.

November 9: Anniversary of the 1923 Beer-Hall Putsch. The holiest day of the Nazi regime. Survivors of the abortive Munich *Putsch* of November 8–9, 1923, reenacted their march through the streets of Munich to the Feldherrn Halle (q.v.), where the Nazi movement had been sanctified in blood. *See also* BEER-HALL PUTSCH.

Winter: Day of the Winter Solstice. A celebration designed to take the place of Christian festivals. It did not, however, supplant the Christmas festival season.

HOLOCAUST. Term used to describe Hitler's attempt to exterminate all European Jews. Roughly equivalent to the coined term *genocide* (q.v.), the holocaust refers to the physical destruction of approximately 6 million Jews in Europe. There had been instances of concentrated persecution of Jews throughout history but never before a state-inspired movement of this magnitude carried through systematically and with such terrible consequences.

The young Hitler roaming the streets of Vienna before

World War I felt the impact of the social Darwinism (q.v.) that had intensified hatred for Jews in the nineteenth and twentieth centuries. He absorbed all the pseudoscientific aspects of anti-Semitism (q.v.) and made them the focal points of his own philosophy. He was determined to allow nothing to stand in the way of eliminating the Jewish danger. It was, he said, a life-and-death struggle not only for Austria and Germany but also for the entire world. He had a shrewd understanding of how anti-Semitism could be exploited for political purposes. In the Twenty-five Points of the Deutsche Arbeiterpartei (q.v.), a manifesto issued on February 25, 1920, points 4 and 5 were aimed at the expulsion of Jews from German life. In *Mein Kampf* (q.v.), the blueprint of his ideology, Hitler condemned the Jews as a culture-destroying race. "If, at the beginning [of World War I], someone had only subjected about 12 or 15,000 of these Hebrew enemies of the people to poison gas . . . then the sacrifice of millions at the front would not have been in vain." Very few Germans or Jews understood the significance of that idea buried in the recesses of Hitler's mind.

Hitler's persecution of the Jews began a month after he became Chancellor on January 30, 1933. His first step was a boycott of Jews in response to the "atrocity campaign" led by Jews abroad against the National Socialists. Within weeks Jewish personnel were being dropped from local governments, law courts, and universities; windows of Jewish shops were broken; and synagogues were wrecked. An act promulgated on April 7, 1933, called for the reestablishment of the career civil service and the dismissal of Jews. Non-Aryan doctors were no longer allowed to work in hospitals, Jews were excluded from the cultural life of the nation on the ground that they had overwhelmed the arts, and Jews were forbidden to engage in certain trades and industry. The regular police made no effort to protect the Jews from attack on the streets.

This early anti-Semitic campaign lasted until September 1935. Hitler released the Nuremberg Laws on citizenship and race (q.v.) at a Nazi party rally (*see* NUREMBERG RALLIES). Despite criticism from foreign countries, the anti-Semitic measures were continued, reflecting the central theme of the Fuehrer's philosophy. On July 23, 1938, every Jew was required to apply to the police for an identity card to be shown to the police on demand. On August 17, 1938, male Jews were ordered to add the name Israel and female Jews the name Sara to their non-Jewish first names. On October 5, 1938, it was announced that passports held by Jews for foreign travel would be valid only if marked *J* for Jew. By this time most German Jews were no longer able to earn a living and had to exist on whatever money they had or on private charity.

Meanwhile, Nazi authorities awaited a pretext to bring about the total exclusion of Jews from German national life. It came with the assassination of Ernst vom Rath, a third secretary of the German Embassy in Paris, by Herschel Grynszpan (q.v.) on November 7, 1938. The *Kristallnacht* (q.v.) pogrom, the Night of the Broken Glass, of November 9–10, 1938, was a new wedge in the campaign to destroy the existence of the Jews in Germany. Hermann Goering (q.v.) began to speak about "our final reckoning with the Jews." On January 30, 1939, on the sixth anniversary of his assumption of political power, Hitler spoke to the Reichstag (q.v.) and publicly made a threat of extermination: "If international-financed Jewry inside and outside Europe should succeed once more in plunging nations into another world war, the consequence will not be world Bolshevism and thereby the triumph of Jewry, but the annihilation [*Vernichtung*] of the Jews in Europe."

The precise moment at which Hitler made up his mind that the Jews had to be destroyed physically cannot be determined from the available evidence, but there are some clues. The concentration camp at Auschwitz (q.v.) was set up originally in May 1940, and its first commandant, Rudolf Franz Hoess (q.v.), later stated that he personally received orders from Heinrich Himmler (q.v.) in May 1941 to proceed with the gassing of Jews. On July 31, 1941, Goering ordered Reinhard Heydrich (q.v.) to proceed: "I herewith instruct you to make all necessary preparations as regards organizational, financial, and military matters with a total solution [*Gesamtlösung*] of the Jewish question within the area of German influence in Europe." At the Wannsee Conference (q.v.), held on January 20, 1942, the details were worked out for the "Final Solution" (*see* ENDLÖSUNG, DIE). Heydrich's specialist at SS (q.v.) headquarters, Adolf Eichmann (q.v.), would be responsible for the administrative problems of genocide. Heydrich informed his audience: "Undoubtedly a great number of Jews will disappear through natural diminution [*natürliche Verminderung*]. The remainder that may be able to survive must be treated accordingly, because these people, representing a natural selection, are to be regarded as the germ cell of a new Jewish development. See the experience of history."

Preparations were made at succeeding conferences to organize a mass movement to the concentration camps and extermination camps (qq.v.). The Gestapo and the SD (qq.v.) went to work in the gradually accelerating program to channel Jews to extermination camps. The elimination of Jews from European life in the midst of World War II became a major undertaking of the Nazi regime. What the readers of *Mein Kampf* had regarded as exaggerated political propaganda now became a precise, highly organized procedure to eliminate the Jews by wholesale slaughter.

At the fulcrum of the extermination system in Poland were the camps at Auschwitz, Maidanek, Treblinka, Chełmno, Belzec, and Sobibór (qq.v.). There were in all more than 400 camp centers, but these included transit and evacuation camps for Poles to be sent to the west for slave labor. Auschwitz was the most notorious of the extermination centers. At the height of its activity Auschwitz could house more than 100,000 men and women and could provide for the gassing and incineration of 12,000 prisoners a day. Two SS doctors on duty met the incoming transports, mostly Jews, and made instant decisions. Those who were fit were sent into the camp; others, including all children, were dispatched immediately to the gas chambers. The Auschwitz gas chambers could accommodate 2,000 prisoners at one time. Rudolf Hoess testified at Nuremberg: "When I set up the extermination building at Auschwitz, I used Zyclon B (*see* ZYKLON-B), which was a crystallized prussic acid which we dropped into the death chamber from a small opening. It took from 3 to 15 minutes to kill the people in the death-chamber, depending on climatic conditions. We knew when the people were dead because their screaming stopped. We usually waited for half-an-hour before we opened the doors and removed the bodies. After the bodies were removed our special commandos [*Sonderkommandos*, q.v., made up of prisoners who were partially trusted] took off the rings and extracted the gold teeth of the corpses."

By the winter of 1944 the extermination camps were being threatened by the advancing Russians. At this time Himmler and his SS comrades were beginning to have some reservations about the whole program. It became more and more difficult to dispose of the great hordes of prisoners. The Russians entered Auschwitz in January 1945. During March and April 1945 Himmler made the gesture of releasing some Jewish prisoners for evacuation to Switzerland under the sponsorship of the International Red Cross, but it was too late to undo the ravages of the holocaust. The British and American armies now learned at first hand the extent of the catastrophe.

There was consternation both inside and outside Germany when the scope of the holocaust was realized. There had been countless episodes of torture, brutality, and execution in the past but nothing to compare with this deliberate mass extermination. The SS, in its efficient way, had kept a vast archive of documents that was captured and used to throw light on the crimes which could not have been witnessed by outsiders.

There is general agreement among historians that the holocaust was one of the worst lapses into barbarism in the entire course of civilization. Not only historians but also psychologists, sociologists, psychiatrists, and psychoanalysts have sought a rational explanation. In colleges and universities, study groups and courses have been initiated for the purpose of understanding the tragic phenomenon. The persecution set into motion by the National Socialist regime with diabolical consistency and implemented with cold-blooded efficiency remains a unique phenomenon in history.

Bibliography. Eugen Kogon, *The Theory and Practice of Hell*, tr. by Heinz Norden, Farrar, Straus & Cudahy, New York, 1950; Gerald Reitlinger, *The Final Solution*, A. S. Barnes and Co., Inc., New York, 1961.

HOLY GROUND AND SOIL. *See* HEILIGER GRUND UND BODEN.

HOME EVENING. *See* HEIMABEND.

HONOR CROSS OF THE GERMAN MOTHER. A medal of honor for fertile German mothers. The idea originated with Reich Medical Leader Dr. Gerhardt Wagner, director of the people's health section of the Reich leadership of the party: "The prolific German mother is to be accorded the same place of honor in the German *Volk* community as the combat soldier, since she risks her body and her life for the people and the fatherland as much as the combat soldier does in the roar and thunder of battle." The suggestion was approved by Hitler. The medal was awarded in three classes: bronze for more than four children, silver for more than six, gold for more than eight. The decoration bore the motto: "The Mother Ennobles the Child." On Mothering Sunday, 1939 (*see* HOLIDAYS, NAZI), some 3 million mothers throughout the country were awarded

Bronze Honor Cross of the German Mother.

the medal of honor by party leaders. The celebration was repeated annually on the second Sunday in May. Wearers were provided with miniature replicas for everyday use; the originals were preserved for ceremonial occasions. Members of all youth organizations were expected to salute wearers of the Mother's Honor Cross.

HONORARY ARYANS. Title accorded the Japanese people by Hitler. The Fuehrer's purpose was to justify the German-Japanese agreement on communism signed in Berlin on November 25, 1936. Although the Japanese were of a different race, they were considered by Hitler to possess qualities similar enough to German Nordic characteristics to warrant the designation.

HONORARY LEADER. *See* EHRENFUEHRER.

HORCHER RESTAURANT INCIDENT. A clash between Dr. Paul Joseph Goebbels and Hermann Goering (qq.v.) on the issue of total war in 1943. On February 18, 1943, Goebbels delivered a speech in the Sportpalast (q.v.) on total war. He followed it up by an order to close Berlin's luxury restaurants and places of amusement. Goering promptly intervened to protect his favorite restaurant, Horcher's, from the edict. Some demonstrators, probably instigated by Goebbels, appeared at the restaurant and smashed its windows. The dispute was settled by closing the restaurant to the public but operating it as a private club for the Luftwaffe (q.v.). The incident was one of a number of examples of bad blood existing between the Propaganda Minister and the head of the Luftwaffe.

HORNEY, KAREN (1885–1952). Psychoanalyst and prominent refugee from the Third Reich. Karen Horney was born Karen Danielsen in Blankensee, a village on the Elbe River, on September 16, 1885. Her father was a Norwegian sea captain who had become a German citizen, and her mother was a Dutchwoman descended from south German gentry. Karen studied medicine at the University of Freiburg and married Oskar Horney, a student of law and social science. In her first psychoanalytic paper, published in 1917, she took issue with the theories and teaching of Sigmund Freud, the father of psychoanalysis, and became numbered among his opponents. As instructor and curriculum organizer at the Berlin Psychoanalytic Institute in 1919, she maintained that there are no innate psychological differences between the sexes that can be accounted for by biology, as Freud claimed, and that both men and women are neurotic for the same reasons. In 1932, when the growing Hitler movement made the future of psychoanalysis, which the Nazis called "the Jewish science," very dim in Gèrmany, Karen Horney emigrated to the United States. She continued a successful career, although she was forced from the ranks of the orthodox Freudian circle. Her friends and former patients established in her honor a clinic that was expanded into a large research and training center. She died in New York on December 4, 1952.

Bibliography. Karen Horney, *The Neurotic Personality of Our Time*, W. W. Norton & Company, Inc., New York, 1937.

"HORST WESSEL LIED" ("Horst Wessel Song"). The official marching song of the Nazi party. Horst Wessel was a young Storm Trooper (*see* SA), a student who had broken with his father, a Protestant military chaplain. He preferred to lead the life of a bohemian with a girlfriend in the slums of Berlin. In early 1930 either a love rival or perhaps a Communist invaded Wessel's room and killed him. Dr. Paul Joseph Goebbels (q.v.), chief propagandist for the Nazi party, praised Horst Wessel as a hero and martyr. The young Storm Trooper wrote the lyrics of a marching song that included many of the party's most familiar slogans, and his verses were set to music borrowed from a North Sea fishermen's song. For Dr. Goebbels the "Horst Wessel Song" was exactly the right sort of tune "whose chords would ring out on the barricades of freedom." The following are the first three stanzas:

1.

Die Fahne hoch, die Reihen dicht geschlossen!
S.A. marschiert mit ruhig festem Schritt.
Kam'raden, die Rotfront und Reaktion erschossen,
Marschieren im Geist in unsern Reihen mit.

2.

Die Strasse frei den braunen Bataillonen!
Die Strasse frei dem Sturmabteilungsmann!
Es schaun aufs Hakenkreuz voll Hoffnung schon Millionen,
Der Tag für Freiheit und für Brot bricht an.

3.

Zum letzten Mal wird nun Appell geblasen!
Zum Kämpfe stehn wir alle schon bereit.
Bald flattern Hitlerfahnen über allen Strassen,
Die Knechtschaft dauert nur noch kurze Zeit! . . .

1.

Hold high the banner! Close the hard ranks serried!
S.A. marches on with sturdy stride.
Comrades, by Red Front and Reaction killed, are buried,
But march with us in image at our side.

2.

Gangway! Gangway! now for the Brown battalions!
For the Storm Troopers clear roads o'er land!
The Swastika gives hope to our entranced millions,
The day for freedom and for bread's at hand.

3.

The trumpet blows its shrill and final blast!
Prepared for war and battle here we stand.
Soon Hitler's banners will wave unchecked at last,
The end of German slav'ry in our land! . . .

Translated by the editor.

HOSSBACH, FRIEDRICH (1894–). Hitler's military adjutant from 1934 to 1938. Friedrich Hossbach was born in Unna on November 21, 1894. Starting as a cadet in 1913, he became a career soldier. He was promoted to lieutenant in 1914. In 1934 he became chief of the Central Section of the General Staff and Wehrmacht (q.v.) as well as adjutant to the Fuehrer. In 1935 he was made lieutenant colonel and in 1937 colonel. On November 5, 1937, he played an important role in the conference at the Wilhelmstrasse between Hitler and his top military leaders (*see* HOSSBACH CONFERENCE). The colonel took careful notes of what Hitler said and five days later wrote the highly secret document since known as the Hossbach Memorandum (*Hossbach Niederschrift*, q.v.). This account, which was revealed at the Nuremberg Trial (q.v.), showed Hitler's plans for aggression. The protocol is regarded by historians as a decisive turning point in the history of the Third Reich.

In January 1938, at the height of the Blomberg-Fritsch crisis (q.v.), Hossbach, defying Hitler's orders to maintain silence, went to the apartment of Col. Gen. Werner Freiherr von Fritsch (q.v.) and informed him that he was to be brought up on charges of homosexuality under Section 175 of the German Criminal Code. Two days later Hossbach was dismissed from his post as adjutant to the Fuehrer.

After the outbreak of World War II in 1939, Hossbach was restored to the General Staff. He was promoted to major general (1942), lieutenant general (1942), and general of infantry (1943) as commander of the 16th Panzer Corps. After taking command of the Fourth Army on the Russian front, he was dismissed abruptly by Hitler on January 30, 1945, because he had withdrawn his troops in East Prussia in defiance of Hitler's orders.

HOSSBACH CONFERENCE. A secret meeting at which Hitler informed his closest advisers that he planned to go to war. In speeches to the Reichstag (q.v.) or to foreign correspondents, Hitler always insisted that he wanted peace, but to his intimates he often spoke of the "duty to war." At a meeting held on November 5, 1937, at the Reich Chancellery, he outlined the steps he intended to take in achieving *Lebensraum* (q.v.), or living space, in the east, and the means he would use to provide for its Germanization. With him at the conference were Col. Friedrich Hossbach (q.v.), his military aide; Field Marshal Werner von Blomberg (q.v.), Minister of War; Gen. Werner Freiherr von Fritsch (q.v.), commander in chief of the armed forces; Adm. Erich Raeder (q.v.), commander in chief of the Navy; Col. Gen. Hermann Goering (q.v.), commander in chief of the Luftwaffe (q.v.); and Constantin Freiherr von Neurath (q.v.), Foreign Minister. After pledging his colleagues to secrecy, Hitler informed them of his decisions and urged them to regard his words as a political testament in the event of his death. Colonel Hossbach wrote the record of this conference, which later came to be known as the *Hossbach Niederschrift* (q.v.).

HOSSBACH NIEDERSCHRIFT (Hossbach Memorandum; also called the Hossbach Protocol). The record of the Hossbach Conference (q.v.) held on November 5, 1937, in the Reich Chancellery. Col. Friedrich Hossbach (q.v.), Hitler's Wehrmacht (q.v.) adjutant, wrote the minutes of the conference from his notes five days later. Dated November 10, 1937, the Hossbach Memorandum was introduced in evidence before the International Military Tribunal at Nuremberg on November 24, 1945.

At the conference Hitler began by asserting that the "solid racial core" of the German nation gave it the right to greater *Lebensraum* (q.v.), or living space. The future of Germany depended on satisfaction of its need for space. Expansion could not take place without destroying resistance, and the problem was how to gain the most at the lowest cost. Once it was decided to use force, timing and execution were to be determined. The latest time would be between 1943 and 1945; a date later than those years would be to Germany's disadvantage.

The complete text of the memorandum[1] is given below. For the role of the Hossbach Memorandum in the Taylor–Trevor-Roper controversy on the origins of World War II, *see* TAYLOR, A. J. P.

Berlin, November 10, 1937

MINUTES OF THE CONFERENCE IN THE REICH CHANCELLERY, BERLIN,
NOVEMBER 5, 1937, FROM 4:15 TO 8:30 P.M.

Present: The Führer and Chancellor,
Field Marshal von Blomberg, War Minister,
Colonel General Baron von Fritsch, Commander in Chief, Army,
Admiral Dr. h.c. Raeder, Commander in Chief, Navy,
Colonel General Göring, Commander in Chief, *Luftwaffe*,
Baron von Neurath, Foreign Minister,
Colonel Hossbach.

The Führer began by stating that the subject of the present conference was of such importance that its discussion would, in other countries, certainly be a matter for a full Cabinet meeting, but he—the Führer—had rejected the idea of making it a subject of discussion before the wider circle of the Reich Cabinet just because of the importance of the matter. His exposition to follow was the fruit of thorough deliberation and the experiences of his 4½ years of power. He wished to explain to the gentlemen present his basic ideas concerning the opportunities for the development of our position in the field of foreign affairs and its requirements, and he asked, in the interests of a long-term German policy, that his exposition be regarded, in the event of his death, as his last will and testament.

The Führer then continued:

The aim of German policy was to make secure and to preserve the racial community [*Volksmasse*] and to enlarge it. It was therefore a question of space.

The German racial community comprised over 85 million people and, because of their number and the narrow limits of habitable space in Europe, constituted a tightly packed racial core such as was not to be met in any other country and such as implied the right to a greater living space than in the case of other peoples. If, territorially speaking, there existed no political result corresponding to this German racial core, that was a consequence of centuries of historical development, and in the continuance of these political conditions lay the greatest danger to the preservation of the German race at its present peak. To arrest the decline of Germanism [*Deutschtum*] in Austria and Czechoslovakia was as little possible as to maintain the present level in Germany itself. Instead of increase, sterility was setting in, and in its train disorders of a social character must arise in course of time, since political and ideological ideas remain effective only so long as they furnish the basis for the realization of the essential vital demands of a people. Germany's future was therefore wholly conditional upon the solving of the need for space, and such a solution could be sought, of course, only for a foreseeable period of about one to three generations.

Before turning to the question of solving the need for space, it had to be considered whether a solution holding promise for the future was to be reached by means of autarchy or by means of an increased participation in world economy.

Autarchy

Achievement only possible under strict National Socialist leadership of the State, which is assumed; accepting its achievement as possible, the following could be stated as results:—

A. In the field of raw materials only limited, not total, autarchy.

(1) In regard to coal, so far as it could be considered as a source of raw materials, autarchy was possible.

(2) But even as regards ores, the position was much more difficult. Iron requirements can be met from home resources and similarly with light metals, but with other raw materials—copper, tin—this was not the case.

(3) Synthetic textile requirements can be met from home resources to the limit of timber supplies. A permanent solution is impossible.

(4) Edible fats—possible.

B. In the field of food the question of autarchy was to be answered by a flat "No."

With the general rise in the standard of living compared with that of 30 to 40 years ago, there has gone hand in hand an increased demand and an increased home consumption even on the part of the producers, the farmers. The fruits of the increased agricultural production had all gone to meet the increased demand, and so did not represent an absolute production increase. A further increase in production by making greater demands on the soil, which already, in consequence of the use of artificial fertilizers, was showing signs of exhaustion, was hardly possible, and it was therefore certain that even with the maximum increase in production, participation in world trade was unavoidable. The not inconsiderable expenditure of foreign exchange to insure food supplies by imports, even when harvests were good, grew to catastrophic proportions with bad harvests. The possibility of a disaster grew in proportion to the increase in

[1] Germany, Auswärtiges Amt, *Documents on German Foreign Policy*, Series D, Government Printing Office, Washington, 1949, vol. I, pp. 29–39.

population, in which, too, the excess of births of 560,-000 annually produced, as a consequence, an even further increase in bread consumption, since a child was a greater bread consumer than an adult.

It was not possible over the long run, in a continent enjoying a practically common standard of living, to meet the food supply difficulties by lowering that standard and by rationalization. Since, with the solving of the unemployment problem, the maximum consumption level had been reached, some minor modifications in our home agricultural production might still, no doubt, be possible, but no fundamental alteration was possible in our basic food position. Thus autarchy was untenable in regard both to food and to the economy as a whole.

Participation in World Economy

To this there were limitations which we were unable to remove. The establishment of Germany's position on a secure and sound foundation was obstructed by market fluctuations, and commercial treaties afforded no guarantee for actual execution. In particular it had to be remembered that since the World War, those very countries which had formerly been food exporters had become industrialized. We were living in an age of economic empires in which the primitive urge to colonization was again manifesting itself; in the cases of Japan and Italy economic motives underlay the urge for expansion, and with Germany, too, economic need would supply the stimulus. For countries outside the great economic empires, opportunities for economic expansion were severely impeded.

The boom in world economy caused by the economic effects of rearmament could never form the basis of a sound economy over a long period, and the latter was obstructed above all also by the economic disturbances resulting from Bolshevism. There was a pronounced military weakness in those states which depended for their existence on foreign trade. As our foreign trade was carried on over the sea routes dominated by Britain, it was more a question of security of transport than one of foreign exchange, which revealed, in time of war, the full weakness of our food situation. The only remedy, and one which might appear to us as visionary, lay in the acquisition of greater living space—a quest which has at all times been the origin of the formation of states and of the migration of peoples. That this quest met with no interest at Geneva or among the satiated nations was understandable. If, then, we accept the security of our food situation as the principal question, the space necessary to insure it can only be sought in Europe, not, as in the liberal-capitalist view, in the exploitation of colonies. It is not a matter of acquiring population but of gaining space for agricultural use. Moreover, areas producing raw materials can be more usefully sought in Europe in immediate proximity to the Reich, than overseas; the solution thus obtained must suffice for one or two generations. Whatever else might prove necessary later must be left to succeeding generations to deal with. The development of great world political constellations progressed but slowly after all, and the German people with its strong racial core would find the most favorable prerequisites for such achievement in the heart of the continent of Europe. The history of all ages—the Roman Empire and the British Empire—had proved that expansion could only be carried out by breaking down resistance and taking risks; setbacks were inevitable. There had never in former times been spaces without a master, and there were none today; the attacker always comes up against a possessor.

The question for Germany ran: where could she achieve the greatest gain at the lowest cost?

German policy had to reckon with two hate-inspired antagonists, Britain and France, to whom a German colossus in the center of Europe was a thorn in the flesh, and both countries were opposed to any further strengthening of Germany's position either in Europe or overseas; in support of this opposition they were able to count on the agreement of all their political parties. Both countries saw in the establishment of German military bases overseas a threat to their own communications, a safeguarding of German commerce, and, as a consequence, a strengthening of Germany's position in Europe.

Because of opposition of the Dominions, Britain could not cede any of her colonial possessions to us. After England's loss of prestige through the passing of Abyssinia into Italian possession, the return of East Africa was not to be expected. British concessions could at best be expressed in an offer to satisfy our colonial demands by the appropriation of colonies which were not British possessions—e.g., Angola. French concessions would probably take a similar line.

Serious discussion of the question of the return of colonies to us could only be considered at a moment when Britain was in difficulties and the German Reich armed and strong. The Führer did not share the view that the Empire was unshakable. Opposition to the Empire was to be found less in the countries conquered than among her competitors. The British Empire and the Roman Empire could not be compared in respect of permanence; the latter was not confronted by any powerful political rival of a serious order after the Punic Wars. It was only the disintegrating effect of Christianity, and the symptoms of age which appear in every country, which caused ancient Rome to succumb to the onslaught of the Germans.

Beside the British Empire there exist today a number of states stronger than she. The British motherland was able to protect her colonial possessions not by her own power, but only in alliance with other states. How, for instance, could Britain alone defend Canada against attack by America, or her Far Eastern interests against attack by Japan!

The emphasis on the British Crown as the symbol of the unity of the Empire was already an admission that, in the long run, the Empire could not maintain its position by power politics. Significant indications of this were:

(*a*) The struggle of Ireland for independence.

(*b*) The constitutional struggles in India, where Britain's half measures had given to the Indians the opportunity of using later on as a weapon against Britain, the nonfulfillment of her promises regarding a constitution.

(*c*) The weakening by Japan of Britain's position in the Far East.

(*d*) The rivalry in the Mediterranean with Italy who—under the spell of her history, driven by necessity and led by a genius—was expanding her power position, and thus was inevitably coming more and more into conflict with British interests. The outcome of the Abyssinian War was a loss of prestige for Britain which Italy was striving to increase by stirring up trouble in the Mohammedan world.

To sum up, it could be stated that, with 45 million Britons, in spite of its theoretical soundness, the position of the Empire could not in the long run be maintained by power politics. The ratio of the population of the Empire to that of the motherland of 9:1, was a warning to us not, in our territorial expansion, to allow the foundation constituted by the numerical strength of our own people to become too weak.

France's position was more favorable than that of Britain. The French Empire was better placed territorially; the inhabitants of her colonial possessions represented a supplement to her military strength. But France was going to be confronted with internal political difficulties. In a nation's life about 10 percent of its span is taken up by parliamentary forms of government and about 90 percent by authoritarian forms. Today, nonetheless, Britain, France, Russia, and the smaller states adjoining them, must be included as factors [*Machtfaktoren*] in our political calculations.

Germany's problem could only be solved by means of force and this was never without attendant risk. The campaigns of Frederick the Great for Silesia and Bismarck's wars against Austria and France had involved unheard-of risk, and the swiftness of the Prussian action in 1870 had kept Austria from entering the war. If one accepts as the basis of the following exposition the resort to force with its attendant risks, then there remain still to be answered the questions "when" and "how." In this matter there were three cases [*Fälle*] to be dealt with:

Case 1: Period 1943–1945

After this date only a change for the worse, from our point of view, could be expected.

The equipment of the army, navy, and *Luftwaffe*, as well as the formation of the officer corps, was nearly completed. Equipment and armament were modern; in further delay there lay the danger of their obsolescence. In particular, the secrecy of "special weapons" could not be preserved forever. The recruiting of reserves was limited to current age groups; further drafts from older untrained age groups were no longer available.

Our relative strength would decrease in relation to the rearmament which would by then have been carried out by the rest of the world. If we did not act by 1943–45, any year could, in consequence of a lack of reserves, produce the food crisis, to cope with which the necessary foreign exchange was not available, and this must be regarded as a "warning point of the regime." Besides, the world was expecting our attack and was increasing its countermeasures from year to year. It was while the rest of the world was still preparing its defenses [*sich abriegeln*] that we were obliged to take the offensive.

Nobody knew today what the situation would be in the years 1943–45. One thing only was certain, that we could not wait longer.

On the one hand there was the great *Wehrmacht*, and the necessity of maintaining it at its present level, the aging of the movement and of its leaders; and on the other, the prospect of a lowering of the standard of living and of a limitation of the birth rate, which left no choice but to act. If the Führer was still living, it was his unalterable resolve to solve Germany's problem of space at the latest by 1943–45. The necessity for action before 1943–45 would arise in cases 2 and 3.

Case 2

If internal strife in France should develop into such a domestic crisis as to absorb the French Army completely and render it incapable of use for war against Germany, then the time for action against the Czechs had come.

Case 3

If France is so embroiled by a war with another state that she cannot "proceed" against Germany.

For the improvement of our politico-military position our first objective, in the event of our being embroiled in war, must be to overthrow Czechoslovakia and Austria simultaneously in order to remove the threat to our flank in any possible operation against the west. In a conflict with France it was hardly to be regarded as likely that the Czechs would declare war on us on the very same day as France. The desire to join in the war would, however, increase among the Czechs in proportion to any weakening on our part and then her participation could clearly take the form of an attack toward Silesia, toward the north or toward the west.

If the Czechs were overthrown and a common German-Hungarian frontier achieved, a neutral attitude on the part of Poland could be the more certainly counted on in the event of a Franco-German conflict. Our agreements with Poland only retained their force as long as Germany's strength remained unshaken. In the event of German setbacks a Polish action against East Prussia, and possibly against Pomerania and Silesia as well, had to be reckoned with.

On the assumption of a development of the situation leading to action on our part as planned, in the years 1943–45, the attitude of France, Britain, Italy, Poland, and Russia could probably be estimated as follows:

Actually, the Führer believed that almost certainly Britain, and probably France as well, had already tacitly written off the Czechs and were reconciled to the fact that this question would be cleared up in due course by Germany. Difficulties connected with the Empire, and the prospect of being once more entangled in a protracted European war, were decisive considerations for Britain against participation in a war against Germany. Britain's attitude would certainly not be without influence on that of France. An attack by France without British support, and with the prospect of the offensive being brought to a standstill on our western fortifications, was hardly probable. Nor was a French march through Belgium and Holland without British support to be expected; this also was a course not to be contemplated by us in the event of a conflict with France, because it would certainly entail the hostility of Britain. It would of course be necessary to maintain a strong defense [*eine Abriegelung*] on our western frontier during the prosecution of our attack on the Czechs and Austria. And in this connection it had to be remembered that the defense measures of the Czechs were growing in strength from year to year, and that the actual worth of the Austrian Army also was increasing in the course of time. Even though the populations concerned, especially of Czechoslovakia, were not sparse, the annexation of Czechoslovakia and Austria would mean an acquisition of foodstuffs for 5 to 6 million people, on the assumption that the compulsory emigration of 2 million people from Czechoslovakia and 1 million people from Austria was practicable. The incorporation of these two States with Germany meant, from the politico-military point of view, a substantial advantage because it would mean shorter and better frontiers, the freeing of forces for other purposes, and the possibility of creating new units up to a level of about 12 divisions, that is, 1 new division per million inhabitants.

Italy was not expected to object to the elimination of the Czechs, but it was impossible at the moment to estimate what her attitude on the Austrian question would be; that depended essentially upon whether the Duce were still alive.

The degree of surprise and the swiftness of our action were decisive factors for Poland's attitude. Poland—with Russia at her rear—will have little inclination to engage in war against a victorious Germany.

Military intervention by Russia must be countered by the swiftness of our operations; however, whether such an intervention was a practical contingency at all was, in view of Japan's attitude, more than doubtful.

Should case 2 arise—the crippling of France by civil war—the situation thus created by the elimination of the most dangerous opponent must be seized upon *whenever it occurs* for the blow against the Czechs.

The Führer saw case 3 coming definitely nearer; it might emerge from the present tensions in the Mediterranean, and he was resolved to take advantage of it whenever it happened, even as early as 1938.

In the light of past experience, the Führer did not see any early end to the hostilities in Spain. If one considered the length of time which Franco's offensives had taken up till now, it was fully possible that the war would continue another 3 years. On the other hand, a 100 percent victory for Franco was not desirable either, from the German point of view; rather were we interested in a continuance of the war and in the keeping up of the tension in the Mediterranean. Franco in undisputed possession of the Spanish Peninsula precluded the possibility of any further intervention on the part of the Italians or of their continued occupation of the Balearic Islands. As our interest lay more in the prolongation of the war in Spain, it must be the immediate aim of our policy to strengthen Italy's rear with a view to her remaining in the Balearics. But the permanent establishment of the Italians on the Balearics would be intolerable both to France and Britain, and might lead to a war of France and England against Italy—a war in which Spain, should she be entirely in the hands of the Whites, might make her appearance on the side of Italy's enemies. The probability of Italy's defeat in such a war was slight, for the road from Germany was open for the supplementing of her raw materials. The Führer pictured the military strategy for Italy thus: on her western frontier with France she would remain on the defensive, and carry on the war against France from Libya against the French North African colonial possessions.

As a landing by Franco-British troops on the coast of Italy could be discounted, and a French offensive over the Alps against northern Italy would be very difficult and would probably come to a halt before the strong Italian fortifications, the crucial point [*Schwerpunkt*] of the operations lay in North Africa. The threat to French lines of communication by the Italian Fleet would to a great extent cripple the transportation of forces from North Africa to France, so that France would have only home forces at her disposal on the frontiers with Italy and Germany.

If Germany made use of this war to settle the Czech and Austrian questions, it was to be assumed that Britain—herself at war with Italy—would decide not to act against Germany. Without British support, a warlike action by France against Germany was not to be expected.

The time for our attack on the Czechs and Austria must be made dependent on the course of the Anglo-French-Italian war and would not necessarily coincide with the commencement of military operations by these three States. Nor had the Führer in mind military agreements with Italy, but wanted, while retaining his own independence of action, to exploit this favorable situation, which would not occur again, to begin and carry through the campaign against the Czechs. This descent upon the Czechs would have to be carried out with "lightning speed."

In appraising the situation Field Marshal von Blomberg and Colonel General von Fritsch repeatedly emphasized the necessity that Britain and France must not appear in the role of our enemies, and stated that the French Army would not be so committed by the war with Italy that France could not at the same time enter the field with forces superior to ours on our western frontier. General von Fritsch estimated the probable French forces available for use on the Alpine frontier at approximately twenty divisions, so that a strong French superiority would still remain on the western frontier, with the role, according to the German view, of invading the Rhineland. In this matter, moreover, the advanced state of French defense preparations [*Mobilmachung*] must be taken into particular account, and it must be remembered apart from the insignificant value of our present fortifications—on which Field Marshal von Blomberg laid special emphasis—that the four motorized divisions intended for the West were still more or less incapable of movement. In regard to our offensive toward the southeast, Field Marshal von Blomberg drew particular attention to the strength of the Czech fortifications, which had acquired by now a structure like a Maginot Line and which would gravely hamper our attack.

General von Fritsch mentioned that this was the very purpose of a study which he had ordered made this winter, namely, to examine the possibility of conducting operations against the Czechs with special reference to overcoming the Czech fortification system; the General further expressed his opinion that under existing circumstances he must give up his plan to go abroad on his leave, which was due to begin on November 10. The Führer dismissed this idea on the ground that the possibility of a conflict need not yet be regarded as so imminent. To the Foreign Minister's objection that an Anglo-French-Italian conflict was not yet within such a measurable distance as the Führer seemed to assume, the Führer put the summer of 1938 as the date which seemed to him possible for this. In reply to considerations offered by Field Marshal von Blomberg and General von Fritsch regarding the attitude of Britain and France, the Führer repeated his previous statements that he was convinced of Britain's nonparticipation, and therefore he did not believe in the probability of belligerent action by France against Germany. Should the Mediterranean conflict under discussion lead to a general mobilization in Europe, then we must immediately begin action against the Czechs. On the other hand, should the powers not engaged in the war declare themselves disinterested, then Germany would have to adopt a similar attitude to this for the time being.

Colonel General Göring thought that, in view of the Führer's statement, we should consider liquidating our military undertakings in Spain. The Führer agrees to this with the limitation that he thinks he should reserve a decision for a proper moment.

The second part of the conference was concerned with concrete questions of armament.

HOSSBACH

CERTIFIED CORRECT:
Colonel (General Staff)

HOUSE OF GERMAN ART. A building constructed in Munich by Hitler to exhibit what he considered to be the best paintings produced by Nazi artists. On October 15, 1933, the Fuehrer solemnly laid the cornerstone for the House of German Art. During the next four years, he worked with one of his favorite younger architects, Albert Speer (q.v.), on the pseudoclassical structure. He was highly elated by its appearance, which he regarded as "unparalleled and inimitable." The building was formally opened in the summer of 1937. In his dedicatory speech, made on July 18, 1937, Hitler denounced "neurotic artists who produce stupid and insolent nonsense. . . . With the opening of this exhibition has come the end of artistic lunacy and the artistic pollution of our people."

The first exhibition showed some 900 works by Nazi artists, selected from 15,000 submitted. Modern German artists of great reputation, including Oskar Kokoschka and George Grosz (qq.v.), were deliberately excluded (*see* ENTARTETE KUNST). Hitler himself made the final selection. It was reported that in viewing examples of modern art he lost his temper and kicked holes in several of them with his jackboot. *See also* ART IN THE THIRD REICH.

HÜBENER, HELMUTH GÜNTHER (1925–1942). A seventeen-year-old youth sentenced to death for listening to foreign broadcasts. Helmuth Günther Hübener was born in Hamburg on January 8, 1925. A locksmith's apprentice, he joined the junior section of the Hitler Jugend (q.v.), the Hitler Youth, in 1938 and later became a member of the Hitler Youth proper. In August 1942 he was arrested for listening to foreign broadcasts and for spreading the news he had heard. He was simultaneously accused of plotting high treason and treacherously supporting the enemy. He was further charged with mimeographing and distributing British bulletins on the war situation. The court casebook stated: "The handbills contained insults and insinuations against the Fuehrer and his lieutenants and inflammatory attacks on the institutions of National Socialism." Young Hübener was executed on October 27, 1942.

HUBER, KURT (1893–1943). Professor of philosophy and psychology who was executed by the Nazi regime. Kurt Huber was born on October 24, 1893, in Chur, Switzerland, where his father was a schoolmaster. After his family moved to Württemberg, Kurt studied music and philosophy at the University of Munich and took his doctorate in 1917. He became a regular lecturer at Munich in 1925 and a professor in 1926. In 1937 he set up a folk song department for German music research but came into disagreement with Nazi officials. Opposed to Nazi *Gleichschaltung* (q.v.), or coordination, he became associated with student Resistance (q.v.) movements, especially with the White Rose group (*see* WEISSE ROSE), which included Hans and Sophie Scholl (q.v.). In early 1943 Huber drafted a leaflet that was scattered in the courtyard of the University of Munich by the Scholls and others: "In the name of German youth we demand of Adolf Hitler that he return to us the personal freedom which is the most valuable possession of each German, and of which he has cheated us in the lowest possible manner." Huber was arrested by the Gestapo (q.v.) and, with two of his students, sentenced to death. He was beheaded on July 13, 1943.

Kurt Huber. [*From Annedore Leber (ed.),* Conscience in Revolt, *tr. by Rosemary O'Neill, Vallentine, Mitchell & Co., Ltd., London, 1957*]

HUCH, RICARDA (1864–1947). Poet, historian, and anti-Nazi intellectual. Ricarda Huch was born in Braunschweig on July 18, 1864. She was awarded her doctorate in history at Zürich in 1892, worked there for a short time in the city library, and then taught in Bremen. A prolific writer, she was a leader of the neoromantic school and opposed naturalistic tendencies in modern German literature. She was known for her tender poems revealing a passionate love for life and for beauty. Later she turned to the production of historical works, including an analysis of the earlier romantic movement and a dynamic treatment of the Thirty Years' War. In 1933, after Hitler became Chancellor, she resigned from the Prussian Academy of Fine Arts in protest against the Nazi dismissal of Jewish members. She spoke plainly in her letter of resignation: "What the present Government prescribes as national beliefs is not my idea of Germanism. Centralization, the use of force, brutal methods, defamation of opponents, and boasting self-praise, are disastrous. My views differ so much from the opinions of the State that I can no longer remain a member of a State Academy." She died in Schönberg im Taunus on November 17, 1947.

HUGENBERG, ALFRED (1865–1951). Industrialist and spokesman for heavy industry in the 1920s. Alfred Hugenberg was born in Hannover on June 19, 1865. An energetic nationalist, he was the cofounder of the Alldeutscher Verband (Pan-German League), devoted to the task of including all Germans in an expanded empire. In 1894 he was on a board in Posen (Poznań) organized to buy land, mainly from the Poles, and settle Germans there. In 1900 he was instrumental in the organization of agricultural societies, and in 1903 he was active in the Prussian Finance Ministry. From 1909 to 1918 he was chairman of the board of the Krupp firm, whose finances he administered with considerable success. Meanwhile, from 1916 on, he built up his own Hugenberg interests. A self-made man, he amassed a fortune by combining business with politics. Buying up newspapers, he gained control of the Scherl publishing house; the Telegraphen Union, another publishing firm; and UFA, a large film company. By this time he was recognized as Germany's Lord of Film and Press.

In 1928 Hugenberg became chairman of the Deutschnationale Volkspartei (German Nationalist People's party), of which he remained the leader until its dissolution. He fought against the parliamentarianism of the Weimar Republic (q.v.), ridiculed its constitution, and assailed the 1928 Young Plan (q.v.) on reparations. On October 11, 1931, with other rightist party members including Hitler's Nazis, he joined the Harzburg Front (q.v.), which failed when Hitler withdrew his support. Hugenberg played an important role in the involved negotiations that eventually led Hitler to the chancellorship. In the elections of July 31, 1932, Hugenberg's Nationalist party, the only one to support Franz von Papen (q.v.), was overwhelmingly defeated. On August 13, 1932, when Hitler insisted that he himself be made Chancellor, Hugenberg withheld his support. Although he served in the Cabinet of Chancellor Kurt von Schleicher (q.v.), Hugenberg then decided to go along with Hitler. The latter used Hugenberg in the days before he became Chancellor, and Hugenberg was rewarded with an appointment as Minister of Agriculture in Hitler's first Cabinet.

In the elections of March 5, 1933, the Nationalists led by Von Papen and Hugenberg were disappointed by a vote of 3,136,760, or a mere 8 percent of votes cast. Hugenberg's hopes of controlling Hitler's new National Socialist government were illusory. On June 26, 1933, after being forsaken by President Paul von Hindenburg (q.v.) and observing Nazi Storm Troopers (*see* SA) attack youngsters who were sympathetic to the Nationalist party, Hugenberg resigned. The Nationalist party, along with others, was dissolved. Hugenberg died in Kükenbruch bei Rinteln on March 12, 1951.

HUMPS, GERTRUD. *See* JUNGE, GERTRUD.

HUNDERTSCHAFTEN (Hundreds). Action squads of Storm Troopers (*see* SA) of the Nazi party existing until 1923. For this private army Hitler recruited followers who would be "as hard as Krupp steel." He set the age range for new recruits at from seventeen to twenty-three. From these units he demanded *Kadavergehorsam* (blind obedience).

HUNTING UNITS. *See* JAGDVERBÄNDE.

I

"I DECIDE WHO IS OR IS NOT A JEW" to IVS

"I DECIDE WHO IS OR IS NOT A JEW." *See* "WER JUDE IST, BESTIMME ICH."

IDEOLOGICAL SCHOOLING. *See* WELTANSCHAULICHE SCHULUNG.

IG FARBEN. Shortened form of Interessen Gemeinschaft Farbenindustrie Aktiengesellschaft (Community of Interests of Dye Industries, Incorporated), also called IG Farbenindustrie, A.G. The "community of interests" part of the name represented in reality the word *monopoly*, or cartel, but the IG firm preferred its own interpretation. The full name was deceptive, for dyestuffs were only a part of IG's chemical production, and chemicals were only a part of IG's total production.

IG Farben was the largest and most powerful German cartel. The cartel was a modern step in a series of business devices designed to control trade and production, stifle competition, and keep prices high. It took the form of an agreement between professedly independent firms. The cartel covered every possible procedure, from the setting of production quotas to the sharing of trademarks and patents and the splitting of profits. Competing monopolies in several countries were obligated to stay within assigned areas and share the market. Above all, they agreed to control prices. The entire cartel system ran counter to the precepts of free trade.

Germany was a late entrant in the industrial arena of the nineteenth century. German merchants found a world that had already been penetrated by the traders of other nations. In the commercial battle against the entrenched industrial nations, Germany had to compete in every possible way Unhampered by obsolescent equipment and methods, Germans were free to take over the processes of the new industry at their best and highest efficiency. Among new methods was the cartel system. The German cartel movement began shortly after the Franco-Prussian War of 1870–1871. The stage was set for an aggressive business approach in capturing foreign markets. In the United States there took place a countermovement against trusts and monopolies, epitomized in the Sherman Antitrust Act and President Theodore Roosevelt's trust-busting, but in Germany there was no such opposition. The cartels did their service for the fatherland in both World War I and World War II. Laws designed to limit the strength of cartels during the Weimar Republic (q.v.) were never effective. After Hitler came to political power in 1933, the German cartel movement reached its final high point. Cartels became compulsory for the entire economy. The state now had the power to force outsiders into existing cartels and to form new ones. Representatives of the cartels acted as efficiently within the Nazi bureaucracy as they had in their own organizations.

IG Farben was the most powerful combine in the Third Reich. During World War II it controlled some 900 chemical factories inside Germany and in the occupied territories, supplied the Wehrmacht (q.v.) with 85 percent of its explosives, and produced almost all the synthetic tires that kept the Nazi war machine rolling. It presented to the government an annual bill of at least $1 billion. IG Farben had at its command an army of scientists, industrialists, statesmen, spies, saboteurs, and conspirators. It was highly experienced in the art of controlling corporations and accumulating stocks of raw materials.

Party to 2,000 cartel agreements distributed throughout the world, IG Farben manufactured forty-three major products which it distributed everywhere. It controlled some 500 firms in ninety-two countries. Its cartel agreements were made with such major companies as Standard Oil of New Jersey, the Aluminum Company of America, Dow Chemical Company, E. I. du Pont de Nemours & Co., Ethyl Export Corporation, Imperial Chemical Industries (Great Britain), Établissements Kuhlmann (France), and Mitsui (Japan). During the late days of the Hitler regime, IG Farben used the extermination camp at Auschwitz (q.v.; *see* EXTERMINATION CAMPS) as a site for one of its synthetic coal oil and rubber plants, which it found suitable especially because of the supply of cheap labor. Its officers were later held accountable for this action (*see* IG FARBEN TRIALS).

Bibliography. Richard Sasuly, *I. G. Farben*, Boni & Gaer, New York, 1947.

IG FARBEN TRIALS. The trials of twenty-four leading officials of IG Farben (q.v.) after World War II. According to Section 12 of the Potsdam Agreement, signed on August 2, 1945, the German economy was to be decentralized "for the purpose of eliminating the present excessive concentration of economic power as exemplified in particular by cartels, syndicates, trusts, and other monopolistic arrangements." Previous to this announcement, a directive (JCS 1067) to Gen. Dwight D. Eisenhower called for the industrial disarmament of Germany. IG Farben was described as a major threat to the peace and security of the postwar world as long as such industries remained under German control. Because IG Farben had been implicated in activities at concentration camps and extermination camps (qq.v.), its directors were brought to trial for willfully engaging in questionable practices that had been deemed indispensable to Germany's war effort. This was the first such indictment against businessmen in history.

The IG Farben directors were charged with the enslavement and mass murder of foreign workers as well as with "the plunder and spoliation of public and private properties in the invaded countries." The trials took place in an atmosphere of tension between the United States and the Soviet Union. Zeal for decartelization had lessened in Washington, where there was a growing realization that the economic potential of Germany must be utilized as a means of halting Russian expansion. The prosecution of IG Farben officials and the entire program of decartelization were allowed to lapse. IG Farben executives, including Max Ilgner, Günther Frank-Fahle, and Georg von Schnitzler, were released from prison.

ILLUSTRIERTER BEOBACHTER (Illustrated Observer). An illustrated magazine used by the Nazi party as a complement to the *Völkischer Beobachter* (q.v.), the Nazi daily newspaper. Published by the Eher Verlag (q.v.), official publishers for the Nazi party throughout its existence, the first edition of the *Illustrierter Beobachter* appeared in November 1926 as a monthly. Composed of a combination of photographs and text, it was designed to appeal to a public that liked picture magazines. The front page of the first edition showed members of the Bamberger Nationalist party marching in front of a synagogue on German Day (October 10, 1926). Inside a photograph of Jacob Rosny Rosenstein, who was being considered for the Nobel Prize for Literature, was distorted to give him the appearance of an ape. The accompanying article denounced him as "a disgrace to German culture." To illustrate an article titled "Der Talmud," one picture showed a religious Jew eyeing a naked woman, and another depicted Jesus nailed to the Cross and a religious Jew setting fire to his feet.

The strongly polemical tone of the *Illustrierter Beobachter* was maintained after Hitler assumed political power. Because of its popularity, it now appeared as a biweekly. The issue of December 30, 1943, was devoted to glorifying German heroes on the Russian front and criticizing the "gangster" behavior of American troops. Several pages were reprinted from the "Jewish" magazine *Life*, revealing how American soldiers were being trained to kill from behind "like a vicious cat," using a knife, a piano wire, or a club. The text explained that American Indians at one time killed their enemies from behind in this fashion.

The final edition of the *Illustrierter Beobachter* appeared on April 13, 1944. Although the Third Reich was on the verge of defeat, the editors still worked hard at the task of maintaining morale in a deteriorating situation. One picture showed a war widow with two happy little children who were to be sent by the government to study medicine at a university when they grew up. Scenes from the Italian front were included as proof that the enemy Allies were destroying cultural monuments and ancient art, such as a picture of *Torso des Benedict* without a head. Theater audiences, mostly women and children, were shown as happy and enthusiastic despite the heavy Allied bombings.

ILONA. Code name for a contemplated attack on Spain in 1942. In a war directive dated May 29, 1942, Hitler issued instructions for operations against Unoccupied France and the Iberian Peninsula. The code names Attila and Isabella had previously been used for these intended operations. Attila was changed to Anton, and Isabella to Ilona.

IN PLAIN GERMAN. *See* AUF GUT DEUTSCH.

INDO-EUROPEAN RACE. *See* RACIAL DOCTRINE.

INDO-GERMANIC RACE. *See* RACIAL DOCTRINE.

INDUSTRIEKLUB (Industry Club). A wealthy and influential organization of industrial magnates in Düsseldorf. On January 27, 1932, Hitler's friends maneuvered industrialist Fritz Thyssen (q.v.) to invite the Nazi leader to address the Industrieklub. For two and one-half hours the up-and-coming politician talked to his initially skeptical audience. He was given a deafening round of applause by the industrialists at the end of his speech. *See also* DÜSSELDORF SPEECH.

INTELLIGENCE AGENT. *See* VERTRAUENSMANN.

INT (International Military Tribunal). *See* NUREMBERG TRIAL.

INTEREST SLAVERY. *See* ZINSKNECHTSCHAFT.

INTERNATIONALE VEREINIGUNG ERNSTER BIBELFORSCHER (IVS; International Organization of Serious Bible Researchers). The German branch of Jehovah's Witnesses, a worldwide religious organization founded by Charles Russell. Established in 1927 during the Weimar Republic (q.v.), the German community numbered 6,034 when Hitler assumed the chancellorship in 1933. Of these, 5,911 were arrested from 1933 to 1935 because of their refusal to be coordinated into the Nazi state, primarily because they declined to take an oath of allegiance to the Fuehrer. They were declared to be enemies of the state, and more than 2,000 members of the organization either were executed or died of ill treatment, disease, or overwork in concentration camps and extermination camps (qq.v.).

IRON CROSS. *See* EISERNES KREUZ.

IRON FRONT. *See* EISERNE FRONT.

IRON GUARD. The Romanian fascist organization.

ISABELLA. Original code name for the operation designed to take over the Iberian Peninsula. The name was later changed to Ilona (q.v.).

IVS. *See* INTERNATIONALE VEREINIGUNG ERNSTER BIBELFORSCHER.

J

JABO
to
JUSTICE IN THE THIRD REICH

JABO. *See* JAGDBOMBER.

JACKSON, ROBERT H[OUGHWOUT] (1892–1954). Chief American prosecutor at the International Military Tribunal in Nuremberg. Robert Houghwout Jackson was born in Spring Creek, Pennsylvania, on February 13, 1892. Educated at Albany Law School, he was admitted to the New York bar in 1913 and began his practice in Jamestown. A member of the firm of Jackson, Herrick, Durkin, and Leet, he served on the New York State Committee to Investigate the Administration of Justice. A Democrat, an Episcopalian, and a Mason, he was sent to Nuremberg to head the American team for the prosecution, which included Brig. Gen. Telford Taylor (q.v.), T. J. Dodd, and other experts.

Jackson, a lawyer with a deep sense of idealism, came to the trial in the belief that aggressive war was a crime and that individuals who acted on behalf of their governments were to be held responsible for what hitherto had been considered acts of state. While the indictments were being prepared, he said in London: "We want this group of nations to stand up and say, as we have said to our people, as President Roosevelt said to the people, as members of the Cabinet said to the people, that launching a war is an act of aggression and that no political or economic situation can justify it. If that is wrong, then we have been wrong in a good many things in the United States which helped the countries under attack before we entered the war."

Prosecutor Jackson delivered the opening address on November 21, 1945. He described the way in which the Nazi party rose to power with the aid of the SA (q.v.), "who terrorized and silenced democratic opposition and were able at length to combine with political opportunists, militarists, industrialists, monarchists, and political reactionaries." Less than a month after the Nazis took power, the Reichstag fire (q.v.) was used as a pretext to give Hitler dictatorial power. Labor unions were abolished, and both Protestants and Catholics were persecuted. Jackson described the crimes against the Jews as "the most savage and numerous crimes planned and committed by the Nazis." Some 60 percent of the Jews in Nazi-dominated Europe—about 5.7 million—were murdered. "History does not record a crime perpetrated against so many victims or ever carried out with such calculated cruelty. . . . Our proof will be disgusting, and you will say I have robbed you of your sleep. But these are the things that have turned the stomach of the world, and set every civilized hand against Nazi Germany." The prosecutor further accused the defendants of murdering prisoners of war and hostages, plundering art treasures in occupied countries, enforcing slave labor and starvation, and carrying on war against civilian populations based on the "master race" ideology. Jackson summed up the moral and legal aspects of the trial: "The real complaining party at your bar is civilization. . . . The refuge of the defendants can be only their hope that international law will lag so far behind the moral sense of mankind that conduct which is a crime in the moral sense must be regarded as innocence in law. We challenge that proposition."

These concepts were stressed by Jackson throughout the trial. Again and again he clashed with Hermann Goering (q.v.). The opening interchange on cross-examination:

> JACKSON: "You are perhaps aware that you are the only living man who can espouse to us the true purposes of the Nazi Party and the inner workings of the leadership?"
>
> GOERING: "I am perfectly aware of that."
>
> JACKSON: "You, from the very beginning, together with those who were associated with you, intended to overthrow and later did overthrow the Weimar Republic [q.v.]?"
>
> GOERING: "That was, as far as I was concerned, my firm intention."

When Jackson asked about preparations for the occupation of the Rhineland that were being kept secret, Goering replied: "I do not think that I can recall beforehand the publication of the mobilization preparations of the United States." Toward the end of the trial Jackson told the court: "It would be a greater catastrophe to acquit the organiza-

Robert H. Jackson. [*Courtesy of the Library of Congress*]

tions [accused of being criminal] than it should be to acquit the entire 22 individual defendants in the box."

In his summation on July 26, 1946, Jackson stated that the accused had been given the kind of trial which they, in the days of their pomp and power, never gave to any man. "We now have before us the tested evidences of criminality and have heard the flimsy excuses and paltry evasions of the defendants. The suspended judgment with which we opened the case is no longer appropriate. The time has come for final judgment and if the case I present seems hard and uncompromising, it is because the evidence makes it so. . . . If you were to say of these men that they are not guilty, it would be true to say there has been no war, there have been no slain, there has been no crime." *See also* NUREMBERG TRIAL.

Bibliography. R. W. Cooper, *The Nuremberg Trial,* Penguin Books, Harmondsworth, England, 1947; Eugene Davidson, *The Trial of the Germans: Nuremberg, 1945–1946,* The Macmillan Company, New York, 1966.

JAFUE. *See* JAGDFLIEGERFUEHRER.

JAGDBOMBER (Jabo; Fighter Bomber). A light bomber aircraft in the Luftwaffe (q.v.).

JAGDFLIEGERFUEHRER (Jafue; Fighter Aircraft Leader). Chief field commander of the Luftwaffe (q.v.).

JAGDGESCHWADER (JG; Fighter Group). A Luftwaffe (q.v.) group composed of three *Gruppen,* or wings (*see* GRUPPE).

JAGDVERBÄNDE (Hunting Units). Units of the SS (q.v.) devoted to sabotage and subversion. They were under the direction of Otto Skorzeny (q.v.).

JAHN, ERICH (1907–). Berlin youth leader. Erich Jahn was born in Berlin on July 23, 1907, the son of a printer. While in his teens he joined the Bismarck Bund, a Berlin youth organization, but turned to the Nazis in 1929. He rose quickly in the leadership of the Hitler Jugend (q.v.), the Hitler Youth, in Greater Berlin and also played a role in the national organization.

JASPERS, KARL (1883–1969). Philosopher and critic of National Socialism. Karl Jaspers was born in Oldenburg on February 23, 1883, the son of a bank director. In 1913 he became a *Privatdozent* (unsalaried lecturer) at the University of Heidelberg and in 1916 professor of psychology and philosophy there. Jaspers was one of the early apostles of existentialism, whose main premise is that because man exists he can shape his own destiny by the exercise of his will in the face of a given set of potentialities. Man has freedom of choice and action, through which he can influence other people; hence, every individual is responsible to humanity as a whole. Such views brought Jaspers into conflict with National Socialism and made him *persona non grata* with Hitler. The Fuehrer was even more deeply disturbed by Jaspers's insistence that Nazi racial theories and mass mysticism had no place in German culture (*see* RACIAL DOCTRINE). To Jaspers Nazism was "a seed of evil that was planted a long time ago." From 1937 to 1945 he was forbidden to teach in Germany. He refused to make any concessions to National Socialism and continued to uphold the traditions of Western civilization. In 1948 he was called to the University of Basel as professor of philosophy. He died in Basel on February 26, 1969.

JESCHONNEK, HANS (1899–1943). Professional soldier and one of the leaders of the Luftwaffe (q.v.). Hans Jeschonnek was born in Hohensalza (now Inowrocław, Poland) on April 9, 1899. In World War I he first served as an officer in the infantry and then was transferred to the Air Force. Promoted to colonel in 1938, he was, with Erhard Milch and Ernst Udet (qq.v.), among the most important subordinates of Hermann Goering (q.v.) in the general planning and centralization of the new Luftwaffe. On February 1, 1939, when he was not quite forty years old, he was made chief of the General Staff of the Luftwaffe. The following August he was promoted to major general, in July 1940 to general of fliers, and on April 1, 1942, to colonel general. He served on the Leadership Staff of the Luftwaffe as the fortunes of Goering's air arm declined. Jeschonnek committed suicide in East Prussia on August 19, 1943.

JEW-CHRISTIAN. *See* JUDEN-CHRISTEN.

JEWISH COUNCILS. *See* JUDENRÄTE.

JEWS' RESERVATION. *See* JUDENRESERVAT.

JG. *See* JAGDGESCHWADER.

JODL, ALFRED (1890–1946). Pro-Hitler general and chief of the Operations Staff of the armed forces from 1939 to 1945. Alfred Jodl was born in Würzburg on May 10, 1890, to a family of intellectuals that produced philosophers, lawyers, and priests as well as soldiers. Brilliant, able, and ambitious, Jodl was one of a trio of high officers, including Wilhelm Keitel and Walther Warlimont (qq.v.), who resented the old-line Prussian officers and military traditions. Imbued since his early days with a Napoleonic hero worship, Jodl was completely subservient to Hitler, whom he regarded as Germany's savior. Throughout the war, as chief of the Wehrmachtfuehrungsstab (q.v.; armed forces Operations Staff), he was Hitler's first adviser on strategic and operations problems. He was aware as early as 1940 that the Fuehrer intended to attack

Colonel General Jodl signs the unconditional surrender agreement at Reims on May 7, 1945. [*Keystone*]

Soviet Russia, and he was involved in the preliminary planning for that operation.

Jodl was made colonel general in 1944, but in the late months of the war his advisory role was limited. On May 7, 1945, he represented Adm. Karl Doenitz (q.v.), Hitler's successor, at Reims, where he signed the German capitulation. Brought to trial before the International Military Tribunal at Nuremberg, he defended himself by stating that he had always been subjected to "superior orders." He was found guilty on all four counts: (1) conspiracy to commit crimes alleged in other counts, (2) crimes against peace, (3) war crimes, and (4) crimes against humanity. He was hanged at Nuremberg on October 16, 1946.

Bibliography. Günther Just, *Alfred Jodl: Soldat ohne Furcht und Tadel,* National Verlag, Hannover, 1971.

JOHST, HANNS (1890–1978). National Socialist writer and dramatist. Hanns Johst was born in Seerhausen bei Riesa, Saxony, on July 8, 1890. Early in his career he wrote such expressionist dramas as *Der junge Mensch*, 1916 *(The Young Man), Der König,* 1920 *(The King),* and *Thomas Paine* (1927). Attracted by Nazi ideology, he turned his pen to the defense of the National Socialist cause, praising Hitler highly and in general taking the Nazi line. His drama *Schlageter* (1933), concerning the foremost Nazi martyr, Albert Leo Schlageter (q.v.), made a strong impression on Hitler and was later performed again and again in theaters of the Third Reich. As a producer of the Prussian State Theater in 1933, Johst used his influence to create a new theater in the spirit of National Socialism. He called for a "reawakening of confidence" as the condition for a new folk art under National Socialist auspices. Johst had a character boast that whenever someone mentioned the word *culture* to him, he was inclined to reach for his revolver. In 1933 he was made president of the Academy for German Poetry, and in 1934 he was named to the Prussian State Council. He became president of the Reich Theater Chamber in 1935.

See also THEATER IN THE THIRD REICH.

JOURNALISM. *See* NEWSPAPERS IN THE THIRD REICH.

JOYCE, WILLIAM (1906–1946). Anglo-American propagandist for the Nazis in World War II, when he was widely known as Lord Haw-Haw. William Joyce was born on Herkimer Street, Brooklyn, New York, in 1906, the son of a naturalized American citizen. At the age of three he was taken to Ireland, where he lived until 1921. He never returned to the United States. In 1933 he joined Sir Oswald Mosley's British Union of Fascists, and in 1939 he moved to Germany, to which he was attracted by Hitler's ideology. Throughout World War II he broadcast from Berlin to England German propaganda in which he mocked British efforts and urged Englishmen to desert their country. Arrested by British soldiers after the war on May 28, 1945, he was judged subject to British jurisdiction because he carried a British passport. He was tried in Old Bailey, London, and sentenced to death. Joyce appealed the verdict, but it was affirmed. He was hanged in London on January 3, 1946.

Bibliography. Rebecca West, *The Meaning of Treason,* The Viking Press, Inc., New York, 1949.

JU-87. *See* JUNKERS-87.

JU-88. *See* JUNKERS-88.

"JUDA VERRECKE!" ("Death to Judaism!"). A favorite Nazi slogan used in graffiti and painted on walls and store windows during the anti-Semitic campaigns in Germany. The German word *verrecken* is a slang term for "to die" (it is usually applied to cattle, sometimes to people).

JUDAS-JUDE (Judas-Jew). In Nazi ideology, a term indicating a connection between Jew and traitor. The resemblance between the German word *Jude* (Jew) and the traitor's name Judas set up a juxtaposition between Jews and treason in the Nazi mind.

JUDEN-CHRISTEN (Jew-Christian). Term applied to persons who could not prove their Aryan ancestry as far back as two or three generations. *See also* ARIERPARAGRAPH.

JUDENFREI (Cleansed of Jews). Term used by Heinrich Himmler (q.v.) and other Nazi leaders to characterize a satisfactory purge of Jews. The word was used interchangeably with *Judenrein* (free of Jews). For example, in the fall of 1942 Himmler decided to make his concentration camps (q.v.) *Judenfrei* by transferring all Jews to the extermination center at Auschwitz (q.v.; *see* EXTERMINATION CAMPS). On May 19, 1943, the city of Berlin was pronounced *Judenrein.*

JUDENRÄTE (Jewish Councils). Special bodies representing Jews vis-à-vis the Nazi government. These councils were set up not only in Germany but throughout German-occupied Europe. Inside Germany the *Judenrat* was called the Reichsvertretung der Deutschen Juden (Reich Representative Council of German Jews). Jewish councils were organized in Austria, Belgium, Czechoslovakia, France, the Netherlands *(Joodse Raad),* Hungary, Poland *(Jedenrat),* and Romania. A special *Judenrat* functioned during the Warsaw ghetto uprising (q.v.).

Bibliography. Isaiah Trunk, *Judenrat,* The Macmillan Company, New York, 1972.

JUDENRESERVAT (Jews' Reservation). A cluster of ghettoes reserved for Jews either in Nazi Germany or in German-occupied countries.

JUDICIARY. *See* JUSTICE IN THE THIRD REICH.

JUGENDHERBERGEN (Youth Hostels). Rest camps set up in 1933 for the Hitler Jugend (q.v.), the Hitler Youth. The purpose was to provide a place where members of the Hitler Youth who were hiking might sleep in return for a modest payment. Rest camps had long existed in Germany, but they were now taken over by the Nazis. By 1934 some 5 million youngsters had taken advantage of the rest camps.

JUGENDSCHUTZKAMMER (Youth Protection Chamber). An official body responsible for adjudicating the rights of young people. It handled such cases as vindicating teachers for face slapping as a disciplinary measure.

JULY PLOT. An attempt on Hitler's life at a war conference held at the *Gästebaracke* (guest barracks) in the Fuehrer's headquarters at Rastenburg, East Prussia, on July 20, 1944. There was dissatisfaction in military circles with Hitler and Nazism in the days before he became Chancellor in 1933. The upper brackets of the High Command of the armed forces in the Bendlerstrasse (q.v.) in Berlin remained *Fuehrertreu* (q.v.; loyal to the Fuehrer). Such high officers as Field Marshal Wilhelm Keitel, Col. Gen. Alfred Jodl, and Maj. Gen. Walther Warlimont (qq.v.) adhered to their oath of loyalty to the Fuehrer, but the lower brackets were riddled with dissent. On October 19, 1938, Col. Gen. Ludwig Beck (q.v.) resigned as chief of the General Staff in protest against Hitler's plan to annex Czechoslovakia. For some time Beck had concentrated on winning the support of high-ranking army officers in a plan to arrest or eliminate Hitler, and he founded a loosely knit organization to achieve this end. Over the next five years discontent proceeded in three stages, from opposition to resistance to conspiracy.

At the center of the plot were such senior officers as Maj. Gen. Henning von Tresckow (q.v.), chief of staff in Army Group Center on the Russian front; Col. Gen. Erich Hoepner (q.v.), the commander of an armored force who had been dismissed by Hitler in December 1941; Col. Gen. Friedrich Olbricht (q.v.), head of the Supply Section of the Reserve Army; Col. Gen. Karl Heinrich von Stuelpnagel (q.v.), military governor in France; Maj. Gen. Hans Oster (q.v.), chief of staff of the Abwehr (q.v.); and Field Marshal Erwin von Witzleben (q.v.), who had been retired from active service in 1942. Added to these senior members were a number of younger officers who believed that the Third Reich was a catastrophe for Germany and were willing to gamble their lives on the outcome of the plot. Among them were Col. Claus Schenk Graf von Stauffenberg (q.v.), chief of staff to Gen. Friedrich Fromm (q.v.), commander of the Reserve Army (who was both in and out of the conspiracy); 1st Lieut. Fabian von Schlabrendorff, staff officer under General von Tresckow on the eastern front; and Lieut. Werner von Haeften (q.v.), Von Stauffenberg's adjutant.

Added to the military were such diplomats as Christian Albrecht Ulrich von Hassell (q.v.), former German Ambassador to Italy; Hans Bernd Gisevius (q.v.), who worked for the Abwehr from his base in Switzerland; and Adam von Trott zu Solz (q.v.), an official in the Foreign Office. On the political side were such figures as Carl Friedrich Goerdeler (q.v.), former lord mayor of Leipzig;

Julius Leber (q.v.), a former Social Democratic member of the Reichstag (q.v.); and Johannes Popitz (q.v.), Prussian Finance Minister. There were such ecclesiastics as Pastor Dietrich Bonhoeffer (q.v.), religious leader, scholar, and teacher; and a Jesuit, Father Alfred Delp (q.v.). There were members of the Kreisau Circle (q.v.), including Helmuth James Graf von Moltke (q.v.), legal adviser to the Abwehr, who counseled nonviolence; and Peter Graf Yorck von Wartenberg (q.v.). There were also such miscellaneous figures as Adm. Wilhelm Canaris (q.v.), leader of the Abwehr; Wolf Heinrich Graf von Helldorf (q.v.), chief of the Berlin Police; and several lawyers, including Carl Langbehn, Klaus Bonhoeffer, Josef Müller, and Joseph Wirmer (qq.v.).

Others knew of the plot but did not take an active role in it. Among them were Field Marshal Erwin Rommel (q.v.), popular war hero; Lieut. Gen. Adolf Heusinger (q.v.), operations chief of the Army High Command; and Field Marshal Günther Hans von Kluge (q.v.), army group commander in France.

By the summer of 1938 definite plans began to crystallize for a coup d'état. Beck's resignation in October 1938 stimulated the move from opposition to resistance. Evidence was gathered to certify Hitler as insane in order to remove him from office before setting up a provisional government. Approaches made to Paris, London, and Washington had little success. The Berlin *Putsch* (q.v.) of September 1938 failed at the critical moment because of weak planning. The conspirators were dealt a heavy blow by the Munich Agreement (q.v.), which heightened Hitler's popularity with the German people. Equally disappointing were the November 1939 Zossen *Putsch* and the January 1943 Stalingrad *Putsch* (qq.v.).

In March 1943 General von Tresckow and his junior officer, 1st Lieutenant von Schlabrendorff, both active in the Beck group, decided that the time had come for action. A British-made time bomb, disguised as a bottle of brandy, was placed on the Fuehrer's plane by Von Schlabrendorff as it took off from Smolensk on a flight back to headquarters in East Prussia. The bomb failed to explode, but by good luck for the plotters it was never discovered (*see* SMOLENSK ATTENTAT). On March 21, 1943, another attempt on Hitler's life, a suicide mission in which two bombs were to be placed in the Fuehrer's overcoat pocket, failed when Hitler changed his schedule at the last moment. Other similar attempts were also frustrated.

In early 1944 Graf von Stauffenberg became the active leader of the anti-Hitler conspirators. In February 1944 the conspiracy received an unexpected reinforcement when it was learned that Field Marshal Rommel, disgusted by Hitler's mismanagement of the war, decided to join the Beck group. General von Tresckow agreed with Von Stauffenberg that the assassination attempt must be made now at all costs: "We must prove to the world and to future generations that the men of the German Resistance movement dared to take the decisive step and wager their lives on it."

Early on the morning of July 20, 1944, Hitler called a conference of his close military advisers at the Wolfsschanze (Wolf's Lair) headquarters at Rastenburg for 12:30 P.M. (*see* RASTENBURG CONFERENCE for a list of those present). The compound was protected by numerous electric fences and barbed wire, with blockhouses and checkpoints. The meeting was held in the *Gästebaracke*, a large wooden hut built on concrete and stone pillars and having a roof of tarred felt. There were three windows and at each end a small table. In the center of the room was a large table covered by situation maps.

Shortly after 10 A.M. Von Stauffenberg arrived at Rastenburg and was admitted after giving the proper password. He had been summoned to give a report on the state of the Home Army. In his briefcase along with papers and reports, was a British time bomb. He set the timer on the bomb and brought it into the conference room. After greeting the Fuehrer, he placed the briefcase on the floor beside Hitler and then excused himself: "I must make a telephone call." Col. Heinz Brandt, deputy to General Heusinger, feeling the briefcase to be in his way, pushed it away from his chair under the map table in such a manner that it rested against the heavy upright support on the side farthest away from Hitler. That move saved the Fuehrer's life.

Several minutes passed as General Heusinger gave his gloomy report on the Russian front. He was in the final stages: "The Russians are pressing with strong forces westward. Their forward troops are already southwest of Dünaburg [Daugavpils]. If now we do not at last withdraw the Army Group from Peipussee [Lake Peipus], there will be a disaster. . . ." At this moment, precisely at 12:50 P.M., a tremendous explosion blasted the room, wrecking the ceiling and shattering the central table. Several bodies flew out of the smashed windows, and thick clouds of smoke rose from the scene.

Of the twenty-four men present, Berger, the stenographer, was killed outright, and three others, Gen. Günther Korten, Gen. Rudolf Schmundt (q.v.), and also Col. Heinz Brandt, died of their wounds later. Of the remainder, several were severely wounded, and many were slightly hurt. Shielded from the full blast, Hitler himself was alive. His hair was set afire, his right arm partially paralyzed, his right leg burned, and his eardrums damaged.

Meanwhile, Von Stauffenberg, certain that all in the hut had been killed, bluffed his way through three guard posts and by 1 P.M. was in a plane bound for Berlin. Arriving at the War Ministry at 4:10 P.M., he learned to his amazement that Hitler had not been killed by the blast. Officers who were in the plot were dismayed and virtually paralyzed into inaction. By 10:30 that night officers loyal to Hitler had taken control of the War Ministry and arrested the conspirators. General Fromm hurried to cover his tracks. At midnight he had four officers (Olbricht, Von Stauffenberg, Von Haeften, and Mertz) shot by a firing squad in the courtyard below. Beck was killed with a *coup de grâce*.

Hitler's vengeance was terrible. Almost all the remaining conspirators were tracked down, handed over to the tortures of the Gestapo (q.v.), and brought before the Volksgericht (q.v.), the dreaded People's Court, under the presidency of Roland Freisler (q.v.). Many more were killed in a massive blood purge. Some were strangled with piano wire and their bodies hanged like animal carcasses on huge hooks. Hitler had the scene photographed and watched movies of it being replayed through-

Hitler only slightly hurt in the bombing at his headquarters, holds his injured right arm. [*National Archives, Washington*]

out the night. Young cadets, forced to view the gruesome films, fainted. General Fromm, who had been active in ordering the executions, could not save himself: he, too, was put to death. All the principal leaders of the conspiracy—Gen. Ludwig Beck, Adm. Wilhelm Canaris, Carl Goerdeler, Ulrich von Hassell, and others—met a barbaric death. Field Marshal Erwin von Witzleben's execution was typical. The old man was pushed into the cellar at Plötzensee Prison in Berlin, placed under the first meat hook, and stripped to the waist. A running noose was placed over the hook and wound around his neck. He was lifted and allowed to fall with the whole weight of his body. Twisting in agony, he was slowly strangled.

The number of those killed as a direct result of the July Plot is estimated at from 180 to 200. The British historian John W. Wheeler-Bennett, in *The Nemesis of Power* (The Macmillan Company, London, 1953, pp. 744–752), gave an incomplete list of 158 names of those who died as a result of Hitler's vengeance. The following list is limited to the major figures in the conspiracy (*see also* separate biographies).

Beck, Ludwig: Colonel general, chief of the General Staff of the Army, 1935–1938. Killed with a *coup de grâce*, in the Bendlerstrasse, July 20, 1944.

Bonhoeffer, Pastor Dietrich: Protestant theologian, director of the preachers' seminar of the Confessional Church at Finkenwalde. Executed at Flossenbürg concentration camp, April 9, 1945.

Canaris, Adm. Wilhelm: Director of the Abwehr. Executed at Flossenbürg, April 9, 1945.

Delp, Father Alfred: Member of the Kreisau Circle. Hanged on February 2, 1945.

Dohnányi, Hans von: Legal expert, member of the Abwehr, brother-in-law of Dietrich Bonhoeffer. Hanged at Flossenbürg, April 8, 1945.

Goerdeler, Dr. Carl Friedrich: Former lord mayor of Leipzig, Price Commissioner. Hanged at Plötzensee Prison, February 2, 1945.

Hassell, Christian Albrecht Ulrich von: Career diplomat, Ambassador in Rome, 1933–1937. Hanged at Plötzensee Prison, September 8, 1944.

Haushofer, Dr. Albrecht: Teacher, poet, dramatist, son of the eminent geopolitician Karl Haushofer. Shot on April 23, 1945, while being transferred from Berlin-Moabit Prison.

Helldorf, Wolf Heinrich Graf von: Police president of Berlin, 1935–1944. Hanged on August 15, 1944.

Hoepner, Erich: Colonel general, commander of armored forces, dismissed by Hitler in December 1941 for disregarding orders. Hanged on August 8, 1944.

Langbehn, Carl: Lawyer. Executed on October 12, 1944.

Leber, Dr. Julius: Social Democratic member of the Reichstag, 1924–1933. Hanged at Plötzensee Prison, January 5, 1945.

Leuschner, Wilhelm: Sculptor, trade union leader. Hanged on September 29, 1944.

Moltke, Helmuth James Graf von: Lawyer, leader of the Kreisau Circle. Executed on January 23, 1945.
Oster, Hans: Major general, chief of staff of the Abwehr. Executed at Flossenbürg Prison, April 9, 1945.
Popitz, Johannes: Professor, Finance Minister for Prussia, 1933–1944. Hanged at Plötzensee Prison, February 2, 1945.
Rommel, Erwin: General field marshal, one of the most popular generals of World War II. Committed suicide on October 14, 1944.
Stauffenberg, Lieut. Col. Claus Schenk Graf von: Chief of staff to Col. Gen. Friedrich Fromm, commander in chief of the Reserve Army. Carried out attempt on Hitler's life on July 20, 1944. Executed at the Bendlerstrasse that same day.
Stuelpnagel, Karl Heinrich von: General of infantry, military governor in France, 1942–1944. Attempted suicide on July 21, 1944; hanged on August 30, 1944.
Tresckow, Henning von: Major general, chief of staff in Army Group Center on the eastern front. Committed suicide on July 21, 1944.
Trott zu Solz, Adam von: Member of the Kreisau Circle, Counselor of Legation in the Foreign Office. Hanged on August 25, 1944.
Wirmer, Joseph: Lawyer, member of the Center party. Executed on September 8, 1944.
Witzleben, Erwin von: General field marshal, one of the older members of the Resistance movement. Hanged on August 8, 1944.
Yorck von Wartenburg, Peter Graf: Member of Kreisau Circle. Hanged on August 8, 1944.

See also RESISTANCE.

Bibliography. Roger Manvell and Heinrich Fraenkel, *The July Plot*, Pan Books, London, 1966.

JUNGBANN (Youngsters). Unit of the Jungvolk (q.v.).

JUNGDEUTSCHER ORDEN (Order of Young Germans). A conservative bourgeois group of young people who joined the liberal forces in the early 1930s to help prevent the rise of Hitler. *See* MAHRUN, ARTUR.

JUNGE, GERTRUD (nee Gertrud Humps; 1920–). Hitler's private secretary. She was born in Munich on March 16, 1920. Frau Junge was present in the bunker during the final days of Hitler's life. He dictated his last will and his political testament to her on the morning of April 29, 1945 (*see* GÖTTERDÄMMERUNG; HITLER'S LAST WILL; HITLER'S POLITICAL TESTAMENT).

JÜNGER, ERNST (1895–). Poet and political writer. Ernst Jünger was born in Heidelberg on March 29, 1895. A volunteer in World War I, he was decorated with the Pour le Mérite medal, Germany's highest military award. After the war he began a career as a writer. At first he specialized in a national activism that became the theme of fascism. He praised war as "an inner experience," denounced parliamentarianism and democracy, and supported the idea of a powerful, aggressive leader. At the same time he was careful not to link himself with the rising Nationalsozialistische Deutsche Arbeiterpartei (q.v.) and in his novels covertly criticized Hitler and the Nazi movement. In World War II he served on the staff of the German military commander in France but was retired in 1944 because of "unsatisfactory military conduct." After the war Jünger turned to a theologically motivated humanism and took up his pen in defense of peace and freedom.

JUNGMÄDEL (Young Girls). An organization of girls below the age of fourteen. *See also* BUND DEUTSCHER MÄDEL.

JUNGSTAHLHELM (Young Steel Helmet). The youth organization of the Stahlhelm (q.v.). On July 25, 1933, the Jungstahlhelm was incorporated into the Hitler Jugend (q.v.), the Hitler Youth.

JUNGVOLK (Young People). The junior division of the Hitler Jugend (q.v.), the Hitler Youth. The Jungvolk consisted of boys from ten to fourteen years of age.

JUNKER CADET SCHOOLS. *See* JUNKERSCHULE.

JUNKERS-87 (Ju-87; Stuka). German single-engine dive bomber that bore the brunt of air attacks in the early days of World War II. Hitler wanted a plane that would be the perfect complementary weapon in the air to his ground *Blitzkrieg* (q.v.). The Stuka was brought into production in 1936. Its specifications included an 1,100-horsepower liquid-cooled engine, a wingspan of 45.2 feet, a top speed of 232 miles per hour, an armament of three 7.9-millimeter machine guns, and the capacity to carry 1,100 pounds of bombs. The famous gull-winged plane was tested in Spain during the civil war (*see* CONDOR LEGION). When World War II began, Hermann Goering (q.v.) sent his Stuka dive bombers to destroy Polish planes and tanks on the ground and accompany the German forces in their surge forward. The Stuka had a strong psychological effect on the enemy: with its crooked wings, square-cut tail, and canopy hump, it had the appearance of a flying vulture and when diving gave a loud and terrifying whine. In his propaganda Dr. Paul Joseph Goebbels (q.v.) boasted that the Stuka was invincible.

However, the easy victories of early campaigns were won in the absence of adequate fighter opposition. Royal Air Force pilots in the Battle of Britain found the Stuka an easy prey. Severe losses in operations throughout August 1940 destroyed the reputation of the Stuka as the all-conquering weapon of the Luftwaffe (q.v.), and it was withdrawn from the spearhead of the attack. Goering continued to use the Stuka on other fronts and on convoy routes.

JUNKERS-88 (Ju-88). Junkers twin-engine medium bomber.

JUNKERSCHULE (Junker Cadet Schools). Special schools set up by the SS (q.v.) to train cadets who could become officers in the organization.

JUSTICE IN THE THIRD REICH. The legal system of the Third Reich was geared to the Fuehrer's attitude toward justice. Hitler had only contempt for the traditional legal system. As Chancellor he wanted no checks or limits on his power. His idea of justice was based on "what is useful to the nation." The human conscience, he said, was a Jewish invention designed to enslave other races. He rejected such conceptions as the Kantian categorical imperative ("Act only on that maxim whereby thou canst at the same time will that it should become a universal law"). However, Hitler was too shrewd to reveal these beliefs publicly and preferred to appear as a firm advocate of law and order. He was careful to cloak all his actions behind a mass of legal verbiage, but in his secret conversations he intimated that law was primarily a means of exercising control over the German people. He would not hesitate, he said, to commit perjury "in cold blood" many times a day if it served his purpose.

As soon as Hitler achieved political power in 1933, he began to revise the German legal system. He had no interest in civil law, such as litigation over wills, torts, and commercial contracts, and allowed it to remain virtually intact. On the other hand, he regarded criminal law as critical for the maintenance of his dictatorship. It was vital to "rid oneself of all enemies." He therefore rejected the legal principle of "no punishment without crime" in favor of "no crime without punishment." In his view punishment was "simply the separating out of alien types and deviant natures." Any opposition to National Socialism was criminal. Hitler decreed a series of draconian laws against all who opposed, resisted, or conspired against his state. The process continued throughout the life of the Third Reich. By 1945 the number of capital crimes had risen to forty-three, and death sentences were almost invariably carried out.

Hitler's first concern was to rid the German legal system of all Jewish elements. Jewish judges were promptly retired, and Jewish lawyers were driven from their profession. In the process of nazification all practicing lawyers were required to join the NS-Rechtswahrerbund (q.v.), the National Socialist Lawyers' Association. This organization maintained a close watch over its members. It had its own "honor" courts with disciplinary power over those who committed such infractions as failing to use the German greeting, *"Heil Hitler!"* Those who did not vote in Reichstag (q.v.) elections or national plebiscites could be disbarred.

In the new Third Reich the *Rechtsstaat* (constitutional state) was replaced by a state grounded on Hitler's views of a legal system. All judges were appointed by the Nazi Minister of Justice. They were cautioned to preserve the existing *voelkisch* community (*see* VOELKISCH MOVEMENT), to punish all anti-Nazi behavior, and to exterminate obstructionists. It was their duty to rationalize any decision from the viewpoint of Nazi *Weltanschauung* (q.v.), or world view. The role of prosecutors in the courts was enhanced, and that of judges and defense reduced. Defense counsel in criminal cases were to serve only with the approval of the court. Judicial procedures in local districts could be influenced by the local *Gauleiter* (q.v.), the district leader, by the *Reichsstatthalter* (q.v.), the provincial governor, or by *Das Schwarze Korps* (q.v.), the newspaper of the SS (q.v.).

Many older jurists were retired because they "did not act in the interest of the National Socialist state." Often young, inexperienced Nazis, who were regarded as more reliable, were appointed to key judicial posts. University students who studied law were subjected to careful supervision and indoctrination in Nazi ideology.

German courts of law became known for coercion and arbitrary, sometimes bizarre decisions. Political prisoners were often sentenced to lunatic asylums. Those found guilty of *Rassenschande* (q.v.), or race defilement, because of intercourse between German and Jew, were punished by verdicts ranging from ten years' imprisonment to death. In 1937 the Ministry of Justice decided that the beating of prisoners was permissible for purposes of intensive interrogation but that such beatings must be restricted to the posterior and must not exceed twenty-five blows. In 1939 a special division of the Supreme Court of Justice, by which the prosecution could bypass the lower courts, was established. Judges were given vague instructions to punish individuals for "contravening the unwritten law of the folk community."

After the outbreak of World War II in 1939 there was an ever greater intensification of the Nazi view of criminal justice. Many thousands of citizens were sentenced for holding unorthodox opinions, for not supporting the war effort, or for criticizing the Fuehrer. A Berlin pastor was put to death for telling an anti-Nazi joke. The number of executions mounted from 926 in 1940 to 5,336 in 1943. Distinctions between adult and juvenile criminals were abolished: by 1941, death sentences could be pronounced on boys from fourteen to sixteen. By April 1942 the last vestige of independent justice vanished when it became standard procedure for judges and public prosecutor to confer before a trial in order to determine the outcome.

To protect his regime from the Resistance (q.v.) movement, Hitler set up the dreaded Volksgericht (q.v.), the People's Court, in Berlin. Under the presidency of Roland Freisler (q.v.), this court became a caricature of a legal institution. The accused had to prove his innocence, and the defense became a farce. From his position behind the judge's desk, Freisler resembled a prosecutor who heaped insults on the prisoners before him. There was no appeal from his death sentence. With the Volksgericht the Nazi legal system degenerated into a tragic farce.

K

KAHR, GUSTAV RITTER VON
to
KZ

KAHR, GUSTAV RITTER VON (1862–1934). Bavarian politician and a central figure in the 1923 Beer-Hall *Putsch* (q.v.) in Munich. Gustav Kahr was born in Weissenburg, Bavaria, on November 29, 1862. From 1890 on he was active in Bavarian local government. His title of nobility (Ritter von) was assumed in 1911. From 1917 to 1924 Von Kahr was *Regierungspräsident* (Government President) of Upper Bavaria. A dedicated monarchist, he worked in the immediate post World War I years for a return of the local Bavarian dynasty and opposed the central government of the Weimar Republic (q.v.) in Berlin. In September 1921, after the Kapp *Putsch* (q.v.), he set up a rightist government in Bavaria. Refusing Berlin's demand that Bavarians turn in their arms, he resigned a year later. In August 1923 Chancellor Gustav Stresemann (q.v.) announced an end to passive resistance against the French in the Ruhr and proposed the resumption of reparations payments to the Allies, policies that angered both monarchists and Nazis in Bavaria. To forestall any attempt to set up an independent state, President Friedrich Ebert (q.v.) declared a state of emergency on September 26, 1923. The same day the Bavarian Cabinet proclaimed its own state of emergency and appointed Von Kahr as *Generalstaatskommissar* (General State Commissioner). With Gen. Otto von Lossow, commander of the German armed forces in Bavaria, and Col. Hans von Seisser, chief of the Bavarian State Police, Von Kahr refused to take orders from Berlin. The three men ignored the government's warning that the armed forces would suppress any uprising.

At this point Hitler decided to lead a rebellion and with his followers attempted the Beer-Hall *Putsch*. Von Kahr, Von Lossow, and Von Seisser became unwilling participants in the attempted coup d'état. They managed to break away from Hitler as the police and the Reichswehr (q.v.) suppressed the uprising. From 1924 to 1927 Von Kahr was president of the Bavarian Verwaltungsgerichthof (Supreme Court). He was murdered in revenge by the Nazis in Munich, on June 6, 1934, during the Blood Purge (q.v.).

Bibliography. Richard Hanser, *Putsch*, Pyramid Books, New York, 1971.

KALTENBRUNNER, ERNST (1903–1946). Austrian National Socialist, lawyer, and police official and successor to Reinhard Heydrich (q.v.) as chief of the SD (q.v.), the Security Service of Heinrich Himmler (q.v.). Ernst Kaltenbrunner was born in Ried im Innkreis, near Hitler's birthplace, on October 4, 1903. The son of a lawyer, he studied at the *Realgymnasium* (semiclassical high school) in Linz and then at the *Technische Hochschule* (technical college) in Graz. After taking a law degree in 1926, he worked for a year at a court in Salzburg and then opened his own law office in Linz. Kaltenbrunner was tall in stature, with a thick neck, piercing eyes, and a deep scar from the left side of his mouth to his nose. A man of consuming ambition, he joined the Austrian National Socialist party in 1932 and by 1935 was the leader of the Austrian SS. At the time of the 1938 *Anschluss* (q.v.) he made it clear to Berlin that the Austrian SS was awaiting orders from the Fuehrer. Hitler rewarded him by making him state secretary for internal security in Vienna.

Kaltenbrunner reached the summit of his career on January 30, 1943, when Hitler named him chief of the Reichssicherheitshauptamt (q.v.), the Reich Central Security Office (RSHA), as successor to Heydrich, who had been fatally wounded by Czech resistance fighters in May 1942. In this capacity Kaltenbrunner, who held a deep hatred for Jews, hunted them down for the gas chambers. Shortly after obtaining his post as head of the RSHA, he rounded up 5,000 Jews under the age of sixty and had them transferred from the relative safety of the Theresienstadt (q.v.) concentration camp to the Auschwitz (q.v.) extermination camp (*see* CONCENTRATION CAMPS; EXTERMINATION CAMPS). During the war he encouraged local people to kill Allied parachutists and ordered all French prostitutes to be executed. In February 1944 he took over the Abwehr (q.v.), the intelligence service of the German High Command, and made it a part of the RSHA. In March 1944 he personally interrogated Adm. Wilhelm Canaris (q.v.), who had long evaded him. Later that year, aware that the war was lost, Kaltenbrunner attempted to arrange talks with the Allies through Allen Welsh Dulles (q.v.) in Switzerland, but with no success.

Ernst Kaltenbrunner. [*Wide World Photos*]

On October 20, 1945, Kaltenbrunner was brought before the International Military Tribunal at Nuremberg with twenty-one other Nazi leaders (*see* NUREMBERG TRIAL). He was accused of the murder of Jews, Allied parachutists, and prisoners of war. Several million Jews had been murdered in extermination camps under the supervision of Kaltenbrunner's RSHA. Kaltenbrunner protested his innocence: "I do not feel guilty of any war crimes. I have only done my duty as an intelligence organ, and I refuse to serve as an *Ersatz* [substitute] for Hitler." He declared that he scarcely knew Adolf Eichmann (q.v.), although they had been boyhood friends in Linz. On November 18, 1945, the day the trial started, Kaltenbrunner had a cerebral hemorrhage, but he attended the sessions intermittently in December and January. He was found guilty on count 3 (war crimes) and count 4 (crimes against humanity) and hanged at Nuremberg on October 16, 1946. As the trap was sprung at 1:39 A.M., he said in a low, calm voice: "Germany, good luck!"

Bibliography. Ernst Kaltenbrunner, *Spiegelbild einer Verschwörung*, Seewald Verlag, Stuttgart, 1961.

KAMERAD (Comrade). The customary form of address within the formations of the National Socialist party.

KAMERADSCHAFTSFUEHRER (Fellowship Leader). An official in the Nationalsozialistischer Deutscher Studentenbund (q.v.), the Nazi student organization.

KAMERADSCHAFTSKLUB (Fellowship Club). A society of German artists that met at Skaggerak Square in Berlin for social occasions. A favorite guest was the heavyweight boxer Max Schmeling (q.v.), who was accompanied by his wife, the actress Anny Ondra. The club's most important member was Propaganda Minister Dr. Paul Joseph Goebbels (q.v.), who, although charged with purging the decadent arts, would listen to orchestras playing condemned American jazz.

KAMPFBUND (Millitant Association). League of Bavarian rightist groups that helped plan the Beer-Hall *Putsch* (q.v.) in Munich in 1923.

KAMPFBUND DES GEWERBLICHEN MITTELSTANDES (Militant Association of Retailers). Nazi organization whose purpose was to arouse public opposition to chain stores, which were said to be dominantly Jewish-controlled.

KAMPFBUND FÜR DEUTSCHE KULTUR (League of Struggle for German Culture). Organization founded by Alfred Rosenberg (q.v.) in 1929. Its opening session was held in the main lecture hall of the University of Munich. The purpose of the league was to promote the beliefs of Hitler on the nature of German *Kultur* and to combat Jewish influence on German cultural life. In *Mein Kampf* (q.v.) Hitler laid down the broad outlines of the German way of life that he preferred. The power of an ideal, he wrote, was all-important. He contrasted idealism with materialism, the latter being symbolized by the teachings of Marxism. Hitler's own view was *voelkisch* (*see* VOELKISCH MOVEMENT), that is, based on the concept that racial principles are fundamental to human life. To Hitler "race" was the true foundation of all culture. All culture is the product of the Aryan: only he can produce the true personalities destined to lead the German people. Materialism, promoted by Jews, can never produce culture. The revolution in *Weltanschauung* (q.v.), or world view, can succeed only if it becomes part of a mass movement.

On July 18, 1937, in a speech at the opening of the House of German Art (q.v.) in Munich, Hitler set the standard for the Kampfbund für Deutsche Kultur:

> During the long years in which I planned the formation of a new Reich I gave much thought to the tasks which would await us in the cultural cleansing of the people's life: there was to be a cultural renaissance as well as political and economic reform. I was convinced that people which have been trodden underfoot by the whole world of their day have all the greater duty consciously to assert their own value before their oppressors, and there is no prouder proof of the highest rights of a people to its own life than immortal cultural achievements.

With Hitler thus setting the tone, the Kampfbund für Deutsche Kultur accepted *Gleichschaltung* (q.v.), the coordination of all cultural activities in the Third Reich to meet the standards set by its Fuehrer.

KAMPFGESCHWADER (KG; Bomber Group). A bombing unit of the Luftwaffe (q.v.).

KAMPFZEIT (Time of Struggle). Term applied to the years of struggle in Munich in the early days of the Nazi movement. Hitler often used the phrase in evening discussions at the Berghof (q.v.), his mountain retreat. Those were the good old days, he said, which he shared with the *Alte Kämpfer* (q.v.), his old comrades. In the Third Reich after 1933 a special course on the *Kampfzeit* was used in school syllabi, and students were expected to be well versed in the subject. Writers and playwrights were encouraged to produce epics on the period. Novelists were told to depict the *Kampfzeit* as an age of heroes, in which early Nazis performed great deeds of glory. The term was also used to describe the general milieu of war, in which all Germans forgot their personal problems in favor of a truly national spirit.

KAPP PUTSCH. A conspiracy against the Weimar Republic (q.v.) by right wing Germans. Its leaders were the journalist Wolfgang Kapp (1868–1922) and the military leader Gen. Walther von Lüttwitz (1859–1942). In March 1920, according to the terms of the Treaty of Versailles, the Germans were obliged to dismiss between 50,000 and 60,000 men from the armed forces. Among the units to be disbanded was a naval brigade commanded by Capt. Hermann Ehrhardt, a leader of the *Freikorps* (q.v.). The brigade had played a role in suppressing the Communist republic set up in Bavaria. On the evening of March 12, 1920, the Ehrhardt brigade went into action. More than 5,000 of its members marched a dozen miles from its military barracks to Berlin. The Minister of Defense, Gustav Noske, had at his disposal only 2,000 men to oppose the rebels. His top military leaders indicated that they were not anxious to defend the republic. Gen. Hans von Seeckt (q.v.) informed him: "Reichswehr does not fire on Reichswehr."

Early the next morning the Ehrhardt brigade made a triumphant entry through the Brandenburg Gate. General von Lüttwitz proclaimed a new government with Kapp as Chancellor. The legal government escaped to the provinces, from which it denounced the attempted *Putsch*. Before leaving Berlin, it called for a general strike: "Strike, stop working, prevent the return of bloody reaction. Not a hand must move, not a single worker must help the military dictatorship. General strike all along the line! Workers, unite!" The strike was effective because without water, gas, electricity, and transportation, Berlin was paralyzed. Five days later Kapp announced his resignation and fled to Sweden.

Although the Kapp *Putsch* was a fiasco, it had important historical significance. The immediate danger of overthrowing the republic from the right was over, but the seeds of political hatred had been sown. Disgruntled militarists were dedicated to destroying the Weimar democracy and its "Bolshevik republicanism." The men of the Ehrhardt brigade brought a new symbol from the Baltic on their helmets, the swastika (*see* HAKENKREUZ).

Bibliography. Johannes Erger, *Der Kapp-Lüttwitz Putsch*, Droste, Düsseldorf, 1967.

KARINHALL. A large, sumptuous estate north of Berlin owned by Hermann Goering (q.v.). When he was Prime Minister of Prussia, Goering converted one of the Prussian domain lands into an estate as his personal property. He named it after Carin von Kantzow Goering (q.v.), nee Baroness Fock, his first wife. For this lavish country seat Goering employed administrators, servants, foresters, and huntsmen at public expense.

KARL LIEBKNECHT HOUSE. Communist headquarters in Berlin. The house was a special target of the Nazis in the battle of the streets in the late 1920s and early 1930s. On February 25, 1933, after Hitler's accession to political power, Storm Troopers (*see* SA) broke into the headquarters and captured what they said was a long list of incriminating documents calling the Communists to arms against Hitler. Two days later the Reichstag fire (q.v.) occurred.

KASERNIERTE HUNDERTSCHAFTEN (Barrack Hundreds). Early SS (q.v.) parapolice units.

KAZETLAGER (KZ). Abbreviated form of *Konzentrations Lager*, or concentration camp (*see* CONCENTRATION CAMPS).

KDF. *See* KRAFT DURCH FREUDE.

KDF WAGEN. *See* VOLKSWAGEN.

KATYN MASSACRE. Mass execution of Polish military officers during World War II. Katyn is a forest near Smolensk, a provincial city in the western Russian S.F.S.R., or Russia proper. When Hitler and Stalin concluded their nonaggression pact just before the outbreak of the war, they divided Poland between themselves. Soon after the beginning of the war in September 1939, Soviet forces occupied Polish territory, mostly east of the Curzon Line. More than 240,000 Polish officers and men fell into Russian hands. Many of them were interned in three Russian camps at Kozelak, Starobelsk, and Ostashkov.

After the Nazi invasion of the Soviet Union on June 22, 1941, the Polish government-in-exile in London and the Soviet government agreed to form a Polish army on Soviet territory. The Polish general Władysław Anders, who was delegated for this task, requested that 10,000 to 15,000 Polish prisoners of war held in the Soviet camps be transferred to his command. Moscow informed him late in December 1941 that this could not be done because most of the Polish prisoners had escaped to Manchuria. Only 448 officers were eventually attached to Anders's army.

Katyn fell under German control in the summer of 1941. In April 1943 the Germans announced that they had discovered in the Katyn forest a mass grave of 4,443 Polish officers and men, all of whom, they said, had been interned by the Russians before April 1940. Soviet authorities responded that the Polish prisoners had been engaged in construction work west of Smolensk in 1941 and that they had been killed by the Germans, who had won control of the area in July 1941.

Dissatisfied with this explanation, the Polish government-in-exile on April 17, 1943, appealed for an international tribunal, specifically the International Committee of the Red Cross, to investigate the matter and determine how the Poles had died. The Red Cross announced from Geneva that it could do nothing without a corresponding request from the Soviet Union. Stalin retorted that the atrocity had been committed, of course, by the Germans. He had no intention of calling for an investigation.

The incident had international repercussions. The Allied war leadership wanted no internal quarrels to disturb the immediate business of destroying Hitler and the Third Reich. Pressed by the British and Americans, the Polish government-in-exile issued a statement generally condemning aggression against Polish citizens without specifying who were the Katyn criminals. Because this statement did not specifically exculpate the Russians, Stalin on April 25, 1943, angrily broke off relations with the Poles in London.

The Germans then instituted their own inquiry. A German committee of experts announced that the corpses of between 13,400 and 14,900 Poles had been found in mass graves. According to documents found on the bodies, added to a study of the age of the trees planted over the graves, the executions had taken place in early 1940, at a time when the entire district of Katyn was under Russian control.

In September 1943 the Smolensk area was reoccupied by the Russians. Soviet authorities now set up their own inquiry on the fate of the Poles. Their report, issued in January 1944, claimed that because of the rapid German advance it had been impossible to evacuate the three prisoner-of-war camps. The Polish prisoners were captured, it was claimed, and systematically slaughtered by the Germans.

Later research by Polish as well as independent authorities in the West leaves little doubt that the Poles were killed by the Soviet secret police. This conclusion is bolstered by wartime Foreign Office documents. If the Russian report of 1944 is to be believed, nearly 15,000 Polish officers and men passed into German hands from spring 1940 to July 1941 and later were killed by the Germans without a single prisoner escaping, reporting to Polish authorities in Russia, or joining the Polish underground. Although the Nazi regime was rightly accused of such atrocities as Guernica and Lidice (qq.v.), it is absolved by most historians of blame for the Katyn massacre. At the most it is probable that Soviet security forces, possibly at the request, recommendation, or demand of German officials, executed the officers and men in early 1940. However, there are no documents or other solid evidence to support this view.

The crime of Katyn has never been investigated in complete detail. It was not brought up officially at the Teheran Conference (November 28–December 1, 1943). Great Britain and the United States, determined to ease the tension caused by the Katyn massacre, paid no attention to Polish protests on the ground that the current overriding goal was to smash the Third Reich. The Polish-Soviet border was set at the Curzon Line, and this boundary settlement was confirmed at the Yalta Conference of February 1945. Nor was the Katyn massacre mentioned at the Nuremberg Trial (q.v.) despite its concern with the treatment of prisoners of war.

In his history of World War II, Winston Churchill adopted an ambivalent position on the Katyn massacre. The Soviet government, he wrote, did not take the opportunity of clearing itself of the horrible and widely believed accusation against it as well as of fastening the guilt conclusively upon the Germans. "Everyone is therefore entitled to form his own opinion."[1] Soviet authorities were not inclined to accept the suggestion that they remove the stain of Katyn. On the contrary, they preferred to end all discussion of the embarrassing matter. In the Soviet Union all mention of Katyn was removed from maps and history textbooks. The reference to Katyn in the 1953 edition of the *Soviet Encyclopedia* was dropped in the 1973 edition.

[1]*The Hinge of Fate*, Houghton Mifflin Company, Boston, 1950, p. 761.

KEITEL, WILHELM [BODEWIN JOHANN] (1882–1946). General field marshal in the armed forces of the Third Reich and Hitler's chief military adviser in World War II. Wilhelm Keitel was born on September 22, 1882, in Helmscherode, in the Harz Mountains. He served as an officer in World War I and was severely wounded. From 1929 to 1934 he was active in matters of Army organization, and from October 1935 on he was connected with the Ministry of War. On February 4, 1938, after scandals involving Gen. Werner von Blomberg and Col. Gen. Werner Freiherr von Fritsch (qq.v.), respectively charged with marrying a woman of questionable virtue and accused of homosexuality, Hitler announced the retirement of the top echelon of the Reichswehr (q.v.) and assumed supreme command himself. He made Keitel *Chef des Oberkommando der Wehrmacht* (chief of the High Command of the armed forces), a newly created military body, but limited his power. In November 1938 Keitel was promoted to full general.

In 1939, at the outbreak of World War II, Keitel ranked No. 5 among the senior officers of the Army. In June 1940 Hitler entrusted him with concluding the armistice with France at Compiègne (q.v.). On July 19, Keitel was made a general field marshal, with eleven other generals, by a triumphant Hitler. Keitel threatened to resign in 1941 in order to discourage Hitler from invading the Soviet Union, but he was unable to prevent the Fuehrer's invasion. Keitel's influence on Hitler became increasingly limited as the war progressed. Yet his belief in Hitler's genius led him to issue such orders as the Nacht- und Nebel Erlass (q.v.), the Night and Fog Decree, which was to place him in jeopardy after the war. In 1945 Keitel was brought before the International Military Tribunal at Nuremberg (*see* NUREMBERG TRIAL) on charges of participating in a conspiracy, crimes against peace, war crimes, and crimes against humanity. He was found guilty on all four counts and sentenced to death. Keitel mounted the gallows in the execution chamber of Nuremberg Prison on October 16, 1946.

Tall and broad-shouldered, with a monocle firmly held in his left eye, Keitel was the apotheosis of the old-line officer. Yet he never felt adequate to his lofty position. There was no question of his loyalty to Hitler. He was unpopular among his peers, who called him "Yes-Keitel" and "the Nodding Ass." Some went so far as to label him *Laikaitel*, a play on words of the German term *Lakai* (lackey, or flunky). Keitel was second only to Hitler in directing the German war machine. "At the bottom of my heart," he wrote in his memoirs, "I was a loyal shield-bearer for Adolf Hitler." He praised the Fuehrer's iron will, his steadfastness, and his unrelenting severity in the Russian campaign, without which "the German Army would inescapably and inevitably have suffered in 1941 the fate of the French in 1812." On the other hand, Keitel resented the way in which he was treated by his master. "I was never permitted to make decisions: the Fuehrer

Field Marshal Keitel before the International Military Tribunal at Nuremberg. [*Wide World Photos*]

reserved that right to himself even in seemingly trivial matters." Keitel never rebelled against this kind of treatment.

Bibliography. *The Memoirs of Field-Marshal Keitel,* ed. by Walter Görlitz and tr. by David Irving, Stein and Day, Incorporated, New York, 1966.

KEMPKA, ERICH (1910–). Hitler's personal chauffeur. Erich Kempka was born on September 16, 1910. After joining the Nazi party, he became a *Sturmbannfuehrer* (major) in the Leibstandarte-SS Adolf Hitler (q.v.), Hitler's personal bodyguard. He served as a transport officer at the Fuehrer's general headquarters and also as Hitler's private chauffeur.

KEPPLER, WILHELM (1882–1960). Industrialist and an early member of the Nationalsozialistische Deutsche Arbeiterpartei (q.v.), the Nazi party. The organizer of the Keppler Circle (q.v.), Keppler hoped to help Hitler financially in his drive for political power. After Hitler became Chancellor, he made Keppler Reich Commissioner of Economic Affairs. In 1936 Keppler became adviser to Hermann Goering (q.v.) on the Four-Year Plan (q.v.). He helped prepare the way for *Anschluss* (q.v.) with Austria and was sent to Vienna in March 1938 as Reich Commissioner. During World War II he served in the Ministry of Foreign Affairs. After the war he was indicted as a war criminal and sentenced to prison for ten years.

KEPPLER CIRCLE. A group of wealthy and conservative businessmen organized to help Hitler. In the autumn of 1931 Hitler suggested to Wilhelm Keppler (q.v.), a strong pro-Nazi and an affluent entrepreneur, that he bring together a group of business leaders who had proved themselves in industry and who would be willing to "advise" the Nazis in their drive for political power. It was not necessary, he said, that the members of the circle be affiliated with the Nationalsozialistische Deutsche Arbeiterpartei (q.v.). The businessmen of the Keppler Circle, who contributed to Nazi coffers, believed that Hitler would be tamed when he became Chancellor and that he could be taught the principles of a sound economy. Expecting to use Hitler for their own purposes, they learned later to their dismay that he was skillful in using them.

KERRL, HANS (1887–1941). Reich Minister without Portfolio in Hitler's original Cabinet of 1933. Hans Kerrl was born in Fallersleben on December 11, 1887, the son of a Lutheran schoolmaster. After attendance at a *Gymnasium* (high school), he served in World War I as a lieutenant and was awarded the Iron Cross (First and Second Classes) and the Braunschweig service medal. When Hitler came to political power in 1933, he made Kerrl Prussian minister of justice and simultaneously Reich Minister without Portfolio. Hitler relied on Kerrl for various legal tasks. Kerrl also served in the Reichstag (q.v.). He died in Berlin on December 15, 1941.

KERSTEN, FELIX (1898–). Physician who treated National Socialist leaders. Felix Kersten was born in Dorpat (Tartu), Estonia, on September 20, 1898. After attending the *Progymnasium* (lower and middle part of a classical high school) in Wenden, Livonia (Cēsis, Latvia), he undertook higher studies in the *Gymnasium* of the Balkan Knighthood in Birkenruh. From 1914 to 1917 he studied at the Agricultural College of Jenfeld in Holstein and on graduation became the manager of a large farm in Anhalt. In 1919 he joined the Finnish Army and fought for the liberation of Finland in the war against Russia. He subsequently acquired Finnish citizenship. In 1922 he went to Berlin, where he studied physiotherapy, took a degree, and started a lucrative practice.

In March 1939 Kersten was summoned to treat Heinrich Himmler (q.v.) for recurrent stomach spasms. His success in relieving the *Reichsfuehrer-SS* of pain led to referrals among the Nazi hierarchy. At Himmler's request Rudolf Hess (q.v.) became a patient of Dr. Kersten. Until that time Hess had held academic medicine in contempt and would not call in a physician to treat him for his gall bladder trouble. Other patients were Robert Ley (q.v.), leader of the Deutsche Arbeitsfront (q.v.), the German Labor Front, a dipsomaniac with a severe liver complaint, and Joachim von Ribbentrop (q.v.), who suffered habitually from severe headaches, vertigo, and disorders of the digestive system.

In his *Memoirs,* Dr. Kersten claimed that Himmler revealed to him Germany's plans for the future: after the war all American Jews would be surrendered to Germany for extermination; the map of Europe would be radically revised; German would be made the official language in all European countries; the fall of Catholicism would be symbolized by the hanging of the Pope; the old Nordic pagan faith would be revived in Germany; German women would be encouraged to breed; and non-German people would be discouraged from having children.

Bibliography. *The Memoirs of Doctor Felix Kersten*, tr. by Ernst Morwitz, Doubleday & Company, Inc., Garden City, N.Y., 1947.

KESSELRING, ALBERT (1885–1960). General field marshal in the Luftwaffe (q.v.). Albert Kesselring was born in Marktsteft, Bavaria, on November 20, 1885, to a middle-class family. He joined the Army in 1904 and served in the artillery. After two years on the western front in World War I, he was called to the General Staff. In 1936 Hitler made him chief of the General Staff of the Luftwaffe with the task of implementing liaison with the Army.

At the opening of World War II Kesselring led Luftflotte (Air Force) I in the Polish campaign in support of the army group of Gen. Fedor von Bock (q.v.). After his successful command in the east he was transferred to the western front as commander of Luftflotte II in the Flanders campaign. On July 19, 1940, after the fall of France, Hitler made Kesselring a general field marshal of the Luftwaffe along with Erhard Milch and Hugo Sperrle (qq.v.). From December 2, 1941, to March 10, 1945, Kesselring was commander in chief of the Armed Forces South in the Mediterranean area (Italy and North Africa). In this capacity he was responsible for the countermeasures adopted by the Germans against the Italians who had surrendered to the Allies. From March 25 to May 6, 1945, he was commander in chief of the Armed Forces South responsible for combat operations in western Germany.

Field Marshal Albert Kesselring. [*Picture Collection, The Branch Libraries, The New York Public Library*]

On May 6, 1947, a British court-martial convicted Kesselring on a charge of having allowed the shooting of 335 Italian civilians in reprisal for an attack by Italian partisans on a German company. He was sentenced to death, but the penalty was commuted to life imprisonment in October 1947. Kesselring was pardoned and freed on October 23, 1952. He died in Bad Nauheim on July 16, 1960.

KETTE (Chain). A combat formation of three aircraft in the Luftwaffe (q.v.).

KG. *See* KAMPFGESCHWADER.

"KIDS, KIRK, KITCHEN." *See* "KINDER, KIRCHE, KÜCHE."

KIEP, OTTO KARL (1886–1944). Lawyer, diplomat, and member of the Resistance (q.v.) movement against Hitler. Otto Karl Kiep was born in Saltcoats, Scotland, on July 7, 1886, the son of a German consul. Continuing the family tradition, he entered the German diplomatic service.

Otto Karl Kiep. [From *Annedore Leber (ed.),* Conscience in Revolt, *tr. by Rosemary O'Neill, Vallentine, Mitchell & Co., Ltd., London, 1957*]

After taking part in conferences on reparations, he was appointed Counselor to the German Embassy in Washington in 1927 and Consul General in New York in 1930. Because Kiep attended a banquet in honor of Albert Einstein (q.v.), he was recalled in 1933. In London at the outbreak of World War II, he chose to return home. He entered the Foreign Department of the Oberkommando der Wehrmacht (q.v.), which became a center for the Resistance movement. He was betrayed to the Gestapo (q.v.) for attending a meeting at the home of Elizabeth von Thadden (q.v.). Arrested on January 16, 1944, he was condemned to death for treason and executed at Plötzensee Prison in Berlin on August 26, 1944.

KILLER UNITS. *See* EINSATZKOMMANDOS.

"KINDER, KIRCHE, KÜCHE" ("Kids, Kirk, Kitchen"). A slogan that originated before the Nazi era but was employed also during the Third Reich. It was used in various other combinations, such as "*Kirche, Küche, Kinder.*" The cry "Women's place is in the home!" was a popular one after Hitler became Chancellor. From the Fuehrer down through the hierarchy, Nazi thinking on the women's question was dogmatically in favor of inequality between the sexes, as positive as the belief in differences between the races. In this view the emancipation of women was indicative of the depravity of parliamentary democracy. Although there were many women's organizations in the Third Reich, they were regarded as auxiliaries ranking below male groups.

KINDERLANDVERSCHICKUNG (KLV; Sending Children to the Country). Official plan to evacuate large groups of children to the countryside during World War II. The KLV policy served the purpose of removing children to areas of safety and also of taking them from their family environment. Parents who refused to give their permission were denounced as unpatriotic. The parents were discouraged from visiting the KLV camps in order not to intensify homesickness and also to avoid a strain on the transportation system.

KINDERSEGEN (Blessed with Children). Emotional term used constantly by Nazi leaders to promote the birthrate. Although the Germans were supposed to be a people without space (*see* "VOLK OHNE RAUM"), Hitler called for an ever-greater population. The regime adopted such eugenic measures as marriage loans (*see* EHESTANDSDARLEHEN), child subsidies, and family allowances. Added to the financial inducements was a strong propaganda campaign to bring about an increase in the birthrate. The term *family* was limited to households with four children or more. Those who refused to have children were denounced as worse than "deserters on the battlefield." There were special honors for mothers who contributed children to the fatherland (*see* HONOR CROSS OF THE GERMAN MOTHER).

KINDERTAGESSTÄTTE (Nursery School). A special Nazi school for children of nursery age.

KIRDORF, EMIL (1847–1938). Rhineland industrialist, coal baron, and early supporter of the National Socialist movement. Emil Kirdorf was born in Mettmann on April 8, 1847. In his mid-twenties he founded, together with F. Grillo and others, the Gelsenkircher Bergwerke–AG (GBAG; Gelsenkircher Mine Works, Inc.) and was instrumental in the creation of the Rheinisch-Westfälischen Kohlensyndikate (Rhine-Westphalian Coal Syndicate) and the Vereingten Stahlwerke A.G. (United Steel Works, Inc.). An extreme nationalist and a promoter of Pan-Germanism, he even criticized Emperor William II as weak and vacillating. Kirdorf controlled the Ruhr Treasury, a political fund set up by mining interests in the Ruhr to protect their industries. He was both hated and feared by German workers as a ruthless employer.

On August 2, 1929, the eighty-two-year-old Kirdorf went to Nuremberg to have a look at Hitler on the third National Socialist Party Day. The billionaire industrialist was delighted by what he saw. He sent Hitler a glowing letter including the following (condensed) passages:

> Dear Herr Hitler: On our return home my wife and I are eager to express our thanks to you for requesting that we attend the Party Day. We shall never forget how overwhelmed we were in attending the memorial celebration for the World War I dead, and the sight of your thousands and thousands of supporters, who hung on your every word and cheered you. At this moment, I, who am filled with despair by the degeneration of the masses, suddenly realized why you believe and trust so zealously in the fulfillment of the task you have set yourself. You may be proud of the honors and homage done you.
>
> Anyone who was privileged to attend this session will recognize the importance of your movement for the rehabilitation of the Fatherland and wish it success. I have taken with me from Nuremberg the consoling certainty that numerous circles will sacrifice themselves to prevent the doom of Germanism. With true German greetings from my wife and self, in friendship,
>
> Yours,
> Kirdorf

From that moment Kirdorf became a heavy contributor to the National Socialist party, which owed much of its success to his support. He died in Mülheim an der Ruhr on July 13, 1938.

KITZELMANN, MICHAEL (1916–1942). Young officer executed for "undermining the German Army." Michael Kitzelmann was born in the Allgäu on January 29, 1916, the son of a farmer. After serving his term in the Reichsarbeitsdienst (q.v.), the State Labor Service, he was called to the Army. World War II began before his two-year service was finished. He was at the front for two years, took part in three campaigns, won a commission, and was awarded the Iron Cross (Second Class). As a company commander during the Russian campaign, he was arrested for critical remarks on the Nazi regime, such as "If these criminals should win, I would have no wish to live any longer." He was sentenced to death by a court-martial and died before a firing squad at Orel on June 11, 1942.

KL. (1) Acronym used by SS (q.v.) guards instead of the more popular KZ (q.v.) to indicate *Konzentrations Lager* (concentration camp). (2) Acronym for *Kreisleitung* (q.v.), circuit leadership.

KLAUSENER, ERICH (1885–1934). Leader of Catholic Action. Erich Klausener was born in Düsseldorf on January 25, 1885. In 1919 he was a farmer in Recklinghausen. In 1924 he became Ministerial Director in the Welfare Ministry at Berlin, and from 1926 to 1933 he worked in the Prussian Ministry of the Interior. He was the leader of the Catholic Action organization in Berlin from 1928 to 1933. In 1933 he was made Reich Communications Director. He incurred Hitler's anger when he contributed to the text of the critical Marburg speech delivered by Franz von Papen (q.v.) on June 17, 1934 (*see* MARBURGER REDE). Although careful not to criticize Hitler publicly, Klausener made it clear in his speeches and writing that the national revolution must be accompanied by "an inner, spiritual revival." To the Nazis this was dangerous dissent. In the Blood Purge (q.v.) of June 30, 1934, Klausener was murdered in his office at the Ministry of Communications by an SS (q.v.) squad. Lawyers who attempted to represent Klausener's widow in her suit for damages against the state were held in Sachsenhausen (q.v.) concentration camp until they formally withdrew the action.

KLAUSING, FRIEDRICH KARL (1920–1944). Adjutant to Claus Schenk Graf von Stauffenberg (q.v.) and member of the Resistance (q.v.) movement. Friedrich Karl Klausing was born on May 24, 1920. After serving in the Hitler Jugend and the Reichsarbeitsdienst (qq.v.; the Hitler Youth and the State Labor Service), he joined the Army in 1938. He took part in the Polish and French campaigns, during which he was promoted to officer rank and won the Iron Cross (First Class). Transferred to the Russian front, he was badly wounded at Stalingrad and promoted to 1st lieutenant. In 1943 he was posted to General Headquarters for home service. Alienated by the Nazi movement, he joined the conspiracy against Hitler. Arrested on the day of the 1944 July Plot (q.v.), he was sentenced to death by the Volksgericht (q.v.), the dreaded People's Court, and executed on August 8, 1944.

Bibliography. Annedore Leber (ed.), *Conscience in Revolt*, tr. by Rosemary O'Neill, Vallentine, Mitchell & Co., Ltd., London, 1957.

KLEE, PAUL (1879–1940). Swiss painter and graphic artist denounced in the Third Reich as a purveyor of degenerate art (*see* ENTARTETE KUNST). Paul Klee was born at Münchenbuchsee, near Bern, on December 18, 1879, the son of a German music teacher. After studying art at Munich from 1898 to 1901, he traveled in Italy and in 1906 returned to Munich. In 1912 he went to Paris, where he met Pablo Picasso. From 1921 on he was a master at the Bauhaus at Weimar and later at Dessau. Dismissed in 1933 when Hitler came to political power, Klee settled in Switzerland. One of the great figures of modern art, Klee was noted for his delicacy of line and his mastery of space. In 1937 Nazi authorities confiscated 102 of his works as unworthy of public display. Klee died in Muralto, near Locarno, on June 29, 1940.

KLEINE VOLKSGENOSSEN (Little Fellow Countrymen). Term used by Hitler in the early days of his movement to describe his followers responsible for the Nazi revolution. The left-wingers who took him at his word and attempted to turn the revolution in the direction of socialism were eliminated in the 1934 Blood Purge (q.v.). *See also* SECOND REVOLUTION.

KLEIST, EWALD VON (1881–1954). General field marshal in the armed forces of the Third Reich. Ewald von Kleist was born in Braunfels an der Lahn on August 8, 1881, to an old-line aristocratic family. A strong monarchist close to the Von Hindenburg family, he served as commander of a cavalry division from 1932 to 1935. He was promoted to general of cavalry on August 1, 1936, and given command of Wehrkreis (Defense District) VIII at Breslau. Temporarily retired, he was recalled in August 1939 at the age of fifty-eight as commanding general of the XXII Corps. In 1940 he led a *Panzer* (q.v.) group on the western front and achieved a decisive breakthrough at a canal near Abbeville. The next year he was sent to the Balkans, where he captured Belgrade. In 1941 he led the First Panzer Army in the invasion of the Soviet Union, but his tanks could make little progress toward Rostov. He blamed this breakdown on the early onset of winter.

In 1942 Hitler sent Von Kleist to the Caucasus with orders to take the oil wells there by autumn. At first Von Kleist made progress in this campaign. Official Nazi policy was to treat the non-Germanic peoples in the east as *Untermenschen* (inferior people racially), an attitude that cost the Germans millions of potential allies. Von Kleist had the foresight to seek the cooperation of the peoples of the Caucasus and used officers who knew them well. As a result he obtained the support of thousands of Azerbaijani, Kalmucks, Ossets, and others, who formed legions to fight with the Germans against the Communists.

Field Marshal Ewald von Kleist. [*Imperial War Museum, London*]

On January 31, 1943, Hitler, in recognition of Von Kleist's services at a time when the Russian campaign was deteriorating, made him a general field marshal. At the end of the war Von Kleist was taken prisoner by the British in Yugoslavia. In 1948 he was transferred to the Soviet Union, where he died in October 1954 in the Vladimirovka camp, about 110 miles from Moscow.

KLEIST-SCHMENZIN, EWALD VON (1890–1945). Lawyer, landowner, and victim of the Nazi regime. Ewald von Kleist-Schmenzin was born in Dubberow, Pomerania (now Dobrowo, Poland), and grew up on his parents' estate. A member of the provincial synod, he leaned toward the Deutschnationale Volkspartei (German Nationalist People's party) and the Stahlhelm (q.v.). In 1932, during the critical period when Hitler was pushing his way to power, Von Kleist-Schmenzin denounced National Socialism as "lunacy" and as "the deadly enemy of our way of life." He spoke out loudly: "National Socialism would never have gained such a flying start if normal and patriotic citizens had openly come out against it." Deeply religious, he called National Socialism a crude form of materialism, "quite incompatible with Christian-

Ewald von Kleist-Schmenzin. [*Ullstein*]

ity." He was arrested twice in 1933 after Hitler took power. In 1944 he invited several Resistance (q.v.) groups to meet at Schmenzin, his country estate. Taken into custody, he was brought to the Gestapo (q.v.)-controlled prison in the Lehrterstrasse in Berlin. On April 9, 1945, only a few weeks before the fall of the Third Reich, Von Kleist-Schmenzin was beheaded at Plötzensee Prison.

KLEMPERER, OTTO (1885–1973). Great musical conductor and refugee from the Third Reich. Otto Klemperer was born in Breslau, now the Polish city of Wrocław, on May 14, 1885. From 1927 to 1933, during the late days of the Weimar Republic (q.v.), he was director of the Kroll Opera, the Berlin State Opera's second house. He gave the first performances of operas by Schoenberg, Stravinsky, Hindemith, Janáček, and other composers. Klemperer was considered to be one of the giants in his field, the survivor of a generation of conductors stretching back to Strauss and Mahler. He regarded Mahler as the guiding light of his career. As a small boy in 1893, he first saw Mahler on the streets of Hamburg, and in 1905 he conducted the offstage orchestra in the Second Symphony in the composer's presence. Klemperer married the opera singer Johanna Geissler (d. 1956).

Klemperer left Germany as an exile in 1933 at the advent of the Hitler regime. From 1933 to 1940 he conducted the Los Angeles Philharmonic Orchestra, and in 1938 he reorganized the Pittsburgh Orchestra. Returning to Europe in 1946, he directed the Budapest Opera from 1947 to 1950. Thereafter, he was active in England and West Germany.

Klemperer's dismissal from his post in Nazi Germany was a classic example of the rejection of a titan in the arts in favor of coordinated mediocrity. Plagued through most of his career by a paralysis resulting from brain surgery, he was often in severe pain while unknowing critics condemned him for his "solemn, intellectual approach." He died in Zürich on July 6, 1973, at the age of eighty-eight.

KLUFT (Clothes). Special name given to the uniform worn by members of the Jungmädel (q.v.), an organization of girls below the age of fourteen.

KLUGE, GÜNTHER HANS VON (1882–1944). General field marshal in the armed forces of the Third Reich. Günther Hans von Kluge was born in Posen (now Poznań), on October 30, 1882. After service in World War I, he was rapidly promoted and by 1935 was a major general assigned to Wehrkreis (Defense District) VI. In 1938 he was one of the generals who were purged because of their support for Gen. Werner Freiherr von Fritsch (q.v.) in his difficulties with Hitler. At the outbreak of World War II in 1939, Von Kluge was recalled at the age of fifty-seven as the eighth-ranking senior officer of the armed forces. He commanded Army Group VI, which occupied the Polish Corridor in the early days of the war, and served on the western front in 1940. Von Kluge was one of the twelve generals to be promoted to general field marshal by Hitler on July 19, 1940, after the fall of France. He was sent to northwestern Russia in 1941 and given command of Army Group Center on the Russian front in 1942.

Von Kluge was familiar with the Resistance (q.v.) movement against Hitler, but he vacillated from one side

Field Marshal Günther Hans von Kluge. [*Picture Collection, The Branch Libraries, The New York Public Library*]

to the other. A non-Nazi rather than an anti-Nazi, he was by nature indecisive. Although he indicated that he might take part in the conspiracy, he relapsed into compliant obedience to Hitler. On Von Kluge's sixtieth birthday, October 30, 1942, Hitler sent him a letter of congratulations plus a substantial sum of cash to enable him to make improvements on his estate. The conspirators obtained a copy of the letter and used it to their advantage in urging Von Kluge to meet with their representatives. Von Kluge agreed to take action as soon as he got word from Berlin about the success of the plot against Hitler's life, but he soon reconsidered and resumed his policy of vacillation. Flattered by the Fuehrer's attention, he withdrew from the plot.

In the autumn of 1943 Von Kluge was seriously injured in an automobile accident while driving from Orsha to Minsk and was incapacitated for some months. On July 2, 1944, Hitler, outraged by the inability of Field Marshal Gerd von Rundstedt (q.v) to stop the Allied invasion of Normandy, dismissed Von Rundstedt in favor of Von Kluge, now recovered from his injuries. Von Kluge himself was removed after the disaster at the Falaise gap and replaced by Field Marshal Walther Model (q.v.), who had been summoned from the Russian front to handle the German retreat to the Rhine. Despondent because of his military misfortunes, Von Kluge committed suicide on August 18, 1944, on a former battlefield of 1870 west of Metz.

KLV. *See* KINDERLANDVERSHICKUNG.

KNAUF, ERICH (1895–1944). Journalist and publicist condemned to death by the Nazi regime. Erich Knauf was born in Saxony on February 21, 1895, to a working-class family. After serving an apprenticeship as a compositor, he wandered in Greece, Italy, and Turkey. He took part in World War I, serving from 1915 to 1918. After the war he turned to political and literary journalism and established a reputation as an author and critic. He resigned from the Gutenberg Book Guild when the Nazis took over in 1933 and was expelled from the Reich Press Association for his critical attitude toward National Socialism. He spent ten weeks in concentration camps (q.v.) at Oranienburg and Lichtenburg. In 1944, toward the close of World War II, he was denounced for referring to Dr. Paul Joseph Goebbels (q.v.) as "this little rat," for saying that "Heinrich Himmler [q.v.] only keeps his job by ordering between 80 and 100 executions a day," and for stating that "a German victory would be the greatest misfortune." Knauf was arrested and brought before the Volksgericht (q.v.), the People's Court, and executed on May 2, 1944. The public prosecutor charged him for an account of 585.74 reichsmarks, which included a 300-mark fee for the death penalty, 44 marks as a "charge for prison maintenance," and 12 pfennigs for postage.

KNIGHT'S CROSS. *See* RITTERKREUZ.

KNOKPLOEGEN. A Dutch resistance organization, similar to the Orde Dienst (q.v.), or Order Service. The Knokploegen, set up shortly after the Nazi invasion of the Netherlands in May 1940, specialized in such tasks as raiding administrative offices to obtain ration books for Dutch citizens who had gone underground. Its members later took part in more serious sabotage.

KOCH, ILSE (1906–1967). Woman called the Witch (*Hexe*) or the Bitch of Buchenwald. Ilse Koch was born in Saxony, the daughter of a laborer. She worked for a time as a librarian. In 1936, at the age of thirty, she married *SS-Standartenfuehrer* (Col.) Karl Koch, a notorious criminal, then commandant of the concentration camp at Sachsenhausen (q.v.). In 1939 she accompanied her husband when he was transferred to Buchenwald (q.v.) as commandant. Here she acquired a reputation as an aggressive sadist. A strapping red-haired woman of ample proportions, she liked to ride on horseback, with whip in hand, through the prison compound, lashing out at any prisoner unfortunate enough to glance in her direction. Her hobby was collecting lampshades, book covers, and gloves made from the skins of dead inmates. On occasion, she gave orders for new prisoners with "interesting tattoos" to be reserved for her. In 1944 her husband was brought before an SS (q.v.) tribunal on charges of racketeering, insubordination, and murder. He was hanged in early 1945. His widow was acquitted of receiving stolen goods. In 1947 an American military tribunal found her guilty of murder and sentenced her to life imprisonment. Gen. Lucius D. Clay reduced her sentence to four years, a decision that aroused international controversy because of its "lack of severity." A United States Senate committee investigated her case and came to the conclusion on December 27, 1948, that she had taken part in killing or beating hundreds of prisoners: "This bestial woman's guilt in specific murders is irrefutably established."

Rearrested in 1949, Ilse Koch was brought to trial before a West German court for crimes against German nationals. On January 15, 1951, she was sentenced to life imprisonment. Asserting her innocence, she appealed in vain for help from the International Human Rights Commission. Psychiatrists who examined her judged her to be "a perverted, nymphomaniacal, hysterical, power-mad demon." Finally giving up hope, she committed suicide on September 1, 1967, at the age of sixty-one, by using a bed sheet latched to the door of her cell in the Bavarian prison of Aichach. In her last note to her son Uwe, born in prison in 1947, she wrote: "I cannot do otherwise. Death is the only deliverance."

KOHN, HANS (1891–1971). American historian and interpreter of the German mind. Hans Kohn was born in Prague on September 15, 1891. Serving with the Austrian Army in World War I, he was captured by the Russians and sent as a prisoner of war to Samarkand and later to Siberia. Returning to Prague, he then spent four years in London and four years in Jerusalem. In 1931 he went to the United States, where he served as professor of history at Smith College (1934–1949) and at the City College of New York (1949–1962). A prolific author, he was a major authority on nationalism, on which he wrote many books including his masterpiece, *The Idea of Nationalism* (1944). Kohn published many scholarly studies on the nature of the German mind and on the intellectual forerunners of National Socialism. He died in Philadelphia on April 16, 1971.

Bibliography. Hans Kohn, *The Mind of Modern Germany: The Education of a Nation*, Charles Scribner's Sons, New York, 1960.

KOKOSCHKA, OSKAR (1886–). Austrian expressionist painter denounced by the Nazis as a purveyor of degenerate art (*see* ENTARTETE KUNST). Oskar Kokoschka was born in Pöchlarn an der Donau on March 1, 1886. From 1920 to 1924 he taught art at Dresden and then traveled extensively through Europe and North Africa. His early paintings were distinguished by a restless energy and an emphasis on psychological tension in face and hands; his later art, by a subdued impressionistic style. In 1937 all his works in Germany were summarily removed from galleries as decadent and unworthy of Nazi approval.

KOLBE, MAXIMILIAN (1894–1941). Catholic priest who chose death in the place of a condemned Polish prisoner at Auschwitz (q.v.). Born Raymond Kolbe, he decided at the age of thirteen to become a priest. Entering the Franciscan order, he studied at the Gregorian University at Rome and by the age of twenty-two had two doctorates, one in philosophy and the other in theology. Returning to Poland, he led a group of friars in establishing in a field about twenty-five miles from Warsaw what was to become the world's largest monastery. By 1939 there were some 750 friars at Niepokalanów. When the Nazis invaded Poland in 1939, Father Kolbe set up a haven for refugees there.

Arrested as an enemy of the Third Reich, Father Kolbe was sent first to a Warsaw jail and then to the concentration camp at Auschwitz. In late July 1941 a prisoner escaped from a labor detail and disappeared. The camp commander, a Colonel Fritsch, announced that if the fugitive was not found within twenty-four hours, in reprisal 10 of the 600 men in his cellblock would be chosen at random and allowed to starve. After the selection was made, Father Kolbe approached Colonel Fritsch and asked to take the place of one of the prisoners. "I am alone in the world. That man, Francis Gajowniczek, has a family to live for." The camp commander replied "Accepted" and turned away. The priest was the last of the 10 men to die.

On October 17, 1971, a ceremony of beatification, a preliminary step to canonization as a Catholic saint, took place for Father Kolbe at St. Peter's Basilica in Rome. Among the 8,000 men and women who journeyed from

Poland to attend the services were Francis Gajowniczek, now a white-haired pensioner, and his wife. Pope Paul VI described the priest as "probably the brightest and most glittering figure to emerge from the inhuman degradation and unthinkable cruelty of the Nazi epoch."

KOLLWITZ, KÄTHE (1867–1945). Renowned artist *persona non grata* in the Third Reich. Born Käthe Schmidt in Königsberg on July 8, 1867, she studied art with Karl Stauffer-Bern in Berlin and with Ludwig Heterich in Munich. Until 1943 she lived in Berlin, where she was a professor at the Academy of Art from 1919 to 1933. Her charcoal drawings, etchings, and lithographs, nearly all devoted to proletarian life, were distinguished by a sharp, concise style that won her worldwide fame. She died in Moritzburg, near Dresden, on April 22, 1945.

KOMMISSAR ERLASS (Commissar Decree). Order issued by Hitler early in March 1941 to the top military command on the manner in which the war would be conducted after the invasion of Soviet Russia:

> The war against Russia cannot be fought in knightly fashion. The struggle is one of ideologies and racial differences and will have to be waged with unprecedented, unmerciful, and unrelenting hardness. All officers will have to get rid of any old-fashioned ideas they may have. I realize that the necessity for conducting such warfare is beyond the comprehension of you generals, but I must insist that my orders be followed without complaint. The commissars hold views directly opposite to those of National Socialism. Hence these commissars must be eliminated. Any German soldier who breaks international law will be pardoned. Russia did not take part in the Hague Convention and, therefore, has no rights under it.

This extraordinary order caused some soul-searching among the older officers, but it was carried out in obedience to the Fuehrer's wishes. The Commissar Decree was the subject of much discussion at the Nuremberg Trial (q.v.).

KOMMUNISTISCHE PARTEI DEUTSCHLANDS (KPD; Communist Party of Germany). Name used by the Communist party of Germany. In the 1920s the party was unsuccessful in the battle of the streets against Nazi Storm Troopers (*see* SA).

KÖNIGSBERGER REDE (Königsberg Speech). An address delivered on August 18, 1935, by Dr. Hjalmar Schacht (q.v.) at Königsberg, East Prussia, in which he condemned indiscriminate violence against the Jews. The speech, like the *Marburger Rede* of Vice-Chancellor Franz von Papen (qq.v.), was designed to discourage the more violent aspects of the Hitler regime. It received little attention in the Nazi-controlled press, which deliberately avoided criticism of this kind. The text was reprinted in a minor Reichsbank publication.

KORDT, ERICH (1903–). Diplomat. After a long preparatory career in the civil service, Erich Kordt was attached to the German Foreign Office in 1934 under Joachim von Ribbentrop (q.v.). In this capacity Kordt took part as an important official in high-level conferences and state visits. He accompanied Von Ribbentrop to London in May 1935 on a disastrous "goodwill" trip. From 1942 to 1945 he served as Minister in the German Embassies in Japan and China (Nanking government). After the war he was exonerated by a denazification (q.v.) court.

Bibliography. Erich Kordt, *Nicht aus den Akten*, Union Deutsche Verlagsgesellschaft, Stuttgart, 1950.

KORDT, THEODOR (1893–). Diplomat, brother of Erich Kordt (q.v.). Theodor Kordt served in various posts abroad. In 1939, before the outbreak of World War II, he was Counselor of Embassy in London. From 1939 to 1945 he was Counselor of the legation at Bern.

KORTNER, FRITZ (1892–). Actor, director, and prominent refugee from the Third Reich. Fritz Kortner was born in Vienna on March 12, 1892. After serving his apprenticeship at Mannheim in 1911, he went to Berlin, where he worked with the famous director Max Reinhardt (q.v.) at the Deutsches Theater. With a group of young actors Kortner rebelled against Reinhardt's methods and developed his own form of expressionism. He became widely known in such roles as Gessler, Shylock, Richard III, Othello, and Oedipus. Forced to leave Germany in 1933, he went to London and subsequently to the United States, where he was featured in many films. He returned to Germany in 1949 and won great success in a series of plays ranging from *Waiting for Godot* (1954) to *Storm* (1968).

KPD. *See* KOMMUNISTISCHE PARTEI DEUTSCHLANDS.

KRAFT DURCH FREUDE (KdF; Strength through Joy). National Socialist recreational organization designed to stimulate morale among workers. Roughly translated, Kraft durch Freude means "more strength through more pleasure." Set up in imitation of a similar Italian organization founded by Mussolini, KdF was the carrot that was to lead the German workers to greater productivity. It was the best-publicized program of industrial relations in the Third Reich. Participants in a new form of mass tourism, KdF holiday makers cruised on luxury liners and traveled by train to the Alps, Venice, Naples, and Lisbon. There were also many tourist trips to Norway. These vacations not only were well received by workers but also brought large profits to rural hotel owners as well as to the Reichsbahn, the state railroad system. The KdF program also included subsidized theater performances, concerts, exhibitions, sports, hiking, folk dancing, and adult education courses.

The Kraft durch Freude organization received huge subsidies from the government (24 million marks in 1933–1934, 17 million in 1935, and 15 million in 1936). It became a big business itself. Within two years after KdF was organized, two ocean liners with single-class accommodations were constructed especially for its tours. The Volkswagen (q.v.), the people's automobile, was known originally as the KdF Wagen. Large governmental subsidies went into its development. Until this time the automobile had been considered a bourgeois status symbol, but now the average worker could pay weekly installments in order to obtain one eventually.

With its multiple functions the KdF was regarded by Nazi leaders as practical proof of benign National Socialist economic and labor policies. Dr. Robert Ley (q.v.), who was responsible for KdF activities, summarized its goal: "The worker sees that we are serious about raising his social position. He sees that it is not the so-called 'educated classes' whom we send out as representative of the new Germany, but himself, the German worker, whom we show to the world." Ley regarded the KdF as proof that there were no longer classes in the Third Reich: "In the years to come the worker will lose the last traces of inferiority feelings he may have inherited from the past."

KRAMER, JOSEF (1907–1945). Commander of the Belsen (q.v.) concentration camp (*see* CONCENTRATION CAMPS). Josef Kramer received his training under Rudolf Franz Hoess at Auschwitz (qq.v.) and later had additional experience at Mauthausen, Dachau, and Birkenau (qq.v.). In 1940 Kramer accompanied Hoess to inspect Auschwitz as a site for a new synthetic coal oil and rubber plant. He became notorious as a harsh taskmaster. Dr. Franz Lucas, one of the defendants at the Frankfurt Trial (q.v.), testified that he tried to avoid assignments given him by Kramer by pleading stomach and intestinal disorders. When Dr. Lucas saw that his name had been added to the list of selecting physicians for a large group of inmates transported from Hungary, he objected strenuously. Kramer reacted sharply: "I know you are being investigated for favoring prisoners. I am now ordering you to go to the ramp, and if you fail to obey the order, I shall have you arrested on the spot."

In August 1943 Kramer received eighty inmates who were to be killed with gas. With the help of SS (q.v.) assistants, Kramer stripped the women and, when they were stark-naked, shoved them in small groups into the gas chamber. "When the door closed they began to scream," he testified later. "I put in a small amount of salt through a tube and looked through a peephole to see what happened. The women breathed about a minute before they fell to the floor." Kramer repeated the performance until all were dead. When asked by his interrogator what his feelings were at the time, he replied: "I had no feelings in carrying out these things because I had received an order. That, incidentally, is the way I was trained."

Josef Kramer after his capture in April 1945. [*Imperial War Museum, London*]

In late 1944 Kramer was transferred from Birkenau to Belsen, near the village of Bergen on the road from Celle to Hamburg. Originally known as a small, privileged camp, Belsen was enlarged to serve as a convalescent depot for sick persons from concentration camps, factories, and farms and for displaced persons from the whole of northwest Europe. There were no gas chambers in Belsen, but so hard was the rule inaugurated by Kramer that he became known as the Beast of Belsen. Within a few months the camp administration began to break down, although Kramer ordinarily never took a step without filling out a form. On March 1, 1945, he wrote a report stating that he had 42,000 inmates in camp and that 250 to 300 had died from "typhus." On March 19, 1945, the number of inmates rose to 60,000; during the week of April 13, some 28,000 prisoners were brought in. Roll calls were stopped, and the inmates were left to their own devices. Corpses rotted in the barracks, and rats attacked the living victims. When British troops came into the camp, Kramer, callous and indifferent, took them on a tour to inspect the scene. Piles of corpses were lying all over the camp, mass graves were filled in, and the huts were crowded with prisoners in every stage of emaciation and disease.

Kramer was tried by a British military court at Lüneburg and was sentenced to death on November 17, 1945. He was executed shortly afterward.

KREIS (Circuit). A county or region, the main subdivision of a *Gau* (q.v.), or district.

KREISAU CIRCLE. A small group of officers and professional civilians formed in 1933 to oppose Hitler and the Nazi movement. Led by Helmuth James Graf von Moltke and Peter Graf Yorck von Wartenburg (qq.v.), the circle met at the Moltke family estate in Kreisau, Silesia (now Krzyzowa, Poland). Its members regarded Hitler as a catastrophe for the fatherland. They agreed that it was necessary to rechristianize their country as a prelude to humanization. Considering themselves to be "planners of the future Germany," they dedicated themselves to the task of overthrowing the Nazi regime and substituting for its philosophy a new political and social ethic. In a document drafted on August 9, 1943, they issued their Basic Principles for the New Order, which outlined their objectives for a new German state.

In 1943 the Kreisau Circle had more than twenty active members, including army officers, academicians, conservatives, liberals, socialists, Catholics, and Protestants. Although they were not Communist, the members looked to the east with sympathy for the Russian people. Those of the group who were closely associated with the July Plot (q.v.) of 1944 were arrested and executed.

KREISLEITER (Circuit Leader). The lowest salaried official of the National Socialist party, responsible for administering a *Kreis,* or circuit. The *Kreisleiter* doubled as a *Landrat* (q.v.), the executive director of a rural county, until 1935.

KREISLEITUNG (KL; Circuit Leadership). The administration responsible for the leadership of a *Kreis*, or circuit.

KRIEGSSCHULDLÜGE (War Guilt Lie). Term often used by Nazi speakers in denouncing Article 231 (q.v.) of the Treaty of Versailles, the provision that placed responsibility on Germany and its allies for causing all the loss and damage of World War I. During the postwar period, every political party in Germany from right to left denounced the treaty as the *Versaillesdiktat* (Dictation of Versailles). It was pointed out that Germany, as a result of the treaty, had lost its colonies, virtually all its investments abroad, 15.5 percent of its arable land, 12 percent of its livestock, nearly 10 percent of its manufacturing plants, two-fifths of its coal reserves, almost two-thirds of its iron ore, and more than half of its lead. Germany's navy was almost wiped out, and its merchant marine was reduced from 5.7 million tons to less than 500,000 tons. The surrender of the colonies meant the loss of access to rubber and oil supplies. In *Mein Kampf* (q.v.), Hitler denounced the Treaty of Versailles as a monstrous injustice. Nazi speakers followed his lead in attacking the *Kriegsschuldlüge* as designed to destroy the German people.

KRIMINALPOLIZEI (KRIPO). The criminal police under the control of the SD (q.v.), the Sicherheitsdienst.

KRISTALLNACHT (Crystal Night; also called the Night of the Broken Glass). The night of November 9, 1938, when terror attacks were made on Jewish synagogues and stores. Two days earlier, Ernst vom Rath, Third Secretary of the German Embassy in Paris, had been assassinated by Herschel Grynszpan (q.v.), a Polish Jew. In retaliation, Reinhard Heydrich (q.v.), chief of the SD (q.v.), ordered the destruction of all Jewish places of worship in Germany and Austria. The assault had been long prepared; the murder of Vom Rath provided an opportunity to begin the attack. In fifteen hours 101 synagogues were destroyed by fire, and 76 were demolished. Bands of Nazis systematically destroyed 7,500 Jewish-owned stores. The pillage and looting went on through the night. Streets were covered with broken glass, hence the name *Kristallnacht*.

Three days later Hermann Goering (q.v.) called a meeting of the top Nazi hierarchy at the Air Ministry to assess the damage done during the night and place responsibility for it. Dr. Paul Joseph Goebbels (q.v.) proposed that Jews no longer be allowed to use the public parks: "We will give the Jews a part of the forest, where animals, which are damnably like Jews—the elk, too, has a hooked nose—can mix with them." It was decided that the Jews would have to pay for the damage they had provoked. A fine of 1 billion marks was levied for the slaying of Vom Rath, and 6 million marks paid by insurance companies for broken windows was to be given to the state coffers. The incident of the *Kristallnacht* and its aftermath generated unfavorable worldwide publicity for the Nazi regime. For the reaction of a German diplomat, *see* GISEVIUS, Hans Bernd.

KROLL OPERA HOUSE. Home of the German Reichstag (q.v.) in Berlin following the Reichstag fire (q.v.) of February 27, 1933.

KRUPP TRIAL. Trial of Krupp defendants after World War II. Gustav Krupp von Bohlen und Halbach (q.v.) was regarded by the victorious Allies as one of the most prominent war criminals. As head of the main armaments firm of Germany and Europe and as one of the Fuehrer's most devoted supporters among German industrialists, the elder Krupp, aged seventy-four at the close of the war, was accused of complicity in Hitler's aggression. The Americans and French were anxious to try either the old man or his son, Alfred Krupp von Bohlen und Halbach (q.v.); the Russians wanted to try either or both. Justice Robert H. Jackson (q.v.) made it plain: "The United States submits that no greater disservice to the future peace of the world would be done than to excuse the entire Krupp family from this trial." The American military tribunal chose a medical panel which reported that the elder Krupp, suffering from senility, could not stand trial because he would be unable to understand the nature of the proceedings. An indictment was held pending in the event that he should recover, but he never did. Later Alfred was tried before an American court and sentenced in 1948 to twelve years' imprisonment. He served three years and was then released. His confiscated property was returned to him.

KRUPP VON BOHLEN UND HALBACH, ALFRED (1907–). Son of Gustav Krupp von Bohlen und Halbach (q.v.). During World War II the younger Krupp took over the management of the great Krupp Works, manufacturers of Germany's tanks, ammunition, and munitions. Because large numbers of prisoners of war and inmates of concentration camps (q.v.) were used in the Krupp factories as slave labor, Alfred Krupp von Bohlen was tried as a war criminal and sentenced in 1948 to twelve years' imprisonment (*see* KRUPP TRIAL). He was released in 1951. In 1953 he was allowed to return to his position as head of the firm provided that he divest himself of his major interests. This condition was never fulfilled. The Krupp Works again became the largest steel producer in Europe.

KRUPP VON BOHLEN UND HALBACH, GUSTAV (1870–1950). Industrialist and patron of Hitler. Gustav Krupp von Bohlen und Halbach was born in The Hague on August 7, 1870, to a well-known banking family. After attending a *Gymnasium* (high school) in Karlsruhe, he took a law degree in Heidelberg in 1893. At first he turned to a diplomatic career and served in the German Legations at Washington, Peking, and the Vatican. In 1906 he married Bertha Krupp and gradually took over control of the Krupp Works at Essen, Kiel, Magdeburg, and elsewhere. The Krupp industries played an important role in World War I. Krupp von Bohlen opposed the rising Hitler movement in the 1920s, and as late as the day before President Paul von Hindenburg (q.v.) appointed Hitler Chancellor, he warned the old field marshal against the move. Within three weeks, however, Germany's munitions king changed from a violent anti-Nazi to an enthusiastic Hitler supporter. He was converted when Hitler, at a meeting on February 20, 1933, assured a gathering of leading industrialists that he would oppose democratic elections and disarmament. At this meeting Krupp von Bohlen rose and thanked Chancellor Hitler "for having given us such a clear picture."

The alliance between Hitler and such industrialists as

Krupp von Bohlen and Fritz Thyssen (q.v.) paved the way for German rearmament. The Fuehrer threw out the Nazi radicals who had attempted to seize control of the employers' associations and restored authority to the industrialists. In May 1933 he appointed Krupp von Bohlen chairman of the Adolf Hitler–Spende (q.v.), a fund raised by industrialists for Nazi benefit. In 1943, in the midst of World War II, the Fuehrer ordered that the Krupp Works, which had been made a public company in 1903, be converted to a family holding. The Krupps, makers of Germany's guns, tanks, and munitions, were later accused of using slave laborers, including prisoners of war and inmates of the concentration camps (q.v.). In 1948 Krupp von Bohlen was supposed to be tried by an American military tribunal, but a medical panel reported that he suffered from senility and could not stand trial (*see* KRUPP TRIAL). He died in Blühnbach bei Salzburg on January 16, 1950.

KUBIZEK, AUGUST (ca. 1889–). Hitler's closest friend when both were in their teens. August Kubizek, an upholsterer's helper in Linz, on the Danube in Upper Austria, met Adolf Hitler at the local opera house in 1904. Before long August began to regard his chance acquaintance as his best friend. The two subsequently became roommates and took frequent walks through the town and went on country excursions. The serious, tense, and meticulous Adolf dominated his friend Gustl, who served as a kind of audience. "His speeches," Kubizek wrote later, "seemed like a volcano erupting. It was as though something quite apart from him was bursting out of him."

Early in 1908 Gustl left his upholsterer's shop and journeyed to Vienna to study the viola at the Academy of Music. Adolf, too, had moved to Vienna to study art. The two roomed together at No. 29 Stumper Alley. Gustl was accepted at the conservatory, but Adolf was turned down by the Academy of Fine Arts, a blow from which he never recovered. Again Gustl found his friend "choking on his catalog of hates," not the least of which was the academy that had rejected him. "He was at odds with the world. I had the impression that Adolf Hitler had become unbalanced." In the summer of 1908, before Gustl went back to Linz for a vacation, he arranged with Adolf to resume their previous plan as roommates in the fall. But when Gustl returned, his landlady informed him that Adolf had moved out, leaving no message or forwarding address. More than thirty years elapsed before the two saw one another again in Bayreuth at the home of Richard Wagner's son Siegfried. By this time Hitler was at the summit of his career.

Bibliography. August Kubizek, *The Young Hitler I Knew*, Houghton Mifflin Company, Boston, 1955.

KUHN, FRITZ. *See* GERMAN-AMERICAN BUND.

KULMHOF. *See* CHEŁMNO.

KULTUR, NAZI (Culture, Nazi). The term *Kultur* can be translated freely as "culture," but it actually means much more. It takes into consideration not only the culture but the entire way of life of a people. Nazi *Kultur* was closely associated with its *Weltanschauung* (q.v.), its world view, or attitude toward life in general.

KZ. Popular abbreviation for *Kazetlager* (q.v.), or *Konzentrations Lager* (concentration camp). *See also* KL.

L

L DAY
to
LUTZE, VIKTOR

L DAY. *See* LACHSFANG.

LABOR CHARTER. National Socialist document that epitomized the economic philosophy of Nazism. Promulgated on January 16, 1934, and entered into force on May 1, 1934, it called for the cooperation of labor and capital. In fact, however, its tendency was to favor the leaders of business enterprises. The most important right that the wage earner retained was to be elected to the *Vertrauensrat* (confidential council). Hitler's Labor Charter was in many respects similar to Mussolini's earlier Charter of Labor (1927).

LABOR COMMUNITY. *See* ARBEITSGEMEINSCHAFT.

LABOR COMMUNITY LEADER. *See* ARBEITSGEMEINSCHAFTSLEITER.

LABOR FRONT. *See* DEUTSCHE ARBEITSFRONT.

"LABOR LIBERATES." *See* "ARBEIT MACHT FREI."

LABOR MAIDS. *See* ARBEITSMAIDEN.

LABOR OFFICE. *See* ARBEITSAMT.

LABOR SERVICE LEADER. *See* ARBEITSDIENSTFUEHRER.

LABOR SUPERVISOR. *See* ARBEITSEINSATZFUEHRER.

LACHSFANG (Salmon Trap). Code name for the contemplated seizure of the Murmansk railway in 1942. In late July 1942, Hitler, encouraged by the success of German arms in the Caucasus, decided to cut the northern supply route that linked Soviet Russia with its Anglo-Saxon allies. The Fuehrer was especially attracted by the Murmansk railroad, on which most supplies from the United States and Great Britain were delivered during the winter months. Accordingly, he issued a directive, dated July 21, 1942, in which he proposed an autumn offensive to seize the Murmansk railway near Kandalaksha. The undertaking was allotted the cover name Lachsfang, and the day of attack was to be called L Day.

LAGARDE, PAUL ANTON DE (1827–1891). German orientalist, philologist, political thinker, and intellectual forerunner of National Socialism. He was born as Paul Bötticher in Berlin on November 2, 1827. Opting for an academic career, he began as a *Privatdozent* (unsalaried university lecturer who received only students' fees) at Halle. For years he had to teach in Berlin public schools to supplement his income. In 1869 he became the successor of G. H. A. Ewald as professor of oriental philosophy at Göttingen. He was well known for his copying and editing of ancient texts in Greek, Aramaic, and Arabic.

As a political writer, Lagarde criticized the materialism of his times. Considering himself a patriot, he called for a moral cleansing of German life. His *Deutsche Schriften, 1878–1881 (German Literature)*, advocated an absolute *voelkisch* nationalism (*see* VOELKISCH MOVEMENT). The German nation, he wrote, could be unified only through the adoption of a national form of Christianity, thus prefiguring positive Christianity (q.v.). Christianity, in his view, had to be purged of its antiquated ideas before it could meet the needs of modern man. Above all, Lagarde called for an end to the spiritual and economic power of the Jews. Responsible for materialism and commercialization, the Jews were "purveyors of decadence," foreign bodies in the state, a nation within the nation. He condemned the use of any "humanitarian principles" to defend the Jews. "One does not have dealings with pests and parasites; one does not rear and cherish them; one destroys them as speedily and thoroughly as possible."

One of the most influential predecessors of National Socialist ideology, Lagarde was held in high esteem by Alfred Rosenberg (q.v.), the party's leading ideologist. His severe strictures against the Jews helped prepare the way for Hitler's policy of genocide (q.v.). Lagarde died in Göttingen on December 22, 1891.

LAGER. A concentration or prison camp.

LAIKAITEL. Sarcastic term used by fellow officers to

describe Gen. Wilhelm Keitel (q.v.). *Laikaitel* was a play on words, using the German term *Lakai* (lackey, or flunky) in combination with Keitel's name to indicate his subservience to Hitler.

LAMMERS, HANS HEINRICH (1879–1962). Jurist, Reich Minister, and head of the Reich Chancellory. Hans Heinrich Lammers was born at Lublinitz (Lubliniec), Upper Silesia, on May 27, 1879. From 1921 to 1933 he served in the Ministry of the Interior and from 1933 to 1945 as Chief of the Reich Chancery. He was accepted as a member of Hitler's inner circle at Obersalzberg (*see* BERGHOF), where for months at a time he and his staff conducted the business of the Chancery. He was often consulted by Hitler on legal problems. In 1937 Hitler appointed Lammers Reich Minister without Portfolio and Chief of the Reich Chancery and in 1939 Ministerial Councillor for the Defense of the Reich. In all these posts Lammers remained one of Hitler's closest legal advisers. In 1940 he was made an *SS-Obergruppenfuehrer* (general).

In 1943 the Fuehrer appointed Lammers, along with Martin Bormann and Field Marshal Wilhelm Keitel (qq.v.), to the Committee of Three (q.v.), the triumvirate designed to take over details and ease Hitler's tasks as Chief of State. An unimaginative bureaucrat, Lammers liked to immerse himself in legal technicalities. He became the victim of Hitler's rage when, on April 23, 1945, Hermann Goering (q.v.) sent a telegram to Hitler in his Berlin bunker stating that he, Goering, was taking over control of the country. Angered, Hitler ordered the arrest not only of Goering but also of Lammers. The Fuehrer had been told that Lammers advised Goering that Hitler's decree of June 29, 1941, naming Goering as his replacement in the event of incapacity, was entirely legal.

At a trial held at Nuremberg in 1949, Lammers was accused of formulating anti-Jewish measures and giving them legal sanction. He pleaded that he knew nothing of such measures until they were revealed at the earlier Nuremberg Trial (q.v.): "I knew that a Fuehrer order was transmitted by Goering to Heydrich. This order was called the 'Final Solution of the Jewish Problem.' But I knew nothing about it." Lammers was given a prison sentence of twenty years, which was commuted in 1951 to ten years. Released from Landsberg Prison in 1952, he died in Düsseldorf on January 4, 1962.

LAND (State). One of the fifteen principal territorial divisions of the Third Reich. This type of organization was taken over by the National Socialist regime from that of the Weimar Republic (q.v.). Each *Land* had its own administration headed by a governor (*see* REICHSSTATTHALTER).

LAND INSPECTOR. *See* LANDESINSPEKTEUR.

LANDBUND (Farmers' Association). The most important agricultural organization in the Third Reich.

LANDESINSPEKTEUR (Land Inspector). Originally one of nine officials just below the *Reichsleitung* (q.v.), the Reich leadership in the upper level of the Nazi party hierarchy. Each *Landesinspekteur* was responsible for the administration of four *Gaue,* or districts (*see* GAU). The post of *Landesinspekteur* began to disappear as Hitler started to appoint all *Gauleiters* directly (*see* GAULEITER). Later, the responsibility for such appointments was assigned to Heinrich Himmler (q.v.).

LANDRAT (Subprefect). Executive director of a rural county, or *Kreis* (q.v.), in Prussia. He was frequently the same man as the Nazi party *Kreisleiter* (q.v.), or circuit leader.

LANDSBERG AM LECH. A fortress-prison in Bavaria to which Hitler was sent after the Beer-Hall *Putsch* (q.v.) of 1923 in Munich. Found guilty of conspiracy to commit high treason, he was sentenced to five years' fortress arrest at the Munich Trial (q.v.) of 1924. Through the indulgence of the authorities, he served only nine months of detention. He was pampered in prison, he read voraciously, he entertained visitors, and in general he regarded his detention as no more than a comfortable interruption of his career. In his cell he dictated to the faithful Rudolf Hess (q.v.) the first volume of his book *Mein Kampf* (q.v.).

LANDTAG (Diet). The chamber of deputies in an individual *Land,* or state, in the days before the Third Reich. The *Landtag* was abolished after the Nazis came to power.

LANDWIRTSCHAFTLICHER GAUFACHBERATER (LGF; Gau Agricultural Expert). *Gau* (district) official of the Agrarpolitischer Apparat (q.v.).

LANGBEHN, CARL (1901–1944). A lawyer and member of the conspiracy who attempted to involve Heinrich Himmler (q.v.) in the plot to overthrow Hitler. Langbehn was acquainted with Himmler socially because their daughters had gone to the same school. Learning that Himmler was not averse to a negotiated peace as early as 1942, Langbehn conducted private inquiries through his American and English contacts in Switzerland about the intention of the Allies. He learned that it was the firm plan of the Allies to demand unconditional surrender (q.v.). Langbehn was arrested in September 1943 and executed on October 12, 1944.

LANGBEHN, JULIUS (1851–1907). Writer and intellectual forerunner of Hitler and National Socialism. Julius Langbehn was born at Hadersleben on March 26, 1851. In 1890 he published anonymously a sensational book, *Rembrandt als Erzieher (Rembrandt as Teacher),* the title of which he borrowed from the third of the *Unzeitgemässen Betrachtungen (Untimely Studies)* of Friedrich Nietzsche (q.v.). As a representative of the younger generation, Langbehn looked for a model hero and found him in the Dutch painter Rembrandt Harmensz van Rijn (1606–1669), whom he appropriated for Germany. To Langbehn the Dutch artist represented the integral German culture, which was menaced by "Americanism." Langbehn lauded Germany's strong, disciplined monarchy, which he believed to be enthroned by the grace of God. A racialist, he described the German Nordic as "the Aryan par excellence" and considered the Aryans as a race destined to dominate the world. The Greater Germany of tomorrow, he said, would govern Europe and, transcending Europe's borders, achieve universal domination. Germany's true religion was not Christianity but Aryanism. Langbehn denounced "one-sided intellectual education" and called for a natural and poetic development of the individual. He set the direction for cultural conservatism and folk art. His views, similar to those of Paul Anton de Lagarde, Adolf Stoecker, Arthur Comte de Gobineau, and Houston Stewart Chamberlain (qq.v.), were later appropriated and exploited by Hitler and Nazi party ideologists. Langbehn died in Rosenheim on April 30, 1907.

LANZ, JOSEF. *See* LIEBENFELS, JÖRG LANZ VON.

LAST WILL, HITLER'S. *See* HITLER'S LAST WILL.

LAVAL, PIERRE (1883–1945). French politician and collaborator with Hitler and the Third Reich. Pierre Laval was born in Châteldon, Puy-de-Dôme, on June 28, 1883, the son of a village butcher and innkeeper. Studying at the Universities of Lyon and Paris, he took degrees in natural history and law and was admitted to the bar at Paris in 1907. Elected a Socialist deputy in 1914, he served reluctantly in World War I. His comrades regarded him as a defeatist. He lost his seat in 1919 but regained it in 1924. In 1925 he won his first Cabinet post, as Minister of Public Works in Premier Paul Painlevé's government. Elected to the Senate in 1926, he became Minister of Justice under Premier Aristide Briand (1926) and Minister of Labor under Premier André Tardieu (1930). In 1931–1932 he was Premier and Minister of the Interior. After the murder of Foreign Minister Jean-Louis Barthou in 1934, Laval took over the leadership of the Ministry of Foreign Affairs. On January 7, 1935, he concluded an agreement with Mussolini that in effect gave Italy a free hand in Ethiopia. He was coauthor of the Hoare-Laval agreement to end the Italo-Ethiopian War at Ethiopia's expense, the first of a series of efforts to appease the dictators at any price.

On the collapse of France in World War II, Laval became Vice-Premier (July 1940) and then Foreign Minister (October 1940) in the Vichy government of Marshal Philippe Pétain (q.v.). Heir apparent to Pétain as Chief of State, Laval began a program of collaboration with Hitler. His intrigues on behalf of Nazi Germany and his ambition to assume power led in December 1940 to his dismissal and arrest. In April 1942 he was released at Hitler's demand and under German pressure made Premier in the place of Adm. Jean-François Darlan. From then until his puppet government was dissolved in 1944, Laval was the main agent of German power in France. He raised a French army for Hitler, allowed Frenchmen to be deported to Germany for forced labor, and made no objections to Nazi plundering in France.

In 1944 French guerrillas opened all-out war on Laval. In August he moved his government to Belfort, and in September to Germany. He kept out of sight until May 2, 1945, when he appeared in Barcelona. Expelled by the Spanish government, he fled to Austria. He was arrested by American troops in Innsbruck on July 31. Charged with treason, he was brought to trial in Paris in a passionately angry atmosphere. After an attempt at suicide, he was shot by a firing squad on October 15, 1945.

Bibliography. Geoffrey Warner, *Pierre Laval and the Eclipse of France,* Eyre & Spottiswoode (Publishers), Ltd., London, 1968.

Pierre Laval. [*Wide World Photos*]

LAW. *See* JUSTICE IN THE THIRD REICH.

LAW FOR PREVENTING OVERCROWDING IN GERMAN SCHOOLS AND COLLEGES. A decree, promulgated on April 25, 1933, which ordered that the number of non-Aryans in relation to the total registration at all schools and colleges must no longer exceed the proportion of non-Aryans to Aryans in the German population as a whole.

LAW TO REMOVE THE DISTRESS OF PEOPLE AND STATE. *See* ENABLING ACT.

LEADER, THE *See* FUEHRER, DER.

LEADER OF A GIRLS' GROUP. *See* GRUPPENLEITERIN.

LEADER OF THE SS. *See* REICHSFUEHRER-SS.

LEADER STATE. *See* FUEHRERSTAAT.

LEADER WORSHIP. *See* FUEHRER WORSHIP.

LEADER'S BUNKER. *See* FUEHRERBUNKER.

LEADERS' CORPS. *See* FUEHRER-KORPS.

LEADER'S FIELD HEADQUARTERS. *See* FUEHRER-HAUPTQUARTIER.

LEADERSHIP PRINCIPLE. *See* FUEHRERPRINZIP.

LEAGUE FOR AERONAUTIC SPORT. *See* LUFTSPORTVERBAND.

LEAGUE FOR COMBAT POLICY. *See* WEHRPOLITISCHE VEREINIGUNG.

LEAGUE FOR GERMANS ABROAD. *See* VOLKSTUM FÜR DAS DEUTSCHTUM IM AUSLAND.

LEAGUE OF GERMAN GIRLS. *See* BUND DEUTSCHER MÄDEL.

LEAGUE OF STRUGGLE FOR GERMAN CULTURE. *See* KAMPFBUND FÜR DEUTSCHE KULTUR.

LEBENSBORN (Fountain of Life). A program organized by Heinrich Himmler (q.v.), *Reichsfuehrer* and head of the SS (q.v.), for the purpose of transforming the German nation into a superrace through selective breeding. Official National Socialist ideology (*see* RACIAL DOCTRINE) stressed the duty of German women to bear racially sound children and held that it was unimportant whether such children were born out of wedlock. German girls, especially those in the Bund Deutscher Mädel (q.v.), were reminded of their duty to the Third Reich. Those who were chosen were encouraged to become pregnant by SS men regarded as racially and politically desirable. After pregnancy the girls were sent to one of twelve special maternity centers, where they were given elaborate medical care.

Recent investigation has brought to light a more sinister aspect of the Lebensborn program, the wholesale kidnapping of foreign children to add to the breeding stock of the Third Reich. During World War II Himmler informed Lebensborn authorities that it was desirable to import "racially acceptable" children from such occupied countries as Poland, France, Norway, Yugoslavia, and Czechoslovakia. On his orders children with Aryan-looking features were selected in mass examinations, brought to Germany for placement in indoctrination centers, and then put up for adoption by "racially trustworthy" German families. It is estimated that several hundred thousand children were taken from their families for this part of the Lebensborn program.

LEBENSRAUM (Living Space). Slogan popular in Germany before World War I and in the early years of the Long Armistice after 1918. It was alleged that Germany was overpopulated in comparison with its arable soil and needed territorial expansion. Before 1914 the term *Lebensraum* was used to justify a desire for additional colonies; after 1919 it expressed a demand for the return of the colonies taken from Germany by the Treaty of Versailles. Hitler appropriated the slogan and used it to claim the extension of German living space into neighboring zones, especially the Ukrainian breadbasket.

LEBER, JULIUS (1891–1945). Leading Social Democrat and one of the central figures in the conspiracy against Hitler. Julius Leber was born in the village of Biesheim, Alsace, on November 16, 1891. His father was a mason,

Julius Leber hears his death sentence at the People's Court. [*From* Das Gewissen steht auf, *Mosaik Verlag, Berlin*]

and his mother a farm worker. In his poverty-stricken youth he had neither books nor shoes. Later he became an apprentice in a rug factory and managed to obtain an education in the nine-year *Oberrealschule* (higher modern school). He studied political economy and history at Freiburg and Strassburg (Strasbourg) while earning his livelihood by tutoring and writing for newspapers. A Social Democrat from his early years, he worked within the Social Democratic party for the rest of his life. In August 1914 he volunteered for service, and by March 1915 he was promoted to officer rank in the German Army. He was wounded and received many combat awards. In 1920 he earned his doctorate at Freiburg. The same year he took part in the overthrow of the rightist Kapp *Putsch* (q.v.) in Berlin, and the next year he began a career in journalism as chief editor of the *Volksbote (People's Messenger)* in Lübeck. In 1924 he served in the Reichstag (q.v.) and remained a delegate until 1933. A firm opponent of Hitler and the National Socialists throughout the 1920s, he was placed at the top of the Nazis' list of dangerous opponents.

On January 31, 1933, the day after Hitler's accession to power, Leber was the target of an assassination attempt. He was wounded in the fray, but a young member of the Reichsbanner Schwarz-Rot-Gold (q.v.), who came to his rescue, killed one of the attackers. On recovering, Leber went to Berlin to take his seat in the Reichstag, only to be arrested, tried, and sentenced to twenty months' imprisonment. He served his term, after which he was rearrested as a "security risk" and sent to concentration camps (q.v.) at Esterwegen and Oranienburg.

After his release in 1937, Leber joined the Kreisau Circle (q.v.). He also became one of the most prominent left-wing men who gathered around Carl Friedrich Goerdeler (q.v.) in the conspiracy against Hitler. Leber was chosen to be Minister of the Interior in the regime to succeed Hitler. He was politically as well as personally close to Claus Schenk Graf von Stauffenberg (q.v.), the young aristocrat who was determined to kill Hitler. Leber urged Von Stauffenberg to make use of the militant left in the plot against the Fuehrer. On June 22, 1944, Leber and Adolf Reichwein (q.v.), a schoolmaster and Social Democrat, acting as intermediaries for Von Stauffenberg, met three Communist agents to see if they would take places in the ranks of the conspiracy. Neither Leber nor Reichwein knew that one of the "Communists" was a Gestapo (q.v.) spy. The two Social Democrats were taken into custody. As a result of their arrest, the proposed date for the July Plot (q.v.) was set forward by the conspirators. Both men were tried before the Volksgericht (q.v.), the People's Court, on October 24, 1944, found guilty of treason, and sentenced to death. One of the journalists who was present wrote that never in his life had he observed such deep earnestness and nobility of character as that shown by Leber at the moment when he was sentenced. Reichwein was executed the same day. Leber was hanged on January 5, 1945, at Plötzensee Prison.

LEEB, WILHELM RITTER VON (1876–1956). General field marshal. Wilhelm Ritter von Leeb was born in Landsberg am Lech, Bavaria, on September 5, 1876. From 1930 to 1933 he commanded Wehrkreis (Defense District) VII and was assigned to Army Group II. In January 1938 he was among sixteen high-ranking officers retired by Hitler during the Blomberg-Fritsch crisis (q.v.). In 1939, at the outbreak of World War II, he was recalled to duty at the age of sixty-three to command Army Group C on the western front. He was among the twelve general field marshals created by Hitler on July 19, 1940, after the victory over France. In March 1941 Hitler assigned Ritter von Leeb, Gen. Gerd von Rundstedt, and Gen. Fedor von Bock (qq.v.) to command three armies for the coming campaign against the Soviet Union. Von Leeb protested that the armed forces were not ready for this gigantic task, but to no avail. From June 1941 to January 1942 he commanded Army Group North on the Russian front. Victorious at first, he later advised the Fuehrer that a retreat from the Leningrad area was vital to shorten his lines for the winter. Hitler disagreed with what he regarded as a challenge to his own military ability and ordered the retirement of his recalcitrant field marshal. Ritter von Leeb died in Hohenschwangau, Bavaria, on April 29, 1956.

Field Marshal Wilhelm Ritter von Leeb. [*Imperial War Museum, London*]

LEERS, JOHANN VON (1902–1965). Prolific Nazi propagandist. Johann von Leers was born in Vietlübbe, Mecklenburg, on January 25, 1902. He studied law at Berlin, Kiel, and Rostock and worked for a time in the Foreign Office. Von Leers joined the Nationalsozialistische Deutsche Arbeiterpartei (q.v.) in 1929 and, as a protégé of Dr. Paul Joseph Goebbels (q.v.), was assigned to write propaganda for the party. There flowed from his pen a long series of books, pamphlets, and articles on the history of National Socialism, on blood and race, and on the Weimar Republic (q.v.), which he called the *Judenrepublik.* In 1933 he published *Juden sehen dich an (Jews Look at You),* which he dedicated to "the gallant, faithful, and undaunted Julius Streicher [q.v.]." In this book photographs of Albert Einstein, Emil Ludwig, and Lion Feuchtwanger (qq.v.) appeared under the caption "Not Hanged Yet!"

During World War II Von Leers devoted himself to the anti-Semitic campaign: "Jews are political assassins and creeping thieves who worm their way into governments of other peoples and bring them down from inside so that world Jewry may then establish its bloody rule of Bolshevism." In 1945 he fled to Italy and in 1950 to the colony of Nazi exiles in Argentina. In the mid-1950s he went to Cairo, established contact with the anti-Semitic former mufti of Jerusalem, and was converted to Islam under the assumed name Omar Arnim von Leers. An apostle of neo-Nazism (q.v.), Von Leers continued his strictures: "I don't believe in glorifying the dead. But what I liked about Hitler was that he fought the Jews, and killed so many of them."

LEGAL SYSTEM. *See* JUSTICE IN THE THIRD REICH.

LEGALITÄTS-EID (Oath of Legality). Hitler's promise to win political power through legal means only. After the failure of the 1923 Beer-Hall *Putsch* (q.v.), Hitler decided that thereafter he would reject force and use only the legal means of the ballot to win political supremacy for the Nazi movement. At the trial of three Nazi officers of the Reichswehr (q.v.) held in Ulm in 1930, Hitler attempted to win credibility for his intention by voluntarily taking an "oath of legality."

LEIBHOLZ, GERHARD (1901–). Jurist and prominent exile from the Third Reich. Gerhard Leibholz was born in Berlin on November 15, 1901, the son of Wilhelm Leibholz, a *Stadtrat* (town councillor). After study at the

Gymnasium (high school) in Berlin-Charlottenburg, he took a doctorate in philosophy at Heidelberg (1921) and another doctorate in jurisprudence at Berlin (1925). Known for his warm and generous nature, he went on to a brilliant career in teaching (Berlin, Greifswald, and Göttingen) and in law. In 1926 he married Sabine Bonhoeffer, the twin sister of Dietrich Bonhoeffer (q.v.), the pastor who was executed at Flossenbürg (q.v.) on April 9, 1945.

From the beginning Leibholz opposed the Nazi regime as a disgrace for his country. In 1936 he was compulsorily retired from his position at the University of Göttingen because his parents were Jewish. In 1939 new Nuremberg legislation required all non-Aryans (*see* NON-ARYAN) to carry the letter *J* on their passports, an order designed to prevent them from leaving the country. On September 9, 1939, Leibholz, his wife and two daughters made a last-minute dash into Switzerland. From 1939 to 1946 he held a fellowship of the World Council of Churches and of Magdalen College, Oxford, for special political tutorials and lectures. The Leibholzes were in England when they received the tragic news of Dietrich Bonhoeffer's death only a few weeks before the end of the war in Europe. They returned to Germany, where Leibholz continued a distinguished career as Associate Justice of the Constitutional Court and professor of law at Göttingen. He retired in 1972.

Bibliography. Gerhard Leibholz, *Politics and Law,* A. W. Sythoff, Leiden, 1965.

LEIBSTANDARTE-SS ADOLF HITLER (SS Bodyguard Regiment Adolf Hitler). The personal militarized formation under orders to protect the person of the Fuehrer. From his early political days Hitler was in constant danger of attack by his enemies. He formed the Stabswache (q.v.), a staff guard composed of SA (q.v.) members. The Stabswache was absorbed first in the Stosstruppe–Adolf Hitler (*see* STOSSTRUPP), shock troops to protect Nazi meetings, and later in the Leibstandarte. When Hitler took power in 1933, he was guarded by a 120-man SS guard (*see* SS), which formed a triple cordon around his person. At the September 1933 Nuremberg party rally (*see* NUREMBERG RALLIES), he transformed this group into the Leibstandarte-SS Adolf Hitler under the command of *SS-Obergruppenfuehrer* (Gen.) Josef (Sepp) Dietrich (q.v.). Two months later, on the tenth anniversary of the 1923 Beer-Hall *Putsch* (q.v.) in Munich, all members of the Leibstandarte were required to take an oath of personal allegiance to the Fuehrer. (Earlier military units had sworn loyalty to the Reich President as commander in chief of the armed forces.)

The Leibstandarte was used both as an instrument of terror and as a military force. Because of Hitler's support it took its place alongside the regular Army as a second army. Its commandos specialized in attacking both anti-Nazis and rival SA Storm Troopers. It inspired Heinrich Himmler (q.v.) to set up similar units in his SS—the *Sonderkommandos* (q.v.), special detachments, and later the *politische Bereitschaften* (q.v.), political alarm squads—to protect himself and other top Nazi leaders. The Leibstandarte played a leading role in the 1934 Blood Purge (q.v.). It was noted for its fighting spirit in World War II, taking part in commando raids on Dunkirk in the west and on Soviet defenses in the Crimea in the east.

LEIBWACHE (Bodyguard). The original assault guard responsible for Hitler's safety, also called the Stabswache (q.v.). Later, it was called the Stosstruppe–Adolf Hitler (*see* STOSSTRUPP), and eventually it became the Leibstandarte-SS Adolf Hitler (q.v.), Hitler's bodyguard regiment.

LEICHENKOMMANDO (Corpse Commando). Ironic term used in the extermination camps (q.v.) to describe an inmate designated as a corpse collector, or undertaker. The *Leichenkommandos* were required to collect the bodies of those who had died during the night. On occasion, as many as 300 to 400 inmates died during the night from starvation or other causes. The *Leichenkommandos* had the privilege of emptying pockets and giving friends whatever crusts of bread they could find.

LEITER DES REICHSBERUFSWETTKAMPFES (Reich Sports Division Leader). An official of the Nationalsozialistischer Deutscher Studentenbund (q.v.), the National Socialist German Students' League.

LENARD, PHILIPP E. A. VON (1862–1947). Professor of theoretical physics at the University of Heidelberg and Nobel laureate (1905) for his work on cathode rays. A follower of Hitler as early as 1924, he was praised by Nazi party leaders for "making science relevant to the political struggle." He divided knowledge into natural and spiritual sciences. The world of the spirit, he said, is determined by racial origins. This was close enough to the Nazi *Weltanschauung* (q.v.), or world view, to be acceptable to ideologists of the Third Reich.

LENYA, LOTTE (1900–1981). Actress, singer, and refugee from the Third Reich. Lotte Lenya was born in Vienna on October 18, 1900. She won a reputation as Pirate Jenny in *Die Dreigroschenoper (The Threepenny Opera)* by Bertolt Brecht (q.v.). With her husband, Kurt Weill (q.v.), she left Germany for the United States after Hitler took political power in 1933. She had a successful career as a Broadway star. In 1955 she returned to Europe, where she continued her career in such plays as Brecht's *Mother Courage and Her Children* (1965). In 1968 she played the main role in the American version of the musical *Cabaret* in New York.

LETTERHAUS, BERNHARD (1894–1944). Leader of the Catholic Labor Organization and member of the Resistance (q.v.) movement against Hitler. Born in the Rhineland on July 10, 1894, he was badly wounded in World War I and was awarded the Iron Cross (First Class). In the postwar era of the Weimar Republic (q.v.) he worked in the Catholic labor movement. While a delegate to the Prussian Landtag (Legislature) in 1928, he criticized Hitler as a demagogue who would lead Germany into an unwanted war. After Hitler came to political power in 1933, Letterhaus worked underground to encourage resistance among Catholics to the Nazi Regime. Resistance leaders considered him for a post in the interim government after Hitler. Arrested after the failure of the July Plot (q.v.) in 1944, he was sentenced to death by the Volksgericht (q.v.), and hanged on November 14, 1944.

Bernhard Letterhaus in the People's Court. [*From Annedore Leber (ed.),* Conscience in Revolt, *tr. by Rosemary O'Neill, Vallentine, Mitchell & Co., Ltd., London, 1957*]

Bibliography. Annedore Leber (ed.), *Conscience in Revolt*, tr. by Rosemary O'Neill, Vallentine, Mitchell & Co., Ltd., London, 1957.

LEUSCHNER, WILHELM (1888–1944). Trade unionist and member of the Resistance (q.v.). Wilhelm Leuschner was born at Bayreuth on June 15, 1888. An engraver by trade, he joined the labor movement while still in his teens and remained with it for the rest of his life. A member of the Hesse Landtag (Legislature), he became deputy chairman of the German Trade Union Association in 1933. A critic of both communism and National Socialism, he was arrested after Hitler came to political power and tortured by his SA (q.v.) guards. After his release he organized trade union resistance against Nazism. To camouflage his political work he started a small purchasing business. Known as Uncle Leuschner among the conspirators, he put aside all personal ambitions in the conspiracy for the overthrow of Hitler. During World War II he worked with Gen. Ludwig Beck and Carl Friedrich Goerdeler (qq.v.) to end the Nazi government and to plan for an interim regime. Arrested after the failure of the July Plot (q.v.) in 1944, Leuschner was sent to the gallows on September 29, 1944.

Wilhelm Leuschner [*Stamp issued by the German Federal Republic*]

Bibliography. Annedore Leber (ed.), *Conscience in Revolt*, tr. by Rosemary O'Neill, Vallentine, Mitchell & Co., Ltd., London, 1957.

LEY, ROBERT (1890–1945). National Socialist politician and head of the German Labor Front (Deutsche Arbeitsfront, q.v.). Robert Ley was born in Niederbreidenbach, Gummersbach District, on February 15, 1890. A chemist by profession, he was an early member of the Nationalsozialistische Deutsche Arbeiterpartei (q.v.). In the struggle for Nazi party leadership, he opposed Gregor Strasser (q.v.) and took the side of Hitler, who never forgot his loyalty and who helped his career from then on (*see* SECOND REVOLUTION). Dr. Paul Joseph Goebbels (q.v.) regarded Ley with hostility: "To appreciate Ley's mentality one has only to remember that he is now immersed in the subject of death rays and is expert with white rabbits. As is to be expected, all his experiments have failed." In 1928 Ley was elected to the Prussian Landtag (Legislature) and in 1930 to the Reichstag (q.v.). From 1931 to 1934 he was a party *Gauleiter* (q.v.), operating out of Cologne in the Rhineland District.

Soon after Hitler became Chancellor in 1933, Ley reached for power in Prussia by attempting to coordinate the Staatsrat (Council of State) with himself as head. He was blocked by Hermann Goering (q.v.), who wanted no rivals in Prussia to take over as Hitler's chief of staff. On May 2, 1933, Ley, with Hitler's consent, led a "committee of action for the protection of German labor" in occupying the offices of all labor unions and imprisoning their leaders. Within a few days all German trade union organizations were coordinated, and Ley became the undisputed dictator of labor as leader of the Deutsche Arbeitsfront. "Workers," he said, "your institutions are sacred and unassailable to us National Socialists. I myself am a poor son of peasants and have known poverty. I swear to you that we shall not only preserve everything you have, we shall extend the rights of the worker in order that he might enter the new National Socialist state as an equal and respected member of the nation." In 1935 Ley claimed that Nazi Germany was the first country in Europe to overcome the class struggle.

On October 20, 1945, Ley, with twenty-one others, was indicted by the International Military Tribunal at Nuremberg (*see* NUREMBERG TRIAL). Emotional and highly unstable, he protested. "How can I prepare a defense?" he asked G. M. Gilbert, the prison psychologist. "Am I sup-

Robert Ley. [*Ullstein*]

posed to defend myself against all these crimes which I knew nothing about? Stand us up against the wall and shoot us—you are the victors." On October 24, he was found strangled in his cell. He had made a noose from the edges of a towel and fastened it to the toilet pipe. In a suicide note he wrote that he was unable any longer to bear the shame.

Bibliography. Robert Ley, *Wir alle helfen dem Fuehrer,* Eher Verlag, Munich, 1940.

LFL. *See* LUFTFLOTTE.

LGF. *See* LANDWIRTSCHAFTLICHER GAUFACHBERATER.

LICHTENBURG, BERNARD (1875–1943). Catholic priest and a victim of the Nazi regime. Bernard Lichtenburg was born in Silesia on December 3, 1875. Ordained in 1899, he served from 1900 on in Berlin. He was a military chaplain during World War I and represented the Catholic Center party on the Berlin City Council after the war. On August 28, 1941, as provost of St. Hedwig's Cathedral in Berlin, he sent an angry letter to Dr. Leonardo Conti (q.v.), chief physician of the Reich, protesting against the willful killing of a large number of people of unsound mind. "I, as a human being, a Christian, a priest and a German, demand of you, the Chief Physician of the Reich, that you answer for the crimes that have been perpetrated at your bidding and with your consent, and which will call forth the vengeance of the Lord on the heads of the German people." The priest sent copies of his letter to the Reich Chancellery, the Reich ministries, and the Gestapo (q.v.). It was a courageous act but, under the circumstances, a dangerous gesture. Lichtenburg was arrested and sentenced to two years' imprisonment, which he served in Berlin-Tegel Prison. At the end of his term he was not released but sent instead to Dachau (q.v.). He died on November 3, 1943, while being taken to the concentration camp.

Bernard Lichtenburg. [*From Annedore Leber (ed.),* Conscience in Revolt, *tr. by Rosemary O'Neill, Vallentine, Mitchell & Co., Ltd., London, 1957*]

LICHTERFELDE BARRACKS. Quarters of the Leibstandarte-SS Adolf Hitler (q.v.), the Fuehrer's bodyguard regiment, near Berlin. The site had formerly been used by the Cadet College. By 1934 the barracks had become notorious because of the number of political opponents of the National Socialist regime who were killed there by firing squads.

LIDICE. Czechoslovakian mining village near Prague. Lidice was the scene of a Nazi reprisal action. In 1941 Reinhard Heydrich (q.v.) was named Deputy Reich Protector for Bohemia and Moravia and began a reign of terror against civilians in the protectorate. Driven to desperation, Czech patriots on May 29, 1942, attempted to assassinate Heydrich. On the escape of the assailants, Nazi authorities declared a state of emergency in the protectorate. Heydrich died of his wounds on June 4, 1942. Six days later the Nazis, alleging that the people of Lidice had aided the men who killed Heydrich, took savage vengeance on the villagers. All the men and older boys, numbering 172, were shot. The women were either killed or sent to concentration camps (q.v.), where many of them died. The children were taken off to the camps or, in some cases, distributed to foster homes. The village itself was systematically destroyed, and its name was erased from official records. Nazi authorities, apparently oblivious to worldwide shock, admitted the massacre.

LIEBENFELS, JÖRG LANZ VON (1874–1954). Religious sectarian and self-described father of National Socialism. Also called Josef Lanz, he assumed his aristocratic title on his own authority. As a novice in the Heiligenkreuz (Holy Cross) Monastery, where he remained for six years, he turned his attention to the study of race. He left the monastery in 1899 and founded the Order of the New Temple (Ordensburg Werfenstein), whose principal aim was to foster the "pure" racial foundations of Aryanism. In his journal *Ostara,* named for the Teutonic god of beauty, he advocated the concept of racial purity. Although irregularly published, the journal eventually reached a circulation of 100,000 in Austria and Germany.

Like Arthur Comte de Gobineau and Houston Stewart Chamberlain (qq.v.), Liebenfels wrote in a turgid, pseudoscientific style and hammered away at his central racialist theme (*see* RACIAL DOCTRINE). On one side he placed the white, blond, blue-eyed Nordic, in whom resided the virtues of blood and breeding. On the other side were the apelike inferiors, subhuman, vicious, worthless, and contemptible. He called the exalted, superhuman Nordics either *Asinge* (German gods), *Heldlinge* (heroes), or *Arioheroiker* (Aryan heroes). He termed all other races of mankind the *Chandalas,* a name used in India for untouchables; these he identified as *Afflinge* (monkey people) or *Schrätlinge* (hobgoblins). All history, he said, was a conflict between these two breeds. It was impossible to improve the Aryan race as long as the *Chandalas* existed. He called for a crusade to destroy these inhuman beasts *(Ausrottung der Tiermenschen).* Along with these ideas, presented again and again in *Ostara,* Liebenfels decorated the journal's pages with symbols from ancient legends and myths, including the swastika (*see* HAKENKREUZ).

When the eighteen-year-old Hitler went to Vienna in September 1907, he was influenced by the journal of the renegade Cistercian monk. He became so enthusiastic about *Ostara* that he sought out its editor for a personal interview and to ask for some back numbers he had missed. Liebenfels gave him a supply of back numbers, which the young vagabond devoured. In the café Zur goldenen Kugel (Golden Bowl) Hitler hotly defended Liebenfels's ideas against skeptics, and in the Viennese Home for Men he spent hours discoursing on the basic theme of *Ostara.* Passage after passage in *Mein Kampf* (q.v.) reads like a paraphrase of an article from the journal which Hitler took seriously.

After 1933, when Hitler rose to power, Liebenfels claimed that he had been Hitler's mentor in Vienna and that he himself should be given credit for the rise of National Socialism. The Fuehrer was not pleased by this assertion. He saw to it that the works of Liebenfels were banned.

Bibliography. Wilfried Daim, *Der Mann, der Hitler die Ideen gab,* Isar Verlag, Munich, 1958.

LIEBERMANN, MAX (1847–1935). Painter and etcher, denounced in the Third Reich as a purveyor of degenerate art (*see* ENTARTETE KUNST). Max Liebermann was born in Berlin on July 20, 1847, the son of a Jewish merchant. Studying art in Paris in 1873, he was influenced mostly by the Barbizon painters. He lived in Munich from 1878 to 1884 and then went to Berlin, where he joined the Sezession movement. He moved from impressionism to naturalism, from accent to dark to light tones. At first he depicted the life of workingmen and peasants but later turned to landscape and outdoor studies. In 1933, when Hitler became Chancellor, Liebermann was forced to resign as president of the Prussian Academy of Art. During the last year of his life his work was exhibited in displays of degenerate art, and he was forbidden to carry on his artistic activities. He died in Berlin on February 8, 1935.

LIGHTNING WAR. *See* BLITZKRIEG.

LILA. Code name for the projected German occupation of the naval port of Toulon and the capture of the French Fleet in World War II. On November 27, 1942, Hitler gave the word for Lila, and German troops raided the port. As soon as the attack began, French crews were ordered to scuttle their ships, thus depriving the Germans of important naval units for the war in the Mediterranean. The scuttling was equally damaging to the Allied side, which also could have used the warships.

LILI MARLEEN. Most popular song among German troops in World War II. The poem *Lili Marleen* was written by Hans Leip in Hamburg in 1923. In its original version the verses told the age-old story of the love of a soldier for his girl. The poem was set to music in 1936 by Norbert Schultze and introduced by Lale Andersen. In World War II *Lili Marleen* became enormously popular when broadcast to troops of the Afrika Korps (q.v.) in the Libyan campaign. British troops adopted it in a translated version titled *Lilli Marlene,* and Anne Sheldon made a best-selling recording in London. The French version, titled *Lily Marlène,* was written by Henry Lemarchand. The song was used in the United States in the film *Lili Marlene* (1944), featuring Marlene Dietrich (q.v.), and was also used in such films as *A Bell for Adano* (1945) and *Judgment at Nuremberg* (1961). The German and English versions are as follows:

1

Vor der Kaserne
vor dem grossen Tor
stand eine Laterne,
und steht sie noch davor,
so wolln wir uns da wiedersehn,
bei der Laterne wolln wir stehn
wie einst, Lili Marleen.

Unsre beiden Schatten
sahn wie einer aus;
dass wir so lieb uns hatten,
das sah man gleich daraus.
Und alle Leute solln es sehn,
wenn wir bei der Laterne stehn
wie einst, Lili Marleen.

3

Schon rief der Posten:
Sie blasen Zapfenstreich;
es kann drei Tage kosten!—
Kam'rad, ich komm ja gleich.
Da sagten wir auf Wiedersehn.
Wie gerne wollt' ich mit dir gehn,
mit dir, Lili Marleen!

4

Deine Schritte kennt sie,
deinen zieren Gang,
alle Abend brennt sie,
mich vergass sie lang.
Und sollte mir ein Leids geschehn,
wer wird bei der Laterne stehn
mit dir, Lili Marleen?

Sheet music of "Lili Marleen." [© *Copyright APOLLO-VERLAG Paul Lincke, Berlin. Sole Distributor for the United States of America and Mexico. EDWARD B. MARKS MUSIC CORPORATION. Used by permission.*]

5

Aus dem stillen Raume,
aus der Erde Grund
hebt mich wie im Traume
dein verliebter Mund.
Wenn sich die späten Nebel drehn,
werd ich bei der Laterne stehn
wie einst, Lili Marleen.

1

Underneath the lantern
By the barrack gate,
Darling I remember
The way you used to wait:
'Twas there that you whispered tenderly,
That you lov'd me,
You'd always be
My Lilli of the lamplight,
My own LILLI MARLENE.

2

Time would come for roll call,
Time for us to part,
Darling I'd caress you;
And press you to my heart;
And there 'neath that far off lantern light,
I'd hold you tight,
We'd kiss "Good-night,"
My Lilli of the lamplight,
My own LILLI MARLENE.

3

Orders came for sailing
Somewhere over there,
All confined to barracks
Was more than I could bear;
I knew you were waiting in the street,
I heard your feet,
But could not meet:
My Lilli of the lamplight,
My own LILLI MARLENE.

4

Resting in a billet
Just behind the line,
Even tho' we're parted
Your lips are close to mine;
You wait where that lantern softly gleams,
Your sweet face seems,
To haunt my dreams
My Lilli of the lamplight,
My own LILLI MARLENE.

LIST, WILHELM (1880–1971). General field marshal. Wilhelm List was born in Oberkirchberg, Württemberg, on May 14, 1880. After a successful early military career, he was promoted in 1935 to general and assigned to Wehrkreis (Defense District) IV, one of the twelve districts of the Wehrmacht (q.v.). List was firmly on the Fuehrer's side at the time of the Blomberg-Fritsch crisis (q.v.). He served Hitler well in the months preceding the *Anschluss* (q.v.) with Austria, after which he was transferred to Vienna to command the new Fourteenth Army Group. At the outbreak of World War II in 1939, he was at the age of fifty-nine No. 6 in seniority among the high-ranking officers and was assigned to command Army Group V. On July 19, 1940, he was one of twelve officers promoted to general field marshal as a result of the Fuehrer's satisfaction in the defeat of France. From June 10, 1941, to October 15, 1941, List served as commander in chief for the southeast (Balkans). On July 15, 1942, he was given command of Army Group A on the Russian front. Hitler blamed him in large part for the Russian fiasco and dismissed him on September 9, 1942. List was condemned to life imprisonment at Nuremberg in February 1946, but he was pardoned and released at Christmas 1952. He died in 1971.

LIST OF RACIAL GERMANS. *See* VOLKSLISTE, DEUTSCHE.

LIST REGIMENT. Unit with which Hitler fought in World War I. Named after its first commander, a Colonel von List, the infantry regiment was composed largely of students and intellectuals who had volunteered for service. Under indifferent leadership the regiment incurred staggering losses. It was said that the flower of Bavarian youth in the regiment was lost in combat. For a time Rudolf Hess (q.v.) also served in the List Regiment, but he and Hitler did not meet while members of the same unit.

LISTENERS TO ENEMY BROADCASTS. *See* FEINDHÖRER.

LITERATURE IN THE THIRD REICH. Literature was the branch of art most seriously affected by the Nazis' coming to power. Hitler sensed that the written word could be dangerous for his regime. After 1933 more than 2,500 writers, including Nobel Prize winners, left Germany either voluntarily or under duress. Within a short time German literature, which had won global acclaim, was reduced to a level of boredom that the German public found distasteful. Whereas previously the works of German writers had been translated into many languages, scarcely a writer active in the Third Reich achieved a reputation beyond its borders.

Hitler placed writers first on his list of detested intellectuals. His attitude became the standard. It was expressed publicly only a little more than three months after the beginning of the National Socialist government. At midnight on May 10, 1933, a torchlight parade of thousands of young Nazis ended on Unter den Linden, opposite the University of Berlin. There torches were put to a large pile of books. Many more volumes were then consigned to the flames, including works by such famous German authors as Thomas Mann, Heinrich Mann, Lion Feuchtwanger, Arnold Zweig, Erich Maria Remarque, and Albert Einstein (qq.v.). There were also non-German authors, dead and living, who were classed as enemies of the Third Reich: Émile Zola, Marcel Proust, Jack London, Maxim Gorky, Arthur Schnitzler, Helen Keller, H. G. Wells, Sigmund Freud, Henri Barbusse, Margaret Sanger, and Upton Sinclair. Nearby the crowd was addressed by Dr. Paul Joseph Goebbels (q.v.), soon to become the powerful Minister for Public Enlightenment and Propaganda, himself an unsuccessful writer. Goebbels denounced "any book which acts subversively on our future." "The soul of the German people," he said, "can express itself again. These flames not only illuminate the end of the old era, they also light up the new." *See also* BOOKS, BURNING OF THE.

Meanwhile, the mass flight of writers had begun. The list of exiles reads like a roll of literary giants. Thomas Mann, Nobel Prize winner and one of the most eminent writers of the twentieth century, became an expatriate. He was joined by his eldest brother, Heinrich Mann, internationally known for his portraits of German social life before and after World War I. Erich Maria Remarque, especially hated by the Nazis for his pacifist best-selling novel *All Quiet on the Western Front* (1929), became an exile. Many others joined the exodus, among them Emil Ludwig (q.v.), author of popular books dealing with historical and political subjects; Arnold Zweig, novelist best known for *The Case of Sergeant Grischa* (1927); Stefan Zweig (q.v.), Austrian playwright and biographer; Ernst Toller (q.v.), a leading expressionist; Franz Werfel (q.v.), known for *The Forty Days of Musa Dagh* (1934); Jakob Wassermann, who was concerned with problems of psychoanalysis; Bruno Frank, historical novelist; and Bertolt Brecht (q.v.), revolutionary poet and playwright.

Many authors who were Jews or liberals left in fear for their lives. Others emigrated because they could not function in a totalitarian state. Most settled in Paris, London, Amsterdam, and New York. Those who did not know foreign languages often went through periods of starvation. Several worked for magazines and small newspapers to earn a living. Exiled writers were subjected to indignities, but they were not silenced. Anti-Nazi novels and plays flowed from their pens. Some, including Ernst Toller and Klaus Mann (q.v.), succumbed to despair and took their lives.

Several authors who seemed favorable to the regime attempted to escape its limitations. The celebrated poet Stefan Anton George (*see* GEORGE KREIS), the high priest of classical aestheticism, emigrated to Switzerland and died there. Nazi authorities thought him to be a friend because of his 1928 poem *Das neue Reich (The New Reich)*, a dithyramb to a charismatic Fuehrer. The able Ernst Jünger (q.v.) rejected the Nazi offer of a seat in the Reichstag (q.v.) but allowed large reprints to be made of his works for Nazi benefit. He managed to avoid close identification with the state by choosing an officer's life as a haven.

Dr. Goebbels did his best to repair the damage to the German literary scene. He turned control of literature over to Department VIII of the Ministry for Public Enlightenment and Propaganda. By 1939 this section had full supervisory power over 2,500 publishing houses, 3,000 authors, and 23,000 bookshops. It controlled 1 million books in print as well as the 20,000 new books published annually. It awarded fifty national literary prizes. Most important of all, it had the right to approve every manuscript of a book or play before publication or performance. Department VIII was careful to promote *Mein Kampf* (q.v.) as the highest form of literary art. By 1940 more than 6 million copies of Hitler's book had been sold.

The Propaganda Ministry established new standards for German literature. Writers were expected to produce works in four major categories: (1) *Fronterlebnis* (q.v.), or front experience, which stressed the camaraderie and homoeroticism of wartime; (2) works reflecting Nazi *Weltanschauung* (q.v.), or world view, expressed by the Fuehrer and Alfred Rosenberg (q.v.); the (3) *Heimatroman* (q.v.), or regional novel, with emphasis on the national mystique of regional Germanness; and (4) *Rassenkunde* (ethnology), specifically the kind of racial doctrine (q.v.) that contrasted the uniquely endowed German Nordic with the biologically defective Jews, French, Russians, Poles, and Africans.

The writers who functioned within this framework were distinguished only by their mediocrity. Werner Bumelburg, specialist in *Fronterlebnis*, wrote sickeningly sentimental novels about the *Kameradschaft* (camaraderie) in the front lines. Agnes Miegel, novelist and poet, devoted herself to the genre of *Heimatdichtung* (regional poetry). Rudolf Binding and Börries von Münchhausen wrote awkward epics about chivalry and manly virtues. One of the most popular writers was Hans Grimm (q.v.), whose *Volk ohne Raum (People without Space)*, a 1926 best seller, gave the Nazis one of their most powerful propaganda slogans. ("The Germans, the cleanest, most honest people, most efficient, and most industrious, live within too narrow frontiers.") Gottfried Benn (q.v.), another able writer, advocated an aesthetic nihilism and primitive atavism ("floods of ancestral vitality"), which he at first professed to see in the Nazi movement. This point of view guaranteed him publication and acceptance, but he later turned critic of the Nazi revolution. The output of Nazi writers made it clear that German literature could not survive the mass flight of intellectuals.

LITTLE FELLOW COUNTRYMEN. *See* KLEINE VOLKSGENOSSEN.

LIVING SPACE. *See* LEBENSRAUM.

LOAN. *See* DARLEHEN.

LOCAL BRANCH LEADER. *See* ORTSGRUPPENLEITER.

LOCAL GROUP. *See* ORTSGRUPPE.

LOCARNO PACT. Agreement in 1925 confirming the inviolability of the Franco-German and Belgo-German frontiers and the demilitarized zone of the Rhineland. This pact played an important role in the career of Hitler, who violated it in March 1936 when he sent his troops into the Rhineland. After British rejection of the Geneva Protocol (1924), European diplomacy became concerned with security arrangements of more limited scope designed to meet specific dangers in particular areas. In 1925 Gustav Stresemann (q.v.), the German Foreign Minister, offered France a pact of mutual guarantee and nonaggression. A conference was held in the Swiss town of Locarno on Lake Maggiore, closing on October 16, 1925, with the signing of a treaty of mutual guarantee and four arbitration treaties between Germany and France, Belgium, Poland, and Czechoslovakia. There were also two treaties of guarantee between France on the one side and Poland and Czechoslovakia on the other.

The "sweetness and light" of Locarno led European statesmen to believe for the first time since World War I that there was a possibility for peace in Europe. Hatred and ill will were to be replaced by mutual understanding. Stresemann set the tone: "We are citizens each of his own country, but we are also citizens of Europe and are joined together by a great conception of civilization. We have the right to speak of a European idea." Locarno was, in effect, a skillfully managed attempt to abolish the psychology of Versailles. The agreements amounted to a diplomatic triumph for Stresemann, Aristide Briand, and Austen Chamberlain. The immediate result of Locarno was the admission of Germany to the League of Nations.

Bibliography. Harold Scott Quigley, *From Versailles to Locarno*, The University of Minnesota Press, Minneapolis, 1927.

LORENZ, KONRAD (1903–). Austrian-born specialist in animal behavior. Konrad Lorenz was born in Vienna on November 7, 1903, the son of an orthopedic surgeon. After attendance at the Schotten Gymnasium (high school), he took doctorates at the University of Vienna in medicine, philosophy, and political science. In 1937 he was appointed *Privatdozent* (unsalaried lecturer who received only students' fees) for comparative anatomy and animal psychology at Vienna. In 1940 he became professor of comparative psychology at the University of Königsberg, East Prussia (now Kaliningrad, U.S.S.R.). Later in World War II he saw military service and was made a prisoner of war in the Soviet Union.

In 1940 Lorenz wrote an article in the *Zeitschrift für Angewandte Psychologie und Charakterkunde (Journal of Applied Psychology and Personality Science)* in which he supported "race-preserving" measures to avoid the "degeneracy" in man that is typical of domesticated animals. The latter, he wrote, unlike their relatives in the wild, were not bred along strictly racial lines and hence turned out to be ugly and degenerate. The danger, he warned, was that "socially inferior human material is enabled . . . to penetrate and finally annihilate the healthy nation. . . . The racial idea as the basis of our state has already accomplished much in this respect." Lorenz later, in 1943, restated and elaborated these ideas in a 174-page article in the *Zeitschrift für Tierpsychologie (Journal of Animal Psychology)*. His views were interpreted as support for the racial doctrine (q.v.) popular in the Third Reich and were used by Nazi authorities to justify legal restrictions on the intermarriage of German Nordics with non-Aryans (*see* NON-ARYAN).

After the war Lorenz headed the Max Planck Institute for Behavioral Physiology at Seewiesen über Starnberg, Bavaria, where his experiments with geese attracted worldwide attention. He wrote many popular books, such as *On Aggression* (1963), which were widely read but were criticized by anthropologists as going too far in equating human and animal behavior. In 1973 he shared the Nobel Prize in physiology and medicine with Nikolaas Tinbergen and Karl von Frisch, also specialists in animal behavior. On announcement of the award, Simon Wiesenthal (q.v.), head of the Documentation Center in Vienna, who made a career of tracking down Nazi war criminals, wrote to Dr. Lorenz and asked him to decline the prize as a gesture of contrition for his writings on racial purity during the Nazi regime. At a news conference in Stockholm in December 1973, Lorenz said: "I deeply regret [these writings]. I have very different notions now concerning the Nazis."

LOYAL TO THE LEADER. *See* FUEHRERTREU.

LUBBE, MARINUS VAN DER (1909–1934). Unemployed vagrant Dutchman who was blamed by the Nazis for setting the Reichstag fire (q.v.). Arrested for carrying out arson on behalf of the Communist party, he was tried at Leipzig beginning on September 21, 1933, found guilty, and beheaded on January 10, 1934. Many believed him to have been an unwitting and naïve victim of Nazis who themselves had planned the burning. *See also* REICHSTAG FIRE TRIAL.

LUDENDORFF, ERICH (1865–1937). World War I military leader and collaborator with Hitler in the 1923 Beer-Hall *Putsch* (q.v.) in Munich. Erich Ludendorff was born in Kruszewnia, near Posen (Poznań), on April 9, 1865, the son of an impoverished landowner. He entered the Army through the Cadet Corps. From 1908 to 1912 he was head of the deployment section of the General Staff responsible for planning an invasion of Belgium and France, and from 1912 to 1914 he commanded an infantry brigade. At the beginning of World War I he was named quartermaster general of the Second Army. The quick capture of the Belgian fortress of Liège was due primarily to his work as liaison officer and his heroism in personally leading the troops infiltrating the garrison.

This exploit brought Ludendorff to the attention of the highest military command. He was appointed chief of staff to Gen. Paul von Hindenburg (q.v.), who had been recalled from retirement to head the Eighth Army on the eastern front. In the organization of the German Army a chief of staff often had greater influence than his commanding officer, and Ludendorff took full advantage of his opportunity. Together, Von Hindenburg and Ludendorff won two great victories over the Russians in August and September 1914. Both men were responsible for the series of German successes on the eastern front until August 1916. Ludendorff, especially, showed tremendous energy and a mastery of detail in carrying out operational plans. On August 29, 1916, Emperor William II dropped Gen. Erich von Falkenhayn as chief of the General Staff and named Von Hindenburg supreme commander, with Ludendorff as his senior quartermaster general. The two managed to ease the situation on the western front, where German losses had been heavy at Verdun and the Somme, by withdrawing their forces to the Hindenburg Line.

By this time Ludendorff was becoming increasingly involved in politics. A brilliant military tactician, he soon revealed that he had little conception of the broader aspects of supreme control. In January 1917 he made the decision to adopt unrestricted submarine warfare. He contributed to the fall of Chancellor Theobald von Bethmann-Hollweg and the appointment of Georg Michaelis in July 1917. Ludendorff was the force behind the harsh Treaty of Brest Litovsk with Bolshevik Russia (March 3, 1918), which gave the Allies an indication of what would be in store for them if Germany were to win the war. After the failure of the German offensive in France in the summer of 1918 and the collapse of the Balkan front, Ludendorff became despondent and began to urge the imperial government to sue for peace. He violently opposed the new government of Prince Max of Baden, who dismissed him from his military post on October 26, 1918.

After the armistice Ludendorff fled in disguise to Sweden, where he wrote his memoirs. In 1919 he returned to Munich. Embittered by defeat, he began to devote himself to right-wing nationalist causes. He took part in the Kapp *Putsch* (q.v.) of 1920, and he collaborated with Hitler in the unsuccessful Beer-Hall *Putsch* on November 8–9, 1923. On the latter occasion he marched straight through the ranks of the police, who respectfully turned their guns away from the great war hero. He was acquitted at the subsequent trial (*see* MUNICH TRIAL). In May 1924 he became a Nationalist Socialist delegate to the Reichstag (q.v.), where he served until 1928. In 1925 he stood unsuccessfully as a National Socialist for the Presidency of the Reich.

Ludendorff was strongly influenced by the right-wing ideas of his second wife, Dr. Mathilde Spiess Ludendorff

Gen. Erich Ludendorff. [*Brown Brothers*]

(1877–1966), a specialist in mental diseases. With her support he founded the Tannenberg Bund (q.v.), which was dedicated to a struggle against what the Ludendorffs called "powers above the state": Jews, Jesuits, Freemasons, and Marxists. Both detested Christianity and urged the formation of a new German religion venerating the old pagan Nordic gods. Ludendorff began to attack his old commanding officer, President von Hindenburg, who was adhering to strict legality in his office. Ludendorff became increasingly eccentric. He paid a swindler named Tausend an enormous fee for a box to manufacture paper money with which German reparations obligations could be paid. The old war-horse became an extreme pacifist. He began to argue with Hitler at the height of Nazi power, and the former collaborators became bitter enemies. Ludendorff died in Tutzing, Bavaria, on December 20, 1937. An attempt was made in 1945 to start a new Ludendorff movement, but it was banned by the Bonn government on May 25, 1961.

Bibliography. Erich Ludendorff, *Auf dem Weg zur Feldherrnhalle*, Ludendorffs Verlag, Munich, 1938; Mathilde Ludendorff, *Erich Ludendorff*, Ludendorffs Verlag, Munich, 1940.

LUDWIG, EMIL (1881–1948). Best-selling author, critic of Nazism, and refugee from the Third Reich. Originally Emil Ludwig Cohn, he was born in Breslau on January 25, 1881, the son of an ophthalmologist. He studied law but in 1914 turned to journalism as London correspondent for the *Berliner Tageblatt*. He was converted to Christianity, but in 1922, after the murder of Walther Rathenau, he renounced his conversion. In 1932 he became a Swiss citizen and in 1941 emigrated to the United States. Ludwig was the author of a series of biographies, rich in psychological analysis, that won him global fame. These included *Bismarck* (1912), *Goethe* (1929), *Michelangelo* (1930), *Schliemann* (1932), *Roosevelt* (1938), *Napoleon* (1939), and *Beethoven* (1943). Reviewers were inclined to dismiss most of his work, with the exception of the *Goethe*, as lacking in scholarship. Throughout his career, Ludwig remained an uncompromising critic of Hitler and the Nazi ideology. He died in Moscia, near Ascona, Switzerland, on September 17, 1948.

LUEGER, KARL (1844–1910). Anti-Semitic mayor of Vienna who strongly influenced Hitler in his early years. Karl Lueger was born in Vienna on October 24, 1844, of humble parentage. Qualifying as a lawyer in 1874, he was elected to the municipal council the following year. Taking part in Viennese politics, he was the cofounder (1889) and leader of a new Catholic party, the Christian Socialists. At first Emperor Francis Joseph refused to confirm Lueger's appointment as mayor of Vienna because of Lueger's anti-Semitism (q.v.) but in 1897 was induced by public opinion to accept him. Lueger held this post until his death on March 10, 1910. Eloquent, domineering, and immensely popular, he exploited prevailing anti-Semitic sentiment for his own demagogic purposes. When Hitler as a young man arrived in Vienna in 1907, he was impressed by Lueger's strictures against the Jews and adopted them as a major pursuit in his own life.

LUFTFLOTTE (Lfl; Air Force). A section of the Luftwaffe (q.v.), the German Air Force.

LUFTHANSA. German civilian air transportation company. Erhard Milch (q.v.), its manager in the early 1920s, built up a small air force within the framework of the Lufthansa in contravention of the Treaty of Versailles.

LUFTKREISE (Air Circuits). Geographical units of the Luftwaffe (q.v.), the German Air Force. Like the Army, the Luftwaffe was organized in six areas. Of these, three were commanded by older generals and three by younger commanders, all of whom were chosen by Hermann Goering (q.v.).

LUFTSPORTVERBAND (League for Aeronautic Sport). A combination of clubs devoted to civilian flying and gliding. The Luftsportverband was used by Hermann Goering (q.v.) to provide secret pilot training for budding air force officers from 1933 to 1935 (*see* LUFTWAFFE).

LUFTWAFFE (Air Force). The German air arm during the Third Reich. Under the terms of the Treaty of Versailles of 1919, military aviation was prohibited in defeated Germany. The construction of civil aircraft also was forbidden until 1922, when it was allowed under certain limitations. At the instigation of Gen. Hans von Seeckt (q.v.), adjutant general of the new Reichswehr (q.v.), the highly centralized German civil aviation was to a great extent controlled by the military. Gliding and flying clubs were popular, and many pilots were trained in the old prewar Lufthansa (q.v.), the commercial line. By the mid-1920s there was a highly efficient aircraft construction industry, including Focke Wulf at Bremen, Dornier at Friedrichshafen, Heinkel at Warnemünde, Junkers at Dessau, and Messerschmitt at Augsburg. While the victorious Allies were still flying obsolete biplanes of wood and fabric, German designers were developing advanced all-metal monoplanes with cantilevered wings, retractable undercarriages, and variable-pitch propellers. The reorganized Lufthansa, with routes now allowed throughout Western Europe, became technically the most advanced airline in the world. In contravention of the Treaty of Versailles, military crews were trained at four Lufthansa flying schools and became proficient in night and all-weather flying.

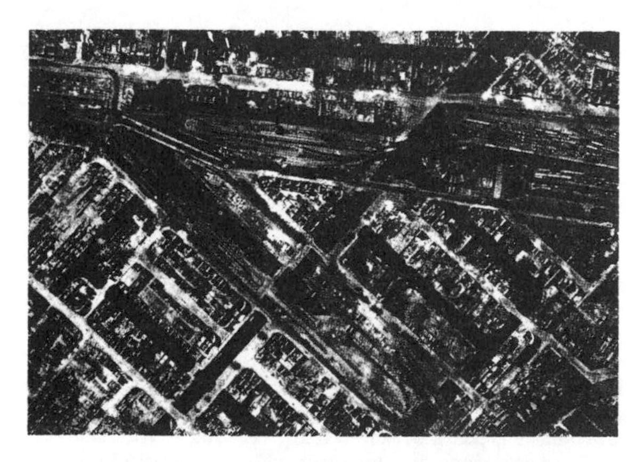

Hamburg after a British air raid in July 1943. A declining Luftwaffe can no longer protect German cities. [*British official photo*]

When Hitler became Chancellor in 1933, he already had the foundations for a military air arm, but much remained to be done. Almost immediately he arranged heavy subsidies for the new Luftwaffe, which he would use to blaze the way to German *Lebensraum* (q.v.), or living space. He appointed his deputy, Hermann Goering (q.v.), the new *Reichskommissar* for Air with instructions to forge a powerful new weapon for the Nazi state. Goering, who held high offices in the Nationalsozialistische Deutsche Arbeiterpartei (q.v.), could not devote as much attention to aviation matters as he would have wished; he therefore called in State Secretary Erhard Milch (q.v.), an efficient businessman who had been director of Lufthansa. Milch proved to be the indispensable man in the development of the Luftwaffe. There was a crisis when it became known that Milch had Jewish forebears, in Hitler's estimation the ultimate sin. In an extraordinary feat of legerdemain, Goering was able to Aryanize Milch's biological background in order to satisfy Hitler's monomania on Jews and at the same time relieve Milch of the onus of this depressing discovery.

Goering and Milch set up the organization of the Luftwaffe. The basic tactical unit was the *Geschwader* (group), each of which was composed of three *Gruppen* (wings), although some bomber formations consisted of six or more wings. Each wing in turn consisted of as many as three *Staffeln* (squadrons), and each squadron had from 12 to 16 aircraft. Thus a wing comprised about 40 planes, and a group about 120. During World War II heavy losses in combat meant that actual numbers varied considerably. Luftwaffe nomenclature included the *Jagdgeschwader* (JG), fighter group; *Kampfgeschwader* (KG), bomber group; *Nachtjagdgeschwader* (NJG), night fighter group; *Schnellkampfgeschwader* (SKG), fast bomber group; *Stukageschwader* (StG), dive bomber group; *Transportgeschwader* (TG), transport group; and *zur besonderen Verwendung* (zbV), special assignment.

Subordinate to Milch as chief of the Air Command Office was Gen. Walther Wever (q.v.), a former infantryman who had been transferred to the new Luftwaffe. Wever was a zealous apostle of National Socialism. Under the leadership of Goering, Milch, and Wever, working in secrecy with the full support of Hitler, new factories for building aircraft, new airfields, and new training schools appeared all over Germany. In March 1935 the Fuehrer felt strong enough to reveal to the world that his new and powerful Luftwaffe comprised 1,888 aircraft of all types and a cadre of 20,000 officers and men. Members of the former gliding and flying clubs and police flying formations were absorbed one by one into the new Air Force. The news of Hitler's powerful air arm aroused consternation outside the Third Reich.

In May 1936 General Wever was killed in an air crash. He was succeeded by Gen. Albert Kesselring (q.v.), another popular commander, who continued to expand the Luftwaffe. In August 1936 the German Air Force went into action for the first time in support of Gen. Francisco Franco's Nationalist forces in the Spanish Civil War. Originally, some twenty Ju-52 transports ferried 10,000 troops loyal to Franco from Morocco to Spain, in the first large airlift in history. By November 1936 the Luftwaffe contingent had been increased to some 200 aircraft and renamed the Condor Legion (q.v.). In a dress rehearsal for World War II the Luftwaffe rejected the old close wing-to-wing formations in favor of a new "figure-four" formation designed as a compromise between concentrated fire power and freedom of action. The Luftwaffe received precious combat experience in Spain but also world contempt for its obliteration of the town of Guernica (q.v.) in a cruel, unnecessary action.

The Luftwaffe was held in abeyance as a threat during the two major crises preceding World War II: the *Anschluss* (q.v.) with Austria in March 1938 and the territorial demand on Czechoslovakia in September 1938. On September 1, 1939, some 1,600 combat aircraft, concentrated mostly in Luftflotten I and IV, were unleashed in Hitler's *Blitzkrieg* (q.v.) on Poland. Polish airfields came under continuing attack by horizontal and dive bombers, especially the extraordinary Stukas (*see* JUNKERS-87). Few Polish pilots managed to get off the ground, and those who did had to face the powerful, speedy Messerschmitts. German planes repeatedly attacked Polish troops and helped their own ground troops by smashing strongpoints and artillery batteries. The Luftwaffe combat units then moved back to rest and refit during the period of the *Sitzkrieg* (q.v.). They went back into action when Hitler struck at Denmark and Norway on April 9, 1940, in the subsequent invasion of the Netherlands and Belgium, and in the Battle of France. While the Luftwaffe kept Allied airfields under bombardment, its dive bombers prepared the way for the *Panzer* (tank) units on the ground. Unable to prevent the evacuation at Dunkirk from May 26 to June 4, 1940, the Luftwaffe turned its attention to supporting the tank units heading toward Paris. For the first time the Luftwaffe had met an air force with equal equipment. Its tired and overworked pilots had received their first setback.

After the fall of France, Hitler turned his eyes toward Britain. Before the German Army could cross the English Channel and invade Britain, the Luftwaffe would have to eliminate the Royal Air Force (RAF). Luftflotten II and III, in position on the channel coast, had 2,600 aircraft for this vital task. In mid-July 1940 they began light probing attacks coupled with mine laying from the air. On August 13, 1940, the Battle of Britain began. On that day the Luftwaffe made 1,000 fighter sorties and 485 bomber runs, losing 45 aircraft. Two days later it made 1,266 fighter sorties and 520 bomber runs, with a loss of 75 planes. Almost immediately it became obvious that the Luftwaffe was in serious trouble. In building his air force, Hitler had wanted quick results to fit *Blitzkrieg* tactics; he therefore relied on speedy fighter planes and never developed heavy bombers. His light bombers were not equipped for the task of subduing Britain, nor did he expect the fierce RAF retaliation he encountered. Throughout late August and early September the Luftwaffe continued its operations with increasingly heavy losses. On September 15, 1940, it lost some 60 aircraft in the last big daylight attack on London. From that day on Luftwaffe activity over Britain decreased.

From September 1940 to the end of the war Hitler's air arm became increasingly unable to carry the fight to the enemy or even to defend the homeland against night saturation bombing attacks by the British and later day precision bombing by the Americans. There were some local successes, such as the May 20, 1941, assault on Crete, but the Luftwaffe could not face the formidable task of halting Allied landings in North Africa. Nor could it support a holding campaign in the west or perform adequately on the long Russian front. By 1943 it was forced on the defensive to protect Germany itself. Through June and July 1944 it struggled to compete with Allied superiority everywhere. The failure of its oil supply because of Allied bombardment and the ineffectual robot attacks on England brought the Luftwaffe close to the end. It made one final effort in the Ardennes offensive of December 1944.

By late February 1945 the Luftwaffe was a beaten air force. It still had more than 3,000 aircraft, but most of these remained on the ground without fuel in their tanks or sufficient trained pilots to fly them. After Hitler's opening *Blitzkrieg* on Poland, the Luftwaffe had lost 44,065 aircrew killed or missing, 28,200 wounded, and 27,610 prisoners or missing. Successful in the early days of the war, it was unable to stop the inexorable Allied advance to victory.

Luftwaffe statisticians made remarkable claims for their fighter pilots. According to official German records, 94 aces of the Luftwaffe shot down 13,997 enemy planes in aerial combat, a staggering claim when compared with the records of Allied airmen. Most German kills were registered on the Russian front. The following list is limited to German aces credited with more than 150 kills.[1]

Erich Hartmann	352
Erich Gerhard Barkhorn	301
Günther Rall	275
Otto Kittel	267
Walther Nowotny	258
Wilhelm Batz	242
Theo Weissenberger	238
Erich Rudorffer	222

[1]Listed in Martin Caldin, *Me-109*, Pan/Ballantine, London, 1973, p. 136.

Heinrich Bär	220
Heinz Ehrler	220
Hans Philipp	213
Walter Schuck	206
Anton Hafner	204
Helmut Lippert	203
Hermann Graf	202
Walter Krupinski	197
Anton Hackl	190
Joachim Brendle	189
Max Stotz	189
Joachim Kirschner	185
Werner Brandle	180
Günther Josten	178
Joh. Steinhoff	176
Günther Schack	174
Heinz Schmidt	173
Emil Lang	173
E. W. Reinert	169
Horst Adameit	166
Wolf D. Wilcke	161
Gordon Gollob	160
Hans-Joachim Marseille	158
Gerhard Thyben	157
Hans Beisswenger	152
Peter Duttmann	152

Bibliography. Werner Baumbach, *The Life and Death of the Luftwaffe,* Coward, McCann, Inc., New York, 1960; Adolf Galland, *The First and the Last,* Henry Holt and Company, Inc., New York, 1954.

LUTINE BELL. A bell at Lloyd's of London rung to announce the loss of a ship at sea. The sound was used in radio broadcasts during World War II to announce a U-boat sinking (*see* U-BOATS).

LUTZE, VIKTOR (1890–1943). Chief of staff of the SA (q.v.). Viktor Lutze was born in Bevergern on December 28, 1890. After serving in the ranks, he was an officer throughout World War I. He joined the Nationalsozialistische Deutsche Arbeiterpartei (q.v.) in 1922 and rapidly rose in the Brownshirt hierarchy. In 1925 he was a deputy *Gauleiter* (district leader) in the Ruhr and in 1928 became senior Fuehrer of the SA. He was elected to the Reichstag (q.v.) in 1930 to represent Hannover-Braunschweig for the Nazi party. In 1933 he was promoted to *SA-Obergruppenfuehrer* (general), appointed police president of Hannover, and designated a member of the Prussian State Council. On June 30, 1934, Hitler summoned Lutze to accompany him to Bad Wiessee to confront Ernst Roehm (q.v.) and other SA leaders in the Blood Purge (q.v.). After the executions Hitler appointed Lutze successor to Roehm as SA chief of staff. The Fuehrer gave Lutze a special twelve-point order directed against drinking bouts, parties, automobile trips, and unnatural lewdness among SA members. Lutze was killed in an automobile accident on May 2, 1943.

M

MACHTERGREIFUNG
to
MYTH OF THE TWENTIETH CENTURY, THE

MACHTERGREIFUNG (Seizure of Power). A term used interchangeably with *Machtübernahme* by the Nazis to indicate the assumption of political power by Hitler on January 30, 1933. Hitler was proud of the fact that his rise to the chancellorship had been achieved by legal means and not by a coup d'état.

MADAGASCAR PLAN. A Nazi plan devised in 1940 to solve the Jewish problem by emigration to Madagascar. The world's fourth-largest island (228,000 square miles), lying about 250 miles from the southeast coast of Africa, Madagascar was a French colony. The plan called for its cession by France to Germany in a peace treaty. The German Navy would be given its choice of bases on the island, while the rest of the island would be made a Jewish reservation under the jurisdiction of Heinrich Himmler (q.v.). Madagascar was considered to be preferable to Palestine, "which belonged to the Christians and Muslims." Moreover, the Jews sent to Madagascar could be held as hostages to ensure the conduct of their "racial comrades" in the United States. The resettlement of Jews on the island would be financed by the expropriation of Jewish property in Europe.

The Madagascar Plan was never implemented. It could not be launched until a peace treaty had been made with France, and that in turn hinged on peace with Great Britain. The next major step in handling the Jewish question was the Wannsee Conference (q.v.), devoted to the *Endlösung*, or Final Solution (*see* ENDLÖSUNG, DIE).

MAGINOT LINE. The elaborate system of fortifications constructed from 1929 to 1934 along the eastern frontier of France from Switzerland to Montmédy. Europe's major fixed frontier, the line took its name from its creator, André Maginot (1877–1932), French Minister of War. It stretched in a series of gigantic pillboxes connecting old fortifications with two great new ones, Hackenberg and Hochwald, covering the iron and industrial region of Lorraine. Into the Maginot Line went the services of a huge work force, $1 billion, and, later, 300,000 troops. At points there were huge underground forts on six levels, quarters for officers and men, power stations for ventilation, miniature railroads, telephone exchanges, hospitals, and rest rooms, all immune to shells and bombs. Aboveground were casemates, served by elevators, with guns pointing only to the east.

There was a major weakness in the construction of the Maginot Line: the fortifications were not continued along the Franco-Belgian frontier because of Belgian objections and because of the assumption by French military strategists that the Germans could not penetrate the Ardennes. The planners of the Maginot Line did not intend it to be more than a partial defense, but the French public assumed that it gave total protection. In 1940 the fast-moving German armies had no trouble in outflanking the supposedly impregnable line. When France signed its armistice with Germany at Compiègne (q.v.), the forts of the Maginot Line were intact. Psychologically, the Maginot Line represented the purely defensive mentality of the French High Command in the Long Armistice between the two world wars.

MAHRUN, ARTUR (1890–1950). Founder of the Jungdeutscher Orden (q.v.) and early political opponent of Hitler. Artur Mahrun was born in Kassel on December 30, 1890. In 1920 he founded the Jungdeutscher Orden (Order of Young Germans), of which he remained the intellectual pivot. It was a conservative bourgeois group of young people who belatedly joined the disintegrating liberal forces at the time of the Nazi landslide in the early 1930s. A democrat by conviction, Mahrun early discerned that Hitler's strength lay in his political behavior and his methods of propaganda: "The leaders of the Nazi Party have understood well how to turn the disgust of the German people over the deep economic depression into the wheels which drive the mills of the Party. The Nazis are allowed to say anything. They believe in the dictatorship which is supposed to save Germany." Mahrun was one of the founders of the German State party in 1932 and, as such, a strong opponent of Hitler and the Nazis. He was imprisoned briefly in 1933 after Hitler came to power. He died in Gütersloh on March 27, 1950.

MAIDANEK. Extermination camp located in German-occupied Poland about 2 miles from Lublin (*see* EXTERMINATION CAMPS). It was regarded as in the same class as Belzec and Sobibór (qq.v.). Like Belzec, Maidanek was originally a labor camp but was transformed into a death camp under the administration of *SS-Brigadefuehrer* Odilo Globocnik (q.v.). Unlike Belzec, it had some industrial activity. Non-Jewish prisoners were admitted. At first death was induced by carbon monoxide asphyxiation, but later hydrocyanic, or prussic, acid fumes (*see* ZYKLON-B) were used following successful tests at Belzec. It is estimated that 1.5 million inmates were gassed at Maidanek. After Russian troops discovered the camp on July 23, 1944, Konstantin Simonov, a Soviet writer, wrote a full account of the death camp for *Pravda*. In a special issue the *London Illustrated News* published photographs of the gas chambers and ovens at Maidanek.

MAILED FIST. *See* EISERNE FAUST.

MAIN PERSONNEL OFFICE. *See* PERSONALHAUPTAMT.

MANN, ERIKA (1905–1969). Author and daughter of Thomas Mann (q.v.). Erika Mann was born in Munich on November 9, 1905. A critic of Hitler and National Socialism, she fled in 1933 from Germany to Switzerland, where she was associated with an anti-Nazi cabaret, the Pfeffermühle (the Pepper Mill). In 1934 she married the English poet W. H. Auden. This marriage of convenience was arranged so that she would have British nationality and not be stateless when the Nazis canceled her German citizenship. Erika Mann went to the United States for the wedding, signed an agreement not to make any financial claims on her husband, and then returned to Europe. She remained active in liberal causes and continued to attack Nazism in her writings. Her *School for Barbarians*, a devastating description of the Nazi educational system, helped alert the world to the nature of National Socialism. She died in Kilchberg, near Zürich, on August 27, 1969.

Bibliography. Erika Mann, *School for Barbarians*, Modern Age Books, Inc., New York, 1938.

MANN, GOLO (1909–). Historian and refugee from the Third Reich. Golo Mann, the younger son of Thomas Mann (q.v.), was born in Munich on March 27, 1909. Like his father, his uncle Heinrich, his sister Erika, and his brother Klaus Mann (qq.v.), he left Germany at the advent of the Nazi regime. After working as a journalist in Switzerland, he went to the United States, where he taught at several colleges. In 1960 he returned to Germany to become professor of political science at Stuttgart Technical College (later University of Stuttgart). Among his publications is *Deutsche Geschichte des neunzehnten und zwanzigsten Jahrhunderts* (1958).

MANN, HEINRICH (1871–1950). Novelist and refugee from the Third Reich. The eldest brother of Thomas Mann (q.v.), Heinrich Mann was born in Lübeck on March 27, 1871. Active in Berlin as an editor, he was named president of the Prussian Academy of Arts (Poetry Division) in 1930. He was forced to relinquish this post in 1933 when Hitler came to power. Emigrating by way of Prague to Paris, he joined André Gide and Henri Barbusse in a literary struggle against fascism and National Socialism. A gifted novelist, he portrayed social life in Germany before and after World War I, with attention to the evils of a vulgar prosperity. His miscellaneous writings include essays on French literature and polemics against the Nazi regime. Heinrich Mann died in Santa Monica, California, on March 12, 1950.

MANN, KLAUS (1906–1949). Writer, son of Thomas Mann and brother of Erika Mann (qq.v.). Klaus Mann was born in Munich on November 18, 1906. A theater critic in Berlin in 1925, he also performed as an actor in a stock company with his sister. Opposed to the Nazi regime, he emigrated from Germany in 1933. With Aldous Huxley, Heinrich Mann (q.v.), and André Gide, he edited the emigrant journal *Die Sammlung (The Collection)*. In 1942 he moved to the United States, where he became editor of *Decision*. He continued to write critically on Hitler and Nazism. Enlisting in the American armed forces, he served as a correspondent for the Army newspaper *Stars and Stripes*. He committed suicide in Cannes on May 21, 1949.

MANN, THOMAS (1875–1955). One of the great novelists of the twentieth century and a dedicated opponent of the Nazi regime. Thomas Mann was born in Lübeck on June 6, 1875. Early in his career he became known for his studies of the psychology of the artist and for his extensive use of philosophic symbolism. His novels show the influence of nineteenth-century German romanticism. In 1914 he was carried away by the contemporary military spirit: "German militarism is inherent in the German soul, its ethical conservatism, its soldier-like morality—an element of demonism and heroism—this is what refuses to recognize the civilian spirit as a final ideal of mankind." Mann later rejected this view and became a passionate defender of liberal causes, particularly the

Thomas Mann. [*Brown Brothers*]

Weimar Republic (q.v.). From his prolific pen there poured a series of novels which in 1929 won him the Nobel Prize for literature.

Mann was in Switzerland when Hitler came to power, and he decided to stay there in exile. The Nazi government deprived him of his German citizenship in early 1936. On December 19, 1936, he was informed that his honorary degree *(Ehrendoktor)* from the University of Bonn had been canceled. The letter sent to him by the dean of the Philosophical Faculty at Bonn and Mann's spirited reply attracted global attention. Mann's letter was a devastating indictment of the Nazi way of life. He continued his anti-Nazi writings until Hitler's suicide. In 1938 he went to the United States, where he taught at Princeton University and wrote a number of essays denouncing Nazism. He returned in 1954 to Zürich, where he died on August 12, 1955.

MANN, SS. A private in the Schutzstaffel (*see* SS).

MANNHEIM, KARL (1893–1947). Austrian sociologist and prominent refugee from the Third Reich. From 1930 to 1933 Karl Mannheim was professor of sociology at the University of Frankfurt am Main. Soon after Hitler assumed political power, Mannheim left Germany and took a post at the London School of Economics. In opposition to current thinking, he was the founder of systematic "scientific sociology." Among his books were *Ideology and Utopia* (Harcourt, Brace and Company, Inc., New York, 1951) and *Freedom, Power, and Democratic Planning* (Oxford University Press, New York, 1950). He died in London on January 9, 1947.

MANSTEIN, [FRIEDRICH] ERICH [VON LEWINSKI] VON (1887–1973). Armored warfare strategist who was the mastermind behind the *Blitzkrieg* (q.v.) against France in 1940. Erich von Manstein was born in Berlin on November 24, 1887, under his original name of Lewinski. On the death of his parents he was adopted by Georg von Manstein, a wealthy landowner. Commissioned in the Imperial Army in 1906, he served in World War I.

In 1935 and 1936 Von Manstein was chief of operations, and until February 1938 he served as senior quartermaster on the Army General Staff. From the opening of World War II in 1939 to February 1940 he was chief of staff for the army group commanded by Gen. Gerd von Rundstedt (q.v.). In this post he established the operations plans for Hitler's successful campaign in the west. He was promoted to general field marshal on July 19, 1940, after the fall of France. Transferred to the eastern front, he commanded the Eleventh Army from September 18 to November 21, 1941. He conquered the Crimea and Sevastopol for the Third Reich. In October and November 1941 he issued orders, along with Gen. Walther von Reichenau (q.v.), "to complete the annihilation of false Bolshevik doctrines of the Soviet State and its armed forces and the pitiless extermination of foreign treachery and cruelty." After the fall of Sevastopol, Hitler dispatched Von Manstein with his staff to complete the reduction of Leningrad while most of his men were sent to support Gen. Friedrich von Paulus (q.v.). From November 28, 1942, to February 14, 1943, Von Manstein held command of Army Group Don. In this capacity he managed to prevent the collapse of the southern wing of the eastern front. He commanded Army Group South from February 14, 1943, to March 30, 1944.

Field Marshal Erich von Manstein. [*Picture Collection, The Branch Libraries, The New York Public Library*]

As early as 1942 Von Manstein had been approached by officers of the Resistance (q.v.) to join them in the plot against Hitler. He intimated that he was not averse to the "strike," provided that he could take Sevastopol. Sevastopol fell on July 3, 1942, after a siege of 250 days. The victorious Von Manstein then placed himself at the disposal of Col. Gen. Ludwig Beck (q.v.) and the Resistance movement. He gave his word that as soon as Stalingrad fell to the German armed forces, he would fly to Hitler's headquarters and demand that he and Gen. Günther Hans von Kluge (q.v.) be given supreme command of the eastern front. Then the conspirators would wrest active command from Hitler. However, Von Manstein was so deeply disgusted with the performance of Von Paulus before Stalingrad that he reaffirmed his allegiance to Hitler. Maj. Gen. Henning von Tresckow (q.v.), at the core of the Resistance, attempted desperately to keep Von Manstein in line, but the latter refused and declined to accept Von Tresckow as his chief of staff. Von Manstein gradually drew away from the plot.

At the close of the war Von Manstein, after captivity in Great Britain, was transferred to Germany for trial. In August 1948 he was brought before a British military court in Hamburg. After a trial lasting four months, he was sentenced to eighteen years' imprisonment. The prosecution introduced an order of the day, issued by Von Manstein on November 20, 1941, in which he reminded each soldier of the Eleventh Army that he was "not merely a fighter according to the rules of the art of war, but also the bearer of a ruthless ideology . . . therefore the soldier should understand the necessity for a severe but just revenge on sub-human Jewry." However, he was acquitted of the charge of having "ordered, authorized, and permitted" mass extermination of Jews and others in Russia.

Subsequently, the sentence was reduced to twelve years. Von Manstein was released on parole in 1952 to enter a hospital for an eye operation; he was finally released in May 1953. He subsequently became a consultant to the West German government, advocating a citizens' army with universal conscription. He died in Irschenhausen, near Munich, on June 12, 1973, at the age of eighty-five.

Bibliography. Erich von Manstein, *Lost Victories*, tr. by Anthony G. Powell, Henry Regnery Company, Chicago, 1958.

MANTEUFFEL, HASSO FREIHERR VON (1897–). General and politician. Hasso von Manteuffel was born in Potsdam on January 14, 1897, the grandnephew of Prussian Field Marshal Edwin Freiherr von Manteuffel (1809–1885). A tough commander, Hasso von Manteuffel distinguished himself on the eastern front at the head of the 7th Panzer Division. In January 1945 he was given command of the 5th Panzer (Grossdeutschland) Division on the western front, with orders to thrust forward to Brussels. Lacking air support and an adequate supply of fuel and munitions and faced with a determined Allied counteroffensive, he appealed in vain to Hitler for help. As the Fuehrer vacillated, Von Manteuffel spoke despairingly of "a corporal's war" and recommended a general retreat to the Rhine. Later he commanded the Third Panzer Army on the eastern front, Hitler's last hope. From 1953 to 1957 Von Manteuffel was a delegate to the Bundestag (Federal Diet) in Bonn.

MARBURGER REDE (Marburg Speech). Speech by Vice-Chancellor Franz von Papen (q.v.), delivered on June 17, 1934, at the University of Marburg. In his talk Von Papen criticized the National Socialist regime and called for greater freedom. He declared the question as to whether the German Reich would remain a Christian state was still open. There must be an end, he warned, to the eternal lecturing to the people. The Germans were in severe economic distress; yet the situation was painted in glowing colors. Propaganda, Von Papen said, was not enough to win the confidence of the people. It must be made clear that the absolute rule of one party was only a transitional step toward a more democratic state. Actually, Von Papen was expressing what millions of Germans were feeling but few dared to state openly. In an angry reply the infuriated Hitler called Von Papen a "worm" and a "ridiculous dwarf" who would be "crushed by the fist of the entire German nation."

MARITA. Code name for the contemplated German attack on Greece in 1941. In a directive dated December 13, 1940, Hitler ordered Operation Marita for the occupation of the Aegean coast and the Salonika Basin. Germany was not at war with Greece, but the Fuehrer's directive indicated that he considered this to be only a temporary state of affairs. The British were helping the Greeks against Italy, and Hitler was determined to keep them from gaining a foothold on the European continent.

MARR, WILHELM (1819–1904). Anti-Semitic journalist and forerunner of National Socialist ideology. Wilhelm Marr spent most of his professional career in sustained attacks on the Jews. He was the first to use the term *anti-Semitism* (q.v.). In 1878 he published a pamphlet, *The Victory of Judaism over Teutonism*, which went through twelve editions in six years. The Jews, he wrote, were a race capable of maintaining their identity over 1,800 years. They were racially inflexible: they could not change themselves, nor could they be changed. They had come into Germany to create a New Palestine, and they were specifically to blame for the 1873 financial crash. They had taken a disproportionate share of government and press in Germany. There must be a struggle between "Germanism" and "the threatening world domination of Judaism." These were precisely the ideas that Hitler accepted and advocated until his death.

MARRIAGE LOAN. *See* EHESTANDSDARLEHEN.

MARSEILLE, HANS-JOACHIM (1909–1942). Ace fighter pilot for the Luftwaffe (q.v.) in the World War II North African campaign. Attached to Jagdgeschwader (Fighter Group) 27, Marseille flew only the Messerschmitt-109 (q.v.) in support of the desert campaign of Gen. Erwin Rommel (q.v.). Luftwaffe statisticians credited Marseille with 388 sorties and the destruction of 158 enemy aircraft in the west, placing him thirty-first on the list of German aces. According to the Luftwaffe organizer Adolf Galland (q.v.), Marseille was "an acknowledged virtuoso among fighter pilots of World War II." He was awarded many high decorations, including the Knight's Cross with Oak Leaves, Swords, and Diamonds (*see* RITTERKREUZ) and the Italian gold medal for bravery.

Next to Rommel, Marseille was the most publicized and popular figure in the North African fighting. The German press referred to him as the African Eagle and the Star of the Desert. Despite his record, however, he was cited for "inefficiency" by Hermann Goering (q.v.), who was depressed by the results of the African campaign. On September 30, 1942, returning from a sweep over Cairo, Marseille notified headquarters: "There is smoke in my cockpit!" He attempted unsuccessfully to bail out and was killed instantly in a crash behind German lines.

MARTYRS, NAZI. The sixteen early followers of Hitler who were killed by the police on November 9, 1923, after the unsuccessful Beer-Hall *Putsch* (q.v.). On October 16, 1924, Hitler, while in prison at Landsberg am Lech (q.v.), dedicated the first volume of *Mein Kampf* (q.v.) to these Nazi martyrs: "So-called national authorities denied a common grave to these dead heroes." The sixteen martyrs were as follows:

Felix Alfarth, merchant (b. July 5, 1901)
Andreas Bauriedl, hat maker (b. May 4, 1879)
Theodor Casella, bank official (b. August 8, 1900)
Wilhelm Ehrlich, bank official (b. August 19, 1894)
Martin Faust, bank official (b. January 27, 1901)
Anton Hechenberger, locksmith (b. September 28, 1902)
Oskar Körner, merchant (b. January 4, 1875)
Karl Kuhn, headwaiter (b. July 26, 1897)
Karl Laforce, student engineer (b. October 28, 1904)
Kurt Neubauer, servant (b. March 27, 1899)
Klaus von Pape, merchant (b. August 16, 1904)
Theodor von der Pfordten, counsel on the State Supreme Court (b. May 14, 1873)
Joh. Rickmers, retired cavalry captain (b. May 7, 1881)
Max Erwin Von Scheubner-Richter, doctor of engineering (b. January 9, 1884)
Lorenz Ritter von Stransky, engineer (b. March 14, 1899)
Wilhelm Wolf, merchant (b. October 19, 1898)

MÄRZGEFALLENE (Those Who Joined in March). Term used sarcastically to describe Germans who hastened to join the National Socialist party in March 1933 after Hitler's accession to power.

MÄRZVEILCHEN (Sweet Violets). Popular term of derision to designate individuals who joined the National Socialist party in a general stampede when the Nazis officially took office in March 1933. *See also* MÄRZGEFALLENE.

MASTER MAN. *See* HERRENMENSCH.

MASTER RACE. *See* HERRENVOLK.

MAURICE, EMIL (1897–1972). Hitler's personal bodyguard, chauffeur, and early crony. Emil Maurice was born in Westermoor on January 19, 1897. A clockmaker by vocation, he was an armed bohemian by preference. In 1919 he joined the German Workers' party (Deutsche Arbeiterpartei, q.v.) and became member No. 19 when it was reorganized as the Nationalsozialistische Deutsche Arbeiterpartei (q.v.), the NSDAP. In 1920, when a tough young butcher named Ulrich Graf (q.v.) organized the *Ordnertruppe* (q.v.), a strong-arm squad of monitor troops whose duty it was to protect Hitler at mass meetings, Maurice joined the group. Both Graf and Maurice subsequently claimed the distinction of being "the first SA [q.v.] man." Maurice later became Hitler's bodyguard.

Maurice was not popular in Nazi party circles. Dark and of French descent, he was accused in the inner entourage of having Jewish blood. In the summer of 1924, while in Landsberg Prison (*see* LANDSBERG AM LECH), Maurice took notes of Hitler's first dictation for *Mein Kampf* (q.v.), a task completed by Rudolf Hess (q.v.). Maurice was friendly with Angela (Geli) Raubal (q.v.), Hitler's niece, and it was believed that he was his employer's rival for her affections before her suicide on September 18, 1931. Maurice played a leading role in the 1934 Blood Purge (q.v.). He was one of the gunmen who executed Edmund Heines (q.v.) and a homosexual boy at Bad Wiessee on June 30, 1934. He also led a murder gang that killed Father Bernhard Stempfle, who had talked too much about the Hitler–Geli Raubal affair. Maurice served as an *SS-Oberfuehrer* (brigadier general) and, in 1937, as head of the Landeshandwerksmeister, a society of professional handicraft workers in Munich. He died on February 6, 1972.

MAUTHAUSEN. Concentration camp located near Linz, Upper Austria, on the north bank of the Danube near Enns (*see* CONCENTRATION CAMPS). During the first weeks after the *Anschluss* (q.v.) between Germany and Austria in 1938, Heinrich Himmler and Reinhard Heydrich (qq.v.) took advantage of their stay in Austria to set up a Jewish emigration center in Vienna and a concentration camp at Mauthausen. It was too much trouble, Himmler said, to transport prisoners all the way north to Germany, and besides Austria needed a camp of its own. In 1941, 1,000 Dutch Jews were deported to Mauthausen for labor in the granite works there. In 1944 some 600 Italian Jews were sent to the camp, to be followed in early 1945 by thousands of Hungarian Jews.

During the six and one-half years of its existence (January 1939–April 1945), Mauthausen held the record for a concentration camp, as opposed to an extermination camp (*see* EXTERMINATION CAMPS), of 36,318 executions duly recorded in its official *Totenbuch* (q.v.), death book. On April 25, 1945, Mauthausen, along with Dachau and Theresienstadt (qq.v.), was cut off from Berlin by Allied troops and its inmates liberated. Thousands of the worst cases were transferred by the International Red Cross to hospitals in Germany, Switzerland, and Sweden.

MAX HEILIGER DEPOSIT ACCOUNT. Cover name for an SS (q.v.) bank account for booty collected in the extermination camps (q.v.). Deposited to the Max Heiliger account were gold fillings from the teeth of gassed inmates, diamonds, gold watches, gold bars, wedding and other rings, silverware, bracelets, and cash. The vaults of the Reichsbank were filled to overflowing with this macabre booty. Dr. Walther Funk (q.v.), president of the Reichsbank, was aware of the origin of this treasure.

MAYER, HELENE (1910–1953). German women's fencing champion. Helene Mayer was born in Offenbach on December 12, 1910, the daughter of Dr. Ludwig Karl Mayer, a physician. In her teens she excelled in riding, swimming, skiing, and fencing. At the age of fifteen she became women's fencing champion of the Weimar Republic (q.v.). In spring, 1928, she won her first international success in London. Competing that summer in the Olympic Games at Amsterdam, she won the gold medal in foils. Later that year she took the national championship in Italy, where she was graciously received by Mussolini. In the international fencing tourney held in Offenbach in 1929 she won all the events in which she was entered. She won the German championship in foils for the sixth time at Mainz in 1930. Unwilling to take part in the European championships held on May 24–31, 1931, because of the death of her father, she relinquished the title to the Belgian Janny Addams.

Shortly after the Nazis came to power in 1933, Propaganda Minister Dr. Paul Joseph Goebbels (q.v.) portrayed Helene Mayer, by this time a national heroine, in glowing terms as the perfect specimen of Nordic womanhood. Tall, thin, and fair, she was described as the apotheosis of German racial purity. The campaign was quietly but abruptly dropped when it was discovered that her line of heredity included Jewish grandparents.

ME-109. *See* MESSERSCHMITT-109.

ME-110. *See* MESSERSCHMITT-110.

ME-262. *See* MESSERSCHMITT-262.

MEDICAL WAR CRIMES. *See* DOCTORS' TRIAL.

MEFO BILLS. Special notes issued by the Reichsbank and guaranteed by the government of the Third Reich. The name was taken as an acronym for Metallurgische Forschung, GmbH (Metallurgical Research, Inc.), indicating the study of metallurgy. The idea was projected by Dr. Hjalmar Schacht (q.v.) as a means of maintaining secrecy in rearmament. Used to pay arms manufacturers, the Mefo bills were accepted by all German banks. However, mention of them was strictly forbidden either orally or in the published statements of banking institutions. From 1935 to the beginning of World War II in 1939 more than 12 billion marks in Mefo bills were issued to finance rearmament.

MEIN KAMPF (My Struggle). Title of a book written by Hitler in which he gave his political program. Regarded inside Germany as the bible of National Socialism, it was an accurate blueprint of what Hitler intended to do in the future. Few readers at the time of its publication believed that the Nazi leader intended to carry out every phase of his stated program. The first part was written in the fortress of Landsberg am Lech (q.v.), a prison in Bavaria to which Hitler had been sent after the abortive 1923 Beer-Hall *Putsch* (q.v.) in Munich. Other Nazis, including Dr. Paul Joseph Goebbels, Gottfried Feder, and Alfred Rosenberg (qq.v.), had already written either pamphlets or books, and Hitler was eager to prove to his colleagues that he, too, despite his meager education, had formed a political philosophy. The milieu at Landsberg for Hitler and some forty other National Socialists was easy and comfortable. Hitler spent much of his time from July 1923 onward dictating the first part of his book to Emil Maurice and Rudolf Hess (qq.v.). The second part was written from 1925 to 1927 after the reconstruction of the Nazi party.

Advertisement for *Mein Kampf* with its original title. [*Courtesy of the Library of Congress*]

Hitler's own original title for the book was *Four and a Half Years of Struggle against Lies, Stupidity, and Cowardice*. His publisher, Max Amann (q.v.), dissatisfied with the long title, changed it to *Mein Kampf*. Crudely written, turgid in style, the first version was filled with long words, awkward expressions, and constant repetition, all reflecting a half-educated man. The novelist Lion Feuchtwanger (q.v.) attributed thousands of grammatical errors to the original edition. The style was improved in later printings, but the basic views were retained. The book was an enormous and profitable success. By 1939 it had sold 5.2 million copies and had been translated into eleven languages. Every German couple about to be married was expected to buy a copy. The huge sales made Hitler a millionaire.

Hitler's basic theme was racial. The Germans, he wrote, should be a racially pure, superior Aryan people (*see* RACIAL DOCTRINE). It was their duty to increase their numbers in order to fulfill their destiny of world supremacy. They had to be reinvigorated despite the defeat of World War I. Only in this way could they take their place as leaders of mankind in the future.

Hitler described the Weimar Republic (q.v.) as "the greatest miscarriage of the 20th century," as "a monstrosity of the human mechanism." He pointed to three prevailing conceptions of the state. First, there were those who saw in the state simply a more or less voluntary collection of people under a government. This was by far the largest group, the "crazy brains" of which created a "state authority" *(Staatsautorität)* and which forced people to serve it instead of serving them. An example was the Bavarian Volkspartei (People's party). The second group, a smaller one, recognized a state authority under certain conditions, such as "liberty," "freedom," and other rights of man. It expected that the state would be run so that the individual's pocketbook would be comfortably filled. This group was recruited mainly from the German bourgeoisie, from liberal democracy. The third and weakest group looked for the unity of all people having the same language. It attempted to obtain nationalization through language. This group, dominated by the Nationalist party, was handicapped by a fundamentally false assumption. The conglomerate peoples of Austria, for example, could never be Germanized. A Negro or a Chinese could never become a German simply because he spoke the German language fluently. "Germanization can take place only on ground, not in language." Nationality and race, Hitler wrote, lay in blood, not in language. The mixture of blood in the German state could be corrected if the lowest elements were weeded out. Equally bad was the mixture in eastern Germany, where Polish elements had contaminated German blood. Germany had placed itself in a bad position because of the prevalent belief in America that immigrants from Germany were Germans. They were, on the contrary, "Jewish imitation Germans."

All three of these views of the state, the voluntary, the liberal democratic, and the nationalistic, said Hitler, were fundamentally false. They did not recognize the key factor, which was that the cultural powers of a state depended in the final analysis upon racial elements. It was the prime duty of the state to preserve and encourage its racial elements. "The fundamental thing is that the State is no end, but a means to an end. It is, indeed, a prerequisite to the development of a high *Kultur,* but not the cause of it. The cause lies exclusively in the existence of a race capable of improving its *Kultur.*" Hitler summarized seven points as "the business of a state":

1. It must place "race" in the center of attention.
2. It must keep the race clean.
3. It must as a duty force the practice of modern birth control. No diseased or weak people should be permitted to have children. The German nation must be prepared for future leadership.
4. It must promote sports among young people to an unprecedented level of efficiency.
5. It must make the Army the final and highest school.
6. It must emphasize the teaching of "racial knowledge" in the schools (*see* RASSENFORSCHUNG).
7. It must awaken patriotism and national pride among its citizens.

Hitler went on to express his ideology of racial nationalism. Repeating the views of Houston Stewart Chamberlain (q.v.), he wrote that the Aryan or Indo-European stocks, especially the German or Teutonic, were actually what the Jews were said to be, "a chosen people," upon whose survival the existence of man on this planet depended. "Everything we admire on the earth, whether in science, technics, or invention, is the creation of only a few nations and, perhaps, originally, of one race. The whole success of our *Kultur* depends on those nations." For him that one race was the Aryan. "History shows in complete clarity that every mixture of blood between the Aryan race with lower races has resulted in the downfall of the bearer of *Kultur.* North America, whose greater proportion of population consists of German elements, which have mixed but little with lower, colored races, shows a civilization and a *Kultur* different from that of Central or South America, where the Romantic immigrants became assimilated to a great extent with the original inhabitants." Germanic North America, on the other hand, had remained "racially clean and unmixed." Any fellow countryman who failed to understand the laws of race would bring misfortune upon himself. Hitler beseeched the Germans to join the parade of victory *(Siegeszug)* of the "best races." Eliminate the Aryan race from the earth, and deep blackness, comparable to the Dark Ages, would descend upon mankind.

Hitler divided all humanity into three classes: (1) founders of civilization *(Kulturbegründer),* (2) bearers of civilization *(Kulturträger),* and (3) destroyers of civilization *(Kulturzerstörer).* In the first group, the founders of civilization, he placed the Aryan race, that is, the Germanic and North American civilizations, as of the greatest importance. The gradual worldwide spread of Aryan civilization to such nations as Japan and other "morally subjugated races" had led to the creation of the second class, or bearers of civilization. Hitler included the Orient generally in this category. Only in their outer form would Japan and other bearers of civilization remain Asiatic; inwardly they would become Aryanized. In his third class, the destroyers of civilization, Hitler placed the Jews at the top.

Again Hitler repeated that just as mankind produced the genius, so did the various races number among them a "genius" race, the Aryan. It was an inborn characteristic, "just as genius is born in the brain of a child." When the Aryan came into contact with lower races, it conquered them and made its will prevail. Instead of keeping his blood clean, however, the Aryan had mixed it with that of natives until he began to adopt the spiritual and bodily characteristics of the lower race. A continuation of this blood mixture meant the destruction of the old civilizations and the loss of the power of resistance *(Widerstandskraft),* which was the possession solely of those of pure blood. The Ayran race had kept its high place in civilization because it understood the meaning of duty; that is, the Aryan individual was always eager to offer his life for the benefit of the majority. This fact revealed a crowning feature of mankind, "the essence of sacrifice."

Hitler devoted many bitter pages to his contempt for Jews. "In strong contrast to the Aryan is the Jew. Scarcely any people on earth has its instinct for self-preservation so well developed as the so-called 'chosen people.' The Jew has never had a *Kultur* of his own; he has always borrowed from others and has developed his intellect from contact with the intellect of other peoples. Unlike the Aryan, the Jew's desire for self-preservation does not go beyond the individual." The Jewish feeling of "belonging together" *(Zusammengehörigkeitsgefühl)* was based on a "very primitive herd instinct." The Jewish race was "nakedly egotistic" and possessed only an imaginary *Kultur.* There was no idealism to be found in it. The Jews were not even a race of nomads, because the nomads had at least an idea of the word *work.*

In Hitler's view, the Jews were parasites in the bodies of other peoples, making a state within a state and refusing to leave. Judaism was not a religion to Hitler: "It is composed of a people with positive racial characteristics. The Talmud is not a religious book dedicated to preparation for immortality, but rather a guide to the practical and endurable life of the present world. The religious teachings of Judaism are devoted to keeping the Jewish blood pure, not to religion itself." The Jewish spirit, Hitler wrote, was working for the ruin of Germany. "The black-haired Jewish youth waits for hours, with satanic joy in his eyes, for the unsuspecting [Aryan] girls, whom he shames with his blood and thereby robs the nation. . . . He seeks to destroy the racial characteristics of the Germans with every means at his command. . . . It was the Jews who brought the Negro to the Rhine, always with the same thought and clear aim in the back of their heads—to destroy the hated white races through 'bastardization,' to tumble them from their cultural and political heights and to raise themselves to the vacant place."

To Hitler's contempt for Jews was added a hatred of Marxism. He saw Marxism and its dictatorship of the proletariat as responsible for the current corruption of national blood and national ideals in Germany. Marxism had overcome German nationalism until he, Hitler, emerged to act in the role of savior. Its evil influence was attributable to the Jews, who wanted to root out "the national bearers of intelligence and make slaves in the land." A terrible example of its effects could be seen in

Russia, "where 30,000,000 were allowed to die of hunger in a truly savage manner, undergoing inhuman torments, while literary Jews and stock-exchange bandits obtain the rule over a great people."

A racially clean people, Hitler wrote, could never be subjugated by the Jews. Everything on earth could be made better. Every defeat could be made the victory of a later epoch. A "rebirth" of the German soul would come if the blood of the German people was kept pure. Germany's defeat in 1918 could be explained racially: 1914 was simply the last attempt of the forces working for national preservation against the steadily advancing pacifist-Marxist crippling of the German national body. What Germany needed was a "Teutonic State of the German Nation."

Hitler's economic theories as expressed in *Mein Kampf* repeated the teachings of Gottfried Feder. National self-sufficiency and economic independence had to replace international trade. The principle of autarchy (*Autarkie*, q.v.) was based on the assumption that economic interests and economic leaders must be subordinated ruthlessly to racial and national considerations. The nations of the world were already erecting higher and higher tariff barriers against commercial intercourse and were cutting imports to a minimum. Hitler recommended even greater extremes. Germany had to cut itself off from the rest of Europe and attain self-sufficiency. Enough food could be raised inside its borders and in the eastern European agricultural countries to ensure the existence of the Reich. This would involve a tremendous economic revolution, but Germany had already been subjected to enough strain to inure itself to it. The struggle against international finance and loan capitalism had become the central point in the program for Germany's independence and freedom. The steel axle of National Socialism was the breaking of interest slavery (*Zinsknechtschaft*, q.v.). Farmers, laborers, the entire bourgeoisie, industrialists, even the nation, which had to borrow foreign capital, were all under the influence of interest slavery. The state and the people had to be freed from interest debts owed to loan capitalism. A national state capitalism should be created. The Reichsbank had to be placed under governmental control. Money for all public works, such as the development of waterpower and roads, had to be obtained through the issue of government coupons (*Staatskassengutscheine*, q.v.), which would bear no interest. Building associations and industrial banks that would grant interest-free loans should be formed. All wealth acquired during World War I should be regarded as criminally acquired. War profits were to be confiscated. Trusts, as combinations in restraint of trade, should be placed under government ownership. All industrial enterprises had to adopt a profit-sharing system. An old-age pension system should be established. Such large department stores as Tietz, Karstadt, and Wertheim should be placed on a cooperative basis and leased to small tradesmen.

In sum, the arguments presented in *Mein Kampf* were dominantly negative and were designed to appeal to dissatisfied elements in Germany. Hitler's views were violently nationalistic, "truly" socialist, anti-Semitic, antidemocratic, antiliberal, antiparliamentary, anti-Catholic, anti-Marxist, and anti-French.

Bibliography. Adolf Hitler, *Mein Kampf*, Houghton Mifflin Company, Boston, 1943.

MEINECKE, FRIEDRICH (1862–1954). Historian and opponent of Nazi ideology. Friedrich Meinecke was born in Salzwedel on October 30, 1862. He was reared in an atmosphere of nationalism at a time when Otto von Bismarck was forging national unity in three wars. As a young man Meinecke observed his self-confident fatherland shift its commercial and industrial interests from the Rhine and the Oder to the channels of world commerce. After studying at the Universities of Bonn and Berlin from 1882 to 1886, he became an official of the Prussian Archives, where he developed a familiarity with the source material he was to utilize later in his academic and writing careers. In 1893 he became an editor of the *Historische Zeitschrift (Historical Journal)*, and he retained his connection with it for forty-two years. Turning to a teaching career, he served successively at the Universities of Berlin (1896–1901), Strassburg (Strasbourg, 1901–1906), Freiburg (1906–1914), and Berlin again (from 1914). Occupying the chair once held by Heinrich von Treitschke, Meinecke was a popular historian who drew hundreds of students from all parts of Germany. A prolific writer and editor, he published many standard historical works that won him international acclaim.

An admirer of Western liberalism, Meinecke was at the same time an advocate of Prussian authoritarianism. He worked energetically to bring the two concepts into harmony, and he failed to understand why anyone could object to this unlikely merger. He gave a brilliantly subtle interpretation of historicism, a view of history regarded partly as a reaction against the abstract principles of the Enlightenment. In contrast to the belief that truth and the meaning of life are to be found in God or reason or the law of nature or the absolute, historicism contended that understanding is to be found in history. There are no absolute principles in history, nor is there any true monistic interpretation. Values and ideas change with periods of history, and what may be considered ethical and moral at one time may be regarded differently at another. Only by "objectively" interpreting the ideology of historical periods in their own frameworks can the true historical picture be obtained. This means that the historian must restore contact with contemporary society and assist it to understand and solve its problems. "Historicism," Meinecke wrote, "is nothing other than the transference to historical life of the new life principles won in the great German movement from Leibnitz to the death of Goethe. The movement continued as a general Occidental movement, and the crown fell to the German spirit." Other historians, especially critics outside Germany, rejected Meinecke's historicism and contended that, stripped of its ponderous verbiage, it was in reality a highly rationalized argument in support of Prussianism and German nationalism.

Meinecke was alienated by Hitler's harsh and arrogant nationalism and spoke out against it until 1933. In 1935 his name was stricken from the cover of the *Historische Zeitschrift*, and he lost his academic post. Throughout World War II he lived in penurious circumstances. Following the collapse of the Third Reich, the American occupation authorities appointed Meinecke to the position of rector (chancellor) of the new Free University in West Berlin. He served in that capacity until his death in Berlin-Dahlem on February 6, 1954.

In *The German Catastrophe* (1950), a small book giving his reflections and reminiscences, Meinecke sought to find the causes for the "catastrophe" that had smashed his beloved fatherland. He began to see the role of the historian in a slightly different light: "The historian has only to write down and evaluate the course of events, and not to take part in determining them. But times of great crisis lead him beyond this mission." He finally admitted the twofold nature of the German soul, one spiritual and one unspiritual, one peaceful and one militaristic. "A higher and lower principle were struggling with one another, and the lower principle won." He denounced that lower and degenerate militarism which became the tool of a Hitler and reached its last vicious peak in Himmler's Waffen-SS (q.v.). At one time Meinecke had argued in favor of power politics; now he professed himself astonished, chagrined, and humiliated by the catastrophe of Hitlerism, which represented in part the outcome of state worship. "Hitler's work," he wrote, "must be reckoned as the eruption of a satanic principle in world history." Critics commented that Meinecke failed to see that ideologically he had been unfortunate enough to place himself in the trap which Hitler had sprung.

Bibliography. Friedrich Meinecke, *The German Catastrophe: Reflections and Recollections*, tr. by Sidney B. Fay, Harvard University Press, Cambridge, Mass., 1950.

MEISSNER, OTTO (1880–1953). National Socialist jurist. Otto Meissner was born in Bischweiler (Bischwiller), Alsace, on March 13, 1880. Entering the civil service at an early age, he served as chief of the Reich Chancellery for twenty-five years, first for President Paul von Hindenburg (q.v.), from 1924 to 1934, and then for Hitler, from 1934 to 1945. Along with Oskar von Hindenburg (q.v.), the President's son, Meissner was an influential member of the camarilla that convinced the old man to name Hitler Chancellor. In reward for his services Meissner was retained as State Secretary in the presidential Chancellery. In 1937 he was named a Reich Minister. On April 11, 1949, he was tried before Military Tribunal No. 4 at Nuremberg and was acquitted of war crimes. He died in Munich on May 27, 1953.

MEITNER, LISE (1878–1968). Austro-Swedish physicist and mathematician, one of the small group of scientists responsible for atomic fission, and a prominent exile from Nazi Germany. Lise Meitner was born in Vienna on November 7, 1878. In 1917 she went to Berlin to join the distinguished chemist Otto Hahn at the Kaiser Wilhelm Institute to work on radioactive substances and the disintegration products of radium, thorium, and actinium. With Hahn she was the codiscoverer of protoactinium, later called protactinium, a rare radioactive chemical element. One of the first women to hold a professorship in Germany, she taught at the University of Berlin from 1926 to 1933.

After the Austrian *Anschluss* in 1938, Lise Meitner left Germany and went to Stockholm, where she became a member of the staff at the Nobel Institute. There she received a letter from Hahn describing a strange discovery: when a uranium atom was disintegrated by a neutron, an atom of barium was produced. She discussed the phenomenon with Niels Bohr, the Danish physicist, and her nephew, Otto Frisch, both of whom recognized its extraordinary significance. It meant that when the uranium atom was split into roughly two parts, the action was accompanied by a tremendous release of energy. Frisch called this *fission*, a term borrowed from biology.

Ironically, Lise Meitner, a Jewish scientist who could not work in Nazi Germany, contributed much to the development of the atomic bomb: Hitler had hoped that such a bomb would be his ultimate weapon. In 1946 Lise Meitner was a visiting professor at the Catholic University of America in Washington. Three years later she returned to Sweden and became a Swedish citizen. She died in Cambridge, England, on October 27, 1968.

MENGELE, JOSEF (1911– ?). Camp doctor at the Auschwitz (q.v.) extermination camp, notorious for his medical experimentation (*see* EXTERMINATION CAMPS). Anne Frank (q.v.) called him "the angel of extermination." Josef Mengele was born in Günzburg, a quaint medieval town of 12,000 inhabitants on the banks of the Danube in Bavaria, on March 16, 1911. His father was the founder of the farm machinery factory of Karl Mengele & Sons, an enterprise employing many townspeople. In the 1920s Josef Mengele went to Munich to study philosophy. There he became acquainted with the racial ideology of Alfred Rosenberg (q.v.), whose Aryan theory impressed him as being scientific truth. He also met Hitler and became one of his most devoted followers. Later he took a medical degree at the University of Frankfurt am Main. Combining studies of philosophy and medicine, Mengele developed a theory that human beings, like dogs, had pedigrees. He would later initiate experiments to breed a race of blue-eyed, blond Nordic giants.

In 1939 Mengele enlisted in the Army and joined the Waffen-SS (q.v.) as an *Untersturmfuehrer* (2d lieutenant). He served as a medical officer in France and Russia. In 1943 he was appointed chief doctor at Auschwitz by Heinrich Himmler (q.v.). There he joined other doctors (König, Thilon, Klein) in the task of choosing employable Jews to operate the industrial machines and sending others to the gas chambers. The selection was haphazard. The inmates were paraded before Mengele, who called

Dr. Josef Mengele.

either "Right!" (work squads) or "Left!" (gas chambers). In addition to this task, Mengele promoted medical experimentation on inmates, especially on twins, to find means of multiplying the German nation. On one occasion he supervised an operation by which two Gypsy children were sewn together to create Siamese twins. The hands of the two children became badly infected where the veins had been resected.

Witnesses at the Frankfurt Trial (q.v.) told of Mengele's standing before his victims with his thumb in his pistol belt and choosing candidates for the gas chambers. When it was reported that one block was infected with lice, Mengele solved the problem by gassing all the 750 women assigned to it. An elderly witness, the seventy-one-year-old Maximilian Sternol, testified: "On the night of July 31, 1944, there were terrible scenes at the liquidation of the Gypsy compound. Women and children were on their knees in front of Mengele and Boger crying 'Take pity on us, take pity on us!' Nothing helped. They were beaten down, brutally trampled upon, and pushed on the trucks. It was a terrible, gruesome sight."

After the war Mengele spent some time in a British internment hospital, but then disappeared and went underground. Apparently using the same route as that employed by Adolf Eichmann (q.v.), he went to Rome in 1949 and from there, with false identification papers as "Gregorio Gregori," moved to Buenos Aires. High on the list of wanted Nazi criminals, he became the object of a search by Interpol (International Police), Israeli agents, and the Nazi hunter Simon Wiesenthal (q.v.). Large rewards were offered for his capture: $5,000 by an organization in Frankfurt am Main (1961) and $50,000 by the Haifa Documentation Center for Josef Mengele (1971). He was variously reported as seen in Brazil (1961 and 1964) and Paraguay (1968 and 1973). On June 7, 1985, gravediggers at Embu, Brazil, smashed open a coffin which investigators believed to be Mengele's body. Some 16 forensic experts (six of them American), announced unanimously that the skeleton was that of Mengele "within a reasonable scientific certainty."

Bibliography. Gerald L. Posner and John Ware, *Mengele: The Complete Story*, New York, McGraw-Hill Book Company, 1986.

MENSUR (Duel). Student duel fought by fraternity members in the pre-Hitler era. The *Mensur* was forbidden during the Weimar Republic (q.v.), but it was legalized by the Nazi regime as a means of instilling students with discipline, courage, and indifference to pain.

MESCHUGGISMUS (Cult of Insanity). Term used by Nazi speech makers to denounced innovators of modern art. The word was borrowed from the Yiddish expression *meschugge* (crazy). Because of Hitler's hostility to modernity in art, members of the Nazi hierarchy competed with one another in excoriating German expressionists, impressionists, Dadaists, and surrealists.

MESSERSCHMITT, WILLY (1898–1978). Aircraft designer, builder, and entrepreneur. Willy Messerschmitt was born in Frankfurt am Main on June 26, 1898. In 1923 he founded the Messerschmitt aircraft plant at Bamberg and in 1926 produced his first all-metal plane. His fighter plane, the Messerschmitt-109 (q.v.), first took to the air in 1935 and later underwent a host of variations and modifications. Throughout World War II it could fly and fight on even terms with the best fighters produced by the Allies. It was rated by experts as one of the most consistently superior aircraft in aviation history. Messerschmitt himself gained a global reputation as one of the outstanding aircraft designers of the twentieth century. After the war he produced prefabricated houses but later turned to designing jet aircraft for the new air force of the Bonn Republic.

MESSERSCHMITT-109 (Me-109). Germany's standard single-seat fighter plane for more than a decade. Originating in 1934 on specifications from the German Air Ministry, which required a fast monoplane to replace the obsolete fighter biplanes for the Luftwaffe (q.v.), the Me-109 was designed and produced by Willy Messerschmitt (q.v.). After performance tests, the first public display of the Me-109 was made at the 1936 Olympic Games (*see* OLYMPIAD XI). Field tests in Spain in support of the Franco forces proved the plane to be a superb fighting machine.

The Messerschmitt-109E. [*US Air Force*]

Wartime Messerschmitts were used with great success in Poland, Scandinavia, and the Low Countries. The model Me-109E had an 1,100-horsepower liquid-cooled engine, a wingspan of 32 feet, a maximum speed of 354 miles per hour, and an armament of two 20-millimeter cannon and two 7.9-millimeter machine guns. Not until it encountered the British Spitfire in the Battle of Britain did the Me-109 meet its match. It was the favorite fighter plane of German pilots, including Maj. Erich Hartmann (q.v.), who scored 352 confirmed victories in World War II.

MESSERSCHMITT-110 (Me-110). A Messerschmitt twin-engine fighter plane.

MESSERSCHMITT-262 (Me-262; Schwalbe). The first military jet-propelled plane to be used in World War II. Work on the plane, which was designed by Willy Messerschmitt (q.v.), began in 1938, and an experimental model was flown in 1941. Specifications included two

1,980-pound turbojet engines, a maximum speed of 540 miles per hour, a wingspan of 41 feet, and an armament of four 30-millimeter cannon and twenty-four 50-millimeter rocket missiles. The Me-262 was intended as a fighter-interceptor, but Hitler, angered by Allied bombings, ordered that it be produced as a bomber. Because of conflicts in the Air Ministry and the Luftwaffe (q.v.), the plane was never produced in quantity. A late product of German aviation, it was unable to affect the course of the war despite its extraordinary speed and performance.

METALLURGISCHE FORSCHUNG, GMBH (Metallurgical Research, Inc.). *See* MEFO BILLS.

METZGER, MAX JOSEF (1887–1944). Catholic priest and a victim of the Nazi regime. Max Josef Metzger was born in the Black Forest area on February 3, 1887. After studying theology at Freiburg, he was ordained in 1911. He became a curate at Mannheim and Karlsruhe. After serving in World War I as a divisional chaplain, he became a chaplain for the People's Welfare Center in Graz. In 1917 he founded the Peace League of German Catholics, of which he was the leading figure to the time of his death. In 1942 Metzger sent the Protestant Archbishop of Uppsala a memorandum calling for a new government for Germany. When this document fell into the hands of the Gestapo (q.v.), Metzger was arrested and condemned for high treason by the Volksgericht (q.v.), the People's Court, "for assisting the enemy." He was executed at Brandenburg on April 17, 1944.

MG-42. German light machine gun considered to be the best weapon of its kind in World War II. Replacing the older MG-34, with which German troops were equipped at the beginning of the war, the MG-42 was first used by the Afrika Korps (q.v.) at Bir Hacheim. It was fired like a rifle, with its barrel braced on a simple tripod mount. Operated by a feed belt, it had a cycling rate of 1,200 rounds per minute and a range of 4,000 yards. It could easily be carried by the individual soldier. The MG-42 was mass-produced throughout the war.

MIDDLE CLASS. *See* MITTELSTAND.

MIESBACHER ANZEIGER. Rightist newspaper founded in 1875 and appearing in Miesbach, a summer and winter sports resort in Upper Bavaria. After World War I the paper won wide popularity for its sharp criticism of the Weimar Republic (q.v.). Because of its rightist viewpoint it was the favorite newspaper of the early Nazis until the adoption of the *Völkischer Beobachter* (q.v.) in 1921 as the official organ of the Nationalsozialistische Deutsche Arbeiterpartei (q.v.). The *Miesbacher Anzeiger* was discontinued in 1945.

MIESSMACHER UND KRITIKASTER (Alarmists and Critics). Catchwords used by Dr. Paul Joseph Goebbels (q.v.), Minister for Public Enlightenment and Propaganda, in his so-called enlightenment campaign. Shortly after Hitler assumed political power in 1933, Goebbels decided to fight criticism of the new regime by a strong campaign against dissenters. The German words *Miessmacher und Kritikaster* are almost untranslatable. *Miessmacher* were considered to be "Jewish-minded" individuals who found fault with everything. *Kritikaster* was invented by Goebbels himself. The campaign, which lasted for two months, was featured at more than 2,000 mass meetings.

MILCH, ERHARD (1892–1972). General field marshal of the Luftwaffe (q.v.) and deputy to Hermann Goering (q.v.). Erhard Milch was born in Wilhelmshaven on March 30, 1892. After service as an airman in World War I, he went into civil aviation. In 1923 he worked with the Junkers aviation firm and from 1926 to 1933 with Lufthansa (q.v.) as director of its finance division. Milch was responsible for creating the Lufthansa network in civil aviation. Meanwhile, he became closely connected with the rising Nazi movement.

In 1933 Goering, who knew Milch and respected his technical ability, had him appointed State Secretary in the Air Ministry (equivalent to an undersecretary in the Cabinet). In addition, Milch was made armament chief of the Luftwaffe. In this post he distributed the management of separate areas of armament production to capable technicians in industrial firms. The creation of the Luftwaffe was the achievement of Goering and Milch, who worked well together. There was a complicating factor: Milch's mother was Jewish, ordinarily an impossible situation for an official of the Nazi regime. Goering solved the problem by having Milch's mother sign a legal affidavit stating that Erhard Milch was a bastard son of his father and not a child of her marriage. Milch did not object to this process of Aryanization. This was a standard procedure for Goering, who never took anti-Semitism (q.v.) as seriously as did the Fuehrer. Goering habitually drew non-Aryan officers to the Luftwaffe if he felt them to be of special value. Milch was an efficient administrator, egocentric and demanding, who cut through red tape and went straight to the core of Luftwaffe problems.

In 1938 Milch was promoted to *Generaloberst* (colonel general). The next year he commanded Luftflotte V in the Norwegian campaign. In 1940, after the fall of France, he was one of three Luftwaffe officers (with Albert Kesselring and Hugo Sperrle, qq.v.) to be promoted to general field marshal. For 1941 to 1944 he also held the title of *Luftzeugmeister* (air inspector general). In the intrigues around the Fuehrer, Milch favored the Dr. Paul Joseph Goebbels–Albert Speer (qq.v.) group opposed to Martin

Field Marshal Erhard Milch. [*Imperial War Museum, London*]

Bormann (q.v.). In 1942 Hitler made Milch and Speer temporary transportation dictators of the Third Reich. The next year Milch attempted unsuccessfully to alert Goering to the dangers of American aircraft production, but the *Reichsmarschall* was not inclined to listen. In 1947 Milch was tried by an international military tribunal and sentenced to life imprisonment. He was released in 1954 and died in 1972.

MILITANT ASSOCIATION. *See* KAMPFBUND.

MILITANT ASSOCIATION OF RETAILERS. *See* KAMPFBUND DES GEWERBLICHEN MITTELSTANDES.

MILITARIZED TROOPS. *See* VERFÜGUNGSTRUPPE.

MISCHLINGE (Individuals of Mixed Race). Half-Jews and quarter-Jews according to Nazi racial doctrine (q.v.). This doctrine defined *Mischlinge* of the first degree as half-Jews who were descended from two Jewish grandparents who did not adhere to the Jewish religion and who were not married to Jews. *Mischlinge* of the second degree, or quarter-Jews, were those descended from one Jewish grandparent. In general, the *Mischlinge* were to be distinguished from Jews and were not to be subject to extermination. Whether a half-Jew was to be considered a Jew or a *Mischling* was said to depend upon his general attitude and conduct. Wilhelm Stuckart, State Secretary in the Ministry of the Interior, who helped draft the Nuremberg Laws on citizenship and race (q.v.), was in principle opposed to deporting *Mischlinge* on the ground that this would mean sacrificing German blood: "I have always considered it dangerous biologically to introduce German blood into the enemy camp. The intelligence and excellent education of the half-Jews, linked to their ancestral Germanic heritage, make them natural leaders outside Germany and therefore very dangerous. I prefer to see the *Mischlinge* die a natural death inside Germany."

The subject of the *Mischlinge* became of major importance at the Wannsee Conference (q.v.) of January 20, 1942, at which the Final Solution (*see* ENDLÖSUNG, DIE) was discussed. The matter was not resolved, and the recommended drastic reclassification was not made. In the end, the *Mischlinge* were neither deported, sterilized, nor exterminated. They remained non-Aryans (*see* NON-ARYAN) under the earlier decrees, but later measures were taken only against "full" Jews. Most *Mischlinge* survived the war.

MISSION OF HISTORIC IMPORTANCE. *See* WELTGESCHICHTLICHE MISSION.

MIT BRENNENDER SORGE (With Deep Anxiety). An alternate title for the papal encyclical *On the Condition of the Church in Germany,* issued by Pope Pius XI (q.v.) on March 14, 1937. *Mit brennender Sorge* were the opening words of the encyclical. In the text the Pope accused the Nazi government of violating the Concordat of 1933 (q.v.) between the Third Reich and the Holy See.

MITARBEITER IN DER STUDENTENFUEHRUNG (Associate Leader of Students). An official in the Nationalsozialistischer Deutscher Studentenbund (q.v.).

MITFORD, UNITY VALKYRIE (1914–1948). English aristocrat and friend of Adolf Hitler. Unity Mitford was born on August 8, 1914, one of the seven children (six daughters and one son) of David Bertram Ogilvy Freeman-Mitford, 2d Baron Redesdale. The father was an excessively eccentric character. The rebellious brood of girls later caused headlines. Nancy, the eldest, became a novelist and historian; Diana became the wife of Sir Oswald Mosley, British fascist leader; Jessica married Esmond Romilly, who was a relative of Winston Churchill and who described himself as a Communist; and Deborah, the youngest, became Duchess of Devonshire. Unity became a great admirer of Hitler.

Unity Mitford was a statuesque blond, lively and eccentric. From 1933 on she was a member of the Fuehrer's salon in Munich, where she was regarded as an outstanding example of Nordic beauty. She fell deeply in love with Hitler and in all probability hoped to become his wife. No one was expected to mention politics at the intimate gatherings, but Miss Mitford often spoke up for her country and pleaded with the Fuehrer to maintain good relations with Britain. Although Hitler was attentive and gracious to his guest, he was reserved on political matters and declined to discuss politics with her despite her persistence. On September 3, 1939, the day when Britain and France declared war on Germany, Miss Mitford tried to kill herself with a small-caliber pistol in the Englischer Garten in Munich. Hitler sent the best specialists in Munich to care for her. As soon as she was able to travel, she was sent home to England by a special railway car via Switzerland. She died unmarried on May 28, 1948, and was buried in the graveyard of St. Mary's Church in the village of Swinbrook. On her grave was placed a stone that read: "Unity Valkyrie Mitford. Say not the struggle nought availeth."

MITTELSTAND (Middle Class). Term used to designate the economic middle class of independent Germans. Composed of shopkeepers and craftsmen, the *Mittelstand* included Hitler's most dependable followers. It was credited with playing a critical role in the Nazi drive for political power.

MITTWOCHSGESELLSCHAFT (Wednesday Club). A group of right-wing conservatives who met each Wednesday in Berlin to discuss history, art, science, and literature. Composed of academics, industrialists, and civil servants, the Wednesday Club acted as a theoretical forum of conservative resistance to the Hitler regime. Among its members were Christian Albrecht Ulrich von Hassell (q.v.), a diplomat, and Johannes Popitz (q.v.), Prussian minister of finance, both of whom were active in the Resistance (q.v.).

MIXED RACE, INDIVIDUALS OF. *See* MISCHLINGE.

MODEL, WALTHER (1891–1945). General field marshal in the armed forces of the Third Reich. Walther Model was born in Genthin on January 24, 1891. As a young officer he made a name for himself by publishing a book on the Prussian general August Wilhelm Anton Graf von Gneisenau (1760–1831). Loyal to Hitler from the beginning, Model never faltered in his faith in the Nazi movement.

Field Marshal Walther Model. [Imperial War Museum, London]

During World War II, on March 1, 1944, he was promoted to general field marshal. After the failure of the July Plot (q.v.) of 1944, he sent an enthusiastic message of support to the Fuehrer, congratulating him on his escape and vowing eternal allegiance. In the late days of the war Hitler was encouraged by Model's firm belief that new and revolutionary weapons were on their way to turn the tide of battle.

Model's loyalty to the Fuehrer eventually brought him a high military post. On August 16, 1944, Hitler issued an order forbidding a retreat in France from the Falaise gap. Despite this order, Field Marshal Günther Hans von Kluge (q.v.), who was in command, allowed his troops to fall back. The next day a furious Hitler dismissed Von Kluge and appointed Model in his stead as commander in chief of the Army West. Astounded and distressed, Von Kluge committed suicide by swallowing poison near Metz. In mid-April 1945, Model's forces were trapped in the ruins of Germany's greatest industrial area. Some 325,000 German troops and thirty generals were captured by the Allies. Rather than become a prisoner, Model shot himself in a forest between Düsseldorf and Duisburg, and died on April 21, 1945.

MOELDERS, WERNER (1913–1941). Fighter ace of the Luftwaffe (q.v.). Werner Moelders was born in Brandenburg on March 18, 1913. After studying at the Dresden Military Academy in 1932, he joined the new Luftwaffe in 1935. For the next three years he was a flight instructor at Wiesbaden. In 1938 he was ordered to Spain as a squadron commander in the Condor Legion (q.v.) just two months before it was disbanded. He was credited with fourteen kills, a total that made him the outstanding German fighter pilot in the Spanish Civil War.

In 1939, at the outbreak of World War II, Moelders was given command of Jagdgeschwader (Fighter Group) 53. From June 1940 to July 1941 he was assigned to command Jagdgeschwader 51, in which capacity he took part in both the Battle of France and the Battle of Britain. On June 5, 1940, he had a narrow escape when a French fighter pilot surprised him over the front at Chantilly and forced him to bail out of his burning Messerschmitt-109 (q.v.). Luftwaffe statisticians credited Moelders with 115 air kills, of which 68 were made in the western theater. He was promoted to general of fighters and posted to the High Command of the Luftwaffe as inspector of fighter aircraft. At the same time he became the first Luftwaffe winner of the Knight's Cross with Oak Leaves, Swords, and Diamonds (*see* RITTERKREUZ). With this award he became the most highly decorated soldier of the Third Reich.

On November 17, 1941, when the fighter ace Ernst Udet (q.v.) committed suicide, Moelders, who was directing air operations in the Crimea, was called home to join the guard of honor at Udet's bier. On November 21, 1941, Moelders took off in an He-111 bomber only to be caught in fog and rain at Breslau. His plane hit the protruding wire of a cable, and he was killed instantly. He was replaced in his post by Adolf Galland (q.v.).

MOELLER VAN DEN BRUCK, ARTHUR (1876–1925). Leader of the young conservative revolutionaries during the Weimar era and one of the intellectual forerunners of Hitler and Nazism. Arthur Moeller van den Bruck was born in Solingen on April 23, 1876. A historian and critic, he was one of the founders of the Juniklub (June Club) in Berlin and its ideological pivot from 1915 to 1925. Antidemocratic, he stressed "the mystique of the national idea" and demanded the formation of "a new German self-consciousness." He was also opposed to Russian communism. To the right and left of Germany he saw nothing but mad egalitarianism, which he believed was reducing the international situation to absurdity. Unwilling to admit the existence of an international order, he prefigured Hitler in his contempt for international law.

Sympathetic to racial doctrine (q.v.), Moeller van den Bruck urged the Germans to support the concept of a superior Nordic race. The future, he said, lay entirely in a union between Prussia and Germany. A "true revolution," he said, would restore the values of the eternal Reich. He urged his countrymen to return to the milieu of primitive and classical times and to show their contempt for Western rationalism. He asked them to identify themselves absolutely with the living *Volkstum*, a kind of mystic totality in which each individual German would sense the "national rhythm." Germany, he said, must be an authoritarian state with completely centralized control and a planned economy. All these ideas were expressed in Moeller van den Bruck's major work, *Das Dritte Reich (The Third Reich)*, originally published in 1923, two years before his death by suicide. Hitler was profoundly influenced by Moeller van den Bruck's ideas and regarded himself as the activist who could implement them. Hitler borrowed the title of Moeller van den Bruck's book for his own use. In addition, he became the personification of the violent dynamism recommended by its author.

Bibliography. Arthur Moeller van den Bruck, *Das Dritte Reich*, Hanseatische Verlagsanstalt, Hamburg, 1931.

MOLTKE, HELMUTH JAMES GRAF VON (1907–1945). Legal adviser to the German High Command and one of the leaders of the Resistance (q.v.) movement. Helmuth von Moltke was born in Kreisau, Silesia (now Krzyżowa, Poland), on March 11, 1907, the son of a German father and an English-African mother, both Christian Scientists. He was the great-grandnephew of Field Marshal Helmuth von Moltke (1800–1891), whose generalship had helped

Helmuth James Graf von Moltke. [*Stamp issued by the German Federal Republic*]

Bismarck in the foundation of the Second Reich. From his mother Helmuth absorbed a preference for Christian, democratic, and international institutions. In his teens he was active in the German youth movement. Von Moltke dedicated himself to social reform. At the age of twenty-three he took over the management of the family estate at Kreisau. Deciding to follow the legal profession, he practiced as an international lawyer in Berlin. A tall man of striking appearance, bearing one of Germany's most respected names, he seemed to be destined for a long and brilliant legal career.

From the beginning Von Moltke opposed the Nazi regime, which he regarded as an unmitigated disgrace for his beloved fatherland. Whenever he could, he gave surreptitious aid to the victims of Nazism, including legal assistance and help in leaving the country. He was the founder and head of the Kreisau Circle (q.v.), a small group of friends and associates who planned a post-Hitler order. The circle was not a tightly organized band of conspirators but rather an informal association of young Germans concerned about the future of their country. They wanted to plan a new Germany to replace the Third Reich. The moving spirit of the group, Von Moltke believed that Germany could have a stable government only after moral rejuvenation based on Christian principles. He called for a fully open society with equal justice for all. His motives were quite different from those of many in the military wing of the Resistance, who wanted the immediate elimination of Hitler and the Nazi regime.

At the beginning of World War II Von Moltke held a second-echelon post as an expert on international law in the Amt/Ausland (Foreign Office) of the German High Command. In this capacity he communicated with the enemy and used his office to help hostages, prisoners of war, and forced laborers. In January 1944 he was taken into custody for warning an associate of impending arrest. From then on the Kreisau Circle lost its driving force. After the July Plot (q.v.) of 1944 Von Moltke was tried for treason, especially for failing to report the early activities of his associates. The real reason for his trial was his status as a man of humanity and conscience. Judge Roland Freisler (q.v.), of the dreaded Volksgericht (q.v.), the People's Court, made it plain: "The mask is off. Only in one respect are we and Christianity alike: we demand the whole man."

Von Moltke was condemned to death on January 11, 1945. In his last letter to his wife he wrote that he did not aim at martyrdom but regarded it as "an inestimable advantage to die for something which (*a*) we really have done and which (*b*) is worthwhile." He was to be killed not for what he had done but for what he had thought. He was executed at Plötzensee Prison on January 23, 1945, at the age of thirty-seven.

Bibliography. Michael Balfour and Julian Frisby, *Helmuth von Moltke: A Leader against Hitler*, St. Martin's Press, Inc., New York, 1972.

MONITOR TROOPS. *See* ORDNERTRUPPE.

MONTE, HILDE (1914–1945). Socialist poet who was killed at the frontier while attempting to return to Germany. Hilde Monte (Hilde Meisel) was born on July 31, 1914, to a Jewish family. At the age of fifteen she was already writing for *Der Funke (The Spark)*, a Berlin paper representing the Socialist International. She was in England when Hitler became Chancellor, and she joined the international campaign of resistance against the Nazi regime. Although physically delicate, she deemed it important to return to her homeland to carry on the struggle against Hitler. In 1939 she got only as far as Lisbon. In 1944 she made her way to Switzerland in the hope of reaching Germany. In early 1945 she was shot and killed by an SS (q.v.) patrol while trying to cross the border into Germany.

MORELL, THEODOR (ca. 1890–1948). Hitler's personal physician *(Leibarzt)* and injection specialist. After obtaining a medical degree, Morell served as a ship's doctor and then set up a practice on the Kurfürstendamm in Berlin as a specialist in skin and venereal diseases for the artistic demimonde. Many well-known actors and film stars were his patients. Later, he claimed to have studied with Ilya Mechnikov (1845–1916), famous Russian biologist and Nobel Prize winner, who, he said, had taught him the art of combatting bacterial infection. In 1935 Heinrich Hoffmann (q.v.), Nazi court photographer, fell critically ill and was cured by Morell with sulfanilamides obtained from Hungary. Hoffmann repeatedly told Hitler how Morell had saved his life. The Fuehrer finally asked the doctor to examine him. Morell's main finding was that Hitler was suffering from complete exhaustion of the intestinal system, which he attributed to overburdening of the nerves. He suggested a year's treatment with vitamins, hormones, phosphorus, and dextrose, mostly by injection. The Fuehrer was delighted: "No one has ever told me precisely what is wrong with me. Morell's method of cure is so logical that I have the greatest confidence in him. I shall follow his prescriptions to the letter." At the beginning of Morell's treatment Hitler developed a rash, which soon disappeared, to be followed by improvement and a sense of well-being. The Fuehrer began to eat more. "What luck I had to meet Morell," he said. "He has saved my life. It is wonderful, the way he has helped me."

The doctor-patient relationship between Morell and Hitler was to last nine years. Convinced of Morell's genius, Hitler forbade any criticism of the physician and urged his associates to go to his new doctor. Among his intimates Hitler never tired of speaking about such medical miracles as bull's testicles and Morell's newest vitamins. Morell always had a supply of his "Multiflor" capsules, composed of intestinal bacteria "raised from the

Dr. Morell being decorated [*National Archives, Washington*]

best stock owned by a Bulgarian peasant." As time went by and Hitler's symptoms returned, Morell poured more and more drugs into him: biologicals from the intestines of male animals and an assortment of twenty-eight drugs, including dangerous amphetamines. Whenever the Fuehrer gave a speech or caught a cold, he received drug injections from Morell. Gradually, Hitler's skin became more and more discolored.

Meanwhile, Morell took advantage of his relationship with his powerful patient to amass a fortune. He built factories where he manufactured patent remedies. His chocolate vitamins were a financial success. The use of Morell Russian Lice Powder was made compulsory for the armed forces. Pleased by his good fortune, Morell went on to claim that he was the true discoverer of penicillin and that his secret had been stolen from him by the British Secret Service.

Morell also accumulated an assortment of enemies. Hermann Goering (q.v.) referred to him contemptuously as "Herr Reich Injection Master." Eva Braun (q.v.) spoke of him as having the habits of a pig and refused to return to him because of the filth in his office. Other physicians, notably Dr. Karl Brandt (q.v.), claimed that Morell was slowly poisoning Hitler by the injection of dangerous drugs. Hitler was developing symptoms similar to those of Parkinson's disease. After the July Plot (q.v.) of 1944, Hitler dropped Morell and turned to Drs. Brandt and Ludwig Stumpfegger (q.v.) as his personal physicians. Morell died at Tegernsee in May 1948.

MORGENTHAU PLAN. A plan for reducing Germany to an agrarian economy after World War II. Sponsored by Secretary of the Treasury Henry Morgenthau, Jr. (1891–1967), the proposal was tentatively approved at the Second Quebec Conference, held on September 11–16, 1944, between President Franklin D. Roosevelt and Prime Minister Winston Churchill. The Morgenthau Plan aimed at preventing "renewed rearmament of Germany" by shutting down and dismantling the industries of the Ruhr and the Saar and by having a world organization "insure that these activities are not started up again by some subterfuge." One statement not contained in Morgenthau's original version was inserted in the communiqué signed by Roosevelt and Churchill. It held that the Allies were "looking forward to converting Germany into a country primarily agricultural and pastoral in character." A month later Roosevelt rejected the proposal, but the damage had been done. Hitler pointed to Morgenthau's "Program to Prevent Germany Starting World War III" as proof that defeat would finally seal the fate of all Germans. The Fuehrer urged Germans to fight to the end to avoid the penalties to be inflicted by the Morgenthau Plan.

MOTHER AND CHILD WELFARE. *See* HILFSWERK MUTTER UND KIND.

MOTHERING SUNDAY. *See* HOLIDAYS, NAZI.

MOUNTED SS. *See* REITER-SS.

MUCHOW, REINHOLD (1905–1933). Nazi organizational leader and author of the much-discussed Muchow Plan (q.v.) for street cells. Reinhold Muchow was born in Neukölln, the workers' quarter in Berlin, on December 21, 1905, the son of a typesetter. An early member of the Nazi movement, which entitled him to status as one of the *Alte Kämpfer* (q.v.), or old guard, he became a leader for the Greater Berlin Gau (District) I in 1925. So successful was he in organizing his area that in 1938 *Gauleiter* (q.v.) Dr. Paul Joseph Goebbels (q.v.), district leader of Berlin, appointed Muchow organizational leader for the entire city. In this post he devised the Muchow Plan for a tightly knit street cell system. Later he was transferred to the Deutsche Arbeitsfront (q.v.), the German Labor Front of Robert Ley (q.v.), for which he set up fourteen new units. Muchow was killed in an accident at Bacharach, in the Rhineland, on September 12, 1933. He was mourned by the Nazi hierarchy as an outstanding expert on party organization.

MUCHOW PLAN. A plan for the organization of the Nazi party in middle-class urban areas. Named after its originator, Reinhold Muchow (q.v.), the organizational leader of the Greater Berlin Gau (District) I, the scheme called for a series of vertical subdivisions of the party, ranging from a section (ten to twenty city blocks) to a cell (about five members). The idea was to preserve personal contacts between lower-echelon Nazis and at the same time retain a large number of militants.

MÜLLER, FRIEDRICH MAX (1823–1900). Anglo-German philologist and Orientalist and unwitting progenitor of Aryan racial theory. Friedrich Max Müller was born in Dessau on December 6, 1823, the son of Wilhelm Müller, poet and ducal librarian. The young man studied under several great teachers. In 1841 he matriculated at the University of Leipzig, where Hermann Brockhaus recommended that he study Sanskrit. In 1844 Müller went to Berlin, where Professor Franz Bopp introduced him to the study of comparative philology and where he learned about the idealistic philosophy of Friedrich von Schelling. On a visit to Paris in 1845, he became acquainted with the work of Eugène Burnouf, the leading Zend scholar of his time, who started him on the study of comparative religion. This discipline was to absorb his attention for the remainder of his life. Determined to issue a new edition of the Rig Veda, he journeyed to England in 1846 to consult manuscripts in the East India House at London and the Bodleian Library at Oxford. His reception was warm and gracious. British scholars, intrigued by the brilliant young German, introduced him to Queen Victoria and the Prince Consort and prevailed on the East India Company to sponsor his edition of the Rig Veda. It was duly published in 1848.

In 1856 Müller was appointed Taylor professor of modern languages at Oxford. Four years later, when the chair in Sanskrit became vacant, Müller hoped to be named to the position, and he was grievously disappointed when it went to Monier-Williams. Despite his scintillating academic career, Müller never became reconciled to what he regarded as an unfair decision. Meanwhile, still in his thirties, he enjoyed a rapidly rising reputation. In the years from 1859 to 1861, aristocratic audiences hastened to the Royal Institution in London to hear Müller's fiery lectures about their anthropological and linguistic background. Covering the disciplines of comparative religion, mythology, and languages, Müller showed little interest in the new anthropology and ethnography. He was convinced that the growth of the human mind must be studied in the history of language. He regarded himself as the "author of the science of language," although some of his theories in comparative philology were disproved by later investigation.

Müller was chiefly responsible for the vogue of Aryanism in the latter half of the nineteenth century. He coined the term *Aryan* to replace the more cumbersome *Indo-European*. Interested in tracing the wanderings of the Aryan nations, he started with Grimm's theory of "irresistible impulse" and went on to describe the migrations of the early Indo-European peoples. Müller told how, like a swarm from a central beehive, the Indo-Europeans surged into northwestern Europe. Unfortunately, his scholarly prestige paved the way for the Aryan theory that confused race with language. Müller himself was shocked by the unexpected use made of his conjectures. In 1888 he warned scholars interested in race that they were wrong: "I have declared again and again that if I say Aryans, I mean neither blood nor bones, nor hair nor skull; I mean simply those who speak an Aryan language. To me an ethnologist who speaks of Aryan race, Aryan blood, Aryan eyes and hair, is as great a sinner as a linguist who speaks of a dolichocephalic dictionary or a brachycephalic grammar. It is worse than a Babylonian confusion of tongues—it is downright theft. We have made our own terminology for the classification of languages; let ethnologists make their own for the classification of skulls, and hair, and blood."[1] *Aryan* in scientific language, Müller insisted, was utterly inapplicable to race. It meant language and nothing but language, and if one were to speak of an Aryan race at all, it should mean nothing more than Aryan speech.

The damage was done. Müller accepted the blame, but his explanations had no effect on racialists. He died at Oxford on October 28, 1900. From his time on the "science" of linguistic paleontology was utilized to prove the existence, purity, and superiority of the Aryan (later Nordic) race. The resulting racialism became the central ideology of the Third Reich. *See also* RACIAL DOCTRINE.

[1]Friedrich Max Müller, *Biographies of Words, and the Home of the Aryas*, Longmans, Green & Co., Ltd., London, 1888, p. 89.

Bibliography. Friedrich Max Müller, *Chips from a German Workshop*, 5 vols., Charles Scribner's Sons, New York, 1869–1881.

MÜLLER, HEINRICH (1901–). Chief of the Gestapo (q.v.) and leading administrator in mass killing operations. *Gruppenfuehrer* (Lieut. Gen.) Heinrich Müller was directly subordinate to Reinhard Heydrich (q.v.). He was one of the fifteen top-ranking Nazi bureaucrats present at the Wannsee Conference (q.v.) on January 20, 1942, when the Final Solution to the Jewish question was arranged (*see* ENDLÖSUNG, DIE). In the fall of 1942 Heinrich Himmler (q.v.) decided to make his concentration camps (q.v.) *Judenrein* (*Judenfrei*, q.v.) and delegated much of the responsibility for the task to Müller. In January 1943 Müller rounded up 45,000 Jews from the Netherlands, 3,000 from Berlin, 30,000 from the Białystok ghetto, and 10,000 from Theresienstadt (q.v.) to be deported to Auschwitz (q.v.) for extermination. In June 1943 he was sent by Himmler to Rome to ascertain why and how Italian Jews were escaping arrest. In the summer of 1944, when the German frontiers were being breached in both east and west, Müller, at Himmler's orders, took terrible vengeance. He sent huge transports of Jews to Auschwitz and the gas chambers. On September 28, 1944, he called for volunteers at Theresienstadt to work in German factories. Some 2,300 inmates took him at his word and soon found themselves in Auschwitz, where 900 were gassed immediately. As late as October 1944 Müller continued his policy of sending Jews to Auschwitz. In 1945, efforts by the International Red Cross to take over the concentration camps from Müller were unsuccessful.

In the final days of the Third Reich Müller was present in the *Fuehrerbunker* (q.v.). Hitler entrusted him with the questioning of Hermann Fegelein (q.v.), Eva Braun's brother-in-law, who had sought to escape from the bunker. By now Müller was almost independent of Himmler and made no secret of his ambition to succeed his superior officer. For some years after the war it was assumed that Müller had been killed when the Russians encircled Berlin. Later he was reported to be in Brazil and Argentina, where he was said to be an "enforcer" among escaped SS (q.v.) criminals. In 1973 he was placed on a list of most wanted Nazis.

MÜLLER, JOSEF (1898–). A Munich lawyer who was one of the fraternity of conspirators working for the assassination of Hitler. A devout Catholic and a confidant of Michael Cardinal von Faulhaber (q.v.), Archbishop of Munich-Freising, Müller made no secret of his contempt for the Nazi Fuehrer. A man of tremendous physique, inexhaustible energy, and raw courage, he reveled in his nickname since his school days, Ochsensepp (Joe the Ox). On the declaration of war in 1939, Müller enlisted in the Abwehr (q.v.) and left Germany to take up his duties in Rome. For three years he maintained contact with British agents. In April 1943 he was arrested and later was taken to the Buchenwald (q.v.) concentration camp. Müller was kept chained hand and foot and given a reduced quantity of normal prison food. He was unable to sleep because the light was never extinguished in his cell or the door closed. A fortunate circumstance was that his files had been destroyed in an air raid. In the closing days of the war

Müller was transferred from camp to camp, including Dachau (q.v.), but he managed to survive. He was liberated by American forces on May 4, 1945.

MÜLLER, LUDWIG (1883–1945). Evangelical theologian, crusading nationalist, and Hitler's choice for Reich bishop. Ludwig Müller was born at Gütersloh on June 23, 1883. A Protestant army chaplain, he was assigned to the First Military Command in Königsberg, East Prussia, in the mid-1920s. There he became known for his preaching of an untrammeled love for the fatherland, for his sermons on the paramount duty of being a German, and for his strongly anti-Semitic feeling (*see* ANTI-SEMITISM). In 1926 he was brought to Hitler's attention by Gen. Werner von Blomberg (q.v.), commander of the East Prussian Military District. Hitler and Müller, holding similar views, were impressed with one another. Müller's career blossomed shortly after Hitler became Chancellor. On April 4, 1933, he was appointed to the post of confidant and plenipotentiary for all problems concerning the Evangelical Church.

From then on Müller was a central figure in the struggle between the German Faith movement (Deutsche Glaubensbewegung, q.v.), which was supported by Hitler, and the new Confessional Church (Bekenntniskirche, q.v.), which was led by Martin Niemoeller (q.v.). In conformity with his policy of *Gleichschaltung* (q.v.), or coordination, Hitler wanted a Reich church that would bring all Protestants together in one easily ruled body. He expected the new church to support his doctrines of race and leadership (*see* FUEHRERPRINZIP; RACIAL DOCTRINE). On July 23, 1933, Müller was elected Reich bishop by a national synod in Wittenberg, and in that capacity he fought Hitler's battles against the Confessional Church. Although he was a fanatical supporter of the Nazi regime, Müller never quite won the Fuehrer's complete confidence. "If only Reibi [Hitler's nickname for the Reich bishop] had some kind of stature. Why do they appoint a nobody of an Army chaplain?" From 1935 on Müller's influence lessened as Hitler turned ecclesiastical problems over to a Reich Church Commission. Müller died in Berlin on July 31, 1945.

MUNICH AGREEMENT. Settlement of the crisis over Czechoslovakia reached on September 29–30, 1938, in a conference at Munich. The ease with which Hitler had achieved *Anschluss* (q.v.) with Austria encouraged him to proceed with his plans against Czechoslovakia. The Republic of Czechoslovakia had been created in 1918–1919 out of the former Austrian territories of Bohemia, Moravia, and Austrian Silesia and the former Hungarian areas of Slovakia and Ruthenia. Led by Tomáš Masaryk and Eduard Beneš (q.v.), it became the most prosperous of the succession states. In the vigorous new nation were located many important industries including the famed Škoda steel and armament works. From the days of its formation, however, Czechoslovakia had been plagued by minority problems. In a population of 14 million there were in addition to Czechs and Slovaks some 3.3 million Germans, 760,000 Magyars, 480,000 Ruthenians, and many Poles and Jews. The German-speaking Czechs in former Bohemia, who were the Sudeten Germans, formed a clamorous minority (*see* SUDETENLAND). They claimed discrimination against them in administration and economic life. Among the nearly 1 million unemployed in the country, almost half were Sudeten Germans. The government at Prague, sensing unrest among the Sudeten Germans, made far-reaching concessions to satisfy them. It gave them full parliamentary representation and equal opportunities in education, but they remained restive.

Hitler was determined to eliminate the Czechoslovak state, but there were formidable obstacles in the way. The Czechs had a strong line of fortifications in the Sudeten Mountains, defended by some thirty-five divisions, and they also had binding commitments from Great Britain and France. The Fuehrer decided to proceed anyway. As early as 1935 a pro-Nazi party formed in Czechoslovakia by Konrad Henlein (q.v.) had demanded "full liberty for Germans to proclaim their Germanism and their adherence to the ideology of Germans." In February 1938 Hitler addressed the Reichstag (q.v.) and called attention to "the horrible conditions of the German brethren in Czechoslovakia." He announced that the Sudeten Germans could depend on the Third Reich to defend them against their

The signers of the Munich Agreement (left to right, Chamberlain, Daladier, Hitler, Mussolini) with Count Galeazzo Ciano. [*Picture Collection, The Branch Libraries, The New York Public Library*]

Czech oppressors.

Meanwhile, the German press denounced Czech atrocities against the Sudeten Germans. When several Germans were killed in a frontier incident, Hitler dispatched German troops to the border. The Czechs, with probably the finest small army in Europe, promptly sent 400,000 troops to face the Germans. When France and the Soviet Union indicated that they would honor their obligations, Hitler withdrew his troops. British Prime Minister Neville Chamberlain (q.v.), however, was careful to say that he would not give assurances that Britain would support France in case the latter were called upon to help Czechoslovakia against German aggression.

Encouraged by Chamberlain's hesitancy, Hitler went forward with his plans to use the Sudeten Germans as a fifth column (q.v.) to destroy the Czechs. He called Henlein to Berlin and ordered him to propose what amounted to an autonomous German province inside the Czech state. Henlein did as he was told, making the announcement at Karlsbad (Karlovy Vary) on April 24, 1938. On May 30 the Fuehrer called a secret meeting of his top generals at the Artillery School at Jüterbog and informed them: "It is my unalterable will to smash [*zerschlagen*] Czechoslovakia by military action in the near future." He then issued a general order fixing October 1, 1938, as the deadline for putting Operation Green into effect (*see* GRÜN).

By this time the threat of war had become so severe that Chamberlain, with the consent of France, sent Viscount Runciman of Doxford to Prague as a kind of unofficial arbiter. Encouraged by Runciman, the Czechs offered generous concessions to Henlein and the Sudeten Germans. They would agree to a division of the country into a set of cantons on the Swiss model. All nationalities would share proportionately in government offices, government enterprises, monopolies, institutions, and other organizations. In addition, the Sudeten Germans would receive immediate economic relief. Hitler had no intention of accepting these concessions. On September 12, 1938, he made a speech in which he stated that he would come to the assistance of the oppressed Sudeten Germans. For the benefit of London and Paris he added that he was constructing in the west the strongest defenses ever made by man. Meanwhile, Henlein and his followers arranged further "incidents," which impelled President Beneš to proclaim martial law.

At this point Chamberlain decided to go to Berchtesgaden (q.v.) and plead with Hitler not to go to war. The British Prime Minister had never flown before. At Berchtesgaden Hitler informed Chamberlain that the Sudetenland must be included in the Third Reich immediately or there would be war. The Fuehrer would agree only to give Chamberlain time to return to London and consult with his ministers. Chamberlain flew home to consult with his divided Cabinet and with Premier Édouard Daladier (q.v.) of France. On September 20 Britain and France, without previously consulting the Czechs, notified Prague that it must "deliver the districts mainly inhabited by the Sudeten Germans" to Hitler in order to avoid a general European war. The Czechoslovak Cabinet decided to yield, then resigned.

With the Czech surrender in his hands, Chamberlain journeyed to a second meeting with Hitler, at Bad Godesberg on the Rhine. He found the Fuehrer in a towering rage. Now Hitler made more demands than he had made at Berchtesgaden. If the Czechs did not agree to his terms by October 1, they would see the German Army march across their borders. He gave the astonished Chamberlain a map on which he had indicated the parts of Czechoslovakia that he was going to take. Chamberlain took the map, agreed to present it to the Czechs, and flew home. Again there were inconclusive conferences with the French. The Czechs indignantly rejected the Bad Godesberg ultimatum.

In the midst of the tension, Mussolini suggested to Hitler that he set up a four-power conference to settle the issue. Hitler agreed, but on September 26, three days before the meeting, he spoke at a mass meeting at the Sportpalast (q.v.) in Berlin. He assured Chamberlain and the whole world that if the Sudeten problem were solved, he would make no further territorial claims in Europe: "We have come now to the last problem which has to be solved. It is the last territorial demand that I have to make in Europe. In 1919, 3,500,000 Germans were torn away from their compatriots by a company of mad statesmen. The Czech state originated in a huge lie and the name of the liar is Beneš."

For the third time Chamberlain made a plane trip to Germany, this time to Munich. He went literally to beg for peace. "I should still say it was right to attempt it. The only alternative is war." The Soviet Union and Czechoslovakia were excluded from the conference. Chamberlain and Daladier accepted Hitler's terms and together put pressure on Czechoslovakia to sign its own death warrant. The agreement drawn up on September 29, 1938, and signed early the next day, was almost the same as the terms demanded by Hitler at Bad Godesberg. The Sudetenland was split into four zones that would be occupied progressively by the German Army between October 1 and 7. The determination of a final fifth zone, to be occupied on October 10, was left to an international commission on which Czechoslovakia was to be represented along with the four signatory powers. The new frontiers of Czechoslovakia were guaranteed. The Third Reich won the adjoining fringe of Bohemia that contained the mountain approaches and the Czech fortifications. The loss left Czechoslovakia defenseless. Chamberlain flew home and happily reported at the airport, while waving a paper of the agreement, that he had brought "peace in our time."

The Munich crisis, pronouncing the death sentence on Czechoslovakia, revealed the helplessness of the West. Chamberlain and Daladier, aware that their countries lagged far behind Germany in military preparedness, believed that there was little they could do other than accept Hitler's terms. Winston Churchill was appalled by the policy of appeasement at Munich: "I will begin by saying what everybody would like to ignore or forget but which nevertheless must be stated, namely, that we have sustained a total and unmitigated defeat, and that France has suffered even more than we have. . . . And do not suppose that this is the end. This is only the beginning of the reckoning. This is only the first sip, the first foretaste of a bitter cup which will be proffered to us year by year unless by a supreme recovery of moral health and martial vigor, we arise again and make our stand for freedom as in the olden time."

General Ludendorff (center) and Hitler after their trial in Munich. Wilhelm Frick is third from the left; Ernst Roehm, second from the right. [*Keystone*]

For Hitler the Munich Agreement was a scintillating success. He was enjoying one success after another: in sending German troops into the Rhineland, in annexing Austria in the *Anschluss,* in stirring up Danzig, and now in incorporating the Bohemian Germans. Munich brought Hitler the strategic keystone of Europe and made him the master of Central Europe.

Bibliography. John W. Wheeler-Bennett, *Munich: Prologue to Tragedy,* The Macmillan Company, New York, 1948.

MUNICH PUTSCH. *See* BEER-HALL PUTSCH.

MUNICH TRIAL. Trial for high treason of leaders of the 1923 Beer-Hall *Putsch* (q.v.) in Munich. The proceedings, which began on February 24, 1924, and lasted twenty-four days, were held in the Infantry Officers School in Munich. The building was protected by barbed wire and patrolled by helmeted guards. The court consisted of two professional judges and three laymen (two insurance men and a dealer in stationery). There were ten defendants, including Hitler, Gen. Erich Ludendorff, Ernst Roehm, and Wilhelm Frick (qq.v.). All were accused of conspiracy to commit treason. The chief witnesses for the prosecution were Gustav Ritter von Kahr (q.v.), General State Commissioner of Bavaria, Gen. Otto von Lossow, commander of the German armed forces in Bavaria, and Col. Hans von Seisser, Chief of the Bavarian State Police. The trial aroused attention throughout Germany and around the world. At least 100 reporters sat at the press table, and large crowds attempted to find seating space in the courtroom.

The accused Hitler wore a cutaway suit with the Iron Cross (First Class) pinned to the left breast. He dominated the proceedings from the start. For the first time the zealous young politician had an audience outside Bavaria, and he took full advantage of the opportunity. He later said: "As though by an explosion, our ideas were hurled over the whole of Germany." Each day the country listened with increasing excitement as the Nazi leader converted the trial into a triumph for himself and his party. His plan was simple: instead of apologizing or admitting his guilt, he took the initiative and in long, impassioned speeches presented his case to the German people. He told the court that in all justice his accusers—Von Kahr, Von Lossow, and Von Seisser—should be sitting with him as prisoners. "One thing is certain: if our enterprise was actually high treason, then during this time Lossow, Kahr, and Seisser must have been committing high treason along with us, for during all these weeks we talked of nothing but the aims of which we are now accused." He took full responsibility upon himself. "But there is no such thing as high treason against the traitors of 1918. I feel myself the best of Germans who wanted the best for the German people."

By this time all Germany was listening to the leader of the National Socialist movement. "The greatest gain of the 8th of November [1923] is this: that it did not lead to depression and discouragement, but contributed to lifting the people to the greatest heights of enthusiasm. I believe that the hour will come when the masses on the streets who to-day stand under our banner, the hooked cross, will unite with those who shot at us on November 9. I believe this: blood will not separate us forever. One day the hour will come when the Reichswehr [q.v.] will be standing at our side, officers and men." Hitler sought to convince his German audience that his *Putsch* was actually a success. He touched on all the German miseries in the Weimar Republic (q.v.)—the *Dolchstosstheorie* (q.v.), the stab-in-the-back theory, the revolution, the inflation, Marxism, decadent Berlin. "I accuse Ebert, Scheidemann, and company of high treason. I accuse them because they destroyed a nation of 70 millions." When he was rebuked by the court for going too far, he paid no attention and went on in the same vein for four hours. His words became even more dramatic:

> I aimed from the first at something a thousand times higher than being a minister. I wanted to become the destroyer of Marxism. I am going to achieve this task, and, if I do, the title of minister will be an absurdity as far as I am concerned. . . .
>
> At one time I believed that perhaps this battle against Marxism could be carried on with the help of the government. In January 1923 I learned that that was just not possible. The hypothesis for the victory of Marxism is not that Germany must be free, but rather Germany will only be free when Marxism is broken. At that time I did not dream that our movement would become great and cover Germany like a flood.
>
> The army that we are building grows from day to day, from hour to hour. Right at this moment I have the proud hope that once the hour strikes these wild troops will merge into battalions, battalions into regiments, regiments into divisions. I have hopes that the old cockade will be lifted from the dirt, that the old colors will be unfurled to flutter again, that expiation will come before the tribunal of God. Then from our bones and from our graves will speak the voice of the only tribunal which has the right to sit in justice over us.
>
> Then, gentlemen, not you will be the ones to deliver the verdict over us, but that verdict will be given by the eternal judgment of history, which will speak out against the accusation that has been made against us. I know what your judgment will be. But that other court will not ask us: Have you committed high treason or not? That court will judge the quartermaster-general of the old army, its officers and soldiers, who as Germans wanted only the best for their people and Fatherland, who fought and who were willing to die. You might just as well find us guilty a thousand times, but the goddess of the eternal court of history will smile and tear up the motions of the state's attorney and the judgment of this court: for she finds us not guilty.

It was one of Hitler's best speeches, and it was effective. Newspapers that had never mentioned Hitler before now devoted columns to him. Millions of Germans were electrified by the man of action who was playing a hero's role in the courtroom at Munich.

The verdict was handed down on April 1, 1924. Ludendorff was acquitted, but the rest were found guilty. The maximum penalty for high treason was life imprisonment, but Hitler was given the minimum, five years' fortress arrest, considered to be the most lenient and dignified of all forms of detention. Hitler served nine months of his sentence at Landsberg am Lech (q.v.).

Bibliography. Richard Hanser, *Putsch,* Pyramid Books, New York, 1971.

MUSIC IN THE THIRD REICH. All cultural forms in Nazi Germany were subjected to *Gleichschaltung* (q.v.), or coordination. Only music, the least political of the arts, fared well under Hitler's dictatorship. It was an isolated phenomenon in what was otherwise a vast cultural wasteland.

German contributions to music in the past had won the admiration of the world. The supreme masters of the late eighteenth century, especially Beethoven, were German. The German *Lied* (song with German words) became almost as important as the symphony. Three great German composers of the early nineteenth century, Mendelssohn, Schumann, and Richard Wagner (q.v.), had enormous influence throughout the musical world. Johannes Brahms composed notable symphonies in the later nineteenth century. The twentieth century brought a radical musical upheaval associated with the name of Schoenberg, an Austrian composer who worked in Berlin.

As soon as Hitler became Chancellor in 1933, he appointed Dr. Paul Joseph Goebbels (q.v.) as head of the Ministry for Public Enlightenment and Propaganda. Under Goebbels's cultural dictatorship, music, along with the press, radio, films, theater, art, and literature, was subjected to control by the Ministry. The works of Wagner were encouraged because of Hitler's fanatical devotion to the composer. The composers Meyerbeer and Mendelssohn were banned because of their Jewish background. German orchestras were forbidden to play the music of Paul Hindemith (q.v.), the nation's leading contemporary composer, who had won international acclaim. Hindemith, far from renouncing tonality, had experimented with new ideas of key relationships of the natural harmonic series. To Hitler, the enthusiastic Wagnerite, Hindemith's work was decadent, and he ordered that it be banned from the concert stage.

Coordination of music meant that all Jewish artists were purged from symphony orchestras and operas. There was a veritable exodus of Jewish composers and musical artists. Among the many musicians who went into exile was Otto Klemperer (q.v.), the great conductor of Mahler's music. The cultural life of other countries was enriched by this parade of artists who left Nazi Germany because they were Jewish and feared for their lives or because they refused to recognize a regime that they regarded as a disgrace to the fatherland.

Some of the leading figures in music, unlike writers, who were more highly politicized, decided to remain in Germany. Some simply carried on with their work, while others offered their services to the government. The latter did not feel oppressed in the Nazi milieu and continued their careers with official sanction. Wilhelm Furtwängler (q.v.), widely recognized as one of the great conductors of the twentieth century, made his peace with the regime. For a time he was out of favor because of his spirited defense of the banned Hindemith, but he continued to hold his posts at the Berlin Philharmonic and the Berlin State Opera. Richard Strauss, one of the world's leading composers and a master of the German *Lied,* remained in the Third Reich and for a time headed the Reich Music Chamber, attached to Goebbels's Ministry of Propaganda.

Walter Gieseking, the eminent pianist, was sent by Goebbels to give concerts in foreign countries.

Concerts inside Germany were well attended throughout the life of the Third Reich. Listeners had to be content with an excess of Wagner, the absence of "degenerate" composers, and the attendance of party functionaries as guests of honor.

MUSSERT, ANTON (1894–1946). Dutch Nazi leader. Anton Mussert was born in Werkendam on May 5, 1894. An engineer, he founded the Nationaal-Socialistisch Beweging, the National Socialist movement in the Netherlands in imitation of the German prototype. In 1940, like Léon Degrelle (q.v.) in Belgium, Mussert began to work closely with German National Socialists. In 1942 the German Reich Commissioner for the Netherlands named him leader of the Dutch people. On May 7, 1945, he was arrested by the Dutch as a collaborator. He was hanged at The Hague on May 7, 1946.

MUSSOLINI, BENITO [AMILCARE ANDREA] (1883–1945). Dictator of Fascist Italy from 1922 to 1943 and ally of Hitler and the Third Reich. Benito Mussolini was born at Dovia, in the commune of Predappio, Forlì Province, on July 29, 1883, the elder son of a socialist blacksmith and a devoutly Catholic mother. For a time he was an elementary school teacher. In 1902 he went to Switzerland, where he worked as a mason and translator. He was arrested for vagrancy. Returning to Italy, he served in a Bersaglieri regiment in 1905–1906. Until the outbreak of World War I he was a convinced Socialist who advocated neutrality. Changing his point of view, he then favored intervention on the Allied side. The Socialist party expelled him in November 1914. After Italy entered the war in May 1915, he volunteered as a private and served until 1917, when he was wounded in a firing exercise.

As editor of *Il Popolo d'Italia* in the postwar years, Mussolini advocated a program of violent nationalism designed to appeal to his compatriots, who were suffering in a serious economic situation. He portrayed fascism as a politico-religious philosophy. "Fascism," he said, "is a religious conception in which man is seen in his immanent relationship with a superior law and with an objective will that transcends the particular individual and raises him to a conscious membership of a spiritual society. . . . Fascism besides being a system of government is also, and above all, a system of thought. . . . Fascism is opposed to all the individualistic abstractions of a materialistic nature like those of the 18th century; and it is opposed to all Jacobin utopias and innovations. . . . Against individualism, the Fascist concept is for the State; and it is for the individual in so far as he coincides with the State, which is the conscience and universal will of man in his historical existence. . . . Liberalism defines the State in the interests of the particular individual; Fascism reaffirms the State as the true reality of the individual."

Italians were impressed by Mussolini's philosophy of fascism. Dissatisfied former soldiers, angered members of the middle class, patriotric youths, hungry farmers, and radical intellectuals joined in a compact political party called the Fascio di Combattimento (Union of Combat). The term *fascism* was derived from the Latin *fasces,* bundles of rods encircling an ax, used in ancient Rome as a symbol of authority. Mussolini portrayed fascism as a unifying factor that would save Italy. By emphasizing the dangers of communism he obtained support from Italian industrialists. Gradually, he acquired the support of police, courts, bureaucracy, and the Army.

Mussolini and Hitler in Salzburg in April 1942. [*Brown Brothers*]

Mussolini's semimilitary bands of Blackshirts began breaking up Socialist headquarters, attacking Communist meetings, and compelling workers to return to their jobs. The Fascists used guns, clubs, and castor oil in the battle of the streets. They were victorious in the savage warfare. By 1921 Mussolini's party had some 30 seats in Parliament. On October 22, 1922, about 50,000 Fascists marched on Rome while Mussolini traveled there in a railway sleeping car. He intimidated the Chamber of Deputies and forced the resignation of Premier Luigi Facta. Several days later King Victor Emmanuel III made Mussolini Prime Minister.

Within a year Mussolini transformed the Italian government, which had been a democracy modeled upon that of Great Britain, into a dictatorship. He took control of the Army and the air and naval forces and directed foreign affairs himself. He created legislation by decree, suspended civil rights, and discouraged his political enemies by imprisoning or exiling their leaders. When Giacomo Matteotti (1885–1924), head of the Socialist party, was found brutally murdered, the Socialists seceded from the Chamber in protest. Mussolini silenced opposition by setting up a rigid censorship, suppressing newspapers, banning public meetings, dismissing university professors, and establishing military tribunals to try all opponents of his regime.

A Grand Council of twenty members drafted new legislation, filled its own vacancies, and appointed ministers. The National Directory, composed of the secretary-general of the party and nine members, was run by Mussolini himself. There were various auxiliary organizations designed to prepare Italians for life in an authoritarian state. The Balilla was established for boys from eight to fourteen, and the Avanguardia for boys from fourteen to eighteen. Young men from eighteen to twenty-one were eligible for membership in the Fascist party. For the Fascist militia, or Blackshirts, military service was compulsory. Mussolini tried to satisfy the Italian thirst for the theatrical by reviving the Roman salute and providing for colorful parades, distinctive uniforms, and the Fascist hymn, *Giovinezza*.

The dictator, in conformity with the views of the syndicalists Georges Sorel and Edmondo Rossoni, set up a corporate state. In 1926 he placed the vast organization of Fascist syndicates under his own control. There were to be no strikes, lockouts, or class warfare but, instead, class discipline, absolute obedience, and "the sacrifice of the individual for society." The National Council of Corporations regulated wages, hours, and conditions of work. A Charter of Labor, enacted on April 21, 1927, proclaimed higher pay for night workers, an annual paid vacation, social services, and free vocational education. In 1928 Mussolini enacted a law that made Italy the first Western state to have a national legislature representing the economic levels of the people. Women were excluded from the national franchise.

Mussolini introduced a long series of reforms. He revised the system of taxation and finance, refunded foreign debts, and stabilized the currency. He enacted high tariffs, expanded the merchant marine, and concluded trade pacts with other countries. He set up an extensive program of public works designed to alleviate unemployment. He encouraged foreign capitalists to invest money in Italy, and he began a campaign to attract tourists. To combat illiteracy he reorganized the educational system. He encouraged large families by offering bonuses and tax exemptions. He banned birth control, divorce, and emigration. To resolve the Roman question, he concluded on February 11, 1929, a treaty and concordat with the Catholic Church. The absolute authority of Pope Pius XI (q.v.) in the small Vatican city-state was recognized in exchange for papal recognition of the Kingdom of Italy. The papacy was reimbursed for territorial losses in 1870 by a large indemnity, part being paid in cash and part in government bonds. In July 1929, after fifty-eight years of "papal imprisonment," Pope Pius emerged into the square at St. Peter's as a sign of the settlement of the Roman question.

Mussolini's foreign policy was colored by a fervent exaltation of nationalism. His goal was to expand the old colonial empire in order to provide an outlet for surplus population and obtain raw materials. He saw the Adriatic and eventually the entire Mediterranean as an Italian lake *(mare nostrum)*. He concluded a series of nonaggression and friendship treaties with neighboring states as a step toward increased Italian power in international relations.

The keystone of Mussolini's foreign policy was close friendship with Adolf Hitler and the Third Reich. Mussolini came to power in 1922; Hitler, not until 1933. In many respects Mussolini's Fascist experience served as a guide for Hitler's National Socialism. At first the Duce considered the Nazi politician an upstart adventurer, but he decided to support Hitler. Mussolini had originally regarded himself as the master and Hitler as his pupil. It soon became obvious, however, that the German dictator was far surpassing his Italian comrade. Mussolini decided to follow his German ally because most of their interests were identical, but there were some differences. Mussolini had to abandon Austria, which had been under Italian influence. There were angry repercussions in 1934 when Hitler prepared to march on Austria in order to implement his dream of *Anschluss* (q.v.). The Italian dictator massed his troops in the Brenner Pass, but the issue was resolved when Hitler withdrew for the time being. The two dictators joined in 1936 to supply Gen. Francisco Franco with aid in the Spanish Civil War. By the end of the 1930s Mussolini was merely an appendage to the Nazi comet.

The Italian dictator held himself aloof when Hitler marched on Austria in 1938. The next year the Rome-Berlin Axis (q.v.) was concluded as a pact of steel. When World War II began, Italy aligned itself with the Third Reich. In 1940–1941 the myth of Italian military strength, blown to enormous proportions by Mussolini's boasts, was shattered on the sands of Libya by British tanks and in Albania by Greek bayonets. Mussolini's prestige waned still further in 1943 with the threat of Allied invasion. In March 1943 Hitler demanded Italian troops to relieve German garrisons in France and the Balkans, but Mussolini was unable to help. Meanwhile, the situation in Italy deteriorated. Mussolini tried to defend the Po Valley and left the rest of the country to its fate.

On July 25, 1943, Mussolini was summoned by King Victor Emmanuel and dismissed. This was effectively the end of the Fascist regime. The fallen dictator was transferred from one detention place to another, eventually to a clinic on Campo Imperatore, near Aquila in the Abruzzi mountains. Hitler hoped to use him as a rallying point for Fascists in northern Italy. Crestfallen, Mussolini tried to escape to Switzerland, but he was captured by Italian partisans together with other Fascist leaders and his mistress, Clara Petacci. All were executed on April 28, 1945. Their bodies were displayed in gruesome fashion in a public square in Milan.

Twenty-three years of fascism demonstrated that Mussolini was operating in the wrong century. Italy's geographic position, which made it the hard core of the old Roman Empire, was outdated in the twentieth century. Italy was now merely a peninsula locked in the Mediterranean. Mussolini's motto—"Believe! Obey! Fight!"—was not suited to the Italian temperament. Rejecting individualism and accepting Hegelian dogma of the state as an ethical whole, Mussolini attempted to remake an entire people in his own image. He denounced democracy as a "putrescent corpse" and insisted that the Italians were incapable of governing themselves. The Italian people, like the Germans, learned painfully about the effects of this kind of political philosophy. Instead of lifting Italy to new heights of glory, Mussolini was responsible for its descent into defeat and misery.

Bibliography. Richard Collier, *Duce: A Biography of*

Benito Mussolini, The Viking Press, Inc., New York, 1971; Laura Fermi, *Mussolini,* The University of Chicago Press, Chicago, 1961; Ivone A. Kirkpatrick, *Mussolini: A Study in Power,* Hawthorn Books, Inc., New York, 1964; Benito Mussolini, *My Autobiography,* tr. by. Richard Washburn Child, Hutchinson & Co. (Publishers), Ltd., London, 1928.

MUTUAL AID ASSOCIATION. *See* HILFSGEMEINSCHAFT AUF GEGENSEITIGKEIT.

MY STRUGGLE. *See* MEIN KAMPF.

MYTH OF THE TWENTIETH CENTURY, THE. *See* ROSENBERG, ALFRED.

N

NACHT DER LANGEN MESSER, DIE
to
NURSERY SCHOOL

NACHT DER LANGEN MESSER, DIE. *See* BLOOD PURGE.

NACHT- UND NEBEL ERLASS (Night and Fog Decree). Order issued on December 7, 1941, by Hitler to seize "persons endangering German security," who were not to be executed immediately but were to vanish without a trace into the night and fog. Gen. Wilhelm Keitel (q.v.), who was given responsibility for carrying out the decree, explained that "in principle the punishment for offenses committed against the German state is the death penalty." The task was assigned to the SD (q.v.). Although the SD files were captured, it is still not known how many Europeans fell victim to the Nacht- und Nebel Erlass. Many indeed vanished into the night and fog without a trace.

NADOLNY, RUDOLF (1873–1953). Professional diplomat active in the first years of the Third Reich. In 1919 he became first State Secretary to the President of the Weimar Republic (q.v.). Later he served as German Ambassador to Turkey and leader of the German delegation to the Disarmament Conference (q.v.) at Geneva. His goal was to improve relations between Berlin and Moscow. In November 1933, after Hitler withdrew from the Disarmament Conference, he appointed Nadolny Ambassador to the Soviet Union. Nadolny stayed there for less than a year because of differences with Joachim von Ribbentrop (q.v.). After World War II Nadolny worked again for an understanding between the Soviet Union and a neutralized Germany.

NAPOLAS. *See* NATIONALPOLITISCHE ERZIEHUNGSANSTALTEN.

NATIONAL BADGE. *See* HOHEITSABZEICHEN.

NATIONAL COMMITTEE FOR A FREE GERMANY. *See* NATIONALKOMITEE FREIES DEUTSCHLAND.

NATIONAL COORDINATING AGENCY FOR THERAPEUTIC AND MEDICAL ESTABLISHMENTS. *See* T-4.

NATIONAL DAY OF MOURNING. *See* HOLIDAYS, NAZI.

NATIONAL DEMOCRATIC PARTY OF GERMANY. *See* NEO-NAZISM.

NATIONAL DRUNKARD IN CHIEF. *See* REICHSTRUNKENBOLD.

NATIONAL HOUR. *See* REICHSSTUNDE.

NATIONAL LABOR DAY. Annual Nazi celebration of labor on May 1 to take the place of May Day. In the towns the workers marched in formation with waving banners. In the countryside there were celebrations including maypole dancing, bonfires, and the proclamation of a May king and queen. The procession of the May queen rode beneath triumphal arches adorned with Nazi symbols including the stylized eagle. Dance and folk song groups in regional costume vied with one another in celebrating the holiday. *See also* HOLIDAYS, NAZI.

NATIONAL POLITICAL TRAINING INSTITUTES. *See* NATIONALPOLITISCHE ERZIEHUNGSANSTALTEN.

NATIONAL REDOUBT. A projected mountain fortress in southern Bavaria and western Austria where Hitler was to make a last stand against the Allies in World War II. In April 1945 the Russians were smashing Berlin by artillery fire from the east, and the Americans were closing in from the west. In his propaganda campaign Dr. Paul Joseph Goebbels (q.v.) hinted at a last stand in an impregnable mountain fortress. However, the so-called National Redoubt never existed except as a figment of Nazi imagination. At the same time it was taken seriously by American intelligence, which feared a prolonged guerrilla war in the Alpine region. Both Gen. Dwight D. Eisenhower and Gen. Omar N. Bradley believed in the possibility of such a threat to Allied victory. In the last days of the war they agreed that an attack might have to be made on a mountain stronghold.

NATIONAL SOCIALIST. *See* NS.

NATIONAL SOCIALIST FLIERS' CORPS. *See* NATIONALSOZIALISTISCHES FLIEGER-KORPS.

NATIONAL SOCIALIST GERMAN. *See* NATIONALSOZIALISTISCHER DEUTSCHER.

NATIONAL SOCIALIST GERMAN DOCTORS' ALLIANCE. *See* NSD-ÄRTZEBUND.

NATIONAL SOCIALIST GERMAN SECONDARY SCHOOL. *See* NATIONALSOZIALISTISCHE DEUTSCHE OBERSCHULE.

NATIONAL SOCIALIST GERMAN STUDENTS' LEAGUE. *See* NATIONALSOZIALISTISCHER DEUTSCHER STUDENTENBUND.

NATIONAL SOCIALIST GERMAN WORKERS' ASSOCIATION. *See* NATIONALSOZIALISTISCHER DEUTSCHER ARBEITERVEREIN.

NATIONAL SOCIALIST GERMAN WORKERS' PARTY. *See* NATIONALSOZIALISTISCHE DEUTSCHE ARBEITERPARTEI.

NATIONAL SOCIALIST JUBILATION THIRD STAGE. *See* NS-JUBEL DRITTE STUFE.

NATIONAL SOCIALIST LAWYERS' ASSOCIATION. *See* NS-RECHTSWAHRERBUND.

NATIONAL SOCIALIST LEAGUE OF EX-SERVICEMEN. *See* STAHLHELM.

NATIONAL SOCIALIST LECTURERS' ALLIANCE. *See* NS-DOZENTENBUND.

NATIONAL SOCIALIST MONTHLY. *See* NATIONALSOZIALISTISCHE MONATSHEFTE.

NATIONAL SOCIALIST MOTOR CORPS. *See* NATIONALSOZIALISTISCHES KRAFTFAHRER-KORPS.

NATIONAL SOCIALIST PEOPLE'S ASSOCIATION. *See* NATIONALSOZIALISTISCHER VOLKSBUND.

NATIONAL SOCIALIST PEOPLE'S WELFARE ORGANIZATION. *See* NATIONALSOZIALISTISCHE VOLKSWOHLFAHRT.

NATIONAL SOCIALIST RELIEF FUND. *See* NS-HILFSKASSE.

NATIONAL SOCIALIST SHOP CELL ORGANIZATION. *See* NATIONALSOZIALISTISCHE BETRIEBSZELLENORGANISATION.

NATIONAL SOCIALIST TEACHERS' ALLIANCE. *See* NS-LEHRERBUND.

NATIONAL SOCIALIST WOMEN'S GROUPS. *See* NS-FRAUENSCHAFT.

NATIONAL SOCIALIST WORKING ASSOCIATION. *See* NATIONALSOZIALISTISCHE ARBEITSGEMEINSCHAFT.

NATIONAL STUDENT WELFARE ORGANIZATION. *See* REICHSSTUDENTENWERK.

NATIONAL SUPERHIGHWAY. *See* REICHSAUTOBAHN.

NATIONAL VOCATIONAL COMPETITION. *See* REICHSBERUFSWETTKAMPF.

NATIONALDEMOKRATISCHE PARTEI DEUTSCHLANDS. *See* NEO-NAZISM.

NATIONALKOMITEE FREIES DEUTSCHLAND (National Committee for a Free Germany). A committee of captured German Army officers, including Gen. Field Marshal Friedrich von Paulus (q.v.), set up inside the Soviet Union to work for the liberation of Germany after the fall of Stalingrad on February 2, 1943.

NATIONALPOLITISCHE ERZIEHUNGSANSTALTEN (Napolas; National Political Training Institutes). The second of three types of schools established by Hitler for the purpose of training a Nazi elite (for the other two types, *see* ADOLF HITLER–SCHULE; ORDENSBURGEN). The special purpose of the *Napolas* was to restore the type of education formerly given in the old Prussian academies and to obtain candidates for high posts in the government of the Third Reich. Outside the normal school system, the *Napolas* were set up in April 1933 under the direction of August Heissmeyer. Roughly equivalent to the *Gymnasien* (high schools), the *Napolas* gave priority to the families of loyal Nazis, members of the Hitler Jugend (q.v.), the Hitler Youth, and sons of old-line officers. Candidates were nominated by an *SS-Obergruppenfuehrer* (general) responsible only to Hitler. Most came from the rural and labor elements of the population. Gradually they came under control of the SS (q.v.), which sought to inculcate the "soldierly spirit, with attributes of courage, sense of duty, and simplicity." By 1938 there were twenty-three *Napolas,* including four in Austria and one in the Sudeten area of Czechoslovakia. Many graduates went directly into the armed forces, and most served during World War II.

NATIONALSOZIALISTISCH. *See* NS.

NATIONALSOZIALISTISCHE ARBEITSGEMEINSCHAFT (NSAG; National Socialist Working Association). A loose union of Nazi *Gauleiters* (*see* GAULEITER) who were active in the north in 1925 and 1926, during the early days of the National Socialist movement.

NATIONALSOZIALISTISCHE BETRIEBSZELLENORGANISATION (NSBO; National Socialist Shop Cell Organization). Organization of Nazi industrial propaganda units in factories, used to replace the old labor unions. According to a typical contemporary joke, NSBO meant "*Noch sind die Bozen oben*" ("The party favorites are still on top").

NATIONALSOZIALISTISCHE DEUTSCHE ARBEITERPARTEI (NSDAP; National Socialist German Workers' Party). The Nazi party created by Hitler to succeed the Deutsche Arbeiterpartei (q.v.), the German Workers'

HIERARCHY OF THE NSDAP

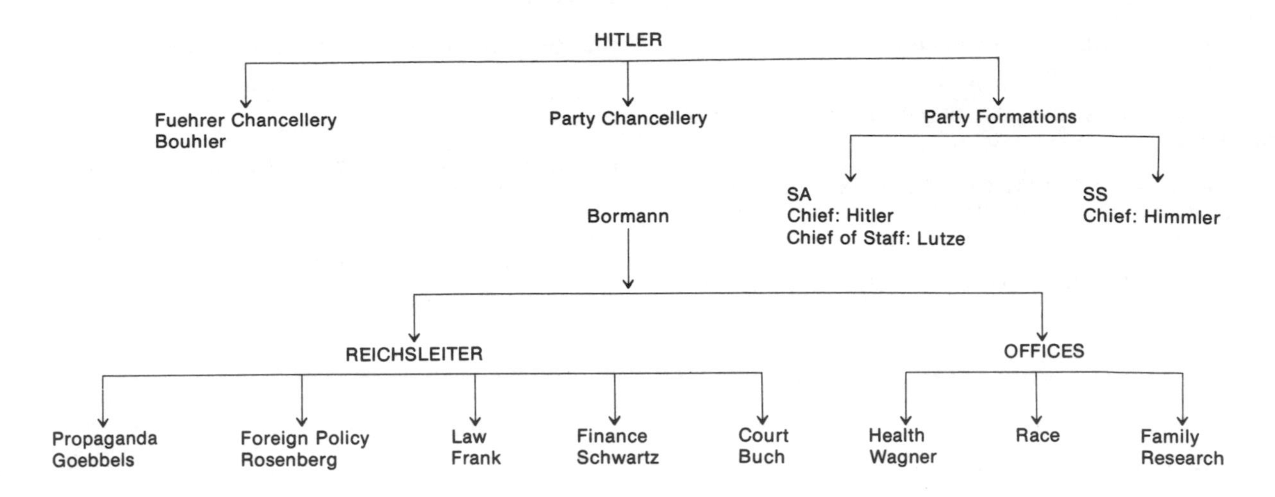

ORGANIZATION OF THE NSDAP

DER FUEHRER ADOLF HITLER (The Leader Adolf Hitler)	Undisputed dictator of the party.
REICHSLEITUNG DER NSDAP (Reich Leadership of the NSDAP)	Several *Reichsleiter* with specific portfolios, such as the party treasurer and the Fuehrer's deputy in charge of party matters.
LANDESINSPEKTEUR (regional inspector)	Originally nine, each of whom was responsible for four *Gaue*. This level gradually became insignificant. *Gauleiter* were appointed at first directly by the Fuehrer and later by Heinrich Himmler.
GAULEITER (district leader)	Leader of a *Gau* (district; plural, *Gaue*), a province such as Saxony or Swabia. There were 36 *Gauleiter* in the old Reich. The number increased with the German annexation of Austria, the Sudetenland, and Danzig.
KREISLEITER (circuit leader)	Leader of a *Kreis* (plural, *Kreise*), the next lower administrative unit, comparable to a rural council.
ORTSGRUPPENLEITER (local group leader)	Leader of an *Ortsgruppe* (local group), responsible for a town section.
ZELLENLEITER (cell leader)	Leader of a party cell based on a neighborhood unit or an employment unit. He was responsible usually for four or five blocks of households.
BLOCKWART (block warden)	Lowest official in the Nazi party above the ordinary member.
PG-PARTEIGENOSSE (party comrade)	Ordinary member.

party. The name was changed in April 1920. The organization and hierarchy of the party in June 1933 are shown in the accompanying tables.

NATIONALSOZIALISTISCHE DEUTSCHE OBERSCHULE (National Socialist German Secondary School). A special school for future leaders located at Feldafing on the Starnberger See. This cadet academy was in direct competition with the *Nationalpolitische Erziehungsanstalten* (q.v.), the *Napolas*.

NATIONALSOZIALISTISCHE MONATSHEFTE (NS-Monatshefte; National Socialist Monthly). A monthly magazine edited by Alfred Rosenberg (q.v.) and devoted to propaganda for Nazi ideology. It was regarded as the monthly equivalent of the *Völkischer Beobachter* (q.v.).

NATIONALSOZIALISTISCHE VOLKSWOHLFAHRT (NSV; National Socialist People's Welfare Organization). An organization allied to the Nazi party and devoted to the welfare of party members and their families, especially mothers and juveniles.

NATIONALSOZIALISTISCHER DEUTSCHER (NSD; National Socialist German). Term denoting citizenship in the Third Reich.

NATIONALSOZIALISTISCHER DEUTSCHER ARBEITERVEREIN (NSDAV; National Socialist German Workers' Association). The legal name of the Nationalsozialistische Deutsche Arbeiterpartei (q.v.), the Nazi party.

NATIONALSOZIALISTISCHER DEUTSCHER STUDENTENBUND (NSDStB; National Socialist German Students' League). Organization devoted to the furtherance of the Nazi way of life among students. It was regarded as a *Gliederung* (limb) of the Nazi party.

NATIONALSOZIALISTISCHER VOLKSBUND (NSVB; National Socialist People's Association). A Nazi party splinter group opposed to Hitler and active in Munich in 1925. The NSVB was beaten by Hitler in the struggle for party power.

NATIONALSOZIALISTISCHES FLIEGER-KORPS (NSFK; National Socialist Fliers' Corps). A special aircraft unit of the Nationalsozialistische Deutsche Arbeiterpartei (q.v.).

NATIONALSOZIALISTISCHES KRAFTFAHRER KORPS (NSKK; National Socialist Motor Corps). A special motorized unit of the Nationalsozialistische Deutsche Arbeiterpartei (q.v.). A paramilitary formation, it oversaw the premilitary training of recruits for the Army's motorized and armored units (*see* PANZER). It was regarded as a *Gliederung* (limb) of the Nazi party.

NAUJOCKS, ALFRED HELMUT (1911–). With Otto Skorzeny (q.v.), one of the most publicized adventurers of Nazi Germany. Described by William L. Shirer (q.v.) as a typical Gestapo (q.v.) product, "a sort of intellectual gangster," Naujocks was the central figure in several escapades. In his teens he worked as a welder. He then studied engineering at Kiel University, where as a young Nazi he first brawled with anti-Nazis. In 1931 he joined the blackshirted SS (q.v.), and in 1934 he became a charter member of the SD (q.v.), the Sicherheitsdienst, as a secret agent.

On or about August 10, 1939, Reinhard Heydrich (q.v.), chief of the SD, summoned Naujocks, now an *SS-Sturmbahnfuehrer* (major), to his office and outlined to him the details for a simulated "Polish" attack on a small German radio station at Gleiwitz, just a mile from the Polish border. The raid was vital, he said, because it would give the Fuehrer justification for his contemplated attack on Poland. Always the happy-go-lucky adventurer, Naujocks accepted the assignment and carried it out as ordered on August 31 (*see* GLEIWITZ RAID). Naujocks's part in this assignment won him a reputation as "the man who triggered World War II."

On November 8, 1939, Naujocks took part in the kidnapping by SS agents of two British agents in the Netherlands near the German border (*see* VENLO INCIDENT). He was implicated in several other bizarre escapades. In May 1940 he was involved in an undertaking in which German troops were disguised in the uniforms of Dutch and Belgian frontier guards. In the SD office he specialized in forging passports. He proposed Operation Bernhard (*see* BERNHARD, OPERATION), a plan to drop forged British banknotes from German planes flying over England. In 1943 he was sent to the eastern front, where he was wounded. The next year he was assigned to duty as an economic administrator in Belgium and then was detailed to ferret out members of the resistance in Denmark. By this time expecting an Allied victory, he deserted to the Americans on October 19, 1944. Still leading a charmed life, he escaped from an internment camp in 1946. Naujocks was never brought to trial for his wartime activities. He settled in Hamburg as a businessman and sold accounts of his exploits to the press as "the man who started World War II."

NAZI. Acronym formed from the first syllable of *NAtional* and the second syllable of *SoZIalist*. Such terms, usually formed from the initial letters or syllables of successive parts of compound names, were popular in the Third Reich. Another typical example was Gestapo (q.v.), or Geheime Staatspolizei (Secret State Police).

NEO-NAZISM. A movement dedicated in part or in whole to the revival of National Socialism after 1945. The German public was profoundly shocked by postwar revelations of the full extent of the Nazi terror. The government of the Federal Republic of Germany enacted a series of stringent laws against the revival of anti-Semitism (q.v.) and paid $1 billion in reparations to Israel, the symbolic home of world Jewry. At the same time, the vast majority of Germans, who had been unwillingly drawn into the Nazi vortex, wanted to forget the past. Pragmatic political leaders of the Bonn Republic tried to furnish the stability that the public seemed to need. They called for German participation as a respected member of the European family. Their work was considerably facilitated by the economic miracle that brought West Germany to the forefront of prosperous nations not only in Europe but in the world.

Meanwhile, there appeared in West Germany a movement which called itself rightist and conservative but which critics denounced as a revival of Nazism. By 1950 there were at least a dozen new political parties that were accused of being neo-Nazi in spirit. One of the most successful of such nationalist movements was the Nationaldemokratische Partei Deutschlands (NPD; National Democratic party of Germany), formed in the early 1960s as an amalgam of several right-wing groups. At its core were a hard group of superpatriots and a cadre of fanatical youngsters. Its strongly nationalist platform included these demands:

1. Recall all foreign troops, including Americans, from German soil.
2. Deport the 1.3 million foreign workers in the country.
3. End the one-sided war crimes trials because "in other countries millions of war crimes against German men, women, and children go unpunished."
4. Destroy all lies about German responsibility for World War II.
5. Put an end to the practice of extorting money from Germany.
6. Return the territories where Germans had lived for centuries (lands beyond the Oder-Neisse line; Austria).
7. Decline any American aid.

The chief architect and leader of the NPD, Adolf von Thadden (q.v.), disavowed any connection with Nazism and attempted to give his movement an air of respectability. An able speaker, he was more polished than the ungrammatical Hitler. He preached the message of nationalism, attacked the war crimes trials as "a national pollution," and urged pensions for all Germans who had fought for their fatherland, including members of the Waffen-SS (q.v.). He urged Germans to regain their lost unity, discipline, and pride by rallying to the NPD flag—flame red, centered with an empty white circle.

Critics who denounced the NPD as neo-Nazi pointed out that a dozen of the eighteen members of its executive board were former card-holding National Socialists and that half of them had held high SS (q.v.) rank and were entitled to the Nazi golden badge (*see* GOLDENES PARTEIABZEICHEN). The party officially denied that it was anti-Semitic, although its speakers often made veiled insults against Jews and Israel. At political rallies NPD leaders revealed the "inside news" that the gas chambers had been constructed by American troops after the war in an effort to throw guilt on innocent Germans.

In 1965 the NPD claimed a membership of 16,298. In the November 1966 state elections it returned twenty-three candidates in Bavaria and Hesse, polling 225,000 votes (2.9 percent) in Hesse and 390,000 (7.4 percent) in Bavaria. In Nuremberg, the former site of Nazi rallies, the NPD received 13.1 percent of the total vote; in Bayreuth, home of Wagnerian traditions, it won 13.9 percent. In April 1967, 6.9 percent of the voters in the Rhineland-Palatinate and 5.8 percent in Schleswig-Holstein cast their ballots for the NPD. From then on the NPD declined in voting power. In the elections of November 1972 it received only 0.6 percent of the total vote. Other nationalist parties favoring a rebirth of Nazism similarly lost voting power.

Bibliography. Kurt P. Tauber, *Beyond Eagle and Swastika*, 2 vols., Wesleyan University Press, Middletown, Conn., 1967.

NERO DECREE. Detailed instructions issued by Hitler on March 19 and 30, 1945, on the implementation of his scorched-earth policy. The decree laid down conditions for the blowing up of bridges, industrial plants, road works, and railway lines.

NEUDECK. Hereditary baronial estate of the Von Hindenburg family in Rosenberg, East Prussia. In 1927, while Gen. Paul von Hindenburg (q.v.) was serving as President of the Weimar Republic (q.v.), Elard von Oldenburg-Janus-Schau, a Junker living in East Prussia, discovered that Neudeck, which had once belonged to the Von Hindenburg and Von Beneckendorff family, was for sale. He approached other Junkers and some friendly industrialists and collected funds from them. On Von Hindenburg's eightieth birthday, October 2, 1927, the Stahlhelm (q.v.) presented to him as its honorary president the estate and castle of Neudeck. In order to avoid death duties, title was given to Oskar von Hindenburg (q.v.), the President's son. On the death of the elder Von Hindenburg, the state would receive no inheritance tax. The incident played a part in the *Osthilfe Skandal* (q.v.). President von Hindenburg died at Neudeck on August 2, 1934.

NEUE FRONT (New Front). Trademark of a cigarette promoted and sold by Nazi merchants and others sympathetic to the Nazi regime. In the campaign before the presidential election of April 1932, the Iron Front (Eiserne Front, q.v.), a union of republican-minded voters, was organized to work for the reelection of President Paul von Hindenburg (q.v.). At that time the Iron Front anti-Nazi emblem showing three arrows was used on such articles as cigarettes, especially the Drei Pfeile (Three Arrows) brand. The Nazis introduced the Neue Front as their own brand to compete with the Eiserne Front packages.

NEUENGAMME. Concentration camp (*see* CONCENTRATION CAMPS) located in the marshy Elbe country southeast of Hamburg and south of Bergedorf. It was set up in 1940 to supply a cheap source of labor for the armaments factories of northwest Germany. By 1942 the number of prisoners had risen to three times as many as the camp was supposed to accommodate. At this time additional space was used in the area to add several camps in what was known as the Neuengamme-Ring. Of the 90,000 prisoners who were sent to Neuengamme, nearly half died from causes induced by unnatural conditions. Inmates were infected with tuberculosis and other diseases in medical experiments. Early in 1945, Jewish, French, and Russian children between the ages of five and twelve were brought to the camp. Of some eighty Dutch prisoners, twenty died of debility and sixty were hanged without trial. In late April 1945 the inmates of Neuengamme were transferred to three ships, the *Cap Arcona*, *Thielbeck*, and *Athena*. In an air-raid attack on May 3, 1945, two of the three ships were sunk by British bombers, causing the loss of several thousand prisoners. German sources estimate that 82,000 prisoners died at Neuengamme.

NEUORDNUNG (New Order). Hitler's concept of a total rearrangement of German life to conform with the Nazi *Weltanschauung* (q.v.), or world view. In June 1933, shortly after his accession to political power, Hitler told his major party leaders that the dynamism of the "national revolution" was still active in Germany, that it must continue, and that it must lead to complete change. Every phase of living in the Third Reich would be subjected to *Gleichschaltung* (q.v.), or coordination, in conformity with Hitler's wishes. Actually, stripped of verbiage, Hitler's *Neuordnung* was an old-fashioned despotism and a totalitarian police state. Both the Reichstag (q.v.) and the Weimar Constitution were already powerless. Government was replaced by administration under the rule of the Fuehrer and the Nazi party. Every agency was ruled from above. In theory the *Neuordnung* was supposed to combine two contradictory forces, nationalism and socialism, but nationalism was dominant and socialism weak and ineffective. Nazi propaganda sought to give the impression that National Socialism was the wave of the future and that the new order would bring prosperity and worldwide recognition to the German people.

NEURATH, CONSTANTIN FREIHERR VON (1873–1956). Diplomat and Hitler's adviser on foreign affairs. Constantin von Neurath was born in Klein Glattbach, Württemberg, on February 2, 1873. He entered government service at the Foreign Office in Berlin in 1901 and subsequently devoted his career to diplomacy. In 1903 he was German Consul General at London, in 1914 Embassy Counselor at Constantinople, and from 1916 to 1918 Cabinet Chief in Württemberg. In 1919 he was German envoy at Copenhagen, in 1922 Ambassador at the Quirinal in Rome, and in 1930 Ambassador at London. On June 1, 1932, he was appointed by Chancellor Franz von Papen (q.v.) to his "Cabinet of barons," a post he retained under Chancellor Kurt von Schleicher (q.v.) and under Hitler. On January 31, 1933, the day after Hitler came to political power, Von Neurath joined the Nazi party and the SS (q.v.) with the rank of *SS-Gruppenfuehrer* (lieutenant general). In June 1943 he was promoted to *SS-Obergruppenfuehrer* (general).

Although Hitler was aware of Von Neurath's conservatism, he appointed him to the first Nazi Cabinet because he was a convenient front man. The Fuehrer was careful not to give Von Neurath complete control of foreign affairs but instead allowed him to compete with Alfred Rosenberg (q.v.), director of the Foreign Affairs Department of the Nazi party, and Joachim von Ribbentrop (q.v.), head of his own Ribbentrop Bureau (Dienststelle Ribbentrop, q.v.). Von Ribbentrop was an aspirant for Von Neurath's post. In his Cabinet position Von Neurath advised Hitler to withdraw from the Disarmament Conference (q.v.) and from the League of Nations (October 14, 1933). In 1936, on behalf of the Fuehrer, Von Neurath denounced the 1925 Locarno Pact (q.v.). On November 5, 1937, he was present at the Hossbach Conference (q.v.), at which Hitler outlined his policy of aggression.

Von Neurath's protest against Hitler's plans for expansion led to his own temporary decline. On February 4, 1938, he was swept out of office along with such experienced diplomats as Christian Albrecht Ulrich von Hassell (q.v.), Ambassador to Rome, and Herbert Dirksen (q.v.), Ambassador to Tokyo, as well as the Fuehrer's two top military leaders, Gen. Werner von Blomberg and Gen. Werner Freiherr von Fritsch (qq.v.; *see* BLOMBERG-FRITSCH CRISIS). To divert attention from his plans, Hitler kept Von Neurath in office as Minister without Portfolio. At the same time Von Neurath was invested with the chairmanship of a new Geheimer Kabinettsrat (q.v.), a secret Cabinet Council that was supposed to guide the Fuehrer in the conduct of foreign policy but was actually a mere paper organization. In accepting these offices, Von Neurath implicated himself in Hitler's aggressive designs, which he had opposed. On March 18, 1939, Von Neurath was appointed Reich Protector of Bohemia and Moravia. In this post he muzzled the press and abolished all opposition, including political parties and trade unions. He relinquished his office on August 25, 1943.

At the International Military Tribunal at Nuremberg Von Neurath defended himself on one aspect of the Nazi regime: "I was always against punishment without the possibility of a defense." On October 1, 1946, the court found him guilty on all four counts of the indictment: count 1, conspiracy to commit crimes alleged in other counts; count 2, crimes against peace; count 3, war crimes; and count 4, crimes against humanity. He was sentenced to fifteen years' imprisonment. Released from Spandau Prison in 1954, he died in Enzweihingen on August 14, 1956.

NEW FRONT. *See* NEUE FRONT.

NEW ORDER. *See* NEUORDNUNG.

NEW WEST WALL. *See* WEST WALL.

NEWSPAPERS IN THE THIRD REICH. From the beginning of the Nazi regime on January 30, 1933, Hitler considered the German press to be one of the prime weapons in the battle to maintain his dictatorship. Along with radio, films, music, theater, sports, art, education, and literature, the entire press of the Third Reich was subjected to *Gleichschaltung* (q.v.), or coordination. Newspapers were placed under the direct control of Dr. Paul Joseph Goebbels (q.v.), who set up a Press Division in his Ministry for Public Enlightenment and Propaganda.

Immediately after the accession of Hitler to political power in 1933, all opposition newspapers were suppressed. The press in the Third Reich became a monolithic structure under rigid National Socialist control. The Reich Press Law of October 4, 1933, called for a "racially clean" journalism. Newspapers were purged of all Jewish or liberal journalists. Reporters and editors who remained had to pass tests of German citizenship and prove that they were not married to Jews. They were expected to be sympathetic to the Nazi cause. A major step in the purge was the expropriation of Jewish-owned newspapers. Pressure was brought to bear on Jewish owners to sell out. If they refused to relinquish control, their papers were banned for a few days, and then for weeks, until they were brought to the verge of ruin. The publishing house of Ullstein, Jewish-owned, found it necessary to sell out to the Eher Verlag (q.v.), the Nazi publishing house centered in Munich. Among the papers acquired by Max Amann (q.v.), head of the Eher Verlag, was the celebrated *Vossische Zeitung*, the liberal newspaper founded in 1703. The *Berliner Tageblatt*, also Jewish-owned, lasted until 1937. Because the German Foreign Office wanted a showpiece to influence world opinion, Goebbels allowed the

Frankfurter Zeitung, which was well known and respected everywhere, to maintain a modicum of independence. However, its Jewish owners were dropped.

Because of their monopoly Nazi-controlled newspapers at first flourished financially. The *Völkischer Beobachter* (q.v.), which had been acquired by the party in the early days of the movement, now became the most important official newspaper in the Third Reich. Edited by Alfred Rosenberg (q.v.), the leading National Socialist philosopher, it appeared in Munich as a morning newspaper and was distributed throughout the country in various editions. Its quality was distinctly below the norm for journalism set in the Weimar Republic (q.v.). Goebbels founded his own newspaper, *Der Angriff* (*The Assault; see* ANGRIFF, DER), which appeared in Berlin in the afternoon. Capitalizing on the previously high estimate of the German press in foreign countries, Goebbels retained the name, makeup, and general appearance of some of the older newspapers. At the same time he saw to it that their columns reflected National Socialist policy. He gave the editorship of the old Berlin *Boersen Zeitung (Stock Exchange Journal)* to Walther Funk (q.v.), Hitler's private tutor on economic and financial affairs, because of Funk's "right connections."

From his office in the Propaganda Ministry, Goebbels supervised more than 3,600 newspapers and hundreds of magazines. Each morning he received the editors of the Berlin daily papers and correspondents from the news services for other cities and towns and gave them precise directives on what was to be featured in the news that day. He sent similar directives by telegram or mail to smaller newspapers throughout the country. Goebbels required all journalists to hew strictly to the party line and, above all, never to challenge the word of the Fuehrer. He expected them to praise Hitler and to show a sympathetic attitude toward members of the party hierarchy trusted by the Propaganda Ministry. He delegated the details to Hans Fritzsche (q.v.), a smooth and efficient newspaperman who was made division chief of the home press in 1937. After the war Fritzsche was one of the defendants at the Nuremberg Trial (q.v.), at which he was found not guilty.

Goebbels was especially careful to seek the goodwill of foreign newspaper correspondents working in Berlin. He assigned them luxurious quarters and entertained them lavishly in order to induce reports favorable to himself and the Third Reich. However, with the exception of a few sycophants, he was never able to win over the foreign press corps.

A special problem for Goebbels was the proliferation of pornographic newspapers. *Der Stürmer (The Stormer; see* STÜRMER, DER), published by Julius Streicher (q.v.), was the most notorious of these scandal sheets. Goebbels realized the harm that it was doing to the regime, but it had won Hitler's support, and that was vital. Despite his own claim of high morality, the Fuehrer read each issue from front to back, primarily because of the paper's persistent fanatical attacks on Jews and its caricatures of "Jewish types." Goebbels was dissatisfied with both the Streicher pornographic sheet and the badly edited *Völkischer Beobachter*. In 1940, after the fall of Poland, the Propaganda Minister founded another weekly publication, *Das Reich*, for each issue of which he was supposed to write an article. The first edition was published on May 26, 1940. Goebbels wrote two lead articles and then nothing; the paper quietly expired. Late in the war, when newsprint became scarce, Goebbels took advantage of the opportunity to express his contempt for Streicher by banning *Der Stürmer*.

German newspaper readers, like radio listeners, became bored by and unimpressed with the regimented press. Between 1933 and 1937 the number of newspapers decreased from 3,607 to 2,671. Official newspapers like the *Völkischer Beobachter* and *Der Angriff* also suffered a loss of many readers. The public gradually realized that there were no independent newspapers in the Third Reich and that it had to accept a diet of Nazi propaganda.

NIEMOELLER, MARTIN (1892–1984). German pastor of the Protestant Evangelical Church and an outspoken anti-Nazi. Born in Lippstadt, Westphalia, on January 14, 1892, Martin Niemoeller served in World War I as a naval lieutenant and U-boat commander. He was awarded the high decoration Pour le Mérite for his services. After the war he studied theology and was ordained in 1924. He served as pastor of the wealthy Berlin-Dahlem Church from 1931 to 1937. A convinced nationalist and an inveterate opponent of communism, he, like many other Protestant pastors, at first welcomed Hitler and National Socialism and joined the Nationalsozialistische Deutsche Arbeiterpartei (q.v.). He was disillusioned when Hitler insisted upon the supremacy of the state over religion and especially when the Fuehrer began to promote his movement for positive Christianity (q.v.). Niemoeller countered these moves by taking over leadership of the Bekenntniskirche (q.v.), the Confessional Church, which remained true to traditional Lutheran principles. To defend the Confessional Church, Niemoeller set up the Pastors' Emergency League (Pfarrenbund, q.v.). In 1934 he helped draw up its Six Principles at the Synod of Barmen. Some 7,000 pastors joined Niemoeller, but their ranks were quickly decimated by Nazi persecution.

On June 27, 1937, Niemoeller preached his final sermon in the Third Reich to a large congregation at Berlin-Dahlem. "No more," he said, "are we ready to keep silent at man's behest when God commands us to speak. We must obey God rather than man!" Hitler was furious when news of Niemoeller's sermon was brought to him. For years he had hated Niemoeller with a passionate intensity. He regarded the pastor's sermons as political and not religious, and he was angered because churchgoers, both Protestant and Catholic, regarded Niemoeller as a kind of

Martin Niemoeller. [*Picture Collection, The Branch Libraries, The New York Public Library*]

folk hero. On July 1, 1937, Niemoeller was arrested and confined to Moabit Prison in Berlin, where he spent the next eight months.

Hitler could have kept Niemoeller confined indefinitely, but he decided to use the legal system instead of the Gestapo (q.v.) to deal with him. After repeated postponements the trial began on March 3, 1938, before a *Sondergericht,* a special court designed to try offenders against the state. In the indictment Niemoeller was accused of "underhanded attacks" against the state. Not content merely with defending himself, Niemoeller turned on his accusers. He was found guilty and sentenced to seven months in a fortress (an honorable prison for officers) and fined 2,000 marks for "abuse of the pulpit" and holding collections in his church.

Hitler was infuriated by what he regarded as a light sentence. He threatened that Niemoeller would "do time until he was blue in the face" and warned the entire court that it might be punished. Niemoeller served eight months, or one month more than his sentence, and was then released, only to be rearrested by the Gestapo at Hitler's order and held in "protective custody." He was confined in concentration camps (q.v.) throughout World War II, at first in Sachsenhausen and then in Dachau (qq.v.). At the latter camp he was a fellow prisoner with the former Austrian chancellor Kurt von Schuschnigg, the bankers Fritz Thyssen and Hjalmar Schacht (qq.v.), and the former princes Philip of Hesse and Frederick of Prussia. He was released in 1945 by Allied troops.

In 1946 Niemoeller admitted Germany's guilt of war crimes in a speech at Geneva. The next year he was elected first bishop of the reformed Evangelical Church of Hesse-Nassau, a post he retained until 1964. His later career was distinguished by a firm pacifism opposed especially to atomic armament. In 1952 he visited Moscow, and in 1967 North Vietnam.

Bibliography. Martin Niemoeller, *Here Stand I,* tr. by Jane Lymburn, Willett, Clark & Co., Chicago, 1937.

NIETZSCHE, FRIEDRICH [WILHELM] (1844–1900). German philosopher, erroneously adopted as an intellectual precursor of National Socialism. Friedrich Wilhelm Nietzsche was born in Röcken, near Lützen, Saxony, on October 15, 1844. Both his father and his grandfather were Protestant pastors. At the University of Bonn he abandoned theology, to the grief of his family, and devoted himself exclusively to philological studies. In his maturity he concerned himself wholly with philosophy and became one of the notable philosophers of the nineteenth century. Uncompromising in his ideal conception of man, he despised the masses, defied organized Christianity, and called for the training of a race of supermen.

In his best-known work, *Also sprach Zarathustrà (Thus Spake Zarathustra),* Nietzsche expounded his theory of the *Übermensch,* the "beyond-man" or "superman," a term that he borrowed from Goethe's *Faust.* Nietzsche believed his *Übermensch* to be perfect in mind and body. There would be no foe to match the *Übermensch* in strength, agility, and intelligence. He would delight in battle, and the more he fought, the more insensitive he would become to pain. There would be no religious doctrines to disturb him: he would be happy in the consciousness of his own strength. Without mercy, strong, and contemptuous of others, he would learn to disdain man-made laws and man-made gods, just as man himself had learned to belittle the type of fear exhibited by lower animals for lions and tigers. "Surpass yourself at the expense of your neighbor!" warned Zarathustra. "What you cannot seize, let no man give you." Man must throw off his sense of morality and be hard. Thus Nietzsche crystallized by means of philosophical speculation, melancholy but firm and clear, the idea of force and strength.

Friedrich Nietzsche. *[Picture Collection, The Branch Libraries, The New York Public Library]*

When Nietzsche spoke of the superman, he envisioned no one special people, least of all the Germans. But to the ideologists of National Socialism, the basic idea was so close to their own conception of the ideal German that they appropriated it without regard for the main tenets of Nietzsche's teachings. Nietzsche was no admirer of the Germans. In a letter dated 1887 he wrote: "It seems to me that Germany for the last 15 years has become a regular school of besotment. Water, rubbish, filth, far and wide—that is what it looks like at a distance. I beg a thousand pardons if I have hurt your nobler feelings by stating this, but for present-day Germany, however much it may bristle hedge-hog like with arms, I have no longer any respect. It represents the stupidest, most depraved and most mendacious form of the German spirit that has ever existed. I forgive no one for compromising with it in any way, even if his name be Richard Wagner [q.v.]." The German soul, Nietzsche said, was complex and indefinable. It possessed "galleries and passages, caverns, hiding places, and dungeons." The Germans preferred the mysterious and the chaotic and loved "all that is cloudy, indistinct, watery, veiled, nebulous, and opaque." German profundity and passion in intellectual matters were declining. German philosophers were "unconscious counterfeiters." French culture was something else again. "All that Europe has known of sensibility, of taste and nobleness, has been the work and creation of France." Nietzsche had only contempt for anti-Semites: "It is the bravery of the Jews under the cloak of wretched submission that surpasses the virtues of the saints." The idea of a pure Teutonic race appeared to Nietzsche as "a mendacious swindle." "It is probable that there are no pure races, but only races which have become purified, and even these are extremely rare."

Nazi ideologists nevertheless appropriated two basic ideas from Nietzsche which they twisted to conform with their own *Weltanschauung* (q.v.), or world view: (1) the concept of a superman applicable to the Nordic German hero; and (2) contempt for Christianity, which they condemned as a religion of Judaistic origins. Accepting only these simplistic versions of Nietzsche's philosophy, they rejected his sympathetic attitude toward the Jews as well as his opposition to nationalism and racialism. Nazi mythmakers utilized Nietzsche's ideas out of context to bolster their own ideology.

Bibliography. Walter Arnold Kaufman, *Nietzsche*, Princeton University Press, Princeton, N.J., 1968.

NIGHT AND FOG DECREE. *See* NACHT- UND NEBEL ERLASS.

NIGHT OF THE BROKEN GLASS. *See* GRYNSZPAN, HERSCHEL; KRISTALLNACHT.

NIGHT OF THE LONG KNIVES. A campaign of assassination unleased by Hitler on the night of June 30, 1934, to strike against the growing power of the SA (q.v.) and to prevent a second revolution (q.v.). (*See* BLOOD PURGE.) The term is also used to describe a number of bloody encounters between Nazis and Communists at the time of the national elections on July 31, 1932. These skirmishes took place primarily in Königsberg. In the preceding month 99 people had been beaten to death, and 1,125 wounded in street battles. Nazi Storm Troopers took a leading role in the street brawls, meeting hall disturbances, bombings, and shootings.

NOLDE, EMIL (1867–1956). Expressionist artist. Emil Nolde (originally Emil Hansen) was born in Nolde, Südtondern, on August 7, 1867. From 1892 to 1898 he taught industrial art at St. Gall, Switzerland, and subsequently traveled throughout Europe. Nolde became known in Germany for his explosively colored canvases featuring supernatural and mystical themes and extreme distortions of shape. He joined the Nazi movement in 1920 but later became the object of Nazi hostility. He failed to understand why he, a party member, should be proscribed. In 1936 about 1,000 of his paintings were confiscated as degenerate art (*see* ENTARTETE KUNST). He died in Seebüll, North Friesland, on April 15, 1956.

NON-ARYAN. Term used in the Third Reich to describe any person who did not possess "Aryan" blood. It was used most often to depict Jews as "a culture-destroying race." *See also* RACIAL DOCTRINE.

NORDIC RACE. *See* RACIAL DOCTRINE.

NORDLICHT (Northern Light). Code name for the projected capture of Leningrad in 1942. In a directive dated July 23, 1942, Hitler ordered Army Group North to prepare for the capture of Leningrad by the beginning of September. The original cover name was Feuerzauber (q.v.; Fire Magic), which was changed ten days later to Nordlicht. Hitler was never able to put Nordlicht into force despite the long siege of Leningrad. The people of Leningrad refused to capitulate. Under bombing and shellfire they continued to work at their jobs. Despite gnawing hunger they repaired the fortifications ringing the city. There was no fuel for cooking; water had to be brought in from the river, wells, and canals; and the food supply diminished to the vanishing point. Yet there was no German occupation of Leningrad.

NOT-, BROT- UND SCHICKSALSGEMEINSCHAFT (Community of Need, Bread, and Fate). Favorite slogan used by Dr. Paul Joseph Goebbels (q.v.) in his propaganda. It combined three ideas: *bread,* representing the biological and material world; explicitly defined *need;* and *fate,* representing a secularized religion.

NOVEMBERVERBRECHER (November Criminals). Sarcastic term used by Nazi speakers to describe those responsible for concluding the armistice on November 11, 1918, at the end of World War I. German leaders who had agreed to a suspension of hostilities pending a definitive peace settlement were denounced as traitors to the fatherland. The implication was that Social Democrats and Jews had been responsible for this "stab in the back" (*see* DOLCHSTOSSTHEORIE) at a time when the German armies had not been completely defeated.

NOWOTNY, WALTHER (1921–1944). Fifth-ranking ace of the Luftwaffe (q.v.) in World War II. In 1942, as a 1st lieutenant, Walther Nowotny was assigned to Jagdgeschwader (Fighter Group) 54, and the next year he was promoted to group captain with that unit. In 1944, as a major, he commanded Jagdgeschwader 52 in Rhine/Hopsten. He was officially credited by Luftwaffe statisticians with 258 kills, of which 255 were on the eastern front. Nowotny was the eighth Luftwaffe winner of the Knight's Cross with Oak Leaves, Swords, and Diamonds (*see* RITTERKREUZ). On November 8, 1944, while flying an Me-262, he was shot down and killed.

NPD. *See* NEO-NAZISM.

NS (Nationalsozialistisch; National Socialist). Prefix to denote a National Socialist background, as in *NS-Briefe (NS Letters).*

NS-BEAMTENBUND. *See* BEAMTENBUND.

NS-BRIEFE (NS Letters). A fortnightly National Socialist newsletter founded by Gregor Strasser (q.v.) in 1924 to keep Nazi officials informed about the proper party line. As editor, Strasser hired a twenty-seven-year-old writer and dramatist, Dr. Paul Joseph Goebbels (q.v.), who took Hitler's side in the Hitler-Strasser feud and soon emerged as one of the most important leaders of the Nazi movement.

NS-DOZENTENBUND (National Socialist Lecturers' Alliance). A professional association of university lecturers established under Nazi party control and designed to keep university teachers in line with National Socialist ideology.

NS-FRAUENSCHAFT (National Socialist Women's Groups). Women's auxiliary of the Nationalsozialistische Deutsche Arbeiterpartei (q.v.). It was regarded as a basic *Gliederung* (limb) of the Nazi party. The purpose of its members was to rear their children as patriots. They were to give "that which is most dear to the Fatherland." They were to sing battle songs for the movement. "It is the duty of all leaders of the NS-Frauenschaft to see to it that all commands of the Fuehrer are unconditionally carried out."

Founded on October 1, 1931, and led for a time by Elsbeth Zander, the organization was generally inactive until Hitler became Chancellor in 1933. It was reorganized under the leadership of Gertrud Bäumer and then under Frau Gertrud Scholtz-Klink (q.v.). Two confidential bulletins presented directions for the leadership:

> The leadership of the NS *Frauenschaft* makes known: (1) *The "bringing-in-line."* The "bringing-in-line" of the women's organizations does not mean a deviation from the clear line of National Socialism. We want no break in unity. The NS *Frauenschaft* must have the leading role in the woman's federation. Through the "bringing-in-line" a new field of activity is open for you: to fill the other women's organizations with the National Socialist spirit. For the NS *Frauenschaft* to be able to fulfill these tasks it must to its last member be schooled in National Socialist thought. . . . In social work the most important places in the country as well as the city must be occupied in proportion to available force. Also the executive bodies of the other women's associations are to be slowly penetrated. However, the best forces of the NS *Frauenschaft* must not be drained away. . . . The religious groups are to be handled with caution. They cannot be brought into line in the same way as the other women's clubs.
>
> In every province a woman commissioner who must be a National Socialist will be appointed by the province leader in collaboration with the province leader of the *Frauenschaft*. This commissioner can be the province leader of the *Frauenschaft* herself. The commissioner is to set up in her province a German *Frauenfront* that consists essentially of those national organizations which have placed themselves under the German *Frauenfront*. . . . The women's professional organizations are, so far as professional interests are represented, to be joined to the parallel men's organizations. As women's groups, however, they belong to the German *Frauenfront*. The commissioner, according to the principle of the last *Information Service*, shall cause the women's organizations themselves to accept a newly chosen leadership. Only when the organization refuses to accept the new staff does the commissioner take over this office. Severity in this connection is to be avoided if possible. The by-laws of the individual organizations shall be demanded only by the Berlin office of the German *Frauenfront*. Treasury books may not be requested from the Commissioner. Above all the individual life of the inner groups is to be interfered with as little as possible.

NS-HILFSKASSE (National Socialist Relief Fund). An accident and insurance plan owned and administered by the Nationalsozialistische Deutsche Arbeiterpartei (q.v.).

NS-JUBEL DRITTE STUFE (National Socialist Jubilation Third Stage). Peak-volume applause and demonstrations at Nazi party meetings. The stage managers of such demonstrations assigned a decibel value for the volume of applause to be used on ritual occasions. Colored lights called for the proper amount of jubilation.

NS-LEHRERBUND (NSLB; National Socialist Teachers' Alliance). A monolithic Nazi party organization for teachers, designed to supersede all professional teachers' groups of the Weimar Republic (q.v.). It was formed on November 1, 1935, in the interest of coordination (*Gleichschaltung*, q.v.), and all its members were subject to strict party control.

NS LETTERS. *See* NS-BRIEFE.

NS-MONATSHEFTE. *See* NATIONALSOZIALISTISCHE MONATSHEFTE.

NS-RECHTSWAHRERBUND (National Socialist Lawyers' Association). A Nazi organization composed of all practicing lawyers, designed to replace all other lawyers' organizations. It had its own honor courts, which were armed with formidable disciplinary powers. Any member who failed to use the German greeting *"Heil Hitler!"* or who failed to vote in Reichstag (q.v.) elections or plebiscites could lose his license to practice.

NSAG. *See* NATIONALSOZIALISTISCHE ARBEITSGEMEINSCHAFT.

NSBO. *See* NATIONALSOZIALISTISCHE BETRIEBSZELLENORGANISATION.

NSD. *See* NATIONALSOZIALISTISCHER DEUTSCHER.

NSD-ÄRTZEBUND (National Socialist German Doctors' Alliance). A physicians' unit allied with the Nazi party. A monolithic organization, it superseded all previous medical associations of the Weimar Republic (q.v.).

NSDAP. *See* NATIONALSOZIALISTISCHE DEUTSCHE ARBEITERPARTEI.

NSDAV. *See* NATIONALSOZIALISTISCHER DEUTSCHER ARBEITERVEREIN.

NSDSTB. *See* NATIONALSOZIALISTISCHER DEUTSCHER STUDENTENBUND.

NSFK. *See* NATIONALSOZIALISTISCHES FLIEGER-KORPS.

NSKK. *See* NATIONALSOZIALISTISCHES KRAFTFAHRER-KORPS.

NSLB. *See* NS-LEHRERBUND.

NSV. *See* NATIONALSOZIALISTISCHE VOLKSWOHLFAHRT.

NSVB. *See* NATIONALSOZIALISTISCHER VOLKSBUND.

NUREMBERG (Nürnberg). German city and favorite showplace of the Nazi regime. Nuremberg is located in the *Land* (state) of Bavaria approximately 92 miles north-northwest of Munich. It stands on the Pegnitz River, which at this point is crossed by a dozen bridges. The earliest settlement at Nuremberg rose around a royal fortress and became important as a junction of medieval trade routes between the Italian states and the East on the one hand and Northern Europe on the other. Citizens of the town amassed great wealth as a result of its favorable location. In 1219 Emperor Frederick II conferred on Nuremberg the rights of a free imperial town. It was the first of the imperial towns to adopt Protestantism. In painting, Nuremberg claimed the great Albrecht Dürer and in literary history Hans Sachs, the cobbler-poet, and other *Meistersänger* (mastersingers). From its workshops came such popular products as silver plate, stoves, watches, and gunlocks. The economic prosperity of Nuremberg declined after the opening of a sea route to India in 1497–1498 and, later, with the destructive effects of the Thirty Years' War (1618–1648).

The streets of Nuremberg were narrow and crooked and were lined by homes of the old patrician families. Most of these houses lacked precision of line, with red-tiled roofs and gables turned toward the streets. There were many beautiful fountains, notably the Schöner Brunnen (Beautiful Fountain), in the form of a large Gothic pyramid, and the Gänsemännchen (Goose Mannikin). The Rathaus (Town Hall), built in the Italian style in the early seventeenth century, had frescoes by Dürer. Among the most notable churches were St. Lorenz, St. Sebald, and the Frauenkirche. The Marthakirche was the meeting place of the *Meistersänger*.

The old medieval town became a favorite haunt of the Nazi hierarchy. Just as Hitler used the Third Reich to indicate the continuity of German history, so did he choose Nuremberg as the scene of the annual Nazi rallies (*see* NUREMBERG RALLIES). There were carefully planned celebrations in the Dutzenreich district to the southeast of the city, where a stadium could hold 50,000 spectators. The old streets of the city reverberated for hours to the sound of marching boots. The name of the city was used for the Nuremberg Laws on citizenship and race (q.v.), directed against the Jews. Nuremberg suffered severe damage from Allied bombing attacks in World War II and from air and land attacks in April 1945. After the war Nuremberg was chosen by the Allies as the site for the trial of Nazi war leaders (*see* NUREMBERG TRIAL).

Nazi anti-Semitism is manifested in the word *Jude* ("Jew") and the swastika scrawled on the front of an optician's store. [*Brown Brothers*]

NUREMBERG LAWS ON CITIZENSHIP AND RACE (also called Ghetto Laws). The Nuremberg Laws were designed by Hitler to define the status of Jews in Germany and to restrict them in political and social life. In his drive for political power Hitler promoted a bitter anti-Semitic campaign (*see* ANTI-SEMITISM) and stirred up extreme hatred against the Jews. After becoming Chancellor, he encouraged his followers to assault and beat Jews, to humiliate them by forcing them to clean the streets, to picket or close Jewish businesses, and to denounce Jews in the professions as rogues, profiteers, and traitors. When accounts of Nazi atrocities were published abroad, a boycott of German goods was urged in retaliation. The result was disastrous for German Jews. Jewish businesses were boycotted, Jewish physicians excluded from hospitals, Jewish judges dismissed, and Jewish students thrown out of the universities. Jews were increasingly barred from all German life. "The Jews can speak only Jewish. When he writes in German, he lies." From September to November 1935 Hitler took steps to define the legal status of Jews in Germany. The Nuremberg Laws withdrew German citizenship from persons of "non-German blood."

NUREMBERG RALLIES (also called Parteitage, or Party Days). Nazi party rallies designed to impress German public opinion and foreigners with the strength and prestige of the Nazi movement. Everything possible was done to publicize the message that National Socialism was the only true religion and Adolf Hitler its messiah. In the spirit of nationalism, most of the rallies were held at Nuremberg (q.v.), with its medieval architecture and artistic trappings, its traditions of *Minnesänger* and *Meistersänger* (troubadours), of Tannhäuser and Walther von der Vogelweide. The high point was invariably a long speech by the Fuehrer, in which he attacked Jews, Marxists, bolshevists, and pacifists and heaped scorn on the Treaty of Versailles, the Weimar Republic (q.v.), France, and Soviet Russia.

The first and smallest rally was held at Munich at the end of January 1923, when 20,000 spectators and party members gathered to celebrate the Nazi cause. There was a modest parade of the *Freikorps* (free corps), the predecessor of the Storm Troops (*see* SA). However, the marchers, called the Gymnastics and Sports Division, had no uniforms or weapons. At this opening rally there took place the first consecration of the flags, a rite that was to be performed at all subsequent rallies. The flags featured red for the blood of the party, white for national purity, and the swastika (*see* HAKENKREUZ) to represent the triumph of Nordicism over Judaism and Marxism.

The second rally was held at Nuremberg in August 1923. The idea for the change came from Julius Streicher (q.v.), the anti Semitic leader, who convinced Hitler that Nuremberg, with its historical traditions and central location (seven railroad lines converged there), was an ideal spot for the celebration. In the presence of Hitler and Gen. Erich Ludendorff (q.v.), a memorial service was held in honor of those who had died during World War I. Then came a two-hour parade of 80,000 Nazis, including a regiment of Uhlans, police, civilians in Bavarian and Tyrolean dress, and Storm Troopers. In the Ausstellungshalle (Exhibition Hall) Hitler gave the same speech four times to audiences of 2,000 each.

Three years passed before the next rally. After the unsuccessful Beer-Hall *Putsch* (q.v.) of November 8–9, 1923, in Munich, Hitler was imprisoned in Landsberg am Lech (q.v.). Following his release he found it necessary to rebuild his shattered party. He was forbidden to speak in most cities, including Nuremberg. Because of this ban the third rally was transferred to Weimar. It began on July 3, 1926, and ended at noon the next day. For the first time the gathering was called a *Parteitag* (party day). The pageantry was reduced to a modest scale. The celebrants were brought to Weimar in special trains draped with swastika banners. The flag consecration ceremony was held in secret, only Storm Troopers being allowed to attend. This rally marked the rise to prominence of Dr. Paul Joseph Goebbels (q.v.), who made a speech filled with praise for Hitler. "I am half-crazy with pride," he wrote later, "that such a genius as Hitler should see eye to eye with me toward the future." Special committees were assigned to attract youth, labor, and women to the party.

Rally No. 4, held in Nuremberg for three days in August 1927, was again a minor celebration. By this time party membership had doubled, to 50,000, but the Nazi appeal to the masses had been lessened by somewhat better economic conditions. The highlight of this rally was a torchlight procession through the narrow streets. The consecration of the flags was held in the open. Now that the ban on his speaking had been lifted, Hitler addressed his followers on the desperate need for racial purity. The rally saw the emergence of Heinrich Himmler (q.v.) to a top position in the Nazi hierarchy.

The next rally, held in Nuremberg from August 2 to 5, 1929, was the first truly spectacular Nazi rally. The theme was "composure." The effect was that of a gigantic stage presentation. All major buildings in Nuremberg, especially the Kulturvereinhaus (House of Culture), were used for meetings. Open spaces, such as the Zeppelinwiese and the Luitpoldhain, were utilized for mighty dramatic spectacles. More than 2,000 delegates assembled to hear speeches by Streicher, Goebbels, and Hitler. The next day a crowd of 150,000 gathered to witness the ceremony. There were ear-piercing Wagnerian overtures, athletes with burning torches, the formation of human swastikas, a two-hour speech by the Fuehrer, and then a dazzling

The 1936 rally in Nuremberg. [*Imperial War Museum, London*]

display of fireworks. On the final day new party flags were consecrated by the *Blutfahne* (q.v.). The rally ended with a seemingly endless march through the streets of the old city.

The 1933 Nuremberg rally, held from August 31 to September 3, was called the Congress of Victory to celebrate Hitler's assumption of power. The planning called for a miracle in logistics: to accommodate half a million Nazis, factories, churches, and public buildings were requisitioned, and huge tent cities, complete with kitchens and outdoor toilets, were set up. A great grandstand was built overnight on the Luitpoldhain for 60,000 people to hear the Fuehrer. On the morning of September 1 came the consecration of the flags. To the sound of muffled drums, a lone SS man (*see* SS) mounted the platform and displayed the *Blutfahne*. The audience stood in silence as the long roll of the dead was read by Ernst Roehm (q.v.), who had no way of knowing that he himself would be sacrificed the next June in the 1934 Blood Purge (q.v.). The next day was devoted to party parades, with immense but ordered phalanxes, followed by a fireworks display. On the final day came the speeches, culminating in Hitler's fiery address, against the enemies of National Socialism.

The 1934 rally, held at Nuremberg from September 3 to 10, was the first to last a full week. This time Hitler entrusted the filming to Leni Riefenstahl (q.v.), an actress and film director. Her *Triumph of the Will* (*Triumph des Willens*, q.v.) was a photographic masterpiece accurately depicting the excitement of the rally: the Wagnerian overture, the opening shots of Nuremberg, Hitler coming to earth in his plane, the 300,000 spectators, the 50,000 men of the Reichsarbeitsdienst (q.v.) with their shovels glittering in the sunlight, the unfurling of 21,000 flags, the rhythmic goose-stepping, and the torchlight processions. The three-hour film was shortened for more effective presentation and distributed by the UFA, the giant film company controlled by Alfred Hugenberg (q.v.).

At the 1935 rally, held in Nuremberg in mid-September, Hitler presented the Nuremberg Laws on citizenship and race (q.v.), directed against the Jews. For the first time he displayed the results of German rearmament, including new tanks, armored cars, and sleek aircraft. The military motif was repeated in the 1936 rally, dedicated to honor and freedom. At this rally some 250,000 party members and 70,000 spectators swarmed to the enlarged Zeppelinwiese. At the 1937 rally Hitler informed his listeners that his Third Reich would last 1,000 years.

The final and greatest Nuremberg rally was held from September 5 to 12, 1938, with the theme of Greater Germany. Each day was dedicated to a separate topic: Welcome, Congress of Labor, Fellowship, Politics, Youth, Storm Troopers, and Armed Forces. All the accumulated experiences of the past were used in the parades, banners, reviews, speeches, torchlight processions, and fireworks. This time more than 1 million people were involved. Hundreds of reporters came from all over the world to record the proceedings in a blaze of publicity. This was the final Nuremberg spectacle: the next year Germany was at war.

Bibliography. Hamilton T. Burden, *The Nuremberg Party Rallies, 1923–1939*, Frederick A. Praeger, Inc., New York, 1967.

NUREMBERG TRIAL. The public trial of twenty-two German principals held at Nuremberg from November 1945 to October 1946. The triumphant Allies came out of World War II flushed with victory but divided upon virtually all policies except one: the German war criminals would be punished. An agreement dated August 8, 1945, between the United States, Great Britain, and the Soviet Union to try the Nazi leaders was subsequently endorsed by nineteen member states of the United Nations. Although special courts had been set up in the past to judge political crimes by extraordinary authority, no such court had ever obtained universal recognition. The Nuremberg court was to judge crimes against peace, against humanity, and against defenseless minorities.

The legality of the trial troubled many jurists who were disturbed by the ex post facto implications of the proceedings. As the proceedings went on and it became clear from the testimony what had happened in Nazi Germany, fewer voices were raised against the trial.

Following are lists of the judges, the members of the prosecution, and the accused (*see also* individual biographies).

THE INTERNATIONAL MILITARY TRIBUNAL

President	Lord Justice Geoffrey Lawrence
British alternate member	Mr. Justice William Norman Birkett
United States member	Mr. Francis Biddle
United States alternate member	Judge John J. Parker
French member	Professor Henri Donnedieu de Vabre
French alternate member	M. Robert Falco
Russian member	Maj. Gen. I. T. Nikitchenko
Russian alternate member	Lieut. Col. A. F. Volchkov

THE PROSECUTION

American	Mr. Justice Robert H. Jackson Mr. T. J. Dodd Brig. Gen. Telford Taylor
British	Sir Hartley Shawcross Sir David Maxwell-Fyfe Mr. G. D. Roberts Col. H. J. Phillimore Lieut. Col. J. M. G. Griffith-Jones Maj. F. Elwyn Jones Mr. J. Harcourt Barrington
French	M. François de Menthon (served until January 14, 1946) M. Edgar Faure M. Auguste Champetier de Ribes M. Charles Dubost
Russian	Lieut. Col. R. A. Rudenko Col. Y. V. Pokrovsky

THE ACCUSED

Hermann Goering	Reich marshal and commander in chief of the Luftwaffe
Rudolf Hess	Deputy to the Fuehrer; top party official
Joachim von Ribbentrop	Reich Foreign Minister
Wilhelm Keitel	Chief of the High Command of the armed forces
Ernst Kaltenbrunner	Chief of the Security Police and SD and head of the RSHA
Alfred Rosenberg	Party philosopher and Reich Minister for the eastern occupied area
Hans Frank	Governor-General of occupied Polish territory
Wilhelm Frick	Former Minister of the Interior; brought the German nation under the complete control of the NSDAP
Julius Streicher	Founder of an anti-Semitic hate sheet, *Der Stürmer*
Walther Funk	President of the Reichsbank, 1939
Hjalmar Schacht	Minister of Economics, 1934–1937; president of the Reichsbank, 1933–1939
Karl Doenitz	Supreme commander of the Navy, 1943; German Chancellor, 1945
Erich Raeder	Supreme commander of the Navy, 1928–1943
Baldur von Schirach	Fuehrer of the Hitler Youth
Fritz Sauckel	Plenipotentiary for Labor Allocation
Alfred Jodl	Chief of the Operations Staff of the armed forces, 1939–1945
Franz von Papen	Chancellor, 1932; Minister and Ambassador in Vienna, 1934–1938; Ambassador in Turkey, 1939–1944
Artur Seyss-Inquart	Minister of the Interior and Reich Governor of Austria following fall of Von Schuschnigg; Reich Commissioner for the occupied Netherlands, 1940–1945
Albert Speer	Minister of Armaments and War Production; Inspector General of Highways
Constantin von Neurath	Minister of Foreign Affairs, 1932–1938; Reich Protector of Bohemia and Moravia, 1939–1943
Hans Fritzsche	Head of the Radio Division of the Propaganda Ministry
Martin Bormann (*in absentia*)	Deputy Fuehrer after Hess's flight to England

Hermann Goering enters a plea of not guilty at Nuremberg on November 21, 1945. Seated next to him are (left to right) Rudolf Hess, Joachim von Ribbentrop, and Field Marshal Wilhelm Keitel. [*Associated Press*]

THE ACCUSED (AGE)	VERDICT	PUNISHMENT
Hermann Goering (53)	Guilty on all four counts	Death
Rudolf Hess (52)	Guilty on counts 1 and 2	Life imprisonment
Joachim von Ribbentrop (53)	Guilty on all four counts	Death
Wilhelm Keitel (64)	Guilty on all four counts	Death
Ernst Kaltenbrunner (43)	Guilty on counts 3 and 4	Death
Alfred Rosenberg (53)	Guilty on all four counts	Death
Hans Frank (46)	Guilty on counts 3 and 4	Death
Wilhelm Frick (69)	Guilty on counts 2, 3, and 4	Death
Julius Streicher (61)	Guilty on count 4	Death
Walther Funk (56)	Guilty on counts 2, 3, and 4	Life imprisonment
Hjalmar Schacht (69)	Not guilty	Acquitted
Karl Doenitz (55)	Guilty on counts 2 and 3	Ten years
Erich Raeder (70)	Guilty on counts 2, 3, and 4	Life imprisonment
Baldur von Schirach (39)	Guilty on count 4	Twenty years
Fritz Sauckel (51)	Guilty on counts 2 and 4	Death
Alfred Jodl (56)	Guilty on all four counts	Death
Franz von Papen (66)	Not guilty	Acquitted
Artur Seyss-Inquart (54)	Guilty on counts 2, 3, and 4	Death
Albert Speer (41)	Guilty on counts 3 and 4	Twenty years
Constantin von Neurath (73)	Guilty on all four counts	Fifteen years
Hans Fritzsche (46)	Not guilty	Acquitted
Martin Bormann (45; *in absentia*)	Guilty on counts 3 and 4	Death

The evidence taken by the Tribunal was enough to fill forty-two bulky volumes. The verdicts condemned the Nazi *Fuehrer-Korps*, the Gestapo, the SS, and the SD (qq.v.) as criminal organizations. The individuals were indicted on four counts: count 1, conspiracy to commit crimes alleged in other counts; count 2, crimes against peace; count 3, war crimes; and count 4, crimes against humanity. Verdicts on individuals are shown above.

NÜRNBERG. *See* NUREMBERG.

NURSERY SCHOOL. *See* KINDERTAGESSTÄTTE.

O

OAK
to
"OUR HONOR IS NAMED LOYALTY"

OAK. *See* EICHE.

OATH OF LEGALITY. *See* LEGALITÄTS-EID.

OATH OF LOYALTY. Solemn declaration of loyalty *(Eid)* to Hitler required of all members of the armed forces. The order to take the oath came on August 2, 1934, the day on which President Paul von Hindenburg (q.v.) died. On that day Hitler also combined the offices of President and Chancellor. The oath read: "I swear by God this sacred oath that I shall render unconditional obedience to Adolf Hitler, the Fuehrer of the German Reich, supreme commander of the armed forces, and that I shall at all times be prepared, as a brave soldier, to give my life for this oath."

With this pledge the military leaders and soldiers of the Third Reich swore allegiance to the person of Hitler instead of to the constitution. For some this oath meant a severe conflict of conscience. Officers in the Resistance (q.v.) movement found it distasteful to break a pledge even if they had been forced to take it. Hitler himself regarded any deviation from this pledge as treason to the state.

OB. *See* OBERBEFEHLSHABER.

OBDH. *See* OBERBEFEHLSHABER DES HEERES.

OBDL. *See* OBERBEFEHLSHABER DER LUFTWAFFE.

OBERABSCHNITT (Higher Section). The main territorial division of the SS (q.v.), usually equivalent to a *Wehrkreis* (q.v.), or military district.

OBERBEFEHLSHABER (Ob; Commander in Chief). Top commander of units in the armed forces.

OBERBEFEHLSHABER DER LUFTWAFFE (ObdL; Commander in Chief of the Air Force). Senior post in the Luftwaffe (q.v.), held by Hermann Goering (q.v.).

OBERBEFEHLSHABER DES HEERES (ObdH; Commander in Chief of the Army). Top post in the Army.

OBERF. *See* OBERFUEHRER-SS.

OBERFOHREN MEMORANDUM. A memorandum supposedly written and circulated by Dr. Ernst Oberfohren. It accused the Nazis of having started the Reichstag fire (q.v.). Oberfohren, who held a degree in political science, abandoned his teaching post at Kiel at the age of forty-three and devoted himself to politics. In 1928, when Alfred Hugenberg (q.v.) became leader of the German Nationalist People's party, he appointed Oberfohren its parliamentary leader. In early 1933 Oberfohren was said to have written in a memorandum what he knew of the burning of the Reichstag (q.v.) and to have sent the report to his friends. The memorandum was first published in the *Manchester Guardian* on April 27, 1933. Soon thereafter, on May 7, Oberfohren was reported to have committed suicide at Kiel.

The Oberfohren Memorandum alleged that Dr. Paul Joseph Goebbels (q.v.), Minister for Public Enlightenment and Propaganda, conceived the idea of setting the fire; that the then Capt. Hermann Goering (q.v.), acting Prussian Minister of the Interior, supervised the arson; and that Wolf Heinrich Graf von Helldorf (q.v.), a Nazi leader in Berlin, and a certain Lieutenant Schultz prepared the preliminary steps. It was further charged that Marinus van der Lubbe (q.v.), a half-witted Dutchman, was led by Nazis through an underground passage from Goering's nearby headquarters to the Reichstag, where he was left to set the fire and be captured.

The Oberfohren Memorandum became the subject of a bitter historical controversy. The Nazis claimed that the Reichstag fire was the work of the Communists. The Communists countered by insisting that the Nazis had started the fire themselves to provide "evidence" of a Communist plot and thus have an excuse for heavy reprisals. The one thing that was clear was that Marinus van der Lubbe could not, as he stated, have started the fire by himself.

The Oberfohren charges appeared in the *Brown Book of the Hitler Terror and the Burning of the Reichstag* (q.v.; Victor Gollancz, Ltd., London, 1933) to show Nazi guilt in the arson. In London a Commission of Inquiry into the Burning of the Reichstag, presided over by an "International Committee of Jurists and Technical Experts," reported on September 30, 1933, that Van der Lubbe was not a member of the Communist party, that no connection whatever could be traced between the Communist party and the burning of the Reichstag, and that the Reichstag was set on fire by, or on behalf of, leading members of the National Socialist party.

This point of view was widely accepted until 1960, when Dr. Fritz Tobias, a German investigator, published in *Der Spiegel* an article holding that Van der Lubbe had acted alone in setting the fire and that the Nazis had not arranged it. He was supported by Professor Hans Mommsen, historian at the Ruhr University in Bochum, as well by several other scholars.

Bibliography. Fritz Tobias, *The Reichstag Fire Trial,* tr. by Arnold Pomerans, G. P. Putnam's Sons, New York, 1964.

OBERFUEHRER-SS (OBERF). Brigadier general in the SS (q.v.).

OBERGRUPPE (Superior Group). A main territorial division of the SA (q.v.).

OBERGRUPPENFUEHRER-SS (OGRUF). General in the SS (q.v.).

OBERKOMMANDO DER LUFTWAFFE (OKL; High Command of the Air Force). The administrative unit responsible for all activities of the Luftwaffe (q.v.).

OBERKOMMANDO DER WEHRMACHT (OKW; High Command of the Armed Forces). The new top command set up by Hitler on February 4, 1938, to replace the old War Ministry (Reichskriegsministerium). From 1934 to 1938 Hitler strengthened his grip on the German armed forces. With the consent of high Army leaders, he made himself supreme commander of the armed forces and required all members of the military to take a new oath of personal loyalty to himself (*see* OATH OF LOYALTY). The OKW was divided into four departments: Wehrmachtfuehrungsamt (q.v.; WFA), responsible for operations; Amt/Ausland Abwehr (q.v.), responsible for foreign intelligence; Wirtschafts- und Rüstungsamt (q.v.), responsible for supply; and Amtsgruppe Allgemeine Wehrmachtangelegenheiten (q.v.), for general purposes. Hitler appointed Gen. Wilhelm Keitel (q.v.) as the responsible officer in charge of the WFA with the title of chief of the High Command of the armed forces. The organization of the Oberkommando der Wehrmacht in three periods from 1934 to 1945 is shown in the chart on page 259.

OBERKOMMANDO DES HEERES (OKH; High Command of the Army). The supreme command of the Army, not to be confused with Oberkommando der Wehrmacht (q.v.), the supreme command of the armed forces.

OBERSALZBERG. *See* BERGHOF.

OBERSTE SA-FUEHRUNG (Supreme SA Leadership). The upper hierarchy of the SA (q.v.).

OBERSTER BEFEHLSHABER DER WEHRMACHT (Oberst. Bef. Wehrm.; Supreme Commander of the Armed Forces). Title assumed by Hitler as the highest responsible leader of the military during World War II.

OBERSTER SA-FUEHRER (OSAF; Supreme Commander of the SA). Title held by Hitler from 1930 on. *See also* SA.

OBERSTES PARTEIGERICHT (Supreme Party Court). The highest court within the Nationalsozialistische Deutsche Arbeiterpartei (q.v.), the Nazi party.

OBERSTGRUPPENFUEHRER-SS (Obstgruf.; SS Colonel General). A high officer of the SS (q.v.).

The High Command of the armed forces salutes Hitler. [*Associated Press*]

ORGANIZATION OF THE OBERKOMMANDO DER WEHRMACHT (HIGH COMMAND OF THE ARMED FORCES) IN THE THIRD REICH

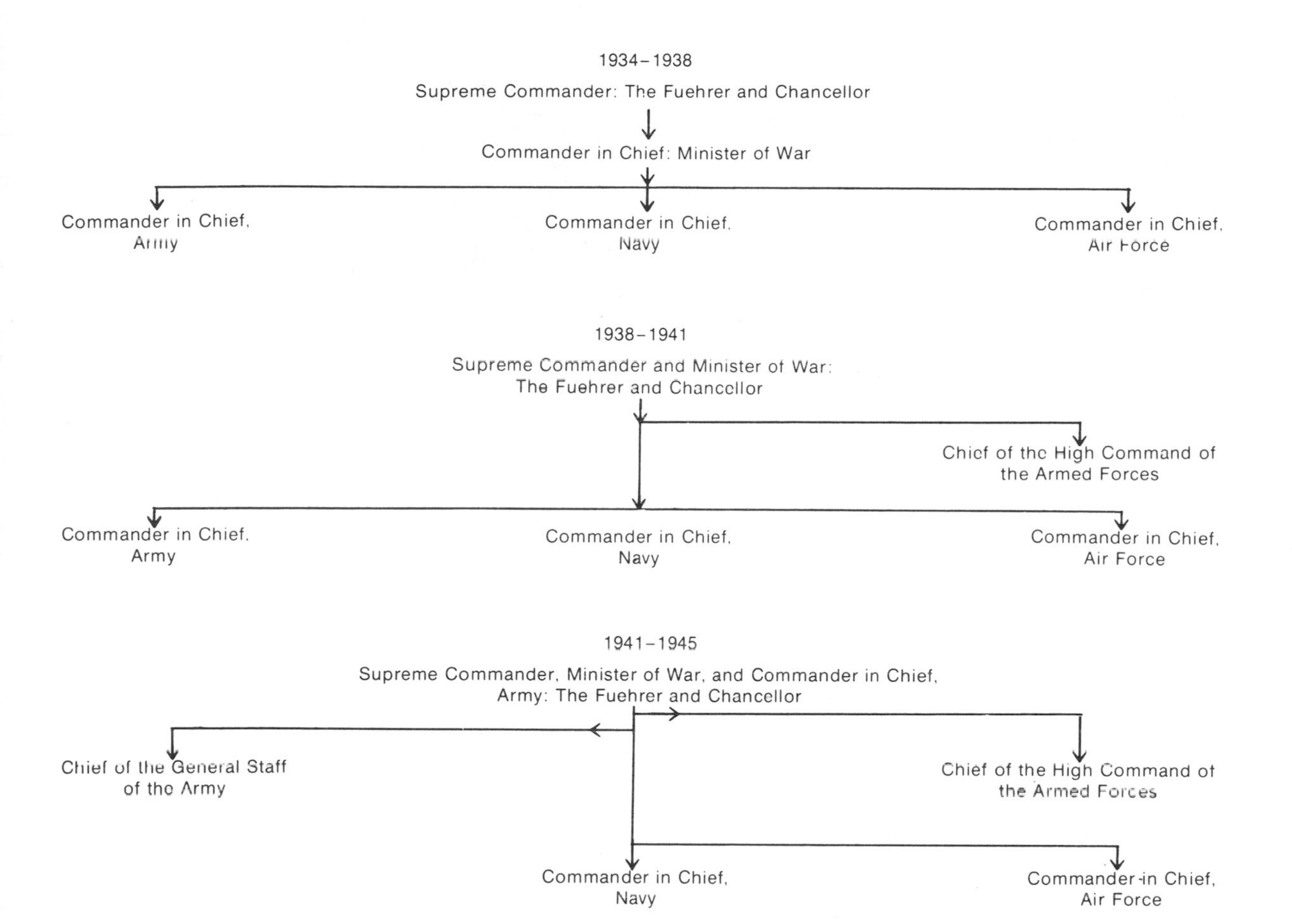

OBERSTURMBANNFUEHRER-SS (Ostubaf.; SS Lieutenant Colonel). A high officer of the SS (q.v.).

OBERSTURMFUEHRER-SS (SS 1st Lieutenant). A lower officer in the SS (q.v.).

OBSTGRUF. *See* OBERSTGRUPPENFUEHRER-SS.

ODESSA. The secret escape organization of the SS (q.v.) underground. A vast clandestine Nazi travel organization was set up after the defeat of the Third Reich in 1945 to enable SS members and other high Nazi functionaries to avoid arrest by the Allies. The main terminal point for Odessa was Buenos Aires, Argentina.

OFFICE FOR AGRICULTURE. *See* AGRARPOLITISCHER APPARAT.

OFFICE FOR DEPUTIES. *See* BÜRO DER ABGEORDNETEN.

OFFICE FOR GENERAL MILITARY AFFAIRS. *See* AMTSGRUPPE ALLGEMEINE WEHRMACHTSANGELEGENHEITEN.

OFFICE OF FOREIGN INTELLIGENCE. *See* AMT/AUSLAND ABWEHR.

OGRUF. *See* OBERGRUPPENFUEHRER-SS.

OHLENDORF, OTTO (1908–1951). Mass executioner of the SS (q.v.) during World War II. Trained in his early years as an economist, Ohlendorf left the Institute of Applied Economic Science in 1936 for a post as head of Amt III of the Reichssicherheitshauptamt (q.v.), or RSHA, under the leadership of Heinrich Himmler (q.v.).

When Himmler organized four *Einsatzgruppen* (q.v.), special extermination units, for service in the Soviet Union, he gave command of Group D to Ohlendorf. The economist relinquished his post for desk work as an *SS-Brigadefuehrer* (major general) assigned to the southernmost sector of the Ukraine and attached to the Eleventh Army. In a little over a year, from June 1941 to July 1942, he was responsible for the liquidation of 90,000 Jews. He then returned quietly to the Wilhelmstrasse in a civilian position on the Central Planning Board in the Department of Overseas Trade, while simultaneously holding his post as head of Amt III of the RSHA. In the late stages of the war he was chosen by Walter Schellenberg (q.v.) as a member of a possible future Himmler Cabinet "presentable to the Allies."

Ohlendorf was brought to trial at Nuremberg on September 15, 1947, in the so-called *Einsatztruppen* case (the Red Jacket defendants). With twenty-one others (five SS generals, five colonels, six lieutenant colonels, three majors, and three junior officers), he was accused of complicity in the murder of 1 million Jews. Ohlendorf readily admitted that he had received reports of executions by his subordinates, but he justified himself on ethical grounds. He cited historical precedents such as the killing of Gypsies in the Thirty Years' War. "I never permitted the shooting of individuals, but ordered that several of the men should shoot at the same time in order to avoid direct personal responsibility. Other group leaders demanded that the victims lie down flat on the ground to be shot through the nape of the neck. I did not approve of these methods because both for the victims and for those who carried out the executions, it was, psychologically, an immense burden to bear." Later, he said, the victims were dispatched in gas vans, but he complained that only fifteen to twenty could be put to death at one time until ovens were used. During the trial love-smitten young women sent bouquets to the cell of the handsome defendant.

Ohlendorf's judges at Nuremberg described him as a Jekyll and Hyde, whose actions were beyond the belief of normal men. On April 10, 1948, they sentenced him, along with thirteen others, to death. Of these, four—Ohlendorf and three other group commanders—were executed on June 8, 1951.

OKH. *See* OBERKOMMANDO DES HEERES.

OKL. *See* OBERKOMMANDO DER LUFTWAFFE.

OKW. *See* OBERKOMMANDO DER WEHRMACHT.

OLBRICHT, FRIEDRICH (1888–1944). One of the key conspirators in the July Plot (q.v.) of 1944. Friedrich Olbricht was born in Leisnig, Saxony, on October 4, 1888. A career soldier, he joined the Imperial Army in 1907 as a *Fahnenjunker* (cadet officer). In 1908 he was promoted to lieutenant and adjutant in the 105th Infantry Regiment. After World War I he served in the Foreign Armies Branch of the Reich Ministry of Defense. In the years after Hitler's rise to political power Olbricht held various important military posts, including that of chief of staff of the Dresdner Division (1933), chief of staff in the Fourth Army Corps in Dresden (1935), Commander of the 24th Infantry Division (1938–1940), chief of the General Staff of the Army High Command (1940), and chief of staff and deputy commander of the Reserve Army (1943). In the two last-named posts he served at the War Office in the Bendlerstrasse (q.v.) in Berlin, a vantage point for the conspirators.

Gen. Friedrich Olbricht. [*Bundesarchiv*]

A deeply religious man, Olbricht regarded the Nazi regime as a disgrace to the German fatherland and worked actively to overthrow it. He carried the main responsibility for initiating and organizing the coup, just as Lieut. Col. Claus Schenk Graf von Stauffenberg (q.v.) had the direct assignment of carrying the bomb. On July 15, 1944, the date originally set for the attack, Olbricht ordered the troops at Berlin to march some two hours before the bomb attempt on Hitler's life was to be made. He was reprimanded by his superiors. Olbricht was at the War Office during the July 20, 1944, attack. Arrested on the spot by Gen. Friedrich Fromm (q.v.), his immediate superior officer, he was shot by a firing squad, along with Von Stauffenberg, a few hours after it became known that Hitler had escaped death.

OLD GUARD (Old Fighters). *See* ALTE KÄMPFER.

OLGA. Code name for the signals office at the temporary headquarters of the Oberkommando der Wehrmacht (q.v.) in Ohrdruf, Thuringia. After the Allies captured Ohrdruf, newspapermen mistakenly believed the name Olga, which they found on a door next to Hitler's private room, to be that of a Nordic mistress of the Fuehrer.

OLYMPIAD XI. The Eleventh Olympic Games, held in Berlin in 1936, three and one-half years after the creation of the Third Reich. The traditional competition had been awarded to Germany before the accession of Hitler to political power. In 1933 the Nazi press denounced the forthcoming games as "a festival dominated by Jews," but criticism ceased as soon as Hitler decided that the Olympics would provide an important showcase for his regime. The preparations were lavish. The Nazi government spent $25 million in building nine arenas including a magnificent Olympic Stadium in Berlin, the scene of the summer competitions. A three-week moratorium on the anti-Jewish campaign was ordered to avoid an unfavorable impression on foreigners who came to Berlin to see the games.

On the opening day a capacity crowd of 110,000 erupted in nationalistic fervor when Hans Woellke, a shot-putter, won the first gold medal and became the first German in history to win an Olympic track-and-field championship. Woellke and another German, Gerhard Stock, who finished third, were brought to Hitler's box to be congratulated personally by the Fuehrer. That morning Tilly Fleischer finished first in the women's javelin competition, bringing further joy to Hitler and the huge crowd. Late that afternoon three Americans, Cornelius Johnson, Dave Albritton, and Delos Thurber, made a clean sweep of the high jump. Johnson and Albritton were blacks. Hitler left the stadium during the finals. Olympic officials discreetly reminded him that he had received winning German athletes in his box and that it would be reasonable to honor all winners in this fashion whenever the Fuehrer was present. Hitler replied that he would refrain from receiving any more winners.

Then came a series of embarrassing events for Hitler. On the third day of competition, Jesse Owens, a black sprinter from Ohio State University who had picked cotton as a child in Alabama, won the 100-meter dash, winning his semifinal heat in 10.2 seconds (not made official because of a following wind) and equaling the Olympic record of 10.3 seconds in the final. The next morning Owens won his second gold medal with a jump of 26 feet 2⁵⁄₁₆ inches. In this event Owens defeated Luz Long of Germany by almost 5 inches. The German athlete was a gracious loser. The following day Owens was awarded his third gold medal with another world record of 20.7 seconds in the 200-meter race. On the final day of the games he won a fourth gold medal and contributed to still another world record as a member of the 400-meter relay team. The great crowd joined in deafening applause for the superb American athlete, by this time the hero of the games.

The scintillating performance of Owens and the other nine black athletes on the American team presented Hitler with a problem. In accordance with Aryan racial theory (*see* RACIAL DOCTRINE), he regarded blacks along with Jews as inferior human beings. People whose ancestors came from the jungle, he explained, were primitive, and their physiques were stronger than those of civilized whites. He intimated that this was in reality unfair competition and that blacks should be excluded from future Olympic Games. The Fuehrer was present on the day when Owens won his third gold medal but pointedly left the stadium before the medals were presented to the winning athletes.

Hitler followed the events with the greatest excitement, especially when German athletes were victorious. There was an additional annoyance for him. When the French athletes marched past his box, they raised their arms in tribute, thereby sending the crowd into a wave of enthusiasm. The long applause indicated to the Fuehrer a desire upon the part of the German public for peace and conciliation with Germany's neighbor to the west. This was disturbing to Hitler, who apparently hoped for a more satisfactory military solution to the problem of Franco-German rivalry.

"ONE PEOPLE! ONE GOVERNMENT! ONE LEADER!" *See* "EIN VOLK! EIN REICH! EIN FUEHRER!"

ONE-POT MEAL. *See* EINTOPF.

OPEN-AIR MEDLEYS. *See* THINGSPIELSTÄTTEN.

OPERATION HIMMLER. *See* GLEIWITZ RAID.

OPERATION REINHARD. Procedure by which the property of murdered Jews was sequestered. Operation Reinhard was planned after the fatal wounding on May 29, 1942, of Reinhard Heydrich (q.v.), Deputy Reich Protector of Bohemia and Moravia, and named for him.

OPERATIONAL HEADQUARTERS-SS. *See* FUEHRUNGS-HAUPTAMT-SS.

OPPOSITION. *See* WIDERSTAND.

OQUIV. Abbreviation for the intelligence section of the General Staff of the Oberkommando des Heeres (q.v.), the High Command of the Army.

ORDE DIENST (Order Service). The original Dutch resistance group. Organized a few weeks after Hitler's invasion of the Netherlands in May 1940, the Orde Dienst was set up to send military information to London and to arrange, when the time came, for a transitional government to maintain order after the defeat of the Third Reich. By November 1940 it had a national membership. *See also* KNOKPLOEGEN.

ORDENSBURGEN (Order Castles). The highest residential academies for the training of the Nazi elite. Hitler established three types of schools for training future leaders of the party: the *Adolf Hitler–Schule* (q.v.), the Adolf Hitler Schools, closely associated with the Hitler Jugend (q.v.), the Hitler Youth; the *Nationalpolitische Erziehungsanstalten* (q.v.), the National Political Training Institutes, also called the *Napolas;* and the *Ordensburgen.* The last two were under control of the Nazi party. The ultimate destination for the top level of the Adolf Hitler alumni was the Order Castles, the finishing schools for future party leadership. Those chosen formed a kind of party university, an institutional core of Nazi brothers united in mysticism. "My teaching will be hard," Hitler said. His purpose was to create a violently active, dominating, brutal youth. It was to be indifferent to pain, without weakness and tenderness. "I want to see once more in its eyes the gleam of pride and independence of the beast of prey."

The Order Castles received their name from the medieval fortresses built by the Teutonic Knights and other orders. Four *Ordensburgen* were established, at Crössinsee, Sonthofen, Vogelsang, and Marienburg, in out-of-the-way, romantic settings. Each one accommodated 1,000 students called Junkers. Supervision was in the hands of 500 instructors, administrative staff, and grooms. The executive official was Robert Ley (q.v.), organizational chief of the Nazi party, who set its standards ("There must be great attention to riding because it gives the Junkers the feeling of being able to dominate a living creature entirely"). Entrants were chosen from among those who had spent six years between the ages of twelve and eighteen at the Adolf Hitler Schools, two and one-half years in the State Labor Service (Reichsarbeitsdienst, q.v.), and another four years in such activity as full-time party work. The candidates were usually in their mid-twenties when chosen for the Order Castles. Students went to each of the four *Ordensburgen* for a year at a time. At the first academy, at Crössinsee, the emphasis was on athletics, such as boxing, riding, and gliding; at Sonthofen the stress was on mountain climbing and skiing; at Vogelsang there was a year of physical training; and at Marienburg the students were expected to obtain their final political indoctrination. The Junkers were subjected to rigorous discipline and were expected to be obedient and respectful. There were severe punishments for the slightest infractions. Live ammunition was used in war games.

The selection of candidates was controlled by high party functionaries. Those who were chosen regarded it as a distinct honor. Intellectual standards were low: only 1 in 10 Junkers possessed the *Abitur,* the certificate for university entrance, and only 1 in 100 was a university graduate. The *Ordensburgen* often failed to attract a full complement of students despite the financial inducement and the honor of attendance. The graduates were expected to enter the higher echelons of the Nazi party. Many entered the armed forces during World War II, going straight from the *Ordensburgen* into the Wehrmacht (q.v.), the regular Army, or the Luftwaffe (q.v.), the Air Force.

ORDER OF YOUNG GERMANS. *See* JUNGDEUTSCHER ORDEN.

ORDER POLICE. *See* ORDNUNGSPOLIZEI.

ORDER SERVICE. *See* ORDE DIENST.

ORDNERTRUPPE (Monitor Troops). Strong-arm squads enlisted by Hitler in the early days of the Nazi movement. In 1920, soon after he had added the words "National Socialist" to "German Workers' party," Hitler organized a group of tough war veterans to keep order at Nazi political meetings and to break up those of other parties, especially the Communist party. Members of Hitler's squads included Ulrich Graf and Emil Maurice (qq.v.). At first the *Ordnertruppe* called themselves the Gymnastics and Sports Division of the party in order to avoid suppression by the police. In October 1921 they were officially absorbed into the SA (q.v.) as Storm Troopers.

ORDNUNGSPOLIZEI (Orpo; Order Police). The major uniformed police force of the Third Reich. It consisted of various types of police units.

ORGANISATION DER GEWERBLICHEN WIRTSCHAFT (Organization of the Industrial Economy). A new economic organization set up by laws of February 27 and November 27, 1934. In this reorganization the powers of the Cartel Tribunal of November 2, 1923, which controlled relations between cartelized industries and between cartels and consumers, were transferred to the Ministry of National Economy, that is, to the government itself. From this time on all firms were grouped within a double organization, both vertical and horizontal:

1. There were seven vertical *Reichsgruppen* (Reich groups): industry, artisans, banking, commerce, insurance, power, and transport. Each group was in turn divided into *Hauptgruppen* (main groups), *Wirtschaftsgruppen* (economic groups), and *Fachgruppen* (professional groups). There was no democratic control: all directors were chosen by the government. Membership in all these groups was compulsory.

2. The horizontal groups, called economic chambers, included all industrial, commercial, and artisan enterprises. Each chamber was coterminous with a *Gau* (q.v.), or territorial division. The director of each chamber was a loyal Nazi businessman and was regarded as an adviser to the *Gauleiter* (q.v.), the district leader.

Both groups and chambers were expected to maintain close ties with the Nazi party. They were to receive the general directives of the government and implement them. In effect, they represented the substantial unity of the Hitler dictatorship with big business, finance, and industry.

ORGANISATION TODT (OT; Todt Organization). A semimilitary governmental unit set up in 1938 for the purpose of constructing military installations and special highways suitable for armored vehicles. It was administered by Dr. Fritz Todt (q.v.) until his death in 1942 and then by Albert Speer (q.v.), Reich Minister for Armaments and War Production and General Plenipotentiary for Armaments under the Four-Year Plan (q.v.).

ORGANIZATION FOR FOREIGNERS. *See* AUSLANDSORGANISATION.

ORGANIZATION OF NATIONAL SOCIALIST SHOP CELLS. *See* NATIONALSOZIALISTISCHE BETRIEBSZELLENORGANISATION.

ORGANIZATION OF THE INDUSTRIAL ECONOMY. *See* ORGANISATION DER GEWERBLICHEN WIRTSCHAFT.

ORPO. *See* ORDNUNGSPOLIZEI.

ORTSGRUPPE (Local Group). Local group of the Nationalsozialistische Deutsche Arbeiterpartei (q.v.), responsible for a town section.

ORTSGRUPPENLEITER (Local Branch Leader). A Nazi party official in charge of one or more parts of a town. He was subordinate to a *Kreisleiter* (q.v.), or circuit leader. Until 1935 the *Ortsgruppenleiter* often doubled as a town mayor.

OSAF. *See* OBERSTER SA-FUEHRER.

OSSIETZKY, CARL VON (1889–1938). German journalist and pacifist. Carl von Ossietzky was born in Hamburg on October 3, 1889. While serving in World War I, he was so angered by the terrible loss of life he witnessed that he became an active pacifist for the remainder of his life. After the war he settled in Berlin. In 1928 he became editor of *Die Weltbühne (The World Stage),* a periodical with pacifist tendencies. In 1929 an article in the journal accused the Reichswehr (q.v.) of secretly arming in defiance of the Treaty of Versailles. Editor Ossietzky and his

Carl von Ossietzky in the Sachsenhausen concentration camp. [*Ullstein*]

contributor were arrested and sentenced to eighteen months' imprisonment. Again, in 1931, he was sentenced to prison for treason because of continued criticism of the armed forces. He was pardoned and released, only to be arrested again in 1933 after Hitler came to power and interned in a concentration camp (*see* CONCENTRATION CAMPS) as an enemy of the state. While an inmate he was awarded the Nobel Peace Prize for 1935. He was forbidden by the Nazi government to accept the award. Ossietzky died in Berlin on May 3, 1938, of tuberculosis, which he had contracted in the unfavorable environment of his concentration camp.

Bibliography. Carl von Ossietzky, *The Stolen Republic*, ed. by Bruno Frei and tr. by John Peet, Lawrence & Wishart, Ltd., London, 1971.

OSTARBEITER (Eastern Worker). Polish or Russian slave worker in the occupied countries during World War II. Such workers were required to wear an identification patch with an *O*. Because they were regarded as subhuman, they were ordered to be separated from Germans. Those who tried to escape were hanged where other workers could see their bodies.

OSTER, HANS (1888–1945). Chief of Staff of the Abwehr (q.v.) and principal organizer of the Resistance (q.v.) movement against Hitler. Hans Oster was born in Dresden on August 9, 1888. From 1933 to 1944, first under Maj. Gen. Kurt von Bredow and then under Adm. Wilhelm Canaris (q.v.), he served as chief of staff and deputy controller of the German military intelligence department. A firm opponent of the National Socialist regime, he was a driving force among officers in the Resistance and conspiracy against Hitler. In the winter of 1939–1940 he informed both the Dutch and the Norwegians about the aggression Hitler planned against them. Described by his colleagues as "a man after God's heart," as without personal ambition, Oster had deep religious convictions and held the Nazi movement to be anti-Christian. In April 1943 he was suspended from duty and a year later was dismissed from the Army. He was arrested after the July Plot (q.v.) of 1944 and executed, along with Admiral Canaris and Pastor Dietrich Bonhoeffer (q.v.), at Flossenbürg (q.v.) concentration camp on April 9, 1945.

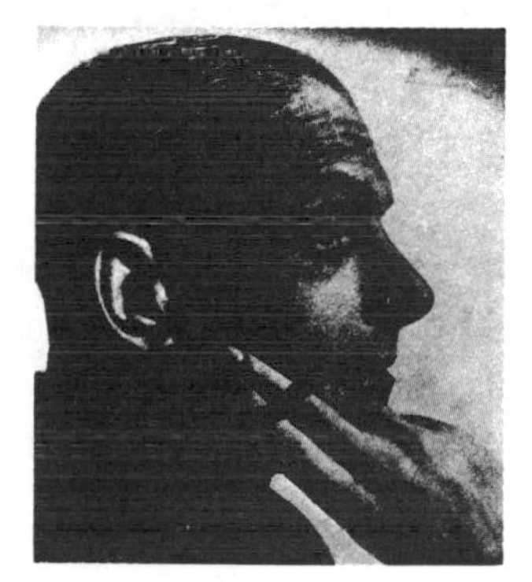

Hans Oster. [*Bundesarchiv*]

OSTHILFE SKANDAL (East Subvention Scandal). A political scandal involving the governmental organization for subsidizing estates east of the Elbe. A program of aid for the maintenance of the great landed estates in East Prussia was instituted in the early 1930s by the Reichstag (q.v.). The agricultural interests of the eastern provinces were suffering distress in part because of their separation from Germany by the Polish Corridor instituted by the

Treaty of Versailles. There were serious financial abuses involving Junker owners of large estates. The scandal led in early 1933 to difficulties for President Paul von Hindenburg and subsequently to the fall of Chancellor Kurt von Schleicher (qq.v.). The Nazis used the scandal to good advantage in their drive for power. It was rumored at the time that one of the reasons impelling Von Hindenburg to name Hitler Chancellor was a Nazi threat to bring the *Osthilfe Skandal* into the open. Oskar von Hindenburg (q.v.), the President's son, represented the interests of the agrarians in the *Osthilfe* affair. Linked with the scandal was the estate of Neudeck (q.v.), which was presented to Von Hindenburg in the name of his son to avoid inheritance taxes.

OSTINDUSTRIE GMBH (Eastern Industries, Ltd.). An establishment set up by the SS (q.v.) in March 1943 for the purpose of utilizing slave labor in Poland. Directed by *Brigadefuehrer* (Maj. Gen.) Odilo Globocnik (q.v.), it ran special factories in the Lublin area. The majority of the workers were Jewish prisoners.

OSTMARK (Eastern March). Name applied to Austria following the *Anschluss* (q.v.), or union between Germany and Austria to form a part of Greater Germany in 1938. The century-old name Österreich was abolished and replaced by the archaic Ostmark.

OSTMEDAILLE (Eastern Medal). Decoration given to those who served on the eastern front during World War II. In soldier's parlance the award was often called the Frost Medal or the Order of Chilled Beef *(Gefrierfleischorden)* because of the cold conditions that were encountered by the Nazi armies fighting in Soviet Russia.

OSTUBAF. *See* OBERSTURMBANNFUEHRER-SS.

OŚWIĘCIM. *See* AUSCHWITZ.

OT. *See* ORGANISATION TODT.

OTTO. Code name in a directive issued under Hitler's order for armed intervention against Austria. Named after Otto of Hapsburg, youthful pretender to the throne of Austria, who was then in exile in Belgium, Operation Otto called for armed intervention by German forces in Austria in the event of a restoration of the monarchy. "Making use of domestic dissension among the Austrian people," the directive noted, "there will be a march toward the general direction of Vienna, and all resistance will be smashed." Later, a top-secret directive made it clear that the German ultimatum to Austria had not been effective, and "to avoid further bloodshed in Austrian cities," the German Army was ordered to move at daybreak on March 12, 1938.

OTTO-PROGRAMME (Otto Program). A special program of the Wehrmacht (q.v.), the armed forces, for the development of rail and road facilities leading through Central and Eastern Europe to the Soviet border (*Otto* stood for *Ost*, meaning "east"). The *Otto-Programme* was initiated on October 1, 1940, and completed on May 10, 1941, apparently for the coming invasion of the Soviet Union.

"OUR HONOR IS NAMED LOYALTY." *See* "UNSERE EHRE HEISST TREUE."

P

PACT OF STEEL
to
PZK

PACT OF STEEL. *See* ROME-BERLIN AXIS.

PALACE. *See* SCHLOSS.

PANTHER TANK (SdKfz-171). One of the most formidable weapons of World War II. When Hitler invaded the Soviet Union in June 1941, he used in his *Blitzkrieg* (q.v.) the effective PZKW-III and PZKW-IV tanks that had been put to use elsewhere. The early victories seemed to bear out the Fuehrer's expectation of victory by winter, but the German failure to take Moscow and the Soviet counteroffensive changed the picture entirely. Suddenly the Russians sent into action their first-rate T-34 medium tanks, which slowed the German advance to a crawl and finally stopped it completely. Hitler hurriedly ordered his technological designers to plan a competing war vehicle. The result was the Panther, a medium-heavy tank that performed with notable success against the Russian T-34s, the British Churchills, and the American Shermans. The specifications of the Panther were impressive: a combat weight of 49 tons, a top speed of 30 miles per hour, a 700-horsepower Maybach V-12 cylinder engine, synchromesh transmission and torsion-bar suspension, 4.3-inch turret armor, a 75-millimeter gun, two 7.9-millimeter machine guns, and a five-man crew. The Panther was used not only against the Russians but also in defense of the western front against the Anglo-American invasion of Normandy on June 6, 1944. The Panther was probably the best tank built by any nation during the war.

A Panther tank knocked out by American guns in France. [*US Army*]

PANZER (Pz; Tank). German armored vehicle used by the Wehrmacht (q.v.). Under the terms of the Treaty of Versailles, Germany was forbidden the use of tanks in the armed forces of the Weimar Republic (q.v.). Because of this restriction Col. Gen. Hans von Seeckt (q.v.), who was responsible for postwar military reconstruction, turned his attention to the creation of a small, highly mobile force. His subordinate, Capt. (later Gen.) Heinz Guderian (q.v.), stressed the use of tanks for both assault and exploitation. As early as 1928, tanks were built secretly and tested in Russia. After Hitler occupied the Rhineland in 1936, he ordered the manufacture of tanks in defiance of treaty restrictions. *Panzers* were tested in the Spanish Civil War (1936), the Austrian *Anschluss* (q.v.; 1938), and the annexation of Czechoslovakia (1939). They played an important role in the *Blitzkrieg* (q.v.) against Poland (1939) and also against France (1940). Success lay in a combination of assault power and mobility. In integrated formations infantry in armored vehicles were always ready to clear pockets of resistance left by the armor. *Panzers* worked in close coordination with artillery and dive bombers. This was the height of German military success in the war. From 1943 on, the *Panzer* forces were generally on the defensive.

Panzer divisions were formed originally from the infantry. On mobilization in 1939 each tank battalion was reduced to three companies, one of medium and two of light tanks. For the invasion of France in 1940, ten *Panzer* divisions were employed with thirty-five tank battalions between them. Later the number of *Panzer* divisions was doubled by halving the number of tanks in each division and increasing the infantry components. In February 1941 some armored units were sent to Libya to help the Italians. The 21st and 15th Panzer Divisions were combined to form the celebrated Afrika Korps (q.v.). Despite the military genius of Gen. Erwin Rommel (q.v.), the *Panzer* units in North Africa found themselves in severe difficulties because of the excessively long lines of communications. The Afrika Korps ceased to exist after it surrendered in Tunisia in 1943. There were heavy tank losses on the Soviet front in 1942 and 1943. The year 1943 saw the creation of the first SS (q.v.) *Panzer* divisions. There were some spectacular victories in the Soviet Union, where the terrain favored armored divisional operations. *Panzer* forces were close to final victory but never managed to defeat the Russians.

See also PANTHER TANK.

Franz von Papen *[Picture Collection, The Branch Libraries, The New York Public Library]*

PAPEN, FRANZ VON (1879–1969). Politician and statesman who played a major role in Hitler's drive to power. Franz von Papen was born in Werl, Westphalia, on October 29, 1879, to a wealthy, noble family. Choosing a military career, he became a lieutenant in a cavalry regiment in 1907 and was transferred as a captain to the General Staff in 1913. After serving as a military attaché in Mexico, he was sent to a similar post in Washington during World War I. There he became notorious for his clumsy secret service activities and was expelled as *persona non grata*. In 1918 he was sent as a lieutenant general to serve as chief of staff with the Turkish Fourth Army in Palestine.

After the war Von Papen resigned his commission and entered politics. From 1921 to 1932, as a member of the extreme right wing of the Catholic Center party, he represented the agrarian interests of his constituency in the Prussian Landtag (Legislature). Failing to win a seat in the German Reichstag (q.v.), he joined the industrialist Florian Klückner in acquiring control of *Germania*, the leading Catholic daily newspaper. He became chairman of its management committee. At the same time his marriage to the daughter of a Saar industrialist brought him valuable connections as well as access to a large fortune.

Scarcely a technically proficient professional, Von Papen was never taken seriously in politics. His ambition was clouded by his indifference and a happy-go-lucky air. A man of impeccable social grace, he was also a confirmed reactionary who thought in outdated terms. He identified his own interests as a member of the upper echelon of society with those of the state and supported the antiparliamentarian, antirepublican right. He clothed both his monarchism and his nationalism in a kind of pseudo-Christian vocabulary, which won him little popular understanding or support. Von Papen was a member of the highly conservative Herrenklub (q.v.), the Gentlemen's Club, which regarded itself as fitted by divine right, position, and wealth to control the destinies of Germany. He took as much advantage as he could of his links to the clergy as a Catholic nobleman, to the Reichswehr (q.v.) as a former General Staff officer, and to Rhineland industrialists through his wife's family.

In the presidential elections of 1932 Von Papen supported not the candidate of his own political party but Field Marshal Paul von Hindenburg (q.v.). On June 1, 1932, despite his lack of experience in administration, he was appointed, with the support of Gen. Kurt von Schleicher (q.v.), to the chancellorship to succeed Heinrich Bruening (q.v.). When the news was confirmed, André François-Poncet, the French Ambassador at Berlin, wrote: "It was greeted at first with incredulous amazement. Everyone smiled. There is something about Von Papen that prevents either his friends or his enemies from taking him entirely seriously. He bears the stamp of frivolity. He is not a personality of the first rank." Von Papen formed a conservative Cabinet composed of four barons and a count, none of whom had majority support in the Reichstag. Ridiculed for his "Cabinet of barons," Von Papen made it clear that he intended to return German society to its traditional class foundations.

Meanwhile, Von Papen had to face the annoying problem of what to do with Hitler. In conformity with a pledge by Von Schleicher, Von Papen lifted the ban on the SA (q.v.) and called for new elections to the Reichstag. In June–July 1932 he managed to bring an end to reparations, an achievement prepared by Bruening. On July 20, in a show of strength, he deposed the Social Democratic administration of Otto Braun (q.v.) in Prussia and assumed control himself as Reich Commissioner for Prussia. He was unable to win a majority vote in the Reichstag elections of November 6, 1932. His Minister of Defense, Von Schleicher, alienated by Von Papen's increasingly reactionary policies, refused to support him any longer. Von Schleicher convinced Von Hindenburg that he should dismiss Von Papen from all his offices on December 3, 1932. The President then requested Von Schleicher himself to form a new Cabinet.

Von Papen was determined to strike back at Von Schleicher. On January 4, 1933, he had a historic interview with Hitler at the Cologne home of an intermediary, the wealthy banker Kurt Freiherr von Schroeder (q.v.). Angered by Von Schleicher's treatment, Von Papen prevailed upon the elderly Von Hindenburg to make Hitler Chancellor on January 30, 1933. Von Papen became Vice-Chancellor. In placing himself at the disposal of the Nazis, Von Papen believed that he could control Hitler and once again rise to a position of supreme political power. This was a grotesque miscalculation.

As Vice-Chancellor, Von Papen had to participate, though unwillingly, in Hitler's consolidation of control. On June 17, 1934, in a speech at the University of Marburg, he called for a halt to Nazi excesses, the end of the revolution, and the restoration of normal decencies in the country (*see* MARBURGER REDE). He was horrified by the Blood Purge (q.v.) of June 30, 1934, in which some of his closest colleagues were killed and from which he barely escaped with his own life. Recovering in typical fashion, within a month he accepted from Hitler an appointment as Minister (from 1936, as Ambassador) to Vienna, where he worked for *Anschluss* (q.v.), union between Germany and Austria. He made certain to undermine the position of Austrian Chancellor Kurt von Schuschnigg (q.v.). Von Papen was recalled on March 10, 1938. From April 1939 to August 1944 he served as Ambassador to Turkey.

In April 1945 Von Papen was arrested in the Ruhr by troops of the United States Ninth Army. The next year he was brought to trial before the International Military Tribunal at Nuremberg (*see* NUREMBERG TRIAL). Disassociating himself from Nazi guilt, he claimed to be astonished by the indictment. "I believe that paganism and the years of totalitarianism bear the main guilt. Through both of these Hitler became a pathological liar in the course of the years." The court denounced him for his "intrigue and bullying" in the campaign for *Anschluss* but on October 1, 1946, acquitted him on all counts because "such offenses against political morality, however bad they may be, were not criminal." Once again Von Papen had come through a grave crisis unscathed. However, in February 1947 a German denazification court sentenced him to eight months' imprisonment as a major Nazi war criminal. He appealed, and in January 1949 he was found guilty only in a secondary degree and released. Von Papen died in Obersasbach, Baden, on May 2, 1969.

Bibliography. Tibor Koeves, *Satan in Top Hat: The Biography of Franz von Papen,* Alliance Book Corporation, New York, 1941; Franz von Papen, *Memoirs,* E. P. Dutton & Co., Inc., New York, 1953.

PAPENBURG. A concentration camp on Oldenburg Heath (*see* CONCENTRATION CAMPS). Nominally, Papenburg remained under control of the old law enforcement agencies because only criminals were supposed to be sent there. However, the exemption from SS (q.v.) administration was only temporary. Papenburg, too, eventually received political prisoners.

PARACHUTE TROOPS. *See* FALLSCHIRMTRUPPEN.

PARLIAMENT. *See* REICHSTAG.

PARTEIGENOSSE (Pg; Party Comrade). An ordinary member of the Nazi party in good standing.

PARTEIGERICHTE (Party Courts). Party tribunals of the Nationalsozialistische Deutsche Arbeiterpartei (q.v.), the Nazi party. These tribunals existed both during the years of Hitler's rise to power in Germany and in the days when the party ruled the Third Reich. Established by Hitler in 1921, the *Parteigerichte* developed from comparatively unimportant judicial committees into powerful bureaucratic mechanisms for controlling party members. They were set up at the *Gau* (q.v.), or district, level. The courts were expected to guard and maintain the purity of the Nordic race. They served to protect the political unity of the Third Reich by dealing with such "enemies of the state" as Jews, Communists, and liberals. They also had authority to hold party members in line by subjecting them to loss of employment, social banishment, and prison terms.

In many ways the *Parteigerichte* were the key to the party's control over its members. Much of the courts' effectiveness was due to the party's chief justice, Walter Buch, who played an important role in party leadership as the highest disciplinary authority after the Fuehrer. The system of party courts revealed justice as an instrument of political power and the special interests of Hitler as the leader of a charismatic and totalitarian movement.

PARTEITAGE (Party Days). *See* NUREMBERG RALLIES.

PARTY COMRADE. *See* PARTEIGENOSSE.

PARTY COURTS. *See* PARTEIGERICHTE.

PARTY GOLDEN BADGE OF HONOR. *See* GOLDENES PARTEIABZEICHEN.

PARTY SCHOOL FOR ORATORS. *See* REDNERSCHULE DER NSDAP.

PASTORS' EMERGENCY LEAGUE. *See* PFARRENBUND.

PATROL SERVICE. *See* STREIFENDIENST.

PATRON MEMBER OF THE SS. *See* FÖRDERNDE MITGLIED DER SS.

PAULUS, FRIEDRICH (1890–1957). General field marshal in the armed forces and the losing commander at the Battle of Stalingrad. Friedrich Paulus was born in Breitenau, Melsungen District, on September 23, 1890. From September 1940 to January 1942 he was *Oberquartiermeister* 1 (senior quartermaster) in operations of the Oberkommando des Heeres (q.v.). From December 30, 1941, to February 1, 1943, he was in command of the Sixth Army in its assault on Stalingrad as *Generalleutnant* (lieutenant general). Caught in the Stalingrad pocket under severe Russian pressure, Paulus saw his supplies cut off and his ammunition dwindling. He recommended a temporary retreat, but Hitler refused to allow him to move an inch backward: "I have considered the situation carefully. My conclusion remains unaltered. The Sixth Army will stay where it is. I am not leaving the Volga."

On news of the defeat at Stalingrad, Hitler went into a fury and ordered that the epaulets be torn from the uniform of a corps commander, who was then to be thrown into jail. On January 31, 1943, he made Paulus a general field marshal and issued a new order: "The forces of the Sixth Army will henceforth be known as Fortress Stalingrad." By this time Paulus's Sixth Army, which in 1940 smashed the Netherlands and Belgium, had been cut to pieces with 100,000 casualties. From the cellars and caves of Stalingrad streamed the last 12,000 ragged and hungry German troops, including Paulus and his staff. The angered Fuehrer insisted that Paulus was afraid of suicide: he and his troops, said Hitler, should have closed ranks and died to the last man. After the war Paulus joined the Nationalkomitee Freies Deutschland (q.v.), the National Committee for a Free Germany, a Soviet puppet organization. After his release from a Russian prison in 1953 he settled in the German Democratic Republic (DDR).

PEENEMÜNDE. Wooded island in the Baltic where German scientists worked on the *Vergeltungswaffen* (q.v.), the secret reprisal weapons of World War II. In May 1942, Allied photographic reconnaissance planes revealed that some kind of long-range rocket experimentation was going on at Peenemünde. The island was given top priority as a target. In August 1943 a huge force of Royal Air Force bombers blasted the island. Allied air attacks were also made on rail-served rocket-launching sites along the French coast between Calais and Cherbourg. *See also* BRAUN, Wernher Freiherr von.

PEIPER, JOCHEN (1915–). *Sturmbannfuehrer* (major) in the SS (q.v.). Peiper commanded a combat group of Waffen-SS (q.v.), which killed seventy-one American prisoners at Malmédy crossroads on December 17, 1944. He was condemned to death on July 16, 1946, but was later reprieved.

PEOPLE BECOMING ITSELF. *See* VOLKWERDUNG.

PEOPLE WITHOUT SPACE. *See* VOLK OHNE RAUM.

PEOPLE'S APARTMENT. *See* VOLKSWOHNUNG.

PEOPLE'S ARMY. *See* VOLKSSTURM.

PEOPLE'S CAR. *See* VOLKSWAGEN.

PEOPLE'S COURT. *See* VOLKSGERICHT.

PEOPLE'S OFFICER. *See* VOLKSOFFIZIER.

PERSONALHAUPTAMT (Main Personnel Office). Department responsible for the records of all SS (q.v.) officers.

PÉTAIN, [HENRI] PHILIPPE [BENONI OMER JOSEPH] (1856–1951). Marshal of France, hero of World War I, and collaborator with the Third Reich in World War II. Philippe Pétain was born in Cauchy-la-Tour, Pas-de-Calais, on May 24, 1856, to a peasant family. After his graduation from the military academy at Saint-Cyr in 1878, he was commissioned in the Army. He studied at the École de Guerre and held various staff appointments. In 1910 he was promoted to colonel. In the opening weeks of World War I he acquitted himself with distinction while commanding an infantry regiment. As a reward he was given command first of a brigade and then of a division. In May 1915 he led his troops through German defenses near Arras. In February 1916 he was assigned the task of stopping the Germans at Verdun. It was largely due to his organizational ability and energy that Verdun was saved. From then on his name was associated with the slogan *"Ils ne passeront pas!"* ("They shall not pass!"). On May 15, 1916, Pétain was promoted to commander in chief of the French armies in the field. He prepared the great offensives of August 8 and September 26, 1918, against the Germans. On November 21, 1918, he was awarded the baton of *maréchal de France* (marshal of France). Pétain also received high honors from the Allied governments. He was now regarded throughout France as one of the great heroes of French history.

Marshal Philippe Pétain. [Life, *April 29, 1940*]

Pétain's reputation was shattered in World War II. In May 1940 he was called into the Cabinet as Vice-Premier. By this time he had come to the conclusion that a Hitler victory was inevitable. He urged an immediate capitulation so that France could obtain favorable terms from the Nazi Fuehrer. He warned that if France continued to fight against superior German forces, it faced a total collapse. On June 16, 1940, he formed a Cabinet and asked Hitler for an armistice. On June 26, he told the French people of the humiliating terms imposed by Hitler.

Pétain now became Chief of State, a post in which he acted as a collaborator with the Third Reich. Together with Pierre Laval (q.v.), he abolished the republican constitution and set up a dictatorship in conquered France. On July 10, 1940, the National Assembly at Vichy gave him the right to rule France along authoritarian lines. He began the task of purging the country of "moral decadence." When German troops overran France in November 1942 as a response to Allied landings in North Africa, Pétain became little more than a German puppet. He retired from active duty by the end of 1943.

At the end of the war Pétain's name was detested by most Frenchmen. He never ceased to claim that he had saved his countrymen from a terrible fate by collaborating with Hitler and the Nazis. When the Allied invasion of France took place on June 6, 1944, Pétain appealed to all Frenchmen to "remain out of it." Under German threats he was forced to leave Vichy and accompany the Germans eastward, first to Belfort and then to Sigmaringen. In April 1945 he returned voluntarily to France, where he was arrested and interned. In July 1945 he was tried for treason by the French High Court of Justice. He was found guilty and sentenced to death, but the punishment was commuted to life imprisonment. Taken to the Île d'Yeu, he died in Port-Joinville on July 23, 1951. To his last day he insisted that he had saved his people. "The French people will never forget that I saved them [at Vichy] as I had saved them at Verdun."

Bibliography. Richard Griffiths, *Marshal Pétain*, Constable & Co., Ltd., London, 1970.

PFARRENBUND (Pastors' Emergency League). An organization of pastors set up by Dr. Martin Niemoeller (q.v.) in 1934 to defend the Lutheran Church against the inroads of Hitler's proposed German Faith movement (Deutsche Glaubensbewegung, q.v.).

PFLEGE (Care). A special eugenics and hygiene course held in schools for Nazi girls.

PG. *See* PARTEIGENOSSE.

PHILISTINE. *See* SPIESSER.

PHONY WAR. *See* SITZKRIEG.

PIEFKE. A derisory epithet used by Nazis to describe north Germans.

PIMPF. A member of the Jungvolk (q.v.), the branch of the Hitler Jugend (q.v.), the Hitler Youth, for boys ten to fourteen years of age. Each *Pimpf* was required to undergo an initiation test, which consisted of condensed versions of Nazi dogma (*Schwertworte*, q.v.), all the verses of the "Horst Wessel Lied" (q.v.), running 60 meters in twelve seconds, and taking part in a cross-country hike of a day and a half. As a *Pimpf* he was expected to learn to read semaphore signals, to lay telephone wires, and also to participate in small arms drill. After various tests he was eligible for the Hitler Youth proper.

PIMPFENPROBE (Boys' Examination). A special promotion examination for the *Pimpfe* (*see* PIMPF).

PISCATOR, ERWIN (1893–1966). Director, theater manager, and prominent refugee from the Third Reich. Erwin Piscator was born in Ulm, Wetzlar District, on December 17, 1893. In 1920, as a Communist and pacifist, he established the Proletarian Theater in Berlin. After its failure he became senior director of the Berlin Volksbühne (People's Stage). There he introduced such revolutionary techniques as film projections and loudspeakers to accompany stage dialogue. Piscator was among the first directors to present classical plays in modern dress and to introduce the so-called documentary theater. Sensing a Hitler victory as early as 1931, he left Berlin and became active at theaters in Moscow, Paris, and New York. In New York he presented the works of Arthur Miller and Tennessee Williams in his unique style. After the fall of the Third Reich he returned to West Germany. From 1962 until his death he renewed his form of political documentary for the Theater der Freien Volksbühne (Theater of the Free People's Stage) in Berlin. He died at Starnberg on March 30, 1966.

Erwin Piscator. [*Picture Collection, The Branch Libraries, The New York Public Library*]

Pope Pius XI. [*Brown Brothers*]

PIUS XI (1857–1939). Pope of the Catholic Church from 1922 to 1939. Achille Ratti was born in Desio, near Milan, on May 31, 1857. After study at the Lombard College in Rome, he won a triple doctorate in philosophy, theology, and law. From 1882 to 1886 he taught theology in Milan. Beginning in 1888 he served as director of the Ambrosian Library in Milan, and in 1912 he was called to Rome to administer the Vatican Library. In 1918 he became Apostolic Nuncio to Poland and in 1919 titular Archbishop of Lepanto. In 1921 he was named Archbishop of Milan and then Cardinal. Cardinal Ratti was elected Pope in 1922. A brilliant scholar, Pius XI extended the diplomatic relationships of the Holy See. He resolved the Roman question in 1929 by the Lateran Treaty with Mussolini and a concordat between the church and the Italian government whereby the temporal power of the papacy was restored. Two years later he issued a famous letter, *Non abbiamo bisogno*, protesting against the pagan worship of the state by Italian Fascists. With the assistance, among others, of Eugenio Pacelli, his Cardinal Secretary of State (*see* PIUS XII), he concluded eighteen concordats and treaties, among them those with Bavaria (1924), Prussia (1929), Baden (1932), the Third Reich (1933), and Austria (1934).

On March 14, 1937, Pius XI issued an extraordinary encyclical on the condition of the church in Germany. Titled *With Deep Anxiety* (*Mit brennender Sorge*, q.v.), it protested against the violations of natural law and justice in Nazi Germany. The Pope reminded Hitler that man as a human being possessed rights that must be preserved against every attempt by the community to deny, suppress, or hinder them. He accused Nazi Germany of violating the terms of the Concordat of 1933 (q.v.) and deplored the illegal and inhuman persecution of Catholics. The same week he condemned atheistic communism in a letter titled *Divini redemptoris*. Pius XI died in Rome on February 10, 1939.

PIUS XII (1876–1958). Pope of the Catholic Church from 1939 to 1958. Eugenio Pacelli was born in Rome on March 2, 1876. From 1904 to 1914 he was professor of ecclesiastical diplomacy at Rome. In 1917 he became titular Archbishop of Sardis and Nuncio to Bavaria (until 1925), and in 1920 Nuncio to Germany as a whole (until 1929). Made a Cardinal in 1929, he became Secretary of State in 1930. A master diplomat, Cardinal Pacelli was instrumental in

Pope Pius XII granting a private audience in the Vatican to men of the Allied forces. [*US Army*]

concluding on behalf of Pope Pius XI (q.v.) a series of concordats and treaties. He was the chief adviser to Pius XI on an anti-Nazi stand, and his election as Pius's successor was widely interpreted as a continuation of the Vatican's attitude toward the Hitler regime.

Pius XII made vain efforts to prevent World War II by mediation. In December 1939 he denounced "premeditated aggression and the contempt for freedom and human life which originate acts crying to God for vengeance." In his Christmas message of 1942 he spoke of his sorrow for "the hundreds of thousands of people who, through no fault of their own and solely because of their nation or their race, have been condemned to death or progressive extinction." On April 30, 1943, he sent a letter to the Archbishop of Berlin: "It is superfluous to say that Our paternal love and solicitude are greater today toward non-Aryan or semi-Aryan Catholics, children of the Church like the others, when their outward existence is collapsing and they are going through moral distress. Unhappily, in present circumstances, We cannot offer them effective help other than through our prayers." In the fall of 1943 the Nazis began rounding up 8,000 Jews in Rome, 1,000 of whom, mostly women and children, were sent off to the extermination center at Auschwitz (q.v.). Some 7,000 Jews went into hiding, 4,000 in monasteries. The Vatican remained silent. This silence continued when an Italian law promulgated on December 1, 1943, provided for the internment of all Jews and the confiscation of their property. Pius XII died in Castel Gandolfo on October 9, 1958.

After the war Pius XII was subjected to criticism because of his silence in the face of Nazi mass murder. Rolf Hochhuth's play *Der Stellvertreter* (*The Deputy*, 1963) aroused international controversy. Publication of documents by various official sources since the war indicated that the Pope had received repeated reports through diplomatic and other channels concerning the mass slaughter of Jews in occupied Poland and deportations to death camps from Germany, France, the Netherlands, and other countries. It was charged that he did not view the plight of the Jews with an expected sense of moral outrage or real urgency. Furthermore, it was said that he ignored calls for the excommunication of Hitler. Those who defended the Pope insisted that public protests would have been unsuccessful in helping the Jews and might well have caused additional danger for Catholics in Nazi-occupied Europe. It was necessary, they said, that the Vatican preserve its good name with the Germans, and it could not risk the charge that it lacked a sense of neutrality. Moreover, it was said, the Vatican did not wish to undermine the German struggle against Soviet Russia. The controversy over the "silence" of Pius XII has not been resolved and continues to the present day.

Bibliography. Saul Friedländer, *Pius XII and the Third Reich: A Documentation*, Alfred A. Knopf, Inc., New York, 1966.

PK. *See* PROPAGANDA-KOMPAGNIEN.

PLANCK, ERWIN (1893–1945). Civil servant and member of the Resistance (q.v.) movement. Erwin Planck was born in Berlin on March 12, 1893, the son of Max Planck, the internationally known physicist. Wounded in World War I, he was taken prisoner by the French and exchanged as a prisoner of war in 1917. Turning to the civil service, he worked in various positions. He became Undersecretary in the Reich Chancellery in 1932 and in this post served Chancellors Franz von Papen and Kurt von Schleicher (qq.v.). When Hitler came to political power in 1933, Planck resigned and turned to the private study of economics, political science, and history, accepting a post with a business firm. He was arrested on July 23, 1944, after the failure of the July Plot (q.v.). Found guilty of treason by the Volksgericht (q.v.), the People's Court, he was executed at Plötzensee Prison in Berlin on January 23, 1945.

PLATTFUSSINDIANERN (Flatfoot Indians). Term of derision applied to Jews by Nazi speakers. It was a favorite term of Hans Frank (q.v.), Governor-General of occupied Poland.

PLÖTZENSEE. A prison in Berlin. Many conspirators of the July Plot (q.v.) of 1944, including Christian Albrecht Ulrich von Hassell, Johannes Popitz, Helmuth James Graf von Moltke, and Julius Leber (qq.v.), were executed at Plötzensee.

POELZL, KLARA. *See* HITLER, KLARA POELZL.

POHL, OSWALD (1892–1951). *SS-Obergruppenfuehrer* (general) in charge of works projects for inmates of concentration camps (q.v.). Oswald Pohl was born in Duisburg on June 30, 1892. He joined the Nazi party in 1926.

While serving as a naval officer, he joined the SA (q.v.), the Storm Troopers, in 1929. In 1934 he left his post as a senior paymaster in the Navy to become chief administrative officer of the Reichssicherheitshauptamt (q.v.), the Reich Central Security Office. In 1939 he was made a ministerial director. At this time he became a member of the Circle of Friends of Heinrich Himmler (Freundeskreis Heinrich Himmler, q.v.). From 1942 to 1945 he was a general in the Waffen-SS (q.v.). During these years he also served as chief of the Wirtschafts- und Verwaltungshauptamt (q.v.), the Economic and Administrative Central Office of the SS (q.v.). In this post he had charge of all concentration camps and was responsible for all works projects. He saw to it that valuables taken from Jewish inmates were returned to Germany (*see* CANADA) and supervised the melting down of gold teeth taken from inmates (*see* MAX HEILIGER DEPOSIT ACCOUNT).

After the defeat of the Third Reich, Pohl went into hiding. Arrested in May 1946 while disguised as a farmhand, he was tried on November 3, 1947, by a United States military tribunal and sentenced to death. He was hanged at Landsberg Prison on June 8, 1951.

"POLISH BUSINESS." *See* "POLNISCHE WIRTSCHAFT."

POLITICAL ALARM SQUADS. *See* POLITISCHE BEREITSCHAFTEN.

POLITICAL TESTAMENT, HITLER'S. *See* HITLER'S POLITICAL TESTAMENT.

POLITISCHE BEREITSCHAFTEN (Political Alarm Squads). Units set up by Heinrich Himmler (q.v.) to protect himself and other Nazi leaders.

POLITISCHE ZENTRALKOMMISSION (PZK; Central Political Commission). A general Nazi party commission established during the reorganization of the party in December 1932.

"POLNISCHE WIRTSCHAFT" ("Polish Business"). Metaphor used by Nazi leaders before and after 1933 to indicate a milieu of chaos in Poland. Stress was placed on the "bleeding frontiers of the east," a reference to the loss of territory in Prussia brought about by the formation of the Polish Corridor by the Treaty of Versailles. To Hitler and his followers the Poles were subhuman Slavic racial types. According to Nazi ideology, an independent Poland stood directly in the way of legitimate German expansion.

POPITZ, JOHANNES (1884–1945). Jurist, Prussian minister of finance, and leading civilian member of the Resistance (q.v.) movement. Johannes Popitz was born in Leipzig on December 2, 1884. A brilliant scholar, he studied law, economics, and political science and embarked on a highly successful career in legal administration. In 1919 he served as Privy Councillor and in 1925 as State Secretary in the Reich Ministry of Finance. An honorary professor at the University of Berlin, he was also a member of the Wednesday Club (Mittelwochgesellschaft, q.v.), a small group of intellectuals who met weekly to discuss common interests. In 1933 Hitler named Popitz Minister without Portfolio and Reich Commissioner for the Prussian Ministry of Finance. Until 1944 Popitz held the posts of Prussian state minister and minister of finance. The Fuehrer regarded his services as so valuable that he awarded him the Party Golden Badge of Honor (*Goldenes Parteiabzeichen*, q.v.).

On his side, however, Popitz had only contempt for Hitler and secretly traveled the road from opposition to resistance to conspiracy. A monarchist, he attempted unsuccessfully to persuade his fellow conspirators to support the Hohenzollern Crown Prince as successor to Hitler (*see* WILHELM, Crown Prince). Popitz even proposed the name of Heinrich Himmler (q.v.) for that role and initiated careful negotiations with Himmler on behalf of the plotters.

In the summer of 1943 Popitz, together with Carl Langbehn (q.v.), visited Himmler and attempted to gain his support for a coup d'état. Popitz described Hitler as a genius but insisted that the war was lost and that Himmler must join in an attempt to negotiate a satisfactory peace. Himmler said nothing. Later Langbehn was arrested, but Popitz was allowed his freedom so that the Gestapo (q.v.), on the Fuehrer's orders, could watch him and collect "incriminating evidence."

Popitz was arrested the day after the tragic fiasco of the 1944 July Plot (q.v.). He was condemned to death before the Volksgericht (q.v.), the People's Court, on October 3, 1944. His execution was delayed for four months, primarily through the intercession of Himmler, who sensed that Popitz might be useful to him as a possible intermediary with the Western Allies through Sweden and Switzerland. Himmler's intervention ultimately failed, and Popitz was hanged at Plötzensee Prison on February 2, 1945.

POSITIVE CHRISTIANITY. Religious philosophy professed by Alfred Rosenberg (q.v.), intellectual leader of the Third Reich, in the early days of the Nazi movement. Rosenberg never explained his thesis adequately, but he regarded his concept of Christianity as a transitional stage toward the complete rejection of both Catholicism and Protestantism. The goal of positive Christianity, he said, was to purify the German Nordic race, harmonize belief in Christ with "the laws of blood and soil," restore the old pagan Nordic values, and substitute the spirit of the hero for that of the Crucifixion. Christianity would then become one with the old Norse paganism as a new religion. The symbol of positive Christianity was the orb of the sun. Hitler, who was violently opposed to Christian ethics, was careful not to take a public stand in defense of the new religion, but he was sympathetic to it and gave it his approval. In 1934, after Hitler became Chancellor, the German Faith movement (Deutsche Glaubensbewegung, q.v.), which emphasized the goals of positive Christianity, came into existence.

POTEMPA CASE. A notorious political murder openly approved by Hitler. On the night of August 9, 1932, in the village of Potempa in Upper Silesia, five Nazis armed with revolvers broke into the home of a Communist miner, Konrad Pietrzuch. The entire family, including Pietrzuch, his mother, and his brother, were in bed. The intruders pulled Pietrzuch out of bed, threw him to the floor, and trampled him to death. The five assailants were caught and sentenced to death. Hitler sent them a telegram: "My comrades! I am bound to you in unlimited loyalty in the face of this most hideous blood sentence. You have my picture hanging in your cells. How could I forsake you?" Hitler denounced Pietrzuch as not only a Communist but also a Pole and, therefore, an enemy of Germany: "Anyone who struggles, lives, fights, and, if need be, dies for Germany, has the right on his side." On March 21, 1934, Nazi authorities decreed an amnesty for crimes committed "for the good of the Reich during the Weimar Republic." The five slayers of Pietrzuch were released from prison.

POTSDAM PUTSCH. Unsuccessful attempt by high military officers to seize political power in January 1933 just before Hitler became Chancellor. After the resignation of Chancellor Heinrich Bruening (q.v.) on May 30, 1932, Franz von Papen (q.v.) headed a Nationalist Cabinet with the support of Gen. Kurt von Schleicher (q.v.), an influential Army leader. In December 1932 Von Schleicher brought about Von Papen's downfall and succeeded him as Chancellor. Von Schleicher, too, was compelled to resign a month later. On January 30, 1933, by legal means, Hitler became Chancellor of the German Republic. During this critical period, the generals who hated Hitler planned the Potsdam *Putsch*. They intended to proclaim a state of emergency, declare martial law, and set up a military dictatorship for a limited period. They expected to use Hitler and a modified form of National Socialism to obtain the support of the masses and then get rid of him. Indifferently organized, the contemplated coup d'état was unsuccessful.

POUR LE SÉMIT (For the Semite). A cynical punning of Pour le Mérite, the coveted high German military decoration awarded for merit. *Pour le Sémit* was used to describe the yellow star that Jews were required to wear on their clothing as a means of identification.

PREMILITARY TRAINING CAMPS. *See* WEHRERTÜCHTIGUNGSLAGER.

PRESS. *See* NEWSPAPERS IN THE THIRD REICH.

PREUSSEN, AUGUST WILHELM HEINRICH GÜNTHER, PRINZ VON (1887–1949). Hohenzollern prince and member of the Nationalsozialistische Deutsche Arbeiterpartei (q.v.), the Nazi party. Prince August Wilhelm, who was popularly known as Auwi, was born at the *Schloss* (palace) in Potsdam on January 29, 1887, the fourth of six sons (Crown Prince Wilhelm [q.v.], Eitel Friedrich, Adalbert, August Wilhelm, Oskar, and Joachim) of the Hohenzollern Prince Wilhelm. The latter was the Hohenzollern who in 1888 ascended the throne as Emperor William II. August Wilhelm attended schools at Potsdam and Plön, took his doctorate in political science, and passed state examinations in law. He served as a colonel in World War I. After the war he held many administrative posts in Prussia. In 1927 he joined the Stahlhelm (q.v.), the society of combat veterans, but resigned in 1929 after differences with its leaders. That year he joined the Nazi party.

August Wilhelm toured Germany lecturing on behalf of Hitler and the Nazi movement. In the spring of 1931 he was beaten during a police raid in Königsberg. He maintained his affiliation with Nazi organizations, especially the SA (q.v.), throughout his career. He advanced from *SS-Standartenfuehrer* (colonel) in 1931 to *SA-Oberfuehrer* (brigadier general) in 1933, *SA-Gruppenfuehrer* (lieutenant general) in 1932, and *SA-Obergruppenfuehrer* (general) in 1943. In 1932 he represented the Nazi party in the Prussian Landtag (Legislature) and in 1933 was elected a delegate to the Reichstag (q.v.) for Wahlkreis (Electoral District) Potsdam. Hitler named him to the Prussian State Council in 1933. Many leaders of the Resistance (q.v.) movement, who as monarchists wanted a restoration of the Hohenzollern dynasty, rejected August Wilhelm as their candidate because he remained a dedicated Nazi.

Deeply in awe of Hitler, August Wilhelm always addressed him as "*Mein Fuehrer.*" Although he was aware of Hitler's hostility to the former royal family and to princes in general, he nevertheless hoped to become the Hohenzollern regent. His oldest brother, the Crown Prince (1882–1951), openly approved Hitler's candidacy in the presidential elections of 1932. Prince Oskar, on the other hand, a member of the Stahlhelm before 1933, resigned in protest when it threw its support to Hitler. August Wilhelm died in Stuttgart on March 25, 1949.

PRIEN, GÜNTHER (1909–1941). Highly publicized U-boat commander and national hero in World War II. Günther Prien was born in Osterfeld and at the age of fifteen joined the Navy. He subsequently served as an officer for the Hamburg-Amerika Line but resigned in 1931. In 1933, on the accession of Hitler to political power, Prien was recalled to the Navy as an officer. On October 13–14, 1939, as a U-boat commander, he brought his craft through the bight at Scapa Flow, home port of the British Royal Navy in the Orkney Islands, and sank the battleship *Royal Oak* in one of the most spectacular exploits of the war.

At the close of World War I two U-boat commanders had attempted the identical feat of penetrating Scapa Flow, but both were destroyed in the process. From the start of World War II Adm. Karl Doenitz (q.v.) considered the possibility of attacking the British Fleet at its anchorage. Intelligence agents attached to the German High Command reported that aerial photographs revealed that an entry was possible by way of the narrow Kirk Sound passage. Doenitz chose Prien, then a lieutenant commander, to command the *U-47* for the task and swore him to secrecy. On the morning of October 13, 1939, while his U-boat lay on the seabed near the Orkneys, Prien briefed his crew. At nightfall he went ahead on his daring assignment. Although no moon was visible, the northern lights of the aurora borealis lit the sky.

In treacherous tides Prien navigated past the sunken ships that blocked Kirk Sound. He ran aground once but managed to get afloat and went through the sound at 12:27 A.M. on October 14. To the north he saw two battleships and several destroyers at anchor. Moving in close to the British ships, he fired three torpedoes from his bow tubes. One struck the *Royal Oak* but with little damage. Astonished by the lack of depth charges, which he had expected to be hurled at him from protective destroyers, Prien turned away. The *U-47* stayed on the surface while its crew hurriedly reloaded the torpedo tubes. At 1:16

Günther Prien. [*Imperial War Museum, London*]

A.M., Prien moved back and fired a second salvo, this time with devastating effect. Within fifteen minutes the giant *Royal Oak* turned on her side and sank; 24 officers and 800 men went down with her.

While the entire fleet at Scapa Flow stirred into action, Prien ordered full speed ahead. With incredibly good luck he was able to avoid an oncoming British destroyer by holding to the coast to protect his silhouette. He reached the narrows of Kirk Sound and managed to steer the *U-47* through the south side of the passage.

Prien and his crew reached their base safely. Prien was awarded the Iron Cross (First Class), and each member of the crew the Iron Cross (Second Class). The same day they were flown to Berlin to be received in audience with the Fuehrer. The feat was hailed with delight throughout Germany, and Prien was elevated to the status of a national hero. On March 17, 1941, while attacking a convoy, Prien was drowned in the Atlantic.

PRINZ ALBRECHTSTRASSE. The street in Berlin on which the headquarters of the Gestapo (q.v.) was located. In popular parlance Prinz Albrechtstrasse was used as a synonym for the Gestapo. Nazi authorities employed the term to arouse a sense of fear and dread in their listeners.

PRINZ REGENTENSTRASSE. Street in Munich where Hitler kept an apartment.

PRISONERS IN LIMITED-TERM PREVENTIVE CUSTODY. *See* BEFRISTETE VORBEUGUNGSHÄFTLINGE.

PRISONERS IN SECURITY CUSTODY. *See* SICHERUNGSVERWAHRTE.

PROPAGANDA, NAZI. In the National Socialist drive for political power and throughout the life of the Third Reich from 1933 to 1945 an intensive propaganda campaign was directed by Dr. Paul Joseph Goebbels (q.v.), Minister for Public Enlightenment and Propaganda. Much of the success won by Hitler and his movement was due to the remarkable talents of his Propaganda Minister. In the early days Goebbels made a thorough study of American advertising and promotion methods and applied them to his homeland. A keen student of the psychology of propaganda, he believed that it should always be used as a means to an end. He felt that propaganda that produced the desired results was good and that all other kinds were bad. Propaganda, he said, was by no means a second-rate profession; on the contrary, it was an art. It was far more effective when people did not know that they were being influenced. "Propaganda," said Goebbels, "can be taught by the average person, like playing a violin. But there comes a point at which one can say: 'This is where you stop. What remains to be learned can be achieved only by a genius!' What else was Jesus Christ? Did he not make propaganda? Did he write books or did he preach? And what about Muhammad? Did he compose sophisticated essays, or did he go to the people to tell them what he wanted? Were not Buddha and Zoroaster propagandists?"

In the National Socialist drive Goebbels transformed political rallies into pageants with music, flags, and parades, all dedicated to the idea that Hitler was a superman destined to save Germany (*see* NUREMBERG RALLIES). From his pen came a flood of slogans such as "The Jews are our misfortune" (*"Die Juden sind unser Unglück"*), "Blood and Soil" (*"Blut und Boden,"* q.v.), and "People without Space" (*"Volk ohne Raum,"* q.v.). His task was to keep the movement at fever pitch, and in this he was highly successful. In March 1933 Hitler created the Ministry for Public Enlightenment and Propaganda, with Goebbels as Minister and Cabinet member. The Propaganda Ministry was housed in the remodeled Leopold Palast opposite the Chancellery in Berlin. Insatiable for power, Goebbels took complete control of every means of molding the minds of Germans—press, radio, books, plays, music, art, commercial activities, and tourism. He sent propaganda attachés to all German embassies and legations abroad and also used special propaganda agents for special tasks. At least 300 officials and 500 employees worked for him on shifts through twenty-four hours a day. So well organized and effective was his work that a popular witticism held that the German government had become a subdivision of the Propaganda Ministry.

In World War II Goebbels was assigned the tasks of exploiting German victories in the early days of the conflict and of maintaining morale as the Allies gradually attained superiority. He directed the propaganda machine to explain the campaign against Poland, justify aggression against the Soviet Union, disparage the military strength of the United States, and demolish the characters of Winston Churchill and Franklin D. Roosevelt.

Goebbels's adroitness is revealed in this sample propaganda pamphlet written by him in 1930 when the Nazis were driving to political power. The capitalization recalls a similar practice in editorials written in a section of the American press.

> WHY ARE WE NATIONALISTS?
> WE are NATIONALISTS because we see in the NATION the only possibility for the protection and the furtherance of our existence.
> The NATION is the organic bond of a people for the protection and defense of their lives. He is nationally minded who understands this IN WORD AND IN DEED.
> Today, in GERMANY, NATIONALISM has degenerated into BOURGEOIS PATRIOTISM, and its power exhausts itself in tilting at windmills. It says GERMANY and means MONARCHY. It proclaims FREEDOM and means BLACK-WHITE-RED.

A German propaganda war poster: "Victory will be ours!" [*Imperial War Museum, London*]

Young nationalism has its unconditional demands. BELIEF IN THE NATION is a matter of all the people, not for individuals of rank, a class, or an industrial clique. The eternal must be separated from the contemporary. The maintenance of a rotten industrial system has nothing to do with nationalism. I can love Germany and hate capitalism; not only CAN I do it, I also MUST do it. The germ of the rebirth of our people LIES ONLY IN THE DESTRUCTION OF THE SYSTEM OF PLUNDERING THE HEALTHY POWER OF THE PEOPLE.

WE ARE NATIONALISTS BECAUSE WE, AS GERMANS, LOVE GERMANY. And because we love Germany, we demand the protection of its national spirit and we battle against its destroyers.

WHY ARE WE SOCIALISTS?

We are SOCIALISTS because we see in SOCIALISM the only possibility for maintaining our racial existence and through it the reconquest of our political freedom and the rebirth of the German state. SOCIALISM has its peculiar form first of all through its comradeship in arms with the forward-driving energy of a newly awakened nationalism. Without nationalism it is nothing, a phantom, a theory, a vision of air, a book. With it, it is everything, THE FUTURE; FREEDOM, FATHERLAND!

It was a sin of the liberal bourgeoisie to overlook THE STATE-BUILDING POWER OF SOCIALISM. It was the sin of MARXISM to degrade SOCIALISM to a system of MONEY AND STOMACH.

We are SOCIALISTS because for us THE SOCIAL QUESTION IS A MATTER OF NECESSITY AND JUSTICE, and even beyond that A MATTER FOR THE VERY EXISTENCE OF OUR PEOPLE.

SOCIALISM IS POSSIBLE ONLY IN A STATE WHICH IS FREE INSIDE AND OUTSIDE.

DOWN WITH POLITICAL BOURGEOIS SENTIMENT: FOR REAL NATIONALISM!

DOWN WITH MARXISM: FOR TRUE SOCIALISM!

UP WITH THE STAMP OF THE FIRST GERMAN NATIONAL SOCIALIST STATE!

AT THE FRONT THE NATIONAL SOCIALIST GERMAN WORKERS' PARTY! . . .

WHY DO WE OPPOSE THE JEWS?

We are ENEMIES OF THE JEWS, because we are fighters for the freedom of the German people. THE JEW IS THE CAUSE AND THE BENEFICIARY OF OUR MISERY. He has used the social difficulties of the broad masses of our people to deepen the unholy split between Right and Left among our people. He has made two halves of Germany. He is the real cause for our loss of the Great War.

The Jew has no interest in the solution of Germany's fateful problems. He CANNOT have any. FOR HE LIVES ON THE FACT THAT THERE HAS BEEN NO SOLUTION. If we would make the German people a unified community and give them freedom before the world, then the Jew can have no place among us. He has the best trumps in his hands when a people lives in inner and outer slavery. THE JEW IS RESPONSIBLE FOR OUR MISERY AND HE LIVES ON IT.

That is the reason why we, AS NATIONALISTS and AS SOCIALISTS, oppose the Jew. HE HAS CORRUPTED OUR RACE, FOULED OUR MORALS, UNDERMINED OUR CUSTOMS, AND BROKEN OUR POWER.

THE JEW IS THE PLASTIC DEMON OF THE DECLINE OF MANKIND.

THE JEW IS UNCREATIVE. He produces nothing. HE ONLY HANDLES PRODUCTS. As long as he struggles against the state, HE IS A REVOLUTIONARY; as soon as he has power, he preaches QUIET AND ORDER, so that he can consume his plunder at his convenience.

ANTI-SEMITISM IS UN-CHRISTIAN. That means, then, that he is a Christian who looks on while the Jew sews straps around our necks. TO BE A CHRISTIAN MEANS: LOVE THY NEIGHBOR AS THYSELF! MY NEIGHBOR IS ONE WHO IS TIED TO ME BY HIS BLOOD. IF I LOVE HIM, THEN I MUST HATE HIS ENEMIES. HE WHO THINKS GERMAN MUST DESPISE THE JEWS. The one thing makes the other necessary.

WE ARE ENEMIES OF THE JEWS BECAUSE WE BELONG TO THE GERMAN PEOPLE. THE JEW IS OUR GREATEST MISFORTUNE.

It is not true that we eat a Jew every morning at breakfast.

It is true, however, that he SLOWLY BUT SURELY ROBS US OF EVERYTHING WE OWN.

THAT WILL STOP, AS SURELY AS WE ARE GERMANS.

PROPAGANDA-KOMPAGNIEN (PK; Propaganda Units). Propaganda battalions used by Dr. Paul Joseph Goebbels (q.v.) to make World War II alive and fascinating on the home front. Before the outbreak of war Goebbels compiled a list of all newspapermen considered suitable for duty as war correspondents. These reporters attended an eight-week training course that included techniques of war reporting. During the opening years of Nazi victories Goebbels's propagandists wrote glamorous reports of magnificent victories. In the last year of the war the PK units were ordered to send in stories to raise morale on the home front. Goebbels described his special journalists as "cold-blooded and fearless" and as just as much exposed to danger as the man with the flame-thrower.

PROPERTY-OWNING BOURGEOISIE. *See* BESITZBÜRGERTUM.

PROTECTIVE CUSTODY. *See* SCHUTZHAFT.

PROTEKTORAT (Protectorate). Nazi-occupied Bohemia and Moravia.

PROTOCOLS OF THE ELDERS OF ZION. A famous forged publication used by Hitler in his campaign against the Jews. Most of it was copied from a French pamphlet published in 1864 as a polemic against Napoleon III. In Czarist Russia the secret political police used the *Protocols* to justify the government's persecution of the Jews. The *Protocols,* comprising twenty-four sections (in one version, twenty-seven), was supposed to be an authentic report of the minutes of a secret Zionist congress aiming at the overthrow of Christian civilization. The document professed to contain the program of one of the annual meetings held by an international Jewish government in Basel, Switzerland, simultaneously with the First Zionist Congress in 1897. The delegates were accused of entering into a conspiracy to blow up major buildings in the capitals of Europe, destroy the Aryan race, and set up a Jewish world state.

At the time of the Kishinev pogrom in Russia in 1903, a shortened form of the *Protocols* was published in the newspaper *Znania.* In 1905 Sergei Nilus edited a longer version, which was republished in 1907. After World War I the *Protocols* was translated into every European language as well as into Japanese, Chinese, and Arabic. Many editions appeared in Paris. In the United States the forgery appeared in Henry Ford's *Dearborn Independent.* The industrialist ceased publication after a lawsuit.

In 1921 *The Times* of London pronounced the *Protocols* a clumsy forgery compiled by the Czarist Okrana, the secret police, and based on the original pamphlet directed against Napoleon III. Historians and lawyers throughout the world, especially in Switzerland and South Africa, denounced the *Protocols.* On May 14, 1935, a law court in Bern described the publication as a forgery. Despite such decisions new editions of the *Protocols* appeared again and again in many languages.

In Nazi Germany the *Protokolle der Weisen von Zion* was used consistently in the drive against the Jews. Alfred Rosenberg (q.v.), leading advocate of Nazi philosophy, edited a German version. In *Mein Kampf* (q.v.), Hitler declared that "the entire being of these people [the Jews] rests on a continuing lie, as shown in unparalleled form in the *Protocols of the Elders of Zion,* so interminably hated by the Jews." In the Third Reich the *Protocols* was officially recommended by Nazi authorities for use in schools.

Bibliography. John S. Curtiss, *An Appraisal of the Protocols of Zion,* Columbia University Press, New York, 1942.

PROVISIONAL GOVERNMENT. The intended temporary regime to be set up by members of the Resistance (q.v.) in Germany after Hitler had been removed from office and executive power placed in the hands of the armed forces. After much discussion the various groups in the conspiracy agreed on common action. Included were Col. Gen. Ludwig Beck (q.v.), representing the older officers; another group under Col. Claus Schenk Graf von Stauffenberg (q.v.) and the younger officers; Dr. Carl Friedrich Goerdeler (q.v.) and the civilians; and members of the Kreisau Circle (q.v.). All groups had suggestions on the composition of the leadership of the new Reich. In one version the provisional government was to include the following:

Regent *(Reichsverweser)*: Col. Gen. Ludwig Beck
State Secretary to the Regent: Ulrich-Wilhelm Schwerin von Schwanenfeld
Chancellor: Dr. Carl Friedrich Goerdeler
State Secretary to the Chancellor: Peter Graf Yorck von Wartenburg
Vice-Chancellor: Wilhelm Leuschner (Social Democratic party)
Deputy Vice-Chancellor: Jacob Kaiser (Christian Trade Unions)
Minister for War: Gen. Friedrich Olbricht
Commander in chief, armed forces: Field Marshal Erwin von Witzleben
Commander in chief, Army: Col. Gen. Erich Hoepner
Minister of the Interior: Julius Leber (Social Democratic party)
State Secretary to the Minister of the Interior: Dr. Paul Lejeune-Jung
Minister of Justice: Joseph Wirmer (Center party)
Minister of Finance: Ewald Loeser (Nationalist party)
Minister of Education: Eugen Bolz (Center party)
Minister of Agriculture: Andreas Hermes
Minister of Information: Theodor Haubach (Social Democratic party)
Minister of Reconstruction: Bernhard Letterhaus (Christian Trade Unions)

PUBLIC PEACE. *See* BURGFRIEDE.

PUBLIC TRUSTEES OF LABOR. *See* TREUHÄNDER DER ARBEIT.

PUNISHMENT. Hitler's code name for his attack on the city of Belgrade. On March 27, 1941, the Fuehrer issued War Directive 25, in which he ordered: "As soon as we have sufficient forces available and the weather permits it, the ground installations of the Yugoslav Air Force and the city of Belgrade will be destroyed from the air by continual day and night attack." Accordingly, the Luftwaffe (q.v.) early on the morning of April 6, 1941, struck at Belgrade and reduced it to a mass of rubble. The city had no antiaircraft guns. A week later German and Hungarian troops entered the battered Yugoslav capital.

PZ. *See* PANZER.

PZK. *See* POLITISCHE ZENTRALKOMMISSION.

Q

QUESTIONNAIRE, THE
to
QUISLING, VIDKUN

QUESTIONNAIRE, THE. *See* FRAGEBOGEN, DER.

QUISLING, [LAURITZ] VIDKUN [ABRAHAM] (1887–1945). Norwegian politician widely regarded as the prototype of the puppet-traitor. Vidkun Quisling was born in Fyresdal, Telemarken, on July 18, 1887. In 1911 he was graduated from the Norwegian Military Academy as a junior officer. From 1922 to 1926 he worked for Fridtjof Nansen the celebrated explorer and scientist, and for the League of Nations, primarily in Russia. Returning to Norway in 1929, he entered politics as an anti-Communist. In 1931 he became Foreign Minister. Gradually gravitating toward fascism, he founded the Nasjonal Samling party in 1933. In December 1939 he warned Hitler about the possibility of a British occupation of Norway and advised him to forestall an invasion by occupying the country himself.

On April 9, 1940, on the German invasion of Norway, Quisling proclaimed himself Prime Minister. At first he was opposed by the Germans, who found that his fellow citizens refused to follow his orders. There was a change in policy in September 1940, when his party was declared the only legal one in Norway. On February 1, 1942, Hitler made Quisling his puppet Prime Minister. In this post Quisling took sharp measures against his opponents, and he quarreled openly with Josef Terboven (q.v.), the Nazi plenipotentiary for Norway.

Vidkun Quisling. *[Associated Press]*

On May 9, 1945, shortly after Germany's surrender in World War II, Quisling was arrested, tried, and sentenced to death. He was shot in Oslo on October 24, 1945. Because of his cooperation with Hitler, his name became synonymous with *traitor* not only in Norway but throughout the world.

Bibliography. Ralph Hewins, *Quisling: Prophet without Honor*, W. H. Allen & Co., Ltd., London, 1965.

R

RACE DEFILEMENT to RYAN, HERMINE BRAUNSTEINER

RACE DEFILEMENT. *See* RASSENSCHANDE.

RACE RESEARCH. *See* RASSENFORSCHUNG.

RACIAL COMMUNITY. *See* VOLKSGEMEINSCHAFT.

RACIAL COMRADES. *See* VOLKSGENOSSEN.

RACIAL DOCTRINE. The idea of racialism at the core of Hitler's *Weltanschauung* (q.v.), or world view. Racial doctrine played an important role in the history of the Third Reich. Emerging in the nineteenth century in the midst of a rising nationalism and its concomitant romanticism, German racialism acquired political and cultural significance. Not satisfied with proclaiming the superiority of the white over the colored races, racialists erected a hierarchy within the white race itself. To meet this need they developed the myth of Aryan superiority. This in turn became the source of secondary myths such as Teutonism (Germany), Anglo-Saxonism (England and the United States), and Celticism (France). The first step was the confusion of the Indo-European group of languages with a so-called Indo-European race. The term Indo-European was soon replaced by Indo-Germanic. This in turn became the Aryan, the creation of Friedrich Max Müller (q.v.) to designate a language group. Müller rejected the identification of race with language, but the damage was done. From this point on, racialists insisted that Aryan meant nobility of blood, incomparable beauty of form and mind, and a superior breed. Every worthwhile achievement in history, they said, was made by the Aryan race. All civilization, in their view, was the result of a struggle between the creative Aryan and the uncreative non-Aryan.

Racialism found a fruitful soil in Germany, where it became identified with nationalism. Early-nineteenth-century romanticism, with its accent on the vague, the mysterious, the emotional, and the imaginative, as opposed to reason, made a deep impression upon German intellectuals. Herder, Fichte, and other German romantics disagreed sharply with the *philosophes* of the Enlightenment, who used reason as a touchstone. The Germans held that each people had its own particular genius which, though deeply embedded in the past, would express itself ultimately in the national spirit, or *Volksgeist*. It was intimated that the *Volksgeist* was incontestably superior and had its own moral universe whose outward form was a distinctive national culture. This type of irrationalism, which took a strong hold on the German mind, stressed such vague concepts as thinking with the blood. Two non-German ideologists contributed much to this type of thinking, the Frenchman Arthur Comte de Gobineau and the Englishman Houston Stewart Chamberlain (qq.v.). Quite as influential in promoting this kind of racialism was the German composer Richard Wagner (q.v.), who insisted that the German hero spirit was inborn in those with Nordic blood. German racialists held that the Nordic was the best of the Aryan race. It followed that lower cultures could not prevail against the biologically ingrained combination of the Nordic mind, spirit, and physique.

Adolf Hitler, who worshiped at the Wagnerian shrine, made racial doctrine the cultural core of his Third Reich. In the stormy prose of *Mein Kampf* (q.v.) he condemned all of opposing opinions on race as "liars and traitors to civilization." History, he said, had proved with terrible clarity how each time Aryan blood became mixed with that of inferior peoples, the result was the end of the "culture-sustaining race." Germans, he warned, must not fall into the shame of race mixture. He spoke glowingly of a future German order, which he saw as a brotherhood of templars around the holy grail of pure blood. Bastardization of the German race was to be avoided; the main task of the state must be the preservation of ancient racial elements. The Aryan-Nordic, Hitler said, was the founder and maintainer of civilization; the Jews were the destroyers. Therefore, Germans must unite racially for a struggle between Nordic and Jewish races.

Hitler's racialism was legalized in the Nuremberg Laws on citizenship and race (q.v., issued in 1935). Citizenship was granted to "all subjects of German or kindred blood" but not permitted anyone classified as belonging to the Jewish race. With these laws racialism, hitherto distinguished mostly by vagueness, became for the first time the legal basis of a modern nation. It was responsible eventually for Hitler's Final Solution of the Jewish question (*see* ENDLÖSUNG, DIE). Inside Germany Hitler supported the discipline of *Rassenforschung* (q.v.), or race research. The new subject was to be investigated by Nazi scholars, and it was to be taught in all schools of the Third Reich from the lowest grades to the universities. Little attention was paid to the fact that German scholars who gave papers on race at world anthropological congresses were ridiculed by their peers.

At the base of Nazi racialism was the concept of racial purity. The decay of any nation, it was said, was always the result of race mixture: the fate of a nation depended upon the ability to maintain its racial purity. This notion, charged with emotion and vigorously defended, has no scientific basis. The peoples of the world have become so intermingled that there is scarcely a possibility of the existence of a pure race anywhere. Leading ethnologists and anthropologists, without important exceptions, agree that the juxtaposition of races has resulted in an inextricable tangle in which it is impossible to find a pure race. Most scientists agree that world society is an ethnological melting pot composed of energetic mongrels. They regard every civilized group of which we have record as hybrid, a fact contradicting the thesis that hybrid peoples are inferior to purebred ones. Jean Finot put it simply: *"La purité de sang n'est pas ainsi qu'un myth"* ("Purity of blood is nothing but a myth").

Equally untenable is the Nazi notion of racial superiority. The idea of ruling stocks is as old as history itself, but before the nineteenth century it was based on cultural, not racial, differences. Modern notions of racial superiority are motivated by the same psychological roots: fear and scorn of the unfamiliar. The sentiment is based on the instinct for self-preservation. Individuals and nations, like animals, tend to look upon the stranger as a natural enemy. Thus to some it becomes a matter of importance to develop a sense of racial superiority.

Competent biologists, ethnologists, and anthropologists agree that loose usage of the term race has led to confusion. Employing the word to justify Hitler's national ambitions is an example. Actually, there never was a German race but rather a German nation. There never was an Aryan race, but there were Aryan languages. There was no Roman race, but there was a Roman civilization. There never was a Jewish race, but there is a Jewish religion or culture. Outside the discipline of biology the word race tends to become meaningless. Race expresses the continuity of a physical type, representing an essentially biological grouping, and has nothing in common with the nationality, languages, or customs of historically developed social groups. In the biological sense a race is a group of related intermarrying individuals, a population that differs from other populations in the relative similarity of certain hereditary traits, of which color is only one characteristic. In the political sense, it takes on the quality of a meaningless fraud.

Even in its proper sense the word race still retains a vagueness difficult to overcome. Scientists have made many attempts to arrange the peoples of the world in some ordered classification, but they have been hampered by the fact that distinct lines of demarcation do not exist between the races. All such classifications are subjective and arbitrary. The first attempts to classify races on the basis of simple biological differences were inconclusive. Equally unsatisfactory were classifications by geography (by observing populations in given areas and searching for common characteristics), by history (by studying migrations of peoples), or by culture ("racial mentality") derived from cultural conditions. Examples of the last-named approach are Carl Gustav Carus's division into four races: European, African, Mongoloid, and American, based on "day, night, Eastern dawn, and Western dawn," and Gustav Friedrich Klemm's division into active (male) and passive (female) races, a division later accepted and elaborated by Gobineau. The development of anthropology in the nineteenth century introduced quantitative methods of distinguishing between races. The first step was the introduction in 1842 of the cephalic index, the percentage ratio of the length to the breadth of the skull, by the Swedish comparative anatomist Anders Adolf Retzius. Further attempts at classification were made in studies of somatic differentiations in skin color, hair, stature, eyes, nose, and face. The most impressive classification in the popular mind was the differentiation between five major types by color: white, black, brown, red, and yellow. This grouping of mankind became a convenient framework, but even here the variations within each group made it extremely difficult to ascertain sharp, clear-cut differentiations. Anatomical, linguistic, mental, and cultural traits are so deeply intertwined that it is hard to make any meaningful distinctions between the races. Even somatic characteristics may be influenced by environment acting directly through limitation of food supply, natural or artificial selection, habits of life, or chance. Certainly no one somatic quality is sufficient to demonstrate demarcation lines between races.

None of this type of thinking on a highly complex subject had the least influence on Hitler. So strongly convinced was the Fuehrer of his intuitions on a subject that has baffled scientists that he ordered a search for scientific and historical facts to rationalize his position. He rejected, as inconsequential, facts that destroyed Nazi racial doctrine at its roots. It is in the nature of modern dictatorships that their leaders, in addition to asserting political power, can set the tone for cultural coordination. In the Third Reich an entire nation was forced to accept the intuitions of a badly educated politician whose theories on racial matters actually belonged in a theater of the absurd.

Bibliography. Frank H. Hankins, *The Racial Basis of Civilization*, Alfred A. Knopf, Inc., New York, 1926; M. F. Ashley-Montagu, *Man's Most Dangerous Myth: The Fallacy of Race*, Columbia University Press, New York, 1946; Louis L. Snyder, *Race: A History of Modern Ethnic Theories*, Longmans, Green & Co., Ltd., New York, 1939.

RACIAL GROUP. *See* VOLKSGRUPPE.

RACIAL OBSERVER. *See* VÖLKISCHER BEOBACHTER.

RAD. *See* REICHSARBEITSDIENST.

RADIKALINSKIS. Term of derision applied to the radical,

or leftist, members of the Nazi hierarchy (*see* SECOND REVOLUTION).

RADIO. *See* RUNDFUNK.

RADIO IN THE THIRD REICH. Like all other means of communication in Nazi Germany, radio was subjected to *Gleichschaltung* (q.v.), or coordination. Soon after Hitler became Chancellor in 1933, he made Dr. Paul Joseph Goebbels (q.v.) Minister for Public Enlightenment and Propaganda, with full control of radio broadcasting. Asserting that the spoken word was much more effective than the printed word, Goebbels considered radio his No. 1 weapon in maintaining the Nazi state. "What the press has been in the nineteenth century," he said, "radio will be for the twentieth century."

In the Weimar Republic (q.v.), as in most of Europe, broadcasting had been a monopoly of the state. In March 1933 Goebbels transferred control of radio from the Postmaster General's office to his own Ministry of Propaganda. From then until the fall of the Third Reich in 1945, the German radio was controlled down to the smallest detail by Goebbels and his corps of propagandists. He placed the system under the supervision of an assistant, Eugen Hadamowsky, who was named head of the Chamber of Radio, a department of the Ministry. On August 16, 1933, Hadamowsky issued a report on what had been accomplished in a little more than a month: "We National Socialists must show enough dynamism and enthusiasm coupled with lightning speed to impress Germany and the whole world. Party comrade Dr. Goebbels ordered me on July 13 [1933], to purge the German radio of influence opposed to our cause. I can now report that the work has been done thoroughly."

Throughout the day and evening the German public heard broadcasts portraying the Fuehrer as the nation's most precious asset, describing the Nazi way of life as desirable, and emphasizing patriotism, nationalism, and the great mission of the Nordic Germans. Every listener was required to pay 2 marks a month (approximately $6 a year) for a license. At first Goebbels hoped to use this fund to make his Ministry of Propaganda self-supporting, but the effort failed when the Ministry developed into a colossus.

Goebbels also used the German radio as a propaganda weapon abroad. He was anxious to convey an impression of harmlessness in foreign countries. In 1933 he set up a five-year plan for foreign broadcasting. At first he ordered the shortwave system to feature operatic performances from Berlin, Dresden, and Munich and symphonic concerts from Leipzig. Then he gradually introduced subtle propaganda favorable to Nazism. Foreign countries were swamped with special broadcasts: Alsace-Lorraine was covered by radio from Frankfurt am Main; Belgium, by the Cologne transmitter; Denmark, by broadcasts from Hamburg and Bremen; Czechoslovakia, by shortwave from Breslau and Gleiwitz; and Austria, by radio from Munich. The rest of the world was reached by a huge broadcasting studio operating on 100,000 kilowatts from Seesen, near Berlin. Broadcasting began to the United States (1933); South Africa, South America, and East Asia (1934); and Central America and South Asia (1938). By this time shortwave broadcasts were being transmitted from Germany in twelve languages at every minute of the day and night.

At the beginning of World War II Goebbels was faced with a serious radio problem. Many Germans, bored with reiterative propaganda and suspecting slanted news, came to depend more and more on the British Broadcasting Corporation (BBC) for accurate news. Listening to these broadcasts was regarded as treasonable and was strictly forbidden. Most such listeners were never caught, but in the first year of the war more than 1,500 Germans were sent to concentration camps (q.v.) or to jail at hard labor for listening to London. In 1942 Hans Fritzsche (q.v.), former head of the Press Section of the Propaganda Ministry, returned from the eastern front to take control of the Radio Division. "Radio," he said, "must reach all or it will reach none."

Later in the war Moscow developed a method of synchronizing wavelengths so that Soviet radio experts could break in on the Deutschlandsender (q.v.; Transmitter Germany), the national broadcasting system. German listeners would suddenly hear an excited voice shouting "Lies! Lies!" and then a rapid explanation of what was claimed to be the "real truth." There were excellent imitations of the voices of Hitler and Goebbels. Frantic German studio staffs would generally interrupt their programs and substitute patriotic music. Most effective was the Russian promise to read the names of German prisoners of war, a technique that won large audiences for Russian shortwave broadcasts.

RAEDER, ERICH (1876–1960). Grand admiral and commander in chief of the German Navy. Erich Raeder was born in Wandsbek, near Hamburg, on April 24, 1876. His father was a language teacher at a secondary school, and his mother was the daughter of a musician. His middle-class origin did not prevent him from pursuing a successful career in the German Navy, which, unlike the Army, did not place a premium on a Prussian Junker background. Raeder attended the Naval Academy at Kiel for two years and as a young officer made a cruise to the Orient with a flotilla of warships. He was also assigned for duty on Emperor William II's yacht *Hohenzollern.* In the opening months of World War I he took part in mining operations and hit-and-run raids on the British coast. On May 31, 1916, he served in the Battle of Jutland, in which the British failed to destroy the German Fleet but managed to maintain their supremacy in the North Sea. In

Grand Adm. Erich Raeder. [*Life, April 29, 1940*]

1928 he was named *Chef der Marineleitung* (chief of the Naval Command).

Raeder was not a devoted Nazi such as Adm. Karl Doenitz (q.v.), but he was impressed by Hitler when he met him in 1933. He was made *Oberbefehlshaber der Kriegsmarine* (commander in chief of the Navy), a post he held until his retirement in 1943. In this capacity he played a central role in building and directing the new German Navy. When Hitler ordered his troops to march into the Rhineland in 1936, he was opposed by Raeder, who later admitted his mistake: "We won because Hitler had the stronger nerves and stuck it out." In 1937 Raeder accepted the National Socialist *Goldenes Parteiabzeichen* (q.v.) with the comment that National Socialism stemmed from the spirit of the German fighting soldier. He praised its "clear and unsparing summons to fight Bolshevism and intellectual Jewry, whose race-destroying actions we have suffered—the parasites of a foreign race." Raeder was one of the five men present at the Hossbach Conference (q.v.) on November 5, 1937, when Hitler bared his aggressive designs.

After declining the honor several times, Raeder finally accepted the rank of grand admiral in early 1939. In the first months of World War II he recommended to Hitler a projected invasion of Norway. In 1941 he opposed Hitler's attack on the Soviet Union, but once the decision was made, he sent his forces to harass Russian shipping in the Baltic Sea. His differences with Hitler gradually grew unbearable. He was retired on the Fuehrer's orders on January 30, 1943.

At the Nuremberg Trial (q.v.) before the International Military Tribunal, Raeder was accused of being, until his retirement, a major factor in building and directing the German Navy. He admitted that the German Navy had violated the Treaty of Versailles "as a matter of honor." Raeder was found guilty on three counts: count 1, conspiracy to commit crimes alleged in other counts; count 2, crimes against peace; and count 3, war crimes. He was sentenced to life imprisonment. Released on September 26, 1955, because of ill health, he died in Kiel on November 6, 1960.

Bibliography. Erich Raeder, *My Life*, tr. by Henry W. Drexel, United States Naval Institute, Annapolis, Md., 1960.

RAINBOW. *See* REGENBOGEN.

RALL, GÜNTHER (1918–). Ace fighter pilot for the Luftwaffe (q.v.) in World War II. Günther Rall was born in Gaggenau on March 10, 1918. He originally flew in Jagdgeschwader (Fighter Group) 52 with Maj. Erich Gerhard Barkhorn (q.v.) and later served with Group 11 and others. Rall was officially credited by Luftwaffe statisticians with 275 kills, of which 271 were on the eastern front. This was the third highest record of air victories after those of Maj. Erich Hartmann (q.v.) and Major Barkhorn. Like Hartmann and Barkhorn, Rall survived the war.

RANKS IN THE THIRD REICH. Comparative ranks in the German Army, the SS (q.v.), the Nationalsozialistische

GERMAN ARMY	SS	NSDAP	GERMAN POLICE	UNITED STATES ARMY
Generalfeldmarschall	*Reichsfuehrer-SS*	*Reichsleiter*		General of the army
Generaloberst	*SS-Oberstgrupenfuehrer*[1]	*Reichsleiter*	*Generaloberst der Polizei*	No exact equivalent
General	*SS-Obergruppenfuehrer*	*Gauleiter*	*General der Polizei*	General
Generalleutnant	*SS-Gruppenfuehrer*	*Deputy Gauleiter*	*Generalleutnant der Polizei*	Lieutenant general
Generalmajor	*SS-Brigadefuehrer*	*Deputy Gauleiter*	*Generalmajor der Polizei*	Major general
Oberst	*SS-Oberfuehrer*	*Deputy Gauleiter*	*Oberst der Schutzpolizei*	Brigadier general
Oberst	*SS-Standartenfuehrer*	*Deputy Gauleiter*	*Reichskriminaldirektor*	Colonel
Oberstleutnant	*SS-Obersturmbannfuehrer*	*Kreisleiter*	*Oberstleutnant der Gendarmerie*	Lieutenant colonel
Major	*SS-Sturmbannfuehrer*	*Kreisleiter*	*Major der Gendarmerie*	Major
Hauptmann (Rittmeister)	*SS-Hauptsturmfuehrer*	*Ortsgruppenleiter*	*Hauptmann der Gendarmerie*	Captain
Oberleutnant	*SS-Obersturmfuehrer*	*Zellenleiter*	*Oberstleutnant der Gendarmerie*	1st lieutenant
Leutnant	*SS-Untersturmfuehrer*	*Blockleiter*	*Leutnant der Gendarmerie*	2d lieutenant
Stabsfeldwebel	*SS-Sturmscharfuehrer*	*Hauptbereitschaftsleiter*	*Meister*	Sergeant major
Hauptfeldwebel	*SS-Stabsscharfuehrer*	*Hauptbereitschaftsleiter*	*Hauptwachtmeister*	Sergeant major
Oberfeldwebel	*SS-Hauptscharfuehrer*	*Oberbereitschaftsleiter*	*Kompaniehauptwachtmeister*	Master sergeant
Feldwebel	*SS-Oberscharfuehrer*	*Bereitschaftsleiter*	*Revieroberwachtmeister*	Technical sergeant
Unterfeldwebel	*SS-Scharfuehrer*	*Bereitschaftsleiter*	*Oberwachtmeister*	Staff sergeant
Unteroffizier	*SS-Unterscharfuehrer*	*Hauptarbeitsleiter*	*Wachtmeister*	Sergeant
Gefreiter	*SS-Rottenfuehrer*	*Oberarbeitsleiter*	*Rottwachtmeister*	Corporal
Oberschütze	*SS-Sturmmann*	*Arbeitsleiter*	*Unterwachtmeister*	Private 1st class
Schütze	*SS-Mann*	*Helfer*	*Anwärter*	Private

[1]1942 on.

Deutsche Arbeiterpartei, q.v. (NSDAP), the police, and the United States Army are shown in the table on page 280.

RASSE- UND SIEDLUNGSHAUPTAMT (RuSHA; Central Office for Race and Resettlement). One of the five key branches of the SS (q.v.). The RuSHA began as an SS marriage bureau with the purpose of authenticating the Aryan ancestry of would-be SS brides, but it was later extended to control the racial purity of the entire SS. It was also responsible for organizing the settlement and welfare of SS colonists in the conquered and occupied countries in the east.

RASSENFORSCHUNG (Race Research). The study of race as encouraged by Hitler for schools and universities in the Third Reich. The research was to fit Hitler's ideas on race (*see* RACIAL DOCTRINE). The new discipline conformed closely with *Rassenkunde*, the study of races, or ethnology. The level of this research can be judged by the following passage by Professor Hermann Gauch, a specialist in *Rassenforschung:*

> Generally speaking, the Nordic race alone can emit sounds of untroubled clearness, whereas among non-Nordic men and races, the pronunciation is impurer, the individual sounds more confused and more like the noises made by animals, such as barking, snoring, sniffing, and squeaking. That birds can learn to talk better than other animals is explained by the fact that their mouths are Nordic in structure—that is to say, high, narrow, and short-tongued. The shape of the Nordic gum allows a superior movement of the tongue, which is the reason why Nordic talking and singing are fuller.

This passage may be compared with the following description of "Jewish sounds" by the composer Richard Wagner (q.v.), spiritual forerunner of National Socialism and the venerated master of Adolf Hitler:

> The Jew speaks the language of the nation in whose midst he dwells from generation to generation, but he always speaks it as an alien. Our whole European art and civilization have remained to the Jew a foreign tongue. In this speech, this art, the Jew can only after-speak and after-patch—not truly make a poem of his words, an artwork of his doings. In the peculiarities of Semitic pronunciation the first thing that strikes our ear as quite outlandish and unpleasant, in the Jew's production of the voice-sounds, is a creaking, squeaking, buzzing snuffle [*ein zischender, schrillender, summsender und murksender Lautausdruck*]. . . . This mode of speaking acquires at once the character of an intolerably jumbled blabber [*eines unertraglich verwirrten Geplappers*]. The cold indifference of his peculiar blubber [*Gelabber*] never by chance rises to the ardor of a higher heartfelt passion.

RASSENKUNDE. *See* RASSENFORSCHUNG.

RASSENSCHANDE (Race Defilement). Term used to describe forbidden cohabitation between German Aryans and Jews. The Nuremberg Law on race of September 15, 1935 (*see* NUREMBERG LAWS), banned marriage of a German national and a Jew. The purpose was to prevent interbreeding between the two "racial strains." Cases of such forbidden sexual intercourse received tremendous publicity in the press, such as this story printed on October 9, 1936:

> A nineteen-year-old Jewish defendant appeared before the criminal court charged with violation of race purity. He had become acquainted in May with a twenty-one-year-old Aryan household employee in a café labeled German Business and entered into an intimate relation with her which continued until his arrest at the end of July. The girl alleged not to have known that the affair involved a Jew, since he had occasionally shown her a police registration certificate on which he was designated as Protestant. The prosecuting attorney urging a prison sentence stressed that the accused had no right to have anything to do with a resort designated as above. Had the accused heeded this fundamental rule he would not have made himself liable for punishment. The previously unpunished accused was sentenced to prison for a year and a half minus the time involved in investigation.

RASTENBURG CONFERENCE. Meeting of Hitler and his close military advisers held at his field headquarters, also called the Wolfsschanze (Wolf's Lair), at 12:30 P.M. on July 20, 1944. This was the scene of the July Plot (q.v.), the attempted assassination of Hitler. In the center of the *Gästebaracke* (guest barracks) was a large table covered with situation maps. Surrounding the table were the following, in order:

1. Hitler
2. Lieut. Gen. Adolf Heusinger, chief of operations, OKH
3. Gen. Günther Korten, chief of the General Staff, Luftwaffe
4. Col. Heinz Brandt, deputy to General Heusinger
5. Gen. Karl Bodenschatz, chief of staff, Luftwaffe
6. Gen. Rudolf Schmundt, Hitler's adjutant
7. Colonel Borgman, General Staff, OKH
8. Vice Adm. Jesco von Puttkamer, naval adjutant to the Fuehrer
9. Berger, stenographer
10. Capt. Kurt Assmann, naval adjutant to the Fuehrer
11. Maj. Gen. Walther Scherff, chief of historical section, OKW
12. Lieut. Gen. Walther Buhle, General Staff, OKH
13. Vice Adm. Hans Voss, naval liaison officer at field headquarters
14. SS-Brig. Gen. Hermann Fegelein, representative of the Waffen-SS
15. Col. Nicholaus von Below, Luftwaffe adjutant to the Fuehrer
16. SS-Maj. Otto Günsche, adjutant to the Fuehrer
17. Stenographer
18. Lieutenant Colonel von John, adjutant to Field Marshal Keitel
19. Maj. Herbert Büchs, adjutant to Colonel General Jodl
20. Lieutenant Colonel Waizenegger, adjutant to Field Marshal Keitel
21. Counselor von Sonnleithner, Ministry of Foreign Affairs

22. Maj. Gen. Walther Warlimont, deputy to Colonel General Jodl in Operations
23. Col. Gen. Alfred Jodl, chief of operations, OKW
24. Field Marshal Wilhelm Keitel, chief of the High Command of the armed forces

See JULY PLOT for details of the assassination attempt.

RATH, ERNST VOM. *See* GRYNSZPAN, HERSCHEL; KRISTALLNACHT.

RAUBAL, ANGELA (GELI) (1908–1931). Hitler's niece and reputedly the only deep love of his life. In 1925 Hitler's half sister, Angela Raubal, went to Berchtesgaden (q.v.) to keep house for him. With her came two daughters, Friedl and a seventeen-year-old also named Angela, or Geli for short. Geli Raubal was a pretty girl with an immense crown of blond hair and a pleasant voice. Hitler fell in love with his attractive niece. In 1929 he rented a large apartment on the Prinz Regentenstrasse in Munich and brought the Raubals there to be with him. He took Geli with him everywhere—to meetings, conferences, cafés, and theaters. He rode through the countryside and delighted in showing his blond niece to his friends. Geli looked forward to a career as a singer and expected that her uncle would make things easy for her. But Hitler, who apparently wanted her for himself alone, discouraged her hopes for an operatic career.

The lovers' quarrels became more and more violent. When Geli heard rumors that Hitler intended to marry Frau Winifred Wagner (q.v.), the widow of Siegfried Wagner and daughter-in-law of the composer Richard Wagner (q.v.), she became hysterical. The angered Hitler fumed and cursed. On his side, Hitler, who may have intended to marry his niece, suspected that she had had a clandestine love affair with Emil Maurice (q.v.), his bodyguard.

In the summer of 1931 Geli, who continued to object to her uncle's tyranny, made up her mind to go to Vienna. Resisting violently, Hitler forbade her to leave. On September 17, as he left for Hamburg, Hitler again ordered his niece to give up any plans to go to Vienna. All day the distracted girl, carrying a dead canary that she intended to bury, moved around the apartment. She kept insisting that the next day she would travel to Berchtesgaden to see her mother and bury her pet. The next morning, September 18, 1931, Geli was found shot to death. It was a terrible blow for Hitler, who wept copiously at her grave. Struck down by grief, he did not recover for a long time.

The mystery of Geli's death has never been explained. One rumor had it that Hitler murdered her in a rage. Another held that Heinrich Himmler (q.v.) saw to it that the girl was eliminated because she was embarrassing to the Nazi party. Those who were implicated in the matter fared badly. Father Bernhard Stempfle, who had helped edit Hitler's *Mein Kampf* (q.v.) and who made the mistake of talking too much about the relationship between Hitler and Geli, was found dead in a forest near Munich. There were three bullets in his heart.

RAUSCHNING, HERMANN (1887–). National Socialist politician, later a critic of Hitler and Nazism. Hermann Rauschning was born in Thorn, West Prussia (now Toruń, Poland), on August 7, 1887, the son of an active officer and manorial lord of an old farming family. After attending cadet schools at Potsdam and Berlin-Lichterfelde, he studied music, history, and Germanics at Munich and Berlin. In World War I he served as an infantryman with the rank of lieutenant and was wounded in action. After the war he led a German cultural group in Poland and then moved to the Danzig free state. He joined the Nationalsozialistische Deutsche Arbeiterpartei (q.v.) in 1932 and soon became a trusted confidant of Hitler.

At the May 28, 1932, elections for the Danzig Volkstag (Parliament), the National Socialists received an absolute, though scant, majority of votes (50.03 percent). Hitler made his friend Rauschning President of the Danzig Senate. The appointment annoyed the Nazi *Alte Kämpfer* (q.v.), the old guard, who were themselves eager for political office. Rauschning was denounced as a latecomer, one of those who had joined Hitler only when he was on the verge of success. On August 5, 1933, Rauschning, on behalf of Danzig and after negotiations with Józef Beck, the Polish Foreign Minister, signed a treaty with Poland governing future relations. Until then Danzig had been under the wing of the League of Nations, which Hitler regarded with disfavor. Rauschning put forward the new German line for Hitler in Danzig, but within a year he was alienated from National Socialism, and in 1936 he fled to Switzerland.

In a series of books Rauschning revealed the ruthless character of Hitler and Nazism: *The Revolution of Nihilism* (1939); *The Voice of Destruction* (1940); *The Conservative Revolution* (1941); *Time of Delirium* (1946). His name was placed on the *Sonderfahndungsliste-GB* (q.v.), the *Special Search List—Great Britain* of Heinrich Himmler (q.v.), the Nazi black book of enemies listing all the names of Britons and others living in England who were slated for arrest by the Gestapo (q.v.). From 1948 on Rauschning lived in Gaston, Oregon, as a farmer.

RAVENSBRÜCK. Concentration camp specializing in women inmates (*see* CONCENTRATION CAMPS). Ravensbrück was located 50 miles north of Berlin, near Lake Fürstenberg. It was surrounded by swampland. Established in 1938, the camp became a place of internment for Red Cross nurses, Russian women captured on the battlefields, French nationals, members of the Resistance (q.v.), and slave workers. The main camp was supposed to accommodate some 6,000 prisoners, but from 1944 on there were never fewer than 12,000 and in January 1945 there were at least 36,000. About 50,000 prisoners perished in Ravensbrück. Polish women were subjected to transplantation of human bones in experiments carried out there. All ordinary furs expropriated in other concentration camps were sent to the Ravensbrück clothing plant to be remodeled. On April 25, 1945, Ravensbrück was captured by the Allies, and its remaining prisoners were liberated.

RED. *See* ROT.

RED BEARD. *See* BARBAROSSA.

RED FRONT FIGHTERS' ASSOCIATION. *See* ROTFRONTKÄMPFERBUND.

RED-LETTER DAYS. *See* HOLIDAYS, NAZI.

RED ORCHESTRA. *See* ROTE KAPELLE.

REDNERSCHULE DER NSDAP (Party School for Orators). A training institute for Nazi speakers. In 1928 Fritz Reinhardt (q.v.), *Gauleiter* (district leader) of Upper Bavaria–Swabia, founded a school for training local speakers. When the subsequent elections revealed the party's great appeal to voters in this rural area, Hitler made Reinhardt's school a national organization. Here Nazi leaders were trained in the art of public speaking. Often they memorized speeches and answers to possible questions.

REGENBOGEN (Rainbow). Code name for the projected scuttling of the German U-boat fleet (*see* U-BOATS) at the close of World War II. After Hitler's suicide his successor, Adm. Karl Doenitz (q.v.), who hoped to obtain a quick end to the war, refused to give the order for Regenbogen. U-boat commanders, angered by the possibility of their submarine fleet's falling into enemy hands, took it upon themselves to send the code word Regenbogen by radio to all U-boats in German ports. In response crews managed to scuttle 231 U-boats in early May 1945.

REGIONAL NOVEL. *See* HEIMATROMAN.

REICH AIR TRAVEL MINISTRY. *See* REICHSLUFTFAHRTMINISTERIUM.

REICH BANNER BLACK-RED-GOLD. *See* REICHSBANNER SCHWARZ-ROT-GOLD.

REICH CENTRAL SECURITY OFFICE. *See* REICHSSICHERHEITSHAUPTAMT.

REICH CHAMBER OF CULTURE. *See* REICHSKULTURKAMMER.

REICH CHAMBER OF VISUAL ARTS. *See* ART IN THE THIRD REICH.

REICH CIVIL ADMINISTRATION FOR OCCUPIED SOVIET TERRITORIES IN THE EAST. *See* REICHSKOMMISSARIAT FÜR DAS OSTLAND.

REICH COMMISSIONER FOR THE SUPERVISION OF PUBLIC OPINION. *See* REICHSKOMMISSAR FÜR DIE ÜBERWACHUNG DER ÖFFENTLICHEN MEINUNG.

REICH COMMISSIONERS. *See* REICHSKOMMISSARE.

REICH DISTRICT. *See* REICHSGAU.

REICH FILM CHAMBER. *See* REICHSFILMKAMMER.

REICH GOVERNOR. *See* REICHSSTATTHALTER.

REICH HIGH COMMAND OF THE SS. *See* REICHSFUEHRUNG-SS.

REICH LEADER. *See* REICHSLEITER.

REICH LEADER-SS. *See* REICHSFUEHRER-SS.

REICH LEADERSHIP OF THE NSDAP. *See* REICHSLEITUNG DER NSDAP.

REICH LITERARY CHAMBER. *See* REICHSSCHRIFTUMSKAMMER.

REICH MARSHAL. *See* REICHSMARSCHALL.

REICH MINISTRY FOR PUBLIC ENLIGHTENMENT AND PROPAGANDA. *See* REICHSMINISTERIUM FÜR VOLKSAUFKLÄRUNG UND PROPAGANDA.

REICH OFFICE FOR THE CONSOLIDATION OF GERMAN NATIONHOOD. *See* REICHSKOMMISSARIAT FÜR DIE FESTIGUNG DES DEUTSCHEN VOLKSTUMS.

REICH PROPAGANDA LEADERSHIP. *See* REICHSPROPAGANDALEITUNG.

REICH PROPAGANDA OFFICE. *See* REICHSPROPAGANDAAMT.

REICH REPRESENTATIVE COUNCIL OF GERMAN JEWS. *See* JUDENRÄTE.

REICH SCHOOL FOR LEADERS. *See* REICHSFUEHRERSCHULE.

REICH SPORTS DIVISION LEADER. *See* LEITER DES REICHSBERUFSWETTKAMPFES.

REICH SPORTS LEAGUE. *See* REICHSSPORTBUND.

REICH SS LEADER AND CHIEF OF THE GERMAN POLICE. *See* REICHSFUEHRER-SS UND CHEF DER DEUTSCHEN POLIZEI.

REICH TEACHERS' LEAGUE. *See* REICHSLEHRERBUND.

REICH YOUTH DEDICATION CEREMONY. *See* REICHSJUGENDWEIHE.

REICH YOUTH LEADER. *See* REICHSJUGENDLEITER.

REICH YOUTH OFFICE. *See* REICHSJUGENDAMT.

REICHENAU, WALTHER VON (1884–1942). General field marshal in the armed forces of the Third Reich. Walther von Reichenau was born in Karlsruhe on August 16, 1884. Entering the Army at an early age, he served in World War I as a pupil of Max Hoffmann, the military genius behind Generals Paul von Hindenburg and Erich Ludendorff (qq.v.) in the victory at Tannenberg on August 26–29, 1914. By 1933 Reichenau was chief of staff to Gen. Werner von Blomberg (q.v.). Although he had no great opinion of Hitler, the ambitious Reichenau broke off relations with the Prussian military caste and gave his support to the Fuehrer. He acted as liaison officer in dealing with the Nazis and soon became a favorite of the party.

On January 10, 1935, Reichenau was promoted to general. Later that year, restless and tired of his desk job, he

Field Marshal Walther von Reichenau. [*Picture Collection, The Branch Libraries, The New York Public Library*]

was transferred to the field as commander of Wehrkreis (Defense District) VII in Munich to replace Gen. Wilhelm Adam (q.v.). In 1939, at the age of fifty-five, he was No. 14 in seniority among the leading generals and was given command of Army Group IV. He supported Hitler in his war plans at a time when other generals warned of a possible military disaster. After serving in Poland in 1939 and in France in 1940, he was made a field marshal following the fall of France. In December 1941 he was given command of an army group. Reichenau died in an air crash on January 17, 1942.

REICHSARBEITSDIENST (RAD; State Labor Service). Required labor service for all able-bodied citizens of the Third Reich. In speeches before he came to power, Hitler promised that he would overcome *Arbeitslosigkeit* (unemployment). His cure was simple: first he placed the jobless in labor battalions, and then he found places for them in the armed forces. A law promulgated on June 26, 1935, made it obligatory for all citizens to serve in the Reichsarbeitsdienst. All Germans between the ages of nineteen and twenty-five were required to work in labor camps. The first annual contingents numbered 200,000 men, organized into two units, each functioning for six months. Most of the men were assigned to farms, where they worked in accordance with a strict disciplinary code under authoritarian leaders. No distinction was made as to occupation. Intellectuals, workers, artisans, peasants, all were subject to common tasks. Women were drawn into the labor service to do housework in peasant homes while the men worked in the fields.

Hitler regarded the State Labor Service as a necessary step to rearmament: the men who shouldered shovels would one day carry guns. The plan had the additional advantages of providing a large cheap labor supply and of withdrawing the unemployed from the labor market. In September 1936 Hitler announced before a party congress that the number of jobless had been reduced from 6 million to 1 million. This report increased Hitler's popularity in a country burdened for years by unemployment.

REICHSAUTOBAHN (National Superhighway). An advanced system of highways constructed by Hitler as "an overture to peace" but obviously undertaken to permit the rapid movement of troops in war. The work of constructing superhighways had begun as early as 1924. In 1932, a year before Hitler became Chancellor, a highway linking Cologne and Bonn was opened for traffic. Hitler continued the practice. In September 1933 he ordered the construction of new highways under the direction of Dr. Fritz Todt (q.v.). More than 30,000 workers were supplied for the task, and within the next several years the labor force was increased to 70,000. Hitler was especially interested in east-west highways in order to meet the demands of a two-front war. His goal was a network of 7,300 miles of four-lane highways. A quarter of this network was completed by 1938. Today many Germans remember Hitler primarily as "the man who built the Autobahn."

REICHSBANNER SCHWARZ-ROT-GOLD (Reich Banner Black-Red-Gold). A uniformed but unarmed formation of Social Democratic ex-servicemen in the Weimar Republic (q.v.) in the 1920s and early 1930s. It was customary at the time for political groups to march in uniform and in formation to their rallies and to set out on maneuvers in the countryside. A private army of the majority of trade union workers, the Reichsbanner played a role like that of the Stahlhelm (q.v.), representing the war veterans; the Rotfrontkämpferbund (q.v.), the Communist formations; and the Storm Troopers (*see* SA), the Nazi paramilitary units.

REICHSBERUFSWETTKAMPF (National Vocational Competition). An annual competition among workers on their understanding of the nature of their work and its connection with the Nazi way of life. The idea was to demonstrate the loyalty of workers to the regime. Introduced in 1933 as a typical Nazi creation, the competition was extended in 1938 to include virtually all forms of employment in industry, handicrafts, civil service, and white-collar occupations as well as students. Winners were treated like Olympic athletes and brought to Berlin to be presented to Dr. Robert Ley (q.v.), leader of the Deutsche Arbeitsfront (q.v.), the German Labor Front, and to Hitler himself.

REICHSBUND DEUTSCHER BEAMTER. *See* BEAMTENBUND.

REICHSFILMKAMMER (Reich Film Chamber). Organization that controlled the entire German film industry in the Third Reich. In 1937 the Ministry for Public Enlightenment and Propaganda, led by Dr. Paul Joseph Goebbels (q.v.), assumed control of UFA, the last independent German film company. The financial side of film production was centralized under firm Nazi control. It was ordered that all German films portray "genuine Aryan femininity" instead of the supposed materialistic degeneracy depicted by Hollywood. *See also* FILMS IN THE THIRD REICH.

REICHSFUEHRER-SS (RFSS; Reich Leader-SS). Title used by Heinrich Himmler (q.v.) as head of the SS (q.v.).

REICHSFUEHRER-SS UND CHEF DER DEUTSCHEN POLIZEI (Reich SS Leader and Chief of the German

Police). The full title used by Heinrich Himmler (q.v.) after June 1936 as the leader of the SS (q.v.).

REICHSFUEHRERSCHULE (RFS; Reich School for Leaders). A special school for the training of future leaders of the Nazi party.

REICHSFUEHRUNG-SS (Reich High Command of the SS). The leadership of Heinrich Himmler (q.v.) and his personal staff in the SS (q.v.).

REICHSGAU (Reich District). One of the eleven districts formed from territories annexed after 1939 and administered by a *Reichsstatthalter* (q.v.) as governor.

REICHSJUGENDAMT (Reich Youth Office). The office responsible for the administration and training of Nazi youth.

REICHSJUGENDLEITER (Reich Youth Leader). Title reserved for the Nazi chief of youth.

REICHSJUGENDWEIHE (Reich Youth Dedication Ceremony). A pagan ceremony sponsored by the German Faith movement (Deutsche Glaubensbewegung, q.v.).

REICHSKOMMISSAR FÜR DIE ÜBERWACHUNG DER ÖFFENTLICHEN MEINUNG (RKoln; Reich Commissioner for the Supervision of Public Opinion). Functionary responsible for suppressing any open dissent in the National Socialist state.

REICHSKOMMISSARE (Reich Commissioners). High Nazi officials who served as governors of occupied territories during World War II.

REICHSKOMMISSARIAT FÜR DAS OSTLAND (Reich Civil Administration for Occupied Soviet Territories in the East). A special unit organized to administer the affairs of the occupied lands in the east after the outbreak of World War II. Alfred Rosenberg (q.v.) was named head of this office.

REICHSKOMMISSARIAT FÜR DIE FESTIGUNG DES DEUTSCHEN VOLKSTUMS (RKFDV; Reich Office for the Consolidation of German Nationhood). One of the five main branches of the SS (q.v.). This office coordinated two other SS agencies, the Rasse- und Siedlungshauptamt and the Volksdeutsche Mittelstelle (qq.v.). Created by Hitler in 1939 under Heinrich Himmler (q.v.), the RKFDV was responsible for the program of resettlement of *Volksdeutsche* (q.v.; ethnic Germans), the expropriation and displacement of Slavs in the occupied countries, and the consignment of racially undesirable types to forced labor, concentration camps (q.v.), or extermination camps (q.v.).

REICHSKULTURKAMMER (Reich Chamber of Culture). Organization founded by a law dated September 22, 1933, to encourage all forms of artistic creation from the Nazi point of view. It was closely linked to the Ministry for Public Enlightenment and Propaganda under the leadership of Dr. Paul Joseph Goebbels (q.v.). The Reich Chamber of Culture was divided originally into seven subordinate chambers, for literature, music, films, theater, radio, fine arts, and press. All were directed by Goebbels. Membership was compulsory. Persons denied membership were in effect excluded from their professions.

REICHSLEHRERBUND (RLB; Reich Teachers' League). An organization of teachers devoted to the ideals of National Socialism. It was carefully watched by high Nazi officials.

REICHSLEITER (Reich Leader). Official term for Hitler's position as leader of the Third Reich. In the late stage of his career Hitler designated Martin Bormann (q.v.) as *Reichsleiter* to succeed him with authority to implement all policies inaugurated by the Fuehrer. The term was also used to describe members of the Executive Committee and departmental heads of the Nationalsozialistische Deutsche Arbeiterpartei (q.v.). The designation of *Reichsleiter* was highly regarded by the Nazi hierarchy.

REICHSLEITUNG DER NSDAP (Reich Leadership of the NSDAP). Term applied collectively to several officials high in Nazi party affairs, such as the party treasurer.

REICHSLUFTFAHRTMINISTERIUM (RLM; Reich Air Travel Ministry). The national central office for aviation. It was established by Hermann Goering (q.v.) in 1933 before the denunciation of the Treaty of Versailles and the unveiling of the Luftwaffe (q.v.) in March 1935. Unlike the Army and the Navy in the Third Reich, the Luftwaffe was under the control of a civilian ministry.

REICHSMARSCHALL (Reich Marshal). Special title created for Hermann Goering (q.v.) as second in command and successor to Hitler. On April 23, 1945, Goering sent a telegram to Hitler in his Berlin bunker asking him to agree to Goering's immediate assumption of total leadership in the Third Reich. The angered Fuehrer dismissed Goering from all his offices, including that of *Reichsmarschall*, and especially from his right of succession to political power. *See also* GÖTTERDÄMMERUNG.

REICHSMINISTERIUM FÜR VOLKSAUFKLÄRUNG UND PROPAGANDA (RMVP; Reich Ministry for Public Enlightenment and Propaganda). Official ministry responsible for all propaganda in support of the Nazi regime. It was under the direction of Dr. Paul Joseph Goebbels (q.v.).

REICHSPROPAGANDAAMT (RPA; Reich Propaganda Office). Office of the Reichsministerium für Volksaufklärung und Propaganda (q.v.) that was concerned with all cultural activities in the Third Reich.

REICHSPROPAGANDALEITUNG (RPL; Reich Propaganda Leadership). The special national leadership unit responsible for supervising Nazi propaganda. This leadership group formed a small percentage of the membership of the Propaganda Ministry, which by the middle of 1933 had 300 officials and 500 employees.

REICHSSCHRIFTUMSKAMMER (Reich Literary Cham-

ber). National Nazi literary guild. The organization included all National Socialist writers, publishers, and librarians. Headed by Hanns Johst (q.v.), it subjected all its members to directions from above, and it expected all to contribute their share to Nazi *Gleichschaltung* (q.v.), or coordination. The chamber banned the work of all anti-Nazi writers.

REICHSSICHERHEITSHAUPTAMT (RSHA; Reich Central Security Office). The main security department of the Nazi government. It was set up in 1939 to combine all the existing police forces, including the Gestapo (q.v.), the secret police; the Kriminalpolizei (q.v.), the criminal police; and the SD (q.v.), the SS (q.v.) security service. Its chief was Reinhard Heydrich (q.v.), who served until his death on June 4, 1942. The RSHA was responsible for taking into custody all enemies of the state and turning them over to Oswald Pohl (q.v.), administrator of the concentration camps (q.v.). It served as a central office for both the Reich leadership of the SS and the Reich Ministry of the Interior. The dreaded subbranch of the RSHA, called Amt VI (Office VI), was the responsibility of Adolf Eichmann (q.v.) and was commissioned to bring about the Final Solution (*see* ENDLÖSUNG, DIE).

REICHSSPORTBUND (Reich Sports League). Organization for the promotion of sports among Nazi party members. *See also* SPORTS IN THE THIRD REICH.

REICHSSTATTHALTER (Reich Governor). The governor of a *Reichsgau* (q.v.), one of the eleven districts formed from territories annexed by the Third Reich after 1939. In many cases the local *Reichsstatthalter* was also the *Gauleiter* (q.v.), the ranking Nazi party official of one of the forty-three *Gaue,* or territorial divisions, of the Nationalsozialistische Deutsche Arbeiterpartei (q.v.).

REICHSSTUDENTENWERK (National Student Welfare Organization). A national organization devoted to helping Nazi students. Its objective was to give assistance to "the most virtuous students in the sense of National Socialist demands." According to a law of March 27, 1934, the Reichstudentenwerk and all other training organizations such as the Hitler Jugend and the Bund Deutscher Mädel (qq.v.) were to stress four goals: physical *(körperlich),* moral *(charakterlich),* intellectual *(geistig),* and eugenic *(voelkisch; see* VOELKISCH MOVEMENT).

REICHSSTUNDE (National Hour). Hour set aside for special celebrations by patriotic organizations. Thus, the 1,000 members of the National League of Wearers of the Life-saving Medal celebrated their *Reichstunde* by a parade through the Lustgarten in Berlin.

REICHSTAG (Parliament). The central German legislative body. Although Hitler abolished the *Landtag* (q.v.; legislature) in the individual German states, he retained the Reichstag in the Third Reich. However, he deprived it of all legislative power by the Enabling Act (q.v.) of March 24, 1933.

REICHSTAG FIRE. Burning of the imposing building in Berlin housing the German Parliament. The event signaled the beginning of the Nazi dictatorship. At approximately ten o'clock on the evening of February 27, 1933, a cold, raw night with crusts of caked snow on the streets, a telephone message came from a Berlin citizen to the police: "The dome of the Reichstag building is burning in brilliant flames!" It turned out to be a correct report.

The Berlin Fire Department appeared on the scene with astonishing speed, but the flames were already gutting the great four-square mass of the building. The Reichstag was built like a block of stone into which tunnels had been bored and wooden cubes set: the tunnels were the lobbies and corridors, and the cubes were the timber-paneled session chamber, committee rooms, restaurant, and similar rooms. The main structure was fireproof, but the wood-paneled halls and rooms could be burned. At the Brandenburg Gate and on both sides of the Spree River a crowd of several thousand Berliners pressed against police barriers set up in a wide circle around the Reichstag. The people looked on in amazement as the crackling flames reached into the night sky.

When the fire was discovered, Chancellor Hitler was dining with Dr. Paul Joseph Goebbels (q.v.) at the latter's flat in the Reichskanzlerplatz. Apprised of the news by telephone, Goebbels at first took it for an ill-timed joke, hooked up the receiver, and only on a second call informed Hitler. The two, accompanied by August Wilhelm Heinrich Günther, Prinz von Preussen (q.v.), a member of the Hohenzollern family, Vice-Chancellor Franz von Papen (q.v.), and several others, were taken with great speed to the Reichstag. There they conferred with Police President von Levetzow, Lord Mayor Salm, and other officials. Hermann Goering (q.v.), who had been at work in the nearby Prussian Ministry of the Interior, hastened to the Reichstag. Goering immediately informed Hitler and Goebbels: "This is a Communist outrage. One of the Communist culprits has been arrested." Hitler, even as the Reichstag was burning, proclaimed the fire "a sign from heaven." Now everyone would know what would have happened to Germany if "these gentry" had obtained power. He, the Fuehrer, would rescue Germany from this danger. He was convinced, he added, that the fire was a *Fanal* (beacon or signal) set by Communists to start their revolution in Germany.

Meanwhile, the police, already aware that the fire had been started by arson, arrested an incoherent, hysterical, half-naked young Dutchman named Marinus van der Lubbe (q.v.) inside the flaming building. Taken to the police station at the Brandenburg Gate, he was interrogated. The police claimed that they found on his person an identification card of the Dutch Communist party bearing his name. The prisoner confessed that he alone had started the fire.

At 11:30 P.M., as the fire died down, members of the Berlin and foreign press, who had been waiting outside the Reichstag, were led by police and firemen into the building to see for themselves what damage had been done. The reception hall, though untouched by flames, had water a foot deep on its floor. Fire-fighting apparatus stretched everywhere. Smoke was still pouring through the doors of the meeting hall, which was a mass of ruins. The roof of the hall, now a skeleton, was about to fall. Other rooms, including the restaurant and the workroom of the Reichstag delegates, were heavily damaged. Police established that some twenty bundles of incendiary materials had been scattered throughout the building, although not all were set on fire. Virtually all the journalists on this guided tour came to the conclusion that it would have been impossible for one arsonist to have set the fires by himself. The *Frankfurter Zeitung* went to the heart of the issue when it spoke of "some doubt as to whether the imprisoned man could have done it all by himself."

The police, puzzled by the tremendous amount of incendiary material brought into the Reichstag, began to look for confederates of the half-witted Dutchman. They decided that the arsonists had entered and escaped from the building by means of a tunnel leading from Goering's office to the Reichstag building. Originally the tunnel had been part of the central heating system of the Reichstag. The incendiaries apparently had gotten in and out of the Reichstag through the backyard of Goering's offices. From that time on there were rumors that the Nazis themselves had burned the building and that Van der Lubbe was an innocent dupe.

Van der Lubbe was not the only one to be arrested. Ernst Torgler (q.v.), chairman of the Communist bloc in the Reichstag, voluntarily gave himself up to the police when he heard that they were looking for him. Later, three Bulgarian Communists, Georgi M. Dimitrov (q.v.), Blagoi Popov, and Vassili Tanev, were arrested after a suspicious waiter in a Berlin café informed the police that they had been acting strangely. *See also* REICHSTAG FIRE TRIAL.

In his capacity as police minister in Prussia, Goering began to take drastic action, approved by Hitler, against the Communists. In addition to Torgler, he arrested the 100 Communist deputies to the Reichstag. He proclaimed a state of virtual siege. The press was prepared for grave action. The Preussische Pressedienst (Prussian Press Service) announced that "this act of incendiarism is the most monstrous act of terrorism carried out by Bolshevism in Germany." The *Vossische Zeitung* stated that "the government is of the opinion that the situation is such that a danger to the state and nation existed and still exists." The police moved not only against Communists but against pacifists, liberals, and democrats. "When Germany awoke," wrote Douglas Reed, a British reporter, "a man's home was no longer his castle. He could be seized by private individuals, could claim no protection from the police, could be indefinitely detained without preferment of charge; his property could be seized, his verbal and written communications overheard and perused; he no longer had the right to foregather with his fellow countrymen, and his newspapers might no longer freely express their opinions." The Reichstag fire produced exactly the result that Hitler had anticipated. The Germany of the Weimar Constitution went up in flames, and from its ashes rose the Third Reich.

Those who were convinced that the Nazis had set the fire themselves on the principle that the end justified the means point to the realities of the political situation. As the new Chancellor, Hitler had only three of his followers in his Cabinet, as opposed to eight belonging to the Von Papen–Hugenberg group. He needed a clear majority of Reichstag seats in the coming March 5, 1933, elections, and it was certain that the Communists would obtain at least 100 seats among the 600 deputies. Hitler controlled some 250 seats, not a clear majority. If he could wipe out the critical 100 Communist seats, he would win his battle for power. Nazi authorities had already raided the Karl Liebknecht House (q.v.), headquarters of the Communist party in Berlin, but they had failed to incriminate the Communists in a revolutionary conspiracy as a pretext for silencing them. They had to think of something else because the date for a national election was fast approaching. The motive for arson at the Reichstag, said the accusers, was clear. Some months later, a prominent nationalist deputy named Ernst Oberfohren circulated a paper asserting that the Nazis were the real incendiaries (*see* OBERFOHREN MEMORANDUM).

The burned-out Reichstag. [*National Archives, Washington*]

A controversy on the origins of the fire has persisted to the present day. In 1960 a German investigator, Dr. Fritz Tobias, published in the news magazine *Der Spiegel* the results of his investigation, which showed that Van der Lubbe had acted alone in setting the fire. This thesis was supported by Professor Hans Mommsen, historian at the Ruhr University in Bochum. Both held that Van der Lubbe, in the days before the fire, had tried without success to burn other public buildings. Both agreed that there was no Nazi participation whatever. In March 1973 a Swiss historian, Professor Walter Hofer of Bern Univer-

Confrontation of Hermann Goering (back to camera) and Georgi M. Dimitrov (standing in front of police officer) at the Reichstag Fire Trial. [*Picture Collection, The Branch Libraries, The New York Public Library*]

sity, accused Tobias and Mommsen of resorting to "non-scientific methods" in upholding the lone-arsonist theory. Hofer contended that his international team, formed in 1969, possessed documentary proof that the detectives in charge of the Tobias inquiry had worked for the Third Reich and that some of them had made common cause with the Nazis before the fire. Mommsen refused to retreat: "Professor Hofer's rather helpless statement that the accomplices of Van der Lubbe 'could only have been Nazis' is tacit admission that the committee did not actually obtain any positive evidence in regard to the alleged accomplices' identity."

Bibliography. Douglas Reed, *The Burning of the Reichstag*, Covici-Friede, Inc., New York, n.d.

REICHSTAG FIRE TRIAL. The trial of five defendants accused of setting the Reichstag fire (q.v.) on February 27, 1933. On arriving at the scene, Hermann Goering (q.v.), the No. 2 Nazi, pronounced the conflagration "a Communist outrage." This became the official position of the Nazi party. In July 1933 the German authorities decided that a trial must be held to prove to the world that the arson had been a Communist plot and not a Nazi scheme originating in Goering's offices. The proceedings began on September 21 and ended on December 23, 1933. The court sat for fifty-seven days. The trial was held in Leipzig before the Fourth Penal Chamber of the Supreme Court of the German Reich under the presiding judge, Dr. Wilhelm Bünger, president of the Fourth Criminal Court. The accused were Marinus van der Lubbe, a Dutch laborer, born in Leiden on January 13, 1909; Ernst Torgler (q.v.), a Communist commercial employee and former Reichstag deputy, born in Berlin on April 15, 1893; Georgi M. Dimitrov (q.v.), a Communist writer, born in Radomir, Bulgaria, on June 18, 1882; Blagoi Popov, a Communist student, born at Drjan, near Sofia, Bulgaria, on November 28, 1902; and Vassili Tanev, a Communist shoemaker, born in Gevgelija, Macedonia, on November 21, 1897.

The opening of the indictment read:

> That in Berlin, within the legal period of limitation, namely on February 25 and February 27, [the accused] have been guilty of the following connected offenses, partially committed in common:
>
> 1. All the accused,
>   *a.* that they attempted to alter the German constitution by the use of violence, and
>   *b.* that they set fire with malice aforethought to a building that was used for human habitation and inside which people were actually present, namely the *Reichstag* building, and that they committed the aforesaid arson with the intention of provoking a rebellion the outbreak of which was to be facilitated thereby.
> 2. The accused van der Lubbe,
>   *c.* that he implemented his intention of setting fire to a building which was the property of other people, that is, the welfare office in Neukölln, Berlin, by carrying out acts in which he began to carry out his intentions but did not proceed to complete his said intention;
>   *d.* further, that he set fire with malice aforethought to buildings used for human habitation, *i.e.*, the Town Hall and the Palace in Berlin, and that he committed these aforesaid arsons with the intention of provoking a rebellion the outbreak of which was to be facilitated thereby.

The trial began at 8:45 A.M. on September 21, when Van der Lubbe, a dim-witted, slobbering young man, was brought into the courtroom in chains, while the other accused were unfettered. First came a reading of the charges. The next day the interrogation of Van der Lubbe began. He stood with head forward, his mouth half agape, his tangled hair falling over his forehead. It was almost impossible to obtain from him a coherent account of his early life. In 1927, then a builder's apprentice, he had received in his eyes a splash of lime that permanently impaired his sight. He drifted from the Netherlands in September 1931 and then wandered through Austria, Yugoslavia, and Hungary. When asked about his communism, he replied that he had left the party in 1931 but that he was still inclined to Communist ideas. The prosecution then attempted to show a relationship between the German Communist Torgler and the other defendants. Witnesses were presented against the Bulgarians Popov and Tanev.

The examination of Dimitrov began on the third day. From that moment he won the attention of a worldwide audience. When warned by the president of the court that he must behave himself, he replied: "Herr President, if you were a man as innocent as myself and you have passed seven months in prison, five of them in chains night and day, you would understand it if one perhaps becomes a little strained." Nothing could move Dimitrov from the course he regarded as necessary for his own defense and that of the Communist party. He challenged and debated, attacked the witnesses, and defiantly moved out and back as he was expelled from and returned to the proceedings. Reporters from the foreign press declared that he had turned the proceedings into a trial of the National Socialists themselves.

The high point of the trial came on November 4, 1933, when Dimitrov confronted Goering in cross-examination, a dramatic event that attracted attention throughout the world. Excerpts from their duel follow:

> DIMITROV: Herr Prime Minister Goering stated on February 28 that when arrested the "Dutch Communist van der Lubbe had on his person his passport and a membership card of the Communist Party." From whom was this information taken?
>
> GOERING: The police search all common criminals, and report the result to me.
>
> DIMITROV: The three officials who arrested and examined van der Lubbe all agreed that no membership card of the Communist Party was found on him. I should like to know where the report that such a card had been found came from.
>
> GOERING: I was told by an official. Things which were reported to me on the night of the fire . . . could not be tested or proved. The report was made to me by a responsible official and was accepted as a fact, and as it could not be tested immediately it was announced as a fact. When I issued the first report to the press on the morning after the fire the interrogation of van der Lubbe had not been concluded. In any case I do not see that anyone has any right to complain because it seems to be proved in this trial that van der Lubbe had no such card on him.
>
> DIMITROV: I would like to ask the Minister of the Interior what steps he took to make sure that van der Lubbe's route to Hennigsdorf, his stay and his meetings with other people there were investigated by the police in order to assist them in tracking down van der Lubbe's accomplices?
>
> GOERING: As I am not an official myself but a responsible Minister it was not important that I should trouble myself with such petty, minor matters. It was my task to expose the Party and the mentality which was responsible for the crime.
>
> DIMITROV: Is the Reich Minister aware of the fact that those that possess this alleged criminal mentality to-day control the destiny of a sixth part of the world—the Soviet Union?
>
> GOERING: I don't care what happens in Russia. I know that the Russians pay with bills and I should prefer to know that their bills are paid. I care about the Communist Party here in Germany and about Communist crooks who come here to set the *Reichstag* on fire.
>
> DIMITROV: This criminal mentality rules the Soviet Union, the greatest and best country in the world. Is *Herr* Prime Minister aware of that?
>
> GOERING: I shall tell you what the German people already know. They know that you are behaving in a disgraceful manner. They know that you are a Communist crook who came to Germany to set the *Reichstag* on fire. In my eyes you are nothing but a scoundrel, a crook who belongs on the gallows.

The verdict came on December 23, 1933. The accused Dimitrov, Torgler, Popov, and Tanev were acquitted. Van der Lubbe, found guilty of high treason, insurrectionary arson, and attempted common arson, was sentenced to death and to the perpetual loss of civil rights. The costs of the trial fell upon the convicted man. Van der Lubbe, shambling with sunken head to the guillotine, was executed on January 10, 1934, three days before his twenty-fifth birthday. His family was refused permission to remove his body to the Netherlands. He was buried at Leipzig.

Bibliography. *The Reichstag Fire Trial: The Second Brown Book of the Hitler Terror*, John Lane, The Bodley Head, Ltd., London, 1934; Fritz Tobias, *The Reichstag Fire Trial*, tr. by Arnold Pomerans, G. P. Putnam's Sons, New York, 1964.

REICHSTRUNKENBOLD (National Drunkard in Chief). Surreptitious name used in private conversations to describe "Professor" Heinrich Hoffmann (q.v.), Hitler's official photographer and art expert. Alcoholism was widely recognized as a form of Nazi self-indulgence, and many Nazi leaders were dipsomaniacs. There was an inordinate amount of drinking at annual celebrations of the old guard (*Alte Kämpfer*, q.v.) and party stalwarts.

REICHSVERTRETUNG DER DEUTSCHEN JUDEN. *See* JUDENRÄTE.

REICHSWEHR (Rw; Defensive Land Forces). Name of the standing army during the era of the Weimar Republic (q.v.) and the opening years of the Third Reich, from 1920 to 1935. The term Reichswehr referred to the 100,000-man Army to which Germany was restricted by the Treaty of Versailles. Hitler was commander in chief of the Reichswehr from 1933 to 1935. In the latter year the name was changed by a *Wehrgesetz* (defense regulation) to Wehrmacht (q.v.), the armed forces of the Third Reich.

REICHSWERKE HERMANN GOERING (Hermann Goering National Works). A giant corporation created and capitalized by the National Socialist regime as a means of keeping big industry in line. A basic objective of the Four-Year Plan (q.v.) was increased iron and steel production. The steel industry, reluctant to take the risk of expansion while available capacity was still unused, resisted and declined to develop low-quality domestic ore. Hitler countered by creating the Reichswerke Hermann Goering (Goering-Werke) as a quasi-socialized organ of production. The government claimed some 70 percent of the capital for itself and controlled the voting rights of its shares. The steel industry was required to buy the remaining shares. In Hitler's estimate steel production, vital for rearmament, was to be controlled by the state.

REICHWEIN, ADOLF (1898–1944). University professor executed by the Nazis. Adolf Reichwein was born in Oberasbach on October 8, 1898. After being seriously wounded in World War I, he earned a doctorate in 1920 and became professor of history at the Halle Teachers College in 1930. In 1933 he was removed from his teaching position by Nazi authorities and was forced by circumstances to teach school in a village near Berlin. Opposed to the Hitler movement, he became a link between the Kreisau Circle (q.v.) and other Resistance (q.v.) groups,

Adolf Reichwein in the People's Court. [*From Annedore Leber (ed.),* Conscience in Revolt, *tr. by Rosemary O'Neill, Vallentine, Mitchell & Co., Ltd., London, 1957*]

including those among industrial workers. Denounced by the Gestapo (q.v.), Reichwein was arrested in 1944 and tried before the Volksgericht (q.v.), the People's Court. He was condemned to death by the court president, Roland Freisler (q.v.). Described as a gentle man of rare intellectual and human qualities, Reichwein met his death with dignity and courage.

Bibliography. Annedore Leber (ed.), *Conscience in Revolt,* tr. by Rosemary O'Neill, Vallentine, Mitchell & Co., Ltd., London, 1957.

REINHARD, OPERATION. *See* OPERATION REINHARD.

REINHARD POOL. *See* EINSATZ REINHARD.

REINHARDT, FRITZ (1895–1969). Leader of the Nazi party's school for orators (*see* REDNERSCHULE DER NSDAP). Fritz Reinhardt was born in Ilmenau on April 3, 1895. A schoolmaster, he joined the Nazi party and in 1928 was appointed *Gauleiter* (q.v.), or district leader, for Upper Bavaria. At the same time he became head of the party's training school for orators. In this post he was responsible for supplying speakers for party use as well as the contents of speeches to be memorized by Nazi orators. From 1930 to 1933 he served as a delegate to the Reichstag (q.v.) for Wahlkreis (Electoral District) Upper Bavaria–Swabia. In April 1933 he was appointed State Secretary in the Reich Ministry of Finance, where he did important work in financing the armament of the Wehrmacht (q.v.). He was the author of the so-called Reinhardt program, which advocated a tax to be used for the benefit of workers. On September 1, 1933, he was appointed *SA-Gruppenfuehrer* (lieutenant general) on the staff of the supreme leader of the SA (q.v.) and in 1937 was promoted to *SA-Obergruppenfuehrer* (general).

REINHARDT, MAX (1873–1943). Austrian-born theatrical director and a prominent refugee from the Third Reich. Max Reinhardt was born as Max Goldmann in Baden, southwest of Vienna, on September 9, 1873. At first a bank clerk, he began an acting career in 1893 in Salzburg and the next year appeared at the Deutsches Theater in Berlin. He performed as a character actor until 1902. From 1903 to 1906 he was active at the Neues Theater, where he staged the plays of Schiller, Wilde, and Gorky. From 1905 to 1920, and again from 1924 to 1933, he directed plays at the Deutsches Theater. An advocate of naturalistic theater, he introduced such new devices as the apron stage to ensure intimacy with the audience. His unique productions of Shakespeare, Shaw, Ibsen, Molière, and Strindberg aroused interest throughout the world. Reinhardt's theater in Berlin became a kind of clearinghouse for new tendencies and techniques from many countries. His

Max Reinhardt. [*Der grosse Brockhaus*]

most popular experiment was *The Miracle,* a medieval pageant set against a background merging both actors and audience. Unable to work in Nazi Germany and perceiving the future closed to him there, he gave the Deutsches Theater, which he owned, to the German people and went into exile, first in England and then in the United States. He opened an acting school in Los Angeles and became an American citizen in 1940. He died in New York on October 30, 1943.

REITER-SS (Mounted SS). Special cavalry units of the SS (q.v.).

REITSCH, HANNA (1912–1979). Leading German aviatrix and one of the last visitors to the *Fuehrerbunker* (q.v.) during Hitler's final days. Hanna Reitsch was born in Hirschberg, Silesia (now Jelenia Góra, Poland), the daughter of an ophthalmologist. In her early years she hoped to become a flying missionary physician but turned instead to professional flying. She became Germany's leading woman stunt pilot and flier, setting many European records. In 1937 Gen. Ernst Udet (q.v.) appointed her a test pilot for the new Luftwaffe (q.v.). During World War II she was the only woman to win the Iron Cross (First and Second Classes).

From April 26 to 29, 1945, Hanna Reitsch accompanied Gen. Robert Ritter von Greim (q.v.) on a three-day visit to Hitler's bunker in Berlin. A zealous follower of Nazism who worshiped Hitler and saw in him the apotheosis of German honor, she begged the Fuehrer to allow her to stay and die with him. Hitler, however, ordered her to leave with Von Greim, the newly appointed commander in chief of the Luftwaffe. The British historian H. R. Trevor-Roper (q.v.) described Fräulein Reitsch's character as "well suited to the atmosphere in that last subterranean madhouse at Berlin."

RELIEF FUND. *See* HILFSKASSE.

RELIGION IN THE THIRD REICH. Although Hitler was born a Catholic, he rejected Christianity as an alien idea, foreign to the racialist pattern of German life. "Antiquity," he said, "was better than modern times because it did not know Christianity and syphilis." His criticism had many facets:

1. Christianity was a religion that defended the weak and the low.
2. It was purely Jewish and Oriental in origin. It forced people "to bend their backs to the sound of church bells and crawl to the cross of a foreign God."
3. It began 2,000 years ago among sick, exhausted, and despairing men who had lost their belief in life.
4. The Christian tenets of forgiveness of sin, resurrection, and salvation were plain nonsense.
5. The Christian idea of mercy was a dangerous, un-German idea.
6. Christian love was a silly concept because love paralyzed men.
7. The Christian idea of equality protected the racially inferior, the ill, the weak, and the crippled.

During the Nazi drive for political power Alfred Rosenberg (q.v.) placed positive Christianity (q.v.) on the party program. This movement rejected most of the "Oriental" principles of Christianity and substituted for them such "positive" aspects as racialism (*see* RACIAL DOCTRINE), the reestablishment of the old Nordic values, and an emphasis on the spirit of the hero. At this time Hitler held ambivalent views on the subject. When he became Chancellor in 1933, he insisted again and again that his government aimed at creating favorable conditions for religion and that he placed the greatest value on friendly relations with the churches. Many Germans at this time believed that the Fuehrer had rescued Christianity from "Red persecutions" and that he would allow the free exercise of all religions.

On July 20, 1933, Hitler concluded a concordat with the Catholic Church (*see* CONCORDAT OF 1933). He guaranteed the integrity of the Catholic faith and agreed to safeguard its rights and privileges. Catholic schools, youth groups, and cultural societies were not to be disturbed if they kept out of politics. In concluding the agreement, the Fuehrer hoped to assure himself of an atmosphere of confidence by impressing world public opinion. He was deeply proud of his first diplomatic success. As later events indicated, however, he intended to fulfill his obligations only as long as they were useful to him.

From the beginning of the Third Reich, Hitler failed to come to an understanding with the Protestant Church. During the early years of the Nazi regime there was a call for the rejection of Protestantism and the formation of a new "German" religion that would accommodate ideas of blood and soil (*Blut und Boden,* q.v.) and leadership (*see* DEUTSCHE GLAUBENSBEWEGUNG, the German Faith movement). In 1934 Professor Ernst Bergmann issued his Twenty-five Points of the German Religion. The new German religion stressed these beliefs:

1. The Jewish Old Testament as well as parts of the New Testament are not suitable for the new Germany.
2. Christ was not Jewish but a Nordic martyr put to death by the Jews, a warrior whose death rescued the world from Jewish influence.
3. Adolf Hitler is the new messiah sent to earth to save the world from the Jews.
4. The swastika succeeds the sword as the symbol of German Christianity.
5. German land, German blood, German soul, German art—these are the sacred assets of German Christians.

Speaking for the German national church, Bergmann said: "Either we have a German God or none at all. The international God flies with the strongest squadrons—and they are not on the German side. We cannot kneel to a God who pays more attention to the French than to us. We Germans have been forsaken by the Christian God. He is not a just, supernatural God, but a political party God of the others. It is because we believed in him and not in our German God that we were defeated in the struggle of the nations."

Christians all over the world were repelled by these views. Inside Germany the German Faith movement produced its antithesis, the Bekenntniskirche (q.v.), the Confessional Church, which worked to maintain the purity of the Evangelical faith. The Confessional Church declined to obey the Reich bishop appointed by Hitler and instead convoked a fraternal council of the Evangelical Church in Germany. It declared that Christian doctrine was incompatible with Nazi *Weltanschauung* (q.v.), or world view, and politics.

Meanwhile, Hitler decreed the supremacy of the Nazi state over the Protestant Church. He closed church schools and took over church property, and he drove pastors from their pulpits and forbade others to preach. He hoped to destroy the strength of Protestant opposition by a slow process of erosion. Some Protestant pastors decided to go along with the regime, but many others refused to bow. The theologian Dr. Karl Barth (q.v.), who declined to take an oath of loyalty to Hitler, was removed from his post. "I was a professor of theology for ten years at Bonn University on the Rhine," Barth wrote later in Switzerland, "until I refused to open my lectures each day by raising my arm and saying *'Heil Hitler!'* I could not do that. It would have been blasphemy." The outspoken Dr. Martin Niemoeller (q.v.), pastor in the wealthy Berlin suburb of Dahlem, was arrested and tried secretly on a charge of sedition. Niemoeller, who had been a submarine officer in World War I, was cleared of all major charges, but he was arrested again and sent to a concentration camp (*see* CONCENTRATION CAMPS).

The Catholic Church did not long enjoy the peace that it had been promised by the Concordat of 1933. Catholic bishops attempted to remain on good terms with Hitler and the Nazis, but underneath there was hostility as one by one Hitler broke the terms of the concordat. Monks and nuns were arrested and accused of smuggling gold out of Germany. The Catholic press was censored. Religious processions were banned, and pastoral letters were forbidden. Monasteries were closed, monks subjected to show trials, and priests tried on faked charges of immorality. The propaganda machine led by Dr. Paul Joseph Goebbels (q.v.), Minister for Public Enlightenment and Propaganda, attempted to arouse disgust among the German people for the "moral excesses" of Catholic churchmen.

Catholic theologians fought back. Michael Cardinal von Faulhaber (q.v.), Archbishop of Munich-Freising, defied the Nazi state. To forestall his arrest Rome made him a papal legate, which gave him diplomatic immunity. On March 21, 1937, Pope Pius XI (q.v.) issued an encyclical titled *Mit brennender Sorge (With Deep Anxiety)*, which was read from every Catholic pulpit in Germany. It accused Hitler of breaking his agreement with the church and charged that he had exposed Catholics to "violence as illegal as it is inhuman." Hitler's reply was to subject priests, monks, and lay brothers to a new series of trials.

Hitler's struggle with the churches ended with the outbreak of World War II. He deemed it best to ease his campaign against religion, which might have impaired the morale of his soldiers. But he did not forget his final goal of annihilating both Catholic and Protestant faiths. At the same time he was careful not to come openly to the support of the new paganism. Although he was sympathetic with its approach, he was too shrewd a politician to give his personal support to the new German Faith movement.

REMAGEN BRIDGE. Bridge across the Rhine River and scene of a major disaster for the Third Reich in World War II. In the late days of the war neither the German High Command nor the Allies expected an easy crossing of the treacherous waters of the Rhine. No one had crossed the river in time of war since Napoleon in 1805, but Germany's river barriers were on the verge of collapse in the first week of March 1945. The United States First Army took Cologne after a heavy bombardment by planes and artillery. The Germans retreated across the Hohenzollern Bridge spanning the Rhine and then blew it up. At the same time the United States Third Army, led by Maj. Gen. George S. Patton, reached the Rhine near Koblenz. The 4th Armored Division of the Third Army covered 65 miles in fifty-eight hours. The First Army then turned south to join up with the Third Army.

Then came one of the most extraordinary strokes of fortune in military history. The Rhine barrier was strongest at its center, where steep mountains rose from the east bank of the river, from which the Germans could maintain a powerful defense. Gen. Dwight D. Eisenhower urged all his units to seize any chance to cross the river and shorten the war. On March 7, 1945, Sgt. Alexander A. Drabik, a butcher from Holland, Ohio, serving in the 9th Armored Division, led his platoon through a metal screen of fire to his objective, the town of Remagen, between Bonn and Koblenz. His platoon was ordered to hold a defensive position while troops to the north prepared for an assault crossing of the river.

Meanwhile, German troops were busy blowing up bridges along the Rhine as their comrades retreated into Germany proper. Orders went to Capt. Willi Bratke to destroy the Ludendorff Bridge across the Rhine at Remagen at exactly 4 P.M. on March 7. Half an hour earlier a preliminary charge was exploded, blowing a crater in the western flooring of the span. The charge was not strong enough, and the bridge remained intact. Drabik and his platoon reached the western end of the span at 3:50 P.M. Without pausing, the Americans began to cross the bridge in a catlike line through a hail of bullets. As the platoon surged across, a second preliminary explosion knocked out one of the main supports, but strangely the main charge of 500 pounds of TNT, placed by German experts, failed to go off. It was possible that a lucky hit from an American tank had broken the wrist-thick cable connected to the exploding charge. Sergeant Drabik later told the story: "We ran down the middle of the bridge, shouting as we went. I didn't stop because I knew that if I kept moving they couldn't hit me. My men were in squad column and not one of them was hit. We took cover in some bomb craters. Then we just sat and waited for the others to come. That's the way it was."

By 4 P.M. more than 100 Americans had moved across the bridge. Combat engineers, working speedily and efficiently, installed heavy planking and supporting beams to enable Allied tanks, trains, and trucks to move over the Rhine. Within twenty-four hours more than 8,000 troops and supporting hardware were across the river. At the same time, engineers built a pontoon bridge nearby in twenty-nine and one-half hours and a floating treadway bridge in thirty-nine and one-half hours.

News of the disaster infuriated Hitler. He ordered the Luftwaffe (q.v.) to send twenty-one of its new jet dive bombers to attack all three spans across the Rhine. All except five of the planes crashed or were shot down in the unsuccessful attack. At least a dozen V-2 rockets (*see*

VERGELTUNGSWAFFEN) exploded harmlessly nearby. There was jubilation on the Allied side. "This was one of my happy moments of the war," said General Eisenhower. "This was completely unforeseen. We were across the Rhine, on a permanent bridge; the traditional defensive barrier to the heart of Germany was pierced." "While the bridge lasted," added Lieut. Gen. Walter Bedell Smith, "it was worth its weight in gold." From Washington a delighted Gen. George C. Marshall, who was responsible for American conduct of the war, spoke of the Remagen Bridge incident as a windfall that had been hoped for but not expected: "The prompt seizure and exploit of the crossing demonstrated American initiative and adaptability at its best, from the daring action of the platoon commander to the Army commander who quickly redirected all his moving columns in a demonstration of brilliant staff management."

Germany had been opened as if by a surgeon's scalpel. Hitler later admitted that the Normandy beachhead and the Remagen bridgehead had sealed the fate of the Third Reich. He ordered severe punishment for four officer considered responsible for the disaster. All four were brought before a drumhead court-martial and summarily executed. Captain Bratke, to whom the faulty demolition wires were attributed, survived because he had the good fortune to be captured by the Americans. The Fuehrer removed Field Marshal Gerd von Rundstedt (q.v.), commander in chief of the German armies in the west, and replaced him with Field Marshal Albert Kesselring (q.v.), who was brought up from the Italian front.

Ten days later the central span of the bridge, attacked repeatedly by Luftwaffe planes and weakened by long-range artillery shells, collapsed. Twenty-seven American engineers died, and sixty-three were wounded in the wreckage. By this time several divisions of Americans had crossed the bridge. In another two weeks the bridgehead was expanded to a depth of 8 miles and a length of 25 miles.

After the war Hermann Goering (q.v.) said: "The capture of the Remagen bridge made a long Rhine defense impossible and upset our entire defense scheme along the river. We had to rush reserves to the Remagen bridgehead, as a result of which the Rhine was badly protected between Mainz and Mannheim." The Germans were outmaneuvered by the Americans. In a matter of days 75,000 American combat engineers built sixty-two bridges, including forty-six pontoon, eleven fixed highway, and three railway bridges, across the Rhine. One of the new floating treadways, 330 yards long and capable of sustaining heavy artillery loads, was set in the record time of ten hours eleven minutes. By March 25, 1945, seven armies were across the Rhine and moving against understrength and demoralized German divisions.

REMARQUE, ERICH MARIA (1898–1970). German novelist, *persona non grata* in the Third Reich. Erich Maria Remarque was born in Osnabrück on June 22, 1898, under the name Remark. He was drafted in 1916, wounded in 1917 and saw no further action. He was appalled by what he regarded as a useless loss of life. After the war he held several jobs until the great success of his first novel won him worldwide fame. His dramatic and realistic account of the devastation of the war, *Im Westen nichts Neues* (*All Quiet on the Western Front*), appeared in Germany in 1929 and immediately became a best seller. It sold half a million copies in some four months. Devoid of all romanticism, describing the situation in searing prose, the book was alive with pathos. In the United States it was dramatized as a highly successful motion picture. In later novels, such as *Der Weg zurück*, 1931 *(The Road Back)*, and *Drei Kameraden*, 1937 *(Three Comrades)*, Remarque continued with the same theme of a world in which the lowly individual was crushed by blind and irrational hatred.

Nazi ideologists were angered by Remarque's pacifism, antimilitarism, and antifascism. He left Germany as early as 1931 to live in Switzerland. In 1938 the National Socialist authorities canceled his German citizenship. The next year he went to the United States, of which he later became a citizen. His novel *Arch of Triumph* (1946), concerning the fate of refugees from Nazi Germany, won wide approval. In 1948 he returned to Europe and settled in Porto Ronco, Switzerland. He died in Ascona, Switzerland, on September 25, 1970.

REMER, OTTO-ERNST (1912–). Nazi anti-Resistance hero who played a leading role in thwarting the July Plot (q.v.) of 1944. A career officer, Maj. Otto-Ernst Remer was wounded eight times in the early years of World War II and received from Hitler the Knight's Cross with Oak Leaves (*see* RITTERKREUZ). On July 20, 1944, Remer was in command of Wachbataillon Grossdeutschland (Greater Germany Guard Battalion), a crack unit stationed at Döberitz, near Berlin, with instructions to take over the security of the capital in the event of a revolt of any kind, but especially one of foreign workers. On being alerted from Berlin, Remer moved into the city and sealed off the ministries in the Wilhelmstrasse. To prove that Hitler was not dead, Propaganda Minister Paul Joseph Goebbels (q.v.) put Remer on the telephone to the Fuehrer at Rastenburg. Hitler ordered Remer to place himself under Heinrich Himmler (q.v.), now commander in chief of the Home Army, and suppress all resistance with ruthless energy.

Until that moment Remer had not known which way to turn; now he wholeheartedly became the nemesis of the conspiracy. With 500 men he occupied the command post on Unter den Linden, sent out patrols to halt other troops, and supported Gen. Friedrich Fromm (q.v.) in arresting

Otto-Ernst Remer. [dpa Bild]

the conspirators. For his work in suppressing the July Plot, Remer was promoted to major general.

After the fall of the Third Reich in 1945, Remer became a living symbol of Nazi loyalty. In 1950 he founded the Neo-Nazi Sozialistische Reichspartei (SRP; Socialist Reich party). This new party attacked the Bonn regime and sought to revive the Nazi movement (*see* NEO-NAZISM). On March 15, 1952, the German High Court at Braunschweig sentenced Remer to three months' imprisonment for slandering the participants of the July Plot as traitors. On September 12, 1952, the Constitutional Court of the Federal Republic issued an interim injunction declaring the SRP unconstitutional. The party was formally dissolved on October 23, 1952. Remer, whose party had received comparatively little public support, disappeared from the political scene.

RENN, LUDWIG (1889–1979). Leftist anti-Nazi writer. Ludwig Renn (original name, Arnold Vieth von Golsenau) was born in Dresden on April 22, 1889. As an officer in World War I, he commanded successively a company and a battalion. After retiring from the Army in 1920, he studied economics, law, and the Russian language at Göttingen and Munich. Later he studied art history, archaeology, and Chinese history. A prolific writer, he served from 1928 to 1932 as secretary of the Alliance of Proletarian Revolutionary Writers. He also edited the journal *Linkskurve (Left Trajectory).* His novel *Der Krieg,* 1928 *(The War),* won him wide attention. In 1929 he went to the Soviet Union as a sympathetic observer. On the evening of the Reichstag fire (q.v.), February 27, 1933, he was arrested by the Nazi authorities and sentenced to two and one-half years in prison. Renn fled to Switzerland in 1936. In the Spanish Civil War he served as chief of staff of the International Brigade. Arrested in France in 1940, he was sent to prison and released the next year. He then went successively to England, the United States, and Mexico, where he became professor of European languages and history at the University of Morelia. From 1941 to 1946 he was the foremost figure in the Free German movement and took part in the Latin American Conference of Free Germans. In 1947 he settled in the German Democratic Republic (DDR), where he became professor of anthropology at the *Technische Hochschule* (technical college) in Dresden.

REPRISAL WEAPONS. *See* VERGELTUNGSWAFFEN.

RESISTANCE. The movement inside Germany that worked for the overthrow of Hitler and the Third Reich. Originally the Resistance took the form of opposition, to be followed by conspiracy. Early antagonisms inside the Nazi party were crushed in the 1934 Blood Purge (q.v.). Subsequently there emerged several centers of opposition. After Hitler came to power, attempts were made in governmental circles to discourage the more violent aspects of Nazi rule. On June 17, 1934, Vice-Chancellor Franz von Papen (q.v.) made his *Marburger Rede* (q.v.), a speech pleading for greater freedom of thought and expression. On August 18, 1935, Dr. Hjalmar Schacht (q.v.), in his *Königsberger Rede* (q.v.), deplored violence against the Jews. This kind of feeble criticism had no effect on either Hitler or his followers.

Once the policy of *Gleichschaltung* (q.v.) was begun to coordinate all German life, the most consistent opposition came from the churches. Despite the Concordat of 1933 (q.v.) between the papcy and the Third Reich, Nazi authorities continued to accuse Catholic priests and nuns of immoral behavior, violations of monetary regulations, and treason. The papal encyclical *Mit brennender Sorge* (q.v.; *With Deep Anxiety*), issued on March 21, 1937, denounced the persecution of Catholics. Michael Cardinal von Faulhaber (q.v.), despite past expressions of support for the Nazi regime, delivered sermons in defense of the Old Testament. The great majority of Protestant pastors settled for political obedience, but a small group headed by Dr. Martin Niemoeller and Pastor Dietrich Bonhoeffer (qq.v.) established the Bekenntniskirche (q.v.), the Confessional Church, to defend Protestantism and resist the pressures of dictatorship. Intellectuals, notably the Heidelberg group of Karl Jaspers and the Freiburg Circle (q.v.) around the historian Gerhard Ritter (q.v.), resisted the Nazi way of life and provided several members for the Resistance. Added to these were the Christian- and socialist-oriented members of the Kreisau Circle (q.v.). A small student group, led by Hans and Sophie Scholl (q.v.) and assisted by Professor Kurt Huber (q.v.), issued leaflets denouncing Hitler. They were arrested and executed in 1943.

Resistance was solidified by three developments: the Czech crisis of 1938, the outbreak of World War II in 1939, and the downward turn in Nazi fortunes in 1942. Several levels of opposition coalesced into the Resistance. The movement now drew its strength from three main sources: in the Foreign Office and governmental administration; among civilians; and, most important, inside the Wehrmacht (q.v.). Governmental administrators included Christian Albrecht Ulrich von Hassell (q.v.), former German Ambassador to Italy, and Professor Johannes Popitz (q.v.), Prussian minister of finance from 1933 to 1944. Among the more energetic civilian leaders were Dr. Carl Friedrich Goerdeler (q.v.), former mayor of Leipzig and for a time Price Commissioner in Hitler's government; Julius Leber (q.v.), Social Democratic delegate to the Reichstag (q.v.) from 1924 to 1933; and such church leaders as the Jesuit Father Alfred Delp (q.v.) and Pastor Bonhoeffer. Active on the technical side of the conspiracy were high army officers, including Gen. Ludwig Beck (q.v.), chief of the Army General Staff; Field Marshal Erwin von Witzleben (q.v.), one of the older conspirators; and several young officers, notably Col. Claus Schenk Graf von Stauffenberg (q.v.). Added to these were two important intelligence officers: Maj. Gen. Hans Oster (q.v.), chief of staff of the Abwehr (q.v.), and Adm. Wilhelm Canaris (q.v.), director of the counterintelligence department of the High Command.

In early 1938 Goerdeler went to London to inform British and French authorities of Hitler's aggressive plans and of the existence of a conspiracy to overthrow him. Any possible help from outside the Third Reich was thwarted by the Munich Agreement (q.v.). In February 1940 Von Hassell attempted to open negotiations with the Allies through a British agent. In May 1942 Pastor Bonhoeffer met with the Anglican Bishop of Chichester in Stockholm to apprise him of the Resistance plans. Later contacts were established in Switzerland with Allen Welsh Dulles (q.v.)

of the United States Office of Strategic Services. After much discussion, agreement was reached between General Beck and the older officers, Von Stauffenberg and the younger officers, Goerdeler and the civilians, and the Kreisau Circle on the composition and leadership of the new government once Hitler had been removed from the scene (*see* PROVISIONAL GOVERNMENT). The planning ultimately culminated in the ill-fated July Plot (q.v.) of 1944, after which the leading conspirators were arrested and executed.

The Resistance failed primarily because it never extended beyond a small circle of conspirators and because it came far too late to be effective. An additional unfavorable factor was the inability of the conspirators to win outside support. There was some sentiment in favor of Hitler in the democracies until the outbreak of war in 1939 made clear his aggressive intentions.

Bibliography. Roger Manvell and Heinrich Fraenkel, *The July Plot*, Pan Books, Ltd., London, 1966; Hans Rothfels, *The German Opposition to Hitler*, tr. by Lawrence Wilson, Henry Regnery Company, Chicago, 1962.

RETINUE. *See* GEFOLGSCHAFT.

RETURN OF THE GERMAN COLONIES. *See* RÜCKGABE DER DEUTSCHEN KOLONIEN.

REVENTLOW, ERNST [CHRISTIAN EINAR LUDWIG DETLEV] GRAF ZU (1869–1943). Pan-German leader who became a National Socialist. Ernst zu Reventlow was born in Husum, Schleswig-Holstein, then a part of Prussia, on August 18, 1869. In the opening decade of the twentieth century he was a writer on political and naval subjects and a leading member of the strongly nationalist Pan-German League. In 1913 he was forced to resign his commission as a naval officer after publishing *Der Kaiser und die Monarchisten (The Emperor and the Monarchists)*, which displeased William II. From 1920 on he edited the *Reichswart (Reich Observer)*. In 1924 he was elected to the Reichstag (q.v.), and three years later he joined the National Socialist party. From 1928 on he represented the Nazi party as a Reichstag deputy. He died in Munich on November 21, 1943.

RFS. *See* REICHSFUEHRERSCHULE.

RFSS. *See* REICHSFUEHRER-SS.

RHEIN. Code name for an earlier version of Operation Danzig (1939), meaning "Proceed with offensive in the west." *See* DANZIG.

RIBBENTROP, JOACHIM VON (1893–1946). National Socialist statesman and Hitler's Minister for Foreign Affairs. Joachim Ribbentrop was born in Wesel on April 30, 1893, to a middle-class officer's family. Educated at Kassel and Metz, he went to Canada as a commercial representative and returned to Germany shortly after the outbreak of World War I. At first he served on the eastern front, but in 1915 he was attached to the German military mission in Turkey. According to later critics, his Iron Cross (First Class) was awarded retroactively as a result of his own petition. After the war he worked as a wine salesman. Ribbentrop joined the lower ranks of Berlin café society, from which he was rescued by marrying the daughter of a wealthy champagne producer. At this time he took advantage of a change in the law to get himself adopted by a distant relative of the same name who had been knighted in 1884. He now took on the noble prefix "von."

Joachim von Ribbentrop. [*Imperial War Museum, London*]

On May 1, 1932, Von Ribbentrop joined the Nationalsozialistische Deutsche Arbeiterpartei (q.v.) and was named a *Standartenfuehrer* (colonel) in the SS (q.v.). Other Nazis regarded him as an ambitious upstart who had come late to the party. Hitler, on the other hand, was impressed by him. Ribbentrop's palatial home in Berlin-Dahlem served Hitler as a meeting place in the final negotiations for the formation of his first Cabinet.

Vain, domineering, and self-important, Von Ribbentrop was disliked both inside and outside the party. His obviously forced manners earned him the nickname Von Ribbensnob. His one outstanding characteristic was absolute subservience to Hitler. He became the Fuehrer's shadow. Foreign policy he understood to mean anything in foreign relations that was approved by the Fuehrer. He took great pains to learn beforehand exactly what was on Hitler's mind before he approached him with any problem or recommendation. His desire to please the Fuehrer was matched only by his inordinate ambition. His colleagues in the party, especially those who had risked their lives for the movement, had only contempt for the fawning flatterer. Among the estimates of his character was that by Paul Joseph Goebbels (q.v.): "Von Ribbentrop bought his name, he married his money, and he swindled his way into office."

As soon as he became Chancellor, Hitler, alienated by his conservative Foreign Office, decided to use the more compliant Von Ribbentrop as his adviser on foreign affairs. He set up the so-called Ribbentrop Bureau (Dienststelle Ribbentrop, q.v.) as a rival of the Foreign Office. As head of the new office, Von Ribbentrop, with Hitler's acquiescence, carried on a prolonged war with the pedantic Foreign Office. In 1934 Hitler appointed Von Ribbentrop a special commissioner for disarmament and sent him on a tour of foreign capitals to prepare the way for German rearmament.

As Ambassador-at-Large, Von Ribbentrop negotiated the Anglo-German naval agreement of June 18, 1935. On

August 11, 1936, he was made Ambassador to Great Britain, a post in which he hoped to encourage an Anglo-German understanding as envisioned by Hitler in *Mein Kampf* (q.v.). His mission failed partly because of his own awkward behavior. At a court reception in 1937 he committed a *faux pas* by greeting the King with a Nazi salute. It was a classic example of diplomatic bungling. Offended because English society rejected him, he became a pronounced Anglophobe. After the failure of his London mission he pushed the Berlin-Rome-Tokyo Axis (*see* ROME-BERLIN AXIS), obviously directed at Britain. When Hitler, on February 4, 1938, reshuffled both Army and administrative leadership, he made Von Ribbentrop Reich Minister for Foreign Affairs. During the successive crises of 1938 and 1939, Von Ribbentrop, still angry about his London mission, gave the Fuehrer misleading information. Britons, he said, were so lethargic and paralyzed that they would accept without complaint any aggressive moves by Nazi Germany. Hitler, he said, need not fear any effective British support for Poland.

On August 23, 1939, Von Ribbentrop went to Moscow to sign with Soviet Foreign Minister Vyacheslav M. Molotov a nonaggression agreement containing a secret clause providing for the partition of Poland (*see* HITLER-STALIN PACT). The pact opened the way for Hitler's attack on Poland and the subsequent outbreak of World War II. On September 28, 1939, Von Ribbentrop signed a second German-Soviet treaty readjusting the partition. He held his post to the end of the war, but he received less and less attention from the Fuehrer.

Von Ribbentrop disappeared in April 1945, but he was arrested by the British on June 14. Called before the International Military Tribunal at Nuremberg (*see* NUREMBERG TRIAL), he was accused of participating in Hitler's aggressive plans, particularly for Czechoslovakia and Poland, and of playing an important role in the Final Solution of the Jewish question (*see* ENDLÖSUNG, DIE). He complained: "The indictment is directed against the wrong people." In prison he sustained his sense of subservience even to the dead Hitler: "Even with all I know, if in this cell Hitler should come to me and say: 'Do this!' I would still do it." His performance in the courtroom was pathetic: pale, stooped, and beaten, he sobbed and pleaded his innocence. All the brash pompousness and arrogance were gone. The court stated: "It is because Hitler's policy and plans coincided with his own ideas that Ribbentrop served him so willingly to the end." Von Ribbentrop was found guilty on all four counts: count 1, conspiracy to commit crimes alleged in other counts; count 2, crimes against peace; count 3, war crimes; and count 4, crimes against humanity. He was hanged at Nuremberg at 11 minutes past 1 A.M. on the morning of October 16, 1946. He was the first of the condemned Nazis to mount the gallows.

Bibliography. Joachim von Ribbentrop, *The Ribbentrop Memoirs,* tr. by Oliver Watson, Weidenfeld and Nicolson, London, 1954; Paul Schwartz, *This Man Ribbentrop: His Life and Times,* Julian Messner, Publishers, Inc., New York, 1943.

RIBBENTROP BUREAU. *See* DIENSTSTELLE RIBBENTROP.

RICHARD. Code name adopted in 1936 for possible war complications with a future Communist Spain. Richard was to be implemented in the event that the Loyalists were victorious in the Spanish Civil War.

RICHTHOFEN, WOLFRAM FREIHERR VON (1895–1945). Outstanding officer of the Luftwaffe (q.v.) in World War II. Born on October 10, 1895, Wolfram von Richthofen was a cousin of Manfred Freiherr von Richthofen (1892–1918), the famous World War I flying ace. A junior member of the Flying Circus, Wolfram von Richthofen studied engineering after World War I and resumed his Army career in 1923. He was sent as a military attaché to Rome, where he was befriended by Italo Balbo, the Italian aviator. In 1936 he served as chief of staff to both Gen. Hugo Sperrle and his successor, Maj. Gen. Helmuth Volkmann (qq.v.), commanders of the Condor Legion (q.v.) of the new Luftwaffe. In November 1938, as brigadier general, he became the final commander of that unit.

In the opening months of World War II Von Richthofen led Stuka (q.v.) formations with great success in the *Blitzkrieg* (q.v.) against Poland and later against France. In July 1940, on the eve of the Battle of Britain, he commanded Fliegerkorps (Air Corps) VIII, a specialized corps consisting of three squadrons of Stukas and reconnaissance planes, with headquarters at Deauville. His unit suffered severe losses in combat with the Royal Air Force. It was moved to the Pas-de-Calais to be used in support of Operation Sea Lion (Seelöwe, q.v.), the projected invasion of Great Britain that never took place. Von Richthofen died on July 12, 1945.

RIEFENSTAHL, LENI (1902–   ). German film actress, director, and producer. Leni Riefenstahl was born in Berlin on August 22, 1902, the daughter of Alfred and Bertha Riefenstahl. She began her career as a dancer, studying at the Berlin School of Crafts, and was a ballet dancer with the Russian Ballet and with Mary Wigman. She was employed by Max Reinhardt (q.v.) for dance performances and had many other engagements from 1923 to 1926. Her first films, including *Der heilige Berg (The Holy Mountain),* used Alpine and mountain backgrounds. She starred in *S.O.S. Eisberg* with the pilot Ernst Udet (q.v.). Founding her own film company in 1931, she wrote, directed, produced, and played the leading role in *Das blaue Licht (The Blue Light),* which was awarded a gold medal at the Venice Biennale in 1932.

Hitler appointed Fräulein Riefenstahl to the post of director and producer in charge of making films for the Nazi party. She produced the Nuremberg rally film *Triumph des Willens* (q.v.; *Triumph of the Will*). On April 20, 1938, she released a masterpiece, *Olympia,* which was given a gala premiere on the occasion of the Fuehrer's forty-ninth birthday with Hitler in the audience. The film presented the 1936 Olympic Games in Berlin (*see* OLYMPIAD XI). It was released in two parts, each running approximately two hours, the *Fest der Völker (Festival of the Nations)* and the *Fest der Schönheit (Festival of Beauty).* Both won first prizes at the Venice Biennale. Hitler said of Leni Riefenstahl: "She has given the film of our time its mission and destination. It is a unique and incomparable glorification of the strength and beauty of our Party." In 1948 the International Olympic Committee gave her an award for the two Olympic films.

In interviews after the fall of the Third Reich, Leni Riefenstahl contended that she was a political illiterate who did not understand Hitler's motivation and plans. She defended herself vigorously against charges of political and romantic complicity with Hitler. "All they have written about me," she said, "it is nothing. I had no high position and no love story with Hitler. It was 1934. Women did not have a big position in film or anything. There was no law against Jews. Nobody knew what was going to happen." Other film makers described her as "a genius glorifying the wrong cause." *See also* FILMS IN THE THIRD REICH.

RITTER, GERHARD (1888–1967). Historian and opponent of Nazism. Gerhard Ritter was born in Bad Sooden an der Werra on April 6, 1888. A brother of the Orientalist Hellmut Ritter, he embarked on a distinguished career as one of Germany's leading historians. After teaching at Hamburg in 1924, he was called to the University of Freiburg the next year and remained there until 1956. A prolific writer, he published many books ranging from a history of Heidelberg to biographies of Luther, Frederick the Great, Vom Stein, and Gneisenau. A zealous Protestant, Ritter had a pronounced distaste for Hitler and Nazism. He joined the Bekenntniskirche (q.v.), the Confessional Church, as soon as it was formed, and he was the central figure in the Freiburg Kreis (q.v.), a conservative nationalist group that worked actively in the Resistance (q.v.) movement against Hitler. Together with his close friend Carl Friedrich Goerdeler (q.v.), civilian leader of the conspiracy against Hitler, Ritter envisioned a future Germany that would be a peaceful partner in a stable European community of nations. Ritter was arrested in 1944 and held in prison until he was released the following year by the Soviet Army. He died in Freiburg on July 1, 1967.

RITTERKREUZ (Knight's Cross). Hitler's variation of the Iron Cross (*Eisernes Kreuz,* q.v.), awarded for bravery. On September 1, 1939, the Fuehrer, as was customary at the beginning of a new war, revived the Iron Cross decoration, but he changed the grading, design, and ribbon. He abolished award of the medal for noncombatant service and established a new grade, the *Ritterkreuz,* to bridge the gap between the Iron Cross (First Class) and the Grand Cross. The *Ritterkreuz* came in the following ascending grades:

1. *Ritterkreuz* (Knight's Cross).
2. *Ritterkreuz mit Eichenlaub* (Knight's Cross with Oak Leaves).
3. *Ritterkreuz mit Eichenlaub und Schwerten* (Knight's Cross with Oak Leaves and Swords). The first to receive this decoration was Lieut. Gen. Adolf Galland of the Luftwaffe (qq.v.), after twenty victories in the Battle of Britain.
4. *Ritterkreuz mit Eichenlaub, Schwerten, und Brillianten* (Knight's Cross with Oak Leaves, Swords, and Diamonds). The first to receive this medal was Luftwaffe Maj. Werner Moelders (q.v.), who was credited with 115 air kills. Among other Luftwaffe officers who were given this decoration were, in order, General Galland and Col. Gordon Gollob, Capt. Hans-Joachim Marseille, Maj. Walther Nowotny, and Maj. Erich Hartmann (qq.v.).
5. *Ritterkreuz mit goldenen Eichenlaub, Schwerten, und Brillianten* (Knight's Cross with Golden Oak Leaves, Swords, and Diamonds). This medal was awarded only once, to Col. Hans-Ulrich Rudel (q.v.), who survived World War II.
6. *Grosskreuz* (Grand Cross of the Iron Cross). The only recipient in World War II was Hermann Goering (q.v.), after the Battle of France.

The Knight's Cross with Oak Leaves and Swords.

RKFDV. *See* REICHSKOMMISSARIAT FÜR DIE FESTIGUNG DES DEUTSCHEN VOLKSTUMS.

RKOIN. *See* REICHSKOMMISSAR FÜR DIE ÜBERWACHUNG DER ÖFFENTLICHEN MEINUNG.

RLB. *See* REICHSLEHRERBUND.

RLM. *See* REICHSLUFTFAHRTMINISTERIUM.

RMVP. *See* REICHSMINISTERIUM FÜR VOLKSAUFKLÄRUNG UND PROPAGANDA.

ROEHM (RÖHM), ERNST (1887–1934). Nazi politician and chief of the SA (q.v.). Ernst Roehm was born in Munich on November 28, 1887, to an old Bavarian family of civil servants. He became a professional soldier and was commissioned just prior to 1914. A fanatical, simple-minded swashbuckler, he was delighted by the camaraderie of war and suffered numerous wounds in the process. After 1918 he was a member of the lost generation that turned to extreme adventurism in such armed nationalist associations as the *Freikorps* (q.v.). An obese little man with a bullet-scarred and slightly red face and a weakness for young males, he divided people into soldiers and civilians, into friends and enemies. "Since I am an immature and wicked man," he said, "war and unrest appeal to me more than good bourgeois order." He was involved in the plot led by Franz Xaver Ritter von Epp (q.v.) against the left-wing government in Munich. As a captain in Reichswehr (q.v.) Group Headquarters 4 in Munich, Roehm was one of a number of ambitious officers who, after returning from the front, sought to exploit the helplessness of public officials in chaotic times. He had stored near Munich a secret cache of weapons, which he used as a means of achieving power among those sworn to destroy the radical government in Bavaria.

Attracted by Hitler's oratory, Roehm became one of the original members of the Nazi party. He was one of Hitler's closest friends, and the two were on the familiar *du* (thou) basis in conversation. Roehm was at Hitler's side during the 1923 Beer-Hall *Putsch* (q.v.) in Munich. Jailed, he was released on probation immediately after the trial, while Hitler was sent to prison at Landsberg am Lech (q.v.). Hitler learned from the unsuccessful *Putsch* that the crude idea of a head-on conquest of the state was impractical, but the happy-go-lucky Roehm was not convinced. Meanwhile, in difficult times Roehm worked as a traveling salesman for a publisher of patriotic works and, for two months, in a machine factory. Bored and disgusted, he accepted an invitation to go to Bolivia as a military instructor.

Following Nazi victories in the elections of September 14, 1930, Roehm was called back to Germany by Hitler to take charge of organizing and training Nazi Storm Troopers. Both he and his assistants were required to take an oath of allegiance to Hitler. Roehm was fascinated by his work. Within three months he had 170,000 men under his command, and by the end of 1933 there were more than 2 million. A brutal boss, Roehm gathered around him a dissolute crew of adventurers. His tough followers easily won the battle of the streets against the Communists.

Hitler rewarded Roehm by appointing him to the Reich Cabinet, but the two were at odds in deciding whether the SA was to be incorporated in the regular Army. Roehm wanted his private SA force to be combined with the armed forces to make a great "people's army" under his command. He was bitterly opposed by high-ranking officers of the Reichswehr, who did not want the Army to be corrupted by the SA bully boys. Hitler was caught in the middle, between his warm friendship for Roehm and his pragmatic sense of reality. He was fond of Roehm, but he needed the support of the generals in the decisive task of consolidating the Nazi regime. On New Year's Day, 1934, Hitler wrote to Roehm thanking him for his "immeasurable services rendered to the National Socialist movement and to the German people."

Hitler later alleged that his trusted friend Roehm had entered a conspiracy to take over political power. The Fuehrer was told, possibly by one of Roehm's jealous colleagues, that Roehm intended to use the SA to bring a socialist state into existence. On June 4, 1934, Hitler sent for Roehm and, in the course of a five-hour man-to-man conversation, warned him not to start a second revolution (q.v.). The Fuehrer admitted that he had no intention of dissolving the SA, to which he owed so much, but he ordered it on leave for the month of August, during which time no uniforms were to be worn. Hitler had now come to his final decision to eliminate the socialist element in the party. A list of hundreds of victims was prepared.

On June 30, 1934, Hitler flew to Munich and then went by car to Bad Wiessee, where Roehm and other SA leaders were vacationing. The Fuehrer confronted Roehm and ordered his arrest. Two days later, a gun was placed in Roehm's cell, and he was ordered to take the "honorable" way out. Unbelieving, Roehm refused, whereupon a murder squad shot him down. Dr. Paul Joseph Goebbels (q.v.), Minister for Public Enlightenment and Propaganda, reported in the controlled press that in this moment of rebellion the Fuehrer had become one with Germany and had acted as its avenging arm against traitors. Goebbels charged, and Hitler repeated the accusation in an address before the Reichstag (q.v.) on July 13, 1934, that the homosexual Roehm had joined Gregor Strasser and Gen. Kurt von Schleicher (qq.v.) in a conspiracy against Hitler and the Third Reich. All three had lost their lives in the Blood Purge (q.v.) that began on June 30.

Bibliography. Jean François, *L'affaire Röhm-Hitler*, Éditions Gallimard, Paris, 1939.

ROEHM PURGE (Roehm Affair). *See* BLOOD PURGE.

ROEHM'S AVENGERS. A secret group that dedicated itself to striking back for the execution of Ernst Roehm (q.v.) in the 1934 Blood Purge (q.v.). In the second half of 1934 and in early 1935 at least 155 SS (q.v.) leaders were murdered in retaliation by members of this group. Roehm's avengers identified their unit on a slip of paper pinned to the body of each victim.

RÖHM, ERNST. *See* ROEHM, ERNST.

ROLLAND, ROMAIN (1866–1944). French author known for his idealism. Romain Rolland was a strong opponent of the Third Reich. From 1904 to 1912 he published ten volumes of a remarkable work, *Jean-Christophe,* stressing the period of German culture represented by Beethoven and Goethe. For this extraordinary work he was awarded the Nobel Prize for Literature in 1915 and the Grand Prize of the French Academy. During World War I his uncompromising pacifist attitude led to accusations that he was pro-German. Rolland never denied his sympathy and respect for Germany, but the Nazi regime repelled him. On May 14, 1933, he sent a letter to the *Kölnische Zeitung* in which he denounced "the Germany of the swastika."

ROME-BERLIN AXIS. Formal agreement between Italy and Germany, the so-called pact of steel, signed on May 22, 1939. Mussolini and Hitler collaborated closely during the Spanish Civil War in 1936 and thereafter until the closing days of World War II. The metaphor Rome-Berlin Axis was used by Mussolini in a speech in Milan on November 1, 1936: "The Berlin-Rome line is not a diaphragm but rather an axis." Mussolini's son-in-law, Count Galeazzo Ciano, Italian Foreign Minister, visited Hitler and arranged a loose understanding (October Protocols) between the two countries. The formal alliance followed. The Rome-Berlin Axis was extended into the tripartite Berlin-Rome-Tokyo Axis on September 27, 1940.

ROMMEL, ERWIN (1891–1944). General field marshal, the famous Desert Fox of World War II. Erwin Rommel was born in Heidenheim, northeast of Ulm, on November 15, 1891. Entering the Army as a cadet in 1910, he became a professional soldier and devoted his life to that profession. He served in World War I as a lieutenant in an Alpine battalion in Romania and at Caporetto in Italy. In 1915 he was awarded the Iron Cross (First Class). After the war he remained in the Army as an infantry regimental officer and as an instructor at the Infantry School in Dresden. He met Hitler in 1935. In 1938, after reading Rommel's book *Infanterie greift an (Infantry Attacks),* Hitler appointed Rommel commander of his personal bodyguard battalion.

In World War II Rommel won a reputation as Germany's most popular general. At the same time he was regarded by many Allied officers as a master of desert warfare and as a fair-minded military professional. In 1940 he was assigned to command the 7th Panzer (Armored) Division on the western front under Gen. Gerd von Rundstedt (q.v.). On February 6, 1941, Hitler gave him command of the new Afrika Korps (q.v.) in North Africa with the task of pushing the British back into Egypt.

Rommel's campaign started successfully. On March 21, he defeated the British under Gen. Archibald Wavell at El Agheila and advanced to Tobruk. In late 1941 the British counterattacked and moved back to Benghazi. Rommel was promoted to full general in January 1942. On May 27, 1942, he struck swiftly in a renewed offensive and soon had the British reeling back toward the Egyptian frontier. On June 21, he captured Tobruk, the key to the British defenses. The next day Hitler made him a general field marshal. By the end of June 1942 Rommel was at El Alamein, 60 miles from Alexandria and the Nile Delta. It was one of the darkest moments of the war for the Allies.

Rommel's drive was halted by the end of October 1942 because of a combination of logistical difficulties and the buildup of Allied strength. Flown back to Germany for medical treatment, he returned to North Africa only after the Battle of El Alamein was lost (*see* EL ALAMEIN). Within two weeks he had to fall back 700 miles with the remnants of his African army. He was recalled from Tunis on March 9, 1943.

In mid-1943 Rommel was given command of Army Group B in northern Italy to prevent an Italian defection and to counter an Allied invasion of southern Europe. In January 1944 he was transferred to command of an army group in northern France. On two occasions, on June 17 and 29, 1944, Rommel and Von Rundstedt saw Hitler and attempted to convince him that he should end the war while considerable German forces still existed. The pale and shaken Fuehrer met their frankness with angry diatribes. On July 17, 1944, after the Allied invasion of Normandy, Rommel was severely injured when his automobile was strafed by a British plane, and he was sent home to Ulm to recover.

Field Marshal Erwin Rommel. [*Imperial War Museum, London*]

By this time Rommel had become increasingly disillusioned not only by Hitler's unrealistic military leadership but also by the worldwide reaction to Nazi atrocities. The bluff, simple military man began to turn to politics. He opposed the projected assassination attempt on Hitler's life on the ground that this action would only create a martyr. He suggested that it was better to place the Fuehrer on trial to reveal his crimes to the nation. Rommel never took an active role in the July Plot (q.v.), although the conspirators wanted him as Chief of State after the elimination of Hitler. After the failure of the plot, one of the conspirators, before he died in agony on a meat hook, blurted out Rommel's name to his tormentors. Rommel's doom was sealed. The Fuehrer sent two officers to Rommel's home at Herrlingen bei Ulm on October 14, 1944, to give him the choice of suicide or trial. "I shall die in fifteen minutes," Rommel told his wife. He then took poison. Hitler ordered burial with full military honors. In his funeral oration Von Rundstedt said: "A pitiless destiny snatched him from us. His heart belonged to the Fuehrer."

Bibliography. Desmond Young, *Rommel: The Desert Fox,* Harper & Brothers, New York, 1950.

ROSENBERG, ALFRED (1893–1946). Leading proponent of National Socialist ideology. Alfred Rosenberg was born in Reval (Tallinn), Estonia, on January 12, 1893, the son of an Estonian mother and a Lithuanian father. He took his first examination for an engineer's diploma at the *Technische Hochschule* (college of technology) in Riga. During World War I he lived for a time in Paris and in 1918 returned to Reval. Emigrating to Germany, he became a German citizen and settled in 1920 in Munich. There he met Hitler, who was fascinated by the young man's seemingly vast fund of knowledge. In 1921 Hitler made Rosenberg editor of the *Völkischer Beobachter* (q.v.), the newspaper of the rising Nazi movement.

Rosenberg's first pamphlet, *The Trace of Jews in the History of the World,* contained much of the pseudoscientific verbiage that was to appear in his later work. Next he reissued the spurious *Protocols of the Elders of Zion* (q.v.). This kind of specialization won him a reputation as the spiritual leader of National Socialism. He was at Hitler's side in 1923 in the unsuccessful Beer-Hall *Putsch* (q.v.) in Munich. He founded the German People's Publishing House in 1926, published a monthly magazine called *The World Struggle,* and in 1929 organized the Kampfbund für Deutsche Kultur (q.v.). After Hitler became Chancellor in 1933, Rosenberg was placed in charge of the party office for foreign politics, whose agents were active in Nazi intrigue abroad. He controlled a network of foreign branches, and he also administered the German Academic Exchange Service. In 1934 he was given responsibility for training all Nazi party members in National Socialist ideology.

On July 17, 1941, Hitler appointed Rosenberg Reich Minister for the Eastern Occupied Territories. In this post Rosenberg promoted the Germanization of Eastern peoples under brutal conditions, supervised slave labor, and arranged the extermination of Jews. He was responsible

Alfred Rosenberg at Nuremberg. [*Official United States photo*]

for rounding up quotas of workers and sending them to the Reich (*see* HEU AKTION).

At the Nuremberg Trial (q.v.), Rosenberg was found guilty on all four counts and sentenced to death by hanging. He was executed at Nuremberg on October 16, 1946. It was reported that he looked at the chaplain but said nothing. In ninety seconds he was dead, in the swiftest execution of the condemned men.

Rosenberg was moody and retiring but glibly persuasive. Ruthlessly ambitious, he edged into Hitler's inner coterie and managed to stay there. The Fuehrer had so much confidence in him that he sent him to London on May 1, 1933, for the purpose of explaining to British leaders the peaceable, defensive nature of the Nazi movement. The outcome was deplorable. The sight of the morose figure did much to intensify British distrust of the new Nazi regime. Because a hostile press and repeated public incidents made his stay in England unbearable, he soon departed. At the Nuremberg Trial the philosopher of Nazism was reduced to a shaking hulk. Reporters commented on his extreme nervousness in the dock and on the way in which, with his hands shaking, he lurched forward as he strained to hear every word.

Rosenberg worked on his magnum opus, *Mythus des XX. Jahrhunderts (The Myth of the Twentieth Century)*, for eight years and finished it in 1925. It was published in Munich in 1930 with the subtitle *A Valuation of the Spiritual-Intellectual Conflicts of Our Time*. The publisher called the author "an inspired and endowed seer" and praised the book as "a fountainhead of fundamental precepts in the field of human history, religion, and cultural philosophy, almost overwhelming in magnitude." The title was explained: "The *Mythus* is the Myth of the Blood, which, under the sign of the Swastika, released the World Revolution. It is the Awakening of the Soul of the Race, which, after a period of long slumber, victoriously put an End to Racial Chaos." The book quickly became a best seller, second only to *Mein Kampf* (q.v.). By December 1936, 500,000 copies had been sold; by 1943 the sales reached 750,000, and in 1944 1 million copies were in print. In the Third Reich the *Mythus* was regarded as a kind of National Socialist bible.

A melodramatic depiction of history as a perennial struggle between the glorious Nordic spirit and the corrupting influence of inferior races, the book filled a need for Hitler. Rosenberg's first concern was to give a "scientific" justification for the Nazi blood myth. Each race, he said, had its own soul and its own religion. It is necessary to understand, Rosenberg wrote, that race is at the top of a hierarchy of values embracing the state, religion, and art. The so-called unity of races is an absurd hypothesis and a simple abstraction. Actually, said Rosenberg, there is a plurality of races, which differ from one another in the hereditary composition of the blood. Each race has its own conception of beauty, morality, and religion. The superior, creative race, the Nordic, came from a vanished continent to the north of Europe, where it had taken on the spiritual qualities of a semi-Arctic environment of blue water and gleaming ice. Its branches could be recognized in the Amorites of the Middle East, the Aryans of India, the early Greeks and Romans, and, finally, the Germanic peoples. These peoples created all the states in the West.

The Germanic element of the Nordic race, Rosenberg wrote, brought order out of chaos to India, Persia, Greece, the Roman Empire, France, England, and the United States. The highest value of the Nordic race is honor, a special attribute of the German people. The spirit of the Nordic race is personified in the god Wotan: honor and heroism, the art of song, the protection of right, and the eternal striving for wisdom. Wotan's spirit could be found in such Nordics as Luther, Dante, Frederick the Great, Bismarck, and Hitler. Christianity, the Renaissance, and the Enlightenment were not progressive movements but rather sources of disintegration of Nordic truth. Rosenberg warned that when Nordic blood was mixed with inferior stocks, civilization deteriorated: witness "the decline of the West, the certain result of criminal bastardization of race and de-nordicization." He stated: "To-day a new faith awakens: the myth of the blood, the faith that by defending his blood we defend also the divine nature of man. The faith, embodied in scientific clarity, that the Nordic blood represents the mystery which has replaced and conquered the ancient sacraments."

Rosenberg denounced Christianity as a dangerous product of the Semitic-Latin spirit and a disintegrative Judaistic concept. Christian churches, he wrote, especially the Roman Catholic Church, are "prodigious, conscious, and unconscious falsifications." The Old Testament should be abandoned as a book of religion, because it was responsible for "our present Jewish domination." For the Old Testament cattle breeders Rosenberg would substitute the Nordic sagas and fairy tales. Instead of what he called the murdering messiahship he would have "the dream of honor and freedom rekindled by the Nordic, Germanic sagas." The true picture of Christ, he asserted, had been distorted by Jewish fanatics like Matthew, by materialistic rabbis like Paul, by African jurists like Tertullian, and by mongrel half-breeds like St. Augustine. The real Christ, Rosenberg insisted, was an Amorite Nordic, aggressive and courageous, a revolutionary who opposed the Jewish and Roman systems with sword in hand, bringing not peace but war. Popes and Jesuits, in Rosenberg's view, had made Christianity unrecognizable, and the heroic Luther and Calvin had been frustrated by their followers.

Rosenberg reserved his utmost contempt for the Roman Catholic Church. It had kept civilization in slavery, and it remained a pitiless force working against the Nordic ideal. Roman Catholicism, he wrote, was an even greater menace than Judaism because its roots were tenacious in history. It had made the fundamental error of taking into its fold any human being regardless of his racial origin—a crime against the ideal of racial purity. The Catholic doctrines of love and pity were directly contrary to the Germanic virtues of heroism and honor. There were irreconcilable differences between the Catholic and the Christian mentalities. Catholicism sprang from Oriental races in Judea and Syria and was therefore alien to the spirit of Nordicism. Spiritually, the Catholic clergy was a continuation of the old Etruscan priesthood. The Pope was merely a medicine man, and church history only a series of atrocities, swindles, and forgeries.

As a Nazi ideologist, Rosenberg demanded that the "white race" be freed from the disruptive Etruscan-Syrio-Judaic-Asiatic-Catholic influence. This influence was, he charged, a monstrous perversion of truth. The German people must turn away from the medicine man Pope and his voodoo practices, from mongrelized Catholicism, from the Old Testament, from the decadent morals of the Sermon on the Mount, and from the doctrine of sin and salvation. These should be replaced by the swastika (*Hakenkreuz,* q.v.) as the living symbol of race and blood. The warrior syndrome of the early Teutons should be revived. The universal spirit of Christianity, Rosenberg charged, had led only to the internationalism of Karl Marx. It had prefigured the false concept of liberty, equality, and fraternity, creations of Judaistic-Christian decadence and "idiotic principles designed to enslave the Nordic peoples."

Rosenberg projected what he called positive Christianity (q.v.), which would purify the Nordic race, reestablish the old pagan values, and substitute the spirit of the hero for the Crucifixion. The new Christianity would become one with the old Norse paganism. The old idea of Christian world citizenship would disappear in favor of a healthy and heroic race-conscious devotion.

The *Mythus* was devastating in its indictment of Jews: whereas the Nordics were noble, creative, and constructive, the Jews were ignoble, parasitic, and destructive. In attacking the Jews, the *Mythus* restated the doctrines projected in *Mein Kampf* (q.v.). Rosenberg, like Hitler, attributed all evil to the Jews. The Jewish spirit, Rosenberg wrote, had seeped into Christianity and thus was responsible for all the evils that Christianity had brought to the world.

Rosenberg added to his anti-Semitism (q.v.) an attack on Freemasonry as an impossible universalist dream. The Freemasons had made the mistake of trying to create a religion of humanity by fusing all ethnic and national ideas. They did not understand the German spirit. For the Marxists, Rosenberg had complete contempt. Germans, he said, must struggle alike against the democratic shopkeeper ideal of the bourgeoisie and the Marxist idea of the dictatorship of the proletariat.

In essence, Rosenberg's *Mythus* was a rehash of the racial doctrine of Arthur Comte de Gobineau and Houston Stewart Chamberlain (qq.v.; *see* RACIAL DOCTRINE). Rosenberg differed in part from his predecessors in his emotional denunciation of Christianity (both Gobineau and Chamberlain had professed their attachment to Christianity), but his racial ideology came directly from them. Rosenberg's myth of the blood marked the transition of German irrationalism to extreme Nazi mysticism. What was left of German humanism was dissolved in a new, confused neoromanticism. Firmly supported by Hitler, Rosenberg's *Mythus* of the blood became the official philosophy of the Third Reich. Millions of Germans accepted it as the essence of wisdom.

Bibliography. Alfred Rosenberg, *Selected Writings,* Jonathan Cape, Ltd., London, 1970.

ROSENBERG TASK FORCE. *See* EINSATZSTAB ROSENBERG.

ROSSBACH GROUP. One of the many freebooter *Freikorps* (q.v.) companies in the immediate post-World War I years. Commanded by a former 1st lieutenant named Gerhard Rossbach, the group saw its mission as the liberation of the fatherland from the "traitors and weaklings" who had been responsible for Germany's defeat. On occasion, the Rossbach group resorted to killing for the cause. Among its members were Edmund Heines (q.v.), a close associate of Ernst Roehm (q.v.), the leader of the SA (q.v.), and of Rudolf Franz Hoess (q.v.), the future commandant of Auschwitz (q.v.). *See also* SCHLAGETER, Albert Leo.

ROT (Red). Code name for possible German action in the Czechoslovakian crisis of 1937–1938. Hitler ordered all three of his military services to prepare for two major eventualities. The first assumed the opening of a war by a surprise French attack, in which case the Wehrmacht (q.v.), the regular Army, was to deploy its principal strength in the west. The plan to meet the attack was given the cover name Red, known in German staff circles as Fall Rot (Case Red). The second plan, Fall Grün (Case Green), concerned a surprise German attack against Czechoslovakia "in order to counter the imminent attack of a superior enemy coalition." *See also* GRÜN.

ROTE KAPELLE (Red Orchestra). A group of about 100 pro-Soviet Germans who set up a widespread espionage system for Moscow inside Germany. Among its leaders were Harro Schulze-Boysen, a grandson of Adm. Alfred von Tirpitz, the World War I naval hero, and Arvid Harnack, a nephew of the celebrated theologian Adolf von Harnack. The Rote Kapelle managed to penetrate important military and civilian offices in Berlin. The network was discovered by the Abwehr (q.v.), the counterintelligence agency, in 1942, and most of its leaders, including Schulze-Boysen and Harnack, were executed for treason in a new method of slaughter, the strangulation of victims attached to meat hooks.

ROTFRONTKÄMPFERBUND (Red Front Fighters' Association). The unofficial army of the Communists during the Weimar Republic (q.v.). From 1930 on it faced Nazi Storm Troopers (*see* SA) in a continual bloody battle of the streets. Many on both sides were killed in these clashes. Calling themselves antifascists, the Communists, sometimes trained by Russian instructors, used the slogan: "Strike the fascists wherever you find them!" On February 1, 1933, directly after Hitler's assumption of political power, the Hamburg Rotfrontkämpferbund issued a call to arms: "The day is not far distant when our victorious Red Army that needs no police to protect it, weapon in hand, will drive the deadly enemy of the working class to the devil." After the Enabling Act of March 24, 1933 (q.v.), the Communist party and its unofficial army ceased to exist.

ROTTENFUEHRER-SS. Corporal in the SS (q.v.).

RPA. *See* REICHSPROPAGANDAAMT.

RPL. *See* REICHSPROPAGANDALEITUNG.

RSHA. *See* REICHSSICHERHEITSHAUPTAMT.

RUBLEE PLAN. An unsuccessful proposal for the rescue of Jews from Nazi Germany. At a conference convened in Évian, France, in the summer of 1938, the Intergovernmental Committee for Political Refugees, under the chairmanship of an American, George Rublee, proposed that the emigration of Jews from the Third Reich be linked with the promotion of German exports in such a way that Jews could transfer their ledger credits abroad. On January 2, 1939, Hjalmar Schacht (q.v.), president of the Reichsbank, spoke to Hitler over the violent protests of both Hermann Goering and Joachim von Ribbentrop (qq.v.), each of whom considered the matter within his jurisdiction. The Fuehrer was skeptical, but he gave Schacht permission to go ahead.

In the middle of January 1939 Schacht and Rublee met in Berlin to discuss the emigration of 150,000 Jews (450,000 with their families) whose age (fifteen to forty-five) and state of health would make it possible for them to earn a living abroad. The plan would be completed within three or, at the most, five years. The Jews would have to place 25 percent of their assets in a cash fund to be used for their support until they emigrated; this fund would then be transferred to the Reich.

While these negotiations were going on, Schacht and Hitler clashed on the matter of financing rearmament. The Reichsbank president insisted that Goering's expenditures were bankrupting the country and that the reserves of money would soon be exhausted. Hitler, who would allow nothing to stand in the way of a powerful rearmed Germany, dismissed Schacht on January 30, 1939. Within a few days Rublee resigned his post. His scheme to rescue Jews was abruptly dropped.

RÜCKGABE DER DEUTSCHEN KOLONIEN (Return of the German Colonies). Phrase stressed by Nazi orators. It called for the return to Germany of all colonies taken from it after World War I by the Treaty of Versailles. When Rudolf Hess (q.v.) flew to Scotland on May 10, 1941, he used this phrase in discussions with British authorities. He urged the British to stop the "civil war" between the two Germanic peoples, let each stay in its own sphere, and give Germany its colonies. *See* HESS FLIGHT.

RUDEL, HANS-ULRICH (1916–). The most highly decorated soldier in the Third Reich and the only holder of the Knight's Cross with Golden Oak Leaves, Swords, and Diamonds (*see* RITTERKREUZ). Hans-Ulrich Rudel attended military school at Wildpark. In 1938 he was posted to a Stuka (q.v.) formation in the Luftwaffe (q.v.) as an engineering officer. During World War II he was promoted from lieutenant (1939) to colonel (1945). In September 1941 he sank a cruiser and the battleship *Marat*. Shot down and captured by the Russians in March 1944, he escaped. In January 1945 he was awarded the highest *Ritterkreuz* decoration, the only participant in the war to receive the award with golden oak leaves. A month later he was shot down again, this time losing his right leg. By the end of the war, which he survived, he was credited officially with 2,530 operations and 532 tank kills.

In 1953 Rudel returned from a self-imposed exile in Argentina as a candidate for the Deutsche Reichspartei, the neo-Nazi German Reich party. An irreconcilable nationalist, he called for a return to the old military virtues of chivalry and obedience.

RUHR. German mining and manufacturing region. The greatest part of Germany's coal, iron, and steel production is in the Ruhr area. By 1914 Bochum, Dortmund, and Essen in the Ruhr Basin had become essential as the source of German armaments. The growth of Essen was due for the most part to the Krupp family. When Germany informed the Allies in 1923 that it could no longer pay reparations, it had to look on as French and Belgian troops marched into the Ruhr. To obstruct the occupation as much as possible the Germans adopted passive resistance. Albert Leo Schlageter (q.v.), later to become a Nazi folk hero, was killed in the Ruhr district during the occupation. The basin was evacuated by the French and Belgians in 1925.

In 1933 the war industry of the Ruhr was reestablished,

at first in secret, by Rhineland industrialists who were cooperating with the new Third Reich. During World War II the Ruhr area became a target for Allied bombing raids. The entire Ruhr Basin was encircled by American troops in mid-April 1945.

RUNDFUNK (Radio). The domestic German radio system. *See also* RADIO IN THE THIRD REICH.

RUNDSTEDT, GERD VON (1875–1953). General field marshal in the armed forces of the Third Reich and one of its highest-ranking officers. Gerd von Rundstedt was born in Aschersleben on December 12, 1875. He was promoted to the rank of *Generaloberst* (colonel general) in 1932 and given command of Army Group I in Berlin. In February 1938, with fourteen other senior officers, he was purged from the Army as a result of the Blomberg-Fritsch crisis (q.v.). As a retired officer available for duty at the outbreak of World War II, he was recalled in August 1939 as commander in chief of Army Group South. In May and June 1940 he was commander in chief of the German armies in the west. In this capacity he led the main thrust of the campaign against France. In recognition of his services Hitler promoted Von Rundstedt on July 19, 1940, to general field marshal, along with eleven other generals.

On the invasion of Soviet Russia in 1941, Von Rundstedt was given command of Army Group South with instructions to clear the Black Sea coast, take Rostov, seize the Maikop oil fields, and then push on to Stalingrad on the Volga to sever Stalin's last link with the Caucasus. Coming into conflict with Hitler on strategy in Russia, Von Rundstedt was relieved on December 12, 1941. On March 1, 1942, he was appointed commander in chief of the Army West to replace Gen. Erwin von Witzleben (q.v.); except for two short intervals in 1944 he served in that capacity until March 1945. On July 2, 1944, Hitler, angered by Von Rundstedt's failure to stop the Anglo-American invasion of Normandy, dismissed him and replaced him temporarily with Field Marshal Günther Hans von Kluge (q.v.).

As early as 1942 Von Rundstedt knew about the Resistance (q.v.) movement against Hitler among high-ranking officers of the armed forces, but although he was never a convinced Nazi, he refused to commit himself to the conspiracy. He informed Gen. Erwin Rommel (q.v.): "You are young and you are popular with the people. You must do it." That was as far as Von Rundstedt would go in the conspiracy. After the unsuccessful July Plot (q.v.) of 1944, Von Rundstedt followed his oath of allegiance to Hitler and presided over the military court of honor that found the conspirators guilty and expelled them from the armed forces prior to their appearance before the Volksgericht (q.v.), the People's Court. Von Rundstedt's last gamble, the Ardennes offensive in December 1944, failed to halt the Allied advance into Germany. He died in Hannover on February 24, 1953.

Field Marshal Gerd von Rundstedt. [*US Army*]

Bibliography. Günther Blumentritt, *Von Rundstedt, the Soldier and the Man,* tr. by Cuthbert Reavely, Odhams Press, Ltd., London, 1952.

RURAL HOME GUARD. *See* WACHDIENST.

RUSHA. *See* RASSE- UND SIEDLUNGSHAUPTAMT.

RUSSIAN LICE POWDER. A disinfectant manufactured by Dr. Theodor Morell (q.v.), Hitler's personal physician. Its use was made compulsory by Hitler's order throughout the armed forces, and the construction of factories for its manufacture was given high priority during World War II.

RUST, BERNHARD (1883–1945). Reich Minister for Science, Education, and Culture in Hitler's Cabinet from 1933 to 1945. Bernhard Rust was born in Hannover on September 30, 1883, to a farm family of Lower Saxony that could trace its lineage for centuries. After attending a *Gymnasium* (high school) in Hannover, he studied Germanics, philosophy, philology, art history, and music at several universities, including Munich, Göttingen, Berlin, and Halle. In 1908 he passed the state examinations for secondary teaching, and the next year he became an *Oberlehrer* (senior teacher) at the *Realgymnasium* (secondary school with emphasis on science) in Hannover. He served for four years in World War I, winning the Iron Cross (First and Second Classes) and the Hohenzollern Order.

After the war Rust joined the National Socialists and was made *Gauleiter* (district leader) for Hannover-Braunschweig. In 1930 he was elected to the Reichstag (q.v.) as a Nazi delegate. In February 1933, after Hitler assumed power, Rust was appointed Prussian minister of culture. The next year the Fuehrer named him to his Cabinet as Reich Minister for Science, Education, and Culture. From then until the fall of the Third Reich, Rust was in charge of the educational and cultural system of Nazi Germany. He committed suicide in May 1945.

RW. *See* REICHSWEHR.

RYAN, HERMINE BRAUNSTEINER. *See* BRAUNSTEINER, HERMINE.

S

SA
to
SWORD WORDS

SA (Sturmabteilung; Storm Detachment). The early private army, the Storm Troopers, of the Nationalsozialistische Deutsche Arbeiterpartei (q.v.), the Nazi party. It was designed originally to protect National Socialist mass meetings and oppose rival political parties. Hitler started the SA by organizing squads of young roughnecks brought in largely from the *Freikorps* (q.v.; free corps), the post-World War I nationalistic freebooters. The name Sturmabteilung was adopted in late 1921. The SA was led at first by a non-Nazi, a Captain Pfeiffer von Salomon, who used his troops like a Renaissance mercenary. In January 1931 the organization was taken over by Capt. Ernst Roehm (q.v.), who had returned from service in the Bolivian Army the previous October. Roehm brought in large numbers of veterans, outfitted them in brown uniforms (hence their nickname Brownshirts), and used them as guards at Nazi meetings. He modeled the SA on the German Army, with a general staff, headquarters, and a training college in Munich. The formations of the SA as of June 1933 are shown in the accompanying chart.

The SA was assigned the task of winning the battle of the streets against the Communists on the assumption that "possession of the streets is the key to the power of the state." It was also used to keep the people in a permanent state of excitement. By 1931 it numbered 100,000 men, and by 1932 its ranks had risen to 400,000. In the presidential election campaign of 1932 President Paul von Hindenburg (q.v.) banned the SA. Hitler was annoyed by this action, but, determined to win power legally, he obeyed and ordered the SA to respect the ban.

From its earliest days Hitler regarded the SA as a political and not as a military force. He considered his Brownshirts shock troops for a revolution that was never to be made. His problem was to maintain the spirit of the SA without allowing it to move into revolutionary action. Above all, he was determined to keep it from a conflict

FORMATIONS OF THE SA

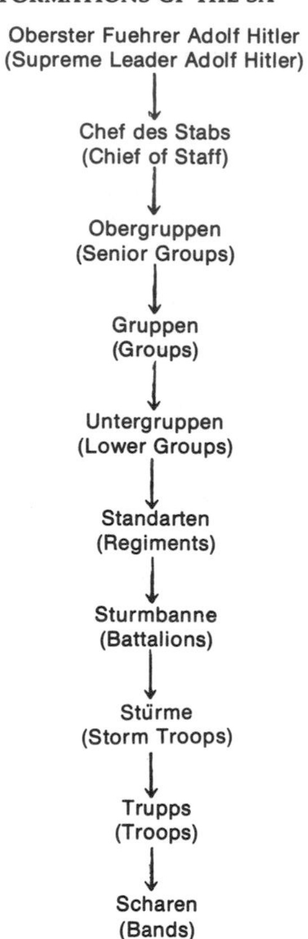

with the Army. Roehm, on the other hand, saw the SA not only as the backbone of the Nazi movement but as the nucleus of a revolutionary army like the conscripts for Napoleon. Roehm hoped that the SA would be combined eventually with the armed forces under his own command. He would stress the socialist aspect of National Socialism, even as Hitler was interested primarily in the nationalist side. The Reichswehr (q.v.) command opposed the SA as a motley bunch of street brawlers, thugs, and hooligans who understood nothing of Army traditions.

A Nazi poster extolling the Storm Troopers: "Service with the SA raises one to comradeship, toughness, and strength!" *[Imperial War Museum, London]*

As soon as Hitler became Chancellor in 1933, he called on the SA, the SS, and the Stahlhelm (qq.v.) to act as auxiliary police. A day after the Nazis came to political power, Storm Troopers broke into Communist headquarters in Berlin to search for incriminating evidence. Some SA leaders began to demand that they supplant regular army officers. The issue came to a head in the 1934 Blood Purge (q.v.), when Roehm and other SA leaders were purged. The decline of the SA began with the purge. In 1935 it was reorganized. An attempt was made to improve the quality of the Storm Troopers; members from eighteen to thirty-five years of age were called to active service, those from thirty-five to forty-five were placed on reserve, and those over forty-five were assigned to the Landsturm (local militia). The organization was divided into twenty-one groups, and these in turn into ninety-seven brigades, with 627 *Standarten* (regiments), each comprising between 1,000 and 2,000 men.

In October 1935, Dr. Paul Joseph Goebbels (q.v.), Minister for Public Enlightenment and Propaganda, stated: "The SA is an historic fact and no one can imagine its disappearance. There are some organizations which act simply by their presence. An army is not obliged to demonstrate its *raison d'être* by making war. By its mere presence it often prevents war." Hitler added that the SA was to maintain internal order, just as the armed forces were required to provide external order.

The International Military Tribunal at Nuremberg (*see* NUREMBERG TRIAL) found the *Fuehrer-Korps* (q.v.) of the Nazi party, the SD, and the *Gestapo* (qq.v.) to be criminal but rejected the cases against the Reich Cabinet, the High Command of the armed forces, and the SA. Its judgment on the SA follows:

> Up until the purge beginning on June 30, 1934, the SA was a group composed in large part of ruffians and bullies who participated in the outrages of that period. It has not been shown, however, that these atrocities were part of a specific plan to wage aggressive war, and the Tribunal therefore cannot hold that these activities were criminal under the Charter. After the purge the SA was reduced to the status of unimportant Nazi hangers-on. Although in specific instances some units of the SA were used for the commission of war crimes and crimes against humanity, it cannot be said that the members participated in, or even knew of, the criminal acts. For these reasons the Tribunal does not declare the SA to be a criminal organization within the meaning of Article 9 of the Charter.

SA-LIEDERBUCH (SA Songbook). A 294-page pocket-size booklet published in 1933 by the Joseph C. Huber Verlag, of Diessen am Ammersee, near Munich, with an introduction by the SA chief of staff, Ernst Roehm (q.v.). The songbook included poetry by Dietrich Eckart (q.v.) and others; SA songs; soldier, freedom, and marching songs; fatherland, folk, and home songs; songs of devotion and prayer songs; humorous songs; and bugle songs of the SA ("Streets Free!"; "Adjutant Call"; "Fuehrer Call"). In the back of the booklet were blank pages on which texts of special songs and poems could be added.

SA-MANN BRAND. A Nazi film produced early in the career of Dr. Paul Joseph Goebbels (q.v.), Minister for Public Enlightenment and Propaganda. This film and others such as *Hitlerjunge Quex* and *Hans Westmar* were greeted enthusiastically by Nazi party members, but they were box-office failures. The German public as a whole was never attracted by such propaganda films. *See also* FILMS IN THE THIRD REICH.

SA RESERVE NO. 1. *See* STAHLHELM.

SA RESERVE NO. 2. *See* STAHLHELM.

SA SONGBOOK. *See* SA-LIEDERBUCH.

SAALSCHLACHTEN (Hall Battles). Organized assaults on rival political meetings in Munich by Nazi Storm Troopers (*see* SA) in the early 1920s. The battles were fought with beer mugs, blackjacks, and chair legs. The favorite targets of the Nazis were Communists and Socialists. The Socialists organized a strong-arm squad called the Erhard Auer Guards (after a Socialist party leader who nearly lost his life in a shooting in the Bavarian Parliament at the time of the Kurt Eisner assassination on February 21, 1919). In the battles the halls were left strewn with wreckage and covered with the blood of the rival factions.

SAAR (Saarland). A German district in the Saar Basin, covering almost 1,000 square miles along the Saar River, between the French Department of the Moselle and the German Rhineland-Palatinate. After World War I, from 1919 to 1935, it was administered by the League of Nations, with the valuable mines under French control because of the damage done by German troops to French coalfields during the war. In 1935 the population of the Saar decided by plebiscite to return to Germany, and the district reverted to the Third Reich. During World War II the Saar was taken by troops of the United States Seventh Army. In 1945 the French again occupied the area and administered it until 1957, when, after another plebiscite, it became German territory again. The importance of the Saar district derives from its rich coalfields, which are utilized by the German iron and steel industry.

SACHSENHAUSEN. Concentration camp located north of Berlin, near Oranienburg (*see* CONCENTRATION CAMPS). Sachsenhausen was one of three camps set up in 1933 to form the nucleus of a penal camp system: Sachsenhausen in the north, Dachau (q.v.) in the south, and Buchenwald (q.v.) in central Germany. Like other camps, Sachsenhausen was commanded by an *SS-Standartenfuehrer* (colonel) and administered by a staff headed by a *Sturmbannfuehrer* (major).

SALMON TRAP. *See* LACHSFANG.

SALOMON, ERNST VON (1902–1972). Author and political activist. Ernst von Salomon was born in Kiel in 1902 to a family of Huguenot extraction. He was educated as a cadet at the royal military academies in Karlsruhe and Berlin-Lichterfelde. His hopes and ideals were shattered by the defeat of Germany in 1918. Later, in his novel *The Outlaws* (1930), he described his feelings of despair and bitter resentment. Soon after the war he joined a unit of the *Freikorps* (q.v.), a voluntary paramilitary group of freebooters distinguished for their rejection of the normal conventions of civilian life and obedient only to their chosen leaders. Von Salomon took part in the street fighting in Berlin in early 1919. For his part in the murder of Walther Rathenau, the German Foreign Minister, on June 24, 1922, Von Salomon was sentenced to five years' imprisonment. After his release he helped organize peasants' revolts in Schleswig-Holstein.

During the era of the Third Reich, Von Salomon did not play an active role in Nazi affairs. He announced his retirement from politics and worked as a scriptwriter for UFA, the German film company. His writings, however, were approved by the National Socialist regime as "documents portraying the struggle for the rebirth of the nation." In 1945 he was arrested by the Allied military government and interned at Plattling until 1946.

In 1951 Von Salomon published *Der Fragebogen (The Questionnaire)*, a long, contemptuous, and satirical response to 131 questions submitted by the Allied military government in its campaign of denazification (q.v.). It was a brilliant tour de force as a response to an awkward and somewhat naïve questionnaire. The book was highly successful in Germany but was denounced elsewhere as evidence that the deep-rooted nationalism which Hitler had exploited still existed in Germany to an alarming extent. *See also* FRAGEBOGEN, DER.

SANITÄTSDIENSTGEFREITER (SDG; Deputy Health Service Officer). Officer in the extermination camps (q.v.) responsible for executing inmates in the gas chambers. Because there was never a stock of gas in the crematoria, supplies of poison gas were brought in from the outside in an automobile bearing the insignia of the International Red Cross. Accompanied by an SS (q.v.) officer, the SDG usually brought in four green sheet-iron canisters. The two men advanced across the grass to a spot where at every 30 yards short concrete pipes jutted from the ground. Donning a gas mask, the SDG lifted the concrete lid of the pipe, opened one of the cans, and poured the granulated contents into the opening. The gas thus produced soon filled the room where the inmates were placed. In five minutes all were dead. The two executioners waited another five minutes and then drove off.

SAUCKEL, FRITZ (1894–1946). National Socialist politician and chief of slave labor recruitment. Ernst Friedrich Christoph Sauckel (shortened to Fritz Sauckel) was born in Hassfurt am Main on October 27, 1894, the son of a postman and a seamstress. He attended a *Gymnasium* (high school) until the age of fifteen and then became a seaman, serving on German, Norwegian, and Swedish steamers. After World War I he studied engineering for two years and held various jobs as a factory construction worker. An early member of the new Nazi movement, holding party card No. 1395, he was noted for his unconditional loyalty to Hitler. A devoted family man, he was the father of ten children, two of whom were killed in World War II. Because of his indefatigable work for the party, he was appointed *Gauleiter* (district leader) for Thuringia in 1927. He served in the Thuringian Landtag (Legislature) from 1927 to 1933. When Hitler became Chancellor in 1933, he made Sauckel *Reichsstatthalter* (governor) of Thuringia. In 1933 Sauckel was elected to the Reichstag (q.v.).

During the period of rearmament from 1935 to 1939, thousands of Dutch, Polish, and French workers were imported into Germany to work in the booming industries and to help supply the new Wehrmacht (q.v.). At the outbreak of World War II in 1939, Hitler, on the recommendation of Martin Bormann (q.v.), made Sauckel a Reich defense commissioner with a special post as Plenipotentiary for Labor Allocation. Assured by the Fuehrer that he was doing the job of "a good soldier," Sauckel was delighted by what he regarded as a high honor.

In a decree dated March 21, 1942, Hitler called for the mobilization of German and foreign workers. Sauckel, starting his work in humane fashion, ordered that workers be treated with consideration. "All these people must be fed, housed, and treated in such a way that with the least possible outlay the greatest possible results will be achieved." The assignment proved to be a difficult one as more and more workers were needed to satisfy the insatiable demands of the war machine. With additional authority from Hitler, Sauckel began to operate what turned out to be the greatest slave trade in history. Tirelessly and efficiently he directed a brutal hunt for workers. His "protection squads" rounded up hundreds of workers at a time from the streets or from motion picture theaters. In all, more than 5 million such workers were imported, many of them under conditions of extreme cruelty.

On November 20, 1945, Sauckel, together with twenty-one other Nazi leaders, was indicted by the International Military Tribunal at Nuremberg for his work as chief of slave labor recruitment (*see* NUREMBERG TRIAL). He found it difficult to reconcile the charge with what he believed to be his own love for the workers. "The abyss between the ideal of a social community, which I imagined and advocated as a former seaman and worker, and the terrible happenings at the concentration camps, has shaken me deeply." His defense was that he only did his duty for the fatherland in time of war. He had believed, he said, that the war was forced on Germany by the Bolshevik-Jewish-capitalist world but finally realized that this was propaganda. He insisted that he had had nothing to do with the concentration camps (q.v.). When the atrocity films were shown, he trembled and exclaimed: "I'd choke myself with these hands if I thought that I had the slightest thing to do with those murders. It is a shame! It is a disgrace for us and our children!" He claimed innocence of any wrongdoing: "I just supplied workers to places like the Krupp works at Hitler's orders. It was like a seaman's agency. If I supply hands for a ship, I am not responsible for cruelty that may be exercised aboard ship without my knowledge."

His judges were not convinced. Sauckel was found guilty on two counts: count 2, war crimes; and count 4, crimes against humanity. He was hanged at Nuremberg on October 16, 1946. Wearing a sweater with no coat, he was defiant at the end. Gazing around the room from the gallows platform, he suddenly screamed: "I am dying innocent. The sentence is wrong. God protect Germany and make her great again! God protect my family!"

SAUERBRUCH, FERDINAND (1875–1951). The most famous physician in Germany during the era of the Third Reich. Ferdinand Sauerbruch was born in Barmen on July 3, 1875. After studying medicine, he pursued a distinguished career culminating in such posts as chief surgeon with the rank of lieutenant general of the German Army and director of the Charité Hospital in Berlin. In the fall of 1933 he joined Martin Heidegger (q.v.), the existentialist philosopher, and 960 other leading professionals in taking a public vow to support Hitler and the Nazi party. Sauerbruch was the attending physician during the final illness of President Paul von Hindenburg (q.v.) in August 1934. As the country's leading surgeon, he was often called upon to operate on important figures of the Nazi hierarchy. In 1940 he removed a growth from Hitler's throat. When, in April 1943, Claus Schenk Graf von Stauffenberg (q.v.) was gravely wounded in North Africa by bullets from a low-flying plane, losing his left eye, right hand, and part of a leg, he was saved medically by Dr. Sauerbruch's expert supervision at a Munich hospital.

Sauerbruch later became an anti-Nazi and joined the Resistance (q.v.) movement. He was interrogated by the Gestapo (q.v.) but was not arrested. After World War II he was cleared by a denazification court (*see* DENAZIFICATION), but the East German government dismissed him from all his posts. Sauerbruch died in Berlin on July 2, 1951.

SCHACHT, HJALMAR [HORACE GREELEY] (1877–1970). Financier, president of the Reichsbank, and economic expert behind German rearmament. Hjalmar Horace Greeley Schacht was born in Tingleff, Schleswig (now Tinglev, Denmark), on January 22, 1877, to a family of Danish background. In the early 1870s his parents emigrated to the United States, where his father became an American citizen. They returned to Germany because of enhanced opportunities in the victorious Second Reich after the Franco-Prussian War. The Schachts named their son for Horace Greeley in tribute to "the free enlightened man of the New World."

A caricature of Dr. Hjalmar Schacht. [*Ullstein*]

Young Schacht attended a *Gymnasium* (high school) in Berlin and then studied medicine at Kiel, German philology at Berlin, and political science at Munich before taking his doctorate in economics at Berlin. For more than a decade he worked for the Dresdner Bank and then headed a private bank of his own. In World War I he worked in the economic section of the German occupation in Belgium. In 1916, at the age of thirty-nine, he became a director of the National Bank for Germany (later, Darmstädter und National Bank). Egotistical, ambitious, and able, he made his way rapidly to the forefront of banking circles. In 1919, although professedly a monarchist, he helped found the German Democratic party.

In 1923 Schacht, as special currency commissioner in the Finance Ministry, was primarily responsible for ending the disastrous inflation and setting up the *Rentenmark* as the basis for a new currency backed by German land values and foreign loans. In December 1923 he was appointed president of the Reichsbank, Germany's leading financial institution. By now he had won a reputation as a financial wizard (later it was revealed at Nuremberg that he had the highest IQ among the prominent accused on trial). In March 1930 he resigned his post at the Reichsbank in protest against the Young Plan (q.v.), against continued German reparations payments, and against the growing foreign debt of the Weimar government. A fervent nationalist, he was outraged by what he called unfair economic and political treatment by the Allies.

In 1930, after reading *Mein Kampf* (q.v.), Schacht decided that Hitler was a political genius who, unlike the inept Weimar politicians, might rescue Germany by supporting "a sound economy in a strong state." Schacht was even more deeply impressed when the Nazis won a major victory in the September 14, 1930, elections and became the second strongest party in the Reichstag (q.v.). When Hitler needed financial support, Schacht helped to bring him to the attention of wealthy Rhineland industrialists. With other old-line conservatives he joined the Harzburg Front (q.v.) on October 11, 1931, in an effort to win Hitler to their side in the struggle against the Weimar Republic. "I am no National Socialist," Schacht said during this period, "but the basic ideas of National Socialism contain a great deal of truth." He was solidly behind Hitler in the involved negotiations that preceded the Nazi rise to political power.

In March 1933 a grateful Hitler reappointed Schacht to the presidency of the Reichsbank. From August 1934 to November 1937, as Reich Minister of Economics, Schacht played an important role in the vigorous rearmament program by using the facilities of the Reichsbank to the fullest extent. His greatest problem was to discourage inflation during the process of rearmament.

Publicly Schacht proclaimed that he would support Hitler and the Third Reich as long as he had breath in his body, but privately he began to have doubts about them both. He was alienated by the 1934 Blood Purge (q.v.), by the 1938 Blomberg-Fritsch crisis (q.v.), and by increasing persecution of the Jews. Nevertheless, he continued to work in the belief that Hitler's economic policies could be made consistent with his own. In November 1937 he resigned his posts as Minister of Economics and Plenipotentiary General for the War Economy. Hitler retained him as Minister without Portfolio (1937–1943) and renamed him to the presidency of the Reichsbank in March 1938.

When it became clear that Hitler was bent on war, Schacht turned to the Resistance (q.v.) movement but was careful to do nothing to endanger his own life or his family. On July 21, 1944, the day after the unsuccessful July Plot (q.v.), Schacht was arrested on suspicion of conspiracy; he was imprisoned in three concentration camps, Ravensbrück, Flossenbürg, and Dachau (qq.v.). In 1945, American troops took him into custody at Pustertal, Austria.

Brought before the Nuremberg Tribunal (*see* NUREMBERG TRIAL) in 1946, Schacht protested: "I do not understand at all why I have been accused." He claimed innocence throughout his trial. On one occasion, when films of concentration camps (q.v.) were shown in the courtroom, he folded his arms and angrily turned his back to the screen. The verdict stated that although Schacht was active in organizing Germany for war, rearmament was not of itself a criminal act. "The Tribunal has considered the whole of this evidence with great care, and comes to the conclusion that this necessary inference [plan to wage aggressive war] has not been established beyond a reasonable doubt." Schacht was acquitted. Later he was brought to trial in a German court and sentenced to eight years' imprisonment as a major offender under the denazification (q.v.) laws. The decision was reversed on appeal, and Schacht was freed on September 2, 1948. He was cleared for the fifth and final time on September 13, 1950. In 1953 he founded a private banking house, Schacht & Co., in Düsseldorf. Schacht died in Munich on June 3, 1970.

Bibliography. Henri Bertrand, *Le docteur Schacht*, Éditions Gallimard, Paris, 1939; Hjalmar Schacht, *Confessions of "the Old Wizard,"* Houghton Mifflin Company, Boston, 1956.

SCHAMIL. Code name for a parachute attack on Maikop. In a war directive dated July 11, 1942, Hitler called for the continuation of operations in the Crimea. Included among the special operations ordered was a parachute drop of a commando detachment on the oil installations in the Maikop area to the east of the Black Sea.

SCHELLENBERG, WALTER (1910–1952). No. 2 man in the Gestapo (q.v.) after Heinrich Himmler (q.v.). Walter Schellenberg was born in Saarbrücken on January 16, 1900. After receiving a degree in law, he joined the Nationalsozialistische Deutsche Arbeiterpartei (q.v.) in 1923. From 1939 to 1942 he was Deputy Leader of the dreaded Amt VI of the Reich Central Security Office (Reichssicherheitshauptamt, q.v.) and personal aide to Himmler. In early November 1939 Schellenberg played an important role in the Venlo incident (q.v.), in which he led a commando unit across the Dutch border to kidnap two British agents accused by Himmler of leading an unsuccessful bombing attempt on Hitler's life. In 1940 Schellenberg was charged with drawing up the *Sonderfahndungsliste-GB* (q.v.), a special search list of 2,300 prominent persons in Great Britain to be arrested after the projected German invasion, Operation Sea Lion (Seelöwe, q.v.). He was also sent on a mission to Portugal to kidnap the Duke and Duchess of Windsor and induce them to work with Hitler for a peace settlement with Britain. Foreign Minister Joachim von Ribbentrop (q.v.) adopted the plan with enthusiasm and ordered Schellenberg to prevent the Windsors from leaving Portugal for the Duke's post as Governor in the Bahamas. In the ensuing comic opera Schellenberg accomplished little other than delaying the Duke's baggage for a few hours.

Walter Schellenberg. [*Ullstein*]

During World War II Schellenberg served as a *Brigadefuehrer* (major general) in the Waffen-SS (q.v.). From 1942 to 1944 he held a high post in the political secret service for foreign countries as *Leiter Amt VI* of the Reichssicherheitshauptamt. In the final years of the Third Reich he urged Himmler to negotiate with Swedish Count Folke Bernadotte of Wisborg (q.v.) on the surrender of the German Army to the Western Allies. Tried by the International Military Tribunal at Nuremberg, he was sentenced to six years' imprisonment. Released in 1950, he died in Italy in 1952.

Bibliography. *The Schellenberg Memoirs*, ed. and tr. by Louis Hagen, André Deutsch, London, 1956.

SCHEMANN, LUDWIG (1852–1938). Racialist writer. Ludwig Schemann was born in Cologne on October 16, 1852. A librarian at the University of Göttingen, he founded the Gobineau Vereinigung (Gobineau Society) in Germany in 1891. He translated the *Essay on the Inequality of Human Races*, by Arthur Comte de Gobineau (q.v.), as *Die Rasse in der Geisteswissenschaft* (1928–1931). Schemann was known as one of Germany's foremost advocates of racial doctrine (q.v.). He died on February 13, 1938.

SCHICKELGRUBER, ALOIS. *See* HITLER, ALOIS SCHICKELGRUBER.

SCHIRACH, BALDUR VON (1907–1974). Reich Youth Leader. Baldur von Schirach was born in Berlin on March 9, 1907, the first of four children of a well-to-do family. His father, Carl Bailer-Norris von Schirach, an officer in the Garde-Kürassier-Regiment Wilhelm II (William II Guard Cuirassier Regiment), resigned in 1908 to become a theater director, first in Weimar and then in Vienna. His mother was an American, Emma Tillou, who claimed two signers of the Declaration of Independence among her ancestors. Baldur von Schirach grew up in a milieu of music, theater, and literature and early showed talent for poetry. A romantic and sentimental lad, somewhat plump in physique, he longed for adventure. He joined the Young German League at the age of ten and took much joy in its hikes, camp life, and singing sessions. As a student he was obliged to resign from a *Verbindung* (fraternity) under unpleasant circumstances. From then on he had only contempt for his country's former ruling class. In turn he was regarded as a renegade by his peers. A violent critic of Christianity, he became an anti-Semite after reading Henry Ford's *The International Jew* and *The Foundations of the Nineteenth Century*, by Houston Stewart Chamberlain (q.v.).

In 1924, at the age of seventeen, Von Schirach went to Munich, where he studied art history and Germanic folklore. He encountered small groups of National Socialists, whose *Weltanschauung* (q.v.) conformed closely to his own philosophy of life. Within a year he joined the Nazi party and served in an SA (q.v.) unit. He became known as the party's poet laureate. He campaigned to win Hitler's attention by writing flattering verses on "Germany's greatest son" and "a genius grazing the stars":

> That is the greatest thing about him,
> That he is not only our Leader and a great hero,
> But himself, upright, firm and simple,
> . . . in him rest the roots of our world.
> And his soul touches the stars,
> And yet he remains a man like you and me.

The Fuehrer, attracted by such devotion, was even better pleased by the young aristocrat's rejection of his own social caste. He found admirable Von Schirach's contention that the altar of Christianity was not his church, but was rather the steps of the Feldherrn Halle (q.v.) in Munich, drenched in blood during the 1923 Beer-Hall *Putsch* (q.v.). The Fuehrer referred to his young protégé as "a true follower and a dependable lad." He was delighted when Von Schirach married Henny Hoffmann, the daughter of the photographer Heinrich Hoffmann (q.v.).

In 1929 Von Schirach was appointed head of the National Socialist German Students' League, with the task of bringing the entire university system under Nazi control. In 1931 Hitler made him Reich youth leader of the National Socialist party, a post in which he proved himself to be a master organizer. The next year he directed a massive youth demonstration in Potsdam, at which more

Baldur von Schirach surrounded by members of the Hitler Youth. *[Ullstein]*

than 100,000 youngsters marched past the Fuehrer for seven hours. On June 1, 1933, Chancellor Hitler conferred on Von Schirach, then twenty-six years of age, the title of Youth Leader of the German Reich. Von Schirach then sought to reeducate German youth in the spirit of National Socialism. He announced that the generation gap had been closed by National Socialism and that loyal German parents rejoiced to see their children in the ranks of the Hitler Jugend (q.v.), the Hitler Youth. Von Schirach would permit no opposition to his plans. As early as February 1933 he had led a surprise raid of fifty boys on the office of the rival Central Committee of Youth Organizations and confiscated its records.

By 1936 Hitler had banned all youth organizations other than the Hitler Youth and decreed that all German youngsters must belong to it. He called on Von Schirach "to project National Socialism through German youth into eternity." Honors came to the Reich Youth Leader. Ranking at the top level of the Nazi hierarchy, he was presented to the German public as a kind of demigod embodying all that was fine and noble in German youth. His pictures were second only to Hitler's in displays throughout Germany and were used more widely than those of either Hermann Goering or Rudolf Hess (qq.v.).

Meanwhile, Von Schirach's enemies started a campaign of vilification against him. Jokes about his effeminate behavior, especially concerning his preference for a "girlish" bedroom in white, became a national pastime. He was ridiculed as a transplanted Berliner in Bavarian leather breeches *(Lederhosen)*. In July 1941 Hitler decided to appoint him *Gauleiter* (district leader) of Vienna, a much less important post. On July 25, 1942, Von Schirach made a speech defending the deportation of thousands of Jews to the ghettoes of the east as "a contribution to European culture."

At the Nuremberg Trial (q.v.) the Tribunal found that Von Schirach, while not originating the policy of deporting Jews from Vienna, participated in the deportation, and that bulletins describing the extermination of Jews were discovered in his office. He was found guilty on count 4 (crimes against humanity) and sentenced to twenty years' imprisonment. Released in 1966, he died in Kröv on August 8, 1974.

Bibliography. Baldur von Schirach, *Ich glaubte an Hitler,* Mosaik Verlag, Hamburg, 1967.

SCHLAGETER, ALBERT LEO (1894–1923). One of the most important martyrs in the Nazi lexicon. Born in Schönau im Wiesental, Baden, on August 12, 1894, Schlageter lived as a young *Freikorps* (q.v.) officer in the Ruhr (q.v.) region during the French occupation after World War I. Active in opposing French authority, he was arrested by the French criminal police, tried for espionage and sabotage, and executed on May 26, 1923, on Golzheimer Heath, near Düsseldorf.

In the early days of the Nazi movement Schlageter was accepted as a hero who had given his life for his country. "The German people," said Hitler when he was informed of Schlageter's death, "don't deserve this sacrifice. They are not truly worthy to possess a Schlageter!" The Rossbach group (q.v.), one of the many *Freikorps* units, resolved to avenge Schlageter's death. An execution squad, which was believed to have included Martin Bormann (q.v.), later to become Hitler's most trusted assistant, and Rudolf Franz Hoess (q.v.), the future commandant at the Auschwitz (q.v.) concentration camp, killed Walther Kadow, the man who allegedly had betrayed Schlageter to the French.

Schlageter was elevated to the level of a folk hero. In 1931 a monument was erected to him, but it was removed after World War II. The Nazi movement accepted him as the perfect specimen of the "new man." A special edition of his letters was published during the Nazi regime. Lothar Müthel, a well-known German actor, portrayed Schlageter in a drama written by Hanns Johst (q.v.). The play was originally staged in 1933 and revived many times thereafter throughout Germany. "Albert Leo Schlageter's War Song" became one of the most popular Nazi refrains:

> Though at first we are but few,
> You perhaps, we, a couple of others still,
> The road is broad, the aim is clear;
> Forward, step by step!
> Courage, come along!
> Though at first we are but few,
> We shall carry it off, nonetheless!

Bibliography. Friedrich Glombowski, *Frontiers of Terror: The Fate of Schlageter and His Comrades,* tr. by Kenneth Kirkness, Hurst & Blackett, Ltd., London, 1935.

SCHLAWIENER (Viennese Slavs). A derisory epithet used by Nazis to describe the Austrians. The *Anschluss* (q.v.), the union of Austria and Germany in 1938, and the creation of a Greater Germany did not halt the currency of sarcastic names for those who lived outside Germany.

Kurt von Schleicher. [*E. Bieber*]

SCHLEICHER, KURT VON (1882–1934). Army officer and last Chancellor of the Weimar Republic (q.v.). Kurt von Schleicher was born in Brandenburg on April 7, 1882, to an old Prussian military family. In 1903 he joined the 3d Foot Guards, Gen. Paul von Hindenburg's (q.v.) old regiment, as a subaltern, and in 1913 he was attached to the General Staff in the rank of captain. Von Schleicher became a close friend of Oskar von Hindenburg (q.v.). During the early years of World War I, he continued to serve on the General Staff, and in 1918 he became personal assistant to Quartermaster General Wilhelm Groener (q.v.) in the political section of General Headquarters. At this time he played an important role in helping to organize the illegal *Freikorps* (q.v.). In 1923 and 1924 he worked with Gen. Hans von Seeckt (q.v.), chief of the Army Command (Heeresleitung), which had replaced the General Staff. In February 1926, Colonel von Schleicher was made head of the Armed Forces Division of the Reichswehr Ministry.

In 1929 General Groener, now Minister of Defense, appointed Von Schleicher, now a major general, chief of a new office in the Reichswehr Ministry. In this post Von Schleicher engaged increasingly in politics and worked in the background to aid the Reichswehr (q.v.). An unscrupulous master of political intrigue, vain and ambitious, he sought to promote his own influence and that of the Army. From 1929 to 1933 he, along with General Groener, President von Hindenburg, and Chancellor Heinrich Bruening (q.v.), played a determining role in the political affairs of the declining Weimar Republic. Von Schleicher convinced Von Hindenburg that he should appoint Bruening to the chancellorship on March 28, 1930, and then prevailed on the old President to dismiss Bruening on May 30, 1932, in favor of Franz von Papen (q.v.). Von Schleicher became Minister of Defense and on December 3, 1932, succeeded Von Papen as Chancellor.

In his post as Chancellor, Von Schleicher attempted to contain the Nazis by combining the Reichswehr and the trade unions against them. Both he and Von Papen hoped to take advantage of Hitler's increasing popularity to strengthen their own positions. Von Schleicher offered to support a National Socialist government provided Hitler would appoint him to his Cabinet and allow him to direct the Reichswehr. Angered by Von Schleicher's role in his own dismissal as Chancellor, Von Papen met Hitler secretly and promised him the financial support of the Rhineland industrialists. Von Papen won out in the political infighting. On January 30, 1933, the President appointed Hitler Chancellor, with Von Papen as Vice-Chancellor.

Von Schleicher retired to private life, but he was to become the victim of Hitler's vengeance under especially brutal circumstances during the Blood Purge (q.v.). The Fuehrer was convinced that Von Schleicher was involved in a conspiracy to overthrow the Nazi regime. On June 30, 1934, six assassins in mufti appeared at the Von Schleicher villa outside Berlin, rang the bell, broke in, and shot the former Chancellor in front of his wife and stepdaughter. Frau von Schleicher, whom he had married eighteen months earlier, died a half hour later from her wounds. The murderers reported to Hitler that Von Schleicher had reached for his gun and that they had killed in self-defense.

Bibliography. Kurt Caro and Walter Oehme, *Schleichers Aufstieg*, Rowohlt Verlag, Berlin, 1933; Thilo Vogelsang, *Reichswehr, Staat und NSDAP*, Deutsche Verlagsanstalt, Stuttgart, 1962.

SCHLEICHER, RÜDIGER (1895–1945). Civil servant, teacher, and member of the conspiracy against Hitler. Rüdiger Schleicher was born in Württemberg on January 14, 1895, the son of a civil servant. Later he worked in the Ministry of Transport and Communications. Schleicher lost his post when Hitler became Chancellor in 1933. He then took a part-time position at the Institute for Aviation Law of the University of Berlin, where his office became a meeting place for members of the Resistance (q.v.). After the arrest of his brothers-in-law, Dietrich Bonhoeffer and Hans von Dohnányi (qq.v.), Schleicher continued his work in the underground. After the failure of the July Plot (q.v.) in 1944, he was taken into custody and sentenced to death by the Volksgericht (q.v.), the People's Court, as a traitor. He was kept in chains despite war wounds and was shot by an SS (q.v.) firing squad on the night of April 22–23, 1945.

Rüdiger Schleicher. [*From Annedore Leber (ed.), Conscience in Revolt, tr. by Rosemary O'Neill, Vallentine, Mitchell & Co., Ltd., London, 1957*]

SCHLEIFEREI (Grinding). Term used at camps of the Hitler Jugend (q.v.), the Hitler Youth, to describe the excessive drilling of young recruits. Many youngsters broke down under the grueling conditions, but most were proud of their ability to meet exacting standards.

SCHLOSS (Palace). The royal palace in Berlin.

SCHMAUS, ANTON (1910–1934). German youth, a victim of the Nazi terror. Anton Schmaus was born in Berlin-Köpenick on April 19, 1910, the son of a trade union official who was also a member of the Reichsbanner Schwarz-Rot-Gold (q.v.). He served his apprenticeship as a carpenter and attended evening classes at a technical school for builders. A Socialist, he was a member of the youth organization of the Reichsbanner.

On June 21, 1933, the Storm Troopers (*see* SA) of Köpenick seized several hundred people. Schmaus was in bed when the Brownshirts forced their way into his home, knocked down his mother, and moved toward the young man. Schmaus, who had said that he had no intention of spending his time permanently in hiding, told the Storm Troopers to leave the house; otherwise he would shoot. When they closed in on him, he pulled out a pistol and badly wounded three of them. A fourth was fatally wounded by a shot from one of his colleagues. Schmaus jumped out of the window and gave himself up to the police. While he was being transferred to police headquarters in Berlin by two constables, he was surrounded by thirty or forty Storm Troopers and shot. Paralyzed by an injury to his spinal cord, he died in a police hospital in January 1934.

SCHMELING, MAX [SIEGFRIED] (1905–). Germany's most successful heavyweight boxer and champion of the world from 1930 to 1932. Max Schmeling was born in Klein Luckow, Uckermark, Brandenburg, on September 28, 1905. In 1926 he won the German light-heavyweight championship; in 1927, the European light-heavyweight title; and in 1928, the German heavyweight championship. On June 12, 1930, at the age of twenty-four, Schmeling won the world's heavyweight championship in New York on a foul in the fourth round in a bout with the incumbent, Jack Sharkey. Schmeling was 6 feet 1 inch tall and had a weight range of 185 to 196 pounds and a reach of 76 inches. Of a total of seventy fights, he won fifty-six, lost ten, and drew four. He won thirty-nine bouts by knockouts and was knocked out five times himself.

Schmeling held the world title for two years and then

lost it back to Sharkey on June 21, 1932, by a decision in fifteen rounds. Almost everyone in the arena in Long Island City thought that Schmeling had won, but it was Sharkey's hand that was raised in victory. Schmeling became the only fighter to win the title lying down and lose it standing up. Max Jacobs, Schmeling's manager, shouted over the radio: "We wuz robbed!" In 1933 Schmeling married the film actress Anny Ondra. On June 19, 1936, he astounded the boxing world by knocking out Joe Louis, the sensational Brown Bomber, in the twelfth round of their bout at Yankee Stadium in New York (42,088 spectators; gate, $547,541). It was a dramatic setback for the supposedly invincible but overconfident Louis.

From that point on Schmeling became a display figure for Nazi propagandists, who hailed his victory as a triumph for the Nordic race over inferior black athletes. Louis won the title in 1937 but said that he could not be the real champion until he had defeated Schmeling. A return engagement was arranged at Yankee Stadium on June 22, 1938 (70,043 spectators; gate, $1,015,012). In this grudge fight Louis hurled himself at the German with unrestrained fury. Schmeling was counted out in two minutes four seconds of the first round, in the second shortest championship fight in heavyweight history. In 1939 Schmeling regained his title as European heavyweight champion.

Schmeling enlisted in the German Army in World War II. On May 20, 1941, he was one of the parachutists who jumped from transport planes to occupy Crete in a brilliant assault. From 1957 on he was the owner of an American Coca-Cola franchise in Hamburg-Wandsbek. He retained his popularity as a great sports figure in both Germany and the United States. In 1969 Nat Fleischer, the boxing expert, rated Schmeling No. 9 in his all-time ranking of the world's heavyweight boxers.

SCHMIDT, PAUL (1899–1970). Diplomat and professional interpreter. Paul Schmidt was born in Berlin on June 23, 1899. From 1924 to 1945 he was head of the Secretariat and chief interpreter in the German Foreign Office, and he served as Hitler's personal interpreter from 1935 to 1945. Schmidt's main function was to translate and record what he heard at important meetings of high officials in the Third Reich. He was the official interpreter at the Munich Conference of September 29–30, 1938 (*see* MUNICH AGREEMENT).

In his memoirs Schmidt gave a valuable picture of the leading personalities of the Third Reich. He described Hitler as an absentminded brooder, pale from sleeplessness, who would suddenly fly into a rage. The Fuehrer, he wrote, was always averse to precise statements and had an extraordinary capacity for self-destruction. Schmidt condemned Foreign Minister Joachim von Ribbentrop (q.v.) for his "inferiority complex with an assumed brusqueness," his "monstrously suspicious nature," his persistence and obstinacy, and his slavish repetition of what he believed Hitler wanted him to say. In 1952 Schmidt became director of the Munich Language and Interpreter Institute. He died in Munich on April 21, 1970.

Bibliography. Paul Schmidt, *Hitler's Interpreter: The Secret History of German Diplomacy, 1935–1945*, The Macmillan Company, New York, 1951.

SCHMIDT, PAUL KARL (1911–). Press chief in the Third Reich. Paul Karl Schmidt served as acting director of the News Service and Press Department in the Reich Foreign Office from 1940 to 1945. After World War II, under the pen name Paul Carell, he wrote a series of best-selling books on the history of the war, including *Unternehmen Barbarossa (Undertaking Barbarossa),* which appeared in Germany in 1963 and in the United States as *Hitler Moves East: 1941–1943* (Little, Brown and Company, Boston, 1965).

SCHMITT, CARL (1888–1985). Legal and political thinker. Carl Schmitt was born in Plettenberg, Westphalia, on July 11, 1888. After receiving a doctorate in 1910, he embarked on a successful career as a teacher and writer. Schmitt served as professor of public law at Bonn (1922), Berlin (1926), Cologne (1933), and again Berlin (1933). He won national attention with works on subjects ranging from constitutional to literary questions. His ideas were rooted in the concept that one who possesses power makes the laws. A persistent critic of the Weimar Constitution, he wrote a devastating critique of the post-World War I Reichstag (q.v.). On May 1, 1933, soon after Hitler came to power, he joined the Nationalsozialistische Deutsche Arbeiterpartei (q.v.) after deciding to be the self-appointed theorist of the Nazi state. However, in 1936 the Nazis attacked him as politically unreliable, and he was warned "to cease posing as a Nazi theorist." After the fall of the Third Reich he was denounced by scholars as one of the small group of intellectuals who had rallied to Hitler's standard and accused of giving specious but impressive respectability to the Nazi regime. Other scholars defended him against the charge of political opportunism and insisted that his devotion to Nazism was at best lukewarm.

SCHMITT, KURT (1886–1950). Reich Minister of Economics in Hitler's original Cabinet. Kurt Schmitt was born in Heidelberg on October 7, 1886, the son of a physician. From 1896 to 1902 he attended the *Progymnasium* (lower and middle part of a classical high school) at Bad Dürkheim and the *Gymnasium* (high school) at Neustadt, and from 1905 to 1907 he studied law at the University of Munich. Schmitt performed his one-year volunteer military service as a lieutenant with the Infantry Leib Division Munich in 1911 and passed his assessor's examination the following year. He was badly wounded in World War I, in which he received the Iron Cross (Second Class). In 1921, at the age of thirty-five, he became general director of the Allianz Versicherurgs A.G., a large insurance company. Named Reich Minister of Finance by Chancellor Franz von Papen (q.v.) in 1932, he was appointed to the same post by Hitler on June 29, 1933. Schmitt died in Heidelberg on November 11, 1950.

SCHMUNDT, RUDOLF (1896–1944). Chief adjutant of the armed forces to Hitler. Rudolf Schmundt was born in Metz on August 13, 1896. A career officer, he eventually became adjutant to Hitler, a post he held until his death. From October 1942 to June 1944 he was also chief of Army personnel. He was promoted to lieutenant colonel in 1938, colonel in 1939, major general in 1942, lieutenant general in 1943, and general of infantry in 1944. Schmundt was present at the Fuehrer's military conferences before and after the outbreak of World War II. The notes that he took at the conference of May 3, 1939, at the Chancellery, in which Hitler stated that war was inevitable, were confiscated by the Allies after the war. Schmundt was present at Rastenburg on July 20, 1944, when the most serious attempt was made on Hitler's life by Claus Schenk Graf von Stauffenberg (q.v.; *see* JULY PLOT). He was grievously wounded by the bomb that was supposed to kill Hitler and died of his wounds on October 1, 1944.

SCHOERNER, FERDINAND (1892–1973). Last general field marshal appointed by Hitler. Ferdinand Schoerner was born in Munich on June 12, 1892. In World War I he received the Pour le Mérite decoration. In 1923, as a 1st lieutenant, he helped suppress the Beer-Hall *Putsch* (q.v.) in Munich, although he sympathized with the new National Socialist movement and belonged to several racial organizations. Later he became one of Hitler's favorites, in part because of his plebeian background, and won rapid promotion. Throughout his career he insisted that there was no difference between military and intellectual leadership. "The soldier of today," he said in the midst of the Russian campaign, "will achieve victory by his world view [*Weltanschauung,* q.v.]."

One of Hitler's most trusted officers in the Wehrmacht (q.v.), Schoerner served the Fuehrer as chief of the National Socialist Leadership Staff of the armed forces. In 1942 and 1943 he commanded Mountain Corps XIX in Lapland, and until February 1, 1944, Panzer Corps XL in southern Russia. On April 7, 1944, he was made supreme commander of Army Group South in the Ukraine; on July 25, 1944, supreme commander of Army Group North; and on January 16, 1945, supreme commander of the German Central Zone, including Berlin. In each of these posts he took harsh measures to maintain morale under conditions of disintegration.

During his last days in the *Fuehrerbunker* (q.v.), Hitler, by this time issuing orders to units that existed only in his imagination, gave Schoerner command of a nonexistent army group and promoted him to general field marshal. The Fuehrer ordered Martin Bormann (q.v.) to send copies of his last will and political testament to Adm. Karl Doenitz (q.v.), his designated successor, and to Schoerner "to assure their preservation for the people." Hitler trusted Schoerner to the last day of his life. *See also* HITLER'S LAST WILL; HITLER'S POLITICAL TESTAMENT.

As the German armies crumbled, Schoerner changed into civilian clothes and flew to the American zone in Austria in his own light plane. The Americans handed him over to the Soviet Union. For some time Schoerner had been a leading name on the Soviet list of war criminals. Sentenced to prison, he was released ten years later, in April 1955, the first former field marshal whom the Russians allowed to return to West Germany. The Association of Returned Prisoners of War charged him with murdering thousands of German soldiers in his drumhead courts in the last stages of the war on the eastern front.

In 1957 a German court in Munich sentenced Schoerner to four and one-half years' imprisonment on a charge of manslaughter. He was accused of having ordered the execution without trial of a German corporal found drunk at the wheel of an army truck. Schoerner died in Munich on July 6, 1973, at the age of eighty-one.

SCHOLL, HANS (1918–1943), and SCHOLL, SOPHIE (1921–1943). Martyrs of the anti-Nazi movement. Hans and Sophie Scholl, brother and sister, were born in Forchtenberg, Württemberg, the children of the local mayor. They grew up with three brothers and sisters. Both became students at the University of Munich, where the movement for revolt against Hitler was especially pronounced. Hans was a medical student, and Sophie majored in biology. Encouraged by Dr. Kurt Huber (q.v.), a professor of philosophy, the two students were instrumental in organizing a resistance group known as the Weisse Rose (q.v.; White Rose) "to strive for the renewal of the mortally wounded German spirit." They kept in close touch with similar student groups at other universities. Using small duplicating machines, the students defied an enormously powerful state apparatus. The password White Rose was designed to symbolize a Christian spirit which loved every thing that was noble and beautiful and opposed the "dictatorship of evil" in National Socialist Germany.

In mid-February 1943, the Scholls, helped by other students, took part in a demonstration on the streets of Munich, the first protest of its kind in the Third Reich. They also dropped leaflets from a balcony of the university's inner court. The handbills read in part: "Germany's name will remain disgraced forever unless German youth finally rises up immediately, takes revenge, and atones, smashes its torturers, and builds a new, spiritual Europe." The Scholls were reported to the Gestapo (q.v.) by a building superintendent. Both were arrested, along with four others, and brought before the Volksgericht (q.v.), the People's Court.

After a hasty trial the Scholls were sentenced to death. Sophie Scholl showed rare courage in prison: "Thousands will be stirred and awakened by what we have done." On February 22, 1943, she was executed by beheading. Hans Scholl was executed the same day, and Professor Huber on July 13. In East Germany a commemorative stamp was issued in 1961 in honor of both Scholls. Another stamp in tribute to the brother and sister appeared in the Federal Republic in 1964.

Sophie and Hans Scholl. [*Stamp issued by the German Democratic Republic*]

SCHOLTZ-KLINK, GERTRUD (1902–). Women's leader in the Third Reich. Gertrud Scholtz-Klink was born in Adelsheim on February 9, 1902. In her early career she worked with the German Red Cross in Berlin. Although it was claimed that the status of women had changed in Nazi Germany, actually the traditional place of women in German society, symbolized by the slogan *"Kinder, Kirche, Küche"* (q.v.; "Kids, Kirk, Kitchen") was maintained. Germany was ruled by the Nazi party, in which women had little influence.

In 1934 Frau Scholtz-Klink, formerly deputy leader of the National Socialist *Frauenschaft* (woman's organization), was promoted to Fueherin (woman leader) of all National Socialist women. An able, energetic worker and the mother of four children, she had originally been a district leader and had been active in labor organizations until called to her high office. In theory she was the head of all women's organizations including the Frauenwerk (a federal organization of women), the Women's League of the Red Cross, the Women's Bureau in the Deutsche Arbeitsfront (q.v.; German Labor Front), and the Woman's Labor Service. Behind all these groups was a strong masculine authority. Frau Scholtz-Klink was expected to step softly, avoid controversial issues, and hold conciliatory opinions. Hitler was firm in his contention that women were to perform their most important task by producing future leaders of the party.

Frau Scholtz-Klink stated the goal of women in the Third Reich: "Woman is entrusted in the life of the nation with a great task, the care of man, soul, body, and mind. It is the mission of woman to minister in the home and in her profession to the needs of life from the first to the last moment of man's existence. Her mission in marriage is . . . comrade, helper and womanly complement of man—this is the right of woman in the New Germany." She was described in this interview in *The New York Times* of September 26, 1937:

> One meets her surrounded by Nazi flags and uniforms. Her gentle femininity is a startling contrast to the military atmosphere. She is a friendly woman in her middle thirties, blonde, blue-eyed, regular featured, slender. She sits in a wicker chair on her little balcony and chats with her visitor. Her complexion is so fresh and clear that she dares to do without powder or rouge. She talks, and one notes that her own, capable hands have known hard work. Her first husband died and left her with six children. Two of the children died. She worked to bring up the others. She married again, this time a doctor. She has had little time for education; her training for her present position came through hard work and party experience.
>
> What does she hope to accomplish for German women in the next ten years? She laughs and cannily refuses to commit herself. She turns to the orthodox National Socialist viewpoint when birth control is mentioned, education for women, the old Feminist movement and working women's problems. Does she feel that her hard-won accomplishments for German women will be swept away in another war? Again she will not commit herself.
>
> A final question. How does she feel about the possibility of Germany's going to war?
>
> She glances up at the swastikas and across at the black boots of the uniformed men beyond the doorway and she turns quickly away to hide the tears in her eyes. "I have sons," she says quietly. Her eyes are as sad as the eyes of many other German mothers who know so well the German Labor Camp motto which says so plainly that sons must "fight stubbornly and die laughing."

SCHÖNERER, GEORG RITTER VON (1842–1921). Austrian nationalist politician who strongly influenced the mind of the young Hitler. Georg Ritter von Schönerer was born in Vienna on July 17, 1842. A landowner, he was a member of the Austrian House of Delegates from 1873 on. In 1879 he helped found the Pan-German Nationalist party. Active in the struggle against liberalism and clericalism, he became known for his extreme anti-Semitism (q.v.). Opposed to the Hapsburg dynasty, he called for a close union with Germany. In 1888, because he had commited acts of violence against his political opponents, he was jailed, stripped of his title of nobility, and ejected from the House of Delegates. From 1897 to 1907 he again served in that legislative body. He was the founder of the *Los von Rom* (Away from Rome) movement.

When the young Hitler went to Vienna in October 1907 and remained there for five years, he took no active part in politics but closely followed the activities of the major political parties. Opposing the Social Democrats and the Christian Socialists, he felt an affinity for the Pan-German Nationalist party. He was attracted by Schönerer, who had come from the same region near Spital in Lower Austria as had his own family. Hitler enthusiastically embraced Schönerer's program of fervid nationalism, anti-Semitism, and antisocialism. To the young man Schönerer was a "deep thinker" who was absolutely correct in his opposition to the Jews, the papacy, and the Hapsburgs. Hitler gave his allegiance to Schönerer's party. Later, in *Mein Kampf* (q.v.), Hitler wrote about his debt to Schönerer but criticized his party as lacking a firm mass basis. It had erred, he wrote, in trying to bring change through parliamentary means. Schönerer died in Schloss Rosenau, near Zwettl, Lower Austria, on December 14, 1921.

SCHROEDER, KURT FREIHERR VON (1889–1965). Wealthy banker and early patron of Hitler and the Nazi movement. Kurt von Schroeder was born in Hamburg on November 24, 1889, the son of the banker Friedrich von Schroeder. He attended *Gymnasien* (high schools) in Hamburg and Gütersloh and the University of Bonn, where he was active in the Corps Borussia, a student fraternity. He served early in World War I in a Bonn unit, the Königshusaren (King's Hussars), and later as a captain on the General Staff. After the war he became a banker in Cologne, Hannover, and Berlin and amassed a fortune as the leading figure in the firm of J. H. Stein.

Von Schroeder contributed large sums to the empty coffers of the Nazi party from its earliest days in the belief that Hitler would protect Germany from communism. In the weeks just before Hitler's assumption of power, Von Schroeder won attention as "the midwife of Nazism" by bringing Hitler and Franz von Papen (q.v.) together for a historic interview. On January 4, 1933, Von Schroeder invited Hitler and Von Papen to his home in Cologne for a discussion that led to a National Socialist government. The interview was supposed to be secret, but news about it leaked out and caused a political sensation.

After Hitler became Chancellor, he made Von Schroeder president of the Rhineland Industrial Chamber. At the same time Von Schroeder served as head of the Fachgruppe Privatbankiers (Trade Association of Private Bankers). After 1945 he was imprisoned in a British internment camp at Eselheide. On November 12, 1947, he was brought to trial before a German court at Bielefeld and charged with crimes against humanity. He was sentenced to three months' imprisonment and fined.

SCHULTZE, WALTHER (1894–). Reich Leader of Teachers. Walther Schultze was born in Hersbruck on January 1, 1894. After taking a degree in medicine, he served in early SA (q.v.) units as a physician. In 1933 he was appointed state commissioner and leader of physical education in the Bavarian State Ministry and president of the State Academy of Medicine in Munich. In 1934 he was made an honorary professor at the University of Munich and the next year was named *Reichsdozentenfuehrer* (Reich Leader of Teachers).

SCHUPOS. The urban constabulary, the ordinary policemen on foot patrol.

SCHUSCHNIGG, KURT VON (1897–1977). Austrian Federal Chancellor and victim of Hitler's aggression. Born in Riva, South Tyrol, on December 14, 1897, he was educated at Freiburg and Innsbruck. A lawyer and a member of the Christian Social party, he served as a deputy to the Austrian Nationalrat (National Council) in 1927. He worked in various ministries and served as Minister of Justice under Chancellor Engelbert Dollfuss (q.v.) from 1932 to 1934. Von Schuschnigg became Federal Chancellor following the assassination of Dollfuss in 1934. By supporting an authoritarian constitution and an estate system, he attempted to maintain Austrian independence.

Von Schuschnigg did his best to resist Hitler's demand for the annexation of Austria, but he was called to the Fuehrer's residence and compelled to sign an agreement clearing the way to *Anschluss* (q.v.) under Nazi control. On returning to Vienna, he tried to organize a plebiscite against Hitler but was stopped by the Nazi invasion of his country. Von Schuschnigg was imprisoned in a concentration camp throughout World War II (*see* CONCENTRATION CAMPS). After the war he became a professor of political science at St. Louis University and in 1956 was naturalized as a United States citizen.

Bibliography. Kurt von Schuschnigg, *Austrian Requiem*, tr. by Franz von Hildebrand, G. P. Putnam's Sons, New York, 1946.

SCHÜTZE-SS. A private in the SS (q.v.).

SCHUTZHAFT (Protective Custody). Nazi euphemism for internment in a concentration camp (*see* CONCENTRATION CAMPS).

SCHUTZSTAFFEL. *See* SS.

SCHWALBE. *See* MESSERSCHMITT-262.

SCHWANENFELD, ULRICH-WILHELM SCHWERIN VON (1902–1944). Member of the Resistance (q.v.) movement and a victim of the Nazi regime. Ulrich-Wilhelm Schwerin von Schwanenfeld was born in Copenhagen, the son of a German diplomat. While a student in Munich in 1923, he witnessed the abortive Beer-Hall *Putsch* (q.v.) and developed a deep dislike for National Socialism. After Hitler came to power in 1933, Von Schwanenfeld joined such members of the Resistance as Hans Oster, Hans von Dohnányi, and Adam von Trott zu Solz (qq.v.) with the goal of liberating Germany from the National Socialists by the death of Hitler. Called up at the outbreak of war in 1939, he served with Gen. Erwin von Witzleben (q.v.) as an assistant adjutant, acting as Von Witzleben's liaison with other generals in the conspiracy against Hitler.. Von Schwanenfeld was arrested after the July Plot of 1944, brought before the Volksgericht (q.v.), the People's Court, sentenced to death for treason, and executed on September 8, 1944.

SCHWARZ, FRANCIS XAVER (b. 1875). Treasurer of the Nationalsozialistische Deutsche Arbeiterpartei (q.v.). Francis Xaver Schwarz was born in Günzburg on November 27, 1875. He attended the *Gymnasium* (high school) there and in 1914 served in the Army. Joining the Nazi party in Munich in 1922, he was made its *Reichsschatzmeister* (national treasurer) three years later and held this post until 1945. In 1929 he was elected to the Munich City Council, and in 1933 he became a delegate to the German Reichstag (q.v.), representing Wahlkreis (Electoral District) Franconia. In 1935, in recognition of his services, he was named a *Reichsleiter* (Reich leader), and in 1943 he became an *SS-Obergruppenfuehrer* (general).

SCHWARZ (Black). Code name for one of four operations ordered by Hitler on July 31, 1943, to meet the expected invasion by Allied forces of the mainland of Italy (*see also* ACHSE; EICHE; STUDENT). Operation Schwarz called specifically for the military occupation of all Italy.

SCHWARZE FRONT (Black Front). Organization of dissident National Socialists. Also called the Union of Revolutionary National Socialists, the Schwarze Front was formed in May 1930 by Otto Strasser (q.v.) and Walther Stennes (*see* STENNES REVOLT) after they had been expelled from the Nationalsozialistische Deutsche Arbeiterpartei (q.v.). With headquarters in Prague, the Schwarze Front was designed to represent "truly National Socialist views" and led the activities of Nazi émigrés against Hitler. It was never successful in its rivalry with the dominant Hitler hierarchy.

SCHWARZE KORPS, DAS (The Black Corps). The official weekly newspaper of the Schutzstaffel (SS, q.v.), Hitler's black-shirted elite guard. The paper, a kind of house organ of the National Socialist movement, was a strong defender of revolutionary Nazism. The journalistic quality was low in comparison with that of the press of the Weimar Republic (q.v.). *Das Schwarze Korps* was actually the personal mouthpiece of *SS-Reichsleiter* Heinrich Himmler (q.v.), Reich leader of the SS, and it reflected his views and opinions. In its columns Himmler would often threaten business firms that had not appointed Nazis to directorships—a practice close to blackmail. In conformity with the racial doctrine (q.v.) that pure-blooded Nordics must be bred in the Third Reich, Himmler used the newspaper to promote his theory that "illegitimate children are the most beautiful in the world." Each issue of the paper carried announcements of illegitimate births. Every week there were a half-dozen obituary notices of young SS members who had been killed in training. When, in March 1938, the *Anschluss* (q.v.), or union with Austria, was completed, *Das Schwarze Korps* commended the Austrians for their anti-Semitism (q.v.): "In Austria a boycott of the Jews does not need organization—the people themselves have instituted it with honest joy."

As time passed, *Das Schwarze Korps* assumed an increasingly censorious role in national affairs. It kept a close eye on the rest of the German press as well as on German citizens in general. A typical issue showed a photograph of a village group giving the Nazi salute; the title identified one person in the background as Pastor Erich Gans of the Bekenntniskirche (q.v.), the Confessional Church, who had failed to raise his right arm in the German greeting. When, in 1934, a minuscule cabaret in Berlin called the Katakombe was closed down by official order, *Das Schwarze Korps* reported the closure under the headline "Brothel Closed Down."

Every issue of the newspaper featured an attack upon some element of German society that did not meet Himmler's exacting standards. The paper attacked intellectuals because of their mania for self-improvement, their social climbing, and their unwillingness to produce children for the Third Reich. It labeled such distinguished scientists as Werner Heisenberg and Max Planck "white Jews in the sphere of science." It excoriated students for any hint of anti-Nazi conduct. In 1935 it called for the dissolution of student fraternities after printing a report that members of the Corps Saxo-Borussia at a Heidelberg tavern had questioned Hitler's understanding of the proper method of eating asparagus. The paper condemned modern jazz for "promoting the wiggling of one's hips like a lustful homosexual."

No phase of national life escaped the attention of the editors. One issue attacked housemaids who insisted on taking up service in childless homes while mothers of large families were on the verge of nervous breakdowns. During World War II, *Das Schwarze Korps*, like the rest of the German press, devoted its columns to reports of victories and to the maintenance of morale. Its favorite subject was a demand that dealers in black-market goods be "shortened by a head" if their offenses were repeated.

See also ANGRIFF, DER; ILLUSTRIERTER BEOBACHTER; NEWSPAPERS IN THE THIRD REICH; STÜRMER, DER; VÖLKISCHER BEOBACHTER.

SCHWEINFURT RAIDS. Air attacks by the United States Army Air Forces in World War II with the aim of destroying the capacity of the Third Reich to wage war. Schweinfurt is a small industrial city on the north bank of the Main River as it curves through the hill country of Franconia, the northern region of Bavaria. It is 65 miles due east of Frankfurt am Main and 50 miles northwest of Nuremberg. Schweinfurt was famous for its beer, its dyes, and, most important of all, its ball bearings, critical necessities for the modern industrial machine. In 1943 most German ball bearings were produced in the western industrial complex of Schweinfurt. Five major factories there were involved in producing ball bearings: Kugelfischer-Werke (all types of bearings), VKF Werke I (assembly plant), VKF Werke II (balls and races), Deutsche Star Kugelhalter (ball-bearing cages), and Fichtel und Sachs AG (aircraft parts and bearings; motorcycles). Connecting the five factories were a large railway station and marshaling yards. The United States Strategic Bombing Command reasoned that if its force of bombers could penetrate the strong German defenses, it could wreck the heart of the Nazi war effort, shorten the war, and thereby save countless lives.

On August 17, 1943, some 229 Flying Fortresses were dispatched to attack Schweinfurt. Eight weeks later came another raid, this time with 291 bombers. Each time bomber crews had to fight doggedly through a mass of Luftwaffe (q.v.) attackers, including Junkers-87 (q.v.; Stuka) dive bombers and twin-engine He-111s, along a running course extending 200 miles to the target. In the first attack the Americans lost 36 heavy bombers, in the second 60, as well as 950 trained crewmen. The losses ran to about 1 in 5 of the men and machines committed to the Schweinfurt strikes.

Both sides claimed victory in the Schweinfurt confrontation. The Americans reported severe damage to the ball-bearing factories. The raids, they said, resulted in a rapid dispersion of the ball-bearing factories after a production lag of three months. The Schweinfurt raids, said the Americans, had an immediate effect on Hitler's war effort and on German morale because work in many kinds of factories was suspended owing to a lack of ball bearings. American plane losses were soon replaced. As a result of the raids the Americans, although they still held to the concept of daylight bombing, took the precaution of developing the P-51 Mustang as a high-performance fighter plane to accompany bombers on subsequent raids inside Germany. The Strategic Bombing Command regarded this one factor as a key lesson learned from the Schweinfurt raids. Marshal Hermann Goering (q.v.), head of the Luftwaffe, later admitted that the appearance of the P-51 as a long-range fighter escort meant that Germany had lost the war.

The Germans, on the other hand, regarded the Schweinfurt raids as a great gamble that had failed. Admittedly, some structural damage had been done to the Schweinfurt plants, but ball-bearing production had not been adversely affected. One German source even claimed that production had increased during the final quarter of 1943. Moreover, huge stocks of ball bearings were held in reserve. To be on the safe side, the Germans dispersed ball-bearing factories, reduced the number of types of bearings, and began to use many smaller factories. At the same time, German scientists began to work on means of dispensing with ball bearings altogether. Albert Speer (q.v.), Minister of Armaments and War Production, spoke in July 1944 of the *Kugellagerdämmerung* (twilight of ball bearings) and intimated that the attacks on Schweinfurt were impractical and without real results for the Allies.

Allied strategists were not convinced and ordered further raids on Schweinfurt. In all there were sixteen raids on the city. On February 24–25, 1944, American bombers, defended by P-51s, attacked by day, and the Royal Air Force (RAF) continued the raids at night. There was another heavy RAF mission on the night of April 26–27, 1944. While claiming the unimportance of Schweinfurt, the Germans nevertheless defended it with heavy flak and fighter planes. Again the attackers lost heavily, but by this time the tide of war had turned strongly in favor of the Allies.

SCHWERIN VON KROSIGK, LUTZ GRAF (1887–1952). Member of Hitler's original Cabinet as Reich Minister of Finance. Lutz Schwerin von Krosigk was born in Rathmannsdorf, Anhalt, on August 22, 1887. After attending the Klosterschule (Cloister School) Rossleben, he studied law and politics at Lausanne. He then became a Rhodes scholar at Oxford. In 1909 he passed his *Referendarexam* (junior barrister examination) and began a legal career. He performed his one-year volunteer military service in 1909–1910 with the 2d Pomeranian Uhlans Regiment No. 9 in Demmin. In World War I he served as an officer in the field, was wounded, and was awarded the Iron Cross (First and Second Classes). After 1918 he became a government assessor in Hindenburg, Upper Silesia (now Zabrze, Poland). From 1921 to 1932 he worked in various capacities in the Ministry of Finance.

On June 2, 1932, Chancellor Franz von Papen (q.v.) named Von Krosigk Finance Minister in his coalition Cabinet. Von Krosigk retained this post throughout the life of the Third Reich until its collapse in 1945. Hitler relied on Von Krosigk to finance the rearmament of Germany. In February 1935 a special law authorized the Minister of Finance to raise resources by means of credit in order to rearm the country, "the figure for which is to be fixed by the Chancellor and Fuehrer on the advice of the Minister of Finance." During the next three years Von Krosigk denounced the Mefo bills (q.v.), issued by Hjalmar Schacht (q.v.) to raise money for armaments, as merely another way of printing money. Von Krosigk regarded Hitler's anti-Semitic campaign as justified. On November 10, 1938, the day after the *Kristallnacht* (q.v.), the Night of the Broken Glass, he said: "We must do all we can to shove Jews into other countries." In May 1945, Adm. Karl Doenitz (q.v.), successor to Hitler, ignored both Artur Seyss-Inquart and Joachim von Ribbentrop (qq.v.), both named by the Fuehrer, and accepted Von Krosigk instead in the now almost nonexistent post of Foreign Minister. In 1949 Von Krosigk was brought before the International Military Tribunal at Nuremberg, found guilty of war crimes, and sentenced to ten years' imprisonment. He was released in 1951 and died the next year.

SCHWERTWORTE (Sword Words). Highly compressed synopses of National Socialist dogma. The *Schwertworte* had to be memorized and repeated constantly by every *Pimpf* (q.v.), or member of the Jungvolk, the branch of the Hitler Jugend (qq.v.) for boys ten to fourteen years of age.

SD (Sicherheitsdienst; Security Service). The intelligence branch of the SS (q.v.), under the leadership of Reinhard Heydrich (q.v.). Composed of what was said to be the elite of the elite, the SD was responsible for the security of Hitler, the Nazi hierarchy, the National Socialist party, and the Third Reich. It was formed in March 1934, when Heinrich Himmler (q.v.), motivated by the huge growth of the black-uniformed SS (from 30,000 to 100,000 men), decided to create his own security service. Originally the SD was to be a kind of auxiliary police force, but it soon outgrew that designation. "The SD," Himmler said, "will discover the enemies of the National Socialist concept and it will initiate countermeasures through the official police authorities." In theory the SD was supposed to be under Wilhelm Frick (q.v.), Minister of the Interior, but actually it was under the control of Himmler and Heydrich. It was not subservient to the Gestapo (q.v.), the German secret police, but was rather a new instrument of Nazi thought and culture directed against "enemies of the state." Responsible for the entire security of the Third Reich, the SD comprised several active police forces, including the Sicherheitspolizei (SIPO; Security Police); the Kriminalpolizei (KRIPO); the Reichssicherheitshauptamt (RSHA; Reich Central Security Office); and even the *Schupos,* the urban constabulary (qq.v.).

The SD was manned largely by professionals who did their jobs mechanically and methodically. Those who worked in the field seldom knew the identity of other SD men. They were divided into five classes: V-men, or *Vertrauensleute* (q.v.; confidants), those who were trusted; A-men, or *Agenten* (q.v.; agents); Z-men, or *Zubringer* (q.v.; informants); H-men, or *Helfershelfer* (q.v.; secondary informants), persons who acted from selfish motives; and U-men, or *Unzuverlässige* (q.v.; unreliables), those who were corrupt and had to be watched carefully.

The vast power of this intelligence network was concentrated in ferreting out all enemies of the state. Day after day the SD men contributed individual reports on the private lives of ordinary citizens and members of the government or the party. Copies were kept for the local secret files, and main reports were sent to the central office. Heydrich, a perfectionist in surveillance, had at his command a large corps of quick-witted lawyers whose chief task was to demonstrate the legality of any arbitrary SD action. The average citizen was powerless against SD machinations. Heydrich could order immediate arrests and preventive detention, and he could send any persons to concentration camps (q.v.) at any time. He was the absolute master of life and liberty in the Third Reich. Anyone condemned by the People's Court (Volksgericht, q.v.) could be picked up by SD agents waiting in the courtroom. Few could escape this monolithic organ of the Hitler terror. Its victims included Jews, Communists, pacifists, Seventh-Day Adventists, political criminals, professional criminals, beggars, antisocials, "the work-shy," beggars, homosexuals, prostitutes, drunkards, swindlers, and psychopaths. SD men were called on for such major tasks as arresting 67,000 "enemies of the state" in Vienna during the occupation of Austria in 1938.

During World War II the SD was responsible for reporting on the morale of the civilian population. It was active against partisans in the occupied countries and executed thousands of prisoners. From occupied France the SD reported that near Lyon it had closed down an orphanage, taken forty-one children between the ages of three and thirteen into custody, and found "no articles of value." Along with the SS, it helped clear the ghettoes in the east and reported in December 1942 that 80 percent of all Jews in occupied Poland had been transported to extermination camps (q.v.). The guards who witnessed the burning of Hitler's body in Berlin on April 30, 1945, were SD men.

At the Nuremberg Trial (q.v.) the SD was indicted as the intelligence arm of the National Socialist party and as an organization that had developed a network of terror over Europe and the occupied countries. It was found to be a crime to have been a member of the SD, but members were to be tried individually. The judgment specifically linked the SD with the Gestapo (q.v.) for its criminal activities:

> They were first linked together on June 26, 1936, by the appointment of Heydrich, who was the Chief of the S.D., to the position of Chief of the Security Police, which was defined to include both the Gestapo and the Criminal Police.
>
> From a functional point of view the Gestapo and the S.D. were important and closely related groups within the organization of the Security Police and the S.D. The Security Police and S.D. was under a single command, that of Heydrich and later Kaltenbrunner, as Chief of the Security Police and S.D.; it had a single headquarters, the R.S.H.A.; it had its own command channels and worked as one organization both in Germany, in occupied territories and in the areas immediately behind the front lines. During the period with which the Tribunal is primarily concerned applicants for positions in the Security Police and S.D. received training in all its components, the Gestapo, Criminal Police and S.D.
>
> The Security Police and S.D. was a voluntary organization. It is true that many civil servants and administrative officials were transferred into the Security Police. The claim that this transfer was compulsory amounts to nothing more than the claim that they had to accept the transfer or resign their positions, with a possibility of having incurred official disfavour. During the war a member of the Security Police and S.D. did not have a free choice of assignments within that organization, and the refusal to accept a particular position, especially when serving in occupied territory, might have led to serious punishment. The fact remains, however, that all members of the Security Police and S.D. joined the organization voluntarily under no other sanction than the desire to retain their positions as officials.
>
> The Gestapo and S.D. were used for purposes which were criminal under the Charter involving the persecution and extermination of the Jews, brutalities and killings in concentration camps, excesses in the administration of occupied territories, the administration of the slave labour programme and the mistreatment and murder of prisoners-of-war. The defendant Kaltenbrunner, who was a member of this organization, was among those who used it for these purposes. In dealing with the Gestapo the Tribunal includes all executive and administrative officials of Amt IV of the R.S.H.A. or concerned with Gestapo administration in other departments of the R.S.H.A. and all local Gestapo officials serving both inside and outside of Germany, including the members of the Frontier Police, but not including the members of the Border and Customs Protection or the Secret Field Police, except such members as have been specified above. At the suggestion of the prosecution the Tribunal does not include persons employed by the Gestapo for purely clerical, stenographic, janitorial or similar unofficial routine tasks. In dealing with the S.D. the Tribunal includes Amts III, VI and VII of the R.S.H.A. and all other members of the S.D., including all local representatives and agents, honorary or otherwise, whether they were technically members of the S.D. or not.
>
> The Tribunal declares to be criminal within the meaning of the Charter the group composed of those members of the Gestapo and S.D. holding the positions enumerated in the preceding paragraph who became or remained members of the organization with knowledge that it was being used for the commission of acts declared criminal by Article 6 of the Charter, or who were personally implicated as members of the organization in the commission of such crimes. The basis for this finding is the participation of the organization in war crimes and crimes against humanity connected with the war; this group declared criminal cannot include, therefore, persons who had ceased to hold the positions enumerated in the preceding paragraph prior to September 1, 1939.

SDG. *See* SANITATSDIENSTGEFREITER.

SDKFZ-171. *See* PANTHER TANK.

SDP. *See* SUDETEN DEUTSCHE PARTEI.

SEA LION. *See* SEELÖWE.

SECOND BOOK. *See* ZWEITES BUCH.

SECOND REVOLUTION. The attempt in the first year of the Nazi regime to extend the movement on its socialist side. The idea of National Socialism was composed of two apparently contradictory elements, nationalism and socialism. In the early stages of the movement Hitler wavered between nationalism (plus capitalism and the Army) on the one side and socialism on the other. He chose the way of nationalism. Gregor Strasser and Ernst Roehm (qq.v.), leaders of the drive for a second revolution, were liquidated in the Blood Purge (q.v.) of 1934.

SECONDARY INFORMANTS. *See* HELFERSHELFER.

SECRET CABINET COUNCIL. *See* GEHEIMER KABINETTSRAT.

SECRET FIELD POLICE. *See* GEHEIME FELDPOLIZEI.

SECRET STATE POLICE. *See* GESTAPO.

SECTION. *See* ABSCHNITT.

SECURITY POLICE. *See* SICHERHEITSPOLIZEI.

SECURITY SERVICE. *See* SD.

SEECKT, HANS VON (1866–1936). Ranking officer of the Reichswehr (q.v.) responsible for suppressing the Hitler-Ludendorff *Putsch* in Munich in 1923 (*see* BEER-HALL PUTSCH). Hans von Seeckt was born in Silesia on April 22, 1866, the son of a general. At nineteen he joined his father's regiment, the 1st Grenadier Guards, as an ensign *(Fahnenjunker)*, and in 1897 he was appointed to the General Staff of the 3d Army Corps in Berlin. At the outbreak of World War I in August 1914, he served as a lieutenant colonel and on January 27, 1915, was promoted to colonel.

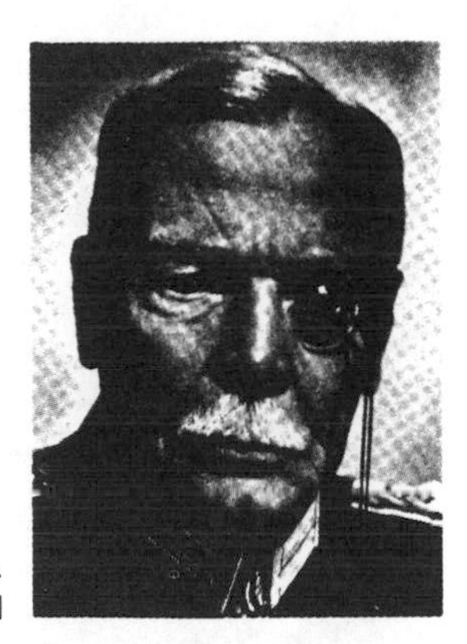

Col. Gen. Hans von Seeckt. [*Tita Binz*]

The following May he played a prominent role in planning the breakthrough of the Central Powers between Gorlice and Tarnów and the subsequent invasion of Serbia. In June 1916 he was appointed chief of the General Staff of the Austrian archduke Charles, and in December 1917 he became chief of staff of the Turkish Army. He returned to Germany in 1918. During his war service he acquired a reputation as an able officer who understood the political implications of military problems. Trim, precise, almost dainty in his well-tailored uniform, he became known as the Sphinx with the monocle.

Under the Weimar Republic (q.v.), Von Seeckt was appointed *Chef des Truppenamtes* (adjutant general) of the new Reichswehr. On June 15, 1920, three months after the failure of the Kapp *Putsch* (q.v.), he took over command of the Army (Heeresleitung). Distrusting traditional theories of mass armies and trench warfare, he remodeled the Reichswehr as a mobile shock force of thirty-five divisions with officers trained to function at higher levels. He supported liaison with Soviet Russia and sent German tank crews and pilots there for training.

In September 1923 Von Seeckt was attacked by the *Völkischer Beobachter* (q.v.), the organ of the rising Nazi movement, as "an enemy of the *völkisch* idea, a lackey of the Weimar Republic, and a pawn of sinister Jewish-Masonic elements." Even worse, he was charged with being under the influence of his wife, who was Jewish ("nee Jacobsohn"). When word came to Berlin of the attempted Hitler-Ludendorff *Putsch* in Munich, President Friedrich Ebert (q.v.) asked Von Seeckt: "Tell us, please, whom does the Army obey—the government or the mutineers?" "Herr Reich President," Von Seeckt replied, "the Army obeys me." Although he had mixed feelings about the attempted coup in Munich, he sent a telegram to Gen. Otto von Lossow, commander of the armed forces in Bavaria, to suppress the Nazi uprising at once. From then until December 28, 1924, Von Seeckt was responsible for security against domestic political dangers, especially the Hitler movement. He was promoted to general, but on October 8, 1926, he was dismissed for two errors: he had issued an order recognizing dueling among officers, and he had offered Prince Wilhelm of Prussia, son of former Crown Prince Wilhelm (q.v.), a military training post.

After his retirement Von Seeckt served in the Reichstag (q.v.) from 1930 to 1932. In 1934 and 1935 he was military adviser to Generalissimo Chiang Kai-shek in China. Von Seeckt wrote many treatises on military affairs. Although he had opposed the Nazi party in its early days, he was inclined to accept National Socialism once it achieved political power. He died in Berlin on December 29, 1936.

SEELE, GERTRUD (1917–1945). Nurse and social worker executed for "defeatist statements designed to undermine the morale of the people." Gertrud Seele was born in Berlin on September 22, 1917, to a working-class family. After service in the Reichsarbeitsdienst (q.v.), the State Labor Service, she turned to a career in public health and social service. During a conversation at a party in wartime Berlin, she openly expressed her indignation against the Nazis, whom she loathed. On several occasions she helped Jews to escape Nazi persecution. In late 1944 she was arrested as "a recognized enemy of the state," tried before the Volksgericht (q.v.), the People's Court, in Potsdam, and executed at Plötzensee Prison in Berlin on January 12, 1945.

SEELÖWE (Sea Lion). Code name for the projected invasion of England in 1940. With France fallen, most of Norway occupied, and German troops in control of the Netherlands and Belgium, Hitler had only one remaining obstacle to his goal of dominating Europe. He would have to invade England. In early July 1940 he decided that a landing on the island kingdom was possible provided he could maintain air supremacy "and other conditions." Accordingly, he issued a war directive for the preparation of a landing operation, which was to be called Seelöwe. Full instructions were given to Hermann Goering (q.v.), head of the Luftwaffe (q.v.), to reduce the British Royal Air Force, clear mine-free channels for German ships, seal off the harbor of Dover, tie down the British Navy, and make a surprise crossing of the English Channel in an area from Ramsgate to the Isle of Wight. The scheme seemed entirely feasible in view of the extent of Nazi triumphs to that point. Preparations were made throughout the summer of 1940.

Meanwhile, Goering's planes strove mightily to set the stage for invasion. But the essential prerequisite of air superiority was never attained. Great air battles over Britain culminated in the smashing defeat of Hitler's air armada on September 15, 1940. The Luftwaffe never recovered from this beating. Gradually Hitler became convinced that the invasion was impossible. On January 9, 1941, he gave orders to discontinue preparations for undertaking Seelöwe. Later he mentioned the possibility of reverting to Seelöwe, but he made the suggestion with little enthusiasm. Hitler, like Napoleon, was destined never to cross the channel and occupy England.

Bibliography. Peter Fleming, *Operation Sea Lion*, Simon and Schuster, New York, 1957.

SEIZURE OF POWER. *See* MACHTERGREIFUNG.

SELBSTGLEICHSCHALTER (Self-Coordinator). An individual who willingly and without pressure from the regime accepted Nazi ideology as binding. After Hitler assumed political power, every conceivable activity, from education to the press, theater, music, literature, business, and law, was subjected to *Gleichschaltung* (q.v.), or coordination. The *Selbstgleichschalter* initiated his own coordination in his discipline or activity.

SELBSTSCHUTZ (Self-Defense). A semimilitary defense unit composed of Germans living in Poland.

SELDTE, FRANZ (1882–1947). Member of Hitler's original Cabinet as Reich Minister of Labor. Franz Seldte was born in Magdeburg on June 29, 1882. After attending the *Realgymnasium* (semiclassical secondary school) in Magdeburg, he studied chemistry in Braunschweig and then embarked on travel in foreign countries. In 1906 he served as a one-year volunteer in the Infantry Regiment 66 Magdeburg. In World War I, in which he served as a captain in the same unit, he lost an arm in combat and was awarded the Iron Cross (First and Second Classes).

On December 23, 1918, with Lieut. Col. Theodor Duesterberg (q.v.), formerly an officer of the General Staff, Seldte founded the Stahlhelm (q.v.), the veterans' organization. In an initial statement Seldte said that the organization had been formed to utilize "the spirit of the frontline soldier" against "the swinish revolution." The field-gray formations of the Stahlhelm became well known in Germany during the 1920s. In 1930 the increasing rivalry between the Stahlhelm and the Nazi Storm Troopers (*see* SA) led to a meeting between Hitler, Seldte, and Duesterberg, at which Hitler declared that when he came to power, the nation would arm immediately and that he would have any man shot who opposed him.

On October 11, 1931, Seldte represented the Stahlhelm in the Harzburg Front (q.v.), the conference of rightist groups that failed because Hitler refused to share power with others. Seldte became a member of the short-lived Papen-Hitler coalition Cabinet as Minister of Labor in 1932. The next year, when Hitler became Chancellor, he appointed Seldte to the same post, which he retained until the fall of the Third Reich. His special assignment was to see to the coordination of Prussia with the Third Reich. He was indicted at Nuremberg but died in Fürth in April 1947.

SELF-COORDINATOR. *See* SELBSTGLEICHSCHALTER.

SELF-DEFENSE. *See* SELBSTSCHUTZ.

SENDING CHILDREN TO THE COUNTRY. *See* KINDERLANDVERSCHICKUNG.

SEPTEMBERLINGS. Contemptuous name given by Dr. Paul Joseph Goebbels (q.v.) to the host of new members who joined the Nazi party after the elections of September 1930. Goebbels warned the party in 1931 that these bourgeois intellectuals from the propertied and educated classes were not to be trusted as much as the *Alte Kämpfer* (q.v.), the old guard: "They believe that the movement had been brought to greatness by the talk of mere demagogues, and are now prepared to take it over themselves and provide it with leadership and expertise. That is what they think!"

SEYSS-INQUART, ARTUR (1892–1946). Austrian National Socialist politician and Reich Commissioner for the Netherlands. Artur Seyss-Inquart was born in Stannern, near Iglau, Bohemia (now Jihlava, Czechoslovakia), on July 22, 1892. In World War I he served in a Tyrolean *Kaiserjäger* (Emperor's rifleman) regiment and was severely wounded. After 1918 he became a fervent advocate of *Anschluss* (q.v.), union between Austria and Germany. An ambitious young lawyer in Vienna, he believed that the best chance for union of the two countries would come through the National Socialist movement. He did not join the Austrian Nazi party, but he became a front man for its activities.

Artur Seyss-Inquart. [*Associated Newspaper Group Ltd.*]

In 1937 Chancellor Kurt von Schuschnigg (q.v.), who was impressed with Seyss-Inquart as a respectable churchgoer, appointed him *Staatsrat* (State Councillor) as a means of establishing connections with the national opposition. On February 12, 1938, a raging Hitler, in confrontation with Von Schuschnigg, forced the Austrian Chancellor to lift his ban against Austrian Nazis, proclaim amnesty for all Nazis held in jail, and agree to appoint the pro-Nazi Seyss-Inquart Minister of the Interior. In this capacity Seyss-Inquart "agreed" to a German invasion of Austria. After Von Schuschnigg's resignation, Seyss-Inquart turned his country over to Hitler and announced the end of Article 88 of the Treaty of Saint-Germain-en-Laye, which proclaimed that Austrian independence was inalienable.

Until April 30, 1939, Seyss-Inquart served as *Reichsstatthalter* (Reich Governor) of the Ostmark (Austria). When Hitler, on October 12, 1939, established the General Government of Poland, he appointed Hans Frank (q.v.) as Governor-General and Seyss-Inquart as his deputy. From 1940 to 1945 Seyss-Inquart served Hitler as *Reichskommissar* (Reich Commissioner) for the occupied Netherlands. His attempts to negotiate with the Dutch were not successful. In his final days in the *Fuehrerbunker* (q.v.) in Berlin, Hitler proposed as his successors Dr. Paul Joseph Goebbels (q.v.) for Chancellor, Martin Bormann (q.v.) for the new post of Party Minister, and Seyss-Inquart for Foreign Minister.

At the Nuremberg Trial (q.v.), Seyss-Inquart was accused of participating directly in the deportation and shooting of hostages. In his final statement to the Tribunal he admitted the "fearful excesses" of the Nazi regime and stated that he must take responsibility in part for what had happened. A few days after receiving the death sentence, he was given the news that his son, who had been missing in the U.S.S.R., had been found alive. Seyss-Inquart was hanged at Nuremberg on October 16, 1946.

SHARPSHOOTER CORPS. *See* FELDJÄGERKORPS.

SHELL HOUSE RAID. A British Royal Air Force (RAF) attack on March 3, 1945, on the Gestapo (q.v.) headquarters in Copenhagen. Late in the spring of 1944 Heinrich Himmler (q.v.) requisitioned the modern office building of the Shell Petroleum Company in the center of the Danish city. In the basement Danish citizens were subjected to torture. The ground floor and the next two floors were used as vast record rooms where dossiers were kept on Danish Jews and resisters. Only the sixth story was empty because it lacked a heating system; here the Gestapo installed twenty-two flimsy concrete-block partitions to house prisoners.

In December 1944 the Danish resistance radio communicated with London and requested the RAF to smash the Shell House before a purge took place. It would be a difficult task to destroy the records without harming the prisoners on the top floor, but the British were interested. The Danes furnished complete architects' plans of the building, with full details on every room. At the time there were about thirty-two prisoners of the resistance and several informers in the Shell House.

On March 3, 1945, a British force composed of eighteen Mosquito bombers and twenty-eight American P-51 Mustangs took off from scattered airfields and crossed the North Sea in the direction of Jutland. Maintaining a tight formation, they descended to 15 feet above the sea, which was churning in a gale. Reaching the South Jutland coast, they rose to 150 feet and headed toward Copenhagen. Then came one of the most dangerous and effective low-level bombings of World War II. The airmen destroyed the Shell House without taking the lives of all the prisoners on the top floor. Four Mosquitos and five Mustangs were lost with ten airmen. Several hundred Nazis were killed, while only six prisoners in the attic lost their lives. The Danes managed to get the rest to Sweden. There was a tragic side effect. The raiders bombed the Jeanne d'Arc School in error, with casualties among nuns and children. After the liberation the British airmen who bombed the Shell House were welcomed in Copenhagen as heroes.

Bibliography. David Lampe, *The Danish Resistance,* Ballantine Books, Inc., New York, 1957.

SHIRER, WILLIAM L[AWRENCE] (1904–). American journalist and historian, author of *The Rise and Fall of the Third Reich* (Simon and Schuster, New York, 1960), the most successful study of the Third Reich published in the United States. Born in Chicago in 1904, William L. Shirer attended Coe College in Cedar Rapids, Iowa. Working his way to Europe on a cattle boat for the summer, he remained there for the next fifteen years. From 1925 to 1932 he was European correspondent for the Chicago *Tribune,* covering assignments in Western Europe, the Near East, and India. He became chief of the Berlin bureau of Universal News Service in 1934. At the same time he began to broadcast for the Columbia Broadcasting System and to keep the daily journal that became the basis for his *Berlin Diary* (Alfred A. Knopf, Inc., New York, 1941). Shirer's remarkable broadcast of June 21, 1940, describing the meeting of the triumphant Hitler and a humiliated French commission at Compiègne (q.v.), was widely hailed as a masterpiece of reporting. Shirer went back to Europe on assignments in 1943, 1944, and 1945 and reported the Nuremberg Trial (q.v.). He also covered the San Francisco Conference and meetings of the United Nations. His book *The Rise and Fall of the Third Reich,* a best seller for many years, went through twenty printings in the first year after publication.

SHOCK TROOP. *See* STOSSTRUPP.

SICHERHEITSDIENST. *See* SD.

SICHERHEITSHAUPTAMT. *See* REICHSSICHERHEITSHAUPTAMT.

SICHERHEITSPOLIZEI (SIPO; Security Police). The security police unit consisting of the Gestapo and the Kriminalpolizei (qq.v.) under Reinhard Heydrich (q.v.).

SICHERUNGSVERWAHRTE (SV; Prisoners in Security Custody). A category of concentration camp prisoners (*see* CONCENTRATION CAMPS) classified by the Gestapo (q.v.) as criminals. This group consisted of convicts who were serving sentences in the camps. Nearly all were dregs of society. They managed to win a dominant position in the concentration camps and ruthlessly exploited the other inmates.

"SIEG HEIL!" ("Hail to Victory!"). Popular rallying cry used at Nazi party meetings (*see* NUREMBERG RALLIES). Huge audiences screamed the slogan in unison, repeating each word again and again in strongly accented tones. After Hitler made one of his speeches, he generally remained standing silently as Rudolf Hess (q.v.), the No. 3 Nazi, with his eyes fixed adoringly on the Fuehrer, commenced the "*Sieg Heil*" chant. The slogan was similar to the Japanese "*Banzai!*" (literally, "Ten Thousand Years!"), a hurrah or shout of honor or joy. The effect produced was much like that of a student cheering section at an American football game.

SIEGFRIED LINE. Term used by the Allies in World War II to describe the West Wall (q.v.), the German defensive line. In World War I the Hindenburg Line stretched like a long serpent inside French territory between the North Sea and Switzerland. Sections of the line were given the names of legendary gods and heroes such as Wotan, Hagen, Brunhilde, and Kriemhilde. The section running south from Dracourt, near Lille, to just south of Saint-Quentin was called the Siegfried Line. In World War II the Germans never employed the term Siegfried Line and regarded its use by the Allies as ridicule and polemic. *See also* "WASHING ON THE SIEGFRIED LINE, WE'RE GONNA HANG OUT THE."

SIPO. *See* SICHERHEITSPOLIZEI.

SIPPENBUCH (Clan Book). A special identification

booklet carried by every member of the SS (q.v.) from 1932 on as proof of his racial purity. Introduced by Heinrich Himmler (q.v.) after his conversion to the "religion of the blood," the *Sippenbuch* attested to the "pure" descent of its holder from Aryan stock (*see* RACIAL DOCTRINE). It was necessary to prove that Aryan blood was uncontaminated as far back as 1750. The *Sippenbuch* gave the individual's genealogical table and was used to obtain a certificate of approval for any girl whom the holder chose to marry. Although the Rasse- und Siedlungshauptamt (q.v.), the Central Office for Race and Resettlement, kept careful records of all the clan books, it was unable to prevent bribery and corruption leading to false entries. During World War II the entire system began to break down and survived only as a topic of amusement.

SITZKRIEG (Sit-down War). German term for the period of inactivity on the western front from September 1939 to May 1940. The British and French forces were strung along the Maginot Line (q.v.), while the German armies were occupied in Poland and the east. There was little action in the west in what the British called the phony war. The world awaited the coming contest between the irresistible force, the German Army, and the supposedly immovable Allied forces. Suddenly, the Germans struck at the Low Countries and France, broke through the gateway at Sedan, outflanked the Maginot Line, drove the British forces from the Continent at Dunkirk, captured Paris, and forced France to sign an armistice at Compiègne (q.v.) on June 22, 1940.

SKORZENY, OTTO (1908–1975). The most publicized adventurer of Nazi Germany, who won worldwide attention for his exploits. Otto Skorzeny was born in Vienna on June 12, 1908, the son of an engineer. While studying engineering, he joined the *Freikorps* (q.v.; free corps), the freebooters of the early post-World War I era. Later he joined the Heimwehr (Home Guard). He became a Nazi in 1930. In the years just before World War II he worked as a business manager for a building contractor. In 1939 he was appointed to Hitler's personal bodyguard. Later he served with the Waffen-SS (q.v.), the armed SS (q.v.), in France and Russia. In April 1943 he began work as an *SS-Standartenfuehrer* (colonel) with Section VI of the Reich Central Security Office (Reichssicherheitshauptamt, q.v.) under Walter Schellenberg (q.v.). His special assignment was to direct secret agents in foreign and neutral countries.

A giant 6 feet 4 inches tall who was known among his comrades as Scarface, Skorzeny won a reputation for reckless courage. On July 29, 1943, just after Mussolini's fall, Hitler summoned Skorzeny and assigned him the task of rescuing the Italian dictator from captivity. Mussolini had been taken to a hotel on the Gran Sasso d'Italia, high in the Abruzzi Apennines and accessible only by a funicular railway. On September 13, Skorzeny led an airborne force of commandos by glider to a dangerous landing near the mountainside hotel. Within a few minutes he placed the astonished Mussolini, who had been contemplating suicide, in a tiny Fieseler-Storch plane and, after a remarkable takeoff from a rocky field, flew him to Rome. Then the Italian dictator was transported to Vienna by a Luftwaffe (q.v.) plane. It was a daring rescue that won Skorzeny instant fame. *See also* EICHE.

Otto Skorzeny with Hitler. [*National Archives, Washington*]

On July 20, 1944, the day of the attempt on Hitler's life at Rastenburg (*see* JULY PLOT), Skorzeny boarded a train at Berlin for Vienna and proceeded as far as the suburb of Lichterfelde, where he learned of the crisis. He hurried back to the Bendlerstrasse (q.v.), where he found chaos. He immediately gave his assistance to the officers loyal to Hitler. The following October, Skorzeny kidnapped Adm. Miklós Horthy, the Hungarian Regent, who had wanted to surrender his country to the advancing Russians. In the Ardennes offensive of December 1944 it was rumored that Skorzeny had planned to kidnap Gen. Dwight D. Eisenhower, but the report was probably exaggerated. Hitler did assign him to lead Operation Greif (*see* GREIF), in which some 2,000 English-speaking Germans, dressed in American uniforms, were sent in captured tanks and jeeps to create havoc behind American lines until the arrival of German armored units. But it was far too late: many of Skorzeny's commandos were caught and summarily shot. In January 1945 he led a diversionary unit on the eastern front.

Skorzeny was arrested by American troops on May 15, 1945, in Steiermark. In September 1947 he was tried before an American military tribunal at Dachau (q.v.) and acquitted. For a short time he worked in a historical section of the United States Army. Arrested by German authorities, he escaped from a camp in Darmstadt in July 1948. From 1949 on, under the name of Robert Steinbacher, he turned his energies to helping his SS comrades. Supported by funds from leftover Nazi concerns, he founded a secret organization, Die Spinne (the Spider), which helped some 500 former SS members to escape from Germany. Under the protection of the Franco regime, he settled in Spain, where he was active in export-import businesses and real estate. In 1959 he bought a country estate in County Kildare, Ireland, where he spent the summer months, and a house in Mallorca. He died in Madrid on July 5, 1975.

Bibliography. Charles Whiting, *Otto Skorzeny*, Ballantine Books, Inc., New York, 1972.

SMOLENSK ATTENTAT (also called Operation Flash). An attempt on Hitler's life on March 13, 1943, on the Russian front. Maj. Gen. Henning von Tresckow (q.v.) and his staff officer, 1st Lieut. Fabian von Schlabrendorff, liaison agents on the eastern front for the Resistance (q.v.) circle in Berlin, planned to kill Hitler with a delayed-action time bomb concealed in his airplane during a return flight from Smolensk to his headquarters in Rastenburg. On March 13, the Fuehrer's private air cavalcade arrived at Smolensk, and the conference took place without incident. At lunch Von Tresckow asked one of the officers accompanying Hitler, Col. Heinz Brandt, who in 1936 had been a leading member of the German Army equestrian team at the Olympic Games (*see* OLYMPIAD XI), to take a couple of bottles of brandy to an old friend, Gen. Helmuth Stieff (q.v.). The unsuspecting Brandt agreed. As the Fuehrer boarded his plane, Von Schlabrendorff started the time fuse to go off in half an hour and handed the parcel to Brandt. The two conspirators then signaled Berlin that the main part of their plan had succeeded.

The judgment was premature. After two and one-half hours word came from Rastenburg that Hitler had arrived safely. Von Schlabrendorff now faced the critical problem of retrieving the faulty bomb. Von Tresckow telephoned Brandt to hold the gift: the date was wrong. He arrived in Rastenburg bringing two bottles of real brandy and took back the original bomb package. That night he dismantled the bomb in a railway car and reported to the conspirators in Berlin that the detonator had been defective.

SNATCH. *See* GREIF.

SOBIBÓR. Extermination camp located near the Bug River on the border of the German-occupied eastern territories (*see* EXTERMINATION CAMPS). Sobibór and Chelmno, Belzec, and Treblinka (qq.v.) were four large death camps in the Lublin district of Poland. All four were under the command of *SS-Brigadefuehrer* (Maj. Gen.) Odilo Globocnik (q.v.). Sobibór was a killing center for Jews, including children, and no selections were made for work or death. There was some minor industrial activity linked to the war effort, but the main work was the execution of inmates. Victims were brought to the camp in unventilated transports, and all but a handful were gassed after arrival. On October 14, 1943, about 150 inmates broke out in a desperate riot, which was quickly subdued. Some 35,000 Dutch Jews, originally assigned to Auschwitz (q.v.), were sent to Sobibór. Most of their corpses were burned in open pits. Sobibór, along with Treblinka and Belzec, was evacuated in the fall of 1943.

SOCIAL DARWINISM. The ideology behind Hitler's policy of genocide (q.v.). In 1859 the English naturalist Charles Darwin, in his *Origin of Species*, projected the concept of evolution as part of a long, gradual development from a lower to a higher form of life. In the struggle for existence, the stronger and more efficient element always prevailed. The species continually progressed in a process of natural selection. Darwinian theory denied the existence of any essential differences between men and animals. It was not long before students of the social order went a step farther and derived from Darwin's basic theory the idea that human society also was a biological organism. The biological factor, it was said, was the one absolute in every sphere of life. Men, like all other animals, must fight for their existence.

The term *social Darwinism* was applied to the use of Darwin's teachings for political and social purposes. It appeared in most countries as a concomitant of integral nationalism. Social Darwinists held that a modern nation should have a sense of its own identity and even of its superiority when measured against other peoples. Everything in the social order must be subordinated to overriding needs in the struggle for existence. In Germany social Darwinism was elevated to the status of a *Weltanschauung* (q.v.), a philosophy stressing a world view of life. German ideologists argued that the modern state, instead of devoting its energy to protecting the weak, should reject its inferior population in favor of the strong, healthy elements. More Germans than Frenchmen were impressed by the *Essay on the Inequality of Human Races* (Paris, 1853–1855) of Arthur Comte de Gobineau (q.v.), which preceded Darwin's classic by a few years but stressed the same basic theme. German social Darwinists were delighted by Gobineau's praise of "the true creative power of the Germanic Nordic race."

Social Darwinism had a profound and long-lasting effect on the mind of Adolf Hitler. He expressed its ideas in simplified form in the pages of *Mein Kampf* (q.v.), and he made it the theme of most of his major speeches. The thinking was always the same: nature teaches us that it is governed by the principle of selection; victory goes to the strong, and the weak must be eliminated; nature knows nothing of humanitarianism, which holds that the weak must be preserved at the cost of the strong; war is an unalterable law of life—the prerequisite for the natural development of the strong and the precedent for the elimination of the weak; and struggle has always been at the core of existence.

From these ideas to the policy of genocide was a tragic step. Only the National Socialist state, said Hitler, could appreciate the necessity for halting the deterioration of the selective process. The German Nordics were an elite, and they should become a unifying element for all humanity. On the other hand, the Jews, "the culture-destroying race," must be eliminated not only from German life but from the world community. In the struggle for existence Germans must follow the principles of sound breeding (*see* RACIAL DOCTRINE). In accordance with these assumptions, Hitler at first used social Darwinism to intensify hatred for the Jews and eventually projected a Final Solution (*see* ENDLÖSUNG, DIE) to eliminate them altogether from human society.

SOCIETY FOR RESEARCH AND TEACHING OF ANCESTRAL HERITAGE. *See* AHNENERBE FORSCHUNGS- UND LEHRGEMEINSCHAFT.

SOLF TEA PARTY. A tea party held on September 10, 1943, which led to the dissolution of the Solf Kreis (Solf Circle), a peripheral group in the conspiracy against Hitler. The group was led by the widow of Wilhelm Solf, for years Colonial Minister under Emperor William II. Solf had served the Weimar Republic (q.v.) and had long warned against the dangers of National Socialism. He fought the Nazi regime from its inception to the day of his death. After he died, Frau Solf and her daughter, Gräfin Ballestrem, continued to work in opposition to Hitler, especially in helping Jews persecuted by the Nazis. Frau Solf, her daughter, and Fräulein Elizabeth von Thadden (q.v.), former headmistress of a well-known girls' school near Heidelberg, became the center of a small group of Anglophile intellectuals.

On September 10, 1943, a tea party held at Fräulein von Thadden's home was attended by many of the conspirators. Also present was a Dr. Reckze, a young physician from the Charité Hospital, who posed as a Swiss national but was actually a spy for the Gestapo (q.v.). Reckzeh invited Frau Solf to give him a letter that she wanted to send to Switzerland and then promptly informed the Gestapo. The secret police waited four months and then, in January 1944, arrested all who had been present at the fatal tea party, including Frau Solf and her daughter, Helmuth James Graf von Moltke (q.v.), and others. The Solf Circle was smashed. The arrest of Von Moltke also meant the dissolution of the Kreisau Circle (q.v.).

All the guests were executed with the exception of Frau Solf and her daughter, both of whom survived. They were being tried before the Volksgericht (People's Court) on February 3, 1945, when an American bomb fell on the courtroom and destroyed the entire dossier of the Solf case. The dreaded judge Roland Freisler (q.v.) was killed in the bombing. Frau Solf and her daughter were released from Moabit Prison on April 23, 1945, through an oversight.

SOLMITZ, FRITZ (1893–1933). Socialist journalist beaten to death in a concentration camp (*see* CONCENTRATION CAMPS). Fritz Solmitz was born in Berlin on October 22, 1893, the son of well-to-do parents. After studying political economy at the University of Freiburg, he served in World War I. His experiences made him a pacifist. After the war he entered the field of journalism as the political editor of the *Lübecker Volksbote*. For the last nine years of his life he was a severe critic of Hitler and the Nazis. Arrested two weeks after Hitler came to political power, he was sent to Fuhlsbüttel concentration camp, near Hamburg, where he was brutally beaten. He died of his injuries on September 19, 1933.

SONDERBEHANDLUNG (Special Treatment). Nazi term used to describe the treatment of undesirable racial groups in the Third Reich. It was actually a euphemism for liquidation. The term was also given the connotation of discriminatory treatment. *See also* SONDERKOMMANDOS.

SONDERFAHNDUNGSLISTE-GB (Special Search List —Great Britain). A list of prominent Britons and others who were to be arrested immediately after the projected German invasion of the British Isles in World War II. The list was drawn up by an assistant to Heinrich Himmler (q.v.), Walter Schellenberg (q.v.), chief of counterespionage of the Reichssicherheitshauptamt (q.v.), the Reich Central Security Office. It contained the names of 2,300 persons, mostly Britons but also German refugees, all of whom were to be arrested by the Gestapo (q.v.) and subjected to its interrogations.

The list was headed by Prime Minister Winston Churchill as the "archcriminal" of the British establishment. Among other names were those of the scholars Harold Laski, Bertrand Russell, and Beatrice Webb; the authors H. G. Wells, Virginia Woolf, Aldous Huxley, and Norman Angell; the journalists Rebecca West and Douglas Reed (Reed's dispatches on the Reichstag fire, q.v., had displeased the Nazis); and the entertainer Noël Coward. Prominent on the list were such non-English names as Chaim Weizmann, Ignace Paderewski, Eduard Beneš (q.v.), and Jan Masaryk. Conspicuous among the Nazi refugees from the Third Reich were the names of Ernst Franz Sedgwick (Putzi) Hanfstaengel and Hermann Rauschning (qq.v.). The *Special Search List—Great Britain,* also called the Nazi black book, was among the "invasion documents" found in the Himmler papers after the war.

SONDERGERICHT (Special Court). One of the special secret courts established by the Nazis to try offenders against the state. *See also* NIEMOELLER, Martin.

SONDERKOMMANDOS (Special Detachments). (1) Special units of the SS (q.v.) employed for police and political tasks in the occupied territories of the east during World War II. (2) More frequently a term used to describe detachments of male Jews designated for special work in the extermination camps (q.v.). Their main task was body disposal. Controlled by SS guards, the *Sonderkommandos* were bribed to perform their macabre work. At Auschwitz (q.v.) shifts of about 100 prisoners worked in the gas chambers and crematoria. They led the naked prisoners into the execution chamber. The inmates, listening to piped-in music, believed that they were going into bathrooms. When all were inside, the *Sonderkommandos* quietly left and sealed the prisoners into the room. Then trucks bearing the insignia of the Red Cross brought up supplies of Zyklon-B (q.v.) crystals, which were dropped into vents in the roof. After an interval of twenty minutes, during which the deadly fumes were extracted by ventilators, the *Sonderkommandos,* wearing protective clothing and gas masks, hosed down the corpses and loaded them on elevators for descent to the crematorium below. Originally, the bodies were buried in huge trenches, but this practice was discontinued after the arrival of patented crematoria. The *Sonderkommandos* were allowed to live in comparative luxury during a duty period of four months, after which they were shot and cremated with the new prisoners. There were to be no witnesses to this ghastly work.

SONNENBLUME (Sunflower). Code name for German reinforcements in Tripoli in World War II. In a war council held on January 11, 1941, Hitler directed that Operation Sonnenblume be implemented in mid-February 1942. German forces were to be sent to Tripoli and to go into action wherever there was British resistance. The new Afrika Korps (q.v.), with its powerful armored vehicles, was designated for this task.

SORGE, RICHARD (1895–). German master spy and double agent during World War II. Richard Sorge was born at Baku, the son of a mining engineer working for the Imperial Russian Oil Company. He was also a grandson of a secretary to Karl Marx. At the age of three he was brought back to Germany. He volunteered in October 1914 for service on the western front and was severely wounded. During the last two years of World War I he studied at the Universities of Berlin, Kiel, and Hamburg. Sorge became a member of the Communist party and after the war was active as an agent for the Comintern. He went to China and worked in Shanghai until 1928 as the editor of a German news service. He then went to Tokyo as correspondent for the *Frankfurter Zeitung*. Tall, gaunt, and unkempt, he became a well-known member of the German community in Tokyo. An alcoholic, he lived in a filthy apartment in a slum district. He joined the Nazi party and maintained close contact with the German Embassy as an espionage agent. Sorge's eccentric behavior disguised the fact that he was a double agent working for a Communist spy ring directed from Moscow.

Four months before the Germans invaded the Soviet Union on June 22, 1941, Sorge informed the Russians of Hitler's intentions. He was arrested in Tokyo on October 16, 1941, along with a Japanese assistant. It was reported that he was hanged in Tokyo on November 7, 1944, but no evidence has been produced of his death.

Bibliography. *The Schellenberg Memoirs*, ed. and tr. by Louis Hagen, André Deutsch, London, 1956.

SOVIET-GERMAN NONAGGRESSION PACT. *See* HITLER-STALIN PACT.

SOZIALDEMOKRATISCHE PARTEI DEUTSCHLANDS. *See* SPD.

SPANDAU. Fortress prison in West Berlin at the mouth of the Spree River. It was used for the internment of seven Nazi prisoners convicted at the Nuremberg Trial (q.v.). Constructed originally to hold 600 convicts, Spandau consists of a decaying central building set in 8 acres forming an island. The prison is encircled by a fence inside which is a second electrified barrier set in a mined area. There is a high wall with nine concrete towers housing armed guards twenty-four hours a day. The guards press a button every 10 minutes for an electronic time check in the commandant's office. Entrance to and exit from the prison can be made only through the main gate.

Spandau Prison was set aside for the exclusive use of the Nazi leaders given prison terms at the Nuremberg

Spandau Prison. [*UPI*]

Trial. The four Allied powers were obligated to keep the prisoners in close captivity. Each was required to maintain Spandau for a month: France in January, Great Britain in February, the U.S.S.R. in March, and the United States in April. The cycle was repeated in May and September. Each country provided a prison commandant, two doctors, cooks, and other personnel. The upkeep was paid for by the city of Berlin and the federal government in Bonn.

On July 18, 1947, after waiting for nine months while Spandau was prepared for them, the seven prisoners were moved from Nuremberg to the Berlin prison. They were given numbers from 1 to 7: No. 1 was Baldur von Schirach (twenty years); No. 2, Grand Adm. Karl Doenitz (ten years); No. 3, Constantin Freiherr von Neurath (fifteen years); No. 4, Grand Adm. Erich Raeder (life); No. 5, Albert Speer (twenty years); No. 6, Walther Funk (life); and No. 7, Rudolf Hess (life; qq.v.). The prison regime was harsh. The prisoners were allowed thirty minutes twice a day for exercise in the open air, one letter of 1,200 words to their families each week, strictly limited visits, a choice from the restricted prison fare, and a small amount of selected reading material. The guards were under military law and were forbidden to talk to the prisoners. The daily routine was fixed and precise: up at 6 A.M.; lights out at 10 P.M.

In 1954, after serving seven years of his fifteen-year sentence, Von Neurath was released. In 1955, after serving nine years of his life sentence, Raeder was set free because of his age and weak health. In 1956, after completing his ten years, Doenitz was given his freedom. In 1957, after serving nearly eleven years of his life sentence, Funk was released. In 1966, after completing their twenty years, Speer and Von Schirach were freed. Only Hess remained as the last prisoner, guarded by a small army of warders. The governments of the United States, Britain, and France repeatedly urged his release, but the Russians, unmoved by public opinion, vetoed the request. In the Russian view a life sentence for Hess meant exactly that.

SPANN, OTHMAR (1878–1950). Austrian economist, sociologist, and advocate of the German version of the corporate state. Othmar Spann was born in Vienna on October 1, 1878. Turning to an academic career, he became a professor at the University of Brünn (Brno) in 1909 and at Vienna in 1919. Influenced by the romanticism of Adam Müller, Fichte, and List, Spann projected an economic and theoretical sociological universalism in contrast to the teachings of Adam Smith and David Ricardo. Spann emphasized the relation of the individual to class and nationality. He supported the idea of an interventionist state capable of defending the rights of the peasants and the middle class against trusts and cartels. The state, he said, must be directed by a new elite imbued with romantic sentiment and willing to give youth a real share in direction. He opposed scientific Marxism and all varieties of liberalism. In effect, Spann presented a German version of the corporate state as envisioned by Mussolini and based on the ideas of Georges Sorel and Edmondo Rossoni.

Those who agreed with Spann's theories of the corporative state joined the Nationalsozialistische Deutsche Arbeiterpartei (q.v.) because point 25 of the party program provided for the formation of corporative and professional chambers. Fritz Thyssen (q.v.), a representative of big industry and a financial supporter of Hitler, embraced Spann's theories of a corporative society. In 1929 Spann was invited by Alfred Rosenberg (q.v.), who had just founded his Kampfbund für Deutsche Kultur (q.v.; League of Struggle for German Culture), to give the main lecture at the University of Munich calling for the reorganization of German society on a corporate basis. Spann's theories coincided closely with such National Socialist concepts as opposition to class warfare, defense of private property, and integral nationalism. He died in Neustift, Burgenland, on July 8, 1950.

SPARTACISTS. Forerunners of the German Communist party in the Weimar Republic (q.v.).

SPD (Sozialdemokratische Partei Deutschlands; German Social Democratic Party). One of the major political parties in the Weimar Republic (q.v.).

SPECIAL COURT. *See* SONDERGERICHT.

SPECIAL DETACHMENTS. *See* SONDERKOMMANDOS.

SPECIAL SEARCH LIST—GREAT BRITAIN. *See* SONDERFAHNDUNGSLISTE-GB.

SPECIAL TREATMENT. *See* SONDERBEHANDLUNG.

SPEER, ALBERT (1905–). Hitler's personal architect and city planner. Albert Speer was born in Mannheim on March 15, 1905. After studying architecture, he became an assistant at the Berlin Technical College. In 1931 he joined the Nationalsozialistische Deutsche Arbeiterpartei (q.v.) as party member No. 474,481 and in 1932 became a member of the SS (q.v.). After performing several minor architectural commissions for the office of the Berlin *Gauleiter* (q.v.), he was entrusted with technical arrangements for a giant party rally at Tempelhof Field on May 1, 1933. His skill in the use of rapidly erected flagpoles and unusual lighting effects gave the Nazi mass rallies the style that they later employed. In 1934 he was commissioned to design the party rally grounds at Nuremberg (*see* NUREMBERG RALLIES).

Albert Speer. [*Wide World Photos*]

These successes brought Speer, still under thirty, to Hitler's notice. Along with this attention came a collection of offices and commissions. A frustrated architect himself, the Fuehrer saw in Speer a means of fulfilling his own youthful dreams. He became strongly attached to his able assistant. Hitler made Speer a section leader of the Deutsche Arbeitsfront (q.v.), the German Labor Front, and appointed him to the Deputy Fuehrer's staff. In 1937 Speer became General Architectural Inspector of the Reich, with instructions to "turn Berlin into a real and true capital of the German Reich." Speer worked tirelessly to convert Hitler's grandiose words into stone. He designed state offices, stadia, superpalaces, monuments, and supercities for the future Greater Germany. Speer professed great admiration for his patron's ideas, which other architects called "insane sentimentality" appropriate for the year 1890. Hitler, the failed art student, stood transfixed for hours as he admired the sketches and models Speer prepared for him. In 1938 he conferred the party's Golden Badge of Honor (*Goldenes Parteiabzeichen,* q.v.) on him.

Speer continued his work after the outbreak of World War II. In 1941 he was elected a delegate to the Reichstag (q.v.) to represent Wahlkreis (Electoral District) Berlin-West. The next year he was given the important post of Minister of Armaments and War Production, succeeding Dr. Fritz Todt (q.v.), who had been killed in a plane accident. With this appointment Speer changed from a master architect to a complete technocrat. He held many other important posts: member of the Central Planning Bureau, General Inspector of Water and Energy, chief of the Organisation Todt and the Nationalsozialistische Kraftfahr Korps (qq.v.), and leader of the party's main office for technology. For a time he was the second most important man in the Third Reich and the virtual dictator of the German war economy. His production miracles, achieved in the midst of opposition from other Nazi leaders and under heavy Allied bombing, undoubtedly prolonged the course of the war. Toward the end he showed some interest in the conspiracy to assassinate Hitler but never became closely connected with the July Plot (q.v.) of 1944. In the final weeks of the war he opposed Hitler's orders to leave chaos and destruction because the German people were unworthy of the Fuehrer's genius.

Brought before the International Military Tribunal at Nuremberg (*see* NUREMBERG TRIAL) in 1946, Speer was the only one of the defendants to admit his guilt in the crimes of the Third Reich. "This trial is necessary," he said. "There is a common responsibility for such horrible crimes in an authoritarian system." He admitted: "I suppose that if Hitler ever had a friend, I would have been that friend," intimating that even he could not affect the ultimate coldness of the Fuehrer. Speer maintained that his work was "technological and economic," not political, that he was an architect, and that all he knew about law was what he read in the papers. In his testimony he repudiated violence, not on humanitarian grounds but on the practical point that it hindered his efforts to increase production. The Tribunal limited its judgment entirely to Speer's participation in the slave labor program. "In mitigation, it must be recognized that . . . in the closing stages of the war he was one of the few men who had the courage to tell Hitler that the war was lost and to take steps to prevent the senseless destruction of production facilities." Speer was found guilty on count 3 (war crimes) and count 4 (crimes against humanity). On October 1, 1946, he was sentenced to twenty years' imprisonment at Spandau (q.v.) Prison in Berlin. He was released in 1966.

In 1970 Speer published *Inside the Third Reich,* which became a worldwide best seller. He wrote the first draft in Spandau, smuggled out the pages bit by bit, and then organized the material into a publishable manuscript. Characterized by the historian Golo Mann (q.v.) as "one of the foremost political memoirs of all time," the book showed how Hitler's unlimited power was combined with new devices provided by modern technology. It described the Third Reich as far from being a monolithic totalitarian state but rather a patchwork of fiefdoms controlled by local politicos, such as Dr. Paul Joseph Goebbels (q.v.), the cynical Propaganda Minister, Heinrich Himmler (q.v.), the colorless Gestapo (q.v.) chief, and Hermann Goering (q.v.), head of the Luftwaffe (q.v.). Each one defended his own private interests and strove for personal gain no matter what the cost to the war effort. Speer insisted that he personally had not participated in the horrors that his work made possible. He confessed that he had made a pact with the devil and realized far too late the implications of his agreement.

Bibliography. Albert Speer, *Inside the Third Reich,* tr. by Richard and Clara Winston, Weidenfeld and Nicolson, London, 1970.

SPEIDEL, HANS (1897–). General in the Wehrmacht (q.v.) and member of the Resistance (q.v.) movement. Hans Speidel was born in Metzingen, Württemberg, on October 28, 1897. Like his friend Gen. Karl Heinrich von Stuelpnagel (q.v.), he had a successful military career before and after Hitler became Chancellor of the Third Reich. During World War II, from 1940 to 1944, he held high posts on the General Staff both in France and on the Russian front. On April 15, 1944, while he was serving as chief of staff of the Eighth Army in the east, he was summoned by Gen. Erwin Rommel (q.v.), an old frontline comrade and a fellow Württemberger, to France as his chief of staff for Army Group B. From that moment on Rommel's headquarters in France became a nerve center for the plot against Hitler. Speidel and Von Stuelpnagel worked together to draw Rommel into the conspiracy, but Rommel, though sympathetic, did not play an important role in the cabal, which was directed from Berlin. In May 1944 Speidel and Von Stuelpnagel put the final touches on a projected armistice agreement with the Allies.

Gen. Hans Speidel. *[Picture Collection, The Branch Libraries, The New York Public Library]*

After the failure of the July Plot (q.v.), Field Marshal Wilhelm Keitel (q.v.) removed Speidel from his post. Speidel was interrogated by Ernst Kaltenbrunner (q.v.) of the Gestapo (q.v.), but he admitted nothing and betrayed no one. His denials led to his acquittal before a court of honor, even though Keitel informed the court that Hitler believed him to be guilty. In 1955 Speidel represented the West German Republic in the North Atlantic Treaty Organization. Beginning on November 22, 1955, he served as chief of the Armed Forces Department of the Defense Ministry of the Federal Republic.

SPENGLER, OSWALD (1880–1936). Philosopher of history. Oswald Spengler was born in Blankenburg, in the Harz Mountains, on September 25, 1880. He studied natural history and mathematics, together with history and art, an unusual combination that became the basis of his later work. From 1908 to 1911 he was a *Gymnasiumoberlehrer* (senior high school teacher) in Hamburg and after 1911 a free-lance writer in Munich. His major work, *Der Untergang des Abendlandes* (2 vols., 1918–1922), published in English as *The Decline of the West,* won him a worldwide reputation and also caused great controversy. In what he called his morphology of world history, he presented the pessimistic theory that the different cultures of the world came to life, developed to their climax, declined, and fell in identical cycles. Civilization, he wrote, went through the same seasonal fluctuations, from spring to summer to fall to winter. The West was now on the downward curve

Oswald Spengler. [*German Information Center, New York*]

of a historical cycle such as that which involved the ruin of the Roman Empire and its civilization. Cosmos turns to chaos, and civilization reverts to barbarism. Spengler saw his current age as one of disillusionment and despair. In this deterministic view of history he described the continuing urbanization and materialism of European society as leading to decay. He predicted wars of extermination, the primitivization of political forms, and a coming phase of Caesarism.

Spengler's political influence was based on his smaller works, such as *Preussentum und Sozialismus*, 1919 *(Prussianism and Socialism)*, in which he distinguished between Marxism and the socialism he saw in classical Prussianism. He was an outspoken opponent of the Weimar Republic (q.v.). In his *Jahre der Entscheidung (Years of Decision)*, published shortly after Hitler took political power in 1933, Spengler called for European resurrection under Prusso-German leadership. He enthusiastically welcomed the emergence of National Socialism. "No one could have longed more for the national revolution than I. I hated the filthy revolution of 1918 from its inception. . . . Something *had* to happen, in any form, to liberate the deepest instincts in our blood."

Spengler was quickly disillusioned by National Socialism. To him race meant a human and manly type formed through tradition, and he was depressed to discover the unscientific and primitive aberrations of Hitler's racialism (*see* RACIAL DOCTRINE). He was appalled by the Fuehrer's mounting hysteria in the campaign against the Jews, and he disassociated himself from the rising anti-Semitism (q.v.). Spengler began to speak out with increasing bitterness against the Nazi regime. A movement that had begun with great promise, he warned, would end in tragedy. For their part, Nazi leaders, who at first had praised Spengler, now attacked him for his pessimistic doctrines. His main work was suppressed, and he was ignored. Independently wealthy, he managed to exist in his homeland, although under a dark cloud and condemned to public silence. In 1936 he wrote to a friend that in ten years "the German Reich will probably no longer exist." He died in Munich on May 8, 1936.

Bibliography. John F. Fennelly, *Twilight of the Evening Lands: Oswald Spengler—a Half Century Later*, Brookdale Press, New York, 1972.

SPERRLE, HUGO (1885–1953). General field marshal in the Luftwaffe (q.v.). Hugo Sperrle served in the armed forces during World War I and did some flying in the early combat aircraft of that conflict. In 1933, after Hitler's accession to political power, Sperrle was transferred as a senior army officer to the Air Force. Gigantic and energetic, he soon became one of the best-known leaders of the Luftwaffe and in 1934 was promoted to *Generalmajor* (brigadier general). In 1936 he was detailed by Hermann Goering (q.v.) to command the Condor Legion (q.v.) in Spain. In conjunction with the German Mediterranean Fleet, which shelled the coastal town of Almería, Sperrle let loose his Junkers-87 (q.v.) bombers on Spanish towns and villages behind the Loyalist lines, including Guernica (q.v.). His work in Spain led to his promotion to *Generalleutnant* (lieutenant general) and then to *General der Flieger* (general of fliers). In 1937 he was given command of Luftflotte (Air Force) III in the south bordering on Austria. The next year he used hundreds of his planes for demonstration purposes to convince the Czechs of Germany's overwhelming air power.

At the outbreak of World War II in 1939, Sperrle was in command of one of the four *Luftflotte* (Berlin—Kesselring; Braunschweig—Felmy; Vienna—Loehr; Munich—Sperrle). His planes took part in the attack on France. On July 19, 1940, Sperrle, along with Erhard Milch and Albert Kesselring (qq.v.), was created a general field marshal of the Luftwaffe. Before the Battle of Britain, Sperrle joined Kesselring in advising Hitler that the British Royal Air Force had to be destroyed before successful bomber attacks could be staged on British soil. Detailed to Paris in 1944, Sperrle, who was loyal to the Fuehrer, carefully watched those in his office who were sympathetic to the conspiracy against Hitler (*see* JULY PLOT). Sperrle died in Munich just before Easter, 1953, and was buried there on April 7, 1953.

SPIESSER (Philistine). Term used in the vocabulary of National Socialism to describe members of the middle class. It was employed alternately with *Bürger* or *bourgeois*. *Spiesser* was a favorite word in the vocabulary of morals and moralizing of Dr. Paul Joseph Goebbels (q.v.), Minister for Public Enlightenment and Propaganda. He often spoke of the uncultured, unenlightened, and prosaic *Bürger*, of bourgeois selfishness and stupidity, and of "*Spiesser* middle-class order and calm."

SPORTPALAST (Sports Palace). An indoor sports arena in the center of Berlin where Hitler, Dr. Paul Joseph Goebbels (q.v.), and other leaders could speak to an audience of 15,000 Nazi functionaries or officials.

SPORTS DIVISION LEADER. *See* LEITER DES REICHSBERUFSWETTKAMPFES.

SPORTS IN THE THIRD REICH. Throughout the forty-seven years of the Second Reich and the fourteen years of the Weimar Republic (q.v.) the German people were enthusiastically sports-minded. This interest in virtually every kind of sporting activity continued unabated during the twelve years of the Third Reich. Although averse to any kind of exercise for himself, Hitler regarded sports as essential for a healthy national state. In *Mein Kampf* (q.v.) he referred to sports as the fourth point of his seven requirements of "the business of the State." "The State," he said, "must promote sports to an unheard level of efficiency." He called for a physically hard youth to continue the racial struggle. After attaining political power in 1933, he used sports as a means of promoting national enthusiasm on the domestic scene and of enhancing German prestige abroad. Youth must be trained to win on the sporting field. If this was not possible, then at least the winner should be Aryan (*see* RACIAL DOCTRINE). The physical superiority of the German-Aryan should be demonstrated for the world to see.

The German public liked Hitler's attitude toward sports. Huge crowds attended such outdoor events as football (soccer) in stadia throughout the country. Indoor contests also drew millions of spectators. Before and after 1933 Hitler and Nazi leaders were careful to choose such arenas as the Sportpalast (q.v.; Sports Palace) in Berlin as the scene of mass meetings and rallies.

By far the most popular figure in German sports was Max Schmeling (q.v.), the only German to hold the heavyweight championship of the world. Schmeling's victory over Joe Louis, the American Brown Bomber, in New York in the summer of 1936 was greeted with an explosion of joy in the Third Reich. Most experts had predicted that the black boxer would have no trouble with the aging German. Nazi propagandists, however, insisted that the strongest man in a nation that regarded itself as the strongest on earth could not be beaten by a Negro. Both Hitler and Dr. Paul Joseph Goebbels (q.v.), Minister for Public Enlightenment and Propaganda, sent Schmeling telegrams of congratulations. An extraordinary welcome was arranged for the German boxer on his return home. German boxing fans were crushed when word was received that in a return bout on June 22, 1938, Louis gave Schmeling a fearful beating in the second shortest fight in heavyweight history. The consternation was matched by another disappointment when it was revealed that Helene Mayer (q.v.), the tall, blond, big-boned German women's fencing champion, who was regarded as the ideal specimen of Aryan womanhood, was actually Jewish.

As soon as the Nazis won political power, all sports were subjected to *Gleichschaltung* (q.v.), or coordination. Enormous emphasis was placed on sports prowess and endurance. All Germans, boys and girls, men and women, were encouraged to participate actively in sports of every description. Unprecedented attention was given to the young. During the early years of the Nazi regime, physical training was allotted two to three periods per week in the schools. In 1938 the schedule was increased to five periods each week at the expense of religious education. Efficiency in sports was required both for entrance to schools and for the school-leaving certificate. Teachers of physical training were now to be regarded as the most important members of the staff, and many were promoted to posts as assistant principals. Boxing was made compulsory for students in the upper classes. Students who were persistently unsatisfactory in sports could be expelled and barred from further study. At the *Napolas* (*Nationalpolitische Erziehungsanstalten*, q.v.), Nazi elite schools, students were expected to learn such sports as rowing, sailing, gliding, shooting, driving motorcycles and automobiles, and boxing. The overemphasis placed on physical training in all schools encouraged young boys to reckless endurance tests that overtaxed their physical resources. Many nervous youngsters were forced to seek medical attention.

Adults, too, were infected by the sports craze. Sports were officially promoted at factories, and workers were given time off during the day for mass calisthenics. Appointment to a job in the national railway system was contingent on possession of the national sports medal. At the height of World War II there were 5 million holders of sports certificates issued by the Strength through Joy movement (Kraft durch Freude, q.v.). This preoccupation with sports could not but have a beneficial effect upon many adults, but for others it was hazardous. One edict called for severe tests for men up to the age of fifty-five, including throwing a 6½-pound medicine ball a distance of 6.15 meters, a broad jump of 2.8 meters, and a run of 1,000 meters in six minutes.

The Olympic Games of 1936 were awarded to Germany in 1932 before Hitler became Chancellor. After the Nazis won political power in 1933, there were many protests against holding the contests in a nation controlled by men who believed themselves to be superior by race. Dr. Goebbels countered that sports had nothing to do with politics and that it would be unsportsmanlike to make a last-minute change. The Propaganda Minister was anxious to impress his fellow Germans with the fact that the Nazi regime was universally accepted. At the same time he would put on a proper show for the entire world. The summer games took place at the scheduled time in a magnificent new stadium in Berlin. The extraordinary spectacle, highly publicized throughout the world, was depicted on film in a superb documentary directed by Leni Riefenstahl (q.v.). The Berlin Olympics were marred by Hitler's refusal to greet Jesse Owens, a black American athlete who won four gold medals. *See also* OLYMPIAD XI.

SPORTS PALACE. *See* SPORTPALAST.

SPRING AWAKENING. *See* FRÜHLINGSERWACHEN.

SQUADRON. *See* STAFFEL.

SS (Schutzstaffel; Elite Guard). Originally the black-shirted personal guard of Hitler but later transformed by its leader, Heinrich Himmler (q.v.), into a mass army on which was to rest the ultimate exercise of Nazi power. Schutzstaffel literally means "defense echelon." The name was universally abbreviated to SS, not in Roman or Gothic letters but written as a lightning flash in imitation of ancient runic characters. The SS was known as the Black Order.

The SS served as a political police and was later assigned the duty of administering concentration camps and extermination camps (qq.v.). It was widely regarded as a *Gliederung* (limb) of the Nazi party. Shortly after Hitler became Chancellor in 1933, the SS, SA, and Stahlhelm (qq.v.) were all authorized to act as auxiliary police units. The formations of the SS in June 1933 are shown in the accompanying chart.

FORMATIONS OF THE SS

Oberster Fuehrer Adolf Hitler
(Supreme Leader Adolf Hitler)
↓
Reichsfuehrer der SS
(Reich Leader of the SS—Heinrich Himmler)
↓
Obergruppen
(Senior Groups)
↓
Grupen
(Groups)
↓
Abschnitte
(Sections)
↓
Standarten
(Regiments)
↓
Sturmbanne
(Battalions)
↓
Stürme
(Storm Troops)
↓
Trupps
(Troops)
↓
Scharen
(Bands)

After the Blood Purge (q.v.) of 1934, when Hitler liquidated Ernst Roehm (q.v.) and his coterie of the SA High Command, the SS emerged as the chief police arm of the Nazi party. Under the leadership of Heinrich Himmler the SS was designed to find, fight, and destroy all open and secret enemies of the Fuehrer, the National Socialist movement, and "our racial resurrection." In 1943 it played a major role in suppressing the Warsaw ghetto uprising (q.v.), when some 60,000 Jews were killed in what was called a military action. The SS lost 16 men in the process. With Hitler's agreement Himmler formed an SS economic empire that controlled business and manufacturing enterprises.

Essentially, the SS was a police organization dedicated to maintaining the principles of National Socialism. In 1929 it numbered only 280 men, all of whom were regarded as especially trustworthy. The original formation was called the Allgemeine-SS (q.v.), the General SS, which by 1939 grew into a corps of 240,000 men organized in divisions and regiments. The main branch was the Waffen-SS (q.v.), which was primarily a military organization. Members of the Waffen-SS had the underside of the upper arm tattooed with the lightning SS insignia. Later, the mark identified them to Allied troops. The Waffen-SS won a reputation as fanatical combat soldiers in World War II.

At the Nuremberg Trial (q.v.) the International Military Tribunal made a sweeping judgment on the SS. It found the organization guilty of persecuting and exterminating Jews, of brutalities and killings in concentration camps, of excesses in the administration of occupied territories, of administration of the slave labor program, and of mistreatment and murder of prisoners of war. All members of the SS were declared to be war criminals who had participated in the planning of war crimes and crimes against humanity connected with the war.

Bibliography. Gerald Reitlinger, *The SS: Alibi of a Nation*, William Heinemann, Ltd., London, 1957.

SS BODYGUARD REGIMENT ADOLF HITLER. *See* LEIBSTANDARTE-SS ADOLF HITLER.

SS 1ST LIEUTENANT. *See* OBERSTURMFUEHRER-SS.

SS GENERAL. *See* OBERSTGRUPPENFUEHRER-SS.

SS LIEUTENANT COLONEL. *See* OBERSTURMBANNFUEHRER-SS.

SS-MANN (SS Man). A private in the Schutzstaffel (*see* SS).

SS RESERVES. *See* SS-VERFÜGUNGSTRUPPE.

SS-TOTENKOPFVERBÄNDE (SSTV; SS-Death's Head Formations). Concentration camp guard units (*see* CONCENTRATION CAMPS) formed from the original *Wachmannsschaft* (q.v.), a guard unit, and similar formations. In April 1934 Heinrich Himmler (q.v.), who led the Prussian Secret State Police, appointed Theodor Eicke (q.v.) inspector of concentration camps and SS guard formations. Eicke set down precise regulations for the maintenance of discipline and order for inmates, escorts, and guards. SS guards, who were recruited from the toughest Nazi elements, received the name SS-Death's Head Formations from the skull-and-bones insignia on their black tunics. At the outbreak of World War II in 1939 these formations provided the nucleus for the SS-Panzerdivision-Totenkopf, one of the original field units of the Waffen-SS (q.v.).

SS-VERFÜGUNGSTRUPPE (SS Reserves). The reserve unit of the SS (q.v.). Socially and educationally, these troops were well below the standard of the Wehrmacht (q.v.), the regular Army. Before 1939 only 2 out of 5 SS subalterns possessed the *Abitur*, the matriculation certificate for universities.

SS-WIRTSCHAFTS- UND VERWALTUNGSHAUPTAMT. *See* WIRTSCHAFTS- UND VERWALTUNGSHAUPTAMT.

SSTV. *See* SS-TOTENKOPFVERBÄNDE.

ST. *See* STAFFEL.

STAATSKASSENGUTSCHEINE (Government Coupons). Projected substitute for money advocated by Gottfried Feder (q.v.), Hitler's economics adviser in the early days of Nazism. Feder urged that the international usage of loans and finance capital be eliminated. In the new National Socialist state, money would be obtained for public works through the issue of special government coupons that would bear no interest. In addition, there would be no interest on loans. Hitler never adopted Feder's suggestions.

STAB-IN-THE-BACK THEORY. *See* DOLCHSTOSSTHEORIE.

STABSWACHE (Headquarters Guard). The original headquarters guard unit formed from SA (q.v.) members after the 1923 Beer-Hall *Putsch* (q.v.) in Munich. It was organized to protect Hitler and other Nazi leaders, especially at mass meetings. The Stabswache was replaced by the Leibstandarte-SS Adolf Hitler (q.v.), a bodyguard regiment, and the oldest of the SS (q.v.) military formations initiated in 1933 after Hitler became Chancellor.

STAF. *See* STANDARTENFUEHRER-SS.

STAFF POOL. *See* EINSATZSTAB.

STAFFEL (St; Squadron). Basic Luftwaffe (q.v.) formation of twelve to sixteen planes.

STAHLHELM (Steel Helmet). Nationalist ex-servicemen's organization. The Stahlhelm was formed on December 23, 1918, by Franz Seldte (q.v.), a reserve officer in Magdeburg, and Theodor Duesterberg (q.v.), a former officer of the General Staff. Their purpose was to oppose the German revolution. Stahlhelm members wore field-gray uniforms in their marching formations. Most were strongly nationalist, and many called for a restoration of the Hohenzollern monarchy. Some were attracted into the ranks of the Reichswehr (q.v.), the new German Army.

The Stahlhelm played a prominent role in politics in the 1920s and early 1930s. In the presidential elections of March 13, 1932, cofounder Duesterberg won 2,557,729 votes as an independent Nationalist candidate, but he withdrew to support Hitler on the runoff ballot of April 10. Once in political power, Hitler wanted no opposition of any kind in his coordinated Third Reich. Accordingly, by a decree issued on December 1, 1933, he incorporated all members of the Stahlhelm up to the age of thirty-five into the SA (q.v.), the Storm Troopers. All older members of the Stahlhelm were formed into units called the SA Reserve. This was not a popular decision, for there was antagonism between former Stahlhelm members and the Storm Troopers. On occasion, they attacked one another at meetings or in street battles. On February 17, 1934, the Stahlhelm was given a new name, the National Socialist League of Ex-Servicemen. Its leader, Franz Seldte, was retained in the Cabinet as Reich Minister of Labor until the end of World War II. In 1951 the Stahlhelm was revived in more modest form with headquarters at Cologne.

Bibliography. Volker Rölf Berghahn, *Der Stahlhelm*, Droste, Düsseldorf, 1966.

STALAG. Term used to describe a detention camp for prisoners of war captured by the Germans in World War II. The acronym is derived from *Stammlager* (*Stamm*, stem, trunk, something stable or constant, and *Lager*, camp). Prisoners of various nationalities were held in such camps. The name became familiar to the American public through a play written by Donald Bevan and Edmund Trzcinski, who had been prisoners for two years in a German war camp. The scene was laid in the barracks of Stalag 17, somewhere in Germany during World War II. Staged and produced by José Ferrer, it opened at the Forty-eighth Street Theater in New York on May 8, 1951. It appeared later as a film.

STALINGRAD PUTSCH. Unsuccessful attempt made in January 1943 to overthrow Hitler. The Stalingrad debacle in November 1942 made it clear both to the generals who opposed Hitler and to the German people that the war was lost. The conspirators (*see* BERLIN PUTSCH) once again decided that the overthrow of Hitler and the dissolution of the Nazi regime had to be accomplished while the German Army was relatively intact. The Stalingrad *Putsch* was designed to achieve this goal. Col. Gen. Ludwig Beck (q.v.), leader of the Resistance (q.v.) movement, dispatched an aide to Gen. Friedrich von Paulus (q.v.), then about to be surrounded at Stalingrad, and begged him to issue a manifesto to the German Army and people calling on them to depose Hitler and his regime, which had sacrificed the flower of German youth. At this moment Hitler refused Von Paulus permission to surrender and promoted him to general field marshal to protect "Fortress Stalingrad." Von Paulus, however, did not give the signal requested by Beck, nor did others who were expected to help the conspirators make a move. Once again Hitler through good fortune had outwitted his enemies inside Germany.

STAND AGAINST. *See* WIDERSTAND.

STANDARTE (Standard; Ensign). A unit of the SA or SS (qq.v.) comprising 1,200 to 3,000 men, roughly equivalent to an army regiment.

STANDARTENFUEHRER-SS (STAF). A colonel in the SS (q.v.).

STANDGERICHT (Court-Martial). A special court set up by Franz Gürtner (q.v.) in the early months of World War II to try Poles and Jews in the occupied lands in the east.

STARHEMBERG, ERNST RÜDIGER FÜRST (1899–1956). Austrian politician who first worked with Hitler and then opposed him. Ernst Starhemberg was born in Eferding, Upper Austria, on May 10, 1899, to one of Austria's oldest aristocratic families. After World War I he became a member of the German *Freikorps* (q.v.), the free corps units that were responsible for many political assassinations. He took part in the abortive Beer-Hall *Putsch* (q.v.) in Munich in 1923. Later he became the leading organizer of Austrian fascism. Starhemberg held such posts as Minister of the Interior, Vice-Chancellor, and leader of the Heimwehr (Home Guard). He was regarded as one of those responsible for the destruction of parliamentarianism in Austria. During the decade preceding *Anschluss* (q.v.) between Germany and Austria, Starhemberg became an ardent defender of Austrian independence and an outspoken enemy of Nazism. After the occupation of Austria by the Germans in 1938, he left his country and lost his citizenship as well as his valuable property. The next year he joined the French Air Force as a volunteer in the struggle against Hitler. From 1942 to 1955 he lived in South America. He died in Schruns, Vorarlberg, on March 15, 1956.

Bibliography. Ernst Rüdiger Fürst Starhemberg, *Between Hitler and Mussolini*, Harper & Brothers, New York, 1942.

STARK, JOHANNES (1874–1951). Physicist and Nobel laureate in 1919 for his work on electromagnetism. In 1922 Stark was forced to relinquish his chair at the University of Würzburg because of his furious attacks on Albert Einstein (q.v.) and the theory of relativity. According to Stark, German science was factual, as opposed to "Jewish science," which he claimed to be opinionated. His emphasis on racial doctrine (q.v.) made him acceptable as a scientist to the Nazi hierarchy. He was made president of the Deutsche Forschungsgemeinschaft (German Research Society) and held that post during the life of the Third Reich.

STARK, JONATHAN (1926–1944). An eighteen-year-old Jehovah's Witness who was hanged in a concentration camp (*see* CONCENTRATION CAMPS). Jonathan Stark was born on July 8, 1926. At the age of seventeen he was ordered to report for labor service. Loyal to his faith, he refused to take the required oath of allegiance to Hitler. He was arrested by the Gestapo (q.v.) and taken to the concentration camp at Sachsenhausen (q.v.). When the hangman hesitated on the scaffold, young Stark asked: "Why do you hesitate? Bear witness for Jehovah and Gideon!" He was executed in the closing days of October 1944.

STATE. *See* LAND.

STATE LABOR SERVICE. *See* REICHSARBEITSDIENST.

STATUTE OF LIMITATIONS. Subject of a debate in post-Hitler Germany in which people differed on whether a date should be set for ending the prosecution of crimes committed by Nazis, especially in concentration camps and extermination camps (qq.v.). Roman and Anglo-Saxon laws are based on the principle of *tempus non occurrit regi* (the passage of time has no effect on the prosecution of crime). This means that there is no statute of limitation for murder. In postwar Germany there was a call for an end to the prosecution of crimes during the Nazi regime. The debate came to a head in 1964, when there was much discussion about whether the existing statute of limitations should be extended. By this time some 65,000 Nazi criminals had been sentenced, but prosecution of more than 10,000 had not yet taken place. Members of the rightist National Democratic party of Germany (*see* NEO-NAZISM) argued that the law should be allowed to lapse because most of the important Nazis had already been arrested and sentenced. After a long debate the Bundestag (Federal Diet) voted to consider September 21, 1949, the day when West Germany became a sovereign state, the starting point for a twenty-year statute of limitations. This extended the suspension date to September 21, 1969.

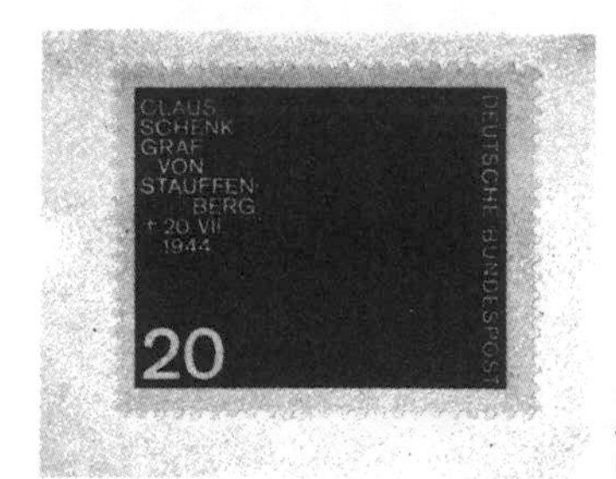

Claus Schenk Graf von Stauffenberg. [*Stamp issued by the German Federal Republic*]

STAUFFENBERG, CLAUS SCHENK GRAF VON (1907–1944). Lieutenant colonel on the General Staff and central figure among the conspirators of the July Plot (q.v.) of 1944. Claus Schenk von Stauffenberg was born in Greiffenstein Castle, Upper Franconia, on November 15, 1907, to a family that had served the royal houses of Württemberg and Bavaria. His father was Privy Chamberlain to the King of Bavaria, and his mother was a granddaughter of the Prussian general August Wilhelm Anton Graf von Gneisenau (1760–1831). A strikingly handsome young man, Claus was nicknamed the Bamberger Reiter because of his extraordinary resemblance to the famous thirteenth-century statue in the Cathedral of Bamberg. Reared in a milieu of monarchist conservatism and Catholic piety, he later turned to the left in political thought and preferred a socialist society to that of the bourgeois Weimar Republic (q.v.).

In the early part of World War II Von Stauffenberg served with distinction as an officer in a Bavarian cavalry regiment in Poland, France, and North Africa. In April 1943 he was wounded in the face, in both hands, and in the knee by fire from a low-flying Allied plane. He feared that he might lose his eyesight completely, but he kept one eye and lost his right hand, half the left hand, and part of his leg. He was saved by the expert supervision of Dr. Ferdinand Sauerbruch (q.v.), Germany's most famous physician. Reporting back for service, he was appointed chief of staff of the Army Ordnance Department.

During his convalescence Von Stauffenberg revised his attitude. He made no secret of his utter contempt for Hitler and Nazism. He resented any form of totalitarianism, especially National Socialism, and criticized Hitler as the Antichrist and as the "Master of Vermin." Von Stauffenberg decided to join the conspirators against Hitler with the goal of liquidating the Nazi regime and replacing it with a new social state that would maintain the good name of the fatherland. He became closely connected with the Kreisau Circle (q.v.) through his cousin Peter Graf Yorck von Wartenburg (q.v.). When Helmuth James Graf von Moltke (q.v.) was arrested in January 1944, Von Stauffenberg hoped to carry on the work of the Kreisau Circle. Always impelled by Christian morality and angered by the excesses of Nazism, Von Stauffenberg became the leader of the conspiracy. In this capacity he commanded the devotion of both soldiers and civilians.

On July 20, 1944, the fiery young officer carried an explosive in a briefcase to the *Gästebaracke* (guest barracks) in the Fuehrer's headquarters at Rastenburg, East

Prussia, shortly after midday. Although the explosion took place, Hitler survived. After the failure of the plot Von Stauffenberg was shot at the Bendlerstrasse (q.v.) that same day.

Bibliography. Joachim Kramarz, *Stauffenberg: The Architect of the Famous July 20th Conspiracy to Assassinate Hitler,* tr. by R. H. Barry, The Macmillan Company, New York, 1967.

STEEL HELMET. *See* STAHLHELM.

STEIN, EDITH (1891–1942). A Catholic nun of Jewish background and a victim of the Nazi regime. Edith Stein was born in Breslau on October 12, 1891, the daughter of a Jewish timber merchant. After studying philosophy, literature, and history at Breslau and Göttingen, she took her doctorate in philosophy at Freiburg in 1916. Her philosophical studies led her to become a Catholic in 1922. From 1922 to 1931 she was a teacher in Speyer and at the same time published several works on philosophy, especially on Thomas Aquinas. In 1932 she was appointed a lecturer at the German Institute for Scientific Pedagogy but later was dismissed because of her Jewish parents. She then entered the Carmelite convent in Cologne as Sister Benedicta. She refused to vote in the national elections of 1933 and was prohibited from voting in the 1938 elections. At the end of 1938 she was transferred to a convent in Echt, the Netherlands, where she was arrested by the Gestapo (q.v.) in January 1942 and again in August 1942. She was sent to Auschwitz (q.v.), where on August 9, 1942, she was asphyxiated in a gas chamber.

STELLBRINK, KARL FRIEDRICH (1894–1943). Protestant theologian and victim of the Nazi regime. Karl Friedrich Stellbrink was born on October 28, 1894, the son of a customs official. After World War I he was ordained in the Protestant Church of Prussia and served for eight years among German settlers in Brazil. He returned to Germany in 1929 to become a pastor in Steinsdorf, Thuringia. On April 7, 1942, he was arrested by the Gestapo (q.v.), along with three Catholic priests, with whom he was tried for treason before the Volksgericht (q.v.), the People's Court, in Berlin. He was accused of disseminating the letters of Archbishop Clemens August Graf von Galen (q.v.), who had spoken out against National Socialism. On November 10, 1943, all four churchmen were executed in Hamburg.

STEMPFLE, BERNHARD. *See* RAUBAL, ANGELA.

STENNES REVOLT. An unsuccessful rebellion in 1931 in the Nationalsozialistische Deutsche Arbeiterpartei (q.v.), the Nazi party. On February 20, 1931, Hitler, who was determined to win power legally, issued a proclamation to the SA (q.v.), his Storm Troopers, to refrain from street fighting. "I understand your distress and your rage, but you must not bear arms." The order provoked a mutiny among the Storm Troop detachments in Berlin, who regarded it as a betrayal of the basic revolutionary principles of the party. Walther Stennes, *Oberster SA-Fuehrer* (supreme SA leader), who had become increasingly dissatisfied with Hitler's leadership, denounced both the decree and Hitler's decision to abide by it. It was, he said, a fundamental betrayal of the party's principles. With the support of Dr. Paul Joseph Goebbels (q.v.), now *Gauleiter* (district leader) of Greater Berlin, Hitler quelled the revolt and expelled Stennes from the party for insubordination and mutiny.

Stennes continued to fight for what he regarded as the revolutionary principles of National Socialist ideology. Angered by the direction that the movement was taking, he and Otto Strasser (q.v.) had already formed the Black Front (*see* SCHWARZE FRONT) with headquarters in Prague. This organization spearheaded the activities of Nazi émigrés against Hitler. In 1934 Stennes sued Hitler for libel after *Der Angriff* (*see* ANGRIFF, DER) had printed a story charging Stennes with being a police spy in the party. At the trial Hitler testified: "I could only come to the conclusion that anyone opposed to me or my movement must have been a paid agent." Stennes later went to China, where he served as commander of Chiang Kai-shek's personal bodyguard.

STG. *See* STURZKAMPFGESCHWADER.

STIEFF, HELMUTH (1901–1944). One of the main conspirators of the unsuccessful July Plot (q.v.) of 1944. Helmuth Stieff was born in Deutsch-Eylau (now Iława, Poland) on June 6, 1901. A career soldier, he joined the Imperial Army in 1917 and served in the 71st Field Artillery until 1918. On April 1, 1922, he was commissioned in the 3d Artillery Regiment. Promoted to captain in 1934, he was subsequently assigned to the General Staff (1938–1940). In 1942 he was made a colonel and chief of the Organization Branch of the Army High Command. On January 30, 1944, he was promoted to major general.

A short, slightly hunchbacked man (Heinrich Himmler, q.v., called him a "little poisoned dwarf"), Stieff was a key officer in the plot to murder Hitler. As early as September 1943 he arranged to plant a bomb at Rastenburg, Hitler's field headquarters on the eastern front, but he withdrew at the last moment. A few days later several English plastic bombs, which he had placed in a water tower at Rastenburg, exploded prematurely. On this occasion Hitler ordered an investigation but made the mistake of assigning for the task an Abwehr (q.v.), or counterintelligence, officer who was a member of the conspiracy. For the July 20, 1944, plot Stieff worked closely with Lieut. Col. Claus Schenk Graf von Stauffenberg (q.v.), supplying him with the bomb and flying with him to Rastenburg.

Gen. Helmuth Stieff. [*Bundesarchiv*]

Stieff was arrested along with Gen. Erich Fritz Fellgiebel (q.v.) at Rastenburg shortly after the explosion. He was brought before the Volksgericht (q.v.), the People's Court, along with Field Marshal Erwin von Witzleben, Gen. Erich Hoepner (qq.v.), and others on August 7, 1944. The defendants, broken by their treatment in Gestapo (q.v.) cellars, were humiliated by being forced to appear in decrepit clothes, unshaven, and without belts or suspenders. All were insulted and degraded by the judge, Roland Freisler (q.v.). The next day, August 8, 1944, Stieff and seven other officers were hanged like cattle on meat hooks at Plötzensee Prison.

STINGING NETTLE, THE. *See* BRENNESSEL, DIE.

STINNES, HUGO (1870–1924). Industrial magnate, creator of the Stinnes Combine, and with Fritz Thyssen and Emil Kirdorf (qq.v.) among the early financial backers of the Nationalsozialistische Deutsche Arbeiterpartei (q.v.). Hugo Stinnes was born in Mühlheim on February 12, 1870, the youngest son of Mathias Stinnes, the owner of lucrative coal ships. After an education as a mining engineer, Hugo Stinnes founded a company of his own in 1892 with a capital of 50,000 marks. The business expanded rapidly to include coal mines, coal depots, barges, and seagoing ships. Stinnes also established iron and steel factories. He was the chief figure in the Rheinisch-Westfälische Elektrizitätswerk A.-G., which supplied many towns with gas and electricity. During World War I he increased his fortune considerably by acquiring a large share of the industry required for the German war effort, including iron mines, shipping, and hotels. Stinnes achieved great power in German economic life. He made a practice of buying newspapers whose democratic point of view he then modified in consonance with his own conservative views. From 1920 to 1924 he was a member of the Reichstag (q.v.) as a delegate of the German People's party. He was one of the main financial supporters of Hitler in the earliest stages of the Nazi party. He died at Berlin on April 10, 1924.

At the time of Stinnes's death his largest concern, the Siemens-Rhein-Elbe-Schuckert Union, and several others ran into financial difficulties. The business, which was being conducted by his sons, rapidly shrank, and slowly the great organization was liquidated. In October 1925 a new company was formed in Hamburg, with the Stinnes family retaining 40 percent of the shares. Under Hitler it became one of the more important components of the armament and engineering industries, which built the war machine of the Third Reich.

STOECKER, ADOLF (1835–1909). Anti-Semitic court chaplain to Emperors William I and William II and forerunner of Hitler and Nazism. Adolf Stoecker was born in Halberstadt on December 11, 1835, the son of a subaltern army quartermaster. After theological studies in Halle and Berlin, he became a pastor in several small communities. At the beginning of the Franco-Prussian War in 1870, he was sent to Metz as a field chaplain. One of his sermons on the battlefield attracted the attention of the Prussian king William I, who later as German Emperor called the young man to Berlin as court chaplain (1874–1879). In 1878 Stoecker founded the Christian Social Workers' party to combat social democracy and Judaism, the overriding objects of his hatred. He hoped to win workingmen to "national Christian thought" and at the same time carry on a struggle against the Jews. He was the foremost anti-Semite of his time (*see* ANTI-SEMITISM).

From 1879 to 1898 Stoecker served in the Prussian Landtag (Legislature), and from 1881 to 1893 and again from 1898 to 1908 he held a seat in the German Reichstag (q.v.). A gifted orator, he defended ecclesiastical orthodoxy, monarchism, and nationalism while attacking capitalism, social democracy, and Jews. Repeated scandalous affairs at mass meetings, frequent libel suits, and quarrels with Chancellor Otto von Bismarck tended to make his position at court untenable. He paid little heed to the warnings of William I. After the latter's death in March 1888, Stoecker's fate seemed to be sealed because the liberal Frederick III was repelled by him. His stock rose again for a time after William II, who wanted to be popular with labor, ascended the throne on the death of his father in June 1888. William abandoned Stoecker shortly after Bismarck's dismissal in 1890 by ignoring him at the marriage of Princess Victoria, the Emperor's sister. Stoecker submitted his resignation on November 5, 1891, and William accepted it without the courtesy of a reply.

Despite the royal affront Stoecker continued his activities. He turned his attention to the Inner Mission in Berlin, through which he hoped to convert workingmen to Christianity. He called for socialism as depicted in the New Testament, opposed to "social democracy and radicalism, materialism and belief." He died in Gries, near Bozen (now Bolzano), on February 7, 1909.

Stoecker prefigured many of Hitler's beliefs: integral nationalism, hatred of social democracy, populism and courting of the masses, and uncompromising anti-Semitism. However, the Nazi leader rejected Stoecker's monarchism and orthodox Christianity. Stoecker's contempt for Judaism set the standard for Hitler's own extremism. Stoecker believed it to be impossible for Jews to understand the Christian *Weltanschauung* (q.v.), its world view, or the spirit of German ideas. He regarded Judaism as "a foreign drop of blood in our national body: it is a destructive power. We must nurse again the peculiarities of our national genius—German Spirit, industriousness, and piety, our national heritages." He believed the Germans to be fools if they let Jews cripple national life: "The Jews are a nation within the nation, a state within the state, a race in the midst of another race. They are in direct contrast to the German Spirit." When, in 1888, a statue was to be erected to Heinrich Heine, Stoecker opposed the proposal: "It ought to be made of mud. Heine—the Jew—was a rascal [*Lump*]." At mass meetings Stoecker attacked the Jews with charges like this: "Ladies and Gentlemen: Recently a body was found in the vicinity. It was examined: present were the Jewish town physician, a Jewish doctor, a Jewish coroner, a Jewish lawyer—only the body was German." The struggle with the Jews, he said, was a veritable racial war, because "Judaism wants to rule, to attack our best possessions, our Christian religion, our *Kultur,* and our German Spirit."

Stoecker's form of anti-Semitism reemerged in the early days of the Weimar Republic (q.v.) to become the launching pad of the Hitler movement. In Vienna young Hitler had become a voracious reader of anti-Semitic literature.

The many German *voelkisch* clubs (*see* VOELKISCH MOVEMENT) utilized Stoecker's views in their pamphlets. Stoecker's strictures against the Jews appeared almost word for word in Hitler's *Mein Kampf* (q.v.). The anti-Semitism that Stoecker had presented as theory was translated by Hitler from a symbol of debate into an activism that led to the attempted Final Solution of the "Jewish problem" in Europe (*see* ENDLÖSUNG, DIE).

Bibliography. Dietrich von Oertzen, *Adolf Stoecker: Lebensbild und Zeitgeschichte im Auftrage der Familie,* F. Bahn, Schwerin in Mecklenburg, 1912.

STOLZ, ROBERT (1880–). Austrian composer and prominent refugee from Nazism. Robert Stolz was born in Graz on August 25, 1880. A composer in the tradition of Johann Strauss, he emigrated to the United States in 1938 to escape the milieu of National Socialism. He continued to compose operettas, waltzes, and film music.

STORM. *See* STURM.

STORM BATTALION. *See* STURMBANN.

STORM DETACHMENT. *See* SA.

STORM SONG. The oldest National Socialist song, written by Dietrich Eckart (q.v.). The first verse follows:

> Storm! Storm! Storm!
> The serpent, the dragon from Hell has broken loose!
> Stupidities and lies his chains have burst asunder,
> Lust for gold in the dreadful couch,
> Red as with blood are the Heavens in flames,
> The roof-tops collapsed, a sight to appal.
> One after another, the chapel goes too!
> Howling with rage, the dragon dashes it to pieces!
> Ring out for the assault now or never!
> Germany awake!

STORM TROOP LEADER. *See* STURMTRUPPENLEITER.

STORM TROOPERS. *See* SA.

STORMER, THE. *See* STÜRMER, DER.

STOSSTRUPP (Shock Troop). Assault unit. The term, which was first used in World War I, was adopted by the Nazis in their early days. Battle groups of this type were used to guard the stages on which Hitler spoke to his followers. The members would move silently forward and deliver rabbit punches to hecklers and then frog-march them out of the hall. The Stosstrupp–Adolf Hitler became well known in Munich streets in the days when Hitler was fighting for political power.

STRASSENZELLEN (Street Cells). A system of groups used by the Nazi party in the early 1920s. Borrowed from the Communist organization, the *Strassenzellen* were small groups of four or five men, one of whom, the *Obman,* or chairman, made sure that each man in his group knew the party program and was reliable. The *Obman* was required to report any change of political views in his cell. Orders came from above in the form of military commands and were transmitted in the same form. All members were pledged to strict obedience and were not expected to ask questions in carrying out a command. The *Strassenzellen* system was designed to win the battle of the streets against the Communists.

STRASSER, GREGOR (1892–1934). Nazi populist and early rival of Hitler for the leadership of the National Socialist party. Gregor Strasser was born in Geisenfeld, Lower Bavaria, on May 31, 1892. He served during World War I, advancing in rank to lieutenant, and was awarded the Iron Cross (First and Second Classes). After the war he settled in Landshut as an apothecary. In the 1923 Beer-Hall *Putsch* (q.v.), Strasser led a group of volunteers from Landshut to Munich but arrived too late to be of much use to Hitler. During Hitler's imprisonment in Landsberg am Lech (q.v.), Strasser acted as cochairman of the National Socialist party. In this capacity he proved to be an able organizer, an indefatigable if weak speaker, a shrewd politician, and a lover of action.

In 1924 Strasser sold his apothecary shop and used the money to devote himself wholly to the party. He founded a newspaper, the *Berliner Arbeiter Zeitung (Berlin Workers' Paper),* edited by his brother, Otto Strasser (q.v.). At the same time he set up the newsletter *NS-Briefe* (q.v.), which was designed to keep party officials informed of the correct political line. He called in young Dr. Paul Joseph Goebbels (q.v.) as editor. In 1924 he was elected a delegate to the Bavarian Landtag (Legislature). Using his parliamentary immunity to protect him from libel suits and holding a free railway pass, he turned his energy to seeking the highest post in the National Socialist party. He would push Hitler aside and replace him. Strasser regarded himself as a proud intellectual who had far more to offer the party than the emotional and unstable Hitler.

From the beginning Gregor Strasser and his brother represented the socialist wing of National Socialism. An urban revolutionary, Gregor believed in "undiluted socialist principles." National Socialism, he said, must hasten the destruction of capitalism in any way possible, including cooperation with Bolshevik Russia. At the Bamberg Party Congress (q.v.) held on February 14, 1926, he represented the radical socialist wing. He was supported at first by his protégé Goebbels. Strasser waged a battle of words with Hitler concerning the extent of socialism in the movement, a struggle that was to last for eight years. At Bamberg, Goebbels, sensing strength on Hitler's side, deserted the Strasser brothers, to their chagrin and anger. Gregor Strasser began to call his protégé "the scheming dwarf."

In 1932 Hitler made Strasser *Reichsorganisationsleiter* (Reich organization leader) of the Nazi party. The two quarreled. In the July 31, 1932, elections the Nazis returned 230 deputies, which made them the strongest party in the Reichstag (q.v.). Hitler could have appointed Strasser to the presiding office of the Reichstag but instead chose Hermann Goering (q.v.). On December 7, 1932, Chancellor Kurt von Schleicher (q.v.), aiming to split the Nazis by giving some of them a share of responsibility, suggested that Strasser accept the position of Vice-Chancellor and Premier of Prussia. Hitler, who secretly wanted Goering in those posts, was infuriated. He and Strasser met at the Kaiserhof to discuss the offer. Hitler accused Strasser of trying to cheat him of the chancellorship and of seeking to split the party. Strasser countered that, on the contrary, he wanted to save the party but that Hitler had stabbed him in the back. Angered, Strasser resigned his post in the party leadership in December 1932 and informed his friends that he would take his wife and children to Italy to bask in the sun. A depressed Hitler, deserted not only by the Strasser brothers but also by Gottfried Feder (q.v.) and fearful that he was losing his hold on the party, broke down and wept. Recovering, he used his best oratory to overpower the recalcitrant left-wingers.

Meanwhile, Strasser disappeared, only to be seen again as an adviser on labor problems for a chemical company. Hitler dismissed him as head of the political organization of the party and appointed Rudolf Hess (q.v.) as head of the party's new Central Political Commission. Gregor Strasser remained politically inactive. He was arrested at noon on June 30, 1934, and killed by bullets fired through the windows of his prison cell; he was the most prominent victim of the Blood Purge (q.v.). Hitler had not forgotten his most dangerous rival.

Bibliography. Gregor Strasser, *Mein Kampf*, Heine Verlag, Frankfurt am Main, 1969.

STRASSER, OTTO (1897–1974). Brother of Gregor Strasser (q.v.) and a leader of the left wing of the Nationalsozialistische Deutsche Arbeiterpartei (q.v.) in the 1920s. Otto Strasser was born in Windsheim, Middle Franconia, on September 10, 1897. Originally a Social Democrat, he was a member of the Nazi party from 1925 to 1930. Like his brother he took seriously the words "Socialist" and "Workers" in the party's title. He wanted the party to turn to socialist principles. He relegated the Wittelsbachs and other German dynasties to "history's rubbish heap" and called for the nationalization of industry, banks, and land. As editor of the *Berliner Arbeiter Zeitung (Berlin Workers' Paper)*, founded by his brother in 1924, he encouraged strikes by trade unions and professed a strong sympathy for the Soviet Russian regime.

Hitler was annoyed by the activities of both brothers. He denounced Otto as a "parlor Bolshevik" and labeled his followers "doctrinaire fools, uprooted literati, and political boy scouts." In Hitler's mind Otto Strasser was the victim of the "cardinal sins of democracy and liberalism." The Fuehrer, who needed the support of the Rhineland industrialists, was angered by his recalcitrant socialists. He bought stock in the Strasser publishing business, closed the firm, and discontinued printing the newspapers. Otto was left without an outlet for his ideology. After a quarrel with his brother, the *Berliner Arbeiter Zeitung* was changed from a daily to a weekly, while at the same time an up-and-coming Dr. Paul Joseph Goebbels (q.v.) saw his successful newspaper *Der Angriff* (*see* ANGRIFF, DER) transformed from a weekly into a popular daily publication.

On May 21, 1930, Hitler demanded a showdown. Otto Strasser would have to submit completely to party discipline and do as he was told. He refused, whereupon Hitler ordered Goebbels to expel him and his friends from the party. Claiming that he was the true National Socialist, Otto Strasser formed a splinter party, the Union of Revolutionary National Socialists, which came to be known as the Black Front (Schwarze Front, q.v.). He continued to attack Hitler as "the betrayer of the revolution," but he was never able to command any voting strength. Leaving Germany, he moved first to Prague and then to Canada. In 1935 he wrote a book on the Blood Purge (q.v.), which had taken his brother's life (*Die deutsche Bartholomäusnacht*, Reso-Verlag, Zürich, 1935). In 1955, after winning back his citizenship, he returned to West Germany. He died in Munich on August 27, 1974, at the age of seventy-six.

Bibliography. Otto Strasser, *Hitler and I*, Jonathan Cape, Ltd., London, 1940.

STREET CELLS. *See* STRASSENZELLEN.

STREICHER, JULIUS (1885–1946). National Socialist politician widely known as the principal baiter of Jews. Julius Streicher was born in the village of Fleinhausen, Upper Bavaria, on February 12, 1885, the ninth child of a Roman Catholic primary school teacher. Little is known of his early life beyond the fact that he too became a teacher, in 1909 in a Nuremberg suburb. In serving as a one-year volunteer before World War I, he behaved so badly that it was stated in his paybook that he was never to be given a commission in the Army. Despite this warning his record in a Bavarian unit during the war was so impressive (he earned the Iron Cross, First and Second Classes) that he was given the rank of lieutenant. After the war he returned to teach in an elementary school in Nuremberg and began to play a role in right-wing politics.

In 1919 Streicher formed a political party based solely on anti-Semitism (q.v.). Two years later he joined the Nationalsozialistische Deutsche Arbeiterpartei (q.v.; NSDAP), to which he presented the entire membership of his own party. In 1923 he founded his own organ, *Der Stürmer* (*see* STÜRMER, DER), which was to gain a reputation as Germany's most violent anti-Semitic journal. In 1925 he was named *Gauleiter* (district leader) of the NSDAP for Franconia, with headquarters in Nuremberg. Streicher began to have increasing difficulties in his teaching post. He insisted that his pupils greet him each day with *"Heil Hitler!"* He continually denounced the government of the Weimar Republic (q.v.) and on one occasion took sick leave to attend a Nazi rally in Munich. In 1928, charges were brought against him, and he was dismissed for conduct unbecoming a teacher. Later he expressed great pride in this "achievement." In 1929 he was elected to the Bavarian Landtag (Legislature) as a Nazi delegate from Franconia.

Streicher became a master rabble-rouser for the party. In speeches and articles, week after week and month after month, he urged his audience to fight the Jews. He filled the columns of his paper with anti-Semitic articles and cartoons, stories of ritual murders, pornography, and letters to the editor denouncing Jews. Young men wrote in to reveal the names of girls who danced with Jews; a dentist complained that a Jewish colleague had used dental plates that disintegrated; an inmate of a mental hospital complained that he was the victim of a Jewish conspiracy. The paper attributed the destruction of the Zeppelin *Hindenburg* at Lakehurst, New Jersey, in May 1937, to a Jewish plot. Editorials announced the discovery that Christ was not a Jew. Hitler eagerly read each issue from beginning to end.

In January 1933 Streicher was elected to the Reichstag (q.v.) as a Nazi delegate from Thuringia. At the same time he was given the title of leader of the Central Committee for Counteracting Jewish Atrocity Tales and Boycotts. He was promoted to *SS-Gruppenfuehrer* (lieutenant general) in 1934. Meanwhile, he was acquiring a national reputation as an eccentric. Carrying a riding whip, he strode through his district like an avenging master. He took pleasure in beating people in the presence of witnesses. On one occasion he visited the Nuremberg jail, where before two friends he administered a severe beating to a young prisoner. He acquired a fortune by appropriating Jewish property in his district and permitted friends to buy Jewish homes and businesses at 10 percent of their value. He was charged with rape, and he was sued many times for libel.

Streicher's hatred for the Jews amounted to a fixation. On April 3, 1925, he stated: "For thousands of years the Jews have been destroying peoples; make a beginning today so that we can destroy the Jews." He took charge of a boycott against the Jews on April 1, 1933. He strongly advocated the 1935 Nuremberg Laws on citizenship and race (q.v.), which were directed against the Jews. In 1937 he said: "The Jew always lives from the blood of other peoples; he needs murders and sacrifices. Victory will only be achieved when the whole world is free of Jews." On November 10, 1938, he spoke publicly in support of the nationwide pogrom against the Jews then taking place (*see* KRISTALLNACHT). On August 10, 1939, he urged the demolition of the synagogue in Nuremberg. During World War II he called for the extermination of Jews in the eastern occupied territories. On January 6, 1944, he wrote in *Der Stürmer:* "Developments since the rise of National Socialism make it probable that the Continent will be freed from its Jewish destroyers of peoples and exploiters forever."

Streicher's followers were fanatical in their devotion. In others he aroused extreme loathing. He was an obnoxious individual by any standard. Brutal, violent, and sadistic, he advocated force as the solution to any problem. Streicher heaped scorn on all his enemies both inside and outside the party. He was unable to understand the views of others and would accept no compromise with his own opinions. He was absolutely certain that his estimate of the Jews was correct. Dishonest and corrupt, he had no use for laws that barred his way to riches. His sexual appetite bordered on the psychopathic. The pornographic side of his propaganda accounted for much of his popularity with a certain element of the public. His presence in the high Nazi hierarchy undoubtedly discouraged moderate and conservative Germans who otherwise saw in National Socialism a possible solution to their problems.

By 1939 even Hitler, who had long supported Streicher's campaign against the Jews, began to be annoyed by his colleague's disreputable dealings. Several times the Fuehrer reluctantly reprimanded Streicher for his conduct. Something had to be done now that party officials were beginning to complain about Streicher's erratic behavior. Hermann Goering (q.v.) had never forgotten Streicher's charge that Edda, Goering's daughter, had been conceived by artificial insemination. Streicher retracted the accusation, but Goering was not appeased. Hitler at last placed a *Redeverbot* (speaking ban) on

Julius Streicher [*Ullstein*]

Streicher. In 1940 Goering appointed a commission to examine Streicher's personal life and business transactions. The result was that Streicher was dismissed from party posts. Unmoved, he continued his activities along the same lines.

At the Nuremberg Trial (q.v.) Streicher was indicted for writing and publishing his "propaganda of death": "Streicher's incitement to murder and extermination, at the time when the Jews in the East were being killed under the most horrible conditions, constitutes persecution on political and racial grounds in connection with war crimes and constitutes a crime against humanity." A restless prisoner, Streicher called his trial "a triumph for world Jewry." He was found not guilty of having conspired to wage aggressive warfare because he had taken no part in the plans for invasions and had not been a military, political, or diplomatic adviser to Hitler. He was found guilty on count 4 (crimes against humanity) and sentenced to death. On October 16, 1946, he was brought to the gallows at Nuremberg Prison. As he mounted the scaffold, he shouted bitterly: *"Purimfest!"* (He referred to the Jewish festival celebrating the defeat of Haman, the oppressor of the Jews in biblical times.) Streicher's last words were *"Heil Hitler!"*

Bibliography. Julius Streicher, *Kampf dem Weltfeind*, Verlag Der Stuermer, Nuremberg, 1938.

STREIFENDIENST (Patrol Service). A special force of the Hitler Jugend (q.v.), the Hitler Youth. The unit was organized in 1934. In 1938, by an agreement between Baldur von Schirach and Heinrich Himmler (qq.v.), service in the Streifendienst was to be regarded as a prerequisite for entrance into an SS (q.v.) unit. The members of the Streifendienst were trained to the age of eighteen by officers of the SS.

STRENGTH THROUGH JOY. *See* KRAFT DURCH FREUDE.

STRESEMANN, GUSTAV (1878–1929). Parliamentarian and statesman responsible for the restoration of Germany's international status after World War I. Gustav Stresemann was born in Berlin on May 10, 1878, the son of an innkeeper. He took his doctorate in 1902 with a dissertation on the development of the Berlin bottled-beer

Gustav Stresemann. [*Picture Collection, The Branch Libraries, The New York Public Library*]

trade. After a successful commercial career he turned to politics. A monarchist, he was not attracted by the democracy of the Weimar Republic (q.v.), but he accepted the reality of a republican Germany.

On August 13, 1923, Stresemann became Chancellor of the Reich at the head of a coalition government. Countering assaults on the republic from both left and right, he sent troops to put down Communist insurrections in Saxony and Thuringia and restored the authority of his government after the failure of Hitler's Beer-Hall *Putsch* (q.v.) in Munich. When the Social Democrats deserted his coalition government, Stresemann was forced to resign as Chancellor on November 23, 1923.

Stresemann remained Foreign Minister of the Weimar Republic and its most important statesman until his death. In this capacity he guided the return of Germany to international status. He supported closer relations with the Western Powers by fulfilling most of the obligations set forth in the Treaty of Versailles and by negotiating for better terms. Stresemann worked for conciliation with France through Aristide Briand (the two statesmen shared the Nobel Peace Prize in 1926). He accepted the Dawes Plan (q.v.) on reparations in 1924 and the Locarno Pact (q.v.) in 1925, led Germany into the League of Nations in 1926, and supported the Young Plan (q.v.) on reparations in 1929. Adolf Hitler and the Nazis, in their struggle for power, fought Stresemann on every one of these policies. Hitler regarded Stresemann, despite the latter's nationalist and rightist sympathies, as a traitor to the German cause. Quite as despicable in Hitler's mind was the fact that Stresemann was married to the Jewish daughter of the Berlin industrialist Adolf Kreefeld. Stresemann died suddenly in Berlin on October 3, 1929.

Both before and after his death Stresemann was the subject of controversy. During the era of the Third Reich he was ignored, but after 1945 historians paid him renewed attention. On the one hand he was praised as a proponent of the Pan-European idea; on the other, he was characterized as an unscrupulous but masterful politician who used such slogans as "League of Nations" and "Spirit of Locarno" to mask his primary goal of reasserting German nationalism, militarism, and imperialism.

Bibliography. Rudolf Olden, *Stresemann*, tr. by R. T. Clark, E. P. Dutton & Co., Inc., New York, 1930.

STROHKOPF (Straw Head). Hitler's favorite vernacular term to describe a person of low intelligence. Angered when his armies were halted on the Russian front in December 1941, Hitler called Gen. Wilhelm Keitel (q.v.), chief of the High Command of the armed forces, a *Strohkopf* to his face. Humiliated, Keitel walked away without a word. His colleague Gen. Alfred Jodl (q.v.) found Keitel sitting at his desk, a pistol in front of him, writing his resignation. Jodl quietly removed the weapon and persuaded his fellow officer to remain in Hitler's service.

STROOP, JÜRGEN (1895–1951). *Brigadefuehrer* (major general) in the SS (q.v.). Stroop was police leader during the ghetto rebellion of 1943 (*see* WARSAW GHETTO UPRISING). In 1943 he was appointed SS and political leader of Greece, where he served until 1944. On March 22, 1947, he was condemned to death by an American tribunal in Dachau and on September 8, 1951, was executed in Warsaw.

STU-75. A highly successful German self-propelled 75-millimeter gun. A powerful mobile weapon used initially in the Polish campaign early in World War II and subsequently on other fronts, the Stu-75 consisted of a short gun mounted on a standard tank chassis. Extremely low in silhouette, the self-propelled gun presented a difficult target and could cause much damage to the enemy. Later the frontal areas were fitted with 4 inches of auxiliary armor.

STUBAF. *See* STURMBANNFUEHRER-SS.

STUDENT. Code name for one of four operations ordered by Hitler on July 31, 1943, to meet the expected invasion of Allied forces on the mainland of Italy (*see also* ACHSE; EICHE; SCHWARZ). Operation Student called for the occupation of Rome and the restoration of Mussolini's regime.

STUDY OF GERMAN CULTURE. *See* DEUTSCHKUNDE.

STUELPNAGEL, KARL HEINRICH VON (1886–1944). Military governor of occupied France and principal agent in Paris of the conspiracy against Hitler. Karl Heinrich von Stuelpnagel was born in Darmstadt on January 2, 1886. He pursued a successful military career both before and after Hitler became Chancellor in 1933. Described by his colleagues as a chivalrous gentleman schooled in philosophy, Von Stuelpnagel was opposed from its inception to the Nazi regime, which with many fellow officers he regarded as a stain on the honor of his country. From November 1938 to June 1940 he served as senior quartermaster on the Army General Staff. In December 1940, after the fall of France, he was chairman of the German-French Armistice Commission. He commanded the Seventeenth Army from the invasion of the Soviet Union on June 22 until October 1941. From February 1942 to July 1944 he was military governor in Paris.

In his Paris post Von Stuelpnagel protested against the operations of the agents of Alfred Rosenberg (q.v.), who sequestered Jewish property without compensation. While in France, Von Stuelpnagel became involved in the conspiracy of army officers to unseat Hitler, and he tried to persuade his close friend Gen. Erwin Rommel (q.v.) to use his influence to end the war in the west before the expected Allied invasion. His preparations in Paris for the coup d'état were far better organized than those inside Germany. His subordinates knew exactly what to do. At the signal for Operation Valkyrie (*see* VALKYRIE), Von Stuelpnagel's staff in a single stroke arrested 1,200 key Gestapo and SS (qq.v.) men without encountering any resistance. When word came from Berlin that the plot had misfired, Von Stuelpnagel, facing certain arrest, calmly prepared for the inevitable and destroyed his papers.

On July 21, 1944, Field Marshal Wilhelm Keitel (q.v.) ordered Von Stuelpnagel to return to Berlin by air. After dining leisurely, Von Stuelpnagel's party started out by car. Thirty miles east of Paris, the automobile broke down, and the group had to await a replacement. After sleeping in a garage, the party drove through the dangerous woods of the Argonne. Near Sedan, where so many of his comrades had fallen in World War I, Von Stuelpnagel stopped the car, saying that he wanted to walk a little. His escort went on for a short distance but stopped when a shot was heard. In a canal nearby they saw Von Stuelpnagel with his hands clutching his throat. One of his eyes had been blown away, but he had survived a suicide attempt. He was hanged in Berlin on August 30, 1944.

STUKA. *See* JUNKERS-87.

STUMPFEGGER, LUDWIG (ca. 1915–1945). One of Hitler's personal physicians, who remained with him during the last days in the *Fuehrerbunker* (q.v.) in Berlin. Ludwig Stumpfegger was a competent orthopedic surgeon who worked in a clinic in Hohenlychen under Professor Dr. Karl Gebhardt. The latter, at the suggestion of Heinrich Himmler (q.v.), sent Dr. Stumpfegger to Hitler's headquarters on the eastern front on October 31, 1944. A man of huge stature, Stumpfegger admired Hitler and gave him unconditional loyalty. He was careful never to criticize or quarrel with Dr. Theodor Morell (q.v.), the physician whose drugs were undermining Hitler's health.

During the final days, from April 20 to 30, 1945, Stumpfegger remained in his two rooms on the lower level of the bunker. On April 28 he dressed the injured foot of Gen. Robert Ritter von Greim (q.v.), who had flown in under dangerous circumstances to be named successor to Hermann Goering (q.v.) as head of the Luftwaffe (q.v.). Stumpfegger was among the small group that tried to escape from the bunker after Hitler's suicide. Artur Axmann (q.v.), Reich Youth Leader, later claimed that on May 1, 1945, he had seen the corpse of Stumpfegger, along with that of Martin Bormann (q.v.), behind the bridge where the Invalidenstrasse crossed the railway line. Both bodies, he said, lay outstretched on their backs with the moonlight on their faces. Apparently, he added, they had been killed by the Russians. *See also* GÖTTERDÄMMERUNG.

STURM (Storm). A unit of either the SA or the SS (qq.v.), roughly equivalent to a company.

STURMABTEILUNG. *See* SA.

STURMBANN (Storm Battalion). A unit of either the SA or the SS (qq.v.), roughly equivalent to a battalion.

STURMBANNFUEHRER-SS (STUBAF). A major in the SS (q.v.).

STÜRMER, DER (The Stormer). Illustrated newspaper owned and published by Julius Streicher (q.v.), Nazi party militant in Franconia. A pornographic sheet, it was an example of journalism at its worst. The columns were filled with reports of sexual scandals and almost hysterical paeans to Hitler and Nazism. Illustrations invariably included exaggerated cartoons of Jewish faces and drawings of such subjects as Christian girls being raped by Jewish men. Streicher claimed that his newspaper was the only one that Hitler read from the first page to the last.

STURMTRUPPENLEITER (Storm Troop Leader). An officer of the SA (q.v.).

STURZKAMPFGESCHWADER (StG; Dive Bomber Group). A unit of the Luftwaffe (q.v.).

SUBHUMANS. *See* UNTERMENSCHEN.

SUBPREFECT. *See* LANDRAT.

SUDETEN DEUTSCHE PARTEI (SdP; Sudeten German Party). Political party composed of the Sudeten Germans in Czechoslovakia. The SdP was formed in 1933 under the leadership of Konrad Henlein (q.v.), a gymnastics teacher. By 1935 the party was being heavily subsidized by the German Foreign Office, and within a few years it had captured the majority of Sudeten Germans. Taking orders from Berlin, Henlein led the party on the road to union with the Third Reich. Hitler regarded the SdP as a satellite party useful in developing opposition to the Czechoslovak government as a preliminary to a take-over by the Third Reich. *See also* MUNICH AGREEMENT.

SUDETENLAND. An area in Bohemia adjoining Germany that was awarded to Czechoslovakia by the Treaty of Saint-Germain-en-Laye between Austria and the Allies in 1919. The Sudetenland had formerly been Austrian territory, and some 3 million German-speaking people lived there. It contained rich mineral resources as well as an important munitions factory in Pilsen (Plzeň). Two years after Hitler became Chancellor, the Nazi Sudeten Deutsche Partei (q.v.), led by Konrad Henlein (q.v.), began an intensive campaign against the Czechoslovak government, which it accused of suppressing the German minority in the Sudetenland. After the *Anschluss* (q.v.) between Germany and Austria in March 1938, Henlein and his followers increased their agitation. The Munich Agreement (q.v.) of September 1938 assigned the Sudetenland to Germany as a part of the general settlement. In 1945 all German-speaking inhabitants of the area were expelled, and the Sudetenland was resettled by Czechs from other areas of Czechoslovakia.

SUNFLOWER. *See* SONNENBLUME.

SUPERIOR GROUP. *See* OBERGRUPPE.

SUPREME COMMANDER OF THE ARMED FORCES. *See* OBERSTER BEFEHLSHABER DER WEHRMACHT.

SUPREME COMMANDER OF THE SA. *See* OBERSTER SA-FUEHRER.

SUPREME PARTY COURT. *See* OBERSTES PARTEIGERICHT.

SUPREME SA LEADERSHIP. *See* OBERSTE SA-FUEHRUNG.

SV. *See* SICHERUNGSVERWAHRTE.

SWASTIKA. *See* HAKENKREUZ.

SWEET VIOLETS. *See* MÄRZVEILCHEN.

SWORD WORDS. *See* SCHWERTWORTE.

T

T-4 to TYPHOON

T-4. Code name for the National Coordinating Agency for Therapeutic and Medical Establishments, an organization created to administer the euthanasia program to exterminate European Jewry. T-4 referred to the organization's address at Tiergartenstrasse 4 in Berlin. Hitler gave full power to implement the program to Philip Bouhler (q.v.), chief of chancellery of the Nationalsozialistische Deutsche Arbeiterpartei (q.v.), and Dr. Karl Brandt (q.v.), the Fuehrer's personal physician. In two years, from 1939 to 1941, more than 50,000 persons were killed by gas or lethal injections.

TABLE TALK, HITLER'S. The unguarded, all night, off-the-record talk of the Fuehrer, taken down in shorthand by his party associates. The talks were later published as *Hitler's Secret Conversations, 1941–1944* (Farrar, Straus & Co., New York, 1953). Self-educated, Hitler held forth on hundreds of subjects, from food to world politics, from music to military tactics. He paid some attention to ideas but preferred to issue dicta and ukase. He often dismissed as insane anyone who disagreed with his judgments and disconnected dialogues. The subject of most interest to him was racialism, and he insisted that it was the duty of all Germans to arouse the forces that slumbered in their blood. He spoke in extravagant terms of his own worth, and he indicated that when anyone entered the Reich Chancellery he should have the feeling that he was meeting "the master of the world." Again and again he intimated that both Churchill and Roosevelt were "sick brains." He also made certain to ridicule the fighting qualities of such people as the Americans.

In his table talk Hitler often paraphrased the works of Arthur Comte de Gobineau, Houston Stewart Chamberlain, Friedrich Nietzsche, Karl Haushofer (qq.v.), Arthur Schopenhauer, and Thomas Carlyle. His voice usually remained calm and low-pitched until the mere mention of the word "Jew" would sent him into hysterical denunciation. This monomania remained with him to the last day of his life, when in his political testament (*see* HITLER'S POLITICAL TESTAMENT) he denounced international Jewry as "the real criminal of this murderous struggle." Those who were present at these all-night table talks agreed that no one subject could arouse Hitler to greater paroxysms of rage than "international Jewry and its helpers." Anyone who dared to intervene on behalf of a Jew was promptly ordered to cease making such requests.

TAIFUN (Typhoon). Code name for the German attack on Moscow ordered on September 19, 1941. While the Leningrad area was being encircled, Hitler ordered an attack against Marshal Semyon K. Timoshenko's army group in the Moscow area. The Fuehrer was anxious to defeat the Russians and annihilate them there before the onset of winter.

TANK. *See* PANZER.

TANNENBERG. Hitler's military headquarters from June 28 to July 6, 1940, located west of Freudenstadt in the Black Forest. Tannenberg was named after a famous German victory in World War I. At the Battle of Tannenberg on August 26–29, 1914, a Russian army under Gen. Aleksandr V. Samsonov was trapped by the Germans. On June 25, 1940, the day the armistice with France became effective in World War II, the Fuehrer closed his headquarters at Brûly-de-Pêche, where he was annoyed by gnats, and moved to the new location between Strasbourg and Freudenstadt. On July 6, 1940, he broke up the Tannenberg headquarters and returned to Berlin for a triumphant reception.

TANNENBERG BUND. A rightist organization of nationalist veterans of World War I active in 1926. It was headed by Gen. Erich Ludendorff (q.v.). Its name was taken from the Battle of Tannenberg, fought on August 26–29, 1914, in which a Russian army under Gen. Aleksandr V. Samsonov stumbled into a German trap. More than 90,000 Russian troops surrendered, and the unhappy Samsonov shot himself. The victorious German Eighth Army was commanded by Gen. Paul von Hindenburg (q.v.) with Ludendorff as his chief of staff.

The Tannenberg Bund, reflecting Ludendorff's philosophy, was fiercely nationalistic, anti-Semitic, anti-Communist, anti-Socialist, and anti-Masonic. It was directed against what Ludendorff believed to be *"die überstaatlichen Mächte"* (powers above the state). Among its members were many officers who had fought under Ludendorff during the war. The Tannenberg Bund never succeeded in winning a mass base. Most of its members turned to Hitler and National Socialism.

TASK FORCES. *See* EINSATZGRUPPEN.

TATKREIS (Action Circle). One of the many *voelkisch* movements active during the era of the Weimar Republic (q.v.; *see* VOELKISCH MOVEMENT). Members of the Tatkreis were neoconservatives of the radical right who considered themselves to be conservative revolutionaries. Combining nationalism and racialism, they attacked modern democracy as outmoded. They were opposed to the equality of classes and religions, to "disputatious and irresponsible parliaments," and to anything connected with the Weimar Republic ("corrupt and sterile beyond repair"). They denounced traditional reason and discussion as obsolete and welcomed political chaos as inevitable, because only in this way could there be "rebirth and freedom" in the German fatherland.

In the place of a disintegrating liberal and democratic society, the Tatkreis called for an intellectual elite open to talent but isolated from popular pressures. Members were quite willing to lead the coming national revolution themselves. They made an elaborate attempt to combine the educated class with the *Mittelstand* (q.v.; middle class), which comprised 45 percent of the German people. The Tatkreis extolled youth as the model on which the future German society would be built. Adherents called for the end of capitalism and its replacement by a planned national economy, a neomercantilist self-sufficiency that would put an end to German obligations to outsiders.

In the 1920s the Tatkreis rallied around its official publication, *Die Tat (Action)*. The periodical's guiding spirit was Hans Zehrer, who became editor in 1928 and raised its circulation from 1,000 to 30,000. *Die Tat* became the best-known *voelkisch* publication in Germany.

Hitler, who regarded his own movement of National Socialism as basically *voelkisch*, was strongly influenced by the Tatkreis, especially by its right-wing elitism and anticapitalism. For their part, members of the Tatkreis at first were not attracted by this lower-class Austrian, and many were convinced that the disruption of the Nazi party in 1932 signified a permanent trend. When Hitler assumed political power in 1933, some members of the Tatkreis were disillusioned, and several lost their lives in opposing the Nazis. Zehrer, disgusted with Nazi excesses, resigned as editor of *Die Tat*. Many other members of the Tatkreis, pleased that Hitler had accepted at least some of their demands, recognized the National Socialist regime by becoming party members. The Fuehrer himself, however, wanted no independent-minded individuals among the rightist elite any more than among his leftist enemies. The Tatkreis gradually disintegrated in the milieu of Nazi coordination *(Gleichschaltung*, q.v.).

Bibliography. Fritz Stern, *The Politics of Cultural Despair*, Doubleday & Company, Inc., Garden City, N.Y., 1965.

TAUBER, RICHARD (1891–1948). Austrian lyric tenor and prominent refugee from Nazism. Richard Tauber was born in Linz on May 16, 1891. Originally an actor in Graz and Linz, he won global fame as a lyric tenor specializing in Lehár operettas and Mozart operas. He was also known as a composer of such operettas as *Old Chelsea*, film music, and *Lieder*. He died in London on January 8, 1948.

TAUSENDJÄHRIGE REICH. *See* THOUSAND-YEAR REICH.

TAYLOR, A[LAN] J[OHN] P[ERCIVALE] (1906–). English historian and author of an early revisionist interpretation of the origins of World War II. Alan John Percivale Taylor was born in Birkdale, Lancashire, on March 25, 1906. He attended Bootham School in York and Oriel College, Oxford. Taylor began his academic career at Manchester University (1930–1938). He was a fellow and tutor at Magdalen College, Oxford, from 1938 to 1963 and a lecturer in international history at Oxford from 1953 to 1963. A prolific writer, he published works on German colonial policy, the Hapsburg monarchy, European diplomacy, World Wars I and II, and recent English history. His *The Course of German History* (Coward-McCann, Inc., New York, 1946), which traces German development from the time of the French Revolution to the present day, is considered by many historians to be one of the most brilliant interpretations of German history ever written.

In 1961 Taylor published *The Origins of the Second World War* (Atheneum Publishers, New York), which became the first important revisionist work on the causes of the conflict. He implied that Hitler was not guilty of having been the prime instigator of the war and attempted to counter the verdict of the Nuremberg Trial (q.v.) that Hitler bore the main responsibility for the outbreak of the war. The responsibility, according to Taylor, lay chiefly with others, notably Prime Minister Neville Chamberlain (q.v.), who by their own errors pushed Hitler to aggression. Taylor held that British mistakes brought on a war that Hitler never wanted and that there were no Nazi plans for world conquest. Hitler himself, said Taylor, was a blunderer who was pressed into aggression by outsiders under circumstances utterly beyond his control. Hitler was no better and no worse than other contemporary statesmen. He never wanted the annexation of either Austria or Czechoslovakia. He was maneuvered into the Czechoslovak crisis by Chamberlain. He never intended to implement the blueprint indicated in *Mein Kampf* (q.v.). Taylor deprecated the importance of the critical Hossbach Conference (q.v.) and argued that this was merely an occasion on which Hitler dissimulated to confuse his opponents.

Taylor's book created a storm of controversy. Other historians, notably H. R. Trevor-Roper (q.v.) and G. F. Hudson, considered Taylor's revisionism too painful to be accepted by any person of academic standing. Virtually all historians writing on World War II were in agreement that the chief impetus for the war had come from Hitler, that he had outlined his plans carefully in *Mein Kampf*, and that the Hossbach Memorandum (*Hossbach Niederschrift*, q.v.) was in itself overwhelming proof of his plans and objectives. The vast majority of scholars on the war saw Hitler as deliberately starting it and not stumbling into it by mistake. How could it have been possible, they asked, for Hitler to blunder into a war on September 1, 1939, when he had informed his generals on May 23, 1939, that there would be a war over Poland? Critics refused to accept Taylor's theses that Hitler only wanted a free hand to destroy conditions in the east which Westerners regarded as intolerable and that the Fuehrer had no ambitions directed against Britain and France. Had Hitler had his way, said one critic, Taylor himself would long ago have perished in Buchenwald or Dachau.

TAYLOR, TELFORD (1908–). American Chief of Counsel for War Crimes at the Nuremberg Trial (q.v.). Telford Taylor was born in Schenectady, New York, on February 24, 1908. He took an undergraduate degree at Williams College in 1928 and a bachelor of laws degree at Harvard in 1932. After teaching history and political science at Williams for a year, he started his legal career as a law clerk in New York (1932–1933) and as Assistant Solicitor, United States Department of the Interior (1933–1934). He was General Counsel for the Federal Communications Commission from 1940 to 1942. From April 1943 to May 1945 he served as a military intelligence officer in the European theater of operations, specializing in matters concerning the German High Command.

Brig. Gen. Telford Taylor. [*UPI*]

From June 1945 to October 1946, Taylor served as Chief of Counsel for War Crimes at the Nuremberg Trial. In this post he played a major role in unraveling the tangled details of the charges against the top hierarchy of Nazi leaders on trial. He was promoted to brigadier general in April 1946. Later he became a professor of law at Columbia University and a visiting lecturer at Yale Law School. Among his publications on subjects concerned with the Third Reich are *Sword and Swastika: Generals and Nazis in the Third Reich* (Simon and Schuster, New York, 1952) and *The Breaking Wave: World War II in the Summer of 1940* (Simon and Schuster, New York, 1967).

TECHNISCHE NOTHILFE (Technical Emergency Corps). An auxiliary police unit belonging to the Ordnungspolizei (q.v.), the Order Police, and consisting of specialists in construction work.

TEPPICHFRESSER (Carpet Chewer). Sarcastic term used to describe Hitler throughout his career. It was claimed that in moments of fury Hitler would drop to the floor and chew the carpet in a rage. This charge, for which there is no evidence, has been made against several historical figures, notably King John I of England, who was said to have reacted precisely in this way when he was forced by his barons to sign the Magna Charta in 1215.

TERBOVEN, JOSEF (1898–1945). Reich Commissioner for Norway. Josef Terboven was born in Essen on May 23, 1898. A bank employee, he joined the Nazi party and in 1930 was elected to the Reichstag (q.v.) as a National Socialist deputy for Wahlkreis (Electoral District) Düsseldorf-West. In 1933 he was appointed to the Prussian State Council and was also designated a *Gauleiter* (district leader) of the Nationalsozialistische Deutsche Arbeiterpartei (q.v.) for Essen. His place in party circles was recognized when, on June 28, 1934, the Fuehrer attended Terboven's wedding in Essen. On February 5, 1935, Terboven was named senior president of the Rhine Province, and in September 1939 he was appointed Reich defense commissioner for Wehrkreis (Defense District) VI.

After the Nazis invaded Norway on April 9, 1940, Hitler deemed it necessary to appoint a reliable proconsul for the country. The Fuehrer was dissatisfied with the Norwegian Vidkun Quisling (q.v.), who was unable to obtain support from the Norwegians, and dismissed him on April 15, just six days after Quisling had proclaimed himself Norwegian Prime Minister. At first there was an administrative council of six leading Norwegian citizens, including Bishop Eivind Berggrav, head of the Norwegian Lutheran Church, and Paal Berg, president of the Supreme Court (who later became head of the Norwegian resistance movement). Hitler distrusted this council and on April 24, 1940, named Terboven *Reichskommissar für Norwegen* (Reich Commissioner for Norway) and *SA-Obergruppenfuehrer* (general). The appointment was opposed by Gen. Wilhelm Keitel (q.v.), who wanted the administration of occupied Norway to remain in the hands of the military. When Hitler informed Keitel that he nevertheless would name *Gauleiter* Terboven to the office, Keitel threw his briefcase on the table and walked out of the room.

Terboven's cruel conduct in his Norwegian post was similar to that of Reinhard Heydrich (q.v.) in Czechoslovakia. During the opening months of his regime Terboven took measures which gave the impression that Norwegian Jews would not be molested, but little by little the predicament of the Jews grew worse. In June 1941, soon after the Germans invaded the Soviet Union, Terboven rounded up all the Jews in Tromsø and other towns in northern Norway and deported them to Germany. Others arrested in Trondheim were executed. The Jews in Oslo were unharmed, but on February 2, 1942, Terboven forced all of them to wear the Jewish star and have their documents stamped with a *J*.

Terboven distrusted all Norwegians. While in his post he performed such tasks as seeing that natural stone was sent to Germany to be used for heroic statues of Hitler planned by Albert Speer (q.v.). Terboven died in May 1945, presumably a suicide.

TEREZÍN. *See* THERESIENSTADT.

TESTAMENT, HITLER'S POLITICAL. *See* HITLER'S POLITICAL TESTAMENT.

THADDEN, ADOLF VON (1921–). Conservative nationalist leader very active in post-World War II West Germany. Adolf von Thadden was born in Trieglaff, Pomerania, on July 7, 1921, the scion of an old Junker family. He was the half brother of the Christian conservative Elizabeth von Thadden (q.v.), who was executed for defeatism and attempted treason during the era of the Third Reich. After attending a *Gymnasium* (high school) in Greifenberg, he served as a first lieutenant in World War II and was wounded several times. From 1948 to 1960 he was a member of the Göttingen City Council, and from 1949 to 1953 a member of the Bundestag of the Federal Republic. In 1961 he became chairman of the Deutsche Rechts-Partei (q.v.; German Rightist party) in Lower Saxony. In 1964 he joined the Nationaldemokratische Partei Deutschlands (NPD; National Democratic party of Germany) and in 1967 became its chairman.

A young man of quick wit and demagogic talent, known to his friends as Bubi, Von Thadden hoped to make conservative nationalism respectable in postwar Germany. Critics accused him of neo-Nazism (q.v.), a charge that he heatedly denied. He attracted much attention by his defense of Germany on the subject of war guilt:

> There is no German guilt which is not at the same time the guilt of other peoples. There is no German injustice that has not been committed partly or wholly by others as well. Therefore, there can be no confession of guilt by the Germans only, but rather a worldwide confession of guilt. . . . The constantly renewed digging around in concentration-camp atrocities borders on psychic self-flagellation whose result must be the prevention of moral recovery by the German body social [*Volkskörper*].

Adolf von Thadden. [*Courtesy of the Library of Congress*]

THADDEN, ELIZABETH VON (1890–1944). Pomeranian teacher who was active in the anti-Hitler movement. Elizabeth von Thadden was born in Mohrungen, East Prussia (now Morąg, Poland), on July 29, 1890, the daughter of the chairman of the local council. In 1927 she founded a Protestant boarding school at Schloss Wieblingen, near Heidelberg. Although her school flourished, she was forced by new state regulations to resign in 1941. She then turned to work with the Red Cross while at the same time joining the Resistance (q.v.). On September 10, 1943, she invited a number of people to her home to discuss the Nazi regime. Among them was a young man invited by an old friend in Switzerland. The young man reported her and her guests to the Gestapo (q.v.; *see* SOLF TEA PARTY), which arrested them all. Elizabeth von Thadden was sentenced to death by the Volksgericht (q.v.), the People's Court, and was executed on September 8, 1944. Her last words were "Put an end, O Lord, to all our sufferings."

Elizabeth von Thadden. [*From Annedore Leber (ed.),* Conscience in Revolt, *tr. by Rosemary O'Neill, Vallentine, Mitchell & Co., Ltd., London, 1957*]

THAELMANN, ERNST (1886–1944). German Communist politician high on Hitler's list of enemies. Ernst Thaelmann was born in Hamburg on April 16, 1886. A transport worker, he became a member of the Social Democratic party in 1903. During World War I he was an Independent Socialist, and in 1919 he joined the Communist party. He was elected that year to the Hamburg City Council. From 1924 to 1933 Thaelmann was a member of the German Reichstag (q.v.). As chairman of the Communist party from 1925 on, he was responsible, despite formidable opposition, for bringing the German Communist movement in line with Moscow's directives. In 1925 and again in 1932 he ran for the Reich Presidency. In the elections of March 13, 1932, he received 4,983,197 votes

Ernst Thaelmann (Thälmann). [*Stamp issued by the German Democratic Republic*]

against 18,650,730 for Paul von Hindenburg (q.v.), 11,339,285 for Hitler, and 2,557,729 for Theodor Duesterberg (q.v.). In the runoff elections of April 10, he received 3,706,655 votes against Von Hindenburg's winning total of 19,359,650 and Hitler's 13,418,011. Hitler bitterly hated his Communist rival. Thaelmann was arrested on February 28, 1933, the day after the Reichstag fire (q.v.), and with many of his party comrades was sent to a concentration camp (*see* CONCENTRATION CAMPS). He was shot in Buchenwald (q.v.) on August 28, 1944.

THEATER IN THE THIRD REICH. From 1919 to 1933, during the era of the Weimar Republic (q.v.), the German theater achieved a high reputation for excellence. Playwrights, directors, and actors brought great creative energy to both tragedy and comedy. All forms of theater, from the classics to radical expressionism, were produced with maximum effect. There were impressive productions about human destiny as well as brilliantly staged plays about the lighter side of human nature. All the world laughed at the winning satire of *Der Hauptmann von Köpenick (The Captain of Köpenick)*, by Carl Zuckmayer (q.v.), staged in Germany in 1931 and produced thereafter in translation in many other countries.

The installation of the Nazi regime in 1933 caused a sharp decline in the German theater. Under the cultural leadership of Dr. Paul Joseph Goebbels (q.v.), head of the Ministry for Public Enlightenment and Propaganda, the theater, along with films, radio, art, literature, and the press, was subjected to *Gleichschaltung* (q.v.), or coordination. The first step was to remove all Jewish producers, directors, and actors, many of whom were active in films as well as in the theater (*see* FILMS IN THE THIRD REICH). The famous director Max Reinhardt (q.v.), head of the Deutsches Theater in Berlin, left Germany for exile. The Bavarian neorealistic playwright Bertolt Brecht (q.v.), whose epic dramas had been highly popular in the Weimar Republic, left his homeland in 1933 and went to Denmark. Later, in the United States, Brecht wrote several anti-Nazi plays, including *The Resistible Rise of Arturo Ui*, which described the propaganda tactics used by Hitler in his rise to political power, and *The Private Life of the Master Race*, which predicted that the political stupidity of the Nazis would lead to their ruin. Another refugee playwright, Ernst Toller (q.v.), wrote *Pastor Hall*, a drama about a German clergyman who defied Hitler's Brownshirts (*see* SA). Similarly, Friedrich Wolf's *Professor Mamlock*, performed in New York in 1937, told the story of a Jewish surgeon who, slandered, mistreated, and driven from his practice, committed suicide. These plays, produced outside the Third Reich by prominent refugee playwrights, gave a striking picture of the Nazi terror and the lack of moral fiber of the artists who remained inside Germany and failed to oppose the Nazi regime.

Inside the Third Reich an attempt was made to maintain the interest of a public that had been accustomed to a high quality of stage performances. Goebbels named Hanns Johst (q.v.), a playwright of little talent, head of the Reich Theater Chamber, which was controlled by the Propaganda Ministry. Johst's drama *Schlageter*, produced in 1933, was written in praise of Albert Leo Schlageter (q.v.), the Nazi martyr who had been killed in 1923 while opposing the French occupation of the Rhineland. The dedication of the play ("Written for Adolf Hitler, in affectionate veneration and unchanging loyalty") won Johst the Fuehrer's attention and a place in the Nazi hierarchy. Johst presented two goals for the German theater. First, "the German must be born of the blood and essence of Germanism." Second, "the theater is the last pedagogical possibility to save the German people from the complete materialism of a purely realistic world." Johst set the tone for the new Nazi drama by repeating a line from his *Schlageter*: "When I hear the word '*Kultur*' ['culture'], I loosen the safety catch of my revolver."

The only established playwright of talent to remain in Germany during the era of the Third Reich was Gerhart Hauptmann (q.v.). A gifted author who represented naturalism as well as symbolism and classicism in the theater, Hauptmann made his peace with National Socialism. His plays continued to be performed. In addition, there were good performances of plays by Goethe, Schiller, and Shakespeare. Bernard Shaw's dramas were retained because they satirized the British aristocracy and democracy. The German public, hungry for entertainment, accepted these classics as long-time favorites.

On the other hand, the theatergoing public rejected the boring propaganda-ridden plays that the Propaganda Ministry regarded as satisfactory. The tone of Nazi drama was heroic. Friedrich Bethge's *Marsch der Veteranen (March of the Veterans)*, produced in 1935, told the story of how veterans of the Napoleonic Wars found a leader and patriots rose from the dead to march once more. Kurt Heynicke's *Der Weg ins Reich (The Road to Empire)*, staged in 1938, portrayed an aggressive Nazi who destroyed a traitor and united the German people. Richard Euringer's *Deutsche Passion (German Passion Play)*, which appeared in 1936, featured an unknown soldier who sought a better world by combating capitalists and intellectuals. Eberhard Wolfgang Müller's *Panamaskandal (Panama Scandal)*, produced in 1936, which showed how a democracy was destroyed by corrupt politicians, was actually an attack on the Weimar Republic. Other Nazi playwrights won Goebbels's approval to transfer racial doctrine (q.v.) to the stage. They failed to attract audiences.

THERESIENSTADT (Terezín). A concentration camp located in northern Bohemia, about 35 miles from Prague (*see* CONCENTRATION CAMPS). It was situated on a gently sloping plain among meadows and low hills. From 1780 to 1882 there was a fortress on the spot. In November 1941 Reinhard Heydrich (q.v.) ordered the evacuation of 7,000 persons living at a garrison in Theresienstadt and constructed a special concentration camp for Jews. Originally, Theresienstadt had the reputation of an especially humane detention center. Jews from Prague who were taken there in thousands believed that they were safe in a "model ghetto." Among the Jewish inmates were elderly men and women, war veterans, discharged officials, and Jews married to Aryans. Some went so far as to bribe Gestapo (q.v.) agents for the privilege of being sent to Theresienstadt.

The legend of a humane concentration camp died as Heydrich designated Theresienstadt a transit station on the way to the extermination camps (q.v.; *see* ENDLÖSUNG, DIE). The Sephardic Jews of Amsterdam, who were regarded at first by Nazi authorities as having no affinity to Eastern Jewry, lost their exemption in February 1944. They, too, were sent to Theresienstadt for eventual transportation in cattle cars to extermination camps, especially to Auschwitz (q.v.). Theresienstadt was liberated and then destroyed in 1945.

THIERACH, OTTO GEORG (1889–1946). Reich Minister of Justice from 1942 to 1945. Otto Georg Thierach was born in Würzen to a middle-class family that could trace its origins to 1633. After attending a humanistic *Gymnasium* (high school), he studied law and political science at Marburg and Leipzig. He took a law degree in February 1914. In World War I he served as a lieutenant and was awarded the Iron Cross (Second Class). After the war he pursued a legal career. In 1933 he was appointed minister of justice for Saxony and in 1942 was named Reich Minister of Justice. On October 26, 1946, while a case was being prepared against him in Nuremberg, he committed suicide by hanging at Neumünster camp.

THINGSPIELSTÄTTEN (Open-Air Medleys). Nazi outdoor agitprop (agitation-propaganda) presentations. The celebrations were held in rudimentary natural theaters incorporating hilly slopes and ancient ruins. The Nazis revived the *Thing*, an old Teutonic tribal assembly, as a support for National Socialist ideology. The *Thingspiel* was a special show that included military tattoos, pagan oratorios, exhibitions of horsemanship, and circus acts. Entire battalions of the Hitler Jugend (q.v.), the Hitler Youth, engaged in battle scenes featuring swordplay. Special attention was given to pagan belief in earth, air, fire, and water. In addition, Nazi martyrs were honored at the medleys. This sort of presentation was the only contribution of the Nazis to theatrical art forms.

THIRD REICH (Third Empire). The official Nazi designation for the regime in power in Germany from January 1933 to May 1945. Hitler regarded his government as a logical extension of two previous German empires. The First Reich was the Holy Roman Empire of the German Nation, which began in A.D. 962 with the coronation in Rome of Otto the Great, the second ruler of the Saxon line. The First Reich was ultimately abolished by Napoleon in 1806. The Second Reich was the empire founded by Otto von Bismarck in 1871, which lasted until 1918 and the end of the Hohenzollern dynasty. In 1923 a German nationalist writer, Arthur Moeller van den Bruck (q.v.), used *Das dritte Reich (The Third Reich)* as a title for one of his books. The term was enthusiastically adopted by Hitler in the early 1920s to signify his intention of establishing a new empire. The Fuehrer regarded his Third Reich as the greatest of all German empires and as an institution that would last 1,000 years. He was also attracted by the term because of its connection with the mysticism of the Middle Ages, when a "third realm" was regarded as the millennium.

THIRD REICH, THE. *See* DRITTE REICH, DAS.

THOMPSON, DOROTHY (1894–1961). American journalist and one of the strongest anti-Nazi voices in the United States. Born in Lancaster, New York, on July 9, 1894, Dorothy Thompson became a foreign correspondent for the Curtis-Martin newspaper chain, which she represented in Vienna from 1920 to 1924 and in Berlin as chief of its Central European Service from 1924 to 1928. She early developed an antipathy toward Hitler and Nazism, both of which she denounced in polemical prose. Expelled from Germany in 1934 by Hitler's personal order, she returned to the United States to pour forth warnings against the Third Reich. In her thrice-weekly column, syndicated in some 130 newspapers throughout the country, as well as in her regular weekly broadcasts, she undertook to arouse Americans to "the truth about Nazism." She became a columnist and broadcaster only after she had been forced to leave Germany. Her *I Saw Hitler* (Farrar & Rinehart, New York, 1932) was one of the first books on Hitler published in the United States. She was forcibly ejected from Madison Square Garden during a mass meeting of the German-American Bund (q.v.), when she laughed loudly during a speech by Fritz Kuhn, Fuehrer of the American Nazi party. Her broadcasts to the German people ("Listen Hans!") were designed to alert them to foreign opinion on the Hitler regime. She died in Lisbon on January 31, 1961.

THOSE WHO JOINED IN MARCH. *See* MÄRZGEFALLENE.

THOUSAND-YEAR REICH (Tausendjährige Reich). Hitler's conception of the duration of the National Socialist state. In September 1934 at Nuremberg the Fuehrer declared the revolution over. "This revolution has achieved without exception all that was expected of it. . . . In the next thousand years there will be no new revolution in Germany." From that point on the term *Thousand-Year Reich* was popular in National Socialist Germany.

THULE GESELLSCHAFT (Thule Society). A *voelkisch* circle (*see* VOELKISCH MOVEMENT) in Munich during the early post-World War I years. Outwardly an innocent club composed of persons who wanted to study and promote old Germanic literature, it was actually devoted to extreme nationalism, race mysticism, occultism, and anti-Semitism (q.v.). The society was an offshoot of the Germanenorder, or Teutonic Order, whose base was in Berlin and whose branches throughout Germany were patterned after the Masonic lodges. The Munich branch received its name from Thule, the legendary kingdom of Nordic mythology which was supposed to be the homeland of the ancient German race that had come down from the north.

The Thule Society in Munich was founded during World War I by an emissary from Berlin, Rudolf Freiherr von Sebottendorf, who enlisted 250 members in Munich and another 1,500 elsewhere in Bavaria. Among the members were journalists, poets, professors, and army officers. The membership list included Dietrich Eckart (q.v.), an elderly journalist; Rudolf Hess (q.v.), a member of the Nationalsozialistische Deutsche Arbeiterpartei (q.v.), the NSDAP, from 1920 on; and Alfred Rosenberg (q.v.), the Nazi philosopher. The objectives of the society were mainly *voelkisch,* embracing especially the concepts of racial superiority and anti-Semitism. The group supported the Pan-German dream of a new, powerful German Reich. Like other such societies in Bavaria and Germany as a whole, the Thule Society used mystical symbols such as the swastika (*Hakenkreuz,* q.v.) and elaborate rituals. Its motto was *"Gedenke, dass Du ein Deutscher bist. Halte dein Blut rein!"* ("Remember that you are a German. Keep your blood pure!"). Thule agents infiltrated the armed formations of the Communist regime in Munich and stored caches of arms and munitions to help destroy it. Members of the society decided to kill Kurt Eisner, leader of the Bavarian Communist revolution, but they were beaten to the deed by Anton Graf Arco-Valley, a young officer of Jewish descent who had been rejected for membership by the Thulists. Arco-Valley, determined to shame his insulters by an example of courage, killed Eisner in February 1919.

Members of the Thule Society approached Anton Drexler (q.v.), who worked in the Munich railroad yards, to serve as a liaison to the working class. Drexler founded the Deutsche Arbeiterpartei (q.v.), the German Workers' party, which eventually became the NSDAP. Many Thulists joined the German Workers' party and, eventually, the Nazi party.

THYSSEN, FRITZ (1873–1951). Heir to the Thyssen fortune and early supporter of Hitler and National Socialism. Son of the industrialist August Thyssen, who became enormously wealthy during the era of Emperor William II, Fritz Thyssen was born on November 9, 1873, in Mülheim an der Ruhr. A firm nationalist, he was angered by French occupation of the Ruhr in 1923 and gave large sums to such anti-French patriots as Albert Leo Schlageter (q.v.). He himself was arrested and faced a French military court. Thyssen had little use for the Weimar Republic (q.v.): "In Germany democracy represents nothing." In 1923 he was attracted to a budding politician, Adolf Hitler, who convinced him that he would smash communism in the streets. For the next decade Thyssen contributed more than 1 million marks to the National Socialist party. Later he reported that Hitler had given him the impression that he would work to clear the way for a restoration of the Hohenzollern dynasty.

In 1928 Thyssen was the founder, along with his father, and the chief shareholder of the powerful cartel Vereinigte Stahlwerke (United Steel Works). That year he became *Vorsitzender der International Rohstahlgenossenschaft* (chairman of the International Steel Society). He joined the Nationalsozialistische Deutsche Arbeiterpartei (q.v.) in 1931. Thyssen invited Hitler to speak before a meeting of Düsseldorf industrialists on January 27, 1932. The Nazi Fuehrer spoke for more than two and one-half hours and

Fritz Thyssen. [Life, *April 29, 1940*]

helped to solidify his party's finances (*see* DÜSSELDORF SPEECH). In the presidential elections of 1932 Thyssen voted for Hitler: "I am firmly convinced that he is the only man who can and will rescue Germany from ruin and disgrace." After Hitler became Chancellor in 1933, Thyssen was chosen to direct an institute of studies devoted to research on the corporate state. The Nazi hierarchy regarded him as a leading economic expert.

By 1935 Thyssen began having doubts about the Nazi movement. In 1938 he resigned from the Prussian Staatsrat (Council of State) in protest against Nazi persecution of Jews. Although his business interests were helped by the pace of German rearmament, he was alienated by the leaders of the Nazi hierarchy. He denounced Dr. Robert Ley (q.v.), head of the German Labor Front (Deutsche Arbeitsfront, q.v.), as "a stammering drunkard." In 1939 he protested in a Reichstag (q.v.) speech against the coming of war. On December 28, 1939, after leaving Germany for Switzerland, he sent a long letter to Hitler that contained the following passages:

> My conscience is clear. I feel free of any guilt. My sole error was that I believed in you, Adolf Hitler, the Fuehrer, and in the movement you led. I believed with all the ardor of one passionately German. Since 1923 I have made the heaviest sacrifices for the National Socialist movement. I solicited membership for the Party and fought for it, without ever wishing or asking anything for myself. I was always inspired by the hope that our endeavors would rescue our unfortunate German people. When the National Socialist Party came into power, the initial developments seemed to justify my belief, at least as long as Mr. von Papen was still Vice Chancellor. The same Mr. von Papen to whom you owed your appointment to the Chancellorship of the Reich, by its President, General von Hindenburg. The same Mr. von Papen, in front of whom you took a solemn oath in a sacred place—the Church of the Garrison of Potsdam—to uphold the Constitution. Don't forget that your rise was not the result of some great revolutionary action, but was due to the country's liberal constitution, to which you are bound by your oath.
>
> In the course of time, however, a disastrous change took place. At an early stage already I felt it necessary to voice my protest against the persecution of Christianity, against the brutalization of its priests, against the desecration of its churches.
>
> When on Nov. 9, 1938, the Jews were robbed and tortured in the most cowardly and most brutal man-

ner, and their synagogues destroyed all over Germany, I protested once more. As an outward expression of my repugnance, I resigned my position of State Councilor. All my protests obtained no reply and no remedy. . . .

Now you have concluded a pact with Communism. Your Propaganda Ministry even dares to state that the good Germans who voted for you, the professed opponent of Communism, are, in essence, identical with those beastly anarchists who have plunged Russia into tragedy, and who were described by you yourself as "bloodstained common criminals" *(Mein Kampf, p. 750)*. . . . Stop the useless bloodshed and Germany will obtain peace with honor, and will thus preserve her unity.

I have been pressed for an explanation of the reasons that prompted me to leave Germany. I have not spoken as yet. All the documents out of a struggle of more than 15 years are kept secret. I do not intend, at a time when my Fatherland is struggling so hard, to furnish the enemy with moral weapons. I am, and always shall be, German with all my heart, with all my thoughts and endeavors. I profess proudly and loudly my German nationality and shall continue to do so to my last breath. Because I am German, I neither desire nor do I have the right to speak at this moment of deepest national distress. Some day this will become necessary and justifiable for the sake of truth. Listen to me and you will hear the voice of the tormented German nation that is crying out to you: "Turn back, let freedom, right and humaneness rise again in the German Reich."

I shall keep silent. I shall wait to see what you are going to do. I demand that this letter shall not be kept from the German people. I am waiting. Should the German nation, however, be prevented from hearing my words, which are the words of a free and upright German, then I shall call upon the conscience of the world, and shall let the world pass judgment. I am waiting.

Heil Germany!
FRITZ THYSSEN

Thyssen never received an acknowledgment of his letter to the Fuehrer. Instead, five weeks later the German newspapers announced his denationalization and the confiscation of his property. He was arrested in France and with his wife was kept in concentration camps (q.v.) until 1945. He died in Buenos Aires on February 8, 1951. His wife, Amalie, and his daughter, Countess Anita Zichy-Thyssen, live in Argentina as heirs of the Thyssen fortune.

Bibliography. Fritz Thyssen, *I Paid Hitler*, Farrar & Rinehart, Inc., New York, 1941.

TILLICH, PAUL [JOHANNES] (1886–1965). Theologian and prominent refugee from Nazism. Paul Tillich was born in Starzeddel, Guben District, on August 20, 1886, the son of a Lutheran minister. After study at the Universities of Berlin, Tübingen, Halle, and Dresden, he became a lecturer on theology at Berlin (1919–1924), professor of theology at Marburg (1924–1925), professor of the philosophy of religion at Dresden and Leipzig, and professor and *Dekan* (dean) at Frankfurt am Main. In Berlin he was a cofounder of a movement known as religious socialism. An ordained minister of the Evangelical Lutheran Church, Tillich projected a theological system based on the "Protestant principle," according to which every Yes had to have a corresponding No. He saw no human truth as ultimate. In his system he incorporated depth psychology, which he regarded as essential for the elaboration of Christian doctrine. In 1933 he was dismissed from the University of Frankfurt am Main for opposing Nazi regulations. He then went to New York at the invitation of Reinhold Niebuhr and served as professor of philosophy at the Union Theological Seminary. In 1955 he became a university professor at Harvard. From 1956 to 1958 he held posts at Berlin and Hamburg, and from 1962 on at the University of Chicago. Tillich died in Chicago on October 22, 1965.

Bibliography. Rollo May, *Paulus: A Personal Portrait of Paul Tillich*, Harper & Row, Publishers, Incorporated, New York, 1973; Hannah Tillich, *From Time to Time*, Stein and Day Incorporated, New York, 1973.

TIME OF STRUGGLE. *See* KAMPFZEIT.

"TODAY GERMANY! TOMORROW THE WORLD!" *See* "HEUTE DEUTSCHLAND! MORGEN DIE WELT!"

TODT, FRITZ (1891–1942). Reich Minister for Armament and Munitions. Fritz Todt was born in Pforzheim, Baden, on September 4, 1891, the son of the owner of a jewelry factory. After attending the humanist *Gymnasium* (high school) in his birthplace, he studied at a *Technische Hochschule* (college of technology) in Munich (1911–1914) and in Karlsruhe (1918–1920). During World War I, from 1914 to 1916, he served on the western front. He was a flying observer from 1916 to 1918 and was wounded in an air battle. After the war he worked as a construction engineer. Todt joined the Nationalsozialistische Deutsche Arbeiterpartei (q.v.), the Nazi party, in 1923. In 1931 he was made an *SS-Standartenfuehrer* (colonel) on the staff of Heinrich Himmler (q.v.). Named leader of the Organisation Todt (q.v.) in 1933, he was assigned to important construction work, including military fortifications and superhighways (*see* REICHSAUTOBAHN). At the same time he was designated a leader of the Four-Year Plan (q.v.). In 1938 he was given the task of building the fortifications of the West Wall (q.v.). From 1940 to 1942 he served as Reich Minister for Armament and Munitions. Todt died on

Fritz Todt. *[Imperial War Museum, London]*

February 8, 1942, in an airplane accident at Rastenburg, the Fuehrer's headquarters on the eastern front. He was succeeded by Albert Speer (q.v.), Hitler's favorite architect, as Reich Minister for Armaments and Munitions.

TODT ORGANIZATION. *See* ORGANISATION TODT.

TOLLER, ERNST (1893–1939). German poet and playwright. Ernst Toller was born in Samotschin, Posen (now Szamocin, Poland), on December 1, 1893, the son of a Jewish merchant. He volunteered for service in World War I but later in the conflict helped to organize strikes to stop the war. He took part in the revolution in Bavaria after the war and was elected President of the Bavarian Soviet Republic. After the suppression of the revolution he was imprisoned for five years. Many of his best-known works were written while he was in prison. His plays, marked by deep indignation at injustice, are concerned primarily with the destiny of working people in an industrial civilization as well as with the horrors of war. He made liberal use of expressionistic techniques in his stagecraft. Among his dramatic works are *Masse Mensch*, 1920 *(Masses and Man)*; *Die Maschinenstürmer*, 1922 *(The Machine Wreckers)*; *Nie wieder Friede!*, 1936 *(No More Peace!)*; and *Pastor Hall* (1939). After Hitler came to power in 1933, Toller's books were burned, and he was deprived of German citizenship. He emigrated to the United States and became active in the antifascist movement. In despair apparently because of conditions in his homeland, he committed suicide in New York on May 22, 1939.

Ernst Toller. [*Picture Collection, The Branch Libraries. The New York Public Library*]

TORGAU. A town on the Elbe River about 75 miles south of Berlin. Here, on April 25, 1945, Allied and Soviet armies were joined. Patrols of the 69th Division of the United States V Corps greeted elements of the Soviet 58th Guards Division, commanded by Marshal Ivan S. Konev. The next day, while columns of German troops moved westward to escape Russian vengeance, Americans and Russians staged riotous celebrations. "It was like the finale of a circus," said one eyewitness. "The men saluted one another regardless of rank, drank toasts in liberated German champagne, whooped, yelled, and slapped backs in mutual joy." Moscow hailed the Torgau meeting with twenty-four salvos from 324 guns, while happy crowds celebrated in Times Square in New York.

TORGLER, ERNST (1893–). Communist politician and defendant at the Reichstag Fire Trial (q.v.). Ernst Torgler was born in Berlin on April 15, 1893. His father was a laborer in the gasworks, and his mother was a member of the Social Democratic party and a friend of August Bebel. As a young man he was taught the principles of socialism. Twenty-one years old at the outbreak of World War I, he enlisted in the Army and served throughout the conflict. During his Army service he transferred his allegiance from the Social Democratic party to the Independent Social Democrats. In 1920 he adhered to the majority decision of the latter to join the Communists. Entering the Reichstag (q.v.) in 1924 as a representative of the Communist party, he held his seat until the party was outlawed in 1933. A formidable debater, he was known for his biting sarcasm and his criticism of "the tyranny of fascism." His duties as chairman of the Communist parliamentary group required him to pass the greater part of his days attending sessions of the Reichstag and working in his office there. This role led to a major crisis in his life.

Torgler was arrested on February 28, 1933, and accused of complicity in setting the Reichstag fire (q.v.). For seven months he was held for preliminary investigation, during five months of which he was fettered day and night. He was one of five defendants in the three-month trial. The case against him included three main charges: (1) that he took part in the arson; (2) that he was associated with the Dutchman Marinus van der Lubbe (q.v.), two Bulgarians, Georgi M. Dimitrov (q.v.) and Blagoi Popov, and a Macedonian, Vassili Tanev; and (3) that he acted on the instructions of the German Communist party. He was easily able to establish an alibi, although Nazi witnesses testified that he had been seen with the other defendants and that he had not left the Reichstag until 8:40 or 8:45 P.M. on the night of the fire. Defense witnesses proved that he had left about 8:15 P.M., arrived at the Aschinger Restaurant at the Friedrichstrasse Station about 8:30 P.M., and eaten a three-course dinner until 9 P.M. He defended the Communist party: "I must categorically state that the fight for Socialism has been the content and meaning of my life. I have fought for the interests of the working class with all the idealism of which man is capable and I declare that I shall not cease to give of my best to the workers of Germany."

The case against Torgler was so weak that the court had to acquit him, partly as a result of the moral pressure of world opinion. At the close of the trial he was rearrested as "a prisoner of the Third Reich for his own protection against the Communists." In 1935 he was expelled from the Communist party, presumably because he had registered with the police against party orders. He joined the Social Democratic party.

TOTAL SS. *See* GESAMT-SS.

TOTENBUCH (Death Book). Official ledger used in concentration camps and extermination camps (qq.v.) to record the names of those who were executed.

TOTENBURGEN (Castles of the Dead). Monumental soldiers' memorials that Hitler planned to construct on the Atlantic coast facing west as an "eternal monument for the liberation of the Continent from British influence." The Fuehrer planned to build similar massive towers on Germany's eastern flank as symbols of the conquest by the Third Reich of "the chaotic forces of the East." None of this planned monumental masonry was completed. *See also* ARCHITECTURE IN THE THIRD REICH.

TOTENKOPFVERBÄNDE. *See* SS-TOTENKOPFVERBÄNDE.

TOTENVÖGEL (Birds of Death). Popular term for local party leaders who were charged with informing the families of soldiers that their next of kin had been killed on the battlefield. They were also charged with organizing subsequent ceremonies to honor the fallen heroes. In this way the party hoped to take the place of religion in giving solace at a difficult time. The term *Birds of Death* was employed satirically as a nickname because of the use of the German eagle on most uniforms. *See also* GOLDFASANEN.

TRANSMITTER GERMANY. *See* DEUTSCHLANDSENDER.

TREASON LAW. *See* HEIMTÜCKE GESETZ.

TREBLINKA. Extermination camp (*see* EXTERMINATION CAMPS) located at Małkinia Górna, on the Bug River in Poland. With Chełmno, Belzec, and Sobibór (qq.v.), it was one of four main Polish camps used as receiving centers primarily for Jews. Treblinka was almost exclusively a death center. At first inmates were killed by exhaust gas from internal combustion engines of captured tanks and trucks, which were often faulty. Later more efficient Zyklon-B (q.v.) gas was utilized. More than 80,000 prisoners were gassed at Treblinka in the six months preceding the spring of 1942. Mass expulsions of Jews from Warsaw began on July 22, 1942, with one train a day bringing 5,000 Jews to Treblinka. Some of the prisoners were diverted from Sobibór.

After being unloaded from trains, the prisoners were told that they were to be bathed and then classified under various signs—Tailors, Hatmakers, Carpenters, Road Workers. Instead, they were taken to the "bath houses of Treblinka," where they were sprayed with gas instead of water. The bath hoax did not always work: some prisoners suffered nervous shock, crying and laughing alternately, until they were forced into the execution rooms by irritated guards using whips. On August 2, 1943, after secreting hand grenades and rifles stolen from the camp arsenal, the prisoners rushed the guards. About 150 to 200 of the 700 inmates then in the camp got away, but they were hunted down one by one. Only about 12 survived. The knowledge of certain death at Treblinka was responsible in part for the Warsaw ghetto uprising (q.v.).

TRESCKOW, HENNING VON (1901–1944). A leading member of the Resistance (q.v.) movement. Descended from a line of Prussian soldiers, Henning von Tresckow born in Magdeburg on January 10, 1901, to a family with a military background. A gentleman farmer in Pomerania, he later turned his attention to banking and the stock market. At first he embraced National Socialism because he believed that it might help liberate his country from the chains of the Treaty of Versailles, but he was soon disillusioned and turned first to opposition, then to resistance, and finally to conspiracy. At the beginning of World War II he served with distinction in Poland and France. He was promoted to major general and then served as an assistant to Gen. Fedor von Bock (q.v.) on the Russian front. Convinced that the Russian campaign was doomed to disaster, he attempted without success to obtain Von Bock's help in eliminating the Nazi regime. He was involved in the Smolensk *attentat* (q.v.) on Hitler's life on March 13, 1943. In late 1943 Gen. Friedrich Erich von Manstein (q.v.) ruined Von Tresckow's further chances of working for the Resistance in the east by refusing to appoint him his chief of staff, with the excuse that Von Tresckow's attitude toward National Socialism was in doubt. Had he been accepted by Von Manstein, Von Tresckow undoubtedly would have had access to Hitler's headquarters and with it additional opportunities to kill the Fuehrer. Von Tresckow attempted again and again to have himself transferred to Rastenburg, but without success.

Maj. Gen. Henning von Tresckow. [*From Annedore Leber (ed.),* Conscience in Revolt, *tr. by Rosemary O'Neill, Vallentine, Mitchell & Co., Ltd., London, 1957*]

Lieut. Col. Claus Schenk Graf von Stauffenberg (q.v.), at the center of the July Plot (q.v.) of 1944, advised Von Tresckow to remain in the east until he was summoned to Berlin by the conspirators. He himself, Von Stauffenberg said, would lead the assassination attempt at Rastenburg. On July 20, 1944, Von Tresckow, together with Lieut. Fabian von Schlabrendorff, waited with Army Group

Center for news. They were told by telephone from Berlin that the plot had been successful, but soon they learned from the radio that the Fuehrer was safe. Despairing, Von Tresckow resolved on suicide. Von Schlabrendorff attempted to deter him. "They will soon find out about me," said Von Tresckow. "They will try to extract from me the names of our companions. To prevent them I shall have to take my life."

On July 21, 1944, Von Tresckow set out alone toward the front lines. Moving away from his escort, he fired his revolver into the air, apparently in an attempt to stimulate an exchange of shots. He then killed himself with a hand grenade. His final words later became well known throughout Germany:

> We have done the right thing. In a few hours I shall stand before my God, responsible for my actions and for my omissions. I believe I shall be able to say with a clear conscience that I have done my best in the struggle against Hitler. God once promised Abraham to spare Sodom should there be ten just men in the city. He will, I hope, spare Germany because of what we have done, and not destroy her. None of us can complain. Whoever joined the Resistance put on the shirt of Nessus. The worth of a man is certain only if he is prepared to sacrifice his life for what he believes.

TREUHANDER (Trustees). An organization of trustees set up in 1940 to exploit conquered Poland and to achieve its rapid assimilation into the Third Reich. From their headquarters in Berlin the *Treuhänder* confiscated peasant holdings and forcibly sent 500,000 Poles to Germany to work as agricultural laborers and 100,000 Poles into German factories. University professors, lawyers, and doctors were imprisoned. Manuals of the Polish language and literature were destroyed, and the university library in Warsaw was razed.

TREUHÄNDER DER ARBEIT (Public Trustees of Labor). Officials designated to replace workers' trade unions and employers' organizations in concluding work contracts. Instituted by a law of May 19, 1933, the *Treuhänder der Arbeit* numbered thirteen, corresponding to the thirteen economic regions of the Third Reich. They were named by the central government and were responsible to it. In practice this meant that the arbiters of last resort between employers and workers were Hitler's trusted followers.

TREVIRANUS, GOTTFRIED (1891–1971). Parliamentarian of the era of the Weimar Republic (q.v.). Gottfried Treviranus was born in Schieder, Lippe, on March 20, 1891. A naval officer in World War I, he served as a delegate to the Reichstag (q.v.) from 1924 to 1932 as a representative of the German Nationalist party. Opposed to the leadership of Alfred Hugenberg (q.v.), who was inclined to work with Hitler, Treviranus left the party in 1930 and formed his own group, the People's Conservative Union. From 1930 to 1932 he served in various minor capacities in the Cabinet of Chancellor Heinrich Bruening (q.v.). Treviranus remained a firm opponent of Hitler and the Nazis. On June 30, 1934, the day of the Blood Purge (q.v.), he escaped over a garden wall as two carloads of SS (q.v.) men drew up to his home. Later he made his way to England and then to Canada. He returned to Germany in 1948 and became active in industry.

TREVOR-ROPER, H[UGH] R[EDWALD] (1914–). English historian and authority on the history of the Third Reich. Hugh Redwald Trevor-Roper was born in Northumberland on January 15, 1914. He was educated at Charterhouse and Christ Church, Oxford, where he took first-class honors in modern history. In his academic career he rose to be Regius professor of modern history at Oxford. Although he specialized in the sixteenth and seventeenth centuries, with emphasis upon the Reformation, he was interested in the history of the Third Reich and produced several major works on it. His *The Last Days of Hitler* (Macmillan & Co., Ltd., London, 1947) is considered the definitive study of the so-called Nazi *Götterdämmerung* (q.v.), the final days in the *Fuehrerbunker* (q.v.) in Berlin. In September 1945, when many people wondered if Hitler was really dead, Trevor-Roper undertook to learn the truth about the last days of the Fuehrer. His book is a fascinating account of what happened in the bomb shelter. It describes the mounting hysteria, the wishful thinking, the blood lust, and the general air of lunacy. Trevor-Roper's *Hitler's War Directives, 1939–1945* (Sidgwick & Jackson, Ltd., London, 1964) is a notable contribution to the documentation of World War II. The superb editing places the directives in the wider context of Hitler's personality and strategy.

Trevor-Roper was involved in a classic confrontation with A. J. P. Taylor (q.v.) on the origins of World War II. In his controversial book *The Origins of the Second World War* (Atheneum Publishers, New York, 1961), Taylor asserted the systems that were attributed to Hitler were really those of Hugh Trevor-Roper, Elizabeth Wiskemann, and Alan Bullock, all specialists on the Third Reich. Trevor-Roper replied in a strong indictment of Taylor's theses, which he refuted by a detailed examination of the evidence. In Trevor-Roper's view Taylor's performance was a painful one, amounting to an apologia for Hitler, that was based upon a questionable interpretation of the facts.

TRIUMPH DES WILLENS (Triumph of the Will). An extraordinary film celebrating Hitler's leadership of the German people as revealed at the annual National Socialist party congress held in Nuremberg in September 1934. Directed and produced by Leni Riefenstahl (q.v.) under Hitler's sponsorship, it appeared in 1936 and immediately won recognition in Germany and throughout the world as a masterpiece of film technique. After the premiere at the UFA-Palast cinema in Berlin, the film received a National State Prize, a gold medal at the Venice Film Festival, and a Grand Prix of the French government at the Paris Film Festival.

In her book about the making of the film, *Hinter der Kulissen des Reichsparteitag,* 1935 *(Behind the Scenes of the Reich Party Congress),* Leni Riefenstahl claimed that the careful preparations of the party congress took into account her plans for making the film. She assembled thirty cameramen and a large staff of technical workers. Tracks were constructed for traveling shots, elevators were built to use for panoramic views, and special holes for cameras were dug in front of the speaker's platform.

Leni Riefenstahl directing *Triumph des Willens.* [*From David Stewart Hull,* Film in the Third Reich, *Simon and Schuster, New York, 1973, page 75*]

The Fuehrer was so greatly impressed with Leni Riefenstahl's work that he commissioned her for the film without checking first with Dr. Paul Joseph Goebbels (q.v.), his Propaganda Minister and jealous guardian of all cultural activities in the Third Reich. The result was that Goebbels did whatever he could to sabotage the film and placed one barrier after another in the way of its director. Despite his opposition Leni Riefenstahl produced an extraordinary film, which converted what could have been a merely boring depiction of parades and speeches into a remarkable, awe-inspiring tribute to the Fuehrer. The following is an outline of the script as condensed by Roger Manvell and Heinrich Fraenkel:[1]

> Prolonged orchestral play-in, Wagnerian style. Slow fade-up, of the German eagle, and the title, "Triumph des Willens," and the caption:
>
> "Made by order of the Führer 20 years since the outbreak of the World War, 16 years after the beginning of the German misery, 19 months after the beginning of the German Renaissance: 1934, the Party Congress."
>
> The Führer approaches through the clouds, his plane weaving through the white masses. The music is soft and romantic, the effect godlike. Nuremberg appears below. The Horst Wessel Nazi anthem starts. The shadow of Hitler's plane passes up a long line of marching men in the street below. Shot by shot, we descend nearer to the streets and the city full of marching columns.
>
> The airport. The plane taxis in. The welcoming crowds crane forward, their arms a sea of Nazi salutes. The Leader emerges. The crowd surges with enthusiasm. Goebbels in a raincoat follows the Führer grinning with pleasure.
>
> The drive into Nuremberg. The camera is behind Hitler in the car, angled up, concentrating on his arm extended in salute. The crowds are lining the streets and saluting him. Montage of Hitler's arm and the crowds as the car drives along the endless streets thronged with people. The music builds, reflecting the emotion of welcome. Hitler's car stops for a mother and her little girl to present flowers to the Führer. During the journey there are frequent shots of people in the crowds, people at the windows above, even a cat on a beflagged balcony.
>
> Nuremberg, its Gothic roofs, its medieval fountains, its Nazi flags. Hitler's face is now stiff and set, now as near smiling as he can be. Soldiers are shown with handsome faces turned sideways to the sun. Lines of jackboots. "Sieg Heil," the crowds shout. Hitler arrives, and stands out on the balcony above the crowds, smiling.
>
> The first night of the Rally. Torches; martial music; bonfires. Pictorial effects with streams of smoke lit by floodlights. Silhouettes of helmeted heads. The transparent veils of the flags and banners lit from behind in the night.
>
> Dawn over the roofs of Nuremberg. The great Rally camp for youth. Slow "dawn" music accompanies the rousing of the sleepers. Camp scenes. Food. Wrestling matches. The laughing boys. Procession of men and girls in folk costume, parading in the streets of Nuremberg. A little girl gnaws an apple. Cut from the little girl to Hitler, the father of his people. He shakes hands with chosen young delegates in their folk costumes. Close-ups reveal Hitler's searching interest in what is going on. He talks to the representatives of the youth movement. A little boy presses his fingers in his mouth as he watches the Führer.
>
> The Congress Hall filled with a vast perspective of people. Light floods onto their heads; onto the sym-

[1]From *The German Cinema* by Roger Manvell and Heinrich Fraenkel, published in 1971 by Praeger Publishers, Inc., New York. Reprinted by permission.

bolic eagles. Hess speaks: "We think of the dead. We greet our foreign guests. We see the revival of the Wehrmacht under the Führer. The greatness of the future; only then will the Führer be appreciated as he should be. The Führer is Germany; when he judges, the nation judges [reference to Roehm purge]. Germany is home for all Germans from all over the world."

Wagnerian music. The leaders come forward to pay their tributes to Hitler. Rosenberg is sweating. Dietrich—"we want the truth to be presented about the German people." Streicher wants to see racial purity. Goebbels: "The flame of our enthusiasm gives life and warmth; it comes from the deep-down roots of our people. It is good to have guns and bayonets, but better to have the hearts of the nation." Hitler is acclaimed.

Hitler addresses the Labour Force, who stand marshalled in ranks with their spades. The ceremony is staged like a religious service, the men chanting in unison. "We stand here. We are ready." A roll is called of the Districts represented. The chanting is resumed. "Ein Volk. Ein Reich. Ein Führer. We plant trees. We build streets. We give the farmers new acres. For Germany." To slow music, the flags are ceremonially lowered. The spades are held in line beneath the great skeleton of the German Eagle mounted over the Nuremberg Stadium. Hitler watches with grimly benevolent concentration. Then he addresses them. "Earth and labour unite us all. The entire nation goes through your school. Germany is happy to see her sons marching."

Night again. The torches flare behind silhouetted figures. Lutze (the successor to Roehm as head of the S.A.) addresses the Storm Troops. Fireworks and bonfires. Singing in the night.

Daylight. The parade of the Hitler Youth. Drum and fife music. Boys not on parade strain on tip-toe to see the Führer. Arrival of Hitler and Schirach, the Youth Leader. Goebbels is there, in uniform. Schirach speaks: "This hour makes us proud and happy. We know no differences of class." He turns to Hitler: "Loyalty. We'll be loyal to you for ever and ever." Hitler comes forward to address the youth, whose patterned ranks make wonderful shots to cut in with the Führer while he speaks. "You are only part of the millions who are not here. You must educate yourself to obedience. [The boys' faces are seen in a sunlit soft focus.] Be peaceloving and brave. Don't be effeminate. Be hard and tough. Live austerely. We will die, but you are the future. The flag we have raised from nothing we shall hand on to you, flesh of our flesh. Follow us everywhere. Before us, around us, behind us is Germany." Drum beats are synchronized with the applause, the drums seen in close-up. Hitler drives away through the ranks of cheering youth.

There are massed bands and singing.

A military display. (The Army being in its infancy, it is not very impressive.)

Massed flags in silhouette at night. Long procession in floodlight. A great spectacular assembly before Hitler, who stands on a flood-lit dais in the Stadium. The German eagle is floodlit. Hitler speaks: "All are here because their hearts are loyal. No one can understand us who has not suffered as we have suffered. The State does not order us, but we the State. The State has not created us but we the State. The movement exists like a rock. So long as any one of us can breathe, our movement will never be destroyed." The pictorial effect of the massed ranks is like some spectacular shot in an epic film of classical Rome. There are close-ups of Hitler on his floodlit dais. He says: "We will never give up what we have built with so much sacrifice." The applause is accompanied by synchronized drumrolls. The figure of Hitler orating is seen through the serried lines of men. Every hour, he says, we think of nothing but the German Reich. It is an impressive scene in the smoking light of the torches and the searchlights. Hitler gives the salute, bringing his fist right back to his chest.

The German eagle leads into a great perspective shot of the three minute figures (Hitler, Himmler, Lutze) marching up the wide space between the assembled ranks in the Stadium. It is daytime again, and the music is slow and solemn; it is a salute to the fallen. The three figures pay their tribute, turn and march back again.

Next, a procession with the eagled banners with the swastika, like tall Roman emblems. A mass movement of banners and flags. Lutze addresses the Führer before this assembly of the Storm Troops: "We know nothing but the need to execute the orders of the Führer." Hitler stands, a lone figure on the rostrum, silhouetted against the sky. He says: "We have thrown away what turned out to be bad. Now the Storm Troops are as good as ever they have been. Whoever sins against the spirit of my Storm Troops will be punished. [All this a direct reference to the Roehm purge.] Only a madman would think that we will dissolve what we have built. We live only for Germany. You [the Storm Troops] are still the most loyal hands in Germany." There follows the ceremony of the blood flag, the official flag stained with the blood of the Nazi martyrs. When new flags are presented to the Storm Troops, Hitler touches these new flags with the old in a kind of baptism. Guns are fired as he presents each new flag to the Storm Troopers. He stares at them, his face set and grim. There is solemn music, with Nazi banners on the screen.

There follows a march-past of the assembled rally. Hitler stands on a dais in the street. The leaders, including Goering, also march; as they pass they leave the procession and stand beneath Hitler. The army passes along the streets and over the picturesque bridges of Nuremberg. Crowds line the route, and offer the camera innumerable portrait shots. Hitler stands saluting, seen from below.

The final assembly in the Congress Hall. The floodlights; the eagle banners. Hitler makes his biggest speech from a script, his face sweating, his arms gesticulating. He is evidently roused, excited, almost laughing to himself now and then with sheer pleasure in his power to stir so much applause and enthusiasm. His eyelids flicker with excitement as he pauses for the roar of appreciation. He cannot suppress the triumphant laughter his face reveals in close shot. He is much more volatile than in any previous speech when he had no script. He says that all the best racial Germans have joined the movement. Now he is here for ever. He is determined to keep the leadership and never let it go. "More is required of you," he says, "than from others. I not only believe, I fight. Only the best shall become members of the Party." (At moments there seems to be a touch of contempt in his expression.) "We must purge whatever is bad," he continues. "The Reich is to last now for a thousand years." (He gives a triumphant stare, and his lips stir with a proud laugh.) "The youth is ours," he shouts. (He breathes heavily, sweating in the floodlight, and clasps his arms to his chest.) "The highest aim of nationalism is strength and toughness. We carry on our shoulders the State and the People."

"Sieg Heil!" shouts the audience. Hitler ends by referring to the glorious tradition of the Army and the movement. He retires to his place amid thunderous applause; Hess comes forward, waiting for the applause to stop. Eventually he shouts, "The Party is Hitler. Hitler is Germany." The Horst Wessel anthem starts again. The swastikas fade up on the screen and blend in a dissolve into the marching men behind them.
See also NUREMBERG RALLIES.

TROOP TASK FORCE. *See* EINSATZTRUPP.

TROOST, PAUL LUDWIG (1878–1934). Hitler's favorite architect. Paul Ludwig Troost was born in Wuppertal-Eberfeld on August 17, 1878. A tall, thin Westphalian with a closely shaved head, he won a reputation when he designed the fittings of the German passenger liner *Europa*. His architectural style combined a kind of spartan traditionalism with a lean approach, almost devoid of ornamentation and leaning to classical forms. In 1930 Hitler commissioned Troost to rebuild the Barlow Palace in Munich for a complex of buildings to house the new party headquarters (*see* BRAUNES HAUS). Hitler was delighted with Troost's work and from that time on considered him to be Germany's finest architect. The Fuehrer believed that Troost could do no wrong and often visited the architect at his studio to observe his latest work. Troost planned many structures, including the Haus der Deutschen Kunst (House of German Art, q.v.) in Munich. Any architect who dared criticize Troost's work was immediately declared ineligible for work on any public project. Troost died in Munich on March 21, 1934. He was succeeded as Hitler's favorite architect by Albert Speer (q.v.).

Adam von Trott zu Solz in the People's Court. [*From Annedore Leber (ed.),* Conscience in Revolt, *tr. by Rosemary O'Neill, Vallentine, Mitchell & Co., Ltd., London, 1957*]

TROTT ZU SOLZ, ADAM VON (1909–1944). Official in the Foreign Office and one of the more important figures in the conspiracy against Hitler. The son of a former Prussian minister of education, Adam von Trott zu Solz had an American grandmother, Anna Jay von Schweinitz, who was the great-granddaughter of Chief Justice John Jay. He took his *Abitur* from the Gymnasium in Hannoversch-Münden near Kassel, having attended school earlier in Kassel and at the French *Gymnasium* in Berlin. In 1929 he went to Mansfield College, Oxford, as a Rhodes scholar. He returned to Germany in 1933 as an intern undergoing practical legal training.

From the beginning Von Trott zu Solz opposed the Nazi regime. He was a member of the small Kreisau Circle (q.v.), which hoped to overthrow the Nazis and restore Germany to the social ethic of Christianity. In 1935 he published a new edition of the works of Heinrich von Kleist, accompanied by a commentary that related the poet's attack on Napoleonic tyranny to contemporary events. Von Kleist, he wrote, had become a rebel "because the divine destiny of man has been trampled into the dust" and Von Kleist had set his hopes on "the sense of decency of the individual citizen."

In 1937–1938 Von Trott zu Solz was in China under the auspices of the Rhodes Trust on a postponed third year of his original Rhodes Scholarship. At the outbreak of World War II he was brought into the German Office after the intercession of friends. At this time he decided to enter the inner circle of the conspiracy against Hitler.

Von Trott zu Solz went to Washington in October 1939 as a member of the International Secretariat of the Institute of Pacific Relations to participate in a conference at Virginia Beach. One of his goals was to establish political contacts for the German Resistance. In 1939 he went on a similar mission to London. The idealistic young German was unsuccessful in obtaining either American or British support. After the July Plot (q.v.), he was arrested, sentenced to death, and executed on August 26, 1944.

TRUSTEES. *See* TREUHÄNDER.

TWENTY-FIVE POINTS. The original program of the Deutsche Arbeiterpartei (q.v.), the German Workers' party.

TWILIGHT OF THE GODS. *See* GÖTTERDÄMMERUNG.

TYPHOON. *See* TAIFUN.

U

U-BOATS to USCHLA

U-BOATS. Germany's undersea arm in World Wars I and II. In 1914 the British Fleet swept German commerce from the seas, bottled up the German battleships at Kiel, and began the task of eliminating German submarines. German U-boats took a grave toll of Allied shipping, nearly winning the war for Germany until the Allies began using a convoy system of grouping ships under a naval escort. Britain's superior Navy enabled it to set up a blockade, protect the British Isles, transport troops, and safeguard Allied commerce. The defeat of the U-boats contributed much to the ultimate collapse of Germany and its allies.

At the outbreak of World War II Hitler's surface fleet again was inferior to that of Britain. The Fuehrer realized that he would have to attack Britain from either below the surface of the seas or from the air. His U-boats, already at their stations in the Atlantic, would strike at once. Then Britain, with its imports curtailed, its factories closed, and its people starving, would yield to the Third Reich. It was a big task for what proved to be a modest U-boat fleet. At the beginning of the war Germany had 57 U-boats, of which only 22 were equipped for Atlantic operations. There were varied types, including Type VII, with a displacement of 600 to 1,000 tons, a surface speed of 16 to 17 knots, and a submerged speed of 8 knots; and Type IX, with a displacement of 740 tons, a surface speed of 18 knots, and a submerged speed of 7.3 to 7.7 knots. The remainder were mostly Type II, the so-called dugouts, averaging 250 tons, with a surface speed of 13 knots and a submerged speed of 6.9 knots. These were intended for coastal duty or for training rather than for operations. With this modest underseas fleet, Hitler was going to challenge the might of Allied navies and merchant marines. He gave orders also for immediate additions to the U-boat fleet.

To the Allies, Hitler's U-boat personnel were treacherous monsters of the deep who lay in wait for their prey and then without warning hurled their torpedoes at helpless victims. To Germans the submarine crews were heroic sons of the fatherland who risked their lives in dangerous battle. In the early days of World War I, U-boat captains had attempted to give warning to ships they hoped to sink. The practice was abruptly discontinued when several slow-moving U-boats were rammed by their intended victims. The new practice was to hit hard without warning and run.

Life aboard a submarine was difficult and dangerous. The crews were subjected to psychological tensions. The complement, averaging forty-six men, had to sleep in shifts. For months they were lodged in close quarters because every inch of space was needed for machinery, supplies, and torpedoes. The air was heavy with odors from bilges, diesel oil, and unwashed bodies. The craft rolled and pitched and heeled over in heavy seas. The men faced sudden death from depth charges, aerial bombing attacks, or the sharp bow of a swift destroyer.

The architect of Hitler's U-boat campaign was Adm. Karl Doenitz (q.v.). In 1935 Grand Adm. Erich Raeder (q.v.) chose Doenitz, who had commanded a submarine in the closing days of World War I and served months of confinement in British prison camps, to command the new U-boat arm of the rebuilt German Navy. Given a free hand, Doenitz performed his work with enthusiasm. There had been no German submarines for fifteen years, and only a handful of submariners remained. Doenitz was able to devise and exploit his own theories.

The opening attacks were deadly. At least a dozen British ships were sent to the bottom of the Atlantic during the first week of the war. At least 67 Allied ships were sunk during the first two months. This was an impressive performance, but the Germans paid for it with a loss of 20 of their original 57 U-boats.

In response to the U-boat menace the Allies adopted the convoy system that had been successful in the late days of World War I. A large group of merchant ships would sail together. Near the shore they were guarded by aircraft, and in the open sea by escorts of destroyers and heavier warships. The convoy was circled constantly by a destroyer screen. As soon as a U-boat was sighted or detected by new scientific devices, the ships in the convoy scattered while the destroyers went to the attack. The ships then met again at a prearranged rendezvous. Once again the convoy system was proving to be an effective response to the submarine.

In June 1941 Doenitz devised a new plan to counter the convoy system. He believed that he could achieve only minimal results unless his U-boats operated in groups. He therefore organized a system of wolf packs, by which the U-boats could roam in a wide concave curve that the enemy could penetrate. The first U-boat captain to make a sighting would then fall back, maintain contact, and communicate the position of the victim to others in the formation. These submarines would close in on the prey from the flanks and from behind as if they formed the jaws of a huge trap. To facilitate the work of the wolf packs, special fleet supply ships were maintained at sea for refueling and repairs. In this way the U-boats could keep a convoy under attack for days and nights. Contributing to the success of the pack system was the existence of submarine pens along the coast from Schleswig-Holstein to Spain, which had been built after the fall of France in 1940.

Meanwhile, the construction of new U-boats continued at a record-breaking pace. During the first six months of 1942 Hitler raised his U-boat strength to 101, of which an average of 19 were always on station and waiting for prey. In these six months the German submarines sank 503 ships, aggregating more than 3 million tons. In early 1943 the wolf packs sank 90 ships in 20 days.

Then suddenly, between March and June 1943, an extraordinary change took place. The Allies began to win the war against Hitler's submarines in the Battle of the Atlantic. By this time the technique of underwater warfare had advanced far beyond that used in the opening months of the war. The Allies pitted thousands of ships, hundreds of thousands of sailors, and billions of dollars in the campaign against the undersea craft. As early as December 1943, Doenitz admitted the grave turn in events: "The enemy has rendered the U-boat war ineffective. He has achieved his object not through superior tactics or strategy but through superiority in the field of science; this finds its expression in the modern battle weapon: detection. By this means he has torn our sole offensive weapon in the war against the Anglo-Saxons from our hands."

Hitler eventually found it impossible to maintain submarine construction against his losses. He could not cope with the growing skill, the increasing numbers, and the technical superiority of the Allies on the high seas. It was the end of a skillful but unsuccessful attempt by the Fuehrer to bring the Allies to their knees by severing the ocean routes on which their lives depended. The fight had been a close call, just as in World War I. In the early months of World War II the Allies were losing up to 750,000 tons of shipping monthly, and it seemed for a time that they might be throttled by their losses at sea. But the balance eventually swung against the Third Reich. Not even the German introduction of snorkel-fitted U-boats (the snorkel allowed the submarine to breathe through a tube while batteries were being recharged) could change the situation to Germany's advantage.

The cost was great on both sides. In the six years of the war, the Germans, by their own statistics, destroyed more than 2,000 British, Allied, and neutral ships in the Atlantic and Indian Oceans and the Mediterranean Sea. This amounted to a total of 13.5 million tons of shipping. In addition, the Germans claimed 175 Allied naval vessels. However, there was a heavy toll of U-boats. Hitler had built 1,162 submarines, of which 783 were lost. Of the 41,000 men recruited into the submarine service, between 28,000 and 32,000 lost their lives, and 5,000 were taken prisoner. Doenitz himself lost his only two sons as well as a son-in-law. The British, too, paid heavily, losing a large proportion of the Royal Navy's full wartime strength of 70,000 and more than 30,000 men of the British merchant marine.

The battle for the sea-lanes was one of the most critical aspects of the war. Prime Minister Winston Churchill later admitted his real concern: "The only thing that really frightened me during the war was the U-boat peril. Our life line, even across the broad oceans, was endangered. I was even more anxious about this battle than I had been about the glorious air fight called the Battle of Britain." Still later Churchill added: "The U-boat attack was our worst evil. It would have been wise for the Germans to stake all on it."

Bibliography. David Mason, *U-Boat: The Secret Menace*, Pan/Ballantine, New York, 1972.

"U-BOATS." Name given by Austrians to the 3,000 Jews who survived World War II in Vienna by going underground and remaining hidden from the Nazis. About 200,000 Jews had lived in the Austrian capital before 1939. Most of them emigrated from Austria or were captured and deported to extermination camps (q.v.).

U-MEN. *See* UNZUVERLÄSSIGE.

UDET, ERNST (1896–1941). Air fighter, stunt flier, and racing pilot. Ernst Udet was born in Frankfurt am Main on April 26, 1896. A flying ace in World War I, he was credited with sixty-two confirmed victories, second only to the eighty attributed to Baron Manfred von Richthofen. During the era of the Third Reich he was, with Hermann Goering and Erhard Milch (qq.v.), one of the most important planners of the Luftwaffe (q.v.). In 1936 he was made chief of the Technical Office of the Air Ministry. In February 1938 he was appointed *Generalluftzeugmeister* (chief air inspector general), in charge of aircraft design, production, and inspection. Because of his experience as a fighter pilot in fast evasive tactics, he preferred to concentrate on fighter planes, such as the Messerschmitt-109, the dive-bombing Junkers-87 (Stuka), and the medium bomber Junkers-88 (qq.v.). These light planes were produced at the expense of heavy bombers, in which the Luftwaffe remained deficient throughout the war. Udet had a gift for design, but he lacked the administrative hardness necessary for his critical job.

Both Hitler and Goering held Udet responsible for the unsuccessful air war on Britain. At a conference on August 1, 1940, a pilot reported to Goering that the British Spitfires which he had encountered over England were fully as good as German fighter planes. "If that is so," Goering replied, "I would have to send my *Luftzeugmeister* before the firing squad." Udet smiled and touched his neck with his hand, but he was unable to forget the slight.

When Rudolf Hess (q.v.) flew to Scotland on May 10, 1941 (*see* HESS FLIGHT), Hitler called Udet and asked if the plane Hess was using could reach Scotland safely. Udet replied that Hess was bound to fail because of the prevailing trade winds and would probably fly past England into empty space. Hitler never forgave Udet for his advice. When it became obvious that the Luftwaffe could no longer help Hitler in his disastrous Russian campaign, Udet, anguished and depressed, shot himself on November 17, 1941.

ULBRICHT, WALTHER (1893–1973). Communist politician and architect of the German Democratic Republic (DDR; East Germany) after World War II. Walther Ulbricht was born in Leipzig on June 30, 1893, the son of a tailor. His anticlerical parents introduced him early to socialism, and as a young boy he distributed leaflets for the Socialist youth movement. Joining the Socialist party in 1912, he became one of its most active workers in Leipzig. At the end of World War I he joined a group that founded the German Communist party. Ulbricht then went to Soviet Russia, where he underwent a long and extensive course of training. He returned to Germany to introduce Stalin's cell system to the German Communists, and in 1928 he was elected to the Reichstag (q.v.) to represent South Westphalia. He was an active opponent of Hitler during the years of the Nazi drive for power.

In 1933, when Hitler destroyed the Communist party and sent many of its leaders to concentration camps (q.v.), Ulbricht managed to obtain false identity papers and was smuggled out of the country. In Paris he led a group of exiles called the Auslandskomitee (Foreign Committee) and there perfected a method of eliminating potential rivals in the party hierarchy. In Spain, from 1936 to 1938, he was entrusted by Moscow with the liquidation of all Communist party members suspected of disloyalty. Returning to Germany in 1945 in the uniform of a Soviet Army colonel, Ulbricht immediately began to set up the framework of a Communist administration in the Soviet zone of defeated Germany. He eliminated the Social Democrats, Christian Democrats, and all other non-Communist political parties. Soon he was the most hated and feared political leader in Eastern Europe. He was the moving force behind the creation of the German Democratic Republic in 1949.

Walther Ulbricht. [*London Daily Telegraph*]

In August 1961 the situation in East Berlin deteriorated rapidly, as the number of refugees from East to West Germany increased to 2,000 daily. Ulbricht countered by building the Berlin Wall, which with 840 miles of barriers, barbed wire, and minefields served to isolate his country from the West. The wall aroused criticism throughout the world, but it led to a dramatic improvement in the economic fortunes of East Germany.

One of the last Stalinist leaders in Eastern Europe and a stalwart friend of the Soviet Union, Ulbricht opposed a rapprochement between East and West Germany. In May 1971, pleading old age, he resigned his post as first secretary of the German Socialist Unity party in East Germany. He died in East Berlin on February 1, 1973. *The Times* of London commented editorially:

> It is difficult to mourn Herr Ulbricht as a politician because he added little or nothing to the sum of human happiness. It is difficult to mourn him as a human being because he showed so few signs of being one. He was, in fact, one of the least likable men to appear on the stage of European history. Yet in a curious way he filled very effectively the role he was chosen to play. He created a new German state in Europe, and although he did so under the control and protection of the Soviet Union he managed to give it his own very personal German stamp.
>
> He was one of the world's most remarkable survivors, combining luck with skill in backing the right man at the right time or playing off his rivals against each other. He survived the decimation of the German Communist Party by the Nazis, the Moscow purges of the 1930s, the Second World War, and even the death of his great mentor Stalin, for although he resisted de-Stalinization for as long as he could he was probably saved after the workers' uprising of 1953 by Moscow's fear of change. The Russians disliked him but felt he was the best man available to hold the fragile frontline of their empire.

UNCONDITIONAL SURRENDER. Policy announced by President Franklin D. Roosevelt and Prime Minister Winston Churchill at the Casablanca Conference in North Africa, held from January 14 to 24, 1943. On behalf of the Allies the two war leaders insisted upon the "unconditional surrender" of the Third Reich and Japan. Roosevelt explained the decision: "It means not the destruction of the populace but the destruction of a philosophy which is based on conquest and subjugation of other people." The term infuriated Hitler and the top Nazi hierarchy, who used it in an attempt to convince the Germans that they must fight to the end. Germany accepted unconditional surrender on May 7, 1945.

UNION. *See* ANSCHLUSS.

UNION OF REVOLUTIONARY NATIONAL SOCIALISTS. *See* SCHWARZE FRONT.

UNIVERSITIES IN THE THIRD REICH. For generations the German university system had been a model for higher education throughout the world. Its professors were respected, and its students functioned at a high level of competence. A *cause célèbre* that aroused German public opinion in 1837 was the dismissal of seven professors from the University of Göttingen because they had pro-

Cover of the German university guide for 1936.

tested against the abrogation of the constitution by King Ernst August, the new ruler of Hannover. The incident stimulated a tradition of academic freedom that rebelled against outside interference with the university system. At the same time, the German universities, despite their great achievements, never quite solved the problem of the interrelationship between *Geist* (spirit) and *Macht* (power). The higher institutions of learning were strongholds of nationalism. In 1915 a statement of German war aims was signed by 450 university professors. Many academicians refused to acknowledge Germany's defeat in 1918 and were either hostile or indifferent to the democratic Weimar Republic (q.v.).

With this mixed background the German university system became easy prey for Nazi *Gleichschaltung* (q.v.), or coordination. Hitler distrusted professors and regarded the universities as dangerous obstacles to the kind of compliant society he wanted to build. He would replace the old humanist university with politico-racial institutions dedicated to militarism and territorial expansion. In the process he received much unsolicited support from academicians.

The purge began almost immediately after Hitler became Chancellor in 1933. Within a short time 1,200 university teachers, or about one-tenth of the teaching force, mostly Jews, liberals, and Social Democrats, were dismissed. Included among them was the Göttingen circle of quantum physicists. This was a critical loss for Germany, which had held a position of world leadership in science. The Orientalist Paul Kahle, who was discovered helping a Jewish friend sweep up her shop, suffered such harassment that he emigrated to England. The theologian Karl Barth (q.v.) was expelled, and the educationalist Eduard Spranger resigned his chair. The historian Hermann Oncken, no friend of the Weimar Republic, was relieved of his professorship when he published *L'Incorruptible*, a study of the dictatorial Robespierre. The historian Friedrich Meinecke (q.v.), though a fervent nationalist, was deprived of his post as editor of the *Historische Zeitschrift*. Others resigned their positions and emigrated from the Third Reich.

The pace of coordination was stimulated by academicians who supported the new regime. During the years of struggle for political power many professors scorned Nazism, but their attitude changed after Hitler became Chancellor. When James Frank, a Jewish Nobel Prize winner, refused a university chair in protest against official anti-Semitism (q.v.), thirty-three professors and lecturers at Göttingen condemned his gesture as an act of sabotage. The existentialist philosopher Martin Heidegger (q.v.) praised Nazi innovations: "The duty of students as well as professors is to serve the people under the triple form of labor service, military service, and scientific service." The surgeon Dr. Ferdinand Sauerbruch (q.v.) took a public stand in support of National Socialism.

The new university administration functioned under the *Fuehrerprinzip* (q.v.), the leadership principle. The traditional representative and self-governing system was scrapped in favor of dictatorship by the *Rektor*, the university chancellor. Such posts were awarded to reliable Nazis. At the University of Berlin the new *Rektor* was a Storm Trooper (*see* SA) and a veterinarian who promptly introduced eighty-six courses in his specialty as well as twenty-five new offerings in *Rassenkunde*, or "racial science" (*see* RASSENFORSCHUNG). As older professors resigned or retired, their positions were taken by young Nazis, many of whom were inexperienced and unqualified. All professors and lecturers were expected to adjust their teaching to the requirements of the regime. No one could take an academic post without first completing a six-week training course at an NS-Dozentenbund (q.v.; National Socialist Lecturers' Alliance) camp. There they were indoctrinated with National Socialist philosophy and were required to pass tests in military drill and physical training.

The new curriculum stressed the basic elements of Nazi ideology: racialism (*see* RACIAL DOCTRINE), nationalism, and Germanics. Professors and lecturers were expected to emphasize *German* physics, *German* chemistry, and *German* mathematics. Modern physics in general was denounced as an instrument of world Jewry working for the destruction of German science. The theory of relativity by Albert Einstein (q.v.) was described as a Jewish plot to achieve world rule and reduce German manhood to slavery.

German universities lost their reputation for excellence during the years of the Third Reich as a result of the "reforms" instituted by Hitler to bring the system into line with his theories of education. The decline in the qualification of teachers led to the deterioration of standards. The number of university students dropped from 127,820 in 1933 to 58,325 in 1939. The Nazi loss resulting from the purge of university professors was a gain for the free world. The denigration of intellectuals was catastrophic for Germany. By an irony of fate the atomic bomb was developed by the contributions of such exiles as Einstein and Lise Meitner (q.v.).

See also EDUCATION IN THE THIRD REICH.

Bibliography. Edward Yarnell Hartshorne, *The German Universities and National Socialism,* Harvard University Press, Cambridge, Mass., 1937.

"UNSERE EHRE HEISST TREUE" ("Our Honor Is Named Loyalty"). Motto on the belt buckles of all members of the SS (q.v.). This phrase was chosen in imitation of the *"Gott mit uns"* ("God with us") legend engraved on army buckles under Emperor William II.

UNTERMENSCHEN (Subhumans). Term used in Nazi propaganda to describe non-Germanic peoples in the occupied Soviet Union. Rigid adherence to racial doctrine (q.v.) cost the Germans the support of millions of individuals who were strongly anti-Communist and could have helped the invaders in their campaign against bolshevism.

UNTERSCHARFFUEHRER-SS. A sergeant in the SS (q.v.).

UNTERSTURMFUEHRER-SS. A 2d lieutenant in the SS (q.v.).

UNTERSUCHUNGS- UND SCHLICHTUNGS-AUSSCHÜSSE (USCHLA; Committees for Examination and Adjustment). National Socialist party courts established by Hitler in 1926 to deal with internal accusations of all kinds. In setting up his dictatorship, the Fuehrer encouraged feuds among his followers. He devised the USCHLA as a means of keeping order among the unruly hierarchy. Offenses against discipline were examined and punished, in some cases with expulsion from the party. The ultimate crime was disobedience or lack of respect for the Fuehrer. The courts were not concerned with such private offenses as dishonest business practices, immorality, gambling, or home difficulties, all of which were considered to be trivial matters when compared with party discipline. The USCHLA turned their complete attention to the necessity of maintaining the Nazi dictatorship.

UNZUVERLÄSSIGE (U-Men; Unreliables). Those members of the SD (q.v.), the security service, who were regarded as corrupt and had to be watched carefully.

"UPROOTED AND DISINHERITED." Favorite phrase used by Hitler in his early speeches to describe contemporary Germans. In a speech delivered in October 1923 he hammered at this theme: "The fate of Germany has slipped from the hands of the former ruling classes into the hands of the uprooted and disinherited. The Germans who have faith in the fatherland will go back to the battlefields and return to the place where the old German Reich was founded and where it was smashed by the slimy bandits who set their signatures to the Versailles Peace Treaty." According to Hitler, the "uprooted and disinherited" would "raise the new Germany from the bloody baptismal font."

USCHLA. *See* UNTERSUCHUNGS- UND SCHLICHTUNGS-AUSSCHÜSSE.

V

V-MEN
to
VOMI

V-MEN. *See* VERTRAUENSLEUTE.

V-1 AND V-2. *See* VERGELTUNGSWAFFEN.

VALKYRIE. Code name for two distinct operations. In Norse-Teutonic mythology Valkyrie were the beautiful and awe-inspiring maidens who were said to have hovered over the ancient battlefields choosing those who were to be killed. Hitler set up an Operation Valkyrie that designated the Home Army to take over the security of Berlin and other large cities in the event of a revolt by the millions of imported foreign workers. With most able-bodied men away at the frontlines, the suspicious Hitler feared a revolt on the home front.

There was a second meaning for Valkyrie. The conspirators of the July Plot (q.v.) of 1944 appropriated the name Valkyrie as a perfect cover because it enabled them openly to draw up plans for the Home Army and take over the large industrial centers. For them the Valkyrie maidens provided a code name for the intended assassination of Hitler.

VANSITTART, ROBERT GILBERT (1st Baron Vansittart of Denham) (1881–1957). English diplomat and critic of National Socialism and the Third Reich. Robert Gilbert Vansittart was born in Farnham on June 25, 1881, the eldest son of R. A. Vansittart. His mother was the only daughter of an American general, William C. Heppenheimer. After studying at Eton, he entered the diplomatic service in 1902 as an attaché. He served in Cairo (1909), Stockholm (1915), and Paris (1919). From 1920 to 1924 he was secretary to Earl Curzon, the Secretary of State for Foreign Affairs. From 1930 to 1938 he was Permanent Undersecretary of State for Foreign Affairs, and from 1938 to 1941 Chief Diplomatic Adviser to the Foreign Secretary.

As Great Britain's ranking diplomat during the era of the Third Reich, Vansittart developed an antipathy to Hitler and Nazism so strong that the term *Vansittartism* was used to describe it. In May 1935 he was assigned the task of welcoming Joachim von Ribbentrop (q.v.), head of the Dienststelle Ribbentrop (q.v.; the special Nazi bureau established as a rival to the German Foreign Office), whom he later described as "a ponderous lightweight." In 1936 he visited the Olympic Games in Berlin (*see* OLYMPIAD XI), met Hitler, and informed him through the interpreter Dr. Paul Schmidt (q.v.) that "the next war will be a war not of nations, but of ideologies." In London in 1937 Vansittart greeted the temporarily retired Gen. Ewald von Kleist (q.v.), who urged a firm declaration by Britain that it would oppose any aggression by Hitler. On May 12, 1938, Vansittart received Konrad Henlein (q.v.), leader of the Sudeten Germans in Czechoslovakia, who denied that he was influenced in any way by Berlin.

In *To the Bitter End* (Houghton Mifflin Company, Boston, 1947), Hans Bernd Gisevius (q.v.), a member of the Resistance (q.v.) movement, complained that Vansittart did not take seriously the tips passed on to him by anti-Hitler Germans: "Instead this permanent Under Secretary of the British Foreign Office felt it incumbent to soothe the alarmists. The British knew what was going on, he assured us; they would anticipate it and conclude an agreement with Russia in good time. . . . But Sir Robert Vansittart was bluffing. Unfortunately, he was not bluffing Hitler. He was deceiving the German Opposition." Vansittart died in Denham on February 14, 1957.

VB. *See* VÖLKISCHER BEOBACHTER.

VENLO INCIDENT. A clash between German and British military intelligence units at the beginning of World War II. The contest was won by the Germans. In early September 1939, British intelligence agents at The Hague received word from a German refugee in the Netherlands that German officers representing a military conspiracy against the Nazi regime wanted to make contact with British authorities. London assigned Capt. S. Payne Best and Maj. R. H. Stevens to meet the Germans. After complicated secret maneuvers, the British agents met three German officers, including a Major Schaemel. The latter told them that high officers in Germany were appalled by the losses suffered in Poland, that they wanted peace, and that they were prepared to take Hitler into custody and open peace negotiations.

On November 8, 1939, Best and Stevens arrived at the little frontier town of Venlo, where they were supposed to meet a German general high in the ranks of the conspiracy. Instead, they were kidnapped by a detachment of armed Germans from across the frontier and brought to Berlin. There they found to their dismay that "Major Schaemel" was Maj. Walter Schellenberg (q.v.), chief of the counterespionage division of the Gestapo (q.v.). For his coup Schellenberg was decorated by Hitler and promoted to SS major general in charge of all intelligence operations at home and abroad.

For Hitler the Venlo incident was important because he could claim that Dutchmen were involved and that the Netherlands had violated neutrality; this gave the Fuehrer an excuse for invading the Netherlands. Captain Best and Major Stevens remained prisoners of the Germans until the end of the war, when they were liberated by American troops.

Bibliography. S. Payne Best, *The Venlo Incident*, Hutchinson & Co. (Publishers), Ltd., London, 1950.

VERFALLSKUNST (Degenerate Art). A name for the art forms opposed by Hitler and the Nazis. *See also* ENTARTETE KUNST.

VERFÜGUNGSTRUPPE (Militarized Troops). Formations of the SS (q.v.). At the outbreak of World War II in 1939 they were absorbed by the Waffen-SS (q.v.).

VERGELTUNGSWAFFEN (Reprisal Weapons). The secret *Wunderwaffen* (wonder weapons) used by Hitler in the closing days of World War II. The Fuehrer was told that these weapons would be the means of assuring victory. Both the V-1 and the V-2 were developed at Peenemünde (q.v.). On June 12, 1944, D Day plus 6, the first V-1 was launched from a base along the French coast in the Pas-de-Calais area. It descended upon a startled London. The V-1 was a small pilotless jet-propelled plane that moved at a speed of 400 miles per hour on a predetermined course. It carried a ton of explosives that detonated on contact. Because of its peculiar sound Londoners dubbed it the buzz bomb. From June 12 to 20, 1944, more than 8,000 V-1s crashed on the British capital. Many were shot down as vulnerable prey to swift fighter planes, and others were hit by antiaircraft fire. At least 630 V-1s were exploded in the air. The cost to the British was heavy: 5,479 people killed, 40,000 injured, and 75,000 buildings destroyed.

Three months later Hitler unveiled the V-2, an even more sophisticated and deadly weapon. On September 8, 1944, the first V-2 descended on Chiswick and buried itself deep in the ground before it exploded. The V-2 was a supersonic rocket launched from bases in the Netherlands. It was 48 feet long and 5.5 feet in diameter and weighed 13 tons, including a 1-ton explosive warhead. It carried 4 tons of liquid alcohol fuel and 5 tons of liquid oxygen for combustion. The reaction engine delivered a 52,000-pound thrust equal to 600,000 horsepower. The V-2 could reach a speed of 3,500 miles per hour with a range of 225 miles and a 116-mile ceiling. Unlike its predecessor, the V-2 could not be seen, heard, or intercepted in flight. More than 1,000 V-2s fell on England; of these 600 hit London and caused about 10,000 casualties.

Both weapons were terrifying, but there were far too few of them to bring Hitler victory. Had they been used in greater numbers earlier in the war, they might well have changed the final outcome. The *Vergeltungswaffen* led eventually to the American and Soviet space programs and the development of intercontinental ballistic missiles.

A V-2 rocket being refueled. [*Imperial War Museum, London*]

VERSAILLES DIKTAT (Versailles Dictation). Popular slogan used in the Third Reich. The *Versailles Diktat* meant that the Treaty of Versailles, concluded at the end of World War I, was a deliberate Carthaginian peace designed to destroy Germany. To Hitler the treaty was "a shame and an outrage," a dictated peace. Throughout his drive for political power Hitler utilized this slogan as a core argument for national regeneration. All other German political parties during the Weimar Republic (q.v.) were opposed to the peace treaty, but the Nazis made it a special object of attack.

VERTRAUENSLEUTE (V-Men; Confidants). Members of the SD (q.v.), the security service, who were regarded as meriting the trust of their superiors.

VERTRAUENSMANN (Intelligence Agent). A spy or an informer.

VIENNESE SLAVS. *See* SCHLAWIENER.

VIRUS HOUSE. Term used to designate the German nuclear research laboratory in Berlin in World War II. German efforts to produce an atomic bomb were minuscule when compared with the activity in the United States. The pace of American research was dictated by the fear that Hitler might win the race. The theory of atomic energy was well known in Germany at the time. Otto Hahn, a German scientist, discovered atomic fission. Many able physicists chose to remain in Nazi Germany and work for the regime. In the long run, however, the loss by exile of such scientists as Albert Einstein, Max Born, and Lise Meitner (qq.v.) was critically important in the competition.

VISUAL ARTS. *See* ART IN THE THIRD REICH.

VOELKERCHAOS (Chaos of Peoples). In Nazi ideology all impure races, especially those in the Mediterranean area. *See also* RACIAL DOCTRINE.

VOELKISCH MOVEMENT. Ideological groups, unions, societies, and federations, most of which were founded after World War I and which had a strong influence on the practical political program of Hitler and the National Socialists. The closest equivalent to the term *voelkisch* is *national,* but the word denotes something more: the eagerness to cultivate the features typical of the nation and at the same time eliminate the material and spiritual influences of other peoples. There were similar nationalistic patriotic organizations in the imperial era, including the All-Deutscher Verein (Pan-German League) and the Ostmarkverein (Eastern Provinces Association), that stressed *voelkisch* ideas. By the end of World War I there were about seventy-five *voelkisch* organizations working within the Weimar Republic (q.v.) on behalf of a feverish nationalist extremism. The movement advocated race mysticism (*see* RACIAL DOCTRINE), pseudobiology, and anti-Semitism (q.v.). Its literature emphasized the idea of recasting history as a primeval battle between the blond Nordic hero and the Jew.

The *voelkisch* movement provided the historical roots and constituted the organizational as well as the ideological starting point of National Socialism. In Munich Hitler was deeply impressed by the Thule Gesellschaft (q.v.), the local group of the German Voelkisch Protection and Defense League, which included among its members Gottfried Feder and Alfred Rosenberg (qq.v.). In *Mein Kampf* (q.v.) Hitler wrote: "The basic ideas of the National Socialist movement are *voelkisch* and the *voelkisch* ideas are National Socialist." At the same time, as a political propagandist, he made certain to dissociate National Socialism from the typical *voelkisch* clubs, which he regarded as sectarian groups run by bourgeois philistines. The older *voelkisch* movement, he said, did not understand that an idea had no value as long as it was not turned into action. He himself would take a sterile and powerless idea and transform it by the use of political power. In essence this was the theme of Hitler's career.

See also TATKREIS.

"VOLK OHNE RAUM" ("People without Space"). Slogan used to describe Germany as a country without sufficient land to support its increasing population. The term was borrowed by Nazi propagandists from Hans Grimm (q.v.), who in 1926 published a highly popular book titled *Volk ohne Raum.* The Nazis used the slogan to justify aggression as a means of obtaining their share of territory on the globe. They made it plain that if other nations did not freely grant the right of Nazi Germany to seek *Lebensraum* (q.v.), or living space, they would take matters into their own hands in order to find the space to which they were entitled.

VÖLKISCHER BEOBACHTER (VB; Racial Observer). The official newspaper of the Nationalsozialistische Deutsche Arbeiterpartei (q.v.; NSDAP). Before World War I the *Münchener Beobachter (Munich Observer)* was a weekly gossip sheet devoted to scandalmongering. After 1919 its name was changed to *Völkischer Beobachter,* to represent the *voelkisch* (q.v.) views (*see* VOELKISCH MOVEMENT) of the Thule Gesellschaft (q.v.). It appeared twice a week. A typical issue on March 10, 1920, featured a front-page story headlined *"Macht Ganze Arbeit mit den Juden"* ("Clean Out the Jews Once and for All"). The text urged a "final solution" of the Jewish problem by "sweeping out the Jewish vermin with an iron broom." This idea of a Final Solution (*see* ENDLÖSUNG, DIE) was to be implemented during the Nazi regime. The article also urged the construction of concentration camps (q.v.) to house Germany's Jewish population. At first the paper was cool to Hitler and his friends because of personal quarrels, but this attitude was to change drastically.

By the end of 1920 the run-down newspaper was badly in debt. However, its point of view attracted the attention of Dietrich Eckart and Ernst Roehm (qq.v.), members of the German Workers' party (Deutsche Arbeiterpartei, q.v.). They persuaded Maj. Gen. Franz Xaver Ritter von Epp (q.v.), Roehm's commanding officer in the Reichswehr (q.v.), the regular Army, and a member of a small political group in Munich, to raise 60,000 marks in order to acquire the anti-Semitic sheet as a party newspaper. Von Epp managed to obtain the money from his wealthy friends and, probably, secret Army funds. Among the contributors were Frau Helene Bechstein, wife of a wealthy piano manufacturer, and Frau Gertrud von Seidlitz, wife of an affluent Balt. Hitler took over control of the paper in 1921, when he became head of the NSDAP.

In February 1923 Hitler, thanks to financial assistance against a mortgage from Ernst Franz Sedgwick (Putzi) Hanfstaengel (q.v.), made the *Völkischer Beobachter* a daily newspaper with a new and larger format. His chief editor was Alfred Rosenberg (q.v.), the party's unofficial philosopher, who for five years issued the newspaper almost singlehandedly. Rosenberg filled its columns with popular versions of racial doctrine (q.v.). He reproduced the *Protocols of the Elders of Zion* (q.v.) and other anti-Semitic material such as the anti-Jewish poetry of Josef Czerny. Rosenberg praised the Nordic "race" and attacked "colored subhumanity," especially the "French Negro armies." His greatest trial was the opposition of Max Amann (q.v.), treasurer of both the party and the *Völkischer Beobachter,* who had been Hitler's first sergeant in the List Regiment. Rosenberg wanted to politicize his readers by stressing the Nazi way of life, while Amann called for a sensational newspaper that would make money for the party: "I spit on Party members, business comes first." In the shabby Munich office Rosenberg worked zealously on editorials, while Amann exploited the reporters at starvation wages. Rosenberg and Amann

Süddeutsche Ausgabe / Ausgabe A

Ausgabe A / Süddeutsche Ausgabe

München, Dienstag, 27 Juni 1933

VÖLKISCHER BEOBACHTER

Kampfblatt der national-sozialistischen Bewegung Großdeutschlands

Die Aktion gegen die Bayerische Volkspartei

Die amtliche Mitteilung über die Verhaftungen der Bayerischen Volkspartei-Führer – Abrechnung des bayerischen Innenministers mit der Hinterhältigkeit der B.V.P.-Politik – Dr. Goebbels über die deutsch-französischen Beziehungen

50 Millionen Mark Marxisten-Diäten in vierzehn Jahren

Die schwarzen Saboteure in Schutzhaft

50 Millionen in 14 Jahren

Was die Marxisten an Diäten schluckten

„Wir sind die Vollstrecker des Volkswillens"

The June 27, 1933, issue of the *Völkischer Beobachter*, with the headline "The Battle against the Bavarian People's Party."

often had furious arguments that ended with each throwing scissors and inkwells at the other.

In late September 1923 the *Völkischer Beobachter* attacked Gen. Hans von Seeckt (q.v.), chief of staff of the German armed forces, as an enemy of the *voelkisch* movement and described his wife as Jewish (nee Jacobsohn). At the same time it excoriated the Weimar Republic (q.v.) as a pawn of Jewish-Masonic interests. Angered, Von Seeckt ordered Gen. Otto von Lossow, ranking army officer in Munich, to ban publication of the newspaper by force if necessary. Von Lossow consulted Gustav Ritter von Kahr (q.v.), Premier of Bavaria, who refused to carry out the order on the ground that it would endanger public security. After the Beer-Hall *Putsch* (q.v.) of November 8–9, 1923, the *Völkischer Beobachter* reported "Hitler's triumph" on its front page and priced the issue at 8 billion marks a copy, as an ironic reminder of the current inflation.

In 1924, when Hitler was in prison at Landsberg am Lech (q.v.) and the party was at a low ebb, the *Völkischer Beobachter* was banned. It reappeared on February 26, 1925, with a long editorial written by Hitler and titled "A New Beginning": "I do not consider it a task for the political leader to attempt to improve, or even fuse together, the human material ready to his hand." Hitler was commenting on party disputes between leftist and rightist groups within the Nazi movement. In August 1926 Dr. Paul Joseph Goebbels (q.v.) publicly broke with Gregor and Oto Strasser (qq.v.), leaders of the socialist wing of the party, with a ringing denunciation in the columns of the *Völkischer Beobachter:* "Only now do I recognize you for what you are: revolutionaries in speech but not in deed. We bow to the Fuehrer. We feel that he is a greater man than all of us, greater than you or I. He is the instrument of the divine will who shapes hisotory with a fresh, creative passion."

This type of fawning flattery became commonplace in the columns of the *Völkischer Beobachter*. During the Nazi drive for political power Hitler used the paper to stress his special interests. He ordered a special Army edition in which he warned of the consequences if the Communists instead of the National Socialists won political power. Goebbels also used its columns mostly for articles in which he described in the third person his own amazing achievements. In 1927 Goebbels founded his own newspaper, *Der Angriff* (*see* ANGRIFF, DER), in Berlin. The *Völkischer Beobachter* appeared in the mornings in Munich and reached Berlin within twelve hours, and *Der Angriff* came to the streets in the afternoons. *See also* ILLUSTRIERTER BEOBACHTER.

In 1932 the *Völkischer Beobachter* again ran into financial difficulties. In November and December the printer, Adolf Müller, threatened several times to cease printing the paper unless he was paid overdue bills. "The *Völkischer Beobachter* is ruining me," Müller complained, "but luckily I am doing good business printing Catholic Church notices." An anxious Hitler was rescued by Gen. Kurt von Schleicher (q.v.), who promised him that the Reichswehr would pay the huge debts of the NSDAP as well as the payroll and printer's bills of its party newspaper.

In the early days of World War II it was the task of the *Völkischer Beobachter* to report glowing victories. The paper was not distinguished for accuracy. The October 23, 1939, issue, for example, had a huge headline: "Churchill Sank the *Athenia*." When the tide turned against Hitler, the *Völkischer Beobachter* was used in a desperate attempt to maintain the morale of the German people. In the issue of May 24, 1944, Goebbels wrote an editorial in which he stated that "Germany must be made more desolate than the Sahara." In the September 7, 1944, issue, Hitler ordered an extraordinary editorial: "Not a German stalk of wheat is to feed the enemy, not a German mouth to give him information, not a German hand to give him help. He is to find every footbridge destroyed, every road blocked—nothing but death, annihilation, and hatred will meet him." The *Völkischer Beobachter* expired along with Hitler and the Third Reich in 1945.

VOLKMANN, HELMUTH (1889–1940). General of infantry and former commander of the Condor Legion (q.v.). Helmuth Volkmann was born in Diedenhofen (Thionville) on February 28, 1889. After attending the Cadet Academy, he joined the Imperial Army as a *Fahnrich* (cadet) on March 4, 1907. Commissioned on August 18, 1908, he served in World War I and was promoted to lieutenant colonel on October 1, 1932. On April 1, 1934, he was made a department chief in the Reichswehr (q.v.) Ministry. He then joined the Luftwaffe (q.v.) with the rank of colonel.

From October 6, 1936, to November 1937, Volkmann served as chief of the Luftwaffe Administration Department with the rank of major general. On November 1, 1937, he succeeded Hugo Sperrle (q.v.) as commander of the Condor Legion in Spain and held that post until October 31, 1938. From April to September 1939 he commanded the Luftwaffe War Academy with the rank of general of fliers. He was then transferred from the Luftwaffe to the Wehrmacht (q.v.), the regular Army. On August 25, 1939, he was promoted to general of infantry, and for the next year he commanded the 95th Infantry Division. He was killed in an automobile accident on August 21, 1940.

VOLKSDEUTSCHE (Ethnic Germans). Persons who were classified as Germans by race. The *Volksdeutsche* brought back to the Third Reich from various Balkan countries, whose dialects were strange to German ears, were victims of doubt as to their ethnic authenticity. *See also* RACIAL DOCTRINE.

VOLKSDEUTSCHE MITTELSTELLE (VOMI; German Racial Assistance Office). An office charged with caring for the welfare of Germans settled abroad. The assumption was that all Germans who lived in other countries were biologically linked with the pure Nordics of the Third Reich. VOMI was one of the five key divisions of the SS (q.v.). Is chief was *SS-Obergruppenfuehrer* (Gen.) Werner Lorenz. Later it was combined with the Rasse- und Siedlungshauptamt (q.v.), the Central Office for Race and Resettlement, to form the Reichskommissariat für die Festigung des Deutschen Volkstums (q.v.), the Reich Office for the Consolidation of German Nationhood.

VOLKSGEMEINSCHAFT (Racial Community). The National Socialist ideological image of a racially superior, harmonized community. *See also* RACIAL DOCTRINE.

VOLKSGENOSSEN (Racial Comrades). Term favored by Nazi orators and ideologues to describe those Germans who belonged to the community by race. A more exact translation is "fellow countrymen," but in Nazi ideology the emphasis was always on ethnic considerations. *See also* RACIAL DOCTRINE.

VOLKSGERICHT (People's Court). A dreaded court set up in Berlin to render quick verdicts for accused traitors of the Third Reich. The Volksgericht met in the plenary chamber of the Berlin Law Courts. The courtroom was decorated with three large swastika banners and busts of Frederick the Great and Hitler. Bright lights blazed for the benefit of film cameras. At a long table sat two professional judges and five others selected from among party officials, the SS (q.v.), and the armed forces. The two professional judges could outvote the others. At the center of the table sat Roland Freisler (q.v.), presiding officer of the court. From his position of power Freisler shouted abuse at the defendants, denouncing them for treason and threatening dire punishment. The sessions were held *in camera*, and there was no appeal from the verdicts.

A long series of accused, including the conspirators of the July Plot (q.v.), appeared before the People's Court. It sat almost without interruption from midsummer 1944 into 1945, pronouncing one death sentence after another. On the morning of February 3, 1945, just as the defendant Fabian von Schlabrendorff was being led into the courtroom, a bomb from a United States Army Air Forces plane fell on the building and demolished it. Among those killed was Freisler. Von Schlabrendorff managed to escape with his life and was eventually freed by the Americans.

VOLKSGRUPPE (Racial Group). Term used inside the Third Reich to describe a minority of *Volksdeutsche* (q.v.; ethnic Germans) in another country. *See also* RACIAL DOCTRINE.

VOLKSLISTE, DEUTSCHE (List of Racial Germans). A special list of Germans living in foreign countries. It was introduced by decree in defeated Poland in 1941 and was later extended to other occupied territories. The list designated persons eligible for citizenship in the Third Reich, those who were Germans by naturalization (Germans on approval), and those who held provisional citizenship (Germans on trial). *See also* RACIAL DOCTRINE.

VOLKSOFFIZIER (People's Officer). A new category of officer in the Wehrmacht (q.v.), the armed forces, after its reorganization in 1935. With the expansion of the Wehrmacht the older officers of the old Reichswehr (q.v.) were submerged by a flood of reactivated officers, reserve officers, and SA (q.v.) men. The lowering of educational and social standards was considered by Hitler and the Nazi hierarchy to be the implementation of the desired folk community. To the caste-conscious senior officers, this *Verwässerung* (dilution) of the armed forces was a source of dismay and disgust. Among older officers and even in popular parlance, these new officers with Nazi background were ridiculed with the acronym VOMAG (*Volksoffizier mit Arbeitergesicht*, or people's officer with a proletarian face).

VOLKSSCHÄDLINGE (Enemies of the People). Citizens declared to be enemies of the people during wartime. Toward the end of World War II the judicial extermination of *Volksschädlinge* was accompanied by summary action by SS (q.v.) units. In October 1944 seventeen post office employees in Vienna who were found to have taken chocolate or soap from badly wrapped Wehrmacht (q.v.) gift packages were marched to a public square and publicly executed. The legal category of *Volksschädlinge* included *Feindhörer* (q.v.), those who listened to banned enemy broadcasts.

VOLKSSTURM (People's Army). German home guard in World War II, raised as a last defense in the winter of 1944–1945. The Volkssturm consisted of all able-bodied Germans (freely interpreted) who were not in the armed forces. This local defense militia was brought into existence by a decree of Hitler on September 25, 1944. The basic unit was the battalion, which included men from sixteen to sixty years of age, mostly veterans invalided out of service or otherwise considered unfit for regular military duties. They were supposed to be used only in their own districts, but many ended up on either the western or the eastern front. *See also* WACHDIENST.

VOLKSTUM FÜR DAS DEUTSCHTUM IM AUSLAND (League for Germans Abroad). An organization formed before the Nazi era to deal with German minorities in foreign countries. It was taken over by the Nationalsozialistische Deutsche Arbeiterpartei (q.v.) and placed under the jurisdiction of the SS (q.v.).

VOLKSWAGEN (People's Car). A small, air-cooled, brilliantly designed automobile that Hitler promised would be available eventually for the masses. Known originally as the *KdF Wagen*, after the Kraft durch Freude (q.v.), the Strength through Joy organization, the Volkswagen never was used for civilian purposes in the Third Reich. It was an all-purpose vehicle employed by the armed forces in World War II. Hitler had wanted to make the automobile a status symbol for the working class, as a protest against the identification of the automobile with a bourgeois society. At the same time the Volkswagen served to help the financial liquidity of the government with weekly installment payments from prospective owners.

After the fall of the Third Reich and the rebuilding of the German economy, the Volkswagen was produced on a huge scale, not only in Germany but in subsidiary factories throughout the world. Complete assembly plants were constructed in other countries. The Volkswagen became one of the world's most popular automobiles. Some contemporary Germans speak of Hitler only as the "man who made the Volkswagen."

VOLKSWOHNUNG (People's Apartment). A dwelling favored by the Nazi administration. There had been a severe housing shortage in Germany since the end of World War I. Some new apartment houses had been constructed during the Weimar Republic (q.v.), from 1919 to 1933, but the National Socialist regime was careful to extend the average annual output of flats. However, the new *Volkswohnung* was considerably smaller than the units built in the pre-Nazi era.

VOLKWERDUNG (People Becoming Itself). Term used by Nazi speakers to describe the events of 1933 as Hitler took political power. In Nazi semantics, the word *Volk* denoted both the "people" in the democratic sense and the "folk" in the racial sense. The implication was that the new Nazi "folk community" would be a society that was no longer divided into haves and have-nots. The slogan *Volkwerdung* was used constantly to remind the German people that at long last it had instituted a superior form of society.

VOMAG. *See* VOLKSOFFIZIER.

VOMI. *See* VOLKSDEUTSCHE MITTELSTELLE.

WACHDIENST
to
WVHA

WACHDIENST (Rural Home Guard). A special unit for home protection in which mostly elderly men were enrolled. The Wachdienst should not be confused with the military Volksturm (q.v.), the People's Army. The Wachdienst was used for duty in village fire brigades as well as in search parties for insects that destroyed crops.

WACHENFELS. Hitler's house in Berchtesgaden (q.v.) in the middle 1920s.

WACHMANNSCHAFT (Guard Unit). An early SS (q.v.) concentration camp unit (*see* CONCENTRATION CAMPS). Among other such ad hoc units were the *Wachsturm* (guard company), the *Wachtruppe* (guard troops), and the *Wachverbände* (guard formations). All four units were eventually combined in the *SS-Totenkopfverbände* (q.v.), the Death's Head formations.

WAFFEN-SS (Armed SS). The military arm and the largest of the major branches of the SS (q.v.). Although Hitler regarded the Wehrmacht (q.v.), the traditional armed forces, as indispensable, he suspected the loyalty of much of its leadership. He preferred to place his trust in a special armed force trained in Nazi ideology and certain to carry out his plans with blind obedience. For this purpose he set up the Waffen-SS, a heterogeneous organization that eventually numbered thirty-nine divisions and through whose ranks nearly 1 million men of fifteen nationalities passed. Waffen-SS troops took part in a dozen major battles and became noted for their tough fighting qualities.

The standards established for the Waffen-SS were closely allied with Nazi ideology. The goal was Hitler's version of the superman of Friedrich Nietzsche (q.v.): "To judge morality properly, it must be replaced by two concepts borrowed from zoology: the *taming* of a beast and the *breeding* of a species." The SS man must be hard, unemotional, fiercely loyal: "The SS man's basic attitude must be that of a fighter for fighting's sake; he must be unquestionably obedient and become emotionally hard; he must have contempt for all 'racial inferiors' and for those who do not belong to the order; he must feel the strongest bonds of comradeship with those who do belong, particularly his fellow soldiers, and he must think nothing impossible."

The idea of the Waffen-SS had its origins in the immediate post-World War I years in the *Freikorps* (q.v.), the emergency units of demobilized servicemen who remained loyal to the authoritarian creed of the Imperial Army. Nationalist and revanchist, the *Freikorps* expected continued military privileges and a voice in national affairs. Many early Nazis came from the ranks of the *Freikorps*. When the SS was formed in 1925, it had two militarized formations, the *Verfügungstruppe* (q.v.), the militarized troops, and the *SS-Totenkopfverbände* (q.v.), the Death's Head formations. Both were eventually combined to form the Waffen-SS. Another militarized formation was the Leibstandarte-SS Adolf Hitler (q.v.), the SS Bodyguard Regiment Adolf Hitler, formed in 1933 to include the Stabswache (q.v.), the Headquarters Guard originally set up in 1923. All these militarized units were eventually absorbed in the newly named Waffen-SS in 1939.

The Waffen-SS contingent played only a small role in the opening campaign against Poland in World War II. Immediately after the opening *Blitzkrieg* (q.v.), the lightning war, Heinrich Himmler (q.v.) obtained Hitler's permission to increase the number of SS divisions from one to three. These were organized in the months of the so-called phony war (*see* SITZKRIEG). By March 1940 service in the Waffen-SS was regarded as a military duty for Nazi party members. Three Waffen-SS *Panzer* (q.v.), or tank, divisions—the Leibstandarte Adolf Hitler, Das Reich, and Totenkopf—drew attention by leading the way in a lightning thrust into the Netherlands and by participating in the Battle of France. In the reports of the Wehrmacht (q.v.), the regular Army, from the western front there were scarcely any references to the Waffen-SS units. However, the Waffen-SS soon received recognition for its exploits. During the winter of 1940–1941, Himmler reorganized his Waffen-SS divisions, four of which were ready in the spring of 1941 for Barbarossa (q.v.), the

ORDER OF BATTLE OF THE WAFFEN-SS

	TITLE[1]	DATE OF ORIGIN	COMPOSITION	FINAL DISPOSITION
I	SS-Panzerdivision-Leibstandarte Adolf Hitler	1933	Germans	Surrendered, 1945
II	SS-Panzerdivision-Das Reich	1939	Germans	Surrendered, 1945
III	SS-Panzerdivision-Totenkopf	1940	Germans	Surrendered, 1945
IV	SS-Polizei-Panzergrenadierdivision-Polizei Division	1940	Germans	Surrendered, 1945
V	SS-Panzerdivision-Wiking	1940	Germans	Surrendered, 1945
VI	SS-Gebirgsdivision-Nord	1940	Germans	Surrendered, 1945
VII	SS-Freiwilligen-Gebirgsdivision-Prinz Eugen	1942	Ethnic Germans	Surrendered, 1945
VIII	SS-Kavalieriedivision-Florian Geyer	1942	Germans/ethnic Germans	Surrendered, 1945
IX	SS-Panzerdivision-Hohenstaufen	1943	Germans	Surrendered, 1945
X	SS-Panzerdivision-Frundsberg	1943	Germans	Surrendered, 1945
XI	SS-Freiwilligen-Panzergrenadierdivision-Nordland	1942	Germans/Scandinavians	Surrendered, 1945
XII	SS-Panzerdivision-Hitler Jugend	1943	Germans	Surrendered, 1945
XIII	Waffen-Gebirgsdivision der SS-Handschar	1943	Yugoslavs	Dissolved, 1944
XIV	Waffen-Grenadierdivision der SS-Galizische No. 1	1943	Ukrainians	Surrendered, 1945
XV	Waffen-Grenadierdivision der SS-Lettische No. 1	1943	Latvians/Germans	Surrendered, 1945
XVI	SS-Panzergrenadierdivision-Reichsfuehrer-SS	1943	Germans/ethnic Germans	Surrendered, 1945
XVII	SS-Panzergrenadierdivision-Götz von Berlichingen	1943	Germans/ethnic Germans	Surrendered, 1945
XVIII	SS-Freiwilligen-Panzergrenadierdivision-Horst Wessel	1944	Germans/ethnic Germans	Surrendered, 1945
XIX	Waffen-Grenadierdivision der SS-Lettische No. 2	1944	Latvians	Surrendered, 1945
XX	Waffen-Grenadierdivision der SS-Estnische No. 1	1944	Estonians	Surrendered, 1945
XXI	Waffen-Gebirgsdivision der SS-Albanische No. 1-Skanderberg	1944	Albanians	Dissolved, 1944
XXII	SS-Freiwilligen-Kavalieriedivision-Maria Theresa	1944	Ethnic Germans/Germans	Surrendered, 1945
XXIII-a	Waffen-Gebirgsdivision der SS-Kama	1944	Yugoslavs	Dissolved, 1944
XXIII-b	SS-Freiwilligen-Panzerdivision-Nederland	1945	Dutch	Surrendered, 1945
XXIV	Waffen-Gebirgsdivision der SS-Karstjäger	1944	Italians/ethnic Germans	Dissolved, 1945
XXV	Waffen-Grenadierdivision der SS-Hunyadi No. 1	1944	Hungarians	Vanished
XXVI	Waffen-Grenadierdivision der SS-Hunyadi No. 2	1944	Hungarians	Vanished
XXVII	SS-Freiwilligen-Grenadierdivision-Langemarck	1945	Flemish/Belgians	Surrendered, 1945
XXVIII	SS-Freiwilligen-Grenadierdivision-Wallonie	1945	Walloons/Belgians	Surrendered, 1945
XXIX-a	Waffen-Grenadierdivision der SS-Russische No.1	1944	Russians	Made part of Vlasov Army, 1944
XXIX-b	Waffen-Grenadierdivision der SS-Italische No. 1	1945	Italians	Vanished, 1945
XXX	Waffen-Grenadierdivision der SS-Russische No. 2	1944	Russians	Made part of Vlasov Army, 1945
XXXI	SS-Freiwilligen-Grenadierdivision	1945	Germans	Surrendered, 1945
XXXII	SS-Freiwilligen-Panzerdivision-Böhmen-Mahren	1945	Germans/ethnic Germans	Surrendered, 1945
XXXIII	Waffen-Grenadierdivision der SS-January 30	1945	Germans	Surrendered, 1945
XXXIV	Waffen-Grenadierdivision der SS-Charlemagne	1945	French	Defeated at Berlin, 1945
XXXV	SS-Freiwilligen-Grenadierdivision-Landstorm Nederland	1945	Dutch	Dissolved, 1945
XXXVI	SS-Polizei-Grenadierdivision der SS	1945	German policemen	Dissolved, 1945
XXXVII	Waffen-Grenadierdivision-Dirlewanger	1945	Germans	Surrendered, 1945
XXXVIII	SS-Freiwillingen-Kavalieriedivision-Lützow	1945	Ethnic Germans	Surrendered, 1945
XXXIX	SS-Panzergrenadierdivision-Nibelungen	1945	SS cadets	Surrendered, 1945

[1]Division titles often had a patriotic connotation and sometimes were based on ethnic composition. The SS Division was composed of German volunteers; the *SS-Freiwilligendivision*, of ethnic Germans or Germanic volunteers; the *Division der Waffen-SS*, of East Europeans. The main categories included the *Grenadierdivision* (infantry division); *Panzergrenadier-division* (motorized infantry division); *Gebirgsdivision* (mountain division); and *Kavalierledivision* (cavalry division).

assault on the U.S.S.R. Motorized Waffen-SS units were moved from their stations along the Soviet frontier to meet an anti-Nazi outbreak in the Balkans.

Hitler was pleased by the performance of the Waffen-SS divisions at the beginning of the Russian campaign. The SS troops were well trained in antibolshevism and racial doctrine (q.v.). Himmler set the pace: "This is an ideological battle and a struggle of races. National Socialism is

Capture of a Waffen-SS officer in April 1945. [*Imperial War Museum, London*]

based on the value of our Germanic, Nordic blood—a beautiful, decent, socially equal society. On the other side stands a population of 180 millions, a mixture of races, whose very names are unpronounceable, and whose physique is such that one can shoot them down without pity or compassion. These animals have been welded by the Jews into one religion, one ideology that is called bolshevism." Permeated with this ideology, the Waffen-SS fought furiously in the opening victorious months of the Russian campaign. By the following summer the Waffen-SS divisions had been withdrawn one by one to France. Stalingrad, fortunately for the reputation of the Waffen-SS, was not to be its battle: the regular Wehrmacht was trapped there by Russian resistance.

From the beginning Himmler hoped to make the Waffen-SS an international organization that would include racialists who were in agreement with Nazi ideology. By attracting "Nordic blood" to his cause, he would make certain that "never again will Nordic or Germanic blood fight against us." His desire to set up "foreign legions" of Waffen-SS units was intensified by the reluctance of the Wehrmacht to release enough Germans from the manpower pool to fill out his own divisions. Dutch, Norwegian, Danish, and Belgian legions were set up in July 1941. In 1942 these foreign units were utilized on the Russian front. In March 1943 the auxiliary formations, with the exception of the Belgian, were combined to form the 11th SS Volunteer Panzer Grenadier Division Nordland. Its ranks were filled with native Germans to be used on the western front. Other Waffen-SS foreign units used Romanians, Hungarians, Yugoslavs, and even Muslims. It is difficult to assess the fighting quality of the foreign units because most of them were combined eventually in units with native-born Germans. Himmler's experiment of a superior international military force was not successful. Most of his foreign formations counted for little in the overall military picture. On the other hand, the elite units of the Waffen-SS were unquestionably of the highest military quality and compared favorably with the best of the Wehrmacht. The order of battle of the thirty-nine Waffen-SS divisions in World War II is shown in the table on page 367.

At the Nuremberg Trial (q.v.) the SS and the Waffen-SS were both indicted as criminal organizations. The leaders of the Wehrmacht who were on trial insisted that all atrocities in combat were committed by the Waffen-SS and certainly not by regular Army units, which had been trained carefully in the art of traditional warfare. The older officers charged that Himmler's soldiers, nurtured on racialism and the superman ethic, went to extremes in attempts to achieve their goal of biological purification. Members of the Waffen-SS who claimed that they knew nothing of atrocities pointed out that the Nuremberg verdict was directed at the SS as a whole and did not establish individual guilt.

Bibliography. Gerald Reitlinger, *The SS: Alibi of a Nation*, William Heinemann, Ltd., London, 1957.

WAGNER, ADOLF (1890–1944). Nazi leader in Bavaria. Adolf Wagner was born at Algringen (Algrange), Lorraine, on October 1, 1890. During World War I he served as an officer. An early member of the Nationalsozialistische Deutsche Arbeiterpartei (q.v.), he was appointed *Gauleiter* (district leader) for Upper Bavaria. In 1933 he was made minister of the interior and deputy premier of Bavaria and also served as a delegate to the Reichstag (q.v.), representing Wahlkreis (Electoral District) Upper Bavaria–Swabia. Two years later he was appointed to the personal staff of Hitler at the Brown House (Braunes Haus, q.v.) in Munich. He was made Bavarian minister for education and culture in 1936. In September 1939, shortly after the outbreak of World War II, he was appointed Reich defense commissioner for Military Districts VII and XIII.

WAGNER, [WILHELM] RICHARD (1813–1883). German composer, dramatist, essayist, and influential forerunner of Nazi ideology. Richard Wagner was born in Leipzig on May 22, 1813. After studying at the Kreuzschule in Dresden and the Nicolaischule in Leipzig, he matriculated in 1830 at the University of Leipzig, where he studied composition. In 1833 he became conductor of the Magdeburg Opera. In 1839 he went to Paris, where he lived in abject poverty until 1842. Gradually he perfected a musical style that brought him worldwide fame. His major works, though often called operas, were rather *Gesammtkunstwerke* (works of all arts in one), combining poetry, music, and dance. He died in Venice on February 13, 1883.

Wagner's magnificent operas and his general view of

life had an enormous influence on Hitler. From the days of his youth Hitler worshiped the composer. He never tired of hearing the music dramas, with their accent on Teutonic and German mythology, the splendor of life and the nobility of death, and the sense of destiny. Each year he attended the Bayreuth Festival (q.v.). He made many visits to Haus Wahnfried, the composer's home, to meet the Wagner family (*see* WAGNER, Winifred). It was rumored that Hitler's attachment to the Wagnerian circle was so deep that he would eventually marry Winifred Wagner. "I remember," Hitler said, "my emotion the first time I entered Wahnfried. To say I was moved is an understatement."

Wagner considered his music to be essentially German. It was his task, he believed, to lead German music away from cosmopolitan confusion to the highest point of real national drama, to free it from every foreign influence, and to build on the foundations of German hero legends. He was certain that until he had appeared there was no real German music, no German theater, no German style. German operas had borrowed from all sources except German. True, there was the genius of Beethoven, who had reached the height of sterling art and who had evoked the spiritually energetic and the profoundly passionate in matchless expression. In addition, there was Johann Sebastian Bach, who had incorporated in his own incomparable figure the strength and meaning of the German spirit. But Germans, Wagner complained, had not really learned from Beethoven and Bach the meaning of their own heritage. These two great composers became *cosmopolitan* heroes. What was needed, Wagner asserted, was a typically German style.

Wagner tried to capture the spirit of German music in his masterpiece, *Der Ring des Nibelungen*, a series of four music dramas inspired by the *Nibelungenlied*, the old German epic. Wagner's heroes, heroines, and villains—Siegfried, Kriemhild, Brunhild, and Hagen—were enthusiastically received by the Germans, who considered them to be truly representative of the German spirit. Hitler was entranced by the entire mythology. So intense was his belief in it that, consciously or unconsciously, he recapitulated the final scenes of the *Götterdämmerung* (q.v.) in his own life. In the *Ring* Valhalla is set on fire by Wotan and goes up in flames in an orgy of self-destruction. In 1945, trapped in the smoke and chaos of his Berlin bunker (*see* FUEHRERBUNKER), Hitler too died a Wagnerian death. At the same time he cried out that the German people had not been worthy of him and that they must go down to annihilation in shell and flame.

Wagner's passion for the German spirit in music was matched by his contempt for Jewish music. He was repelled by what he called the physical aspect of Jewish speech: "The first thing that strikes our ears as quite outlandish and unpleasant, in the Jew's production of the voice-sounds, is a creaking, squeaking, buzzing snuffle: add thereto an employment of words in a sense quite foreign to our nation's tongue, and an arbitrary twisting of the structure of our phrases—and this mode of speaking acquires at once the character of an intolerably jumbled blabber" (*see also* RASSENFORSCHUNG). Jewish music in the synagogues aroused in Wagner a feeling of revulsion, "of horror mingled with the absurd, at hearing that sense-and-sound confounding gurgle, yodel, and cackle, which no unintentional caricature can make more repugnant than as offered here in full." Jewish works of music impressed him "as though a poem of Goethe's were being rendered in the Jewish jargon." The Jewish musician simply threw together all forms of music in a motley chaos and called it his own; he had no real passion for art creation.

Wagner was contemptuous of two rivals, Felix Mendelssohn and Giacomo Meyerbeer. Mendelssohn, in Wagner's opinion, never revealed "that deep heart-searching effect which we await from Art." "Whereas Beethoven, the last in the great chain of our true music-heroes, strove with highest longing, and wonder-working faculty, for the clearest, most certain expression of an unsayable content through a sharp-cut, plastic shaping of his tone-pictures, Mendelssohn, on the contrary, reduces these achievements to vague, fantastic shadow-forms, midst whose indefinite shimmer our freakish fancy is indeed aroused, but our inner, purely human yearning for distinct artistic right is hardly touched with even the merest hopes of a fulfillment." Wagner labeled Meyerbeer "a far-famed Jewish tone-setter," whom he found utterly boring, a composer who offered his admirers a peculiar jargon of thrilling situations and emotional catastrophes: "He writes operas for Paris, and sends them touring around the world—the surest means to-day of earning oneself an art-renown albeit not the name of an artist."

Throughout his prose works, comprising many volumes, Wagner emphasized his sense of extreme nationalism. As a glowing patriot he worshiped his fatherland. He constantly used the phrase "German *Herrlichkeit*" ("German glory"). German earnestness, he said, was proverbial, as were German solidity, the natural, easygoing Germanic manner, German depth, and German fidelity. "Whereas the Romance nations abandon themselves to a dubious life of the moment, and, strictly speaking, have a sense of nothing but what the immediate present offers them, the German builds the world of the present out of motives from all zones and ages. His enjoyment of the beautiful is consequently more reflective than in the case of his Romance neighbors."

Wagner had high praise for what he called the German spirit, an innate quality that distinguished Germans from all other peoples. German folk blood and folk spirit, he wrote, emanated from the German spirit. There was a

Richard Wagner. *Picture Collection, The Branch Libraries, The New York Public Library*]

resurrection of German art in the Middle Ages. Those German princes who, like Frederick the Great, deprecated the *esprit allemand* in favor of French culture and who Frenchified or attempted to Frenchify Germany would lose in the end. The German spirit was born in the War of Liberation against Napoleon: "A new life of wonders was won for German feeling." Even Frenchmen, disgusted with their own way of life, had flocked to Goethe and Schiller. The great German masters of the theater—Goethe, Schiller, Heinrich von Kleist—had awakened the consciousness of Germans and had stretched the hand of understanding to Aeschylus and Sophocles across 2,000 years. They had constructed the pillars of "the German Spirit's only veritable Hall of Fame." The German political system must recognize the German spirit and "give this Spirit a fitting habitation in the system of the German State." Wagner regarded monarchy as the ideal form of government to express the German spirit. He denounced "Franco-Judaic-German democracy" for pretending that it had a German mien.

The Germans, Wagner said, had a great mission about which other nations knew scarcely anything. Germany's mission lay in extricating the world from the material civilization of the French. It was not strictly a "national mission" but rather a universal mission: the world and not Germany alone must be rescued from this pernicious material influence. The goal must be achieved through national means: "We will do things *Germanly* and grandly; from its rising to its setting the sun shall look upon a beautiful free Germany, and on the borders of the daughter-lands, as on the frontiers of their mother, no downtrod, unfree folk shall dwell; the rays of *German freedom* and *German gentleness* [*Milde*] shall light and warm the French and Cossacks, the Bushmen and Chinese."

Wagner's racial doctrine (q.v.) was borrowed from two non-German sources, the Frenchman Arthur Comte de Gobineau and the Englishman Houston Stewart Chamberlain (qq.v.). He was delighted by Gobineau's contention that the Germans were probably the best of all Aryans. Similarly, he was attracted by Chamberlain's belief that the way to be rid of Jewish influence lay in Teutonic culture, that the Germans were the most civilized people on earth, and that they had the inalienable right to be masters of the world. Wagner never relented in his anti-Semitism (q.v.). He attacked Heinrich Heine as "the conscience of Judaism, just as Judaism is the evil conscience of our modern civilization." In Wagner's view Ludwig Börne had attempted to become a man by renouncing Judaism for Christianity, but for Wagner this was not enough. On September 3-6, 1850, Wagner published "Judaism in Music" in the *Neue Zeitschrift für Musik (New Journal for Music)*, under the pseudonym K. Freigedank (K. Free Thought). The polemic aroused much comment, especially after it became known that Wagner was the author. Many pamphlets were written in response, some of them attributing his anti-Semitism to envy of Meyerbeer and Mendelssohn. Others called Wagner the victim of a persecution complex, and still others intimated that he had stepped over the borderline into insanity.

For Hitler and Nazi ideologists Wagner was the perfect hero. The composer epitomized Germany's greatness. In Hitler's view Wagner's music justified German nationalism. Wagnerian triumphs were produced by the German mind in a German way for the German people. Hitler regarded Wagner as his spiritual master: "At every stage of my life I come back to Wagner." The closeness of the views of Wagner and Hitler is illustrated by the following précis:

THE STATE

WAGNER: In the State the unit must offer a part of his own egoism for the welfare of the majority.

—The intrinsic object of the State *is stability*, the maintenance of quiet.

HITLER: The State is only a means towards an end. Its highest aim is the care and maintenance of those primeval racial elements [*Urelemente*] which create the beauty and dignity of a higher civilization.

VOLK

WAGNER: The *Volk* consists of those who think instinctively.

—The *Volk* deals unconsciously and, for that very reason, from a Nature-instinct.

HITLER: The dead mechanism [of the old State] must be replaced by a living organism based on the herd instinct, which appears when all are of one blood.

THE LEADER

WAGNER: We must now seek the Hero of the future, who turns against the ruin of his race.

—Barbarossa-Siegfried will some day return to save the German people in time of deepest need.

HITLER: One must never forget it: the majority can never replace the leader. It [the majority] is not only stupid but cowardly. You cannot get one wise man out of a hundred fools, and a heroic decision cannot come out of a hundred cowards.

GERMAN SUPERIORITY

WAGNER: The true foundation of continued renovation has remained the German nature.

—In *something* EVERY German is akin to his great masters.

Genius and the German people have a certain something in common.

HITLER: It ought to be a greater honor to be a street-cleaner of the German Reich than king of a foreign power.

THE JEWS

WAGNER: The Jew is the plastic demon of the decline of mankind.

HITLER: The Jews are parasites on the bodies of other peoples; they make states within the State.

ANTIRATIONALISM

WAGNER: We must be brave enough to deny our intellect.

—The *Volk* must burst the chain of hindering consciousness.

HITLER: The educational system of the Folkish-State finds its crowning work in burning into the brains and heart of the youth intrusted to it an instinctual and understanding sense of race and race feeling.

DEMOCRACY

WAGNER: Democracy is totally un-German, a translated thing from elsewhere.

—Franco-Judaico-German democracy is a disgusting thing.

HITLER: Democracy is a rule by crazy brains.

—The German Republic is a monstrosity of human mechanism.

FRANCE

WAGNER: Germany's mission lies in extricating the world from the materialistic civilization of the French.

HITLER: France is and remains the inexorable enemy of Germany.

—France has made so much progress in her Negroization [*in seiner Venegerung*] that one can in fact speak of the creation of an African state on European territory.

Wagner remained a controversial figure even after the fall of the Third Reich. As late as June 1974 a planned performance of his music, which had been so admired by Hitler, produced harsh discord between Israeli music lovers and those Jews who could not forget Wagner's spiritual association with Nazism. Complaints were so bitter that the Israel Philharmonic Orchestra canceled a concert that was to have included works by the German composer. The incident revealed the continuing acute grief suffered by Jews who had lost relatives and friends in the extermination camps (q.v.). At the same time, it showed that music lovers, especially among the younger generations, felt that there was a cultural loss in excluding Wagnerian music.

Bibliography. Ernest Newman, *The Life of Richard Wagner*, 4 vols., Alfred A. Knopf, Inc., New York, 1933–1946; Leon Stein, *The Racial Thinking of Richard Wagner*, Philosophical Library, Inc., New York, 1950.

WAGNER, WINIFRED (1894–). The daughter-in-law of Richard Wagner (q.v.), the widow of the composer's son Siegfried, and a special friend of Adolf Hitler. Born in England as Winifred Williams, she was the adopted daughter of Karl Klindworth, a pupil of Franz Liszt. In 1915 she married Siegfried Wagner, who was twenty-five years her senior. In the spring of 1923 she met Hitler, then an aspiring politician. In the fall of that year Hitler visited Haus Wahnfried, the Wagner home in Bayreuth, where he met Cosima Wagner, the aged mistress of Bayreuth; Houston Stewart Chamberlain (q.v.); Siegfried Wagner, the composer's heir; and Winifred Wagner. Hitler remained a close friend of the family, especially after 1930, when Siegfried died. It was rumored that Hitler intended to marry Winifred, whose children he treated as his own, but nothing developed along this line. Each year Hitler attended the Bayreuth Festival (q.v.), and he saw to it that the opera house in Bayreuth received governmental assistance.

WAHLKREIS (Electoral District). A voting area. For example, a deputy to the Reichstag (q.v.) might represent Wahlkreis Berlin-Dahlem.

WALDECK-PYRMONT, JOSIAS ERBPRINZ VON (1896–1967). *Obergruppenfuehrer* (general) in the SS (q.v.). A hereditary prince, Waldeck-Pyrmont was the first member of the old nobility to be recruited for the SS by Heinrich Himmler (q.v.). He joined the Nazi movement in 1929. From 1939 on he served as police leader for the district of Kassel-Mainfranken. On August 14, 1947, because of his jurisdiction over the Buchenwald (q.v.) concentration camp (*see* CONCENTRATION CAMPS), he was sentenced to life imprisonment. He began serving his term at Landsberg Prison.

WALTER, BRUNO (1876–1962). Orchestra conductor and refugee from Nazism. Bruno Walter Schlesinger was born in Berlin on September 15, 1876. In his early career he came under the influence of the composer Gustav Mahler. From 1913 to 1922 Walter was music director of the State Opera in Munich, and from 1936 to 1938 conductor of the State Opera and the Philharmonic in Vienna. In 1938 he emigrated to France and in 1940 to the United States. From 1947 to 1949 he conducted the New York Philharmonic. Walter won a global reputation as an interpreter of Mahler and Mozart. He died in Beverly Hills, California, on February 17, 1962.

WANDERVÖGEL (Birds of Passage). A group that initiated the German youth movement. In 1901 several students and other young men in Berlin started a club and called themselves the *Wandervögel*. Annoyed by the fact that many Germans had migrated from the countryside to the cities, the young men decided to help reverse the process. In essence, they were disgusted with the materialism of the day. Protesting against the burgeoning industrial life, they communed with nature in the woods at lakeside refuges. Their goal was to revive romantic Teutonic idealism and, at the same time, to stress nationalism and anti-Semitism (q.v.).

The movement spread rapidly. By 1914 there were 25,000 members of various *Wandervögel* groups. Some 7,000 *Wandervögel* were killed in World War I. After the war the *Wandervögel* were succeeded by the better-organized *Bünde* (leagues). By this time the youth movement had taken on a political coloration. Youngsters took part in street brawls to fight out the political issues of the day. Typical was the *Knappenschaft* (Young Novitiates), whose members denounced the iniquities of the Treaty of Versailles and attacked Jews and Marxists. From the beginning the Hitler movement was anxious to win control over German youth through such organizations, a goal in which it was highly successful.

Bibliography. Howard Becker, *German Youth: Bond or Free*, Oxford University Press, New York, 1946.

WANNSEE CONFERENCE. A meeting held on January 20, 1942, in the Berlin suburb of Grossen-Wannsee, where the decision was made to adopt the Final Solution, the contemplated extermination of the Jews (*see* ENDLÖSUNG, DIE). On July 31, 1941, Hermann Goering (q.v.) issued orders to Reinhard Heydrich (q.v.), chief of the SD (q.v.), the security service, to submit a comprehensive plan for "a final solution of the Jewish question." The meeting was originally scheduled for December 8, 1941, but it was postponed until noon on January 20, 1942. It was to be followed by a luncheon. Fifteen leading Nazi bureaucrats were present:

SS-Obergruppenfuehrer (General) Heydrich, chairman, RSHA

Gauleiter (*Gau* Leader) Dr. Meyer, East Ministry

Reichsamtsleiter (Reich Office Leader) Dr. Leibrandt, East Ministry

Staatssekretär (State Secretary) Dr. Stuckart, Minister of the Interior

Staatssekretär (State Secretary) Neumann, Office of the Four-Year Plan
Staatssekretär (State Secretary) Dr. Freisler, Ministry of Justice
Staatssekretär (State Secretary) Dr. Buhler, General Government of Poland
Unterstaatssekretär (Under State Secretary) Luther, Foreign Office
SS-Oberfuehrer (Brigadier General) Klopfer, Party Chancellery
Ministerialdirektor (Ministerial Director) Kritzinger, Reich Chancellery
SS-Obergruppenfuehrer (General) Hoffmann, RuSHA
SS-Gruppenfuehrer (Lieutenant General) Müller, RSHA, Amt IV
SS-Obersturmbannfuehrer (Lieutenant Colonel) Eichmann, RSHA, Amt IV-B-4
SS-Oberfuehrer (Brigadier General) Dr. Schöngarth, General Government of Poland
SS-Sturmbannfuehrer (Major) Dr. Lange, KdS Latvia

The conference was opened by Heydrich, who declared that he was the plenipotentiary for "the final solution of the Jewish question." He then reviewed the emigration problem. Until this time a plan had been held in readiness to deport all Jews to the island of Madagascar, off the coast of Africa, but the Madagascar Plan (q.v.) had fallen through after the invasion of the U.S.S.R. on June 22, 1941. There was no longer any possibility of transporting Jews in this fashion. Instead of emigration the Fuehrer had given his sanction *(Genehmigung)* for the evacuation of all Jews to the east as a "solution possibility" *(Lösungsmöglichkeit)*. The evacuees would be organized into huge labor columns. Undoubtedly, a majority would "fall through natural diminution." The survivors of "this natural selection process," actually the hard core of Jewry and the most dangerous because they could rebuild Jewish life, would be "treated accordingly." Although Heydrich did not elaborate the phrase "treated accordingly," the plain meaning was that, in the course of time, with insufficient food and exhausting work, the survivors would be weakened and ready for the specially equipped extermination camps (q.v.).

The conferees then became involved in a lengthy discussion of the problem of the *Mischlinge* (q.v.), the individuals of mixed race, and that of Jews in mixed marriages. About half the time was taken up with this special discussion, but no drastic reclassification of the *Mischlinge* was made.

Then the conferees adjourned for lunch. Thirty copies of the record (*see* WANNSEE PROTOCOL) were made and circulated in the ministries and SS (q.v.) offices. News of the Final Solution traveled quickly through the Nazi bureaucracy. Within a few months the first gas chamber camps were set up in Poland.

WANNSEE PROTOCOL. Minutes of the meeting at the Wannsee Conference (q.v.), held on January 20, 1942, to plan the Final Solution of the Jewish question (*see* ENDLÖSUNG, DIE). The protocol read in part:

> As a further possibility of solving the question, the evacuation of the Jews to the east can now be substituted for emigration, after obtaining permission from the Fuehrer to that effect. However, these actions are merely to be considered as alternative possibilities, even though they will permit us to make all those practical experiences which are of great importance for the future final solution of the Jewish question.
>
> The Jews should in the course of the Final Solution be taken in a suitable manner to the east for use as labor. In big labor gangs, separated by sex, the Jews capable of work will be brought to these areas for road building, in which task undoubtedly a large number will fall through natural diminution. The remnant that is finally able to survive all this—since this is undoubtedly the part with the strongest resistance—must be treated accordingly, since these people, representing a natural selection, are to be regarded as the germ cell of a new Jewish development, in case they should succeed and go free (as history has proved). In the course of the execution of the Final Solution, Europe will be combed from west to east.

WAR GUILT LIE. *See* KRIEGSSCHULDLÜGE.

"WAR SONG AGAINST ENGLAND." A popular song in the Third Reich during the early months of World War II. Composed by H. Niels in 1940 when invasion of England was considered to be imminent, the "War Song against England" was a streamlined version of the old "Hasslied" ("Song of Hate") directed against England in World War I. The text of the "War Song against England" follows:

> We challenge the lion of England,
> For the last and decisive cup.
> We judge and we say
> An Empire breaks up.
> This sure is our proudest day.
> Comrade, Comrade,
> The orders are here, we start right away.
>
> Go, get on, get on,
> The motto is known;
> Get on to the foe, get on to the foe.
> BOMBS ON ENGLAND!
>
> Listen to the engine singing—get on to the foe!
> Listen, in your ears it's ringing—get on to the foe.
> BOMBS, OH BOMBS, OH BOMBS ON ENGLAND!

WARLIMONT, WALTHER (1895–). Major general and one of Hitler's trusted officers. Walther Warlimont was one of a trio, including Generals Wilhelm Keitel and Alfred Jodl (qq.v.), who remained loyal to the Fuehrer throughout their careers. All three, of bourgeois background, subconsciously resented the Prussian military caste, and all three, eager for promotion, remained at Hitler's side. A jovial Rhinelander, Warlimont complemented the cold mediocrity of Keitel and the academic reserve of Jodl. In 1937, while colonel in the Wehrmachtamt (Office of the Armed Forces) of the War Ministry, Warlimont and a colleague, Colonel Müller-Lübnitz, prepared a memorandum calling for a reorganization of the armed forces under one staff and one supreme commander (*see* WARLIMONT MEMORANDUM). The recommendation won the attention of Hitler, who was anxious at the time to reduce the powers of the Army elite. The project became the basis for Hitler's reorganization of the armed forces. It won for Warlimont a post first as deputy, then as successor, and again as deputy to Jodl in the Wehrmachtsfuehrungsstab (q.v.), the armed forces Operations Staff.

Maj. Gen. Walther Warlimont. [*Picture Collection, The Branch Libraries. The New York Public Library*]

On December 6, 1940, Jodl and Warlimont were ordered by Hitler to prepare a preliminary general plan for the invasion of the Soviet Union. Together they drew up Directive 21 (q.v.), initially identified by the code name Fritz (q.v.), which was changed a few days later to Operation Barbarossa (*see* BARBAROSSA). On July 20, 1944, the day of the July Plot (q.v.) on Hitler's life, Warlimont was among the officers in the hut at Rastenburg when the bomb exploded. He was not injured.

WARLIMONT MEMORANDUM. A 1937 report calling for the reorganization of the armed forces of the Third Reich under one staff unit and one supreme commander. Conceived largely by Walther Warlimont (q.v.), then an ambitious colonel in the Wehrmachtamt (Office of the Armed Forces) of the War Ministry, the plan was to limit the power of the high officer caste in favor of the Fuehrer. On the basis of this memorandum, Hitler developed the Oberkommando der Wehrmacht (q.v.), the High Command of the armed forces, with himself as supreme commander and Gen. Wilhelm Keitel (q.v.) as his deputy. Warlimont was rewarded with a post as deputy to Gen. Alfred Jodl (q.v.) in the Wehrmachtsfuehrungsstab (q.v.), the armed forces Operations Staff.

WARSAW GHETTO UPRISING. A final struggle of 1,000 Jews against German troops and police in occupied Warsaw, Poland. In late September 1939, after the invasion of Poland, Reinhard Heydrich (q.v.), chief of the Gestapo (q.v.), began to place all Polish Jews in ghettos, where they could slowly die of hunger and disease. The campaign was to be administered by the Waffen-SS (q.v.), the party's military formations that fought as integral units in the armed forces. The Warsaw ghetto was the largest of these segregated areas established by the Nazis in Poland.

In the summer of 1940 Heydrich, using the excuse that the spread of typhus had to be contained, set up a special section 11 miles in circumference enclosed by a brick wall

Jews of the Warsaw ghetto. [*Ullstein*]

10 feet high. The cost was paid by the Judenrat, the Jewish Council of twenty-four members, which was in charge of Jewish affairs inside the ghetto (*see* JUDENRÄTE).

In September 1940 more than 80,000 gentile Poles living in the "infected area" were ordered to leave, and the next month about 140,000 Jews living elsewhere in the city were moved in with the 240,000 still in the ghetto. Some 360,000 Jews, a third of Warsaw's population, were herded into a 3.5-square-mile area. Meanwhile, Gestapo agents removed all Jews from the economic and cultural life of the city, from factories, shops, theaters, and libraries. On November 15, 1940, the ghetto was sealed and its twenty-two entrances closed. No one was allowed to leave or enter: there was to be no contact with the outside world.

The Judenrat, working against heavy odds, attempted to distribute rations equitably. With refugees coming in from Łódź, Cracow, and other cities, the situation soon became critical. Jews fought for jobs in the ghetto, including work with the labor battalions organized by the Nazis. Those unable to find work tried to exist by selling jewels, clothing, or anything else to obtain food. From 300 to 400 died daily in the Warsaw trap. More than 43,000 starved to death during the first year, and 37,000 in the first nine months of 1942. Children crazed by hunger crawled through the sewers to the non-Jewish sectors of the city to smuggle in a bit of food. People were no longer moved by the sight of men and women falling dead on the streets.

The Nazi authorities began "intensified measures" on July 22, 1942. As a memorial to Heydrich, who had expired of wounds on the preceding June 4, Heinrich Himmler (q.v.) ordered all Jews except those already in concentration camps (q.v.) to be deported by the end of the year. The ghetto and all labor camps would then be destroyed. Mass deportations to the gas chambers of Treblinka began. In two months 300,000 Jews were eliminated. The Judenrat was ordered to deliver 6,000 Jews daily for deportation. Each day thousands were driven by guards through the gates.

By this time the truth had become known to the remaining Jews: they were all to be annihilated. Young Zionists, pioneers training to go to Palestine, mobilized first, to be followed by members of the Polish Workers' party, which had replaced the former Communist party. On July 28, 1942, the Jewish Combat Organization, consisting of about 1,000 men and boys, was formed. All resolved to kill as many of their tormentors as they could before they died. Desperate appeals went out for arms. A brisk smuggling business was carried on with Poles outside the ghetto, who themselves resented the German occupation.

On September 5, 1942, orders went out to the remaining 120,000 Jews to register. All knew the meaning of this decision. By the end of September about 60,000 Jews remained in the ghetto. In early January 1943 the Jewish Combat Organization struck back, fighting from rooftops, cellars, and attics. In four days twenty Germans were killed and fifty wounded. The astonished Nazi guards retreated. Poles outside the ghetto now began to send in more revolvers, grenades, and dynamite. From January to April 1943 the guerrillas, divided into twenty-two groups, built an intricate network of underground cellars and tunnels, linked with command posts and leading to streets on the gentile side.

At 2 A.M. on the morning of April 19, 1943, German and Polish troops and police moved in on the ghetto to send all who were left to Treblinka in a "final action." Within minutes the guerrillas were at their fighting stations. First came the armed trucks, then tanks and armored cars. Artillery was drawn up at the walls. At 4 A.M. the ghetto fighters poured a hail of bullets, grenades, and bombs on the troops and police. The German plan was to annihilate the ghetto in three days, but the fighting went on for twenty-eight days. The guerrillas fought to the last. Many committed suicide at the moment before capture.

As the fighting ebbed, the Germans dragged survivors from the cellars and rubble. Fewer than 100 escaped, and of these only a handful survived the war. By mid-May the ghetto was no longer in existence. The last 60,000 Jews had been exterminated or killed in the explosions and fires. Polish sources reported that the ghetto fighters had killed 300 Germans and wounded about 1,000. From Warsaw Jewish resistance moved to the swamps and forests.

Bibliography. Raul Hilberg, *The Destruction of the European Jews*, Quadrangle Books, Inc., Chicago, 1961.

WARTHEGAU. The official name of western Poland after its annexation by the Third Reich. This area became a *Gau* (district) of the Nazi state.

"WASHING ON THE SIEGFRIED LINE, WE'RE GONNA HANG OUT THE." Immensely popular British war song during the winter of 1939–1940. Shortly after the outbreak of war on September 3, 1939, the British sent all available troops to France: some 150,000 in the first five months. Despite the relative weakness of the German defenses in the west, the Allied and German Armies faced one another without much offensive action, in what the British called the phony war and the Germans described as a *Sitzkrieg* (q.v.), a sit-down war. At this time two British songwriters, Jimmy Kennedy and Michael Carr, wrote a song titled "We're Gonna Hang Out the Washing on the Siegfried Line," which reflected the boring days of the phony war. The song was featured in London by Ambrose and His Orchestra with much success.[1]

FIRST VERSE

Mother, dear, I'm writing you from somewhere in France,
Hoping this finds you well,
Sergeant says I'm doing fine: "A soldier and a half"—
Here's the song that we'll all sing,
It'll sure make you laugh:

CHORUS

We're gonna hang out the washing on the Siegfried Line,
Have you any dirty washing, Mother dear?
We gonna hang out the washing on the Siegfried Line,

'Cos the washing day is here.
Whether the weather may be wet or fine,
We'll just rub along without a care,
We're gonna hang out the washing on the Siegfried Line,
If the Siegfried Line's still there.

SECOND VERSE

Everybody's mucking in and doing their job,
Wearing a great big smile,
Everybody's got to keep their spirits up to-day!
If you want to keep in swing,
Here's the song to sing!

CHORUS

WASSERFALL (Waterfall). Code for ground-air offensive rocket. This weapon had already been developed in 1942. There was a possibility of mass production, but the scientists at Peenemünde (q.v.), working under Dr. Wernher von Braun (q.v.), were busy with long-range rockets. About 25 feet long, the Waterfall rocket could carry 660 pounds of explosives along a directional beam up to 50,000 feet and hit enemy bombing planes with great accuracy. It was not affected by unfavorable weather. Albert Speer (q.v.) was certain that in mass production these small rockets would have beaten back the Allied air offensive against German industry from the spring of 1944 on. In contrast, the long-range rockets, which were expensive to build, proved to be an almost total failure. "It was," said Speer, "a mistaken investment."

W.BEF. *See* WEHRMACHTSBEFEHLSHABER.

"WE MOVE AGAINST ENGLAND." *See* "WIR FAHREN GEGEN ENGLAND."

WEDNESDAY CLUB. *See* MITTWOCHSGESELLSCHAFT.

WEHRERTÜCHTIGUNGSLAGER (Premilitary Training Camps). Special training camps set up in 1944, late in World War II, for newly inducted conscripts. Because of the heavy loss of life during the opening years of the war there were increasing calls for recruits in the armed forces. Despite intensive measures to improve the health of young people by physical training courses, German youths were beset by increasing nervousness and ill health. The new *Wehrertüchtigungslager* were designed to bring recruits to a minimum standard of fitness by special exercises, additional food, and medical attention before they were sent to basic training camps.

WEHRKREIS (Wkr.; Defense District). An army district in the Third Reich, equivalent to the peacetime *Korps* area. It was designated by a roman numeral. Ordinarily in peacetime a *Wehrkreis* contained the headquarters, formations, and subordinate formations of one active infantry corps. The commander of the corps was also the *Wehrkreis* commander.

WEHRMACHT (Wehrm.; Armed Forces). The official name of the combined Army, Navy, and Air Force in the Third Reich. Under the *Wehrgesetz* (defense law) decreed by the Fuehrer on May 21, 1935, the term Reichswehr (q.v.), used to describe the 100,000-man Army of the Weimar Republic (q.v.), was replaced by Wehrmacht. The ten senior generals in 1939 are listed below.

SENIOR GENERALS OF THE OFFICER CORPS IN 1939

	Date of birth	Command
Walther von Brauchitsch	1881	Commander in chief of the Army
Gerd von Rundstedt	1875	In temporary retirement
Fedor von Bock	1880	Army Group I
Wilhelm Ritter von Leeb	1876	In temporary retirement
Wilhelm Keitel	1882	Chief of the High Command of the armed forces (OKW)
Wilhelm List	1880	Army Group V
Johannes Blaskowitz	1883	Army Group III
Günther Hans von Kluge	1882	Army Group VI
Erwin von Witzleben	1881	Army Group II
Friedrich Dollmann	1882	Corps IX

WEHRMACHTSBEFEHLSHABER (W.Bef.; Armed Forces Commander). Military title of the commander of the armed forces in occupied territory. The *Wehrmachtsbefehlshaber* was responsible to the Oberkommando der Wehrmacht (q.v.; OKW), the High Command of the armed forces.

WEHRMACHTSFUEHRUNGSAMT (WFA; Armed Forces Operations Office). Branch of the Oberkommando der Wehrmacht (q.v.) responsible for military operations. This office, created on February 4, 1938, was placed under the jurisdiction of Gen. Wilhelm Keitel (q.v.) as chief of the High Command of the armed forces.

WEHRMACHTSFUEHRUNGSSTAB (WFSt.; Armed Forces Operations Staff). The section of the Oberkommando der Wehrmacht (q.v.; OKW), the High Command of the armed forces, devoted to operations. It was headed by Gen. Alfred Jodl (q.v.).

WEHRPOLITISCHE VEREINIGUNG (League for Combat Policy). A private officers' club formed by Ernst Roehm (q.v.) in the mid-1920s as a nucleus for Hitler's future army. The league was ostensibly devoted to the theoretical study of military questions, but it was actually intended to support Hitler in his drive for power. Roehm traveled around the countryside, especially in Bavaria, and enlisted his old comrades for the club, which he assured them would have an attractive future. The Wehrpolitische Vereinigung was regarded by both Hitler and Roehm as a kind of general staff for the future German Army under Nazi control.

WEHRWIRTSCHAFT (Defense Economy). The Nazi term for a war economy. All economic forces were to be geared deliberately and systematically for waging war. The *Wehrwirtschaft* was inaugurated by Hitler soon after he became Chancellor in 1933.

WEHRWIRTSCHAFTSAMT (Defense Economy Office). The staff of the armed forces that was devoted to economic matters.

WEHRWOLF. With the Stahlhelm (q.v.), one of the two most important *Wehrverbände* (defense formations) in the years before Hitler became Chancellor. The Wehrwolf, with its national headquarters in Thuringia, had far fewer members than the Stahlhelm, but there was a relatively larger percentage of working-class members on its rolls. In the late 1920s Hitler was anxious to use both groups for his own Nazi movement.

WEICHS, MAXIMILIAN FREIHERR VON (1881–1954). General field marshal. Born in Bavaria on November 12, 1881, Maximilian von Weichs turned early to a military career. In January 1938 he held a post as general in command of Wehrkreis (Defense District) XIII, with headquarters at Nuremberg. At that time he was among the sixteen high-ranking officers relieved from duty by Hitler because of the Blomberg-Fritsch crisis (q.v.). Within a short time, however, he was recalled to active service. During the months preceding the *Anschluss* (q.v.) between Germany and Austria, he was sent into the field to be ready to command his unit on the march to Vienna. At the outbreak of World War II in 1939, he held the rank, at the age of fifty-eight, of general of cavalry and was thirteenth in rank among the senior officers of the armed forces. Von Weichs was assigned to the Russian front. In January 1943 he was promoted to general field marshal. The appointment came through just at the moment when Hitler, angered by the failure of the campaign against the Soviet Union, declared: "No more field marshals." Von Weichs died in Rösberg-Cologne. His death was announced on September 27, 1954.

WEILL, KURT (1900–1950). Composer and refugee from the Third Reich. Kurt Weill was born in Dessau on March 2, 1900. In 1928 he composed the celebrated *Die Dreigroschenoper (The Threepenny Opera)*, with a text by Bertolt Brecht (q.v.). Based on a theme about proletarian life, it utilized modern jazz rhythms. As a ballad opera it achieved worldwide success. Labeled by Nazi officialdom as a degenerate intellectual, Weill emigrated from Germany in 1933 and settled in New York, where he did much to develop American folk opera, including *Knickerbocker Holiday* (1938), *Street Scene* (1947), and *Down in the Valley* (1948). He died in New York on April 3, 1950.

WEIMAR REPUBLIC. The German republic lasting from 1918 to 1933. In early 1919, after the defeat of World War I, a National Constituent Assembly was convened in Weimar, the home of Goethe, which was noted for its liberal traditions. The new Weimar Constitution provided for a President serving seven years, a bicameral legislature, and proportional representation. Although it was widely considered to be one of the most advanced constitutions ever written, its value was weakened by the existence of Article 48 (q.v.). Friedrich Ebert (q.v.), the first President

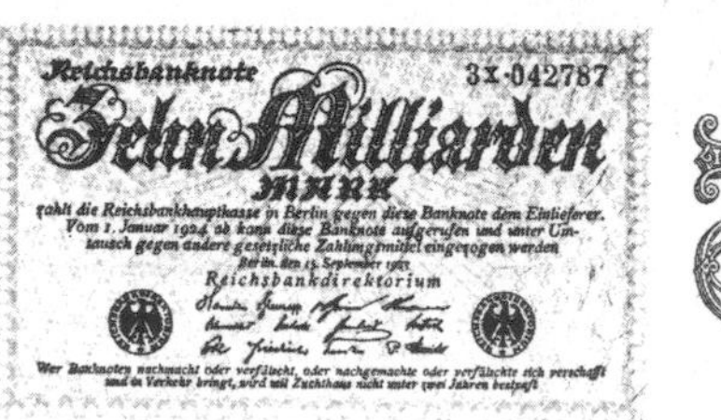

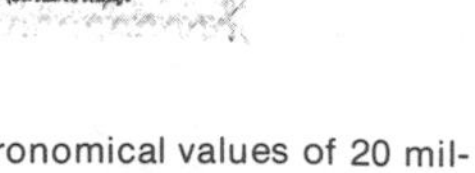

German currency in the astronomical values of 20 million marks and 10 billion marks issued during the runaway inflation of 1923–1924. [*Author's collection*]

of the Republic, served from February 1919 until his death in February 1925.

From the beginning the Weimar Republic suffered from political confusion and economic difficulties caused in part by the continued Allied blockade and the burden of reparations. The inflation of 1923 was a severe blow to the middle class, from whose ranks later came millions of Hitler's followers. The Depression of 1929 was accompanied by mass unemployment, and the fledgling Nationalsozialistische Deutsche Arbeiterpartei (q.v.), the Nazi party, took full advantage of the chaotic situation. After a series of attempts by delicately balanced political coalitions to rule the country, Hitler was appointed Chancellor on January 30, 1933.

The story of the Weimar Republic is a study in political frustration. During the later years of World War I the German people, hungry and miserable, hoped for a miracle to bring the hotly desired victory. They lived in a curious dream world, believing that somehow there would be a joyful end to the war. The official communiqués still referred to triumphs on the battlefields, and not a square inch of German territory had been taken by the enemy. Then, seemingly overnight, came the news of defeat. Emperor William II abdicated, and the Republic was proclaimed.

From the day of its inception the Weimar Republic was in serious trouble. The triumphant Allies occupied German territory, war prisoners were not sent home, and the naval blockade was maintained. In the German mind these depressing conditions were associated with the new government. To them the Weimar Republic was the illegitimate child of defeat. The new regime was born without adequate planning, almost as an afterthought. The architects of Weimar worked hurriedly to produce a government which the Allies would regard with favor and which might bring Germany an easier peace. There was little mass support. To many Germans the Republic was an artificial creation, a kind of stopgap or caretaker government pending the recall of the Hohenzollern dynasty. The Weimar Republic, from its opening days, was unwanted and unloved. It was doomed to die unhonored and unsung.

Not only was the Weimar Republic unwanted by the German people, but it was also misunderstood by other countries. The Allies showed little sympathy for the new Republic, nor did they do much to help it. In the heat of war propaganda the Allies had made a careful distinction between the German people and their reactionary rulers. That fine distinction was dropped as soon as the war was won. Those Germans who believed that they had laid down their arms on the basis of the Wilsonian Fourteen Points cried out that they had been the victims of a gigantic hoax. They had placed their trust in an Allied propaganda statement and had been treated ignominiously as soon as they surrendered.

The Weimar Republic was sabotaged by friends and foes alike. The men who tried to make it work were too hesitant, too reluctant to cast aside the traditions of yesterday. Honest and well-meaning, they made one mistake after another. Inexperienced in wielding political power, they tried to share it with Prussian militarists and industrial plutocrats, both of whom had only contempt for the new Republic and its way of life. This kind of coalition was headed inevitably for ruin. The government was besieged from two sides, by wild nationalists on the right and by equally fanatical internationalists on the left. The blundering, tortuous course of the Weimar statesmen satisfied few Germans. With internal chaos and no help from the outside, the Weimar Republic was doomed. It was wide open for attack by unscrupulous politicians. What had begun as a bold experiment in democracy degenerated into the nightmare of Hitlerism.

Bibliography. Erich Eyck, *A History of the Weimar Republic*, tr. by Harlan P. Hanson and Robert G. L. Waite, Harvard University Press, Cambridge, Mass., 1962; S. William Halperin, *Germany Tried Democracy*, W. W. Norton & Company, Inc., New York, 1965.

WEISS (White). Code name for the attack on Poland on September 1, 1939. In 1934 Hitler temporarily adjusted difficulties with Poland by concluding a ten-year military and commercial pact with the Polish government. Five years later he broke the agreement by insisting upon the annexation of Danzig and by demanding a roadway between Germany and East Prussia. After Hitler violated the Munich Agreement (q.v.), Great Britain and France guaranteed the independence of Poland and made it plain that Nazi aggression there would be a direct challenge to war. On April 3, 1939, Hitler issued a directive to Field Marshal Wilhelm Keitel (q.v.), chief of the High Command of the armed forces, on preparations for war. Annexed to the directive was a document containing details of Fall Weiss for a projected attack on Poland. In the document the Fuehrer explained that in spite of the existing treaty with Poland it might be necessary "to settle the account." He would smash the Polish armed forces and proclaim Danzig part of Germany. In the directive he gave precise instructions to the three branches of the armed forces to ensure surprise when the attack was ordered. On August 23, 1939, the Hitler-Stalin Pact (q.v.) was signed. Thus secured against attack from the east, Hitler gave orders for Fall Weiss to be implemented.

WEISSE ROSE (White Rose). An organization of students formed at the University of Munich in 1942 to oppose Hitler and the Nazi regime. It proposed "to knock down the iron wall of fear and terror." *See also* HUBER, Kurt; SCHOLL, Hans, and SCHOLL, Sophie.

WEIZSACKER, ERNST FREIHERR VON (1882–1951). Diplomat. Born in Stuttgart on May 12, 1882, he joined the Imperial Navy in 1910, served in World War I, and ended the war with the rank of commander. After entering the Foreign Office in 1920, he served in various consular and diplomatic posts, culminating in appointments as Minister to Norway, from 1931 to 1933, and Minister to Switzerland, from 1933 to 1936. Shortly after the appointment of Joachim von Ribbentrop (q.v.) as Foreign Minister in 1938, Von Weizsäcker was given the vacant post of State Secretary. He served the Third Reich in the Munich, Czechoslovakia, and Polish crises and throughout World War II. From 1943 to 1945 he was German Ambassador to the Holy See and received sanctuary in Rome after the war. Arrested by Allied authorities as a war criminal, he was placed on trial in 1947. In 1949 an American military tribunal at Nuremberg sentenced him to seven years for complicity in crimes of the Nazi regime. The sentence was later commuted to five years; in 1950 he was released under a general amnesty.

In his memoirs Von Weiszäcker insisted that he had always opposed Hitler's foreign policy and that he had made every effort to keep Nazi officials out of the foreign service. He claimed that he had repeatedly threatened to resign and be allowed to return to the Navy but that he was forced to give up in disgust and abandon his hopeless cause. He insisted that he had become a member of the Nazi party only "for decorative reasons" and had similarly accepted honorary rank in the SS (q.v.). He died in Lindau am Bodensee on August 4, 1951.

Bibliography. Ernst von Weizsäcker, *Memoirs*, tr. by John Andrews, Henry Regnery Company, Chicago, 1951.

WELS, OTTO (1873–1939). Social Democratic politician during the Weimar Republic (q.v.). Otto Wels was born in Berlin on September 15, 1873. An upholsterer by trade, he was a lifelong member and leader of the Social Democratic party (SPD). From 1931 on he was a member of the party's Central Committee, and he was one of its representatives in the Reichstag (q.v.) from 1912 to 1918 and again from 1920 to 1933. From 1931 to 1933 he served as chairman of the SPD. On March 23, 1933, he addressed the Reichstag in a long speech that explained why the SPD rejected Hitler's proposed Enabling Act (q.v.), which would grant the Fuehrer dictatorial powers. Shortly afterward he went into exile, first to Prague and then, in 1938, to Paris, where he led the SPD in exile. He died in Paris on September 16, 1939.

WELTANSCHAULICHE SCHULUNG (Ideological Schooling). Course of study devoted to instilling the Nazi

Weltanschauung (q.v.), or world view, in young pupils.

WELTANSCHAUUNG (World View). Favorite word in the Third Reich to denote the National Socialists' conception of the world, or their philosophy of life. The term was used by Hitler again and again in speeches and writings. In March 1934 he told a meeting of old party comrades that his victory was nothing more than a change of government. Only the victory of a *Weltanschauung* was a revolution. The National Socialist revolution would achieve its final victory only when it was accepted by all Germans. Thus the Nazi *Weltanschauung* must become the exclusive German *Weltanschauung*. Because of Hitler's constant stress on the word, it was often employed by the entire Nazi hierarchy. In the National Vocational Competition (*Reichsberufswettkampf*, q.v.), which included such questions as "What are the tasks of the cartels in National Socialist Germany?" the contestant's *Weltanschauung* counted for 20 of 120 points in the total score. *See also* RACIAL DOCTRINE.

Bibliography. George L. Mosse, *The Crisis of German Ideology: Intellectual Origins of the Third Reich*, Grosset & Dunlap, Inc., New York, 1964.

WELTGESCHICHTLICHE MISSION (Mission of Historic Importance). Catchwords used by Dr. Paul Joseph Goebbels (q.v.), Minister for Public Enlightenment and Propaganda. Germany's mission, according to Goebbels, was to enlighten the world on the supreme importance of racial doctrine (q.v.). He always preferred to use language with a historical connotation. He spoke often of "the German soul," "the soul of the German worker," and "the coming Reich." Over and over again he used the vague word *Idee* (idea). "We manure [*düngen*] with our whole being and with our whole life for the idea." Most important in the lexicon of the National Socialist idea was the German mission to impress the rest of the world with the positive quality of racialism.

"WELTMACHT ODER NIEDERGANG" ("World Power or Ruin"). Slogan used by Hitler to designate his original program. If world power was unattainable, then like Samson at Gaza, he would die in the cataclysm. "Even if we could not conquer," he said in 1934, "we should drag half the world into destruction with us." In his final days he turned on the German people and denounced them because they had failed to implement his designs (*see* GÖTTERDÄMMERUNG).

"WENN DIE SS UND DIE SA AUFMARSCHIERT" ("When the SS and the SA March Up"). A marching song popular in the early days of the Nazi movement. It was supposed to show the brotherly unity of the SS (q.v.), the black-shirted elite guards, and the SA (q.v.), the brown-shirted Storm Troopers. Actually, the SS, led by Heinrich Himmler (q.v.), and the SA, under the leadership of Ernst Roehm (q.v.), were not as close as the marching song claimed.

"WER JUDE IST, BESTIMME ICH" ("I Decide Who Is or Is Not a Jew"). Statement attributed to Hermann Goering (q.v.), the No. 2 Nazi and the head of the Luftwaffe (q.v.). In its basic opportunism this statement was as truly National Socialist as the accusation by Dr. Paul Joseph Goebbels (q.v.) that the Jews were at the root of all evil. Goering on many occasions appointed non-Aryan officers to Luftwaffe posts. One of his chief assistants, Erhard Milch (q.v.), had a Jewish mother. Goering had the mother sign an affidavit declaring that Erhard was the illegitimate son of his father and not her own child, thereby Aryanizing the officer. Hitler, too, revealed this opportunistic streak. In the presidential elections of March 13, 1932, Theodor Duesterberg (q.v.), one of the founders of the Stahlhelm (q.v.), the veterans' organization, was denounced by Nazi propagandists for having a Jewish grandfather. When Hitler became Chancellor on January 30, 1933, he apologized to Duesterberg for the calumnies of the Nazi papers. When Duesterberg failed to comply with Hitler's wishes, his Jewish grandfather promptly reappeared, to be used again as a token of racial disgrace.

WEREWOLF. *See* WERWOLF.

WERFEL, FRANZ (1890–1945). Austrian writer and refugee from Nazism. Franz Werfel was born in Prague on September 10, 1890. He studied at the University of Prague and after World War I went to Vienna, where he married the widow of the composer Gustav Mahler. A lyric poet, dramatist, and novelist, he produced works ranging in style from psychological realism to expressionsim. His large-scale novel *Die vierzig Tage des Musa Dagh*, 1933 (*The Forty Days of Musa Dagh*), an account of the Armenian massacres, won him global attention. In 1938, after the Nazi occupation of Austria, he went into exile to France and, after the fall of France in 1940, to the United States. He died in Beverly Hills, California, on August 26, 1945.

WERWOLF (Werewolf). An organization of guerrilla fighters set up in the closing days of World War II, when Germany was on the verge of defeat. Its leader at the time of the surrender was *SS-Obergruppenfuehrer* (Gen.) Hans Pruetzmann. The Werwolf members regarded themselves as a resistance movement similar to the underground armies that had fought against the Germans in Poland, France, Italy, and the Balkans. They expected to fight in uniform and, if captured, to claim the rights of prisoners of war. They also looked upon themselves as a paramilitary auxiliary of the Wehrmacht (q.v.), the regular Army. They hoped to fight behind the Allied lines to create diversions.

In the late days of the war the Werwolf issued crude pamphlets threatening revenge on those who refused to support them. "We shall punish every traitor and his entire family. Our revenge will be deadly!" Despite such threats the Werwolf never became an effective fighting force. In his first speech as successor to Hitler, Adm. Karl Doenitz (q.v.) ordered all members of the organization to cease operations. The order was obeyed.

WESERÜBUNG (Weser Exercise). Code name for the invasion of Denmark and Norway in early 1940. The destruction of the *Graf Spee* (q.v.) on December 17, 1939, made it clear to Hitler that he was dependent on submarines, which had to have safe anchorage in Norwegian territorial waters. In addition, the German war machine needed Swedish ore, which had to be brought in winter from the Norwegian port of Narvik through the same territorial waters. Immediately after the sinking of the *Graf Spee*, the Fuehrer consulted with Vidkun Quisling (q.v.), his Norwegian puppet, on the critical matter of using Norwegian ports. On March 1, 1940, Hitler issued a directive: "The development of the situation in Scandinavia makes it necessary to prepare for the occupation of Denmark and Norway by formations of the Armed Forces. This would serve to anticipate English action against Scandinavia and the Baltic, would secure our lines of supply of ore from Sweden, and would provide the Navy and Air Force with expanded bases for operations against England." Fall Weserübung was activated on April 9, 1940, with the Nazi invasion of Denmark and Norway.

WESSEL, HORST (1907–1930). Student and martyr of the National Socialist movement. Born in Bielefeld on September 9, 1907, Horst Wessel joined the Nazi party in 1926. He wrote the lyrics for the "Horst Wessel Lied" (q.v.), the song that was adopted as a national anthem alongside "Deutschland über Alles" (q.v.). Wessel was killed in a brawl in Berlin on February 23, 1930. He was elevated by Nazi propaganda to the level of a national hero.

Horst Wessel. [*Courtesy of the Library of Congress*]

WEST GERMAN OBSERVER. *See* WESTDEUTSCHER BEOBACHTER.

WEST WALL. A line of German fortifications extending from Luxemburg in the north to Switzerland in the south. It was designed to protect the Third Reich in the west. Hitler believed that the French Army was conditioned to a Maginot Line (q.v.) defensive mentality, while he preferred the fast movement of a *Blitzkrieg* (q.v.). However, he needed a stationary line for possible defense. At the time of the Czechoslovak crisis in 1938 he ordered his armed forces to prepare not only for an invasion of Czechoslovakia but also for a two-front war. At the same time he ordered the immediate construction of a defense line facing the Maginot Line.

The West Wall was a series of fortifications of which the key point was the rebuilt fortress of Listen, opposite the French Mulhouse. It was never so elaborate as the Maginot Line, and portions of it consisted merely of concrete teeth set in the earth. Construction was supervised by Dr. Fritz Todt (q.v.), then Inspector General of Highways. A million men were mobilized to expedite the work, and many families were evicted to make way for the line of fortifications. Hitler took a personal interest in the progress of the work and often visited the line on tours of inspection.

In War Directive 1, issued on August 31, 1939, Hitler stated: "The Army will occupy the West Wall and will take steps to secure it from being outflanked in the north by the Western powers from Belgian or Dutch territory." In 1940, Anglo-French troops in the Maginot Line faced the Germans in the West Wall (*see* SITZKRIEG; "WASHING ON THE SIEGFRIED LINE, WE'RE GONNA HANG OUT THE"). Construction of the West Wall continued after the death of Dr. Todt and throughout the war. On August 25, 1944, the day Paris fell to the Allies, Hitler issued a war directive calling for the building of a "new West Wall" for the defense of the Third Reich. *See also* SIEGFRIED LINE.

WESTDEUTSCHER BEOBACHTER (West German Observer). A Nazi newspaper with headquarters in Cologne.

WESTFELDZUG (Western Campaign). Hitler's military campaign in the Low Countries and France in 1940.

WEVER, WALTHER (ca. 1890–1936). The first chief of the Air Command Office of the Luftwaffe (q.v.). Originally Wever was assigned to the Reichswehr (q.v.) as director of infantry training. His work in that post was so effective that in the new Wehrmacht (q.v.) he was transferred to the Luftwaffe in 1936. Wever was an unswerving disciple of National Socialism. The Luftwaffe, he said, either would be National Socialist or would not exist at all. An able staff officer, Wever did much to smooth the way for the new Air Force. In May 1936 he was killed in an air crash. His death was a severe blow to his superior, Hermann Goering (q.v.), who said later: "He was an inspiring example to us all—straightforward, modest, and yet a great man and a fine officer. His contribution cannot be described adequately with mere words. The fact that the Luftwaffe exists to-day is due to his untiring work." Wever was succeeded by Gen. Alfred Kesselring (q.v.) in a post now called chief of the General Staff of the Luftwaffe.

WFA. *See* WEHRMACHTSFUEHRUNGSAMT.

WFST. *See* WEHRMACHTSFUEHRUNGSSTAB.

"WHEN THE SS AND THE SA MARCH UP." *See* "WENN DIE SS UND DIE SA AUFMARSCHIERT."

WHITE. *See* WEISS.

WHITE BOOK OF THE PURGE. A book on the Blood Purge (q.v.) of 1934. Published in Paris by German refugees, the White Book gave details of the bloody summer weekend in which Hitler eliminated the leftist wing of the Nazi party. The book identified the names of 166 persons who had been killed in the purge.

WHITE ROSE. *See* WEISSE ROSE.

WIDERSTAND (Opposition; Stand Against). The early movement of opposition to Hitler after his assumption of political power in 1933. Included among its members were Social Democrats, Communists, churchmen, intellectuals, and high army officers—all those who regarded the Hitler regime with disfavor. The movement later developed into Resistance (q.v.) under military leadership, although its members continued to use the term *Widerstand* as a reminder that resistance inside the Third Reich was necessarily different from that in conquered countries. The term *Widerstand* was applied to Helmuth James von Moltke and the Kreisau Circle (qq.v.), whose stand against the Nazi regime was moral rather than practical. Eventually opposition merged into resistance and then into conspiracy. *See also* JULY PLOT.

WIEDEMANN, FRITZ (1891–1970). Hitler's battalion adjutant in World War I. Fritz Wiedemann was born in Augsburg on August 16, 1891. Embarking on an Army career, he served in 1910 in the 3d Bavarian Infantry Regiment at Augsburg and the next year at the War School in Munich. In 1912 he was promoted to lieutenant. In 1914 he was battalion adjutant of the 17th Bavarian Infantry Regiment, known as the List Regiment. Lance Corporal Adolf Hitler, a dispatch bearer on the staff of this regiment, developed an attachment to Wiedemann as his superior officer. After the war Wiedemann retired as a captain and became a farmer in the Allgäu. In 1934 he joined the Nationalsozialistische Deutsche Arbeiterpartei (q.v.) and became personal adjutant to Hitler. He was sent to San Francisco as German Consul General in 1939 and returned to Germany in 1944. At Nuremberg after World War II, he was sentenced to twenty-eight months' imprisonment.

WIENER, ALFRED (1885–1964). Arabist, scholar, anti-Nazi refugee, and founder of the Wiener Library. Alfred Wiener was born in Potsdam on March 16, 1885, the son of a merchant. He attended the Evangelical Grammar School in Bentschen, Posen (now Zbąszyń, Poland), and from 1896 to 1905, the Viktoria Gymnasium in Potsdam. From 1905 to 1910 he studied philosophy and Jewish theology at the Universities of Berlin and Heidelberg. After World War I he worked for the Central Council of German Citizens of Jewish Faith in Berlin, for which he organized an extensive information service. For years he warned about the coming danger to the Jews of Germany. Forced to leave Germany in 1933, he went to Amsterdam, where he founded the Jewish Center Information Office. He collected a mass of information on Hitler and the Nazis. The center was subsequently transferred to London and renamed the Wiener Library. During World War II the Wiener Library was the main source of information on Nazi Germany for newspapers as well as governmental officials. It has remained a valuable repository of source material for historians and students.

WIESENTHAL, SIMON (1908–   ). Founder of the Documentation Center in Vienna, devoted to tracking down Nazis who attempted to escape punishment. Born in Galicia, later a part of independent Poland, Simon Wiesenthal became an architect. Hounded by Nazi functionaries through more than a dozen concentration camps (q.v.), he managed to survive. After World War II he worked for the United States Army in its search for war criminals in Austria and was later employed by the United States Office of Strategic Services and the Counterintelligence Corps. In 1947 he opened a small Documentation Center in Linz to help trace the thousands of Nazi killers still at large. In 1960 he played an important role in helping the Israeli government find Adolf Eichmann (q.v.), the Nazi expert designated to carry out the Final Solution (*see* ENDLÖSUNG, DIE). Wiesenthal reopened his Documentation Center in Vienna in 1961 and gathered a card index of 22,500 names on his wanted list. At this time he also served as head of the Federation of Jewish Victims of the Nazi Regime.

Wiesenthal's detective work supplemented similar efforts in the German Federal Republic, especially those of the Central Agency of State Administration of Justice for the Prosecution of National Socialist Crimes of Violence, set up by the various states of West Germany in 1948.

Bibliography. Simon Wiesenthal, *The Murderers among Us*, McGraw-Hill Book Company, New York, 1967.

WILDE LAGER (Wild Camps). Unauthorized camps set up by individual Nazis. The concentration camp system (*see* CONCENTRATION CAMPS) was initiated as early as March 1933, a month after Hitler became Chancellor. The camps were supposed to be rehabilitation centers for the politically unreliable. The growing thousands placed under arrest made normal imprisonment impossible. The early camps authorized by Nazi officials were supplemented immediately by the so-called *wilde Lager* established by individual Nazis. One such camp was built by Edmund Heines (q.v.), commissioner of police at Breslau, and another by Karl Ernst (q.v.), a member of the supreme leadership of the SA (q.v.), at Berlin. (Both Heines and Ernst were liquidated in the 1934 Blood Purge, q.v.) At the Nuremberg Trial (q.v.), Hermann Goering (q.v.) testified that he had had both these camps closed.

WILFRED. Code name used by the Allied Supreme War Council for the mining of Norwegian waters on April 8, 1940. The purpose was to cut off vital ore shipments from Narvik to the Third Reich. Wilfred was to be used in conjunction with Plan R-4, the occupation of Trondheim, Bergen, and Stavanger by a small Anglo-French force.

WILHELM, CROWN PRINCE (1882–1951). Eldest son of Emperor William II and Hohenzollern heir to the throne of the German Reich and the Kingdom of Prussia. Wilhelm was born in Potsdam on May 6, 1882. After early military training he studied at the University of Bonn (1901–1903). In World War I he commanded the Fifth Army and, in 1916, an army group named after him. He resigned on November 11, 1918, and went into exile in the Netherlands. Within three weeks he surrendered all his rights to the German throne. In November 1923, at the invitation of Chancellor Gustav Stresemann (q.v.), he returned to his homeland. Because of his unswerving loyalty to his deposed father, he was unable to win significant political support in the Weimar Republic (q.v.).

Crown Prince Wilhelm. [*dpa Bild*]

Throughout his life Wilhelm remained in the shadow of his domineering father. As a youth he suffered under the *System des Dritten* (system of the third), by which he was allowed communication with his father only through intermediaries. The Emperor usually left his son's letters unanswered. During his exile in the Netherlands Prince Wilhelm was unable to understand why he was regarded with contempt. He made it plain to the leaders of the Weimar Republic that he was available for a restoration or would be pleased to be elected President of the republic. In 1932 he supported Hitler in his candidacy for the Presidency.

Unlike his brother August Wilhelm (*see* PREUSSEN, AUGUST WILHELM HEINRICH GÜNTHER, PRINZ VON), Crown Prince Wilhelm did not become an active member of the Nazi party, but he twice announced his unconditional allegiance to Hitler and ostentatiously wore the swastika badge. The Fuehrer, however, had no intention of recalling the Hohenzollern dynasty. Crown Prince Wilhelm was not the ogre depicted by war propaganda, but he lacked the qualities necessary to take on the role of a people's Kaiser, a constitutional sovereign, or even a puppet ruler for Hitler. He died in Hechingen on July 20, 1951.

WILHELMSTRASSE. The street in Berlin on which the Reich Chancellery was located during the Hitler era. In popular parlance the Wilhelmstrasse was used as a synonym for the Chancellery building or for the German government.

WILL, HITLER'S LAST. *See* HITLER'S LAST WILL.

WING. *See* GRUPPE.

WINTERHILFE (Winter Relief). Annual charity collection to help finance the National Socialist People's Welfare Organization (Nationalsozialistische Volkswohlfahrt, q.v.), the official Nazi private charitable organization. Hitler described the Winterhilfe as a means of educating the people in the direction of National Socialism, and he hoped to display the government as a benevolent guardian of the public. Once a year on a Sunday, all Nazi organizations were expected to make their personnel available for an extensive street collection. Functionaries of the party, along with stars of the theater and screen, appeared at centrally located spots in the cities to collect money for the fund. Contributors placed coins in collection boxes and received buttons for their lapels. Jewish owners of department stores in the early days of the Nazi regime were expected to make disproportionately large contributions. The *Völkischer Beobachter* (q.v.), the party's newspaper, reported the amount of collections in big headlines. Those who refused to contribute were denounced as bourgeois *Spiesser* (q.v.; philistines).

"WIR FAHREN GEGEN ENGLAND" ("We Move against England"). A popular march. During World War II any victory against the British was announced on the air with a blast of fanfares, followed by the playing of "Wir fahren gegen England."

WIRMER, JOSEPH (1901–1944). A Berlin lawyer who played a leading role in the July Plot (q.v.) of 1944 against Hitler. Known for his skill as a negotiator, Wirmer mediated between the right and left wings of the conspiracy, between Carl Friedrich Goerdeler (q.v.) on the right and Claus Schenk Graf von Stauffenberg and Julius Leber (qq.v.) on the left. Arrested after the failure of the plot, Wirmer was executed on September 8, 1944. In a last letter from Fürstenberg Prison he wrote: "It is not at all easy to die. I hope to keep up my spirit to the end. All I can say is, love one another, be kind to one another, help one another."

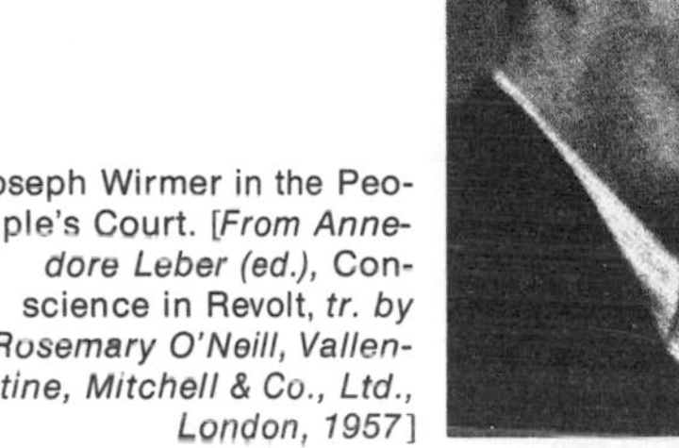

Joseph Wirmer in the People's Court. [*From Annedore Leber (ed.),* Conscience in Revolt, *tr. by Rosemary O'Neill, Vallentine, Mitchell & Co., Ltd., London, 1957*]

Bibliography. Annedore Leber (ed.), *Conscience in Revolt*, tr. by Rosemary O'Neill, Vallentine, Mitchell & Co., Ltd., London, 1957.

WIRTSCHAFTS- UND RÜSTUNGSAMT (WiRü Amt; Economic and Armament Office). Branch of the Oberkommando der Wehrmacht (q.v.) responsible for military supplies.

WIRTSCHAFTS- UND VERWALTUNGSHAUPTAMT

(WVHA; Economic and Administrative Central Office). One of the five key branches of the SS (q.v.). Organized in 1942, the WVHA controlled all the economic enterprises of the SS and administered the concentration camps and extermination camps (qq.v.). Its chief administrative officer was *Obergruppenfuehrer* (Gen.) Oswald Pohl (q.v.). Its activities resulted in the death of all but a handful of the millions of people under its control.

WIRÜ AMT. *See* WIRTSCHAFTS- UND RÜSTUNGSAMT.

WISLICENY, DIETER (d. 1948). *Sturmbannfuehrer* (major) in the SS (q.v.). Wisliceny served as an official in the Reich Central Office of Jewish Emigration under Adolf Eichmann (q.v.). In this post he was active in seeking to bargain for Jewish lives in Hungary, Slovakia, and Greece. He was hanged at Bratislava in July 1948.

WITH DEEP ANXIETY. *See* MIT BRENNENDER SORGE.

WITZLEBEN, ERWIN VON (1881–1944). General field marshal in the armed forces of the Third Reich and leading member of the conspiracy against Hitler. Erwin von Witzleben was born in Breslau on December 4, 1881. In 1935, as a senior officer assigned to Wehrkreis (Defense District) III, he was promoted to Generalleutnant (lieutenant general). From the outbreak of World War II in 1939 until October 1940, he was in command of the First Army. On July 19, 1940, after the defeat of France, he was one of twelve new general field marshals named by Hitler. Until March 1941 Von Witzleben was in command of Army Group D, and until February 1942 he was *Oberbefehlshaber West* (commander in chief of the Army West) in France. He was retired from active service in 1942.

Field Marshal Erwin von Witzleben. [*Keystone*]

One of the older members of the Resistance (q.v.) movement, Von Witzleben was slated to become commander in chief of the armed forces after the removal of Hitler. He was arrested as one of the principal conspirators against Hitler's life. Von Witzleben was condemned to death by the Volksgericht (q.v.), the People's Court, on August 8, 1944, and executed on the same day. *See also* JULY PLOT.

WKR. *See* WEHRKREIS.

WOLFF, KARL (1906–1975). *Oberstgruppenfuehrer* (colonel general) in the SS (q.v.) and the liaison officer of Heinrich Himmler (q.v.) with Hitler until 1943. Wolff was German military governor of north Italy and plenipotentiary to Mussolini during the latter's days of decline. Toward the end of World War II he attempted unsuccessfully to surrender his troops to the Allies. Arrested after the war, he was freed from prison in August 1949.

WOLF'S GLEN. *See* WOLFSSCHLUCHT.

WOLFSSCHANZE (Wolf's Lair). Hitler's field headquarters at Rastenburg, East Prussia, during the late days of World War II. *See also* JULY PLOT; RASTENBURG CONFERENCE.

WOLFSSCHLUCHT (Wolf's Glen). Code name for Hitler's headquarters at Brûly-de-Pêche from June 6 to 25, 1940.

WOMEN'S CAMP. *See* FRAUENLAGER.

WOMEN'S FRONT. *See* FRAUENSCHAFTEN.

WOMEN'S ORGANIZATIONS. *See* FRAUENSCHAFTEN.

WONDER WEAPONS. *See* VERGELTUNGSWAFFEN.

WORK. *See* ARBEITERTUM.

WORKERS' EDUCATIONAL CAMPS. See ARBEITSERZIEHUNGSLAGER.

"WORLD POWER OR RUIN." *See* "WELTMACHT ODER NIEDERGANG."

WORLD VIEW. *See* WELTANSCHAUUNG.

WUNDERWAFFEN. *See* VERGELTUNGSWAFFEN.

WVHA. *See* WIRTSCHAFTS- UND VERWALTUNGSHAUPTAMT.

X-REPORT

X-REPORT. A secret memorandum drawn up for the Resistance (q.v.) movement by Hans von Dohnányi (q.v.) concerning the activities in Rome of Dr. Josef Müller (q.v.). In October 1939, only a short time after the outbreak of World War II, there were reports in London that the papacy was willing to support the idea of a soft peace with a non-Nazi Germany. Müller, with excellent contacts in Rome, drew up a report on the situation. Von Dohnányi added to it and submitted it to the leaders of the conspiracy, Col. Gen. Ludwig Beck and Christian Albrecht Ulrich von Hassell (qq.v.). Known as the X-Report, the memorandum declared that the Pope was prepared to act as an intermediary between Germany and Great Britain on these terms: (1) the removal of the Nazi regime, (2) the formation of a new German government, (3) no attack in the west by either side, and (4) a settlement in the east in Germany's favor.

The X-Report was submitted through an intermediary to Gen. Walther von Brauchitsch (q.v.), commander in chief of the armed forces, who was known to be opposed to an attack in the west. Von Brauchitsch rejected the idea as "plain treason" but did not inform Hitler about it. Leaders of the Resistance then made an attempt to win support from Col. Gen. Franz Halder (q.v.), who replied that the action would be "a breach of my oath to the Fuehrer and could not possibly be justified." By failing to take advantage of the X-Report, the generals lost their last opportunity to win a peace favorable to Germany.

Y

YELLOW
to
YOUTH PROTECTION CHAMBER

YELLOW. *See* GELB.

YORCK VON WARTENBURG, PETER GRAF (1903–1944). Member of the Resistance (q.v.) movement against Hitler. Peter Yorck von Wartenburg was born in Klein Oels, Silesia (now Oleśnica, Poland), on November 13, 1904, the great-great-grandson of Gen. Hans David Ludwig Yorck von Wartenburg, who had won fame in the Napoleonic Wars. After studying law and political science at Bonn and Breslau, he took civil service posts at Breslau and Berlin. He served in the Polish campaign at the opening of World War II and then joined the opposition to Hitler (*see* WIDERSTAND). With Helmuth James Graf von Moltke (q.v.) he was one of the founders of the Kreisau Circle (q.v.). Working in the War Office in the Bendlerstrasse (q.v.), he was one of the first of the conspirators to be arrested after the failure of the July Plot (q.v.) of 1944. His last letter to his wife contained this passage: "It must be regarded as one of God's inscrutable decisions which I myself accept in all humility. I believe I have gone some way to atone for the guilt which is our heritage." He was executed on August 8, 1944.

Graf Yorck von Wartenburg in the People's Court. [*From Annedore Leber (ed.),* Conscience in Revolt, *tr. by Rosemary O'Neill, Vallentine, Mitchell & Co., London, 1957*]

YOUNG GIRLS. *See* JUNGMÄDEL.

YOUNG PEOPLE. *See* JUNGVOLK.

YOUNG PLAN. The second major attempt to solve the problem of German reparations following World War I. Despite National Socialist criticism of the first attempt, the Dawes Plan (q.v.), as solidifying international control of Germany's finances, the country made a spectacular recovery from 1924 to 1929. During these years of relative prosperity the Germans promptly met their obligations under the Dawes Plan. Chancellor Gustav Stresemann (q.v.), however, was anxious to effect a new settlement before the standard annuity payment in 1928–1929. As a result, the Young Committee, led by the American financier Owen D. Young, formulated a new series of recommendations: (1) a fixed capital value of reparations of $8 billion payable in 58½ annual installments, (2) the identity of the number of installments with the number of inter-Allied debt installments, and (3) provision for a Bank of International Settlements (BIS) to handle all payments.

The Young Plan was well received everywhere except in Germany. The Nazis began a strong campaign against it. Contending that the accusation of war guilt was a lie, Hitler asked why Germans must continue payments for

58½ years, or until 1988. Why should generations unborn, he asked, be saddled with the debts of their elders? When Dr. Hjalmar Schacht (q.v.), in protest, resigned his post as head of the Reichsbank, he won the approval of Hitler and the National Socialists. German Nationalists and Communists joined the Nazis in denouncing the Young Plan. But the Reichstag (q.v.) voted acceptance, and on March 13, 1930, President Paul von Hindenburg (q.v.) signed the bill. Before the first payment was due under the Young Plan, there appeared unmistakable signs of an economic depression. Hitler and the National Socialists took advantage of the worsening economic situation to pursue their own plans for German recovery.

YOUNG STEEL HELMET. *See* JUNGSTAHLHELM.

YOUNGSTERS. *See* JUNGBANN.

YOUTH HOSTELS. *See* JUGENDHERBERGEN.

YOUTH PROTECTION CHAMBER. *See* JUGENDSCHUTZKAMMER.

Z

Z-MEN to ZYKLON-B

Z-MEN. *See* ZUBRINGER.

Z-PLAN. A plan, devised by Hitler in 1938, whereby German naval strength was to be increased steadily until it approached that of Great Britain by 1945. The outbreak of World War II in September 1939 came far too early to permit the implementation of the Z-Plan.

ZEITZLER, KURT (1895–1963). Chief of the General Staff of the Oberkommando des Heeres (q.v.; OKH), the High Command of the Army, from 1942 to 1944. Kurt Zeitzler was born in Cossmar-Luckau on June 9, 1895. A career officer, he served in World War I as commander of the 72d Infantry Regiment. He held many important posts during the Hitler era. In 1937–1938, as a lieutenant colonel, he was attached to the Heeresleitung (Army Command); from April to September 1939, as a colonel, he commanded the 60th Infantry Division; from September 1939 to March 1940 he was chief of staff of the XXII Army Corps; from March 1940 to April 1942 he was chief of staff of Panzer Group A; and in 1942, as a major general, he was chief of staff of Army Group D.

On September 22, 1942, Hitler, disgusted with the performance of the old military leadership in the Russian campaign, dismissed Gen. Franz Halder (q.v.) as chief of the General Staff of the Army and appointed Zeitzler in his place. Zeitzler did his best to convince the Fuehrer that the German position in the Soviet Union was precarious and that it was necessary to retreat temporarily. Hitler refused to accept this advice. Zeitzler retired from the Army on January 31, 1945.

ZELLENLEITER (Cell Leader). A Nazi party official responsible for four or five blocks of households in an urban area.

ZENTRALKOMITEE DER KOMMUNISTISCHEN PARTEI (ZK; Central Committee of the Communist Party). The guiding group of the German Communist party and the supreme political enemy of the Nationalsozialistische Deutsche Arbeiterpartei (q.v.), the Nazi party.

ZEPPELIN. Code word for the headquarters of the Oberkommando des Heeres (q.v.; OKH), the High Command of the Army.

ZETKIN, KLARA (1857–1933). Leader of the international socialist women's movement and an energetic foe of Hitler and Nazism. Klara Zetkin was born in Wiederau, Saxony, on July 5, 1857. An early Social Democrat, she helped prepare the Second International in 1889 and took part in all its congresses until 1914. For a time she worked closely with Karl Liebknecht and Rosa Luxemburg. After 1914, with other leaders of the German left, she fought against the "imperialist war" and the "bourgeois position" of the right-wing Social Democrats. In March 1915 she was jailed for working with Russian Bolsheviks in organizing an international socialist women's conference against the war. From October 1919 on she was a member of the Central Committee of the German Communist party and an active leader of the Spartacus Bund. She supported the revolution in Russia in November 1917 and visited Moscow in 1920. A member of the Reichstag (q.v.)

Klara Zetkin. [*Stamp issued by the German Democratic Republic*]

from 1920 to 1933, she was a leader in the political struggle against Hitler and the rising Nazi party.

In August 1932, presiding over the Reichstag by reason of seniority, Klara Zetkin opened the proceedings with a slashing attack on the National Socialists. Despite warnings and threats on her life, she called for a united front of workers against what she denounced as a fascist menace. She died on June 20, 1933, a few months after Hitler became Chancellor. Her ashes were placed in the wall of the Kremlin in Moscow.

ZIEGENBERG. Fortified complex of shelters used as Hitler's operational headquarters during the closing days of World War II. Situated at one end of a grassy valley near Bad Nauheim, Hesse, Ziegenberg was a manorial estate in Goethe's time. In 1939 Albert Speer (q.v.) was assigned to fit out a combat headquarters for the Fuehrer at this spot in the foothills of the Taunus range. The complex was to be used for Fall Gelb (*see* GELB), the attack in the west in 1940. After investing millions of marks in construction, Hitler abruptly decided that the place was too luxurious for him. Nevertheless, he returned to it during the final months of the war. In November 1944 he transferred his headquarters from the Wolfsschanze (q.v.) in the east to Ziegenberg in the west to meet the advancing Allies. He directed the Ardennes offensive from the massive bunkers of Ziegenberg.

ZINSKNECHTSCHAFT (Interest Slavery). An economic theory advanced by Gottfried Feder (q.v.), one of the early National Socialists. According to Feder, the breaking of interest slavery was a prime requirement for the future of Germany. The following is Feder's own explanation of his system:

> Breaking of interest-slavery is our cry on the field of battle. I know that this principle has not been rightly understood in its unheard of and fundamental importance, even in our own ranks. One sees for example how seldom our speakers dare to come to this root problem. Indeed most of them feel it to be a fundamental question; in the treasury of words of our comrades is the motto: "Fight against exchange and loan capitalism." But just what "breaking of interest-slavery" means, how it works in the practical life of the individual and the nation, what technically financial occurrences make the nation "slaves of interest," or what practical steps are necessary to carry out the breaking of interest-slavery, and what the results will be for the entire population when this interest-slavery is broken—these all are vague.
>
> What does one understand by "interest-slavery"? The condition of people who live under the money rule or the interest rule of the almighty Jewish high finance.
>
> In interest-slavery is the farmer, who, in order to finance his farm, must take "credit," at so high a rate of interest, that the interest almost eats up the profits of his work, or who has made or must make debts and must drag the mortgage debts with him as an eternal ball of lead.
>
> In interest-slavery is the workingman, who labors in the factories and workshops for insufficient wages, while the stockholder collects interest and dividends—without worry or work.
>
> In interest-slavery is the entire bourgeoisie, which to-day must work practically speaking to pay for the interest on bank loans.
>
> In interest-slavery are all who must earn their bread through bodily or mental work, while standing opposite them a class—without care and without work—obtains huge incomes through interest on loaned money, through profits on the markets and in the banks, and through financial transactions.—We do not speak of the small independent men or the men with savings-accounts, even though they collect small profits through a fundamentally unsound system but throughout their lives a hundred times the amount of their small savings are taken away from them in some manner, through taxes, pensions, etc., so that in old age they may be given a part of what has been taken away from them before.
>
> In interest-slavery is the industrialist, who has built up his business through the hardest of work, then, according to the principle of keeping up with the times, has changed his business into a corporation; he is now no longer his own boss, but he must satisfy the insatiable greed for profits of the "members of the board and the stockholders"—if he doesn't want to be fired from his own business.
>
> In interest-slavery is every nation that covers its need for money through "loans."
>
> In interest-slavery every nation is destroyed, every nation that gives its most important domestic sovereign rights to the money-power—the bankers, its financial interests, its railroads, and the control of the most important taxes and tariffs, as Germany has done through acceptance of the Dawes Plan.
>
> In interest-slavery are all nations and all governments that bend before the power of loan-capital.
>
> In interest-slavery is all creative work, that has lost its place to gold, so that to-day money has become the most brutal tyrant over work.
>
> Interest-slavery is the correct term for the contrasts "capital vs. work," "blood vs. money," "power of creation vs. profiteering."
>
> The demand for breaking of interest-slavery is of such gigantic proportions, of such fundamental importance for our nation, for our race, that the rebirth of our nation out of the depths of slavery and shame is dependent upon the solution of the problem, indeed the happiness, prosperity and civilization of the world is dependent upon it.
>
> BREAKING OF INTEREST-SLAVERY IS THE STEEL AXLE ABOUT WHICH EVERYTHING TURNS. IT IS MUCH MORE THAN A FINANCIAL, POLITICAL DEMAND; . . . IT GOES INTO THE PERSONAL LIFE OF EVERYONE. IT DEMANDS THE DECISION FROM EVERYONE: SERVING FOR THE PEOPLE OR LIMITLESS PRIVATE WEALTH. IT MEANS THE SOLUTION OF THE SOCIAL QUESTION.

ZK. *See* ZENTRALKOMITEE DER KOMMUNISTISCHEN PARTEI.

ZOSSEN. Army command headquarters about 20 miles south of Berlin.

ZOSSEN PUTSCH. An attempt to overthrow the Hitler regime shortly after the outbreak of World War II. Leaders of the Resistance (q.v.) were disheartened by the failure of the 1938 Berlin *Putsch* (q.v.) but resolved on another attempt. The generals in the conspiracy were pleased by the quick victory over Poland and now hoped for an equally prompt peace. They were soon disillusioned. The

Fuehrer began talking about "killing without mercy all men, women, and children of Polish race and language." Even in the flush of victory he was insisting that "our strength is in our ruthlessness and brutality." It was clear that Hitler intended to go ahead and launch his offensive against the west.

This time the conspirators planned the Zossen *Putsch,* named after the village in which they met. Once again the plot was wrecked by hesitancy and poor planning. The *Putsch* was supposed to take place during the early days of November 1939, but it was never implemented. At the psychological moment Hitler called in his commander in chief, Gen. Walther von Brauchitsch (q.v.), and began to berate him and his generals for cowardice and defeatism. He heaped insult upon insult on the astonished military leaders. His pride in the National Socialist training of German youths, he shouted, had been destroyed. The generals who were aware of the conspiracy made no reply but resolved not to go ahead with the plot. Hitler had won another moral victory over his generals. Within a few days, on November 8, 1939, came still another attempt on the life of the Fuehrer (*see* BÜRGERBRÄU KELLER ATTENTAT).

ZUBRINGER (Z-Men; Informants). Special agents who brought information to the SD (q.v.), the security service.

ZUCKMAYER, CARL (1896–). Writer, dramatist, and prominent refugee from the Third Reich. Carl Zuckmayer was born on December 27, 1896, in Nachenheim, Rheinhessen. After serving as an officer in World War I, he became an outstanding dramatist in the Weimar Republic (q.v.). The best known of his plays is *Der Hauptmann von Köpenick,* 1931 *(The Captain of Köpenick),* a satire directed against Prussian militarism, worship of the uniform, and corpselike obedience *(Kadavergehorsam).* The highly popular play was based on an incident in 1906, when a local citizen, angered by an overbearing bureaucracy, used a uniform greatcoat plus a commanding voice to take over the town treasury. In 1938, after the *Anschluss* (q.v.) between Austria and Germany, Zuckmayer emigrated as a refugee to the United States, where he was active as a farmer and writer. He returned to Europe after World War II.

ZWEIG, ARNOLD (1896–1977). Writer and refugee from Nazism. Arnold Zweig was born in Glogau, Silesia (now Głogów, Poland), on November 10, 1887, the son of a harness maker. As a writer he was noted for his realistic novels, including *Der Streit um den Sergeanten Grischa,* 1927 *(The Case of Sergeant Grischa),* which won worldwide attention. A Zionist, he was denaturalized after the beginning of the Nazi regime. He went to Palestine and returned to East Germany in 1948. From 1950 to 1953 he was president of the German Academy of Arts in the German Democratic Republic (DDR).

ZWEIG, STEFAN (1881–1942). Austrian biographer, novelist, and poet and refugee from Nazism. Stefan Zweig was born in Vienna on November 28, 1881, to a well-to-do Jewish family. From 1919 on he lived in Salzburg. Passionately pacifist and humanitarian, he advocated a Pan-European union. He won a global reputation with his psychologically oriented biographies of Marie Antoinette, Erasmus, Mary Queen of Scots, Magellan, and Balzac. In 1934 he went into exile to London. In 1941, with his second wife, he emigrated to Brazil, where both committed suicide in Petropolis, near Rio de Janiero, on February 22, 1942.

ZWEITES BUCH (Second Book). A contemplated sequel to *Mein Kampf* (q.v.). It was reported that Hitler had written a new volume after 1928. A book titled *Hitlers Zweites Buch* was published in Stuttgart in 1960 by the Deutsche Verlagsanstalt, but there is doubt as to whether it is genuine.

ZYKLON-B. A poison gas used in the chambers of the extermination camps (q.v.). Inmates or new arrivals in the camps were brought to what they believed to be *Brausebäder* (shower baths). Amethyst-blue crystals of hydrogen cyanide were dropped through the vents of the chambers to form hydrocyanic, or prussic, acid fumes. Then the vents were sealed. The special process of Zyklon-B was originally patented by IG Farben (q.v.) as a strong disinfectant. The process was similar to that first used in 1782 from the substance known as prussian blue. The material was formed by decomposing chemicals in almonds and other vegetable substances. Rights to manufacture the gas crystals were acquired by Tesch und Stabenow of Hamburg and Degesch of Frankfurt am Main, which supplied tons of Zyklon-B for the extermination camps. *See also* HOLOCAUST.

BIBLIOGRAPHY

BOOKS ON OR CONCERNING THE THIRD REICH

Abetz, Otto: *Das offene Problem: Ein Rückblick auf zwei Jahrzehnte deutscher Frankreichpolitik,* Greven-Verlag, Cologne, 1951.

Abrahamson, Irving (ed.): *Against Silence: The Voice of Elie Weisel,* Holocaust Library, 1985.

Abshagen, Karl Heinz: *Canaris,* tr. by Alan Houghton Brodrick, Hutchinson & Co. (Publishers), Ltd., London, 1956.

Absolon, Rudolf: *Wehrgesetz und Wehrdienst, 1935–1945,* H. Boldt, Boppard, 1959.

Abzug, Robert H.: *Inside the Vicious Heart,* Oxford University Press, New York, 1985.

Achille-Delmas, François: *Adolf Hitler: Essai de biographie psycho-pathologique,* Librairie Marcel Rivère et Cie, Paris, 1946.

Ackermann, Nathan W., and Marie Jahoda: *Anti-Semitism and Emotional Disorder: A Psychoanalytical Interpretation,* Harper & Brothers, New York, 1950.

Addington, Larry H.: *The Blitzkrieg Era and the German General Staff, 1865–1941,* Rutgers University Press, New Brunswick, N.J., 1971.

Adler, H. G.: *Theresienstadt, 1941–1945: Das Antlitz einer Zwangsgemeinschaft, Geschichte, Soziologie, Psychologie,* J. C. B. Mohr (Paul Siebeck), Tübingen, 1955.

Adorno, T. W., Else Frenkel-Brunswik, et al.: *The Authoritarian Personality,* Harper & Brothers, New York, 1950.

Alfieri, Dino: *Dictators Face to Face,* New York University Press, New York, 1955.

Aloisi, Pompeo: *Journal (25 juillet 1932–14 juin 1936),* tr. by Maurice Vaussard, Librairie Plon, Paris, 1957.

Alquen, Gunter d': *Die SS: Geschichte, Aufgabe und Organisation der Schutzstaffel der NSDAP,* Junker und Dünnhaupt, Berlin, 1939.

Alter, Junius (Franz Sontag): *Nationalisten,* K. F. Koehler, Leipzig, 1930.

Amè, Cesare: *Guerra segreta in Italia, 1940–1943,* Gherardo Casini, Rome, 1954.

Anders, Wladysław: *Hitler's Defeat in Russia,* Henry Regnery Company, Chicago, 1953.

Andics, Hellmut: *Der Staat, den keiner wollte,* Herder & Co., Vienna, 1962.

Andreas-Friedrich, Ruth (Ruth Seitz): *Berlin Underground, 1938–1945,* tr. by Barrows Mussey, Henry Holt and Company, Inc., New York, 1947.

Anfuso, Filippo: *Rom-Berlin im diplomatischen Spiegel,* tr. by Egon Hyman, Pohl, Essen, 1951.

Ansel, Walter: *Hitler Confronts England,* Duke University Press, Durham, N.C., 1960.

Arad, Yitzhak: *Belzec, Sobibor, Treblinka,* Indiana University Press, Bloomington, 1987.

Arendt, Hannah: *Eichmann in Jerusalem: A Report on the Banality of Evil,* The Viking Press, Inc., New York, 1963.

———: *The Origins of Totalitarianism,* Harcourt, Brace and Company, Inc., New York, 1951.

Aretin, Erwein Freiherr von: *Fritz Michael Gerlich: Ein Märtyrer unserer Tage,* Verlag Schnell & Steiner, Munich, 1949.

———: *Krone und Ketten,* Süddeutscher Verlag, Munich, 1955.

Armstrong, John A. (ed.): *Soviet Partisans in World War II,* The University of Wisconsin Press, Madison, 1964.

Assmann, Kurt: *Deutsche Schicksalsjahre: Historische Bilder aus dem zweiten Weltkrieg und seiner Vorgeschichte,* Eberhard Brockhaus, Wiesbaden, 1950.

———: *Deutsche Seestrategie in zwei Weltkriegen,* Kurt Vowinckel, Heidelberg, 1957.

Ausgewählte Reden des Fuehrers, Centralverlag der NSDAP, Munich, 1938.

Balfour, Michael, and Julian Frisby: *Helmuth von Moltke: A Leader against Hitler,* St. Martin's Press, Inc., New York, 1972.

Ball-Kaduri, Kurt Jakob: *Das Leben der Juden in Deutschland im Jahre 1933,* Europäische Verlagsanstalt, Frankfurt am Main, 1963.

Banse, Ewald: *Germany Prepares for War,* tr. by Alan Harris, Harcourt, Brace and Company, Inc., New York, 1934.

Bartz, Karl: *Swastika in the Air,* William Kimber & Co., Ltd., London, 1956.

Baschwitz, Kurt: *Der Massenwahn,* C. H. Beck, Munich, 1932.

Baum, Rainer C.: *The Holocaust and the German Elite,* Rowman & Littlefield, Totowa, N.J., 1981.

Baumbach, Werner: *The Life and Death of the Luftwaffe,* Coward-McCann, Inc., New York, 1960.

Bäumler, Alfred: *Alfred Rosenberg und der Mythus des 20. Jahrhunderts,* Hoheneichen-Verlag, Munich, 1943.

Baumont, Maurice, et al.: *The Third Reich,* Frederick A. Praeger, Inc., New York, 1955.

Baur, Hans: *Ich flog Mächtige der Erde,* A. Pröpster, Kempten, 1956; tr. by Edward Fitzgerald as *Hitler's Pilot,* Frederick Muller, Ltd., London, 1958.

Beck, Earl R.: *Verdict on Schacht,* Florida State University Studies, No. 20, Tallahassee, 1955.

Becker, Howard: *German Youth: Bond or Free,* Oxford University Press, New York, 1946.

Bekker, Cajus (Hans-Dieter Berenbrok): *The Luftwaffe War Diaries,* Doubleday & Company, Inc., Garden City, N.Y., 1968; Eng. tr. of *Angriffshöhe 4000,* G. Stalling, Hamburg, 1964.

Belgion, Montgomery: *Victor's Justice,* Henry Regnery Company, Chicago, 1949.

Beloff, Max: *The Foreign Policy of Soviet Russia, 1929–1941,* 2 vols., Oxford University Press, London, 1945–1948.

Beneš, Eduard: *Memoirs of Dr. Eduard Beneš: From Munich to New War and New Victory,* Houghton Mifflin Company, Boston, 1954.

Bennecke, Heinrich: *Hitler und die SA,* G. Olzog, Munich and Vienna, 1962.

———: *Die Reichswehr und der "Röhm Putsch,"* G. Olzog, Munich and Vienna, 1964.

Benneckenstein, Paul-Meyer (ed.): *Dokumente der deutschen Politik, 1933–1944,* Junker und Dünnhaupt, Berlin, 1939–1944.

Benoist-Méchin, Jacques G. P.: *History of the German Army since the Armistice,* tr. by Eileen R. Taylor, Scientia, Zürich, 1939.

Benton, Wilbourn E., and George Grimm (eds.): *Nuremberg: German Views of the War Trial,* Southern Methodist University Press, Dallas, 1955.

Benze, Rudolf: *Erziehung im grossdeutschen Reich,* Verlag Moritz Diesterweg, Frankfurt am Main, 1943.

Berghahn, Volker Rölf: *Der Stahlhelm,* Droste, Düsseldorf, 1966.

Bergsträsser, Ludwig: *Geschichte der politischen Parteien in Deutschland,* Isar Verlag, Munich, 1952.

Bernadotte, Count Folke: *The Curtain Falls,* Alfred A. Knopf, Inc., New York, 1945.

Berndt, Alfred Ingemar: *Meilensteine des Dritten Reiches,* Eher Verlag, Munich, 1938.

Bertrand, Henri: *Le docteur Schacht,* Éditions Gallimard, Paris, 1939.

Besgen, Achim: *Der stille Befehl: Medizinalrat Kersten und das Dritte Reich,* Nymphenburger Verlagshandlung, Munich, 1960.

Best, S. Payne: *The Venlo Incident,* Hutchinson & Co. (Publishers), Ltd., London, 1950.

Best, Werner: *Die deutsche Polizei,* L. C. Wittich Verlag, Darmstadt, 1941.

Bethell, Nicholas: *The War Hitler Won: The Fall of Poland, September 1939,* Holt, Rinehart and Winston, Inc., New York, 1973.

Bethge, Eberhard: *Dietrich Bonhoeffer,* tr. by Eric Mosbacher and others, Harper & Row, Publishers, Incorporated, New York, 1970.

Bettelheim, Bruno: *The Informed Heart: Autonomy in a Mass Age,* Avon Book Division, The Hearst Corporation, New York, 1971.

Bewley, Charles: *Hermann Goering and the Third Reich,* The Devin-Adair Company, Inc., New York, 1962.

Binion, Rudolph: *Hitler Among the Germans,* Elsevier, New York, 1976.

Bird, Eugene K.: *Prisoner #7, Rudolf Hess: The 30 Years in Jail of Hitler's Deputy Führer,* The Viking Press, Inc., New York, 1974.

Biss, Andreas: *Der Stopp der Endlösung: Kampf gegen Himmler und Eichmann in Budapest,* Seewald Verlag, Stuttgart, 1966.

Black, Peter S.: *Ernst Kaltenbrunner,* Princeton University Press, Princeton, N.J., 1984.

Blau, George E.: *The German Campaign in Russia: Planning and Operations (1940–1942),* United States Department of the Army, Washington, 1955.

Bleuel, Hans Peter: *Sex and Society in Nazi Germany,* tr. by J. Maxwell Brownjohn, J. B. Lippincott Company, Philadelphia, 1973.

Blond, Georges: *The Death of Hitler's Germany,* tr. by Frances Frenaye, The Macmillan Company, New York, 1954.

Blücher, Wipert von: *Gesandter zwischen Diktatur und Demokratie: Erinnerungen aus den Jahren 1935–1944,* Limes Verlag, Wiesbaden, 1951.

Blum, John Morton (ed.): *From the Morgenthau Diaries,* 3 vols., Houghton Mifflin Company, Boston, 1959–1967.

Blumentritt, Günther: *Von Rundstedt, the Soldier and the Man,* tr. by Cuthbert Reavely, Odhams Press, Ltd., London, 1952.

Boelcke, Willi A.: *Deutschlands Rüstung im zweiten Weltkrieg,* Akademische Verlagsgesellschaft Athenaion, Frankfurt am Main, 1969.

———: *Kriegspropaganda, 1939–1941: Geheime Ministerkonferenzen im Reichspropagandaministerium,* Deutsche Verlagsanstalt, Stuttgart, 1966.

Boldt, Gerhard: *Hitler: The Last Ten Days,* Coward, McCann & Geoghegan, Inc., New York, 1973; tr. from the German edition, *Die letzten Tage der Reichskanzlei,* Rówohlt Verlag, Hamburg, 1947.

Bonhoeffer, Dietrich: *Gesammelte Schriften,* vol. I, C. Kaiser, Munich, 1958.

Bonnin, Georges: *Le putsch de Hitler à Munich en 1923,* Les Sables-d'Olonne, 1966.

Bor, Peter (Paul Egon Heinrich Lüth): *Gespräche mit Halder,* Limes Verlag, Wiesbaden, 1950.

Borchard, Edwin, and William Potter Lage: *Neutrality for the United States,* Yale University Press, New Haven, Conn., 1937.

Borinski, Friedrich, and Werner Milch: *Jugendbewegung: The Story of German Youth, 1896–1933,* German Educational Reconstruction, nos. 3, 4, London, 1945.

Bormann, Martin: *Le testament politique de Hitler,* Librairie Arthème Fayard, Paris, 1945.

Borowski, Tadeusz: *This Way for the Gas, Ladies and Gentleman and Other Stories,* tr. by Barbara Vedder, Jonathan Cape, Ltd., London, 1967.

Bosanquet, Mary: *The Life and Death of Dietrich Bonhoeffer,* Harper & Row, Publishers, Incorporated, New York, 1968.

Bossenbrook, William J.: *The German Mind,* Wayne State University Press, Detroit, 1961.
Bouthillier, Yves: *Le drame de Vichy,* 2 vols., Librairie Plon, Paris, 1950.
Boveri, Margaret: *Treason in the Twentieth Century,* G. P. Putnam's Sons, New York, 1963.
Bowen, Ralph H.: *German Theories of the Corporative State,* McGraw-Hill Book Company, New York, 1947.
Bracher, Karl-Dietrich: *Die Auflösung der Weimarer Republik,* Ring-Verlag, Düsseldorf, 1957.
———: *The German Dictatorship,* tr. by Jean Steinberg, Frederick A. Praeger, Inc., New York, 1970.
———, Wolfgang Sauer, and Gerhard Schulz: *Die nationalsozialistische Machtergreifung: Studien zur Errichtung des totalitären Herrschaftssystems in Deutschland, 1933–1934,* Westdeutscher Verlag, Cologne, 1960.
Brand, Joel, and Alex Weissberg: *Desperate Mission,* Criterion Books, Inc., New York, 1958.
Brandmyer, Balthasar: *Mit Hitler Meldegänger, 1914–1918,* F. Walter, Überlingen, 1940.
Braubach, Max: *Der Weg zum 20. Juli 1944,* Westdeutscher Verlag, Cologne, 1953.
Braun, Otto: *Von Weimar zu Hitler,* Europa Verlag, New York, 1940.
Braunbuch Kriegs- und Nazi Verbrecher in der Bundesrepublik, Archivverwaltung der DDR, Berlin, 1965.
Bronder, Dietrich: *Bevor Hitler kam,* H. Pfeiffer, Hannover, 1964.
Bross, Werner: *Gespräche mit Goering während des Nürnberger Prozesses,* Wolff Verlag, Flensburg and Hamburg, 1950.
Broszat, Martin: "The Concentration Camps," tr. by Dorothy Lang and Marian Jackson, in *Anatomy of the SS State,* William Collins Sons & Co., Ltd., London, 1966.
———: *German National Socialism, 1919–1945,* ABC-Clio, Santa Barbara, Calif., 1966.
———: *Nationalsozialistische Polenpolitik, 1919–1935,* Deutsche Verlagsanstalt, Stuttgart, 1961.
Brown Book of the Hitler Terror and the Burning of the Reichstag, Victor Gollancz, Ltd., London, 1933.
Brown Book of the Hitler Terror, Second, The Bodley Head, Ltd., London, 1934.
Das Buch der NSDAP, Schoenfeld, Berlin, 1934.
Buchheim, Hans: *Das Dritte Reich: Grundlagen und politische Entwicklung,* Kösel-Verlag, Munich, 1958.
———: *Glaubenskrise im Dritten Reich,* Deutsche Verlagsanstalt, Stuttgart, 1953.
———: *SS und Polizei im NS-Staat,* Studiengesellschaft für Zeitprobleme, Duisdorf bei Bonn, 1964.
———: *Totalitäre Herrschaft,* Kösel-Verlag, Munich, 1962.
Buchheit, Gert: *Der deutsche Geheimdienst,* P. List, Munich, 1966.
———: *Soldatentum und Rebellion,* Grote'sche Verlagsbuchhandlung, Rastatt, 1961.
Buckreis, Adam: *Politik des 20. Jahrhunderts,* 3 vols., Panorama Verlag, Nuremberg, n.d.
Bullock, Alan: *Hitler: A Study in Tyranny,* Harper & Row, Publishers, Incorporated, New York, 1964.
Burckhardt, Carl J.: *Meine Danziger Mission, 1937–1939,* G. D. W. Callwey, Munich, 1960.
Burns, James MacGregor: *Roosevelt: The Lion and the Fox,* Harcourt, Brace & World, Inc., New York, 1956.
Butler, Rohan D'Olier: *The Roots of National Socialism, 1783–1933,* E. P. Dutton & Co., Inc., New York, 1942.
Cahen, Fritz Max: *Men against Hitler,* Jarrolds Publishers, Ltd., 1939.
Caldin, Martin: *Me 109,* Pan/Ballantine, London, 1973.
Calic, Édouard: *Himmler et son empire,* Série Témoins de Notre Temps, Stock, Paris, 1966.
———: *Le Reichstag brûle!* Série Témoins de Notre Temps, Stock, Paris, 1969.
Cameron, John (ed.): "The Peleus Trial," in David Maxwell-Fyffe (ed.), *War Crimes Trials,* William Hodge & Co., Ltd., London, 1948.
Carell, Paul (Paul Karl Schmidt): *Hitler Moves East: 1941–1943,* Little, Brown and Company, Boston, 1965.
———: *Hitler's War on Russia,* tr. by Ewald Osers, George G. Harrap & Co., Ltd., London, 1940.
———: *Verbrannte Erde,* Ullstein-Verlag, Berlin, 1966.
Caro, Kurt, and Walter Oehme: *Schleichers Aufstieg,* Rowohlt Verlag, Berlin, 1933.
Carr, Edward Hallett: *German-Soviet Relations between the Two World Wars, 1919–1939,* The Johns Hopkins Press, Baltimore, 1951.
Carsten, Francis L.: *Die Reichswehr und Politik, 1918–1933,* Kiepenheuer & Witsch, Cologne and Berlin, 1964.
Castell, Clementine zu (ed.): *Glaube und Schönheit: Ein Bildbuch von den 17–21 jährigen Mädeln,* Centralverlag der NSDAP, Munich, n.d.
Cecil, Robert: *The Myth of the Master Race: Alfred Rosenberg and Nazi Ideology,* Dodd, Mead & Company, Inc., New York, 1972.
Celovsky, Boris: *Das Münchener Abkommen von 1938,* Deutsche Verlagsanstalt, Stuttgart, 1938.
Churchill, Winston S.: *The Second World War,* 6 vols., Cassell & Co., Ltd., London, 1948–1954.
Cianfarra, Camille M.: *The Vatican and the War,* E. P. Dutton & Co., Inc., New York, 1944.
Ciano, Galeazzo: *The Ciano Diaries, 1939–1943,* Doubleday & Company, Inc., Garden City, N.Y., 1946.
Clark, Alan: *Barbarossa: The Russian-German Conflict, 1941–45,* William Morrow & Company, Inc., New York, 1965.
Clarke, Comer: *Eichmann: The Man and His Crimes,* Ballantine Books, Inc., New York, 1960.
Clay, Lucius D.: *Decision in Germany,* Doubleday & Company, Inc., Garden City, N.Y., 1950.
Coblitz, Wilhelm: *Theodor von der Pfordten,* Eher Verlag, Munich, 1937.
Cohen, Elie A.: *Human Behavior in the Concentration Camp,* tr. by M. H. Braaksma, W. W. Norton Company, Inc., New York, 1953.
Collier, Basil: *The Battle of Britain,* B. T. Batsford, Ltd., London, 1962.
———: *Eagle Day,* Hodder & Stoughton, Ltd., London, 1966.
Colvin, Ian: *Admiral Canaris: Chief of Intelligence,* Victor Gollancz, Ltd., London, 1951.
Compton, James V.: *The Swastika and the Eagle,* Houghton Mifflin Company, Boston, 1967.
Conway, John S.: *The Nazi Persecution of the Churches, 1933–45,* Basic Books, Inc., Publishers, New York, 1968.
Cooper, R. W.: *The Nuremberg Trial,* Penguin Books, Harmondsworth, England, 1947.
Coulondre, Robert: *De Staline à Hitler: Souvenirs de deux ambassades, 1936–1939,* Librairie Hachette, Paris, 1950.

Craig, Gordon A.: *The Politics of the Prussian Army, 1640–1945*, Clarendon Press, Oxford, 1945.
Crankshaw, Edward: *The Gestapo*, Putnam & Co., Ltd., London, 1956.
Crippen, Harlan R. (ed.): *Germany: A Self-Portrait*, Oxford University Press, New York, 1942.
Czech-Jochberg, Erich: *Adolf Hitler und sein Stab*, Gerhard Stalling, Oldenburg, 1933.
———: *Hitler: Eine deutsche Bewegung*, Gerhard Stalling, Oldenburg, 1930.
D'Abernon, Viscount (Edgar Vincent): *Ambassador of Peace*, 3 vols., Hodder & Stoughton, Ltd., London, 1929.
Dahlerus, Birger: *Der letzte Versuch*, Nymphenburger Verlagshandlung, Munich, 1948.
Daim, Wilfried: *Der Mann, der Hitler die Ideen gab*, Isar Verlag, Munich, 1958.
Dallin, Alexander: *German Rule in Russia, 1941–1945: A Study in Occupation Policies*, St. Martin's Press, Inc., New York, 1957.
Dallin, David J.: *Soviet Russia's Foreign Policy*, Yale University Press, New Haven, 1942.
Daniel, J.: *Le problème du châtiment des crimes de guerre d'après les enseignements de la deuxième guerre mondiale*, R. Schindler, Cairo, 1946.
Datner, Szymon: *Crimes against POWs*, Zachodnia Agencja Prasowa, Warsaw, 1964.
Davidson, Eugene: *The Death and Life of Germany*, Alfred A. Knopf, Inc., New York, 1959.
———: *The Trial of the Germans: Nuremberg, 1945–1946*, The Macmillan Company, New York, 1966.
Davignon, Jacques: *Berlin, 1936–40: Souvenirs d'une mission*, Éditions Universitaires, Paris, 1951.
Deakin, Frederick William: *The Brutal Friendship: Mussolini, Hitler and the Fall of Italian Fascism*, Harper & Brothers, New York, 1962.
——— and Richard Storry: *The Case of Richard Sorge*, Harper & Row, Publishers, Incorporated, New York, 1966.
De Gaulle, Charles: *Memoirs: Call to Honor*, William Collins Sons & Co., Ltd., London, 1955.
———: *Unity*, Weidenfeld and Nicolson, London, 1959.
Degrelle, Léon: *Die verlorene Legion*, Veritas Verlag, Stuttgart, 1955.
Delarue, Jacques: *The History of the Gestapo*, tr. by Mervyn Savill, MacDonald & Co., Publishers, Ltd., London, 1964.
Demeter, Karl: *Das deutsche Offizierkorps in Gesellschaft und Stadt, 1650–1945*, Bernard & Graefe, Frankfurt am Main, 1962.
Denne, Ludwig: *Das Danzig-Problem in der deutschen Aussenpolitik, 1934–39*, L. Röhrscheid, Bonn, 1959.
Desroches, Alain: *La campagne de Russie d'Adolf Hitler (juin 1941–mai 1945)*, Maisonneuve et Larose, Paris, 1964.
Detwiler, Donald S.: *Hitler, Franco und Gibraltar: Die Frage des spanischen Eintritts in der zweiten Weltkrieg*, F. Steiner, Wiesbaden, 1962.
Deuel, Wallace R.: *People under Hitler*, Harcourt, Brace, and Company, Inc., New York, 1942.
Deuerlein, Ernst: *Der Hitler-Putsch*, Deutsche Verlagsanstalt, Stuttgart, 1962.
Deutsch, Harold C.: *The Conspiracy against Hitler in the Twilight War*, The University of Minnesota Press, Minneapolis, 1968.
———: *Hitler and His Generals: The Hidden Crisis, January–June 1938*, The University of Minnesota Press, Minneapolis, 1974.
Diamond, Sandor A.: *The Nazi Movement in the United States*, Cornell University Press, Ithaca, N.Y., 1973.
Dickinson, John K.: *German and Jew: The Life and Death of Sigmund Stein*, Quadrangle Books, Inc., Chicago, 1967.
Diels, Rudolf: *Lucifer ante portas: Es spricht der erste Chef der Gestapo*, Deutsche Verlagsanstalt, Stuttgart, 1950.
Diesel, Eugen: *Germany and the Germans*, tr. by W. D. Robson-Scott, The Macmillan Company, New York, 1931.
Dietrich, Otto: *The Hitler I Knew*, Methuen & Co., Ltd., London, 1955.
———: *Mit Hitler in die Macht*, Eher Verlag, Munich, 1938.
Dimitroff contra Goering, Editions du Carrefour, Paris, 1934.
Dimitrov, Georgi: *Der Reichstagbrandprozess*, Verlag Neuer Weg, Berlin, 1946.
Dippel, Martin: *Houston Stewart Chamberlain*, Deutscher Volksverlag, Munich, 1938.
Dirksen, Herbert von: *Moskau-Tokio-London: Erinnerungen und Betrachtungen zu 20 Jahren deutscher Aussenpolitik, 1919–1939*, W. Kohlhammer, Stuttgart, 1950.
Dissman, Willi, and Max Wegner (eds.): *Jungen und Mädel im Krieg*, F. Schneider, Berlin and Leipzig, 1941.
Documents on German Foreign Policy, 1918–1945, Series D, 11 vols., Government Printing Office, Washington, 1937–1945.
Dodd, Martha: *Through Embassy Eyes*, Harcourt, Brace and Company, Inc., New York, 1939.
Dodd, William E.: *Ambassador Dodd's Diary, 1933–1938*, ed. by William E. Dodd, Jr., and Martha Dodd, Harcourt, Brace and Company, Inc., New York, 1941.
Doeberl, Michael, et al. (eds.): *Das akademische Deutschland*, 2 vols., C. A. Weller, Berlin, 1930–1931.
Doenitz, Karl: *Ten Years and Twenty Days*, tr. by R. H. Stevens, Weidenfeld and Nicolson, London, 1959.
Dokumente und Materialien aus der Vorgeschichte des zweiten Weltkrieges aus dem Archiv des Deutschen Auswärtigen Amtes, 1937–38, Ministerium für Auswärtige Angelegenheiten der UdSSR, Berlin, n.d.
Dollmann, Eugen: *The Interpreter*, Hutchinson Publishing Group, Ltd., London, 1967.
Domarus, Max: *Hitler: Reden und Proklamationen, 1932–1945*, 4 vols., Süddeutscher Verlag, Munich, 1965.
Donat, Alexander: *The Holocaust Kingdom*, Holt, Rinehart and Winston, Inc., New York, 1965.
Donohoe, James: *Hitler's Conservative Opponents in Bavaria, 1930–1945*, E. J. Brill, NV, Leiden, 1961.
Dornberg, John: *Schizophrenic Germany*, The Macmillan Company, New York, 1961.
Dorpalen, Andreas: *Hindenburg and the Weimar Republic*, Princeton University Press, Princeton, N.J., 1964.
Douglas-Hamilton, James: *Motive for a Mission*, The Macmillan Company, London, 1971.
Douglas-Home, Charles: *Rommel*, Saturday Review Press, New York, 1973.
Douglass, Paul F.: *God among the Germans*, University of Pennsylvania Press, Philadelphia, 1935.

Drechsler, Karl: *Deutschland-China-Japan, 1933–1939,* Akademie-Verlag GmbH, East Berlin, 1964.

Duesterberg, Theodor: *Der Stahlhelm und Hitler,* Wolfenbüttel Verlagsanstalt, Wolfenbüttel, 1949.

Dulles, Allen Welsh: *The Craft of Intelligence,* Harper & Row, Publishers, Incorporated, New York, 1963.

———: *Germany's Underground,* The Macmillan Company, New York, 1947.

———: *The Secret Surrender,* Harper & Row, Publishers, Incorporated, New York, 1966.

Dumbach, Annette E., and Jud Newborn: *The Story of the White Rose,* Little, Brown & Co., Boston, 1986.

Ebeling, Hans: *The German Youth Movement: Its Past and Future,* New Europe Publishing Company, Ltd., London, 1945.

Eckart, Dietrich: *Der Bolschewismus von Moses bis Lenin: Zwiegespräch zwischen Adolf Hitler und mir,* Hoheneichen-Verlag, Munich, 1924.

Eden, Anthony: *The Memoirs of Anthony Eden: Facing the Dictators,* Houghton Mifflin Company, Boston, 1962.

Eggers, Reinhold: *Colditz: The German Viewpoint,* tr. by Howard Gee, Robert Hale, Ltd., London, 1961.

Ehlers, Dieter: *Technik und Moral einer Verschwörung, 20. Juli 1944,* Athenäum-Verlag, Frankfurt am Main and Bonn, 1964.

Ehrenthal, Günther: *Die deutschen Jugendbünde,* Zentral-Verlag, Berlin, 1929.

Eichstädt, Ulrich: *Von Dollfuss zu Hitler,* F. Steiner, Wiesbaden, 1955.

Eisenhower, Dwight D.: *Crusade in Europe,* Doubleday & Company, Inc., Garden City, N.Y., 1948.

Ensor, R. C. K.: *Self-Disclosure in* Mein Kampf, Oxford University Press, London, 1939.

Erbe, René: *Die nationalsozialistische Wirtschaftspolitik 1933–1939 im Lichte der modernen Theorie,* Polygraphischer Verlag, Zürich, 1958.

Die Erhebung der österreichischen Nationalsozialisten im Juli 1934, Akten der Historischen Kommission des Reichsfuehrers SS, Europa Verlag, Vienna, 1965.

Ettlinger, Harold: *The Axis on the Air,* The Bobbs Merrill Company, Inc., Indianapolis, 1943.

Eubank, Keith: *Munich,* University of Oklahoma Press, Norman, 1963.

Eyck, Erich: *Geschichte der Weimarer Republik,* 2 vols., E. Rentsch, Erlenbach-Zürich and Stuttgart, 1956.

Fabricius, Hans: *Reichsinnenminister Dr. Frick: Der revolutionäre Staatsmann,* Verlag Deutsche Kultur-Wacht, Berlin, 1939.

Fabricius, Wilhelm: *Die deutsche Corps,* Deutsche Corps Zeitung, Frankfurt am Main, 1926.

Fabry, Philipp W.: *Der Hitler-Stalin Pakt, 1939–1941,* Fundus Verlag, Darmstadt, 1962.

Farago, Ladislas: *The Game of the Foxes,* David McKay Company, Inc., New York, 1971.

———: *Aftermath: Martin Bormann and the Fourth Reich,* Simon and Schuster, New York, 1974.

Faulhaber, Michael von: *Judaism, Christianity, and Germany,* tr. by G. D. Smith, The Macmillan Company, New York, 1935.

Faure, Edgar: *La condition humaine sous la domination nazie,* Office Francais d'Édition, Paris, 1946.

Feder, Gottfried: *Hitler's Official Programme and Its Fundamental Ideas,* George Allen & Unwin, Ltd., London, 1934.

———: *Kampf gegen die Hochfinanz,* Eher Verlag, Munich, 1933.

Feingold, Henry L.: *The Politics of Rescue: The Roosevelt Administration and the Holocaust, 1938–1945,* Rutgers University Press, New Brunswick, N.J., 1971.

Fernández Artucio, Hugo, *The Nazi Underground in South America,* Farrar & Rinehart, Inc., New York, 1942.

Fest, Joachim C.: *The Face of the Third Reich,* tr. by Michael Bullock, Random House, Inc., New York, 1970.

———: *Hitler,* tr. by Richard and Clara Winston, Harcourt Brace Jovanovich, New York, 1974.

Fishman, Jack: *The Seven Men of Spandau,* W. H. Allen & Co., Ltd., London, 1954.

Fitzgibbon, Constantine: *20 July,* W. W. Norton & Company, Inc., New York, 1956.

Flandin, Pierre-Étienne: *Politique française 1919–1940,* Éditions Nouvelles, Paris, 1947.

Flannery, Harry W.: *Assignment to Berlin,* Alfred A. Knopf, Inc., New York, 1942.

Fleming, Peter: *Operation Sea Lion,* Simon and Schuster, New York, 1957.

Flicke, W. F.: *Die Rote Kapelle,* Neptun-Verlag, Kreuzlingen, 1949.

Foerster, Wolfgang: *Generaloberst Ludwig Beck: Ein General kämpft gegen den Krieg,* Isar Verlag, Munich, 1953.

Foertsch, Hermann: *Schuld und Verhängnis: Die Fritsch-Krise im Frühjahr 1938,* Deutsche Verlagsanstalt, Stuttgart, 1951.

Foreign Relations of the United States: The Conference of Berlin (the Potsdam Conference) 1945, 2 vols., Government Printing Office, Washington, 1960.

Forester, C. S.: *The Last Nine Days of the Bismarck,* Little, Brown and Company, Boston, 1959.

Fotitch, Constantin: *The War We Lost,* The Viking Press, Inc., New York, 1948.

Fraenkel, Heinrich: *The German People versus Hitler,* George Allen & Unwin, Ltd., London, 1940.

———: *The Other Germany,* Lindsay Drummond, Ltd., London, 1942.

——— and Roger Manvell: *Der 20. Juli,* Ullstein-Verlag, Berlin, 1964.

François-Poncet, André: *The Fateful Years,* tr. by Jacques Le Clercq, Victor Gollancz, Ltd., London, 1948.

Frank, Hans: *Im Angesicht des Galgens,* F. A. Beck, Munich, 1953.

———: *Neues deutsches Recht,* Eher Verlag, Munich, 1936.

———: *Die Technik des Staates,* Der Rechtsverlag, Berlin, Leipzig, and Vienna, 1942.

Frank, Walther: *Franz Ritter von Epp,* Hanseatische Verlagsanstalt, Hamburg, 1934.

Franz-Willing, Georg: *Die Hitlerbewegung,* R. V. Decker, Hamburg, 1962.

Fredborg, Arvid: *Behind the Steel Wall: A Swedish Journalist in Berlin, 1941–1943,* The Viking Press, Inc., New York, 1944.

Freedman, Philip: *Auschwitz,* Sociedad Hebraica Argentina, Buenos Aires, 1952.

Freiden, Seymour, and William Richardson (eds.): *The Fatal Decisions,* William Sloane Associates, New York, 1956.

Freksa, Friedrich: *Kapitän Ehrhardt,* A. Scherl, Berlin, 1924.

Frick, Wilhelm: *Freiheit und Bindung der Selbstverwaltung*, Eher Verlag, Munich, 1937.
———: *Germany Speaks*, Butterworth & Co. (Publishers), Ltd., London, 1938.
———: *Die Nationalsozialisten im Reichstag, 1924–1928*, Eher Verlag, Munich, 1928.
———: *Die Rassengesetzgebung des Dritten Reiches*, Eher Verlag, Munich, 1934.
Friedländer, Saul: *Hitler et les États-Unis, 1939–41*, Librairie Droz, Geneva, 1963.
———: *Pius XII and the Third Reich: A Documentation*, tr. by Charles Fullman, Alfred A. Knopf, Inc., New York, 1966.
Friedlander, W., and Earl Dewey Myers: *Child Welfare in Germany before and after Nazism*, The University of Chicago Press, Chicago, 1940.
Friedrich, Carl J.: *Totalitarianism*, Grosset & Dunlap, Inc., New York, 1934.
Friedrich, G., and F. Lang: *Vom Reichstagsbrand zur Entfachung des Weltbrandes*, Prométhée, Paris, 1938.
Friedrich, Julius: *Wer spielte falsch? Hitler, Hindenburg, der Kronprinz, Hugenberg, Schleicher*, H. Laatzen, Hamburg, 1949.
Frischauer, Willi: *Goering*, Odhams Press, Ltd., London, 1960.
———: *Himmler*, Odhams Press, Ltd., London, 1953.
Fritsche, Hans: *Es sprach Hans Fritsche*, Thiele, Stuttgart, 1949.
———: *Krieg den Kriegshetzern*, Brunnen-Verlag Bischoff, Berlin, 1940.
———: *Zeugen gegen England*, Völkischer Verlag, Düsseldorf, 1941.
Fromm, Bella: *Blood and Banquets: A Berlin Social Diary*, Harper & Brothers, New York, 1942.
Frye, Alton: *Nazi Germany and the Western Hemisphere, 1933–1941*, Yale University Press, New Haven, Conn., 1967.
Fuehrerlexikon, Das deutsche, Verlagsanstalt Otto Stollberg, Berlin, 1934–1935.
Fuller, J. F. C.: *The Second World War, 1939–1945*, Eyre & Spottiswoode (Publishers), Ltd., London, 1948.
Funk, Walther: *Grundsätze der deutschen Aussenpolitik und das Problem der internationalen Verschuldung*, Junker und Dünnhaupt, Berlin, 1938.
———: *Wirtschaftsordnung im neuen Europa*, Südost Echo Verlagsgesellschaft, Vienna, 1941.
Galland, Adolf: *The First and the Last*, Henry Holt and Company, Inc., New York, 1954.
———: *The Luftwaffe at War, 1939–1945*, tr. by D. and I. Dunbar, Ian Allan, Ltd., London, 1972.
Gallentz, Otto H. von der: *Die Tragödie des Preussentums*, Hanfstaengel, Munich, 1948.
Gallin, Mary Alice: *German Resistance to Hitler: Ethical and Religious Factors*, Catholic University of America Press, Washington, 1962.
Gallo, Max: *The Night of Long Knives*, tr. by Lili Emmet, Harper & Row, Publishers, Incorporated, New York, 1972.
Gamm, Hans-Jochen: *Der braune Kult*, Rütten & Loening, Hamburg, 1962.
Gangulee, Nagendranath (ed.): *The Mind and Face of Nazi Germany*, John Murray (Publishers), Ltd., London, 1942.
Gartner, Margarete: *Botschafterin des guten Willens: Aussenpolitische Arbeit, 1914–1950*, Athenäum-Verlag, Bonn, 1955.
Gasman, Daniel: *The Scientific Origins of National Socialism*, American Elsevier Publishing Company, Inc., New York, 1971.
Gay, Peter: *Weimar Culture: The Outsider as Insider*, Alfred A. Knopf, Inc., New York, 1968.
Gehl, Jürgen: *Austria, Germany, and the Anschluss, 1931–1938*, Oxford University Press, London, 1963.
Gemzell, Carl-Axel: *Raeder, Hitler und Skandinavien*, C. W. K. Gleerup, Lund, 1965.
Georg, Enno: *Die wirtschaftlichen Unternehmungen der SS*, Deutsche Verlagsanstalt, Stuttgart, 1963.
Gessler, Otto: *Reichswehrpolitik in der Weimarer Zeit*, Deutsche Verlagsanstalt, Stuttgart, 1958.
Geyde, G. E. R.: *Betrayal in Central Europe: Austria and Czechoslovakia, the Fallen Bastions*, Harper & Brothers, New York, 1939.
Gilbert, Felix: *Hitler Directs His War*, Oxford University Press, New York, 1950.
Gilbert, G. M.: *Nuremberg Diary*, Farrar, Straus & Young, Inc., New York, 1947.
———: *The Psychology of Dictatorship*, The Ronald Press Company, New York, 1950.
Gilbert, Martin: *The Macmillan Atlas of the Holocaust*, Macmillan, New York, 1982.
Gisevius, Hans Bernd: *Adolf Hitler*, Rütten & Loening, Munich, 1963.
———: *To the Bitter End*, tr. by Richard and Clara Winston, Houghton Mifflin Company, Boston, 1947.
Gisselbrecht, André: *Le fascisme hitlérien*, Éditions de la Nouvelle Critique, Paris, 1972.
Glueck, Sheldon: *The Nuremberg Trial and Aggressive War*, Alfred A. Knopf, Inc., New York, 1946.
———: *War Criminals: Their Prosecution and Punishment*, Alfred A. Knopf, Inc., New York, 1944.
Glum, Friedrich: *Philosophen im Spiegel und Zerrspiegel: Deutschlands Weg in den Nationalismus und Nationalsozialismus*, Isar Verlag, Munich, 1954.
Goebbels, Paul Joseph: *The Early Goebbels Diaries*, ed. by Helmut Heiber, Weidenfeld and Nicolson, London, 1962.
———: *The Goebbels Diaries*, ed. and tr. by Louis P. Lochner, Hamish Hamilton, Ltd., London, 1948.
———: *Vom Kaiserhof zum Reichskanzlei*, Eher Verlag, Munich, 1934.
———: *Wetterleuchten*, Eher Verlag, Munich, 1943.
Goering, Hermann: *Aufbau einer Nation*, E. S. Mittler & Sohn, Berlin, 1934.
Goldstein, Bernard: *The Stars Bear Witness*, The Viking Press, Inc., New York, 1949.
Goldston, Robert: *The Life and Death of Nazi Germany*, The Bobbs-Merrill Company, Inc., Indianapolis, 1967.
Gordon, Harold J., Jr.: *Hitler and the Beer-Hall Putsch*, Princeton University Press, Princeton, N.J., 1972.
Görlitz, Walter: *Adolf Hitler*, Musterschmidt Wissenschaftlicher Verlag, Göttingen, 1960.
———: *Der deutsche Generalstab*, Verlag der Frankfurter Hefte, Frankfurt am Main, 1950.
———: *Generalfeldmarschall Keitel: Verbrecher oder Offizier?* Musterschmidt Wissenschaftlicher Verlag, Göttingen, 1961.

———: *Maréchal Paulus, Stalingrad,* Édito-Service, Geneva, 1972.
———: *Paulus and Stalingrad: A Life of Field Marshal Friedrich Paulus with Notes, Correspondence and Documents from His Papers,* The Citadel Press, New York, 1963.
———: *Der zweite Weltkrieg,* 2 vols., Steingrüben-Verlag, Stuttgart, 1951–1952.
——— and Herbert A. Quint: *Adolf Hitler: Eine Biographie,* Steingrüben-Verlag, Stuttgart, 1952.
Gosset, Pierre, and Renée Gosset: *Adolf Hitler,* R. Julliard, Paris, 1961.
Gostner, Erwin: *1000 Tage im KZ,* Wagner'sche Universitäts-Buchdruckerei, Innsbruck, 1945.
Graber, G. S.: *Stauffenberg: Resistance Movement within the General Staff,* Ballantine Books, Inc., New York, 1973.
Graml, Hermann: "Die aussenpolitischen Vorstellungen des deutschen Widerstandes," in *Der deutsche Widerstand gegen Hitler: Vier historisch-kritische Studien,* Kiepenheuer & Witsch, Cologne and Berlin, 1966, pp. 15–72.
——— et al.: *The German Resistance to Hitler,* tr. by Peter and Betty Ross, B. T. Batsford, Ltd., London, 1970.
Grebing, Helga: *Der Nationalsozialismus,* Isar Verlag, Munich, 1959.
Greene, Nathaniel (ed.): *Fascism: An Anthology,* Thomas Y. Crowell Company, New York, 1968.
Greiner, Helmuth: *Die oberste Wehrmachtsfuehrung, 1939–1943,* Limes Verlag, Wiesbaden, 1951
Greiner, Josef: *Das Ende des Hitler-Mythos,* Amalthea-Verlag, Vienna, 1947.
Grewe, Wilhelm, and O. Kuester: *Nürnberg als Rechtsfrage: Eine Diskussion,* E. Klett, Stuttgart, 1947.
Gritzbach, Erich: *Hermann Goering: Werk und Mensch,* Eher Verlag, Munich, 1941.
Groppe, Theodor: *Ein Kampf um Recht und Sitte,* Paulinus-Verlag, Trier, 1947.
Gros, Otto: *850 Worte "Mythus des XX Jahrhunderts,"* Hoheneichen-Verlag, Munich, 1938.
Grunberger, Richard: *Hitler's SS,* Dell Publishing Co., Inc., New York, 1973.
———: *The 12-Year Reich: A Social History of Nazi Germany, 1933–1945,* Holt, Rinehart and Winston, Inc., New York, 1971.
Grunfeld, Frederic V.: *The Hitler File: A Social History of Germany and the Nazis,* Random House, New York, 1974.
Guderian, Heinz: *Erinnerungen eines Soldaten,* Kurt Vowinckel, Heidelberg, 1951.
———: *Panzer Leader,* tr. by Constantine Fitzgibbon, Michael Joseph, Ltd., London, 1952.
Gumbel, E. J.: *Vom Fehmemord zur Reichskanzlei,* L. Schneider, Heidelberg, 1962.
Gun, Nerin E.: *Eva Braun, Hitler's Mistress,* Leslie Frewin (Publishers) Ltd., London, 1969.
Günzenhauser, Max: *Geschichte der geheimen Nachrichtendienst: Spionage, Sabotage, und Abwehr,* Bernard & Graefe, Frankfurt am Main, 1968.
Gurian, Waldemar: *Hitler and the Christians,* Sheed & Ward, Inc., New York, 1936.
Haensel, Carl: *Das Organisationsverbrechen,* Biederstein Verlag, Munich and Berlin, 1947.
Hagemann, Walther: *Publizistik im Dritten Reich,* Hamburger Gildenverlag, Hamburg, 1948.
Hagen, Hans W.: *Zwischen Eid und Befehl,* Türmer Verlag, Munich, 1959.
Hagen, Walter: *Die geheime Front,* Nibelungen-Verlag, Linz, 1950.
Halder, Franz: Diary: Aug. 14, 1939–Sept. 24, 1942, 7 vols., cyclostyled, 1947.
———: *Hitler als Feldherr,* Dom Verlag, Munich, 1949.
———: *Kriegstagebuch,* ed. by Hans-Adolf Jacobsen, 3 vols., W. Kohlhammer, Stuttgart, 1962–1964.
Hale, Oron J.: *The Captive Press in the Third Reich,* Princeton University Press, Princeton, N.J., 1973.
Halperin, S. William: *Germany Tried Democracy: A Political History of the Reich from 1918 to 1932,* Thomas Y. Crowell Company, New York, 1946; W. W. Norton & Company, Inc., New York, 1965.
Hamilton, James Douglas: *Motive for a Mission: The Story behind Hess's Flight to Britain,* St. Martin's Press, Inc., New York, 1971.
Hanfstaengel, Ernst: *Hitler: The Missing Years,* Eyre & Spottiswoode (Publishers), Ltd., London, 1957.
———: *Unheard Witness,* J. B. Lippincott Company, Philadelphia, 1957.
Hanser, Richard: *Putsch,* Pyramid Books, New York, 1971.
Harper, Glenn T.: *German Economic Policy in Spain during the Spanish Civil War, 1936–1939,* Mouton & Co., N.V., Publishers, The Hague, 1967.
Harris, Whitney R.: *Tyranny on Trial: The Evidence at Nuremberg,* Southern Methodist University Press, Dallas, 1954.
Hart, S. T.: *Alfred Rosenberg,* Lehmanns Verlag, Munich, 1933.
Hart, W. E.: *Hitler's Generals,* Cresset Press, Ltd., London, 1944.
Hartlieb, Wladimir Freiherr von: *Parole. Das Reich,* A. Luser, Vienna and Leipzig, 1939.
Hartshorne, Edward Yarnell: *The German Universities and National Socialism,* Harvard University Press, Cambridge, Mass., 1937.
Hassell, Ulrich von: *The Von Hassell Diaries,* Doubleday & Company, Inc., Garden City, N.Y., 1947.
Haupt, Hermann, and Paul Wentzcke: *Hundert Jahre deutscher Burschenschaft,* C. Winter, Heidelberg, 1921.
Hauser, Gideon: *Justice in Jerusalem,* Quadrangle Books, Inc., Chicago, 1961.
Hauser, Paul: *Waffen-SS im Einsatz,* Plesse Verlag, Göttingen, 1953.
Hedin, Sven A.: *German Diary, 1935–1942,* Euphorion Books, Dublin, 1951.
Heer, Friedrich: *Der Glaube des Adolf Hitler,* Bechtle Verlag, Munich, 1968.
Heiber, Helmut: *Adolf Hitler: Eine Biographie,* Colloquium Verlag, Berlin, 1960.
———: *Joseph Goebbels,* Colloquium Verlag, Berlin, 1962.
———(ed.): *Hitlers Lagebesprechungen,* Deutsche Verlagsanstalt, Stuttgart, 1962.
Heiden, Konrad: *Der Fuehrer,* tr. by Ralph Manheim, Houghton Mifflin Company, Boston, 1948.
———: *Hitler: A Biography,* Constable & Co., Ltd., London, 1936.
Heinz, Heinz A.: *Germany's Hitler,* Hurst & Blackett, Ltd., London, 1934.
Heinze, Kurt, and Karl Schilling (eds.): *Die Rechtsprech-*

ung der Nürnberger Militärtribunale, W. Girardet, Bonn, 1952.
Helwig, Werner: *Die blaue Blume des Wandervogels*, S. Mohn, Gütersloh, 1960.
Henkys, Reinhard: *Die nationalsozialistischen Gewaltverbrechen*, Kreuz-Verlag, Stuttgart, 1964.
Herrmann, Wolfgang: *Der neuen Nationalismus und seine Literatur*, Städtische Volksbüchereien, Breslau, 1933.
Hertzmann, Lewis: *DNVP: Right-Wing Opposition in the Weimar Republic, 1918–1924*, University of Nebraska Press, Lincoln, 1963.
Herzog, Robert: *Die Volksdeutschen in der Waffen-SS*, Institut für Besatzungsfragen, Tübingen, 1955.
Hess, Ilse: *England—Nürnberg—Spandau: Ein Schicksal in Briefen*, Druffel Verlag, Leoni am Starnberger See, 1952.
———: *Gefangener des Friedens: Neue Briefe aus Spandau*, Druffel Verlag, Leoni am Starnberger See, 1955.
Hess, Rudolf: *Reden*, Eher Verlag, Munich, 1937.
Heusinger, Adolf: *Befehl im Widerstreit, 1923–45*, R. Wunderlich, Tübingen, 1950.
Hewins, Ralph: *Quisling: Prophet without Honor*, W. H. Allen & Co., Ltd., London, 1965.
Heydebreck, Peter von: *Wir Wehr-Wölfe*, K. F. Koehler, Leipzig, 1931.
Heydecker, Joe J., and Johannes Leeb: *The Nuremberg Trials*, William Heinemann, Ltd., London, 1962.
Hierl, Konstantin: *Im Dienst für Deutschland*, Kurt Vowinckel, Heidelberg, 1954.
Higgins, Trumbull: *Hitler and Russia: The Third Reich in a Two-Front War, 1937–1943*, The Macmillan Company, New York, 1966.
Hilberg, Raul: *The Destruction of the European Jews*, Quadrangle Books, Inc., Chicago, 1961.
Hildebrandt, Klaus: *Vom Reich zum Weltreich: Hitler, NSDAP und koloniale Frage, 1919–1945*, Fink Verlag, Munich, 1969.
Hilger, Gustav, and Alfred G. Meyer: *The Incompatible Allies: A Memoir History of German-Soviet Relations, 1918–1941*, The Macmillan Company, New York, 1953.
Hillgruber, Andreas: *Hitlers Strategie: Politik und Kriegführung, 1940–1941*, Bernard & Graefe, Frankfurt am Main, 1965.
Himmler, Heinrich: *"Himmler Rede": Sammelheft ausgewählte Vorträge und Reden*, Eher Verlag, Munich, 1939.
———: *Die Schutzstaffel als antibolschewistische Kampforganisation*, Eher Verlag, Munich, 1936.
Hinsley, F. H.: *Hitler's Strategy*, Cambridge University Press, London, 1951.
Hippe, Ewald (ed.): *Joachim Nehring—Neo-Nazismus?* E. Hippe, Munich, 1950.
Hirsch, Kurt: *SS, Gestern, Heute und . . .*, Progress-Verlag Fladung, Darmstadt, 1960.
Hirsch, Phil (ed.): *Fighting Generals*, Pyramid Books, New York, 1960.
Hirszowicz, Lukasz: *The Third Reich and the Arab East*, Routledge & Kegan Paul, Ltd., London, 1966.
History of the United Nations War Crimes Commission, comp. by the United Nations War Crimes Commission, His Majesty's Stationery Office, London, 1948.
Hitler, Adolf: *Es sprach der Führer*, S. Mohn, Gütersloh, 1948.
———: *Hitler's War Directives*, Pan Books, London, 1966.
———: *Hitlers Zweites Buch*, Deutsche Verlagsanstalt, Stuttgart, 1960.
———: *Mein Kampf*, Houghton Mifflin Company, Boston, 1943.
———: *The Speeches of Adolf Hitler, 1922–1939*, 2 vols., Oxford University Press, London, 1942.
———: *The Testament of Adolf Hitler*, Cassell & Co., Ltd., London, 1961.
———: *Tischgespräche im Führerhauptquartier, 1941–42*, Seewald Verlag, Stuttgart, 1965.
Hoensch, Jörg K.: *Die Slowakei und Hitlers Ostpolitik*, Böhlau, Cologne, 1965.
Hoess, Rudolf: *Commandant at Auschwitz*, Popular Library, Inc., New York, 1961.
Hofer, Walther (ed.): *Der Nationalsozialismus: Dokumente, 1933–1945*, Fischer Bücherei, Frankfurt am Main, 1957.
Hoffmann, Heinrich: *Hitler in seiner Heimat*, Zeitgeschichte Verlag, Berlin, 1938.
———: *Hilter über Deutschland*, Eher Verlag, Munich, 1932.
———: *Hitler Was My Friend*, tr. by R. H. Stevens, Burke Pub. Co., Ltd., London, 1955.
Hofmann, Hans Hubert: *Der Hitlerputsch*, Nymphenburger Verlagshandlung, Munich, 1961.
Hofmann, Heinrich: *Das unbekannte Amerika: Die Entzauberung des Kontinents*, Pöppinghaus, Bochum, 1939.
Hohlfeld, Johannes: *Dokumente der deutschen Politik*, Junker und Dünnhaupt, Berlin, 1933–1943.
Höhne, Heinz: *The Order of the Death's Head*, tr. by Richard Barry, Coward-McCann, Inc., New York, 1969.
——— and Hermann Zolling: *Network*, Martin Secker & Warburg, Ltd., London, 1972.
Hoover, Calvin B.: *Germany Enters the Third Reich*, The Macmillan Company, New York, 1933.
Humbert, Manuel: *Hitlers Mein Kampf: Dichtung und Wahrheit*, Pariser Tageblatt, Paris, 1936.
Hutton, Joseph Bernard: *Hess: The Man and His Mission*, The Macmillan Company, New York, 1970.
Irving, David: *The Destruction of Dresden*, Holt, Rinehart and Winston, Inc., New York, 1963.
———: *The Rise and Fall of the Luftwaffe*, Little, Brown and Company, Boston, 1974.
——— (ed.): *Breach of Security: The German Secret Intelligence File on Events Leading to the Second World War*, William Kimber & Co., Ltd., London, 1968.
Ismay, Baron: *Memoirs*, William Heinemann, Ltd., London, 1960.
Jäckel, Eberhard: *Frankreich in Hitlers Europa*, Deutsche Verlagsanstalt, Stuttgart, 1966.
Jackson, Robert H.: *The Nuremberg Case*, Alfred A. Knopf, Inc., New York, 1947.
———: *Report*, Department of State Publication 2420, Government Printing Office, Washington, 1945.
———: *Report to the International Conference on Military Trials, London, 1945*, Department of State Publication 3080, Government Printing Office, Washington, 1949.
Jacobsen, Hans-Adolf: *Fall Gelb*, F. Steiner, Wiesbaden, 1957.
———: *Kriegstagebuch des Oberkommandos der Wehrmacht*, Bernard & Graefe, Frankfurt am Main, 1961–1965.
———: *Nationalsozialistische Aussenpolitik, 1933–1938*, A. Metzner, Frankfurt am Main, 1968.
——— (ed.): *Dokumente zum Westfeldzug, 1940*, Musterschmidt Wissenschaftlicher Verlag, Göttingen, 1960.

——— and Werner Jochmann (eds.): *Ausgewählte Dokumente zur Geschichte des Nationalsozialismus, 1933–1945,* Verlag Neue Gesellschaft, Bielefeld, 1961.

Jäger, Jörg-Johannes: *Die wirtschaftliche Abhändigkeit des Dritten Reiches vom Ausland dargestellt am Beispiel der Stahlindustrie,* Berlin Verlag, Berlin, 1969.

Jansen, Jon, and Stefan Weyl: *The Silent War,* J. B. Lippincott Company, Philadelphia, 1943.

Jaspers, Karl: *The Question of German Guilt,* tr. by E. B. Ashton, The Dial Press, Inc., New York, 1947.

Jedlicka, Ludwig: *Der 20. Juli 1944 in Österreich,* Herold, Vienna and Munich, 1965.

Jenks, William A.: *Vienna and the Young Hitler,* Columbia University Press, New York, 1960.

Jetzinger, Franz: *Hitler's Youth,* tr. by Lawrence Wilson, Hutchinson & Co. (Publishers), Ltd., London, 1958.

Jochmann, Werner: *Nationalsozialismus und Revolution: Ursprung und Geschichte der NSDAP in Hamburg, 1922–1933,* Europäische Verlagsanstalt, Frankfurt am Main, 1962.

John, Otto: *Twice through the Lines,* Harper & Row, Publishers, Incorporated, New York, 1973.

Johnson, Chalmers: *An Instance of Treason: Ozuki Hotsumi and the Sorge Spy Ring,* Stanford University Press, Stanford, Calif., 1964.

Jong, G. T. J. de: *De Brand,* Blik, Amsterdam, 1934.

Jong, Louis de: *The German Fifth Column in the Second World War,* The University of Chicago Press, Chicago, 1956.

Jung, Rudolf: *Der nationale Sozialismus: Seine Grundlagen, sein Werdegang und seine Ziele,* Deutsche Volksverlag, Munich, 1922.

Jünger, Ernst: *Jahre der Okkupation,* E. Klett, Stuttgart, 1958.

Just, Günther: *Alfred Jodl: Soldat ohne Furcht und Tadel,* National Verlag, Hannover, 1971.

Kallenbach, Hans: *Mit Adolf Hitler auf Festung Landsberg,* Kress & Hornung, Munich, 1939.

Kamenetski, Ihor: *Hitler's Occupation of the Ukraine,* Marquette University Press, Milwaukee, 1956.

"Kameraden bis zum Ende": History of 4 "DF" SS- Panzergrenadier-Regiment, 1939–1945, Plesse Verlag, Göttingen, 1962.

Kann, Robert A.: *The Hapsburg Empire: A Study in Integration and Disintegration,* Frederick A. Praeger, Inc., New York, 1957.

Katz, Robert: *Black Sabbath,* The Macmillan Company, New York, 1969.

Keegan, John: *Barbarossa: Invasion of Russia, 1941,* Ballantine Books, Inc., New York, 1970.

———: *Waffen SS: The Asphalt Soldiers,* Ballantine Books, Inc., London, 1970.

Keitel, Wilhelm: *The Memoirs of Field-Marshal Keitel,* ed. by Walter Görlitz and tr. by David Irving, Stein and Day, Incorporated, New York, 1966.

Kelley, Douglas M.: *22 Cells in Nuremberg,* Greenberg: Publisher, Inc., New York, 1947.

Kempner, Robert M. W.: *Eichmann und Komplizen,* Europa Verlag, Zürich, 1961.

———: *SS im Kreuzverhör,* Rütten & Loening, Munich, 1964.

Kern, Erich (Erich Kernmayr): *Dance of Death,* William Collins Sons & Co., Ltd., London, 1951.

Kersten, Felix: *The Kersten Memoirs, 1940–1945,* tr. by Constantine Fitzgibbon and James Oliver, Hutchinson & Co. (Publishers), Ltd., London, 1956.

Kesselring, Albert: *A Soldier's Record,* William Morrow & Company, Inc., New York, 1954.

Kielmansegg, Johann Adolf: *Der Fritschprozess, 1938,* Hoffmann und Campe, Hamburg, 1949.

Killinger, Manfred von: *Ernstes und heiteres aus dem Putschleben,* Centralverlag der NSDAP, Munich, ca. 1927.

Kindt, Karl: *Der Führer als Redner,* Hanseatische Verlagsanstalt, Hamburg, 1934.

Kirkpatrick, Clifford: *Nazi Germany: Its Women and Family Life,* Bobbs-Merrill Company, Inc., Indianapolis, 1938.

Klee, Karl: *Das Unternehmen "Seelöwe": Die geplante deutsche Landung in England, 1940,* Musterschmidt Wissenschaftlicher Verlag, Göttingen, 1958.

Kleist, Peter: *Zwischen Hitler und Stalin, 1939–1945,* Athenäum-Verlag, Bonn, 1950.

Klönne, Arno: *Gegen den Strom: Bericht über den Jugendwiderstand im Dritten Reich,* O. Goedel, Hannover, 1957.

———: *Hitlerjugend,* O. Goedel, Hannover, 1956.

Kloss, Ergard (ed.): *Reden des Führers,* Deutscher Taschenbuchverlag, Munich, 1967.

Knieriem, August von: *The Nuremberg Trials,* Henry Regnery Company, Chicago, 1959.

Knight-Patterson, W. M. (W. Kulski): *Germany from Defeat to Conquest,* George Allen & Unwin, Ltd., London, 1945.

Knütter, Hans-Helmuth: *Ideologien des Rechtsradikalismus im Nachkriegsdeutschland: Eine Studie uber die Nachwirkungen der Nationalsozialismus,* L. Röhrscheid, Bonn, 1961.

Kochan, Lionel: *Pogrom: 10 November 1938,* André Deutsch, Ltd., London, 1957.

Koehl, Robert L.: *RKFVD: German Resettlement and Population Policy, 1939–1943,* Harvard University Press, Cambridge, Mass., 1957.

Koerber, Adolf-Viktor von: *Hitler: Sein Leben und seine Reden,* Deutscher Volksverlag, Munich, 1924.

Koeves, Tibor: *Satan in Top Hat: The Biography of Franz von Papen,* Alliance Book Corporation, New York, 1941.

Kogon, Eugen: *Der SS-Staat,* Europäische Verlagsanstalt, Frankfurt am Main, 1965.

———: *The Theory and Practice of Hell,* tr. by Heinz Norden, Farrar, Straus & Cudahy, New York, 1950.

Kohn, Hans: *The Mind of Modern Germany: The Education of a Nation,* Charles Scribner's Sons, New York, 1960.

Kolb, Eberhard: *Bergen-Belsen,* Verlag für Literatur und Zeitgeschehen, Hannover, 1962.

Koonz, Claudia: *Mothers in the Fatherland,* St. Martin's Press, New York, 1988.

Kordt, Erich: *Nicht aus den Akten,* Union Deutsche Verlagsgesellschaft, Stuttgart, 1950.

———: *Wahn und Wirklichkeit,* Union Deutsche Verlagsgesellschaft, Stuttgart, 1948.

Kosthorst, Erich: *Die deutsche Opposition gegen Hitler zwischen Polen- und Frankreichfeldzug,* Bundeszentralle für Heimatdienst, Bonn, 1955.

Kramarz, Joachim: *Stauffenberg: The Architect of the Famous July 20th Conspiracy to Assassinate Hitler,* tr. by R. H. Barry, The Macmillan Company, New York, 1967.

Krämer, Gerhard F.: *The Influence of National Socialism on the Courts of Justice and the Police in the Third Reich,*

Weidenfeld and Nicolson, London, 1955.
Krannhals, Hanns von: *Der Warschauer Aufstand 1944*, Bernard & Graefe, Frankfurt am Main, 1962.
Kranzbühler, Otto: *Rückblick auf Nürnberg*, Zeit Verlag E. Schmidt, Hamburg, 1940.
Krause, Karl Wilhelm: *Zehn Jahre Kammerdiener bei Hitler*, H. Laatzen, Hamburg, n.d.
Krausnick, Helmut, and Martin Broszat: *Anatomy of the SS State*, William Collins Sons & Co., Ltd., London, 1968.
Krebs, Albert: *Tendenzen und Gestalten der NSDAP*, Deutsche Verlagsanstalt, Stuttgart, 1959.
Kris, Ernst, and Hans Speier: *German Radio Propaganda*, Oxford University Press, London, 1944.
Kroch, Hugo: *Rosenberg und die Bibel*, Fritsch, Leipzig, 1935.
Kruck, Alfred: *Geschichte des alldeutschen Verbandes, 1890–1939*, F. Steiner, Wiesbaden, 1954.
Krüger, Alf: *10 Jahre Kampf um Volk und Land*, Verlag Deutsche Kultur-Wacht, Berlin, 1934.
Krummacher, F. A., and Helmut Lange: *Krieg und Frieden*, Bechtle Verlag, Munich, 1970.
Kubizek, August: *The Young Hitler I Knew*, tr. by E. V. Anderson, Houghton Mifflin Company, Boston, 1955.
Kuttner, Erich: *Der Reichstagbrand*, Graphia, Karlovy Vary, 1934.
Lampe, David: *The Danish Resistance*, Cassell & Co., Ltd., London, 1957.
Lange, Karl: *Hitlers unbeachtete Maximen*, W. Kohlhammer, Stuttgart, 1968.
Langer, Walter C.: *The Mind of Adolf Hitler: The Secret Wartime Reports*, Basic Books, Inc., Publishers, New York, 1972.
Langer, William L.: *The Undeclared War*, Harper & Brothers, New York, 1953.
Laqueur, Walter Z.: *Russia and Germany: A Century of Conflict*, Weidenfeld and Nicolson, London, 1965.
———: *Young Germany: A History of the German Youth Movement*, Routledge & Kegan Paul, Ltd., London, 1962.
Latour, Conrad F.: *Südtirol und die Achse Berlin-Rom*, Deutsche Verlagsanstalt, Stuttgart, 1962.
Leasor, James: *Rudolf Hess: The Uninvited Envoy*, George Allen & Unwin, Ltd., London, 1962.
Leber, Annedore (ed.): *Conscience in Revolt: Sixty-four Stories of Resistance in Germany, 1933–45*, tr. by Rosemary O'Neill, Vallentine, Mitchell & Co., Ltd., London, 1957.
Ledeen, Michael Arthur: *Universal Fascism: The Theory and Practice of the Fascist International, 1928–1936*, Howard Fertig, Inc., New York, 1972.
Lee, Asher: *The German Air Force*, Gerald Duckworth & Co., Ltd., London, 1947.
Leers, Johann von: *Adolf Hitler*, R. Kittler, Leipzig, 1932.
Leiser, Erwin: *Mein Kampf: Eine Dokumentation*, Fischer Bücherei, Frankfurt am Main, 1961.
Lend, Evelyn: *The Underground Struggle in Germany*, League for Industrial Democracy, New York, 1938.
Leonhard, Jakob: *Als Gestapoagent im Dienste der Schweizer Gegenspionage*, Europa Verlag, Zürich, 1946.
Leonhardt, Hans I.: *Nazi Conquest of Danzig*, The University of Chicago Press, Chicago, 1942.
Leschnitzer, Adolf: *The Magic Background of Modern Anti-Semitism: An Analysis of the German-Jewish Relationship*, International Universities Press, Inc., New York, 1956.
Les lettres secrètes exchangées par Hitler et Mussolini, Éditions du Pavois, Paris, 1946.
Leur, Salvatore S. L.: *Crimini di guerra e delitti contro l'umanità*, Editizioni La Civilità Cattolica, Rome, 1948.
Leverkuehn, Paul: *German Military Intelligence*, tr. by R. H. Stevens and Constantine Fitzgibbon, Weidenfeld and Nicolson, London, 1954.
Levy, Alan: *Wanted: Nazi Criminals at Large*, Berkley Publishing Corporation, New York, 1962.
Lewy, Guenter: *The Catholic Church and Nazi Germany*, McGraw-Hill Book Company, New York, 1962.
Ley, Robert: *Wir alle helfen dem Fuehrer*, Eher Verlag, Munich, 1940.
Lichtenberger, Henri: *The Third Reich*, tr. by Koppel S. Pinson, Greystone Press, New York, 1937.
Liddell Hart, B. H.: *The German Generals Talk*, William Morrow & Company, Inc., New York, 1948.
Lifton, Robert Jay: *Medical Killing and the Psychology of Genocide*, Basic Books, New York, 1986.
Lilge, Frederic: *The Abuse of Learning: The Failure of the German University*, The Macmillan Company, New York, 1948.
Lippe, Viktor Freiherr von der: *Nürnberger Tagebuchnotizen, November 1945 bis Oktober 1946*, F. Knapp, Frankfurt am Main, 1951.
Liptzin, Solomon: *Germany's Stepchildren*, Jewish Publication Society of America, Philadelphia, 1944.
Littel, Franklin Hamlin: *The German Phoenix: Man and Movements in the Church in Germany*, Doubleday & Company, Inc., Garden City, N.Y., 1960.
Lochner, Louis P.: *Always the Unexpected: A Book of Reminiscences*, The Macmillan Company, New York, 1956.
———: *What about Germany?* Dodd, Mead & Company, Inc., New York, 1942.
Loebsack, Wilhelm: *Danziger Gauleiter Albert Forster*, Hanseatische Verlagsanstalt, Hamburg, 1934.
Lohalm, Uwe: *Völkischer Radikalismus*, Leibniz-Verlag, Hamburg, 1970.
Long, Dorothy: *Anatomy of the SS State*, William Collins Sons & Co., Ltd., London, 1968.
Long, Olivier: *Les Etats-Unis et la Grande-Bretagne devant le Troisième Reich, 1934–1939*, Imprimerie du Journal de Genève, Geneva, 1943.
Lossberg, Bernhard von: *Im Wehrmachtsführungsstab*, H. H. Nölke, Hamburg, 1950.
Lüdde-Neurath, Walter: *Regierung Dönitz: Die letzten Tage des Dritten Reiches*, Musterschmidt Wissenschaftlichen Verlag, Göttingen, 1953.
Ludecke, Kurt G. W.: *I Knew Hitler*, Charles Scribner's Sons, New York, 1957, 1982.
Ludendorff, Erich: *Auf dem Weg zur Feldherrnhalle*, Ludendorffs Verlag, Munich, 1938.
———: *Der totale Krieg*, Ludendorffs Verlag, Munich, 1936.
Ludendorff, Mathilde: *Erich Ludendorff*, Ludendorffs Verlag, Munich, 1940.
Luia, Radomir: *The Transfer of the Sudeten Germans*, New York University Press, New York, 1964.
Lurker, Otto: *Hitler hinter Festungsmauern*, E. S. Mittler & Sohn, Berlin, 1933.

McGovern, James: *Martin Bormann*, Arthur Barker, Limited, London, 1968.
McGovern, William M.: *From Luther to Hitler*, Houghton Mifflin Company, Boston, 1941.
Macksey, K. J.: *Afrika Korps*, Pan/Ballantine, London, 1972.
———: *Panzer Division: The Mailed Fist*, Ballantine Books, Inc., New York, 1968.
Macmillan, Norman: *The Royal Air Force in the World War*, George G. Harrap & Co., Ltd., London, 1944.
McSherry, James E.: *Stalin, Hitler and Europe*, vol. 2, *The Imbalance of Power*, The World Publishing Company, Cleveland, 1970.
Maltitz, Horst von: *The Evolution of Hitler's Germany*, McGraw-Hill Book Company, New York, 1973.
Manstein, Erich von: *Aus einem Soldatenleben, 1887–1939*, Athenäum-Verlag, Bonn, 1958.
———: *Lost Victories*, tr. by Anthony G. Powell, Henry Regnery Company, Chicago, 1958.
Manvell, Roger, and Heinrich Fraenkel: *Doctor Goebbels: His Life and Death*, Simon and Schuster, New York, 1960.
——— and ———: *Gestapo*, Pan/Ballantine, London, 1972.
——— and ———: *Heinrich Himmler*, William Heinemann, Ltd., London, 1965.
———and———: *Hermann Göring*, William Heinemann, Ltd., London, 1962.
———and———: *Hess: A Biography*, McGibbon & Kee, London, 1971.
——— and ———: *The July Plot*, The Bodley Head, Ltd., London, 1964.
Martiensen, Anthony: *Hitler and His Admirals*, Martin Secker & Warburg, Ltd., London, 1948.
Martin, Hermann: *Die Legende vom Hause Ludendorff*, Lang, Rosenheim, 1949.
———: *Zehn Jahre Stahlhelm: Denkschrift*, Fleischer, Leipzig, 1929.
Marton, Kati: *Wallenberg*, Random House, New York, 1982.
Maschke, Hermann M.: *Das Krupp-Urteil*, Musterschmidt Wissenschaftlicher Verlag, Göttingen, 1951.
Maser, Werner: *Die Frühgeschichte der NSDAP: Hitlers Weg bis 1924*, Athenäum-Verlag, Frankfurt am Main, 1965.
———: *Hitler: Legend, Myth and Reality*, tr. by Peter and Betty Ross, Harper & Row, Publishers, Incorporated, New York, 1973.
———: *Hitler's* Mein Kampf, tr. by Richard Barry, Faber & Faber, Ltd., London, 1970.
Mason, David: *U-Boat: The Secret Menace*, Pan/Ballantine, London, 1972.
Mason, John Brown: *The Danzig Dilemma*, Stanford University Press, Stanford, Calif., 1946.
Matthias, Erich, and Rudolf Morsey (eds.): *Das Ende der Parteien, 1933*, Droste, Düsseldorf, 1960.
Maugham, Viscount: *UNO and War Crimes*, John Murray (Publishers), Ltd., London, 1951.
Mayer-Loewenschwerdt, Erwin: *Schoenerer der Vorkämpfer: Eine politische Biographie*, Universitäts-Verlag, Vienna and Leipzig, 1938.
Meinck, Gerhard: *Hitler und die deutsche Aufrüstung*, F. Steiner, Wiesbaden, 1959.
Meissner, Boris: *Russland, die Westmächte und Deutschland: Die sowjetische Deutschlandpolitik, 1943–1953*, H. Nölke, Hamburg, 1953.
Meissner, Otto: *Als Staatssekretär unter Ebert, Hindenburg und Hitler*, Hoffmann und Campe, Hamburg, 1950.
——— and Harry Wilde: *Die Machtergreifung*, J. G. Cotta'sche Buchhandlung, Stuttgart, 1958.
Mellenthin, F. W.: *Panzer Battles: A Study of the Deployment of Armor in the Second World War*, tr. by H. Betzler, Ballantine Books, Inc., New York, 1971.
Melnikow, Daniil: *20 Juli 1944*, Deutscher Verlag der Wissenschaft, East Berlin, 1964.
Die Memoiren des Stabchefs Röhm, Uranus-Verlag, Saarbrücken, 1934.
Mend, Hans: *Adolf Hitler im Felde, 1914–1918*, J. C. Huber, Munich, 1931.
Merker, Manfred: *Die deutsche Politik gegenüber dem spanischen Bürgerkrieg, 1936–1939*, L. Röhrscheid, Bonn, 1961.
Merle, Marcel: *Le procès de Nuremberg et le châtiment des criminels de guerre*, Éditions A. Pedone, Paris, 1949.
Meskill, Johanna M.: *Hitler and Japan: The Hollow Alliance*, Atherton Press, Inc., New York, 1966.
Metnitz, Gustav Adolf von: *Die deutsche Nationalbewegung, 1871–1933*, Junker and Dünnhaupt, Berlin, 1939.
Meyer, Adolf: *Mit Adolf Hitler im Bayrischen Reserve-Infanterie-Regiment 16 List*, G. Aupperle, Neustadt-Aisch, 1934.
Meyer, Henry Cord: *Mitteleuropa in German Thought and Action*, Martinus Nijhoff's Boekhandel, The Hague, 1955.
Meyrowitz, Henri: *La répression par les tribunaux allemands des crimes contre l'humanité*, Librairie Générale de Droit et de Jurisprudence, Paris, 1960.
Miltenberg, Weigland von: *Adolf Hitler—Wilhelm III*, Rowohlt Verlag, Berlin, 1930.
Mitscherlich, Alexander, and Fred Mielke: *Doctors of Infamy*, tr. by Heinz Norden, Henry Schuman, Inc., Publishers, New York, 1949.
——— and ———: *Medizin ohne Menschlichkeit*, Fischer Bücherei, Frankfurt am Main, 1960.
Moeller van den Bruck, Arthur: *Das Dritte Reich*, Hanseatische Verlagsanstalt, Hamburg, 1931.
Möller, Kurt Detlev: *Die letzte Kapitel: Dokumente der Kapitulation Hamburgs*, Hoffmann und Campe, Hamburg, 1947.
Morse, Arthur D.: *While Six Million Died: A Chronicle of American Apathy*, Random House, Inc., New York, 1967.
Mosley, Leonard: *The Reich Marshal*, Doubleday & Company, Inc., Garden City, N.Y., 1974.
Mosse, George L.: *The Crisis of German Ideology: Intellectual Origins of the Third Reich*, Grosset & Dunlap, Inc., New York, 1964.
Mowrer, Edgar Ansel: *Triumph and Turmoil: A Personal History of Our Times*, Weybright & Talley, Inc., New York, 1968.
Mueller-Hillebrand, Burkhart: *Das Heer, 1933–1945*, 2 vols, E. S. Mittler & Sohn, Frankfurt am Main, 1954–1956.
Müller, Karl Alexander: *Im Wandel der Zeit*, Süddeutscher Verlag, Munich, 1966.
Müller, Klaus-Jürgen: *Das Heer und Hitler: Armee und nationalsozialistisches Regime, 1933–1940*, Deutsche Verlagsanstalt, Stuttgart, 1969.

Munske, Hilde: *Mädel im Dritten Reich*, Freiheitsverlag, Berlin, 1935.

Münzenberg, Willi: *Propaganda als Waffe*, Éditions du Carrefour, Paris, 1937.

Murawski, Erich: *Der deutsche Wehrmachtbericht, 1939–1945*, H. Boldt, Boppard, 1962.

Namier, Lewis B.: *Diplomatic Prelude, 1938–1939*, Methuen & Co., Ltd., London, 1948.

———: *In the Nazi Era*, The Macmillan Company, London, 1952.

Naumann, Bernd: *Auschwitz*, tr. by Jean Steinberg, Frederick A. Praeger, Inc., New York, 1966.

Nazi Conspiracy and Aggression, 10 vols., Government Printing Office, Washington, 1946.

Nazi-Soviet Relations, 1939–1941: Documents from the Archives of the German Foreign Office, United States Department of State, Washington, 1948.

Nelte, Otto: *Das Nürnberger Urteil und die Schuld der Generale*, Verlag das Andere Deutschland, Hannover, 1947.

Neuhäusler, Johann Bapt: *Kreuz und Hakenkreuz*, 2 vols., Katholische Kirche Bayerns, Munich, 1946.

Neumann, Franz: *Behemoth: The Structure and Practice of National Socialism, 1933–1934*, Oxford University Press, New York, 1944.

Neumann, Sigmund: *Die deutschen Parteien: Wesen und Wandel nach dem Kriege*, Junker und Dünnhaupt, Berlin, 1932.

Neurohr, Jean F.: *Der Mythos vom Dritten Reich*, J. G. Cotta'sche Buchhandlung, Stuttgart, 1957.

Neusüss-Hunkel, Ermenhild: *Die SS*, Norddeutsche Verlagsanstalt, Hannover, 1956.

Nicholls, A. J.: *Weimar and the Rise of Hitler*, The Macmillan Company, New York, 1968.

——— and Erich Matthias (eds.): *German Democracy and the Triumph of Hitler*, George Allen & Unwin, Ltd., London, 1971.

Niclauss, Karlheinz: *Die Sowjetunion und Hitlers Machtergreifung*, L. Röhrscheid, Bonn, 1966.

Niemoeller, Martin: *Here Stand I*, tr. by Jane Lymburn, Willett, Clark & Co., Chicago, 1937.

Niethammer, Lutz: *Entnazifizierung in Bayern*, S. Fischer, Frankfurt am Main, 1972.

Nolte, Ernst: *Three Faces of Fascism*, tr. by Leila Vennewitz, Holt, Rinehart and Winston, Inc., New York, 1966.

Norden, Günther van: *Kirche in der Krise: Die Stellung der evangelischen Kirche zum nationalsozialistischen Staat im Jahre 1933*, Presseverband der Evangelischen Kirche im Rhineland, Düsseldorf, 1964.

Nyiszli, Miklós: *Auschwitz: A Doctor's Eyewitness Account*, Fawcett Publications, Greenwich, Conn., 1960.

Obbergen, Paulus van (Johann von Leers): *The Oberfohren Memorandum*, German Information Bureau, London, 1933.

Oertzen, Friedrich Wilhelm von: *Die deutschen Freikorps, 1918–1923*, F. Bruckmann, Munich, 1939.

Olden, Rudolf: *Hitler the Pawn*, tr. by Walter Ettinghausen, Victor Gollancz, Ltd., London, 1936.

O'Neill, Robert J.: *The German Army and the Nazi Party, 1933–1939*, Cassell & Co., Ltd., London, 1966.

Orb, Heinrich (pseudonym): *Nationalsozialismus: 13 Jahre Machtrausch*, O. Walter, Olten, 1945.

Orlow, Dietrich: *The Nazis in the Balkans*, University of Pittsburgh Press, Pittsburgh, 1968.

Ossietzky, Carl von: *The Stolen Republic*, ed. by Bruno Frei and tr. by John Peet, Lawrence & Wishart, Ltd., London, 1971.

Oven, Wilfred von: *Mit Goebbels bis zum Ende*, Dürer-Verlag, Buenos Aires, 1949.

Paetel, Karl Otto: *Das Bild vom Menschen in der deutschen Jugendführung*, H. Voggenreiter, Bad Godesberg, 1954.

———: *Jugendbewegung und Politik*, H. Voggenreiter, Bad Godesberg, 1963.

Paget, R. T.: *Manstein: His Campaigns and His Trial*, William Collins Sons & Co., Ltd., London, 1951.

Paikert, G. C.: *The Danube Swabians: German Populations in Hungary, Rumania and Yugoslavia and Hitler's Impact on Their Patterns*, Martinus Nijhoff's Boekhandel, The Hague, 1967.

Papen, Franz von: *Europa was nun?* Göttinger Verlagsanstalt, Göttingen, 1954.

———: *Memoirs*, E. P. Dutton & Co., Inc., New York, 1953.

———: *Vom Scheitern einer Demokratie, 1930–1933*, Verlag Hase & Koehler, Munich, 1968.

———: *Die Wahrheit eine Gasse*, P. List, Munich, 1952.

Payne, Robert: *The Life and Death of Adolf Hitler*, Frederick A. Praeger, Inc., New York, 1973.

Pechel, Rudolf: *Deutscher Widerstand*, E. Rentsch, Erlenbach-Zürich, 1947.

Peis, Günter: *Naujocks, l'homme qui déclencha la guerre*, B. Arthaud, Paris, 1962.

Perrault, Giles (Jacques Peyroles), *The Red Orchestra*, Simon and Schuster, New York, 1969.

Pétain et les Allemands: Un mémorandum d'Abetz sur les rapports franco-allemands, Gaucher, Paris, 1946.

Peterson, Edward N.: *Hjalmar Schacht: For and Against Hitler*, Christopher Publishing House, Boston, 1954.

Pfundtner, Hans: *Dr. Wilhelm Frick und sein Ministerium*, Eher Verlag, Munich, 1937.

Philippi, Alfred: *Der Feldzug gegen Sowjetrussland, 1941 bis 1945*, W. Kohlhammer, Stuttgart, 1962.

Phillips, Raymond (ed.): *Trial of Josef Kramer and Forty-four Others (The Belsen Trial)*, William Hodge & Co., Ltd., London, 1949.

Picard, Max: *Hitler in Ourselves*, tr. by Heinrich Hauser, Henry Regnery Company, Chicago, 1947.

Picker, Henry: *Hitlers Tischgespräche im Fuehrerhauptquartier*, Seewald Verlag, Stuttgart, 1963.

——— and Heinrich Hoffmann: *Hitler Close-Up*, tr. by Nicholas Fry, The Macmillan Company, New York, 1974.

Pinson, Koppel J.: *Modern Germany*, The Macmillan Company, New York, 1934.

——— (ed.): *Essays on Anti-Semitism*, Conference on Jewish Relations, New York, 1946.

Piotrowski, Stanisław (ed.): *Hans Frank's Diary*, Pańtswowe Wydawn Naukowe, Warsaw, 1961.

Poliakov, Léon, and Josef Wulf: *Das Dritte Reich und die Juden*, Arani Verlag, Berlin, 1955.

——— and ———: *Das Dritte Reich und seine Denker*, Arani Verlag, Berlin, 1959.

——— and ———: *Das Dritte Reich und seine Diener*, Arani Verlag, Berlin, 1956.

Polnische Dokumente zur Vorgeschichte des Krieges, Eher Verlag, Munich, 1940.

Pompe, C. A.: *Aggressive War an International Crime*, Martinus Nijhoff's Boekhandel, The Hague, 1953.
Poole, Kenyon E.: *German Financial Policies, 1932–1939*, Harvard University Press, Cambridge, Mass., 1940.
Presseisen, Ernst L.: *Germany and Japan: A Study in Totalitarian Diplomacy, 1933–1941*, Martinus Nijhoff's Boekhandel, The Hague, 1958.
Presser, Jacob: *The Destruction of the German Jews*, tr. from the Dutch by Arnold Pomerans, E. P. Dutton & Co., Inc., New York, 1969.
Price, Alfred: *Luftwaffe*, Pan/Ballantine, London, 1973.
Price, George Ward: *I Knew These Dictators*, Henry Holt and Company, Inc., New York, 1938.
Priepke, Manfred: *Die evangelische Jugend im Dritten Reich, 1933–1936*, Norddeutsche Verlagsanstalt O. Goedel, Hannover, 1960.
Prittie, Terence: *Germans against Hitler*, Hutchinson & Co. (Publishers), Ltd., London, 1964.
Pross, Harry: *Jugend—Eros—Politik: Die Geschichte der deutschen Jugendverbände*, Scherz, Bern, 1964.
———: *Vor und nach Hitler: Zur deutschen Sozialpathologie*, O. Walter, Olten, 1962.
Pulzer, Peter G. J.: *The Rise of Political Anti-Semitism in Germany and Austria*, John Wiley & Sons, Inc., New York, 1964.
Pünder, Hermann: *Politik in der Reichskanzlei: Aufzeichnungen aus den Jahren 1929–1932*, Deutsche Verlagsanstalt, Stuttgart, 1961.
Punishment for War Crimes: The Interallied Documents Signed at St. James' Palace, London, 13 January 1942, and Relative Documents, His Majesty's Stationery Office, London, 1942.
Puttkamer, Jesko Heinrich von: *Irrtum und Schuld: Die Geschichte des National-Komitees "Freies Deutschland,"* Michael-Verlag, Neuwied, 1948.
Rabitsch, Hugo: *Aus Adolf Hitlers Jugendzeit*, Deutscher Volksverlag, Munich, 1938.
Raeder, Erich: *My Life*, tr. by Henry W. Drexel, United States Naval Institute, Annapolis, Md., 1960.
Rauschenbach, Gerhard: *Der Nürnberger Prozess gegen die Organisationen*, L. Röhrscheid, Bonn, 1954.
Rauschning, Hermann: *The Revolution of Nihilism*, Longmans, Green & Company, Inc., New York, 1939.
———: *The Voice of Destruction*, G. P. Putnam's Sons, New York, 1940.
Recktenwald, Johann: *Woran hat Adolf Hitler gelitten?* E. Reinhardt, Munich, 1963.
Reed, Douglas: *The Burning of the Reichstag*, Victor Gollancz, Ltd., London, 1934.
———: *Nemesis? The Story of Otto Strasser*, Houghton Mifflin Company, Boston, 1940.
———: *The Prisoner of Ottawa: Otto Strasser*, Jonathan Cape, Ltd., London, 1953.
Rees, J. R. (ed.): *The Case of Rudolf Hess: A Problem in Diagnosis and Forensic Psychiatry*, William Heinemann, Ltd., London, 1947.
Reich, Albert: *Aus Adolf Hitlers Heimat*, Eher Verlag, Munich, 1933.
———: *Dietrich Eckart*, Eher Verlag, Munich, 1934.
Reichsjugendfuehrer (ed.): *HJ im Dienst*, Bernard & Graefe, Berlin, 1940.
———: *Jahrbuch des BDM Werkes Glaube und Schönheit, 1943*, Eher Verlag, Munich, 1943.
Reichmann, Eva G.: *Hostages of Civilization: The Social Sources of National Socialist Anti-Semitism*, Beacon Press, Boston, 1951.
Reichsarchiv: *Darstellungen aus den Nachkriegskämpfe deutscher Truppen und Freikorps*, 9 vols., E. S. Mittler & Sohn, Berlin, 1936–1940.
Reile, Oscar: *Geheime Ostfront: Die deutsche Abwehr im Osten, 1921–1945*, Verlag Weisermühl, Munich, 1963.
Reitlinger, Gerald: *The Final Solution*, A. S. Barnes and Co., Inc., New York, 1961.
———: *The House Built on Sand: The Conflicts of German Policy in Russia, 1939–1945*, Weidenfeld and Nicolson, London, 1960.
———: *The SS: Alibi of a Nation*, William Heinemann, Ltd., London, 1957.
Remer, Otto-Ernst: *20. Juli 1944*, H. Siep, Hamburg, 1951.
Reuter, Franz: *Schacht*, Deutsche Verlagsanstalt, Stuttgart, 1937.
Reynolds, Quentin: *Minister of Death: The Eichmann Story*, The Viking Press, Inc., New York, 1960.
Ribbentrop, Annaliese von: *Verschwörung gegen den Frieden*, Druffel Verlag, Leoni am Starnberger See, 1962.
Ribbentrop, Joachim von: *The Ribbentrop Memoirs*, tr. by Oliver Watson, Weidenfeld and Nicolson, London, 1954.
Rich, Norman, *Hitler's War Aims: The Establishment of the New Order*, W. W. Norton & Company, Inc., New York, 1974.
Riess, Curt: *Joseph Goebbels: A Biography*, Doubleday & Company, Inc., Garden City, N.Y., 1948.
Ritter, Gerhard: *The German Resistance: Carl Goerdeler's Struggle against Tyranny*, tr. by R. I. Clark, Frederick A. Praeger, Inc., New York, 1958.
Roberts, Stephen H.: *The House That Hitler Built*, Harper & Brothers, New York, 1938.
Robertson, Esmonde M.: *Hitler's Pre-War Policy and Military Plans, 1933–1939*, Longmans, Green & Co., Ltd., London, 1963.
Robinson, Jacob, and Philip G. Friedman: *Guide to Jewish History under Nazi Impact*, YIVO Institute for Jewish Research, Inc., New York, 1960.
Roeder, M.: *Die Rote Kapelle*, H. Siep, Hamburg, 1952.
Roehm, Ernst: *Die Geschichte eines Hochverräters*, Eher Verlag, Munich, 1933.
Röhrs, Hans Dietrich: *Hitler: Die Zerstörung einer Persönlichkeit*, Kurt Vowinckel, Neckargemünd, 1965.
Roloff, Ernst-August: *Bürgertum und Nationalsozialismus, 1930–1933: Braunschweigs Weg ins Dritte Reich*, Verlag für Literatur und Zeitgeschehen, Hannover, 1963.
Rönnefarth, Helmuth K.: *Die Sudetenkrise in der internationalen Politik*, F. Steiner, Wiesbaden, 1961.
Rosenberg, Alfred: *Blut und Ehre*, Centralverlag der NSDAP, Munich, 1934.
———: *Letzte Aufzeichnungen*, Plesse Verlag, Göttingen, 1955.
———: *Memoirs*, tr. by Eric Posselt, Ziff-Davis Publishing, New York, 1949.
———: *Der Mythus des 20. Jahrhunderts*, Hoheneichen-Verlag, Munich, 1930.
———: *Die Protokolle der Weisen von Zion und die jüdische Weltpolitik*, Deutscher Volksverlag, Munich, 1923.
———: *Selected Writings*, Jonathan Cape, Ltd., London, 1970.

———: *Die Spur der Juden im Wandel der Zeiten,* Deutscher Volksverlag, Munich, 1920.
———: *Der staatsfeindliche Zionismus,* Eher Verlag, Munich, 1938.
———: *Unmoral im Talmud,* Deutscher Volksverlag, Munich, 1920.
Rosinski, Herbert: *The German Army,* The Hogarth Press, Ltd., London, 1940.
Ross, Dieter: *Hitler und Dollfuss,* Leibniz-Verlag, Hamburg, 1966.
Roth, Guenther, and Kurt H. Wolff: *The American Denazification of Germany,* Ohio State University, Columbus, 1954.
Rothfels, Hans: *The German Opposition to Hitler,* tr. by Lawrence Wilson, Henry Regnery Company, Chicago, 1963.
———: *The Political Legacy of the German Resistance Movement,* Inter-Nationes, Bad Godesberg, 1969.
Royce, Hans: *Germans against Hitler,* tr. by Allan and Lieselotte Yahraes, Berto-Verlag, Bonn, 1960.
Ruge, Friedrich: *Der Seekrieg, 1939–1945,* K. F. Koehler, Stuttgart, 1954.
Rühle, Gerd: *Das Dritte Reich,* Hummel-Verlag, Berlin, 1936.
Russell, William: *Berlin Embassy,* E. P. Dutton & Co., Inc., New York, 1941.
Russell of Liverpool, Baron: *The Scourge of the Swastika,* Cassell & Co., Ltd., London, 1954.
Sack, Alfons: *Der Reichstagsbrand Prozess,* Ullstein-Verlag, Berlin, 1934.
Sadila-Mantau, Hans Heinz: *Unsere Reichsregierung,* C. A. Weller, Berlin, 1936.
——— (ed.): *Deutsche Führer: Deutsches Schicksal,* Riegler, Berlin, 1933.
Sagitz, Walter: *Bibliographie des Nationalsozialismus,* A. Heine, Cottbus, 1933.
Salomon, Ernst von: *Der Fragebogen,* Rohwolt Verlag, Hamburg, 1951.
Sanders, Marion K.: *Dorothy Thompson: A Legend in Her Time,* Houghton Mifflin Company, Boston, 1973.
Sandvoss, Ernst: *Hitler und Nietzsche,* Musterschmidt Wissenschaftlicher Verlag, Göttingen, 1967.
Sartre, Jean-Paul: *Anti-Semite and Jew,* tr. by George Becker, Grove Press, Inc., New York, 1962.
Sastamoinen, Armas: *Hitlers sevnska förtrupper,* Federativs Förlag, Stockholm, 1947.
———: *Nynazismen,* Federativs Förlag, Stockholm, 1961.
Sasuly, Richard: *I. G. Farben,* Boni & Gaer, New York, 1947.
Sautter, Reinhold: *Hitlerjugend,* C. Röhrig, Munich, 1942.
Sayers, Michael, and Albert Kahn: *Sabotage: The Secret War against America,* Harper & Brothers, New York, 1942.
Schacht, Hjalmar: *Account Settled,* Weidenfeld and Nicholson, London, 1949.
———: *Confessions of "the Old Wizard,"* Houghton Mifflin Company, Boston, 1956.
Schaumburg-Lippe, Friedrich Christian Prinz zu: *Dr. Goebbels,* Limes Verlag, Wiesbaden, 1964.
Schechtman, Joseph B.: *The Mufti and the Fuehrer: The Rise and Fall of Haj Amin el-Husseini,* Thomas Yoseloff, Ltd., New York, 1965.
Scheid, Othon: *Les mémoires de Hitler et le programme nationalsozialiste,* Éditions Olivier Perrin, Paris, 1933.
Schellenberg, Walter: *The Labyrinth,* Harper & Brothers, New York, 1956.
Scheurig, Bodo: *Freies Deutschland: Das Nationalkomitee und der Bund Deutscher Offiziere in der Sowjetunion, 1943-1945,* Nymphenburger Verlagshandlung, Munich, 1960.
Schirach, Baldur von: *Die Feier der neuen Front,* Deutsche Volksverlag, Munich, n.d.
———: *Ich glaubte an Hitler,* Mosaik Verlag, Hamburg, 1967.
———: *Rede zur Eröffnung der Mozart Woche,* Gesellschaft der Bibliophilen, Weimar, 1943.
———: *Revolution der Erziehung,* Eher Verlag, Munich, 1938.
———: *Das wiener Kulturprogramm,* Eher Verlag, Vienna, 1941.
———: *Wille und Macht,* Eher Verlag, Munich, 1938.
Schirach, Max von: *Geschichte der Familie von Schirach,* W. de Gruyter, Berlin, 1939.
Schirmer, Friedrich: *Celler Soldatenbuch,* Pohl, Celle, 1937.
Schlabrendorff, Fabian von: *Offiziere gegen Hitler,* Europa Verlag, Zürich, 1946.
———: *The Secret War against Hitler,* tr. by Hilda Simon, Hodder & Stoughton, Ltd., London, 1961.
Schmidt, Matthias: *Albert Speer: The End of a Myth,* St. Martin's Press, New York, 1984.
Schmidt, Paul: *Hitler's Interpreter: The Secret History of German Diplomacy, 1936–1945,* The Macmillan Company, New York, 1951.
———: *Statist auf diplomatischen Bühne, 1923–1945,* Athenäum-Verlag, Bonn, 1950.
Schmitthenner, Walter A., and Hans Buchheim (eds.): *Der deutschen Widerstand gegen Hitler,* Kiepenheuer & Witsch, Cologne, 1966.
Schnee, Heinrich: *Georg Ritter von Schönerer,* F. Kraus, Reichenberg, 1943.
———: *Karl Lueger,* Duncker & Humblot, Berlin, 1960.
Schoenbaum, David: *Hitler's Social Revolution: Class and Status in Nazi Germany, 1933–1939,* Doubleday and Company, Inc., Garden City, N.Y., 1967.
Schoenbirner, Gerhard, *The Yellow Star,* tr. by Susan Sweet, Bantam Books, Inc., New York, 1973.
Schonauer, Franz: *Deutsche Literatur im Dritten Reich,* O. Walter, Olten, 1961.
Schorn, Hubert: *Der Richter im Dritten Reich,* V. Klostermann, Frankfurt am Main, 1959.
Schramm, Percy Ernst: *Kriegstagebuch des OKW,* Bernard & Graefe, Frankfurt am Main, 1961.
Schramm, Wilhelm von: *Conspiracy among Generals,* tr. by Robert Thomas Clarke, George Allen & Unwin, Ltd., London, 1936.
———: *Der 20. Juli in Paris,* Kindler und Schiermeyer, Bad Wörishofen, 1953.
Schricker, Rudolf: *Rotmord über München,* Verlags und Vertriebs-Gesellschaft, Berlin, 1935.
Schröter, Heinz: *Stalingrad,* tr. by Constantine Fitzgibbon, E. P. Dutton & Co., Inc., New York, 1958.
Schubert, Günter: *Anfänge nationalsozialistischer Aussenpolitik,* Verlag Wissenschaft und Politik, Cologne, 1963.

Schüddekopf, Otto-Ernst: *Revolutions of Our Time: Fascism*, Frederick A. Praeger, Inc., New York, 1973.
Schuschnigg, Kurt von: *Austrian Requiem*, tr. by Franz von Hildebrand, G. P. Putnam's Sons, New York, 1946.
———: *My Austria*, tr. by John Segrue, Alfred A. Knopf, Inc., New York, 1938.
Schwartz, Paul: *This Man Ribbentrop: His Life and Times*, Julian Messner, Publishers, Inc., New York, 1943.
Schweitzer, Arthur: *Big Business in the Third Reich*, Indiana University Press, Bloomington, 1964.
Schweppenburg, Leo Geyr von: *Erinnerungen eines Militärattaches, London, 1933–1937*, Deutsche Verlagsanstalt, Stuttgart, 1949.
Schwerin von Krosigk, Lutz Graf: *Es geschah in Deutschland*, R. Wunderlich, Tübingen, 1951.
Scott, William E.: *Alliances against Hitler*, The Duke University Press, Durham, N.C., 1962.
Seabury, Paul: *The Wilhelmstrasse: A Study of German Diplomats under the Nazi Regime*, University of California Press, Berkeley, 1954.
Sebottendorf, Rudolf Freiherr von: *Bevor Hitler kam*, Grassinger, Munich, 1933.
Seibert, Theodor: *Das amerikanische Rätsel: Die Kriegspolitik der USA unter Roosevelt*, Eher Verlag, Berlin, 1941.
Semmler, Rudolf: *Goebbels: The Man Next to Hitler*, John Westhouse (Publishers) Ltd., London, 1947.
Seraphim, Hans-Günther: *Das politische Tagebuch Alfred Rosenbergs, 1934–1935 und 1939–1940*, Musterschmidt Wissenschaftlicher Verlag, Göttingen, 1956.
Sereny, Gitta: *Into That Darkness: From Mercy Killing to Mass Murder*, McGraw-Hill Book Company, New York, 1974.
Seth, Ronald: *Operation Barbarossa: The Battle for Moscow*, Anthony Blond, Ltd., London, 1964.
Sharf, Andrew: *The British Press and Jews under Nazi Rule*, Oxford University Press, London, 1964.
Shepherd, Gordon: *Dollfuss*, The Macmillan Company, New York, 1961.
Sherwood, Robert E.: *Roosevelt and Hopkins*, Harper & Brothers, New York, 1948.
Shirer, William L.: *Berlin Diary*, Alfred A. Knopf, Inc., New York, 1943.
———: *End of a Berlin Diary*, Alfred A. Knopf, Inc., New York, 1947.
———: *The Rise and Fall of the Third Reich*, Simon and Schuster, New York, 1960.
Sichrovsky, Peter: *Born Guilty*, tr. by Jean Steinberg, Basic Books, New York, 1988.
Siemer, Pat: *Two Thousand and Ten Days of Hitler*, Harper & Brothers, New York, 1940.
Simoni, Leonardo (Michele Lanza): *Berlino: Ambasciata d'Italia, 1939–1943*, Migliaresi Editore, Rome, 1946.
Sington, Derrick, and Arthur Weidenfeld: *The Goebbels Experiment*, John Murray (Publishers), London, 1942.
Skorzeny, Otto: *Skorzeny's Special Missions*, Robert Hale, Ltd., London, 1957.
Smith, Arthur L.: *The Deutschtum of Nazi Germany and the United States*, Martinus Nijhoff's Boekhandel, The Hague, 1965.
Smith, Bradley F.: *Adolf Hitler: His Family, Childhood, and Youth*, Stanford University Press, Stanford, Calif., 1967.
———: *Heinrich Himmler: A Nazi in the Making*, Stanford University Press, Stanford, Calif., 1971.
Smith, Howard K.: *Last Train from Berlin*, Alfred A. Knopf, Inc., New York, 1962.
Smith, Marcus J.: *The Harrowing of Hell: Dachau*, The University of New Mexico Press, Albuquerque, 1972.
Snyder, Louis L.: *From Bismarck to Hitler: The Background of German Nationalism*, Bayard Press, Williamsport, Pa., 1935.
———: *German Nationalism: The Tragedy of a People*, Stackpole Co., Harrisburg, Pa., 1952.
———: *Hitler and Nazism*, Bantam Books, Inc., New York, 1967.
———: *Hitlerism: The Iron Fist in Germany*, Mohawk Press, Inc., New York, 1932.
———: *The War: A Concise History, 1939–1945*, Julian Messner, Inc., New York, 1960.
———: *The Third Reich, 1933–1945: A Bibliographical Guide to German National Socialism*, Garland Publishing, New York, 1987.
———: *The Weimar Republic*, D. Van Nostrand Company, Inc., Princeton, N.J., 1966.
Sontheimer, Kurt: *Antidemokratischen Denken in der Weimarer Republik*, Nymphenburger Verlagshandlung, Munich, 1962.
Sorge, Martin W.: *The Other Price of Hitler's War*, Greenwood Press, Inc., Westport, Conn., 1986.
Speer, Albert: *Inside the Third Reich*, tr. by Richard and Clara Winston, Macmillan, New York, 1970.
——— (ed.): *Neue deutsche Baukunst*, Volk und Reich Verlag, Berlin, 1940.
Speidel, Hans: *We Defended Normandy*, tr. by Ian Colvin, Herbert Jenkins, Ltd., London, 1951.
Spiegelbild einer Verschwörung: Die Kaltenbrunner-Berichte an Bormann und Hitler über das Attentat vom 20. Juli 1944, Seewald Verlag, Stuttgart, 1961.
Starhemberg, Ernst Rudiger Fürst: *Between Hitler and Mussolini*, Harper & Brothers, New York, 1942.
Stein, George H.: *Hitler*, Great Lives Observed Series, Prentice-Hall, Inc., Englewood Cliffs, N.J., 1968.
———: *The Waffen-SS*, Cornell University Press, Ithaca, N.Y., 1966.
Steinbauer, Werner: *Joseph Goebbels: Dämon oder Diktatur*, Union Deutsche Verlagsgesellschaft, Stuttgart, 1949.
Steiner, Jean-François: *Treblinka*, tr. by Helen Weaver, Simon and Schuster, New York, 1967.
Stern, Fritz: *The Failure of Illiberalism*, Alfred A. Knopf, Inc., New York, 1972.
Stern, Werner: *The Politics of Cultural Despair: A Study of the Rise of the Germanic Ideology*, University of California Press, Los Angeles, 1961.
Stevenson, William: *The Bormann Brotherhood*, Harcourt Brace Jovanovich, Inc., New York, 1973.
Stirk, Samuel D.: *The Prussian Spirit*, Faber & Faber, Ltd., London, 1941.
Stockhorst, Erich: *Fünftausendköpfe*, Blick & Bild Verlag, Velbert and Kettwig, 1967.
Stodte, Hermann: *Der Wegbereiter des Nationalsozialismus*, Rathgens, Lübeck, 1936.
Strasser, Bernard P.: *Gregor und Otto Strasser*, Stössel, Külsheim, Baden, 1954.
Strasser, Gregor: *Mein Kampf*, Heine Verlag, Frankfurt am Main, 1969.

Strasser, Otto: *Aufbau des deutschen Sozialismus*, Heinrich Grunov, Prague, 1936.

———: *Die deutsche Bartolomäusnacht*, Reso-Verlag, Zürich, 1935.

———: *History in My Time*, tr. by Douglas Reed, Jonathan Cape, Ltd., London, 1941.

———: *Hitler and I*, Jonathan Cape, Ltd., London, 1940.

Strawson, John: *Hitler's Battle for Europe*, Charles Scribner's Sons, New York, 1971.

Strothmann, Dietrich: *Nationalsozialistische Literaturpolitik: Ein Beitrag zur Publizistik im Dritten Reich*, H. Bouvier, Bonn, 1963.

Streicher, Julius: *Kampf dem Weltfeind: Reden aus der Kampfzeit*, Verlag Der Stürmer, Nuremberg, 1938.

Strik-Strikfeldt, Wilfried: *Against Hitler and Stalin*, The John Day Company, Inc., New York, 1973.

Tauber, Kurt P.: *Beyond Eagle and Swastika*, 2 vols., Wesleyan University Press, Middletown, Conn., 1967.

Taylor, A. J. P.: *The Origins of the Second World War*, Hamish Hamilton, Ltd., London, 1961.

Taylor, Telford: *Final Report to the Secretary of the Army on the Nuremberg War Crimes Trials under Council Law No. 10*, Government Printing Office, Washington, 1949.

———: *Sword and Swastika: Generals and Nazis in the Third Reich*, Simon and Schuster, New York, 1952.

Tec, Nachama: *When Light Pierced the Darkness*. Oxford University Press, New York, 1985.

Tenenbaum, Joseph: *Race and Reich*, Twayne Publishers, Inc., New York, 1956.

Thalmann, Rita, and Emmanuel Feinermann: *Crystal Night*, Thames & Hudson, Ltd., London, 1974.

Thomas, Katherine: *Women in Nazi Germany*, Victor Gollancz, Ltd., London, 1943.

Thomsen, Erich: *Deutsche Besatzungspolitik in Dänemark, 1940–1945*, Bertelsmann Universitätsverlag, Düsseldorf, 1971.

Thyssen, Fritz: *I Paid Hitler*, Farrar & Rinehart, Inc., New York, 1941.

Tobias, Fritz: *The Reichstag Fire Trial*, tr. by Arnold Pomerans, G. P. Putnam's Sons, New York, 1964.

Toland, John: *The Last 100 Days*, Random House, Inc., New York, 1965.

Tolischus, Otto D.: *They Wanted War*, Reynal & Hitchcock, Inc., New York, 1940.

Toynbee, Arnold J., and Veronica M. Toynbee (eds.): *Eve of the War, 1939*, Oxford University Press, London, 1952.

——— and ——— (eds.): *The Initial Triumph of the Axis*, Oxford University Press, London, 1958.

Trainin, Aron N.: *Hitlerite Responsibility under Criminal Law*, tr. by Andrew Rothstein, Hutchinson & Co. (Publishers), Ltd., London, 1945.

Trefousse, Hans L.: *Germany and American Neutrality, 1939–1941*, Bookman Associates, Inc., New York, 1951.

Treviranus, Gottfried Reinhold: *Das Ende von Weimar*, Econ-Verlag, Düsseldorf, 1960.

Trevor-Roper, H. R. *The Bormann Letters*, Weidenfeld and Nicolson, London, 1954.

———: *The Last Days of Hitler*, The Macmillan Company, New York, 1947.

——— (ed.): *Hitler's War Directives, 1939–1945*, Sidgwick & Jackson, Ltd., London, 1964.

Trial of the Major War Criminals before the International Military Tribunal, Nuremberg, 14 November, 1945–1 October, 1946, 42 vols., International Military Tribunal, Nuremberg, 1947–1949.

Trials of War Criminals before the Nuremberg Military Tribunals, under Control Council Law No. 10, October 1946–April 1949, 15 vols., Government Printing Office, Washington, 1946–1949.

Truckenbrodt, Walter: *Deutschland und die Völkerbund: Die Behandlungen reichdeutscher Angelegenheiten im Völkerbundsrat von 1920–1939*, Essener Verlagsanstalt, Essen, 1941.

Trunk, Isaiah: *Judenrat*, The Macmillan Company, New York, 1972.

Turner, Henry Ashby, Jr.: *German Big Business and the Rise of Hitler*, Oxford University Press, New York, 1985.

———: *Hitler: Memoirs of a Confidant*, Yale University Press, New Haven, Conn., 1985.

Tushnet, Leonard: *The Pavement of Hell: Three Leaders of the Judenrat*, St. Martin's Press, Inc., New York, 1974.

United States House of Representatives Select Committee on the Katyn Forest Massacre: *Hearings*, 82d Congress, 1st and 2d Sessions, 1951–1952, Government Printing Office, Washington, 1952.

Valtin, Jan (Richard Krebs): *Out of the Night*, William Heinemann, Ltd., London, 1941.

Viereck, Peter: *Metapolitics: The Roots of the Nazi Mind*, Capricorn Books, G. P. Putnam's Sons, New York, 1961.

Vogel, Rolf: *Ein Weg aus der Vergangenheit*, Ullstein-Verlag, Frankfurt am Main, 1969.

Vogelsang, Carl Walther: *Dieter lernt Fliegen*, Dege, Leipzig, 1943.

Voggenreiter, Heinrich (ed.): *Taschenbuch für den deutschen Jugendführer*, H. Voggenreiter, Potsdam, n.d.

Vogt, Hannah: *The Burden of Guilt: A Short History of Germany, 1914–1945*, tr. by Herbert Strauss, Oxford University Press, New York, 1964.

Vojtech, Mastny, *The Czechs under Nazi Rule: The Failure of National Resistance, 1939–1942*, Columbia University Press, New York, 1971.

Volz, Hans: *Daten der Geschichte der NSDAP*, A. G. Ploetz, Leipzig, 1938.

Wagner, Ludwig: *Hitler: Man of Strife*, tr. by Charlotte La Rue, W. W. Norton & Company, Inc., New York, 1942.

Waite, Robert G. L.: *Vanguard of Nazism: The Free Corps Movement in Post-War Germany, 1918–1923*, Harvard University Press, Cambridge, Mass., 1952.

Warlimont, Walter: *Inside Hitler's Headquarters*, tr. by Richard H. Barry, Weidenfeld and Nicolson, London, 1964.

Warmbruun, Werner: *The Dutch under German Occupation, 1940–1945*, Stanford University Press, Stanford, Calif., 1963.

Wassermann, Jacob: *My Life as German and Jew*, Coward-McCann, Inc., New York, 1933.

Weberstedt, Hans, and Karl Langner: *Gedenkhalle für die Gefallenen des Dritten Reiches*, Eher Verlag, Munich, 1935.

Weinberg, Gerhard L.: *The Foreign Policy of Hitler's Germany: Diplomatic Revolution in Europe, 1933–1936*, The University of Chicago Press, Chicago, 1970.

———: *Germany and the Soviet Union, 1939–1941*, E. J. Brill, NV, Leiden, 1954.

Weinreich, Max: *Hitler's Professors: The Part of Scholarship*

in Germany's Crimes against the Jewish People, Yiddish Scientific Institute, New York, 1946.
Weinstein, Adelbert: *Armee ohne Pathos: Die deutsche Wiederbewaffnung im Urteil ehemaligen Soldaten,* Köllen-Verlag, Bonn, 1951.
Weiszäcker, Ernst von: *Memoirs,* tr. by John Andrews, Henry Regnery Company, Chicago, 1951.
Welles, Sumner: *The Time for Decision,* Harper & Brothers, New York, 1944.
Wendt, Hans: *Hitler regiert,* E. S. Mittler & Sohn, Berlin, 1933.
West, Rebecca: *The Meaning of Treason,* The Viking Press, Inc., New York, 1949.
Westphal, Siegfried: *The German Army in the West,* Cassell & Co., Ltd., London, 1951.
Wetterstetten, Rudolph, and A. M. K. Watson: *The Biography of President von Hindenburg,* The Macmillan Company, New York, 1930.
Whaley, Barton: *Codeword Barbarossa,* The M.I.T. Press, Cambridge, Mass., 1973.
Wheatley, Ronald: *Operation Sea Lion,* Clarendon Press, Oxford, 1958.
Wheeler-Bennett, John W.: *The Nemesis of Power: The German Army in Politics, 1918–1945,* The Macmillan Company, London, 1953.
Whittlesey, Derwent: *German Strategy of World Conquest,* Farrar & Rinehart, Inc., New York, 1942.
White Book on the Executions of 30th June, 1934, Éditions du Carrefour, Paris, 1934.
Whiteside, Andrew G.: *Austrian National Socialism before 1918,* Martinus Nijhoff's Boekhandel, The Hague, 1962.
Whiting, Charles: *Gehlen: Germany's Master Spy,* Ballantine Books, Inc., New York, 1973.
———: *The Hunt for Martin Bormann,* Ballantine Books, Inc., New York, 1973.
———: *Otto Skorzeny,* Ballantine Books, Inc., New York, 1972.
Wiedemann, Fritz: *Der Mann, der Feldherr werden wollte,* Blick & Bild Verlag, Velbert, 1964.
Wiener, Jan G.: *The Assassination of Heydrich,* Grossman Pubs., New York, 1969.
Wiesenthal, Simon: *The Murderers among Us,* McGraw-Hill Book Company, New York, 1967.
Wighton, Charles: *Heydrich, Hitler's Most Evil Henchman,* Odhams Press, Ltd., London, 1962.
——— and Günter Peis: *Hitler's Spies and Saboteurs,* Henry Holt and Company, Inc., New York, 1938.
Wilmot, Chester: *The Struggle for Europe,* Harper & Brothers, New York, 1952.
Wilmowsky, Tilo Freiherr von: *Warum wurde Krupp verurteilt?* Econ-Verlag, Düsseldorf, 1962.
Winkler, Franz: *Die Diktatur in Oesterreich,* Orell Füssli, Zürich, 1935.
Wiskemann, Elizabeth: *The Rome-Berlin Axis,* William Collins Sons & Co., Ltd., London, 1966.
Wolfers, Arnold: *Britain and France between Two Wars,* Harcourt, Brace and Company, Inc., New York, 1940.
Wolff, Richard: *Der Reichstagbrand 1933,* supplement to *Das Parlament,* Bonn, January 18, 1956.
Wucher, Albert: *Eichmanns gab es viele,* Drömische Verlagsanstalt, Munich, 1961.
Wuescht, Johann: *Jugoslawien und das Dritte Reich,* Seewald Verlag, Stuttgart, 1968.
Wulf, Josef: *Die bildenen Künste im Dritten Reich,* S. Mohn, Gütersloh, 1963.
———: *Das Dritte Reich und seine Vollstrecker,* Arani Verlag, Berlin, 1961.
———: *Heinrich Himmler,* Arani Verlag, Berlin, 1960.
———: *Martin Bormann—Hitlers Schatten,* S. Mohn, Gütersloh, 1962.
———: *Presse und Funk im Dritten Reich,* S. Mohn, Gütersloh, 1964.
Wykes, Alan: *Nuremberg Rallies,* MacDonald & Co., Publishers, Ltd., London, 1970.
Wyman, David S.: *The Abandonment of the Jews: America and the Holocaust, 1941-1945,* Pantheon, New York, 1984.
Yahil, Leni: *The Rescue of Danish Jewry,* Jewish Publication Society of America, Philadelphia, 1969.
Young, Desmond: *Rommel: The Desert Fox,* Harper & Brothers, New York, 1950.
Zahn, Gordon C.: *German Catholics and Hitler's Wars: A Study in Social Control,* Sheed & Ward, Inc., New York, 1962.
Zeman, Z. A. B.: *Nazi Propaganda,* Galaxy Books, Oxford University Press, New York, 1973.
Ziehm, Ernst: *Aus meiner politischen Arbeit in Danzig, 1914–1939,* Herder Institut, Marburg, 1960.
Ziemer, Gregor: *Education for Death,* Oxford University Press, New York, 1941.
Ziemke, Earl F.: *Battle for Berlin: End of the Third Reich,* MacDonald & Co., Publishers, Ltd., London, 1969.
Zink, Harold: *The United States in Germany, 1944–1955,* D. Van Nostrand Company, Inc., Princeton, N.J., 1957.
Ziptel, Friedrich: *Gestapo und Sicherheitsdienst,* Arani Verlag, Berlin, 1960.
Zoller, A. (ed.): *Hitler privat, Erlebnis bericht seiner Geheimsekretärin,* Droste, Düsseldorf, 1949.
Zur Geschichte der deutschen antifaschistischen Widerstandsbewegung, 1933–1945, Verlag des Ministeriums für Nationale Verteidigung, Berlin, 1958.

PERIODICAL LITERATURE

Adler, H. G.: "Ideas toward a Sociology of the Concentration Camp," *American Journal of Sociology,* vol. LXIII, no. 5, pp. 513–522, March 1958.
Adler, Les K., and Thomas G. Paterson: "Red Fascism: The Merger of Nazi Germany and Soviet Russia in the American Image of Totalitarianism," *American Historical Review,* vol. LXXV, no. 4, pp. 1046–1064, April 1970.
Ainszstein, Reuben: "Stalin and June 22, 1941: Some New Soviet Views," *International Affairs,* vol. XL, no. 4, pp. 666–672, London, October 1966.
Angres, Werner T., and Bradley F. Smith: "Diaries of Heinrich Himmler's Early Years," *Journal of Modern History,* vol. XXXI, pp. 206–224, June 1959.
Arendt, Hannah: "Social Science Techniques and the Study of Concentration Camps," *Jewish Social Studies,* vol. XII, no. 1, pp. 49–64, January 1950.
Ascher, Abraham, and Guenther Lewy: "National Bolshevism in Weimar Germany: Alliance of Political Extremes against Democracy," *Social Research,* vol. XXIII, no. 4, pp. 450–480, Winter, 1956.
Assmann, Kurt: "The Battle for Moscow," *Foreign Affairs,* vol. XXVIII, pp. 309–326, January 1950.

Baum, Walter: "Marine, Nationalsozialismus und Widerstand," *Vierteljahrshefte für Zeitgeschichte*, vol. XI, no. 1, pp. 16–18, January 1963.

Baumgart, Winfried: "Zur Ansprache Hitlers vor den Führern der Wehrmacht am 22. August 1939: Eine quellenkritische Untersuchung," *Vierteljahrshefte für Zeitgeschichte*, vol. XVI, pp. 120–149, 1968.

Bayer, Oswald: "Neonazismo en la Argentina," *Commentario*, October–December 1956, in *Wiener Library Bulletin*, vol. XI, nos. 1, 2, p. 10, London, January–April 1957.

Bayne, E. A.: "Resistance in the German Foreign Office," *Human Events*, vol. III, no. 14, pp. 1–8, 1946.

Beard, Charles: "Education under the Nazis," *Foreign Affairs*, vol. XIV, pp. 407–423, 437–452, 1936.

Berezhkov, Valentin Mikhailovich: "On the Eve of Hitler's Invasion," *Atlas*, vol. II, no. 1, pp. 10–15, January 1966.

Biesanz, John: "Nazi Influence on German Youth Hostels," *Social Forces*, vol. XIX, no. 4, pp. 554–559, May 1941.

Bloch, Edward: "My Patient Hitler," *Collier's*, vol. CVII, no. 1, pp. 11, 35, March 15, 1941; no. 2, pp. 69–73, March 22, 1941.

Blum, Günther: "Widerstand und Antifaschismus in Marxistisch-Leninischen Geschichtsauffassung," *Vierteljahrshefte für Zeitgeschichte*, vol. IX, no. 1, pp. 50–65, January 1961.

Bodensieck, Heinrich: "Nationalsozialismus in revisionistischer Sicht," *Aus Politik und Zeitgeschichte*, supplement to *Das Parlament*, pp. 175–180, Bonn, March 19, 1961.

Boelcke, Rolf: "Die Spaltung der Nationalsozialisten," *Tat*, vol. XXII, pp. 357–367, August 1930.

Bogomolov, Aleksandr: "Wartime Diplomatic Missions," *International Affairs*, no. 6, pp. 70–79, no. 7, pp. 90–97, no. 8, pp. 69–76, Moscow, 1961.

Bracher, Karl-Dietrich: "Stufen totalitärer Gleichschaltung: Die Befestigung der nationalsozialistischen Herrschaft, 1933/34," *Vierteljahrshefte für Zeitgeschichte*, vol. IV, no. 1, pp. 31–42, January 1956.

Brecht, Arnold: "Die Auflösung der Weimarer Republik und die politische Wissenschaft," *Zeitschrift für Politik*, new series, vol. II, pp. 291–308, 1955.

Bromberg, Norbert: "Totalitarian Ideology as a Defense Technique," *Psychoanalytic Study of Society*, vol. I, pp. 26–38, 1961.

Broszat, Martin: "Das sudetendeutsche Freikorps," *Vierteljahrshefte für Zeitgeschichte*, vol. IX, no. 1, pp. 30–49, January 1961.

———: "Die völkische Ideologie unter denNationalsozialismus," *Deutsche Rundschau*, vol. LXXXIV, no. 1, pp. 53–68, January 1958.

———: "Zum Streit um den Reichstagsbrand," *Vierteljahrshefte für Zeitgeschichte*, vol. VIII, no. 3, pp. 275–279, July 1960.

Bruening, Heinrich: "Ein Brief," *Deutsche Rundschau*, vol. LXX, pp. 1–22, 1947.

Buchheim, Hans: "Die SS in der Verfassung des Dritten Reiches," *Vierteljahrshefte für Zeitgeschichte*, vol. III, no. 2, pp. 127–157, April 1955.

Buck, Gerhard: "Das Führerhauptquartier: Seine Darstellung in der deutschen Literatur," *Jahresbibliographie der Bibliothek für Zeitgeschichte*, vol. XXXVIII, pp. 549–566, Weltkriegesbücherei Stuttgart, Frankfurt am Main, 1968.

Carsten, Francis L.: "The Reichswehr and the Red Army, 1920–1933," *Survey*, no. 44/45, pp. 114–132, October 1962.

———: "Stauffenberg's Bomb," *Encounter*, vol. XXIII, no. 3, pp. 64–67, September 1964.

———: "What German Historians Say about the Nazis," *Listener*, pp. 415–417, March 10, 1955.

Castellan, Georges: "Von Schleicher, Von Papen et l'avènement de Hitler," *Cahiers d'Histoire de la Guerre*, vol. I, pp. 25–37, 1949.

Celovsky, Boris: "The Transferred Sudeten Germans and Their Political Activity," *Journal of Central European Affairs*, vol. XVII, no. 2, pp. 127–149, July 1957.

Conze, Werner: "Die Krise des Parteienstaates in Deutschland, 1929–30," *Historische Zeitschrift*, vol. CLXXVIII, pp. 47–83, 1934.

———: "Zum Sturze Brünings," *Vierteljahrshefte für Zeitgeschichte*, vol. I, pp. 261–288, 1953.

Craig, Gordon A.: "Briefe Schleichers an Groener," *Die Welt als Geschichte*, vol. XI, pp. 122–133, 1951.

Dawidowicz, Lucy S.: "Toward a History of the Holocaust," *Commentary*, vol. XLVII, no. 4, pp. 51–56, April 1969.

Deist, Wilhelm: "Brüning, Herriot, und die Abrüstungs Gespräche von Bessinge 1932," *Vierteljahrshefte für Zeitgeschichte*, vol. V, pp. 265–272, 1957.

Delcour, Roland: "Néonazis, Parti des Réfugiés Parti Allemand," *Allemagne d'Aujourd'hui*, pp. 76–88, May–September 1957.

Deuerlein, Ernst: "Hitlers Eintritt in die Politik und die Reichswehr," *Vierteljahrshefte für Zeitgeschichte*, vol. VII, no. 2, pp. VII, 177-227, April 1959.

Dickmann, Fritz: "Die Regierungsbildung in Thüringen als Modell der Machtbegreifung," *Vierteljahrshefte für Zeitgeschichte*, vol. XIV, no. 3, pp. 454–464, October 1966.

Dietz, Peter: "Das Attentat auf Hitler am 20. Juli 1944," *Der Schweizer Soldat*, vol. XL, pp. 600–602, 1964.

———: "Mut und Angst: Zum Attentat in der 'Wolfschanze' am 20. Juli 1944," *Allgemeine Schweizerische Militärzeitschrift*, vol. CXXX, pp. 442-444, 1964.

Dorpalen, Andreas: "Hitler—Twelve Years After," *Review of Politics*, vol. XIX, pp. 486–506, 1957.

Drobisch, Klaus: "Flick und die Nazis," *Zeitschrift für Geschichtswissenschaft*, vol. XIV, no. 3, pp. 378–397, 1966.

———: "Die Freundeskreis Himmlers," *Zeitschrift für Geschichtswissenschaft*, vol. VIII, no. 2, pp. 304–328, 1960.

Ebeling, Hans: "Unvergessen: Theo Hespers, katholische und treue Jugendbewegung im Widerstand gegen das NS-System," *Graue Blätter*, vol. I, no. 1, pp. 12–44, 1956.

Eder, Peter G.: "Deutschland, deine Helden, 21 Jahre danach: Wer war was am 20. Juli 1944? Zeitung sprach mit Zeugen des Aufstandes," *Zeitung*, pp. 17–21, July 19, 1965.

Edinger, J.: "German Social Democracy and Hitler's 'National Revolution,'" *World Politics*, vol. V, pp. 330–367, April 1953.

"Ein 'Plan Lanz' war Rommel bekannte," *Passauer Neue Presse,* p. 3, July 21, 1949.

"Entscheidende Minuten am 20. Juli," *Hamburger Allgemeine Zeitung,* pp. 1, 2, July 20, 1949.

Epstein, Fritz: "National Socialism and French Colonialism," *Journal of Central European Affairs,* vol. III, no. 1, pp. 52–64, April 1943.

Erfurth, Waldemar: "Generaloberst a.D. Halder zum 70. Geburtstag," *Wehrwissenschaftliche Rundschau,* vol. IV, pp. 241–251, 1954.

Erikson, Erik: "Hitler's Imagery and German Youth," *Psychiatry,* vol. III, pp. 475–493, 1942.

Eschenburg, Theodor: "Franz von Papen," *Vierteljahrshefte für Zeitgeschichte,* vol. I, no. 2, pp. 153–169, 1953.

———: "Die Rolle der Persönlichkeit in der Krise der Weimarer Republik: Hindenburg, Brüning, Groener, Schleicher," *Vieteljahrshefte für Zeitgeschichte,* vol. IX, pp. 1–29, 1961.

———: "Zum Ermordung des Generals von Schleicher," *Vierteljahrshefte für Zeitgeschichte,* vol. I, no. 1, pp. 71–95, 1953.

Feiser, Werner: "Educational Failure of the Weimar Republic," *School and Society,* vol. LVIII, pp. 289–292, October 16, 1943.

Fenichel, Otto: "Psychoanalysis of Anti-Semitism," *American Imago,* vol. I, no. 2, pp. 24–39, March 1940.

Fodor, M. W.: "Austrian Roots of Hitlerism," *Foreign Affairs,* vol. XIV, no. 4, pp. 685–691, July 1936.

Ford, Franklin L.: "Der 20. Juli," *Die Amerikanische Rundschau,* vol. III, pp. 5–17, 1947.

Fox, John P.: "Japanese Reaction to Nazi Germany's Racial Legislation," *Wiener Library Bulletin,* vol. XXIII, nos. 2, 3, pp. 46–50, London, 1969.

Franz, Georg: "Munich: Birthplace and Center of the National Socialist German Workers' Party," *Journal of Modern History,* vol. XXIX, pp. 319–334, December 1957.

Frenkel-Brunswik, Else, and R. Novitt Sanford: "Some Personality Factors in Anti-Semitism," *Journal of Psychology,* vol. XX, no. 2, pp. 271–291, 1945.

Garraty, John A.: "The New Deal, National Socialism, and the Great Depression," *American Historical Review,* vol. LXXVIII, no. 4, pp. 907–944, October 1973.

Gastorowski, Zygmund J.: "Did Pilsudski Attempt to Initiate a Preventive War in 1933?" *Journal of Modern History,* vol. XXVII, no. 2, pp. 135–151, June 1955.

———: "The German-Polish Nonaggression Pact of 1934," *Journal of Central European Affairs,* vol. XV, no. 1, pp. 3–29, 1955.

Gatzke, Hans W.: "Hitler and Psychohistory," review-article, *American Historical Review,* vol. LXXVIII, no. 2, pp. 394–401, April 1973.

———: "Russo-German Military Collaboration during the Weimar Republic," *American Historical Review,* vol. XLIII, no. 3, pp. 565–597, April 1953.

"Genocide," *Yale Law Journal,* vol. LVIII, pp. 1142–1157, 1949.

Gentzen, Felix-Heinrich: "Die Rolle der 'Deutschen Stiftung' bei der Vorbereitung der Annexion des Memellandes im März 1939," *Jahrbuch für Geschichte der UdSSR und der Volksdemokratischen Länder Europas,* vol. V, pp. 71–94, 1961.

Gerth, Hans H.: "The Nazi Party: Its Leadership and Composition," *American Journal of Sociology,* vol. XLV, pp. 517–541, January 1940.

Gies, Horst: "NSDAP und landwirtschaftliche Organisationen in der Endphase der Weimarer Republik," *Vierteljahrshefte für Zeitgeschichte,* vol. XV, pp. 341–376, October 1967.

Gimbel, John: "American Denazification and German Local Politics, 1945–1949: A Case Study in Marburg," *American Political Science Review,* vol. LIV, no. 1, pp. 83–105, March 1960.

Graml, Hermann: "Die deutsche Militäropposition vom Sommer 1940 bis zum Frühjahr 1943," *Vollmacht des Gewissens,* vol. III, pp. 411–474, Europäischen Publikation e.V., Frankfurt am Main and Berlin, 1965.

Groote, Wolfgang von: "Bundeswehr und 20. Juli," *Vierteljahrshefte für Zeitgeschichte,* vol. XII, no. 3, pp. 285–299, July 1964.

Haffner, Sebastian: "Beinahe: Die Geschichte des 20. Juli 1944," *Neue Auslese,* vol. II, no. 8, pp. 1–12, 1947.

Hale, Oron J. (ed.): "Gottfried Feder Calls Hitler to Order," *Journal of Modern History,* vol. XXX, pp. 360 ff., 1958.

Hall, M.: "German Youth: A Lost Generation?" *Christian Century,* vol. LXI, pp. 1098–1100, September 27, 1944.

Hamilton, Alice: "The Youth Who Are Hitler's Strength: A Study of the Nazi Followers and the Appeal That Has Aroused Them," *The New York Times Magazine,* pp. 3–16, October 8, 1933.

Hammerschmidt, Helmut: "Ist der Nationalsozialismus tot?" *Club republikanischer Publizisten: CrP-Information,* p. 37, April 1957.

Hammerstein, Kunrat Freiherr von: "Schleicher, Hammerstein und die Machtübernahme, 1933," *Frankfurter Hefte,* vol. XI, pp. 11–18, 117–128, 163–176, January–March 1956.

Hanisch, Reinhold: "I Was Hitler's Buddy," *New Republic,* vol. XCVIII, no. 1270, pp. 239–242, April 5, 1939; no. 1271, pp. 270–272, April 12, 1939; no. 1272, pp. 297–300, April 19, 1939.

Harnack, Axel von: "Arvid und Mildred Harnack: Erinnerungen an ihren Prozess 1942/43," *Die Gegenwart,* vol. II, nos. 1/2, pp. 15–18, 1947.

Harrigan, William H.: "Nazi Germany and the Holy See, 1933–1936: The Historical Background of *Mit brennender Sorge,*" *Catholic Historical Review,* vol. XLVII, no. 2, pp. 164–173, July 1961.

Heiden, Konrad: "Portrait of the Artist as a Young Man," *Saturday Review,* vol. XXVI, no. 19, pp. 6–9, December 4, 1943.

Helmreich, Ernst C.: "The Arrrest and Freeing of the Protestant Bishops of Württemberg and Bavaria, September—October, 1934," *Central European History,* vol. II, no. 2, pp. 159–169, June 1969.

Herz, John H.: "The Fiasco of Denazification in Germany," *Political Science Quarterly,* vol. LXIII, no. 4, pp. 569–594, December 1948.

Hiller, R. L. H.: "German Youth Will Gladly Die," *Survey Graphic,* vol. XXX, pp. 68–81, February 1941.

Hoffmann, Peter: "The Attempt to Assassinate Hitler on March 21, 1943," *Canadian Journal of History,* vol. II, pp. 67–83, 1967.

———: "Claus Graf Stauffenberg und Stefan George: Der Weg zur Tat," *Jahrbuch der Deutschen Schillergesell-*

schaft, vol. XII, pp. 520–542, 1968.
———: "Zu dem Attentat in Führerhauptquartier 'Wolfschanze' am 20 Juli 1944," *Vierteljahrshefte für Zeitgeschichte*, vol. XII, pp. 254-284, 1964.
———: "Zum Ablauf des Staatsstreichversuches des 20. Juli 1944 in den Wehrkreisen," *Wehrwissenschaftliche Rundschau*, vol. XIV, pp. 377–397, 1964.
Hook, Sidney: "Hitlerism: A Non-metaphysical View," *Contemporary Jewish Record*, vol. VII, pp. 146–155, April 1944.
Hornick, M. P.: "Had Hitler Jewish Blood?" *Contemporary Review*, vol. CXCIV, pp. 28–31, July 1958.
Hossbach, Friedrich: "Die Entwickelung des Oberbefehls über das Heer in Brandenburg-Preussen und im Deutschen Reich von 1655–1945," part II, 1918–1945, *Jahrbuch der Albertus-Universität zu Konigsberg/Pr.*, vol. VIII, pp. 194–280, 1958.
Jasper, Gotthard: "Über die Ursachen des zweiten Weltkrieges: Zu den Büchern von A. J. P. Taylor und David L. Hoggan," *Vierteljahrshefte für Zeitgeschichte*, vol. X, no. 3, pp. 311–340, July 1962.
Jensen, Karl: "SS-Treffpunkt Kairo—Eine dicke Ente!" *Die Brücke*, vol. IV, no. 18, pp. 6–8, October 15, 1957.
Joesten, Joachim: "The Menace of Neo-Nazism," *New Germany Reports*, no. 15, pp. 16–17, September 1950.
Kahn, Lothar: "The Swastika in German Novels," *Wiener Library Bulletin*, vol. XIV, no. 2, p. 29, London, 1960.
Kann, R. A.: "German-speaking Jewry during Austria-Hungary's Constitutional Era," *Jewish Social Studies*, vol. X, no. 3, pp. 239–256, July 1948.
Kecsemeti, Paul, and Nathan Leites: "Some Psychological Hypotheses on Nazi Germany," *Journal of Social Psychology*, vol. XXVI, no. 2, pp. 141-183, 1947; vol. XXVII, no. 1, pp. 91-117, 241-270, 1948; vol. XXVII, no. 2, pp. 141-164, 1948.
Kitsikis, Dimitri: "La Grêce entre l'Angleterre et l'Allemagne de 1936 à 1941," *Revue historique*, vol. CCXXXVIII, pp. 85–116, July–September, 1967.
Kleist-Schmenzin, Ewald von: "Die letzte Möglichkeit: Zur Ernennung Hitlers zum Reichskanzler am 30. January 1933," *Politische Studien*, vol. X, pp. 89–92, 1959.
Kluke, Paul: "Nationalsozialistische Europa-Ideologie," *Vierteljahrshefte für Zeitgeschichte*, vol. III, no. 3, pp. 240–275, July 1955.
Kochan, Lionel: "Russia and Germany, 1935–1937: A Note," *Slavonic and East European Review*, vol. XL, pp. 518–520, 1962.
Krausnick, Helmut: "Legende um Hitlers Aussenpolitik," *Vierteljahrshefte für Zeitgeschichte*, vol. II, no. 3, pp. 217–239, July 1954.
Krecker, Lothar: "Die diplomatischen Verhandlungen über der Viererpakt vom 15. Juli, 1933," *Die Welt als Geschichte*, vol. XXI, pp. 227–237, 1961.
Kubala, Wolfgang: "Mit dem Lastwagen voller SS-Bücher geflüchtet," *Süddeutsche Zeitung*, no. 106, p. 5, Munich, May 4, 1965.
Kuehnelt-Leddihn, Erik R. von: "The Bohemian Background of German National Socialism: DAP, DNSAP, and NSDAP," *Journal of the History of Ideas*, vol. LX, no. 3, pp. 339–371, June 1948.
Kühne, Horst: "Zur Kolonialpolitik des faschistischen deutschen Imperialismus, 1933–1939," *Zeitschrift für Geschichtswissenschaft*, vol. IX, pp. 514–537, 1961.
Kurth, Gertrude M.: "The Jew and Adolf Hitler," *Psychoanalytic Quarterly*, vol. XVI, pp. 11–32, 1947.
Kvaček, Robert: "Československo-německá jednáni v noce 1936 [Czech-German Negotiations in 1936]," *Historie a Vojenstvi*, vol. V, pp. 721–754, 1965.
Laqueur, Walter Z.: "Nazism and the Nazis," *Encounter*, vol. XXII, no. 4, pp. 39–46, April 1964.
Lewy, Guenter: "Pius XII, the Jews, and the German Catholic Church," *Commentary*, vol. XXXVII, no. 2, pp. 23–25, February 1964.
Loeblowitz-Lennard, Henry: "The Jew as Symbol," *Psychoanalytic Quarterly*, vol. XVI, pp. 33–37, 1947.
Loock, Hans-Dietrich: "Zur 'Grossgermanischen Politik' des Dritten Reiches," *Vierteljahrshefte für Zeitgeschichte*, vol. VIII, no. 1, pp. 37–63, January 1960.
Lowenberg, Peter, "The Psychohistorical Origins of the Nazi Youth Cohort," *American Historical Review*, vol. LXXVI, no. 5, pp. 1457–1502, December 1971.
———: "The Unsuccessful Adolescence of Heinrich Himmler," *American Historical Review*, vol. LXXVI, no. 3, pp. 612–641, June 1971.
Maier, Hedwig: "Die SS und der 20. Juli 1944," *Vierteljahrshefte für Zeitgeschichte*, vol. XIV, pp. 299–316, 1966.
Mann, Klaus: "Cowboy Mentor of the Fuehrer," *Living Age*, vol. CLIV, pp. 217-222, November 1940.
Matthias, Erich: "Der Untergang der Sozialdemokratie, 1933," *Vierteljahrshefte für Zeitgeschichte*, vol. IV, no. 2, pp. 179–226, April 1956; vol. IV, no. 3, pp. 250–286, July 1956.
Mau, Hermann: "Die deutsche Jugendbewegung," *Zeitschrift für Religion und Geistesgeschichte*, vol. I, pp. 135–149, 1948.
———: "Die 'Zweite Revolution': Der 30. Juni 1934," *Vierteljahrshefte für Zeitgeschichte*, pp. 119–127, April 1953.
Mierendorff, Carl: "Gesicht und Charakter der Nationalsozialistischen Bewegung," *Die Gesellschaft*, vol. VII, pp. 489–504, June 1930.
Mommsen, Hans: "Der nationalsozialistische Polizeistaat und die Judenverfolgung von 1938," *Vierteljahrshefte für Zeitgeschichte*, vol. X, no. 1, pp. 68–87, January 1962.
———: "Pläne und Träume zum Tag X," *Der Spiegel*, no. 36, pp. 94–97, August 28, 1967.
———: "Der Reichstagbrand und seine politischen Folgen," *Vierteljahrshefte für Zeitgeschichte*, vol. XII, pp. 351–413, 1964.
Morsey, Rudolf: "Hitler als Braunschweiger Regierungsrat," *Vierteljahrshefte für Zeitgeschichte*, vol. VIII, no. 4, pp. 419–448, 1960.
———: "Hitlers Verhandlungen mit der Zentrumsführung am 31. Januar 1933," *Vierteljahrshefte für Zeitgeschichte*, vol. IX, no. 2, pp. 182-210, April 1961.
Muehl, Anita: "Factors Influencing Hitler's Life," reprint from *Transactions of the Medical Guild of St. Luke*, pp. 1–18, March 1941.
Napoli, J. F.: "Denazification from an American's Viewpoint," *Annals of the American Academy of Political and Social Science*, vol. CCLXIV, pp. 115–123, July 1949.
Nemitz, Kurt: "Das Régime der Mitläufer: Soziologische Notizen zur Renazifizierung," *Die Neue Gesellschaft*, vol. II, no. 3, pp. 39–45, May–June 1955.
Olsen, Arthur J.: "Rightists Honor Hitler Defender," *The New York Times*, p. 9, col. 1, May 5, 1964.

Orlow, Dietrich: "The Organizational History and Structure of the NSDAP, 1919–1923," *Journal of Modern History*, vol. XXXVII, pp. 208–226, June 1965.

Pachter, Henry M.: "The Legend of the 20th of July 1944," *Social Research*, vol. XXIX, pp. 109–113, Spring, 1962.

Paetel, Karl Otto; "Otto Strasser und die "Schwarze Front,'" *Politische Studien*, vol. VIII, no. 92, pp. 269–281, December 1957.

———: "Die SS: Ein Beitrag zur Soziologie des Nationalsozialismus," *Vierteljahrshefte für Zeitgeschichte*, vol. II, no. 1, pp. 1–33, January 1954.

Paret, Peter: "An Aftermath of the Plot against Hitler: The Lehrterstrasse Prison in Berlin, 1944–45," *Bulletin of the Institute of Historical Research*, vol. XXXII, pp. 88–102, 1959.

Pechel, Rudolf: "Die Deutschen in Europa," *Deutsche Rundschau*, vol. LXXV, no. 8, pp. 673–679, August 1949.

Pese, Walter Werner: "Hitler und Italien," *Vieteljahrshefte für Zeitgeschichte*, vol. III, no. 2, pp. 113–126, April 1955.

Petersen, Jens: "Deutschland und Italien im Sommer 1935," *Geschichte in Wissenschaft und Unterricht*, vol. XX, no. 6, pp. 330–341, June 1969.

Petzina, Dieter: "Germany and the Great Depression," *Journal of Contemporary History*, vol. IV, pp. 59–74, 1969.

———: "Hauptprobleme der deutschen Wirtschaftspolitik, 1932–1933," *Vierteljahrshefte für Zeitgeschichte*, vol. XV, no. 1, pp. 18–55, January 1967.

Phelps, Reginald H.: "Hitler and the Deutsche Arbeiter Partei," *American Historical Review*, vol. LXVIII, no. 4, pp. 974–986, July 1963.

Plischke, Elmer: "Denazification Law and Procedure," *American Journal of International Law*, vol. XLI, pp. 807–827, October 1947.

Puchert, Berthold: "Die deutsch-polnische Nichtangrifferklärung und die Aussenwirtschaftspolitik des deutschen Imperialismus gegenüber Polen bis 1939," *Jahrbuch für Geschichte der UdSSR und der Volksdemokratischen Länder Europas*, vol. XII, pp. 339–354, 1968.

Raymond, Jack: "Nazi Peril Is Cited in U.S. House Unit," *The New York Times*, p. 5, col. 5, November 24, 1951.

Remak, Joachim: "Friends of the New Germany: The Bund and German-American Relations," *Journal of Modern History*, vol. XXIX, no. 1, pp. 38–41, March 1957.

———: "Hitlers Amerikapolitik," *Aussenpolitik*, vol. VI, pp. 13–33, 1955.

Rhode, Gotthold: "Die Präventivkriegspläne Pilsudskis von 1933," *Vierteljahrshefte für Zeitgeschichte*, vol. III, no. 4, pp. 344–363, October 1955.

Romoser, George K.: "The Politics of Uncertainty: The German Resistance Movement," *Social Research*, vol. XXXI, no. 1, pp. 73–79, Spring, 1964.

Rose, Arnold: "Anti-Semitism's Root in City-Hatred: A Clue to the Jew's Position as Scapegoat," *Commentary*, vol. VI, pp. 374–378, October 1948.

Rothfels, Hans: "The German Resistance in Its International Aspects," *International Affairs*, vol. XXXIV, pp. 477–489, 1958.

———: "Die Roten Kämpfer: Zur Geschichte einer linken Widerstandsgruppe," *Vierteljahrshefte für Zeitgeschichte*, vol. VII, pp. 438–460, 1959.

———: "Zerrspiegel des 20. Juli," *Vierteljahrshefte für Zeitgeschichte*, vol. X, pp. 62–67, 1962.

———: "Zerrspiegel historische Wahrheit," *Die Zeit*, p. 3, October 21, 1961.

——— and Henry M. Pachter: "Forum—The German Resistance Movement," *Social Research*, vol. XXIX, no. 4, pp. 441–448, Winter, 1962.

Schmitz-Esser, Winfried: "Hitler-Mussolini: Das südtiroler Abkommen von 1939," *Aussenpolitik*, vol. XIII, no. 6, pp. 397–409, June 1962.

Scholder, Klaus: "Die evangelische Kirche in der Sicht der nationalsozialistischen Fuhrung bis zum Kriegsausbruch," *Vierteljahrshefte für Zeitgeschichte*, vol. XVI, no. 1, pp. 15-35, January 1968.

Schweitzer, Arthur: "Der ursprüngliche Vierjahresplan," *Jahrbücher für Nationalökonomie und Statistik*, vol. CLXVIII, pp. 348–396, 1957.

———: "Die wirtschaftliche Wiederaufrüstung Deutschlands von 1934–1936," *Zeitschrift für die Gesamte Staatswissenschaft*, vol. CXIV, no. 4, pp. 594–637, 1958.

Seraphim, Hans-Günther: "SS-Verfügungstruppe und Wehrmacht," *Wehrwissenschaftliche Rundschau*, vol. V, no. 12, pp. 569–585, December 1955.

Shabecoff, Philip: "Nazi SS Veterans Cheer Former General at Meeting," *The New York Times*, p. 1, cols. 4-6, p. 17, cols, 3-8, October 25, 1965.

———: "Party Called Neo-Nazi Gains in Bavarian Elections," *The New York Times*, p. 14, cols. 4–6, March 15, 1966.

Sodeikat, Ernst: "Der Nationalsozialismus und die Danziger Opposition," *Vierteljahrshefte für Zeitgeschichte*, vol. XIV, no. 2, pp. 139–174, April 1966.

Skilling, Gordon H.: "Austrian Origins of National Socialism," *University of Toronto Quarterly*, vol. X, no. 4, pp. 482–492, July 1941.

Sohl, Klaus: "Die Kriegsvorbereitungen des deutschen Imperialismus in Bulgarien am Vorabend des zweiten Weltkrieges," *Jahrbücher für Geschichte der UdSSR und der volksdemokratischen Länder Europas*, vol. III, pp. 91–119, 1959.

Sontag, Raymond: "The Origins of the Second World War," *Review of Politics*, vol. XXV, no. 4, pp. 497–508, October 1963.

Speidel, Hans: "Reichswehr und Rote Armee," *Vierteljahrshefte für Zeitgeschichte*, vol. I, no. 1, pp. 9-45, January 1953.

Stammler, Eberhard: "Die politische Bildung und das Hakenkreuz," *Deutsche Jugend*, vol. VIII, no. 2, pp. 63–68, February 1960.

Strasser, Otto: "German Youth as a Postwar Problem," *Catholic World*, vol. CLVI, pp. 530–532, February 1943.

Strothmann, Dietrich: "Kriminelle Kriminalisten? Gestern SS-Sturmbannfuehrer—heute Polizeidirektor," *Freiheit und Recht*, vol. VIII, no. 7, pp. 14–15, Düsseldorf, July 1962.

Syrkin, Marie: "The Literature of the Holocaust," *Midstream*, vol. XII, pp. 3-20, May 1966.

Szymański, Antoni: "Als politischer Militärattache in Berlin, 1932–1939," *Politische Studien*, vol. XIII, no. 141, pp. 42–51, 1962.

Tarachow, Sidney: "A Note on Anti-Semitism," *Psychiatry*, vol. IX, no. 2, pp. 131–132, May 1946.

Tenenbaum, Joseph: "The Einsatzgruppen," *Jewish Social*

Studies, vol. XVII, no. 1, pp. 43–64, January 1955.
Thomas, Norman: "Labor under the Nazis," *Foreign Affairs*, vol. XIV, pp. 424–436, 1936.
Toscano, Mario: "Problemi particolari della storia della Secunda Guerra Mondiale," *Rivista di Studi Politici Internazionali*, vol. XVII, no. 3, pp. 388–398, 1950.
Treue, Wilhelm: "Das Dritte Reich und die Westmächte auf dem Balkan," *Vierteljahrshefte für Zeitgeschichte*, vol. I, no. 1, pp. 45–64, January 1953.
Trevor-Roper, H. R.: "The Germans Reappraise the War," *Foreign Affairs*, vol. XXXI, no. 2, pp. 225–237, January 1953.
———: "Hitlers Kriegsziele," *Vierteljahrshefte für Zeitgeschichte*, vol. VIII, no. 2, pp. 121–133, April 1960.
Trischen, Theo: "Das fromme Märchen vom 'unpolitischen Stahlhelm," *Neue Ruhr Zeitung*, no. 38, p. 1, Essen, September 18, 1953.
Turner, Ewart Edmund: "To Hitler via Two Men," *American Scholar*, vol. VI, no. 1, pp. 3–16, 1937.
Turner, Henry Ashby, Jr.: "Big Business and the Rise of Hitler," *American Historical Review*, vol. LXXV, no. 1, pp. 56-70, October 1969.
———: "Emil Kirdorf and the Nazi Party," *Journal of Central European History*, vol. I, pp. 324–344, December 1968.
———: "Hitler's Secret Pamphlet for Industrialists," *Journal of Modern History*, vol. XL, pp. 348–374, September 1968.
Vagts, Alfred: "'Unconditional Surrender' vor und nach 1945," *Vierteljahrshefte für Zeitgeschichte*, vol. VII, no. 3, pp. 280–309, July 1959.
Vogelsang, Thilo: "Neue Dokumente zur Geschichte der Reichswehr, 1930–1933," *Vierteljahrshefte für Zeitgeschichte*, vol. II, pp. 397–436, 1954.
———: "Zur Politik Schleichers gegenüber der NSDAP," *Vierteljahrshefte für Zeitgeschichte*, vol. VI, pp. 86–118, 1958.
Volbracht, Adolf: "Dokumente zum roten und braunen Faschismus," *Kontakte*, vol. I, no. 8, pp. 9–10, January 1952.
Wagner, Walter: "Politische Justiz in der Weimarer Republik: Der Feind von Links," *Politische Meinung*, vol. VI, no. 60, pp. 48–61, 1961.
———: "Politische Justiz in der Weimarer Republik: Der Feind von Rechts," *Politische Meinung*, vol. VI, no. 58, pp. 50–63, 1961.
Waite, Robert G. L.: "Adolf Hitler's Guilt Feelings: A Problem in History and Psychology," *Journal of Interdisciplinary History*, vol. I, pp. 229–249, 1971.
Walsh, Edmund A.: "Die Tragödie Karl Haushofers," *Neue Auslese*, vol. II, no. 3, pp. 19–29, 1947.
Watt, Donald C.: "The Anglo-German Naval Agreement of 1935: An Interim Judgment," *Journal of Modern History*, vol. XXVIII, no. 2, pp. 155–175, June 1956.
———: "Christian Essay in Appeasement," *Wiener Library Bulletin*, vol. XIV, no. 2, London, 1960.
Waugh, Martin: "National Socialism and the Genocide of the Jews," *International Journal of Psycho-Analysis*, vol. XLV, pp. 386–395, 1954.
Weinberg, Gerhard L.: "Deutsch-japanische Verhandlungen über das Südseemandat, 1937–1938," *Vierteljahrshefte für Zeitgeschichte*, vol. IV, no. 4, pp. 390–398, October 1956.
———: "Hitler's Image of the United States," *American Historical Review*, vol. LXIX, no. 4, pp. 1006–1021, July 1964.
———: "A Proposed Compromise over Danzig in 1939?" *Journal of Central European Affairs*, vol. XIV, no. 4, pp. 334–338, January 1955.
———: "Schachts Besuch in den USA im Jahre 1933," *Vierteljahrshefte für Zeitgeschichte*, vol. XI, no. 2, pp. 166–180, April 1963.
———: "Secret Hitler-Beneš Negotiations in 1936–37," *Journal of Central European Affairs*, vol. XIX, no. 4, pp. 366–374, January 1960.
Weinland, Viktor H.: "Wiedergeburt des Nationalsozialismus?" *Echo der Woche*, vol. III, no. 76, p. 2, Munich, January 7, 1949.
Weniger, Erich: "Zur Vorgeschichte des 20. Juli 1944: Heinrich von Stülpnagel," *Die Sammlung*, vol. IV, pp. 475–492, 1949.
Werdau, Hermann: "Die Jünger der braunen und roten Diktatur," *PZ-Archiv*, pp. 38 ff., February 5, 1952.
Werner, Alfred: "Trotzky of the Nazi Party," *Journal of Central European Affairs*, vol. XI, no. 1, pp. 39–46, January–April 1951.
Wewer, Heinz: "Die Hiag der Waffen-SS," *Frankfurter Hefte*, vol. XVII, no. 7, pp. 448–458, July 1962.
Whiteside, Andrew G.: "The Deutsche Arbeiterpartei, 1904–1918: A Contribution to the Origins of Fascism," *Austrian History News Letter*, no. 4, pp. 3–14, 1963.
———: "The Nature and Origins of National Socialism," *Journal of Central European Affairs*, vol. XVII, no. 1, pp. 48–73, April 1957.
Wilcke, Gerd: "Some Ex-Nazis Quit Courts on Bonn Deadline," *The New York Times*, p. 8, cols. 3–7, July 3, 1962.
Woerden, A. V. N. van: "Hitler Faces England," *Acta Historiae Neerlandica*, vol. III, pp. 141–159, 1968.
Wohlfeil, Rainer: "Der spanische Bürgerkrieg, 1936–1939: Zur Deutung und Nachwirkung," *Vierteljahrshefte für Zeitgeschichte*, vol. XVI, no. 2, pp. 101–119, April 1968.
Wunderlich, Frieda: "Education in Nazi Germany," *Social Research*, vol. IV, pp. 342–369, 1937.
Wyschogrod, Michael: "Faith and the Holocaust," *Judaism*, vol. XX, no. 3, pp. 268–294, Summer, 1971.